Essentials of
Business Analytics
2e

Jeffrey D. Camm
Wake Forest University

James J. Cochran
University of Alabama

Michael J. Fry
University of Cincinnati

Jeffrey W. Ohlmann
University of Iowa

David R. Anderson
University of Cincinnati

Dennis J. Sweeney
University of Cincinnati

Thomas A. Williams
Rochester Institute
of Technology

CENGAGE
Learning·

Australia · Brazil · Japan · Korea · Mexico · Singapore · Spain · United Kingdom · United States

**Essentials of Business Analytics,
Second Edition**
Jeffrey D. Camm, James J. Cochran,
Michael J. Fry, Jeffrey W. Ohlmann,
David R. Anderson, Dennis J. Sweeney,
Thomas A. Williams

Vice President, General Manager: Science,
Math & Quantitative Business: Balraj Kalsi

Product Director: Mike Schenk

Product Team Manager: Joe Sabatino

Product Manager: Aaron Arnsparger

Content Developer: Anne Merrill

Senior Marketing Manager: Nate Anderson

Content Project Manager: Jana Lewis

Media Developer: Chris Valentine

Manufacturing Planner: Ron Montgomery

Production Service: MPS Limited

Sr. Art Director: Michelle Kunkler

Internal Designer: Beckmeyer Design

Cover Designer: Beckmeyer Design

Cover Image: iStockphoto.com/alienforce

Intellectual Property Analyst: Brittani Morgan

Intellectual Property Project Manager:
Nick Barrows

Library of Congress Control Number: 2015958527

Package ISBN: 978-1-305-62773-4

Cengage Learning
20 Channel Center Street
Boston, MA 02210
USA

Cengage Learning is a leading provider of customized learning solutions with employees residing in nearly 40 different countries and sales in more than 125 countries around the world. Find your local representative at **www.cengage.com**.

Cengage Learning products are represented in Canada by Nelson Education, Ltd.

To learn more about Cengage Learning Solutions, visit **www.cengage.com**

Purchase any of our products at your local college store or at our preferred online store **www.cengagebrain.com**

Printed in Canada
Print Number: 01   Print Year: 2016

Brief Contents

Contents

Jeffrey D. Camm. Jeffrey D. Camm is the Inmar Presidential Chair and Associate Dean of Analytics in the School of Business at Wake Forest University. Born in Cincinnati, Ohio, he holds a B.S. from Xavier University (Ohio) and a Ph.D. from Clemson University. Prior to joining the faculty at Wake Forest, he was on the faculty of the University of Cincinnati. He has also been a visiting scholar at Stanford University and a visiting professor of business administration at the Tuck School of Business at Dartmouth College.

Dr. Camm has published over 30 papers in the general area of optimization applied to problems in operations management and marketing. He has published his research in *Science*, *Management Science*, *Operations Research*, *Interfaces*, and other professional journals. Dr. Camm was named the Dornoff Fellow of Teaching Excellence at the University of Cincinnati and he was the 2006 recipient of the INFORMS Prize for the Teaching of Operations Research Practice. A firm believer in practicing what he preaches, he has served as an operations research consultant to numerous companies and government agencies. From 2005 to 2010 he served as editor-in-chief of *Interfaces*.

James J. Cochran. James J. Cochran is Professor of Applied Statistics and the Rogers-Spivey Faculty Fellow at The University of Alabama. Born in Dayton, Ohio, he earned his B.S., M.S., and M.B.A. degrees from Wright State University and a Ph.D. from the University of Cincinnati. He has been at The University of Alabama since 2014 and has been a visiting scholar at Stanford University, Universidad de Talca, the University of South Africa, and Pole Universitaire Leonard de Vinci.

Professor Cochran has published over three dozen papers in the development and application of operations research and statistical methods. He has published his research in *Management Science, The American Statistician, Communications in Statistics—Theory and Methods, Annals of Operations Research, European Journal of Operational Research, Journal of Combinatorial Optimization. Interfaces, Statistics and Probability Letters*, and other professional journals. He was the 2008 recipient of the INFORMS Prize for the Teaching of Operations Research Practice and the 2010 recipient of the Mu Sigma Rho Statistical Education Award. Professor Cochran was elected to the International Statistics Institute in 2005 and named a Fellow of the American Statistical Association in 2011. He also received the Founders Award in 2014 and the Karl E. Peace Award in 2015 from the American Statistical Association. A strong advocate for effective operations research and statistics education as a means of improving the quality of applications to real problems, Professor Cochran has organized and chaired teaching effectiveness workshops in Montevideo, Uruguay; Cape Town, South Africa; Cartagena, Colombia; Jaipur, India; Buenos Aires, Argentina; and Nairobi, Kenya. He has served as an operations research consultant to numerous companies and not-for profit organizations. He served as editor-in-chief of *INFORMS Transactions on Education* from 2006–2012 and is on the editorial board of *Interfaces, International Transactions in Operational Research*, and *Significance*.

Michael J. Fry. Michael J. Fry is Professor and Head of the Department of Operations, Business Analytics, and Information Systems in the Carl H. Lindner College of Business at the University of Cincinnati. Born in Killeen, Texas, he earned a B.S. from Texas A&M University, and M.S.E. and Ph.D. degrees from the University of Michigan. He has been at the University of Cincinnati since 2002, where he has been named a Lindner Research Fellow and has served as Assistant Director and Interim Director of the Center for Business Analytics. He has also been a visiting professor at the Samuel Curtis Johnson Graduate School of Management at Cornell University and the Sauder School of Business at the University of British Columbia.

Professor Fry has published over twenty research papers in journals such as *Operations Research, M&SOM, Transportation Science, Naval Research Logistics, IIE Transactions,* and *Interfaces.* His research interests are in applying quantitative management methods to the areas of supply chain analytics, sports analytics, and public-policy operations. He has worked with many different organizations for his research, including Dell, Inc., Copeland Corporation, Starbucks Coffee Company, Great American Insurance Group, the Cincinnati Fire Department, the State of Ohio Election Commission, the Cincinnati Bengals, and the Cincinnati Zoo. In 2008, he was named a finalist for the Daniel H. Wagner Prize for Excellence in Operations Research Practice, and he has been recognized for both his research and teaching excellence at the University of Cincinnati.

Jeffrey W. Ohlmann. Jeffrey W. Ohlmann is Associate Professor of Management Sciences and Huneke Research Fellow in the Tippie College of Business at the University of Iowa. Born in Valentine, Nebraska, he earned a B.S. from the University of Nebraska, and M.S. and Ph.D. degrees from the University of Michigan. He has been at the University of Iowa since 2003.

Professor Ohlmann's research on the modeling and solution of decision-making problems has produced over a dozen research papers in journals such as *Operations Research, Mathematics of Operations Research, INFORMS Journal on Computing, Transportation Science,* the *European Journal of Operational Research,* and *Interfaces.* He has collaborated with companies such as Transfreight, LeanCor, Cargill, the Hamilton County Board of Elections, and three National Football League franchises. Due to the relevance of his work to industry, he was bestowed the George B. Dantzig Dissertation Award and was recognized as a finalist for the Daniel H. Wagner Prize for Excellence in Operations Research Practice.

David R. Anderson. David R. Anderson is Professor Emeritus of Quantitative Analysis in the Carl H. Lindner College of Business at the University of Cincinnati. Born in Grand Forks, North Dakota, he earned his B.S., M.S., and Ph.D. degrees from Purdue University. Professor Anderson has served as Head of the Department of Quantitative Analysis and Operations Management and as Associate Dean of the College of Business Administration. In addition, he was the coordinator of the College's first Executive Program.

At the University of Cincinnati, Professor Anderson has taught introductory statistics for business students as well as graduate-level courses in regression analysis, multivariate analysis, and management science. He has also taught statistical courses at the Department of Labor in Washington, D.C. He has been honored with nominations and awards for excellence in teaching and excellence in service to student organizations.

Professor Anderson has coauthored 10 textbooks in the areas of statistics, management science, linear programming, and production and operations management. He is an active consultant in the field of sampling and statistical methods.

Dennis J. Sweeney. Dennis J. Sweeney is Professor Emeritus of Quantitative Analysis and Founder of the Center for Productivity Improvement at the University of Cincinnati. Born in Des Moines, Iowa, he earned a B.S.B.A. degree from Drake University and his M.B.A. and D.B.A. degrees from Indiana University, where he was an NDEA Fellow. During 1978–1979, Professor Sweeney worked in the management science group at Procter & Gamble; during 1981–1982, he was a visiting professor at Duke University. Professor Sweeney served as Head of the Department of Quantitative Analysis and as Associate Dean of the College of Business Administration at the University of Cincinnati.

Professor Sweeney has published more than 30 articles and monographs in the areas of management science and statistics. The National Science Foundation, IBM, Procter & Gamble, Federated Department Stores, Kroger, and Cincinnati Gas & Electric have funded his research, which has been published in *Management Science, Operations Research, Mathematical Programming, Decision Sciences,* and other journals.

Professor Sweeney has coauthored 10 textbooks in the areas of statistics, management science, linear programming, and production and operations management.

Thomas A. Williams. Thomas A. Williams is Professor Emeritus of Management Science in the College of Business at Rochester Institute of Technology. Born in Elmira, New York, he earned his B.S. degree at Clarkson University. He did his graduate work at Rensselaer Polytechnic Institute, where he received his M.S. and Ph.D. degrees.

Before joining the College of Business at RIT, Professor Williams served for seven years as a faculty member in the College of Business Administration at the University of Cincinnati, where he developed the undergraduate program in Information Systems and then served as its coordinator. At RIT he was the first chairman of the Decision Sciences Department. He teaches courses in management science and statistics, as well as graduate courses in regression and decision analysis.

Professor Williams is the coauthor of 11 textbooks in the areas of management science, statistics, production and operations management, and mathematics. He has been a consultant for numerous *Fortune* 500 companies and has worked on projects ranging from the use of data analysis to the development of large-scale regression models.

Essentials of Business Analytics 2E is designed to introduce the concept of business analytics to undergraduate and graduate students. This textbook contains one of the first collections of materials that are essential to the growing field of business analytics. In Chapter 1 we present an overview of business analytics and our approach to the material in this textbook. In simple terms, business analytics helps business professionals make better decisions based on data. We discuss models for summarizing, visualizing, and understanding useful information from historical data in Chapters 2 through 6. Chapters 7 through 9 introduce methods for both gaining insights from historical data as well as predicting possible future outcomes. Chapter 10 covers the use of spreadsheets for examining data and building decision models. In Chapters 11 through 12 we discuss optimization models to help decision makers choose the best decision based on the available data. Chapter 13 presents material that some may consider more advanced forms of optimization (nonlinear optimization models), although these models are extremely useful and widely applicable to many business situations. In any case, some instructors may choose to omit covering Chapter 13. In Chapter 14 we introduce the concept of simulation models for understanding the effect of uncertainty on decisions. Chapter 15 is an overview of decision analysis approaches for incorporating a decision maker's views about risk into decision making. In Appendix A we present optional material for students who need to learn the basics of using Microsoft Excel. The use of databases and manipulating data in Microsoft Access is discussed in Appendix B.

This textbook can be used by students who have previously taken a course on basic statistical methods as well as students who have not had a prior course in statistics. The expanded material in the second edition of Essentials of Business Analytics also makes it amenable to a two-course sequence in business statistics and analytics. All statistical concepts contained in this textbook are presented from a business analytics perspective using practical business examples. Chapters 2, 5, 6 and 7 provide an introduction to basic statistical concepts that form the foundation for more advanced analytics methods. Chapters 3, 4 and 9 cover additional topics of data visualization and data mining that are not traditionally part of most introductory business statistics courses, but they are exceedingly important and commonly used in current business environments. Chapter 10 and Appendix A provide the foundational knowledge students need to use Microsoft Excel for analytics applications. Chapters 11 through 15 build upon this spreadsheet knowledge to present additional topics that are used by many organizations that are leaders in the use of prescriptive analytics to improve decision making.

Updates in the Second Edition

The second edition of *Essentials of Business Analytics* is a major revision of the first edition. We have added several new chapters, expanded the coverage of existing chapters, and updated all chapters based on changes in the software used with this textbook. Stylistically, the 2nd edition of *Essentials of Business Analytics* also has an entirely new look. We have added full-color figures throughout the textbook that make many chapters much more meaningful and easier to read.

- **New Chapters on Probability and Statistical Inference.** Chapters 5 and 6 are new to this edition. Chapter 5 covers an introduction to probability for those students who are not familiar with basic probability concepts such as random variables, conditional probability, Bayes' theorem, and probability distributions. Chapter 6 presents statistical inference topics such as sampling, sampling distributions, interval estimation, and hypothesis testing. These two chapters extend the basic statistical coverage of *Essentials of Business Analytics* (in conjunction with Chapter 2 on Descriptive Statistics and Chapter 7 on Linear Regression) so that the textbook includes a full coverage of introductory business statistics for students who are unfamiliar with these concepts.

- **Expanded Data Mining Coverage.** The Data Mining chapter from the first edition has been broken into two chapters: Chapter 4 on Descriptive Data Mining and Chapter 9 on Predictive Data Mining. This allows us to cover additional material related to these concepts and to also clearly delineate the different forms of data mining based on their intended result. Chapter 4 on Descriptive Data Mining covers unsupervised learning methods such as clustering and association rules where the user is interested in identifying relationships among observations rather than predicting specific outcome variables. Chapter 4 also covers very important topics related to data preparation including missing data, outliers, and variable representation. Chapter 9 on Predictive Data Mining introduces supervised learning methods that are used to predict an outcome based on a set of input variables. The methods covered in Chapter 9 include logistic regression, *k*-nearest neighbors clustering, and classification and regression trees. Additional data preparation methods such as data sampling and data portioning are also covered in this chapter.

- **Revision of Linear Regression Chapter.** Based on user feedback from the first edition, Chapter 7's coverage of linear regression has been substantially revised to streamline the exposition with a focus on intuitive understanding without sacrificing technical accuracy. The appendix of this chapter has been expanded to demonstrate the construction of prediction intervals using the Analytic Solver Platform software.

- **New Appendix to Chapter 8.** Chapter 8 on Time Series Analysis and Forecasting now includes an appendix on Excel 2016's new Forecast Sheet tool for implementing Holt-Winters additive seasonal smoothing model.

- **Revision of Simulation Chapter.** As with all other chapters, the coverage of Analytics Solver Platform has been moved to the appendix. All material in the body of the chapter uses only native Excel to implement Monte Carlo simulations.

- **Coverage of Analytic Solver Platform (ASP) Moved to Chapter Appendices.** All coverage of the Excel add-in, Analytics Solver Platform, has been moved to the chapter appendices. This means that instructors can now cover all the material in the bodies of the chapters using only native Excel functionality. ASP is used most heavily in the data mining and simulation chapters, so the result of this change is that the chapter appendices are quite long for Chapters 4, 9, and 14. However, this change makes it easier for an instructor to tailor a course's coverage of data mining concepts and the execution of these concepts.

- **Updates to ASP.** All examples, problems, and solutions have been updated in response to changes in the ASP software. Frontline Systems, the developer of ASP, implemented a major rewrite of the code base that powers ASP shortly after the release of the first edition of *Essentials of Business Analytics*. This new code base is much faster and more stable than the previous releases of ASP, but it also completely changed the output given by ASP in many cases. All the material related to ASP is updated to correspond to Analytic Solver Platform V2016 (16.0.0).

- **Incorporation of Excel 2016.** Most updates in Excel 2016 are relatively minor as they relate to its use for statistics and analytics. However, Excel 2016 does have new options for creating Charts in Excel and for implementing forecasting methods. Excel 2016 allows for the creation of box plots, tree maps, and several other data visualization tools that could not be created in previous versions of Excel. Excel's new Forecast Sheet tool implements a time series forecasting model known as the Holt-Winters additive seasonal smoothing model; this is covered in the appendix to Chapter 8. Several other minor updates to the Ribbon and tabs have also been made in Excel 2016. All material in the second edition of this textbook is easily accessible for students using earlier versions of Excel. For Excel tools that are only implementable in Excel 2016, we include these either in a chapter appendix (such as Forecast Sheet in Chapter 8 appendix) or with margin notes explaining how the same action can be executed in Excel 2013.

- **Additional Excel Features Incorporated.** Several other features that were introduced in Excel 2013 have been more fully incorporated in this edition. Chapter 2 introduces the Quick Analysis button in Excel, and Chapter 3 now makes full use of the Chart Buttons in Excel. The Quick Analysis button is a shortcut method for accomplishing many common Excel formatting and other tasks. The Chart Buttons make it much easier to format, edit, and analyze charts in Excel. Chapter 3 also now also includes coverage of the Recommended PivotTables and Recommended Charts tools in Excel.

- **New Style and More Color.** The second edition of *Essentials of Business Analytics* includes full color figures and a new color template throughout the text. This makes much of the material covered, such as Chapter 3 on Data Visualization, much easier for students to interpret and understand.

Continued Features and Pedagogy

The style of this textbook is based on the other classic textbooks written by the Anderson, Sweeney, and Williams (ASW) team. Some of the specific features that we use in this textbook are listed below.

- **Integration of Microsoft Excel:** Excel has been thoroughly integrated throughout this textbook. For many methodologies, we provide instructions for how to perform calculations both by hand and with Excel. In other cases where realistic models are practical only with the use of a spreadsheet, we focus on the use of Excel to describe the methods to be used.

- **Notes and Comments:** At the end of many sections, we provide Notes and Comments to give the student additional insights about the methods presented in that section. These insights include comments on the limitations of the presented methods, recommendations for applications, and other matters. Additionally, margin notes are used throughout the textbook to provide additional insights and tips related to the specific material being discussed.

- **Analytics in Action:** Each chapter contains an Analytics in Action article. These articles present interesting examples of the use of business analytics in practice. The examples are drawn from many different organizations in a variety of areas including healthcare, finance, manufacturing, marketing, and others.

- **DATAfiles and MODELfiles:** All data sets used as examples and in student exercises are also provided online as files available for download by the student. DATAfiles are Excel files that contain data needed for the examples and problems given in the textbook. MODELfiles contain additional modeling features such as extensive use of Excel formulas or the use of Excel Solver or Analytic Solver Platform.

- **Problems and Cases:** With the exception of Chapter 1, each chapter contains an extensive selection of problems to help the student master the material presented in that chapter. The problems vary in difficulty and most relate to specific examples of the use of business analytics in practice. Answers to even-numbered problems are provided in an online supplement for student access. With the exception of Chapter 1, each chapter also includes an in-depth case study that connects many of the different methods introduced in the chapter. The case studies are designed to be more open-ended than the chapter problems, but enough detail is provided to give the student some direction in solving the cases.

MindTap

MindTap is a customizable digital course solution that includes an interactive eBook, auto-graded exercises from the textbook, and author-created video walkthroughs of key chapter concepts and select examples that use Analytic Solver platform. All of these materials offer students better access to understand the materials within the course. For more information on MindTap, please contact your Cengage representative.

For Students

Online resources are available to help the student work more efficiently. The resources can be accessed through **www.cengagebrain.com**.

- **Analytic Solver Platform:** Instructions to download an educational version of Frontline Systems' Analytic Solver Platform are included with the purchase of this textbook. These instructions can be found within the inside front cover of this text.

For Instructors

Instructor resources are available to adopters on the Instructor Companion Site, which can be found and accessed at **www.cengage.com**, including:

- **Solutions Manual:** The Solutions Manual, prepared by the authors, includes solutions for all problems in the text. It is available online as well as print.
- **Solutions to Case Problems:** These are also prepared by the authors and contain solutions to all case problems presented in the text.
- **PowerPoint Presentation Slides:** The presentation slides contain a teaching outline that incorporates figures to complement instructor lectures.
- **Test Bank:** Cengage Learning Testing Powered by Cognero is a flexible, online system that allows you to:
  - author, edit, and manage test bank content from multiple Cengage Learning solutions,
  - create multiple test versions in an instant, and
  - deliver tests from your LMS, your classroom, or wherever you want. The Test Bank is also available in Microsoft Word.

Acknowledgements

We would like to acknowledge the work of our reviewers, who provided comments and suggestions for improvement of this text. Thanks to:

Matthew D. Bailey
Bucknell University

Phillip Beaver
Daniels College of Business University of Denver

M. Khurrum S. Bhutta
Ohio University

Q B. Chung
Villanova University

Elizabeth A. Denny
University of Kentucky

Mike Taein Eom
University of Portland

Yvette Njan Essounga
Fayetteville State University

Lawrence V. Fulton
Texas State University

Ed Wasil
American University

Paolo Catasti
Virginia Commonwealth University

James F. Hoelscher
Lincoln Memorial University

Eric Huggins
Fort Lewis College

Faizul Huq
Ohio University

Marco Lam
York College of Pennsylvania

Ram Pakath
University of Kentucky

Susan Palocsay
James Madison University

Dothan Truong
Embry-Riddle Aeronautical University

Kai Wang
Wake Technical Community College

We are indebted to our product director Joe Sabatino and our product manager, Aaron Arnsparger; our marketing manager, Nathan Anderson, and our content developer, Anne Merrill; our content project manager, Jana Lewis; our media developer, Chris Valentine; and others at Cengage Learning for their counsel and support during the preparation of this text.

Jeffrey D. Camm
James J. Cochran
Michael J. Fry
Jeffrey W. Ohlmann
David R. Anderson
Dennis J. Sweeney
Thomas A. Williams

Chapter 1

Introduction

You apply for a loan for the first time. How does the bank assess the riskiness of the loan it might make to you? How does Amazon.com know which books and other products to recommend to you when you log in to their web site? How do airlines determine what price to quote to you when you are shopping for a plane ticket? How can doctors better diagnose and treat you when you are ill or injured?

You may be applying for a loan for the first time, but millions of people around the world have applied for loans before. Many of these loan recipients have paid back their loans in full and on time, but some have not. The bank wants to know whether you are more like those who have paid back their loans or more like those who defaulted. By comparing your credit history, financial situation, and other factors to the vast database of previous loan recipients, the bank can effectively assess how likely you are to default on a loan.

Similarly, Amazon.com has access to data on millions of purchases made by customers on its web site. Amazon.com examines your previous purchases, the products you have viewed, and any product recommendations you have provided. Amazon.com then searches through its huge database for customers who are similar to you in terms of product purchases, recommendations, and interests. Once similar customers have been identified, their purchases form the basis of the recommendations given to you.

Prices for airline tickets are frequently updated. The price quoted to you for a flight between New York and San Francisco today could be very different from the price that will be quoted tomorrow. These changes happen because airlines use a pricing strategy known as revenue management. Revenue management works by examining vast amounts of data on past airline customer purchases and using these data to forecast future purchases. These forecasts are then fed into sophisticated optimization algorithms that determine the optimal price to charge for a particular flight and when to change that price. Revenue management has resulted in substantial increases in airline revenues.

Finally, consider the case of being evaluated by a doctor for a potentially serious medical issue. Hundreds of medical papers may describe research studies done on patients facing similar diagnoses, and thousands of data points exist on their outcomes. However, it is extremely unlikely that your doctor has read every one of these research papers or is aware of all previous patient outcomes. Instead of relying only on her medical training and knowledge gained from her limited set of previous patients, wouldn't it be better for your doctor to have access to the expertise and patient histories of thousands of doctors around the world?

A group of IBM computer scientists initiated a project to develop a new decision technology to help in answering these types of questions. That technology is called Watson, named after the founder of IBM, Thomas J. Watson. The team at IBM focused on one aim: how the vast amounts of data now available on the Internet can be used to make more data-driven, smarter decisions.

Watson became a household name in 2011, when it famously won the television game show, *Jeopardy!* Since that proof of concept in 2011, IBM has reached agreements with the health insurance provider WellPoint (now part of Anthem), the financial services company Citibank, and Memorial Sloan-Kettering Cancer Center to apply Watson to the decision problems that they face.

Watson is a system of computing hardware, high-speed data processing, and analytical algorithms that are combined to make data-based recommendations. As more and more data are collected, Watson has the capability to learn over time. In simple terms, according to IBM, Watson gathers hundreds of thousands of possible solutions from a huge data bank, evaluates them using analytical techniques, and proposes only the best solutions for consideration. Watson provides not just a single solution, but rather a range of good solutions with a confidence level for each.

For example, at a data center in Virginia, to the delight of doctors and patients, Watson is already being used to speed up the approval of medical procedures. Citibank is beginning to explore how to use Watson to better serve its customers, and cancer specialists at more than a dozen hospitals in North America are using Watson to assist with the diagnosis and treatment of patients.[1]

This book is concerned with data-driven decision making and the use of analytical approaches in the decision-making process. Three developments spurred recent explosive growth in the use of analytical methods in business applications. First, technological advances—such as improved point-of-sale scanner technology and the collection of data through e-commerce, Internet social networks, and data generated from personal electronic devices—produce incredible amounts of data for businesses. Naturally, businesses want to use these data to improve the efficiency and profitability of their operations, better understand their customers, price their products more effectively, and gain a competitive advantage. Second, ongoing research has resulted in numerous methodological developments, including advances in computational approaches to effectively handle and explore massive amounts of data, faster algorithms for optimization and simulation, and more effective approaches for visualizing data. Third, these methodological developments were paired with an explosion in computing power and storage capability. Better computing hardware, parallel computing, and, more recently, cloud computing (the remote use of hardware and software over the Internet) have enabled businesses to solve big problems more quickly and more accurately than ever before.

In summary, the availability of massive amounts of data, improvements in analytic methodologies, and substantial increases in computing power have all come together to result in a dramatic upsurge in the use of analytical methods in business and a reliance on the discipline that is the focus of this text: business analytics. Figure 1.1 shows the job trend for analytics from 2006 to 2015. The chart from indeed.com shows the percentage of job ads that contain the word *analytics* and illustrates that demand has grown and continues to be strong for analytical skills.

Business analytics is a crucial area of study for students looking to enhance their employment prospects. It has been predicted that by 2018 there will be a shortage of more than 1.5 million business managers with adequate training in analytics in the United States alone.[2] As stated in the Preface, the purpose of this text is to provide

It is difficult to know for sure the cause of the large spike in analytics job ads in 2008. We do note, however, that the thought-provoking book Competing on Analytics by Davenport and Harris was published in 2007.

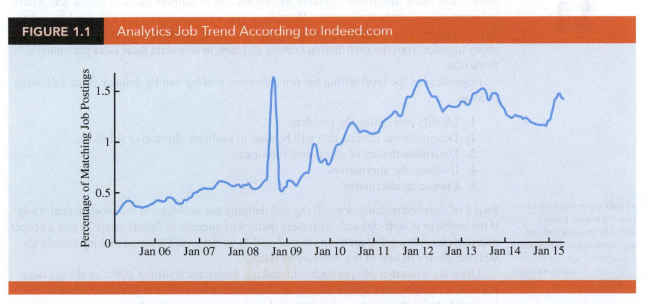

FIGURE 1.1   Analytics Job Trend According to Indeed.com

[1]"IBM's Watson Is Learning Its Way to Saving Lives," Fastcompany web site, December 8, 2012; "IBM's Watson Targets Cancer and Enlists Prominent Providers in the Fight," ModernHealthcare web site, May 5, 2015.
[2]J. Manyika et al., "Big Data: The Next Frontier for Innovation, Competition and Productivity," McKinsey Global Institute Report, 2011.

students with a sound conceptual understanding of the role that business analytics plays in the decision-making process. To reinforce the applications orientation of the text and to provide a better understanding of the variety of applications in which analytical methods have been used successfully, Analytics in Action articles are presented throughout the book. Each Analytics in Action article summarizes an application of analytical methods in practice.

1.1 Decision Making

It is the responsibility of managers to plan, coordinate, organize, and lead their organizations to better performance. Ultimately, managers' responsibilities require that they make strategic, tactical, or operational decisions. **Strategic decisions** involve higher-level issues concerned with the overall direction of the organization; these decisions define the organization's overall goals and aspirations for the future. Strategic decisions are usually the domain of higher-level executives and have a time horizon of three to five years. **Tactical decisions** concern how the organization should achieve the goals and objectives set by its strategy, and they are usually the responsibility of midlevel management. Tactical decisions usually span a year and thus are revisited annually or even every six months. **Operational decisions** affect how the firm is run from day to day; they are the domain of operations managers, who are the closest to the customer.

Consider the case of the Thoroughbred Running Company (TRC). Historically, TRC had been a catalog-based retail seller of running shoes and apparel. TRC sales revenues grew quickly as it changed its emphasis from catalog-based sales to Internet-based sales. Recently, TRC decided that it should also establish retail stores in the malls and downtown areas of major cities. This strategic decision will take the firm in a new direction that it hopes will complement its Internet-based strategy. TRC middle managers will therefore have to make a variety of tactical decisions in support of this strategic decision, including how many new stores to open this year, where to open these new stores, how many distribution centers will be needed to support the new stores, and where to locate these distribution centers. Operations managers in the stores will need to make day-to-day decisions regarding, for instance, how many pairs of each model and size of shoes to order from the distribution centers and how to schedule their sales personnel's work time.

Regardless of the level within the firm, *decision making* can be defined as the following process:

1. Identify and define the problem.
2. Determine the criteria that will be used to evaluate alternative solutions.
3. Determine the set of alternative solutions.
4. Evaluate the alternatives.
5. Choose an alternative.

If I were given one hour to save the planet, I would spend 59 minutes defining the problem and one minute resolving it.

—Albert Einstein

Step 1 of decision making, identifying and defining the problem, is the most critical. Only if the problem is well-defined, with clear metrics of success or failure (step 2), can a proper approach for solving the problem (steps 3 and 4) be devised. Decision making concludes with the choice of one of the alternatives (step 5).

There are a number of approaches to making decisions: tradition ("We've always done it this way"), intuition ("gut feeling"), and rules of thumb ("As the restaurant owner, I schedule twice the number of waiters and cooks on holidays"). The power of each of these approaches should not be underestimated. Managerial experience and intuition are valuable inputs to making decisions, but what if relevant data were available to help us make more informed decisions? With the vast amounts of data now generated and stored electronically, it is estimated that the amount of data stored by businesses more than doubles every two years. How can managers convert these data into knowledge that they can use to be more efficient and effective in managing their businesses?

1.2 Business Analytics Defined

What makes decision making difficult and challenging? Uncertainty is probably the number one challenge. If we knew how much the demand will be for our product, we could do a much better job of planning and scheduling production. If we knew exactly how long each step in a project will take to be completed, we could better predict the project's cost and completion date. If we knew how stocks will perform, investing would be a lot easier.

Another factor that makes decision making difficult is that we often face such an enormous number of alternatives that we cannot evaluate them all. What is the best combination of stocks to help me meet my financial objectives? What is the best product line for a company that wants to maximize its market share? How should an airline price its tickets so as to maximize revenue?

Some firms and industries use the simpler term, analytics. Analytics is often thought of as a broader category than business analytics, encompassing the use of analytical techniques in the sciences and engineering as well. In this text, we use business analytics and analytics synonymously.

Business analytics is the scientific process of transforming data into insight for making better decisions.[3] Business analytics is used for data-driven or fact-based decision making, which is often seen as more objective than other alternatives for decision making.

As we shall see, the tools of business analytics can aid decision making by creating insights from data, by improving our ability to more accurately forecast for planning, by helping us quantify risk, and by yielding better alternatives through analysis and optimization. A study based on a large sample of firms that was conducted by researchers at MIT's Sloan School of Management and the University of Pennsylvania, concluded that firms guided by data-driven decision making have higher productivity and market value and increased output and profitability.[4]

1.3 A Categorization of Analytical Methods and Models

Business analytics can involve anything from simple reports to the most advanced optimization techniques (methods for finding the best course of action). Analytics is generally thought to comprise three broad categories of techniques: descriptive analytics, predictive analytics, and prescriptive analytics.

Descriptive Analytics

Descriptive analytics encompasses the set of techniques that describes what has happened in the past. Examples are data queries, reports, descriptive statistics, data visualization including data dashboards, some data-mining techniques, and basic what-if spreadsheet models.

Appendix B at the end of this book describes how to use Microsoft Access to conduct data queries.

A **data query** is a request for information with certain characteristics from a database. For example, a query to a manufacturing plant's database might be for all records of shipments to a particular distribution center during the month of March. This query provides descriptive information about these shipments: the number of shipments, how much was included in each shipment, the date each shipment was sent, and so on. A report summarizing relevant historical information for management might be conveyed by the use of descriptive statistics (means, measures of variation, etc.) and data-visualization tools (tables, charts, and maps). Simple descriptive statistics and data-visualization techniques can be used to find patterns or relationships in a large database.

---

[3]We adopt the definition of analytics developed by the Institute for Operations Research and the Management Sciences (INFORMS).

[4]E. Brynjolfsson, L. M. Hitt, and H. H. Kim, "Strength in Numbers: How Does Data-Driven Decisionmaking Affect Firm Performance?" (April 18, 2013). Available at SSRN, http://papers.ssrn.com/sol3/papers.cfm?abstract_id=1819486.

Data dashboards are collections of tables, charts, maps, and summary statistics that are updated as new data become available. Dashboards are used to help management monitor specific aspects of the company's performance related to their decision-making responsibilities. For corporate-level managers, daily data dashboards might summarize sales by region, current inventory levels, and other company-wide metrics; front-line managers may view dashboards that contain metrics related to staffing levels, local inventory levels, and short-term sales forecasts.

Data mining is the use of analytical techniques for better understanding patterns and relationships that exist in large data sets. For example, by analyzing text on social network platforms like Twitter, data-mining techniques (including cluster analysis and sentiment analysis) are used by companies to better understand their customers. By categorizing certain words as positive or negative and keeping track of how often those words appear in tweets, a company like Apple can better understand how its customers are feeling about a product like the Apple Watch.

Predictive Analytics

Predictive analytics consists of techniques that use models constructed from past data to predict the future or ascertain the impact of one variable on another. For example, past data on product sales may be used to construct a mathematical model to predict future sales. This mode can factor in the product's growth trajectory and seasonality based on past patterns. A packaged-food manufacturer may use point-of-sale scanner data from retail outlets to help in estimating the lift in unit sales due to coupons or sales events. Survey data and past purchase behavior may be used to help predict the market share of a new product. All of these are applications of predictive analytics.

Linear regression, time series analysis, some data-mining techniques, and simulation, often referred to as risk analysis, all fall under the banner of predictive analytics. We discuss all of these techniques in greater detail later in this text.

Data mining, previously discussed as a descriptive analytics tool, is also often used in predictive analytics. For example, a large grocery store chain might be interested in developing a targeted marketing campaign that offers a discount coupon on potato chips. By studying historical point-of-sale data, the store may be able to use data mining to predict which customers are the most likely to respond to an offer on discounted chips by purchasing higher-margin items such as beer or soft drinks in addition to the chips, thus increasing the store's overall revenue.

Simulation involves the use of probability and statistics to construct a computer model to study the impact of uncertainty on a decision. For example, banks often use simulation to model investment and default risk in order to stress-test financial models. Simulation is also often used in the pharmaceutical industry to assess the risk of introducing a new drug.

Prescriptive Analytics

Prescriptive analytics differs from descriptive or predictive analytics in that **prescriptive analytics** indicates a best course of action to take; that is, the output of a prescriptive model is a best decision. The airline industry's use of revenue management is an example of a prescriptive analytics. Airlines use past purchasing data as inputs into a model that recommends the best pricing strategy across all flights in order to maximize revenue.

Other examples of prescriptive analytics are portfolio models in finance, supply network design models in operations, and price-markdown models in retailing. Portfolio models use historical investment return data to determine which mix of investments will yield the highest expected return while controlling or limiting exposure to risk. Supply-network design models provide data about plant and distribution center locations that will

TABLE 1.1	Coverage of Business Analytics Topics in This Text			
Chapter	Title	Descriptive	Predictive	Prescriptive
1	Introduction	●	●	●
2	Descriptive Statistics	●		
3	Data Visualization	●		
4	Descriptive Data Mining	●		
5	Probability: An Introduction to Modeling Uncertainty	●		
6	Statistical Inference	●		
7	Linear Regression		●	
8	Time Series and Forecasting		●	
9	Predictive Data Mining		●	
10	Spreadsheet Models	●		
11	Linear Optimization Models			●
12	Integer Optimization Models			●
13	Nonlinear Optimization Models			●
14	Simulation		●	●
15	Decision Analysis			●

minimize costs while still meeting customer service requirements. Given historical data, retail price markdown models yield revenue-maximizing discount levels and the timing of discount offers when goods have not sold as planned. All of these models are known as **optimization models**, that is, models that give the best decision subject to the constraints of the situation.

Another type of modeling in the prescriptive analytics category is **simulation optimization**, which combines the use of probability and statistics to model uncertainty with optimization techniques to find good decisions in highly complex and highly uncertain settings. Finally, the techniques of **decision analysis** can be used to develop an optimal strategy when a decision maker is faced with several decision alternatives and an uncertain set of future events. Decision analysis also employs **utility theory**, which assigns values to outcomes based on the decision maker's attitude toward risk, loss, and other factors.

In this text we cover all three areas of business analytics: descriptive, predictive, and prescriptive. Table 1.1 shows how the chapters cover the three categories.

1.4 Big Data

Walmart handles over 1 million purchase transactions per hour. Facebook processes more than 250 million picture uploads per day. Six billion cell-phone owners around the world generate vast amounts of data by calling, texting, tweeting, and browsing the web on a daily basis.[5] As Google CEO Eric Schmidt has noted, the amount of data currently created every 48 hours is equivalent to the entire amount of data created from the dawn of civilization until the year 2003. It is through technology that we have truly been thrust into the data age. Because data can now be collected electronically, the amounts of it available are staggering. The Internet, cell phones, retail checkout scanners, surveillance video, and sensors on everything from aircraft to cars to bridges allow us to collect and store vast amounts of data in real time.

---

[5]SAS White Paper, "Big Data Meets Big Data Analytics," SAS Institute, 2012.

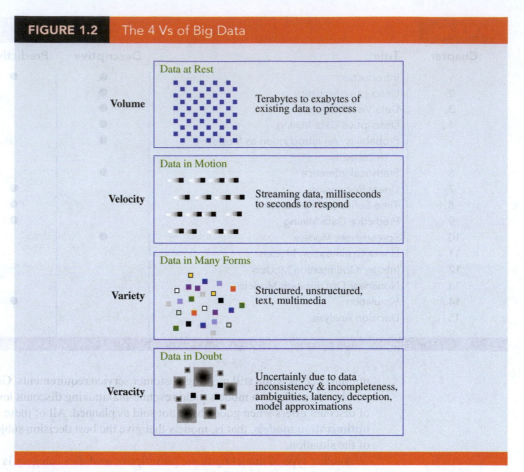

FIGURE 1.2   The 4 Vs of Big Data

Data at Rest

Volume — Terabytes to exabytes of existing data to process

Data in Motion

Velocity — Streaming data, milliseconds to seconds to respond

Data in Many Forms

Variety — Structured, unstructured, text, multimedia

Data in Doubt

Veracity — Uncertainty due to data inconsistency & incompleteness, ambiguities, latency, deception, model approximations

Source: *IBM*

In the midst of all of this data collection, the new term *big data* has been created. There is no universally accepted definition of big data. However, probably the most accepted and most general definition is that **big data** is any set of data that is too large or too complex to be handled by standard data-processing technics and typical desktop software. IBM describes the phenomenon of big data through the four Vs: volume, velocity, variety, and veracity, as shown in Figure 1.2.[6]

Volume

Because data are collected electronically, we are able to collect more of it. To be useful, these data must be stored, and this storage has led to vast quantities of data. Many companies now store in excess of 100 terabytes of data (a terabyte of data is 100,000 gigabytes).

Velocity

Real-time capture and analysis of data present unique challenges both in how data are stored and the speed with which those data can be analyzed for decision making. For example, the New York Stock Exchange collects 1 terabyte of data in a single trading session, and having current data and real-time rules for trades and predictive modeling are important for managing stock portfolios.

[6]IBM web site: http://www.ibmbigdatahub.com/sites/default/files/infographic_file/4-Vs-of-big-data.jpg.

Variety

In addition to the sheer volume and speed with which companies now collect data, more complicated types of data are now available and are proving to be of great value to businesses. Text data are collected by monitoring what is being said about a company's products or services on social media platforms such as Twitter. Audio data are collected from service calls (on a service call, you will often hear "this call may be monitored for quality control"). Video data collected by in-store video cameras are used to analyze shopping behavior. Analyzing information generated by these nontraditional sources is more complicated in part because of the processing required to transform the data into a numerical form that can be analyzed.

Veracity

Veracity has to do with how much uncertainty is in the data. For example, the data could have many missing values, which makes reliable analysis a challenge. Inconsistencies in units of measure and the lack of reliability of responses in terms of bias also increase the complexity of the data.

Businesses have realized that understanding big data can lead to a competitive advantage. Although big data represents opportunities, it also presents challenges in terms of data storage and processing, security and available analytical talent.

The four Vs indicate that big data creates challenges in terms of how these complex data can be captured, stored, and processed; secured; and then analyzed. Traditional databases more or less assume that data fit into nice rows and columns, but that is not always the case with big data. Also, the sheer volume (the first V) often means that it is not possible to store all of the data on a single computer. This has led to new technologies like **Hadoop**—an open-source programming environment that supports big data processing through distributed storage and distributed processing on clusters of computers. Essentially, Hadoop provides a divide-and-conquer approach to handling massive amounts of data, dividing the storage and processing over multiple computers. **MapReduce** is a programming model used within Hadoop that performs the two major steps for which it is named: the map step and the reduce step. The map step divides the data into manageable subsets and distributes it to the computers in the cluster (often termed nodes) for storing and processing. The reduce step collects answers from the nodes and combines them into an answer to the original problem. Without technologies like Hadoop and MapReduce, and relatively inexpensive computer power, processing big data would not be cost-effective; in some cases, processing might not even be possible.

While some sources of big data are publicly available (Twitter, weather data, etc.), much of it is private information. Medical records, bank account information, and credit card transactions, for example, are all highly confidential and must be protected from computer hackers. **Data security**, the protection of stored data from destructive forces or unauthorized users, is of critical importance to companies. For example, credit card transactions are potentially very useful for understanding consumer behavior, but compromise of these data could lead to unauthorized use of the credit card or identity theft. Data security company Datacastle estimated that the average cost of a data breach for a company in 2012 was $7.2 million. Since 2014, companies such as Target, Anthem, JPMorgan Chase, and Home Depot have faced major data breaches costing millions of dollars.

The complexities of the 4 Vs have increased the demand for analysts, but a shortage of qualified analysts has made hiring more challenging. More companies are searching for **data scientists**, who know how to effectively process and analyze massive amounts of data because they are well trained in both computer science and statistics. Next we discuss three examples of how companies are collecting big data for competitive advantage.

Kroger Understands Its Customers[7]   Kroger is the largest retail grocery chain in the United States. It sends over 11 million pieces of direct mail to its customers each quarter. The quarterly mailers each contain 12 coupons that are tailored to each household based on several years of shopping data obtained through its customer loyalty card program. By collecting and analyzing consumer behavior at the individual household level and better matching its coupon offers to shopper interests, Kroger has been able to realize a far higher redemption rate on its coupons. In the six-week period following distribution of the mailers, over 70% of households redeem at least one coupon, leading to an estimated coupon revenue of $10 billion for Kroger.

MagicBand at Disney[8]   The Walt Disney Company has begun offering a wristband to visitors to its Orlando, Florida, Disney World theme park. Known as the Magic-Band, the wristband contains technology that can transmit more than 40 feet and can be used to track each visitor's location in the park in real time. The band can link to information that allows Disney to better serve its visitors. For example, prior to the trip to Disney World, a visitor might be asked to fill out a survey on his or her birth date and favorite rides, characters, and restaurant table type and location. This information, linked to the MagicBand, can allow Disney employees using smartphones to greet you by name as you arrive, offer you products they know you prefer, wish you a happy birthday, have your favorite characters show up as you wait in line or have lunch at your favorite table. The MagicBand can be linked to your credit card, so there is no need to carry cash or a credit card. And during your visit, your movement throughout the park can be tracked and the data can be analyzed to better serve you during your next visit to the park.

General Electric and the Internet of Things[9]   The **Internet of Things (IoT)** is the technology that allows data, collected from sensors in all types of machines, to be sent over the Internet to repositories where it can be stored and analyzed. This ability to collect data from products has enabled the companies that produce and sell those products to better serve their customers and offer new services based on analytics. For example, each day General Electric (GE) gathers nearly 50 million pieces of data from 10 million sensors on medical equipment and aircraft engines it has sold to customers throughout the world. In the case of aircraft engines, through a service agreement with its customers, GE collects data each time an airplane powered by its engines takes off and lands. By analyzing these data, GE can better predict when maintenance is needed, which helps customers to avoid unplanned maintenance and downtime and helps ensure safe operation. GE can also use the data to better control how the plane is flown, leading to a decrease in fuel cost by flying more efficiently. In 2014, GE realized approximately $1.1 billion in revenue from the IoT.

Although big data is clearly one of the drivers for the strong demand for analytics, it is important to understand that in some sense big data issues are a subset of analytics. Many very valuable applications of analytics do not involve big data, but rather traditional data sets that are very manageable by traditional database and analytics software. The key to analytics is that it provides useful insights and better decision making using the data that are available—whether those data are "big" or "small."

---

[7]Based on "Kroger Knows Your Shopping Patterns Better Than You Do," Forbes.com, October 23, 2013.
[8]Based on "Disney's $1 Billion Bet on a Magical Wristband," Wired.com, March 10, 2015.
[9]Based on "G.E. Opens Its Big Data Platform," NYTimes.com, October 9, 2014.

1.5 Business Analytics in Practice

Business analytics involves tools as simple as reports and graphs to those that are as sophisticated as optimization, data mining, and simulation. In practice, companies that apply analytics often follow a trajectory similar to that shown in Figure 1.3. Organizations start with basic analytics in the lower left. As they realize the advantages of these analytic techniques, they often progress to more sophisticated techniques in an effort to reap the derived competitive advantage. Therefore, predictive and prescriptive analytics are sometimes referred to as **advanced analytics**. Not all companies reach that level of usage, but those that embrace analytics as a competitive strategy often do.

Analytics has been applied in virtually all sectors of business and government. Organizations such as Procter & Gamble, IBM, UPS, Netflix, Amazon.com, Google, the Internal Revenue Service, and General Electric have embraced analytics to solve important problems or to achieve a competitive advantage. In this section, we briefly discuss some of the types of applications of analytics by application area.

Financial Analytics

Applications of analytics in finance are numerous and pervasive. Predictive models are used to forecast financial performance, to assess the risk of investment portfolios and projects, and to construct financial instruments such as derivatives. Prescriptive models are used to construct optimal portfolios of investments, to allocate assets, and to create optimal capital budgeting plans. For example, GE Asset Management uses optimization models to decide how to invest its own cash received from insurance policies and other financial products, as well as the cash of its clients, such as Genworth Financial. The estimated benefit from the optimization models was $75 million over a five-year period.[10] Simulation is also often used to assess risk in the financial sector; one example is the deployment by

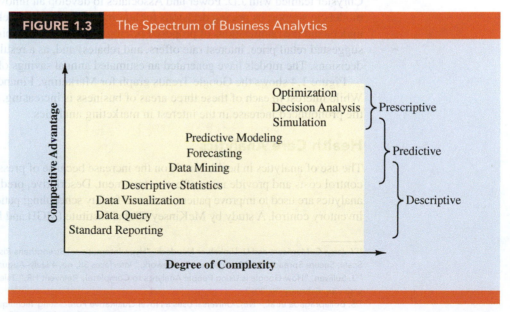

FIGURE 1.3   The Spectrum of Business Analytics

Source: *Adapted from SAS.*

---

[10]L. C. Chalermkraivuth et al., "GE Asset Management, Genworth Financial, and GE Insurance Use a Sequential-Linear Programming Algorithm to Optimize Portfolios," *Interfaces* 35, no. 5 (September–October 2005): 370–80.

Hypo Real Estate International of simulation models to successfully manage commercial real estate risk.[11]

Human Resource (HR) Analytics

A relatively new area of application for analytics is the management of an organization's human resources (HR). The HR function is charged with ensuring that the organization: (1) has the mix of skill sets necessary to meet its needs, (2) is hiring the highest-quality talent and providing an environment that retains it, and (3) achieves its organizational diversity goals. Google refers to its HR Analytics function as "people analytics." Google has analyzed substantial data on their own employees to determine the characteristics of great leaders, to assess factors that contribute to productivity, and to evaluate potential new hires. Google also uses predictive analytics to continually update their forecast of future employee turnover and retention.[12]

Marketing Analytics

Marketing is one of the fastest-growing areas for the application of analytics. A better understanding of consumer behavior through the use of scanner data and data generated from social media has led to an increased interest in marketing analytics. As a result, descriptive, predictive, and prescriptive analytics are all heavily used in marketing. A better understanding of consumer behavior through analytics leads to the better use of advertising budgets, more effective pricing strategies, improved forecasting of demand, improved product-line management, and increased customer satisfaction and loyalty. For example, each year, NBCUniversal uses a predictive model to help support its annual upfront market—a period in late May when each television network sells the majority of its on-air advertising for the upcoming television season. Over 200 NBC sales and finance personnel use the results of the forecasting model to support pricing and sales decisions.[13]

In another example of high-impact marketing analytics, automobile manufacturer Chrysler teamed with J.D. Power and Associates to develop an innovative set of predictive models to support its pricing decisions for automobiles. These models help Chrysler to better understand the ramifications of proposed pricing structures (a combination of manufacturer's suggested retail price, interest rate offers, and rebates) and, as a result, to improve its pricing decisions. The models have generated an estimated annual savings of $500 million.[14]

Figure 1.4 shows the Google Trends graph for Marketing, Financial, and HR Analytics. While interest in each of these three areas of business is increasing, the graph clearly shows the pronounced increase in the interest in marketing analytics.

Health Care Analytics

The use of analytics in health care is on the increase because of pressure to simultaneously control costs and provide more effective treatment. Descriptive, predictive, and prescriptive analytics are used to improve patient, staff, and facility scheduling; patient flow; purchasing; and inventory control. A study by McKinsey Global Institute (MGI) and McKinsey & Company[15]

---

[11]Y. Jafry, C. Marrison, and U. Umkehrer-Neudeck, "Hypo International Strengthens Risk Management with a Large-Scale, Secure Spreadsheet-Management Framework," *Interfaces* 38, no. 4 (July–August 2008): 281–88.

[12]J. Sullivan, "How Google Is Using People Analytics to Completely Reinvent HR," Talent Management and HR web site, February 26, 2013.

[13]S. Bollapragada et al., "NBC-Universal Uses a Novel Qualitative Forecasting Technique to Predict Advertising Demand," *Interfaces* 38, no. 2 (March–April 2008): 103–11.

[14]J. Silva-Risso et al., "Chrysler and J. D. Power: Pioneering Scientific Price Customization in the Automobile Industry," *Interfaces* 38, no. 1 (January–February 2008): 26–39.

[15]J. Manyika et al., "Big Data: The Next Frontier for Innovation, Competition and Productivity," McKinsey Global Institute Report, 2011.

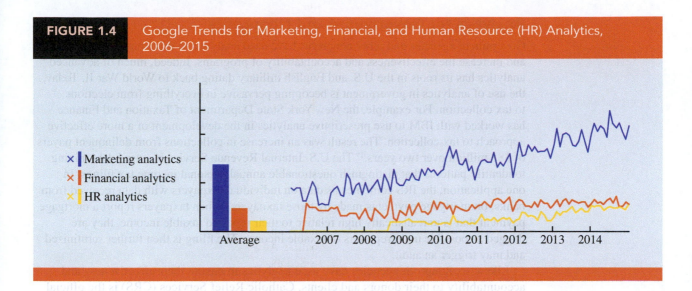

FIGURE 1.4 Google Trends for Marketing, Financial, and Human Resource (HR) Analytics, 2006–2015

estimates that the health care system in the United States could save more than $300 billion per year by better utilizing analytics; these savings are approximately the equivalent of the entire gross domestic product of countries such as Finland, Singapore, and Ireland.

The use of prescriptive analytics for diagnosis and treatment is relatively new, but it may prove to be the most important application of analytics in health care. For example, working with the Georgia Institute of Technology, Memorial Sloan-Kettering Cancer Center developed a real-time prescriptive model to determine the optimal placement of radioactive seeds for the treatment of prostate cancer.[16] Using the new model, 20–30% fewer seeds are needed, resulting in a faster and less invasive procedure.

Supply-Chain Analytics

One of the earliest applications of analytics was in logistics and supply-chain management. The core service of companies such as UPS and FedEx is the efficient delivery of goods, and analytics has long been used to achieve efficiency. The optimal sorting of goods, vehicle and staff scheduling, and vehicle routing are all key to profitability for logistics companies such as UPS and FedEx.

Companies can benefit from better inventory and processing control and more efficient supply chains. Analytic tools used in this area span the entire spectrum of analytics. For example, the women's apparel manufacturer Bernard Claus, Inc., has successfully used descriptive analytics to provide its managers a visual representation of the status of its supply chain.[17] ConAgra Foods uses predictive and prescriptive analytics to better plan capacity utilization by incorporating the inherent uncertainty in commodities pricing. ConAgra realized a 100% return on their investment in analytics in under three months—an unheard of result for a major technology investment.[18]

---

[16]E. Lee and M. Zaider, "Operations Research Advances Cancer Therapeutics," *Interfaces* 38, no. 1 (January–February 2008): 5–25.

[17]T. H. Davenport, ed., *Enterprise Analytics* (Upper Saddle River, NJ: Pearson Education Inc., 2013).

[18]"ConAgra Mills: Up-to-the-Minute Insights Drive Smarter Selling Decisions and Big Improvements in Capacity Utilization," IBM Smarter Planet Leadership Series. Available at: http://www.ibm.com/smarterplanet/us/en/leadership/conagra/, retrieved December 1, 2012.

Analytics for Government and Nonprofits

Government agencies and other nonprofits have used analytics to drive out inefficiencies and increase the effectiveness and accountability of programs. Indeed, much of advanced analytics has its roots in the U.S. and English military dating back to World War II. Today, the use of analytics in government is becoming pervasive in everything from elections to tax collection. For example, the New York State Department of Taxation and Finance has worked with IBM to use prescriptive analytics in the development of a more effective approach to tax collection. The result was an increase in collections from delinquent payers of $83 million over two years.[19] The U.S. Internal Revenue Service has used data mining to identify patterns that distinguish questionable annual personal income tax filings. In one application, the IRS combines its data on individual taxpayers with data received from banks, on mortgage payments made by those taxpayers. When taxpayers report a mortgage payment that is unrealistically high relative to their reported taxable income, they are flagged as possible underreporters of taxable income. The filing is then further scrutinized and may trigger an audit.

Likewise, nonprofit agencies have used analytics to ensure their effectiveness and accountability to their donors and clients. Catholic Relief Services (CRS) is the official international humanitarian agency of the U.S. Catholic community. The CRS mission is to provide relief for the victims of both natural and human-made disasters and to help people in need around the world through its health, educational, and agricultural programs. CRS uses an analytical spreadsheet model to assist in the allocation of its annual budget based on the impact that its various relief efforts and programs will have in different countries.[20]

Sports Analytics

The use of analytics in sports has gained considerable notoriety since 2003 when renowned author Michael Lewis published *Moneyball*. Lewis' book tells the story of how the Oakland Athletics used an analytical approach to player evaluation in order to assemble a competitive team with a limited budget. The use of analytics for player evaluation and on-field strategy is now common, especially in professional sports. Professional sports teams use analytics to assess players for the amateur drafts and to decide how much to offer players in contract negotiations;[21] professional motorcycle racing teams use sophisticated optimization for gearbox design to gain competitive advantage; [22] and teams use analytics to assist with on-field decisions such as which pitchers to use in various games of a Major League Baseball playoff series.

The use of analytics for off-the-field business decisions is also increasing rapidly. Ensuring customer satisfaction is important for any company, and fans are the customers of sports teams. The Cleveland Indians professional baseball team used a type of predictive modeling known as conjoint analysis to design its premium seating offerings at Progressive Field based on fan survey data. Using prescriptive analytics, franchises across several major sports dynamically adjust ticket prices throughout the season to reflect the relative attractiveness and potential demand for each game.

---

[19]G. Miller et al., "Tax Collection Optimization for New York State," *Interfaces* 42, no. 1 (January–February 2013): 74–84.

[20]I. Gamvros, R. Nidel, and S. Raghavan, "Investment Analysis and Budget Allocation at Catholic Relief Services," *Interfaces* 36. no. 5 (September–October 2006): 400–406.

[21]N. Streib, S. J. Young, and J. Sokol, "A Major League Baseball Team Uses Operations Research to Improve Draft Preparation," *Interfaces* 42, no. 2 (March–April 2012): 119–30.

[22]J. Amoros, L. F. Escudero, J. F. Monge, J. V. Segura, and O. Reinoso, "TEAM ASPAR Uses Binary Optimization to Obtain Optimal Gearbox Ratios in Motorcycle Racing," *Interfaces* 42, no. 2 (March–April 2012): 191–98.

Web Analytics

Web analytics is the analysis of online activity, which includes, but is not limited to, visits to web sites and social media sites such as Facebook and LinkedIn. Web analytics obviously has huge implications for promoting and selling products and services via the Internet. Leading companies apply descriptive and advanced analytics to data collected in online experiments to determine the best way to configure web sites, position ads, and utilize social networks for the promotion of products and services. Online experimentation involves exposing various subgroups to different versions of a web site and tracking the results. Because of the massive pool of Internet users, experiments can be conducted without risking the disruption of the overall business of the company. Such experiments are proving to be invaluable because they enable the company to use trial-and-error in determining statistically what makes a difference in their web site traffic and sales.

SUMMARY

This introductory chapter began with a discussion of decision making. Decision making can be defined as the following process: (1) identify and define the problem; (2) determine the criteria that will be used to evaluate alternative solutions; (3) determine the set of alternative solutions; (4) evaluate the alternatives; and (5) choose an alternative. Decisions may be strategic (high-level, concerned with the overall direction of the firm), tactical (midlevel, concerned with how to achieve the strategic goals of the firm), or operational (day-to-day decisions that must be made to run the company).

Uncertainty and an overwhelming number of alternatives are two key factors that make decision making difficult. Business analytics approaches can assist by identifying and mitigating uncertainty and by prescribing the best course of action from a very large number of alternatives. In short, business analytics can help us make better-informed decisions.

There are three categories of analytics: descriptive, predictive, and prescriptive. Descriptive analytics describes what has happened and includes tools such as reports, data visualization, data dashboards, descriptive statistics, and some data-mining techniques. Predictive analytics consists of techniques that use past data to predict future events and include regression, data mining, forecasting, and simulation. Prescriptive analytics uses data to determine a best course of action. This class of analytical techniques includes simulation, decision analysis, and optimization. Descriptive and predictive analytics can help us better understand the uncertainty and risk associated with our decision alternatives. Predictive and prescriptive analytics, also often referred to as advanced analytics, can help us make the best decision when facing a myriad of alternatives.

Big data is a set of data that is too large or too complex to be handled by standard data-processing techniques or typical desktop software. The increasing prevalence of big data is leading to an increase in the use of analytics. The Internet, retail scanners, and cell phones are making huge amounts of data available to companies, and these companies want to better understand these data. Business analytics is helping them understand these data and use them to make better decisions.

We concluded this chapter with a discussion of various application areas of analytics. Our discussion focused on financial analytics, human resource analytics, marketing analytics, health care analytics, supply-chain analytics, analytics for government and nonprofit organizations, sports analytics, and web analytics. However, the use of analytics is rapidly spreading to other sectors, industries, and functional areas of organizations. Each remaining chapter in this text will provide a real-world vignette in which business analytics is applied to a problem faced by a real organization.

GLOSSARY

Advanced analytics Predictive and prescriptive analytics.

Big data Any set of data that is too large or too complex to be handled by standard data-processing technics and typical desktop software.

Business analytics The scientific process of transforming data into insight for making better decisions.

Data dashboard A collection of tables, charts, and maps to help management monitor selected aspects of the company's performance.

Data mining The use of analytical techniques for better understanding patterns and relationships that exist in large data sets.

Data query A request for information with certain characteristics from a database.

Data scientists Analysts trained in both computer science and statistics who know how to effectively process and analyze massive amounts of data.

Data security Protecting stored data from destructive forces or unauthorized users.

Decision analysis A technique used to develop an optimal strategy when a decision maker is faced with several decision alternatives and an uncertain set of future events.

Descriptive analytics Analytical tools that describe what has happened.

Hadoop An open-source programming environment that supports big data processing through distributed storage and distributed processing on clusters of computers.

Internet of Things (IoT) The technology that allows data collected from sensors in all types of machines to be sent over the Internet to repositories where it can be stored and analyzed.

MapReduce Programming model used within Hadoop that performs the two major steps for which it is named: the map step and the reduce step. The map step divides the data into manageable subsets and distributes it to the computers in the cluster for storing and processing. The reduce step collects answers from the nodes and combines them into an answer to the original problem.

Operational decision A decision concerned with how the organization is run from day to day.

Optimization model A mathematical model that gives the best decision, subject to the situation's constraints.

Predictive analytics Techniques that use models constructed from past data to predict the future or to ascertain the impact of one variable on another.

Prescriptive analytics Techniques that analyze input data and yield a best course of action.

Simulation The use of probability and statistics to construct a computer model to study the impact of uncertainty on the decision at hand.

Simulation optimization The use of probability and statistics to model uncertainty, combined with optimization techniques, to find good decisions in highly complex and highly uncertain settings.

Strategic decision A decision that involves higher-level issues and that is concerned with the overall direction of the organization, defining the overall goals and aspirations for the organization's future.

Tactical decision A decision concerned with how the organization should achieve the goals and objectives set by its strategy.

Utility theory The study of the total worth or relative desirability of a particular outcome that reflects the decision maker's attitude toward a collection of factors such as profit, loss, and risk.

Chapter 2

Descriptive Statistics

CONTENTS

U.S. Census Bureau

The Bureau of the Census is part of the U.S. Department of Commerce and is more commonly known as the U.S. Census Bureau. The U.S. Census Bureau collects data related to the population and economy of the United States using a variety of methods and for many purposes. These data are essential to many government and business decisions.

Probably the best-known data collected by the U.S. Census Bureau is the decennial census, which is an effort to count the total U.S. population. Collecting these data is a huge undertaking involving mailings, door-to-door visits, and other methods. The decennial census collects categorical data such as the sex and race of the respondents, as well as quantitative data such as the number of people living in the household. The data collected in the decennial census are used to determine the number of representatives assigned to each state, the number of Electoral College votes apportioned to each state, and how federal government funding is divided among communities.

The U.S. Census Bureau also administers the Current Population Survey (CPS). The CPS is a cross-sectional monthly survey of a sample of 60,000 households used to estimate employment and unemployment rates in different geographic areas. The CPS has been administered since 1940, so an extensive time series of employment and unemployment data now exists. These data drive government policies such as job assistance programs. The estimated unemployment rates are watched closely as an overall indicator of the health of the U.S. economy.

The data collected by the U.S. Census Bureau are also very useful to businesses. Retailers use data on population changes in different areas to plan new store openings. Mail-order catalog companies use the demographic data when designing targeted marketing campaigns. In many cases, businesses combine the data collected by the U.S. Census Bureau with their own data on customer behavior to plan strategies and to identify potential customers. The U.S. Census Bureau is one of the most important providers of data used in business analytics.

In this chapter, we first explain the need to collect and analyze data and identify some common sources of data. Then we discuss the types of data that you may encounter in practice and present several numerical measures for summarizing data. We cover some common ways of manipulating and summarizing data using spreadsheets. We then develop numerical summary measures for data sets consisting of a single variable. When a data set contains more than one variable, the same numerical measures can be computed separately for each variable. In the two-variable case, we also develop measures of the relationship between the variables.

2.1 Overview of Using Data: Definitions and Goals

Data are the facts and figures collected, analyzed, and summarized for presentation and interpretation. Table 2.1 shows a data set containing 2013 information for stocks in the Dow Jones Industrial Index (or simply "the Dow"). The Dow is tracked by many financial advisors and investors as an indication of the state of the overall financial markets and the economy in the United States. The share prices for the 30 companies listed in Table 2.1 are the basis for computing the Dow Jones Industrial Average (DJI), which is tracked continuously by virtually every financial publication.

A characteristic or a quantity of interest that can take on different values is known as a **variable**; for the data in Table 2.1, the variables are Symbol, Industry, Share Price, and Volume. An **observation** is a set of values corresponding to a set of variables; each row in Table 2.1 corresponds to an observation.

Practically every problem (and opportunity) that an organization (or individual) faces is concerned with the impact of the possible values of relevant variables on the business outcome. Thus, we are concerned with how the value of a variable can vary; **variation** is the difference in a variable measured over observations (time, customers, items, etc.).

TABLE 2.1	Data for Dow Jones Industrial Index Companies			
Company	Symbol	Industry	Share Price ($)	Volume
Apple	AAPL	Technology	124.50	42,162,332
American Express	AXP	Financial	75.90	8,639,908
Boeing	BA	Manufacturing	144.06	2,454,976
Caterpillar	CAT	Manufacturing	76.10	9,175,903
Cisco Systems	CSCO	Technology	28.40	39,471,714
Chevron Corporation	CVX	Chemical, Oil, and Gas	90.60	11,158,429
DuPont	DD	Chemical, Oil, and Gas	56.94	5,352,510
Walt Disney	DIS	Entertainment	118.91	4,320,854
General Electric	GE	Conglomerate	25.75	31,124,222
Goldman Sachs	GS	Financial	207.35	2,453,880
The Home Depot	HD	Retail	113.59	4,427,770
IBM	IBM	Technology	159.75	3,778,186
Intel	INTC	Technology	28.06	31,621,031
Johnson & Johnson	JNJ	Pharmaceuticals	99.15	6,524,173
JPMorgan Chase	JPM	Banking	68.91	12,413,896
Coca-Cola	KO	Food and Drink	40.44	10,912,528
McDonald's	MCD	Food and Drink	96.10	5,554,624
3M	MMM	Conglomerate	149.33	3,433,648
Merck	MRK	Pharmaceuticals	57.41	7,847,073
Microsoft	MSFT	Technology	45.94	21,428,146
Nike	NKE	Consumer Goods	112.99	2,983,621
Pfizer	PFE	Pharmaceuticals	34.26	21,428,146
Procter & Gamble	PG	Consumer Goods	80.29	5,660,786
Travelers	TRV	Insurance	105.27	1,604,998
UnitedHealth Group	UNH	Healthcare	117.94	3,840,567
United Technologies	UTX	Conglomerate	99.31	6,588,011
Visa	V	Financial	74.80	21,196,114
Verizon	VZ	Telecommunications	46.04	19,528,682
Wal-Mart	WMT	Retail	71.58	5,951,117
ExxonMobil	XOM	Chemical, Oil, and Gas	79.94	14,888,464

The role of descriptive analytics is to collect and analyze data to gain a better understanding of variation and its impact on the business setting. The values of some variables are under direct control of the decision maker (these are often called decision variables, as discussed in Chapters 11, 12, and 13). The values of other variables may fluctuate with uncertainty because of factors outside the direct control of the decision maker. In general, a quantity whose values are not known with certainty is called a **random variable**, or **uncertain variable**. Random variables are discussed in greater detail in Chapters 5 and 14. When we collect data, we are gathering past observed values, or realizations of a variable. By collecting these past realizations of one or more variables, our goal is to learn more about the variation of a particular business situation.

2.2 Types of Data

Population and Sample Data

To ensure that the companies in the Dow form a representative sample, companies are periodically added and removed from the Dow. It is possible that the companies in the Dow today have changed from what is shown in Table 2.1.

Data can be categorized in several ways based on how they are collected and the type collected. In many cases, it is not feasible to collect data from the **population** of all elements of interest. In such instances, we collect data from a subset of the population known as a **sample**. For example, with the thousands of publicly traded companies in the United States, tracking and analyzing all of these stocks every day would be too time consuming and expensive. The Dow represents a sample of 30 stocks of large public companies based in the United States, and it is often interpreted to represent the larger population of all publicly traded companies. It is very important to collect sample data that are representative of the population data so that generalizations can be made from them. In most cases (although not true of the Dow), a representative sample can be gathered by **random sampling** from the population data. Dealing with populations and samples can introduce subtle differences in how we calculate and interpret summary statistics. In almost all practical applications of business analytics, we will be dealing with sample data.

Quantitative and Categorical Data

Data are considered **quantitative data** if numeric and arithmetic operations, such as addition, subtraction, multiplication, and division, can be performed on them. For instance, we can sum the values for Volume in the Dow data in Table 2.1 to calculate a total volume of all shares traded by companies included in the Dow. If arithmetic operations cannot be performed on the data, they are considered **categorical data**. We can summarize categorical data by counting the number of observations or computing the proportions of observations in each category. For instance, the data in the Industry column in Table 2.1 are categorical. We can count the number of companies in the Dow that are in the telecommunications industry. Table 2.1 shows three companies in the financial industry industry: American Express, Goldman Sachs, and Visa. We cannot perform arithmetic operations on the data in the Industry column.

Cross-Sectional and Time Series Data

For statistical analysis, it is important to distinguish between cross-sectional data and time series data. **Cross-sectional data** are collected from several entities at the same, or approximately the same, point in time. The data in Table 2.1 are cross-sectional because they describe the 30 companies that comprise the Dow at the same point in time (July 2015). **Time series data** are collected over several time periods. Graphs of time series data are frequently found in business and economic publications. Such graphs help analysts understand what happened in the past, identify trends over time, and project future levels for the time series. For example, the graph of the time series in Figure 2.1 shows the DJI value from January 2005 to June 2015. The figure illustrates that the DJI was between 10,000 and 11,000 in 2005 and climbed to above 14,000 in 2007. However, the financial crisis in 2008 led to a significant decline in the DJI to between 6,000 and 7,000 by 2009. Since 2009, the DJI has been generally increasing and topped 18,000 in 2015.

Sources of Data

Data necessary to analyze a business problem or opportunity can often be obtained with an appropriate study; such statistical studies can be classified as either experimental or observational. In an *experimental study*, a variable of interest is first identified. Then one or more other variables are identified and controlled or manipulated to obtain data about how these variables influence the variable of interest. For example, if a pharmaceutical firm conducts an experiment to learn about how a new drug affects blood pressure, then blood pressure is the variable of interest. The dosage level of the new drug is another variable

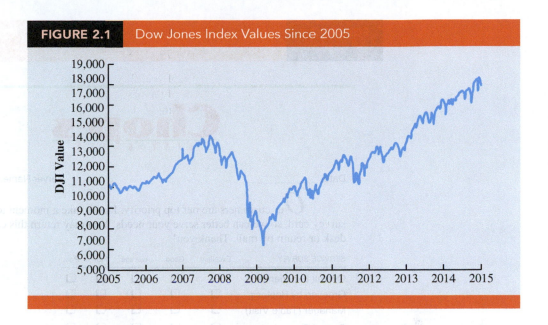

FIGURE 2.1   Dow Jones Index Values Since 2005

that is hoped to have a causal effect on blood pressure. To obtain data about the effect of the new drug, researchers select a sample of individuals. The dosage level of the new drug is controlled by giving different dosages to the different groups of individuals. Before and after the study, data on blood pressure are collected for each group. Statistical analysis of these experimental data can help determine how the new drug affects blood pressure.

Nonexperimental, or *observational*, *studies* make no attempt to control the variables of interest. A survey is perhaps the most common type of observational study. For instance, in a personal interview survey, research questions are first identified. Then a questionnaire is designed and administered to a sample of individuals. Some restaurants use observational studies to obtain data about customer opinions with regard to the quality of food, quality of service, atmosphere, and so on. A customer opinion questionnaire used by Chops City Grill in Naples, Florida, is shown in Figure 2.2. Note that the customers who fill out the questionnaire are asked to provide ratings for 12 variables, including overall experience, the greeting by hostess, the table visit by the manager, overall service, and so on. The response categories of excellent, good, average, fair, and poor provide categorical data that enable Chops City Grill management to maintain high standards for the restaurant's food and service.

In some cases, the data needed for a particular application exist from an experimental or observational study that has already been conducted. For example, companies maintain a variety of databases about their employees, customers, and business operations. Data on employee salaries, ages, and years of experience can usually be obtained from internal personnel records. Other internal records contain data on sales, advertising expenditures, distribution costs, inventory levels, and production quantities. Most companies also maintain detailed data about their customers.

Anyone who wants to use data and statistical analysis to aid in decision making must be aware of the time and cost required to obtain the data. The use of existing data sources is desirable when data must be obtained in a relatively short period of time. If important data are not readily available from a reliable existing source, the additional time and cost involved in obtaining the data must be taken into account. In all cases, the decision maker should consider the potential contribution of the statistical analysis to the decision-making process. In Chapter 15 we discuss methods for determining the value of additional information that can be provided by collecting data. The cost of data acquisition and the subsequent statistical analysis should not exceed the savings generated by using the information to make a better decision.

FIGURE 2.2 Customer Opinion Questionnaire Used by Chops City Grill Restaurant

Chops CITY GRILL

Date: ____________ Server Name: ____________

*O*ur customers are our top priority. Please take a moment to fill out our survey card, so we can better serve your needs. You may return this card to the front desk or return by mail. Thank you!

SERVICE SURVEY	Excellent	Good	Average	Fair	Poor
Overall Experience	❑	❑	❑	❑	❑
Greeting by Hostess	❑	❑	❑	❑	❑
Manager (Table Visit)	❑	❑	❑	❑	❑
Overall Service	❑	❑	❑	❑	❑
Professionalism	❑	❑	❑	❑	❑
Menu Knowledge	❑	❑	❑	❑	❑
Friendliness	❑	❑	❑	❑	❑
Wine Selection	❑	❑	❑	❑	❑
Menu Selection	❑	❑	❑	❑	❑
Food Quality	❑	❑	❑	❑	❑
Food Presentation	❑	❑	❑	❑	❑
Value for $ Spent	❑	❑	❑	❑	❑

What comments could you give us to improve our restaurant?

____

____

Thank you, we appreciate your comments. —The staff of Chops City Grill.

NOTES + COMMENTS

1. Organizations that specialize in collecting and maintaining data make available substantial amounts of business and economic data. Companies can access these external data sources through leasing arrangements or by purchase. Dun & Bradstreet, Bloomberg, and Dow Jones & Company are three firms that provide extensive business database services to clients. Nielsen and Ipsos are two companies that have built successful businesses collecting and processing data that they sell to advertisers and product manufacturers. Data are also available from a variety of industry associations and special-interest organizations.

2. Government agencies are another important source of existing data. For instance, the web site data.gov was launched by the U.S. government in 2009 to make it easier for the public to access data collected by the U.S. federal government. The data.gov web site includes hundreds of thousands of data sets from a variety of U.S. federal departments and agencies. In general, the Internet is an important source of data and statistical information. One can obtain access to stock quotes, meal prices at restaurants, salary data, and a wide array of other information simply by performing an Internet search.

2.3 Modifying Data in Excel

Projects often involve so much data that it is difficult to analyze all of the data at once. In this section, we examine methods for summarizing and manipulating data using Excel to make the data more manageable and to develop insights.

Sorting and Filtering Data in Excel

Excel contains many useful features for sorting and filtering data so that one can more easily identify patterns. Table 2.2 contains data on the 20 top-selling automobiles in the United States in March 2011. The table shows the model and manufacturer of each automobile as well as the sales for the model in March 2011 and March 2010.

Figure 2.3 shows the data from Table 2.2 entered into an Excel spreadsheet, and the percent change in sales for each model from March 2010 to March 2011 has been calculated. This is done by entering the formula =(D2-E2)/E2 in cell F2 and then copying the contents of this cell to cells F3 to F20. (We cannot calculate the percent change in sales for the Ford Fiesta because it was not being sold in March 2010.)

Suppose that we want to sort these automobiles by March 2010 sales instead of by March 2011 sales. To do this, we use Excel's Sort function, as shown in the following steps.

Step 1. Select cells A1:F21
Step 2. Click the **Data** tab in the Ribbon

DATA *file*
Top20Cars

TABLE 2.2	20 Top-Selling Automobiles in United States in March 2011			
Rank (by March 2011 Sales)	Manufacturer	Model	Sales (March 2011)	Sales (March 2010)
1	Honda	Accord	33,616	29,120
2	Nissan	Altima	32,289	24,649
3	Toyota	Camry	31,464	36,251
4	Honda	Civic	31,213	22,463
5	Toyota	Corolla/Matrix	30,234	29,623
6	Ford	Fusion	27,566	22,773
7	Hyundai	Sonata	22,894	18,935
8	Hyundai	Elantra	19,255	8,225
9	Toyota	Prius	18,605	11,786
10	Chevrolet	Cruze/Cobalt	18,101	10,316
11	Chevrolet	Impala	18,063	15,594
12	Nissan	Sentra	17,851	8,721
13	Ford	Focus	17,178	19,500
14	Volkswagon	Jetta	16,969	9,196
15	Chevrolet	Malibu	15,551	17,750
16	Mazda	3	12,467	11,353
17	Nissan	Versa	11,075	13,811
18	Subaru	Outback	10,498	7,619
19	Kia	Soul	10,028	5,106
20	Ford	Fiesta	9,787	0

Source: *Manufacturers and Automotive News Data Center*

FIGURE 2.3   Data for 20 Top-Selling Automobiles Entered into Excel with Percent Change in Sales from 2010

DATA *file*

Top20CarsPercent

	A	B	C	D	E	F
1	Rank (by March 2011 Sales)	Manufacturer	Model	Sales (March 2011)	Sales (March 2010)	Percent Change in Sales from 2010
2	1	Honda	Accord	33616	29120	15.4%
3	2	Nissan	Altima	32289	24649	31.0%
4	3	Toyota	Camry	31464	36251	−13.2%
5	4	Honda	Civic	31213	22463	39.0%
6	5	Toyota	Corolla/Matrix	30234	29623	2.1%
7	6	Ford	Fusion	27566	22773	21.0%
8	7	Hyundai	Sonata	22894	18935	20.9%
9	8	Hyundai	Elantra	19255	8225	134.1%
10	9	Toyota	Prius	18605	11786	57.9%
11	10	Chevrolet	Cruze/Cobalt	18101	10316	75.5%
12	11	Chevrolet	Impala	18063	15594	15.8%
13	12	Nissan	Sentra	17851	8721	104.7%
14	13	Ford	Focus	17178	19500	−11.9%
15	14	Volkswagon	Jetta	16969	9196	84.5%
16	15	Chevrolet	Malibu	15551	17750	−12.4%
17	16	Mazda	3	12467	11353	9.8%
18	17	Nissan	Versa	11075	13811	−19.8%
19	18	Subaru	Outback	10498	7619	37.8%
20	19	Kia	Soul	10028	5106	96.4%
21	20	Ford	Fiesta	9787	0	-----

Step 3. Click **Sort** in the **Sort & Filter** group

Step 4. Select the check box for **My data has headers**

Step 5. In the first **Sort by** dropdown menu, select **Sales (March 2010)**

Step 6. In the **Order** dropdown menu, select **Largest to Smallest** (see Figure 2.4)

Step 7. Click **OK**

The result of using Excel's Sort function for the March 2010 data is shown in Figure 2.5. Now we can easily see that, although the Honda Accord was the best-selling automobile in March 2011, both the Toyota Camry and the Toyota Corolla/Matrix outsold the Honda Accord in March 2010. Note that while we sorted on Sales (March 2010), which is in column E, the data in all other columns are adjusted accordingly.

Now let's suppose that we are interested only in seeing the sales of models made by Toyota. We can do this using Excel's Filter function:

Step 1. Select cells A1:F21

Step 2. Click the **Data** tab in the Ribbon

Step 3. Click **Filter** in the **Sort & Filter** group

Step 4. Click on the **Filter Arrow** ▾ in column B, next to **Manufacturer**

Step 5. If all choices are checked, you can easily deselect all choices by unchecking (**Select All**). Then select only the check box for **Toyota**.

Step 6. Click **OK**

FIGURE 2.4 Using Excel's Sort Function to Sort the Top-Selling Automobiles Data

	A	B	C	D	E	F	G
1	Rank (by March 2011 Sales)	Manufacturer	Model	Sales (March 2011)	Sales (March 2010)	Percent Change in Sales from 2010	
2	1	Honda	Accord	33616	29120	15.4%	
3	2	Nissan	Altima	32289	24649	31.0%	
4	3	Toyota	Camry	31464	36251	−13.2%	
5	4	Honda	Civic	31213	22463	39.0%	
6	5	Toyota	Corolla/Matrix	30234	29623	2.1%	
7	6	Ford					
8	7	Hyundai					
9	8	Hyundai					
10	9	Toyota					
11	10	Chevrolet					
12	11	Chevrolet					
13	12	Nissan					
14	13	Ford					
15	14	Volkswagon					
16	15	Chevrolet					
17	16	Mazda					
18	17	Nissan					
19	18	Subaru	Outback	10498	7619	37.8%	
20	19	Kia	Soul	10028	5106	96.4%	
21	20	Ford	Fiesta	9787	0	-----	

Sort dialog box:
Add Level | Delete Level | Copy Level | ▲ ▼ | Options... | ☑ My data has headers
Column — Sort by: Sales (March 2010) | Sort On: Values | Order: Largest to Smallest
OK | Cancel

The result is a display of only the data for models made by Toyota (see Figure 2.6). We now see that of the 20 top-selling models in March 2011, Toyota made three of them. We can further filter the data by choosing the down arrows in the other columns. We can make all data visible again by clicking on the down arrow in column B and checking (**Select All**) and clicking **OK**, or by clicking **Filter** in the **Sort & Filter** Group again from the **Data** tab.

Conditional Formatting of Data in Excel

Conditional formatting in Excel can make it easy to identify data that satisfy certain conditions in a data set. For instance, suppose that we wanted to quickly identify the automobile models in Table 2.2 for which sales had decreased from March 2010 to March 2011. We can quickly highlight these models:

Step 1. Starting with the original data shown in Figure 2.3, select cells F1:F21
Step 2. Click the **Home** tab in the Ribbon
Step 3. Click **Conditional Formatting** in the **Styles** group
Step 4. Select **Highlight Cells Rules**, and click **Less Than** from the dropdown menu
Step 5. Enter *0%* in the **Format cells that are LESS THAN:** box
Step 6. Click **OK**

FIGURE 2.5	Top-Selling Automobiles Data Sorted by Sales in March 2010 Sales

	A	B	C	D	E	F
1	Rank (by March 2011 Sales)	Manufacturer	Model	Sales (March 2011)	Sales (March 2010)	Percent Change in Sales from 2010
2	3	Toyota	Camry	31464	36251	−13.2%
3	5	Toyota	Corolla/Matrix	30234	29623	2.1%
4	1	Honda	Accord	33616	29120	15.4%
5	2	Nissan	Altima	32289	24649	31.0%
6	6	Ford	Fusion	27566	22773	21.0%
7	4	Honda	Civic	31213	22463	39.0%
8	13	Ford	Focus	17178	19500	−11.9%
9	7	Hyundai	Sonata	22894	18935	20.9%
10	15	Chevrolet	Malibu	15551	17750	−12.4%
11	11	Chevrolet	Impala	18063	15594	15.8%
12	17	Nissan	Versa	11075	13811	−19.8%
13	9	Toyota	Prius	18605	11786	57.9%
14	16	Mazda	3	12467	11353	9.8%
15	10	Chevrolet	Cruze/Cobalt	18101	10316	75.5%
16	14	Volkswagon	Jetta	16969	9196	84.5%
17	12	Nissan	Sentra	17851	8721	104.7%
18	8	Hyundai	Elantra	19255	8225	134.1%
19	18	Subaru	Outback	10498	7619	37.8%
20	19	Kia	Soul	10028	5106	96.4%
21	20	Ford	Fiesta	9787	0	-----

FIGURE 2.6	Top-Selling Automobiles Data Filtered to Show Only Automobiles Manufactured by Toyota

	A	B	C	D	E	F
1	Rank (by March 2011 Sales) ▾	Manufacturer ⊤	Model ▾	Sales (March 2011) ▾	Sales (March 2010) ▾	Percent Change in Sales from 2010 ▾
2	3	Toyota	Camry	31464	36251	−13.2%
3	5	Toyota	Corolla/Matrix	30234	29623	2.1%
13	9	Toyota	Prius	18605	11786	57.9%

The results are shown in Figure 2.7. Here we see that the models with decreasing sales (Toyota Camry, Ford Focus, Chevrolet Malibu, and Nissan Versa) are now clearly visible. Note that Excel's Conditional Formatting function offers tremendous flexibility. Instead of highlighting only models with decreasing sales, we could instead choose **Data Bars**

FIGURE 2.7	Using Conditional Formatting in Excel to Highlight Automobiles with Declining Sales from March 2010

	A	B	C	D	E	F
1	Rank (by March 2011 Sales)	Manufacturer	Model	Sales (March 2011)	Sales (March 2010)	Percent Change in Sales from 2010
2	1	Honda	Accord	33616	29120	15.4%
3	2	Nissan	Altima	32289	24649	31.0%
4	3	Toyota	Camry	31464	36251	−13.2%
5	4	Honda	Civic	31213	22463	39.0%
6	5	Toyota	Corolla/Matrix	30234	29623	2.1%
7	6	Ford	Fusion	27566	22773	21.0%
8	7	Hyundai	Sonata	22894	18935	20.9%
9	8	Hyundai	Elantra	19255	8225	134.1%
10	9	Toyota	Prius	18605	11786	57.9%
11	10	Chevrolet	Cruze/Cobalt	18101	10316	75.5%
12	11	Chevrolet	Impala	18063	15594	15.8%
13	12	Nissan	Sentra	17851	8721	104.7%
14	13	Ford	Focus	17178	19500	−11.9%
15	14	Volkswagon	Jetta	16969	9196	84.5%
16	15	Chevrolet	Malibu	15551	17750	−12.4%
17	16	Mazda	3	12467	11353	9.8%
18	17	Nissan	Versa	11075	13811	−19.8%
19	18	Subaru	Outback	10498	7619	37.8%
20	19	Kia	Soul	10028	5106	96.4%
21	20	Ford	Fiesta	9787	0	-----

from the **Conditional Formatting** dropdown menu in the **Styles** Group of the **Home** tab in the Ribbon. The result of using the **Blue Data Bar Gradient Fill** option is shown in Figure 2.8. Data bars are essentially a bar chart input into the cells that shows the magnitude of the cell values. The widths of the bars in this display are comparable to the values of the variable for which the bars have been drawn; a value of 20 creates a bar twice as wide as that for a value of 10. Negative values are shown to the left side of the axis; positive values are shown to the right. Cells with negative values are shaded in red, and those with positive values are shaded in blue. Again, we can easily see which models had decreasing sales, but Data Bars also provide us with a visual representation of the magnitude of the change in sales. Many other Conditional Formatting options are available in Excel.

Bar charts and other graphical presentations will be covered in detail in Chapter 3. We will see other uses for Conditional Formatting in Excel in Chapter 3.

The **Quick Analysis** button is a feature available in Excel 2013 and Excel 2016. The button appears just outside the bottom-right corner of a group of selected cells whenever you select multiple cells. Clicking the **Quick Analysis** button gives you shortcuts for Conditional Formatting, adding Data Bars, and other operations. Clicking on this button gives you the options shown in Figure 2.9 for **Formatting**. Note that there are also tabs for **Charts**, **Totals**, **Tables**, and **Sparklines**. Many of these functions will be covered in Chapter 3.

FIGURE 2.8 Using Conditional Formatting in Excel to Generate Data Bars for the Top-Selling Automobiles Data

	A	B	C	D	E	F
1	Rank (by March 2011 Sales)	Manufacturer	Model	Sales (March 2011)	Sales (March 2010)	Percent Change in Sales from 2010
2	1	Honda	Accord	33616	29120	15.4%
3	2	Nissan	Altima	32289	24649	31.0%
4	3	Toyota	Camry	31464	36251	−13.2%
5	4	Honda	Civic	31213	22463	39.0%
6	5	Toyota	Corolla/Matrix	30234	29623	2.1%
7	6	Ford	Fusion	27566	22773	21.0%
8	7	Hyundai	Sonata	22894	18935	20.9%
9	8	Hyundai	Elantra	19255	8225	134.1%
10	9	Toyota	Prius	18605	11786	57.9%
11	10	Chevrolet	Cruze/Cobalt	18101	10316	75.5%
12	11	Chevrolet	Impala	18063	15594	15.8%
13	12	Nissan	Sentra	17851	8721	104.7%
14	13	Ford	Focus	17178	19500	−11.9%
15	14	Volkswagon	Jetta	16969	9196	84.5%
16	15	Chevrolet	Malibu	15551	17750	−12.4%
17	16	Mazda	3	12467	11353	9.8%
18	17	Nissan	Versa	11075	13811	−19.8%
19	18	Subaru	Outback	10498	7619	37.8%
20	19	Kia	Soul	10028	5106	96.4%
21	20	Ford	Fiesta	9787	0	-----

FIGURE 2.9 Excel Quick Analysis Button Formatting Options

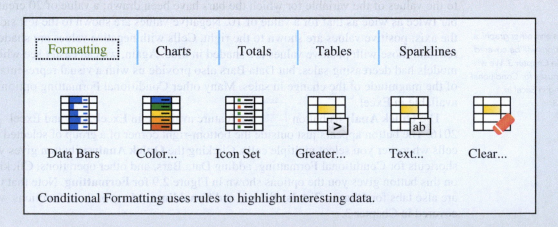

| Formatting | Charts | Totals | Tables | Sparklines |

Data Bars   Color...   Icon Set   Greater...   Text...   Clear...

Conditional Formatting uses rules to highlight interesting data.

2.4 Creating Distributions from Data

Distributions help summarize many characteristics of a data set by describing how often certain values for a variable appear in that data set. Distributions can be created for both categorical and quantitative data, and they assist the analyst in gauging variation.

Frequency Distributions for Categorical Data

Bins for categorical data are also referred to as classes.

It is often useful to create a frequency distribution for a data set. A **frequency distribution** is a summary of data that shows the number (frequency) of observations in each of several nonoverlapping classes, typically referred to as **bins**. Consider the data in Table 2.3, taken from a sample of 50 soft drink purchases. Each purchase is for one of five popular soft drinks, which define the five bins: Coca-Cola, Diet Coke, Dr. Pepper, Pepsi, and Sprite.

To develop a frequency distribution for these data, we count the number of times each soft drink appears in Table 2.3. Coca-Cola appears 19 times, Diet Coke appears 8 times, Dr. Pepper appears 5 times, Pepsi appears 13 times, and Sprite appears 5 times. These counts are summarized in the frequency distribution in Table 2.4. This frequency distribution provides a summary of how the 50 soft drink purchases are distributed across the 5 soft drinks. This summary offers more insight than the original data shown in Table 2.3. The frequency distribution shows that Coca-Cola is the leader, Pepsi is second, Diet Coke is third, and Sprite and Dr. Pepper are tied for fourth. The frequency distribution thus summarizes information about the popularity of the five soft drinks.

We can use Excel to calculate the frequency of categorical observations occurring in a data set using the COUNTIF function. Figure 2.10 shows the sample of 50 soft drink purchases in an Excel spreadsheet. Column D contains the five different soft drink categories as the bins. In cell E2, we enter the formula =COUNTIF($A$2:$B$26, D2), where A2:B26 is the range for the sample data, and D2 is the bin (Coca-Cola) that we are trying to match. The COUNTIF function in Excel counts the number of times a certain value appears in the indicated range. In this case we want to count the number of times

DATA *file*
SoftDrinks

TABLE 2.3	Data from a Sample of 50 Soft Drink Purchases	
Coca-Cola	Sprite	Pepsi
Diet Coke	Coca-Cola	Coca-Cola
Pepsi	Diet Coke	Coca-Cola
Diet Coke	Coca-Cola	Coca-Cola
Coca-Cola	Diet Coke	Coca-Cola
Coca-Cola	Coca-Cola	Pepsi
Dr. Pepper	Sprite	Dr. Pepper
Diet Coke	Pepsi	Coca-Cola
Pepsi	Coca-Cola	Diet Coke
Pepsi	Coca-Cola	Pepsi
Coca-Cola	Coca-Cola	Pepsi
Dr. Pepper	Pepsi	Pepsi
Sprite	Coca-Cola	Pepsi
Coca-Cola	Sprite	Coca-Cola
Diet Coke	Dr. Pepper	Dr. Pepper
Coca-Cola	Pepsi	Pepsi
Coca-Cola	Diet Coke	Sprite

TABLE 2.4	Frequency Distribution of Soft Drink Purchases
Soft Drink	**Frequency**
Coca-Cola	19
Diet Coke	8
Dr. Pepper	5
Pepsi	13
Sprite	5
Total	50

See Appendix A for more information on absolute versus relative references in Excel.

Coca-Cola appears in the sample data. The result is a value of 19 in cell E2, indicating that Coca-Cola appears 19 times in the sample data. We can copy the formula from cell E2 to cells E3 to E6 to get frequency counts for Diet Coke, Pepsi, Dr. Pepper, and Sprite. By using the absolute reference $A$2:$B$26 in our formula, Excel always searches the same sample data for the values we want when we copy the formula.

FIGURE 2.10	Creating a Frequency Distribution for Soft Drinks Data in Excel

	A	B	C	D	E
1	**Sample Data**			**Bins**	
2	Coca-Cola	Coca-Cola		**Coca-Cola**	19
3	Diet Coke	Sprite		**Diet Coke**	8
4	Pepsi	Pepsi		**Dr. Pepper**	5
5	Diet Coke	Coca-Cola		**Pepsi**	13
6	Coca-Cola	Pepsi		**Sprite**	5
7	Coca-Cola	Sprite			
8	Dr. Pepper	Dr. Pepper			
9	Diet Coke	Pepsi			
10	Pepsi	Diet Coke			
11	Pepsi	Pepsi			
12	Coca-Cola	Coca-Cola			
13	Dr. Pepper	Coca-Cola			
14	Sprite	Diet Coke			
15	Coca-Cola	Pepsi			
16	Diet Coke	Pepsi			
17	Coca-Cola	Pepsi			
18	Coca-Cola	Coca-Cola			
19	Diet Coke	Dr. Pepper			
20	Coca-Cola	Sprite			
21	Coca-Cola	Coca-Cola			
22	Coca-Cola	Coca-Cola			
23	Sprite	Pepsi			
24	Coca-Cola	Dr. Pepper			
25	Coca-Cola	Pepsi			
26	Diet Coke	Pepsi			

Relative Frequency and Percent Frequency Distributions

A frequency distribution shows the number (frequency) of items in each of several nonoverlapping bins. However, we are often interested in the proportion, or percentage, of items in each bin. The *relative frequency* of a bin equals the fraction or proportion of items belonging to a class. For a data set with n observations, the relative frequency of each bin can be determined as follows:

The percent frequency of a bin is the relative frequency multiplied by 100.

$$\text{Relative frequency of a bin} = \frac{\text{Frequency of the bin}}{n}$$

A **relative frequency distribution** is a tabular summary of data showing the relative frequency for each bin. A **percent frequency distribution** summarizes the percent frequency of the data for each bin. Table 2.5 shows a relative frequency distribution and a percent frequency distribution for the soft drink data. Using the data from Table 2.4, we see that the relative frequency for Coca-Cola is 19/50 = 0.38, the relative frequency for Diet Coke is 8/50 = 0.16, and so on. From the percent frequency distribution, we see that 38% of the purchases were Coca-Cola, 16% were Diet Coke, and so on. We can also note that 38% + 26% + 16% = 80% of the purchases were the top three soft drinks.

A percent frequency distribution can be used to provide estimates of the relative likelihoods of different values for a random variable. So, by constructing a percent frequency distribution from observations of a random variable, we can estimate the probability distribution that characterizes its variability. For example, the volume of soft drinks sold by a concession stand at an upcoming concert may not be known with certainty. However, if the data used to construct Table 2.5 are representative of the concession stand's customer population, then the concession stand manager can use this information to determine the appropriate volume of each type of soft drink.

Frequency Distributions for Quantitative Data

We can also create frequency distributions for quantitative data, but we must be more careful in defining the nonoverlapping bins to be used in the frequency distribution. For example, consider the quantitative data in Table 2.6. These data show the time in days required to complete year-end audits for a sample of 20 clients of Sanderson and Clifford, a small public accounting firm. The three steps necessary to define the classes for a frequency distribution with quantitative data are:

1. Determine the number of nonoverlapping bins.
2. Determine the width of each bin.
3. Determine the bin limits.

TABLE 2.5	Relative Frequency and Percent Frequency Distributions of Soft Drink Purchases	
Soft Drink	**Relative Frequency**	**Percent Frequency (%)**
Coca-Cola	0.38	38
Diet Coke	0.16	16
Dr. Pepper	0.10	10
Pepsi	0.26	26
Sprite	0.10	10
Total	1.00	100

TABLE 2.6	Year-End Audit Times (Days)		
12	14	19	18
15	15	18	17
20	27	22	23
22	21	33	28
14	18	16	13

DATA *file*
AuditData

Let us demonstrate these steps by developing a frequency distribution for the audit time data in shown Table 2.6.

Number of bins Bins are formed by specifying the ranges used to group the data. As a general guideline, we recommend using from 5 to 20 bins. For a small number of data items, as few as 5 or 6 bins may be used to summarize the data. For a larger number of data items, more bins are usually required. The goal is to use enough bins to show the variation in the data, but not so many that some contain only a few data items. Because the number of data items in Table 2.6 is relatively small ($n = 20$), we chose to develop a frequency distribution with 5 bins.

Width of the bins Second, choose a width for the bins. As a general guideline, we recommend that the width be the same for each bin. Thus the choices of the number of bins and the width of bins are not independent decisions. A larger number of bins means a smaller bin width and vice versa. To determine an approximate bin width, we begin by identifying the largest and smallest data values. Then, with the desired number of bins specified, we can use the following expression to determine the approximate bin width.

APPROXIMATE BIN WIDTH

$$\frac{\text{Largest data value} - \text{smallest data value}}{\text{Number of bins}} \qquad (2.1)$$

The approximate bin width given by equation (2.1) can be rounded to a more convenient value based on the preference of the person developing the frequency distribution. For example, an approximate bin width of 9.28 might be rounded to 10 simply because 10 is a more convenient bin width to use in presenting a frequency distribution.

For the data involving the year-end audit times, the largest data value is 33, and the smallest data value is 12. Because we decided to summarize the data with five classes, using equation (2.1) provides an approximate bin width of $(33 - 12)/5 = 4.2$. We therefore decided to round up and use a bin width of five days in the frequency distribution.

In practice, the number of bins and the appropriate class width are determined by trial and error. Once a possible number of bins is chosen, equation (2.1) is used to find the approximate class width. The process can be repeated for a different number of bins. Ultimately, the analyst judges the combination of the number of bins and bin width that provides the best frequency distribution for summarizing the data.

For the audit time data in Table 2.6, after deciding to use five bins, each with a width of five days, the next task is to specify the bin limits for each of the classes.

Bin limits Bin limits must be chosen so that each data item belongs to one and only one class. The lower bin limit identifies the smallest possible data value assigned to the bin. The upper bin limit identifies the largest possible data value assigned to the class. In developing

TABLE 2.7	Frequency, Relative Frequency, and Percent Frequency Distributions for the Audit Time Data		
Audit Times (days)	**Frequency**	**Relative Frequency**	**Percent Frequency**
10–14	4	0.20	20
15–19	8	0.40	40
20–24	5	0.25	25
25–29	2	0.10	10
30–34	1	0.05	5

DATA *file*
AuditData

Although an audit time of 12 days is actually the smallest observation in our data, we have chosen a lower bin limit of 10 simply for convenience. The lowest bin limit should include the smallest observation, and the highest bin limit should include the largest observation.

frequency distributions for qualitative data, we did not need to specify bin limits because each data item naturally fell into a separate bin. But with quantitative data, such as the audit times in Table 2.6, bin limits are necessary to determine where each data value belongs.

Using the audit time data in Table 2.6, we selected 10 days as the lower bin limit and 14 days as the upper bin limit for the first class. This bin is denoted 10–14 in Table 2.7. The smallest data value, 12, is included in the 10–14 bin. We then selected 15 days as the lower bin limit and 19 days as the upper bin limit of the next class. We continued defining the lower and upper bin limits to obtain a total of five classes: 10–14, 15–19, 20–24, 25–29, and 30–34. The largest data value, 33, is included in the 30–34 bin. The difference between the upper bin limits of adjacent bins is the bin width. Using the first two upper bin limits of 14 and 19, we see that the bin width is $19 - 14 = 5$.

With the number of bins, bin width, and bin limits determined, a frequency distribution can be obtained by counting the number of data values belonging to each bin. For example, the data in Table 2.6 show that four values—12, 14, 14, and 13—belong to the 10–14 bin. Thus, the frequency for the 10–14 bin is 4. Continuing this counting process for the 15–19, 20–24, 25–29, and 30–34 bins provides the frequency distribution shown in Table 2.7. Using this frequency distribution, we can observe that:

- The most frequently occurring audit times are in the bin of 15–19 days. Eight of the 20 audit times are in this bin.
- Only one audit required 30 or more days.

Other conclusions are possible, depending on the interests of the person viewing the frequency distribution. The value of a frequency distribution is that it provides insights about the data that are not easily obtained by viewing the data in their original unorganized form. Table 2.7 also shows the relative frequency distribution and percent frequency distribution for the audit time data. Note that 0.40 of the audits, or 40 percent, required from 15 to 19 days. Only 0.05 of the audits, or 5 percent, required 30 or more days. Again, additional interpretations and insights can be obtained by using Table 2.7.

We define the relative frequency and percent frequency distributions for quantitative data in the same manner as for qualitative data.

Frequency distributions for quantitative data can also be created using Excel. Figure 2.11 shows the data from Table 2.6 entered into an Excel Worksheet. The sample of 20 audit times is contained in cells A2:D6. The upper limits of the defined bins are in cells A10:A14. We can use the FREQUENCY function in Excel to count the number of observations in each bin.

Pressing CTRL+SHIFT+ENTER in Excel indicates that the function should return an array of values.

Step 1. Select cells B10:B14
Step 2. Type the formula =FREQUENCY(A2:D6, A10:A14). The range A2:D6 defines the data set, and the range A10:A14 defines the bins.
Step 3. Press **CTRL+SHIFT+ENTER** after typing the formula in Step 2.

◢	A	B	C	D
1	**Year-End Audit Times (in Days)**			
2	12	14	19	18
3	15	15	18	17
4	20	27	22	23
5	22	21	33	28
6	14	18	16	13
7				
8				
9	**Bin**	**Frequency**		
10	14	=FREQUENCY(A2:D6,A10:A14)		
11	19	=FREQUENCY(A2:D6,A10:A14)		
12	24	=FREQUENCY(A2:D6,A10:A14)		
13	29	=FREQUENCY(A2:D6,A10:A14)		
14	34	=FREQUENCY(A2:D6,A10:A14)		

◢	A	B	C	D
1	**Year-End Audit Times (in Days)**			
2	12	14	19	18
3	15	15	18	17
4	20	27	22	23
5	22	21	33	28
6	14	18	16	13
7				
8				
9	**Bin**	**Frequency**		
10	14	4		
11	19	8		
12	24	5		
13	29	2		
14	34	1		

Because these were the cells selected in Step 1 above (see Figure 2.11), Excel will then fill in the values for the number of observations in each bin in cells B10 through B14.

Histograms

A common graphical presentation of quantitative data is a **histogram**. This graphical summary can be prepared for data previously summarized in either a frequency, a relative frequency, or a percent frequency distribution. A histogram is constructed by placing the variable of interest on the horizontal axis and the selected frequency measure (absolute frequency, relative frequency, or percent frequency) on the vertical axis. The frequency measure of each class is shown by drawing a rectangle whose base is the class limits on the horizontal axis and whose height is the corresponding frequency measure.

Figure 2.12 is a histogram for the audit time data. Note that the class with the greatest frequency is shown by the rectangle appearing above the class of 15–19 days. The height of the rectangle shows that the frequency of this class is 8. A histogram for the relative or percent frequency distribution of these data would look the same as the histogram in Figure 2.12, with the exception that the vertical axis would be labeled with relative or percent frequency values.

Histograms can be created in Excel using the Data Analysis ToolPak. We will use the sample of 20 year-end audit times and the bins defined in Table 2.7 to create a histogram using the Data Analysis ToolPak. As before, we begin with an Excel Worksheet in which

FIGURE 2.12   Histogram for the Audit Time Data

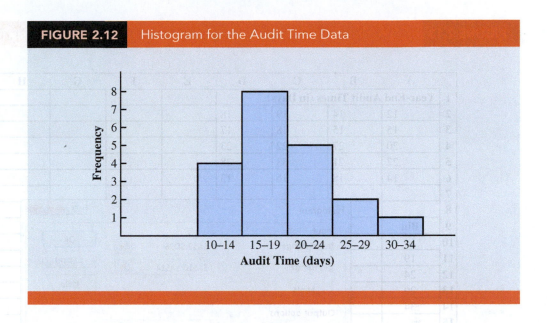

the sample of 20 audit times is contained in cells A2:D6, and the upper limits of the bins defined in Table 2.7 are in cells A10:A14 (see Figure 2.11).

The Data Analysis ToolPak can be found in the Analysis group in versions of Excel prior to Excel 2016.

Step 1. Click the **Data** tab in the Ribbon
Step 2. Click **Data Analysis** in the **Analyze** group
Step 3. When the **Data Analysis** dialog box opens, choose **Histogram** from the list of **Analysis Tools**, and click **OK**

In the **Input Range:** box, enter *A2:D6*
In the **Bin Range:** box, enter *A10:A14*
Under **Output Options:**, select **New Worksheet Ply:**
Select the check box for **Chart Output** (see Figure 2.13)
Click **OK**

The text "10-14" in cell A2 can be entered in Excel as '10-14. The single quote indicates to Excel that this should be treated as text rather than a numerical or date value.

The histogram created by Excel for these data is shown in Figure 2.14. We have modified the bin ranges in column A by typing the values shown in Figure 2.14 into cells A2:A6 so that the chart created by Excel shows both the lower and upper limits for each bin. We have also removed the gaps between the columns in the histogram in Excel to match the traditional format of histograms. To remove the gaps between the columns in the histogram created by Excel, follow these steps:

Step 1. Right-click on one of the columns in the histogram

Select **Format Data Series…**

Step 2. When the **Format Data Series** pane opens, click the **Series Options** button,

Set the **Gap Width** to 0%

One of the most important uses of a histogram is to provide information about the shape, or form, of a distribution. **Skewness**, or the lack of symmetry, is an important characteristic of the shape of a distribution. Figure 2.15 contains four histograms constructed from relative frequency distributions that exhibit different patterns of skewness. Panel A shows the histogram for a set of data moderately skewed to the left. A histogram is said to be skewed to the left if its tail extends farther to the left than to the

FIGURE 2.13   Creating a Histogram for the Audit Time Data Using Data Analysis ToolPak in Excel

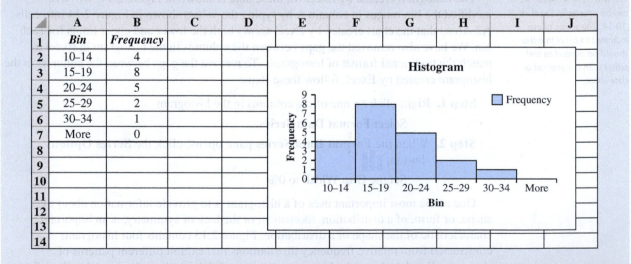

▲	A	B	C	D	E	F	G	H	I
1	**Year-End Audit Times (in Days)**								
2	12	14	19	18					
3	15	15	18	17					
4	20	27	22	23					
5	22	21	33	28					
6	14	18	16	13					
7									
8									
9	**Bin**								
10	14								
11	19								
12	24								
13	29								
14	34								
15									
16									
17									
18									
19									
20									
21									
22									

Histogram dialog box:

Input
Input Range: $A$2:$D$6
Bin Range: $A$10:$A$14
☐ Labels

Output options
○ Output Range:
◉ New Worksheet Ply:
○ New Workbook
☐ Pareto (sorted histogram)
☐ Cumulative Percentage
☑ Chart Output

OK   Cancel   Help

FIGURE 2.14   Completed Histogram for the Audit Time Data Using Data Analysis ToolPak in Excel

▲	A	B	C	D	E	F	G	H	I	J
1	*Bin*	*Frequency*								
2	10–14	4								
3	15–19	8								
4	20–24	5								
5	25–29	2								
6	30–34	1								
7	More	0								
8										
9										
10										
11										
12										
13										
14										

Histogram chart (within figure):

Histogram

☐ Frequency

Y-axis: Frequency (0–9)
X-axis: Bin (10–14, 15–19, 20–24, 25–29, 30–34, More)

FIGURE 2.15	Histograms Showing Distributions with Different Levels of Skewness

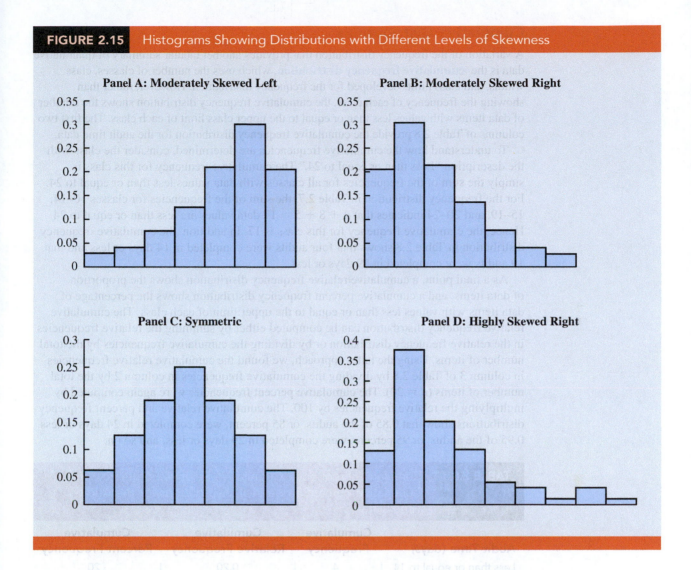

In Excel 2016, histograms can also be created using the new Histogram chart which can be found by clicking on the **Insert** tab in the Ribbon, clicking **Insert Statistic Chart** in the **Charts** group and selecting **Histogram**. Excel automatically chooses the number of bins and bin sizes, but this can be changed using **Format Axis**.

right. This histogram is typical for exam scores, with no scores above 100 percent, most of the scores above 70 percent, and only a few really low scores.

Panel B shows the histogram for a set of data moderately skewed to the right. A histogram is said to be skewed to the right if its tail extends farther to the right than to the left. An example of this type of histogram would be for data such as housing prices; a few expensive houses create the skewness in the right tail.

Panel C shows a symmetric histogram, in which the left tail mirrors the shape of the right tail. Histograms for data found in applications are never perfectly symmetric, but the histogram for many applications may be roughly symmetric. Data for SAT scores, the heights and weights of people, and so on lead to histograms that are roughly symmetric.

Panel D shows a histogram highly skewed to the right. This histogram was constructed from data on the amount of customer purchases in one day at a women's apparel store. Data from applications in business and economics often lead to histograms that are skewed to the right. For instance, data on housing prices, salaries, purchase amounts, and so on often result in histograms skewed to the right.

Cumulative Distributions

A variation of the frequency distribution that provides another tabular summary of quantitative data is the **cumulative frequency distribution**, which uses the number of classes, class widths, and class limits developed for the frequency distribution. However, rather than showing the frequency of each class, the cumulative frequency distribution shows the number of data items with values less than or equal to the upper class limit of each class. The first two columns of Table 2.8 provide the cumulative frequency distribution for the audit time data.

To understand how the cumulative frequencies are determined, consider the class with the description "Less than or equal to 24." The cumulative frequency for this class is simply the sum of the frequencies for all classes with data values less than or equal to 24. For the frequency distribution in Table 2.7, the sum of the frequencies for classes 10–14, 15–19, and 20–24 indicates that $4 + 8 + 5 = 17$ data values are less than or equal to 24. Hence, the cumulative frequency for this class is 17. In addition, the cumulative frequency distribution in Table 2.8 shows that four audits were completed in 14 days or less and that 19 audits were completed in 29 days or less.

As a final point, a cumulative relative frequency distribution shows the proportion of data items, and a cumulative percent frequency distribution shows the percentage of data items with values less than or equal to the upper limit of each class. The cumulative relative frequency distribution can be computed either by summing the relative frequencies in the relative frequency distribution or by dividing the cumulative frequencies by the total number of items. Using the latter approach, we found the cumulative relative frequencies in column 3 of Table 2.8 by dividing the cumulative frequencies in column 2 by the total number of items ($n = 20$). The cumulative percent frequencies were again computed by multiplying the relative frequencies by 100. The cumulative relative and percent frequency distributions show that 0.85 of the audits, or 85 percent, were completed in 24 days or less, 0.95 of the audits, or 95 percent, were completed in 29 days or less, and so on.

TABLE 2.8	Cumulative Frequency, Cumulative Relative Frequency, and Cumulative Percent Frequency Distributions for the Audit Time Data

Audit Time (days)	Cumulative Frequency	Cumulative Relative Frequency	Cumulative Percent Frequency
Less than or equal to 14	4	0.20	20
Less than or equal to 19	12	0.60	60
Less than or equal to 24	17	0.85	85
Less than or equal to 29	19	0.95	95
Less than or equal to 34	20	1.00	100

NOTES + COMMENTS

1. If Data Analysis does not appear in your Analyze group (or Analysis group in versions of Excel prior to Excel 2016), then you will have to include the Data Analysis ToolPak Add-In. To do so, click on the **File** tab and choose **Options**. When the **Excel Options** dialog box opens, click **Add-Ins**. At the bottom of the **Excel Options** dialog box, where it says **Manage: Excel Add-ins**, click **Go...**. Select the check box for **Analysis ToolPak**, and click **OK**.

2. Distributions are often used when discussing concepts related to probability and simulation because they are used to describe uncertainty. In Chapter 5 we will discuss probability distributions, and then in Chapter 14 we will revisit distributions when we introduce simulation models.

2.5 Measures of Location

Mean (Arithmetic Mean)

The most commonly used measure of location is the **mean (arithmetic mean)**, or average value, for a variable. The mean provides a measure of central location for the data. If the data are for a sample (typically the case), the mean is denoted by $\bar{x}$. The sample mean is a point estimate of the (typically unknown) population mean for the variable of interest. If the data for the entire population are available, the population mean is computed in the same manner, but denoted by the Greek letter μ.

In statistical formulas, it is customary to denote the value of variable x for the first observation by x_1, the value of variable x for the second observation by x_2, and so on. In general, the value of variable x for the ith observation is denoted by x_i. For a sample with n observations, the formula for the sample mean is as follows.

If the data set is not a sample, but is the entire population with N observations, the population mean is computed directly by: $\mu = \dfrac{\Sigma x_i}{N}$.

SAMPLE MEAN

$$\bar{x} = \frac{\Sigma x_i}{n} = \frac{x_1 + x_2 + \cdots + x_n}{n} \qquad (2.2)$$

To illustrate the computation of a sample mean, suppose a sample of home sales is taken for a suburb of Cincinnati, Ohio. Table 2.9 shows the collected data. The mean home selling price for the sample of 12 home sales is

$$\bar{x} = \frac{\Sigma x_i}{n} = \frac{x_1 + x_2 + \cdots + x_{12}}{12}$$
$$= \frac{138,000 + 254,000 + \cdots 456,250}{12}$$
$$= \frac{2,639,250}{12} = 219,937.50$$

The mean can be found in Excel using the AVERAGE function. Figure 2.16 shows the Home Sales data from Table 2.9 in an Excel spreadsheet. The value for the mean in cell E2 is calculated using the formula =AVERAGE(B2:B13).

TABLE 2.9	Data on Home Sales in a Cincinnati, Ohio, Suburb	
	Home Sale	**Selling Price ($)**
	1	138,000
	2	254,000
	3	186,000
	4	257,500
	5	108,000
	6	254,000
	7	138,000
	8	298,000
	9	199,500
	10	208,000
	11	142,000
	12	456,250

DATA *file*

HomeSales

FIGURE 2.16   Calculating the Mean, Median, and Modes for the Home Sales Data Using Excel

	A	B	C	D	E
1	Home Sale	Selling Price ($)			
2	1	138,000		Mean:	=AVERAGE(B2:B13)
3	2	254,000		Median:	=MEDIAN(B2:B13)
4	3	186,000		Mode 1:	=MODE.MULT(B2:B13)
5	4	257,500		Mode 2:	=MODE.MULT(B2:B13)
6	5	108,000			
7	6	254,000			
8	7	138,000			
9	8	298,000			
10	9	199,500			
11	10	208,000			
12	11	142,000			
13	12	456,250			

	A	B	C	D	E
1	Home Sale	Selling Price ($)			
2	1	138,000		Mean:	$ 219,937.50
3	2	254,000		Median:	$ 203,750.00
4	3	186,000		Mode 1:	$ 138,000.00
5	4	257,500		Mode 2:	$ 254,000.00
6	5	108,000			
7	6	254,000			
8	7	138,000			
9	8	298,000			
10	9	199,500			
11	10	208,000			
12	11	142,000			
13	12	456,250			

Median

The **median**, another measure of central location, is the value in the middle when the data are arranged in ascending order (smallest to largest value). With an odd number of observations, the median is the middle value. An even number of observations has no single middle value. In this case, we follow convention and define the median as the average of the values for the middle two observations.

Let us apply this definition to compute the median class size for a sample of five college classes. Arranging the data in ascending order provides the following list:

$$32 \quad 42 \quad 46 \quad 46 \quad 54$$

Because $n = 5$ is odd, the median is the middle value. Thus, the median class size is 46 students. Even though this data set contains two observations with values of 46, each observation is treated separately when we arrange the data in ascending order.

Suppose we also compute the median value for the 12 home sales in Table 2.9. We first arrange the data in ascending order.

108,000 138,000 138,000 142,000 186,000 199,500 208,000 254,000 254,000 257,500 298,000 456,250

Middle Two Values

Because $n = 12$ is even, the median is the average of the middle two values: 199,500 and 208,000.

$$\text{Median} = \frac{199{,}500 + 208{,}000}{2} = 203{,}750$$

The median of a data set can be found in Excel using the function MEDIAN. In Figure 2.16, the value for the median in cell E3 is found using the formula =MEDIAN(B2:B13).

Although the mean is the more commonly used measure of central location, in some situations the median is preferred. The mean is influenced by extremely small and large data values. Notice that the median is smaller than the mean in Figure 2.16. This is because the one large value of $456,250 in our data set inflates the mean but does not have the same effect on the median. Notice also that the median would remain unchanged if we replaced the $456,250 with a sales price of $1.5 million. In this case, the median selling price would remain $203,750, but the mean would increase to $306,916.67. If you were looking to buy a home in this suburb, the median gives a better indication of the central selling price of the homes there. We can generalize, saying that whenever a data set contains extreme values or is severely skewed, the median is often the preferred measure of central location.

Mode

A third measure of location, the **mode**, is the value that occurs most frequently in a data set. To illustrate the identification of the mode, consider the sample of five class sizes.

32   42   46   46   54

The only value that occurs more than once is 46. Because this value, occurring with a frequency of 2, has the greatest frequency, it is the mode. To find the mode for a data set with only one most often occurring value in Excel, we use the MODE.SNGL function.

Occasionally the greatest frequency occurs at two or more different values, in which case more than one mode exists. If data contain at least two modes, we say that they are *multimodal*. A special case of multimodal data occurs when the data contain exactly two modes; in such cases we say that the data are *bimodal*. In multimodal cases when there are more than two modes, the mode is almost never reported because listing three or more modes is not particularly helpful in describing a location for the data. Also, if no value in the data occurs more than once, we say the data have no mode.

The Excel MODE.SNGL function will return only a single most-often-occurring value. For multimodal distributions, we must use the MODE.MULT command in Excel to return more than one mode. For example, two selling prices occur twice in Table 2.9: $138,000 and $254,000. Hence, these data are bimodal. To find both of the modes in Excel, we take these steps:

We must press CTRL+SHIFT+ENTER because the MODE.MULT function returns an array of values.

Step 1. Select cells E4 and E5
Step 2. Type the formula =MODE.MULT(B2:B13)
Step 3. Press **CTRL+SHIFT+ENTER** after typing the formula in Step 2.

Excel enters the values for both modes of this data set in cells E4 and E5: $138,000 and $254,000.

Geometric Mean

The **geometric mean** is a measure of location that is calculated by finding the nth root of the product of n values. The general formula for the sample geometric mean, denoted $\bar{x}_g$, follows.

The geometric mean for a population is computed similarly but is defined as μ_g to denote that it is computed using the entire population.

SAMPLE GEOMETRIC MEAN

$$\bar{x}_g = \sqrt[n]{(x_1)(x_2)\cdots(x_n)} = [(x_1)(x_2)\cdots(x_n)]^{1/n} \qquad (2.3)$$

The geometric mean is often used in analyzing growth rates in financial data. In these types of situations, the arithmetic mean or average value will provide misleading results.

To illustrate the use of the geometric mean, consider Table 2.10, which shows the percentage annual returns, or growth rates, for a mutual fund over the past 10 years. Suppose we want to compute how much $100 invested in the fund at the beginning of year 1 would be worth at the end of year 10. We start by computing the balance in the fund at the end of year 1. Because the percentage annual return for year 1 was −22.1 percent, the balance in the fund at the end of year 1 would be:

$$\$100 - 0.221(\$100) = \$100(1 - 0.221) = \$100(0.779) = \$77.90$$

The growth factor for each year is 1 plus 0.01 times the percentage return. A growth factor less than 1 indicates negative growth, whereas a growth factor greater than 1 indicates positive growth. The growth factor cannot be less than zero.

We refer to 0.779 as the **growth factor** for year 1 in Table 2.10. We can compute the balance at the end of year 1 by multiplying the value invested in the fund at the beginning of year 1 by the growth factor for year 1: $100(0.779) = $77.90.

The balance in the fund at the end of year 1, $77.90, now becomes the beginning balance in year 2. So, with a percentage annual return for year 2 of 28.7 percent, the balance at the end of year 2 would be:

$$\$77.90 + 0.287(\$77.90) = \$77.90(1 + 0.287) = \$77.90(1.287) = \$100.26$$

Note that 1.287 is the growth factor for year 2. By substituting $100(0.779) for $77.90, we see that the balance in the fund at the end of year 2 is:

$$\$100(0.779)(1.287) = \$100.26$$

In other words, the balance at the end of year 2 is just the initial investment at the beginning of year 1 times the product of the first two growth factors. This result can be generalized to show that the balance at the end of year 10 is the initial investment times the product of all 10 growth factors.

$$\$100[(0.779)(1.287)(1.109)(1.049)(1.158)(1.055)(0.630)(1.265)(1.151)(1.021)]$$
$$= \$100(1.335) = \$133.45$$

TABLE 2.10	Percentage Annual Returns and Growth Factors for the Mutual Fund Data	
Year	**Return (%)**	**Growth Factor**
1	−22.1	0.779
2	28.7	1.287
3	10.9	1.109
4	4.9	1.049
5	15.8	1.158
6	5.5	1.055
7	−37.0	0.630
8	26.5	1.265
9	15.1	1.151
10	2.1	1.021

MutualFundsReturns

So a $100 investment in the fund at the beginning of year 1 would be worth $133.45 at the end of year 10. Note that the product of the ten growth factors is 1.335. Thus, we can compute the balance at the end of year 10 for any amount of money invested at the beginning of year 1 by multiplying the value of the initial investment by 1.335. For instance, an initial investment of $2,500 at the beginning of year 1 would be worth $2,500(1.335), or approximately $3,337.50, at the end of year 10.

What was the mean percentage annual return or mean rate of growth for this investment over the 10-year period? The geometric mean of the 10 growth factors can be used to answer this question. Because the product of the 10 growth factors is 1.335, the geometric mean is the 10th root of 1.335, or:

$$\bar{x}_g = \sqrt[10]{1.335} = 1.029$$

The geometric mean tells us that annual returns grew at an average annual rate of $(1.029 - 1)$ 100, or 2.9 percent. In other words, with an average annual growth rate of 2.9 percent, a $100 investment in the fund at the beginning of year 1 would grow to $100(1.029)^{10} =$ $133.09 at the end of 10 years. We can use Excel to calculate the geometric mean for the data in Table 2.10 by using the function GEOMEAN. In Figure 2.17, the value for the geometric mean in cell C13 is found using the formula =GEOMEAN(C2:C11).

It is important to understand that the arithmetic mean of the percentage annual returns does not provide the mean annual growth rate for this investment. The sum of the 10 percentage annual returns in Table 2.10 is 50.4. Thus, the arithmetic mean of the 10 percentage returns is 50.4/10 = 5.04 percent. A salesperson might try to convince you to invest in this fund by stating that the mean annual percentage return was 5.04 percent. Such a statement is not only misleading, it is inaccurate. A mean annual percentage return of 5.04 percent corresponds to an average growth factor of 1.0504. So, if the average growth factor were really 1.0504, $100 invested in the fund at the beginning of year 1 would have grown to $100(1.0504)^{10} =$ $163.51 at the end of 10 years. But, using the 10 annual percentage returns in Table 2.10, we showed that an initial $100 investment

FIGURE 2.17   Calculating the Geometric Mean for the Mutual Fund Data Using Excel

	A	B	C	D
1	Year	Return (%)	Growth Factor	
2	1	−22.1	0.779	
3	2	28.7	1.287	
4	3	10.9	1.109	
5	4	4.9	1.049	
6	5	15.8	1.158	
7	6	5.5	1.055	
8	7	−37.0	0.630	
9	8	26.5	1.265	
10	9	15.1	1.151	
11	10	2.1	1.021	
12				
13		Geometric Mean:	1.029	
14				

is worth $133.09 at the end of 10 years. The salesperson's claim that the mean annual percentage return is 5.04 percent grossly overstates the true growth for this mutual fund. The problem is that the arithmetic mean is appropriate only for an additive process. For a multiplicative process, such as applications involving growth rates, the geometric mean is the appropriate measure of location.

While the application of the geometric mean to problems in finance, investments, and banking is particularly common, the geometric mean should be applied any time you want to determine the mean rate of change over several successive periods. Other common applications include changes in the populations of species, crop yields, pollution levels, and birth and death rates. The geometric mean can also be applied to changes that occur over any number of successive periods of any length. In addition to annual changes, the geometric mean is often applied to find the mean rate of change over quarters, months, weeks, and even days.

2.6 Measures of Variability

In addition to measures of location, it is often desirable to consider measures of variability, or dispersion. For example, suppose that you are a considering two financial funds. Both funds require a $1,000 annual investment. Table 2.11 shows the annual payouts for Fund A and Fund B for $1,000 investments over the past 20 years. Fund A has paid out exactly $1,100 each year for an initial $1,000 investment. Fund B has had many different payouts, but the mean payout over the previous 20 years is also $1,100. But would you consider the payouts of Fund A and Fund B to be equivalent? Clearly, the answer is no. The difference between the two funds is due to variability.

TABLE 2.11	Annual Payouts for Two Different Investment Funds	
Year	Fund A ($)	Fund B ($)
1	1,100	700
2	1,100	2,500
3	1,100	1,200
4	1,100	1,550
5	1,100	1,300
6	1,100	800
7	1,100	300
8	1,100	1,600
9	1,100	1,500
10	1,100	350
11	1,100	460
12	1,100	890
13	1,100	1,050
14	1,100	800
15	1,100	1,150
16	1,100	1,200
17	1,100	1,800
18	1,100	100
19	1,100	1,750
20	1,100	1,000
Mean	1,100	1,100

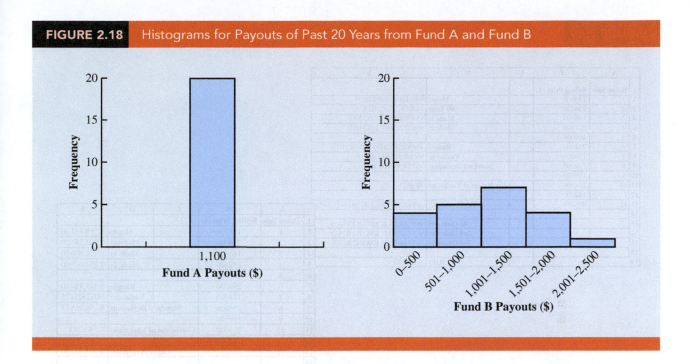

FIGURE 2.18   Histograms for Payouts of Past 20 Years from Fund A and Fund B

Figure 2.18 shows a histogram for the payouts received from Funds A and B. Although the mean payout is the same for the two funds, their histograms differ in that the payouts associated with Fund B have greater variability. Sometimes the payouts are considerably larger than the mean, and sometimes they are considerably smaller. In this section, we present several different ways to measure variability.

Range

The simplest measure of variability is the **range**. The range can be found by subtracting the smallest value from the largest value in a data set. Let us return to the home sales data set to demonstrate the calculation of range. Refer to the data from home sales prices in Table 2.9. The largest home sales price is $456,250, and the smallest is $108,000. The range is $456,250 − $108,000 = $348,250.

Although the range is the easiest of the measures of variability to compute, it is seldom used as the only measure. The reason is that the range is based on only two of the observations and thus is highly influenced by extreme values. If, for example, we replace the selling price of $456,250 with $1.5 million, the range would be $1,500,000 − $108,000 = $1,392,000. This large value for the range would not be especially descriptive of the variability in the data because 11 of the 12 home selling prices are between $108,000 and $298,000.

The range can be calculated in Excel using the MAX and MIN functions. The range value in cell E7 of Figure 2.19 calculates the range using the formula =MAX(B2:B13) − MIN(B2:B13). This subtracts the smallest value in the range B2:B13 from the largest value in the range B2:B13.

Variance

The **variance** is a measure of variability that utilizes all the data. The variance is based on the *deviation about the mean*, which is the difference between the value of each

FIGURE 2.19   Calculating Variability Measures for the Home Sales Data in Excel

	A	B	C	D	E
1	Home Sale	Selling Price ($)			
2	1	138000		Mean:	=AVERAGE(B2:B13)
3	2	254000		Median:	=MEDIAN(B2:B13)
4	3	186000		Mode 1:	=MODE.MULT(B2:B13)
5	4	257500		Mode 2:	=MODE.MULT(B2:B13)
6	5	108000			
7	6	254000		Range:	=MAX(B2:B13)-MIN(B2:B13)
8	7	138000		Variance:	=VAR.S(B2:B13)
9	8	298000		Standard Deviation:	=STDEV.S(B2:B13)
10	9	199500			
11	10	208000		Coefficient of Variation:	=E9/E2
12	11	142000			
13	12	456250			
14					
15				85th Percentile:	=PERCENTILE.EXC(B2:B13,0.85)
16				1st Quartile:	=QUARTILE.EXC(B2:B13,1)
17				2nd Quartile:	=QUARTILE.EXC(B2:B13,2)
18				3rd Quartile:	=QUARTILE.EXC(B2:B13,3)
19				IQR:	=E17-E15

	A	B	C	D	E
1	Home Sale	Selling Price ($)			
2	1	138000		Mean:	$ 219,937.50
3	2	254000		Median:	$ 203,750.00
4	3	186000		Mode 1:	$ 138,000.00
5	4	257500		Mode 2:	$ 254,000.00
6	5	108000			
7	6	254000		Range:	$ 348,250.00
8	7	138000		Variance:	9037501420
9	8	298000		Standard Deviation:	$ 95,065.77
10	9	199500			
11	10	208000		Coefficient of Variation:	43.22%
12	11	142000			
13	12	456250		85th Percentile:	$ 305,912.50
14					
15				1st Quartile:	$ 139,000.00
16				2nd Quartile:	$ 203,750.00
17				3rd Quartile:	$ 256,625.00
18					
19				IQR:	$ 117,625.00

observation (x_i) and the mean. For a sample, a deviation of an observation about the mean is written ($x_i - \bar{x}$). In the computation of the variance, the deviations about the mean are squared.

In most statistical applications, the data being analyzed are for a sample. When we compute a sample variance, we are often interested in using it to estimate the population variance, σ^2. Although a detailed explanation is beyond the scope of this text, for a random sample, it can be shown that, if the sum of the squared deviations about the sample mean is divided by $n - 1$, and not n, the resulting sample variance provides an unbiased estimate of the population variance.[1]

For this reason, the sample variance, denoted by s^2, is defined as follows:

If the data are for a population, the population variance, σ^2, can be computed directly (rather than estimated by the sample variance). For a population of N observations and with μ denoting the population mean, population variance is computed by $\sigma^2 = \dfrac{\Sigma(x_i - \mu)^2}{N}$.

SAMPLE VARIANCE

$$s^2 = \frac{\Sigma(x_i - \bar{x})^2}{n - 1} \tag{2.4}$$

To illustrate the computation of the sample variance, we will use the data on class size from page 40 for the sample of five college classes. A summary of the data, including the computation of the deviations about the mean and the squared deviations about the mean,

---

[1]Unbiased means that if we take a large number of independent random samples of the same size from the population and calculate the sample variance for each sample, the average of these sample variances will tend to be equal to the population variance.

TABLE 2.12	Computation of Deviations and Squared Deviations About the Mean for the Class Size Data			
	Number of Students in Class (x_i)	**Mean Class Size ($\bar{x}$)**	**Deviation About the Mean ($x_i - \bar{x}$)**	**Squared Deviation About the Mean ($x_i - \bar{x})^2$**
	46	44	2	4
	54	44	10	100
	42	44	−2	4
	46	44	2	4
	32	44	−12	144
			0	256
			$\Sigma(x_i - \bar{x})$	$\Sigma(x_i - \bar{x})^2$

is shown in Table 2.12. The sum of squared deviations about the mean is $\Sigma(x_i - \bar{x})^2 = 256$. Hence, with $n - 1 = 4$, the sample variance is:

$$s^2 = \frac{\Sigma(x_i - \bar{x})^2}{n-1} = \frac{256}{4} = 64$$

Note that the units of variance are squared. For instance, the sample variance for our calculation is $s^2 = 64$ (students)^2. In Excel, you can find the variance for sample data using the VAR.S function. Figure 2.19 shows the data for home sales examined in the previous section. The variance in cell E8 is calculated using the formula =VAR.S(B2:B13). Excel calculates the variance of the sample of 12 home sales to be 9,037,501,420.

Standard Deviation

The **standard deviation** is defined to be the positive square root of the variance. We use s to denote the sample standard deviation and σ to denote the population standard deviation. The sample standard deviation, s, is a point estimate of the population standard deviation, σ, and is derived from the sample variance in the following way:

SAMPLE STANDARD DEVIATION

$$s = \sqrt{s^2} \tag{2.5}$$

If the data are for a population, the population standard deviation σ is obtained by taking the positive square root of the population variance: $\sigma = \sqrt{\sigma^2}$. To calculate the population variance and population standard deviation in Excel, we use the functions =VAR.P and =STDEV.P.

The sample variance for the sample of class sizes in five college classes is $s^2 = 64$. Thus, the sample standard deviation is $s = \sqrt{64} = 8$.

Recall that the units associated with the variance are squared and that it is difficult to interpret the meaning of squared units. Because the standard deviation is the square root of the variance, the units of the variance, (students)^2 in our example, are converted to students in the standard deviation. In other words, the standard deviation is measured in the same units as the original data. For this reason, the standard deviation is more easily compared to the mean and other statistics that are measured in the same units as the original data.

Figure 2.19 shows the Excel calculation for the sample standard deviation of the home sales data, which can be calculated using Excel's STDEV.S function. The sample standard deviation in cell E9 is calculated using the formula =STDEV.S(B2:B13). Excel calculated the sample standard deviation for the home sales to be $95,065.77.

Coefficient of Variation

In some situations we may be interested in a descriptive statistic that indicates how large the standard deviation is relative to the mean. This measure is called the **coefficient of variation** and is usually expressed as a percentage.

COEFFICIENT OF VARIATION

$$\left(\frac{\text{Standard deviation}}{\text{Mean}} \times 100 \right)\% \tag{2.6}$$

For the class size data on page 40, we found a sample mean of 44 and a sample standard deviation of 8. The coefficient of variation is $(8/44 \times 100) = 18.2$ percent. In words, the coefficient of variation tells us that the sample standard deviation is 18.2 percent of the value of the sample mean. The coefficient of variation for the home sales data is shown in Figure 2.19. It is calculated in cell E11 using the formula =E9/E2, which divides the standard deviation by the mean. The coefficient of variation for the home sales data is 43.22 percent. In general, the coefficient of variation is a useful statistic for comparing the relative variability of different variables, each with different standard deviations and different means.

2.7 Analyzing Distributions

In Section 2.4 we demonstrated how to create frequency, relative, and cumulative distributions for data sets. Distributions are very useful for interpreting and analyzing data. A distribution describes the overall variability of the observed values of a variable. In this section we introduce additional ways of analyzing distributions.

Percentiles

A **percentile** is the value of a variable at which a specified (approximate) percentage of observations are below that value. The pth percentile tells us the point in the data where approximately p percent of the observations have values less than the pth percentile; hence, approximately $(100 - p)$ percent of the observations have values greater than the pth percentile.

Colleges and universities frequently report admission test scores in terms of percentiles. For instance, suppose an applicant obtains a raw score of 54 on the verbal portion of an admission test. How this student performed in relation to other students taking the same test may not be readily apparent. However, if the raw score of 54 corresponds to the 70th percentile, we know that approximately 70% of the students scored lower than this individual, and approximately 30% of the students scored higher.

To calculate the pth percentile for a data set containing n observations we must first arrange the data in ascending order (smallest value to largest value). The smallest value is in position 1, the next smallest value is in position 2, and so on. The location of the pth percentile, denoted L_p, is computed using the following equation:

Several procedures can be used to compute the location of the pth percentile using sample data. All provide similar values, especially for large data sets. The procedure we show here is the procedure used by Excel's PERCENTILE.EXC function as well as several other statistical software packages.

Location of the pth Percentile

$$L_p = \frac{p}{100}(n + 1) \tag{2.7}$$

Once we find the position of the value of the pth percentile, we have the information we need to calculate the pth percentile.

To illustrate the computation of the pth percentile, let us compute the 85th percentile for the home sales data in Table 2.9. We begin by arranging the sample of 12 starting salaries in ascending order.

108,000	138,000	138,000	142,000	186,000	199,500	208,000	254,000	254,000	257,500	298,000	456,250
Position 1	2	3	4	5	6	7	8	9	10	11	12

The position of each observation in the sorted data is shown directly below its value. For instance, the smallest value (108,000) is in position 1, the next smallest value (138,000) is in position 2, and so on. Using equation (2.7) with $p = 80$ and $n = 12$, the location of the 85th percentile is

$$L_{85} = \frac{p}{100}(n + 1) = \left(\frac{85}{100}\right)(12 + 1) = 11.05$$

The interpretation of $L_{85} = 11.05$ is that the 85th percentile is 5% of the way between the value in position 11 and the value in position 12. In other words, the 85th percentile is the value in position 11 (298,000) plus 0.05 times the difference between the value in position 12 (456,250) and the value in position 11 (298,000). Thus, the 85th percentile is

$$85\text{th percentile} = 298,000 + 0.05(456,250 - 298,000) = 298,000 + 0.05(158,250)$$
$$= 305,912.50$$

Therefore, \$305,912.50 represents the 85th percentile of the home sales data.

The pth percentile can also be calculated in Excel using the function PERCENTILE.EXC. Figure 2.19 shows the Excel calculation for the 85th percentile of the home sales data. The value in cell E13 is calculated using the formula =PERCENTILE.EXC(B2:B13,0.85); B2:B13 defines the data set for which we are calculating a percentile, and 0.85 defines the percentile of interest.

Quartiles

It is often desirable to divide data into four parts, with each part containing approximately one-fourth, or 25 percent, of the observations. These division points are referred to as the **quartiles** and are defined as:

Q_1 = first quartile, or 25th percentile
Q_2 = second quartile, or 50th percentile (also the median)
Q_3 = third quartile, or 75th percentile.

To demonstrate quartiles, the home sales data are again arranged in ascending order.

108,000	138,000	138,000	142,000	186,000	199,500	208,000	254,000	254,000	257,500	298,000	456,250
Position 1	2	3	4	5	6	7	8	9	10	11	12

We already identified Q2, the second quartile (median) as 203,750. To find Q1 and Q3 we must find the 25th and 75th percentiles.

For Q1,

$$L_{25} = \frac{p}{100}(n + 1) = \left(\frac{25}{100}\right)(12 + 1) = 3.25$$

$$25\text{th percentile} = 138,000 + 0.25(142,000 - 138,000) = 138,000 + 0.25(4000)$$
$$= 139,000$$

For Q3,

$$L_{75} = \frac{p}{100}(n+1) = \left(\frac{75}{100}\right)(12+1) = 9.75$$

75th percentile $= 254{,}000 + 0.75(257{,}500 - 254{,}000) = 254{,}000 + 0.75(3500)$
$$= 256{,}625$$

Therefore, the 25th percentile for the home sales data is $139,000 and the 75th percentile is $256,625.

The quartiles divide the home sales data into four parts, with each part containing 25 percent of the observations.

108,000	142,000	208,000	257,500
138,000	186,000	254,000	298,000
138,000	199,500	254,000	456,250

$$Q_1 = 139{,}000 \qquad Q_2 = 203{,}750 \qquad Q_3 = 256{,}625$$

The difference between the third and first quartiles is often referred to as the **interquartile range**, or IQR. For the home sales data, IQR $= Q_3 - Q_1 = 256{,}625 - 139{,}000 = 117{,}625$. Because it excludes the smallest and largest 25 percent of values in the data, the IQR is a useful measure of variation for data that have extreme values or are badly skewed.

A quartile can be computed in Excel using the function QUARTILE.EXC. Figure 2.19 shows the calculations for first, second, and third quartiles for the home sales data. The formula used in cell E15 is =QUARTILE.EXC(B2:B13,1). The range B2:B13 defines the data set, and 1 indicates that we want to compute the 1st quartile. Cells E16 and E17 use similar formulas to compute the second and third quartiles.

z-Scores

A *z-score* allows us to measure the relative location of a value in the data set. More specifically, a *z*-score helps us determine how far a particular value is from the mean relative to the data set's standard deviation. Suppose we have a sample of n observations, with the values denoted by $x_1, x_2, \ldots, x_n$. In addition, assume that the sample mean, $\bar{x}$, and the sample standard deviation, s, are already computed. Associated with each value, x_i, is another value called its *z*-score. Equation (2.8) shows how the *z*-score is computed for each x_i:

z-SCORE

$$z_i = \frac{x_i - \bar{x}}{s} \tag{2.8}$$

where

z_i = the z-score for x_i
$\bar{x}$ = the sample mean
s = the sample standard deviation

The *z*-score is often called the *standardized value*. The *z*-score, z_i, can be interpreted as the number of standard deviations, x_i, is from the mean. For example, $z_1 = 1.2$ indicates that x_1 is 1.2 standard deviations greater than the sample mean. Similarly, $z_2 = -0.5$ indicates that x_2 is 0.5, or 1/2, standard deviation less than the sample mean. A *z*-score greater than zero occurs for observations with a value greater than the mean, and a *z*-score

TABLE 2.13	*z*-Scores for the Class Size Data		
No. of Students in Class (x_i)	Deviation About the Mean $(x_i - \bar{x})$		z-Score $\left(\dfrac{x_i - \bar{x}}{s}\right)$
46	2		2/8 = .25
54	10		10/8 = 1.25
42	−2		−2/8 = −.25
46	2		2/8 = .25
32	−12		−12/8 = −1.50

less than zero occurs for observations with a value less than the mean. A *z*-score of zero indicates that the value of the observation is equal to the mean.

The *z*-scores for the class size data are computed in Table 2.13. Recall the previously computed sample mean, $\bar{x} = 44$, and sample standard deviation, $s = 8$. The *z*-score of −1.50 for the fifth observation shows that it is farthest from the mean; it is 1.50 standard deviations below the mean.

The *z*-score can be calculated in Excel using the function STANDARDIZE. Figure 2.20 demonstrates the use of the STANDARDIZE function to compute *z*-scores for the home sales data. To calculate the *z*-scores, we must provide the mean and standard deviation for the data set in the arguments of the STANDARDIZE function. For instance, the *z*-score in cell C2 is calculated with the formula =STANDARDIZE(B2, $B$15, $B$16), where cell B15 contains the mean of the home sales data and cell B16 contains the standard deviation of the home sales data. We can then copy and paste this formula into cells C3:C13.

Empirical Rule

When the distribution of data exhibits a symmetric bell-shaped distribution, as shown in Figure 2.21, the **empirical rule** can be used to determine the percentage of data values that are within a specified number of standard deviations of the mean. Many, but not all, distributions of data found in practice exhibit a symmetric bell-shaped distribution.

EMPIRICAL RULE

For data having a bell-shaped distribution:

- Approximately 68% of the data values will be within 1 standard deviation of the mean.
- Approximately 95% of the data values will be within 2 standard deviations of the mean.
- Almost all of the data values will be within 3 standard deviations of the mean.

The height of adult males in the United States has a bell-shaped distribution similar to that shown in Figure 2.21, with a mean of approximately 69.5 inches and standard deviation of approximately 3 inches. Using the empirical rule, we can draw the following conclusions.

- Approximately 68% of adult males in the United States have heights between 69.5 − 3 = 66.5 and 69.5 + 3 = 72.5 inches.

FIGURE 2.20	Calculating z-Scores for the Home Sales Data in Excel

	A	B	C
1	Home Sale	Selling Price ($)	z-Score
2	1	138000	=STANDARDIZE(B2,$B$15,$B$16)
3	2	254000	=STANDARDIZE(B3,$B$15,$B$16)
4	3	186000	=STANDARDIZE(B4,$B$15,$B$16)
5	4	257500	=STANDARDIZE(B5,$B$15,$B$16)
6	5	108000	=STANDARDIZE(B6,$B$15,$B$16)
7	6	254000	=STANDARDIZE(B7,$B$15,$B$16)
8	7	138000	=STANDARDIZE(B8,$B$15,$B$16)
9	8	298000	=STANDARDIZE(B9,$B$15,$B$16)
10	9	199500	=STANDARDIZE(B10,$B$15,$B$16)
11	10	208000	=STANDARDIZE(B11,$B$15,$B$16)
12	11	142000	=STANDARDIZE(B12,$B$15,$B$16)
13	12	456250	=STANDARDIZE(B13,$B$15,$B$16)
14			
15	Mean:	=AVERAGE(B2:B13)	
16	Standard Deviation:	=STDEV.S(B2:B13)	

	A	B	C
1	Home Sale	Selling Price ($)	z-Score
2	1	138,000	−0.862
3	2	254,000	0.358
4	3	186,000	−0.357
5	4	257,500	0.395
6	5	108,000	−1.177
7	6	254,000	0.358
8	7	138,000	−0.862
9	8	298,000	0.821
10	9	199,500	−0.215
11	10	208,000	−0.126
12	11	142,000	−0.820
13	12	456,250	2.486
14			
15	Mean:	$ 219,937.50	
16	Standard Deviation:	$ 95,065.77	

FIGURE 2.21	A Symmetric Bell-Shaped Distribution

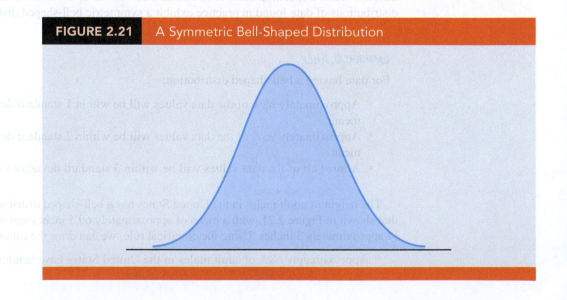

- Approximately 95% of adult males in the United States have heights between 63.5 and 75.5 inches.
- Almost all adult males in the United States have heights between 60.5 and 78.5 inches.

Identifying Outliers

Sometimes a data set will have one or more observations with unusually large or unusually small values. These extreme values are called **outliers**. Experienced statisticians take steps to identify outliers and then review each one carefully. An outlier may be a data value that has been incorrectly recorded; if so, it can be corrected before the data are analyzed further. An outlier may also be from an observation that doesn't belong to the population we are studying and was incorrectly included in the data set; if so, it can be removed. Finally, an outlier may be an unusual data value that has been recorded correctly and is a member of the population we are studying. In such cases, the observation should remain.

Standardized values (z-scores) can be used to identify outliers. Recall that the empirical rule allows us to conclude that for data with a bell-shaped distribution, almost all the data values will be within 3 standard deviations of the mean. Hence, in using z-scores to identify outliers, we recommend treating any data value with a z-score less than -3 or greater than $+3$ as an outlier. Such data values can then be reviewed to determine their accuracy and whether they belong in the data set.

Box Plots

A **box plot** is a graphical summary of the distribution of data. A box plot is developed from the quartiles for a data set. Figure 2.22 is a box plot for the home sales data. Here are the steps used to construct the box plot:

Box plots are also known as box-and-whisker plots.

1. A box is drawn with the ends of the box located at the first and third quartiles. For the home sales data, $Q1 = 139,000$ and $Q3 = 256,625$. This box contains the middle 50% of the data.
2. A vertical line is drawn in the box at the location of the median (203,750 for the home sales data).

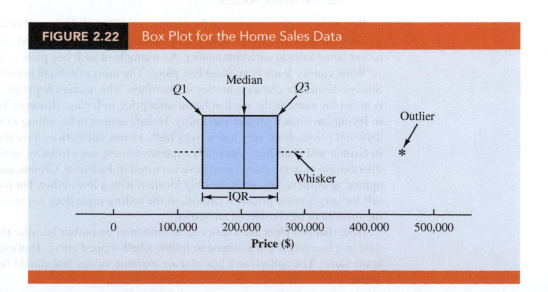

FIGURE 2.22	Box Plot for the Home Sales Data

Box plots can be drawn horizontally or vertically. Figure 2.22 shows a horizontal box plot, and Figure 2.23 shows vertical box plots.

FIGURE 2.23   Box Plots Comparing Home Sale Prices in Different Communities

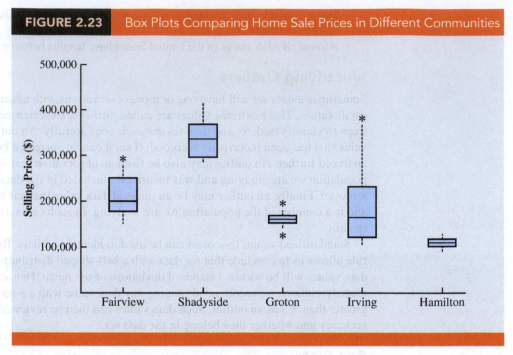

Clearly, we would not expect a home sales price less than 0, so we could also define the lower limit here to be $0.

3. By using the interquartile range, IQR = $Q3 - Q1$, limits are located. The limits for the box plot are 1.5(IQR) below $Q1$ and 1.5(IQR) above $Q3$. For the home sales data, IQR = $Q3 - Q1$ = 256,625 − 139,000 = 117,625. Thus, the limits are 139,000 − 1.5(117,625) = −37,437.5 and 256,625 + 1.5(117,625) = 433,062.5. Data outside these limits are considered outliers.

4. The dashed lines in Figure 2.22 are called *whiskers*. The whiskers are drawn from the ends of the box to the smallest and largest values inside the limits computed in Step 3. Thus, the whiskers end at home sales values of 108,000 and 298,000.

5. Finally, the location of each outlier is shown with an asterisk (*). In Figure 2.22, we see one outlier, 456,250.

Box plots are also very useful for comparing different data sets. For instance, if we want to compare home sales from several different communities, we could create box plots for recent home sales in each community. An example of such box plots is shown in Figure 2.23.

What can we learn from these box plots? The most expensive houses appear to be in Shadyside and the cheapest houses in Hamilton. The median home sales price in Groton is about the same as the median home sales price in Irving. However, home sales prices in Irving have much greater variability. Homes appear to be selling in Irving for many different prices, from very low to very high. Home sales prices have the least variation in Groton and Hamilton. Unusually expensive home sales (relative to the respective distribution of home sales vales) have occurred in Fairview, Groton, and Irving, which appear as outliers. Groton is the only location with a low outlier, but note that most homes sell for very similar prices in Groton, so the selling price does not have to be too far from the median to be considered an outlier.

Note that box plots use a different definition of an outlier because the distribution of the data in a box plot is not assumed to follow a bell-shaped curve. However, the interpretation is the same. The outliers in a box plot are extreme values that should be investigated to ensure data accuracy.

NOTES + COMMENTS

1. Versions of Excel prior to Excel 2010 use the functions PERCENTILE and QUARTILE to calculate a percentile and quartile, respectively. However, these Excel functions can produce odd results for small data sets. Although these functions are still accepted in later versions of Excel, we do not recommend their use; instead we suggest using PERCENTILE.EXC and QUARTILE.EXC.

2. The empirical rule applies only to distributions that have an approximately bell-shaped distribution because it is based on properties of the Normal probability distribution, which we will discuss in Chapter 5. For distributions that do not have a bell-shaped distribution, one can use Chebyshev's

theorem to make statements about the proportion of data values that must be within a specified number of standard deviations of the mean. Chebyshev's theorem states that at least $(1 - \frac{1}{z^2})$ of the data values must be within z standard deviations of the mean, where z is any value greater than 1.

3. There is no easy way to generate box plots in versions of Excel prior to Excel 2016. In Excel 2016, you can create a box plot by clicking the **Insert** tab in the Ribbon, clicking **Insert Statistic Chart** ▬▬▬ ▾ in the **Charts** group and choosing **Box and Whisker**. As an alternative, we explain how to generate a box plot with XLMiner in the chapter appendix.

2.8 Measures of Association Between Two Variables

Thus far, we have examined numerical methods used to summarize the data for one variable at a time. Often a manager or decision maker is interested in the relationship between two variables. In this section, we present covariance and correlation as descriptive measures of the relationship between two variables. To illustrate these concepts, we consider the case of the sales manager of Queensland Amusement Park, who is in charge of ordering bottled water to be purchased by park customers. The sales manager believes that daily bottled water sales in the summer are related to the outdoor temperature. Table 2.14 shows data for high temperatures and bottled water sales for 14 summer days. The data have been sorted by high temperature from lowest value to highest value.

TABLE 2.14	Data for Bottled Water Sales at Queensland Amusement Park for a Sample of 14 Summer Days
High Temperature (°F)	**Bottled Water Sales (cases)**
78	23
79	22
80	24
80	22
82	24
83	26
85	27
86	25
87	28
87	26
88	29
88	30
90	31
92	31

DATA *file*

BottledWater

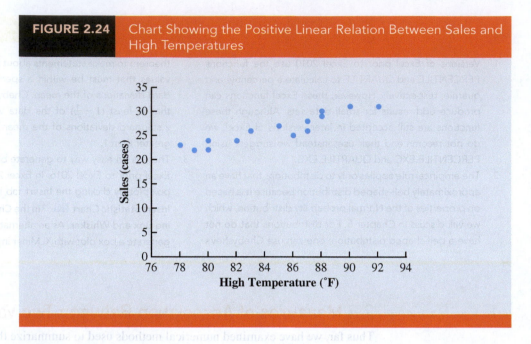

FIGURE 2.24   Chart Showing the Positive Linear Relation Between Sales and High Temperatures

Scatter Charts

A **scatter chart** is a useful graph for analyzing the relationship between two variables. Figure 2.24 shows a scatter chart for sales of bottled water versus the high temperature experienced on 14 consecutive days. The scatter chart in the figure suggests that higher daily high temperatures are associated with higher bottled water sales. This is an example of a positive relationship, because when one variable (high temperature) increases, the other variable (sales of bottled water) generally also increases. The scatter chart also suggests that a straight line could be used as an approximation for the relationship between high temperature and sales of bottled water. We will cover the creation of scatter charts in more detail in Chapter 3.

Covariance

Covariance is a descriptive measure of the linear association between two variables. For a sample of size n with the observations (x_1, y_1), (x_2, y_2), and so on, the sample covariance is defined as follows:

DATA file
BottledWater

If data consist of a population of N observations, the population covariance σ_{xy} is computed by:

$$\sigma_{xy} = \frac{\Sigma(x_i - \mu_x)\Sigma(y_i - \mu_y)}{N}.$$

Note that this equation is similar to equation (2.8), but uses population parameters instead of sample estimates (and divides by N instead of $n - 1$ for technical reasons beyond the scope of this book).

> **SAMPLE COVARIANCE**
>
> $$s_{xy} = \frac{\Sigma(x_i - \bar{x})(y_i - \bar{y})}{n - 1} \qquad (2.9)$$

This formula pairs each x_i with a y_i. We then sum the products obtained by multiplying the deviation of each x_i from its sample mean $(x_i - \bar{x})$ by the deviation of the corresponding y_i from its sample mean $(y_i - \bar{y})$; this sum is then divided by $n - 1$.

To measure the strength of the linear relationship between the high temperature x and the sales of bottled water y at Queensland, we use equation (2.9) to compute the sample covariance. The calculations in Table 2.15 show the computation $\Sigma(x_i - \bar{x})(y_i - \bar{y})$. Note that for our calculations, $\bar{x} = 84.6$ and $\bar{y} = 26.3$.

The covariance calculated in Table 2.15 is $s_{xy} = 12.8$. Because the covariance is greater than 0, it indicates a positive relationship between the high temperature and sales of bottled water. This verifies the relationship we saw in the scatter chart in Figure 2.24 that as the high temperature for a day increases, sales of bottled water generally increase.

TABLE 2.15	**Sample Covariance Calculations for Daily High Temperature and Bottled Water Sales at Queensland Amusement Park**				

	x_i	y_i	$x_i - \bar{x}$	$y_i - \bar{y}$	$(x_i - \bar{x})(y_i - \bar{y})$
	78	23	−6.6	−3.3	21.78
	79	22	−5.6	−4.3	24.08
	80	24	−4.6	−2.3	10.58
	80	22	−4.6	−4.3	19.78
	82	24	−2.6	−2.3	5.98
	83	26	−1.6	−0.3	0.48
	85	27	0.4	0.7	0.28
	86	25	1.4	−1.3	−1.82
	87	28	2.4	1.7	4.08
	87	26	2.4	−0.3	−0.72
	88	29	3.4	2.7	9.18
	88	30	3.4	3.7	12.58
	90	31	5.4	4.7	25.38
	92	31	7.4	4.7	34.78
Totals	1,185	368	0.6	−0.2	166.42

$$\bar{x} = 84.6$$
$$\bar{y} = 26.3$$
$$s_{xy} = \frac{\Sigma(x_i - \bar{x})(y_i - \bar{y})}{n - 1} = \frac{166.42}{14 - 1} = 12.8$$

The sample covariance can also be calculated in Excel using the COVARIANCE.S function. Figure 2.25 shows the data from Table 2.14 entered into an Excel Worksheet. The covariance is calculated in cell B17 using the formula =COVARIANCE.S(A2:A15, B2:B15). A2:A15 defines the range for the x variable (high temperature), and B2:B15 defines the range for the y variable (sales of bottled water).

For the bottled water, the covariance is positive, indicating that higher temperatures (x) are associated with higher sales (y). For a covariance near 0, then the x and y variables are not linearly related. If the covariance is less than 0, then the x and y variables are negatively related, which means that as x increases, y generally decreases. Figure 2.26 demonstrates several possible scatter charts and their associated covariance values.

One problem with using covariance is that the magnitude of the covariance value is difficult to interpret. Larger s_{xy} values do not necessarily mean a stronger linear relationship because the units of covariance depend on the units of x and y. For example, suppose we are interested in the relationship between height x and weight y for individuals. Clearly the strength of the relationship should be the same whether we measure height in feet or inches. Measuring the height in inches, however, gives us much larger numerical values for ($x_i - \bar{x}$) than when we measure height in feet. Thus, with height measured in inches, we would obtain a larger value for the numerator $\Sigma(x_i - \bar{x})(y_i - \bar{y})$ in equation (2.9)—and hence a larger covariance—when in fact the relationship does not change.

Correlation Coefficient

The **correlation coefficient** measures the relationship between two variables, and, unlike covariance, the relationship between two variables is not affected by the units of measurement for x and y. For sample data, the correlation coefficient is defined as follows.

FIGURE 2.25   Calculating Covariance and Correlation Coefficient for Bottled Water Sales Using Excel

	A	B
1	**High Temperature (°F)**	**Bottled Water Sales (cases)**
2	78	23
3	79	22
4	80	24
5	80	22
6	82	24
7	83	26
8	85	27
9	86	25
10	87	28
11	87	26
12	88	29
13	88	30
14	90	31
15	92	31
16		
17	**Covariance:**	=COVARIANCE.S(A2:A15,B2:B15)
18	**Correlation Coefficient:**	=CORREL(A2:A15,B2:B15)

	A	B
1	**High Temperature (°F)**	**Bottled Water Sales (cases)**
2	78	23
3	79	22
4	80	24
5	80	22
6	82	24
7	83	26
8	85	27
9	86	25
10	87	28
11	87	26
12	88	29
13	88	30
14	90	31
15	92	31
16		
17	**Covariance:**	12.80
18	**Correlation Coefficient:**	0.93

If data are a population, the population correlation coefficient is computed by $\rho_{xy} = \dfrac{\sigma_{xy}}{\sigma_x \sigma_y}$. Note that this is similar to equation (2.10) but uses population parameters instead of sample estimates.

SAMPLE CORRELATION COEFFICIENT

$$r_{xy} = \frac{s_{xy}}{s_x s_y} \qquad (2.10)$$

where

r_{xy} = sample correlation coefficient
s_{xy} = sample covariance
s_x = sample standard deviation of x
s_y = sample standard deviation of y

The sample correlation coefficient is computed by dividing the sample covariance by the product of the sample standard deviation of x and the sample standard deviation of y. This scales the correlation coefficient so that it will always take values between -1 and $+1$.

FIGURE 2.26 Scatter Diagrams and Associated Covariance Values for Different Variable Relationships

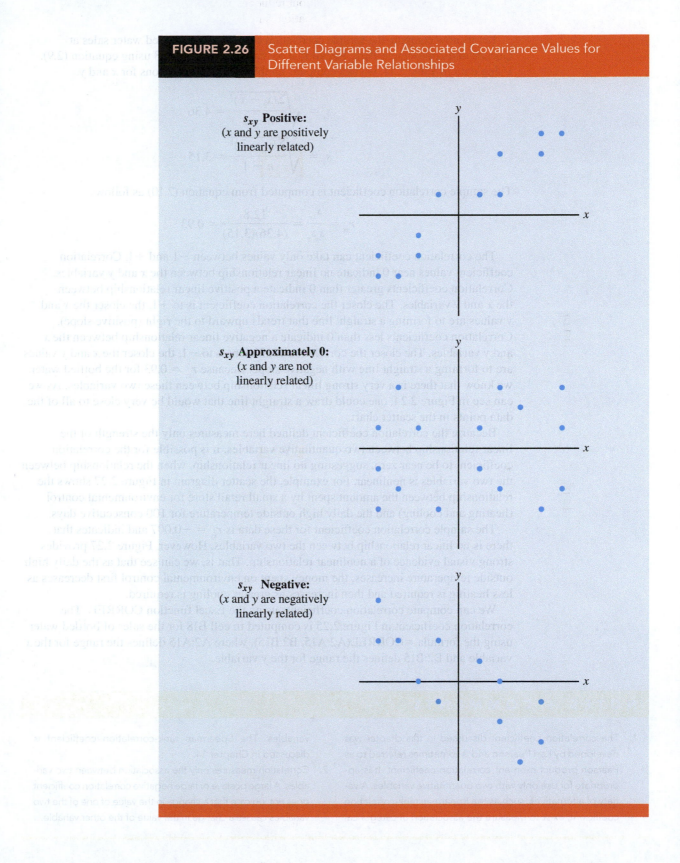

Let us now compute the sample correlation coefficient for bottled water sales at Queensland Amusement Park. Recall that we calculated $s_{xy} = 12.8$ using equation (2.9). Using data in Table 2.14, we can compute sample standard deviations for x and y.

$$s_x = \sqrt{\frac{\Sigma(x_i - \bar{x})^2}{n-1}} = 4.36$$

$$s_y = \sqrt{\frac{\Sigma(y_i - \bar{y})^2}{n-1}} = 3.15$$

The sample correlation coefficient is computed from equation (2.10) as follows:

$$r_{xy} = \frac{s_{xy}}{s_x s_y} = \frac{12.8}{(4.36)(3.15)} = 0.93$$

The correlation coefficient can take only values between -1 and $+1$. Correlation coefficient values near 0 indicate no linear relationship between the x and y variables. Correlation coefficients greater than 0 indicate a positive linear relationship between the x and y variables. The closer the correlation coefficient is to $+1$, the closer the x and y values are to forming a straight line that trends upward to the right (positive slope). Correlation coefficients less than 0 indicate a negative linear relationship between the x and y variables. The closer the correlation coefficient is to -1, the closer the x and y values are to forming a straight line with negative slope. Because $r_{xy} = 0.93$ for the bottled water, we know that there is a very strong linear relationship between these two variables. As we can see in Figure 2.24, one could draw a straight line that would be very close to all of the data points in the scatter chart.

Because the correlation coefficient defined here measures only the strength of the linear relationship between two quantitative variables, it is possible for the correlation coefficient to be near zero, suggesting no linear relationship, when the relationship between the two variables is nonlinear. For example, the scatter diagram in Figure 2.27 shows the relationship between the amount spent by a small retail store for environmental control (heating and cooling) and the daily high outside temperature for 100 consecutive days.

The sample correlation coefficient for these data is $r_{xy} = -0.007$ and indicates that there is no linear relationship between the two variables. However, Figure 2.27 provides strong visual evidence of a nonlinear relationship. That is, we can see that as the daily high outside temperature increases, the money spent on environmental control first decreases as less heating is required and then increases as greater cooling is required.

We can compute correlation coefficients using the Excel function CORREL. The correlation coefficient in Figure 2.25 is computed in cell B18 for the sales of bottled water using the formula =CORREL(A2:A15, B2:B15), where A2:A15 defines the range for the x variable and B2:B15 defines the range for the y variable.

NOTES + COMMENTS

1. The correlation coefficient discussed in this chapter was developed by Karl Pearson and is sometimes referred to as Pearson product moment correlation coefficient. It is appropriate for use only with two quantitative variables. A variety of alternatives, such as the Spearman rank-correlation coefficient, exist to measure the association of categorical variables. The Spearman rank-correlation coefficient is discussed in Chapter 14.

2. Correlation measures only the association between two variables. A large positive or large negative correlation coefficient does not indicate that a change in the value of one of the two variables *causes* a change in the value of the other variable.

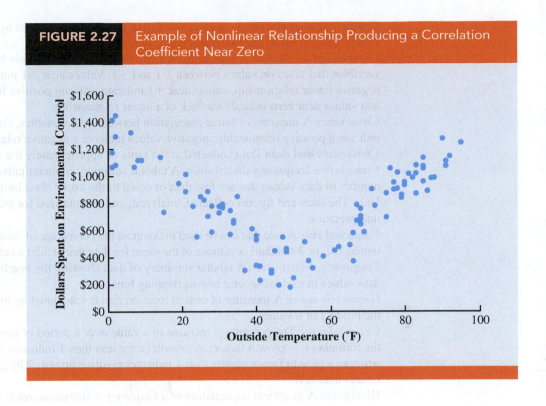

FIGURE 2.27   Example of Nonlinear Relationship Producing a Correlation Coefficient Near Zero

SUMMARY

In this chapter we have provided an introduction to descriptive statistics that can be used to summarize data. We began by explaining the need for data collection, defining the types of data one may encounter, and providing a few commonly used sources for finding data. We presented several useful functions for modifying data in Excel, such as sorting and filtering to aid in data analysis.

We introduced the concept of a distribution and explained how to generate frequency, relative, percent, and cumulative distributions for data. We also demonstrated the use of histograms as a way to visualize the distribution of data. We then introduced measures of location for a distribution of data such as mean, median, mode, and geometric mean, as well as measures of variability such as range, variance, standard deviation, coefficient of variation, and interquartile range. We presented additional measures for analyzing a distribution of data including percentiles, quartiles, and z-scores. We showed that box plots are effective for visualizing a distribution.

Finally, we discussed measures of association between two variables. Scatter plots allow one to visualize the relationship between variables. Covariance and the correlation coefficient summarize the linear relationship between variables into a single number.

GLOSSARY

Bins The nonoverlapping groupings of data used to create a frequency distribution. Bins for categorical data are also known as classes.

Box plot A graphical summary of data based on the quartiles of a distribution.

Categorical data Data for which categories of like items are identified by labels or names. Arithmetic operations cannot be performed on categorical data.

Coefficient of variation A measure of relative variability computed by dividing the standard deviation by the mean and multiplying by 100.

Correlation coefficient A standardized measure of linear association between two variables that takes on values between -1 and $+1$. Values near -1 indicate a strong negative linear relationship, values near $+1$ indicate a strong positive linear relationship, and values near zero indicate the lack of a linear relationship.

Covariance A measure of linear association between two variables. Positive values indicate a positive relationship; negative values indicate a negative relationship.

Cross-sectional data Data collected at the same or approximately the same point in time.

Cumulative frequency distribution A tabular summary of quantitative data showing the number of data values that are less than or equal to the upper class limit of each bin.

Data The facts and figures collected, analyzed, and summarized for presentation and interpretation.

Empirical rule A rule that can be used to compute the percentage of data values that must be within 1, 2, or 3 standard deviations of the mean for data that exhibit a bell-shaped distribution.

Frequency distribution A tabular summary of data showing the number (frequency) of data values in each of several nonoverlapping bins.

Geometric mean A measure of central location that is calculated by finding the nth root of the product of n values.

Growth factor The percentage increase of a value over a period of time is calculated using the formula $(1 - \text{growth factor})$. A growth factor less than 1 indicates negative growth, whereas a growth factor greater than 1 indicates positive growth. The growth factor cannot be less than zero.

Histogram A graphical presentation of a frequency distribution, relative frequency distribution, or percent frequency distribution of quantitative data constructed by placing the bin intervals on the horizontal axis and the frequencies, relative frequencies, or percent frequencies on the vertical axis.

Interquartile range The difference between the third and first quartiles.

Mean (arithmetic mean) A measure of central location computed by summing the data values and dividing by the number of observations.

Median A measure of central location provided by the value in the middle when the data are arranged in ascending order.

Mode A measure of central location, defined as the value that occurs with greatest frequency.

Observation A set of values corresponding to a set of variables.

Outlier An unusually large or unusually small data value.

Percent frequency distribution A tabular summary of data showing the percentage of data values in each of several nonoverlapping bins.

Percentile A value such that approximately p percent of the observations have values less than the pth percentile; hence, approximately (100 - p) percent of the observations have values greater than the pth percentile. The 50th percentile is the median.

Population The set of all elements of interest in a particular study.

Quantitative data Data for which numerical values are used to indicate magnitude, such as how many or how much. Arithmetic operations such as addition, subtraction, and multiplication can be performed on quantitative data.

Quartile The 25th, 50th, and 75th percentiles, referred to as the first quartile, second quartile (median), and third quartile, respectively. The quartiles can be used to divide a data set into four parts, with each part containing approximately 25% of the data.

Random sampling Collecting a sample that ensures that: (1) each element selected comes from the same population and (2) each element is selected independently.

Random (uncertain) variable A quantity whose values are not known with certainty.

Range A measure of variability, defined to be the largest value minus the smallest value.

Relative frequency distribution A tabular summary of data showing the fraction or proportion of data values in each of several nonoverlapping bins.

Sample A subset of the population.

Scatter chart A graphical presentation of the relationship between two quantitative variables. One variable is shown on the horizontal axis and the other on the vertical axis.

Skewness A measure of the lack of symmetry in a distribution.

Standard deviation A measure of variability computed by taking the positive square root of the variance.

Time series data Data that are collected over a period of time (minutes, hours, days, months, years, etc.).

Variable A characteristic or quantity of interest that can take on different values.

Variance A measure of variability based on the squared deviations of the data values about the mean.

Variation Differences in values of a variable over observations.

z-score A value computed by dividing the deviation about the mean ($x_i - x$) by the standard deviation s. A z-score is referred to as a standardized value and denotes the number of standard deviations that x_i is from the mean.

PROBLEMS

1. A *Wall Street Journal* subscriber survey asked 46 questions about subscriber characteristics and interests. State whether each of the following questions provides categorical or quantitative data.
   a. What is your age?
   b. Are you male or female?
   c. When did you first start reading the *WSJ*? High school, college, early career, midcareer, late career, or retirement?
   d. How long have you been in your present job or position?
   e. What type of vehicle are you considering for your next purchase? Nine response categories include sedan, sports car, SUV, minivan, and so on.

2. The following table contains a partial list of countries, the continents on which they are located, and their respective gross domestic products (GDP) in U.S. dollars. A list of 125 countries and their GDPs is contained in the file *GDPlist*.

DATA *file*
GDPlist

Country	Continent	GDP (millions of US$)
Afghanistan	Asia	18,181
Albania	Europe	12,847
Algeria	Africa	190,709
Angola	Africa	100,948
Argentina	South America	447,644
Australia	Oceania	1,488,221
Austria	Europe	419,243
Azerbaijan	Europe	62,321
Bahrain	Asia	26,108
Bangladesh	Asia	113,032
Belarus	Europe	55,483
Belgium	Europe	513,396
Bolivia	South America	24,604
Bosnia and Herzegovina	Europe	17,965
Botswana	Africa	17,570

a. Sort the countries in *GDPlist* from largest to smallest GDP. What are the top 10 countries according to GDP?

b. Filter the countries to display only the countries located in Africa. What are the top 5 countries located in Africa according to GDP?

c. What are the top 5 countries by GDP that are located in Europe?

3. Ohio Logistics manages the logistical activities for firms by matching companies that need products shipped with carriers that can provide the best rates and best service for the companies. Ohio Logistics is very concerned that its carriers deliver their customers' material on time, so it carefully monitors the percentage of on-time deliveries. The following table contains a list of the carriers used by Ohio Logistics and the corresponding on-time percentages for the current and previous years.

DATA *file*

Carriers

Carrier	Previous Year On-Time Deliveries (%)	Current Year On-Time Deliveries (%)
Blue Box Shipping	88.4	94.8
Cheetah LLC	89.3	91.8
Granite State Carriers	81.8	87.6
Honsin Limited	74.2	80.1
Jones Brothers	68.9	82.8
Minuteman Company	91.0	84.2
Rapid Response	78.8	70.9
Smith Logistics	84.3	88.7
Super Freight	92.1	86.8

a. Sort the carriers in descending order by their current year's percentage of on-time deliveries. Which carrier is providing the best service in the current year? Which carrier is providing the worst service in the current year?

b. Calculate the change in percentage of on-time deliveries from the previous to the current year for each carrier. Use Excel's conditional formatting to highlight the carriers whose on-time percentage decreased from the previous year to the current year.

c. Use Excel's conditional formatting tool to create data bars for the change in percentage of on-time deliveries from the previous year to the current year for each carrier calculated in part b.

d. Which carriers should Ohio Logistics try to use in the future? Why?

4. A partial relative frequency distribution is given.

Class	Relative Frequency
A	0.22
B	0.18
C	0.40
D	

a. What is the relative frequency of class D?

b. The total sample size is 200. What is the frequency of class D?

c. Show the frequency distribution.

d. Show the percent frequency distribution.

5. In a recent report, the top five most-visited English-language web sites were google .com (GOOG), facebook.com (FB), youtube.com (YT), yahoo.com (YAH), and wikipedia.com (WIKI). The most-visited web sites for a sample of 50 Internet users are shown in the following table:

YAH	WIKI	YT	WIKI	GOOG
YT	YAH	GOOG	GOOG	GOOG
WIKI	GOOG	YAH	YAH	YAH
YAH	YT	GOOG	YT	YAH
GOOG	FB	FB	WIKI	GOOG
GOOG	GOOG	FB	FB	WIKI
FB	YAH	YT	YAH	YAH
YT	GOOG	YAH	FB	FB
WIKI	GOOG	YAH	WIKI	WIKI
YAH	YT	GOOG	GOOG	WIKI

a. Are these data categorical or quantitative?
b. Provide frequency and percent frequency distributions.
c. On the basis of the sample, which web site is most frequently the most-often-visited web site for Internet users? Which is second?

6. In a study of how chief executive officers (CEOs) spend their days, it was found that CEOs spend an average of about 18 hours per week in meetings, not including conference calls, business meals, and public events. Shown here are the times spent per week in meetings (hours) for a sample of 25 CEOs:

14	15	18	23	15
19	20	13	15	23
23	21	15	20	21
16	15	18	18	19
19	22	23	21	12

a. What is the least amount of time a CEO spent per week in meetings in this sample? The highest?
b. Use a class width of 2 hours to prepare a frequency distribution and a percent frequency distribution for the data.
c. Prepare a histogram and comment on the shape of the distribution.

7. Consumer complaints are frequently reported to the Better Business Bureau. Industries with the most complaints to the Better Business Bureau are often banks, cable and satellite television companies, collection agencies, cellular phone providers, and new car dealerships. The results for a sample of 200 complaints are in the file *BBB*.
a. Show the frequency and percent frequency of complaints by industry.
b. Which industry had the highest number of complaints?
c. Comment on the percentage frequency distribution for complaints.

8. Reports have found that many U.S. adults would rather live in a different type of community than the one in which they are living now. A national survey of 2,260 adults asked: "Where do you live now?" and "What do you consider to be the ideal community?" Response options were City (C), Suburb (S), Small Town (T), or Rural (R). A representative portion of this survey for a sample of 100 respondents is as follows:

Where do you live now?

```
S  T  R  C  R  R  T  C  S  T  C  S  C  S  T
S  S  C  S  S  T  T  C  C  S  T  C  S  T  C
T  R  S  S  T  C  S  C  T  C  T  C  T  C  R
C  C  R  T  C  S  S  T  S  C  C  C  R  S  C
S  S  C  C  S  C  R  T  T  T  C  R  T  C  R
C  T  R  R  C  T  C  C  R  T  T  R  S  R  T
T  S  S  S  S  C  C  R  T
```

DATA *file*

Communities

What do you consider to be the ideal community?

```
S  C  R  R  R  S  T  S  S  T  T  S  C  S  T
C  C  R  T  R  S  T  T  S  S  C  C  T  T  S
S  R  C  S  C  C  S  C  R  C  T  S  R  R  R
C  T  S  T  T  T  R  R  S  C  C  R  R  S  S
S  T  C  T  T  C  R  T  T  T  C  T  T  R  R
C  S  R  T  C  T  C  C  T  T  T  R  C  R  T
T  C  S  S  C  S  T  S  S  R
```

a. Provide a percent frequency distribution and a histogram for each question.
b. Where are most adults living now?
c. Where do most adults consider the ideal community to be?
d. What changes in living areas would you expect to see if people moved from where they currently live to their ideal community?

9. Consider the following data:

DATA *file*

Frequency

```
14   24   18   22
19   18   16   22
24   17   15   16
19   23   24   16
16   26   21   16
20   22   16   12
24   23   19   25
20   25   21   19
21   25   23   24
22   19   20   20
```

a. Develop a frequency distribution using classes of 12–14, 15–17, 18–20, 21–23, and 24–26.
b. Develop a relative frequency distribution and a percent frequency distribution using the classes in part a.

10. Consider the following frequency distribution.

Class	Frequency
10–19	10
20–29	14
30–39	17
40–49	7
50–59	2

Construct a cumulative frequency distribution.

11. The owner of an automobile repair shop studied the waiting times for customers who arrive at the shop for an oil change. The following data with waiting times in minutes were collected over a 1-month period.

2 5 10 12 4 4 5 17 11 8 9 8 12 21 6 8 7 13 18 3

RepairShop

Using classes of 0–4, 5–9, and so on, show:
a. The frequency distribution.
b. The relative frequency distribution.
c. The cumulative frequency distribution.
d. The cumulative relative frequency distribution.
e. The proportion of customers needing an oil change who wait 9 minutes or less.

12. Approximately 1.65 million high school students take the Scholastic Aptitude Test (SAT) each year, and nearly 80 percent of the college and universities without open admissions policies use SAT scores in making admission decisions. The current version of the SAT includes three parts: reading comprehension, mathematics, and writing. A perfect combined score for all three parts is 2400. A sample of SAT scores for the combined three-part SAT are as follows:

SAT

1665	1525	1355	1645	1780
1275	2135	1280	1060	1585
1650	1560	1150	1485	1990
1590	1880	1420	1755	1375
1475	1680	1440	1260	1730
1490	1560	940	1390	1175

a. Show a frequency distribution and histogram. Begin with the first bin starting at 800, and use a bin width of 200.
b. Comment on the shape of the distribution.
c. What other observations can be made about the SAT scores based on the tabular and graphical summaries?

13. Consider a sample with data values of 10, 20, 12, 17, and 16.
a. Compute the mean and median.
b. Consider a sample with data values 10, 20, 12, 17, 16, and 12. How would you expect the mean and median for these sample data to compare to the mean and median for part a (higher, lower, or the same)? Compute the mean and median for the sample data 10, 20, 12, 17, 16, and 12.

14. Consider a sample with data values of 27, 25, 20, 15, 30, 34, 28, and 25. Compute the 20th, 25th, 65th, and 75th percentiles.

15. Consider a sample with data values of 53, 55, 70, 58, 64, 57, 53, 69, 57, 68, and 53. Compute the mean, median, and mode.

16. If an asset declines in value from $5,000 to $3,500 over nine years, what is the mean annual growth rate in the asset's value over these nine years?

17. Suppose that you initially invested $10,000 in the Stivers mutual fund and $5,000 in the Trippi mutual fund. The value of each investment at the end of each subsequent year is provided in the table:

Year	Stivers ($)	Trippi ($)
1	11,000	5,600
2	12,000	6,300
3	13,000	6,900
4	14,000	7,600
5	15,000	8,500
6	16,000	9,200
7	17,000	9,900
8	18,000	10,600

Which of the two mutual funds performed better over this time period?

18. The average time that Americans commute to work is 27.7 minutes (*Sterling's Best Places*, April 13, 2012). The average commute times in minutes for 48 cities are as follows:

Albuquerque	23.3	Jacksonville	26.2	Phoenix	28.3
Atlanta	28.3	Kansas City	23.4	Pittsburgh	25.0
Austin	24.6	Las Vegas	28.4	Portland	26.4
Baltimore	32.1	Little Rock	20.1	Providence	23.6
Boston	31.7	Los Angeles	32.2	Richmond	23.4
Charlotte	25.8	Louisville	21.4	Sacramento	25.8
Chicago	38.1	Memphis	23.8	Salt Lake City	20.2
Cincinnati	24.9	Miami	30.7	San Antonio	26.1
Cleveland	26.8	Milwaukee	24.8	San Diego	24.8
Columbus	23.4	Minneapolis	23.6	San Francisco	32.6
Dallas	28.5	Nashville	25.3	San Jose	28.5
Denver	28.1	New Orleans	31.7	Seattle	27.3
Detroit	29.3	New York	43.8	St. Louis	26.8
El Paso	24.4	Oklahoma City	22.0	Tucson	24.0
Fresno	23.0	Orlando	27.1	Tulsa	20.1
Indianapolis	24.8	Philadelphia	34.2	Washington, D.C.	32.8

CommuteTimes

a. What is the mean commute time for these 48 cities?
b. What is the median commute time for these 48 cities?
c. What is the mode for these 48 cities?
d. What is the variance and standard deviation of commute times for these 48 cities?
e. What is the third quartile of commute times for these 48 cities?

19. Suppose that the average waiting time for a patient at a physician's office is just over 29 minutes. To address the issue of long patient wait times, some physicians' offices are using wait-tracking systems to notify patients of expected wait times. Patients can adjust their arrival times based on this information and spend less time in waiting rooms. The following data show wait times (in minutes) for a sample of patients at offices that do not have a wait-tracking system and wait times for a sample of patients at offices with such systems.

Without Wait-Tracking System	With Wait-Tracking System
24	31
67	11
17	14
20	18
31	12
44	37
12	9
23	13
16	12
37	15

PatientWaits

a. What are the mean and median patient wait times for offices with a wait-tracking system? What are the mean and median patient wait times for offices without a wait-tracking system?
b. What are the variance and standard deviation of patient wait times for offices with a wait-tracking system? What are the variance and standard deviation of patient wait times for visits to offices without a wait tracking system?
c. Create a box plot for patient wait times for offices without a wait-tracking system.

d. Create a box plot for patient wait times for offices with a wait-tracking system.

e. Do offices with a wait-tracking system have shorter patient wait times than offices without a wait-tracking system? Explain.

20. According to the National Education Association (NEA), teachers generally spend more than 40 hours each week working on instructional duties. The following data show the number of hours worked per week for a sample of 13 high school science teachers and a sample of 11 high school English teachers.

DATA file
Teachers

High school science teachers 53 56 54 54 55 58 49 61 54 54 52 53 54

High school English teachers 52 47 50 46 47 48 49 46 55 44 47

a. What is the median number of hours worked per week for the sample of 13 high school science teachers?

b. What is the median number of hours worked per week for the sample of 11 high school English teachers?

c. Create a box plot for the number of hours worked for high school science teachers.

d. Create a box plot for the number of hours worked for high school English teachers.

e. Comment on the differences between the box plots for science and English teachers.

21. Return to the waiting times given for the physician's office in Problem 19.

DATA file
PatientWaits

a. Considering only offices *without* a wait-tracking system, what is the z-score for the 10th patient in the sample (wait time = 37 minutes)?

b. Considering only offices *with* a wait-tracking system, what is the z-score for the 6th patient in the sample (wait time = 37 minutes)? How does this z-score compare with the z-score you calculated for part a?

c. Based on z-scores, do the data for offices without a wait-tracking system contain any outliers? Based on z-scores, do the data for offices without a wait-tracking system contain any outliers?

22. The results of a national survey showed that on average, adults sleep 6.9 hours per night. Suppose that the standard deviation is 1.2 hours and that the number of hours of sleep follows a bell-shaped distribution.

a. Use the empirical rule to calculate the percentage of individuals who sleep between 4.5 and 9.3 hours per day.

b. What is the z-value for an adult who sleeps 8 hours per night?

c. What is the z-value for an adult who sleeps 6 hours per night?

23. Suppose that the national average for the math portion of the College Board's SAT is 515. The College Board periodically rescales the test scores such that the standard deviation is approximately 100. Answer the following questions using a bell-shaped distribution and the empirical rule for the math test scores.

a. What percentage of students have an SAT math score greater than 615?

b. What percentage of students have an SAT math score greater than 715?

c. What percentage of students have an SAT math score between 415 and 515?

d. What is the z-score for student with an SAT math score of 620?

e. What is the z-score for a student with an SAT math score of 405?

24. Five observations taken for two variables follow.

x_i	4	6	11	3	16
y_i	50	50	40	60	30

a. Develop a scatter diagram with x on the horizontal axis.

b. What does the scatter diagram developed in part a indicate about the relationship between the two variables?

c. Compute and interpret the sample covariance.

d. Compute and interpret the sample correlation coefficient.

25. The scatter chart in the following figure was created using sample data for profits and market capitalizations from a sample of firms in the Fortune 500.

DATA *file*
Fortune500

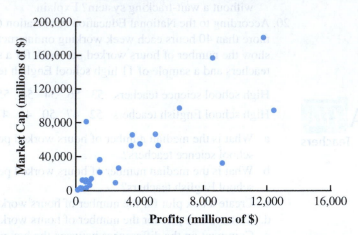

a. Discuss what the scatter chart indicates about the relationship between profits and market capitalization?
b. The data used to produce this are contained in the file *Fortune500*. Calculate the covariance between profits and market capitalization. Discuss what the covariance indicates about the relationship between profits and market capitalization?
c. Calculate the correlation coefficient between profits and market capitalization. What does the correlations coefficient indicate about the relationship between profits and market capitalization?

26. The economic downturn in 2008–2009 resulted in the loss of jobs and an increase in delinquent loans for housing. In projecting where the real estate market was headed in the coming year, economists studied the relationship between the jobless rate and the percentage of delinquent loans. The expectation was that if the jobless rate continued to increase, there would also be an increase in the percentage of delinquent loans. The following data show the jobless rate and the delinquent loan percentage for 27 major real estate markets.

DATA *file*
JoblessRate

Metro Area	Jobless Rate (%)	Delinquent Loans (%)	Metro Area	Jobless Rate (%)	Delinquent Loans (%)
Atlanta	7.1	7.02	New York	6.2	5.78
Boston	5.2	5.31	Orange County	6.3	6.08
Charlotte	7.8	5.38	Orlando	7.0	10.05
Chicago	7.8	5.40	Philadelphia	6.2	4.75
Dallas	5.8	5.00	Phoenix	5.5	7.22
Denver	5.8	4.07	Portland	6.5	3.79
Detroit	9.3	6.53	Raleigh	6.0	3.62
Houston	5.7	5.57	Sacramento	8.3	9.24
Jacksonville	7.3	6.99	St. Louis	7.5	4.40
Las Vegas	7.6	11.12	San Diego	7.1	6.91
Los Angeles	8.2	7.56	San Francisco	6.8	5.57
Miami	7.1	12.11	Seattle	5.5	3.87
Minneapolis	6.3	4.39	Tampa	7.5	8.42
Nashville	6.6	4.78			

Source: *The Wall Street Journal*, January 27, 2009.

a. Compute the correlation coefficient. Is there a positive correlation between the jobless rate and the percentage of delinquent housing loans? What is your interpretation?

b. Show a scatter diagram of the relationship between the jobless rate and the percentage of delinquent housing loans.

CASE PROBLEM: HEAVENLY CHOCOLATES WEB SITE TRANSACTIONS

Heavenly Chocolates manufactures and sells quality chocolate products at its plant and retail store located in Saratoga Springs, New York. Two years ago, the company developed a web site and began selling its products over the Internet. Web-site sales have exceeded the company's expectations, and management is now considering strategies to increase sales even further. To learn more about the web-site customers, a sample of 50 Heavenly Chocolate transactions was selected from the previous month's sales. Data showing the day of the week each transaction was made, the type of browser the customer used, the time spent on the web site, the number of web pages viewed, and the amount spent by each of the 50 customers are contained in the file named *HeavenlyChocolates*. A portion of the data is shown in the table that follows:

DATA *file*

HeavenlyChocolates

Customer	Day	Browser	Time (min)	Pages Viewed	Amount Spent ($)
1	Mon	Chrome	12.0	4	54.52
2	Wed	Other	19.5	6	94.90
3	Mon	Chrome	8.5	4	26.68
4	Tue	Firefox	11.4	2	44.73
5	Wed	Chrome	11.3	4	66.27
6	Sat	Firefox	10.5	6	67.80
7	Sun	Chrome	11.4	2	36.04
.	.	.	.	.	.
.	.	.	.	.	.
.	.	.	.	.	.
.	.	.	.	.	.
48	Fri	Chrome	9.7	5	103.15
49	Mon	Other	7.3	6	52.15
50	Fri	Chrome	13.4	3	98.75

Heavenly Chocolates would like to use the sample data to determine whether online shoppers who spend more time and view more pages also spend more money during their visit to the web site. The company would also like to investigate the effect that the day of the week and the type of browser have on sales.

Managerial Report

Use the methods of descriptive statistics to learn about the customers who visit the Heavenly Chocolates web site. Include the following in your report.

1. Graphical and numerical summaries for the length of time the shopper spends on the web site, the number of pages viewed, and the mean amount spent per transaction. Discuss what you learn about Heavenly Chocolates' online shoppers from these numerical summaries.

2. Summarize the frequency, the total dollars spent, and the mean amount spent per transaction for each day of week. Discuss the observations you can make about Heavenly Chocolates' business based on the day of the week?

3. Summarize the frequency, the total dollars spent, and the mean amount spent per transaction for each type of browser. Discuss the observations you can make about Heavenly Chocolates' business based on the type of browser?

4. Develop a scatter diagram, and compute the sample correlation coefficient to explore the relationship between the time spent on the web site and the dollar amount spent. Use the horizontal axis for the time spent on the web site. Discuss your findings.

5. Develop a scatter diagram, and compute the sample correlation coefficient to explore the relationship between the number of web pages viewed and the amount spent. Use the horizontal axis for the number of web pages viewed. Discuss your findings.

6. Develop a scatter diagram, and compute the sample correlation coefficient to explore the relationship between the time spent on the web site and the number of pages viewed. Use the horizontal axis to represent the number of pages viewed. Discuss your findings.

Chapter 2 Appendix

Appendix 2.1 Creating Box Plots with XLMiner

XLMiner, an Add-in for Excel developed by Frontline Systems, can be used for basic statistical analysis, data visualization, and data mining. In this chapter appendix, we demonstrate the use of XLMiner in making box plots. There are no easy methods for creating box plots in Excel without an Add-in, but XLMiner makes it very easy to create them for single- and multiple-variable data sets.

We demonstrate the use of XLMiner to create a box plot with multiple variables using an expanded form of the home sales data illustrated in Figure 2.23. The data used in generating the box plots in this figure are entered into an Excel Worksheet. In addition to data on the location of the home and selling price, the Excel Worksheet contains data on the type of home sold (detached or condo) and on the size of the home in square feet. Rows 1–20 of this Excel Worksheet are shown in Figure 2.28. To create box plots for the home sales data in Figure 2.23 using XLMiner, following these steps:

DATA *file*
HomeSalesComparison

Step 1. Select a cell containing home sales data (any cell in the range A1:D51)
Step 2. Click the **XLMiner Platform** tab in the Ribbon
Step 3. In the **Data Analysis** group, select **Explore** and click **Chart Wizard**
Step 4. When the **Chart Wizard New Chart** dialog box opens, select **Box Plot**, and click **Next**

FIGURE 2.28 Using XLMiner to Analyze Home Selling Price Comparison Data

	A	B	C	D
1	**Selling Price ($)**	**Size (ft²)**	**Location**	**Type**
2	302,000	2150	Fairview	Detached
3	265,000	1890	Fairview	Detached
4	280,000	1540	Fairview	Detached
5	220,000	1790	Fairview	Detached
6	149,000	1500	Fairview	Detached
7	155,000	1450	Fairview	Detached
8	198,000	1700	Fairview	Condo
9	187,000	1900	Fairview	Condo
10	208,000	1800	Fairview	Detached
11	174,000	1650	Fairview	Detached
12	336,000	1750	Shadyside	Condo
13	398,000	1950	Shadyside	Condo
14	378,000	1780	Shadyside	Condo
15	298,000	1600	Shadyside	Detached
16	425,000	2250	Shadyside	Detached
17	344,000	1780	Shadyside	Condo
18	302,000	1750	Shadyside	Condo
19	300,000	1700	Shadyside	Detached
20	298,000	1540	Shadyside	Detached
21	342,000	1580	Shadyside	Detached
22	152,000	1700	Groton	Detached
23	158,000	1280	Groton	Detached

Chart Wizard dialog box:

New Chart
Please select the data you wish to chart, and a chart type

Data to explore: $A$1:$D$51

- Bar Chart
- Histogram
- Line Chart
- Parallel Coordinates
- ScatterPlot
- Scatterplot Matrix
- Boxplot
- Variable
- Export to PowerBI
- Export to Tableau

Bar charts are useful for comparing a single statistic(e.g. average, count, percentage) across groups.

[< Back] [Next >] [Finish] [Cancel]

Step 5. In the **Y Axis Selection Dialog** box, select **Selling Price ($)** Click **Next**

Step 6. In the **X Axis Selection Dialog** box select **Location** Click **Finish**

The completed box plot appears in Figure 2.29.

Figure 2.29 shows that the most expensive houses appear to be in Shadyside and the cheapest houses in Hamilton. Home selling prices have the least variation in Groton and Hamilton, while there is a large amount of variation in home selling prices in Irving. The percentile and other statistical information shown in Figure 2.29 can be viewed by hovering the pointer over one of the box plots.

XLMiner provides several tools for exploring the data and interacting with the charts created. We can easily adjust the variables being displayed on both the horizontal and vertical axes. To change these values, follow these steps:

Step 1. Click on **Location** below the horizontal axis
Change this value to **Type**

Step 2. Click on **Selling Price ($)** next to the vertical axis
Change this value to **Size (ft2)**

FIGURE 2.29   Box Plots Created Using XLMiner for the Home Sales Comparison Data

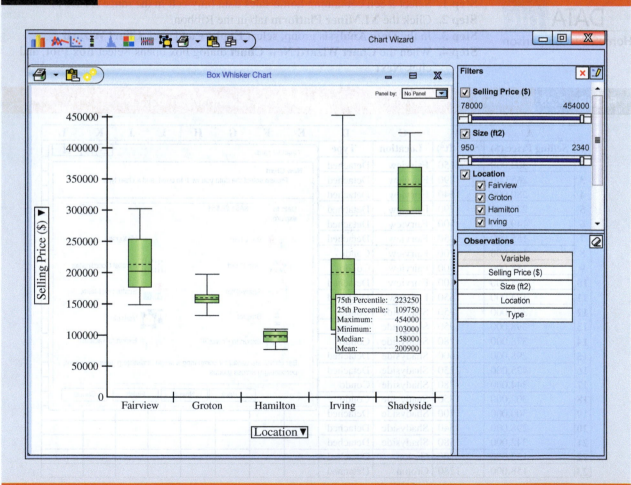

Step 3. In the upper right of the Box Plot, click **No Panel** next to **Panel By:**
Change this value to **Location**

This will now display box plots for Detached and Condo types of home sales versus the size of the homes sold for each location. We can make several interesting comparisons using the chart in Figure 2.30. The figure shows that Hamilton tends to have smaller homes regardless of whether they are condos or detached homes and that detached homes tend to have more variation in size than condos in all locations.

In the **Filters** area of the box plot chart shown in Figure 2.30, we can adjust the data used in constructing the box plots. By unchecking the boxes next to the locations, we can delete all home sales in a particular location from the data used to create the box plots. We can also filter the data displayed within each box plot by adjusting the slider bar handles below Size (ft2) in the **Filters** area. For instance, if we drag the left handle from 950 to 1200 (or by clicking on the value of 950 above the slider handle and replacing it with 1200), all sales of homes less than 1200 square feet in size will not be used in creating the box plots.

FIGURE 2.30 Modified Box Plots Created in XLMiner for the Home Sales Comparison Data

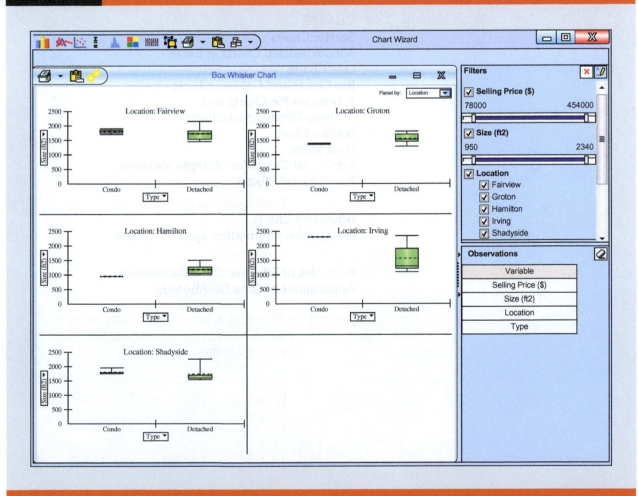

Chapter 3

Data Visualization

CONTENTS

ANALYTICS IN ACTION

Cincinnati Zoo & Botanical Garden[1]

The Cincinnati Zoo & Botanical Garden, located in Cincinnati, Ohio, is the one of the oldest zoos in the United States. To improve decision making by becoming more data-driven, management decided they needed to link the various facets of their business and provide nontechnical managers and executives with an intuitive way to better understand their data. A complicating factor is that when the zoo is busy, managers are expected to be on the grounds interacting with guests, checking on operations, and dealing with issues as they arise or anticipating them.

———
[1]The authors are indebted to John Lucas of the Cincinnati Zoo & Botanical Garden for providing this application.

Therefore, being able to monitor what is happening in real time was a key factor in deciding what to do. Zoo management concluded that a data visualization strategy was needed to address the problem.

Because of its ease of use, real-time updating capability, and iPad compatibility, the Cincinnati Zoo decided to implement its data visualization strategy using IBM's Cognos advanced data visualization software. Using this software, the Cincinnati Zoo developed the set of charts shown in Figure 3.1 (known as a data dashboard) to enable management to track the following key measures of performance:

- Item analysis (sales volumes and sales dollars by location within the zoo)

FIGURE 3.1   Data Dashboard for the Cincinnati Zoo

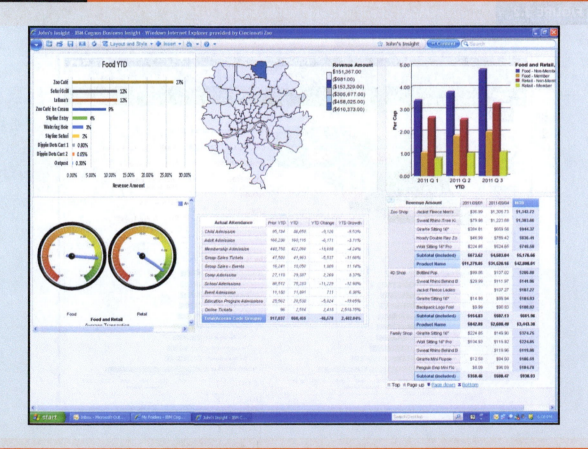

- Geoanalytics (using maps and displays of where the day's visitors are spending their time at the zoo)
- Customer spending
- Cashier sales performance
- Sales and attendance data versus weather patterns
- Performance of the zoo's loyalty rewards program

An iPad mobile application was also developed to enable the zoo's managers to be out on the grounds and still see and anticipate occurrences in real time. The Cincinnati Zoo's iPad application, shown in Figure 3.2, provides managers with access to the following information:

- Real-time attendance data, including what types of guests are coming to the zoo (members, nonmembers, school groups, and so on)

- Real-time analysis showing which locations are busiest and which items are selling the fastest inside the zoo
- Real-time geographical representation of where the zoo's visitors live

Having access to the data shown in Figures 3.1 and 3.2 allows the zoo managers to make better decisions about staffing levels, which items to stock based on weather and other conditions, and how to better target advertising based on geodemographics.

The impact that data visualization has had on the zoo has been substantial. Within the first year of use, the system was directly responsible for revenue growth of over $500,000, increased visitation to the zoo, enhanced customer service, and reduced marketing costs.

FIGURE 3.2   The Cincinnati Zoo iPad Data Dashboard

The first step in trying to interpret data is often to visualize it in some way. Data visualization can be as simple as creating a summary table, or it could require generating charts to help interpret, analyze, and learn from the data. Data visualization is very helpful for identifying data errors and for reducing the size of your data set by highlighting important relationships and trends.

Data visualization is also important in conveying your analysis to others. Although business analytics is about making better decisions, in many cases, the ultimate decision maker is not the person who analyzes the data. Therefore, the person analyzing the data has to make the analysis simple for others to understand. Proper data visualization techniques greatly improve the ability of the decision maker to interpret the analysis easily.

In this chapter we discuss some general concepts related to data visualization to help you analyze data and convey your analysis to others. We cover specifics dealing with how to design tables and charts, as well as the most commonly used charts, and present an overview of some more advanced charts. We also introduce the concept of data dashboards and geographic information systems (GISs). Our detailed examples use Excel to generate tables and charts, and we discuss several software packages that can be used for advanced data visualization. The appendix to this chapter covers the use of XLMiner (an Excel Add-in) for data visualization.

3.1 Overview of Data Visualization

Decades of research studies in psychology and other fields show that the human mind can process visual images such as charts much faster than it can interpret rows of numbers. However, these same studies also show that the human mind has certain limitations in its ability to interpret visual images and that some images are better at conveying information than others. The goal of this chapter is to introduce some of the most common forms of visualizing data and demonstrate when each form is appropriate.

Microsoft Excel is a ubiquitous tool used in business for basic data visualization. Software tools such as Excel make it easy for anyone to create many standard examples of data visualization. However, as discussed in this chapter, the default settings for tables and charts created with Excel can be altered to increase clarity. New types of software that are dedicated to data visualization have appeared recently. We focus our techniques on Excel in this chapter, but we also mention some of these more advanced software packages for specific data-visualization uses.

Effective Design Techniques

One of the most helpful ideas for creating effective tables and charts for data visualization is the idea of the **data-ink ratio**, first described by Edward R. Tufte in 2001 in his book *The Visual Display of Quantitative Information*. The data-ink ratio measures the proportion of what Tufte terms "data-ink" to the total amount of ink used in a table or chart. Data-ink is the ink used in a table or chart that is necessary to convey the meaning of the data to the audience. Non-data-ink is ink used in a table or chart that serves no useful purpose in conveying the data to the audience.

Let us consider the case of Gossamer Industries, a firm that produces fine silk clothing products. Gossamer is interested in tracking the sales of one of its most popular items, a particular style of women's scarf. Table 3.1 and Figure 3.3 provide examples of a table and chart with low data-ink ratios used to display sales of this style of women's scarf. The data used in this table and figure represent product sales by day. Both of these examples are similar to tables and charts generated with Excel using common default settings.

TABLE 3.1   Example of a Low Data-Ink Ratio Table

Scarf Sales by Day			
Day	Sales	Day	Sales
1	150	11	170
2	170	12	160
3	140	13	290
4	150	14	200
5	180	15	210
6	180	16	110
7	210	17	90
8	230	18	140
9	140	19	150
10	200	20	230

In Table 3.1, most of the grid lines serve no useful purpose. Likewise, in Figure 3.3, the horizontal lines in the chart also add little additional information. In both cases, most of these lines can be deleted without reducing the information conveyed. However, an important piece of information is missing from Figure 3.3: labels for axes. Axes should always be labeled in a chart unless both the meaning and unit of measure are obvious.

Table 3.2 shows a modified table in which all grid lines have been deleted except for those around the title of the table. Deleting the grid lines in Table 3.1 increases the data-ink ratio because a larger proportion of the ink used in the table is used to convey the information (the actual numbers). Similarly, deleting the unnecessary horizontal lines

FIGURE 3.3   Example of a Low Data-Ink Ratio Chart

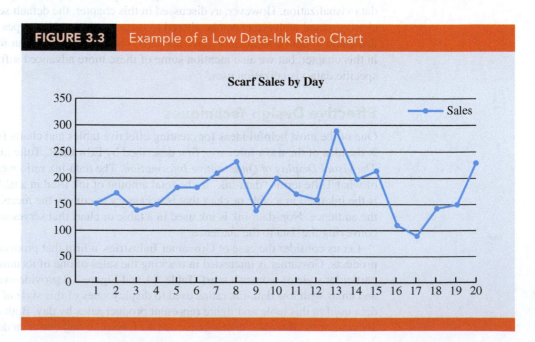

TABLE 3.2	Increasing the Data-Ink Ratio by Removing Unnecessary Gridlines		
Scarf Sales by Day			
Day	**Sales**	**Day**	**Sales**
1	150	11	170
2	170	12	160
3	140	13	290
4	150	14	200
5	180	15	210
6	180	16	110
7	210	17	90
8	230	18	140
9	140	19	150
10	200	20	230

in Figure 3.4 increases the data-ink ratio. Note that deleting these horizontal lines and removing (or reducing the size of) the markers at each data point can make it more difficult to determine the exact values plotted in the chart. However, as we discuss later, a simple chart is not the most effective way of presenting data when the audience needs to know exact values; in these cases, it is better to use a table.

In many cases, white space in a table or chart can improve readability. This principle is similar to the idea of increasing the data-ink ratio. Consider Table 3.2 and Figure 3.4. Removing the unnecessary lines has increased the "white space," making it easier to read both the table and the chart. The fundamental idea in creating effective tables and charts is to make them as simple as possible in conveying information to the reader.

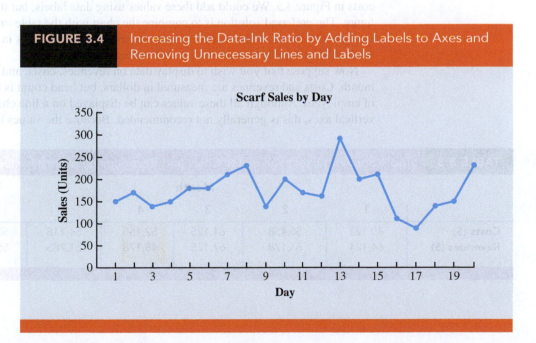

FIGURE 3.4	Increasing the Data-Ink Ratio by Adding Labels to Axes and Removing Unnecessary Lines and Labels

NOTES + COMMENTS

1. Tables have been used to display data for more than a thousand years. However, charts are much more recent inventions. The famous seventeenth-century French mathematician, René Descartes, is credited with inventing the now familiar graph with horizontal and vertical axes. William Playfair invented bar charts, line charts, and pie charts in the late 18th century, all of which we will discuss in this chapter. More recently, individuals such as William Cleveland, Edward R. Tufte, and Stephen Few have introduced design techniques for both clarity and beauty in data visualization.

2. Many of the default settings in Excel are not ideal for displaying data using tables and charts that communicate effectively. Before presenting Excel-generated tables and charts to others, it is worth the effort to remove unnecessary lines and labels.

3.2 Tables

The first decision in displaying data is whether a table or a chart will be more effective. In general, charts can often convey information faster and easier to readers, but in some cases a table is more appropriate. Tables should be used when:

1. The reader needs to refer to specific numerical values.
2. The reader needs to make precise comparisons between different values and not just relative comparisons.
3. The values being displayed have different units or very different magnitudes.

When the accounting department of Gossamer Industries is summarizing the company's annual data for completion of its federal tax forms, the specific numbers corresponding to revenues and expenses are important and not just the relative values. Therefore, these data should be presented in a table similar to Table 3.3.

Similarly, if it is important to know by exactly how much revenues exceed expenses each month, then this would also be better presented as a table rather than as a line chart, as seen in Figure 3.5. Notice that it is very difficult to determine the monthly revenues and costs in Figure 3.5. We could add these values using data labels, but they would clutter the figure. The preferred solution is to combine the chart with the table into a single figure, as in Figure 3.6, to allow the reader to easily see the monthly changes in revenues and costs while also being able to refer to the exact numerical values.

Now suppose that you wish to display data on revenues, costs, and head count for each month. Costs and revenues are measured in dollars, but head count is measured in number of employees. Although all these values can be displayed on a line chart using multiple vertical axes, this is generally not recommended. Because the values have widely different

TABLE 3.3	Table Showing Exact Values for Costs and Revenues by Month for Gossamer Industries						
	Month						
	1	2	3	4	5	6	Total
Costs ($)	48,123	56,458	64,125	52,158	54,718	50,985	326,567
Revenues ($)	64,124	66,128	67,125	48,178	51,785	55,687	353,027

FIGURE 3.5   Line Chart of Monthly Costs and Revenues at Gossamer Industries

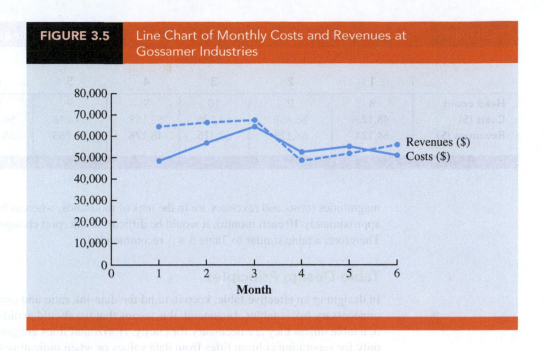

FIGURE 3.6   Combined Line Chart and Table for Monthly Costs and Revenues at Gossamer Industries

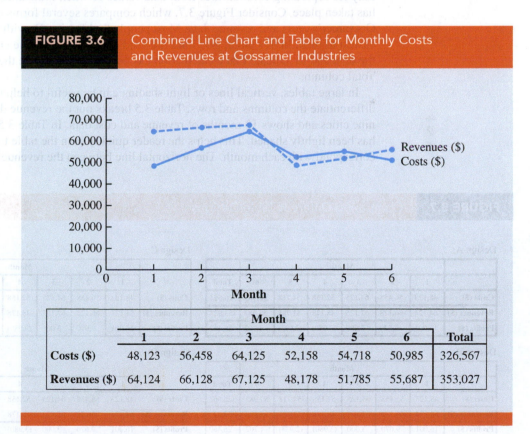

	Month						
	1	**2**	**3**	**4**	**5**	**6**	**Total**
Costs ($)	48,123	56,458	64,125	52,158	54,718	50,985	326,567
Revenues ($)	64,124	66,128	67,125	48,178	51,785	55,687	353,027

TABLE 3.4	Table Displaying Head Count, Costs, and Revenues at Gossamer Industries						
	Month						
	1	2	3	4	5	6	Total
Head count	8	9	10	9	9	9	
Costs ($)	48,123	56,458	64,125	52,158	54,718	50,985	326,567
Revenues ($)	64,124	66,128	67,125	48,178	51,785	55,687	353,027

magnitudes (costs and revenues are in the tens of thousands, whereas head count is approximately 10 each month), it would be difficult to interpret changes on a single chart. Therefore, a table similar to Table 3.4 is recommended.

Table Design Principles

In designing an effective table, keep in mind the data-ink ratio and avoid the use of unnecessary ink in tables. In general, this means that we should avoid using vertical lines in a table unless they are necessary for clarity. Horizontal lines are generally necessary only for separating column titles from data values or when indicating that a calculation has taken place. Consider Figure 3.7, which compares several forms of a table displaying Gossamer's costs and revenue data. Most people find Design D, with the fewest grid lines, easiest to read. In this table, grid lines are used only to separate the column headings from the data and to indicate that a calculation has occurred to generate the Profits row and the Total column.

In large tables, vertical lines or light shading can be useful to help the reader differentiate the columns and rows. Table 3.5 breaks out the revenue data by location for nine cities and shows 12 months of revenue and cost data. In Table 3.5, every other column has been lightly shaded. This helps the reader quickly scan the table to see which values correspond with each month. The horizontal line between the revenue for Academy and the

FIGURE 3.7	Comparing Different Table Designs

Design A:

	Month						
	1	2	3	4	5	6	Total
Costs ($)	48,123	56,458	64,125	52,158	54,718	50,985	326,567
Revenues ($)	64,124	66,128	67,125	48,178	51,785	55,687	353,027
Profits ($)	16,001	9,670	3,000	(3,980)	(2,933)	4,702	26,460

Design B:

	Month						
	1	2	3	4	5	6	Total
Costs ($)	48,123	56,458	64,125	52,158	54,718	50,985	326,567
Revenues ($)	64,124	66,128	67,125	48,178	51,785	55,687	353,027
Profits ($)	16,001	9,670	3,000	(3,980)	(2,933)	4,702	26,460

Design C:

	Month						
	1	2	3	4	5	6	Total
Costs ($)	48,123	56,458	64,125	52,158	54,718	50,985	326,567
Revenues ($)	64,124	66,128	67,125	48,178	51,785	55,687	353,027
Profits ($)	16,001	9,670	3,000	(3,980)	(2,933)	4,702	26,460

Design D:

	Month						
	1	2	3	4	5	6	Total
Costs ($)	48,123	56,458	64,125	52,158	54,718	50,985	326,567
Revenues ($)	64,124	66,128	67,125	48,178	51,785	55,687	353,027
Profits ($)	16,001	9,670	3,000	(3,980)	(2,933)	4,702	26,460

TABLE 3.5 Larger Table Showing Revenues by Location for 12 Months of Data

Revenues by Location ($)	Month 1	2	3	4	5	6	7	8	9	10	11	12	Total
Temple	8,987	8,595	8,958	6,718	8,066	8,574	8,701	9,490	9,610	9,262	9,875	11,058	107,895
Killeen	8,212	9,143	8,714	6,869	8,150	8,891	8,766	9,193	9,603	10,374	10,456	10,982	109,353
Waco	11,603	12,063	11,173	9,622	8,912	9,553	11,943	12,947	12,925	14,050	14,300	13,877	142,967
Belton	7,671	7,617	7,896	6,899	7,877	6,621	7,765	7,720	7,824	7,938	7,943	7,047	90,819
Granger	7,642	7,744	7,836	5,833	6,002	6,728	7,848	7,717	7,646	7,620	7,728	8,013	88,357
Harker Heights	5,257	5,326	4,998	4,304	4,106	4,980	5,084	5,061	5,186	5,179	4,955	5,326	59,763
Gatesville	5,316	5,245	5,056	3,317	3,852	4,026	5,135	5,132	5,052	5,271	5,304	5,154	57,859
Lampasas	5,266	5,129	5,022	3,022	3,088	4,289	5,110	5,073	4,978	5,343	4,984	5,315	56,620
Academy	4,170	5,266	7,472	1,594	1,732	2,025	8,772	1,956	3,304	3,090	3,579	2,487	45,446
Total	64,124	66,128	67,125	48,178	51,785	55,687	69,125	64,288	66,128	68,128	69,125	69,258	759,079
Costs ($)	48,123	56,458	64,125	52,158	54,718	50,985	57,898	62,050	65,215	61,819	67,828	69,558	710,935

Total row helps the reader differentiate the revenue data for each location and indicates that a calculation has taken place to generate the totals by month. If one wanted to highlight the differences among locations, the shading could be done for every other row instead of every other column.

We depart from these guidelines in some figures and tables in this textbook to more closely match Excel's output.

Notice also the alignment of the text and numbers in Table 3.5. Columns of numerical values in a table should be right-aligned; that is, the final digit of each number should be aligned in the column. This makes it easy to see differences in the magnitude of values. If you are showing digits to the right of the decimal point, all values should include the same number of digits to the right of the decimal. Also, use only the number of digits that are necessary to convey the meaning in comparing the values; there is no need to include additional digits if they are not meaningful for comparisons. In many business applications, we report financial values, in which case we often round to the nearest dollar or include two digits to the right of the decimal if such precision is necessary. Additional digits to the right of the decimal are usually unnecessary. For extremely large numbers, we may prefer to display data rounded to the nearest thousand, ten thousand, or even million. For instance, if we need to include, say, $3,457,982 and $10,124,390 in a table when exact dollar values are not necessary, we could write these as 3,458 and 10,124 and indicate that all values in the table are in units of $1,000.

It is generally best to left-align text values within a column in a table, as in the Revenues by Location (the first) column of Table 3.5. In some cases, you may prefer to center text, but you should do this only if the text values are all approximately the same length. Otherwise, aligning the first letter of each data entry promotes readability. Column headings should either match the alignment of the data in the columns or be centered over the values, as in Table 3.5.

Crosstabulation

Types of data such as categorical and quantitative are discussed in Chapter 2.

A useful type of table for describing data of two variables is a **crosstabulation**, which provides a tabular summary of data for two variables. To illustrate, consider the following application based on data from Zagat's Restaurant Review. Data on the quality rating, meal price, and the usual wait time for a table during peak hours were collected for a sample of 300 Los Angeles area restaurants. Table 3.6 shows the data for the first 10 restaurants. Quality ratings are an example of categorical data, and meal prices are an example of quantitative data.

DATA *file*
Restaurant

TABLE 3.6	Quality Rating and Meal Price for 300 Los Angeles Restaurants		
Restaurant	**Quality Rating**	**Meal Price ($)**	**Wait Time (min)**
1	Good	18	5
2	Very Good	22	6
3	Good	28	1
4	Excellent	38	74
5	Very Good	33	6
6	Good	28	5
7	Very Good	19	11
8	Very Good	11	9
9	Very Good	23	13
10	Good	13	1

TABLE 3.7	Crosstabulation of Quality Rating and Meal Price for 300 Los Angeles Restaurants				
	Meal Price				
Quality Rating	**$10–19**	**$20–29**	**$30–39**	**$40–49**	**Total**
Good	42	40	2	0	84
Very Good	34	64	46	6	150
Excellent	2	14	28	22	66
Total	78	118	76	28	300

For now, we will limit our consideration to the quality-rating and meal-price variables. A crosstabulation of the data for quality rating and meal price is shown in Table 3.7. The left and top margin labels define the classes for the two variables. In the left margin, the row labels (Good, Very Good, and Excellent) correspond to the three classes of the quality-rating variable. In the top margin, the column labels ($10–19, $20–29, $30–39, and $40–49) correspond to the four classes (or bins) of the meal-price variable. Each restaurant in the sample provides a quality rating and a meal price. Thus, each restaurant in the sample is associated with a cell appearing in one of the rows and one of the columns of the crosstabulation. For example, restaurant 5 is identified as having a very good quality rating and a meal price of $33. This restaurant belongs to the cell in row 2 and column 3. In constructing a crosstabulation, we simply count the number of restaurants that belong to each of the cells in the crosstabulation.

Table 3.7 shows that the greatest number of restaurants in the sample (64) have a very good rating and a meal price in the $20–29 range. Only two restaurants have an excellent rating and a meal price in the $10–19 range. Similar interpretations of the other frequencies can be made. In addition, note that the right and bottom margins of the crosstabulation give the frequencies of quality rating and meal price separately. From the right margin, we see that data on quality ratings show 84 good restaurants, 150 very good restaurants, and 66 excellent restaurants. Similarly, the bottom margin shows the counts for the meal price variable. The value of 300 in the bottom right corner of the table indicates that 300 restaurants were included in this data set.

PivotTables in Excel

A crosstabulation in Microsoft Excel is known as a **PivotTable**. We will first look at a simple example of how Excel's PivotTable is used to create a crosstabulation of the Zagat's restaurant data shown previously. Figure 3.8 illustrates a portion of the data contained in the file *Restaurant*; the data for the 300 restaurants in the sample have been entered into cells B2:D301.

To create a PivotTable in Excel, we follow these steps:

DATA *file*
Restaurant

Step 1. Click the **Insert** tab on the Ribbon
Step 2. Click **PivotTable** in the **Tables** group
Step 3. When the **Create PivotTable** dialog box appears:
    Choose **Select a Table or Range**
    Enter *A1:D301* in the **Table/Range:** box
    Select **New Worksheet** as the location for the PivotTable Report
    Click **OK**

	A	B	C	D
1	Restaurant	Quality Rating	Meal Price ($)	Wait Time (min)
2	1	Good	18	5
3	2	Very Good	22	6
4	3	Good	28	1
5	4	Excellent	38	74
6	5	Very Good	33	6
7	6	Good	28	5
8	7	Very Good	19	11
9	8	Very Good	11	9
10	9	Very Good	23	13
11	10	Good	13	1
12	11	Very Good	33	18
13	12	Very Good	44	7
14	13	Excellent	42	18
15	14	Excellent	34	46
16	15	Good	25	0
17	16	Good	22	3
18	17	Good	26	3
19	18	Excellent	17	36
20	19	Very Good	30	7
21	20	Good	19	3
22	21	Very Good	33	10
23	22	Very Good	22	14
24	23	Excellent	32	27
25	24	Excellent	33	80
26	25	Very Good	34	9

DATA *file*

Restaurant

The resulting initial PivotTable Field List and PivotTable Report are shown in Figure 3.9. Each of the four columns in Figure 3.8 [Restaurant, Quality Rating, Meal Price ($), and Wait Time (min)] is considered a field by Excel. Fields may be chosen to represent rows, columns, or values in the body of the PivotTable Report. The following steps show how to use Excel's PivotTable Field List to assign the Quality Rating field to the rows, the Meal Price ($) field to the columns, and the Restaurant field to the body of the PivotTable report.

Step 4. In the **PivotTable Fields** task pane, go to **Drag fields between areas below:**
Drag the **Quality Rating** field to the **ROWS** area
Drag the **Meal Price ($)** field to the **COLUMNS** area
Drag the **Restaurant** field to the **VALUES** area

Step 5. Click on **Sum of Restaurant** in the **VALUES** area

Step 6. Select **Value Field Settings** from the list of options

| FIGURE 3.9 | Initial PivotTable Field List and PivotTable Field Report for the Restaurant Data |

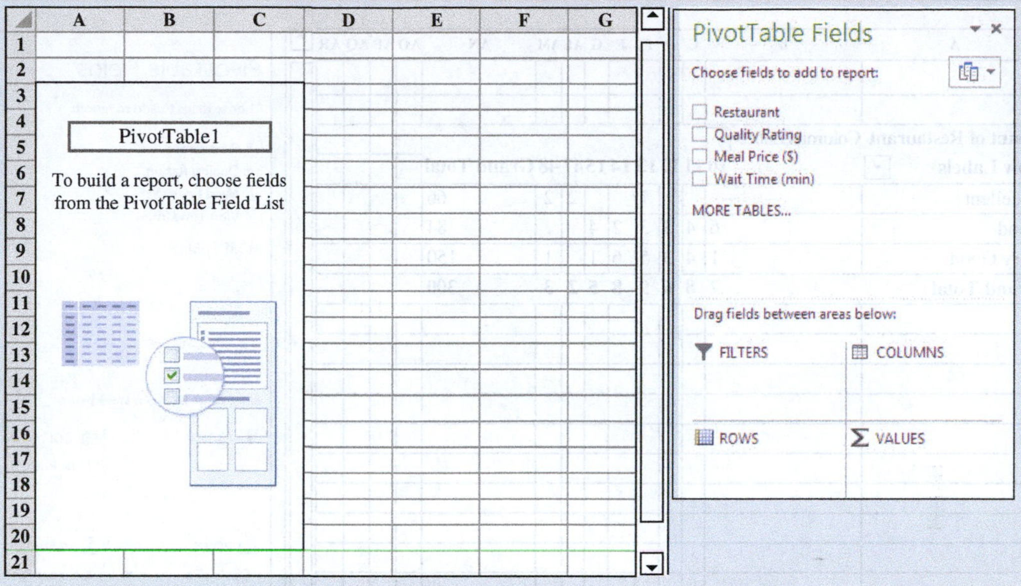

Step 7. When the **Value Field Settings** dialog box appears:
Under **Summarize value field by**, select **Count**
Click **OK**

Figure 3.10 shows the completed PivotTable Field List and a portion of the PivotTable worksheet as it now appears.

To complete the PivotTable, we need to group the columns representing meal prices and place the row labels for quality rating in the proper order:

Step 8. Right-click in cell B4 or any cell containing a meal price column label

Step 9. Select **Group** from the list of options

Step 10. When the **Grouping** dialog box appears:
Enter *10* in the **Starting at:** box
Enter *49* in the **Ending at:** box
Enter *10* in the **By:** box
Click **OK**

Step 11. Right-click on "Excellent" in cell A5

Step 12. Select **Move** and click **Move "Excellent" to End**

The final PivotTable, shown in Figure 3.11, provides the same information as the crosstabulation in Table 3.7.

The values in Figure 3.11 can be interpreted as the frequencies of the data. For instance, row 8 provides the frequency distribution for the data over the quantitative variable of meal price. Seventy-eight restaurants have meal prices of $10 to $19. Column F provides the frequency distribution for the data over the categorical variable of quality. A total of

FIGURE 3.10   Completed PivotTable Field List and a Portion of the PivotTable Report for the Restaurant Data (Columns H:AK Are Hidden)

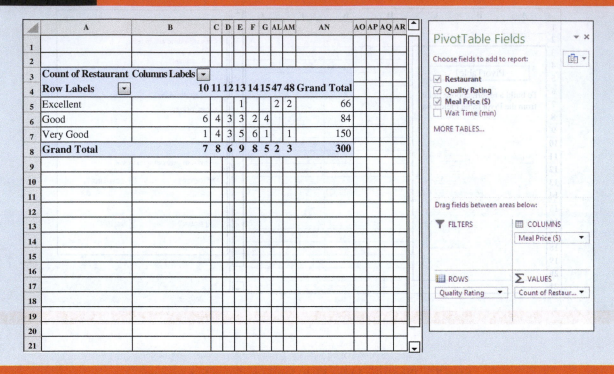

150 restaurants have a quality rating of Very Good. We can also use a PivotTable to create percent frequency distributions, as shown in the following steps:

Step 1. To invoke the **PivotTable Fields** task pane, select any cell in the pivot table

Step 2. In the **PivotTable Fields** task pane, click the **Count of Restaurant** in the **VALUES** area

Step 3. Select **Value Field Settings...** from the list of options

Step 4. When the **Value Field Settings** dialog box appears, click the tab for **Show Values As**

Step 5. In the **Show values as** area, select **% of Grand Total** from the drop-down menu Click **OK**

Figure 3.12 displays the percent frequency distribution for the Restaurant data as a PivotTable. The figure indicates that 50% of the restaurants are in the Very Good quality category and that 26% have meal prices between $10 and $19.

PivotTables in Excel are interactive, and they may be used to display statistics other than a simple count of items. As an illustration, we can easily modify the PivotTable in Figure 3.11 to display summary information on wait times instead of meal prices.

Step 1. To invoke the **PivotTable Fields** task pane, select any cell in the pivot table

Step 2. In the **PivotTable Fields** task pane, click the **Count of Restaurant** field in the **VALUES** area Select **Remove Field**

Step 3. Drag the **Wait Time (min)** to the **VALUES** area

Step 4. Click on **Sum of Wait Time (min)** in the **VALUES** area

Step 5. Select **Value Field Settings...** from the list of options

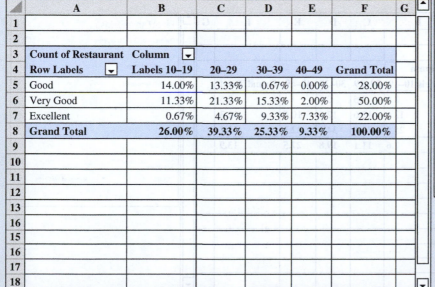

FIGURE 3.11   Final PivotTable Report for the Restaurant Data

	A	B	C	D	E	F	G	H	I
1									
2									
3	Count of Restaurant	Column Labels ▾							
4	Row Labels ▾	10–19	20–29	30–39	40–49	Grand Total			
5	Good	42	40	2		84			
6	Very Good	34	64	46	6	150			
7	Excellent	2	14	28	22	66			
8	Grand Total	78	118	76	28	300			

PivotTable Fields

Choose fields to add to report:

☑ Restaurant
☑ Quality Rating
☑ Meal Price ($)
☐ Wait Time (min)

MORE TABLES...

Drag fields between areas below:

▼ FILTERS   ▦ COLUMNS
                             Meal Price ($) ▾

▦ ROWS   Σ VALUES
Quality Rating ▾   Count of Restaur... ▾

FIGURE 3.12   Percent Frequency Distribution as a PivotTable for the Restaurant Data

	A	B	C	D	E	F	G
1							
2							
3	Count of Restaurant	Column ▾					
4	Row Labels ▾	Labels 10–19	20–29	30–39	40–49	Grand Total	
5	Good	14.00%	13.33%	0.67%	0.00%	28.00%	
6	Very Good	11.33%	21.33%	15.33%	2.00%	50.00%	
7	Excellent	0.67%	4.67%	9.33%	7.33%	22.00%	
8	Grand Total	26.00%	39.33%	25.33%	9.33%	100.00%	

PivotTable Fields

Choose fields to add to report:

☑ Restaurant
☑ Quality Rating
☑ Meal Price ($)
☐ Wait Time (min)

MORE TABLES...

Drag fields between areas below:

▼ FILTERS   ▦ COLUMNS
                             Meal Price ($) ▾

▦ ROWS   Σ VALUES
Quality Rating ▾   Count of Restaurant ▾

Step 6. When the **Value Field Settings** dialog box appears:
Under **Summarize value field by**, select **Average**
Click **Number Format**
In the **Category:** area, select **Number**
Enter *1* for **Decimal places:**
Click **OK**
When the **Value Field Settings** dialog box reappears, click **OK**

The completed PivotTable appears in Figure 3.13. This PivotTable replaces the counts of restaurants with values for the average wait time for a table at a restaurant for each grouping of meal prices ($10–19, $20–29, $30–39, $40–49). For instance, cell B7 indicates that the average wait time for a table at an Excellent restaurant with a meal price of $10–$19 is 25.5 minutes. Column F displays the total average wait times for tables in each quality rating category. We see that Excellent restaurants have the longest average waits of 35.2 minutes and that Good restaurants have average wait times of only 2.5 minutes. Finally, cell D7 shows us that the longest wait times can be expected at Excellent restaurants with meal prices in the $30–$39 range (34 minutes).

*You can also filter data in a PivotTable by dragging the field that you want to filter to the **FILTERS** area in the **PivotTable Fields**.*

We can also examine only a portion of the data in a PivotTable using the Filter option in Excel. To Filter data in a PivotTable, click on the **Filter Arrow** ▾ next to **Row Labels** or **Column Labels** and then uncheck the values that you want to remove from the PivotTable. For example, we could click on the arrow next to Row Labels and then uncheck the Good value to examine only Very Good and Excellent restaurants.

Recommended PivotTables in Excel

Excel also has the ability to recommend PivotTables for your data set. To illustrate Recommended PivotTables in Excel, we return to the restaurant data in Figure 3.8. To create a Recommended PivotTable, follow the steps below using the file *Restaurant*.

FIGURE 3.13   PivotTable Report for the Restaurant Data with Average Wait Times Added

	A	B	C	D	E	F	G
1							
2							
3	Average of Wait Time (min) Column ▾						
4	Row Labels ▾	Labels 10–19	20–29	30–39	40–49	Grand Total	
5	Good	2.6	2.5	0.5		2.5	
6	Very Good	12.6	12.6	12.0	10.0	12.3	
7	Excellent	25.5	29.1	34.0	32.3	32.1	
8	Grand Total	7.6	11.1	19.8	27.5	13.9	
9							
10							
11							
12							
13							
16							
15							
16							
17							

PivotTable Fields

Choose fields to add to report:

☐ Restaurant
☑ Quality Rating
☑ Meal Price ($)
☑ Wait Time (min)

Drag fields between areas below:

▼ FILTERS   ▦ COLUMNS
                 Meal Price ($) ▾

▦ ROWS   Σ VALUES
Quality Rating ▾ Average of Wait Time (... ▾

FIGURE 3.14	Recommended PivotTables Dialog Box in Excel

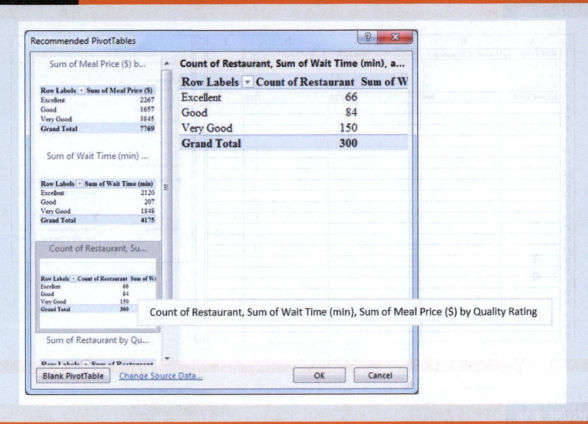

Hovering your pointer over the different options will display the full name of each option, as shown in Figure 3.14.

Step 1. Select any cell in table of data (for example, cell A1)

Step 2. Click the **Insert** tab on the Ribbon

Step 3. Click **Recommended PivotTables** in the **Tables** group

Step 4. When the **Recommended PivotTables** dialog box appears:

Select the **Count of Restaurant, Sum of Wait Time (min), Sum of Meal Price ($) by Quality Rating** option (see Figure 3.14)

Click **OK**

The steps above will create the PivotTable shown in Figure 3.15 on a new Worksheet. The Recommended PivotTables tool in Excel is useful for quickly creating commonly used PivotTables for a data set, but note that it may not give you the option to create the exact PivotTable that will be of the most use for your data analysis. Displaying the sum of wait times and the sum of meal prices within each quality rating category, as shown in Figure 3.15, is not particularly useful here; the average wait times and average meal prices within each quality-rating category would be more useful to us. But we can easily modify the PivotTable in Figure 3.14 to show the average values by selecting any cell in the PivotTable to invoke the **PivotTable Fields** task pane, clicking on **Sum of Wait Time (min)** and then **Sum of Meal Price ($)**, and using the **Value Field Settings…** to change the **Summarize value field by** option to **Average**. The finished PivotTable is shown in Figure 3.16.

FIGURE 3.15 Default PivotTable Created for Restaurant Data Using Excel's Recommended PivotTables Tool

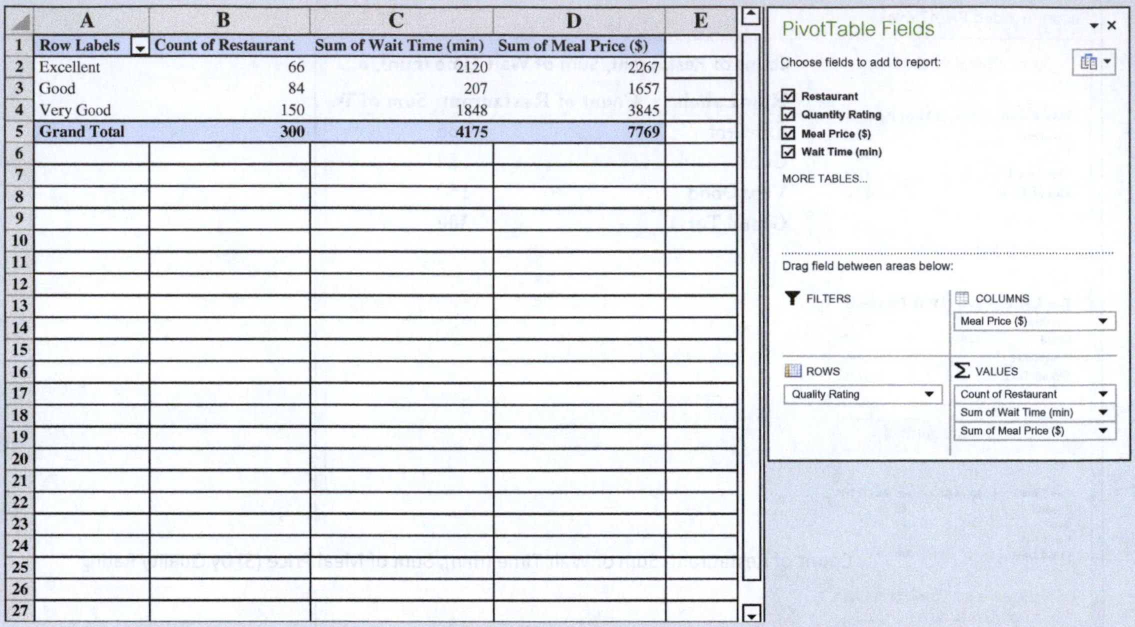

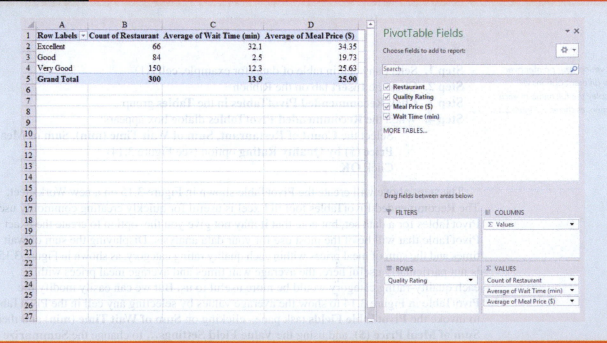

FIGURE 3.16 Completed PivotTable for Restaurant Data Using Excel's Recommended PivotTables Tool

3.3 Charts

Charts (or graphs) are visual methods for displaying data. In this section, we introduce some of the most commonly used charts to display and analyze data including scatter charts, line charts, and bar charts. Excel is the most commonly used software package for creating simple charts. We explain how to use Excel to create scatter charts, line charts, sparklines, bar charts, bubble charts, and heat maps. In the chapter appendix, we demonstrate the use of the Excel Add-in XLMiner to create a scatter-chart matrix and a parallel-coordinates plot.

Scatter Charts

A **scatter chart** (introduced in Chapter 2) is a graphical presentation of the relationship between two quantitative variables. As an illustration, consider the advertising/sales relationship for an electronics store in San Francisco. On 10 occasions during the past three months, the store used weekend television commercials to promote sales at its stores. The managers want to investigate whether a relationship exists between the number of commercials shown and sales at the store the following week. Sample data for the 10 weeks, with sales in hundreds of dollars, are shown in Table 3.8.

We will use the data from Table 3.8 to create a scatter chart using Excel's chart tools and the data in the file *Electronics*:

Step 1. Select cells B2:C11
Step 2. Click the **Insert** tab in the Ribbon
Step 3. Click the **Insert Scatter (X,Y) or Bubble Chart** button in the **Charts** group
Step 4. When the list of scatter chart subtypes appears, click the **Scatter** button
Step 5. Click the **Design** tab under the **Chart Tools** Ribbon
Step 6. Click **Add Chart Element** in the **Chart Layouts** group
  Select **Chart Title**, and click **Above Chart**
  Click on the text box above the chart, and replace the text with *Scatter Chart for the San Francisco Electronics Store*

Hovering the pointer over the chart type buttons in Excel will display the names of the buttons and short descriptions of the types of chart.

TABLE 3.8	Sample Data for the San Francisco Electronics Store		
		No. of Commercials	Sales ($100s)
	Week	x	y
	1	2	50
	2	5	57
	3	1	41
	4	3	54
	5	4	54
	6	1	38
	7	5	63
	8	3	48
	9	4	59
	10	2	46

Step 7. Click **Add Chart Element** in the **Chart Layouts** group
Select **Axis Title**, and click **Primary Vertical**
Click on the text box under the horizontal axis, and replace "Axis Title" with *Number of Commercials*

Step 8. Click **Add Chart Element** in the **Chart Layouts** group
Select **Axis Title,** and click **Primary Horizontal**
Click on the text box next to the vertical axis, and replace "Axis Title" with *Sales ($100s)*

Step 9. Right-click on the one of the horizontal grid lines in the body of the chart, and click **Delete**

Step 10. Right-click on the one of the vertical grid lines in the body of the chart, and click **Delete**

Steps 9 and 10 are optional, but they improve the chart's readability. We would want to retain the gridlines only if they helped the reader to determine more precisely where data points are located relative to certain values on the horizontal and/or vertical axes.

We can also use Excel to add a trendline to the scatter chart. A **trendline** is a line that provides an approximation of the relationship between the variables. To add a linear trendline using Excel, we use the following steps:

Step 1. Right-click on one of the data points in the scatter chart, and select **Add Trendline...**

Step 2. When the **Format Trendline** task pane appears, select **Linear** under **Trendline Options**

Figure 3.17 shows the scatter chart and linear trendline created with Excel for the data in Table 3.8. The number of commercials (*x*) is shown on the horizontal axis, and sales (*y*) are shown on the vertical axis. For week 1, *x* = 2 and *y* = 50. A point is plotted on the scatter chart at those coordinates; similar points are plotted for the other nine weeks. Note that during two of the weeks, one commercial was shown, during two of the weeks, two commercials were shown, and so on.

Scatter charts are often referred to as scatter plots or scatter diagrams.

The completed scatter chart in Figure 3.17 indicates a positive linear relationship (or positive correlation) between the number of commercials and sales: Higher sales are

FIGURE 3.17   Scatter Chart for the San Francisco Electronics Store

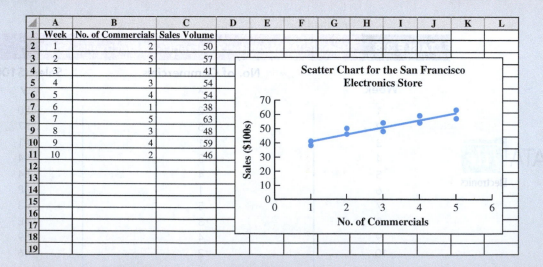

associated with a higher number of commercials. The linear relationship is not perfect because not all of the points are on a straight line. However, the general pattern of the points and the trendline suggest that the overall relationship is positive. From Chapter 2, we know that this implies that the covariance between sales and commercials is positive and that the correlation coefficient between these two variables is between 0 and $+1$.

A new feature in Excel 2013 and Excel 2016 is the inclusion of **Chart Buttons** to quickly modify and format charts. Three new buttons appear next to a chart whenever you click on it to make it active. Clicking on the **Chart Elements** button ➕ brings up a list of check boxes to quickly add and remove axes, axis titles, chart titles, data labels, trendlines, and more. Clicking on the **Chart Styles** button 🖌 allows you to quickly choose from many preformatted styles to change the look of your chart. Clicking on the **Chart Filter** button 🔽 allows you to select the data to be included in your chart. The Chart Filter button is very useful for performing additional data analysis.

The use of Chart Buttons makes it much easier to format charts in Excel, and we use these buttons in our step-by-step instructions for the remainder of the chapter. If you are using an older version of Excel (prior to Excel 2013), most of the formatting instructions described here can be accomplished by clicking on the **Design** tab in the **Chart Tools** Ribbon and then selecting **Add Chart Element** in the **Chart Layouts** group.

Recommended Charts in Excel

Similar to the ability to recommend PivotTables, Excel has the ability to recommend charts for a given data set. The steps below demonstrate the Recommended Charts tool in Excel for the Electronics data.

Step 1. Select cells B2:C11
Step 2: Click the **Insert** tab in the Ribbon
Step 3: Click the **Recommended Charts** button 📊 in the **Charts** group
Step 4: When the **Insert Chart** dialog box appears, select the **Scatter** option (see Figure 3.18)
       Click **OK**

These steps create the basic scatter chart that can then be formatted (using the **Chart Buttons** or **Chart Tools** Ribbon) to create the completed scatter chart shown in Figure 3.17. Note that the Recommended Charts tool gives several possible recommendations for the electronics data in Figure 3.18. These recommendations include scatter charts, line charts, and bar charts, which will be covered later in this chapter. Excel's Recommended Charts tool generally does a good job of interpreting your data and providing recommended charts, but take care to ensure that the selected chart is meaningful and follows good design practice.

Line Charts

A line chart for time series data is often called a time series plot.

Line charts are similar to scatter charts, but a line connects the points in the chart. Line charts are very useful for time series data collected over a period of time (minutes, hours, days, years, etc.). As an example, Kirkland Industries sells air compressors to manufacturing companies. Table 3.9 contains total sales amounts (in $100s) for air compressors during each month in the most recent calendar year. Figure 3.19 displays a scatter chart and a line chart created in Excel for these sales data. The line chart connects

FIGURE 3.18   Insert Chart Dialog Box from Recommended Charts Tool in Excel

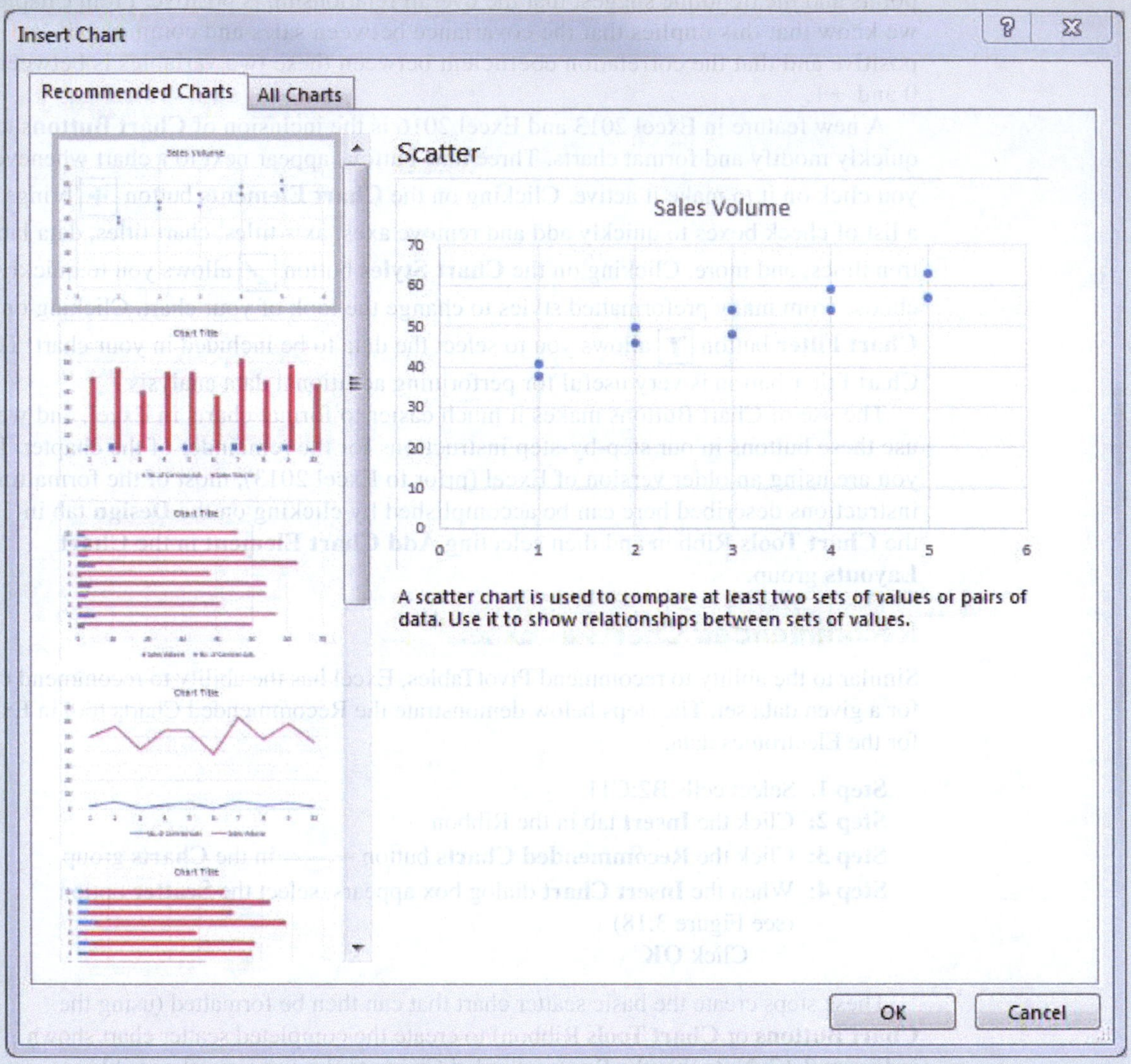

Insert Chart

Recommended Charts   All Charts

Scatter

Sales Volume

A scatter chart is used to compare at least two sets of values or pairs of data. Use it to show relationships between sets of values.

OK   Cancel

the points of the scatter chart. The addition of lines between the points suggests continuity, and it is easier for the reader to interpret changes over time.

To create the line chart in Figure 3.19 in Excel, we follow these steps:

DATA *file*

Kirkland

Step 1. Select cells A2:B13
Step 2. Click the **Insert** tab on the Ribbon
Step 3. Click the **Insert Line Chart** button ⋙ ▾ in the **Charts** group
Step 4. When the list of line chart subtypes appears, click the **Line with Markers** button under **2-D Line**

This creates a line chart for sales with a basic layout and minimum formatting

TABLE 3.9	Monthly Sales Data of Air Compressors at Kirkland Industries	
Month		**Sales ($100s)**
Jan		150
Feb		145
Mar		185
Apr		195
May		170
Jun		125
Jul		210
Aug		175
Sep		160
Oct		120
Nov		115
Dec		120

DATA *file*

Kirkland

Because the gridlines do not add any meaningful information here, we do not select the check box for **Gridlines** *in* **Chart Elements,** *as it increases the data-ink ratio.*

Step 5. Select the line chart that was just created to reveal the **Chart Buttons**

Step 6. Click the **Chart Elements** button ➕

Select the check boxes for **Axes**, **Axis Titles**, and **Chart Title**. **Deselect** the check box for **Gridlines**.

Click on the text box next to the vertical axis, and replace "Axis Title" with *Sales ($100s)*

Click on the text box next to the horizontal axis and replace "Axis Title" with *Month*

Click on the text box above the chart, and replace "Sales ($100s)" with *Line Chart for Monthly Sales Data*

In the line chart in Figure 3.19, we have kept the markers at each data point. This is a matter of personal taste, but removing the markers tends to suggest that the data are continuous when in fact we have only one data point per month.

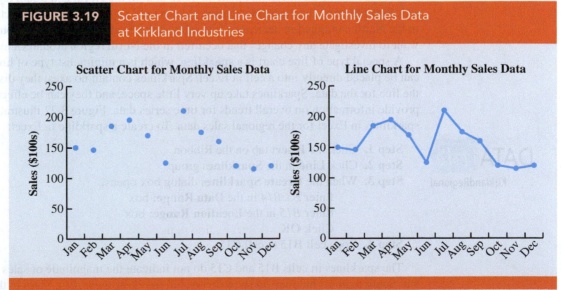

FIGURE 3.19	Scatter Chart and Line Chart for Monthly Sales Data at Kirkland Industries

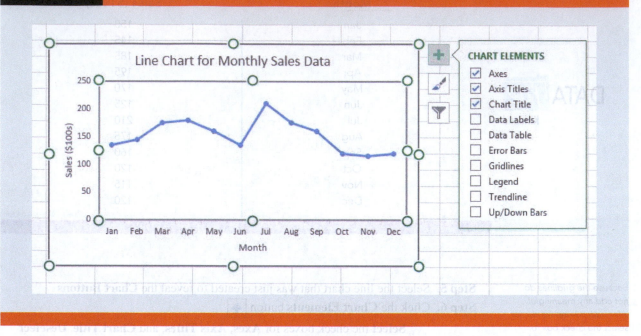

FIGURE 3.20 **Line Chart and Excel's Chart Elements Button Options for Monthly Sales Data at Kirkland Industries**

Figure 3.20 shows the line chart created in Excel along with the selected options for the **Chart Elements** button.

Line charts can also be used to graph multiple lines. Suppose we want to break out Kirkland's sales data by region (North and South), as shown in Table 3.10. We can create a line chart in Excel that shows sales in both regions, as in Figure 3.21 by following similar steps but selecting cells A2:C14 in the file *KirklandRegional* before creating the line chart. Figure 3.21 shows an interesting pattern. Sales in both the North and South regions seemed to follow the same increasing/decreasing pattern until October. Starting in October, sales in the North continued to decrease while sales in the South increased. We would probably want to investigate any changes that occurred in the North region around October.

A special type of line chart is a **sparkline**, which is a minimalist type of line chart that can be placed directly into a cell in Excel. Sparklines contain no axes; they display only the line for the data. Sparklines take up very little space, and they can be effectively used to provide information on overall trends for time series data. Figure 3.22 illustrates the use of sparklines in Excel for the regional sales data. To create a sparkline in Excel:

DATA *file*

KirklandRegional

Step 1. Click the **Insert** tab on the Ribbon
Step 2. Click **Line** in the **Sparklines** group
Step 3. When the **Create Sparklines** dialog box opens,
　　　　　Enter *B3:B14* in the **Data Range:** box
　　　　　Enter *B15* in the **Location Range:** box
　　　　　Click **OK**
Step 4. Copy cell B15 to cell C15

The sparklines in cells B15 and C15 do not indicate the magnitude of sales in the North and South regions, but they do show the overall trend for these data. Sales in the North

TABLE 3.10	Regional Sales Data by Month for Air Compressors at Kirkland Industries	
	Sales ($100s)	
Month	North	South
Jan	95	40
Feb	100	45
Mar	120	55
Apr	115	65
May	100	60
Jun	85	50
Jul	135	75
Aug	110	65
Sep	100	60
Oct	50	70
Nov	40	75
Dec	40	80

DATA *file*

KirklandRegional

appear to be decreasing and sales in the South increasing overall. Because sparklines are input directly into the cell in Excel, we can also type text directly into the same cell that will then be overlaid on the sparkline, or we can add shading to the cell, which will appear as the background. In Figure 3.22, we have shaded cells B15 and C15 to highlight the sparklines. As can be seen, sparklines provide an efficient and simple way to display basic information about a time series.

A bar chart is a graphical display depicting multiple categories of data with the use of horizontal or vertical bars whose lengths are determined by the values associated with each category. Bar charts are useful for comparing categorical data in a way that can be more helpful in making comparisons between items in a time series. Consider the regional supervisor who wants to examine the number of accounts by product for each category. Figure 3.23 shows a bar chart created in Excel displaying sales data for each.

In the line chart in Figure 3.21, we have replaced Excel's default legend with text boxes labeling the lines corresponding to sales in the North and South. This can often make the chart look cleaner and easier to interpret.

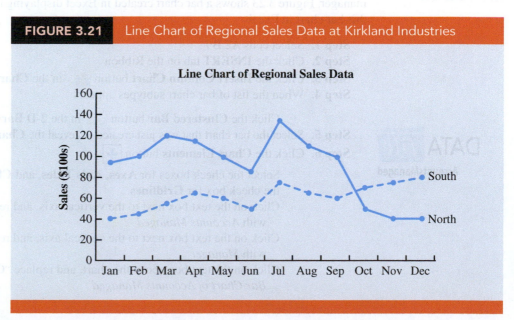

FIGURE 3.21 Line Chart of Regional Sales Data at Kirkland Industries

FIGURE 3.22   Sparklines for the Regional Sales Data at Kirkland Industries

	A	B	C	D	E	F	G	H	I
1		Sales ($100s)							
2	Month	North	South						
3	Jan	95	40						
4	Feb	100	45						
5	Mar	120	55						
6	Apr	115	65						
7	May	100	60						
8	Jun	85	50						
9	Jul	135	75						
10	Aug	110	65						
11	Sep	100	60						
12	Oct	50	70						
13	Nov	40	75						
14	Dec	40	80						
15									

Create Sparklines

Choose the data that you want

Data Range: B3:B14

Choose where you want the sparklines to be placed

Location Range: B15

OK   Cancel

Bar Charts and Column Charts

In versions of Excel prior to Excel 2016, *Insert Bar Chart*  and *Insert Column Chart* each have separate buttons in the *Charts* group, but these are combined under the *Insert Column Chart* button in Excel 2016.

Bar charts and column charts provide a graphical summary of categorical data. **Bar charts** use horizontal bars to display the magnitude of the quantitative variable. **Column charts** use vertical bars to display the magnitude of the quantitative variable. Bar and column charts are very helpful in making comparisons between categorical variables. Consider the regional supervisor who wants to examine the number of accounts being handled by each manager. Figure 3.23 shows a bar chart created in Excel displaying these data. To create this bar chart in Excel:

Step 1. Select cells A2:B9
Step 2. Click the **INSERT** tab on the Ribbon
Step 3. Click the **Insert Column Chart** button in the **Charts** group
Step 4. When the list of bar chart subtypes appears:

Click the **Clustered Bar** button in the **2-D Bar** section
Step 5. Select the bar chart that was just created to reveal the **Chart Buttons**
Step 6. Click the **Chart Elements** button

Select the check boxes for **Axes**, **Axis Titles**, and **Chart Title**. Deselect the check box for **Gridlines**.
Click on the text box next to the vertical axis, and replace "Axis Title" with *Accounts Managed*
Click on the text box next to the vertical axis, and replace "Axis Title" with *Manager*
Click on the text box above the chart, and replace "Chart Title" with *Bar Chart of Accounts Managed*

DATA *file*

AccountsManaged

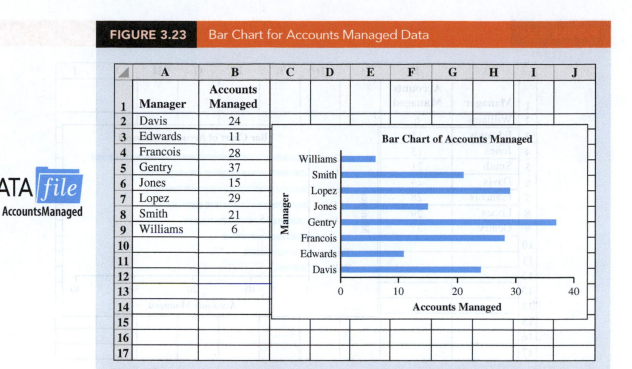

FIGURE 3.23   Bar Chart for Accounts Managed Data

DATA *file*

AccountsManaged

From Figure 3.23 we can see that Gentry manages the greatest number of accounts and Williams the fewest. We can make this bar chart even easier to read by ordering the results by the number of accounts managed. We can do this with the following steps:

Step 1. Select cells A1:B9

Step 2. Right-click any of the cells A1:B9

        Choose **Sort**

        Click **Custom Sort**

Step 3. When the **Sort** dialog box appears:

        Make sure that the check box for **My data has headers** is checked

        Choose **Accounts Managed** in the **Sort by** box under **Column**

        Choose **Smallest to Largest** under **Order**

        Click **OK**

In the completed bar chart in Excel, shown in Figure 3.24, we can easily compare the relative number of accounts managed for all managers. However, note that it is difficult to interpret from the bar chart exactly how many accounts are assigned to each manager. If this information is necessary, these data are better presented as a table or by adding data labels to the bar chart, as in Figure 3.25, which is created in Excel using the following steps:

*Alternatively, you can add Data Labels by right-clicking on a bar in the chart and selecting **Add Data Labels**.*

Step 1. Select the chart to reveal the **Chart Buttons**

Step 2. Click the **Chart Elements** button ➕

        Select the check box for **Data Labels**

This adds labels of the number of accounts managed to the end of each bar so that the reader can easily look up exact values displayed in the bar chart.

FIGURE 3.24   Sorted Bar Chart for Accounts Managed Data

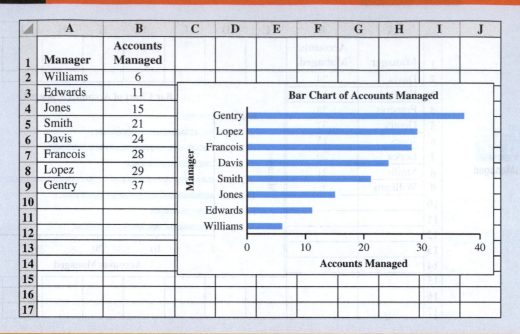

FIGURE 3.25   Bar Chart with Data Labels for Accounts Managed Data

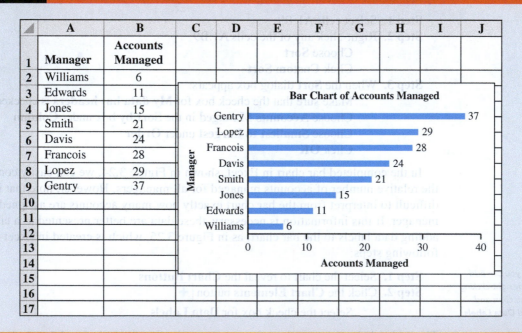

A Note on Pie Charts and Three-Dimensional Charts

Pie charts are another common form of chart used to compare categorical data. However, many experts argue that pie charts are inferior to bar charts for comparing data. The pie chart in Figure 3.26 displays the data for the number of accounts managed in Figure 3.23. Visually, it is still relatively easy to see that Gentry has the greatest number of accounts and that Williams has the fewest. However, it is difficult to say whether Lopez or Francois has more accounts. Research has shown that people find it very difficult to perceive differences in area. Compare Figure 3.26 to Figure 3.24. Making visual comparisons is much easier in the bar chart than in the pie chart (particularly when using a limited number of colors for differentiation). Therefore, we recommend against using pie charts in most situations and suggest instead using bar charts for comparing categorical data.

Because of the difficulty in visually comparing area, many experts also recommend against the use of three-dimensional (3-D) charts in most settings. Excel makes it very easy to create 3-D bar, line, pie, and other types of charts. In most cases, however, the 3-D effect simply adds unnecessary detail that does not help explain the data. As an alternative, consider the use of multiple lines on a line chart (instead of adding a z-axis), employing multiple charts, or creating bubble charts in which the size of the bubble can represent the z-axis value. Never use a 3-D chart when a two-dimensional chart will suffice.

Bubble Charts

A **bubble chart** is a graphical means of visualizing three variables in a two-dimensional graph and is therefore sometimes a preferred alternative to a 3-D graph. Suppose that we want to compare the number of billionaires in various countries. Table 3.11 provides a sample of six countries, showing, for each country, the number of billionaires per 10 million residents, the per capita income, and the total number of billionaires. We can create a bubble chart using Excel to further examine these data:

DATA *file*
Billionaires

Step 1. Select cells B2:D7
Step 2. Click the **Insert** tab on the Ribbon
Step 3. In the **Charts** group, click **Insert Scatter (X,Y) or Bubble Chart** button

In the **Bubble** subgroup, click the **Bubble** button

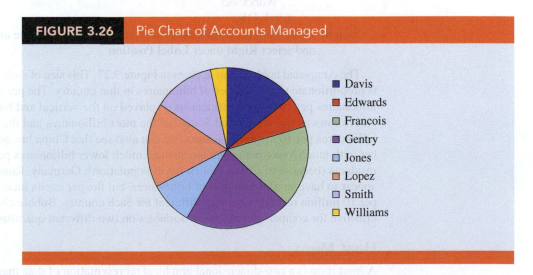

FIGURE 3.26   Pie Chart of Accounts Managed

- Davis
- Edwards
- Francois
- Gentry
- Jones
- Lopez
- Smith
- Williams

Billionaires

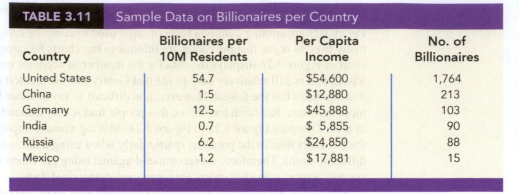

TABLE 3.11	Sample Data on Billionaires per Country		
Country	Billionaires per 10M Residents	Per Capita Income	No. of Billionaires
United States	54.7	$54,600	1,764
China	1.5	$12,880	213
Germany	12.5	$45,888	103
India	0.7	$ 5,855	90
Russia	6.2	$24,850	88
Mexico	1.2	$17,881	15

Step 4. Select the chart that was just created to reveal the **Chart Buttons**

Step 5. Click the **Chart Elements** button ➕
Select the check boxes for **Axes**, **Axis Titles**, **Chart Title** and **Data Labels**. **Deselect** the check box for **Gridlines**.
Click on the text box under the horizontal axis, and replace "Axis Title" with *Billionaires per 10 Million Residents*
Click on the text box next to the vertical axis, and replace "Axis Title" with *Per Capita Income*
Click on the text box above the chart, and replace "Chart Title" with *Billionaires by Country*

Step 6. Double-click on one of the Data Labels in the chart (e.g., the "$54,600" next to the largest bubble in the chart) to reveal the **Format Data Labels** task pane

Step 7. In the **Format Data Labels** task pane, click the **Label Options** icon 📊 and open the **Label Options** area
Under **Label Contains**, select **Value from Cells** and click the **Select Range…** button
When the **Data Label Range** dialog box opens, select cells A2:A8 in the Worksheet
Click **OK**

Step 8. In the **Format Data Labels** task pane, deselect **Y Value** under **Label Contains**, and select **Right** under **Label Position**

The completed bubble chart appears in Figure 3.27. This size of each bubble in Figure 3.27 is proportionate to the number of billionaires in that country. The per capita income and billionaires per 10 million residents is displayed on the vertical and horizontal axes. This chart shows us that the United States has the most billionaires and the highest number of billionaires per 10 million residents. We can also see that China has quite a few billionaires but with much lower per capita income and much lower billionaires per 10 million residents (because of China's much larger population). Germany, Russia, and India all appear to have similar numbers of billionaires, but the per capita income and billionaires per 10 million residents are very different for each country. Bubble charts can be very effective for comparing categorical variables on two different quantitative values.

Heat Maps

A **heat map** is a two-dimensional graphical representation of data that uses different shades of color to indicate magnitude. Figure 3.28 shows a heat map indicating the

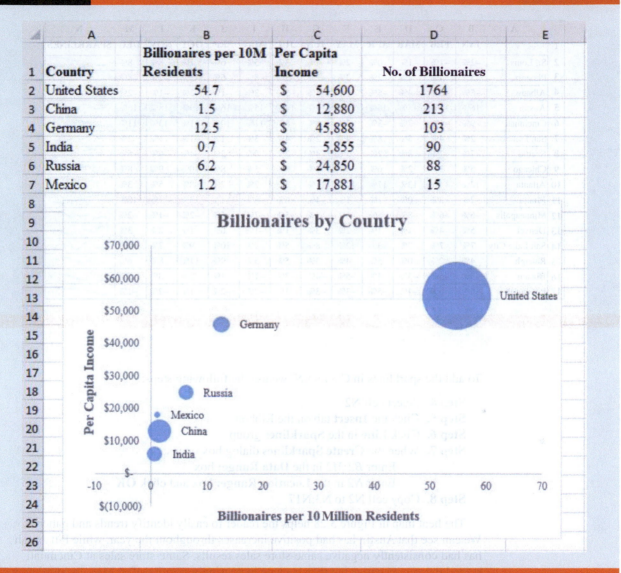

FIGURE 3.27 Bubble Chart Comparing Billionaires by Country

magnitude of changes for a metric called same-store sales, which are commonly used in the retail industry to measure trends in sales. The cells shaded red in Figure 3.28 indicate declining same-store sales for the month, and cells shaded blue indicate increasing same-store sales for the month. Column N in Figure 3.28 also contains sparklines for the same-store sales data.

Figure 3.28 can be created in Excel by following these steps:

SameStoreSales

Step 1. Select cells B2:M17
Step 2. Click the **Home** tab on the Ribbon
Step 3. Click **Conditional Formatting** in the **Styles** group
Choose **Color Scales** and click on **Blue–White–Red Color Scale**

FIGURE 3.28	Heat Map and Sparklines for Same-Store Sales Data

	A	B	C	D	E	F	G	H	I	J	K	L	M	N
1		JAN	FEB	MAR	APR	MAY	JUN	JUL	AUG	SEP	OCT	NOV	DEC	SPARKLINES
2	St. Louis	−2%	−1%	−1%	0%	2%	4%	3%	5%	6%	7%	8%	8%	
3	Phoenix	5%	4%	4%	2%	2%	−2%	−5%	−8%	−6%	−5%	−7%	−8%	
4	Albany	−5%	−6%	−4%	−5%	−2%	−5%	−5%	−3%	−1%	−2%	−1%	−2%	
5	Austin	16%	15%	15%	16%	18%	17%	14%	15%	16%	19%	18%	16%	
6	Cincinnati	−9%	−6%	−7%	−3%	3%	6%	8%	11%	10%	11%	13%	11%	
7	San Francisco	2%	4%	5%	8%	4%	2%	4%	3%	1%	−1%	1%	2%	
8	Seattle	7%	7%	8%	7%	5%	4%	2%	0%	−2%	−4%	−6%	−5%	
9	Chicago	5%	3%	2%	6%	8%	7%	8%	5%	8%	10%	9%	8%	
10	Atlanta	12%	14%	13%	17%	12%	11%	8%	7%	7%	8%	5%	3%	
11	Miami	2%	3%	0%	1%	−1%	−4%	−6%	−8%	−11%	−13%	−11%	−10%	
12	Minneapolis	−6%	−6%	−8%	−5%	−6%	−5%	−5%	−7%	−5%	−2%	−1%	−2%	
13	Denver	5%	4%	1%	1%	2%	3%	1%	−1%	0%	1%	2%	3%	
14	Salt Lake City	7%	7%	7%	13%	12%	8%	5%	9%	10%	9%	7%	6%	
15	Raleigh	4%	2%	0%	5%	4%	3%	5%	5%	9%	11%	8%	6%	
16	Boston	−5%	−5%	−3%	4%	−5%	−4%	−3%	−1%	1%	2%	3%	5%	
17	Pittsburgh	−6%	−6%	−4%	−5%	−3%	−3%	−1%	−2%	−2%	−1%	−2%	−1%	

To add the sparklines in Column N, we use the following steps:

Step 4. Select cell N2

Step 5. Click the **Insert** tab on the Ribbon

Step 6. Click **Line** in the **Sparklines** group

Step 7. When the **Create Sparklines** dialog box opens:
  Enter *B2:M2* in the **Data Range:** box
  Enter *N2* in the **Location Range:** box and click **OK**

Step 8. Copy cell N2 to N3:N17

The heat map in Figure 3.28 helps the reader to easily identify trends and patterns. We can see that Austin has had positive increases throughout the year, while Pittsburgh has had consistently negative same-store sales results. Same-store sales at Cincinnati started the year negative but then became increasingly positive after May. In addition, we can differentiate between strong positive increases in Austin and less substantial positive increases in Chicago by means of color shadings. A sales manager could use the heat map in Figure 3.28 to identify stores that may require intervention and stores that may be used as models. Heat maps can be used effectively to convey data over different areas, across time, or both, as seen here.

Both the heat map and the sparklines described here can also be created using the

***Quick Analysis** button* ▣ *. To display this button, select cells B2:M17. The **Quick Analysis** button will appear at the bottom right of the selected cells. Click the button to display options for heat maps, sparklines, and other data-analysis tools.*

Because heat maps depend strongly on the use of color to convey information, one must be careful to make sure that the colors can be easily differentiated and that they do not become overwhelming. To avoid problems with interpreting differences in color, we can add sparklines as shown in Column N of Figure 3.28. The sparklines clearly show the overall trend (increasing or decreasing) for each location. However, we cannot gauge differences in the magnitudes of increases and decreases among locations using sparklines. The combination of a heat map and sparklines here is a particularly effective way to show both trend and magnitude.

Additional Charts for Multiple Variables

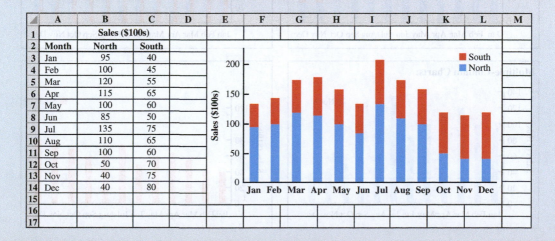

DATA *file*

KirklandRegional

Figure 3.29 provides an alternative display for the regional sales data of air compressors for Kirkland Industries. The figure uses a **stacked-column chart** to display the North and the South regional sales data previously shown in a line chart in Figure 3.21. We could also use a stacked-bar chart to display the same data by using horizontal bars instead of vertical. To create the stacked-column chart shown in Figure 3.29, we use the following steps:

*Note that here we have not included the additional steps for formatting the chart in Excel using the **Chart Elements** button, but the steps are similar to those used to create the previous charts.*

Step 1. Select cells A2:C14

Step 2. Click the **Insert** tab on the Ribbon

Step 3. In the **Charts** group, click the **Insert Column Chart** button

Click the **Stacked Column** button under the **2-D Column**

Stacked-column and stacked-bar charts allow the reader to compare the relative values of quantitative variables for the same category in a bar chart. However, these charts suffer from the same difficulties as pie charts because the human eye has difficulty perceiving small differences in areas. As a result, experts often recommend against the use of stacked-column and stacked-bar charts for more than a couple of quantitative variables in each category. An alternative chart for these same data is called a **clustered-column (or clustered-bar) chart**. It is created in Excel following the same steps but selecting **Clustered Column** under the **2-D Column** in Step 3. Clustered-column and clustered-bar charts are often superior to stacked-column and stacked-bar charts for comparing quantitative variables, but they can become cluttered for more than a few quantitative variables per category.

Clustered-column (bar) charts are also referred to as side-by-side-column (bar) charts.

An alternative that is often preferred to both stacked and clustered charts, particularly when many quantitative variables need to be displayed, is to use multiple charts. For the regional sales data, we would include two column charts: one for sales in the North and one for sales in the South. For additional regions, we would simply add additional column charts. To facilitate comparisons between the data displayed in each chart, it is important to maintain consistent axes from one chart to another. The categorical variables should be

FIGURE 3.29   Stacked-Column Chart for Regional Sales Data for Kirkland Industries

listed in the same order in each chart, and the axis for the quantitative variable should have the same range. For instance, the vertical axis for both North and South sales starts at 0 and ends at 140. This makes it easy to see that, in most months, the North region has greater sales. Figure 3.30 compares the approaches using stacked-, clustered-, and multiple-bar charts for the regional sales data.

Figure 3.30 shows that the multiple-column charts require considerably more space than the stacked- and clustered-column charts. However, when comparing many quantitative variables, using multiple charts can often be superior even if each chart must be made smaller. Stacked-column and stacked-bar charts should be used only when comparing a few quantitative variables and when there are large differences in the relative values of the quantitative variables within the category.

An especially useful chart for displaying multiple variables is the **scatter-chart matrix**. Table 3.12 contains a partial listing of the data for each of New York City's 55 subboroughs (a designation of a community within New York City) on monthly median rent, percentage of college graduates, poverty rate, and mean travel time to work. Suppose we want to examine the relationship between these different categorical variables. Figure 3.31 displays a scatter-chart matrix (scatter-plot matrix) for data related to rentals in New York City.

A scatter-chart matrix allows the reader to easily see the relationships among multiple variables. Each scatter chart in the matrix is created in the same manner as for creating a single scatter chart. Each column and row in the scatter-chart matrix corresponds to one categorical

---

FIGURE 3.30   Comparing Stacked-, Clustered-, and Multiple-Column Charts for the Regional Sales Data for Kirkland Industries

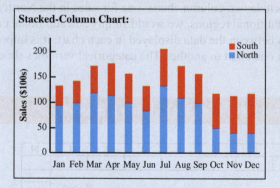

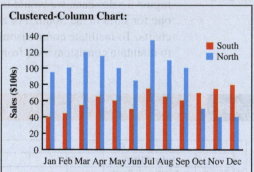

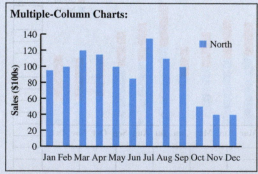

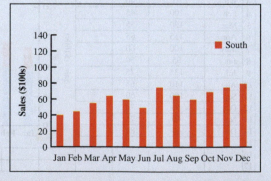

DATA *file*

NYCityData

TABLE 3.12	Data for New York City Subboroughs			
Area	**Median Monthly Rent ($)**	**Percentage College Graduates (%)**	**Poverty Rate (%)**	**Travel Time (min)**
Astoria	1,106	36.8	15.9	35.4
Bay Ridge	1,082	34.3	15.6	41.9
Bayside/Little Neck	1,243	41.3	7.6	40.6
Bedford Stuyvesant	822	21.0	34.2	40.5
Bensonhurst	876	17.7	14.4	44.0
Borough Park	980	26.0	27.6	35.3
Brooklyn Heights/ Fort Greene	1,086	55.3	17.4	34.5
Brownsville/Ocean Hill	714	11.6	36.0	40.3
Bushwick	945	13.3	33.5	35.5
Central Harlem	665	30.6	27.1	25.0
Chelsea/Clinton/ Midtown	1,624	66.1	12.7	43.7
Coney Island	786	27.2	20.0	46.3
⋮	⋮	⋮	⋮	⋮

variable. For instance, row 1 and column 1 in Figure 3.31 correspond to the median monthly rent variable. Row 2 and column 2 correspond to the percentage of college graduates variable. Therefore, the scatter chart shown in row 1, column 2 shows the relationship between median monthly rent (on the *y*-axis) and the percentage of college graduates (on the *x*-axis) in New York City subboroughs. The scatter chart shown in row 2, column 3 shows the relationship between the percentage of college graduates (on the *y*-axis) and poverty rate (on the *x*-axis).

Figure 3.31 allows us to infer several interesting findings. Because the points in the scatter chart in row 1, column 2 generally get higher moving from left to right, this tells us that subboroughs with higher percentages of college graduates appear to have higher median monthly rents. The scatter chart in row 1, column 3 indicates that subboroughs with higher poverty rates appear to have lower median monthly rents. The data in row 2, column 3 show that subboroughs with higher poverty rates tend to have lower percentages of college graduates. The scatter charts in column 4 show that the relationships between the mean travel time and the other categorical variables are not as clear as relationships in other columns.

The scatter-chart matrix is very useful in analyzing relationships among variables. Unfortunately, it is not possible to generate a scatter-chart matrix using native Excel functions. In the appendix at the end of this chapter, we demonstrate how to create a scatter-chart matrix similar to that shown in Figure 3.31 using the Excel Add-in XLMiner. Statistical software packages such as R, NCSS, and SAS can also be used to create these matrixes.

PivotCharts in Excel

DATA *file*

Restaurant

To summarize and analyze data with both a crosstabulation and charting, Excel pairs **PivotCharts** with PivotTables. Using the restaurant data introduced in Table 3.7 and Figure 3.7, we can create a PivotChart by taking the following steps:

Step 1. Click the **Insert** tab on the Ribbon
Step 2. In the **Charts** group, choose **PivotChart**

The scatter charts along the diagonal in a scatter-chart matrix (e.g., in row 1, column 1 and in row 2, column 2) display the relationship between a variable and itself. Therefore, the points in these scatter charts will always fall along a straight line at a 45-degree angle, as shown in Figure 3.31.

FIGURE 3.31   Scatter-Chart Matrix for New York City Rent Data

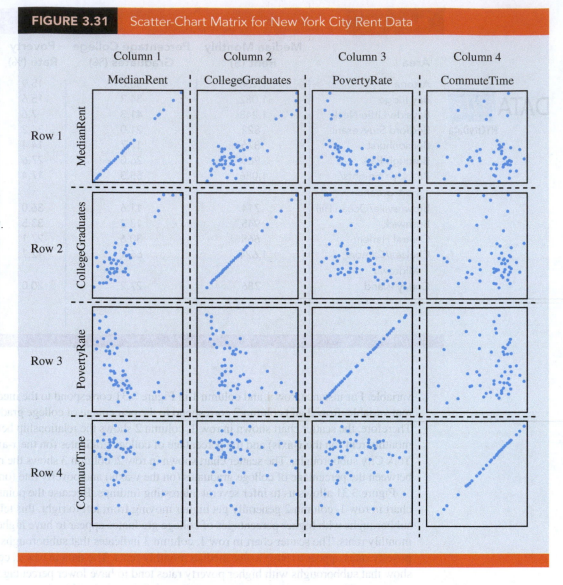

Step 3. When the **Create PivotChart** dialog box appears:

Choose **Select a Table or Range**

Enter *A1:D301* in the **Table/Range:** box

Choose **New Worksheet** as the location for the PivotTable Report

Click **OK**

Step 4. In the **PivotChart Fields** area, under **Choose fields to add to report:**

Drag the **Quality Rating** field to the **AXIS (CATEGORIES)** area

Drag the **Meal Price ($)** field to the **LEGEND (SERIES)** area

Drag the **Wait Time (min)** field to the **VALUES** area

Step 5. Click on **Sum of Wait Time (min)** in the **Values** area

Step 6. Click **Value Field Settings. . .** from the list of options that appear

Step 7. When the **Value Field Settings** dialog box appears:

Under **Summarize value field by**, choose **Average**

Click **Number Format**

In the **Category:** box, choose **Number**

Enter *1* for **Decimal places:**

Click **OK**

When the **Value Field Settings** dialog box reappears, click **OK**

Step 8. Right-click in cell B2 or any cell containing a meal price column label

Step 9. Select **Group** from the list of options that appears

Step 10. When the **Grouping** dialog box appears:

Enter *10* in the **Starting at:** box

Enter *49* in the **Ending at:** box

Enter *10* in the **By:** box

Click **OK**

Step 11. Right-click on "Excellent" in cell A5

Step 12. Select **Move** and click **Move "Excellent" to End**

The completed PivotTable and PivotChart appear in Figure 3.32. The PivotChart is a clustered-column chart whose column heights correspond to the average wait times and are clustered into the categorical groupings of Good, Very Good, and Excellent. The columns are different colors to differentiate the wait times at restaurants in the various meal price ranges. Figure 3.32 shows that Excellent restaurants have longer wait times than Good and Very Good restaurants. We also see that Excellent restaurants in the price range of $30–$39 have the longest wait times. The PivotChart displays the same information as that of the PivotTable in Figure 3.13, but the column chart used here makes it easier to compare the restaurants based on quality rating and meal price.

*Like PivotTables, PivotCharts are interactive. You can use the arrows on the axes and legend labels to change the categorical data being displayed. For example, you can click on the **Quality Rating** horizontal axis label (see Figure 3.32) and choose to look at only Very Good and Excellent restaurants, or you can click on the **Meal Price ($)** legend label and choose to view only certain meal price categories.*

FIGURE 3.32 PivotTable and PivotChart for the Restaurant Data

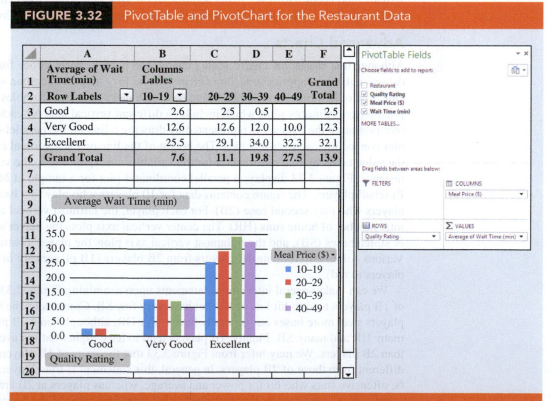

	A	B	C	D	E	F
1	**Average of Wait Time(min)**	**Columns Lables**				**Grand**
2	**Row Labels**	**10–19**	**20–29**	**30–39**	**40–49**	**Total**
3	Good	2.6	2.5	0.5		2.5
4	Very Good	12.6	12.6	12.0	10.0	12.3
5	Excellent	25.5	29.1	34.0	32.3	32.1
6	**Grand Total**	7.6	11.1	19.8	27.5	13.9

1. The steps for modifying and formatting charts were changed in Excel 2013. In versions of Excel prior to 2013, most chart-formatting options can be found in the **Layout** tab in the **Chart Tools** Ribbon. This is where you will find options for adding a **Chart Title**, **Axis Titles**, **Data Labels**, and so on in older versions of Excel.

2. Excel assumes that line charts will be used to graph only time series data. The Line Chart tool in Excel is the most intuitive for creating charts that include text entries for the horizontal axis (e.g., the month labels of Jan, Feb, Mar, etc. for the monthly sales data in Figure 3.19). When the horizontal axis represents numerical values (1, 2, 3, etc.), then it is easiest to go to the **Charts** group under the **Insert** tab in the Ribbon, click the **Insert Scatter (X,Y) or Bubble Chart**

button [⊞] ▾, and then choose the **Scatter with Straight Lines and Markers** button [⊠].

3. Color is frequently used to differentiate elements in a chart. However, be wary of the use of color to differentiate for several reasons: (1) Many people are color-blind and may not be able to differentiate colors. (2) Many charts are printed in black and white as handouts, which reduces or eliminates the impact of color. (3) The use of too many colors in a chart can make the chart appear too busy and distract or even confuse the reader. In many cases, it is preferable to differentiate chart elements with dashed lines, patterns, or labels.

4. Histograms and box plots (discussed in Chapter 2 in relation to analyzing distributions) are other effective data visualization tools for summarizing the distribution of data.

3.4 Advanced Data Visualization

In this chapter, we have presented only some of the most basic ideas for using data visualization effectively both to analyze data and to communicate data analysis to others. The charts discussed so far are those most commonly used and will suffice for most data-visualization needs. However, many additional concepts, charts, and tools can be used to improve your data-visualization techniques. In this section we briefly mention some of them.

Advanced Charts

Although line charts, bar charts, scatter charts, and bubble charts suffice for most data-visualization applications, other charts can be very helpful in certain situations. One type of helpful chart for examining data with more than two variables is the **parallel-coordinates plot**, which includes a different vertical axis for each variable. Each observation in the data set is represented by drawing a line on the parallel-coordinates plot connecting each vertical axis. The height of the line on each vertical axis represents the value taken by that observation for the variable corresponding to the vertical axis. For instance, Figure 3.33 displays a parallel coordinates plot for a sample of Major League Baseball players. The figure contains data for 10 players who play first base (1B) and 10 players who play second base (2B). For each player, the leftmost vertical axis plots his total number of home runs (HR). The center vertical axis plots the player's total number of stolen bases (SB), and the rightmost vertical axis plots the player's batting average. Various colors differentiate 1B players from 2B players (1B players are in blue and 2B players in red).

We can make several interesting statements upon examining Figure 3.33. The sample of 1B players tend to hit lots of HR but have very few SB. Conversely, the sample of 2B players steal more bases but generally have fewer HR, although some 2B players have many HR and many SB. Finally, 1B players tend to have higher batting averages (AVG) than 2B players. We may infer from Figure 3.33 that the traits of 1B players may be different from those of 2B players. In general, this statement is true. Players at 1B tend to be offensive stars who hit for power and average, whereas players at 2B are often faster and more agile in order to handle the defensive responsibilities of the position (traits

The appendix at the end of this chapter describes how to create a parallel coordinates plot similar to the one shown in Figure 3.33 using XLMiner.

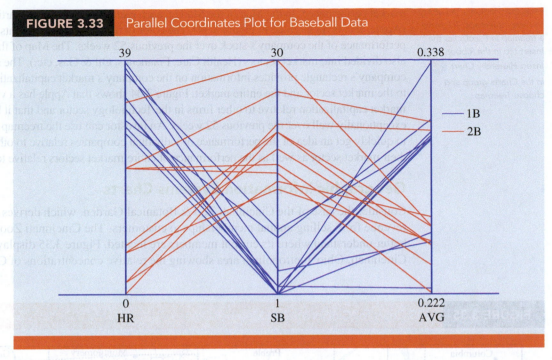

FIGURE 3.33   Parallel Coordinates Plot for Baseball Data

that are not common in strong HR hitters). Parallel-coordinates plots, in which you can differentiate categorical variable values using color as in Figure 3.33, can be very helpful in identifying common traits across multiple dimensions.

A **treemap** is useful for visualizing hierarchical data along multiple dimensions. SmartMoney's Map of the Market, shown in Figure 3.34, is a treemap for analyzing stock

The Map of the Market is based on work done by Professor Ben Shneiderman and students at the University of Maryland Human–Computer Interaction Lab.

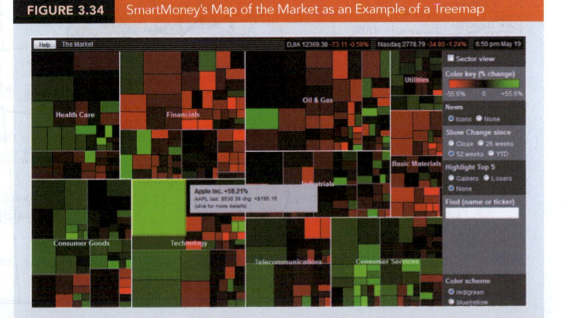

FIGURE 3.34   SmartMoney's Map of the Market as an Example of a Treemap

Excel 2016 includes the ability to create treemaps. To create a treemap in Excel, click the Insert tab in the Ribbon, click Insert Hierarchy Chart in the Charts group and choose Treemap.

market performance. In the Map of the Market, each rectangle represents a particular company (Apple, Inc. is highlighted in Figure 3.34). The color of the rectangle represents the overall performance of the company's stock over the previous 52 weeks. The Map of the Market is also divided into market sectors (Health Care, Financials, Oil & Gas, etc.). The size of each company's rectangle provides information on the company's market capitalization size relative to the market sector and the entire market. Figure 3.34 shows that Apple has a very large market capitalization relative to other firms in the Technology sector and that it has performed exceptionally well over the previous 52 weeks. An investor can use the treemap in Figure 3.34 to quickly get an idea of the performance of individual companies relative to other companies in their market sector as well as the performance of entire market sectors relative to other sectors.

Geographic Information Systems Charts

Consider the case of the Cincinnati Zoo & Botanical Garden, which derives much of its revenue from selling annual memberships to customers. The Cincinnati Zoo would like to better understand where its current members are located. Figure 3.35 displays a map of the Cincinnati, Ohio, metropolitan area showing the relative concentrations of Cincinnati Zoo

FIGURE 3.35   GIS Chart for Cincinnati Zoo Member Data

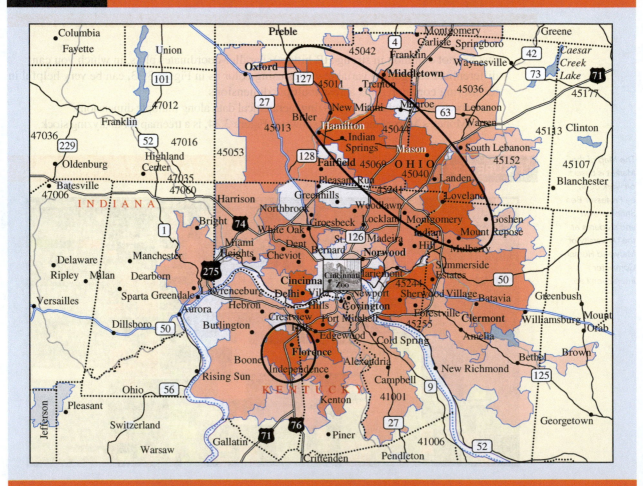

members. The more darkly shaded areas represent areas with a greater number of members. Figure 3.35 is an example of a **geographic information system (GIS)**, which merges maps and statistics to present data collected over different geographic areas. Displaying geographic data on a map can often help in interpreting data and observing patterns.

A GIS chart such as that shown in Figure 3.35 is an example of geoanalytics, the use of data by geographical area or some other form of spatial referencing to generate insights.

The GIS chart in Figure 3.35 combines a heat map and a geographical map to help the reader analyze this data set. From the figure we can see that a high concentration of zoo members in a band to the northeast of the zoo that includes the cities of Mason and Hamilton (circled). Also, a high concentration of zoo members lies to the southwest of the zoo around the city of Florence. These observations could prompt the zoo manager to identify the shared characteristics of the populations of Mason, Hamilton, and Florence to learn what is leading them to be zoo members. If these characteristics can be identified, the manager can then try to identify other nearby populations that share these characteristics as potential markets for increasing the number of zoo members.

N O T E S   +   C O M M E N T S

1. Excel 2016 includes an add-in for creating three-dimensional GIS charts called 3D Maps. This add-in can be found under the **Insert** tab by clicking on **3D Map** in the **Tours** group in Excel 2016. This tool is called Power Map in Excel 2013, but it is not as fully integrated as it is in Excel 2016.

2. Spotfire, Tableau, QlikView, SAS Visual Analytics, and JMP are examples of software that include advanced data visualization capabilities. Many Eyes is a web site developed by IBM Research that allows users to upload data and create data visualizations.

3.5 Data Dashboards

A **data dashboard** is a data-visualization tool that illustrates multiple metrics and automatically updates these metrics as new data become available. It is like an automobile's dashboard instrumentation that provides information on the vehicle's current speed, fuel level, and engine temperature so that a driver can assess current operating conditions and take effective action. Similarly, a data dashboard provides the important metrics that managers need to quickly assess the performance of their organization and react accordingly. In this section we provide guidelines for creating effective data dashboards and an example application.

Principles of Effective Data Dashboards

In an automobile dashboard, values such as current speed, fuel level, and oil pressure are displayed to give the driver a quick overview of current operating characteristics. In a business, the equivalent values are often indicative of the business's current operating characteristics, such as its financial position, the inventory on hand, customer service metrics, and the like. These values are typically known as **key performance indicators (KPIs)**. A data dashboard should provide timely summary information on KPIs that are important to the user, and it should do so in a manner that informs rather than overwhelms its user.

Key performance indicators are sometimes referred to as key performance metrics (KPMs).

Ideally, a data dashboard should present all KPIs as a single screen that a user can quickly scan to understand the business's current state of operations. Rather than requiring the user to scroll vertically and horizontally to see the entire dashboard, it is better to create multiple dashboards so that each dashboard can be viewed on a single screen.

The KPIs displayed in the data dashboard should convey meaning to its user and be related to the decisions the user makes. For example, the data dashboard for a marketing manager may have KPIs related to current sales measures and sales by region, while the data dashboard for a Chief Financial Officer should provide information on the current financial standing of the company, including cash on hand, current debt obligations, and so on.

A data dashboard should call attention to unusual measures that may require attention, but not in an overwhelming way. Color should be used to call attention to specific values to differentiate categorical variables, but the use of color should be restrained. Too many different or too bright colors make the presentation distracting and difficult to read.

Applications of Data Dashboards

To illustrate the use of a data dashboard in decision making, we discuss an application involving the Grogan Oil Company which has offices located in three cities in Texas: Austin (its headquarters), Houston, and Dallas. Grogan's Information Technology (IT) call center, located in Austin, handles calls from employees regarding computer-related problems involving software, Internet, and e-mail issues. For example, if a Grogan employee in Dallas has a computer software problem, the employee can call the IT call center for assistance.

The data dashboard shown in Figure 3.36, developed to monitor the performance of the call center, combines several displays to track the call center's KPIs. The data presented are for the current shift, which started at 8:00 a.m. The line chart in the upper left-hand corner shows the call volume for each type of problem (Software, Internet, or E-mail) over time. This chart shows that call volume is heavier during the first few hours of the shift, that calls concerning e-mail issues appear to decrease over time, and that the volume of calls regarding software issues are highest at midmorning. A line chart is effective here because these are time series data and the line chart helps identify trends over time.

The column chart in the upper right-hand corner of the dashboard shows the percentage of time that call center employees spent on each type of problem or were idle (not working on a call). Both the line chart and the column chart are important displays in determining optimal staffing levels. For instance, knowing the call mix and how stressed the system is, as measured by percentage of idle time, can help the IT manager make sure that enough call center employees are available with the right level of expertise.

The clustered-bar chart in the middle right of the dashboard shows the call volume by type of problem for each of Grogan's offices. This allows the IT manager to quickly identify whether there is a particular type of problem by location. For example, the office in Austin seems to be reporting a relatively high number of issues with e-mail. If the source of the problem can be identified quickly, then the problem might be resolved quickly for many users all at once. Also, note that a relatively high number of software problems are coming from the Dallas office. In this case, the Dallas office is installing new software, resulting in more calls to the IT call center. Having been alerted to this by the Dallas office last week, the IT manager knew that calls coming from the Dallas office would spike, so the manager proactively increased staffing levels to handle the expected increase in calls.

For each unresolved case that was received more than 15 minutes ago, the bar chart shown in the middle left of the data dashboard displays the length of time for which each case has been unresolved. This chart enables Grogan to quickly monitor the key problem cases and decide whether additional resources may be needed to resolve them. The worst case, T57, has been unresolved for over 300 minutes and is actually left over from the previous shift. Finally, the chart in the bottom panel shows the length of time required for resolved cases during the current shift. This chart is an example of a frequency distribution for quantitative data (discussed in Chapter 2).

FIGURE 3.36	Data Dashboard for the Grogan Oil Information Technology Call Center

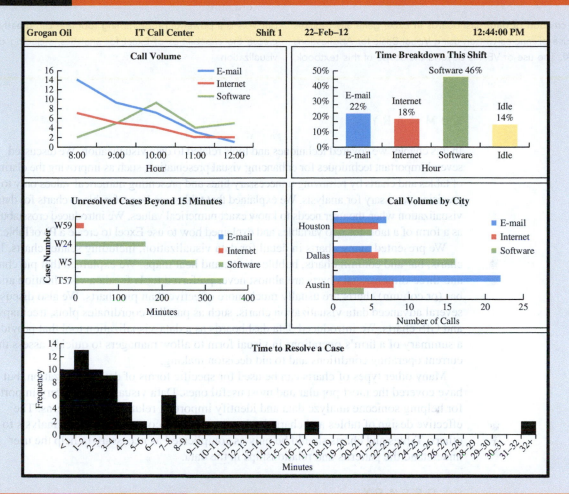

Throughout the dashboard, a consistent color coding scheme is used for problem type (E-mail, Software, and Internet). Because the Time to Resolve a Case chart is not broken down by problem type, dark shading is used so as not to confuse these values with a particular problem type. Other dashboard designs are certainly possible, and improvements could certainly be made to the design shown in Figure 3.36. However, what is important is that information is clearly communicated so that managers can improve their decision making.

The Grogan Oil data dashboard presents data at the operational level, is updated in real time, and is used for operational decisions such as staffing levels. Data dashboards may also be used at the tactical and strategic levels of management. For example, a sales manager could monitor sales by salesperson, by region, by product, and by customer. This would alert the sales manager to changes in sales patterns. At the highest level, a more strategic dashboard would allow upper management to quickly assess the financial health of the company by monitoring more aggregate financial, service-level, and capacity-utilization information.

N O T E S + C O M M E N T S

The creation of data dashboards in Excel generally requires the use of macros written using Visual Basic for Applications (VBA). The use of VBA is beyond the scope of this textbook, but VBA is a powerful programming tool that can greatly increase the capabilities of Excel for analytics, including data visualization.

S U M M A R Y

In this chapter we covered techniques and tools related to data visualization. We discussed several important techniques for enhancing visual presentation, such as improving the clarity of tables and charts by removing unnecessary lines and presenting numerical values only to the precision necessary for analysis. We explained that tables can be preferable to charts for data visualization when the user needs to know exact numerical values. We introduced crosstabulation as a form of a table for two variables and explained how to use Excel to create a PivotTable.

We presented many charts in detail for data visualization, including scatter charts, line charts, bar and column charts, bubble charts, and heat maps. We explained that pie charts and three-dimensional charts are almost never preferred tools for data visualization and that bar (or column) charts are usually much more effective than pie charts. We also discussed several advanced data visualization charts, such as parallel-coordinates plots, treemaps, and GIS charts. We introduced data dashboards as a data-visualization tool that provides a summary of a firm's operations in visual form to allow managers to quickly assess the current operating conditions and to aid decision making.

Many other types of charts can be used for specific forms of data visualization, but we have covered the most popular and most useful ones. Data visualization is very important for helping someone analyze data and identify important relations and patterns. The effective design of tables and charts is also necessary to communicate data analysis to others. Tables and charts should be only as complicated as necessary to help the user understand the patterns and relationships in the data.

G L O S S A R Y

Bar chart A graphical presentation that uses horizontal bars to display the magnitude of quantitative data. Each bar typically represents a class of a categorical variable.

Bubble chart A graphical presentation used to visualize three variables in a two-dimensional graph. The two axes represent two variables, and the magnitude of the third variable is given by the size of the bubble.

Chart A visual method for displaying data; also called a graph or a figure.

Clustered-column (bar) chart A special type of column (bar) chart in which multiple bars are clustered in the same class to compare multiple variables; also known as a side-by-side-column (bar) chart.

Column chart A graphical presentation that uses vertical bars to display the magnitude of quantitative data. Each bar typically represents a class of a categorical variable.

Crosstabulation A tabular summary of data for two variables. The classes of one variable are represented by the rows; the classes for the other variable are represented by the columns.

Data dashboard A data-visualization tool that updates in real time and gives multiple outputs.

Data-ink ratio The ratio of the amount of ink used in a table or chart that is necessary to convey information to the total amount of ink used in the table and chart. Ink used that is not necessary to convey information reduces the data-ink ratio.

Geographic information system (GIS) A system that merges maps and statistics to present data collected over different geographies.

Heat map A two-dimensional graphical presentation of data in which color shadings indicate magnitudes.

Key performance indicator (KPI) A metric that is crucial for understanding the current performance of an organization; also known as a key performance metric (KPM).

Line chart A graphical presentation of time series data in which the data points are connected by a line.

Parallel-coordinates plot A graphical presentation used to examine more than two variables in which each variable is represented by a different vertical axis. Each observation in a data set is plotted in a parallel-coordinates plot by drawing a line between the values of each variable for the observation.

Pie chart A graphical presentation used to compare categorical data. Because of difficulties in comparing relative areas on a pie chart, these charts are not recommended. Bar or column charts are generally superior to pie charts for comparing categorical data.

PivotChart A graphical presentation created in Excel that functions similarly to a PivotTable.

PivotTable An interactive crosstabulation created in Excel.

Scatter chart A graphical presentation of the relationship between two quantitative variables. One variable is shown on the horizontal axis and the other on the vertical axis.

Scatter-chart matrix A graphical presentation that uses multiple scatter charts arranged as a matrix to illustrate the relationships among multiple variables.

Sparkline A special type of line chart that indicates the trend of data but not magnitude. A sparkline does not include axes or labels.

Stacked column (bar) chart A special type of column (bar) chart in which multiple variables appear on the same bar.

Treemap A graphical presentation that is useful for visualizing hierarchical data along multiple dimensions. A treemap groups data according to the classes of a categorical variable and uses rectangles whose size relates to the magnitude of a quantitative variable.

Trendline A line that provides an approximation of the relationship between variables in a chart.

PROBLEMS

1. A sales manager is trying to determine appropriate sales performance bonuses for her team this year. The following table contains the data relevant to determining the bonuses, but it is not easy to read and interpret. Reformat the table to improve readability and to help the sales manager make her decisions about bonuses.

DATA *file*

SalesBonuses

Salesperson	Total Sales ($)	Average Performance Bonus Previous Years ($)	Customer Accounts	Years with Company
Smith, Michael	325000.78	12499.3452	124	14
Yu, Joe	13678.21	239.9434	9	7
Reeves, Bill	452359.19	21987.2462	175	21
Hamilton, Joshua	87423.91	7642.9011	28	3
Harper, Derek	87654.21	1250.1393	21	4
Quinn, Dorothy	234091.39	14567.9833	48	9
Graves, Lorrie	379401.94	27981.4432	121	12
Sun, Yi	31733.59	672.9111	7	1
Thompson, Nicole	127845.22	13322.9713	17	3

2. The following table shows an example of gross domestic product values for five countries over six years in equivalent U.S. dollars ($).

Gross Domestic Product (in US $)						
Country	Year 1	Year 2	Year 3	Year 4	Year 5	Year 6
Albania	7385937423	8105580293	9650128750	11592303225	10781921975	10569204154
Argentina	169725491092	198012474920	241037555661	301259040110	285070994754	339604450702
Australia	704453444387	758320889024	916931817944	982991358955	934168969952	1178776680167
Austria	272865358404	290682488352	336840690493	375777347214	344514388622	341440991770
Belgium	335571307765	355372712266	408482592257	451663134614	421433351959	416534140346

DATA file

GDPyears

a. How could you improve the readability of this table?

b. The file *GDPyears* contains sample data from the United Nations Statistics Division on 30 countries and their GDP values from Year 1 to Year 6 in US$. Create a table that provides all these data for a user. Format the table to make it as easy to read as possible.

Hint: It is generally not important for the user to know GDP to an exact dollar figure. It is typical to present GDP values in millions or billions of dollars.

3. The following table provides monthly revenue values for Tedstar, Inc., a company that sells valves to large industrial firms. The monthly revenue data have been graphed using a line chart in the following figure.

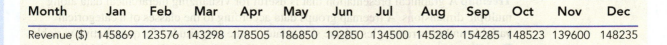

Month	Jan	Feb	Mar	Apr	May	Jun	Jul	Aug	Sep	Oct	Nov	Dec
Revenue ($)	145869	123576	143298	178505	186850	192850	134500	145286	154285	148523	139600	148235

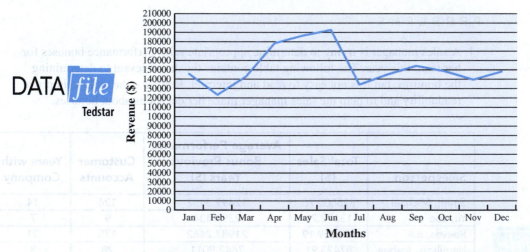

DATA file

Tedstar

a. What are the problems with the layout and display of this line chart?

b. Create a new line chart for the monthly revenue data at Tedstar, Inc. Format the chart to make it easy to read and interpret.

4. In the file *MajorSalary*, data have been collected from 111 College of Business graduates on their monthly starting salaries. The graduates include students majoring in management, finance, accounting, information systems, and marketing. Create a

PivotTable in Excel to display the number of graduates in each major and the average monthly starting salary for students in each major.

a. Which major has the greatest number of graduates?

b. Which major has the highest average starting monthly salary?

c. Use the PivotTable to determine the major of the student with the highest overall starting monthly salary. What is the major of the student with the lowest overall starting monthly salary?

DATA *file*
MajorSalary

5. *Entrepreneur* magazine ranks franchises. Among the factors that the magazine uses in its rankings are growth rate, number of locations, start-up costs, and financial stability. A recent ranking listed the top 20 U.S. franchises and the number of locations as follows:

Franchise	Number of U.S. Locations	Franchise	Number of U.S. Locations
Hampton Inns	1,864	Jan-Pro Franchising Intl. Inc.	12,394
ampm	3,183	Hardee's	1,901
McDonald's	32,805	Pizza Hut Inc.	13,281
7-Eleven Inc.	37,496	Kumon Math & Reading Centers	25,199
Supercuts	2,130	Dunkin' Donuts	9,947
Days Inn	1,877	KFC Corp.	16,224
Vanguard Cleaning Systems	2,155	Jazzercise Inc.	7,683
Servpro	1,572	Anytime Fitness	1,618
Subway	34,871	Matco Tools	1,431
Denny's Inc.	1,668	Stratus Building Solutions	5,018

DATA *file*
Franchises

These data can be found in the file *Franchises*. Create a PivotTable to summarize these data using classes 0–9,999, 10,000–19,999, 20,000–29,999, 30,000–39,999 to answer the following questions. (*Hint:* Use Number of U.S. Locations as the COLUMNS, and use Count of Number of U.S. Locations as the VALUES in the PivotTable.)

a. How many franchises have between 0 and 9,999 locations?

b. How many franchises have more than 30,000 locations?

DATA *file*
MutualFunds

6. The file *MutualFunds* contains a data set with information for 45 mutual funds that are part of the *Morningstar Funds 500*. The data set includes the following five variables:

Fund Type: The type of fund, labeled DE (Domestic Equity), IE (International Equity), and FI (Fixed Income)

Net Asset Value ($): The closing price per share

Five-Year Average Return (%): The average annual return for the fund over the past five years

Expense Ratio (%): The percentage of assets deducted each fiscal year for fund expenses

Morningstar Rank: The risk adjusted star rating for each fund; Morningstar ranks go from a low of 1 Star to a high of 5 Stars.

Note that Excel may display the column headings as 0–10, 10–20, 20–30, etc., but they should be interpreted as 0–9.99, 10–19.99, 20–29.99, etc.

a. Prepare a PivotTable that gives the frequency count of the data by Fund Type (rows) and the five-year average annual return (columns). Use classes of 0–9.99, 10–19.99, 20–29.99, 30–39.99, 40–49.99, and 50–59.99 for the Five-Year Average Return (%).

b. What conclusions can you draw about the fund type and the average return over the past five years?

TaxData

7. The file *TaxData* contains information from federal tax returns filed in 2007 for all counties in the United States (3,142 counties in total). Create a PivotTable in Excel to answer the questions below. The PivotTable should have State Abbreviation as Row Labels. The Values in the PivotTable should be the sum of adjusted gross income for each state.

   a. Sort the PivotTable data to display the states with the smallest sum of adjusted gross income on top and the largest on the bottom. Which state had the smallest sum of adjusted gross income? What is the total adjusted gross income for federal tax returns filed in this state with the smallest total adjusted gross income? (*Hint:* To sort data in a PivotTable in Excel, right-click any cell in the PivotTable that contains the data you want to sort, and select **Sort**.)

   b. Add the County Name to the Row Labels in the PivotTable. Sort the County Names by Sum of Adjusted Gross Income with the lowest values on the top and the highest values on the bottom. Filter the Row Labels so that only the state of Texas is displayed. Which county had the smallest sum of adjusted gross income in the state of Texas? Which county had the largest sum of adjusted gross income in the state of Texas?

   c. Click on **Sum of Adjusted Gross Income** in the **Values** area of the PivotTable in Excel. Click **Value Field Settings…**. Click the tab for **Show Values As**. In the **Show values as** box, choose **% of Parent Row Total**. Click **OK**. This displays the adjusted gross income reported by each county as a percentage of the total state adjusted gross income. Which county has the highest percentage adjusted gross income in the state of Texas? What is this percentage?

   d. Remove the filter on the Row Labels to display data for all states. What percentage of total adjusted gross income in the United States was provided by the state of New York?

FDICBankFailures

8. The file *FDICBankFailures* contains data on failures of federally insured banks between 2000 and 2012. Create a PivotTable in Excel to answer the following questions. The PivotTable should group the closing dates of the banks into yearly bins and display the counts of bank closures each year in columns of Excel. Row labels should include the bank locations and allow for grouping the locations into states or viewing by city. You should also sort the PivotTable so that the states with the greatest number of total bank failures between 2000 and 2012 appear at the top of the PivotTable.

   a. Which state had the greatest number of federally insured bank closings between 2000 and 2012?

   b. How many bank closings occurred in the state of Nevada (NV) in 2010? In what cities did these bank closings occur?

   c. Use the PivotTable's filter capability to view only bank closings in California (CA), Florida (FL), Texas (TX), and New York (NY) for the years 2009 through 2012. What is the total number of bank closings in these states between 2009 and 2012?

   d. Using the filtered PivotTable from part c, what city in Florida had the greatest number of bank closings between 2009 and 2012? How many bank closings occurred in this city?

   e. Create a PivotChart to display a column chart that shows the total number of bank closings in each year 2000 through 2012 in the state of Florida. Adjust the formatting of this column chart so that it best conveys the data. What does this column chart suggest about bank closings between 2000 and 2012 in Florida? Discuss.

(*Hint:* You may have to switch the row and column labels in the PivotChart to get the best presentation for your PivotChart.)

9. The following 20 observations are for two quantitative variables, *x* and *y*.

DATA *file*

Scatter

Observation	x	y	Observation	x	y
1	−22	22	11	−37	48
2	−33	49	12	34	−29
3	2	8	13	9	−18
4	29	−16	14	−33	31
5	−13	10	15	20	−16
6	21	−28	16	−3	14
7	−13	27	17	−15	18
8	−23	35	18	12	17
9	14	−5	19	−20	−11
10	3	−3	20	−7	−22

a. Create a scatter chart for these 20 observations.
b. Fit a linear trendline to the 20 observations. What can you say about the relationship between the two quantitative variables?

10. The file *Fortune500* contains data for profits and market capitalizations from a recent sample of firms in the Fortune 500

DATA *file*

Fortune500

a. Prepare a scatter diagram to show the relationship between the variables Market Capitalization and Profit in which Market Capitalization is on the vertical axis and Profit is on the horizontal axis. Comment on any relationship between the variables.
b. Create a trendline for the relationship between Market Capitalization and Profit. What does the trendline indicate about this relationship?

11. The International Organization of Motor Vehicle Manufacturers (officially known as the Organisation Internationale des Constructeurs d'Automobiles, OICA) provides data on worldwide vehicle production by manufacturer. The following table shows vehicle production numbers for four different manufacturers for five recent years. Data are in millions of vehicles.

DATA *file*

AutoProduction

	Production (millions of vehicles)				
Manufacturer	Year 1	Year 2	Year 3	Year 4	Year 5
Toyota	8.04	8.53	9.24	7.23	8.56
GM	8.97	9.35	8.28	6.46	8.48
Volkswagen	5.68	6.27	6.44	6.07	7.34
Hyundai	2.51	2.62	2.78	4.65	5.76

a. Construct a line chart for the time series data for years 1 through 5 showing the number of vehicles manufactured by each automotive company. Show the time series for all four manufacturers on the same graph.
b. What does the line chart indicate about vehicle production amounts from years 1 through 5? Discuss.
c. Construct a clustered-bar chart showing vehicles produced by automobile manufacturer using the year 1 through 5 data. Represent the years of production

along the horizontal axis, and cluster the production amounts for the four manufacturers in each year. Which company is the leading manufacturer in each year?

12. The following table contains time series data for regular gasoline prices in the United States for 36 consecutive months:

GasPrices

Month	Price ($)	Month	Price ($)	Month	Price ($)
1	2.27	13	2.84	25	3.91
2	2.63	14	2.73	26	3.68
3	2.53	15	2.73	27	3.65
4	2.62	16	2.73	28	3.64
5	2.55	17	2.71	29	3.61
6	2.55	18	2.80	30	3.45
7	2.65	19	2.86	31	3.38
8	2.61	20	2.99	32	3.27
9	2.72	21	3.10	33	3.38
10	2.64	22	3.21	34	3.58
11	2.77	23	3.56	35	3.85
12	2.85	24	3.80	36	3.90

a. Create a line chart for these time series data. What interpretations can you make about the average price per gallon of conventional regular gasoline over these 36 months?

b. Fit a linear trendline to the data. What does the trendline indicate about the price of gasoline over these 36 months?

13. The following table contains sales totals for the top six term life insurance salespeople at American Insurance.

Salesperson	Contracts Sold
Harish	24
David	41
Kristina	19
Steven	23
Tim	53
Mona	39

a. Create a column chart to display the information in the table above. Format the column chart to best display the data by adding axes labels, a chart title, etc.

b. Sort the values in Excel so that the column chart is ordered from most contracts sold to fewest.

c. Insert data labels to display the number of contracts sold for each salesperson above the columns in the column chart created in part a.

14. The total number of term life insurance contracts sold in Problem 13 is 199. The following pie chart shows the percentages of contracts sold by each salesperson.

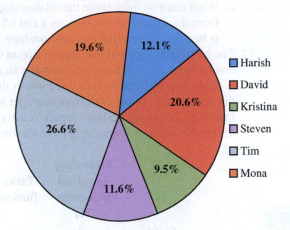

a. What are the problems with using a pie chart to display these data?
b. What type of chart would be preferred for displaying the data in this pie chart?
c. Use a different type of chart to display the percentage of contracts sold by each salesperson that conveys the data better than the pie chart. Format the chart and add data labels to improve the chart's readability.

15. An automotive company is considering the introduction of a new model of sports car that will be available in four-cylinder and six-cylinder engine types. A sample of customers who were interested in this new model were asked to indicate their preference for an engine type for the new model of automobile. The customers were also asked to indicate their preference for exterior color from four choices: red, black, green, and white. Consider the following data regarding the customer responses:

NewAuto

	Four Cylinders	Six Cylinders
Red	143	857
Black	200	800
Green	321	679
White	420	580

a. Construct a clustered-column chart with exterior color as the horizontal variable.
b. What can we infer from the clustered-bar chart in part a?

16. Consider the following survey results regarding smartphone ownership by age:

Smartphone

Age Category	Smartphone (%)	Other Cell Phone (%)	No Cell Phone (%)
18–24	49	46	5
25–34	58	35	7
35–44	44	45	11
45–54	28	58	14
55–64	22	59	19
65+	11	45	44

a. Construct a stacked-column chart to display the survey data on type of cell-phone ownership. Use Age Category as the variable on the horizontal axis.

b. Construct a clustered column chart to display the survey data. Use Age Category as the variable on the horizontal axis.

c. What can you infer about the relationship between age and smartphone ownership from the column charts in parts a and b? Which column chart (stacked or clustered) is best for interpreting this relationship? Why?

17. The Northwest regional manager of Logan Outdoor Equipment Company has conducted a study to determine how her store managers are allocating their time. A study was undertaken over three weeks that collected the following data related to the percentage of time each store manager spent on the tasks of attending required meetings, preparing business reports, customer interaction, and being idle. The results of the data collection appear in the following table:

DATA file
Logan
Locations

	Attending Required Meetings (%)	Tasks Preparing Business Reports (%)	Customer Interaction (%)	Idle (%)
Seattle	32	17	37	14
Portland	52	11	24	13
Bend	18	11	52	19
Missoula	21	6	43	30
Boise	12	14	64	10
Olympia	17	12	54	17

a. Create a stacked-bar chart with locations along the vertical axis. Reformat the bar chart to best display these data by adding axis labels, a chart title, and so on.

b. Create a clustered-bar chart with locations along the vertical axis and clusters of tasks. Reformat the bar chart to best display these data by adding axis labels, a chart title, and the like.

c. Create multiple bar charts in which each location becomes a single bar chart showing the percentage of time spent on tasks. Reformat the bar charts to best display these data by adding axis labels, a chart title, and so forth.

d. Which form of bar chart (stacked, clustered, or multiple) is preferable for these data? Why?

e. What can we infer about the differences among how store managers are allocating their time at the different locations?

18. The Ajax Company uses a portfolio approach to manage their research and development (R&D) projects. Ajax wants to keep a mix of projects to balance the expected return and risk profiles of their R&D activities. Consider a situation in which Ajax has six R&D projects as characterized in the table. Each project is given an expected rate of return and a risk assessment, which is a value between 1 and 10, where 1 is the least risky and 10 is the most risky. Ajax would like to visualize their current R&D projects to keep track of the overall risk and return of their R&D portfolio.

DATA file
Ajax

Project	Expected Rate of Return (%)	Risk Estimate	Capital Invested (Millions $)
1	12.6	6.8	6.4
2	14.8	6.2	45.8
3	9.2	4.2	9.2
4	6.1	6.2	17.2
5	21.4	8.2	34.2
6	7.5	3.2	14.8

a. Create a bubble chart in which the expected rate of return is along the horizontal axis, the risk estimate is on the vertical axis, and the size of the bubbles represents the amount of capital invested. Format this chart for best presentation by adding axis labels and labeling each bubble with the project number.

b. The efficient frontier of R&D projects represents the set of projects that have the highest expected rate of return for a given level of risk. In other words, any project that has a smaller expected rate of return for an equivalent, or higher, risk estimate cannot be on the efficient frontier. From the bubble chart in part a, which projects appear to be located on the efficient frontier?

19. Heat maps can be very useful for identifying missing data values in moderate to large data sets. The file *SurveyResults* contains the responses from a marketing survey: 108 individuals responded to the survey of 10 questions. Respondents provided answers of 1, 2, 3, 4, or 5 to each question, corresponding to the overall satisfaction on 10 different dimensions of quality. However, not all respondents answered every question.

a. To find the missing data values, create a heat map in Excel that shades the empty cells a different color. Use Excel's Conditional Formatting function to create this heat map.

Hint: Click on **Conditional Formatting** in the **Styles** group in the **Home** tab. Select **Highlight Cells Rules** and click **More Rules…**. Then enter **Blanks** in the **Format only cells with:** box. Choose a format for these blank cells that will make them obviously stand out.

b. For each question, which respondents did not provide answers? Which question has the highest nonresponse rate?

20. The following table shows monthly revenue for six different web development companies.

| Company | Revenue ($) | | | | | |
	Jan	Feb	Mar	Apr	May	Jun
Blue Sky Media	8,995	9,285	11,555	9,530	11,230	13,600
Innovate Technologies	18,250	16,870	19,580	17,260	18,290	16,250
Timmler Company	8,480	7,650	7,023	6,540	5,700	4,930
Accelerate, Inc.	28,325	27,580	23,450	22,500	20,800	19,800
Allen and Davis, LLC	4,580	6,420	6,780	7,520	8,370	10,100
Smith Ventures	17,500	16,850	20,185	18,950	17,520	18,580

a. Use Excel to create sparklines for sales at each company.

b. Which companies have generally decreasing revenues over the six months? Which company has exhibited the most consistent growth over the six months? Which companies have revenues that are both increasing and decreasing over the six months?

c. Use Excel to create a heat map for the revenue of the six companies. Do you find the heat map or the sparklines to be better at communicating the trend of revenues over the six months for each company? Why?

21. Zeitler's Department Stores sells its products online and through traditional brick-and-mortar stores. The following parallel-coordinates plot displays data from a sample of 20 customers who purchased clothing from Zeitler's either online or in-store. The data include variables for the customer's age, annual income, and the distance from the customer's home to the nearest Zeitler's store. According to the parallel-coordinates plot, how are online customers differentiated from in-store customers?

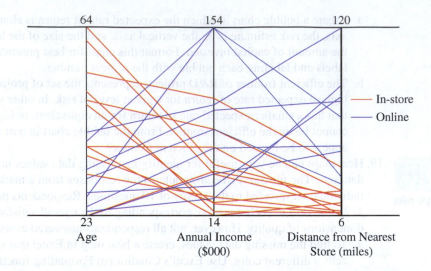

ZeitlersElectronics

22. The file *ZeitlersElectronics* contains data on customers who purchased electronic equipment either online or in-store from Zeitler's Department Stores.
   a. Create a parallel-coordinates plot using XLMiner for these data. Include vertical axes for the customer's age, annual income, and distance from nearest store. Color the lines by the type of purchase made by the customer (online or in-store).
   b. How does this parallel-coordinates plot compare to the one shown in Problem 21 for clothing purchases? Does the division between online and in-store purchasing habits for customers buying electronics equipment appear to be the same as for customers buying clothing?
   c. Parallel-coordinates plots are very useful for interacting with your data to perform analysis. Filter the parallel-coordinates plot in XLMiner so that only customers whose homes are more than 40 miles from the nearest store are displayed. What do you learn from the parallel-coordinates plot about these customers?

23. Aurora Radiological Services is a health care clinic that provides radiological imaging services (such as MRIs, X-rays, and CAT scans) to patients. It is part of Front Range Medical Systems that operates clinics throughout the state of Colorado.
   a. What type of key performance indicators and other information would be appropriate to display on a data dashboard to assist the Aurora clinic's manager in making daily staffing decisions for the clinic?
   b. What type of key performance indicators and other information would be appropriate to display on a data dashboard for the CEO of Front Range Medical Systems who oversees the operation of multiple radiological imaging clinics?

24. Bravman Clothing sells high-end clothing products online and through phone orders. Bravman Clothing has taken a sample of 25 customers who placed orders by phone. The file *Bravman* contains data for each customer purchase, including the wait time the customer experienced when he or she called, the customer's purchase amount, the customer's age, and the customer's credit score. Bravman Clothing would like to analyze these data to try to learn more about their phone customers.
   a. Use XLMiner to create a scatter-chart matrix for these data. Include the variables wait time, purchase amount, customer age, and credit score.
   b. What can you infer about the relationships between these variables from the scatter-chart matrix?

Bravman

CASE PROBLEM ALL-TIME MOVIE BOX-OFFICE DATA

The motion picture industry is an extremely competitive business. Dozens of movie studios produce hundreds of movies each year, many of which cost hundreds of millions of dollars to produce and distribute. Some of these movies will go on to earn hundreds of millions of dollars in box office revenues, while others will earn much less than their production cost.

Data from 50 of the top box-office-receipt-generating movies are provided in the file *Top50Movies*. The following table shows the first 10 movies contained in this data set. The categorical variables included in the data set for each movie are the rating and genre. Quantitative variables for the movie's release year, inflation- and noninflation-adjusted box-office receipts in the United States, budget, and the world box-office receipts are also included.

Title	Year Released	U.S. Box-Office Receipts (inflation-adjusted millions $)	Rating	Genre	Budget (noninflation-adjusted millions $)	World Box-Office Receipts (noninflation-adjusted millions $)	U.S. Box-Office Receipts (noninflation-adjusted millions $)
Gone with the Wind	1939	1,650	G	Drama	3	391	199
Star Wars	1977	1,426	PG	Scifi/fantasy	11	798	461
The Sound of Music	1965	1,145	G	Musical	—	163	163
E.T.	1982	1,132	PG	Scifi/fantasy	—	757	435
Titanic	1997	1,096	PG-13	Drama	200	2,185	659
The Ten Commandments	1956	1,053	G	Drama	14	80	80
Jaws	1975	1,029	PG	Action	12	471	260
Doctor Zhivago	1965	973	PG-13	Drama	11	112	112
The Jungle Book	1967	871	G	Animated	—	206	142
Snow White and the Seven Dwarfs	1937	854	G	Animated	1	185	185

Managerial Report

Use the data-visualization methods presented in this chapter to explore these data and discover relationships between the variables. Include the following in your report:

1. Create a scatter chart to examine the relationship between the year released and the inflation-adjusted U.S. box office receipts. Include a trendline for this scatter chart. What does the scatter chart indicate about inflation-adjusted U.S. box office receipts over time for these top 50 movies?
2. Create a scatter chart to examine the relationship between the budget and the noninflation-adjusted world box office receipts. (*Note:* You may have to adjust the data in Excel to ignore the missing budget data values to create your scatter chart.

You can do this by first sorting the data using Budget and then creating a scatter chart using only the movies that include data for Budget.) What does this scatter chart indicate about the relationship between the movie's budget and the world box office receipts?

3. Create a frequency distribution, percent frequency distribution, and histogram for inflation-adjusted U.S. box office receipts. Use bin sizes of $100 million. Interpret the results. Do any data points appear to be outliers in this distribution?

4. Create a PivotTable for these data. Use the PivotTable to generate a crosstabulation for movie genre and rating. Determine which combinations of genre and rating are most represented in the top 50 movie data. Now filter the data to consider only movies released in 1980 or later. What combinations of genre and rating are most represented for movies after 1980? What does this indicate about how the preferences of moviegoers may have changed over time?

5. Use the PivotTable to display the average inflation-adjusted U.S. box-office receipts for each genre–rating pair for all movies in the data set. Interpret the results.

Chapter 3 Appendix

Appendix 3.1 Creating a Scatter-Chart Matrix and a Parallel-Coordinates Plot with XLMiner

The Excel Add-in XLMiner provides additional functionality for visualizing data in Excel. XLMiner allows the user to create several charts that are not available in Excel without an add-in and allows for additional interactivity with many charts to aid in analyzing data. In this chapter appendix, we discuss two of the most useful charts for analyzing multivariate data that are available in XLMiner but not in Excel: the scatter-chart matrix and the parallel-coordinates plot.

Scatter-Chart Matrix in XLMiner

DATA file
NYCityData

To demonstrate the use of XLMiner to create a scatter-chart matrix similar to Figure 3.31, we will use New York City subboroughs data.

Step 1. Select any cell containing data (any cell in A2:E56)
Step 2. Click the **XLMiner Platform** tab in the Ribbon
Step 3. Click **Explore** in the **Data Analysis** group
　　　　　Click **Chart Wizard**
Step 4. When the **Chart Wizard** dialog box appears (see Figure 3.37), select **Scatterplot Matrix**
　　　　　Click **Next >**
　　　　　In the **Variable Selection Dialog**, select **Median Monthly Rent ($)**, **Percentage College Graduates (%)**, **Poverty Rate (%)**, and **Travel Time (min)**
　　　　　Click **Finish**

| FIGURE 3.37 | XLMiner Chart Wizard Dialog Box |

FIGURE 3.38   Scatter-Chart Matrix Created in XLMiner for the New York City Data

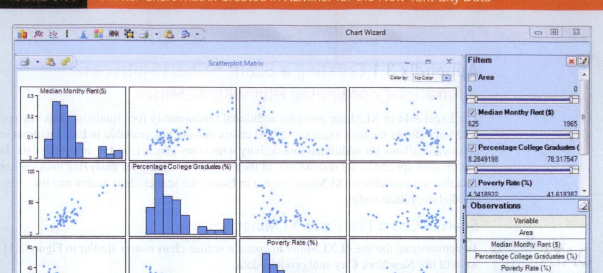

The completed scatter-chart matrix produced by XLMiner is shown in Figure 3.38. Compare this figure to Figure 3.31. We can infer the same relations between variables as in Figure 3.31. For example, median monthly rent increases as the percentage of college graduates increases. Median monthly rent decreases as the poverty rate increases. Notice that XLMiner provides a histogram (discussed in Chapter 2) along the diagonal of the scatter chart matrix and that each histogram shows the distribution of the data for the corresponding variable.

Charts produced using XLMiner are much more interactive than the standard charts produced in Excel. For the scatter-chart matrix in Figure 3.38, we can easily change which variables are displayed by clicking the check boxes in the **Filters** area. We can also filter each variable by clicking and dragging the end points along the lines for each variable in the Filters area. This will change which data points are displayed in the scatter-chart matrix. Only data points with values within the endpoints shown in the lines in the Filters area will be displayed.

Parallel-Coordinates Plot in XLMiner

To demonstrate the use of XLMiner to create a parallel-coordinates plot similar to that in Figure 3.33, we will use the baseball player data.

Step 1. Select any cell containing data (any cell in A1:D21)
Step 2. Click the **XLMiner Platform** tab in the Ribbon

FIGURE 3.39   Parallel-Coordinates Plot Created in XLMiner for Baseball Data

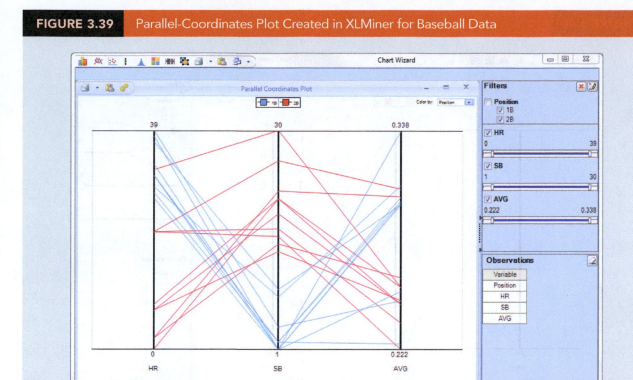

Step 3. Click **Explore** in the **Data Analysis** group
Click **Chart Wizard**

Step 4. When the **Chart Wizard** dialog box appears, select **Parallel Coordinates**
Click **Next >**

Step 5. In the **Variable Selection Dialog**, select **HR, SB, AVG**
Click **Finish**

Step 6. When the **Parallel Coordinates Plot** opens, click **Color by:** in the top right corner of the chart
Select **Position**

The parallel-coordinates plot created by XLMiner is shown in Figure 3.39. The lines corresponding to data for players at the 1B position are in blue; the lines corresponding to data for players at the 2B position are in red. Like the scatter-chart matrix, XLMiner allows for interactive analysis of data through the parallel coordinates plot; we can filter the positions shown by selecting and deselecting the check boxes for **Position** in the **Filters** area. We can also filter the quantitative variable values by using the slider bars for HR, SB, and AVG. To demonstrate this, adjust the left-hand slider bar handle for home runs (**HR**) to 20 (or just type *20* over the 0 on the left-hand side of **HR**). The result is shown in Figure 3.40: Only four players at 2B had more than 20 HRs. Interestingly, these four players also had more stolen bases (SB) than any 1B players, so these players were particularly good at combining speed and power.

FIGURE 3.40   Parallel-Coordinates Plot Filtered to Show Only Those Players with 20 or More HR

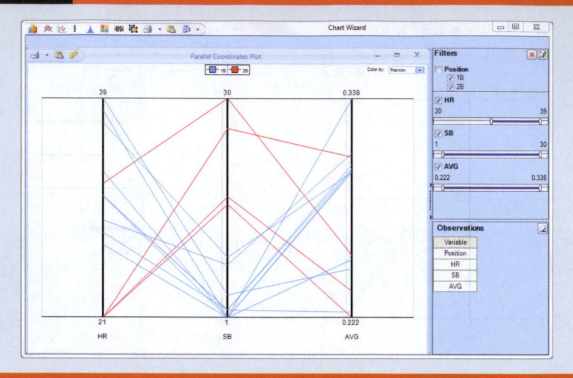

Chapter 4

Descriptive Data Mining

CONTENTS

Advice from a Machine[1]

The proliferation of data and increase in computing power have sparked the development of automated *recommender systems*, which provide consumers with suggestions for movies, music, books, clothes, restaurants, online dating, and whom to follow on Twitter. The sophisticated, proprietary algorithms guiding recommender systems measure the degree of similarity between users or items to identify recommendations of potential interest to a user.

Netflix, a company that provides media content via DVD-by-mail or Internet streaming, provides its users with recommendations for movies and television shows based on each user's expressed interests and feedback on previously viewed content. As its business has shifted from renting DVDs by mail to streaming content online, Netflix has been able to track its customers' viewing behavior more closely. This allows Netflix's recommendations to account for differences in viewing behavior based on the day of the week, the time of day, the device used (computer, phone, television), and even the viewing location.

The use of recommender systems is prevalent in e-commerce. Using attributes detailed by the Music Genome Project, Pandora Internet Radio plays songs with properties similar to songs that a user "likes." In the online dating world, web sites such as eHarmony, Match.com, and OKCupid use different "formulas" to take into account hundreds of different behavioral traits to propose date "matches." Stitch Fix, a personal shopping service for women, combines recommendation algorithms and human input from its fashion experts to match its inventory of fashion items to its clients.

---

[1]"The Science Behind the Netflix Algorithms That Decide What You'll Watch Next," http://www.wired.com/2013/08/qq_netflix-algorithm. Retrieved on August 7, 2013; E. Colson, "Using Human and Machine Processing in Recommendation Systems," *First AAAI Conference on Human Computation and Crowdsourcing* (2013); K. Zhao, X. Wang, M. Yu, and B. Gao, "User Recommendation in Reciprocal and Bipartite Social Networks—A Case Study of Online Dating," *IEEE Intelligent Systems* 29, no. 2 (2014).

Over the past few decades, technological advances have led to a dramatic increase in the amount of recorded data. The use of smartphones, radio-frequency identification (RFID) tags, electronic sensors, credit cards, and the Internet has facilitated the collection of data from phone conversations, e-mails, business transactions, product and customer tracking, business transactions, and web browsing. The increase in the use of data-mining techniques in business has been caused largely by three events: the explosion in the amount of data being produced and electronically tracked, the ability to electronically warehouse these data, and the affordability of computer power to analyze the data. In this chapter, we discuss the analysis of large quantities of data in order to gain insight on customers and to uncover patterns to improve business processes.

We define an **observation**, or record, as the set of recorded values of variables associated with a single entity. An observation is often displayed as a row of values in a spreadsheet or database in which the columns correspond to the variables. For example, in a university's database of alumni, an observation may correspond to an alumnus's age, gender, marital status, employer, position title, as well as size and frequency of donations to the university.

Predictive data mining is discussed in Chapter 9.

In this chapter, we focus on descriptive data-mining methods, also called **unsupervised learning** techniques. In an unsupervised learning application, there is no outcome variable to predict; rather, the goal is to use the variable values to identify relationships between observations. Unsupervised learning approaches can be thought of as high-dimensional descriptive analytics because they are designed to describe patterns and relationships in large data sets with many observations of many variables. Without an explicit outcome (or one that is objectively known), there is no definitive measure of accuracy. Instead, qualitative assessments, such as how well the results match expert judgment, are used to assess and compare the results from an unsupervised learning method.

4.1 Data Preparation

The data in a data set are often said to be "dirty" and "raw" before they have been put into a form that is best suited for a data-mining algorithm. Data preparation makes heavy use of the descriptive statistics and data-visualization methods described in Chapters 2 and 3 to gain an understanding of the data. Common tasks include treating missing data, identifying erroneous data and outliers, and defining the appropriate way to represent variables.

Treatment of Missing Data

It is common to have observations with missing values for one or more variables. The primary options for addressing missing data are: (1) to discard observations (rows) with any missing values, (2) to discard any variable (column) with missing values, (3) to fill in missing entries with estimated values, or (4) to apply a data-mining algorithm (such as classification and regression trees) that can handle missing values.

*XLMiner, data-mining software discussed in the chapter appendix provides a **Missing Data Handling** procedure under **Transform** in the **Data Analysis** group.*

How to deal with missing data requires some understanding of why the data are missing and the impact these missing values might have on the analysis. If the missing value is truly a random occurrence, it is called a data value **missing completely at random** (MCAR). However, the occurrence of some missing values might not be completely at random—they might be correlated with the values of some other variables. These missing values are called **missing at random** (MAR). For data that is MAR, the reason for the missing values may determine its importance. For example if the responses to one survey question collected by a specific employee were lost due to a data entry error, then the treatment of the missing data may be less critical. However, in a health care study, suppose observations corresponding to patient visits are missing the results of a diagnostic tests whenever the doctor deems the patient too sick to undergo the procedure. In this case, the absence of a variable measurement actually provides the additional information about the patient's condition, which may be helpful in understanding other relationships in the data. A third category of missing data is **missing not at random** (MNAR). Data is MNAR if the reason that the value is missing is related to the value of the variable. As an example of MNAR, a survey of households on spending habits and wealth might reveal that records with missing values for annual property taxes paid seem to be associated with expensive house values (and therefore large property taxes).

If a variable is missing measurements for a large number of observations, removing this variable from consideration may be an option. In particular, if the variable to be dropped is highly correlated with another variable that is known for a majority of observations, the loss of information may be minimal. If the number of observations with missing values is small and the missing values seem to be MCAR, discarding these incomplete observations may be a reasonable option.

If a considerable number of observations have missing values, then replacing them with a value that seems reasonable may be useful, as it does not decrease the number of observations. Options for replacing the missing entries for a variable include replacing the missing value with the variable's mode, mean, or median. Imputing values in this manner is truly valid only if variable values are MCAR; otherwise, we may be introducing misleading information into the data. If missing values are particularly troublesome and MAR, it may be possible to build a model to predict a variable with missing values and then to use these predictions in place of the missing entries. How to deal with missing values is fairly subjective, and caution must be used to not induce bias by replacing missing values.

Identification of Outliers and Erroneous Data

Examining the variables in the data set by means of summary statistics, histograms, PivotTables, scatter plots, and other tools can uncover data-quality issues and outliers. For example, negative values for sales may result from a data-entry error or may actually denote a missing value. Closer examination of outliers may reveal an error or a need for further investigation to determine whether the observation is relevant to the current analysis. A conservative approach is to create two data sets, one with and one without outliers, and then construct a model on both data sets. If a model's implications depend on the inclusion or exclusion of outliers, then you should spend additional time to track down the cause of the outliers.

Variable Representation

In many data-mining applications, it may be prohibitive to analyze the data because of the number of variables recorded. In such cases, the analyst may have to first identify variables that can be safely omitted from further analysis before proceeding with a data-mining technique. **Dimension reduction** is the process of removing variables from the analysis without losing any crucial information. One simple method for reducing the number of variables is to examine pairwise correlations to detect variables or groups of variables that may supply similar information. Such variables can be aggregated or removed to allow more parsimonious model development.

XLMiner provides a Transform Categorical procedure under Transform in the Data Analysis group. This procedure provides options to create dummy variables, create ordinal category scores, and reduce categories by combining them into similar groups.

A critical part of data mining is determining how to represent the measurements of the variables and which variables to consider. The treatment of categorical variables is particularly important. Typically, it is best to encode categorical variables with 0–1 dummy variables. Consider a data set that contains the variable Language to track the language preference of callers to a call center. The variable Language with the possible values of English, German, and Spanish would be replaced with three binary variables called English, German, and Spanish. An entry of German would be captured using a 0 for the English dummy variable, a 1 for the German dummy variable, and a 0 for the Spanish dummy variable. Using 0–1 dummy variables to encode categorical variables with many different categories results in a large number of variables. In these cases, the use of PivotTables is helpful in identifying categories that are similar and can possibly be combined to reduce the number of 0–1 dummy variables. For example, some categorical variables (zip code, product model number) may have many possible categories such that, for the purpose of model building, there is no substantive difference between multiple categories, and therefore the number of categories may be reduced by combining categories.

Often data sets contain variables that, considered separately, are not particularly insightful but that, when appropriately combined, result in a new variable that reveals an important relationship. Financial data supplying information on stock price and company earnings may be as useful as the derived variable representing the price/earnings (PE) ratio. A variable tabulating the dollars spent by a household on groceries may not be interesting because this value may depend on the size of the household. Instead, considering the *proportion* of total household spending on groceries may be more informative.

1. In some cases, it may be desirable to transform a numerical variable into categories. For example, if we wish to analyze the circumstances in which a numerical outcome variable exceeds a certain value, it may be helpful to create a binary categorical variable that is 1 for observations with the variable value greater than the threshold and 0 otherwise. In another case, if a variable has a skewed distribution, it may be helpful to categorize the values into quantiles. To facilitate such categorization, XLMiner provides a **Bin Continuous Data** procedure under **Transform** in the **Data Analysis** group on the **XLMINER Platform** tab. However, in general, we advise caution when transforming numerical variables into categories because this causes a loss of information (a numerical variable's category is less informative than a specific numeric value) and increases the number of variables.

2. XLMiner provides functionality to apply a more sophisticated dimension-reduction approach called *principal components analysis*. The **Principal Components** procedure can be found on the **XLMiner Platform** tab under **Transform** in the **Data Analysis** group. Principal-components analysis creates a collection of metavariables (components) that are weighted sums of the original variables. These components are not correlated with each other, and often only a few of them are needed to convey the same information as the large set of original variables. In many cases, only one or two components are necessary to explain the majority of the variance in the original variables. Then the analyst can continue to build a data-mining model using just a few of the most explanatory components rather than the entire set of original variables. Although principal-components analysis can reduce the number of variables in this manner, it may be harder to explain the results of the model because the interpretation of a component that is a linear combination of variables can be unintuitive.

4.2 Cluster Analysis

The goal of clustering is to segment observations into similar groups based on the observed variables. Clustering can be employed during the data-preparation step to identify variables or observations that can be aggregated or removed from consideration. Cluster analysis is commonly used in marketing to divide consumers into different homogeneous groups, a process known as *market segmentation*. Identifying different clusters of consumers allows a firm to tailor marketing strategies for each segment. Cluster analysis can also be used to identify outliers, which in a manufacturing setting may represent quality-control problems and in financial transactions may represent fraudulent activity.

In this section, we consider the use of cluster analysis to assist a company called Know Thy Customer (KTC), a financial advising company that provides personalized financial advice to its clients. As a basis for developing this tailored advising, KTC would like to segment its customers into several groups (or clusters) so that the customers within a group are similar with respect to key characteristics and are dissimilar to customers that are not in the group. For each customer, KTC has an observation consisting of the following variables:

Age   = age of the customer in whole years
Female   = 1 if female, 0 if male
Income   = annual income in dollars
Married   = 1 if married, 0 if not
Children   = number of children
Car Loan   = 1 if customer has a car loan, 0 if not
Mortgage   = 1 if customer has a mortgage, 0 if not

We present two clustering methods using a small sample of data from KTC. We first consider bottom-up **hierarchical clustering** that starts with each observation belonging to its own cluster and then sequentially merges the most similar clusters to create a series of nested clusters. The second method, *k*-means clustering, assigns each observation to one of k clusters in a manner such that the observations assigned to the same cluster are as similar as possible. Because both methods depend on how two observations are similar, we first discuss how to measure similarity between observations.

Measuring Similarity Between Observations

The goal of cluster analysis is to group observations into clusters such that observations within a cluster are similar and observations in different clusters are dissimilar. Therefore, to formalize this process, we need explicit measurements of similarity or, conversely, dissimilarity. Some metrics track similarity between observations, and a clustering method using such a metric would seek to maximize the similarity between observations. Other metrics measure dissimilarity, or distance, between observations, and a clustering method using one of these metrics would seek to minimize the distance between observations in a cluster.

When observations include numerical variables, **Euclidean distance** is the most common method to measure dissimilarity between observations. Let observations $u = (u_1, u_2, \ldots, u_q)$ and $v = (v_1, v_2, \ldots, v_q)$ each comprise measurements of q variables. The Euclidean distance between observations u and v is

$$d_{uv} = \sqrt{(u_1 - v_1)^2 + (u_2 - v_2)^2 + \cdots + (u_q - v_q)^2}$$

Figure 4.1 depicts Euclidean distance for two observations consisting of two variable measurements. Euclidean distance becomes smaller as a pair of observations become more similar with respect to their variable values. Euclidean distance is highly influenced by the scale on which variables are measured. For example, consider the task of clustering customers on the basis of the variables Age and Income. Let observation $u = (23, \$20,375)$ correspond to a 23-year old customer with an annual income of \$20,375 and observation $v = (36, \$19,475)$ correspond to a 36-year old with an annual income of \$19,475. As measured by Euclidean distance, the dissimilarity between these two observations is:

$$d_{uv} = \sqrt{(23 - 36)^2 + (20,375 - 19,475)^2} = \sqrt{169 + 811,441} = 901$$

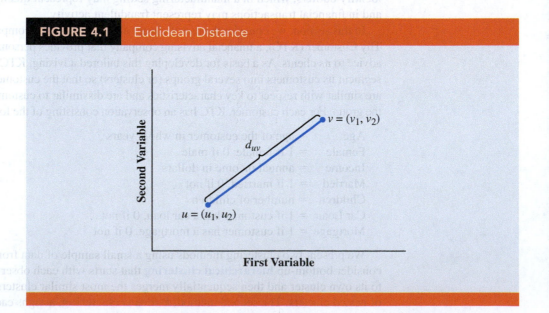

FIGURE 4.1   Euclidean Distance

Refer to Chapter 2 for a discussion of z-scores.

Thus, we see that when using the raw variable values, the dissimilarity between observations is dominated by the Income variable because of the difference in the magnitude of the measurements. Therefore, it is common to standardize the units of each variable j of each observation u. That is, u_j, the value of variable j in observation u, is replaced with its z-score z_j. For the data in *DemoKTC*, the standardized (or normalized) values of observations u and v are $(-1.76, -0.56)$ and $(-0.76, -0.62)$, respectively. The dissimilarity between these two observations based on standardized values is:

$$(standardized)\ d_{uv} = \sqrt{(-1.76 - (-0.76))^2 + (-0.56 - (-0.62))^2}$$
$$= \sqrt{0.994 + 0.004} = 0.998$$

Based on standardized variable values, we observe that observations u and v are actually much more different in age than in income.

Scaling and weighting variable values can be particularly helpful when clustering observations with respect to both numerical and categorical variables.

The conversion to z-scores also makes it easier to identify outlier measurements, which can distort the Euclidean distance between observations. After conversion to z-scores, unequal weighting of variables can also be considered by multiplying the variables of each observation by a selected set of weights. For instance, after standardizing the units on customer observations so that income and age are expressed as their respective z-scores (instead of expressed in dollars and years), we can multiply the income z-scores by 2 if we wish to treat income with twice the importance of age. In other words, standardizing removes bias due to the difference in measurement units, and variable weighting allows the analyst to introduce appropriate bias based on the business context.

When clustering observations solely on the basis of categorical variables encoded as 0–1 (or dummy variables), a better measure of similarity between two observations can be achieved by counting the number of variables with matching values. The simplest overlap measure is called the **matching coefficient** and is computed by

MATCHING COEFFICIENT

$$\frac{\text{number of variables with matching value for observations } u \text{ and } v}{\text{total number of variables}}$$

One weakness of the matching coefficient is that if two observations both have a 0 entry for a categorical variable, this is counted as a sign of similarity between the two observations. However, matching 0 entries do not necessarily imply similarity. For instance, if the categorical variable is Own A Minivan, then a 0 entry in two different observations does not mean that these two people own the same type of car; it means only that neither owns a minivan. To avoid misstating similarity due to the absence of a feature, a similarity measure called **Jaccard's coefficient** does not count matching zero entries and is computed by

JACCARD'S COEFFICIENT

$$\frac{\text{number of variables with matching nonzero value for observations } u \text{ and } v}{(\text{total number of variables}) - (\text{number of variables with matching zero values for observations } u \text{ and } v)}$$

For five customer observations from the file *DemoKTC*, Table 4.1 contains observations of the binary variables Female, Married, Car Loan, and Mortgage and the distance matrixes corresponding to the matching coefficient and Jaccard's coefficient, respectively. Based on the matching coefficient, Observation 1 and Observation 4 are more similar (0.75) than Observation 2 and Observation 3 (0.5) because 3 out of 4 variable values match

TABLE 4.1	Comparison of Similarity Matrixes for Observations with Binary Variables			
Observation	Female	Married	Car Loan	Mortgage
1	1	0	0	0
2	0	1	1	0
3	1	1	1	0
4	1	1	0	0
5	1	1	0	0

Similarity Matrix Based on Matching Coefficient

	1	2	3	4	5
1	1				
2	0	1			
3	0.5	0.5	1		
4	0.75	0.25	0.75	1	
5	0.75	0.25	0.75	1	1

Similarity Matrix Based on Jaccard's Coefficient

	1	2	3	4	5
1	1				
2	0	1			
3	0.333	0.5	1		
4	0.5	0.25	0.667	1	
5	0.5	0.25	0.667	1	1

between Observation 1 and Observation 4 versus just 2 matching values out of 4 for Observation 2 and Observation 3. However, based on Jaccard's coefficient, Observation 1 and Observation 4 are equally similar (0.5) as Observation 2 and Observation 3 (0.5) as Jaccard's coefficient discards the matching zero values for the Car Loan and Mortgage variables for Observation 1 and Observation 4. In the context of this example, choice of the matching coefficient or Jaccard's coefficient depends on whether KTC believes that matching 0 entries imply similarity or not. That is, KTC must gauge whether meaningful similarity is implied if a pair of observations are not female, not married, do not have a car loan, or do not have a mortgage.

Hierarchical Clustering

We consider a bottom-up hierarchical clustering approach that starts with each observation in its own cluster and then iteratively combines the two clusters that are the most similar into a single cluster. Each iteration corresponds to an increased level of aggregation by decreasing the number of distinct clusters. Hierarchical clustering determines the similarity of two clusters by considering the similarity between the observations composing either cluster. Given a way to measure similarity between observations (Euclidean distance, matching coefficients, or Jaccard's coefficients), there are several clustering method alternatives for comparing observations in two clusters to obtain a cluster similarity measure. Using Euclidean distance to illustrate, Figure 4.2 provides a two-dimensional depiction of four methods we will discuss.

When using the **single linkage** clustering method, the similarity between two clusters is defined by the similarity of the pair of observations (one from each cluster) that are the most similar. Thus, single linkage will consider two clusters to be close if an observation in one of the clusters is close to at least one observation in the other cluster. However, a cluster formed by merging two clusters that are close with respect to single linkage may also consist of pairs of observations that are very different. The reason is that there is no consideration of how different an observation may be from other observations in a cluster as long as it is similar to at least one observation in that cluster.

In two dimensions, single linkage clustering can result in long, elongated clusters rather than compact circular clusters. This can occur because single linkage favors merging two different clusters as long as at least one observation in a cluster is very similar to an observation in another cluster.

The **complete linkage** clustering method defines the similarity between two clusters as the similarity of the pair of observations (one from each cluster) that are the most different. Thus, complete linkage will consider two clusters to be close if their most different pair of observations are close. This method produces clusters such that all member observations of a cluster are relatively close to each other. However, clustering created with complete linkage can be distorted by outlier observations.

The single linkage and complete linkage methods define between-cluster similarity based on the single pair of observations in two different clusters that are most similar or least

FIGURE 4.2   Measuring Similarity Between Clusters

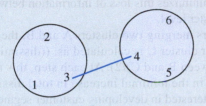

Single Linkage, $d_{3,4}$

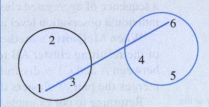

Complete Linkage, $d_{1,6}$

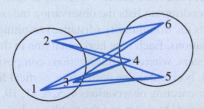

Group Average Linkage,
$$\frac{d_{1,4}+d_{1,5}+d_{1,6}+d_{2,4}+d_{2,5}+d_{2,6}+d_{3,4}+d_{3,5}+d_{3,6}}{9}$$

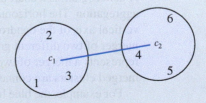

Centroid Linkage, d_{c_1,c_2}

similar. In contrast, the **group average linkage** clustering method defines the similarity between two clusters to be the average similarity computed over *all* pairs of observations between the two clusters. If Cluster 1 consists of n_1 observations and Cluster 2 consists of n_2 observations, the similarity of these clusters would be the average of $n_1 \times n_2$ similarity measures. This method produces clusters that are less dominated by the similarity between single pairs of observations. The **median linkage** method is analogous to group average linkage except that it uses the median of the similarities computed between all pairs of observations between the two clusters. The use of the median reduces the effect of outliers.

Centroid linkage uses the averaging concept of cluster centroids to define between-cluster similarity. The centroid for cluster k, denoted c_k, is found by calculating the average value for each variable across all observations in a cluster; that is, a centroid is the average observation of a cluster. The similarity between two clusters is then defined as the similarity of the centroids of the two clusters.

Ward's method merges two clusters such that the dissimilarity of the observations within the resulting single cluster increases as little as possible. It tends to produce clearly defined clusters of similar size. For a pair of clusters under consideration for aggregation, Ward's method computes the sum of the squared dissimilarity between each individual observation in the union of the two clusters and the centroid of the resulting merged cluster. Representing observations within a cluster with the centroid can be viewed as a loss of information in the sense that the individual differences in these observations will not be captured by the cluster centroid. Hierarchical clustering using Ward's method results in a sequence of aggregated clusters that minimizes this loss of information between the individual observation level and the cluster level.

When **McQuitty's method** considers merging two clusters A and B, the dissimilarity of the resulting cluster AB to any other cluster C is calculated as: ((dissimilarity between A and C) + dissimilarity between B and C)/2). At each step, this method then merges the pair of clusters that results in the minimal increase in total dissimilarity.

Refer to Appendix 4.1 at the end of this chapter for step-by-step instructions on how to execute hierarchical clustering with XLMiner.

Returning to our example, KTC is interested in developing customer segments based on gender, marital status, and whether the customer is repaying a car loan and a mortgage. Using data in the file *DemoKTC*, we base the clusters on a collection of 0–1 categorical variables (Female, Married, Car Loan, and Mortgage). We use the matching coefficient to measure similarity between observations and the group average linkage clustering method to measure similarity between clusters.

Figure 4.3 depicts a **dendrogram** to visually summarize the output from a hierarchical clustering using the matching coefficient to measure similarity between observations and the group average linkage clustering method to measure similarity between clusters. A dendrogram is a chart that depicts the set of nested clusters resulting at each step of aggregation. The horizontal axis of the dendrogram lists the observation indexes. The vertical axis of the dendrogram represents the dissimilarity (distance) resulting from a merger of two different groups of observations. Each blue horizontal line in the dendrogram represents a merger of two (or more) clusters, where the observations composing the merged clusters are connected to the blue horizontal line with a blue vertical line.

For example, the blue horizontal line connecting observations 4, 5, 6, 11, 19, and 28 conveys that these six observations are grouped together and the resulting cluster has a dissimilarity measure of 0. A dissimilarity of 0 results from this merger because these six observations have identical values for the Female, Married, Car Loan, and Mortgage variables. Following the blue vertical line up from the cluster of {4, 5, 6, 11, 19}, another blue horizontal line connects this cluster with the cluster consisting solely of Observation 1. Thus, the cluster {4, 5, 6, 11, 19} and cluster {1} are merged resulting in a dissimilarity of 0.25.

To interpret a dendrogram at a specific level of aggregation, it is helpful to visualize a horizontal line such as one of the black dashed lines we have drawn across Figure 4.3. The

FIGURE 4.3	Dendrogram for KTC

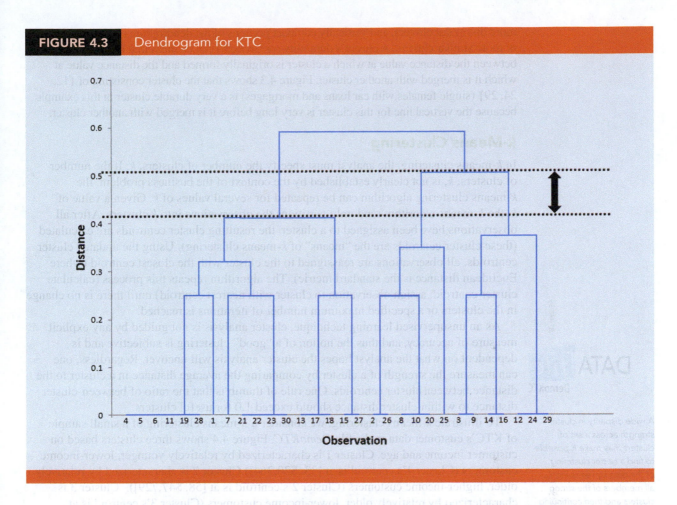

bottom horizontal black dashed line intersects with the vertical branches in the dendrogram three times; each intersection corresponds to a cluster containing the observations connected by the vertical branch that is intersected. The composition of these three clusters is

Cluster 1: {4, 5, 6, 11, 19, 28, 1, 7, 21, 22, 23, 30, 13, 17, 18, 15, 27}
  = mix of males and females, 15 out of 17 married, no car loans, 5 out of 17
  with mortgages
Cluster 2: {2, 26, 8, 10, 20, 25}
  = all males with car loans, 5 out of 6 married, 2 out of 6 with mortgages
Cluster 3: {3, 9, 14, 16, 12, 24, 29}
  = all females with car loans, 4 out of 7 married, 5 out of 7 with mortgages

These clusters segment KTC's customers into three groups that could possibly indicate varying levels of responsibility—an important factor to consider when providing financial advice.

The nested construction of the hierarchical clusters allows KTC to identify different numbers of clusters and assess (often qualitatively) the implications. By sliding a horizontal line up or down the vertical axis of a dendrogram and observing the intersection of the horizontal line with the vertical dendrogram branches, an analyst can extract varying numbers of clusters. Note that sliding up to the position of the top horizontal black line in Figure 4.3 results in merging Cluster 2 with Cluster 3 into a single, more dissimilar, cluster. The vertical distance between the points of agglomeration is the "cost" of merging clusters in terms of decreased homogeneity within clusters. Thus, vertically elongated portions of the dendrogram represent mergers of more dissimilar clusters, and vertically compact portions of the dendrogram represent mergers of more similar clusters. A cluster's durability (or strength) can be measured by the difference between the distance value at which a cluster is originally formed and the distance value at which it is merged with another cluster. Figure 4.3 shows that the cluster consisting of {12, 24, 29} (single females with car loans and mortgages) is a very durable cluster in this example because the vertical line for this cluster is very long before it is merged with another cluster.

k-Means Clustering

In *k*-means clustering, the analyst must specify the number of clusters, *k*. If the number of clusters, *k*, is not clearly established by the context of the business problem, the *k*-means clustering algorithm can be repeated for several values of *k*. Given a value of *k*, the *k*-means algorithm randomly partitions the observations into *k* clusters. After all observations have been assigned to a cluster, the resulting cluster centroids are calculated (these cluster centroids are the "means" of *k*-means clustering). Using the updated cluster centroids, all observations are reassigned to the cluster with the closest centroid (where Euclidean distance is the standard metric). The algorithm repeats this process (calculate cluster centroid, assign observation to cluster with nearest centroid) until there is no change in the clusters or a specified maximum number of iterations is reached.

DATA *file*
DemoKTC

A wide disparity in cluster strength across a set of clusters may make it possible to find a better clustering of the data by removing all members of the strong clusters and then continuing the clustering process on the remaining observations.

As an unsupervised learning technique, cluster analysis is not guided by any explicit measure of accuracy, and thus the notion of a "good" clustering is subjective and is dependent on what the analyst hopes the cluster analysis will uncover. Regardless, one can measure the strength of a cluster by comparing the average distance in a cluster to the distance between cluster centroids. One rule of thumb is that the ratio of between-cluster distance to within-cluster distance should exceed 1.0 for useful clusters.

To illustrate *k*-means clustering, we consider a 3-means clustering of a small sample of KTC's customer data in the file *DemoKTC*. Figure 4.4 shows three clusters based on customer income and age. Cluster 1 is characterized by relatively younger, lower-income customers (Cluster 1's centroid is at [33, $20,364]).Cluster 2 is characterized by relatively older, higher-income customers (Cluster 2's centroid is at [58, $47,729]). Cluster 3 is characterized by relatively older, lower-income customers (Cluster 3's centroid is at [53, $21,416]). As visually corroborated by Figure 4.4, Table 4.2 shows that Cluster 2 is the

Cluster centroids are depicted by circles in Figure 4.4.

Although Figure 4.4 is plotted in the original scale of the variables, the clustering was based on the variables after standardizing (normalizing) their values.

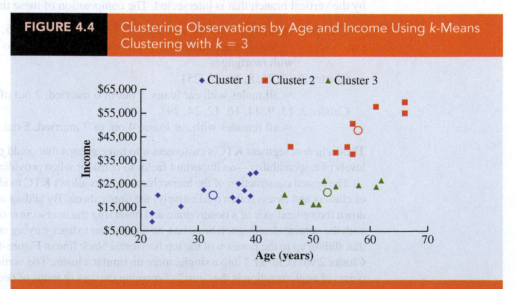

FIGURE 4.4   Clustering Observations by Age and Income Using *k*-Means Clustering with *k* = 3

Tables 4.2 and 4.3 are expressed in terms of normalized coordinates in order to eliminate any distortion resulting from differences in the scale of the input variables.

TABLE 4.2	Average Distances within Clusters	
	No. of Observations	**Average Distance Between Observations in Cluster**
Cluster 1	12	0.622
Cluster 2	8	0.739
Cluster 3	10	0.520

TABLE 4.3	Distances Between Cluster Centroids		
Distance Between Cluster Centroids	**Cluster 1**	**Cluster 2**	**Cluster 3**
Cluster 1	0	2.784	1.529
Cluster 2	2.784	0	1.964
Cluster 3	1.529	1.964	0

smallest, but most heterogeneous cluster. We also observe that Cluster 1 is the largest cluster and Cluster 3 is the most homogeneous cluster. Table 4.3 displays the distance between each pair of cluster centroids to demonstrate how distinct the clusters are from each other. Cluster 1 and Cluster 2 are the most distinct from each other. To evaluate the strength of the clusters, we compare the average distance within each cluster (Table 4.2) to the average distances between clusters (Table 4.3). For example, although Cluster 2 is the most heterogeneous, with an average distance between observations of 0.739, comparing this to the distance between the Cluster 2 and Cluster 3 centroids (1.964) reveals that on average an observation in Cluster 2 is approximately 2.66 times closer to the Cluster 2 centroid than to the Cluster 3 centroid. In general, the larger the ratio of the distance between a pair of cluster centroids and the within-cluster distance, the more distinct the clustering is for the observations in the two clusters in the pair. Although qualitative considerations should take priority in evaluating clusters, using the ratios of between-cluster distance and within-cluster distance provides some guidance in determining k, the number of clusters.

Hierarchical Clustering Versus *k*-Means Clustering

If you have a small data set (e.g., fewer than 500 observations) and want to easily examine solutions with increasing numbers of clusters, you may want to use hierarchical clustering. Hierarchical clusters are also convenient if you want to observe how clusters are nested. However, hierarchical clustering can be very sensitive to outliers, and clusters may change dramatically if observations are eliminated from (or added to) the data set. If you know how many clusters you want and you have a larger data set (e.g., more than 500 observations), you may choose to use *k*-means clustering. Recall that *k*-means clustering partitions the observations, which is appropriate if you are trying to summarize the data with k "average" observations that describe the data with the minimum amount of error. However, *k*-means clustering is generally not appropriate for binary or ordinal data, for which an "average" is not meaningful.

4.3 Association Rules

In marketing, analyzing consumer behavior can lead to insights regarding the location and promotion of products. Specifically, marketers are interested in examining transaction data on customer purchases to identify the products commonly purchased together. In this section, we discuss the development of if–then statements, called **association rules**, which convey the likelihood of certain items being purchased together. Although association rules are an important tool in **market basket analysis**, they are also applicable to disciplines other than marketing. For example, association rules can assist medical researchers in understanding which treatments have been commonly prescribed to certain patient symptoms (and the resulting effects).

Hy-Vee grocery store would like to gain insight into its customers' purchase patterns to possibly improve its in-aisle product placement and cross-product promotions. Table 4.4 contains a small sample of data in which each transaction comprises the items purchased by a shopper in a single visit to a Hy-Vee. An example of an association rule from this data would be "if {bread, jelly}, then {peanut butter}," meaning that "if a transaction includes bread and jelly it also includes peanut butter." The collection of items (or item set) corresponding to the *if* portion of the rule, {bread, jelly}, is called the **antecedent**. The item set corresponding to the *then* portion of the rule, {peanut butter}, is called the **consequent**. Typically, only association rules for which the consequent consists of a single item are considered because these are more actionable. Although the number of possible association rules can be overwhelming, we typically investigate only association rules that involve antecedent and consequent item sets that occur together frequently. To formalize the notion of "frequent," we define the **support count** of an item set as the number of transactions in the data that include that item set. In Table 4.4, the support count of {bread, jelly} is 4. A rule of thumb is to consider only association rules with a support count of at least 20% of the total number of transactions.

If an item set is particularly valuable, then the minimum support count used to filter rules is often lowered.

Support is also sometimes expressed as the percentage of total transactions containing an item set.

The potential impact of an association rule is often governed by the number of transactions it may affect, which is measured by computing the support count of the item set consisting of the union of its antecedent and consequent. Investigating the rule "if {bread, jelly}, then {peanut butter}" from the Table 4.4, we see the support count of {bread, jelly, peanut butter} is 2. By only considering rules involving item sets with a support above a minimum level, inexplicable rules capturing random noise in the data can generally be avoided.

The data in Table 4.4 are in item list format; that is, each transaction row corresponds to a list of item names. Alternatively, the data can be represented in binary matrix format, in which each row is a transaction record and the columns correspond to each distinct item. This is equivalent to encoding each item name with a 0–1 dummy variable.

TABLE 4.4	Shopping-Cart Transactions
Transaction	**Shopping Cart**
1	bread, peanut butter, milk, fruit, jelly
2	bread, jelly, soda, potato chips, milk, fruit, vegetables, peanut butter
3	whipped cream, fruit, chocolate sauce, beer
4	steak, jelly, soda, potato chips, bread, fruit
5	jelly, soda, peanut butter, milk, fruit
6	jelly, soda, potato chips, milk, bread, fruit
7	fruit, soda, potato chips, milk
8	fruit, soda, peanut butter, milk
9	fruit, cheese, yogurt
10	yogurt, vegetables, beer

To help identify reliable association rules, we define the measure of **confidence** of a rule, which is computed as

CONFIDENCE

$$\frac{\text{support of \{antecedent and consequent\}}}{\text{support of antecedent}}$$

This measure of confidence can be viewed as the conditional probability of the consequent item set occurring given that the antecedent item set occurs. A high value of confidence suggests a rule in which the consequent is frequently true when the antecedent is true, but a high value of confidence can be misleading. For example, if the support of the consequent is high—that is, the item set corresponding to the *then* part is very frequent—then the confidence of the association rule could be high even if there is little or no association between the items. In Table 4.4, the rule "if {cheese}, then {fruit}" has a confidence of 1.0 (or 100%). This is misleading because {fruit} is a frequent item; the confidence of *almost any* rule with {fruit} as the consequent will have high confidence. Therefore, to evaluate the efficiency of a rule, we compute the **lift ratio** of the rule by accounting for the frequency of the consequent:

Adjusting the data by aggregating items into more general categories (or splitting items into more specific categories) so that items occur in roughly the same number of transactions often yields better association rules.

LIFT RATIO

$$\frac{\text{confidence}}{\text{support of consequent/total number of transactions}}$$

A lift ratio greater than 1 suggests that there is some usefulness to the rule and that it is better at identifying cases when the consequent occurs than is no rule at all. In other words, a lift ratio greater than 1 suggests that the level of association between the antecedent and consequent is higher than would be expected if these item sets were independent.

For the data in Table 4.4, the rule "if {bread, jelly}, then {peanut butter}" has confidence = 2/4 = 0.5 and a lift ratio = 0.5/(4/10) = 1.25. In other words, identifying a customer who purchased both bread and jelly as one who also purchased peanut butter is 25% better than just guessing that a random customer purchased peanut butter.

An association rule with a high lift ratio and low support may still be useful if the consequent represents a very valuable opportunity.

The utility of a rule depends on both its support and its lift ratio. Although a high lift ratio suggests that the rule is very efficient at finding when the consequent occurs, if it has a very low support, the rule may not be as useful as another rule that has a lower lift ratio but affects a large number of transactions (as demonstrated by a high support).

Based on the data in Table 4.4, Table 4.5 shows the list of association rules that achieve a lift ratio of at least 1.39 while satisfying a minimum support of 4 transactions (out of 10) and a minimum confidence of 50%. The top rules in Table 4.5 suggest that bread, fruit, and jelly are commonly associated items. For example, the sixth rule listed in Table 4.5 states, "If Jelly is purchased, then Bread and Fruit are also purchased." Perhaps Hy-Vee could consider a promotion and/or product placement to leverage this perceived relationship.

Evaluating Association Rules

Although explicit measures such as support, confidence, and lift ratio can help filter association rules, an association rule is ultimately judged on how actionable it is and how well it explains the relationship between item sets. For example, Walmart mined its transactional data to uncover strong evidence of the association rule, "If a customer purchases a Barbie doll, then a customer also purchases a candy bar." Walmart could leverage this relationship in product placement decisions as well as in advertisements and promotions, perhaps by placing a high-margin candy-bar display near the Barbie dolls. However, we must be aware that association rule mining often results in obvious relationships

TABLE 4.5	Association Rules for Hy-Vee					
Confidence (%)	Antecedent (A)	Consequent (C)	Support for A	Support for C	Support for A & C	Lift Ratio
100.0	Bread	Jelly	4	5	4	2.00
100.0	Bread, Fruit	Jelly	4	5	4	2.00
100.0	Bread	Fruit, Jelly	4	5	4	2.00
80.0	Jelly	Bread	5	4	4	2.00
80.0	Fruit, Jelly	Bread	5	4	4	2.00
80.0	Jelly	Bread, Fruit	5	4	4	2.00
100.0	Peanut Butter	Milk	4	6	4	1.67
100.0	Peanut Butter, Fruit	Milk	4	6	4	1.67
100.0	Peanut Butter	Milk, Fruit	4	6	4	1.67
100.0	Potato Chips	Soda	4	6	4	1.67
100.0	Fruit, Potato Chips	Soda	4	6	4	1.67
100.0	Potato Chips	Fruit, Soda	4	6	4	1.67
66.7	Milk	Peanut Butter	6	4	4	1.67
66.7	Milk, Fruit	Peanut Butter	6	4	4	1.67
66.7	Milk	Peanut Butter, Fruit	6	4	4	1.67
66.7	Soda	Potato Chips	6	4	4	1.67
66.7	Fruit, Soda	Potato Chips	6	4	4	1.67
66.7	Soda	Fruit, Potato Chips	6	4	4	1.67
83.3	Soda	Milk	6	6	5	1.39
83.3	Milk	Soda	6	6	5	1.39
83.3	Fruit, Soda	Milk	6	6	5	1.39
83.3	Milk, Fruit	Soda	6	6	5	1.39
83.3	Soda	Milk, Fruit	6	6	5	1.39
83.3	Milk	Fruit, Soda	6	6	5	1.39

such as "If a customer purchases hamburger patties, then a customer also purchases hamburger buns," which may be true but provide no new insight. Association rules with a weak support measure often are inexplicable. For an association rule to be useful, it must be well supported *and* explain an important previously unknown relationship. The support of an association rule can generally be improved by basing it on less specific antecedent and consequent item sets. Unfortunately, association rules based on less specific item sets tend to yield less insight.

SUMMARY

We introduced the descriptive data-mining methods and related concepts. We began with a discussion about preparing data for analysis, including how to handle data errors and missing data. We also presented the issue of reducing or redefining the set of variables to analyze when faced with a data set that includes measurements for an overwhelming number of variables. After introducing similarity measures, we presented two different methods for grouping observations based on the similarity of their respective variable values: hiearchical clustering and *k*-means clustering. Hieararchical clustering begins with each observation in its own cluster and iteratively aggregates clusters. In *k*-means clustering, the analyst specifies *k*, the number of clusters, and then observations are placed into these clusters in an attempt to minimize the dissimilarity within the clusters. We explained the use association rules to identify patterns across transactions.

GLOSSARY

Antecedent The item set corresponding to the *if* portion of an if–then association rule.

Association rule An if–then statement describing the relationship between item sets.

Centroid linkage Uses the averaging concept of cluster centroids to define between-cluster similarity.

Complete linkage Measure of calculating dissimilarity between clusters by considering only the two most dissimilar observations between the two clusters.

Confidence The conditional probability that the consequent of an association rule occurs given the antecedent occurs.

Consequent The item set corresponding to the *then* portion of an if–then association rule.

Dendrogram A tree diagram used to illustrate the sequence of nested clusters produced by hierarchical clustering.

Dimension reduction Process of reducing the number of variables to consider in a data-mining approach.

Euclidean distance Geometric measure of dissimilarity between observations based on the Pythagorean theorem.

Group average linkage Measure of calculating dissimilarity between clusters by considering the distance between each pair of observations between two clusters.

Hierarchical clustering Process of agglomerating observations into a series of nested groups based on a measure of similarity.

Jaccard's coefficient Measure of similarity between observations consisting solely of binary categorical variables that considers only matches of nonzero entries.

k-Means clustering Process of organizing observations into one of k groups based on a measure of similarity.

Lift ratio The ratio of the confidence of an association rule to the benchmark confidence.

Market basket analysis Analysis of items frequently co-occuring in transactions (such as purchases).

Matching coefficient Measure of similarity between observations based on the number of matching values of categorical variables.

McQuitty's method Measure that computes the dissimilarity between a cluster AB (formed by merging clusters A and B) and a cluster C by averaging the distance between A and C and the distance between B and C.

Median linkage Method that computes the similarity between two clusters as the median of the similarities between each pair of observations in the two clusters.

Missing at random The case when data for a variable is missing due to a relationship a relationship between other variables.

Missing completely at random The case when data for a variable is missing purely due to random chance.

Missing not at random The case when data for a variable is missing due to its unrecorded value.

Observation A set of observed values of variables associated with a single entity, often displayed as a row in a spreadsheet or database.

Single linkage Measure of calculating dissimilarity between clusters by considering only the two most similar observations between the two clusters.

Support count The number of times that a collection of items occurs together in a transaction data set.

Unsupervised learning Category of data-mining techniques in which an algorithm explains relationships without an outcome variable to guide the process.

Ward's method Procedure that partitions observations in a manner to obtain clusters with the least amount of information loss due to the aggregation.

PROBLEMS

Problem descriptions may include XLMiner directions. If using alternative software, steps may vary and results may differ depending on algorithm implementation. Due to the realistic size of these data sets, XLMiner may take several minutes to complete execution for some of these problems. Where relevant, we used the default seed of 12345 when applying XLMiner.

1. The Football Bowl Subdivision (FBS) level of the National Collegiate Athletic Association (NCAA) consists of over 100 schools. Most of these schools belong to one of several conferences, or collections of schools, that compete with each other on a regular basis in collegiate sports. Suppose the NCAA has commissioned a study that will propose the formation of conferences based on the similarities of the constituent schools. The file *FBS* contains data on schools belong to the Football Bowl Subdivision (FBS). Each row in this file contains information on a school. The variables include football stadium capacity, latitude, longitude, athletic department revenue, endowment, and undergraduate enrollment.

   a. Apply *k*-means clustering with *k* = 10 using football stadium capacity, latitude, longitude, endowment, and enrollment as variables. Be sure to **Normalize Input Data** and specify 50 iterations and 10 random starts in Step 2 of the XLMiner *k*-Means Clustering procedure. Analyze the resultant clusters. What is the smallest cluster? What is the least dense cluster (as measured by the average distance in the cluster)? What makes the least dense cluster so diverse?

   b. What problems do you see with the plan with defining the school membership of the 10 conferences directly with the 10 clusters?

   c. Repeat part a, but this time do <u>not</u> **Normalize Input Data** in Step 2 of the XLMiner k-Means Clustering procedure. Analyze the resultant clusters. How and why do they differ from those in part a? Identify the dominating factor(s) in the formation of these new clusters.

2. Refer to the clustering problem involving the file *FBS* described in Problem 1. Apply hierarchical clustering with 10 clusters using football stadium capacity, latitude, longitude, endowment, and enrollment as variables. Be sure to **Normalize Input Data** in Step 2 of the XLMiner Hierarchical Clustering procedure. Use Ward's method as the clustering method.

   a. Use a PivotTable on the data in the *HC_Clusters* worksheet to compute the cluster centers for the clusters in the hierarchical clustering.

   b. Identify the cluster with the largest average football stadium capacity. Using all the variables, how would you characterize this cluster?

   c. Examine the smallest cluster. What makes this cluster unique?

   d. By examining the sequence of clustering stages in *HC_Output* worksheet (and the accompanying dendrogram on the *HC_Dendrogram* worksheet), recommend the number of clusters that seems to be the most natural fit based on the distance. By comparing the total distance at the stage with eight clusters to the total distance at the stage with seven clusters, compute the increase in distance if 7 clusters are used instead of 8 clusters.

3. Refer to the clustering problem involving the file *FBS* described in Problem 1. Apply hierarchical clustering with 10 clusters using latitude and longitude as variables. Be sure to **Normalize Input Data** in Step 2 of the XLMiner Hierarchical Clustering procedure. Execute the clustering two times – once with single linkage as the clustering method and once with group average linkage as the clustering method. Use a PivotTable on the data in the respective *HC_Clusters* worksheets to compute the cluster sizes, as well as the minimum and maximum of the latitude and longitude within each cluster. To visualize the clusters, create a scatter plot with longitude as the x-variable and latitude as the y-variable. Compare the results of the two approaches.

4. Refer to the clustering problem involving the file *FBS* described in Problem 1. Apply hierarchical clustering with 10 clusters using latitude and longitude as variables. Be sure to **Normalize Input Data** in Step 2 of the XLMiner Hierarchical Clustering procedure. Execute the clustering two times – once with Ward's method as the clustering method and once with group average linkage as the clustering method. Use a PivotTable on the data in the respective *HC_Clusters* worksheets to compute the cluster sizes, as well as the minimum and maximum of the latitude and longitude within each cluster. To visualize the clusters, create a scatter plot with longitude as the x-variable and latitude as the y-variable. Compare the results of the two approaches.

5. Refer to the clustering problem involving the file *FBS* described in Problem 1. Apply hierarchical clustering with 10 clusters using latitude and longitude as variables. Be sure to **Normalize Input Data** in Step 2 of the XLMiner Hierarchical Clustering procedure. Execute the clustering two times – once with complete linkage as the clustering method and once with Ward's method as the clustering method. Use a PivotTable on the data in the respective *HC_Clusters* worksheets to compute the cluster sizes, as well as the minimum and maximum of the latitude and longitude within each cluster. To visualize the clusters, create a scatter plot with longitude as the x-variable and latitude as the y-variable. Compare the results of the two approaches.

6. Refer to the clustering problem involving the file *FBS* described in Problem 1. Apply hierarchical clustering with 10 clusters using latitude and longitude as variables. Be sure to **Normalize Input Data** in Step 2 of the XLMiner Hierarchical Clustering procedure. Execute the clustering two times – once with centroid linkage as the clustering method and once with group average linkage as the clustering method. Use a PivotTable on the data in the respective *HC_Clusters* worksheets to compute the cluster sizes, as well as the minimum and maximum of the latitude and longitude within each cluster. To visualize the clusters, create a scatter plot with longitude as the x-variable and latitude as the y-variable. Compare the results of the two approaches.

7. Refer to the clustering problem involving the file *FBS* described in Problem 1. Apply hierarchical clustering with 10 clusters using latitude and longitude as variables. Be sure to **Normalize Input Data** in Step 2 of the XLMiner Hierarchical Clustering procedure. Execute the clustering two times – once with median linkage as the clustering method and once with centroid linkage as the clustering method. Use a PivotTable on the data in the respective *HC_Clusters* worksheets to compute the cluster sizes, as well as the minimum and maximum of the latitude and longitude within each cluster. To visualize the clusters, create a scatter plot with longitude as the x-variable and latitude as the y-variable. Compare the results of the two approaches.

8. Refer to the clustering problem involving the file *FBS* described in Problem 1. Apply hierarchical clustering with 10 clusters using latitude and longitude as variables. Be sure to **Normalize Input Data** in Step 2 of the XLMiner Hierarchical Clustering procedure. Execute the clustering two times – once with McQuitty's method as the clustering method and once with group average linkage as the clustering method. Use a PivotTable on the data in the respective *HC_Clusters* worksheets to compute the cluster sizes, as well as the minimum and maximum of the latitude and longitude within each cluster. To visualize the clusters, create a scatter plot with longitude as the x-variable and latitude as the y-variable. Compare the results of the two approaches.

9. From 1946 to 1990, the Big Ten Conference consisted of the University of Illinois, Indiana University, University of Iowa, University of Michigan, Michigan State University, University of Minnesota, Northwestern University, Ohio State University, Purdue University, and University of Wisconsin. In 1990, the conference added Pennsylvania State University. In 2011, the conference added the University of

DATA *file*
BigTen

Nebraska. Even more recently, the University of Maryland and Rutgers University have been added to the conference with speculation of more schools being added. The file *BigTen* contains the similar information as the file *FBS* (see Problem 1 description), except that the variable values for the original 10 schools in the Big 10 conference have been replaced with the respective averages of these variables over these 10 schools. Apply hierarchical clustering with 2 clusters using football stadium capacity, latitude, longitude, endowment, and enrollment as variables. Be sure to **Normalize Input Data** in Step 2 of the XLMiner Hierarchical Clustering procedure. Use complete linkage as the clustering method. By referencing the *HC_Output* worksheet or the *HC_Dendrogram* worksheet, which schools does the clustering suggest would have been the most appropriate to be the eleventh school in the Big Ten? The twelfth and thirteenth schools? What is the problem with using this method to identify the fourteenth school to add to the Big Ten?

10. Refer to the clustering problem involving the file *FBS* described in Problem 1. The NCAA has a preference for conferences consisting of similar schools with respect to their endowment, enrollment, and football stadium capacity, but these conferences must be in the same geographic region to reduce traveling costs. Follow the following steps to address this desire. Apply k-means clustering using latitude and longitude as variables with $k = 3$. Be sure to **Normalize Input Data** and specify 50 iterations and 10 random starts in Step 2 of the XLMiner k-Means Clustering procedure. Using the cluster assignments, separate the original data in the Data worksheet into three separate data sets – one data set for each of the three "regional" clusters.

    a. For Region 1 data set, apply hierarchical clustering with Ward's method to form four clusters using football stadium capacity, endowment, and enrollment as variables. Be sure to **Normalize Input Data** in Step 2 of the XLMiner Hierarchical Clustering procedure. Using a PivotTable on the data in the corresponding *HC_Clusters* worksheet, report the characteristics of each cluster.

    b. For the Region 2 data set, apply hierarchical clustering with Ward's method to form three clusters using football stadium capacity, endowment, and enrollment as variables. Be sure to **Normalize Input Data** in Step 2 of the XLMiner Hierarchical Clustering procedure. Using a PivotTable on the data in the corresponding *HC_Clusters* worksheet, report the characteristics of each cluster.

    c. For the Region 3 data set, apply hierarchical clustering with Ward's method to form two clusters using football stadium capacity, endowment, and enrollment as variables. Be sure to **Normalize Input Data** in Step 2 of the XLMiner Hierarchical Clustering procedure. Using a PivotTable on the data in the corresponding *HC_Clusters* worksheet, report the characteristics of each cluster.

    d. What problems do you see with the plan with defining the school membership of nine conferences directly with the nine total clusters formed from the regions? How could this approach be tweaked to solve this problem?

11. IBM employs a network of expert analytics consultants for various projects. To help it determine how to distribute its bonuses, IBM wants to form groups of employees with similar performance according to key performance metrics. Each observation (corresponding to an employee) in the file *BigBlue* consists of values for: (1) *UsageRate* which corresponds to the proportion of time that the employee has been actively working on high priority projects, (2) *Recognition* which is the number of projects for which the employee was specifically requested, and (3) *Leader* which is the number of projects on which the employee has served as project leader. Apply k-means clustering with for values of $k = 2, \ldots, 7$. Be sure to **Normalize Input Data** and specify 50 iterations and 10 random starts in Step 2 of the XLMiner k-Means

Clustering procedure. How many clusters do you recommend using to categorize the employees? Why?

12. Use the data file *DemoKTC* to conduct the following analysis.
    a. Use hierarchical clustering with the matching coefficient as the similarity measure and the group average linkage as the clustering method to create nested clusters based on the Female, Married, Car Loan, and Mortgage variables as shown in Appendix 4.1. Specify the construction of 3 clusters. Use a PivotTable on the data in *HC_Clusters* to characterize the cluster centers.
    b. Repeat part a, but use Jaccard's coefficient as the similarity measure.
    c. Compare the clusters and explain your observations.
13. Use the data file *DemoKTC* file to conduct the following analysis.
    a. Use k-means clustering with a value of $k = 3$ to cluster based on the Age, Income, and Children variables to reproduce the results in Appendix 4.2.
    b. Repeat the k-means clustering for values of $k = 2, 4, 5$.
    c. How many clusters do you recommend? Why?

14. Attracted by the possible returns from a portfolio of movies, hedge funds have invested in the movie industry by financially backing individual films and/or studios. The hedge fund Gelt Star is currently conducting some research involving movies involving Adam Sandler, an American actor, screenwriter, and film producer. As a first step, Gelt Star would like to cluster Adam Sandler movies based on their gross box office returns and movie critic ratings. Using the data in the file *Sandler*, apply k-means clustering with $k = 3$ to characterize three different types of Adam Sandler movies. Based the clusters on the variables *Rating* and *Box Office*. *Rating* corresponds to movie ratings provided by critics (a higher score represents a movie receiving better reviews). *Box Office* represents the gross box office earnings in 2015 dollars. Be sure to **Normalize Input Data** and specify 50 iterations and 10 random starts in Step 2 of the XLMiner k-Means Clustering procedure. Use the resulting clusters to characterize Adam Sandler movies.

15. Josephine Mater works for a market research firm that specializes in the food industry. She currently is analyzing Trader Joe's, a national chain of specialty grocery stores. Specifically, Josephine would like to gain insight on Trader Joe's future expansion plans (which are closely guarded by the company). Josephine knows that Trader Joe's replenishes its inventory at its retail stores with frequent trucking shipments from its distribution centers. The file *TraderJoes* contains data on the location of Trader Joe's retail stores. To keep costs low, retail stores are typically located near a distribution center. Josephine would like to use k-means clustering to estimate the location and number of Trader Joe's distribution centers (information on Trader Joe's distribution centers is not publicly disclosed). How large must k be so that the average distance to each cluster centroid is less than 8 distance units as measured in the original (non-normalized) coordinates? Be sure to **Normalize Input Data** and specify 50 iterations and 10 random starts in Step 2 of the XLMiner k-Means Clustering procedure.

16. Apple Inc. tracks online transactions at its iStore and is interested in learning about the purchase patterns of its customers in order to provide recommendations as a customer browses its web site. A sample of the "shopping cart" data in binary matrix format resides in the file *AppleCart*. Each row indicates which iPad features and accessories a customer selected.

    Using a minimum support of 10% of the total number of transactions and a minimum confidence of 50%, use XLMiner to generate a list of association rules.
    a. Interpret what the rule with the largest lift ratio is saying about the relationship between the antecedent item set and consequent item set.
    b. Interpret the support count of the item set involved in the rule with the largest lift ratio.
    c. Interpret the confidence of the rule with the largest lift ratio.

d. Interpret the lift ratio of the rule with the largest lift ratio.

e. Review the top 15 rules and summarize what the rules suggest.

17. Cookie Monster Inc. is a company that specializes in the development of software that tracks web browsing history of individuals. A sample of browser histories is provided in the file *CookieMonster*. Using binary matrix format, the entry in row *i* and column *j* indicates whether web site *j* was visited by user *i*.

Using a minimum support of 800 transactions and a minimum confidence of 50%, use XLMiner to generate a list of association rules. Review the top 14 rules. What information does this analysis provide Cookie Monster regarding the online behavior of individuals?

18. A grocery store introducing items from Italy is interested in analyzing buying trends of these new "international" items, namely prosciutto, peroni, risotto, and gelato. The file *GroceryStore* provides data on a collection of transactions in item-list format.

a. Using a minimum support of 100 transactions and a minimum confidence of 50%, use XLMiner to generate a list of association rules. How many rules satisfy this criterion?

b. Using a minimum support of 250 transactions and a minimum confidence of 50%, use XLMiner to generate a list of association rules. How many rules satisfy this criterion? Why may the grocery store want to increase the minimum support required for their analysis? What is the risk of increasing the minimum support required?

c. Using the list of rules from part b, consider the rule with the largest lift ratio that involves an Italian item. Interpret what this rule is saying about the relationship between the antecedent item set and consequent item set.

d. Interpret the support count of the item set involved in the rule with the largest lift ratio that involves an Italian item.

e. Interpret the confidence of the rule with the largest lift ratio that involves an Italian item.

f. Interpret the lift ratio of the rule with the largest lift ratio that involves an Italian item.

g. What insight can the grocery store obtain about its purchasers of the Italian fare?

h. How would you characterize this cluster?

i. Examine the smallest cluster. What makes this cluster unique?

j. By examining the dendrogram on the *HC_Dendrogram* worksheet and the sequence of clustering stages in *HC_Output*, what number of clusters seems to be the most natural fit based on the distance? What is the increase in distance if 7 clusters were used instead of 8 clusters?

k. How many clusters do you recommend? Why?

CASE PROBLEM: KNOW THY CUSTOMER

Know Thy Customer (KTC) is a financial consulting company that provides personalized financial advice to its clients. As a basis for developing this tailored advising, KTC would like to segment its customers into several representative groups based on key characteristics.

Peyton Avery, the director of KTC's fledging analytics division, plans to establish the set of representative customer profiles based on 600 customer records in the file *KnowThyCustomer*. Each customer record contains data on age, gender, annual income, marital status, number of children, whether the customer has a car loan, and whether the customer has a home mortgage. KTC's market research staff has determined that these seven characteristics should form the basis of the customer clustering.

Peyton has invited a summer intern, Danny Riles, into her office so they can discuss how to proceed. As they review the data on the computer screen, Peyton's brow furrows as she realizes that this task may not be trivial. The data contains both categorical variables (Female, Married, Car, Mortgage) and interval variables (Age, Income, and Children).

Managerial Report

Playing the role of Peyton, you must write a report documenting the construction of the representative customer profiles. Because Peyton would like to use this report as a training reference for interns such as Danny, your report should experiment with several approaches and explain the strengths and weaknesses of each. In particular, your report should include the following analyses:

1. Using *k*-means clustering on all seven variables, experiment with different values of *k*. Recommend a value of *k* and describe these *k* clusters according to their "average" characteristics. Why might *k*-means clustering not be a good method to use for these seven variables?
2. Using hierarchical clustering on all seven variables, experiment with using complete linkage and group average linkage as the clustering method. Recommend a set of customer profiles (clusters). Describe these clusters according to their "average" characteristics. Why might hierarchical clustering not be a good method to use for these seven variables?
3. Apply a two-step clustering method:
   a. Apply hierarchical clustering on the binary variables Female, Married, Car, and Mortgage to recommend a set of clusters. Use matching coefficients as the similarity measure and group average linkage as the clustering method.
   b. Based on the clusters from part (a), split the original 600 observations into *m* separate data sets, where *m* is the number of clusters recommended from part (a). For each of these *m* data sets, apply 2-means clustering using Age, Income, and Children as variables. This will generate a total of *2m* clusters. Describe these *2m* clusters according to their "average" characteristics.

   What benefit does this two-step clustering approach have over the approaches in parts (1) and (2)? What weakness does it have?

Chapter 4 Appendix

Appendix 4.1 Hierarchical Clustering with XLMiner

KTC is interested in developing customer segments based on the gender, marital status, and whether the customer is repaying a car loan and a mortgage. Using the file *DemoKTC*, the following steps and Figure 4.5 demonstrate how to use XLMiner to construct hierarchical clusters. We base the clusters on a collection of 0–1 categorical variables (Female, Married, Car Loan, and Mortgage). We use the matching coefficient to measure similarity between observations and the group average linkage clustering method to measure similarity between clusters.

Typically, clustering is executed on "raw" data consisting of observations of variable measurements. However, in some cases, a precomputed distance matrix of pairwise dissimilarity between each pair of observations is used to cluster observations. For these cases, in the Hierarchical Clustering—Step 1 of 3 dialog box, you should select Distance matrix for the Data type: in the Clustering Options area

Step 1. Select any cell in the range of the data
Step 2. Click the **XLMiner Platform** tab in the Ribbon
Step 3. Click **Cluster** in the **Data Analysis** group
Step 4. Click **Hierarchical Clustering**
Step 5. When the **Hierarchical Clustering—Step 1 of 3** dialog box appears:
In the **Data source** area, confirm that the **Worksheet:**, **Workbook:**, and **Data range:** entries correspond to the appropriate data

FIGURE 4.5	XLMiner Steps for Hierarchical Clustering

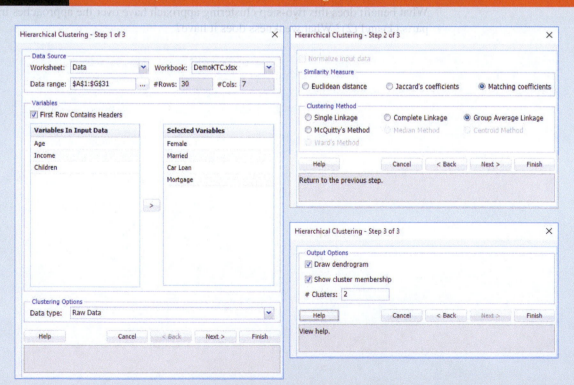

In the **Variables** area, select the checkbox for **First Row Contains Headers**

In the **Variables In Input Data** box of the **Variables** area, select the variables **Female, Married, Car Loan,** and **Mortage,** and click the > button to populate the **Selected Variables** box

In the **Clustering Options** area, select **Raw data** from the drop down window next to **Data type:**

Click **Next** >

Double-clicking on the variable names Female, Married, Car Loan, and Mortage in the Variables box will also move these variables into the Selected variables box.

Step 6. In the **Hierarchical Clustering—Step 2 of 3** dialog box:

In the **Similarity Measure** area, select **Matching coefficients**

In the **Clustering Method** area, select **Group Average Linkage**

Click **Next** >

FIGURE 4.6	HC_Output Worksheet

XLMiner : Hierarchical Clustering

Output Navigator

Predicted Clusters	Dendrogram	Inputs	Clustering Stages

Clustering Stages

Stage	Cluster 1	Cluster 2	Distance
1	4	5	0
2	4	6	0
3	3	9	0
4	8	10	0
5	4	11	0
6	14	16	0
7	13	17	0
8	13	18	0
9	4	19	0
10	8	20	0
11	21	22	0
12	21	23	0
13	12	24	0
14	2	26	0
15	15	27	0
16	4	28	0
17	12	29	0
18	21	30	0
19	1	4	0.25
20	2	8	0.25
21	3	14	0.25
22	13	15	0.25
23	7	21	0.25
24	1	7	0.321429
25	2	25	0.35
26	3	12	0.375
27	1	13	0.4125
28	2	3	0.505952
29	1	2	0.590498

Step 7. In the **Hierarchical Clustering—Step 3 of 3** dialog box:

Select the checkboxes for **Draw dendrogram** and **Show cluster membership**

In the box next to # **Clusters**, enter *3*

Click **Finish**

This procedure generates three worksheets: *HC_Output*, *HC_Clusters*, and *HC_Dendrogram*. As Figure 4.6 shows, *HC_Output* lists the sequence in which clusters are aggregated and the increase in dissimilarity resulting from each merger. For example, at stage 1, Cluster 4 (containing only observation 4) and Cluster 5 (containing only observation 5) are aggregated and the resulting cluster results in a zero increase in dissimilarity because these clusters contain identical observations. When two clusters are merged, the resulting cluster is indexed with the smaller index of the two cluster indices involved in the merger. So when Cluster 4 and Cluster 5 are aggregated, the resulting cluster {4, 5} is labeled Cluster 4 for the next stage.

As Figure 4.7 shows, *HC_Clusters* contains a table showing each observation's cluster at the final level of clustering. For this example, cells B9:B38 list the cluster membership for the final three clusters because we specified 3 for # **Clusters** in the **Hierarchical Clustering - Step 3 of 3** dialog box. As displayed in Figure 4.7, a PivotTable based on the data in the *HC_Clusters* worksheet is often helpful to characterize the clusters. For example, Cluster 1 contains 10 females and 7 males, 15 of the customers are married, none of them have car loans, and 5 have mortgages.

Refer to Chapter 3 to see how to construct a PivotTable.

FIGURE 4.7   HC_Clusters Worksheet

Cluster ID	Sub-Cluster	Female	Married	Car Loan	Mortgage
1	1	1	0	0	0
2	2	0	1	1	1
3	3	1	1	1	0
1	4	1	1	0	0
1	5	1	1	0	0
1	6	1	1	0	0
1	7	0	0	0	0
1	8	0	1	1	0
3	9	1	1	1	0
2	10	0	1	1	0
1	11	1	1	0	0
3	12	1	0	1	1
1	13	1	1	0	1
3	14	1	1	1	1
1	15	0	1	0	1
3	16	1	1	1	1
1	17	1	1	0	1
1	18	1	1	0	1
1	19	1	1	0	0
2	20	0	1	1	0
1	21	0	1	0	0
1	22	0	1	0	0
1	23	0	1	0	0
3	24	1	0	1	1
2	25	0	0	1	0
2	26	0	1	1	1
1	27	0	1	0	1
1	28	1	1	0	0
3	29	1	0	1	1
1	30	0	1	0	0

Row Labels	Sum of Female	Sum of Married	Sum of Car Loan	Sum of Mortgage	Count of Cluster ID
1	10	15	0	5	17
2	0	5	6	2	6
3	7	4	7	5	7
Grand Total	17	24	13	12	30

FIGURE 4.8   HC_Dendrogram Worksheet

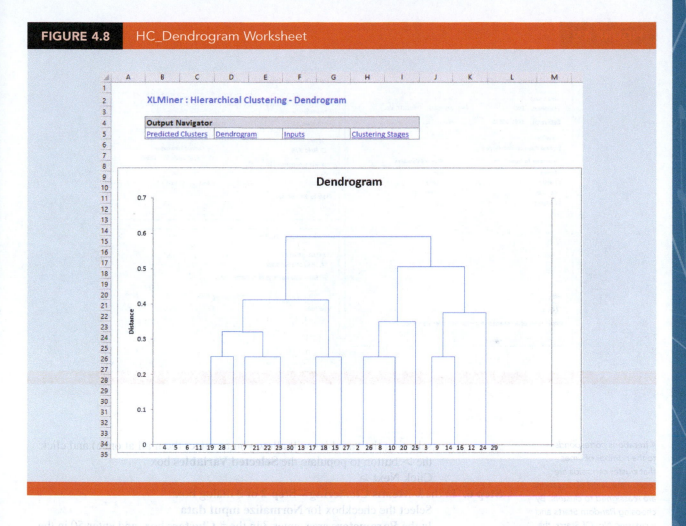

Figure 4.8 shows the dendrogram from *HC_Dendrogram*, visually summarizing the clustering output.

Appendix 4.2 *k*-Means Clustering with XLMiner

KTC is interested in developing customer segments based on age, income, and number of children. Using the file *DemoKTC*, the following steps and Figure 4.9 demonstrate how to execute *k*-means clustering with XLMiner.

Step 1. Select any cell in the range of the data
Step 2. Click the **XLMiner Platform** tab in the Ribbon
Step 3. Click **Cluster** in the **Data Analysis** group
Step 4. Click *k*-**Means Clustering**
Step 5. When the *k*-**Means Clustering—Step 1 of 3** dialog box appears:

In the **Data source** area, confirm the **Worksheet:**, **Workbook:**, and **Data range**: entries correspond to the appropriate data

In the **Variables** area, select the checkbox for **First Row Contains Headers**

In the **Variables In Input Data** box of the **Variables** area, select the variables **Age**, **Income**, and **Children** (pressing the Crtl key while

FIGURE 4.9   XLMiner Steps for *k*-Means Clustering

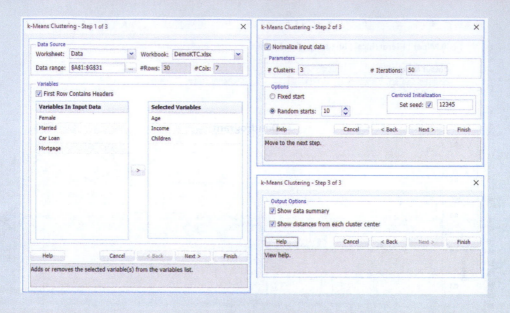

 # Iterations corresponds to the number of times that cluster centroids are recalculated and observations are reassigned to clusters. By choosing Random Starts and increasing No. Of Starts, the k-means algorithm is repeated on multiple randomly generated initial clusters and the best-found cluster set is reported. If the additional run time is not prohibitive, better clusters may result from a larger number of iterations and from a larger number of starts. Setting the seed for Centroid Initialization allows the clustering experiment to be reproduced. If a seed is not set, the clustering results may vary each time the clustering is performed.

selecting the variables will allow you to select them all at once) and click the > button to populate the **Selected Variables** box

Click **Next** >

Step 6. In the ***k*-Means Clustering—Step 2 of 3** dialog box:

Select the checkbox for **Normalize input data**

In the **Parameters** area, enter *3* in the # **Clusters** box, and enter *50* in the # **Iterations** box

In the **Options** area, select **Random Starts:** and enter *10* in the adjacent box

In the **Centroid Initialization** box within the **Options** area, select the checkbox for **Set Seed:** and enter *12345* in the adjacent box

Click **Next** >

Step 7. In the ***k*-Means Clustering—Step 3 of 3** dialog box, click **Finish:**

In the **Output Options** area, select the checkboxes for **Show data summary** and **Show distances from each cluster center**

Click **Finish**

This procedure generates two worksheets, *KMC_Output* and *KMC_Clusters*. Of particular interest on the *KM_Output* worksheet is the **Cluster Centers** information. As shown in Figure 4.10, clicking on the **Cluster Centers** link in the **Output Navigator** area at the top of the *KMC_Output* worksheet brings information describing the clusters into view. In the **Cluster Centers** area, there are two sets of tables. In the first set of tables, the left table lists the cluster centroids in the original units of the input variables and the right table lists the cluster centroids in the normalized units of the input variables. Cluster 1 consists of the youngest customers with largest families and the lowest incomes. Cluster 2 consists of the

FIGURE 4.10 KMC_Output Worksheet

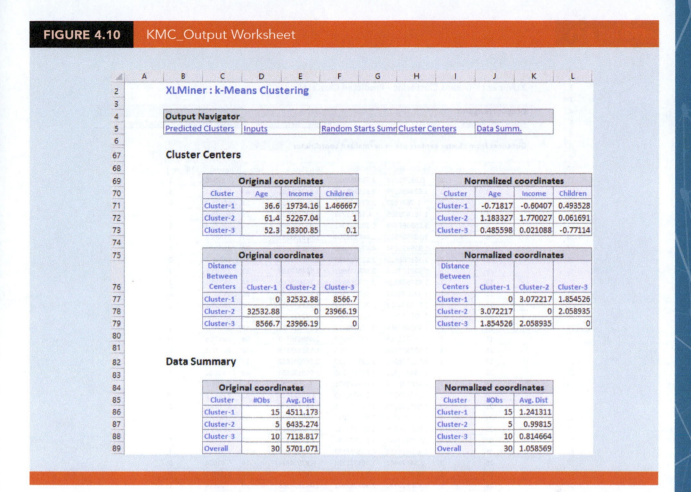

oldest customers with the highest incomes and an average of one child. Cluster 3 consists of older customers with moderate incomes and few children. If KTC decides these clusters are appropriate, they can use them as a basis for creating financial advising plans based on the characteristics of each cluster.

The second set of tables under **Cluster Centers** in Figure 4.10 displays the between-cluster distances between the three cluster centers. The left and right tables express the inter-cluster distances in the original and normalized units of the input variables, respectively. Cluster 1 and Cluster 3 are the most distinct pair of clusters, with a distance of 3.07 units between their respective centroids. Cluster 2 and Cluster 3 are the second most distinct pair of clusters (between-centroid distance of 2.06). Cluster 1 and Cluster 3 are the least distinct (between-centroid distance of 1.85).

The **Data Summary** area of Figure 4.10 displays the within-cluster distances in both the original and normalized units of the input variables, respectively. Referring to the right table expressed in normalized units, we observe that Cluster 3 is the most homogeneous and Cluster 1 is the most heterogeneous. By comparing the normalized between-cluster distance in the bottom right table under **Cluster Centers** to the normalized within-cluster distance in the right table under **Data Summary**, we observe that the observations within clusters are more similar than the observations between clusters. By conducting *k*-means clusters for other values of *k*, we can evaluate how the choice of *k* affects the strength of the clustering as measured by the ratio between the between-cluster and within-cluster distances.

Typically, distance measurements based on the normalized coordinates should be used when making cluster comparisons to avoid the original scale of the input variables skewing the analysis.

FIGURE 4.11 KMC_Clusters Worksheet

XLMiner : k-Means Clustering - Predicted Clusters

Output Navigator

Predicted Clusters	Inputs	Random Starts Summ.	Cluster Centers	Data Summ.

Distances from cluster centers are in normalized coordinates

Record ID	Cluster ID	Dist. Clust-1	Dist. Clust-2	Dist. Clust-3	Age	Income	Children
1	1	0.98792311	2.734158512	1.19091227	48	17546	1
2	1	1.628430379	2.955969211	2.847426201	40	30085.1	3
3	3	1.7646987	2.876825512	0.866409367	51	16575.4	0
4	1	1.761473809	4.18451778	3.547235929	23	20375.4	3
5	2	3.058468348	0.992641041	1.667590968	57	50576.3	0
6	2	2.107506821	1.440136304	1.925798731	57	37869.6	2
7	1	1.929471674	4.473073409	2.72305407	22	8877.07	0
8	3	2.163086915	2.213404825	0.509393351	58	24946.6	0
9	1	0.640107623	2.868415901	2.124907137	37	25304.3	2
10	1	1.459528629	2.317266996	1.788088108	54	24212.1	2
11	2	3.933670152	1.132783988	2.529248044	66	59803.9	0
12	3	1.868574302	2.206364327	0.153137437	52	26658.8	0
13	1	0.770417673	2.981067897	1.392612112	44	15735.8	1
14	2	3.459490964	0.412738412	2.377310051	66	55204.7	1
15	1	1.35811263	3.221133108	1.409030639	36	19474.6	0
16	3	1.374677024	2.97391956	1.183135173	38	22342.1	0
17	1	0.515659563	3.272391017	2.250001888	37	17729.8	2
18	3	2.184811721	1.710157265	1.050178654	46	41016	0
19	3	2.430828697	2.069479576	0.7563163	62	26909.2	0
20	1	1.437973295	3.316736333	1.68923513	31	22522.8	0
21	2	3.390112135	1.012452306	2.862821636	61	57880.7	2
22	1	1.164029752	2.904135826	1.965780278	50	16497.3	2
23	3	2.342344286	1.481686946	0.757448363	54	38446.6	0
24	1	1.574013642	3.872571031	2.15380573	27	15538.8	0
25	1	1.328415143	4.283068598	3.129630608	22	12640.3	2
26	3	2.54373403	1.303721224	0.97594334	56	41034	0
27	3	1.504315206	2.776198332	0.787839774	45	20809.7	0
28	1	0.470226791	2.907788582	1.445834508	39	20114	1
29	1	1.593881128	3.028130438	2.871818915	39	29359.1	3
30	3	1.948348711	2.043313711	1.10683836	61	24270.1	1

The *KMC_Clusters* worksheet (Figure 4.11) lists each observation's assigned cluster in the Cluster ID column as well as the distance (dissimilarity) from the observation to each respective cluster centroid (in normalized units of the input variable). We can use this table to evaluate how well an individual observation fits its assigned cluster relative to the other clusters. For example, Observation 9's assignment to Cluster 1 is quite solid as it is only 0.64 units from Cluster 1's centroid, but 2.12 and 2.87 units from the centroids of Cluster 3 and Cluster 2, respectively. However, Observation 15's assignment to Cluster 1 is not as resolute as it is 1.36 units from Cluster 1's centroid and 1.41 units from Cluster 3's centroid.

Appendix 4.3 Association Rules with XLMiner

DATA *file*
HyVeeDemo

Using the file *HyVeeDemo*, the following steps and Figure 4.12 demonstrate how to examine association rules using XLMiner.

Step 1. Select any cell in the range of the data

Step 2. Click the **XLMiner Platform** tab in the Ribbon

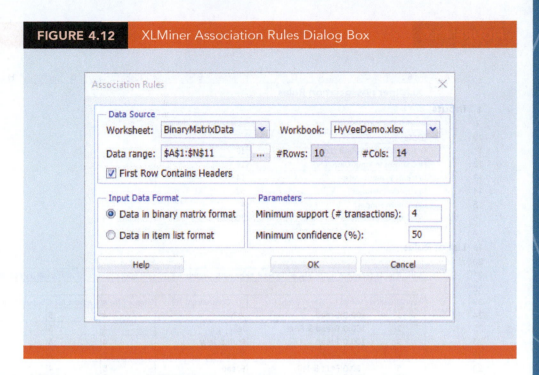

FIGURE 4.12 XLMiner Association Rules Dialog Box

Step 3. Click **Associate** in the **Data Mining** group
Step 4. Click **Association Rules**
Step 5. When the **Association Rules** dialog box appears, in the **Data source** area, confirm that the **Worksheet:**, **Workbook:**, and **Data range:** entries correspond to the appropriate data
Step 6. In the **Data source** area, select the checkbox for **First Row Contains Headers**
Step 7. In the **Input Data Format** area, select **Data in binary matrix format**
Step 8. In the **Parameters** area, enter *4* in the box next to **Minimum support (# transactions)**, and enter *50* in the box next to **Minimum confidence (%)**
Step 9. Click **OK**

Figure 4.13 illustrates a portion of the *AssocRules_Output* worksheet generated by this procedure. For this data, the 52 rules satisfying the minimum support rule of 4 transactions (out of 10) and the minimum confidence of 50% are displayed in decreasing order of lift ratio.

FIGURE 4.13 XLMiner Association Rules Output

	A	B	C	D	E	F	G	H	I
2		**XLMiner : Association Rules**							
8	**Inputs**								
9									
10		**Data**							
11		# Transactions in Input Data			10				
12		# Columns in Input Data			14				
13		# Items in Input Data			14				
14		# Association Rules			52				
15		Minimum Support			4				
16		Minimum Confidence			50.00%				
18									
19	**List of Rules**								
20									
21		Rule: If all Antecedent items are purchased, then with Confidence percentage Consequent items will also be purchased.							
22									

Row ID	Confidence %	Antecedent (A)	Consequent (C)	Support for A	Support for C	Support for A & C	Lift Ratio
1	100.0	Bread	Jelly	4	5	4	2.00
2	100.0	Bread & Fruit	Jelly	4	5	4	2.00
3	100.0	Bread	Fruit & Jelly	4	5	4	2.00
4	80.0	Jelly	Bread	5	4	4	2.00
5	80.0	Fruit & Jelly	Bread	5	4	4	2.00
6	80.0	Jelly	Bread & Fruit	5	4	4	2.00
7	100.0	Peanut Butter	Milk	4	6	4	1.67
8	100.0	Peanut Butter & Fruit	Milk	4	6	4	1.67
9	100.0	Peanut Butter	Milk & Fruit	4	6	4	1.67
10	100.0	Potato Chips	Soda	4	6	4	1.67
11	100.0	Fruit & Potato Chips	Soda	4	6	4	1.67
12	100.0	Potato Chips	Fruit & Soda	4	6	4	1.67
13	66.7	Milk	Peanut Butter	6	4	4	1.67
14	66.7	Milk & Fruit	Peanut Butter	6	4	4	1.67
15	66.7	Milk	Peanut Butter & Fruit	6	4	4	1.67
16	66.7	Soda	Potato Chips	6	4	4	1.67
17	66.7	Fruit & Soda	Potato Chips	6	4	4	1.67
18	66.7	Soda	Fruit & Potato Chips	6	4	4	1.67

Chapter 5

Probability:
An Introduction to
Modeling Uncertainty

CONTENTS

ANALYTICS IN ACTION

National Aeronautics and Space Administration*

WASHINGTON, D.C.

The National Aeronautics and Space Administration (NASA) is the U.S. government agency that is responsible for the U.S. civilian space program and for aeronautics and aerospace research. NASA is best known for its manned space exploration; its mission statement is to "pioneer the future in space exploration, scientific discovery and aeronautics research." With 18,800 employees, NASA is currently working on the design of a new Space Launch System that will take the astronauts farther into space than ever before and provide the cornerstone for future space exploration.

Although NASA's primary mission is space exploration, its expertise has been called on in assisting countries and organizations throughout the world in nonspace endeavors. In one such situation, the San José copper and gold mine in Copiapó, Chile, caved in, trapping 33 men more than 2,000 feet underground. It was important to bring the men safely to the surface as quickly as possible, but it was also imperative that the rescue effort be carefully designed and implemented to save as many miners as possible. The Chilean government asked NASA to provide assistance in developing a rescue method. NASA sent a four-person team consisting of an engineer with expertise in vehicle design, two physicians, and a psychologist with knowledge about issues of long-term confinement.

The probability of success and the failure of various other rescue methods was prominent in the thoughts of everyone involved. Since no historical data were available to apply to this unique rescue situation, NASA scientists developed subjective probability estimates for the success and failure of various rescue methods based on similar circumstances experienced by astronauts returning from short- and long-term space missions. The probability estimates provided by NASA guided officials in the selection of a rescue method and provided insight as to how the miners would survive the ascent in a rescue cage. The rescue method designed by the Chilean officials in consultation with the NASA team resulted in the construction of 13-foot-long, 924-pound steel rescue capsule that would be used to bring up the miners one at a time. All miners were rescued, with the last emerging 68 days after the cave-in occurred.

In this chapter, you will learn about probability as well as how to compute and interpret probabilities for a variety of situations. The basic relationships of probability, conditional probability, and Bayes' theorem will be covered. We will also discuss the concepts of random variables and probability distributions and illustrate the use of some of the more common discrete and continuous probability distributions.

---

*The authors are indebted to Dr. Michael Duncan and Clinton Cragg at NASA for providing this Analytics in Action.

Identifying uncertainty in data was introduced in Chapters 2 and 3 through descriptive statistics and data-visualization techniques, respectively. Uncertainty is an ever-present fact of life for decision makers, and much time and effort are spent trying to plan for, and respond to, uncertainty. Consider the CEO who has to make decisions about marketing budgets and production amounts using forecasted demands. Or consider the financial analyst who must determine how to build a client's portfolio of stocks and bonds when the rates of return for these investments are not known with certainty. In many business scenarios, data are available to provide information on possible outcomes for some decisions, but the exact outcome from a given decision is almost never known with certainty because many factors are outside the control of the decision maker (e.g., actions taken by competitors, the weather, etc.).

In this chapter, we expand on our discussion of modeling uncertainty by formalizing the concept of probability and introducing the concept of probability distributions.

Probability is the numerical measure of the likelihood that an event will occur.[1] Therefore, it can be used as a measure of the uncertainty associated with an event. This measure of uncertainty is often communicated through a probability distribution. Probability distributions are extremely helpful in providing additional information about an event, and as we will see in later chapters in this textbook, they be used to help a decision maker evaluate possible actions and determine the best course of action.

5.1 Events and Probabilities

In discussing probabilities, we often start by defining a **random experiment** as a process that generates well-defined outcomes. Several examples of random experiments and their associated outcomes are shown in Table 5.1.

By specifying all possible outcomes, we identify the **sample space** for a random experiment. Consider the first random experiment in Table 5.1—a coin toss. The possible outcomes are head and tail. If we let S denote the sample space, we can use the following notation to describe the sample space.

$$S = \{\text{Head, Tail}\}$$

Suppose we consider the second random experiment in Table 5.1—rolling a die. The possible experimental outcomes, defined as the number of dots appearing on the upward face of the die, are the six points in the sample space for this random experiment.

$$S = \{1, 2, 3, 4, 5, 6\}$$

Outcomes and events form the foundation of the study of probability. Formally, an **event** is defined as a collection of outcomes. For example, consider the case of an expansion project being undertaken by California Power & Light Company (CP&L). CP&L is starting a project designed to increase the generating capacity of one of its plants in southern California. An analysis of similar construction projects indicates

TABLE 5.1	Random Experiments and Experimental Outcomes
Random Experiment	**Experimental Outcomes**
Toss a coin	Head, tail
Roll a die	1, 2, 3, 4, 5, 6
Conduct a sales call	Purchase, no purchase
Hold a particular share of stock for one year	Price of stock goes up, price of stock goes down, no change in stock price
Reduce price of product	Demand goes up, demand goes down, no change in demand

[1]Note that there are several different possible definitions of probability, depending on the method used to assign probabilities. This includes the classical definition, the relative frequency definition, and the subjective definition of probability. In this text, we most often use the relative frequency definition of probability, which assumes that probabilities are based on empirical data. For a more thorough discussion of the different possible definitions of probability see Chapter 4 of Anderson, Sweeney, Williams, Camm, and Cochran, *An Introduction to Statistics for Business and Economics*, 13e (2017).

TABLE 5.2	Completion Times for 40 CP&L Projects	
Completion Time (months)	No. of Past Projects Having This Completion Time	Probability of Outcome
8	6	6/40 = 0.15
9	10	10/40 = 0.25
10	12	12/40 = 0.30
11	6	6/40 = 0.15
12	6	6/40 = 0.15
Total	40	1.00

that the possible completion times for the project are 8, 9, 10, 11, and 12 months. Each of these possible completion times represents a possible outcome for this project. Table 5.2 shows the number of past construction projects that required 8, 9, 10, 11, and 12 months.

Let us assume that the CP&L project manager is interested in completing the project in 10 months or less. Referring to Table 5.2, we see that three possible outcomes (8 months, 9 months, and 10 months) provide completion times of 10 months or less. Letting C denote the event that the project is completed in 10 months or less, we write:

$$C = \{8, 9, 10\}$$

Event C is said to occur if *any one* of these outcomes occur.

A variety of additional events can be defined for the CP&L project:

L = The event that the project is completed in *less than* 10 months = $\{8, 9\}$

M = The event that the project is completed in *more than* 10 months = $\{11, 12\}$

In each case, the event must be identified as a collection of outcomes for the random experiment.

The **probability of an event** is equal to the sum of the probabilities of outcomes for the event. Using this definition and given the probabilities of outcomes shown in Table 5.2, we can now calculate the probability of the event $C = \{8, 9, 10\}$. The probability of event C, denoted $P(C)$, is given by:

$$P(C) = P(8) + P(9) + P(10) = 0.15 + 0.25 + 0.30 = 0.70.$$

Similarly, because the event that the project is completed in less than 10 months is given by $L = \{8, 9\}$, the probability of this event is given by:

$$P(L) = P(8) + P(9) = 0.15 + 0.25 = 0.40.$$

Finally, for the event that the project is completed in more than 10 months, we have $M = \{11, 12\}$ and thus:

$$P(M) = P(11) + P(12) = 0.15 + 0.15 = 0.30.$$

Using these probability results, we can now tell CP&L management that there is a 0.70 probability that the project will be completed in 10 months or less, a 0.40 probability that it will be completed in less than 10 months, and a 0.30 probability that it will be completed in more than 10 months.

5.2 Some Basic Relationships of Probability

Complement of an Event

The complement of event A is sometimes written as $\bar{A}$ or A′ in other textbooks.

Given an event A, the **complement of A** is defined to be the event consisting of all outcomes that are *not* in A. The complement of A is denoted by A^C. Figure 5.1 shows what is known as a **Venn diagram**, which illustrates the concept of a complement. The rectangular area represents the sample space for the random experiment and, as such, contains all possible outcomes. The circle represents event A and contains only the outcomes that belong to A. The shaded region of the rectangle contains all outcomes not in event A and is by definition the complement of A.

In any probability application, either event A or its complement A^C must occur. Therefore, we have:

$$P(A) + P(A^C) = 1.$$

Solving for $P(A)$, we obtain the following result:

COMPUTING PROBABILITY USING THE COMPLEMENT

$$P(A) = 1 - P(A^C) \tag{5.1}$$

Equation (5.1) shows that the probability of an event A can be computed easily if the probability of its complement, $P(A^C)$, is known.

As an example, consider the case of a sales manager who, after reviewing sales reports, states that 80% of new customer contacts result in no sale. By allowing A to denote the event of a sale and A^C to denote the event of no sale, the manager is stating that $P(A^C) = 0.80$. Using equation (5.1), we see that:

$$P(A) = 1 - P(A^C) = 1 - 0.80 = 0.20.$$

We can conclude that a new customer contact has a 0.20 probability of resulting in a sale.

Addition Law

The addition law is helpful when we are interested in knowing the probability that at least one of two events will occur. That is, with events A and B we are interested in knowing the probability that event A or event B or both occur.

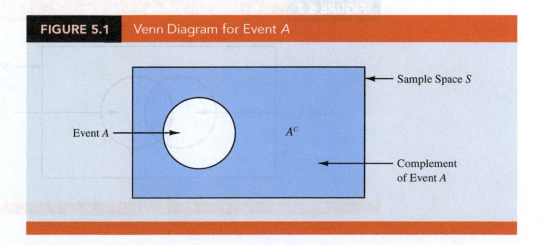

FIGURE 5.1   Venn Diagram for Event A

Sample Space S

Event A

A^C

Complement of Event A

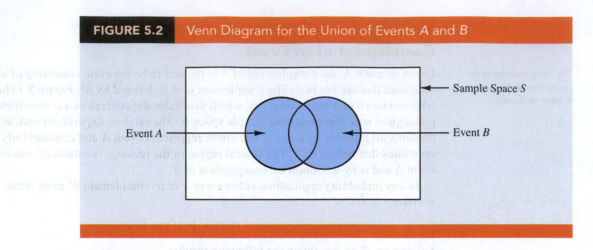

FIGURE 5.2   Venn Diagram for the Union of Events *A* and *B*

Before we present the addition law, we need to discuss two concepts related to the combination of events: the *union* of events and the *intersection* of events. Given two events *A* and *B*, the **union of *A* and *B*** is defined as the event containing all outcomes belonging to *A* or *B* or both. The union of *A* and *B* is denoted $A \cup B$.

The Venn diagram in Figure 5.2 depicts the union of A and B. Note that one circle contains all the outcomes in *A* and the other all the outcomes in *B*. The fact that the circles overlap indicates that some outcomes are contained in both *A* and *B*.

The definition of the **intersection of *A* and *B*** is the event containing the outcomes that belong to both *A* and *B*. The intersection of *A* and *B* is denoted by $A \cap B$. The Venn diagram depicting the intersection of *A* and *B* is shown in Figure 5.3. The area in which the two circles overlap is the intersection; it contains outcomes that are in both *A* and *B*.

The **addition law** provides a way to compute the probability that event *A* or event *B* or both occur. In other words, the addition law is used to compute the probability of the union of two events. The addition law is written as follows:

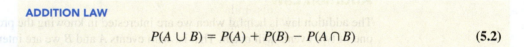

ADDITION LAW

$$P(A \cup B) = P(A) + P(B) - P(A \cap B) \tag{5.2}$$

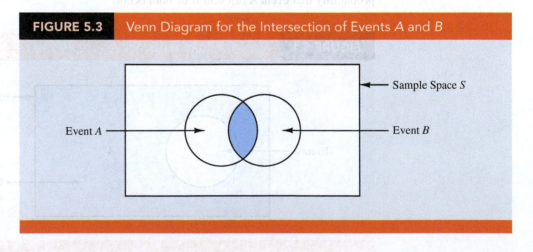

FIGURE 5.3   Venn Diagram for the Intersection of Events *A* and *B*

To understand the addition law intuitively, note that the first two terms in the addition law, $P(A) + P(B)$, account for all the sample points in $A \cup B$. However, because the sample points in the intersection $A \cap B$ are in both A and B, when we compute $P(A) + P(B)$, we are in effect counting each of the sample points in $A \cap B$ twice. We correct for this double counting by subtracting $P(A \cap B)$.

As an example of the addition law, consider a study conducted by the human resources manager of a major computer software company. The study showed that 30% of the employees who left the firm within two years did so primarily because they were dissatisfied with their salary, 20% left because they were dissatisfied with their work assignments, and 12% of the former employees indicated dissatisfaction with *both* their salary and their work assignments. What is the probability that an employee who leaves within two years does so because of dissatisfaction with salary, dissatisfaction with the work assignment, or both?

Let

$$S = \text{the event that the employee leaves because of salary}$$
$$W = \text{the event that the employee leaves because of work assignment}$$

We can also think of this probability in the following manner: What proportion of employees either left because of salary or left because of work assignment?

From the survey results, we have $P(S) = 0.30$, $P(W) = 0.20$ and $P(S \cap W) = 0.12$. Using the addition law from equation (5.2), we have

$$P(S \cup W) = P(S) + P(W) - P(S \cap W) = 0.30 + 0.20 - 0.12 = 0.38.$$

This calculation tells us that there is a 0.38 probability that an employee will leave for salary or work assignment reasons.

Before we conclude our discussion of the addition law, let us consider a special case that arises for **mutually exclusive events**. Events A and B are mutually exclusive if the occurrence of one event precludes the occurrence of the other. Thus, a requirement for A and B to be mutually exclusive is that their intersection must contain no sample points. The Venn diagram depicting two mutually exclusive events A and B is shown in Figure 5.4. In this case $P(A \cap B) = 0$ and the addition law can be written as follows.

ADDITION LAW FOR MUTUALLY EXCLUSIVE EVENTS

$$P(A \cup B) = P(A) + P(B)$$

FIGURE 5.4   Venn Diagram for Mutually Exclusive Events

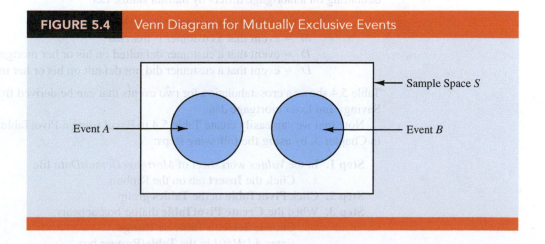

More generally, two events are said to be mutually exclusive if the events have no outcomes in common.

The addition law can be extended beyond two events. For example, the addition law for three events A, B, and C is. $P(A \cup B \cup C) = P(A) + P(B) + P(C) - P(A \cap B) - P(A \cap C) -$ $P(B \cap C) + P(A \cap B \cap C)$. Similar logic can be used to derive the expressions for the addition law for more than three events

5.3 Conditional Probability

Often, the probability of one event is dependent on whether some related event has already occurred. Suppose we have an event A with probability $P(A)$. If we learn that a related event, denoted by B, has already occurred, we take advantage of this information by calculating a new probability for event A. This new probability of event A is called a **conditional probability** and is written $P(A \mid B)$. The notation $\mid$ indicates that we are considering the probability of event A *given* the condition that event B has occurred. Hence, the notation $P(A \mid B)$ reads "the probability of A given B."

To illustrate the idea of conditional probability, consider a bank that is interested in the mortgage default risk for its home mortgage customers. Table 5.3 shows the first 25 records of the 300 home mortgage customers at Lancaster Savings and Loan, a company that specializes in high-risk subprime lending. Some of these home mortgage customers have defaulted on their mortgages and others have continued to make on-time payments. These data include the age of the customer at the time of mortgage origination, the marital status of the customer (single or married), the annual income of the customer, the mortgage amount, the number of payments made by the customer per year on the mortgage, the total amount paid by the customer over the lifetime of the mortgage, and whether or not the customer defaulted on her or his mortgage.

Lancaster Savings and Loan is interested in whether the probability of a customer defaulting on a mortgage differs by marital status. Let

S = event that a customer is single
M = event that a customer is married
D = event that a customer defaulted on his or her mortgage
D^C = event that a customer did not default on his or her mortgage

Table 5.4 shows a crosstabulation for two events that can be derived from the Lancaster Savings and Loan mortgage data.

Note that we can easily create Table 5.4 in Excel using a PivotTable, as was introduced in Chapter 3, by using the following steps:

Step 1. In the *Values* worksheet of *MortgageDefaultData* file
   Click the **Insert** tab on the Ribbon
Step 2. Click **PivotTable** in the **Tables** group
Step 3. When the **Create PivotTable** dialog box appears:
   Choose **Select a Table or Range**
   Enter *A1:H301* in the **Table/Range:** box

TABLE 5.3	Subset of Data from 300 Home Mortgages of Customers at Lancaster Savings and Loan						
Customer No.	Age	Marital Status	Annual Income	Mortgage Amount	Payments per Year	Total Amount Paid	Default on Mortgage?
1	37	Single	$ 172,125.70	$ 473,402.96	24	$ 581,885.13	Yes
2	31	Single	$ 108,571.04	$ 300,468.60	12	$ 489,320.38	No
3	37	Married	$ 124,136.41	$ 330,664.24	24	$ 493,541.93	Yes
4	24	Married	$ 79,614.04	$ 230,222.94	24	$ 449,682.09	Yes
5	27	Single	$ 68,087.33	$ 282,203.53	12	$ 520,581.82	No
6	30	Married	$ 59,959.80	$ 251,242.70	24	$ 356,711.58	Yes
7	41	Single	$ 99,394.05	$ 282,737.29	12	$ 524,053.46	No
8	29	Single	$ 38,527.35	$ 238,125.19	12	$ 468,595.99	No
9	31	Married	$ 112,078.62	$ 297,133.24	24	$ 399,617.40	Yes
10	36	Single	$ 224,899.71	$ 622,578.74	12	$ 1,233,002.14	No
11	31	Married	$ 27,945.36	$ 215,440.31	24	$ 285,900.10	Yes
12	40	Single	$ 48,929.74	$ 252,885.10	12	$ 336,574.63	No
13	39	Married	$ 82,810.92	$ 183,045.16	12	$ 262,537.23	No
14	31	Single	$ 68,216.88	$ 165,309.34	12	$ 253,633.17	No
15	40	Single	$ 59,141.13	$ 220,176.18	12	$ 424,749.80	No
16	45	Married	$ 72,568.89	$ 233,146.91	12	$ 356,363.93	No
17	32	Married	$ 101,140.43	$ 245,360.02	24	$ 388,429.41	Yes
18	37	Married	$ 124,876.53	$ 320,401.04	4	$ 360,783.45	Yes
19	32	Married	$ 133,093.15	$ 494,395.63	12	$ 861,874.67	No
20	32	Single	$ 85,268.67	$ 159,010.33	12	$ 308,656.11	No
21	37	Single	$ 92,314.96	$ 249,547.14	24	$ 342,339.27	Yes
22	29	Married	$ 120,876.13	$ 308,618.37	12	$ 472,668.98	No
23	24	Single	$ 86,294.13	$ 258,321.78	24	$ 380,347.56	Yes
24	32	Married	$ 216,748.68	$ 634,609.61	24	$ 915,640.13	Yes
25	44	Single	$ 46,389.75	$ 194,770.91	12	$ 385,288.86	No

DATA *file*

MortgageDefaultData

Select **New Worksheet** as the location for the PivotTable Report

Click **OK**

Step 4. In the **PivotTable Fields** area go to **Drag fields between areas below:**

Drag the **Marital Status** field to the **ROWS** area

Drag the **Default on Mortgage?** field to the **COLUMNS** area

Drag the **Customer Number** field to the **VALUES** area

Step 5. Click on **Sum of Customer Number** in the **VALUES** area and select **Value Field Settings**

TABLE 5.4	Crosstabulation of Marital Status and if Customer Defaults on Mortgage		
Marital Status	No Default	Default	*Total*
Married	64	79	143
Single	116	41	157
Total	180	120	300

FIGURE 5.5   PivotTable for Marital Status and Whether Customer Defaults on Mortgage

	A	B	C	D	E
1					
2					
3	Count of Customer Number	Column Labels			
4	Row Labels	NO		YES	Grand Total
5	MARRIED		64	79	143
6	SINGLE		116	41	157
7	Grand Total		180	120	300
8					
9					
10					
11					
12					
13					
14					
15					
16					
17					
18					
19					
20					
21					
22					
23					
24					
25					
26					
27					
28					
29					

PivotTable Fields

Choose fields to add to report:

Search

- ☑ Customer Number
- ☐ Age
- ☑ Marital Status
- ☐ Annual Income
- ☐ Mortgage Amount
- ☐ Payments Per Year
- ☐ Total Amount Paid
- ☑ Default on Mortgage?

MORE TABLES...

Drag fields between areas below:

▼ FILTERS

▥ COLUMNS
Default on Mortgage?   ▼

≡ ROWS
Marital Status   ▼

Σ VALUES
Count of Customer Number   ▼

DATA file

MortgageDefaultData

We can also think of this joint probability in the following manner: What proportion of all customers are both married and defaulted on their loans?

Step 6. When the **Value Field Settings** dialog box appears:
Under **Summarize value field by**, select **Count**

These steps produce the PivotTable shown in Figure 5.5.

From Table 5.4 or Figure 5.5, the probability that a customer defaults on his or her mortgage is 120/300 = 0.4. The probability that a customer does not default on his or her mortgage is $1 - 0.4 = 0.6$ (or 180/300 = 0.6). But is this probability different for married customers as compared with single customers? Conditional probability allows us to answer this question.

But first, let us answer a related question: What is the probability that a randomly selected customer does not default on his or her mortgage and the customer is married? The probability that a randomly selected customer is married and the customer defaults on his or her mortgage is written as $P(M \cap D)$. This probability is calculated as $P(M \cap D) = \frac{79}{300} = 0.2633$.

Similarly,

$P(M \cap D^C) = \frac{64}{300} = 0.2133$ is the probability that a randomly selected customer is married and that the customer does not default on his or her mortgage.

$P(S \cap D) = \frac{41}{300} = 0.1367$ is the probability that a randomly selected customer is single and that the customer defaults on his or her mortgage.

We can use the PivotTable from Figure 5.5 to easily create the joint probability table in Excel. To do so, right-click on any of the numerical values in the PivotTable, select *Show Values As*, and choose *% of Grand Total*. The resulting values, which are percentages of the total, can then be divided by 100 to create the probabilities in the joint probability table.

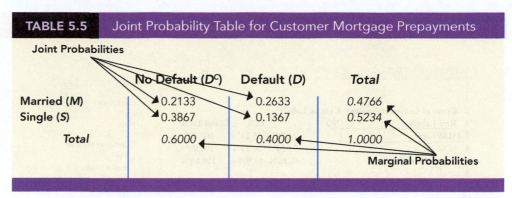

TABLE 5.5 Joint Probability Table for Customer Mortgage Prepayments

Joint Probabilities

	No Default (D^C)	Default (D)	Total
Married (M)	0.2133	0.2633	0.4766
Single (S)	0.3867	0.1367	0.5234
Total	0.6000	0.4000	1.0000

Marginal Probabilities

$P(S \cap D^C) = \frac{116}{300} = 0.3867$ is the probability that a randomly selected customer is single and that the customer does not default on his or her mortgage

Because each of these values gives the probability of the intersection of two events, the probabilities are called **joint probabilities**. Table 5.5, which provides a summary of the probability information for customer defaults on mortgages, is referred to as a joint probability table.

The values in the Total column and Total row (the margins) of Table 5.5 provide the probabilities of each event separately. That is, $P(M) = 0.4766$, $P(S) = 0.5234$, $P(D^C) = 0.6000$, and $P(D) = 0.4000$. These probabilities are referred to as **marginal probabilities** because of their location in the joint probability table. The marginal probabilities are found by summing the joint probabilities in the corresponding row or column of the joint probability table. From the marginal probabilities, we see that 60% of customers do not default on their mortgage, 40% of customers default on their mortgage, 47.66% of customers are married, and 52.34% of customers are single.

Let us begin the conditional probability analysis by computing the probability that a customer defaults on his or her mortgage given that the customer is married. In conditional probability notation, we are attempting to determine $P(D \mid M)$, which is read as "the probability that the customer defaults on the mortgage given that the customer is married." To calculate $P(D \mid M)$, first we note that we are concerned only with the 143 customers who are married (M). Because 79 of the 143 married customers defaulted on their mortgages, the probability of a customer defaulting given that the customer is married is 79/143 = 0.5524. In other words, given that a customer is married, there is a 55.24% chance that he or she will default. Note also that the conditional probability $P(D \mid M)$ can be computed as the ratio of the joint probability $P(D \cap M)$ to the marginal probability $P(M)$.

We can also think of this conditional probability in the following manner: What proportion of all married customers defaulted on their loans?

$$P(D \mid M) = \frac{P(D \cap M)}{P(M)} = \frac{0.2633}{0.4766} = 0.5524$$

The fact that conditional probabilities can be computed as the ratio of a joint probability to a marginal probability provides the following general formula for conditional probability calculations for two events A and B.

CONDITIONAL PROBABILITY

$$P(A \mid B) = \frac{P(A \cap B)}{P(B)} \tag{5.3}$$

or

$$P(B \mid A) = \frac{P(A \cap B)}{P(A)} \tag{5.4}$$

FIGURE 5.6   Using Excel PivotTable to Calculate Conditional Probabilities

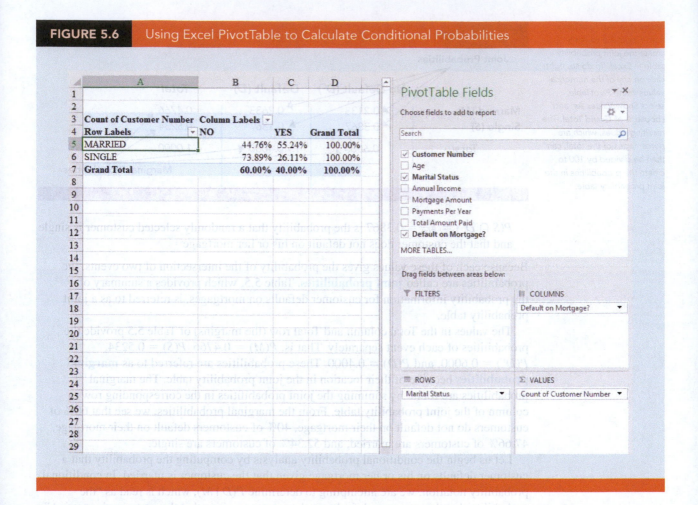

MortgageDefaultData

We have already determined the probability that a customer who is married will default is 0.5524. How does this compare to a customer who is single? In other words, we want to find $P(D \mid S)$. From equation (5.3), we can compute $P(D \mid S)$ as:

$$P(D \mid S) = \frac{P(D \cap S)}{P(S)} = \frac{0.1367}{0.5234} = 0.2611.$$

In other words, the chance that a customer will default if the customer is single is 26.11%. This is substantially less than the chance of default if the customer is married.

Note that we could also answer this question using the Excel PivotTable in Figure 5.5. We can calculate these conditional probabilities by right-clicking on any numerical value in the body of the PivotTable and then selecting **Show Values As** and choosing **% of Row Total**. The modified Excel PivotTable is shown in Figure 5.6.

By calculating the **% of Row Total**, the Excel PivotTable in Figure 5.6 shows that 55.24% of married customers defaulted on mortgages, but only 26.11% of single customers defaulted.

Independent Events

Note that in our example, $P(D) = 0.4000$, $P(D \mid M) = 0.5524$, and $P(D \mid S) = 0.2611$. So the probability that a customer defaults is influenced by whether the customer is married or single. Because $P(D \mid M) \neq P(D)$, we say that events D and M are dependent.

However, if the probability of event D is not changed by the existence of event M—that is, if $P(D \mid M) = P(D)$—then we would say that events D and M are **independent events**. This is summarized for two events A and B as follows:

INDEPENDENT EVENTS

Two events A and B are independent if

$$P(A \mid B) = P(A) \tag{5.5}$$

or

$$P(B \mid A) = P(B) \tag{5.6}$$

Otherwise, the events are dependent.

Multiplication Law

The multiplication law can be used to calculate the probability of the intersection of two events. The multiplication law is based on the definition of conditional probability. Solving equations (5.3) and (5.4) for $P(A \cap B)$, we obtain the **multiplication law**.

MULTIPLICATION LAW

$$P(A \cap B) = P(B)P(A \mid B) \tag{5.7}$$

or

$$P(A \cap B) = P(A)P(B \mid A) \tag{5.8}$$

To illustrate the use of the multiplication law, we will calculate the probability that a customer defaults on his or her mortgage and the customer is married, $P(D \cap M)$. From equation (5.7), this is calculated as $P(D \cap M) = P(M)P(D \mid M)$.

From Table 5.5 we know that $P(M) = 0.4766$, and from our previous calculations we know that the conditional probability $P(D \mid M) = 0.5524$. Therefore,

$$P(D \cap M) = P(M)P(D \mid M) = (0.4766)(0.5524) = 0.2633.$$

This value matches the value shown for $P(D \cap M)$ in Table 5.5. The multiplication law is useful when we know conditional probabilities but do not know the joint probabilities.

Consider the special case in which events A and B are independent. From equations (5.5) and (5.6), $P(A \mid B) = P(A)$ and $P(B \mid A) = P(B)$. Using these equations to simplify equations (5.7) and (5.8) for this special case, we obtain the following multiplication law for independent events.

MULTIPLICATION LAW FOR INDEPDENT EVENTS

$$P(A \cap B) = P(A)P(B) \tag{5.9}$$

To compute the probability of the intersection of two independent events, we simply multiply the probabilities of each event.

Bayes' Theorem

Revising probabilities when new information is obtained is an important aspect of probability analysis. Often, we begin the analysis with initial or **prior probability** estimates for specific events of interest. Then, from sources such as a sample survey or a product test, we obtain additional information about the events. Given this new information, we update

TABLE 5.6	Historical Quality Levels for Two Suppliers	
	% Good Parts	**% Bad Parts**
Supplier 1	98	2
Supplier 2	95	5

the prior probability values by calculating revised probabilities, referred to as **posterior probabilities**. **Bayes' theorem** provides a means for making these probability calculations.

Bayes' theorem is also discussed in Chapter 15 in the context of decision analysis.

As an application of Bayes' theorem, consider a manufacturing firm that receives shipments of parts from two different suppliers. Let A_1 denote the event that the part is from supplier 1 and let A_2 denote the event that a part is from supplier 2. Currently, 65% of the parts purchased by the company are from supplier 1 and the remaining 35% are from supplier 2. Hence, if a part is selected at random, we would assign the prior probabilities $P(A_1) = 0.65$ and $P(A_2) = 0.35$.

The quality of the purchased parts varies according to their source. Historical data suggest that the quality ratings of the two suppliers are as shown in Table 5.6.

If we let G be the event that a part is good and we let B be the event that a part is bad, the information in Table 5.6 enables us to calculate the following conditional probability values:

$$P(G \mid A_1) = 0.98 \quad P(B \mid A_1) = 0.02$$
$$P(G \mid A_2) = 0.95 \quad P(B \mid A_2) = 0.05$$

Figure 5.7 shows a diagram that depicts the process of the firm receiving a part from one of the two suppliers and then discovering that the part is good or bad as a two-step random experiment. We see that four outcomes are possible; two correspond to the part being good and two correspond to the part being bad.

FIGURE 5.7	Diagram for Two-Supplier Example: Step 1 shows that the part comes from one of two suppliers, and step 2 shows whether the part is good or bad.

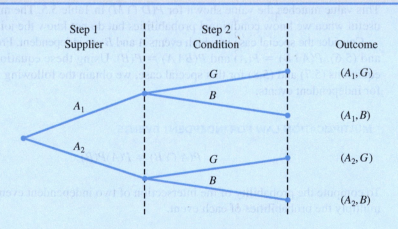

Note: Step 1 shows that the part comes from one of two suppliers, and step 2 shows whether the part is good or bad.

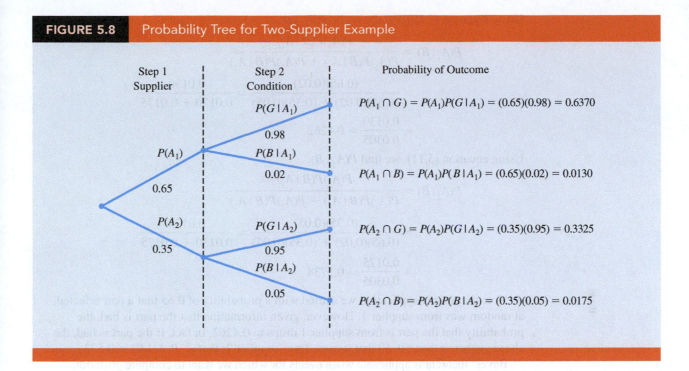

FIGURE 5.8   Probability Tree for Two-Supplier Example

Each of the outcomes is the intersection of two events, so we can use the multiplication rule to compute the probabilities. For instance,

$$P(A_1, G) = P(A_1 \cap G) = P(A_1)P(G \mid A_1).$$

The process of computing these joint probabilities can be depicted in what is called a probability tree (see Figure 5.8). From left to right through the tree, the probabilities for each branch at step 1 are prior probabilities and the probabilities for each branch at step 2 are conditional probabilities. To find the probability of each experimental outcome, simply multiply the probabilities on the branches leading to the outcome. Each of these joint probabilities is shown in Figure 5.8 along with the known probabilities for each branch.

Now suppose that the parts from the two suppliers are used in the firm's manufacturing process and that a machine breaks down while attempting the process using a bad part. Given the information that the part is bad, what is the probability that it came from supplier 1 and what is the probability that it came from supplier 2? With the information in the probability tree (Figure 5.8), Bayes' theorem can be used to answer these questions.

For the case in which there are only two events (A_1 and A_2), Bayes' theorem can be written as:

BAYES' THEOREM (TWO-EVENT CASE)

$$P(A_1 \mid B) = \frac{P(A_1)P(B \mid A_1)}{P(A_1)P(B \mid A_1) + P(A_2)P(B \mid A_2)} \qquad (5.10)$$

$$P(A_2 \mid B) = \frac{P(A_2)P(B \mid A_2)}{P(A_1)P(B \mid A_1) + P(A_2)P(B \mid A_2)} \qquad (5.11)$$

Using equation (5.10) and the probability values provided in Figure 5.8, we have:

$$P(A_1 \mid B) = \frac{P(A_1)P(B \mid A_1)}{P(A_1)P(B \mid A_1) + P(A_2)P(B \mid A_2)}$$

$$= \frac{(0.65)(0.02)}{(0.65)(0.02) + (0.35)(0.05)} = \frac{0.0130}{0.0130 + 0.0175}$$

$$= \frac{0.0130}{0.0305} = 0.4262$$

Using equation (5.11), we find $P(A_2 \mid B)$.

$$P(A_2 \mid B) = \frac{P(A_2)P(B \mid A_2)}{P(A_1)P(B \mid A_1) + P(A_2)P(B \mid A_2)}$$

$$= \frac{(0.35)(0.05)}{(0.65)(0.02) + (0.35)(0.05)} = \frac{0.0175}{0.0130 + 0.0175}$$

$$= \frac{0.0175}{0.0305} = 0.5738$$

Note that in this application we started with a probability of 0.65 that a part selected at random was from supplier 1. However, given information that the part is bad, the probability that the part is from supplier 1 drops to 0.4262. In fact, if the part is bad, the chance is better than 50–50 that it came from supplier 2; that is, $P(A_2 \mid B) = 0.5738$.

Bayes' theorem is applicable when events for which we want to compute posterior probabilities are mutually exclusive and their union is the entire sample space. For the case of n mutually exclusive events $A_1, A_2, \ldots, A_n$, whose union is the entire sample space, Bayes' theorem can be used to compute any posterior probability $P(A_i \mid B)$ as shown in equation 5.12.

If the union of events is the entire sample space, the events are said to be collectively exhaustive.

BAYES' THEOREM

$$P(A_i \mid B) = \frac{P(A_i)P(B \mid A_i)}{P(A_1)P(B \mid A_1) + P(A_2)P(B \mid A_2) + \cdots + P(A_n)P(B \mid A_n)} \qquad (5.12)$$

N O T E S   +   C O M M E N T S

By applying basic algebra we can derive the multiplication law from the definition of conditional probability. For two events A and B, the probability of A given B is $P(A \mid B) = \frac{P(A \cap B)}{P(B)}$. If we multiply both sides of this expression by $P(B)$, the $P(B)$ in the numerator and denominator on the right side of the expression will cancel and we are left with $P(A \mid B)P(B) = P(A \cap B)$, which is the multiplication law.

5.4 Random Variables

Random variables were introduced in Chapter 2 as quantities whose values are not known with certainty. In probability terms, a random variable is a numerical description of the outcome of a random experiment. A random variable can be classified as being either discrete or continuous depending on the numerical values it can assume.

Discrete Random Variables

A random variable that can take on only specified discrete values is referred to as a **discrete random variable**. Table 5.7 provides examples of discrete random variables.

TABLE 5.7	Examples of Discrete Random Variables	
Random Experiment	**Random Variable (x)**	**Possible Values for the Random Variable**
Flip a coin	Face of coin showing	1 if heads; 0 if tails
Roll a die	Number of dots showing on top of die	1, 2, 3, 4, 5, 6
Contact five customers	Number of customers who place an order	0, 1, 2, 3, 4, 5
Operate a health care clinic for one day	Number of patients who arrive	0, 1, 2, 3, . . .
Offer a customer the choice of two products	Product chosen by customer	0 if none; 1 if choose product A; 2 if choose product B

Returning to our example of Lancaster Savings and Loan, we can define a random variable x to indicate whether or not a customer defaults on his or her mortgage. As previously stated, the values of a random variable must be numerical, so we can define random variable x such that $x = 1$ if the customer defaults on his or her mortgage and $x = 0$ if the customer does not default on his or her mortgage. An additional random variable, y, could indicate whether the customer is married or single. For instance, we can define random variable y such that $y = 1$ if the customer is married and $y = 0$ if the customer is single. Yet another random variable, z, could be defined as the number of mortgage payments per year made by the customer. For instance, a customer who makes monthly payments would make $z = 12$ payments per year, a customer who makes payments quarterly would make $z = 4$ payments per year.

Table 5.8 repeats the joint probability table for the Lancaster Savings and Loan data, but this time with the values labeled as random variables.

Continuous Random Variables

A random variable that may assume any numerical value in an interval or collection of intervals is called a **continuous random variable**. Technically, relatively few random variables are truly continuous; these include values related to time, weight, distance, and temperature. An example of a continuous random variable is $x =$ the time between consecutive incoming calls to a call center. This random variable can take on any value $x > 0$ such as $x = 1.26$ minutes, $x = 2.571$ minutes, $x = 4.3333$ minutes, etc. Table 5.9 provides examples of continuous random variables.

As illustrated by the final example in Table 5.9, many discrete random variables have a large number of potential outcomes and so can be effectively modeled as continuous random variables. Consider our Lancaster Savings and Loan example. We can define a random variable $x =$ total amount paid by customer over the lifetime of the mortgage. Because we typically measure financial values only to two decimal places, one could consider this a discrete random variable. However, because in any practical interval there are many possible values for this random variable, then it is usually appropriate to model the amount as a continuous random variable.

TABLE 5.8	Joint Probability Table for Customer Mortgage Prepayments		
	No Default ($x = 0$)	**Default ($x = 1$)**	**$f(y)$**
Married ($y = 1$)	0.2133	0.2633	0.4766
Single ($y = 0$)	0.3867	0.1367	0.5234
$f(x)$	0.6000	0.4000	1.0000

TABLE 5.9	Examples of Continuous Random Variables	
Random Experiment	**Random Variable (x)**	**Possible Values for the Random Variable**
Customer visits a web page	Time customer spends on web page in minutes	$x \geq 0$
Fill a soft drink can (max capacity = 12.1 ounces)	Number of ounces	$0 \leq x \leq 12.1$
Test a new chemical process	Temperature when the desired reaction takes place (min temperature = 150°F; max temperature = 212°F)	$150 \leq x \leq 212$
Invest $10,000 in the stock market	Value of investment after one year	$x \geq 0$

NOTES + COMMENTS

1. In this section we again use the relative frequency method to assign probabilities for the Lancaster Savings and Loan example. Technically, the concept of random variables applies only to populations; probabilities that are found using sample data are only estimates of the true probabilities. However, larger samples generate more reliable estimated probabilities, so if we have a large enough data set (as we are assuming here for the Lancaster Savings and Loan data), then we can treat the data as if they are from a population and the relative frequency method is appropriate to assign probabilities to the outcomes.

2. Random variables can be used to represent uncertain future values. Chapter 14 explains how random variables can be used in simulation models to evaluate business decisions in the presence of uncertainty.

5.5 Discrete Probability Distributions

The **probability distribution** for a random variable describes the range and relative likelihood of possible values for a random variable. For a discrete random variable x, the probability distribution is defined by a **probability mass function**, denoted by $f(x)$. The probability mass function provides the probability for each value of the random variable.

Returning to our example of mortgage defaults, consider the data shown in Table 5.3 for Lancaster Savings and Loan and the associated joint probability table in Table 5.8. From Table 5.8, we see that $f(0) = 0.6$ and $f(1) = 0.4$. Note that these values satisfy the required conditions of a discrete probability distribution that (1) $f(x) \geq 0$ and (2) $\Sigma f(x) = 1$.

We can also present probability distributions graphically. In Figure 5.9, the values of the random variable x are shown on the horizontal axis and the probability associated with these values is shown on the vertical axis.

Custom Discrete Probability Distribution

A probability distribution that is generated from observations such as that shown in Figure 5.9 is called an **empirical probability distribution**. This particular empirical probability distribution is considered a custom discrete distribution because it is discrete and the possible values of the random variable have different values.

A **custom discrete probability distribution** is very useful for describing different possible scenarios that have different probabilities of occurring. The probabilities

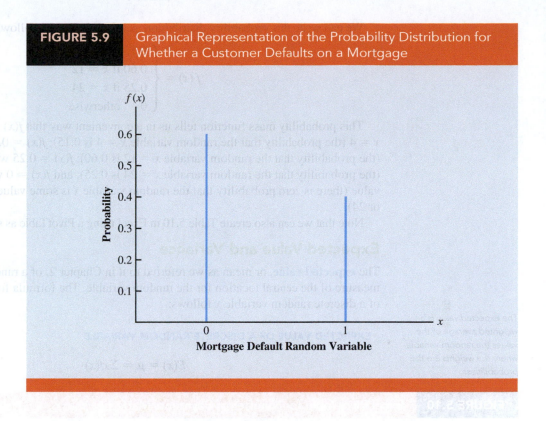

FIGURE 5.9 Graphical Representation of the Probability Distribution for Whether a Customer Defaults on a Mortgage

associated with each scenario can be generated using either the subjective method or the relative frequency method. Using a subjective method, probabilities are based on experience or intuition when little relevant data are available. If sufficient data exist, the relative frequency method can be used to determine probabilities. Consider the random variable describing the number of payments made per year by a randomly chosen customer. Table 5.10 presents a summary of the number of payments made per year by the 300 home mortgage customers. This table shows us that 45 customers made quarterly payments ($x = 4$), 180 customers made monthly payments ($x = 12$), and 75 customers made two payments each month ($x = 24$). We can then calculate $f(4) = 45/300 = 0.15$, $f(12) = 180/300 = 0.60$, and $f(24) = 75/300 = 0.25$. In other words, the probability that a randomly selected customer makes 4 payments per year is 0.15, the probability that a randomly selected customer makes 12 payments per year is 0.60, and the probability that a randomly selected customer makes 24 payments per year is 0.25.

TABLE 5.10 Summary Table of Number of Payments Made per Year

	Number of Payments Made per Year			
	$x = 4$	$x = 12$	$x = 24$	Total
Number of observations	45	180	75	300
$f(x)$	0.15	0.60	0.25	

We can write this probability distribution as a function in the following manner:

$$f(x) = \begin{cases} 0.15 & \text{if } x = 4 \\ 0.60 & \text{if } x = 12 \\ 0.25 & \text{if } x = 24 \\ 0 & \text{otherwise} \end{cases}$$

This probability mass function tells us in a convenient way that $f(x) = 0.15$ when $x = 4$ (the probability that the random variable $x = 4$ is 0.15); $f(x) = 0.60$ when $x = 12$ (the probability that the random variable $x = 12$ is 0.60); $f(x) = 0.25$ when $x = 24$ (the probability that the random variable $x = 24$ is 0.25); and $f(x) = 0$ when x is any other value (there is zero probability that the random variable x is some value other than 4, 12, or 24).

Note that we can also create Table 5.10 in Excel using a PivotTable as shown in Figure 5.10.

Expected Value and Variance

The **expected value**, or mean as we referred to it in Chapter 2, of a random variable is a measure of the central location for the random variable. The formula for the expected value of a discrete random variable x follows:

The expected value is a weighted average of the values the random variable, where the weights are the probabilities.

EXPECTED VALUE OF A DISCRETE RANDOM VARIABLE

$$E(x) = \mu = \Sigma x f(x) \tag{5.13}$$

FIGURE 5.10   Excel PivotTable for Number of Payments Made per Year

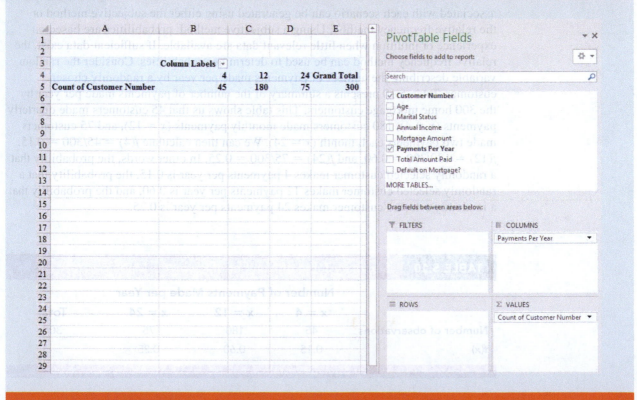

TABLE 5.11	Calculation of the Expected Value for Number of Payments Made per Year by a Lancaster Savings and Loan Mortgage Customer		
x	**f(x)**		**xf(x)**
4	0.15		(4)(0.15) = 0.6
12	0.60		(12)(0.60) = 7.2
24	0.25		(24)(0.25) = 6.0
			13.8 ⟵ $E(x) = \mu = \sum xf(x)$

Both the notations $E(x)$ and μ are used to denote the expected value of a random variable. Equation (5.13) shows that to compute the expected value of a discrete random variable, we must multiply each value of the random variable by the corresponding probability $f(x)$ and then add the resulting products. Table 5.11 calculates the expected value of the number of payments made by a mortgage customer in a year. The sum of the entries in the $xf(x)$ column shows that the expected value is 13.8 payments per year. Therefore, if Lancaster Savings and Loan signs up a new mortgage customer, the expected number of payments per year made by this new customer is 13.8. Obviously, no customer will make exactly 13.8 payments per year, but this value represents our expectation for the number of payments per year made by a new customer absent any other information about the new customer. Some customers will make fewer payments (4 or 12 per year), some customers will make more payments (24 per year), but 13.8 represents the expected number of payments per year based on the probabilities calculated in Table 5.10.

The SUMPRODUCT function in Excel can easily be used to calculate the expected value for a discrete random variable. This is illustrated in Figure 5.11. We can also

FIGURE 5.11	Using Excel SUMPRODUCT Function to Calculate the Expected Value for Number of Payments Made per Year by a Lancaster Savings and Loan Mortgage Customer

FIGURE 5.12   Excel Calculation of the Expected Value for Number of Payments Made per Year by a Lancaster Savings and Loan Mortgage Customer

	A	B	C	D	E	F	G	H
1	Customer Number	Age	Marital Status	Annual Income	Mortgage Amount	Payments Per Year	Total Amount Paid	Prepay Mortgage?
2	1	37	SINGLE	172125.7	473402.96	24	581885.13	YES
3	2	31	SINGLE	108571.04	300468.6	12	489320.38	NO
4	3	37	MARRIED	124136.41	330664.24	24	493541.93	YES
5	4	24	MARRIED	79614.04	230222.94	24	449682.09	YES
6	5	27	SINGLE	68087.33	282203.53	12	520581.82	NO
296	295	37	MARRIED	84791.08	179676.63	24	256361.65	YES
297	296	33	MARRIED	83498.89	235907.5	12	437145.85	NO
298	297	41	SINGLE	16597.53	151972.2	4	171289.87	YES
299	298	30	SINGLE	49293.95	186043.13	12	376694.27	NO
300	299	35	SINGLE	84241.8	194417.84	12	352597.79	NO
301	300	31	MARRIED	94428.15	264175.55	24	434102.49	YES
302								
304					Expected Value:	=AVERAGE(F2:F301)		
305					Variance:	=VAR.P(F2:F301)		
306					Standard Deviation:	=STDEV.P(F2:F301)		

	A	B	C	D	E	F	G	H
1	Customer Number	Age	Marital Status	Annual Income	Mortgage Amount	Payments Per Year	Total Amount Paid	Prepay Mortgage?
2	1	37	SINGLE	$ 172,125.70	$ 473,402.96	24	$ 581,885.13	YES
3	2	31	SINGLE	$ 108,571.04	$ 300,468.60	12	$ 489,320.38	NO
4	3	37	MARRIED	$ 124,136.41	$ 330,664.24	24	$ 493,541.93	YES
5	4	24	MARRIED	$ 79,614.04	$ 230,222.94	24	$ 449,682.09	YES
6	5	27	SINGLE	$ 68,087.33	$ 282,203.53	12	$ 520,581.82	NO
296	295	37	MARRIED	$ 84,791.08	$ 179,676.63	24	$ 256,361.65	YES
297	296	33	MARRIED	$ 83,498.89	$ 235,907.50	12	$ 437,145.85	NO
298	297	41	SINGLE	$ 16,597.53	$ 151,972.20	4	$ 171,289.87	YES
299	298	30	SINGLE	$ 49,293.95	$ 186,043.13	12	$ 376,694.27	NO
300	299	35	SINGLE	$ 84,241.80	$ 194,417.84	12	$ 352,597.79	NO
301	300	31	MARRIED	$ 94,428.15	$ 264,175.55	24	$ 434,102.49	YES
302								
304					Expected Value:	13.8		
305					Variance:	42.360		
306					Standard Deviation:	6.508		

calculate the expected value of the random variable directly from the Lancaster Savings and Loan data using the Excel function AVERAGE, as shown in Figure 5.12. Column F contains the data on the number of payments made per year by each mortgage customer in the data set. Using the Excel formula =AVERAGE(F2:F301) gives us a value of 13.8 for the expected value, which is the same as the value we calculated in Table 5.11.

Note that we cannot simply use the AVERAGE function on the x values for a custom discrete random variable. If we did, this would give us a calculated value of $(4 + 12 + 24)/3 = 13.333$, which is not the correct expected value in this scenario. This is because using the AVERAGE function in this way assumes that each value of the random variable x is equally likely. But in this case, we know that $x = 12$ is much more likely than $x = 4$ or $x = 24$. Therefore, we must use equation (5.13) to calculate the expected value of a custom discrete random variable, or we can use the Excel function AVERAGE on the entire data set, as shown in Figure 5.12.

In Chapter 2 we also introduced **variance** as a measure of variability. Below we define the formula for calculating the variance of a discrete random variable.

VARIANCE OF A DISCRETE RANDOM VARIABLE

The variance is a weighted average of the squared deviations of a random variable from its mean. The weights are the probabilities.

$$\text{Var}(x) = \sigma^2 = \Sigma(x - \mu)^2 f(x) \tag{5.14}$$

As equation (5.14) shows, an essential part of the variance formula is the deviation, $x - \mu$, which measures how far a particular value of the random variable is from the expected value, or mean, μ. In computing the variance of a random variable, the deviations are

TABLE 5.12   Calculation of the Variance for Number of Payments Made per Year by a Lancaster Savings and Loan Mortgage Customer

x	$x - \mu$	$f(x)$	$(x - \mu)^2 f(x)$
4	$4 - 13.8 = -9.8$	0.15	$(-9.8)^2 * 0.15 = 15.606$
12	$12 - 13.8 = -1.8$	0.60	$(-1.8)^2 * 0.60 = 2.904$
24	$24 - 13.8 = 10.2$	0.25	$(10.2)^2 * 0.25 = \underline{24.010}$
			42.360 ◄ $\sigma^2 = \sum (x - \mu)^2 f(x)$

squared and then weighted by the corresponding value of the probability mass function. The sum of these weighted squared deviations for all values of the random variable is referred to as the *variance*. The notations Var(x) and σ^2 are both used to denote the variance of a random variable.

The calculation of the variance of the number of payments made per year by a mortgage customer is summarized in Table 5.12. We see that the variance is 42.360. As in Chapter 2, the **standard deviation**, σ, is defined as the positive square root of the variance. Thus, the standard deviation for the payments made per year by a mortgage customer is $\sqrt{42.360} = 6.508$.

The Excel function SUMPRODUCT can be used to easily calculate equation (5.14) for a custom discrete random variable. We illustrate the use of the SUMPRODUCT function to calculate variance in Figure 5.13.

FIGURE 5.13   Excel Calculation of the Variance for Number of Payments Made per Year by a Lancaster Savings and Loan Mortgage Customer

	A	B	C	D
1	x	$f(x)$	$(x - \mu)^2$	
2	4	0.15	=(A2-$B$6)^2	
3	12	0.6	=(A3-$B$6)^2	
4	24	0.25	=(A4-$B$6)^2	
5				
6	Expected Value:	=SUMPRODUCT(A2:A4,B2:B4)		
7				
8	Variance:	=SUMPRODUCT(B2:B4,C2:C4)		
9				
10	Standard Deviation:	=SQRT(B8)		

	A	B	C	D
1	x	$f(x)$	$(x - \mu)^2$	
2	4	0.15	96.04	
3	12	0.60	3.24	
4	24	0.25	104.04	
5				
6	Expected Value:	13.8		
7				
8	Variance:	42.360		
9				
10	Standard Deviation:	6.508		

Note that here we are using the Excel functions VAR.P and STDEV.P rather than VAR.S and STDEV.S. This is because we are assuming that the sample of 300 Lancaster Savings and Loan mortgage customers is a perfect representation of the population.

We can also use Excel to find the variance directly from the data when the values in the data occur with relative frequencies that correspond to the probability distribution of the random variable. Cell F305 in Figure 5.12 shows that we use the Excel formula =VAR.P(F2:F301) to calculate the variance from the complete data. This formula gives us a value of 42.360, which is the same as that calculated in Table 5.12 and Figure 5.13. Similarly, we can use the formula =STDEV.P(F2:F301) to calculate the standard deviation of 6.508.

As with the AVERAGE function and expected value, we cannot use the Excel functions VAR.P and STDEV.P directly on the x values to calculate the variance and standard deviation of a custom discrete random variable if the x values are not equally likely to occur. Instead we must either use the formula from equation (5.14) or use the Excel functions on the entire data set as shown in Figure 5.12.

Discrete Uniform Probability Distribution

When the possible values of the probability mass function, $f(x)$, are all equal, then the probability distribution is a **discrete uniform probability distribution**. For instance, the values that result from rolling a single, fair die is an example of a discrete uniform distribution because the possible outcomes $y = 1$, $y = 2$, $y = 3$, $y = 4$, $y = 5$, and $y = 6$ all have the same values $f(1) = f(2) = f(3) = f(4) = f(5) = f(6) = 1/6$. The general form of the probability mass function for a discrete uniform probability distribution is given below.

DISCRETE UNIFORM PROBABILITY MASS FUNCTION

$$f(x) = 1/n \tag{5.15}$$

where $n =$ the number of unique values that may be assumed by the random variable.

Binomial Probability Distribution

As an example of the use of the binomial probability distribution, consider an online specialty clothing company called Martin's. Martin's commonly sends out targeted e-mails to its best customers notifying them about special discounts that are available only to the recipients of the e-mail. The e-mail contains a link that takes the customer directly to a web page for the discounted item. The exact number of customers who will click on the link is obviously unknown, but from previous data, Martin's estimates that the probability that a customer clicks on the link in the e-mail is 0.30. Martin's is interested in knowing more about the probabilities associated with one, two, three, etc. customers clicking on the link in the targeted e-mail.

The probability distribution related to the number of customers who click on the targeted e-mail link can be described using a **binomial probability distribution**. A binomial probability distribution is a discrete probability distribution that can be used to describe many situations in which a fixed number (n) of repeated identical and independent trials has two, and only two, possible outcomes. In general terms, we refer to these two possible outcomes as either a success or a failure. A success occurs with probability p in each trial and a failure occurs with probability $1 - p$ in each trial. In the Martin's example, the "trial" refers to a customer receiving the targeted e-mail. We will define a success as a customer clicking on the e-mail link ($p = 0.30$) and a failure as a customer not clicking on the link ($1 - p = 0.70$). The binomial probability distribution can then be used to calculate the probability of a given number of successes (customers who click on the e-mail link) out of a given number of independent trials (number of e-mails sent to customers). Other examples that can often be described by a binomial probability distribution include counting the number of heads resulting from flipping a coin 20 times, the number of customers who click on a particular advertisement link on web site in a day, the number of days on which a particular financial stock increases in value over a month, and the number of nondefective parts produced in a batch.

Whether or not a customer clicks on the link is an example of what is known as a Bernoulli trial—a trial in which: (1) there are two possible outcomes, success or failure, and (2) the probability of success is the same every time the trial is executed. The probability distribution related to the number of successes in a set of n independent Bernoulli trials can be described by a binomial probability distribution.

Equation (5.16) provides the probability mass function for a binomial random variable that calculates the probability of x successes in n independent events.

BINOMIAL PROBABILITY MASS FUNCTION

$$f(x) = \binom{n}{x} p^x (1 - p)^{(n - x)}$$

where

x = the number of successes
p = the probability of a success on one trial
n = the number of trials
$f(x)$ = the probability of x successes in n trials

(5.16)

and

$$\binom{n}{x} = \frac{n!}{x!(n - x)!}$$

n! is read as "n factorial," and
$n! = n \times n - 1 \times n - 2 \times \cdots \times$
2×1. For example, $4! = 4 \times$
$3 \times 2 \times 1 = 24$. The Excel
formula =FACT(n) can be
used to calculate n factorial.

In the Martin's example, use equation (5.16) to compute the probability that out of three customers who receive the e-mail: (1) no customer clicks on the link; (2) exactly one customer clicks on the link; (3) exactly two customers click on the link; and (4) all three customers click on the link. The calculations are summarized in Table 5.13, which gives the probability distribution of the number of customers who click on the targeted e-mail link. Figure 5.14 is a graph of this probability distribution. Table 5.13 and Figure 5.14 show that the highest probability is associated with exactly one customer clicking on the Martin's targeted e-mail link, and the lowest probability is associated with all three customers clicking on the link.

Because the outcomes in the Martin's example are mutually exclusive, we can easily use these results to answer interesting questions about various events. For example, using the information in Table 5.13, the probability that no more than one customer clicks on the link is $P(x \le 1) = P(x = 0) + P(x = 1) = 0.343 + 0.441 = 0.784$.

If we consider a scenario in which 10 customers receive the targeted e-mail, the binomial probability mass function given by equation (5.16) is still applicable. If we want to find the probability that exactly 4 of the 10 customers click on the link and $p = 0.30$, then we calculate:

$$f(4) = \frac{10!}{4!6!} (0.30)^4 (0.70)^6 = 0.2001$$

TABLE 5.13	Probability Distribution for the Number of Customers Who Click on the Link in the Martin's Targeted E-Mail	
x		**f(x)**
0		$\dfrac{3!}{0!3!} (0.30)^0 (0.70)^3 = 0.343$
1		$\dfrac{3!}{1!2!} (0.30)^1 (0.70)^2 = 0.441$
2		$\dfrac{3!}{2!1!} (0.30)^2 (0.70)^1 = 0.189$
3		$\dfrac{3!}{3!0!} (0.30)^3 (0.70)^0 = \dfrac{0.027}{1.000}$

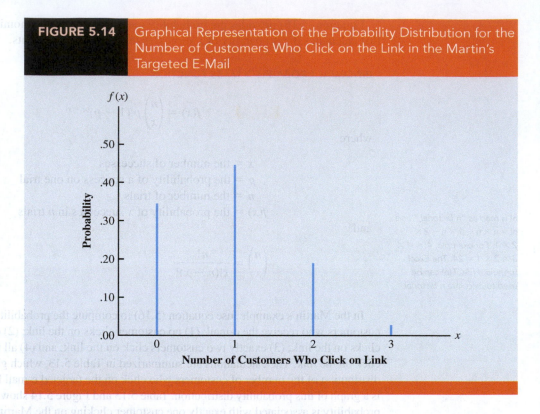

FIGURE 5.14   Graphical Representation of the Probability Distribution for the Number of Customers Who Click on the Link in the Martin's Targeted E-Mail

In Excel we can use the BINOM.DIST function to compute binomial probabilities. Figure 5.15 reproduces the Excel calculations from Table 5.13 for the Martin's problem with three customers.

The BINOM.DIST function in Excel has four input values: the first is the value of x, the second is the value of n, the third is the value of p, and the fourth is FALSE or TRUE. We choose FALSE for the fourth input if a probability mass function value $f(x)$ is desired, and TRUE if a cumulative probability is desired. The formula =BINOM.DIST(A5,$D$1:$D$2,FALSE) has been entered into cell B5 to compute the probability of 0 successes in 3 trials, $f(0)$. Figure 5.15 shows that this value is 0.343, the same as in Table 5.13.

Cells C5:C8 show the cumulative probability distribution values for this example. Note that these values are computed in Excel by entering TRUE as the fourth input in the BINOM.DIST. The cumulative probability for x using a binomial distribution is the probability of x or fewer successes out of n trials. Cell C5 computes the cumulative probability for $x = 0$, which is the same as the probability for $x = 0$ because the probability of 0 successes is the same as the probability of 0 or fewer successes. Cell C7 computes the cumulative probability for $x = 2$ using the formula =BINOM.DIST(A7,$D$1,$D$2,TRUE). This value is 0.973, meaning that the probability that two or fewer customers click on the targeted e-mail link is 0.973. Note that the value 0.973 simply corresponds to $f(0) + f(1) + f(2) = 0.343 + 0.441 + 0.189 = 0.973$ because it is the probability of two or fewer customers clicking on the link, which could be zero customers, one customer, or two customers.

Poisson Probability Distribution

In this section, we consider a discrete random variable that is often useful in estimating the number of occurrences of an event over a specified interval of time or space. For example, the random variable of interest might be the number of patients who arrive at a health care clinic in one hour, the number of computer-server failures in a month, the number of repairs needed in 10 miles of highway, or the number of leaks in 100 miles of pipeline. If the following two

FIGURE 5.15   Excel Worksheet for Computing Binomial Probabilities of the Number of Customers Who Make a Purchase at Martin's

	A	B	C	D
1			Number of Trials (*n*):	3
2			Probability of Success (*p*):	0.3
3				
4	*x*	*f(x)*	Cumulative Probability	
5	0	=BINOM.DIST(A5,$D$1,$D$2,FALSE)	=BINOM.DIST(A5,$D$1,$D$2,TRUE)	
6	1	=BINOM.DIST(A6,$D$1,$D$2,FALSE)	=BINOM.DIST(A6,$D$1,$D$2,TRUE)	
7	2	=BINOM.DIST(A7,$D$1,$D$2,FALSE)	=BINOM.DIST(A7,$D$1,$D$2,TRUE)	
8	3	=BINOM.DIST(A8,$D$1,$D$2,FALSE)	=BINOM.DIST(A8,$D$1,$D$2,TRUE)	

	A	B	C	D
1			Number of Trials (*n*):	3
2			Probability of Success (*p*):	0.3
3				
4	*x*	*f(x)*	Cumulative Probability	
5	0	0.343	0.343	
6	1	0.441	0.784	
7	2	0.189	0.973	
8	3	0.027	1.000	

properties are satisfied, the number of occurrences is a random variable that is escribed by the **Poisson probability distribution**: (1) the probability of an occurrence is the same for any two intervals (of time or space) of equal length; and (2) the occurrence or nonoccurrence in any interval (of time or space) is independent of the occurrence or nonoccurrence in any other interval.

The Poisson probability mass function is defined by equation (5.17).

POISSON PROBABILITY MASS FUNCTION

The number e is a mathematical constant that is the base of the natural logarithm. Although it is an irrational number, 2.71828 is a sufficient approximation for our purposes.

$$f(x) = \frac{\mu^x e^{-\mu}}{x!} \tag{5.17}$$

where

$f(x) =$ the probability of *x* occurrences in an interval
$\mu =$ expected value or mean number of occurrences in an interval
$e \approx 2.71828$

For the Poisson probability distribution, *x* is a discrete random variable that indicates the number of occurrences in the interval. Since there is no stated upper limit for the number of occurrences, the probability mass function $f(x)$ is applicable for values $x = 0, 1, 2, \ldots$ without limit. In practical applications, *x* will eventually become large enough so that $f(x)$ is approximately zero and the probability of any larger values of *x* becomes negligible.

Suppose that we are interested in the number of patients who arrive at the emergency room of a large hospital during a 15-minute period on weekday mornings. Obviously, we do not know exactly how many patients will arrive at the emergency room in any defined interval of time, so the value of this variable is uncertain. It is important for administrators at the hospital to understand the probabilities associated with the number of arriving patients, as this information will have an impact on staffing decisions such as how many nurses and doctors to hire. It will also provide insight into possible wait times for patients to be seen once they arrive at the emergency room. If we can assume that the probability of a patient arriving is the same for any two periods of equal length during this 15-minute period and that the arrival or nonarrival of a patient in any period is independent of the arrival or nonarrival in any other period during the 15-minute period, the Poisson probability mass function is applicable. Suppose these assumptions are satisfied and an analysis of historical data shows that the average number of patients arriving during a 15-minute period of time is 10; in this case, the following probability mass function applies:

$$f(x) = \frac{10^x e^{-10}}{x!}$$

The random variable here is x = number of patients arriving at the emergency room during any 15-minute period.

If the hospital's management team wants to know the probability of exactly five arrivals during 15 minutes, we would set $x = 5$ and obtain:

$$\begin{array}{c}\text{Probability of exactly}\\\text{5 arrivals in 15 minutes}\end{array} = f(5) = \frac{10^5 e^{-10}}{5!} = 0.0378$$

In the preceding example, the mean of the Poisson distribution is $\mu = 10$ arrivals per 15-minute period. A property of the Poisson distribution is that the mean of the distribution and the variance of the distribution are *always equal*. Thus, the variance for the number of arrivals during all 15-minute periods is $\sigma^2 = 10$, and so the standard deviation is $\sigma = \sqrt{10} = 3.16$. Our illustration involves a 15-minute period, but other amounts of time can be used. Suppose we want to compute the probability of one arrival during a 3-minute period. Because 10 is the expected number of arrivals during a 15-minute period, we see that 10/15 = 2/3 is the expected number of arrivals during a 1-minute period and that (2/3)(3 minutes) = 2 is the expected number of arrivals during a 3-minute period. Thus, the probability of x arrivals during a 3-minute period with $\mu = 2$ is given by the following Poisson probability mass function:

$$f(x) = \frac{2^x e^{-2}}{x!}$$

The probability of one arrival during a 3-minute period is calculated as follows:

$$\begin{array}{c}\text{Probability of exactly}\\\text{1 arrival in 3 minutes}\end{array} = f(1) = \frac{2^1 e^{-2}}{1!} = 0.2707$$

One might expect that because (5 arrivals)/5 = 1 arrival and (15 minutes)/5 = 3 minutes, we would get the same probability for one arrival during a 3-minute period as we do for five arrivals during a 15-minute period. Earlier we computed the probability of five arrivals during a 15-minute period as 0.0378. However, note that the probability of one arrival during a 3-minute period is 0.2707, which is not the same. When computing a Poisson probability for a different time interval, we must first convert the mean arrival rate to the period of interest and then compute the probability.

In Excel we can use the POISSON.DIST function to compute Poisson probabilities. Figure 5.16 shows how to calculate the probabilities of patient arrivals at the emergency room if patients arrive at a mean rate of 10 per 15-minute interval.

The POISSON.DIST function in Excel has three input values: the first is the value of x, the second is the mean of the Poisson distribution, and the third is FALSE or TRUE. We choose FALSE for the third input if a probability mass function value $f(x)$ is desired, and TRUE if a cumulative probability is desired. The formula =POISSON.DIST(A4,$D$1,FALSE) has been entered into cell B4 to compute the probability of 0 occurrences, $f(0)$. Figure 5.16 shows that this value (to four decimal places) is 0.0000, which means that it is highly unlikely (probability near 0) that we will have 0 patient arrivals during a 15-minute interval. The value in cell B12 shows that the probability that there will be exactly eight arrivals during a 15-minute interval is 0.1126.

FIGURE 5.16   Excel Worksheet for Computing Poisson Probabilities of the Number of Patients Arriving at the Emergency Room

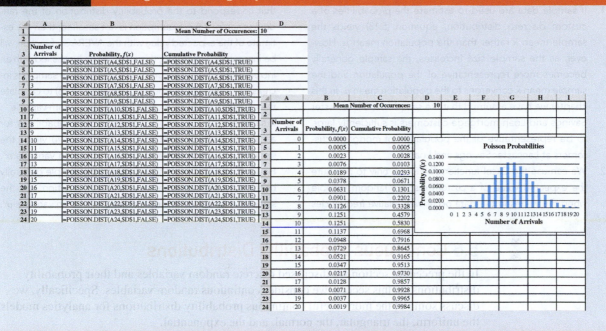

The cumulative probability for x using a Poisson distribution is the probability of x or fewer occurrences during the interval. Cell C4 computes the cumulative probability for $x = 0$, which is the same as the probability for $x = 0$ because the probability of 0 occurrences is the same as the probability of 0 or fewer occurrences. Cell C12 computes the cumulative probability for $x = 8$ using the formula =POISSON.DIST(A12,$D$1,TRUE). This value is 0.3328, meaning that the probability that eight or fewer patients arrive during a 15-minute interval is 0.3328. This value corresponds to:

$$f(0) + f(1) + f(2) + \cdots + f(7) + f(8) = 0.0000 + 0.0005 + 0.0023$$
$$+ \cdots + 0.0901 + 0.1126 = 0.3328.$$

Let us illustrate an application not involving time intervals in which the Poisson distribution is useful. Suppose we want to determine the occurrence of major defects in a highway one month after it has been resurfaced. We assume that the probability of a defect is the same for any two highway intervals of equal length and that the occurrence or nonoccurrence of a defect in any one interval is independent of the occurrence or nonoccurrence of a defect in any other interval. Hence, the Poisson distribution can be applied.

Suppose we learn that major defects one month after resurfacing occur at the average rate of two per mile. Let us find the probability of no major defects in a particular 3-mile section of the highway. Because we are interested in an interval with a length of 3 miles, $\mu = (2 \text{ defects/mile})(3 \text{ miles}) = 6$ represents the expected number of major defects over the 3-mile section of highway. Using equation (5.17), the probability of no major defects is $f(0) = \dfrac{6^0 e^{-6}}{0!} = 0.0025$. Thus, it is unlikely that no major defects will occur in the 3-mile section. In fact, this example indicates a $1 - 0.0025 = 0.9975$ probability of at least one major defect in the 3-mile highway section.

1. If sample data are used to estimate the probabilities of a custom discrete distribution, equation (5.13) yields the sample mean $\bar{x}$ rather than the population mean μ. However, as the sample size increases, the sample generally becomes more representative of the population and the sample mean $\bar{x}$ converges to the population mean μ. In this chapter we have assumed that the sample of 300 Lancaster Savings and Loan mortgage customers is sufficiently large to be representative of the population of mortgage customers at Lancaster Savings and Loan.

2. We can use the Excel function AVERAGE only to compute the expected value of a custom discrete random variable when the values in the data occur with relative frequencies that correspond to the probability distribution of the random variable. If this assumption is not satisfied, then the estimate of the expected value with the AVERAGE function will be inaccurate. In practice, this assumption is satisfied with an increasing degree of accuracy as the size of the sample is increased. Otherwise, we must use equation (5.13) to calculate the expected value for a custom discrete random variable.

3. If sample data are used to estimate the probabilities for a custom discrete distribution, equation (5.14) yields the sample variance s^2 rather than the population variance σ^2. However, as the sample size increases the sample generally becomes more representative of the population and the sample variance s^2 converges to the population variance σ^2.

5.6 Continuous Probability Distributions

In the preceding section we discussed discrete random variables and their probability distributions. In this section we consider continuous random variables. Specifically, we discuss some of the more useful continuous probability distributions for analytics models: the uniform, the triangular, the normal, and the exponential.

A fundamental difference separates discrete and continuous random variables in terms of how probabilities are computed. For a discrete random variable, the probability mass function $f(x)$ provides the probability that the random variable assumes a particular value. With continuous random variables, the counterpart of the probability mass function is the **probability density function**, also denoted by $f(x)$. The difference is that the probability density function does not directly provide probabilities. However, the area under the graph of $f(x)$ corresponding to a given interval does provide the probability that the continuous random variable x assumes a value in that interval. So when we compute probabilities for continuous random variables, we are computing the probability that the random variable assumes any value in an interval. Because the area under the graph of $f(x)$ at any particular point is zero, one of the implications of the definition of probability for continuous random variables is that the probability of any particular value of the random variable is zero.

Uniform Probability Distribution

Consider the random variable x representing the flight time of an airplane traveling from Chicago to New York. The exact flight time from Chicago to New York is uncertain because it can be affected by weather (headwinds or storms), flight traffic patterns, and other factors that cannot be known with certainty. It is important to characterize the uncertainty associated with the flight time because this can have an impact on connecting flights and how we construct our overall flight schedule. Suppose the flight time can be any value in the interval from 120 minutes to 140 minutes. Because the random variable x can assume any value in that interval, x is a continuous rather than a discrete random variable. Let us assume that sufficient actual flight data are available to conclude that the probability of a flight time within any interval of a given length is the same as the probability of a flight time within any other interval of the same length that is contained in the larger interval from 120 to 140 minutes. With every interval of a given length being equally likely, the random variable x is said to have a **uniform probability distribution**. The probability density function, which defines the uniform distribution for the flight-time random variable, is:

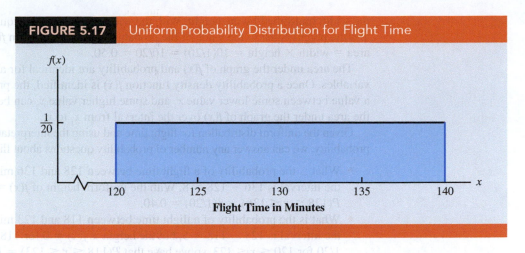

FIGURE 5.17   Uniform Probability Distribution for Flight Time

$$f(x) = \begin{cases} 1/20 & \text{for } 120 \leq x \ \leq 140 \\ 0 & \text{elsewhere} \end{cases}$$

Figure 5.17 shows a graph of this probability density function.

In general, the uniform probability density function for a random variable x is defined by the following formula:

UNIFORM PROBABILITY DENSITY FUNCTION

$$f(x) = \begin{cases} \dfrac{1}{b-a} & \text{for } a \leq x \leq b \\ 0 & \text{elsewhere} \end{cases} \tag{5.18}$$

For the flight-time random variable, $a = 120$ and $b = 140$.

For a continuous random variable, we consider probability only in terms of the likelihood that a random variable assumes a value within a specified interval. In the flight time example, an acceptable probability question is: What is the probability that the flight time is between 120 and 130 minutes? That is, what is $P(120 \leq x \leq 130)$?

To answer this question, consider the area under the graph of $f(x)$ in the interval from 120 to 130 (see Figure 5.18). The area is rectangular, and the area of a rectangle is simply

FIGURE 5.18   The Area Under the Graph Provides the Probability of a Flight Time Between 120 and 130 Minutes

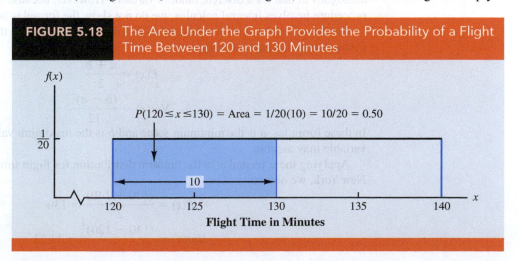

the width multiplied by the height. With the width of the interval equal to $130 - 120 = 10$ and the height equal to the value of the probability density function $f(x) = 1/20$, we have area = width × height = $10(1/20) = 10/20 = 0.50$.

The area under the graph of $f(x)$ and probability are identical for all continuous random variables. Once a probability density function $f(x)$ is identified, the probability that x takes a value between some lower value x_1 and some higher value x_2 can be found by computing the area under the graph of $f(x)$ over the interval from x_1 to x_2.

Given the uniform distribution for flight time and using the interpretation of area as probability, we can answer any number of probability questions about flight times. For example:

- What is the probability of a flight time between 128 and 136 minutes? The width of the interval is $136 - 128 = 8$. With the uniform height of $f(x) = 1/20$, we see that $P(128 \le x \le 136) = 8(1/20) = 0.40$.
- What is the probability of a flight time between 118 and 123 minutes? The width of the interval is $123 - 118 = 5$, but the height is $f(x) = 0$ for $118 \le x < 120$ and $f(x) = 1/20$ for $120 \le x \le 123$, so we have that $P(118 \le x \le 123) = P(118 \le x < 120) + P(120 \le x \le 123) = 2(0) + 3(1/20) = 0.15$.

Note that $P(120 \le x \le 140) = 20(1/20) = 1$; that is, the total area under the graph of $f(x)$ is equal to 1. This property holds for all continuous probability distributions and is the analog of the condition that the sum of the probabilities must equal 1 for a discrete probability mass function.

Note also that because we know that the height of the graph of $f(x)$ for a uniform distribution is $\dfrac{1}{b - a}$ for $a \le x \le b$, then the area under the graph of $f(x)$ for a uniform distribution evaluated from a to a point x_0 when $a \le x_0 \le b$ is width × height = $(x_0 - a) \times (b - a)$. This value provides the cumulative probability of obtaining a value for a uniform random variable of less than or equal to some specific value denoted by x_0 and the formula is given in equation (5.19).

UNIFORM DISTRIBUTION: CUMULATIVE PROBABILITIES

$$P(x \le x_0) = \frac{x_0 - a}{b - a} \quad \text{for } a \le x_0 \le b \tag{5.19}$$

The calculation of the expected value and variance for a continuous random variable is analogous to that for a discrete random variable. However, because the computational procedure involves integral calculus, we do not show the formulas here.

For the uniform continuous probability distribution introduced in this section, the formulas for the expected value and variance are:

$$E(x) = \frac{a + b}{2}$$

$$Var(x) = \frac{(b - a)^2}{12}$$

In these formulas, a is the minimum value and b is the maximum value that the random variable may assume.

Applying these formulas to the uniform distribution for flight times from Chicago to New York, we obtain:

$$E(x) = \frac{(120 + 140)}{2} = 130$$

$$Var(x) = \frac{(140 - 120)^2}{12} = 33.33$$

The standard deviation of flight times can be found by taking the square root of the variance. Thus, for flight times from Chicago to New York, $\sigma = \sqrt{33.33} = 5.77$ minutes.

Triangular Probability Distribution

The triangular probability distribution is useful when only subjective probability estimates are available. There are many situations for which we do not have sufficient data and only subjective estimates of possible values are available. In the **triangular probability distribution**, we need only to specify the minimum possible value a, the maximum possible value b, and the most likely value (or mode) of the distribution m. If these values can be knowledgeably estimated for a continuous random variable by a subject-matter expert, then as an approximation of the actual probability density function, we can assume that the triangular distribution applies.

Consider a situation in which a project manager is attempting to estimate the time that will be required to complete an initial assessment of the new capital project of constructing a new corporate headquarters. The assessment process includes completing environmental-impact studies, procuring the required permits, and lining up all the contractors and subcontractors needed to complete the project. There is considerable uncertainty regarding the duration of these tasks, and generally little or no historical data are available to help estimate the probability distribution for the time required for this assessment process.

Suppose that we are able to discuss this project with several subject-matter experts who have worked on similar projects. From these expert opinions and our own experience, we estimate that the minimum required time for the initial assessment phase is six months and that the worst-case estimate is that this phase could require 24 months if we are delayed in the permit process or if the results from the environmental-impact studies require additional action. While six months represents a best case and 24 months a worst case, the consensus is that the most likely amount of time required for the initial assessment phase of the project is 12 months. From these estimates, we can use a triangular distribution as an approximation for the probability density function for the time required for the initial assessment phase of constructing a new corporate headquarters.

Figure 5.19 shows the probability density function for this triangular distribution. Note that the probability density function is a triangular shape.

The general form of the triangular probability density function is as follows:

TRIANGULAR PROBABILITY DENSITY FUNCTION

$$f(x) = \begin{cases} \dfrac{2(x-a)}{(b-a)(m-a)} & \text{for } a \leq x \leq m \\[2ex] \dfrac{2(b-x)}{(b-a)(b-m)} & \text{for } m < x \leq b \end{cases} \qquad (5.20)$$

where

$$a = \text{minimum value}$$
$$b = \text{maximum value}$$
$$m = \text{mode}$$

In the example of the time required to complete the initial assessment phase of constructing a new corporate headquarters, the minimum value a is six months, the maximum value b is 24 months, and the mode m is 12 months. As with the explanation given for the uniform distribution above, we can calculate probabilities by using the area under the graph of $f(x)$. We can calculate the probability that the time required is less than 12 months by finding the area under the graph of $f(x)$ from $x = 6$ to $x = 12$ as shown in Figure 5.19. The geometry required to find this area for any given value is slightly more

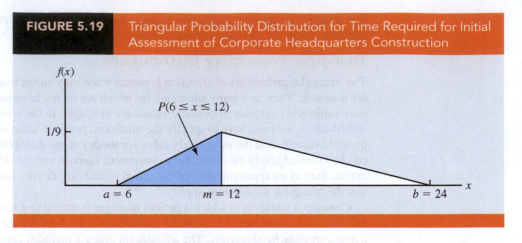

FIGURE 5.19 Triangular Probability Distribution for Time Required for Initial Assessment of Corporate Headquarters Construction

complex than that required to find the area for a uniform distribution, but the resulting formula for a triangular distribution is relatively simple:

TRIANGULAR DISTRIBUTION: CUMULATIVE PROBABILITIES

$$P(x \leq x_0) = \begin{cases} \dfrac{(x_0 - a)^2}{(b - a)(m - a)} & \text{for } a \leq x_0 \leq m \\[2ex] 1 - \dfrac{(b - x_0)^2}{(b - a)(b - m)} & \text{for } m < x_0 \leq b \end{cases}$$

(5.21)

Equation (5.21) provides the cumulative probability of obtaining a value for a triangular random variable of less than or equal to some specific value denoted by x_0.

To calculate $P(x \leq 12)$ we use equation (5.20) with $a = 6$, $b = 24$, $m = 12$, and $x_0 = 12$.

$$P(x \leq 12) = \frac{(12 - 6)^2}{(24 - 6)(12 - 6)} = 0.3333.$$

Thus, the probability that the assessment phase of the project requires less than 12 months is 0.333. We can also calculate the probability that the project requires more than 10 months, but less than or equal to 18 months by subtracting $P(x \leq 10)$ from $P(x \leq 18)$. This is shown graphically in Figure 5.20. The calculations are as follows:

$$P(x \leq 18) - P(x \leq 10) = \left[1 - \frac{(24 - 18)^2}{(24 - 6)(24 - 12)} \right] - \left[\frac{(10 - 6)^2}{(24 - 6)(10 - 6)} \right] = 0.6111$$

Thus, the probability that the assessment phase of the project requires at least 10 months but less than 18 months is 0.6111.

Normal Probability Distribution

One of the most useful probability distributions for describing a continuous random variable is the **normal probability distribution**. The normal distribution has been used in a wide variety of practical applications in which the random variables are heights and weights of people, test scores, scientific measurements, amounts of rainfall, and other similar values. It is also widely used in business applications to describe uncertain quantities such as demand for products, the rate of return for stocks and bonds, and the time it takes to manufacture a part or complete many types of service-oriented activities such as medical surgeries and consulting engagements.

The form, or shape, of the normal distribution is illustrated by the bell-shaped normal curve in Figure 5.21.

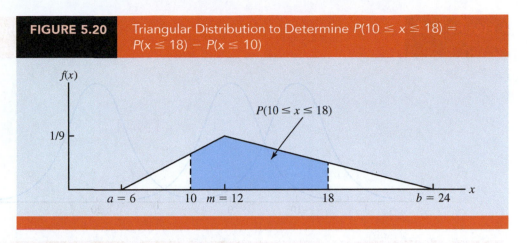

FIGURE 5.20   Triangular Distribution to Determine $P(10 \leq x \leq 18) =$ $P(x \leq 18) - P(x \leq 10)$

The probability density function that defines the bell-shaped curve of the normal distribution follows.

NORMAL PROBABILITY DENSITY FUNCTION

$$f(x) = \frac{1}{\sigma\sqrt{2\pi}} e^{-(x-\mu)^2/2\sigma^2} \tag{5.22}$$

where

μ = mean
σ = standard deviation
$\pi \approx 3.14159$
$e \approx 2.71828$

Although π and e are irrational numbers, 3.14159 and 2.71828, respectively, are sufficient approximations for our purposes.

We make several observations about the characteristics of the normal distribution.

1. The entire family of normal distributions is differentiated by two parameters: the mean μ and the standard deviation σ. The mean and standard deviation are often referred to as the location and shape parameters of the normal distribution, respectively.
2. The highest point on the normal curve is at the mean, which is also the median and mode of the distribution.
3. The mean of the distribution can be any numerical value: negative, zero, or positive. Three normal distributions with the same standard deviation but three different means (-10, 0, and 20) are shown in Figure 5.22.

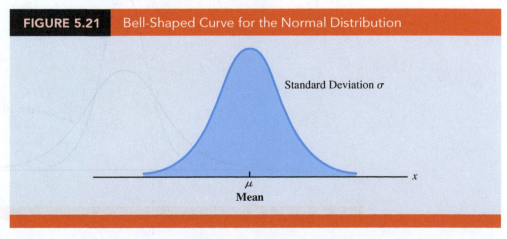

FIGURE 5.21   Bell-Shaped Curve for the Normal Distribution

FIGURE 5.22	Three Normal Distributions with the Same Standard Deviation but Different Means ($\mu = -10$, $\mu = 0$, $\mu = 20$)

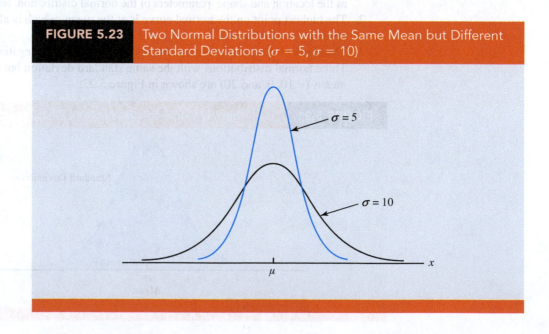

4. The normal distribution is symmetric, with the shape of the normal curve to the left of the mean a mirror image of the shape of the normal curve to the right of the mean.

5. The tails of the normal curve extend to infinity in both directions and theoretically never touch the horizontal axis. Because it is symmetric, the normal distribution is not skewed; its skewness measure is zero.

6. The standard deviation determines how flat and wide the normal curve is. Larger values of the standard deviation result in wider, flatter curves, showing more variability in the data. More variability corresponds to greater uncertainty. Two normal distributions with the same mean but with different standard deviations are shown in Figure 5.23.

7. Probabilities for the normal random variable are given by areas under the normal curve. The total area under the curve for the normal distribution is 1. Because the

FIGURE 5.23	Two Normal Distributions with the Same Mean but Different Standard Deviations ($\sigma = 5$, $\sigma = 10$)

distribution is symmetric, the area under the curve to the left of the mean is 0.50 and the area under the curve to the right of the mean is 0.50.

8. The percentages of values in some commonly used intervals are:
   a. 68.3% of the values of a normal random variable are within plus or minus one standard deviation of its mean.
   b. 95.4% of the values of a normal random variable are within plus or minus two standard deviations of its mean.
   c. 99.7% of the values of a normal random variable are within plus or minus three standard deviations of its mean.

These percentages are the basis for the empirical rule discussed in Section 2.7.

Figure 5.24 shows properties (a), (b), and (c) graphically.

We turn now to an application of the normal probability distribution. Suppose Grear Aircraft Engines sells aircraft engines to commercial airlines. Grear is offering a new performance-based sales contract in which Grear will guarantee that its engines will provide a certain amount of lifetime flight hours subject to the airline purchasing a preventive-maintenance service plan that is also provided by Grear. Grear believes that this performance-based contract will lead to additional sales as well as additional income from providing the associated preventive maintenance and servicing.

From extensive flight testing and computer simulations, Grear's engineering group has estimated that if their engines receive proper parts replacement and preventive maintenance, the mean lifetime flight hours achieved is normally distributed with a mean $\mu = 36{,}500$ hours and standard deviation $\sigma = 5{,}000$ hours. Grear would like to know what percentage of its aircraft engines will be expected to last more than 40,000 hours. In other words, what is the probability that the aircraft lifetime flight hours x will exceed 40,000? This question can be answered by finding the area of the darkly shaded region in Figure 5.25.

The Excel function NORM.DIST can be used to compute the area under the curve for a normal probability distribution. The NORM.DIST function has four input values. The first is the value of interest corresponding to the probability you want to calculate, the second is the mean of the normal distribution, the third is the standard deviation of the normal distribution, and the fourth is TRUE or FALSE. We enter TRUE for the fourth input if we want the cumulative distribution function and FALSE if we want the probability density function.

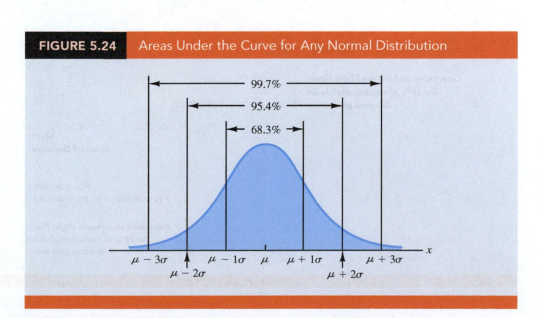

FIGURE 5.24 Areas Under the Curve for Any Normal Distribution

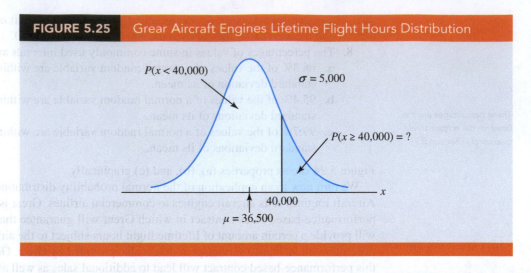

FIGURE 5.25   Grear Aircraft Engines Lifetime Flight Hours Distribution

Figure 5.26 shows how we can answer the question of interest for Grear using Excel—in cell B5, we use the formula =NORM.DIST(40,000, $B$1, $B$2, TRUE). Cell B1 contains the mean of the normal distribution and cell B2 contains the standard deviation. Because we want to know the area under the curve, we want the cumulative distribution function, so we use TRUE as the fourth input value in the formula. This formula provides a value of 0.7580 in cell B5. But note that this corresponds to $P(x \leq 40,000) = 0.7580$. In other words, this gives us the area under the curve to the left of $x = 40,000$ in Figure 5.25, and we are interested in the area under the curve to the right of $x = 40,000$. To find this value, we simply use $1 - 0.7580 = 0.2420$

FIGURE 5.26   Excel Calculations for Grear Aircraft Engines Example

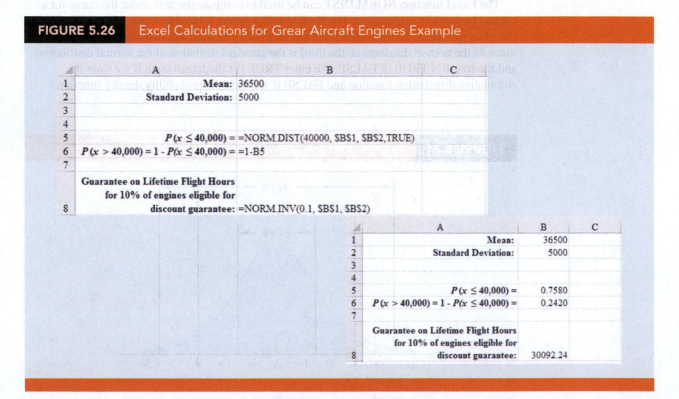

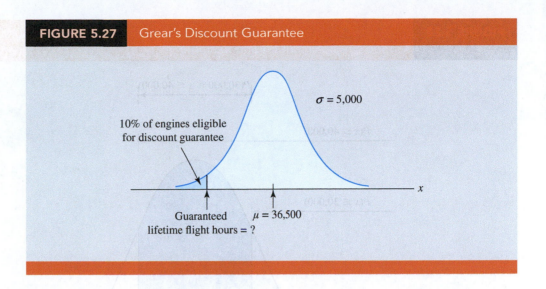

FIGURE 5.27   Grear's Discount Guarantee

(cell B6). Thus, 0.2420 is the probability that x will exceed 40,000 hours. We can conclude that about 24.2% of aircraft engines will exceed 40,000 lifetime flight hours.

Let us now assume that Grear is considering a guarantee that will provide a discount on a replacement aircraft engine if the original engine does not meet the lifetime-flight-hour guarantee. How many lifetime flight hours should Grear guarantee if Grear wants no more than 10% of aircraft engines to be eligible for the discount guarantee? This question is interpreted graphically in Figure 5.27.

According to Figure 5.27, the area under the curve to the left of the unknown guarantee on lifetime flight hours must be 0.10. To find the appropriate value using Excel, we use the function NORM.INV. The NORM.INV function has three input values. The first is the probability of interest, the second is mean of the normal distribution, and the third is the standard deviation of the normal distribution. Figure 5.26 shows how we can use Excel to answer the Grear's question about a guarantee on *With the guarantee set at* lifetime flight hours. In cell B8 we use the formula =NORM.INV(0.10, \$B\$1, \$B\$2), *30,000 hours, the actual* where the mean of the normal distribution is contained in cell B1 and the standard *percentage eligible for* deviation in cell B2. This provides a value of 30,092.24. Thus, a guarantee of 30,092 *the guarantee will be* hours will meet the requirement that approximately 10% of the aircraft engines will be *=NORM.DIST(30000, 36500,* eligible for the guarantee. This information could be used by Grear's analytics team to *5000, TRUE) = 0.0968,* suggest a lifetime flight hours guarantee of 30,000 hours. *or 9.68%.*

Perhaps Grear is also interested in knowing the probability that an engine will have a lifetime of flight hours greater than 30,000 hours but less than 40,000 hours. How do we calculate this probability? First, we can restate this question as follows. What is $P(30{,}000 \leq x \leq 40{,}000)$? Figure 5.28 shows the area under the curve needed to answer this question. The area *Note that we can calculate* that corresponds to $P(30{,}000 \leq x \leq 40.000)$ can be found by subtracting the area *$P(30{,}000 \leq x \leq 40{,}000)$ in a* corresponding to $P(x \leq 30{,}000)$ from the area corresponding to $P(x \leq 40{,}000)$. In other words, *single cell using the formula* $P(30{,}000 \leq x \leq 40{,}000) = P(x \leq 40{,}000) - P(x \leq 30{,}000)$. Figure 5.29 shows how we *=NORM.DIST(40000,* can find the value for $P(30{,}000 \leq x \leq 40{,}000)$ using Excel. We calculate $P(x \leq 40{,}000)$ in *\$B\$1, \$B\$2, TRUE) –* cell B5 and $P(x \leq 30{,}000)$ in cell B6 using the NORM.DIST function. We then calculate *NORM.DIST(30000, \$B\$1,* $P(30{,}000 \leq x \leq 40{,}000)$ in cell B8 by subtracting the value in cell B6 from the value in *\$B\$2, TRUE).* cell B5. This tells us that $P(30{,}000 \leq x \leq 40{,}000) = 0.7580 - 0.0968 = 0.6612$. In other

FIGURE 5.28   Graph Showing the Area Under the Curve Corresponding to $P(30{,}000 \leq x \leq 40{,}000)$ in the Grear Aircraft Engine Example

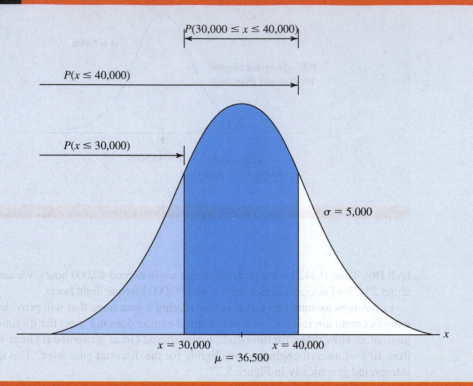

words, the probability that the lifetime flight hours for an aircraft engine will be between 30,000 hours and 40,000 hours is 0.6612.

Exponential Probability Distribution

The **exponential probability distribution** may be used for random variables such as the time between patient arrivals at an emergency room, the distance between major defects in a highway, and the time until default in certain credit-risk models. The exponential probability density function follows.

EXPONENTIAL PROBABILITY DENSITY FUNCTION

$$f(x) = \frac{1}{\mu} e^{-x/\mu} \qquad \text{for } x \geq 0 \qquad (5.23)$$

where

$$\mu = \text{expected value or mean}$$
$$e = 2.71828$$

As an example, suppose that x represents the time between business loan defaults for a particular lending agency. If the mean, or average, time between loan defaults is 15 months ($\mu = 15$), the appropriate density function for x is

$$f(x) = \frac{1}{15} e^{-x/15}$$

FIGURE 5.29 Using Excel to Find $P(30{,}000 \le x \le 40{,}000)$ in the Grear Aircraft Engine Example

	A	B	C
1	Mean:	36500	
2	Standard Deviation:	5000	
3			
4			
5	$P(x \le 40{,}000) =$	=NORM.DIST(40000, $B$1, $B$2,TRUE)	
6	$P(x \le 30{,}000) =$	=NORM.DIST(30000, $B$1, $B$2,TRUE)	
7			
8	$P(30{,}000 \le x \le 40{,}000)$ $= P(x \le 40{,}000) - P(x \le 30{,}000) =$	=B5-B6	

	A	B	C
1	Mean:	36500	
2	Standard Deviation:	5000	
3			
4			
5	$P(x \le 40{,}000) =$	0.7580	
6	$P(x \le 30{,}000) =$	0.0968	
7			
8	$P(30{,}000 \le x \le 40{,}000)$ $= P(x \le 40{,}000) - P(x \le 30{,}000) =$	0.6612	

Figure 5.30 is the graph of this probability density function.

As with any continuous probability distribution, the area under the curve corresponding to an interval provides the probability that the random variable assumes a value in that interval. In the time between loan defaults example, the probability that the time between defaults is 6 months or less, $P(x \le 6)$, is defined to be the area under the curve in Figure 5.30 from $x = 0$ to $x = 6$. Similarly, the probability that the time between defaults will be 18 months or less, $P(x \le 18)$, is the area under the curve from $x = 0$ to $x = 18$. Note also that the probability that the time between defaults will be between 6 months and 18 months, $P(6 \le x \le 18)$, is given by the area under the curve from $x = 6$ to $x = 18$.

To compute exponential probabilities such as those just described, we use the following formula, which provides the cumulative probability of obtaining a value for the exponential random variable of less than or equal to some specific value denoted by x_0.

EXPONENTIAL DISTRIBUTION: CUMULATIVE PROBABILITIES

$$P(x \le x_0) = 1 - e^{-x_0/\mu} \tag{5.24}$$

For the time between defaults example, $x = $ time between business loan defaults in months and $\mu = 15$ months. Using equation (5.24),

$$P(x \le x_0) = 1 - e^{-x_0/15}$$

Hence, the probability that the time between defaults is 6 months or less is:

$$P(x \le 6) = 1 - e^{-6/15} = 0.3297$$

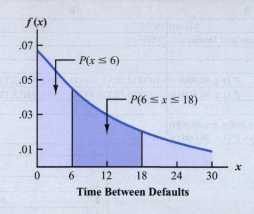

Using equation (5.24), we calculate the probability that the time between defaults is 18 months or less:

$$P(x \leq 18) = 1 - e^{-18/15} = 0.6988$$

Thus, the probability that the time between business loan defaults is 6 months and 18 months is equal to $0.6988 - 0.3297 = 0.3691$. Probabilities for any other interval can be computed similarly.

Figure 5.31 shows how we can calculate these values for an exponential distribution in Excel using the function EXPON.DIST. The EXPON.DIST function has three inputs: the

FIGURE 5.31   Using Excel to Calculate $P(6 \leq x \leq 18)$ for the Time Between Business Loan Defaults Example

	A	B	C
1	Mean, μ =	15	
2			
3	$P(x \leq 18)$ =	=EXPON.DIST(18,1/$B$1, TRUE)	
4	$P(x \leq 6)$ =	=EXPON.DIST(6,1/$B$1, TRUE)	
5	$P(6 \leq x \leq 18) = P(x \leq 18) - P(x \leq 6)$ =	=B3-B4	

	A	B	C
1	Mean, μ =	15	
2			
3	$P(x \leq 18)$ =	0.6988	
4	$P(x \leq 6)$ =	0.3297	
5	$P(6 \leq x \leq 18) = P(x \leq 18) - P(x \leq 6)$ =	0.3691	

first input is x, the second input is $1/m$, and the third input is TRUE or FALSE. An input of TRUE for the third input provides the cumulative distribution function value and FALSE provides the probability density function value. Cell B3 calculates $P(x \le 18)$ using the formula =EXPON.DIST(18, 1/$B$1, TRUE), where cell B1 contains the mean of the exponential distribution. Cell B4 calculates the value for $P(x \le 6)$ and cell B5 calculates the value for $P(6 \le x \le 18) = P(x \le 18) - P(x \le 6)$ by subtracting the value in cell B4 from the value in cell B3.

We can calculate $P(6 \le x \le 18)$ in a single cell using the formula =EXPON.DIST(18, 1/$B$1, TRUE) - EXPON.DIST(6, 1/$B$1, TRUE).

NOTES + COMMENTS

1. The way we describe probabilities is different for a discrete random variable than it is for a continuous random variable. For discrete random variables, we can talk about the probability of the random variable assuming a particular value. For continuous random variables, we can only talk about the probability of the random variable assuming a value within a given interval.

2. To see more clearly why the height of a probability density function is not a probability, think about a random variable with the following uniform probability distribution:

$$f(x) = \begin{cases} 2 & \text{for } 0 \le x \le 0.5 \\ 0 & \text{elsewhere} \end{cases}$$

   The height of the probability density function, $f(x)$, is 2 for values of x between 0 and 0.5. However, we know that probabilities can never be greater than 1. Thus, we see that $f(x)$ cannot be interpreted as the probability of x.

3. The standard normal distribution is the special case of the normal distribution for which the mean is 0 and the standard deviation is 1. This is useful because probabilities for all normal distributions can be computed using the standard normal distribution. We can convert any normal random variable x with mean μ and standard deviation σ to the standard normal random variable z by using the formula $z = \dfrac{x - \mu}{\sigma}$. We interpret z as the number of standard deviations that the normal random variable x is from its mean μ. Then we can use a table of standard normal probability distributions to find the area under the curve using z and the standard normal probability table. Excel contains special functions for the standard normal distribution: NORM.S.DIST and NORM.S.INV. The function NORM.S.DIST is similar to the function NORM.DIST, but it requires only two input values: the value of interest for calculating the probability and TRUE or FALSE, depending on whether you are interested in finding the probability density or the cumulative distribution function. NORM.S.INV is similar to the NORM.INV function, but it requires only the single input of the probability of interest. Both NORM.S.DIST and NORM.S.INV do not need the additional parameters because they assume a mean of 0 and standard deviation of 1 for the standard normal distribution.

4. A property of the exponential distribution is that the mean and the standard deviation are equal to each other.

5. The continuous exponential distribution is related to the discrete Poisson distribution. If the Poisson distribution provides an appropriate description of the number of occurrences per interval, the exponential distribution provides a description of the length of the interval between occurrences. This relationship often arises in queueing applications in which, if arrivals follow a Poisson distribution, the time between arrivals must follow an exponential distribution.

6. Chapter 14 explains how values for discrete and continuous random variables can be generated in Excel for use in simulation models. It also discusses how to use Analytic Solver Platform to assess which probability distribution(s) best describe sample values of a random variable.

SUMMARY

In this chapter we introduced the concept of probability as a means of understanding and measuring uncertainty. Uncertainty is a factor in virtually all business decisions, thus an understanding of probability is essential to modeling such decisions and improving the decision making process.

We introduced some basic relationships in probability including the concepts of outcomes, events, and calculations of related probabilities. We introduced the concept of conditional probability and discussed how to calculate posterior probabilities from prior probabilities using Bayes' theorem. We then discussed both discrete and continuous random variables as well as some of the more common probability distributions related to these types of random variables. These probability distributions included the custom discrete, discrete uniform, binomial, and Poisson probability distributions for discrete random variables, as well as the uniform, triangular, normal, and exponential probability distributions for continuous random variables. We also revisited the concepts of expected values (means) and variance first introduced in Chapter 2.

Probability is used in many chapters that follow in this textbook. The normal distribution is essential to many of the predictive modeling techniques that we introduce in later chapters. Random variables and probability distributions will be seen again in Chapter 6 when we discuss the use of statistical inference to draw conclusions about a population from sample data, Chapter 7 when we discuss regression analysis as a way of estimating relationships between variables, and Chapter 14 when we discuss simulation as a means of modeling uncertainty. Conditional probability and Bayes' theorem will be discussed in Chapter 15 in the context of decision analysis. It is very important to have a basic understanding of probability, such as is provided in this chapter, as you continue to improve your skills in business analytics.

GLOSSARY

Addition law A probability law used to compute the probability of the union of events. For two events A and B, the addition law is $P(A \cup B) = P(A) + P(B) - P(A \cap B)$. For two mutually exclusive events, $P(A \cap B) = 0$, so $P(A \cup B) = P(A) + P(B)$.

Bayes' theorem A method used to compute posterior probabilities.

Binomial probability distribution A probability distribution for a discrete random variable showing the probability of x successes in n trials

Complement of A The event consisting of all outcomes that are not in A.

Conditional probability The probability of an event given that another event already occurred. The conditional probability of A given B is $P(A \mid B) = \dfrac{P(A \cap B)}{P(B)}$.

Continuous random variable A random variable that may assume any numerical value in an interval or collection of intervals. An interval can include negative and positive infinity.

Custom discrete probability distribution A probability distribution for a discrete random variable for which each value x_i that the random variable assumes is associated with a defined probability $f(x_i)$.

Discrete random variable A random variable that can take on only specified discrete values.

Discrete uniform probability distribution A probability distribution in which each possible value of the discrete random variable has the same probability.

Empirical probability distribution A probability distribution for which the relative frequency method is used to assign probabilities.

Event A collection of outcomes.

Expected value A measure of the central location, or mean, of a random variable.

Exponential probability distribution A continuous probability distribution that is useful in computing probabilities for the time it takes to complete a task or the time between arrivals. The mean and standard deviation for an exponential probability distribution are equal to each other.

Independent events Two events A and B are independent if $P(A \mid B) = P(A)$ or $P(B \mid A) = P(B)$; the events do not influence each other.

Intersection of A and B The event containing the outcomes belonging to both A and B. The intersection of A and B is denoted $A \cap B$.

Joint probability The probability of two events both occurring; in other words, the probability of the intersection of two events.

Marginal probability The values in the margins of a joint probability table that provide the probabilities of each event separately.

Multiplication law A law used to compute the probability of the intersection of events. For two events A and B, the multiplication law is $P(A \cap B) = P(B)P(A \mid B)$ or $P(A \cap B) = P(A)P(B \mid A)$. For two independent events, it reduces to $P(A \cap B) = P(A)P(B)$.

Mutually exclusive events Events that have no outcomes in common; $A \cap B$ is empty and $P(A \cap B) = 0$.

Normal probability distribution A continuous probability distribution in which the probability density function is bell-shaped and determined by its mean μ and standard deviation σ.

Poisson probability distribution A probability distribution for a discrete random variable showing the probability of x occurrences of an event over a specified interval of time or space.

Posterior probabilities Revised probabilities of events based on additional information.

Prior probability Initial estimate of the probabilities of events.

Probability A numerical measure of the likelihood that an event will occur.

Probability density function A function used to compute probabilities for a continuous random variable. The area under the graph of a probability density function over an interval represents probability.

Probability distribution A description of how probabilities are distributed over the values of a random variable.

Probability mass function A function, denoted by $f(x)$, that provides the probability that x assumes a particular value for a discrete random variable.

Probability of an event Equal to the sum of the probabilities of outcomes for the event.

Random experiment A process that generates well-defined experimental outcomes. On any single repetition or trial, the outcome that occurs is determined by chance

Random variables A numerical description of the outcome of an experiment.

Sample space The set of all outcomes.

Standard deviation Positive square root of the variance.

Triangular probability distribution A continuous probability distribution in which the probability density function is shaped like a triangle defined by the minimum possible value a, the maximum possible value b, and the most likely value m. A triangular probability distribution is often used when only subjective estimates are available for the minimum, maximum, and most likely values.

Uniform probability distribution A continuous probability distribution for which the probability that the random variable will assume a value in any interval is the same for each interval of equal length.

Union of A and B The event containing the outcomes belonging to A or B or both. The union of A and B is denoted $A \cup B$.

Variance A measure of the variability, or dispersion, of a random variable.

Venn diagram A graphical representation of the sample space and operations involving events, in which the sample space is represented by a rectangle and events are represented as circles within the sample space.

PROBLEMS

1. On-time arrivals, lost baggage, and customer complaints are three measures that are typically used to measure the quality of service being offered by airlines. Suppose that the following values represent the on-time arrival percentage, amount of lost baggage, and customer complaints for 10 U.S. airlines.

Airline	On-Time Arrivals (%)	Mishandled Baggage per 1,000 Passengers	Customer Complaints per 1,000 Passengers
Virgin America	83.5	0.87	1.50
JetBlue	79.1	1.88	0.79
AirTran Airways	87.1	1.58	0.91
Delta Air Lines	86.5	2.10	0.73
Alaska Airlines	87.5	2.93	0.51
Frontier Airlines	77.9	2.22	1.05
Southwest Airlines	83.1	3.08	0.25
US Airways	85.9	2.14	1.74
American Airlines	76.9	2.92	1.80
United Airlines	77.4	3.87	4.24

a. Based on the data above, if you randomly choose a Delta Air Lines flight, what is the probability that this individual flight will have an on-time arrival?

b. If you randomly choose 1 of the 10 airlines for a follow-up study on airline quality ratings, what is the probability that you will choose an airline with less than two mishandled baggage reports per 1,000 passengers?

c. If you randomly choose 1 of the 10 airlines for a follow-up study on airline quality ratings, what is the probability that you will choose an airline with more than one customer complaint per 1,000 passengers?

d. What is the probability that a randomly selected AirTran Airways flight will not arrive on time?

2. Consider the random experiment of rolling a pair of dice. Suppose that we are interested in the sum of the face values showing on the dice.

a. How many outcomes are possible?

b. List the outcomes.

c. What is the probability of obtaining a value of 7?

d. What is the probability of obtaining a value of 9 or greater?

3. Suppose that for a recent admissions class, an Ivy League college received 2,851 applications for early admission. Of this group, it admitted 1,033 students early, rejected 854 outright, and deferred 964 to the regular admission pool for further consideration. In the past, this school has admitted 18% of the deferred early admission applicants during the regular admission process. Counting the students admitted early and the students admitted during the regular admission process, the total class size was 2,375. Let E, R, and D represent the events that a student who applies for early admission is admitted early, rejected outright, or deferred to the regular admissions pool.

a. Use the data to estimate $P(E)$, $P(R)$, and $P(D)$.

b. Are events E and D mutually exclusive? Find $P(E \cap D)$.

c. For the 2,375 students who were admitted, what is the probability that a randomly selected student was accepted during early admission?

d. Suppose a student applies for early admission. What is the probability that the student will be admitted for early admission or be deferred and later admitted during the regular admission process?

4. Suppose that we have two events, A and B, with $P(A) = 0.50$, $P(B) = 0.60$, and $P(A \cap B) = 0.40$.

a. Find $P(A \mid B)$.

b. Find $P(B \mid A)$.

c. Are A and B independent? Why or why not?

5. Students taking the Graduate Management Admissions Test (GMAT) were asked about their undergraduate major and intent to pursue their MBA as a full-time or part-time student. A summary of their responses follows.

		Undergraduate Major			
		Business	Engineering	Other	Totals
Intended Enrollment Status	Full-Time	352	197	251	800
	Part-Time	150	161	194	505
	Totals	502	358	445	1,305

  a. Develop a joint probability table for these data.
  b. Use the marginal probabilities of undergraduate major (business, engineering, or other) to comment on which undergraduate major produces the most potential MBA students.
  c. If a student intends to attend classes full-time in pursuit of an MBA degree, what is the probability that the student was an undergraduate engineering major?
  d. If a student was an undergraduate business major, what is the probability that the student intends to attend classes full-time in pursuit of an MBA degree?
  e. Let F denote the event that the student intends to attend classes full-time in pursuit of an MBA degree, and let B denote the event that the student was an undergraduate business major. Are events F and B independent? Justify your answer.

6. More than 40 million Americans are estimated to have at least one outstanding student loan to help pay college expenses ("40 Million Americans Now Have Student Loan Debt," *CNNMoney*, September 2014). Not all of these graduates pay back their debt in satisfactory fashion. Suppose that the following joint probability table shows the probabilities of student loan status and whether or not the student had received a college degree.

		College Degree		
		Yes	No	
Loan Status	Satisfactory	0.26	0.24	0.50
	Delinquent	0.16	0.34	0.50
		0.42	0.58	

  a. What is the probability that a student with a student loan had received a college degree?
  b. What is the probability that a student with a student loan had not received a college degree?
  c. Given that the student has received a college degree, what is the probability that the student has a delinquent loan?
  d. Given that the student has not received a college degree, what is the probability that the student has a delinquent loan?
  e. What is the impact of dropping out of college without a degree for students who have a student loan?

7. The Human Resources Manager for Optilytics LLC is evaluating applications for the position of Senior Data Scientist. The file *OptilyticsLLC* presents summary data of the applicants for the position.
  a. Use a PivotTable in Excel to create a joint probability table showing the probabilities associated with a randomly selected applicant's sex and highest degree achieved. Use this joint probability table to answer the questions below.

b. What are the marginal probabilities? What do they tell you about the probabilities associated with the sex of applicants and highest degree completed by applicants?

c. If the applicant is female, what is the probability that the highest degree completed by the applicant is a PhD?

d. If the highest degree completed by the applicant is a bachelor's degree, what is the probability that the applicant is male?

e. What is the probability that a randomly selected applicant will be a male whose highest completed degree is a PhD?

8. As was discussed in the Analytics in Action from Chapter 2, the U.S. Census Bureau is a leading source of quantitative data related to the people and economy of the United States. The crosstabulation below represents the number of households (1,000s) and the household income by the highest level of education for the head of household (U.S. Census Bureau web site, 2013). Use this crosstabulation to answer the following questions.

| Highest Level of Education | Household Income | | | | |
	Under $25,000	$25,000 to $49,999	$50,000 to $99,999	$100,000 and Over	Total
High school graduate	9,880	9,970	9,441	3,482	32,773
Bachelor's degree	2,484	4,164	7,666	7,817	22,131
Master's degree	685	1,205	3,019	4,094	9,003
Doctoral degree	79	160	422	1,076	1,737
Total	13,128	15,499	20,548	16,469	65,644

a. Develop a joint probability table.

b. What is the probability the head of one of these households has a master's degree or higher education?

c. What is the probability a household is headed by someone with a high school diploma earning $100,000 or more?

d. What is the probability one of these households has an income below $25,000?

e. What is the probability a household is headed by someone with a bachelor's degree earning less than $25,000?

f. Are household income and educational level independent?

9. Cooper Realty is a small real estate company located in Albany, New York, that specializes primarily in residential listings. The company recently became interested in determining the likelihood of one of its listings being sold within a certain number of days. An analysis of company sales of 800 homes in previous years produced the following data.

| Initial Asking Price | Days Listed Until Sold | | | |
	Under 30	31–90	Over 90	Total
Under $150,000	50	40	10	100
$150,000–$199,999	20	150	80	250
$200,000–$250,000	20	280	100	400
Over $250,000	10	30	10	50
Total	100	500	200	800

a. If A is defined as the event that a home is listed for more than 90 days before being sold, estimate the probability of A.

b. If B is defined as the event that the initial asking price is under $150,000, estimate the probability of B.

c. What is the probability of $A \cap B$?

d. Assuming that a contract was just signed to list a home with an initial asking price of less than $150,000, what is the probability that the home will take Cooper Realty more than 90 days to sell?

e. Are events A and B independent?

10. The prior probabilities for events A_1 and A_2 are $P(A_1) = 0.40$ and $P(A_2) = 0.60$. It is also known that $P(A_1 \cap A_2) = 0$. Suppose $P(B \mid A_1) = 0.20$ and $P(B \mid A_2) = 0.05$.

a. Are A_1 and A_2 mutually exclusive? Explain.

b. Compute $P(A_1 \cap B)$ and $P(A_2 \cap B)$.

c. Compute $P(B)$.

d. Apply Bayes' theorem to compute $P(A_1 \mid B)$ and $P(A_2 \mid B)$.

11. A local bank reviewed its credit-card policy with the intention of recalling some of its credit cards. In the past, approximately 5% of cardholders defaulted, leaving the bank unable to collect the outstanding balance. Hence, management established a prior probability of 0.05 that any particular cardholder will default. The bank also found that the probability of missing a monthly payment is 0.20 for customers who do not default. Of course, the probability of missing a monthly payment for those who default is 1.

a. Given that a customer missed a monthly payment, compute the posterior probability that the customer will default.

b. The bank would like to recall its credit card if the probability that a customer will default is greater than 0.20. Should the bank recall its credit card if the customer misses a monthly payment? Why or why not?

12. RunningWithTheDevil.com created a web site to market running shoes and other running apparel. Management would like a special pop-up offer to appear for female web-site visitors and a different special pop-up offer to appear for male web-site visitors. From a sample of past web-site visitors, RunningWithTheDevil's management learns that 60% of the visitors are male and 40% are female.

a. What is the probability that a current visitor to the web site is female?

b. Suppose that 30% of RunningWithTheDevil's female visitors previously visited LetsRun.com and 10% of male customers previously visited LetsRun.com. If the current visitor to RunningWithTheDevil's web site previously visited LetsRun.com, what is the revised probability that the current visitor is female? Should the RunningWithTheDevil's web site display the special offer that appeals to female visitors or the special offer that appeals to male visitors?

13. An oil company purchased an option on land in Alaska. Preliminary geologic studies assigned the following prior probabilities.

$$P(\text{high-quality oil}) = 0.50$$
$$P(\text{medium-quality oil}) = 0.20$$
$$P(\text{no oil}) = 0.30$$

a. What is the probability of finding oil?

b. After 200 feet of drilling on the first well, a soil test is taken. The probabilities of finding the particular type of soil identified by the test are as follows.

$$P(\text{soil} \mid \text{high-quality oil}) = 0.20$$
$$P(\text{soil} \mid \text{medium-quality oil}) = 0.80$$
$$P(\text{soil} \mid \text{no oil}) = 0.20$$

How should the firm interpret the soil test? What are the revised probabilities, and what is the new probability of finding oil?

14. Suppose the following data represent the number of persons unemployed for a given number of months in Killeen, Texas. The values in the first column show the number of months unemployed and the values in the second column show the corresponding number of unemployed persons.

Months Unemployed	Number Unemployed
1	1,029
2	1,686
3	2,269
4	2,675
5	3,487
6	4,652
7	4,145
8	3,587
9	2,325
10	1,120

Let x be a random variable indicating the number of months a randomly selected person is unemployed.

a. Use the data to develop an empirical discrete probability distribution for x.

b. Show that your probability distribution satisfies the conditions for a valid discrete probability distribution.

c. What is the probability that a person is unemployed for two months or less? Unemployed for more than two months?

d. What is the probability that a person is unemployed for more than six months?

15. The percent frequency distributions of job satisfaction scores for a sample of information systems (IS) senior executives and middle managers are as follows. The scores range from a low of 1 (very dissatisfied) to a high of 5 (very satisfied).

Job Satisfaction Score	IS Senior Executives (%)	IS Middle Managers (%)
1	5	4
2	9	10
3	3	12
4	42	46
5	41	28

a. Develop a probability distribution for the job satisfaction score of a randomly selected senior executive.

b. Develop a probability distribution for the job satisfaction score of a randomly selected middle manager.

c. What is the probability that a randomly selected senior executive will report a job satisfaction score of 4 or 5?

d. What is the probability that a randomly selected middle manager is very satisfied?

e. Compare the overall job satisfaction of senior executives and middle managers.

16. The following table provides a probability distribution for the random variable y.

y	f(y)
2	0.20
4	0.30
7	0.40
8	0.10

a. Compute $E(y)$.
b. Compute $Var(y)$ and σ.

17. The probability distribution for damage claims paid by the Newton Automobile Insurance Company on collision insurance follows.

Payment ($)	Probability
0	0.85
500	0.04
1,000	0.04
3,000	0.03
5,000	0.02
8,000	0.01
10,000	0.01

a. Use the expected collision payment to determine the collision insurance premium that would enable the company to break even.
b. The insurance company charges an annual rate of $520 for the collision coverage. What is the expected value of the collision policy for a policyholder? (*Hint:* It is the expected payments from the company minus the cost of coverage.) Why does the policyholder purchase a collision policy with this expected value?

18. The J.R. Ryland Computer Company is considering a plant expansion to enable the company to begin production of a new computer product. The company's president must determine whether to make the expansion a medium- or large-scale project. Demand for the new product is uncertain, which for planning purposes may be low demand, medium demand, or high demand. The probability estimates for demand are 0.20, 0.50, and 0.30, respectively. Letting x and y indicate the annual profit in thousands of dollars, the firm's planners developed the following profit forecasts for the medium- and large-scale expansion projects.

		Medium-Scale Expansion Profit		Large-Scale Expansion Profit	
		x	f(x)	y	f(y)
	Low	50	0.20	0	0.20
Demand	Medium	150	0.50	100	0.50
	High	200	0.30	300	0.30

a. Compute the expected value for the profit associated with the two expansion alternatives. Which decision is preferred for the objective of maximizing the expected profit?
b. Compute the variance for the profit associated with the two expansion alternatives. Which decision is preferred for the objective of minimizing the risk or uncertainty?

19. Consider a binomial experiment with $n = 10$ and $p = 0.10$.
    a. Compute $f(0)$.
    b. Compute $f(2)$.
    c. Compute $P(x \leq 2)$.
    d. Compute $P(x \geq 1)$.
    e. Compute $E(x)$.
    f. Compute $\text{Var}(x)$ and σ.

20. Many companies use a quality control technique called acceptance sampling to monitor incoming shipments of parts, raw materials, and so on. In the electronics industry, component parts are commonly shipped from suppliers in large lots. Inspection of a sample of n components can be viewed as the n trials of a binomial experiment. The outcome for each component tested (trial) will be that the component is classified as good or defective. Reynolds Electronics accepts a lot from a particular supplier if the defective components in the lot do not exceed 1%. Suppose a random sample of five items from a recent shipment is tested.
    a. Assume that 1% of the shipment is defective. Compute the probability that no items in the sample are defective.
    b. Assume that 1% of the shipment is defective. Compute the probability that exactly one item in the sample is defective.
    c. What is the probability of observing one or more defective items in the sample if 1% of the shipment is defective?
    d. Would you feel comfortable accepting the shipment if one item was found to be defective? Why or why not?

21. A university found that 20% of its students withdraw without completing the introductory statistics course. Assume that 20 students registered for the course.
    a. Compute the probability that 2 or fewer will withdraw.
    b. Compute the probability that exactly 4 will withdraw.
    c. Compute the probability that more than 3 will withdraw.
    d. Compute the expected number of withdrawals.

22. Consider a Poisson distribution with $\mu = 3$.
    a. Write the appropriate Poisson probability mass function.
    b. Compute $f(2)$.
    c. Compute $f(1)$.
    d. Compute $P(x \geq 2)$.

23. Emergency 911 calls to a small municipality in Idaho come in at the rate of one every two minutes. Assume that the number of 911 calls is a random variable that can be described by the Poisson distribution.
    a. What is the expected number of 911 calls in one hour?
    b. What is the probability of three 911 calls in five minutes?
    c. What is the probability of no 911 calls during a five-minute period?

24. A regional director responsible for business development in the state of Pennsylvania is concerned about the number of small business failures. If the mean number of small business failures per month is 10, what is the probability that exactly 4 small businesses will fail during a given month? Assume that the probability of a failure is the same for any two months and that the occurrence or nonoccurrence of a failure in any month is independent of failures in any other month.

25. The random variable x is known to be uniformly distributed between 10 and 20.
    a. Show the graph of the probability density function.
    b. Compute $P(x < 15)$.
    c. Compute $P(12 \leq x \leq 18)$.

d. Compute $E(x)$.

e. Compute $Var(x)$.

26. Most computer languages include a function that can be used to generate random numbers. In Excel, the RAND function can be used to generate random numbers between 0 and 1. If we let x denote a random number generated using RAND, then x is a continuous random variable with the following probability density function:

$$f(x) = \begin{cases} 1 & \text{for } 0 \le x \le 1 \\ 0 & \text{elsewhere} \end{cases}$$

a. Graph the probability density function.

b. What is the probability of generating a random number between 0.25 and 0.75?

c. What is the probability of generating a random number with a value less than or equal to 0.30?

d. What is the probability of generating a random number with a value greater than 0.60?

e. Generate 50 random numbers by entering =RAND() into 50 cells of an Excel worksheet.

f. Compute the mean and standard deviation for the random numbers in part (e).

27. Suppose we are interested in bidding on a piece of land and we know one other bidder is interested.[1] The seller announced that the highest bid in excess of $10,000 will be accepted. Assume that the competitor's bid x is a random variable that is uniformly distributed between $10,000 and $15,000.

a. Suppose you bid $12,000. What is the probability that your bid will be accepted?

b. Suppose you bid $14,000. What is the probability that your bid will be accepted?

c. What amount should you bid to maximize the probability that you get the property?

d. Suppose you know someone who is willing to pay you $16,000 for the property. Would you consider bidding less than the amount in part (c)? Why or why not?

28. A random variable has a triangular probability density function with $a = 50$, $b = 375$, and $m = 250$.

a. Sketch the probability distribution function for this random variable. Label the points $a = 50$, $b = 375$, and $m = 250$ on the x-axis.

b. What is the probability that the random variable will assume a value between 50 and 250?

c. What is the probability that the random variable will assume a value greater than 300?

29. The Siler Construction Company is about to bid on a new industrial construction project. To formulate their bid, the company needs to estimate the time required for the project. Based on past experience, management expects that the project will require at least 24 months, and could take as long as 48 months if there are complications. The most likely scenario is that the project will require 30 months.

a. Assume that the actual time for the project can be approximated using a triangular probability distribution. What is the probability that the project will take less than 30 months?

b. What is the probability that the project will take between 28 and 32 months?

c. To submit a competitive bid, the company believes that if the project takes more than 36 months, then the company will lose money on the project. Management does not want to bid on the project if there is greater than a 25% chance that they will lose money on this project. Should the company bid on this project?

[1]This exercise is based on a problem suggested by Professor Roger Myerson of Northwestern University.

30. Suppose that the return for a particular large-cap stock fund is normally distributed with a mean of 14.4% and standard deviation of 4.4%.
    a.   What is the probability that the large-cap stock fund has a return of at least 20%?
    b.   What is the probability that the large-cap stock fund has a return of 10% or less?

31. A person must score in the upper 2% of the population on an IQ test to qualify for membership in Mensa, the international high IQ society. If IQ scores are normally distributed with a mean of 100 and a standard deviation of 15, what score must a person have to qualify for Mensa?

32. Assume that the traffic to the web site of Smiley's People, Inc., which sells customized T-shirts, follows a normal distribution, with a mean of 4.5 million visitors per day and a standard deviation of 820,000 visitors per day.
    a.   What is the probability that the web site has fewer than 5 million visitors in a single day?
    b.   What is the probability that the web site has 3 million or more visitors in a single day?
    c.   What is the probability that the web site has between 3 million and 4 million visitors in a single day?
    d.   Assume that 85% of the time, the Smiley's People web servers can handle the daily web traffic volume without purchasing additional server capacity. What is the amount of web traffic that will require Smiley's People to purchase additional server capacity?

33. Suppose that Motorola uses the normal distribution to determine the probability of defects and the number of defects in a particular production process. Assume that the production process manufactures items with a mean weight of 10 ounces. Calculate the probability of a defect and the suspected number of defects for a 1,000-unit production run in the following situations.
    a.   The process standard deviation is 0.15, and the process control is set at plus or minus one standard deviation. Units with weights less than 9.85 or greater than 10.15 ounces will be classified as defects.
    b.   Through process design improvements, the process standard deviation can be reduced to 0.05. Assume that the process control remains the same, with weights less than 9.85 or greater than 10.15 ounces being classified as defects.
    c.   What is the advantage of reducing process variation, thereby causing process control limits to be at a greater number of standard deviations from the mean?

34. Consider the following exponential probability density function.

$$f(x) = \frac{1}{3} e^{-x/3} \quad \text{for } x \geq 0$$

    a.   Write the formula for $P(x \leq x_0)$.
    b.   Find $P(x \leq 2)$.
    c.   Find $P(x \geq 3)$.
    d.   Find $P(x \leq 5)$.
    e.   Find $P(2 \leq x \leq 5)$.

35. The time between arrivals of vehicles at a particular intersection follows an exponential probability distribution with a mean of 12 seconds.
    a.   Sketch this exponential probability distribution.
    b.   What is the probability that the arrival time between vehicles is 12 seconds or less?
    c.   What is the probability that the arrival time between vehicles is 6 seconds or less?
    d.   What is the probability of 30 or more seconds between vehicle arrivals?

36. Suppose that the time spent by players in a single session on the *World of Warcraft* multiplayer online role-playing game follows an exponential distribution with a mean of 38.3 minutes.

   a. Write the exponential probability distribution function for the time spent by players on a single session of *World of Warcraft*.

   b. What is the probability that a player will spend between 20 and 40 minutes on a single session of *World of Warcraft*?

   c. What is the probability that a player will spend more than one hour on a single session of *World of Warcraft*?

CASE PROBLEM HAMILTON COUNTY JUDGES

Hamilton County judges try thousands of cases per year. In an overwhelming majority of the cases disposed, the verdict stands as rendered. However, some cases are appealed, and of those appealed, some of the cases are reversed. Kristen DelGuzzi of the *Cincinnati Enquirer* newspaper conducted a study of cases handled by Hamilton County judges over a three-year period. Shown in the table below are the results for 182,908 cases handled (disposed) by 38 judges in Common Pleas Court, Domestic Relations Court, and Municipal Court. Two of the judges (Dinkelacker and Hogan) did not serve in the same court for the entire three-year period.

The purpose of the newspaper's study was to evaluate the performance of the judges. Appeals are often the result of mistakes made by judges, and the newspaper wanted to know which judges were doing a good job and which were making too many mistakes. You are called in to assist in the data analysis. Use your knowledge of probability and conditional probability to help with the ranking of the judges. You also may be able to analyze the likelihood of appeal and reversal for cases handled by different courts.

Total Cases Disposed, Appealed, and Reversed in Hamilton County Courts

Judge	Total Cases Disposed	Appealed Cases	Reversed Cases
Common Pleas Court			
Fred Cartolano	3,037	137	12
Thomas Crush	3,372	119	10
Patrick Dinkelacker	1,258	44	8
Timothy Hogan	1,954	60	7
Robert Kraft	3,138	127	7
William Mathews	2,264	91	18
William Morrissey	3,032	121	22
Norbert Nadel	2,959	131	20
Arthur Ney, Jr.	3,219	125	14
Richard Niehaus	3,353	137	16
Thomas Nurre	3,000	121	6
John O'Connor	2,969	129	12
Robert Ruehlman	3,205	145	18
J. Howard Sundermann	955	60	10
Ann Marie Tracey	3,141	127	13
Ralph Winkler	3,089	88	6
Total	43,945	1,762	199

Continued

Total Cases Disposed, Appealed, and Reversed in Hamilton County Courts (*Continued*)

Domestic Relations Court

Judge	Total Cases Disposed	Appealed Cases	Reversed Cases
Penelope Cunningham	2,729	7	1
Patrick Dinkelacker	6,001	19	4
Deborah Gaines	8,799	48	9
Ronald Panioto	12,970	32	3
Total	30,499	106	17

Municipal Court

Judge	Total Cases Disposed	Appealed Cases	Reversed Cases
Mike Allen	6,149	43	4
Nadine Allen	7,812	34	6
Timothy Black	7,954	41	6
David Davis	7,736	43	5
Leslie Isaiah Gaines	5,282	35	13
Karla Grady	5,253	6	0
Deidra Hair	2,532	5	0
Dennis Helmick	7,900	29	5
Timothy Hogan	2,308	13	2
James Patrick Kenney	2,798	6	1
Joseph Luebbers	4,698	25	8
William Mallory	8,277	38	9
Melba Marsh	8,219	34	7
Beth Mattingly	2,971	13	1
Albert Mestemaker	4,975	28	9
Mark Painter	2,239	7	3
Jack Rosen	7,790	41	13
Mark Schweikert	5,403	33	6
David Stockdale	5,371	22	4
John A. West	2,797	4	2
Total	108,464	500	104

Managerial Report

Prepare a report with your rankings of the judges. Also, include an analysis of the likelihood of appeal and case reversal in the three courts. At a minimum, your report should include the following:

1. The probability of cases being appealed and reversed in the three different courts.
2. The probability of a case being appealed for each judge.
3. The probability of a case being reversed for each judge.
4. The probability of reversal given an appeal for each judge.
5. Rank the judges within each court. State the criteria you used and provide a rationale for your choice.

Chapter 6

Statistical Inference

CONTENTS

ANALYTICS IN ACTION

John Morrell & Company*

CINCINNATI, OHIO

John Morrell & Company, which was established in England in 1827, is considered the oldest continuously operating meat manufacturer in the United States. It is a wholly owned and independently managed subsidiary of Smithfield Foods, Smithfield, Virginia. John Morrell & Company offers an extensive product line of processed meats and fresh pork to consumers under 13 regional brands, including John Morrell, E-Z-Cut, Tobin's First Prize, Dinner Bell, Hunter, Kretschmar, Rath, Rodeo, Shenson, Farmers Hickory Brand, Iowa Quality, and Peyton's. Each regional brand enjoys high brand recognition and loyalty among consumers.

Market research at Morrell provides management with up-to-date information on the company's various products and how the products compare with competing brands of similar products. In order to compare a beef pot roast made by Morrell to similar beef products from two major competitors, Morrell asked a random sample of consumers to indicate how the products rated in terms of taste, appearance, aroma, and overall preference.

In Morrell's independent taste-test study, a sample of 224 consumers in Cincinnati, Milwaukee, and Los Angeles was chosen. Of these 224 consumers, 150 preferred the beef pot roast made by Morrell. Based on these results, Morrell estimates that the population proportion that prefers Morrell's beef pot roast is $\bar{p} = 150/224 = 0.67$. Recognizing that this estimate is subject to sampling error, Morrell calculates the 95% confidence interval for the postulation proportion that prefers Morrell's beef pot roast to be 0.6080 to 0.7312.

Morrell then turned its attention to whether these sample data support the conclusion that Morrell's beef pot roast is the preferred choice of more than 50% of the consumer population. Letting p indicate the proportion of the population that prefers Morrell's product, the hypothesis test for the research question is as follows:

$$H_0: p \leq 0.50$$

$$H_a: p > 0.50$$

The null hypothesis H_0 indicates the preference for Morrell's product is less than or equal to 50%. If the sample data support rejecting H_0 in favor of the alternative hypothesis H_a, Morrell will draw the research conclusion that in a three-product comparison, its beef pot roast is preferred by more than 50% of the consumer population. Using statistical hypothesis testing procedures, the null hypothesis H_0 was rejected. The study provided statistical evidence supporting H_a and the conclusion that the Morrell product is preferred by more than 50% of the consumer population.

In this chapter, you will learn about simple random sampling and the sample selection process. In addition, you will learn how statistics such as the sample mean and sample proportion are used to estimate parameters such as the population mean and population proportion. The concept of a sampling distribution will be introduced and used to compute the margins of error associated with sample estimates. You will then learn how to use this information to construct and interpret interval estimates of a population mean and a population proportion. We then discuss how to formulate hypotheses and how to conduct tests such as the one used by Morrell. You will learn how to use sample data to determine whether or not a hypothesis should be rejected.

*The authors are indebted to Marty Butler, Vice President of Marketing, John Morrell, for providing this Analytics in Action.

In Chapter 2 we presented the following definitions of an element, a population, and a sample.

- An *element* is the entity on which data are collected.
- A *population* is the collection of all the elements of interest.
- A *sample* is a subset of the population.

When collecting data, we usually want to learn about some characteristic(s) of the population from which we are collecting that data. In order to know about some characteristic of a population with certainty, we must collect data from every element in the population of interest; such an effort is referred to as a **census**. However, there are many potential difficulties associated with taking a census:

- A census may be expensive; if resources are limited, it may not be feasible to take a census.
- A census may be time consuming; if the data need be collected quickly, a census may not be suitable.
- A census may be misleading; if the population is changing quickly, by the time a census is completed the data may be obsolete.
- A census may be unnecessary; if perfect information about the characteristic(s) of the population of interest is not required, a census may be excessive.
- A census may be impractical; if observations are destructive, taking a census would destroy the population of interest.

In order to overcome the potential difficulties associated with taking a census, we may decide to take a sample and subsequently use the sample data we collect to make inferences and answer research questions about the population of interest. Therefore, the objective of sampling is to gather data from a subset of the population that is as similar as possible to the entire population so that what we learn from the sample data accurately reflects what we want to understand about the entire population. When we use the sample data we have collected to make estimates of or draw conclusions about one or more characteristics of a population (the value of one or more parameters), we are using the process of **statistical inference**.

A sample that is similar to the population from which it has been drawn is said to be representative of the population.

Sampling is done in a wide variety of research settings. Let us begin our discussion of statistical inference by citing two examples in which sampling was used to answer a research question about a population.

1. Members of a political party in Texas are considering giving their support a particular candidate for election to the U.S. Senate, and party leaders want to estimate the proportion of registered voters in the state that favor the candidate. A sample of 400 registered voters in Texas is selected, and 160 of those voters indicate a preference for the candidate. Thus, an estimate of proportion of the population of registered voters who favor the candidate is $160/400 = 0.40$.

2. A tire manufacturer is considering production of a new tire designed to provide an increase in lifetime mileage over the firm's current line of tires. To estimate the mean useful life of the new tires, the manufacturer produced a sample of 120 tires for testing. The test results provided a sample mean of 36,500 miles. Hence, an estimate of the mean useful life for the population of new tires is 36,500 miles.

A sample mean provides an estimate of a population mean, and a sample proportion provides an estimate of a population proportion. With estimates such as these, some estimation error can be expected. This chapter provides the basis for determining how large that error might be.

It is important to realize that sample results provide only *estimates* of the values of the corresponding population characteristics. We do not expect exactly 0.40, or 40%, of the population of registered voters to favor the candidate, nor do we expect the sample mean of 36,500 miles to exactly equal the mean mileage for the population of all new tires produced. The reason is simply that the sample contains only a portion of the population and cannot be expected to perfectly replicate the population. Some **sampling error** is to be expected. With proper sampling methods, the sample results will provide "good" estimates of the population parameters. But how good can we expect the sample results to be? Fortunately, statistical procedures are available for answering this question.

Let us define some of the terms used in sampling. The **sampled population** is the population from which the sample is drawn, and a **frame** is a list of the elements from which the sample will be selected. In the first example, the sampled population is all registered voters in Texas, and the frame is a list of all the registered voters. Because the number of registered voters in Texas is a finite number, the first example is an illustration of sampling from a finite population.

The sampled population for the tire mileage example is more difficult to define because the sample of 120 tires was obtained from a production process at a particular point in time. We can think of the sampled population as the conceptual population of all the tires that could have been made by the production process at that particular point in time. In this sense the sampled population is considered infinite, making it impossible to construct a frame from which to draw the sample.

In this chapter, we show how simple random sampling can be used to select a sample from a finite population and we describe how a random sample can be taken from an infinite population that is generated by an ongoing process. We then discuss how data obtained from a sample can be used to compute estimates of a population mean, a population standard deviation, and a population proportion. In addition, we introduce the important concept of a sampling distribution. As we will show, knowledge of the appropriate sampling distribution enables us to make statements about how close the sample estimates are to the corresponding population parameters, to compute the margins of error associated with these sample estimates, and to construct and interpret interval estimates. We then discuss how to formulate hypotheses and how to use sample data to conduct tests of a population means and a population proportion.

6.1 Selecting a Sample

The director of personnel for Electronics Associates, Inc. (EAI), has been assigned the task of developing a profile of the company's 2,500 employees. The characteristics to be identified include the mean annual salary for the employees and the proportion of employees having completed the company's management training program.

Using the 2,500 employees as the population for this study, we can find the annual salary and the training program status for each individual by referring to the firm's personnel records. The data set containing this information for all 2,500 employees in the population is in the file named EAI.

A measurable factor that defines a characteristic of a population, process, or system is called a **parameter**. For EAI, the population mean annual salary μ, the population standard deviation of annual salaries σ, and the population proportion p of employees who completed the training program are of interest to us. Using the EAI data and the formulas presented in Chapter 2, we compute the population mean and the population standard deviation for the annual salary data.

$$\text{Population mean:} \quad \mu = \$51,800$$
$$\text{Population standard deviation:} \quad \sigma = \$4,000$$

The data for the training program status show that 1,500 of the 2,500 employees completed the training program. Letting p denote the proportion of the population that completed the training program, we see that $p = 1,500/2,500 = 0.60$. The population mean annual salary ($\mu = \$51,800$), the population standard deviation of annual salary ($\sigma = \$4,000$), and the population proportion that completed the training program ($p = 0.60$) are parameters of the population of EAI employees.

Often the cost of collecting information from a sample is substantially less than the cost of taking a census. Especially when personal interviews must be conducted to collect the information.

Now suppose that the necessary information on all the EAI employees was not readily available in the company's database. The question we must consider is how the firm's director of personnel can obtain estimates of the population parameters by using a sample of employees rather than all 2,500 employees in the population. Suppose that a sample of 30 employees will be used. Clearly, the time and the cost of developing a profile would be substantially less for 30 employees than for the entire population. If the personnel director could be assured that a sample of 30 employees would provide adequate information about the population of 2,500 employees, working with a sample would be preferable to working with the entire population. Let us explore the possibility of using a sample for the EAI study by first considering how we can identify a sample of 30 employees.

Sampling from a Finite Population

Statisticians recommend selecting a probability sample when sampling from a finite population because a probability sample allows you to make valid statistical inferences about the population. The simplest type of probability sample is one in which each sample of size n has the same probability of being selected. It is called a simple random sample. A simple random sample of size n from a finite population of size N is defined as follows.

> **SIMPLE RANDOM SAMPLE (FINITE POPULATION)**
>
> A **simple random sample** of size n from a finite population of size N is a sample selected such that each possible sample of size n has the same probability of being selected.

The random numbers generated using Excel's RAND function follow a uniform probability distribution between 0 and 1.

Procedures used to select a simple random sample from a finite population are based on the use of random numbers. We can use Excel's RAND function to generate a random number between 0 and 1 by entering the formula =RAND() into any cell in a worksheet. The number generated is called a random number because the mathematical procedure used by the RAND function guarantees that every number between 0 and 1 has the same probability of being selected. Let us see how these random numbers can be used to select a simple random sample.

Excel's Sort procedure is especially useful for identifying the n elements assigned the n smallest random numbers.

Our procedure for selecting a simple random sample of size n from a population of size N involves two steps.

Step 1. Assign a random number to each element of the population.
Step 2. Select the n elements corresponding to the n smallest random numbers.

Because each set of n elements in the population has the same probability of being assigned the n smallest random numbers, each set of n elements has the same probability of being selected for the sample. If we select the sample using this two-step procedure, every sample of size n has the same probability of being selected; thus, the sample selected satisfies the definition of a simple random sample.

Let us consider the process of selecting a simple random sample of 30 EAI employees from the population of 2,500. We begin by generating 2,500 random numbers, one for each employee in the population. Then we the select 30 employees corresponding to the 30 smallest random numbers as our sample. Refer to Figure 6.1 as we describe the steps involved.

Step 1. In cell D1, enter the text *Random Numbers*
Step 2. In cells D2:D2501, enter the formula =*RAND()*

FIGURE 6.1   Using Excel to Select a Simple Random Sample

	A	B	C	D	E	F	G
1	Employee	Annual Salary	Training Program	Random Numbers			
2	1	55769.50	No	0.613872			
3	2	50823.00	Yes	0.473204			
4	3	48408.20	No	0.549011			
5	4	49787.50	No	0.047482			
6	5	52801.60	Yes	0.531085			
7	6	51767.70	No	0.994296			
8	7	58346.60	Yes	0.189065			
9	8	46670.20	No	0.020714			
10	9	50246.80	Yes	0.647318			
11	10	51255.00	No	0.524341			
12	11	52546.60	No	0.764998			
13	12	49512.50	Yes	0.255244			
14	13	51753.00	Yes	0.010923			
15	14	53547.10	No	0.238003			
16	15	48052.20	No	0.635675			
17	16	44652.50	Yes	0.177294			
18	17	51764.90	Yes	0.415097			
19	18	45187.80	Yes	0.883440			
20	19	49867.50	Yes	0.476824			
21	20	53706.30	Yes	0.101065			
22	21	52039.50	Yes	0.775323			
23	22	52973.60	No	0.011729			
24	23	53372.50	No	0.762026			
25	24	54592.00	Yes	0.066344			
26	25	55738.10	Yes	0.776766			
27	26	52975.10	Yes	0.828493			
28	27	52386.20	Yes	0.841532			
29	28	51051.60	Yes	0.899427			
30	29	52095.60	Yes	0.486284			
31	30	44956.50	No	0.264628			
32							

The formula in cells D2:D2501 is = RAND().

Note: Rows 32–2501 are not shown.

	A	B	C	D	E
1	Employee	Annual Salary	Training Program	Random Numbers	
2	812	49094.30	Yes	0.000193	
3	1411	53263.90	Yes	0.000484	
4	1795	49643.50	Yes	0.002641	
5	2095	49894.90	Yes	0.002763	
6	1235	47621.60	No	0.002940	
7	744	55924.00	Yes	0.002977	
8	470	49092.30	Yes	0.003182	
9	1606	51404.40	Yes	0.003448	
10	1744	50957.70	Yes	0.004203	
11	179	55109.70	Yes	0.005293	
12	1387	45922.60	Yes	0.005709	
13	1782	57268.40	No	0.005729	
14	1006	55688.80	Yes	0.005796	
15	278	51564.70	No	0.005966	
16	1850	56188.20	No	0.006250	
17	844	51766.00	Yes	0.006708	
18	2028	52541.30	No	0.007767	
19	1654	44980.00	Yes	0.008095	
20	444	51932.60	Yes	0.009686	
21	556	52973.00	Yes	0.009711	
22	2449	45120.90	Yes	0.010595	
23	13	51753.00	Yes	0.010923	
24	2187	54391.80	No	0.011364	
25	1633	50164.20	No	0.011603	
26	22	52973.60	No	0.011729	
27	1530	50241.30	No	0.013570	
28	820	52793.90	No	0.013669	
29	1258	50979.40	Yes	0.014042	
30	2349	55860.90	Yes	0.014532	
31	1698	57309.10	No	0.014539	
32					

The random numbers generated by executing these steps will vary; therefore, results will not match Figure 6.1.

Step 3. In the **HOME** tab on the Ribbon, click **Copy** in the **Clipboard** group

Step 4. In the **HOME** tab on the Ribbon, click the arrow below **Paste** in the **Clipboard** group. When the **Paste** window appears, click **Values** in the **Paste Values** area

Step 5. Select any cell in the range D2:D2501

Step 6. In the **HOME** tab on the Ribbon, click **Sort & Filter** in the **Editing** group and choose **Sort Smallest to Largest**

After completing these steps we obtain a worksheet like the one shown in the foreground of Figure 6.1. The employees listed in rows 2–31 are the ones corresponding to the smallest 30 random numbers that were generated. Hence, this group of 30 employees is a simple random sample. Note that the random numbers shown in the foreground of Figure 6.1 are in ascending order, and that the employees are not in their original order. For instance, employee 812 in the population is associated with the smallest random number and is the first element in the sample, and employee 13 in the population (see row 14 of the background worksheet) has been included as the 22nd observation in the sample (row 23 of the foreground worksheet).

Sampling from an Infinite Population

Sometimes we want to select a sample from a population, but the population is infinitely large or the elements of the population are being generated by an ongoing process for which there is no limit on the number of elements that can be generated. Thus, it is not possible to develop a list of all the elements in the population. This is considered the infinite population case. With an infinite population, we cannot select a simple random sample because we cannot construct a frame consisting of all the elements. In the infinite population case, statisticians recommend selecting what is called a random sample.

RANDOM SAMPLE (INFINITE POPULATION)

A **random sample** of size *n* from an infinite population is a sample selected such that the following conditions are satisfied.

1. Each element selected comes from the same population.
2. Each element is selected independently.

Care and judgment must be exercised in implementing the selection process for obtaining a random sample from an infinite population. Each case may require a different selection procedure. Let us consider two examples to see what we mean by the conditions: (1) Each element selected comes from the same population, and (2) each element is selected independently.

A common quality-control application involves a production process for which there is no limit on the number of elements that can be produced. The conceptual population from which we are sampling is all the elements that could be produced (not just the ones that are produced) by the ongoing production process. Because we cannot develop a list of all the elements that could be produced, the population is considered infinite. To be more specific, let us consider a production line designed to fill boxes with breakfast cereal to a mean weight of 24 ounces per box. Samples of 12 boxes filled by this process are periodically selected by a quality-control inspector to determine if the process is operating properly or whether, perhaps, a machine malfunction has caused the process to begin underfilling or overfilling the boxes.

With a production operation such as this, the biggest concern in selecting a random sample is to make sure that condition 1, the sampled elements are selected from the same population, is satisfied. To ensure that this condition is satisfied, the boxes must be selected at approximately the same point in time. This way the inspector avoids the possibility of selecting some boxes when the process is operating properly and other boxes when the process is not operating properly and is underfilling or overfilling the boxes. With a production process such as this, the second condition, each element is selected independently, is satisfied by designing the production process so that each box of cereal is filled independently. With this assumption, the quality-control inspector need only worry about satisfying the same population condition.

As another example of selecting a random sample from an infinite population, consider the population of customers arriving at a fast-food restaurant. Suppose an employee is asked to select and interview a sample of customers in order to develop a profile of customers who visit the restaurant. The customer-arrival process is ongoing, and there is no way to obtain a list of all customers in the population. So, for practical purposes, the population for this ongoing process is considered infinite. As long as a sampling procedure is designed so that all the elements in the sample are customers of the restaurant and they are selected independently, a random sample will be obtained. In this case, the employee collecting the sample needs to select the sample from people who come into the restaurant and make a purchase to ensure that the same population condition is satisfied. If, for instance, the employee selected for the sample someone who came into the restaurant just to use the restroom, that person would not be a customer and the same population condition would be violated. So, as long as the interviewer selects the sample from people making a purchase at the restaurant, condition 1 is satisfied. Ensuring that the customers are selected independently can be more difficult.

The purpose of the second condition of the random sample selection procedure (each element is selected independently) is to prevent selection bias. In this case, selection bias would occur if the interviewer were free to select customers for the sample arbitrarily. The interviewer might feel more comfortable selecting customers in a particular age group and might avoid customers in other age groups. Selection bias would also occur if the interviewer selected a group of five customers who entered the restaurant together and asked all of them to participate in the sample. Such a group of customers would be likely to exhibit similar characteristics, which might provide misleading information about the population of customers. Selection bias such as this can be avoided by ensuring that the selection of a particular customer does not influence the selection of any other customer. In other words, the elements (customers) are selected independently.

McDonald's, the fast-food restaurant leader, implemented a random sampling procedure for this situation. The sampling procedure was based on the fact that some customers presented discount coupons. Whenever a customer presented a discount coupon, the next customer served was asked to complete a customer profile questionnaire. Because arriving customers presented discount coupons randomly and independently of other customers, this sampling procedure ensured that customers were selected independently. As a result, the sample satisfied the requirements of a random sample from an infinite population.

Situations involving sampling from an infinite population are usually associated with a process that operates over time. Examples include parts being manufactured on a production line, repeated experimental trials in a laboratory, transactions occurring at a bank, telephone calls arriving at a technical support center, and customers entering a retail store. In each case, the situation may be viewed as a process that generates elements from an infinite population. As long as the sampled elements are selected from the same population and are selected independently, the sample is considered a random sample from an infinite population.

NOTES + COMMENTS

1. In this section we have been careful to define two types of samples: a simple random sample from a finite population and a random sample from an infinite population. In the remainder of the text, we will generally refer to both of these as either a *random sample* or simply a *sample*. We will not make a distinction of the sample being a "simple" random sample unless it is necessary for the exercise or discussion.

2. Statisticians who specialize in sample surveys from finite populations use sampling methods that provide probability samples. With a probability sample, each possible sample has a known probability of selection and a random process is used to select the elements for the sample.

Simple random sampling is one of these methods. We use the term *simple* in simple random sampling to clarify that this is the probability sampling method that ensures that each sample of size n has the same probability of being selected.

3. The number of different simple random samples of size n that can be selected from a finite population of size N is:

$$\frac{N!}{n!(N-n)!}$$

In this formula, $N!$ and $n!$ are the factorial formulas discussed in Chapter 4. For the EAI problem with $N = 2,500$ and $n = 30$, this expression can be used to show that approximately 2.75 × 10⁶⁹ different simple random samples of 30 EAI employees can be obtained.

4. In addition to simple random sampling, other probability sampling methods include:
   • stratified random sampling—a method in which the population is first divided into homogeneous subgroups or strata and then a simple random sample is taken from each stratum
   • cluster sampling—a method in which the population is first divided into heterogeneous subgroups or clusters and then simple random samples are taken from some or all of the clusters
   • systematic sampling—a method in which we sort the population based on an important characteristic, randomly select one of the first k elements of the population, and then select every kth element from the population thereafter.

Calculation of sample statistics such as the sample mean $\bar{x}$, the sample standard deviation s, the sample proportion

$\bar{p}$, and so on differ depending on which method of probability sampling is used. See specialized books on sampling such as *Elementary Survey Sampling* (2011) by Scheaffer, Mendenhall, and Ott for more information.

5. Nonprobability sampling methods include:
   • convenience sampling—a method in which sample elements are selected on the basis of accessibility.
   • judgment sampling—a method in which sample elements are selected based on the opinion of the person doing the study.

Although nonprobability samples have the advantages of relatively easy sample selection and data collection, no statistically justified procedure allows a probability analysis or inference about the quality of nonprobability sample results. Statistical methods designed for probability samples should not be applied to a nonprobability sample, and we should be cautious in interpreting the results when a nonprobability sample is used to make inferences about a population.

6.2 Point Estimation

Now that we have described how to select a simple random sample, let us return to the EAI problem. A simple random sample of 30 employees and the corresponding data on annual salary and management training program participation are as shown in Table 6.1. The notation x_1, x_2, and so on is used to denote the annual salary of the first employee in the

TABLE 6.1	Annual Salary and Training Program Status for a Simple Random Sample of 30 EAI Employees		
Annual Salary ($)	**Management Training Program**	**Annual Salary ($)**	**Management Training Program**
$x_1 = 49{,}094.30$	Yes	$x_{16} = 51{,}766.00$	Yes
$x_2 = 53{,}263.90$	Yes	$x_{17} = 52{,}541.30$	No
$x_3 = 49{,}643.50$	Yes	$x_{18} = 44{,}980.00$	Yes
$x_4 = 49{,}894.90$	Yes	$x_{19} = 51{,}932.60$	Yes
$x_5 = 47{,}621.60$	No	$x_{20} = 52{,}973.00$	Yes
$x_6 = 55{,}924.00$	Yes	$x_{21} = 45{,}120.90$	Yes
$x_7 = 49{,}092.30$	Yes	$x_{22} = 51{,}753.00$	Yes
$x_8 = 51{,}404.40$	Yes	$x_{23} = 54{,}391.80$	No
$x_9 = 50{,}957.70$	Yes	$x_{24} = 50{,}164.20$	No
$x_{10} = 55{,}109.70$	Yes	$x_{25} = 52{,}973.60$	No
$x_{11} = 45{,}922.60$	Yes	$x_{26} = 50{,}241.30$	No
$x_{12} = 57{,}268.40$	No	$x_{27} = 52{,}793.90$	No
$x_{13} = 55{,}688.80$	Yes	$x_{28} = 50{,}979.40$	Yes
$x_{14} = 51{,}564.70$	No	$x_{29} = 55{,}860.90$	Yes
$x_{15} = 56{,}188.20$	No	$x_{30} = 57{,}309.10$	No

sample, the annual salary of the second employee in the sample, and so on. Participation in the management training program is indicated by Yes in the management training program column.

To estimate the value of a population parameter, we compute a corresponding characteristic of the sample, referred to as a **sample statistic**. For example, to estimate the population mean μ and the population standard deviation σ for the annual salary of EAI employees, we use the data in Table 6.1 to calculate the corresponding sample statistics: the sample mean and the sample standard deviation s. Using the formulas for a sample mean and a sample standard deviation presented in Chapter 2, the sample mean is:

$$\bar{x} = \frac{\Sigma x_i}{n} = \frac{1,554,420}{30} = \$51,814$$

and the sample standard deviation is

$$s = \sqrt{\frac{\Sigma(x_i - \bar{x})^2}{n-1}} = \sqrt{\frac{325,009,260}{29}} = \$3,384.$$

To estimate p, the proportion of employees in the population who completed the management training program, we use the corresponding sample proportion $\bar{p}$. Let x denote the number of employees in the sample who completed the management training program. The data in Table 6.1 show that $x = 19$. Thus, with a sample size of $n = 30$, the sample proportion is:

$$\bar{p} = \frac{x}{n} = \frac{19}{30} = 0.63$$

By making the preceding computations, we perform the statistical procedure called *point estimation*. We refer to the sample mean $\bar{x}$ as the **point estimator** of the population mean μ, the sample standard deviation s as the point estimator of the population standard deviation σ, and the sample proportion $\bar{p}$ as the point estimator of the population proportion p. The numerical value obtained for $\bar{x}$, s, or $\bar{p}$ is called the **point estimate**. Thus, for the simple random sample of 30 EAI employees shown in Table 6.1, $\$51,814$ is the point estimate of μ, $\$3,348$ is the point estimate of σ, and 0.63 is the point estimate of p. Table 6.2 summarizes the sample results and compares the point estimates to the actual values of the population parameters.

As is evident from Table 6.2, the point estimates differ somewhat from the values of corresponding population parameters. This difference is to be expected because a sample,

TABLE 6.2	Summary of Point Estimates Obtained from a Simple Random Sample of 30 EAI Employees		
Population Parameter	**Parameter Value**	**Point Estimator**	**Point Estimate**
μ = Population mean annual salary	$51,800	$\bar{x}$ = Sample mean annual salary	$51,814
σ = Population standard deviation for annual salary	$4,000	s = Sample standard deviation for annual salary	$3,348
p = Population proportion completing the management training program	0.60	$\bar{p}$ = Sample proportion having completed the management training program	0.63

and not a census of the entire population, is being used to develop the point estimates. In the next chapter, we will show how to construct an interval estimate in order to provide information about how close the point estimate is to the population parameter.

Practical Advice

The subject matter of most of the rest of the book is concerned with statistical inference, of which point estimation is a form. We use a sample statistic to make an inference about a population parameter. When making inferences about a population based on a sample, it is important to have a close correspondence between the sampled population and the target population. The **target population** is the population about which we want to make inferences, while the sampled population is the population from which the sample is actually taken. In this section, we have described the process of drawing a simple random sample from the population of EAI employees and making point estimates of characteristics of that same population. So the sampled population and the target population are identical, which is the desired situation. But in other cases, it is not as easy to obtain a close correspondence between the sampled and target populations.

Consider the case of an amusement park selecting a sample of its customers to learn about characteristics such as age and time spent at the park. Suppose all the sample elements were selected on a day when park attendance was restricted to employees of a large company. Then the sampled population would be composed of employees of that company and members of their families. If the target population we wanted to make inferences about were typical park customers over a typical summer, then we might encounter a significant difference between the sampled population and the target population. In such a case, we would question the validity of the point estimates being made. Park management would be in the best position to know whether a sample taken on a particular day was likely to be representative of the target population.

In summary, whenever a sample is used to make inferences about a population, we should make sure that the study is designed so that the sampled population and the target population are in close agreement. Good judgment is a necessary ingredient of sound statistical practice.

6.3 Sampling Distributions

In the preceding section we said that the sample mean $\bar{x}$ is the point estimator of the population mean μ, and the sample proportion $\bar{p}$ is the point estimator of the population proportion p. For the simple random sample of 30 EAI employees shown in Table 6.1, the point estimate of μ is $\bar{x} = \$51,814$ and the point estimate of p is $\bar{p} = 0.63$. Suppose we select another simple random sample of 30 EAI employees and obtain the following point estimates:

$$\text{Sample mean: } \bar{x} = \$52,670$$

$$\text{Sample proportion: } \bar{p} = 0.70$$

Note that different values of $\bar{x}$ and $\bar{p}$ were obtained. Indeed, a second simple random sample of 30 EAI employees cannot be expected to provide the same point estimates as the first sample.

Now, suppose we repeat the process of selecting a simple random sample of 30 EAI employees over and over again, each time computing the values of $\bar{x}$ and $\bar{p}$. Table 6.3 contains a portion of the results obtained for 500 simple random samples, and Table 6.4 shows the frequency and relative frequency distributions for the 500 $\bar{x}$ values. Figure 6.2 shows the relative frequency histogram for the $\bar{x}$ values.

TABLE 6.3	Values of $\bar{x}$ and $\bar{p}$ from 500 Simple Random Samples of 30 EAI Employees	
Sample Number	**Sample Mean** $(\bar{x})$	**Sample Proportion** $(\bar{p})$
1	51,814	0.63
2	52,670	0.70
3	51,780	0.67
4	51,588	0.53
•	•	•
•	•	•
•	•	•
500	51,752	0.50

The ability to understand the material in subsequent sections of this chapter depends heavily on the ability to understand and use the sampling distributions presented in this section.

In Chapter 2 we defined a random variable as a quantity whose values are not known with certainty. Because the sample mean $\bar{x}$ is a quantity whose values are not known with certainty, the sample mean $\bar{x}$ is a random variable. As a result, just like other random variables, $\bar{x}$ has a mean or expected value, a standard deviation, and a probability distribution. Because the various possible values of $\bar{x}$ are the result of different simple random samples, the probability distribution of $\bar{x}$ is called the **sampling distribution** of $\bar{x}$. Knowledge of this sampling distribution and its properties will enable us to make probability statements about how close the sample mean $\bar{x}$ is to the population mean μ.

Let us return to Figure 6.2. We would need to enumerate every possible sample of 30 employees and compute each sample mean to completely determine the sampling distribution of $\bar{x}$. However, the histogram of 500 $\bar{x}$ values gives an approximation of this sampling distribution. From the approximation we observe the bell-shaped appearance of the distribution. We note that the largest concentration of the $\bar{x}$ values and the mean of the 500 $\bar{x}$ values is near the population mean $\mu = \$51,800$. We will describe the properties of the sampling distribution of $\bar{x}$ more fully in the next section.

The 500 values of the sample proportion $\bar{p}$ are summarized by the relative frequency histogram in Figure 6.3. As in the case of $\bar{x}$, $\bar{p}$ is a random variable. If every possible sample of size 30 were selected from the population and if a value of $\bar{p}$ were computed for

TABLE 6.4	Frequency and Relative Frequency Distributions of $\bar{x}$ from 500 Simple Random Samples of 30 EAI Employees	
Mean Annual Salary ($)	**Frequency**	**Relative Frequency**
49,500.00–49,999.99	2	0.004
50,000.00–50,499.99	16	0.032
50,500.00–50,999.99	52	0.104
51,000.00–51,499.99	101	0.202
51,500.00–51,999.99	133	0.266
52,000.00–52,499.99	110	0.220
52,500.00–52,999.99	54	0.108
53,000.00–53,499.99	26	0.052
53,500.00–53,999.99	6	0.012
Totals	500	1.000

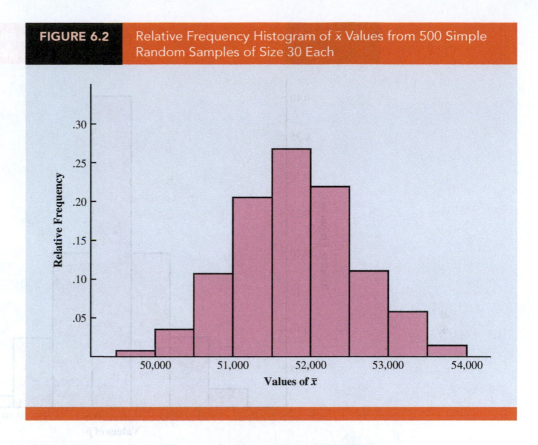

FIGURE 6.2 Relative Frequency Histogram of $\bar{x}$ Values from 500 Simple Random Samples of Size 30 Each

each sample, the resulting probability distribution would be the sampling distribution of $\bar{p}$. The relative frequency histogram of the 500 sample values in Figure 6.3 provides a general idea of the appearance of the sampling distribution of $\bar{p}$.

In practice, we select only one simple random sample from the population. We repeated the sampling process 500 times in this section simply to illustrate that many different samples are possible and that the different samples generate a variety of values for the sample statistics $\bar{x}$ and $\bar{p}$. The probability distribution of any particular sample statistic is called the sampling distribution of the statistic. Next we discuss the characteristics of the sampling distributions of $\bar{x}$ and $\bar{p}$.

Sampling Distribution of $\bar{x}$

In the previous section we said that the sample mean $\bar{x}$ is a random variable and that its probability distribution is called the sampling distribution of $\bar{x}$.

SAMPLING DISTRIBUTION OF $\bar{x}$

The sampling distribution of $\bar{x}$ is the probability distribution of all possible values of the sample mean $\bar{x}$.

This section describes the properties of the sampling distribution of $\bar{x}$. Just as with other probability distributions we studied, the sampling distribution of $\bar{x}$ has an expected value or mean, a standard deviation, and a characteristic shape or form. Let us begin by considering the mean of all possible $\bar{x}$ values, which is referred to as the expected value of $\bar{x}$.

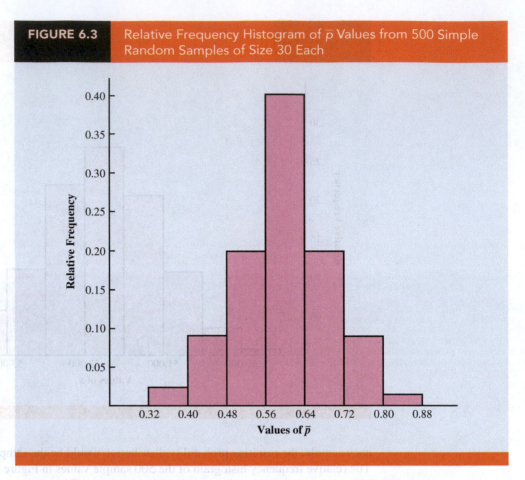

FIGURE 6.3   Relative Frequency Histogram of $\bar{p}$ Values from 500 Simple Random Samples of Size 30 Each

Expected value of $\bar{x}$ In the EAI sampling problem we saw that different simple random samples result in a variety of values for the sample mean $\bar{x}$. Because many different values of the random variable $\bar{x}$ are possible, we are often interested in the mean of all possible values of $\bar{x}$ that can be generated by the various simple random samples. The mean of the $\bar{x}$ random variable is the expected value of $\bar{x}$. Let $E(\bar{x})$ represent the expected value of $\bar{x}$ and μ represent the mean of the population from which we are selecting a simple random sample. It can be shown that with simple random sampling, $E(\bar{x})$ and μ are equal.

The expected value of $\bar{x}$ equals the mean of the population from which the sample is selected.

EXPECTED VALUE OF $\bar{x}$

$$E(\bar{x}) = \mu \tag{6.1}$$

where

$$E(\bar{x}) = \text{the expected value of } \bar{x}$$
$$\mu = \text{the population mean}$$

This result shows that with simple random sampling, the expected value or mean of the sampling distribution of $\bar{x}$ is equal to the mean of the population. In Section 6.1 we saw that the mean annual salary for the population of EAI employees is $\mu = \$51{,}800$. Thus, according to equation (6.1), if we considered all possible samples of size n from the population of EAI employees, the mean of all the corresponding sample means for the EAI study would be equal to $\$51{,}800$, the population mean.

When the expected value of a point estimator equals the population parameter, we say the point estimator is **unbiased**. Thus, equation (6.1) states that $\bar{x}$ is an unbiased estimator of the population mean μ.

The term standard error is used in statistical inference to refer to the standard deviation of a point estimator.

Standard deviation of $\bar{x}$ Let us define the standard deviation of the sampling distribution of $\bar{x}$. We will use the following notation:

$\sigma_{\bar{x}}$ = the standard deviation of $\bar{x}$, or the **standard error** of the mean
σ = the standard deviation of the population
n = the sample size
N = the population size

It can be shown that the formula for the standard deviation of $\bar{x}$ depends on whether the population is finite or infinite. The two formulas for the standard deviation of $\bar{x}$ follow.

STANDARD DEVIATION OF $\bar{x}$

Finite Population	*Infinite Population*	
$\sigma_{\bar{x}} = \sqrt{\dfrac{N-n}{N-1}}\left(\dfrac{\sigma}{\sqrt{n}}\right)$	$\sigma_{\bar{x}} = \dfrac{\sigma}{\sqrt{n}}$	(6.2)

In comparing the two formulas in equation (6.2), we see that the factor $\sqrt{(N-n)/(N-1)}$ is required for the finite population case but not for the infinite population case. This factor is commonly referred to as the **finite population correction factor**. In many practical sampling situations, we find that the population involved, although finite, is "large," whereas the sample size is relatively "small." In such cases the finite population correction factor $\sqrt{(N-n)/(N-1)}$ is close to 1. As a result, the difference between the values of the standard deviation of $\bar{x}$ for the finite and infinite populations becomes negligible. Then, $\sigma_{\bar{x}} = \sigma/\sqrt{n}$ becomes a good approximation to the standard deviation of $\bar{x}$ even though the population is finite. In cases where $n/N > 0.05$, the finite population version of equation (6.2) should be used in the computation of $\sigma_{\bar{x}}$. Unless otherwise noted, throughout the text we will assume that the population size is "large," $n/N \leq 0.05$.

Observe from equation (6.2) that we need to know σ, the standard deviation of the population, in order to compute $\sigma_{\bar{x}}$. That is, the sample-to-sample variability in the point estimator $\bar{x}$, as measured by the standard error $\sigma_{\bar{x}}$, depends on the standard deviation of the population from which the sample is drawn. However, when we are sampling to estimate the population mean with $\bar{x}$, usually the population standard deviation is also unknown. Therefore, we need to estimate the standard deviation of $\bar{x}$ with $s_{\bar{x}}$ using the sample standard deviations as shown in equation (6.3).

ESTIMATED STANDARD DEVIATION OF $\bar{x}$

Finite Population	*Infinite Population*	
$s_{\bar{x}} = \sqrt{\dfrac{N-n}{N-1}}\left(\dfrac{s}{\sqrt{n}}\right)$	$s_{\bar{x}} = \left(\dfrac{s}{\sqrt{n}}\right)$	(6.3)

Let us now return to the EAI example and compute the estimated standard error (standard deviation) of the mean associated with simple random samples of 30 EAI employees. Recall from Table 6.2 that the standard deviation of the sample of 30 EAI employees is $s = 3,348$. In this case, the population is finite ($N = 2,500$), but because $n/N = 30/2,500 = 0.012 < 0.05$, we can ignore the finite population correction factor and compute the estimated standard error as:

$$s_{\bar{x}} = \frac{s}{\sqrt{n}} = \frac{3,348}{\sqrt{30}} = 611.3$$

In this case, we happen to know that the standard deviation of the population is actually $\sigma = 4,000$, so the true standard error is:

$$\sigma_{\bar{x}} = \frac{\sigma}{\sqrt{n}} = \frac{4,000}{\sqrt{30}} = 730.3$$

The difference between $s_{\bar{x}}$ and $\sigma_{\bar{x}}$ is due to **sampling error**, or the error that results from observing a sample of 30 rather than the entire population of 2,500.

Form of the sampling distribution of $\bar{x}$ The preceding results concerning the expected value and standard deviation for the sampling distribution of $\bar{x}$ are applicable for any population. The final step in identifying the characteristics of the sampling distribution of $\bar{x}$ is to determine the form or shape of the sampling distribution. We will consider two cases: (1) The population has a normal distribution; and (2) the population does not have a normal distribution.

Population has a normal distribution In many situations it is reasonable to assume that the population from which we are selecting a random sample has a normal, or nearly normal, distribution. When the population has a normal distribution, the sampling distribution of $\bar{x}$ is normally distributed for any sample size.

Population does not have a normal distribution When the population from which we are selecting a random sample does not have a normal distribution, the central limit theorem is helpful in identifying the shape of the sampling distribution of $\bar{x}$. A statement of the central limit theorem as it applies to the sampling distribution of x follows.

CENTRAL LIMIT THEOREM

In selecting random samples of size n from a population, the sampling distribution of the sample mean $\bar{x}$ can be approximated by a *normal distribution* as the sample size becomes large.

Figure 6.4 shows how the central limit theorem works for three different populations; each column refers to one of the populations. The top panel of the figure shows that none of the populations are normally distributed. Population I follows a uniform distribution. Population II is often called the rabbit-eared distribution. It is symmetric, but the more likely values fall in the tails of the distribution. Population III is shaped like the exponential distribution; it is skewed to the right.

The bottom three panels of Figure 6.4 show the shape of the sampling distribution for samples of size $n = 2$, $n = 5$, and $n = 30$. When the sample size is 2, we see that the shape of each sampling distribution is different from the shape of the corresponding population distribution. For samples of size 5, we see that the shapes of the sampling distributions for populations I and II begin to look similar to the shape of a normal distribution. Even though the shape of the sampling distribution for population III begins to look similar to the shape of a normal distribution, some skewness to the right is still present. Finally, for a sample size of 30, the shapes of each of the three sampling distributions are approximately normal.

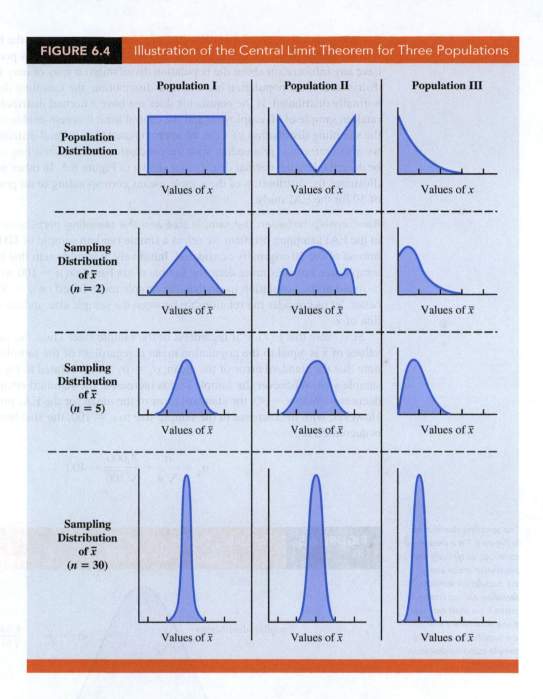

FIGURE 6.4 Illustration of the Central Limit Theorem for Three Populations

From a practitioner's standpoint, we often want to know how large the sample size needs to be before the central limit theorem applies and we can assume that the shape of the sampling distribution is approximately normal. Statistical researchers have investigated this question by studying the sampling distribution of $\bar{x}$ for a variety of populations and a variety of sample sizes. General statistical practice is to assume that, for most applications, the sampling distribution of $\bar{x}$ can be approximated by a normal distribution whenever the sample size is 30 or more. In cases in which the population is highly skewed or outliers are present, sample sizes of 50 may be needed.

Sampling distribution of $\bar{x}$ for the EAI problem Let us return to the EAI problem where we previously showed that $E(\bar{x}) = \$51,800$ and $\sigma_{\bar{x}} = 730.3$. At this point, we do not have any information about the population distribution; it may or may not be normally distributed. If the population has a normal distribution, the sampling distribution of $\bar{x}$ is normally distributed. If the population does not have a normal distribution, the simple random sample of 30 employees and the central limit theorem enable us to conclude that the sampling distribution of $\bar{x}$ can be approximated by a normal distribution. In either case, we are comfortable proceeding with the conclusion that the sampling distribution of $\bar{x}$ can be described by the normal distribution shown in Figure 6.5. In other words, Figure 6.5 illustrates the distribution of the sample means corresponding to all possible sample sizes of 30 for the EAI study.

Relationship between the sample size and the sampling distribution of $\bar{x}$ Suppose that in the EAI sampling problem we select a simple random sample of 100 EAI employees instead of the 30 originally considered. Intuitively, it would seem that because the larger sample size provides more data, the sample mean based on $n = 100$ would provide a better estimate of the population mean than the sample mean based on $n = 30$. To see how much better, let us consider the relationship between the sample size and the sampling distribution of $\bar{x}$.

First, note that $E(\bar{x}) = \mu$ regardless of the sample size. Thus, the mean of all possible values of $\bar{x}$ is equal to the population mean μ regardless of the sample size μ. However, note that the standard error of the mean, $\sigma_{\bar{x}} = \sigma/\sqrt{n}$, is related to the square root of the sample size. Whenever the sample size is increased, the standard error of the mean $\sigma_{\bar{x}}$ decreases. With $n = 30$, the standard error of the mean for the EAI problem is 730.3. However, with the increase in the sample size to $n = 100$, the standard error of the mean is decreased to:

$$\sigma_{\bar{x}} = \frac{\sigma}{\sqrt{n}} = \frac{4,000}{\sqrt{100}} = 400.$$

The sampling distribution in Figure 6.5 is a theoretical construct, as typically the population mean and the population standard deviation are not known. Instead, we must estimate these parameters with the sample mean and the sample standard deviation, respectively.

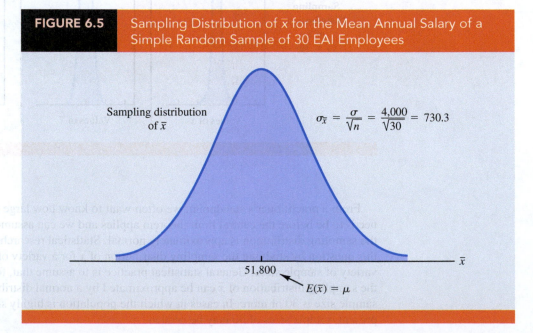

FIGURE 6.5   Sampling Distribution of $\bar{x}$ for the Mean Annual Salary of a Simple Random Sample of 30 EAI Employees

Sampling distribution of $\bar{x}$

$\sigma_{\bar{x}} = \dfrac{\sigma}{\sqrt{n}} = \dfrac{4,000}{\sqrt{30}} = 730.3$

51,800

$E(\bar{x}) = \mu$

$\bar{x}$

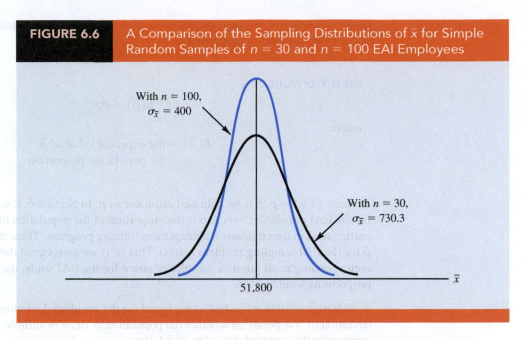

FIGURE 6.6 A Comparison of the Sampling Distributions of $\bar{x}$ for Simple Random Samples of $n = 30$ and $n = 100$ EAI Employees

The sampling distributions of $\bar{x}$ with $n = 30$ and $n = 100$ are shown in Figure 6.6. Because the sampling distribution with $n = 100$ has a smaller standard error, the values of $\bar{x}$ have less variation and tend to be closer to the population mean than the values of $\bar{x}$ with $n = 30$.

The important point in this discussion is that as the sample size increases, the standard error of the mean decreases. As a result, a larger sample size will provide a higher probability that the sample mean falls within a specified distance of the population mean. The practical reason we are interested in the sampling distribution of $\bar{x}$ is that it can be used to provide information about how close the sample mean is to the population mean. The concepts of interval estimation and hypothesis testing discussed in Sections 6.4 and 6.5 rely on the properties of sampling distributions.

Sampling Distribution of $\bar{p}$

The sample proportion $\bar{p}$ is the point estimator of the population proportion p. The formula for computing the sample proportion is:

$$\bar{p} = \frac{x}{n},$$

where

x = the number of elements in the sample that possess the characteristic of interest
n = sample size

As previously noted in this section, the sample proportion $\bar{p}$ is a random variable and its probability distribution is called the sampling distribution of $\bar{p}$.

SAMPLING DISTRIBUTION OF $\bar{p}$

The sampling distribution of $\bar{p}$ is the probability distribution of all possible values of the sample proportion $\bar{p}$.

To determine how close the sample proportion $\bar{p}$ is to the population proportion p, we need to understand the properties of the sampling distribution of $\bar{p}$: the expected value of $\bar{p}$, the standard deviation of $\bar{p}$, and the shape or form of the sampling distribution of $\bar{p}$.

Expected value of $\bar{p}$ The expected value of $\bar{p}$, the mean of all possible values of $\bar{p}$, is equal to the population proportion p.

EXPECTED VALUE OF $\bar{p}$

$$E(\bar{p}) = p, \tag{6.4}$$

where

$$E(\bar{p}) = \text{the expected value of } \bar{p}$$
$$p = \text{the population proportion}$$

Because $E(\bar{p}) = p$, $\bar{p}$ is an unbiased estimator of p. In Section 6.1, we noted that $p = 0.60$ for the EAI population, where p is the proportion of the population of employees who participated in the company's management training program. Thus, the expected value of $\bar{p}$ for the EAI sampling problem is 0.60. That is, if we considered the sample proportions corresponding to all possible samples of size n for the EAI study, the mean of these sample proportions would be 0.6.

Standard deviation of $\bar{p}$ Just as we found for the standard deviation of $\bar{x}$, the standard deviation of $\bar{p}$ depends on whether the population is finite or infinite. The two formulas for computing the standard deviation of $\bar{p}$ follow.

STANDARD DEVIATION OF $\bar{p}$

Finite Population		*Infinite Population*	
$\sigma_{\bar{p}} = \sqrt{\dfrac{N-n}{N-1}}\sqrt{\dfrac{p(1-p)}{n}}$		$\sigma_{\bar{p}} = \sqrt{\dfrac{p(1-p)}{n}}$	(6.5)

Comparing the two formulas in equation (6.5), we see that the only difference is the use of the finite population correction factor $\sqrt{(N-n)/(N-1)}$.

As was the case with the sample mean $\bar{x}$, the difference between the expressions for the finite population and the infinite population becomes negligible if the size of the finite population is large in comparison to the sample size. We follow the same rule of thumb that we recommended for the sample mean. That is, if the population is finite with $n/N \le 0.05$, we will use $\sigma_{\bar{p}} = \sqrt{p(1-p)/n}$. However, if the population is finite with $n/N > 0.05$, the finite population correction factor should be used. Again, unless specifically noted, throughout the text we will assume that the population size is large in relation to the sample size and thus the finite population correction factor is unnecessary.

Earlier in this section, we used the term *standard error of the mean* to refer to the standard deviation of $\bar{x}$. We stated that in general the term *standard error* refers to the standard deviation of a point estimator. Thus, for proportions we use *standard error of the proportion* to refer to the standard deviation of $\bar{p}$. From equation (6.5), we observe that the sample-to-sample variability in the point estimator $\bar{p}$, as measured by the standard error $\sigma_{\bar{p}}$, depends on the population proportion p. However, when we are sampling to compute $\bar{p}$, typically the population proportion is unknown. Therefore, we need to estimate the standard deviation of $\bar{p}$ with $s_{\bar{p}}$ using the sample proportion as shown in equation (6.6).

ESTIMATED STANDARD DEVIATION OF $\bar{p}$

Finite Population	Infinite Population

$$s_{\bar{p}} = \sqrt{\frac{N-n}{N-1}}\sqrt{\frac{\bar{p}(1-\bar{p})}{n}} \qquad\qquad s_{\bar{p}} = \sqrt{\frac{\bar{p}(1-\bar{p})}{n}}$$

(6.6)

Let us now return to the EAI example and compute the estimated standard error (standard deviation) of the mean associated with simple random samples of 30 EAI employees. Recall from Table 6.2 that the sample proportion of EAI employees who completed the management training program is $\bar{p} = 0.63$. Because $n/N = 30/2,500 = 0.012 < 0.05$, we can ignore the finite population correction factor and compute the estimated standard error as:

$$s_{\bar{p}} = \sqrt{\frac{\bar{p}(1-\bar{p})}{n}} = \sqrt{\frac{0.63(1-0.63)}{30}} = 0.0881.$$

In the EAI example, we actually know that the population proportion is $\bar{p} = 0.6$, so we know that the true standard error is:

$$\sigma_{\bar{p}} = \sqrt{\frac{\bar{p}(1-\bar{p})}{n}} = \sqrt{\frac{0.6(1-0.6)}{30}} = 0.0894.$$

The difference between $s_{\bar{p}}$ and $\sigma_{\bar{p}}$ is due to sampling error.

Form of the sampling distribution of $\bar{p}$ Now that we know the mean and standard deviation of the sampling distribution of $\bar{p}$, the final step is to determine the form or shape of the sampling distribution. The sample proportion is $\bar{p} = x/n$. For a simple random sample from a large population, x is a binomial random variable indicating the number of elements in the sample with the characteristic of interest. Because n is a constant, the probability of x/n is the same as the binomial probability of x, which means that the sampling distribution of $\bar{p}$ is also a discrete probability distribution and that the probability for each value of x/n is the same as the binomial probability of the corresponding value of x.

Statisticians have shown that a binomial distribution can be approximated by a normal distribution whenever the sample size is large enough to satisfy the following two conditions:

$$np \geq 5 \quad \text{and} \quad n(1-p) \geq 5.$$

Assuming that these two conditions are satisfied, the probability distribution of x in the sample proportion, $\bar{p} = x/n$, can be approximated by a normal distribution. And because n is a constant, the sampling distribution of $\bar{p}$ can also be approximated by a normal distribution. This approximation is stated as follows:

> The sampling distribution of $\bar{p}$ can be approximated by a normal distribution whenever $np \geq 5$ and $n(1-p) \geq 5$.

Because the population proportion p is typically unknown in a study, the test to see whether the sampling distribution of $\bar{p}$ can be approximated by a normal distribution is often based on the sample proportion, $n\bar{p} \geq 5$ and $n(1 - \bar{p}) \geq 5$.

In practical applications, when an estimate of a population proportion is desired, we find that sample sizes are almost always large enough to permit the use of a normal approximation for the sampling distribution of $\bar{p}$.

Recall that for the EAI sampling problem we know that a sample proportion of employees who participated in the training program is $p = 0.63$. With a simple random sample of size 30, we have $np = 30(0.63) = 18.9$ and $n(1-p) = 30(0.37) = 11.1$. Thus, the sampling distribution of $\bar{p}$ can be approximated by a normal distribution shown in Figure 6.7.

The sampling distribution in Figure 6.7 is a theoretical construct, as typically the population proportion is not known. Instead, we must estimate it with the sample proportion.

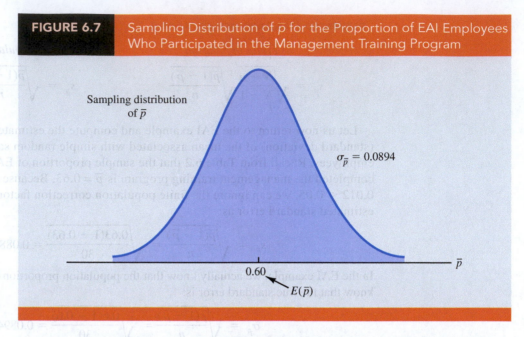

FIGURE 6.7 Sampling Distribution of $\bar{p}$ for the Proportion of EAI Employees Who Participated in the Management Training Program

Sampling distribution of $\bar{p}$

$\sigma_{\bar{p}} = 0.0894$

0.60

$E(\bar{p})$

$\bar{p}$

Relationship between sample size and the sampling distribution of $\bar{p}$ Suppose that in the EAI sampling problem we select a simple random sample of 100 EAI employees instead of the 30 originally considered. Intuitively, it would seem that because the larger sample size provides more data, the sample proportion based on $n = 100$ would provide a better estimate of the population proportion than the sample proportion based on $n = 30$. To see how much better, recall that the standard error of the proportion is 0.0894 when the sample size is $n = 30$. If we increase the sample size to $n = 100$, the standard error of the proportion becomes:

$$\sigma_{\bar{p}} = \sqrt{\frac{0.60(1 - 0.60)}{100}} = 0.0490.$$

As we observed with the standard deviation of the sampling distribution of $\bar{x}$, increasing the sample size decreases the sample-to-sample variability of the sample proportion. As a result, a larger sample size will provide a higher probability that the sample proportion falls within a specified distance of the population proportion. The practical reason we are interested in the sampling distribution of $\bar{p}$ is that it can be used to provide information about how close the sample proportion is to the population proportion. The concepts of interval estimation and hypothesis testing discussed in Sections 6.4 and 6.5 rely on the properties of sampling distributions.

6.4 Interval Estimation

In Section 6.2, we stated that a point estimator is a sample statistic used to estimate a population parameter. For instance, the sample mean $\bar{x}$ is a point estimator of the population mean μ and the sample proportion $\bar{p}$ is a point estimator of the population proportion p. Because a point estimator cannot be expected to provide the exact value of the population parameter, **interval estimation** is frequently used to generate an estimate of the value of a population parameter. In interval estimation, an **interval estimate** is often computed by adding and subtracting a value, called the **margin of error**, to the point estimate. The general form of an interval estimate is as follows:

Point estimate $\pm$ Margin of error.

The purpose of an interval estimate is to provide information about how close the point estimate, provided by the sample, is to the value of the population parameter.

In this section we show how to compute interval estimates of a population mean μ and a population proportion p. The general form of an interval estimate of a population mean is:

$$\bar{x} \pm \text{Margin of error.}$$

Similarly, the general form of an interval estimate of a population proportion is:

$$\bar{p} \pm \text{Margin of error.}$$

The sampling distributions of $\bar{x}$ and $\bar{p}$ play key roles in computing these interval estimates.

Interval Estimation of the Population Mean

In Section 6.3 we showed that the sampling distribution of $\bar{x}$ has a mean equal to the population mean ($E(\bar{x}) = \mu$) and a standard deviation equal to the population standard deviation divided by the square root of the sample size ($\sigma_{\bar{x}} = \sigma/\sqrt{n}$). We also showed that for a sufficiently large sample or for a sample taken from a normally distributed population, the sampling distribution of $\bar{x}$ follows a normal distribution. These results for samples of 30 EAI employees are illustrated in Figure 6.5. Because the sampling distribution of $\bar{x}$ shows how values of $\bar{x}$ are distributed around the population mean μ, the sampling distribution of $\bar{x}$ provides information about the possible differences between $\bar{x}$ and μ.

NORM.S.INV ($p + (1 - p)/2$) computes the number of standard deviations we must go in each direction from the population mean μ in order to include a specified proportion p of all values of a normally distributed variable.

For any normally distributed random variable, 90% of the values lie within 1.645 standard deviations of the mean, 95% of the values lie within 1.960 standard deviations of the mean, and 99% of the values lie within 2.576 standard deviations of the mean. Thus, when the sampling distribution of $\bar{x}$ is normal, 90% of all values of $\bar{x}$ must be within $\pm 1.645\sigma_{\bar{x}}$ of the mean μ, 95% of all values of $\bar{x}$ must be within $\pm 1.96\sigma_{\bar{x}}$ of the mean μ, and 99% of all values of $\bar{x}$ must be within $\pm 2.576\sigma_{\bar{x}}$ of the mean μ.

Figure 6.8 shows what we would expect for values of sample means for 10 independent random samples when the sampling distribution of $\bar{x}$ is normal. Because 90% of all values of $\bar{x}$ are within $\pm 1.645\sigma_{\bar{x}}$ of the mean μ, we expect 9 of the values of $\bar{x}$ for these 10 samples to be within $\pm 1.645\sigma_{\bar{x}}$ of the mean μ. If we repeat this process of collecting 10 samples, our results may not include 9 sample means with values that are within $1.645\sigma_{\bar{x}}$ of the mean μ, but on average, the values of $\bar{x}$ will be within $\pm 1.645\sigma_{\bar{x}}$ of the mean μ for 9 of every 10 samples.

We now want to use what we know about the sampling distribution of $\bar{x}$ to develop an interval estimate of the population mean μ. However, when developing an interval estimate of a population mean μ, we generally do not know the population standard deviation σ, and therefore, we do not know the standard error of $\bar{x}$, $\sigma_{\bar{x}} = \sigma/\sqrt{n}$. In this case, we must use the same sample data to estimate both μ and σ, so we use $s_{\bar{x}} = s/\sqrt{n}$ to estimate the standard error of $\bar{x}$. When we estimate $\sigma_{\bar{x}}$ with $s_{\bar{x}}$, we introduce an additional source of uncertainty about the distribution of values of $\bar{x}$. If the sampling distribution of $\bar{x}$ follows a normal distribution, we address this additional source of uncertainty by using a probability distribution known as the *t* **distribution**.

The standard normal distribution is a normal distribution with a mean of zero and a standard deviation of one. Chapter 5 contains a discussion of the normal distribution and its special case of the standard normal distribution.

The *t* distribution is a family of similar probability distributions; the shape of each specific *t* distribution depends on a parameter referred to as the **degrees of freedom**. The *t* distribution with 1 degree of freedom is unique, as is the *t* distribution with 2 degrees of freedom, the *t* distribution with 3 degrees of freedom, and so on. These *t* distributions are similar in shape to the **standard normal distribution** but are wider; this reflects the additional uncertainty that results from using $s_{\bar{x}}$ to estimate $\sigma_{\bar{x}}$. As the degrees of freedom increase, the difference between $s_{\bar{x}}$ and $\sigma_{\bar{x}}$ decreases and the *t* distribution narrows. Furthermore, because the area under any distribution curve is fixed at 1.0, a narrower *t* distribution will have a higher peak. Thus, as the degrees of freedom increase, the *t* distribution narrows, its peak becomes

FIGURE 6.8   Sampling Distribution of the Sample Mean

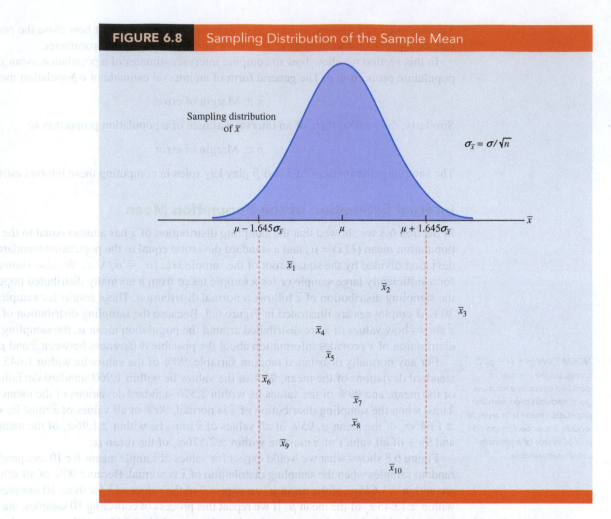

Sampling distribution of $\bar{x}$

$\sigma_{\bar{x}} = \sigma/\sqrt{n}$

$\mu - 1.645\sigma_{\bar{x}}$ μ $\mu + 1.645\sigma_{\bar{x}}$ $\bar{x}$

$\bar{x}_1$

$\bar{x}_2$

$\bar{x}_3$

$\bar{x}_4$

$\bar{x}_5$

$\bar{x}_6$

$\bar{x}_7$

$\bar{x}_8$

$\bar{x}_9$

$\bar{x}_{10}$

higher, and it becomes more similar to the standard normal distribution. We can see this in Figure 6.9, which shows *t* distributions with 10 and 20 degrees of freedom as well as the standard normal probability distribution. Note that as with the standard normal distribution, the mean of the *t* distribution is zero.

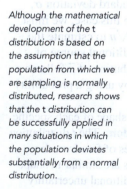

Although the mathematical development of the t distribution is based on the assumption that the population from which we are sampling is normally distributed, research shows that the t distribution can be successfully applied in many situations in which the population deviates substantially from a normal distribution.

FIGURE 6.9   Comparison of the Standard Normal Distribution with *t* Distributions with 10 and 20 Degrees of Freedom

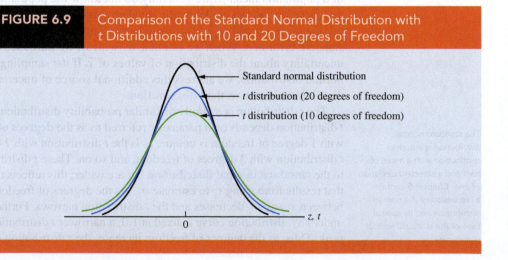

Standard normal distribution

t distribution (20 degrees of freedom)

t distribution (10 degrees of freedom)

0   *z, t*

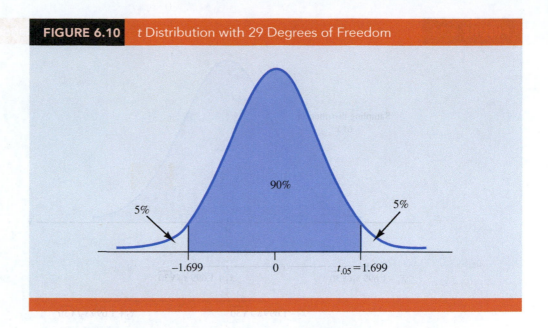

FIGURE 6.10   *t* Distribution with 29 Degrees of Freedom

To use the *t* distribution to compute the margin of error for the EAI example, we consider the *t* distribution with $n - 1 = 30 - 1 = 29$ degrees of freedom. Figure 6.10 shows that for a *t*-distributed random variable with 29 degrees of freedom, 90% of the values are within ± 1.699 standard deviations of the mean and 10% of the values are more than ± 1.699 standard deviations away from the mean. Thus, 5% of the values are more than 1.699 standard deviations below the mean and 5% of the values are more than 1.699 standard deviations above the mean. This leads us to use $t_{0.05}$ to denote the value of *t* for which the area in the upper tail of a *t* distribution is 0.05. For a *t* distribution with 29 degrees of freedom, $t_{0.05} = 1.699$.

To see how the difference between the t distribution and the standard normal distribution decreases as the degrees of freedom increase, use Excel's T.INV.2T function to compute $t_{0.05}$ for increasingly larger degrees of freedom (n − 1) and watch the value of $t_{0.05}$ approach 1.645.

We can use Excel's T.INV.2T function to find the value from a *t* distribution such that a given percentage of the distribution is included in the interval $\pm t$ for any degrees of freedom. For example, suppose again that we want to find the value of *t* from the *t* distribution with 29 degrees of freedom such that 90% of the *t* distribution is included in the interval $-t$ to $+t$. Excel's T.INV.2T function has two inputs: (1) $1 -$ the proportion of the *t* distribution that will fall between $-t$ and $+t$, and (2) the degrees of freedom (which in this case is equal to the sample size $- 1$). For our example, we would enter the formula =T.INV.2T(1 − 0.90, 30 − 1), which computes the value of 1.699. This confirms the data shown in Figure 6.10; for the *t* distribution with 29 degrees of freedom, $t_{0.05} = 1.699$ and 90% of all values for the *t* distribution with 29 degrees of freedom will lie between -1.699 and 1.699.

At the beginning of this section, we stated that the general form of an interval estimate of the population mean μ is $\bar{x} \pm$ margin of error. To provide an interpretation for this interval estimate, let us consider the values of $\bar{x}$ that might be obtained if we took 10 independent simple random samples of 30 EAI employees. The first sample might have the mean $\bar{x}_1$ and standard deviation s_1. Figure 6.11 shows that the interval formed by subtracting $1.699 s_1 / \sqrt{30}$ from $\bar{x}_1$ and adding $1.699 s_1 / \sqrt{30}$ to $\bar{x}_1$ includes the population mean μ. Now consider what happens if the second sample has the mean $\bar{x}_2$ and standard deviation s_2. Although this sample mean differs from the first sample mean, we see in Figure 6.11 that the interval formed by subtracting $1.699 s_2 / \sqrt{30}$ from $\bar{x}_2$ and adding $1.699 s_2 / \sqrt{30}$ to $\bar{x}_2$ also includes the population mean μ. However, consider the third sample, which has the mean $\bar{x}_3$ and standard deviation s_3. As we see in Figure 6.11, the interval formed by subtracting $1.699 s_3 / \sqrt{30}$ from $\bar{x}_3$ and adding $1.699 s_3 / \sqrt{30}$ to $\bar{x}_3$ does

FIGURE 6.11   Intervals Formed Around Sample Means from 10 Independent Random Samples

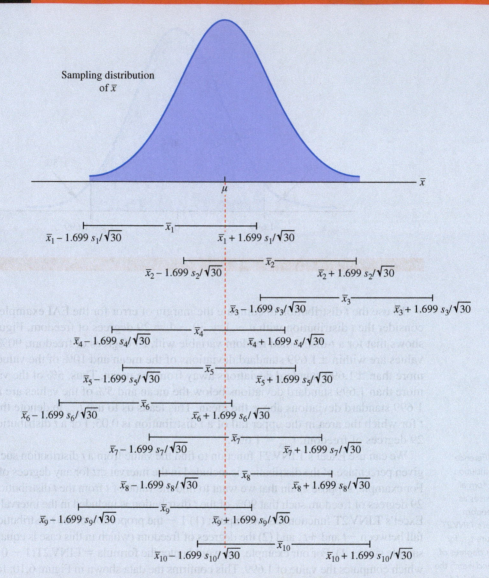

not include the population mean μ. Because we are using $t_{0.05} = 1.699$ to form this interval, we expect that 90% of the intervals for our samples will include the population mean μ, and we see in Figure 6.11 that the results for our 10 samples of 30 EAI employees are what we would expect; the intervals for 9 of the 10 samples of $n = 30$ observations in this example include the mean μ. However, it is important to note that if we repeat this process of collecting 10 samples of $n = 30$ EAI employees, we may find that fewer than 9 of the resulting intervals $\bar{x} \pm 1.699 s_{\bar{x}}$ include the mean μ or all 10 of the resulting intervals $\bar{x} \pm 1.699 s_{\bar{x}}$ include the mean μ. But on average, the resulting intervals $\bar{x} \pm 1.699 s_{\bar{x}}$ for 9 of 10 samples of $n = 30$ observations will include the mean μ.

Now recall that the sample of $n = 30$ EAI employees from Section 6.2 had a sample mean of salary of $\bar{x} = \$51,814$ and sample standard deviation of $s = \$3,340$. Using

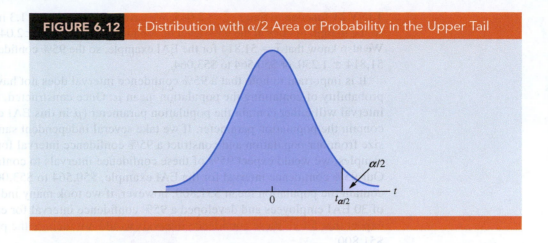

FIGURE 6.12 *t* Distribution with α/2 Area or Probability in the Upper Tail

$\bar{x} \pm 1.699(3340/\sqrt{30})$ to construct the interval estimate, we obtain $51,814 \pm 1,036$. Thus, the specific interval estimate of μ based on this specific sample is \$50,778 to \$52,850. Because approximately 90% of all the intervals constructed using $\bar{x} \pm 1.699(s/\sqrt{30})$ will contain the population mean, we say that we are approximately 90% confident that the interval \$50,778 to \$52,850 includes the population mean μ. We also say that this interval has been established at the 90% **confidence level**. The value of 0.90 is referred to as the **confidence coefficient**, and the interval \$50,564 to \$53,064 is called the 90% **confidence interval**.

Another term sometimes associated with an interval estimate is the **level of significance**. The level of significance associated with an interval estimate is denoted by the Greek letter α. The level of significance and the confidence coefficient are related as follows:

$$\alpha = \text{level of significance} = 1 - \text{confidence coefficient.}$$

The level of significance is the probability that the interval estimation procedure will generate an interval that does not contain μ (such as the third sample in Figure 6.11). For example, the level of significance corresponding to a 0.90 confidence coefficient is $\alpha = 1 - 0.90 = 0.10$.

In general, we use the notation $t_{\alpha/2}$ to represent the value such that there is an area of $\alpha/2$ in the upper tail of the *t* distribution (see Figure 6.12). If the sampling distribution of $\bar{x}$ is normal, the margin of error for an interval estimate of a population mean μ is

$$t_{\alpha/2}s_{\bar{x}} = t_{\alpha/2}\frac{s}{\sqrt{n}}.$$

So if the sampling distribution of $\bar{x}$ is normal, we find the interval estimate of the mean μ by subtracting this margin of error from the sample mean $\bar{x}$ and adding this margin of error to the sample mean $\bar{x}$. Using the notation we have developed, equation (6.7) can be used to find the confidence interval or interval estimate of the population mean μ.

Observe that the margin of error, $t_{\alpha/2}$ (s/√n), varies from sample to sample. This variation occurs because the sample standard deviation s varies depending on the sample selected. A large value for s results in a larger margin of error, while a small value for s results in a smaller margin of error.

INTERVAL ESTIMATE OF A POPULATION MEAN

$$\bar{x} \pm t_{\alpha/2}\frac{s}{\sqrt{n}}, \tag{6.7}$$

where s is the sample standard deviation, $(1 - \alpha)$ is the confidence coefficient, and $t_{\alpha/2}$ is the *t* value providing an area of $\alpha/2$ in the upper tail of the *t* distribution with $n - 1$ degrees of freedom.

If we want to find a 95% confidence interval for the mean μ in the EAI example, we again recognize that the degrees of freedom are $30 - 1 = 29$ and then use Excel's

T.INV.2T function to find $t_{0.025} = 2.045$. We have seen that $s_{\bar{x}} = 611.3$ in the EAI example, so the margin of error at the 95% level of confidence is $t_{0.025} s_{\bar{x}} = \pm 2.045 \,(611.3) = 1{,}250$. We also know that $\bar{x} = 51{,}814$ for the EAI example, so the 95% confidence interval is $51{,}814 \pm 1{,}250$, or \$50,564 to \$53,064.

It is important to note that a 95% confidence interval does not have a 95% probability of containing the population mean μ. Once constructed, a confidence interval will either contain the population parameter (μ in this EAI example) or not contain the population parameter. If we take several independent samples of the same size from our population and construct a 95% confidence interval for each of these samples, we would expect 95% of these confidence intervals to contain the mean μ. Our 95% confidence interval for the EAI example, \$50,564 to \$53,064, does indeed contain the population mean \$51,800; however, if we took many independent samples of 30 EAI employees and developed a 95% confidence interval for each, we would expect that 5% of these confidence intervals would not include the population mean \$51,800.

To further illustrate the interval estimation procedure, we will consider a study designed to estimate the mean credit card debt for the population of U.S. households. A sample of $n = 70$ households provided the credit card balances shown in Table 6.5. For this situation, no previous estimate of the population standard deviation σ is available. Thus, the sample data must be used to estimate both the population mean and the population standard deviation. Using the data in Table 6.5, we compute the sample mean $\bar{x} = \$9{,}312$ and the sample standard deviation $s = \$4{,}007$.

We can use Excel's T.INV.2T function to compute the value of $t_{\alpha/2}$ to use in finding this confidence interval. With a 95% confidence level and $n - 1 = 69$ degrees of freedom, we have that T.INV.2T$(1 - 0.95, 69) = 1.995$, so $t_{\alpha/2} = t_{(1 - 0.95)/2} = t_{.025} = 1.995$ for this confidence interval.

We use equation (6.7) to compute an interval estimate of the population mean credit card balance.

$$9{,}312 \pm 1.995 \frac{4{,}007}{\sqrt{70}}$$

$$9{,}312 \pm 995$$

The point estimate of the population mean is \$9,312, the margin of error is \$955, and the 95% confidence interval is $9{,}312 - 955 = \$8{,}357$ to $9{,}312 + 955 = \$10{,}267$. Thus, we

TABLE 6.5	Credit Card Balances for a Sample of 70 Households				
9,430	14,661	7,159	9,071	9,691	11,032
7,535	12,195	8,137	3,603	11,448	6,525
4,078	10,544	9,467	16,804	8,279	5,239
5,604	13,659	12,595	13,479	5,649	6,195
5,179	7,061	7,917	14,044	11,298	12,584
4,416	6,245	11,346	6,817	4,353	15,415
10,676	13,021	12,806	6,845	3,467	15,917
1,627	9,719	4,972	10,493	6,191	12,591
10,112	2,200	11,356	615	12,851	9,743
6,567	10,746	7,117	13,627	5,337	10,324
13,627	12,744	9,465	12,557	8,372	
18,719	5,742	19,263	6,232	7,445	

DATA *file*

NewBalance

FIGURE 6.13   95% Confidence Interval for Credit Card Balances

▲	A	B	C	D	E
1	NewBalance		*NewBalance*		
2	9430				
3	7535		Mean	9312	
4	4078		Standard Error	478.9281	
5	5604		Median	9466	
6	5179		Mode	13627	
7	4416		Standard Deviation	4007	
8	10676		Sample Variance	16056048	
9	1627		Kurtosis	−0.2960	
10	10112		Skewness	0.1879	
11	6567		Range	18648	
12	13627		Minimum	615	
13	18719		Maximum	19263	
14	14661		Sum	651840	
15	12195		Count	70	
16	10544		Confidence Level(95.0%)	955	
17	13659				
18	7061		Point Estimate	=D3	
19	6245		Lower Limit	=D18−D16	
20	13021		Upper Limit	=D3+D16	
70	9743				
71	10324				
72					

▲	A	B	C	D	E	F
1	NewBalance		*NewBalance*			
2	9430				Point Estimate	
3	7535		Mean	9312		
4	4078		Standard Error	478.9281		
5	5604		Median	9466		
6	5179		Mode	13627		
7	4416		Standard Deviation	4007		
8	10676		Sample Variance	16056048		
9	1627		Kurtosis	−0.2960		
10	10112		Skewness	0.1879		
11	6567		Range	18648		
12	13627		Minimum	615		
13	18719		Maximum	19263		
14	14661		Sum	651840		
15	12195		Count	70		Margin of Error
16	10544		Confidence Level(95.0%)	955		
17	13659					
18	7061		Point Estimate	9312		
19	6245		Lower Limit	8357		
20	13021		Upper Limit	10267		
70	9743					
71	10324					
72						

are 95% confident that the mean credit card balance for the population of all households is between $8,357 and $10,267.

Using Excel   We will use the credit card balances in Table 6.5 to illustrate how Excel can be used to construct an interval estimate of the population mean. We start by summarizing the data using Excel's Descriptive Statistics tool described in Chapter 2. Refer to Figure 6.13 as we describe the tasks involved. The formula worksheet is in the background; the value worksheet is in the foreground.

If you can't find Data Analysis on the Data tab, you may need to install the Analysis Toolpak add-in (which is included with Excel).

Step 1.   Click the **Data** tab on the Ribbon
Step 2.   In the **Analysis** group, click **Data Analysis**
Step 3.   When the **Data Analysis** dialog box appears, choose **Descriptive Statistics** from the list of Analysis Tools
Step 4.   When the Descriptive Statistics dialog box appears:
   Enter A1:A71 in the **Input Range** box
   Select **Grouped By Columns**

Select **Labels in First Row**
Select **Output Range:**
 Enter C1 in the **Output Range** box
Select **Summary Statistics**
Select **Confidence Level for Mean**
 Enter 95 in the **Confidence Level for Mean** box
Click **OK**

The margin of error using the t distribution can also be computed with the Excel function CONFIDENCE.T(alpha, s, n), where alpha is the level of significance, s is the sample standard deviation, and n is the sample size.

The sample mean ($\bar{x}$) is in cell D3. The margin of error, labeled "Confidence Level(95%)," appears in cell D16. The value worksheet shows $\bar{x} = 9{,}312$ and a margin of error equal to 955.

Cells D18:D20 provide the point estimate and the lower and upper limits for the confidence interval. Because the point estimate is just the sample mean, the formula =D3 is entered into cell D18. To compute the lower limit of the 95% confidence interval, $\bar{x} -$ (margin of error), we enter the formula =D18-D16 into cell D19. To compute the upper limit of the 95% confidence interval, $\bar{x} +$ (margin of error), we enter the formula =D18+D16 into cell D20. The value worksheet shows a lower limit of 8,357 and an upper limit of 10,267. In other words, the 95% confidence interval for the population mean is from 8,357 to 10,267.

Interval Estimation of the Population Proportion

In the introduction to this chapter we said that the general form of an interval estimate of a population proportion p is:

$$\bar{p} \pm \text{Margin of error.}$$

The sampling distribution of $\bar{p}$ plays a key role in computing the margin of error for this interval estimate.

In Section 6.3 we said that the sampling distribution of $\bar{p}$ can be approximated by a normal distribution whenever $np \geq 5$ and $n(1 - p) \geq 5$. Figure 6.14 shows the normal

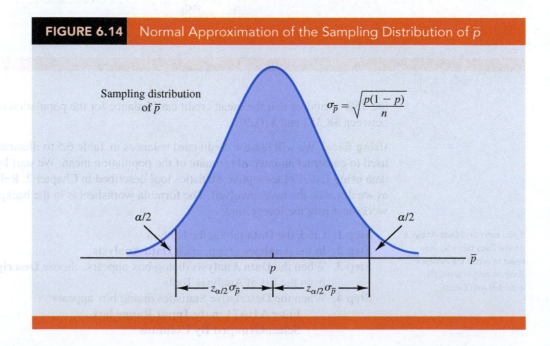

FIGURE 6.14   Normal Approximation of the Sampling Distribution of $\bar{p}$

Sampling distribution of $\bar{p}$

$$\sigma_{\bar{p}} = \sqrt{\frac{p(1 - p)}{n}}$$

$\alpha/2$

$\alpha/2$

p

$\bar{p}$

$z_{\alpha/2}\sigma_{\bar{p}}$ $z_{\alpha/2}\sigma_{\bar{p}}$

approximation of the sampling distribution of $\bar{p}$. The mean of the sampling distribution of $\bar{p}$ is the population proportion p, and the standard error of $\bar{p}$ is:

$$\sigma_{\bar{p}} = \sqrt{\frac{p(1-p)}{n}}. \tag{6.8}$$

The notation $z_{\alpha/2}$ represents the value such that there is an area of $\alpha/2$ in the upper tail of the standard normal distribution (a normal distribution with a mean of zero and standard deviation of one).

Because the sampling distribution of $\bar{p}$ is normally distributed, if we choose $z_{\alpha/2}\sigma_{\bar{p}}$ as the margin of error in an interval estimate of a population proportion, we know that $100(1 - \alpha)\%$ of the intervals generated will contain the true population proportion. But $\sigma_{\bar{p}}$ cannot be used directly in the computation of the margin of error because p will not be known; p is what we are trying to estimate. So we estimate $\sigma_{\bar{p}}$ with $s_{\bar{p}}$ and then the margin of error for an interval estimate of a population proportion is given by:

$$\text{Margin of error} = z_{\alpha/2}s_{\bar{p}} = z_{\alpha/2}\sqrt{\frac{\bar{p}(1-\bar{p})}{n}}. \tag{6.9}$$

With this margin of error, the general expression for an interval estimate of a population proportion is as follows.

INTERVAL ESTIMATE OF A POPULATION PROPORTION

$$\bar{p} \pm z_{\alpha/2}\sqrt{\frac{\bar{p}(1-\bar{p})}{n}}, \tag{6.10}$$

where $1 - \alpha$ is the confidence coefficient and $z_{\alpha/2}$ is the z value providing an area of $\alpha/2$ in the upper tail of the standard normal distribution.

DATA *file*

TeeTimes

The following example illustrates the computation of the margin of error and interval estimate for a population proportion. A national survey of 900 women golfers was conducted to learn how women golfers view their treatment at golf courses in the United States. The survey found that 396 of the women golfers were satisfied with the availability of tee times. Thus, the point estimate of the proportion of the population of women golfers who are satisfied with the availability of tee times is 396/900 = 0.44. Using equation (6.10) and a 95% confidence level:

The Excel formula
=NORM.S.INV(1 − α/2) computes the value of $z_{\alpha/2}$. For example, for α = 0.05, $z_{0.025}$ =NORM.S.INV(1 − .05/2) = 1.96.

$$\bar{p} \pm z_{\alpha/2}\sqrt{\frac{\bar{p}(1-\bar{p})}{n}}$$

$$0.44 \pm 1.96\sqrt{\frac{0.44(1-0.44)}{900}}$$

$$0.44 \pm 0.0324$$

Thus, the margin of error is 0.0324 and the 95% confidence interval estimate of the population proportion is 0.4076 to 0.4724. Using percentages, the survey results enable us to state with 95% confidence that between 40.76% and 47.24% of all women golfers are satisfied with the availability of tee times.

Using Excel Excel can be used to construct an interval estimate of the population proportion of women golfers who are satisfied with the availability of tee times. The responses in the survey were recorded as a Yes or No in the file named *TeeTimes* for each woman surveyed. Refer to Figure 6.15 as we describe the tasks involved in constructing a 95% confidence interval. The formula worksheet is in the background; the value worksheet appears in the foreground.

FIGURE 6.15 95% Confidence Interval for Survey of Women Golfers

	A	B	C	D	E
1	Response		Interval Estimate of a Population Proportion		
2	Yes				
3	No		Sample Size	=COUNTA(A2:A901)	
4	Yes		Response of Interest	Yes	
5	Yes		Count for Response	=COUNTIF(A2:A901,D4)	
6	No		Sample Proportion	=D5/D3	
7	No				
8	No		Confidence Coefficient	0.95	
9	Yes		Level of Significance (alpha)	=1−D8	
10	Yes		z Value	=NORM.S.INV(1−D9/2)	
11	Yes				
12	No		Standard Error	=SQRT(D6*(1−D6)/D3)	
13	No		Margin of Error	=D10*D12	
14	Yes				
15	No		Point Estimate	=D6	
16	No		Lower Limit	=D15−D13	
17	Yes		Upper Limit	=D15+D13	
18	No				
900	Yes				
901	Yes				
902					

	A	B	C	D	E	F	G
1	Response		Interval Estimate of a Population Proportion				
2	Yes						
3	No		Sample Size	900		Enter Yes as the	
4	Yes		Response of Interest	Yes		Response of Interest	
5	Yes		Count for Response	396			
6	No		Sample Proportion	0.44			
7	No						
8	No		Confidence Coefficient	0.95			
9	Yes		Level of Significance	0.05			
10	Yes		z Value	1.96			
11	Yes						
12	No		Standard Error	0.0165			
13	No		Margin of Error	0.0324			
14	Yes						
15	No		Point Estimate	0.44			
16	No		Lower Limit	0.4076			
17	Yes		Upper Limit	0.4724			
18	No						
900	Yes						
901	Yes						
902							

The file TeeTimes displayed in Figure 6.15 can be used as a template for developing confidence intervals about a population proportion p by entering new problem data in column A and appropriately adjusting the formulas in column D.

The descriptive statistics we need and the response of interest are provided in cells D3:D6. Because Excel's COUNT function works only with numerical data, we used the COUNTA function in cell D3 to compute the sample size. The response for which we want to develop an interval estimate, Yes or No, is entered into cell D4. Figure 6.15 shows that Yes has been entered into cell D4, indicating that we want to develop an interval estimate of the population proportion of women golfers who are satisfied with the availability of tee times. If we had wanted to develop an interval estimate of the population proportion of women golfers who are not satisfied with the availability of tee times, we would have entered No in cell D4. With Yes entered in cell D4, the COUNTIF function in cell D5 counts the number of Yes responses in the sample. The sample proportion is then computed in cell D6 by dividing the number of Yes responses in cell D5 by the sample size in cell D3.

Cells D8:D10 are used to compute the appropriate z value. The confidence coefficient (0.95) is entered into cell D8 and the level of significance (α) is computed in cell D9 by entering the formula =1-D8. The z value corresponding to an upper-tail area of $\alpha/2$ is computed by entering the formula =NORM.S.INV(1-D9/2) into cell D10. The value worksheet shows that $z_{0.025} = 1.96$.

Cells D12:D13 provide the estimate of the standard error and the margin of error. In cell D12, we entered the formula =SQRT(D6*(1-D6)/D3) to compute the standard error using the sample proportion and the sample size as inputs. The formula =D10*D12 is entered into cell D13 to compute the margin of error corresponding to equation (6.9).

Cells D15:D17 provide the point estimate and the lower and upper limits for a confidence interval. The point estimate in cell D15 is the sample proportion. The lower and upper limits in cells D16 and D17 are obtained by subtracting and adding the margin of error to the point estimate. We note that the 95% confidence interval for the proportion of women golfers who are satisfied with the availability of tee times is 0.4076 to 0.4724.

NOTES + COMMENTS

1. The reason the number of degrees of freedom associated with the t value in equation (6.7) is $n - 1$ concerns the use of s as an estimate of the population standard deviation σ. The expression for the sample standard deviation is

$$s = \sqrt{\frac{\Sigma(x_i - \bar{x})^2}{n - 1}}.$$

Degrees of freedom refer to the number of independent pieces of information that go into the computation of $\Sigma(x_i - \bar{x})^2$. The n pieces of information involved in computing $\Sigma(x_i - \bar{x})^2$ are as follows: $x_1 - \bar{x}, x_2 - \bar{x}, \ldots, x_n - \bar{x}$. Note that $\Sigma(x_i - \bar{x}) = 0$ for any data set. Thus, only $n - 1$ of the $x_i - \bar{x}$ values are independent; that is, if we know $n - 1$ of the values, the remaining value can be determined exactly by using the condition that the sum of the $x_i - \bar{x}$ values must be 0. Thus, $n - 1$ is the number of degrees of freedom associated with $\Sigma(x_i - \bar{x})^2$ and hence the number of degrees of freedom for the t distribution in equation (6.5).

2. In most applications, a sample size of $n \geq 30$ is adequate when using equation (6.7) to develop an interval estimate of a population mean. However, if the population distribution is highly skewed or contains outliers, most statisticians would recommend increasing the sample size to 50 or more. If the population is not normally distributed but is roughly symmetric, sample sizes as small as 15 can be expected to provide good approximate confidence intervals. With smaller sample sizes, equation (6.7) should be used if the analyst believes, or is willing to assume, that the population distribution is at least approximately normal.

3. What happens to confidence interval estimates of $\bar{x}$ when the population is skewed? Consider a population that is skewed to the right, with large data values stretching the distribution to the right. When such skewness exists, the sample mean x and the sample standard deviation s are positively correlated. Larger values of s tend to be associated with larger values of $\bar{x}$. Thus, when $\bar{x}$ is larger than the population mean, s tends to be larger than σ. This

skewness causes the margin of error, $t_{\alpha/2}(s/\sqrt{n})$, to be larger than it would be with σ known. The confidence interval with the larger margin of error tends to include the population mean more often than it would if the true value of σ were used. But when $\bar{x}$ is smaller than the population mean, the correlation between $\bar{x}$ and s causes the margin of error to be small. In this case, the confidence interval with the smaller margin of error tends to miss the population mean more than it would if we knew σ and used it. For this reason, we recommend using larger sample sizes with highly skewed population distributions.

4. We can find the sample size necessary to provide the desired margin of error at the chosen confidence level. Let E = the desired margin of error. Then:
   - the sample size for an interval estimate of a population mean is $n = \dfrac{(z_{\alpha/2})^2 \sigma^2}{E^2}$, where E is the margin of error that the user is willing to accept, and the value of $z_{\alpha/2}$ follows directly from the confidence level to be used in developing the interval estimate.
   - the sample size for an interval estimate of a population proportion is $n = \dfrac{(z_{\alpha/2})^2 p^*(1 - p^*)}{E^2}$, where the planning value p^* can be chosen by use of: (i) the sample proportion from a previous sample of the same or similar units, (ii) a pilot study to select a preliminary sample, (iii) judgment or a "best guess" for the value of p^*, or (iv) if none of the preceding alternatives apply, use of the planning value of $p^* = 0.50$.

5. The desired margin of error for estimating a population proportion is almost always 0.10 or less. In national public opinion polls conducted by organizations such as Gallup and Harris, a 0.03 or 0.04 margin of error is common. With such margins of error, the sample found with $n = \dfrac{(z_{\alpha/2})^2 p^*(1 - p^*)}{E^2}$ will almost always provide a size that is sufficient to satisfy the requirements of $np \geq 5$ and $n(1 - p) \geq 5$ for using a normal distribution as an approximation for the sampling distribution of p.

6.5 Hypothesis Tests

Throughout this chapter we have shown how a sample could be used to develop point and interval estimates of population parameters such as the mean μ and the proportion p. In this section we continue the discussion of statistical inference by showing how hypothesis testing can be used to determine whether a statement about the value of a population parameter should or should not be rejected.

In hypothesis testing we begin by making a tentative conjecture about a population parameter. This tentative conjecture is called the **null hypothesis** and is denoted by H_0.

We then define another hypothesis, called the **alternative hypothesis**, which is the opposite of what is stated in the null hypothesis. The alternative hypothesis is denoted by H_a. The hypothesis testing procedure uses data from a sample to test the validity of the two competing statements about a population that are indicated by H_0 and H_a.

This section shows how hypothesis tests can be conducted about a population mean and a population proportion. We begin by providing examples that illustrate approaches to developing null and alternative hypotheses.

Developing Null and Alternative Hypotheses

It is not always obvious how the null and alternative hypotheses should be formulated. Care must be taken to structure the hypotheses appropriately so that the hypothesis testing conclusion provides the information the researcher or decision maker wants. The context of the situation is very important in determining how the hypotheses should be stated. All hypothesis testing applications involve collecting a random sample and using the sample results to provide evidence for drawing a conclusion. Good questions to consider when formulating the null and alternative hypotheses are, What is the purpose of collecting the sample? What conclusions are we hoping to make?

Learning to formulate hypotheses correctly will take some practice. Expect some initial confusion about the proper choice of the null and alternative hypotheses. The examples in this section are intended to provide guidelines.

In the introduction to this section, we stated that the null hypothesis H_0 is a tentative conjecture about a population parameter such as a population mean or a population proportion. The alternative hypothesis H_a is a statement that is the opposite of what is stated in the null hypothesis. In some situations it is easier to identify the alternative hypothesis first and then develop the null hypothesis. In other situations it is easier to identify the null hypothesis first and then develop the alternative hypothesis. We will illustrate these situations in the following examples.

The alternative hypothesis as a research hypothesis   Many applications of hypothesis testing involve an attempt to gather evidence in support of a research hypothesis. In these situations, it is often best to begin with the alternative hypothesis and make it the conclusion that the researcher hopes to support. Consider a particular automobile that currently attains a fuel efficiency of 24 miles per gallon for city driving. A product research group has developed a new fuel injection system designed to increase the miles-per-gallon rating. The group will run controlled tests with the new fuel injection system looking for statistical support for the conclusion that the new fuel injection system provides more miles per gallon than the current system.

Several new fuel injection units will be manufactured, installed in test automobiles, and subjected to research-controlled driving conditions. The sample mean miles per gallon for these automobiles will be computed and used in a hypothesis test to determine whether it can be concluded that the new system provides more than 24 miles per gallon. In terms of the population mean miles per gallon μ, the research hypothesis $\mu > 24$ becomes the alternative hypothesis. Since the current system provides an average or mean of 24 miles per gallon, we will make the tentative conjecture that the new system is no better than the current system and choose $\mu \leq 24$ as the null hypothesis. The null and alternative hypotheses are:

$$H_0: \mu \leq 24$$
$$H_a: \mu > 24$$

The conclusion that the research hypothesis is true is made if the sample data provide sufficient evidence to show that the null hypothesis can be rejected.

If the sample results lead to the conclusion to reject H_0, the inference can be made that $H_a: \mu > 24$ is true. The researchers have the statistical support to state that the new fuel injection system increases the mean number of miles per gallon. The production of automobiles with the new fuel injection system should be considered. However, if the sample results lead to the conclusion that H_0 cannot be rejected, the researchers cannot conclude that the new fuel injection system is better than the current system. Production of automobiles with the new fuel injection system on the basis of better gas mileage cannot be justified. Perhaps more research and further testing can be conducted.

Successful companies stay competitive by developing new products, new methods, new systems, and the like that are better than what is currently available. Before adopting something new, it is desirable to conduct research to determine whether there is statistical support for the conclusion that the new approach is indeed better. In such cases, the research hypothesis is stated as the alternative hypothesis. For example, a new teaching method is developed that is believed to be better than the current method. The alternative hypothesis is that the new method is better; the null hypothesis is that the new method is no better than the old method. A new sales force bonus plan is developed in an attempt to increase sales. The alternative hypothesis is that the new bonus plan increases sales; the null hypothesis is that the new bonus plan does not increase sales. A new drug is developed with the goal of lowering blood pressure more than an existing drug. The alternative hypothesis is that the new drug lowers blood pressure more than the existing drug; the null hypothesis is that the new drug does not provide lower blood pressure than the existing drug. In each case, rejection of the null hypothesis H_0 provides statistical support for the research hypothesis. We will see many examples of hypothesis tests in research situations such as these throughout this chapter and in the remainder of the text.

The null hypothesis as a conjecture to be challenged   Of course, not all hypothesis tests involve research hypotheses. In the following discussion we consider applications of hypothesis testing where we begin with a belief or a conjecture that a statement about the value of a population parameter is true. We will then use a hypothesis test to challenge the conjecture and determine whether there is statistical evidence to conclude that the conjecture is incorrect. In these situations, it is helpful to develop the null hypothesis first. The null hypothesis H_0 expresses the belief or conjecture about the value of the population parameter. The alternative hypothesis H_a is that the belief or conjecture is incorrect.

As an example, consider the situation of a manufacturer of soft drink products. The label on a soft drink bottle states that it contains 67.6 fluid ounces. We consider the label correct provided the population mean filling weight for the bottles is *at least* 67.6 fluid ounces. With no reason to believe otherwise, we would give the manufacturer the benefit of the doubt and assume that the statement provided on the label is correct. Thus, in a hypothesis test about the population mean fluid weight per bottle, we would begin with the conjecture that the label is correct and state the null hypothesis as $\mu \geq 67.6$. The challenge to this conjecture would imply that the label is incorrect and the bottles are being underfilled. This challenge would be stated as the alternative hypothesis $\mu < 67.6$. Thus, the null and alternative hypotheses are:

$$H_0: \mu \geq 67.6$$
$$H_a: \mu < 67.6$$

A manufacturer's product information is usually assumed to be true and stated as the null hypothesis. The conclusion that the information is incorrect can be made if the null hypothesis is rejected.

A government agency with the responsibility for validating manufacturing labels could select a sample of soft drink bottles, compute the sample mean filling weight, and use the sample results to test the preceding hypotheses. If the sample results lead to the conclusion to reject H_0, the inference that $H_a: \mu < 67.6$ is true can be made. With this statistical support, the agency is justified in concluding that the label is incorrect and that the bottles are being underfilled. Appropriate action to force the manufacturer to comply with labeling standards would be considered. However, if the sample results indicate H_0 cannot be rejected, the conjecture that the manufacturer's labeling is correct cannot be rejected. With this conclusion, no action would be taken.

Let us now consider a variation of the soft drink bottle-filling example by viewing the same situation from the manufacturer's point of view. The bottle-filling operation has been designed to fill soft drink bottles with 67.6 fluid ounces as stated on the label. The company does not want to underfill the containers because that could result in complaints from customers or, perhaps, a government agency. However, the company does not want to overfill containers either because putting more soft drink than necessary into the containers would be an unnecessary cost. The company's goal would be to adjust the bottle-filling operation so that the population mean filling weight per bottle is 67.6 fluid ounces as specified on the label.

Although this is the company's goal, from time to time any production process can get out of adjustment. If this occurs in our example, underfilling or overfilling of the soft drink bottles will occur. In either case, the company would like to know about it in order to correct the situation by readjusting the bottle-filling operation to result in the designated 67.6 fluid ounces. In this hypothesis testing application, we would begin with the conjecture that the production process is operating correctly and state the null hypothesis as $\mu = 67.6$ fluid ounces. The alternative hypothesis that challenges this conjecture is that $\mu \neq 67.6$, which indicates that either overfilling or underfilling is occurring. The null and alternative hypotheses for the manufacturer's hypothesis test are:

$$H_0: \mu = 67.6$$
$$H_a: \mu \neq 67.6$$

Suppose that the soft drink manufacturer uses a quality-control procedure to periodically select a sample of bottles from the filling operation and computes the sample mean filling weight per bottle. If the sample results lead to the conclusion to reject H_0, the inference is made that $H_a: \mu \neq 67.6$ is true. We conclude that the bottles are not being filled properly and the production process should be adjusted to restore the population mean to 67.6 fluid ounces per bottle. However, if the sample results indicate H_0 cannot be rejected, the conjecture that the manufacturer's bottle-filling operation is functioning properly cannot be rejected. In this case, no further action would be taken and the production operation would continue to run.

The two preceding forms of the soft drink manufacturing hypothesis test show that the null and alternative hypotheses may vary depending on the point of view of the researcher or decision maker. To formulate hypotheses correctly, it is important to understand the context of the situation and to structure the hypotheses to provide the information the researcher or decision maker wants.

Summary of forms for null and alternative hypotheses   The hypothesis tests in this chapter involve two population parameters: the population mean and the population proportion. Depending on the situation, hypothesis tests about a population parameter may take one of three forms: Two use inequalities in the null hypothesis; the third uses an equality in the null hypothesis. For hypothesis tests involving a population mean, we let μ_0 denote the hypothesized value of the population mean and we must choose one of the following three forms for the hypothesis test:

The three possible forms of hypotheses H_0 and H_a are shown here. Note that the equality always appears in the null hypothesis H_0.

$$H_0: \mu \geq \mu_0 \qquad H_0: \mu \leq \mu_0 \qquad H_0: \mu = \mu_0$$
$$H_a: \mu < \mu_0 \qquad H_a: \mu > \mu_0 \qquad H_a: \mu \neq \mu_0$$

For reasons that will be clear later, the first two forms are called one-tailed tests. The third form is called a two-tailed test.

In many situations, the choice of H_0 and H_a is not obvious and judgment is necessary to select the proper form. However, as the preceding forms show, the equality part of the expression (either $\geq$, $\leq$, or $=$) *always* appears in the null hypothesis. In selecting the proper form of H_0 and H_a, keep in mind that the alternative hypothesis is often what the test is attempting to establish. Hence, asking whether the user is looking for evidence to support $\mu < \mu_0$, $\mu > \mu_0$, or $\mu \neq \mu_0$ will help determine H_a.

Type I and Type II Errors

The null and alternative hypotheses are competing statements about the population. Either the null hypothesis H_0 is true or the alternative hypothesis H_a is true, but not both. Ideally the hypothesis testing procedure should lead to the acceptance of H_0 when H_0 is true and the rejection of H_0 when H_a is true. Unfortunately, the correct conclusions are not always possible. Because hypothesis tests are based on sample information, we must allow for the possibility of errors. Table 6.6 illustrates the two kinds of errors that can be made in hypothesis testing.

The first row of Table 6.6 shows what can happen if the conclusion is to accept H_0. If H_0 is true, this conclusion is correct. However, if H_a is true, we made a **Type II error**; that is, we accepted H_0 when it is false. The second row of Table 6.6 shows what can happen if the conclusion is to reject H_0. If H_0 is true, we made a **Type I error**; that is, we rejected H_0 when it is true. However, if H_a is true, rejecting H_0 is correct.

Recall the hypothesis testing illustration in which an automobile product research group developed a new fuel injection system designed to increase the miles-per-gallon rating of a particular automobile. With the current model obtaining an average of 24 miles per gallon, the hypothesis test was formulated as follows:

$$H_0: \mu \leq 24$$
$$H_a: \mu > 24$$

The alternative hypothesis, $H_a: \mu > 24$, indicates that the researchers are looking for sample evidence to support the conclusion that the population mean miles per gallon with the new fuel injection system is greater than 24.

In this application, the Type I error of rejecting H_0 when it is true corresponds to the researchers claiming that the new system improves the miles-per-gallon rating ($\mu > 24$) when in fact the new system is no better than the current system. In contrast, the Type II error of accepting H_0 when it is false corresponds to the researchers concluding that the new system is no better than the current system ($\mu \leq 24$) when in fact the new system improves miles-per-gallon performance.

TABLE 6.6	Errors and Correct Conclusions in Hypothesis Testing		
		Population Condition	
		H_0 True	H_a True
Conclusion	**Do Not Reject H_0**	Correct conclusion	Type II error
	Reject H_0	Type I error	Correct conclusion

For the miles-per-gallon rating hypothesis test, the null hypothesis is $H_0: \mu \leq 24$. Suppose the null hypothesis is true as an equality; that is, $\mu = 24$. The probability of making a Type I error when the null hypothesis is true as an equality is called the **level of significance**. Thus, for the miles-per-gallon rating hypothesis test, the level of significance is the probability of rejecting $H_0: \mu \leq 24$ when $\mu = 24$. Because of the importance of this concept, we now restate the definition of level of significance.

LEVEL OF SIGNIFICANCE

The level of significance is the probability of making a Type I error when the null hypothesis is true as an equality.

The Greek symbol α (alpha) is used to denote the level of significance, and common choices for α are 0.05 and 0.01.

In practice, the person responsible for the hypothesis test specifies the level of significance. By selecting α, that person is controlling the probability of making a Type I error. If the cost of making a Type I error is high, small values of α are preferred. If the cost of making a Type I error is not too high, larger values of α are typically used. Applications of hypothesis testing that only control for the Type I error are called *significance tests*. Many applications of hypothesis testing are of this type.

Although most applications of hypothesis testing control for the probability of making a Type I error, they do not always control for the probability of making a Type II error. Hence, if we decide to accept H_0, we cannot determine how confident we can be with that decision. Because of the uncertainty associated with making a Type II error when conducting significance tests, statisticians usually recommend that we use the statement "do not reject H_0" instead of "accept H_0." Using the statement "do not reject H_0" carries the recommendation to withhold both judgment and action. In effect, by not directly accepting H_0, the statistician avoids the risk of making a Type II error. Whenever the probability of making a Type II error has not been determined and controlled, we will not make the statement "accept H_0." In such cases, only two conclusions are possible: *do not reject H_0* or *reject H_0*.

If the sample data are consistent with the null hypothesis H_0, we will follow the practice of concluding "do not reject H_0." This conclusion is preferred over "accept H_0," because the conclusion to accept H_0 puts us at risk of making a Type II error.

Although controlling for a Type II error in hypothesis testing is not common, it can be done. More advanced texts describe procedures for determining and controlling the probability of making a Type II error.[1] If proper controls have been established for this error, action based on the "accept H_0" conclusion can be appropriate.

Hypothesis Test of the Population Mean

In this section we describe how to conduct hypothesis tests about a population mean for the practical situation in which the sample must be used to develop estimates of both μ and σ. Thus, to conduct a hypothesis test about a population mean, the sample mean $\bar{x}$ is used as an estimate of μ and the sample standard deviation s is used as an estimate of σ.

One-tailed test **One-tailed tests** about a population mean take one of the following two forms:

---

[1]See, for example, D. R. Anderson, D. J. Sweeney, T. A. Williams, J. D. Camm, and J. J. Cochran, *Statistics for Business and Economics*, 13th edition (Mason, OH: Cengage Learning, 2017).

Lower-Tail Test	**Upper-Tail Test**
$H_0: \mu \geq \mu_0$	$H_0: \mu \leq \mu_0$
$H_a: \mu < \mu_0$	$H_a: \mu > \mu_0$

Let us consider an example involving a lower-tail test.

The Federal Trade Commission (FTC) periodically conducts statistical studies designed to test the claims that manufacturers make about their products. For example, the label on a large can of Hilltop Coffee states that the can contains 3 pounds of coffee. The FTC knows that Hilltop's production process cannot place exactly 3 pounds of coffee in each can, even if the mean filling weight for the population of all cans filled is 3 pounds per can. However, as long as the population mean filling weight is at least 3 pounds per can, the rights of consumers will be protected. Thus, the FTC interprets the label information on a large can of coffee as a claim by Hilltop that the population mean filling weight is at least 3 pounds per can. We will show how the FTC can check Hilltop's claim by conducting a lower-tail hypothesis test.

The first step is to develop the null and alternative hypotheses for the test. If the population mean filling weight is at least 3 pounds per can, Hilltop's claim is correct. This establishes the null hypothesis for the test. However, if the population mean weight is less than 3 pounds per can, Hilltop's claim is incorrect. This establishes the alternative hypothesis. With μ denoting the population mean filling weight, the null and alternative hypotheses are as follows:

$$H_0: \mu \geq 3$$
$$H_a: \mu < 3$$

Note that the hypothesized value of the population mean is $\mu_0 = 3$.

If the sample data indicate that H_0 cannot be rejected, the statistical evidence does not support the conclusion that a label violation has occurred. Hence, no action should be taken against Hilltop. However, if the sample data indicate that H_0 can be rejected, we will conclude that the alternative hypothesis, $H_a: \mu < 3$, is true. In this case a conclusion of underfilling and a charge of a label violation against Hilltop would be justified.

Suppose a sample of 36 cans of coffee is selected and the sample mean $\bar{x}$ is computed as an estimate of the population mean μ. If the value of the sample mean $\bar{x}$ is less than 3 pounds, the sample results will cast doubt on the null hypothesis. What we want to know is how much less than 3 pounds must $\bar{x}$ be before we would be willing to declare the difference significant and risk making a Type I error by falsely accusing Hilltop of a label violation. A key factor in addressing this issue is the value the decision maker selects for the level of significance.

As noted in the preceding section, the level of significance, denoted by α, is the probability of making a Type I error by rejecting H_0 when the null hypothesis is true as an equality. The decision maker must specify the level of significance. If the cost of making a Type I error is high, a small value should be chosen for the level of significance. If the cost is not high, a larger value is more appropriate. In the Hilltop Coffee study, the director of the FTC's testing program made the following statement: "If the company is meeting its weight specifications at $\mu = 3$, I do not want to take action against them. But I am willing to risk a 1% chance of making such an error." From the director's statement, we set the level of significance for the hypothesis test at $\alpha = 0.01$. Thus, we must design the hypothesis test so that the probability of making a Type I error when $\mu = 3$ is 0.01.

For the Hilltop Coffee study, by developing the null and alternative hypotheses and specifying the level of significance for the test, we carry out the first two steps required

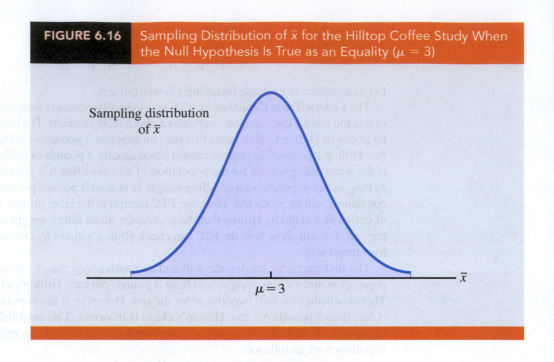

FIGURE 6.16   Sampling Distribution of $\bar{x}$ for the Hilltop Coffee Study When the Null Hypothesis Is True as an Equality ($\mu = 3$)

Sampling distribution
of $\bar{x}$

$\mu = 3$

$\bar{x}$

in conducting every hypothesis test. We are now ready to perform the third step of hypothesis testing: collect the sample data and compute the value of what is called a test statistic.

Test statistic. From the study of sampling distributions in Section 6.3 we know that as the sample size increases, the sampling distribution of $\bar{x}$ will become normally distributed. Figure 6.16 shows the sampling distribution of $\bar{x}$ when the null hypothesis is true as an equality, that is, when $\mu = \mu_0 = 3$.[2] Note that $\sigma_{\bar{x}}$, the standard error of $\bar{x}$, is estimated by $s_{\bar{x}} = s/\sqrt{n} = 0.17\sqrt{36} = 0.028$. Recall that in Section 6.4, we showed that an interval estimate of a population mean is based on a probability distribution known as the t distribution. The t distribution is similar to the standard normal distribution, but accounts for the additional variability introduced when using a sample to estimate both the population mean and population standard deviation. Hypothesis tests about a population mean are also based on the t distribution. Specifically, if $\bar{x}$ is normally distributed, sampling distribution of

The standard error of $\bar{x}$ is the standard deviation of the sampling distribution of $\bar{x}$.

$$t = \frac{\bar{x} - \mu_0}{s_{\bar{x}}} = \frac{\bar{x} - \mu_0}{s/\sqrt{n}} = \frac{\bar{x} - 3}{0.028}$$

is a t distribution with $n - 1$ degrees of freedom. A value of $t = -1$ means that the value of $\bar{x}$ is 1 standard error below the hypothesized value of the mean, a value of $t = -2$ means that the value of $\bar{x}$ is 2 standard errors below the hypothesized value of the mean, and so on. For this lower-tail hypothesis test, we can use Excel to find the lower-tail probability corresponding to any t value (as we show later in this section). For example, Figure 6.17 illustrates that the lower tail area at $t = -3.00$ is 0.0025. Hence, the probability of obtaining a value of t that is three or more standard errors below the mean is 0.0025. As a result, if the null hypothesis is true (that is, if the population mean is 3), the probability of obtaining a value of $\bar{x}$ that is 3 or more standard errors below the hypothesized population

Although the t distribution is based on an conjecture that the population from which we are sampling is normally distributed, research shows that when the sample size is large enough this conjecture can be relaxed considerably.

[2]In constructing sampling distributions for hypothesis tests, it is assumed that H_0 is satisfied as an equality.

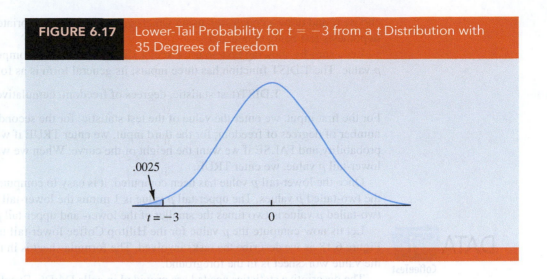

FIGURE 6.17 Lower-Tail Probability for $t = -3$ from a t Distribution with 35 Degrees of Freedom

mean $\mu_0 = 3$ is also 0.0025. Because such a result is unlikely if the null hypothesis is true, this leads us to doubt our null hypothesis.

We use the t-distributed random variable t as a **test statistic** to determine whether $\bar{x}$ deviates from the hypothesized value of μ enough to justify rejecting the null hypothesis. With $s_{\bar{x}} = s/\sqrt{n}$, the test statistic is as follows.

TEST STATISTIC FOR HYPOTHESIS TESTS ABOUT A POPULATION MEAN

$$t = \frac{\bar{x} - \mu_0}{s/\sqrt{n}} \qquad (6.11)$$

The key question for a lower-tail test is, How small must the test statistic t be before we choose to reject the null hypothesis? We will draw our conclusion by using the value of the test statistic t to compute a probability called a **p value**.

A small p value indicates that the value of the test statistic is unusual given the conjecture that H_0 is true.

p VALUE

A p value is a probability that provides a measure of the evidence against the null hypothesis provided by the sample. Smaller p values indicate more evidence against H_0.

The p value is used to determine whether the null hypothesis should be rejected.

Let us see how the p value is computed and used. The value of the test statistic is used to compute the p value. The method used depends on whether the test is a lower-tail, an upper-tail, or a two-tailed test. For a lower-tail test, the p value is the probability of obtaining a value for the test statistic as small as or smaller than that provided by the sample. Thus, to compute the p value for the lower-tail test, we must use the t distribution to find the probability that t is less than or equal to the value of the test statistic. After computing the p value, we must then decide whether it is small enough to reject the null hypothesis; as we will show, this decision involves comparing the p value to the level of significance.

Using Excel Excel can be used to conduct one-tailed and two-tailed hypothesis tests about a population mean. The sample data and the test statistic (t) are used to compute three p values: p value (lower tail), p value (upper tail), and p value (two tail). The user can then choose α and draw a conclusion using whichever *p* value is appropriate for the type of hypothesis test being conducted.

Let's start by showing how to use Excel's T.DIST function to compute a lower-tail *p* value. The T.DIST function has three inputs; its general form is as follows:

T.DIST(test statistic, degrees of freedom, cumulative).

For the first input, we enter the value of the test statistic; for the second input we enter the number of degrees of freedom; for the third input, we enter TRUE if we want a cumulative probability and FALSE if we want the height of the curve. When we want to compute a lower-tail *p* value, we enter TRUE.

Once the lower-tail *p* value has been computed, it is easy to compute the upper-tail and the two-tailed *p* values. The upper-tail *p* value is 1 minus the lower-tail *p* value, and the two-tailed *p* value is two times the smaller of the lower- and upper-tail *p* values.

Let us now compute the *p* value for the Hilltop Coffee lower-tail test. Refer to Figure 6.18 as we describe the tasks involved. The formula sheet is in the background and the value worksheet is in the foreground.

The descriptive statistics needed are provided in cells D4:D6. Excel's COUNT, AVERAGE, and STDEV.S functions compute the sample size, the sample mean, and the sample standard deviation, respectively. The hypothesized value of the population mean (3) is entered into cell D8. Using the sample standard deviation as an estimate of the population standard deviation, an estimate of the standard error is obtained in cell D10 by dividing the sample standard deviation in cell D6 by the square root of the sample size in cell D4. The formula =(D5-D8)/D10 entered into cell D11 computes the value of the test statistic *t* corresponding to the calculation:

$$t = \frac{\bar{x} - \mu_0}{s/\sqrt{n}} = \frac{2.92 - 3}{0.17/\sqrt{36}} = -2.824$$

The degrees of freedom are computed in cell D12 as the sample size in cell D4 minus 1.

To compute the *p* value for a lower-tail test, we enter the following formula into cell D14.

=T.DIST(D11,D12,TRUE)

The *p* value for an upper-tail test is then computed in cell D15 as 1 minus the *p* value for the lower-tail test. Finally, the *p* value for a two-tailed test is computed in cell D16 as two times the minimum of the two one-tailed *p* values. The value worksheet shows that the three *p* values are *p* (lower tail) = 0.0039, *p* (upper tail) = 0.9961, and *p* (two tail) = 0.0078.

The development of the worksheet is now complete. Is $\bar{x} = 2.92$ small enough to lead us to reject H_0? Because this is a lower-tail test, the *p* value is the area under the *t*-distribution curve for values of $t \leq -2.824$ (the value of the test statistic). Figure 6.19 depicts the *p* value for the Hilltop Coffee lower-tail test. This *p* value indicates a small probability of obtaining a sample mean of $\bar{x} = 2.92$ (and a test statistic of -2.824) or smaller when sampling from a population with $\mu = 3$. This *p* value does not provide much support for the null hypothesis, but is it small enough to cause us to reject H_0? The answer depends on the level of significance (α) the decision maker has selected for the test.

Note that the *p* value can be considered a measure of the strength of the evidence against the null hypothesis that is contained in the sample data. The greater the inconsistency between the sample data and the null hypothesis, the smaller the *p* value will be; thus, a smaller *p* value indicates that it is less plausible that the sample could have been collected from a population for which the null hypothesis is true. That is, a smaller *p* value indicates that the sample provides stronger evidence against the null hypothesis.

FIGURE 6.18 Hypothesis Test About a Population Mean

⊿	A	B	C	D
1	Weight		**Hypothesis Test about a Population Mean**	
2	3.15			
3	2.76			
4	3.18		Sample Size	36
5	2.77		Sample Mean	2.92
6	2.86		Sample Standard Deviation	0.170
7	2.66			
8	2.86		Hypothesized Value	3
9	2.54			
10	3.02		Standard Error	0.028
11	3.13		Test Statistic t	-2.824
12	2.94		Degrees of Freedom	35
13	2.74			
14	2.84		p-value (Lower Tail)	0.0039
15	2.60		p-value (Upper Tail)	0.9961
16	2.94		p-value (Two Tail)	0.0078
17	2.93			
18	3.18			
19	2.95			
20	2.86			
21	2.91			
22	2.96			
23	3.14			
24	2.65			
25	2.77			
26	2.96			
27	3.10			
28	2.82			
29	3.05			
30	2.94			
31	2.82			
32	3.21			
33	3.11			
34	2.90			
35	3.05			
36	2.93			
37	2.89			

⊿	A	B	C	D
1	Weight		**Hypothesis Test about a Population Mean**	
2	3.15			
3	2.76			
4	3.18		Sample Size	=COUNT(A2:A37)
5	2.77		Sample Mean	=AVERAGE(A2:A37)
6	2.86		Sample Standard Deviation	=STDEV.S(A2:A37)
7	2.66			
8	2.86		Hypothesized Value	3
9	2.54			
10	3.02		Standard Error	=D6/SQRT(D4)
11	3.13		Test Statistic t	=(D5-D8)/D10
12	2.94		Degrees of Freedom	=D4-1
13	2.74			
14	2.84		p-value (Lower Tail)	=T.DIST(D11,D12,TRUE)
15	2.6		p-value (Upper Tail)	=1-D14
16	2.94		p-value (Two Tail)	=2*MIN(D14,D15)
17	2.93			
18	3.18			
19	2.95			
20	2.86			

As noted previously, the director of the FTC's testing program selected a value of 0.01 for the level of significance. The selection of $\alpha = 0.01$ means that the director is willing to tolerate a probability of 0.01 of rejecting the null hypothesis when it is true as an equality ($\mu_0 = 3$). The sample of 36 coffee cans in the Hilltop Coffee study resulted in $p = 0.0038$, which means that the probability of obtaining a value of $\bar{x} = 2.92$ or less when the null hypothesis is true is 0.0039. Because 0.0039 is less than or equal to $\alpha = 0.01$, we reject H_0. Therefore, we find sufficient statistical evidence to reject the null hypothesis at the 0.01 level of significance.

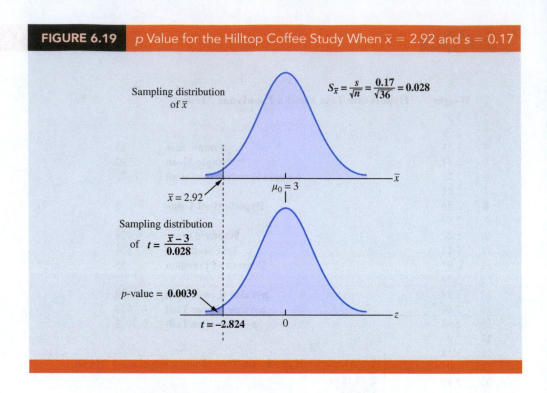

FIGURE 6.19 p Value for the Hilltop Coffee Study When $\bar{x} = 2.92$ and $s = 0.17$

The level of significance α indicates the strength of evidence that is needed in the sample data before we will reject the null hypothesis. If the p value is smaller than the selected level of significance α, the evidence against the null hypothesis that is contained in the sample data is sufficiently strong for us to reject the null hypothesis; that is, we believe that it is implausible that the sample data were collected from a population for which the null hypothesis is true. Conversely, if the p value is larger than the selected level of significance α, the evidence against the null hypothesis that is contained in the sample data is not sufficiently strong for us to reject the null hypothesis; that is, we believe that it is plausible that the sample data were collected from a population for which the null hypothesis is true.

We can now state the general rule for determining whether the null hypothesis can be rejected when using the p value approach. For a level of significance α, the rejection rule using the p value approach is as follows.

REJECTION RULE

Reject H_0 if p value $\leq \alpha$

In the Hilltop Coffee test, the p value of 0.0039 resulted in the rejection of the null hypothesis. Although the basis for making the rejection decision involves a comparison of the p value to the level of significance specified by the FTC director, the observed p value of 0.0039 means that we would reject H_0 for any value of $\alpha \geq 0.0039$. For this reason, the p value is also called the *observed level of significance*.

Different decision makers may express different opinions concerning the cost of making a Type I error and may choose a different level of significance. By providing the p value as part of the hypothesis testing results, another decision maker can compare the reported p value to his or her own level of significance and possibly make a different decision with respect to rejecting H_0.

At the beginning of this section, we said that one-tailed tests about a population mean take one of the following two forms:

Lower-Tail Test	**Upper-Tail Test**
$H_0: \mu \geq \mu_0$	$H_0: \mu \leq \mu_0$
$H_a: \mu < \mu_0$	$H_a: \mu > \mu_0$

We used the Hilltop Coffee study to illustrate how to conduct a lower-tail test. We can use the same general approach to conduct an upper-tail test. The test statistic t is still computed using equation (6.11). But, for an upper-tail test, the p value is the probability of obtaining a value for the test statistic as large as or larger than that provided by the sample. Thus, to compute the p value for the upper-tail test, we must use the t distribution to compute the probability that t is greater than or equal to the value of the test statistic. Then, according to the rejection rule, we will reject the null hypothesis if the p value is less than or equal to the level of significance α.

Let us summarize the steps involved in computing p values for one-tailed hypothesis tests.

> **COMPUTATION OF p VALUES FOR ONE-TAILED TESTS**
>
> 1. Compute the value of the test statistic using equation (6.11).
> 2. **Lower-tail test:** Using the t distribution, compute the probability that t is less than or equal to the value of the test statistic (area in the lower tail).
> 3. **Upper-tail test:** Using the t distribution, compute the probability that t is greater than or equal to the value of the test statistic (area in the upper tail).

Two-tailed test In hypothesis testing, the general form for a **two-tailed test** about a population mean is as follows:

$$H_0: \mu = \mu_0$$
$$H_a: \mu \neq \mu_0$$

In this subsection we show how to conduct a two-tailed test about a population mean. As an illustration, we consider the hypothesis testing situation facing Holiday Toys.

Holiday Toys manufactures and distributes its products through more than 1,000 retail outlets. In planning production levels for the coming winter season, Holiday must decide how many units of each product to produce before the actual demand at the retail level is known. For this year's most important new toy, Holiday's marketing director is expecting demand to average 40 units per retail outlet. Prior to making the final production decision based on this estimate, Holiday decided to survey a sample of 25 retailers to gather more information about demand for the new product. Each retailer was provided with information about the features of the new toy along with the cost and the suggested selling price. Then each retailer was asked to specify an anticipated order quantity.

With μ denoting the population mean order quantity per retail outlet, the sample data will be used to conduct the following two-tailed hypothesis test:

$$H_0: \mu = 40$$
$$H_a: \mu \neq 40$$

If H_0 cannot be rejected, Holiday will continue its production planning based on the marketing director's estimate that the population mean order quantity per retail outlet will be $\mu = 40$ units. However, if H_0 is rejected, Holiday will immediately reevaluate its production plan for the product. A two-tailed hypothesis test is used because Holiday wants to reevaluate the production plan regardless of whether the population mean quantity per retail outlet is less than anticipated or is greater than anticipated. Because it's a new product and therefore, no historical data are available, the population mean μ and the population standard deviation must both be estimated using $\bar{x}$ and s from the sample data.

The worksheet in Figure 6.18 can be used as a template for a hypothesis test about a population mean for other data. Enter the appropriate data in column A, adjust the ranges for the formulas in cells D4:D6, and enter the hypothesized value in cell D8. The standard error, the test statistic, and the three p values will then appear. Depending on the form of the hypothesis test (lower-tail, upper-tail, or two-tailed), we can then choose the appropriate p value to make the decision.

DATA *file*

Orders

The sample of 25 retailers provided a mean of $\bar{x} = 37.4$ and a standard deviation of $s = 11.79$ units. Before going ahead with the use of the t distribution, the analyst constructed a histogram of the sample data in order to check on the form of the population distribution. The histogram of the sample data showed no evidence of skewness or any extreme outliers, so the analyst concluded that the use of the t distribution with $n - 1 = 24$ degrees of freedom was appropriate. Using equation (9.2) with $\bar{x} = 37.4$, $\mu_0 = 40$, $s = 11.79$, and $n = 25$, the value of the test statistic is

$$t = \frac{\bar{x} - \mu_0}{s/\sqrt{n}} = \frac{37.4 - 40}{11.79/\sqrt{25}} = -1.10.$$

The sample mean $\bar{x} = 37.4$ is less than 40 and so provides some support for the conclusion that the population mean quantity per retail outlet is less than 40 units, but this could possibly be due to sampling error. We must address whether the difference between this sample mean and our hypothesized mean is sufficient for us to reject H_0 at the 0.05 level of significance. We will again reach our conclusion by calculating a p value.

Recall that the p value is a probability used to determine whether the null hypothesis should be rejected. For a two-tailed test, values of the test statistic in either tail provide evidence against the null hypothesis. For a two-tailed test the p value is the probability of obtaining a value for the test statistic *at least as unlikely* as the value of the test statistic calculated with the sample given that the null hypothesis is true. Let us see how the p value is computed for the two-tailed Holiday Toys hypothesis test.

To compute the p value for this problem, we must find the probability of obtaining a value for the test statistic at least as unlikely as $t = -1.10$ if the population mean is actually 40. Clearly, values of $t \leq -1.10$ are *at least as unlikely*. But because this is a two-tailed test, all values that are more than 1.10 standard deviations from the hypothesize value μ_0 in either direction provide evidence against the null hypothesis that is at least as strong as the evidence against the null hypothesis contained in the sample data. As shown in Figure 6.20, the two-tailed p value in this case is given by $P(t \leq -1.10) + P(t \geq 1.10)$.

To compute the tail probabilities, we apply the Excel template introduced in the Hilltop Coffee example to the Holiday Toys data. Figure 6.21 displays the formula worksheet in the background and the value worksheet in the foreground.

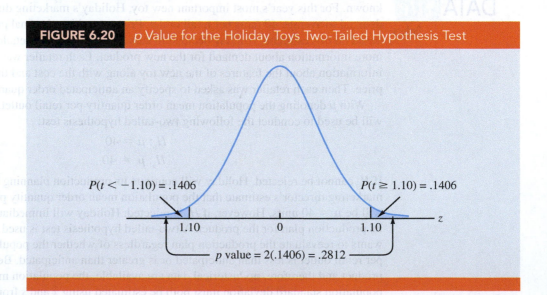

FIGURE 6.20 *p* Value for the Holiday Toys Two-Tailed Hypothesis Test

$P(t < -1.10) = .1406$ $P(t \geq 1.10) = .1406$

-1.10 0 1.10 z

p value $= 2(.1406) = .2812$

FIGURE 6.21 Two-Tailed Hypothesis Test for Holiday Toys

MODEL *file*
OrdersTest

	A	B	C	D
1	Units		Hypothesis Test about a Population Mean	
2	26			
3	23			
4	32		Sample Size	=COUNT(A:A)
5	47		Sample Mean	=AVERAGE(A:A)
6	45		Sample Standard Deviation	=STDEV.S(A:A)
7	31			
8	47		Hypothesized Value	40
9	59			
10	21		Standard Error	=D6/SQRT(D4)
11	52		Test Statistic t	=(D5−D8)/D10
12	45		Degrees of Freedom	=D4−1
13	53			
14	34		p-value (Lower Tail)	=T.DIST(D11,D12,TRUE)
15	45		p-value (Upper Tail)	=1−D14
16	39		p-value (Two Tail)	=2*MIN(D14,D15)
17	52			
18	52			
19	22			
20	22			
21	33			
22	21			
23	34			
24	42			
25	30			
26	28			

	A	B	C	D
1	Units		Hypothesis Test about a Population Mean	
2	26			
3	23			
4	32		Sample Size	25
5	47		Sample Mean	37.4
6	45		Sample Standard Deviation	11.79
7	31			
8	47		Hypothesized Value	40
9	59			
10	21		Standard Error	2.358
11	52		Test Statistic t	−1.103
12	45		Degrees of Freedom	24
13	53			
14	34		p-value (Lower Tail)	0.1406
15	45		p-value (Upper Tail)	0.8594
16	39		p-value (Two Tail)	0.2811
17	52			

Note: Rows 18–24 are hidden.

The file named *OrdersTest* includes a worksheet entitled template that uses the A:A method for entering the data ranges.

To complete the two-tailed Holiday Toys hypothesis test, we compare the two-tailed p value to the level of significance to see whether the null hypothesis should be rejected. With a level of significance of $\alpha = 0.05$, we do not reject H_0 because $p = 0.2811 > 0.05$. This result indicates that Holiday should continue its production planning for the coming season based on the expectation that $\mu = 40$.

The worksheet in Figure 6.21 can be used as a template for any hypothesis tests about a population mean. Just enter the appropriate data in column A, adjust the ranges for the formulas in cells D4:D6, and enter the hypothesized value in cell D8. The standard error, the test statistic, and the three p values will then appear. Depending on the form of the hypothesis test (lower-tail, upper-tail, or two-tailed), we can then choose the appropriate p value to make the rejection decision. We can further simplify the use of Figure 6.21 as a template for other problems by eliminating the need to enter new data ranges in cells D4:D6. To do so we rewrite the cell formulas as follows:

Cell D4: =COUNT(A:A)
Cell D5: =AVERAGE(A:A)
Cell D6: =STDV(A:A)

With the A:A method of specifying data ranges, Excel's COUNT function will count the number of numeric values in column A, Excel's AVERAGE function will compute the average of the numeric values in column A, and Excel's STDEV function will compute the standard deviation of the numeric values in Column A. Thus, to solve a new problem it is necessary only to enter the new data in column A and enter the hypothesized value of the population mean in cell D8.

Let us summarize the steps involved in computing p values for two-tailed hypothesis tests.

COMPUTATION OF p VALUES FOR TWO-TAILED TESTS

1. Compute the value of the test statistic using equation (6.11).
2. If the value of the test statistic is in the upper tail, compute the probability that t is greater than or equal to the value of the test statistic (the upper-tail area). If the value of the test statistic is in the lower tail, compute the probability that t is less than or equal to the value of the test statistic (the lower-tail area).
3. Double the probability (or tail area) from step 2 to obtain the p value.

Summary and practical advice We presented examples of a lower-tail test and a two-tailed test about a population mean. Based on these examples, we can now summarize the hypothesis testing procedures about a population mean in Table 6.7. Note that μ_0 is the hypothesized value of the population mean.

The hypothesis testing steps followed in the two examples presented in this section are common to every hypothesis test.

STEPS OF HYPOTHESIS TESTING

Step 1. Develop the null and alternative hypotheses.
Step 2. Specify the level of significance.
Step 3. Collect the sample data and compute the value of the test statistic.
Step 4. Use the value of the test statistic to compute the p value.
Step 5. Reject H_0 if the $p \leq \alpha$.
Step 6. Interpret the statistical conclusion in the context of the application.

Practical advice about the sample size for hypothesis tests is similar to the advice we provided about the sample size for interval estimation in Section 6.4. In most applications, a sample size of $n \geq 30$ is adequate when using the hypothesis testing procedure described in this section. In cases in which the sample size is less than 30, the distribution of the population from which we are sampling becomes an important consideration. When the population is normally distributed, the hypothesis tests described in this section provide exact results for any sample size. When the population is not normally distributed, these procedures provide approximations. Nonetheless, we find that sample sizes of 30 or more will provide good results in most cases. If the population is approximately normal, small

TABLE 6.7	Summary of Hypothesis Tests About a Population Mean		
	Lower-Tail Test	**Upper-Tail Test**	**Two-Tailed Test**
Hypotheses	$H_0: \mu \geq \mu_0$ $H_a: \mu < \mu_0$	$H_0: \mu \leq \mu_0$ $H_a: \mu > \mu_0$	$H_0: \mu = \mu_0$ $H_a: \mu \neq \mu_0$
Test Statistic	$t = \dfrac{\bar{x} - \mu_0}{s/\sqrt{n}}$	$t = \dfrac{\bar{x} - \mu_0}{s/\sqrt{n}}$	$t = \dfrac{\bar{x} - \mu_0}{s/\sqrt{n}}$
p value	=T.DIST(t, n − 1, TRUE)	=1 − T.DIST(t, n − 1, TRUE)	=2*MIN(T.DIST(t, n − 1, TRUE), 1 − T.DIST(t, n − 1, TRUE))

sample sizes (e.g., $n = 15$) can provide acceptable results. If the population is highly skewed or contains outliers, sample sizes approaching 50 are recommended.

Relationship between interval estimation and hypothesis testing   In Section 6.4 we showed how to develop a confidence interval estimate of a population mean. The $(1 - \alpha)\%$ confidence interval estimate of a population mean is given by:

$$\bar{x} \pm t_{\alpha/2} \frac{s}{\sqrt{n}}.$$

In this chapter we showed that a two-tailed hypothesis test about a population mean takes the following form:

$$H_0: \mu = \mu_0$$
$$H_a: \mu \neq \mu_0$$

where μ_0 is the hypothesized value for the population mean.

Suppose that we follow the procedure described in Section 6.4 for constructing a $100(1 - \alpha)\%$ confidence interval for the population mean. We know that $100(1 - \alpha)\%$ of the confidence intervals generated will contain the population mean and $100\alpha\%$ of the confidence intervals generated will not contain the population mean. Thus, if we reject H_0 whenever the confidence interval does not contain μ_0, we will be rejecting the null hypothesis when it is true ($\mu = \mu_0$) with probability α. Recall that the level of significance is the probability of rejecting the null hypothesis when it is true. So constructing a $100(1 - \alpha)\%$ confidence interval and rejecting H_0 whenever the interval does not contain μ_0 is equivalent to conducting a two-tailed hypothesis test with α as the level of significance. The procedure for using a confidence interval to conduct a two-tailed hypothesis test can now be summarized.

> **A CONFIDENCE INTERVAL APPROACH TO TESTING A HYPOTHESIS OF THE FORM**
>
> $$H_0: \mu = \mu_0$$
> $$H_a: \mu \neq \mu_0$$
>
> 1. Select a simple random sample from the population and use the value of the sample mean $\bar{x}$ to develop the confidence interval for the population mean μ.
>
> $$\bar{x} \pm t_{\alpha/2} \frac{s}{\sqrt{n}}$$
>
> 2. If the confidence interval contains the hypothesized value μ_0, do not reject H_0. Otherwise, reject[3] H_0.

For a two-tailed hypothesis test, the null hypothesis can be rejected if the confidence interval does not include μ_0.

Let us illustrate by conducting the Holiday Toys hypothesis test using the confidence interval approach. The Holiday Toys hypothesis test takes the following form:

$$H_0: \mu = 40$$
$$H_a: \mu \neq 40$$

To test these hypotheses with a level of significance of $\alpha = 0.05$, we sampled 25 retailers and found a sample mean of $\bar{x} = 37.4$ units and a sample standard deviation

---

[3]To be consistent with the rule for rejecting H_0 when $p \leq \alpha$, we would also reject H_0 using the confidence interval approach if μ_0 happens to be equal to one of the endpoints of the $100(1 - \alpha)\%$ confidence interval.

of $s = 11.79$ units. Using these results with $t_{0.025} = \text{T.INV}(1 - (.05/2), 25 - 1) = 2.064$, we find that the 95% confidence interval estimate of the population mean is:

$$\bar{x} \pm t_{.025}\frac{s}{\sqrt{n}}$$

$$37.4 \pm 2.064\frac{11.79}{\sqrt{25}}$$

$$37.4 \pm 4.4$$

or

$$33.0 \text{ to } 41.8.$$

This finding enables Holiday's marketing director to conclude with 95% confidence that the mean number of units per retail outlet is between 33.0 and 41.8. Because the hypothesized value for the population mean, $\mu_0 = 40$, is in this interval, the hypothesis testing conclusion is that the null hypothesis, H_0: $\mu = 40$, cannot be rejected.

Note that this discussion and example pertain to two-tailed hypothesis tests about a population mean. However, the same confidence interval and two-tailed hypothesis testing relationship exists for other population parameters. The relationship can also be extended to one-tailed tests about population parameters. Doing so, however, requires the development of one-sided confidence intervals, which are rarely used in practice.

Hypothesis Test of the Population Proportion

In this section we show how to conduct a hypothesis test about a population proportion p. Using p_0 to denote the hypothesized value for the population proportion, the three forms for a hypothesis test about a population proportion are as follows:

$$H_0: p \geq p_0 \qquad H_0: p \leq p_0 \qquad H_0: p = p_0$$
$$H_a: p < p_0 \qquad H_a: p > p_0 \qquad H_a: p \neq p_0$$

The first form is called a lower-tail test, the second an upper-tail test, and the third form a two-tailed test.

Hypothesis tests about a population proportion are based on the difference between the sample proportion $\bar{p}$ and the hypothesized population proportion p_0. The methods used to conduct the hypothesis test are similar to those used for hypothesis tests about a population mean. The only difference is that we use the sample proportion and its standard error to compute the test statistic. The p value is then used to determine whether the null hypothesis should be rejected.

Let us consider an example involving a situation faced by Pine Creek golf course. Over the past year, 20% of the players at Pine Creek were women. In an effort to increase the proportion of women players, Pine Creek implemented a special promotion designed to attract women golfers. One month after the promotion was implemented, the course manager requested a statistical study to determine whether the proportion of women players at Pine Creek had increased. Because the objective of the study is to determine whether the proportion of women golfers increased, an upper-tail test with H_a: $p > 0.20$ is appropriate. The null and alternative hypotheses for the Pine Creek hypothesis test are as follows:

$$H_0: p \leq 0.20$$
$$H_a: p > 0.20$$

If H_0 can be rejected, the test results will give statistical support for the conclusion that the proportion of women golfers increased and the promotion was beneficial. The course manager specified that a level of significance of $\alpha = 0.05$ be used in carrying out this hypothesis test.

The next step of the hypothesis testing procedure is to select a sample and compute the value of an appropriate test statistic. To show how this step is done for the Pine Creek upper-tail test, we begin with a general discussion of how to compute the value of the test statistic for any form of a hypothesis test about a population proportion. The sampling distribution of $\bar{p}$, the point estimator of the population parameter p, is the basis for developing the test statistic.

When the null hypothesis is true as an equality, the expected value of $\bar{p}$ equals the hypothesized value p_0; that is, $E(\bar{p}) = p_0$. The standard error of $\bar{p}$ is given by:

$$\sigma_{\bar{p}} = \sqrt{\frac{p_0(1 - p_0)}{n}}.$$

In Section 6.3 we said that if $np \geq 5$ and $n(1 - p) \geq 5$, the sampling distribution of $\bar{p}$ can be approximated by a normal distribution.[4] Under these conditions, which usually apply in practice, the quantity

$$z = \frac{\bar{p} - p_0}{\sigma_{\bar{p}}} \tag{6.12}$$

has a standard normal probability distribution. With $\sigma_{\bar{p}} = \sqrt{p_0(1 - p_0)/n}$, the standard normal random variable z is the test statistic used to conduct hypothesis tests about a population proportion.

TEST STATISTIC FOR HYPOTHESIS TESTS ABOUT A POPULATION PROPORTION

$$z = \frac{\bar{p} - p_0}{\sqrt{\dfrac{p_0(1 - p_0)}{n}}} \tag{6.13}$$

DATA *file*

WomenGolf

We can now compute the test statistic for the Pine Creek hypothesis test. Suppose a random sample of 400 players was selected, and that 100 of the players were women. The proportion of women golfers in the sample is

$$\bar{p} = \frac{100}{400} = 0.25$$

Using equation (6.13), the value of the test statistic is

$$z = \frac{\bar{p} - p_0}{\sqrt{\dfrac{p_0(1 - p_0)}{n}}} = \frac{0.25 - 0.20}{\sqrt{\dfrac{0.20(1 - 0.20)}{400}}} = \frac{0.05}{0.02} = 2.50.$$

---

[4]In most applications involving hypothesis tests of a population proportion, sample sizes are large enough to use the normal approximation. The exact sampling distribution of $\bar{p}$ is discrete, with the probability for each value of $\bar{p}$ given by the binomial distribution. So hypothesis testing is a bit more complicated for small samples when the normal approximation cannot be used.

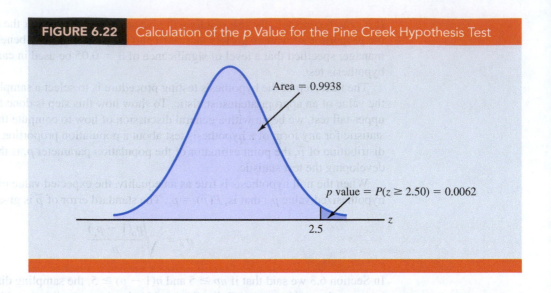

FIGURE 6.22 Calculation of the p Value for the Pine Creek Hypothesis Test

Area = 0.9938

p value $= P(z \geq 2.50) = 0.0062$

2.5

z

The Excel formula = NORM.S.DIST(z, TRUE) computes the area under the standard normal distribution curve that is less than or equal to the value z.

Because the Pine Creek hypothesis test is an upper-tail test, the p value is the probability of obtaining a value for the test statistic that is greater than or equal to $z = 2.50$; that is, it is the upper-tail area corresponding to $z \geq 2.50$ as displayed in Figure 6.22. The Excel formula $= 1 - \text{NORM.S.DIST}(2.5, \text{TRUE})$ computes this upper-tail area of 0.0062.

Recall that the course manager specified a level of significance of $\alpha = 0.05$. A p value $= 0.0062 < 0.05$ gives sufficient statistical evidence to reject H_0 at the 0.05 level of significance. Thus, the test provides statistical support for the conclusion that the special promotion increased the proportion of women players at the Pine Creek golf course.

Using Excel Excel can be used to conduct one-tailed and two-tailed hypothesis tests about a population proportion using the p value approach. The procedure is similar to the approach used with Excel in conducting hypothesis tests about a population mean. The primary difference is that the test statistic is based on the sampling distribution of $\bar{x}$ for hypothesis tests about a population mean and on the sampling distribution of $\bar{p}$ for hypothesis tests about a population proportion. Thus, although different formulas are used to compute the test statistic and the p value needed to make the hypothesis testing decision, the logical process is identical.

MODEL *file*

WomenGolfTest

We will illustrate the procedure by showing how Excel can be used to conduct the upper-tail hypothesis test for the Pine Creek golf course study. Refer to Figure 6.23 as we describe the tasks involved. The formula worksheet is in the background; the value worksheet is in the foreground.

The descriptive statistics needed are provided in cells D3, D5, and D6. Because the data are not numeric, Excel's COUNTA function, not the COUNT function, is used in cell D3 to determine the sample size. We entered Female in cell D4 to identify the response for which we wish to compute a proportion. The COUNTIF function is then used in cell D5 to determine the number of responses of the type identified in cell D4. The sample proportion is then computed in cell D6 by dividing the response count by the sample size.

The hypothesized value of the population proportion (0.20) is entered into cell D8. The standard error is obtained in cell D10 by entering the formula $= \text{SQRT}(\text{D8*}(1-\text{D8})/\text{D3})$. The formula $= (\text{D6-D8})/\text{D10}$ entered into cell D11 computes the test statistic z according to equation (6.13). To compute the p value for a lower-tail test, we enter the formula $= \text{NORM.S.DIST}(\text{D11}, \text{TRUE})$ into cell D13. The p value for an upper-tail test is then computed in cell D14 as 1 minus the p value for the lower-tail test. Finally, the p value for

FIGURE 6.23 Hypothesis Test for Pine Creek Golf Course

	A	B	C	D	E
1	Golfer		Hypothesis Test about a Population Proportion		
2	Female				
3	Male		Sample Size	=COUNTA(A2:A401)	
4	Female		Response of Interest	Female	
5	Male		Count for Response	=COUNTIF(A2:A401,D4)	
6	Male		Sample Proportion	=D5/D3	
7	Female				
8	Male		Hypothesized Value	0.2	
9	Male				
10	Female		Standard Error	=SQRT(D8*(1−D8)/D3)	
11	Male		Test Statistic z	=(D6−D8)/D10	
12	Male				
13	Male		p-value (Lower Tail)	=NORM.S.DIST(D11,TRUE)	
14	Male		p-value (Upper Tail)	=1−D13	
15	Male		p-value (Two Tail)	=2*MIN(D13,D14)	
16	Female				
400	Male				
401	Male				
402					

	A	B	C	D	E	F
1	Golfer		Hypothesis Test about a Population Proportion			
2	Female					
3	Male		Sample Size	400		
4	Female		Response of Interest	Female		
5	Male		Count for Response	100		
6	Male		Sample Proportion	0.25		
7	Female					
8	Male		Hypothesized Value	0.20		
9	Male					
10	Female		Standard Error	0.02		
11	Male		Test Statistic z	2.5000		
12	Male					
13	Male		p-value (Lower Tail)	0.9938		
14	Male		p-value (Upper Tail)	0.0062		
15	Male		p-value (Two Tail)	0.0124		
16	Female					
400	Male					
401	Male					
402						

a two-tailed test is computed in cell D15 as two times the minimum of the two one-tailed *p* values. The value worksheet shows that the three *p* values are as follows: $p = 0.9938$ (lower tail); $p = 0.0062$ (upper tail); and $p = 0.0124$ (two-tailed).

The development of the worksheet is now complete. For the Pine Creek upper-tail hypothesis test, we reject the null hypothesis that the population proportion is 0.20 or less because the $p = 0.0062$ (upper tail) is less than $\alpha = 0.05$. Indeed, with this *p* value we would reject the null hypothesis for any level of significance of 0.0062 or greater.

The procedure used to conduct a hypothesis test about a population proportion is similar to the procedure used to conduct a hypothesis test about a population mean. Although we illustrated how to conduct a hypothesis test about a population proportion only for an upper-tail test, similar procedures can be used for lower-tail and two-tailed tests. Table 6.8 provides a summary of the hypothesis tests about a population proportion. We

TABLE 6.8 Summary of Hypothesis Tests About a Population Proportion

	Lower-Tail Test	Upper-Tail Test	Two-Tailed Test
Hypotheses	$H_0: p \geq p_0$ $H_a: p < p_0$	$H_0: p \leq p_0$ $H_a: p > p_0$	$H_0: p = p_0$ $H_a: p \neq p_0$
Test Statistic	$z = \dfrac{\bar{p} - p_0}{\sqrt{\dfrac{p_0(1 - p_0)}{n}}}$	$z = \dfrac{\bar{p} - p_0}{\sqrt{\dfrac{p_0(1 - p_0)}{n}}}$	$z = \dfrac{\bar{p} - p_0}{\sqrt{\dfrac{p_0(1 - p_0)}{n}}}$
p value	=NORM.S.DIST(z, TRUE)	=1 − NORM.S.DIST(z, TRUE)	2*MIN(NORM.S.DIST(z, TRUE), 1 − NORM.S.DIST(z, TRUE))

assume that $np \geq 5$ and $n(1 - p) \geq 5$; thus the normal probability distribution can be used to approximate the sampling distribution of $\bar{p}$.

Big Data, Statistical Inference, and Practical Significance

In Section 6.4 we saw that the denominator of the standard errors for the sampling distributions of the sample mean $\bar{x}$ and the sample proportion of $\bar{p}$ is $\sqrt{n}$. Thus, for a given level of confidence, the margin of error decreases and interval estimates of the population mean $\bar{x}$ and the population proportion of $\bar{p}$ narrow as the sample size n increases. But how rapidly do these interval estimates narrow? This is a relevant concern for businesses; as we discussed in Chapter 1, technology and electronic (and often automated) data collection make it easy to collect millions, or even billions, of observations in a relatively short time. Businesses are collecting greater volumes of greater varieties of data at a higher velocity that ever, and this is likely to continue.

Suppose you are interested in the average amount of time customers spend when they visit your web site. Advertisers are willing to pay a premium to advertise on web sites that have long average visit times, so this could have a profound impact on your company's profit. Measuring the time of each visit to your web site in seconds, a simple random sample of 100 visits yields a sample mean of $\bar{x} = 82.1$ and a sample standard deviation of $s = 20$. Table 6.9 shows how the 95% margins of error and corresponding interval estimates change based on sample size (assuming that the sample mean and sample standard deviation do not change). One hundred thousand or more visitors might seem unrealistic, but keep in mind that according to quantcast.com, amazon.com had over 76 million visitors in May 2015.

Table 6.9 shows that the 95% margin of error decreases quickly as the sample size n increases, resulting in rapid narrowing of the corresponding interval estimates. At a sample size of $n = 100$, the width of the interval estimate is 7.937 seconds, but at a sample size of $n = 100,000$, the width of interval estimate is only 0.248, or slightly less than one fourth of one second. At a sample size of $n = 1,000,000,000$ the width of the interval estimate is only 0.002 or one five-hundredth of one second.

Now consider the relationship between interval estimation and hypothesis testing that we discussed earlier in this section; if we construct a $100(1 - \alpha)\%$ interval estimate for

TABLE 6.9	Margins of Error and Interval Estimates of the Population Mean at Various Sample Sizes n	
Sample Size n	**Margin of Error** $t_{\alpha/2}(s/\sqrt{n})$	**Interval Estimate** $\bar{x} \pm t_{\alpha/2}(s/\sqrt{n})$
100	3.968	(78.132, 86.068)
500	1.757	(80.343, 83.857)
1,000	1.241	(80.859, 83.341)
10,000	0.392	(81.708, 82.492)
100,000	0.124	(81.976, 82.224)
1,000,000	0.039	(82.061, 82.139)
10,000,000	0.012	(82.088, 82.112)
100,000,000	0.004	(82.096, 82.104)
1,000,000,000	0.001	(82.099, 82.101)

the population mean, we reject H_0: $\mu = \mu_0$ if the $100(1 - \alpha)\%$ interval estimate does not contain μ_0. Thus, for a given level of confidence, as the sample size increases we will reject H_0: $m = m_0$ for increasingly smaller differences between the sample mean $\bar{x}$ and the hypothesized population mean μ_0. We can see that when the sample size n is very large, almost any difference between the sample mean $\bar{x}$ and the hypothesized population mean μ_0 results in rejection of the null hypothesis.

The implication of these results for hypothesis testing is profound. With a sufficiently large sample, even a minuscule and meaningless difference between the sample mean $\bar{x}$ and the hypothesized population mean μ_0 results in rejection of the null hypothesis. Table 6.9 shows that in our example, for a sample of $n = 1{,}000{,}000{,}000$ posts we will reject H_0: $\mu = \mu_0$ for any value of μ_0 outside the interval (82.099, 82.101). Under these circumstances, we would reject the null hypothesis H_0: $\mu = 82.0$ even though the difference between our sample mean $\bar{x}$ and the hypothesized population mean μ_0 is only one-tenth of one second. This result is statistically significant at $\alpha = 0.05$, but is it meaningful? Does this result change any business decisions we might make? If we have been operating under the premise that the mean number of seconds visitors spend at our web site is 82, our sample results may not motivate any action or change in the way we operate our business. On the other hand, if the random variable is the amount of time it takes for a generator to reestablish electricity to an operating room after a power failure, a fraction of a second may be critical. With very large samples, it is particularly important that we consider the practical implications, or **practical significance**, of a statistically significant result in hypothesis testing.

Hypothesis testing is a powerful tool, but no business decision should be based solely on statistical significance. Whenever the results of a hypothesis test are significant, we should also consider the practical significance of the difference between the sample mean $\bar{x}$ and the hypothesized population mean μ_0 or the difference between the sample proportion $\bar{p}$ and the hypothesized population proportion p_0. This is especially true when the sample size n is very large.

NOTES + COMMENTS

1. We have shown how to use p values. The smaller the p value, the stronger the evidence in the sample data against H_0 and the stronger the evidence in favor of H_a. Here are guidelines that some statisticians suggest for interpreting small p values:
   - Less than 0.01—Overwhelming evidence to conclude that H_a is true
   - Between 0.01 and 0.05—Strong evidence to conclude that H_a is true
   - Between 0.05 and 0.10—weak evidence to conclude that H_a is true
   - Greater than 0.10—Insufficient evidence to conclude that H_a is true

2. The procedures for testing hypotheses about the mean that are discussed in this chapter are reliable unless the sample size is small and the population is highly skewed or contains outliers. In these cases, a nonparametric approach such as the sign test can be used. Under these conditions the results of nonparametric tests are more reliable than the hypothesis testing procedures discussed in this chapter. However, this increased reliability comes with a cost; if the sample is large or the population is relatively normally distributed, a nonparametric approach will also reject false null hypotheses less frequently.

3. We have discussed only procedures for testing hypotheses about the mean or proportion of a single population. There are many statistical procedures for testing hypotheses about multiple means or proportions. There are also many statistical procedures for testing hypotheses about parameters other than the population mean or the population proportion.

SUMMARY

In this chapter we presented the concepts of sampling and sampling distributions. We demonstrated how a simple random sample can be selected from a finite population and how a random sample can be selected from an infinite population. The data collected from such samples can be used to develop point estimates of population parameters. Different samples provide different values for the point estimators; therefore, point estimators such as $\bar{x}$ and $\bar{p}$ are random variables. The probability distribution of such a random variable is called a sampling distribution. In particular, we described in detail the sampling distributions of the sample mean $\bar{x}$ and the sample proportion $\bar{p}$. In considering the characteristics of the sampling distributions of x and p, we stated that $E(\bar{x}) = \mu$ and $E(\bar{p}) = p$. After developing the standard deviation or standard error formulas for these estimators, we described the conditions necessary for the sampling distributions of $\bar{x}$ and $\bar{p}$ to follow a normal distribution.

In Section 6.4, we presented methods for developing interval estimates of a population mean and a population proportion. A point estimator may or may not provide a good estimate of a population parameter. The use of an interval estimate provides a measure of the precision of an estimate. Both the interval estimate of the population mean and the population proportion take the form: point estimate $\pm$ margin of error.

We presented the interval estimation procedure for a population mean for the practical case in which the population standard deviation is unknown. The interval estimation procedure uses the sample standard deviation s and the t distribution. The quality of the interval estimate obtained depends on the distribution of the population and the sample size. In a normally distributed population, the interval estimates will be exact in both cases, even for small sample sizes. If the population is not normally distributed, the interval estimates obtained will be approximate. Larger sample sizes provide better approximations, but the more highly skewed the population is, the larger the sample size needs to be to obtain a good approximation.

The general form of the interval estimate for a population proportion is $\bar{p} \pm$ margin of error. In practice, the sample sizes used for interval estimates of a population proportion are generally large. Thus, the interval estimation procedure for a population proportion is based on the standard normal distribution.

In Section 6.5, we presented methods for hypothesis testing, a statistical procedure that uses sample data to determine whether or not a statement about the value of a population parameter should be rejected. The hypotheses are two competing statements about a population parameter. One statement is called the null hypothesis (H_0), and the other is called the alternative hypothesis (H_a). We provided guidelines for developing hypotheses for situations frequently encountered in practice.

In the hypothesis-testing procedure for the population mean, the sample standard deviation s is used to estimate σ and the hypothesis test is based on the t distribution. The quality of results depends on both the form of the population distribution and the sample size; if the population is not normally distributed, larger sample sizes are needed. General guidelines about the sample size were provided in Section 6.5. In the case of hypothesis tests about a population proportion, the hypothesis-testing procedure uses a test statistic based on the standard normal distribution.

The value of the test statistic can be used to compute a p value—a probability that is used to determine whether the null hypothesis should be rejected. If the p value is less than or equal to the level of significance α, the null hypothesis can be rejected.

GLOSSARY

Alternative hypothesis The hypothesis concluded to be true if the null hypothesis is rejected.

Census Collection of data from every element in the population of interest.

Central limit theorem A theorem that enables one to use the normal probability distribution to approximate the sampling distribution of $\bar{x}$ whenever the sample size is large.

Confidence coefficient The confidence level expressed as a decimal value. For example, 0.95 is the confidence coefficient for a 95% confidence level.

Confidence interval Another name for an interval estimate.

Confidence level The confidence associated with an interval estimate. For example, if an interval estimation procedure provides intervals such that 95% of the intervals formed using the procedure will include the population parameter, the interval estimate is said to be constructed at the 95% confidence level.

Degrees of freedom A parameter of the t distribution. When the t distribution is used in the computation of an interval estimate of a population mean, the appropriate t distribution has $n - 1$ degrees of freedom, where n is the size of the sample.

Finite population correction factor The term $\sqrt{(N - n)/(N - 1)}$ that is used in the formulas for $\sigma_{\bar{x}}$ and $\sigma_{\bar{p}}$ whenever a finite population, rather than an infinite population, is being sampled. The generally accepted rule of thumb is to ignore the finite population correction factor whenever $n/N \leq 0.05$.

Frame A listing of the elements from which the sample will be selected.

Hypothesis testing The process of making a conjecture about the value of a population parameter, collecting sample data that can be used to assess this conjecture, measuring the strength of the evidence against the conjecture that is provided by the sample, and using these results to draw a conclusion about the conjecture.

Interval estimate The result of the process of interval estimation, this is an estimate of a population parameter that provides an interval believed to contain the value of the parameter. For the interval estimates in this chapter, it has the form: point estimate $\pm$ margin of error.

Interval estimation The process of using sample data to calculate a range of values that is believed to include the unknown value of a population parameter.

Level of significance The probability that the interval estimation procedure will generate an interval that does not contain the value of parameter being; also the probability of making a Type I error when the null hypothesis is true as an equality.

Margin of error The $\pm$ value added to and subtracted from a point estimate in order to develop an interval estimate of a population parameter.

Null hypothesis The hypothesis tentatively assumed to be true in the hypothesis testing procedure.

One-tailed test A hypothesis test in which rejection of the null hypothesis occurs for values of the test statistic in one tail of its sampling distribution.

Parameter A measurable factor that defines a characteristic of a population, process, or system, such as a population mean μ, a population standard deviation σ, a population proportion p, and so on.

Point estimate The value of a point estimator used in a particular instance as an estimate of a population parameter.

Point estimator The sample statistic, such as $\bar{x}$, s, or $\bar{p}$, that provides the point estimate of the population parameter.

Practical significance The potential impact the result of statistical inference will have on business decisions.

p value A probability that gives a measure of the evidence against the null hypothesis provided by the sample. Smaller p values indicate more evidence against H_0. For a lower-tail test, the p value is the probability of obtaining a value for the test statistic as small as or smaller than that provided by the sample. For an upper-tail test, the p value is the probability of obtaining a value for the test statistic as large as or larger than that provided by the sample. For a two-tailed test, the p value is the probability of obtaining a value for the test statistic at least as unlikely as or more unlikely than that provided by the sample.

Random sample A random sample from an infinite population is a sample selected such that the following conditions are satisfied: (1) Each element selected comes from the same population; and (2) each element is selected independently.

Sample statistic A characteristic of sample data, such as a sample mean $\bar{x}$, a sample standard deviation s, a sample proportion $\bar{p}$, and so on. The value of the sample statistic is used to estimate the value of the corresponding population parameter.

Sampled population The population from which the sample is drawn.

Sampling distribution A probability distribution consisting of all possible values of a sample statistic.

Sampling error The difference between the value of a sample statistic (such as the sample mean, sample standard deviation, or sample proportion) and the value of the corresponding population parameter (population mean, population standard deviation, or population proportion).

Simple random sample A simple random sample of size n from a finite population of size N is a sample selected such that each possible sample of size n has the same probability of being selected.

Standard error The standard deviation of a point estimator.

Standard normal distribution A normal distribution with a mean of zero and standard deviation of one.

Statistical inference The process of making estimates and drawing conclusions about one or more characteristics of a population (the value of one or more parameters) through the analysis of sample data drawn from the population.

t distribution A family of probability distributions that can be used to develop an interval estimate of a population mean whenever the population standard deviation s is unknown and is estimated by the sample standard deviation s.

Test statistic A statistic whose value helps determine whether a null hypothesis should be rejected.

Target population The population for which statistical inferences such as point estimates are made. It is important for the target population to correspond as closely as possible to the sampled population.

Two-tailed test A hypothesis test in which rejection of the null hypothesis occurs for values of the test statistic in either tail of its sampling distribution.

Type I error The error of rejecting H_0 when it is true.

Type II error The error of accepting H_0 when it is false.

Unbiased A property of a point estimator that is present when the expected value of the point estimator is equal to the population parameter it estimates.

PROBLEMS

1. The American League consists of 15 baseball teams. Suppose a sample of 5 teams is to be selected to conduct player interviews. The following table lists the 15 teams and the random numbers assigned by Excel's RAND function. Use these random numbers to select a sample of size 5.

Team	Random Number	Team	Random Number
New York	0.178624	Boston	0.290197
Baltimore	0.578370	Tampa Bay	0.867778
Toronto	0.965807	Minnesota	0.811810
Chicago	0.562178	Cleveland	0.960271
Detroit	0.253574	Kansas City	0.326836
Oakland	0.288287	Los Angeles	0.895267
Texas	0.500879	Seattle	0.839071
Houston	0.713682		

2. The U.S. Golf Association is considering a ban on long and belly putters. This has caused a great deal of controversy among both amateur golfers and members of the Professional Golf Association (PGA). Shown below are the names of the top 10 finishers in the recent PGA Tour McGladrey Classic golf tournament.

1. Tommy Gainey		6. Davis Love III	
2. David Toms		7. Chad Campbell	
3. Jim Furyk		8. Greg Owens	
4. Brendon de Jonge		9. Charles Howell III	
5. D. J. Trahan		10. Arjun Atwal	

Select a simple random sample of 3 of these players to assess their opinions on the use of long and belly putters.

3. A simple random sample of 5 months of sales data provided the following information:

$$\text{Month:} \quad 1 \quad 2 \quad 3 \quad 4 \quad 5$$
$$\text{Units Sold:} \quad 94 \quad 100 \quad 85 \quad 94 \quad 92$$

a. Develop a point estimate of the population mean number of units sold per month.
b. Develop a point estimate of the population standard deviation.

4. Morningstar publishes ratings data on 1,208 company stocks. A sample of 40 of these stocks is contained in the file named *Morningstar*. Use the Morningstar data set to answer the following questions.
a. Develop a point estimate of the proportion of the stocks that receive Morningstar's highest rating of 5 Stars.
b. Develop a point estimate of the proportion of the Morningstar stocks that are rated Above Average with respect to business risk.
c. Develop a point estimate of the proportion of the Morningstar stocks that are rated 2 Stars or less.

5. One of the questions in the Pew Internet & American Life Project asked adults if they used the Internet at least occasionally. The results showed that 454 out of 478 adults aged 18–29 answered Yes; 741 out of 833 adults aged 30–49 answered Yes; and 1,058 out of 1,644 adults aged 50 and over answered Yes.
a. Develop a point estimate of the proportion of adults aged 18–29 who use the Internet.
b. Develop a point estimate of the proportion of adults aged 30–49 who use the Internet.
c. Develop a point estimate of the proportion of adults aged 50 and over who use the Internet.
d. Comment on any apparent relationship between age and Internet use.
e. Suppose your target population of interest is that of all adults (18 years of age and over). Develop an estimate of the proportion of that population who use the Internet.

DATA *file*

EAI

6. In this chapter we showed how a simple random sample of 30 EAI employees can be used to develop point estimates of the population mean annual salary, the population standard deviation for annual salary, and the population proportion having completed the management training program.
   a. Use Excel to select a simple random sample of 50 EAI employees.
   b. Develop a point estimate of the mean annual salary.
   c. Develop a point estimate of the population standard deviation for annual salary.
   d. Develop a point estimate of population proportion having completed the management training program.

7. The College Board reported the following mean scores for the three parts of the SAT:

Critical Reading	502
Mathematics	515
Writing	494

Assume that the population standard deviation on each part of the test is $\sigma = 100$.
   a. For a random sample of 30 test takers, what is the sampling distribution of $\bar{x}$ for scores on the Critical Reading part of the test?
   b. For a random sample of 60 test takers, what is the sampling distribution of $\bar{x}$ for scores on the Mathematics part of the test?
   c. For a random sample of 90 test takers, what is the sampling distribution of $\bar{x}$ for scores on the Writing part of the test?

8. For the year 2010, 33% of taxpayers with adjusted gross incomes between $30,000 and $60,000 itemized deductions on their federal income tax return. The mean amount of deductions for this population of taxpayers was $16,642. Assume that the standard deviation is $\sigma = \$2400$.
   a. What are the sampling distributions of $\bar{x}$ for itemized deductions for this population of taxpayers for each of the following sample sizes: 30, 50, 100, and 400?
   b. What is the advantage of a larger sample size when attempting to estimate the population mean?

9. The Economic Policy Institute periodically issues reports on wages of entry-level workers. The institute reported that entry-level wages for male college graduates were $21.68 per hour and for female college graduates were $18.80 per hour in 2011. Assume that the standard deviation for male graduates is $2.30, and for female graduates it is $2.05.
   a. What is the sampling distribution of $\bar{x}$ for a random sample of 50 male college graduates?
   b. What is the sampling distribution of $\bar{x}$ for a random sample of 50 female college graduates?
   c. In which of the preceding two cases, part (a) or part (b), is the standard error of $\bar{x}$ smaller? Why?

10. The state of California has a mean annual rainfall of 22 inches, whereas the state of New York has a mean annual rainfall of 42 inches. Assume that the standard deviation for both states is 4 inches. A sample of 30 years of rainfall for California and a sample of 45 years of rainfall for New York has been taken.
    a. Show the sampling distribution of the sample mean annual rainfall for California.
    b. Show the sampling distribution of the sample mean annual rainfall for New York.
    c. In which of the preceding two cases, part (a) or part (b), is the standard error of $\bar{x}$ smaller? Why?

11. The president of Doerman Distributors, Inc., believes that 30% of the firm's orders come from first-time customers. A random sample of 100 orders will be used to

estimate the proportion of first-time customers. Assume that the president is correct and $p = 0.30$. What is the sampling distribution of $\bar{p}$ for this study?

12. *The Wall Street Journal* reported that the age at first startup for 55% of entrepreneurs was 29 years of age or less and the age at first startup for 45% of entrepreneurs was 30 years of age or more.

   a. Suppose a sample of 200 entrepreneurs will be taken to learn about the most important qualities of entrepreneurs. Show the sampling distribution of $\bar{p}$ where $\bar{p}$ is the sample proportion of entrepreneurs whose first startup was at 29 years of age or less.

   b. Suppose a sample of 200 entrepreneurs will be taken to learn about the most important qualities of entrepreneurs. Show the sampling distribution of $\bar{p}$ where $\bar{p}$ is now the sample proportion of entrepreneurs whose first startup was at 30 years of age or more.

   c. Are the standard errors of the sampling distributions different in parts (a) and (b)?

13. People end up tossing 12% of what they buy at the grocery store. Assume this is the true population proportion and that you plan to take a sample survey of 540 grocery shoppers to further investigate their behavior. Show the sampling distribution of $\bar{p}$, the proportion of groceries thrown out by your sample respondents.

14. Forty-two percent of primary care doctors think their patients receive unnecessary medical care.

   a. Suppose a sample of 300 primary care doctors was taken. Show the distribution of the sample proportion of doctors who think their patients receive unnecessary medical care.

   b. Suppose a sample of 500 primary care doctors was taken. Show the distribution of the sample proportion of doctors who think their patients receive unnecessary medical care.

   c. Suppose a sample of 1,000 primary care doctors was taken. Show the distribution of the sample proportion of doctors who think their patients receive unnecessary medical care.

   d. In which of the preceding three cases, part (a) or part (b) or part (c), is the standard error of $\bar{p}$ smallest? Why?

15. The International Air Transport Association surveys business travelers to develop quality ratings for transatlantic gateway airports. The maximum possible rating is 10. Suppose a simple random sample of 50 business travelers is selected and each traveler is asked to provide a rating for the Miami International Airport. The ratings obtained from the sample of 50 business travelers follow.

6	4	6	8	7	7	6	3	3	8	10	4	8
7	8	7	5	9	5	8	4	3	8	5	5	4
4	4	8	4	5	6	2	5	9	9	8	4	8
9	9	5	9	7	8	3	10	8	9	6		

Develop a 95% confidence interval estimate of the population mean rating for Miami.

16. A sample containing years to maturity and yield for 40 corporate bonds is contained in the file named *CorporateBonds*.

   a. What is the sample mean years to maturity for corporate bonds and what is the sample standard deviation?

   b. Develop a 95% confidence interval for the population mean years to maturity.

   c. What is the sample mean yield on corporate bonds and what is the sample standard deviation?

   d. Develop a 95% confidence interval for the population mean yield on corporate bonds.

17. Health insurers are beginning to offer telemedicine services online that replace the common office visit. Wellpoint provides a video service that allows subscribers to connect with a physician online and receive prescribed treatments. Wellpoint claims that users of its LiveHealth Online service saved a significant amount of money on a typical visit. The data shown below ($), for a sample of 20 online doctor visits, are consistent with the savings per visit reported by Wellpoint.

92	34	40
105	83	55
56	49	40
76	48	96
93	74	73
78	93	100
53	82	

Assuming that the population is roughly symmetric, construct a 95% confidence interval for the mean savings for a televisit to the doctor as opposed to an office visit.

18. The average annual premium for automobile insurance in the United States is $1,503. The following annual premiums ($) are representative of the web site's findings for the state of Michigan.

1,905	3,112	2,312
2,725	2,545	2,981
2,677	2,525	2,627
2,600	2,370	2,857
2,962	2,545	2,675
2,184	2,529	2,115
2,332	2,442	

Assume the population is approximately normal.
a. Provide a point estimate of the mean annual automobile insurance premium in Michigan.
b. Develop a 95% confidence interval for the mean annual automobile insurance premium in Michigan.
c. Does the 95% confidence interval for the annual automobile insurance premium in Michigan include the national average for the United States? What is your interpretation of the relationship between auto insurance premiums in Michigan and the national average?

19. One of the questions on a survey of 1,000 adults asked if today's children will be better off than their parents. Representative data are shown in the file named *ChildOutlook*. A response of Yes indicates that the adult surveyed did think today's children will be better off than their parents. A response of No indicates that the adult surveyed did not think today's children will be better off than their parents. A response of Not Sure was given by 23% of the adults surveyed.
a. What is the point estimate of the proportion of the population of adults who do think that today's children will be better off than their parents?
b. At 95% confidence, what is the margin of error?
c. What is the 95% confidence interval for the proportion of adults who do think that today's children will be better off than their parents?
d. What is the 95% confidence interval for the proportion of adults who do not think that today's children will be better off than their parents?
e. Which of the confidence intervals in parts (c) and (d) has the smaller margin of error? Why?

20. According to Thomson Financial, last year the majority of companies reporting profits had beaten estimates. A sample of 162 companies showed that 104 beat estimates, 29 matched estimates, and 29 fell short.
    a. What is the point estimate of the proportion that fell short of estimates?
    b. Determine the margin of error and provide a 95% confidence interval for the proportion that beat estimates.
    c. How large a sample is needed if the desired margin of error is 0.05?

21. The Pew Research Center Internet Project conducted a survey of 857 Internet users. This survey provided a variety of statistics on them.
    a. The sample survey showed that 90% of respondents said the Internet has been a good thing for them personally. Develop a 95% confidence interval for the proportion of respondents who say the Internet has been a good thing for them personally.
    b. The sample survey showed that 67% of Internet users said the Internet has generally strengthened their relationship with family and friends. Develop a 95% confidence interval for the proportion of respondents who say the Internet has strengthened their relationship with family and friends.
    c. Fifty-six percent of Internet users have seen an online group come together to help a person or community solve a problem, whereas only 25% have left an online group because of unpleasant interaction. Develop a 95% confidence interval for the proportion of Internet users who say online groups have helped solve a problem.
    d. Compare the margin of error for the interval estimates in parts (a), (b), and (c). How is the margin of error related to the sample proportion?

22. For many years businesses have struggled with the rising cost of health care. But recently, the increases have slowed due to less inflation in health care prices and employees paying for a larger portion of health care benefits. A recent Mercer survey showed that 52% of U.S. employers were likely to require higher employee contributions for health care coverage. Suppose the survey was based on a sample of 800 companies. Compute the margin of error and a 95% confidence interval for the proportion of companies likely to require higher employee contributions for health care coverage.

23. The manager of the Danvers-Hilton Resort Hotel stated that the mean guest bill for a weekend is $600 or less. A member of the hotel's accounting staff noticed that the total charges for guest bills have been increasing in recent months. The accountant will use a sample of future weekend guest bills to test the manager's claim.
    a. Which form of the hypotheses should be used to test the manager's claim? Explain.

$$H_0: \mu \geq 600 \quad H_0: \mu \leq 600 \quad H_0: \mu = 600$$
$$H_a: \mu < 600 \quad H_a: \mu > 600 \quad H_a: \mu \neq 600$$

    b. What conclusion is appropriate when H_0 cannot be rejected?
    c. What conclusion is appropriate when H_0 can be rejected?

24. The manager of an automobile dealership is considering a new bonus plan designed to increase sales volume. Currently, the mean sales volume is 14 automobiles per month. The manager wants to conduct a research study to see whether the new bonus plan increases sales volume. To collect data on the plan, a sample of sales personnel will be allowed to sell under the new bonus plan for a one-month period.
    a. Develop the null and alternative hypotheses most appropriate for this situation.
    b. Comment on the conclusion when H_0 cannot be rejected.
    c. Comment on the conclusion when H_0 can be rejected.

25. A production line operation is designed to fill cartons with laundry detergent to a mean weight of 32 ounces. A sample of cartons is periodically selected and weighed to determine whether underfilling or overfilling is occurring. If the sample data lead to a conclusion of underfilling or overfilling, the production line will be shut down and adjusted to obtain proper filling.
    a. Formulate the null and alternative hypotheses that will help in deciding whether to shut down and adjust the production line.
    b. Comment on the conclusion and the decision when H_0 cannot be rejected.
    c. Comment on the conclusion and the decision when H_0 can be rejected.

26. Because of high production-changeover time and costs, a director of manufacturing must convince management that a proposed manufacturing method reduces costs before the new method can be implemented. The current production method operates with a mean cost of $220 per hour. A research study will measure the cost of the new method over a sample production period.
    a. Develop the null and alternative hypotheses most appropriate for this study.
    b. Comment on the conclusion when H_0 cannot be rejected.
    c. Comment on the conclusion when H_0 can be rejected.

27. Duke Energy reported that the cost of electricity for an efficient home in a particular neighborhood of Cincinnati, Ohio, was $104 per month. A researcher believes that the cost of electricity for a comparable neighborhood in Chicago, Illinois, is higher. A sample of homes in this Chicago neighborhood will be taken and the sample mean monthly cost of electricity will be used to test the following null and alternative hypotheses.

$$H_0: \mu \leq 104$$
$$H_a: \mu > 104$$

    a. Assume the sample data lead to rejection of the null hypothesis. What would be your conclusion about the cost of electricity in the Chicago neighborhood?
    b. What is the Type I error in this situation? What are the consequences of making this error?
    c. What is the Type II error in this situation? What are the consequences of making this error?

28. The label on a 3-quart container of orange juice states that the orange juice contains an average of 1 gram of fat or less. Answer the following questions for a hypothesis test that could be used to test the claim on the label.
    a. Develop the appropriate null and alternative hypotheses.
    b. What is the Type I error in this situation? What are the consequences of making this error?
    c. What is the Type II error in this situation? What are the consequences of making this error?

29. Carpetland salespersons average $8,000 per week in sales. Steve Contois, the firm's vice president, proposes a compensation plan with new selling incentives. Steve hopes that the results of a trial selling period will enable him to conclude that the compensation plan increases the average sales per salesperson.
    a. Develop the appropriate null and alternative hypotheses.
    b. What is the Type I error in this situation? What are the consequences of making this error?
    c. What is the Type II error in this situation? What are the consequences of making this error?

30. Suppose a new production method will be implemented if a hypothesis test supports the conclusion that the new method reduces the mean operating cost per hour.
    a. State the appropriate null and alternative hypotheses if the mean cost for the current production method is $220 per hour.

b. What is the Type I error in this situation? What are the consequences of making this error?

c. What is the Type II error in this situation? What are the consequences of making this error?

31. Which is cheaper: eating out or dining in? The mean cost of a flank steak, broccoli, and rice bought at the grocery store is $13.04. A sample of 100 neighborhood restaurants showed a mean price of $12.75 and a standard deviation of $2 for a comparable restaurant meal.

a. Develop appropriate hypotheses for a test to determine whether the sample data support the conclusion that the mean cost of a restaurant meal is less than fixing a comparable meal at home.

b. Using the sample from the 100 restaurants, what is the p value?

c. At $\alpha = 0.05$, what is your conclusion?

32. A shareholders' group, in lodging a protest, claimed that the mean tenure for a chief executive officer (CEO) was at least nine years. A survey of companies reported in *The Wall Street Journal* found a sample mean tenure of $\bar{x} = 7.27$ years for CEOs with a standard deviation of $s = 6.38$ years.

a. Formulate hypotheses that can be used to challenge the validity of the claim made by the shareholders' group.

b. Assume that 85 companies were included in the sample. What is the p value for your hypothesis test?

c. At $\alpha = 0.01$, what is your conclusion?

33. The national mean annual salary for a school administrator is $90,000 a year. A school official took a sample of 25 school administrators in the state of Ohio to learn about salaries in that state to see if they differed from the national average.

a. Formulate hypotheses that can be used to determine whether the population mean annual administrator salary in Ohio differs from the national mean of $90,000.

b. The sample data for 25 Ohio administrators is contained in the file named *Administrator*. What is the p value for your hypothesis test in part (a)?

c. At $\alpha = 0.05$, can your null hypothesis be rejected? What is your conclusion?

34. The time married men with children spend on child care averages 6.4 hours per week. You belong to a professional group on family practices that would like to do its own study to determine if the time married men in your area spend on child care per week differs from the reported mean of 6.4 hours per week. A sample of 40 married couples will be used with the data collected showing the hours per week the husband spends on child care. The sample data are contained in the file named *ChildCare*.

a. What are the hypotheses if your group would like to determine if the population mean number of hours married men are spending on child care differs from the mean reported by *Time* in your area?

b. What is the sample mean and the p value?

c. Select your own level of significance. What is your conclusion?

35. The Coca-Cola Company reported that the mean per capita annual sales of its beverages in the United States was 423 eight-ounce servings. Suppose you are curious whether the consumption of Coca-Cola beverages is higher in Atlanta, Georgia, the location of Coca-Cola's corporate headquarters. A sample of 36 individuals from the Atlanta area showed a sample mean annual consumption of 460.4 eight-ounce servings with a standard deviation of $s = 101.9$ ounces. Using $\alpha = 0.05$, do the sample results support the conclusion that mean annual consumption of Coca-Cola beverage products is higher in Atlanta?

36. According to the National Automobile Dealers Association, the mean price for used cars is $10,192. A manager of a Kansas City used car dealership reviewed a sample of 50 recent used car sales at the dealership in an attempt to determine whether the population mean price for used cars at this particular dealership differed from the

national mean. The prices for the sample of 50 cars are shown in the file named *UsedCars*.

a. Formulate the hypotheses that can be used to determine whether a difference exists in the mean price for used cars at the dealership.

b. What is the *p* value?

c. At $\alpha = 0.05$, what is your conclusion?

37. What percentage of the population live in their state of birth? According to the U.S. Census Bureau's American Community Survey, the figure ranges from 25% in Nevada to 78.7% in Louisiana. The average percentage across all states and the District of Columbia is 57.7%. The data in the file *Homestate* are consistent with the findings in the American Community Survey. The data are for a random sample of 120 Arkansas residents and for a random sample of 180 Virginia residents.

a. Formulate hypotheses that can be used to determine whether the percentage of stay-at-home residents in the two states differs from the overall average of 57.7%.

b. Estimate the proportion of stay-at-home residents in Arkansas. Does this proportion differ significantly from the mean proportion for all states? Use $\alpha = 0.05$.

c. Estimate the proportion of stay-at-home residents in Virginia. Does this proportion differ significantly from the mean proportion for all states? Use $\alpha = 0.05$.

d. Would you expect the proportion of stay-at-home residents to be higher in Virginia than in Arkansas? Support your conclusion with the results obtained in parts (b) and (c).

38. Last year, 46% of business owners gave a holiday gift to their employees. A survey of business owners indicated that 35% plan to provide a holiday gift to their employees. Suppose the survey results are based on a sample of 60 business owners.

a. How many business owners in the survey plan to provide a holiday gift to their employees?

b. Suppose the business owners in the sample do as they plan. Compute the *p* value for a hypothesis test that can be used to determine if the proportion of business owners providing holiday gifts has decreased from last year.

c. Using a 0.05 level of significance, would you conclude that the proportion of business owners providing gifts has decreased? What is the smallest level of significance for which you could draw such a conclusion?

39. Ten years ago 53% of American families owned stocks or stock funds. Sample data collected by the Investment Company Institute indicate that the percentage is now 46%.

a. Develop appropriate hypotheses such that rejection of H_0 will support the conclusion that a smaller proportion of American families own stocks or stock funds this year than 10 years ago.

b. Assume the Investment Company Institute sampled 300 American families to estimate that the percent owning stocks or stock funds is 46% this year. What is the *p* value for your hypothesis test?

c. At $\alpha = 0.01$, what is your conclusion?

40. According to the University of Nevada Center for Logistics Management, 6% of all merchandise sold in the United States gets returned. A Houston department store sampled 80 items sold in January and found that 12 of the items were returned.

a. Construct a point estimate of the proportion of items returned for the population of sales transactions at the Houston store.

b. Construct a 95% confidence interval for the porportion of returns at the Houston store.

c. Is the proportion of returns at the Houston store significantly different from the returns for the nation as a whole? Provide statistical support for your answer.

DATA *file*
Eagle

41. Eagle Outfitters is a chain of stores specializing in outdoor apparel and camping gear. It is considering a promotion that involves mailing discount coupons to all its credit card customers. This promotion will be considered a success if more than 10% of those receiving the coupons use them. Before going national with the promotion, coupons were sent to a sample of 100 credit card customers.
   a. Develop hypotheses that can be used to test whether the population proportion of those who will use the coupons is sufficient to go national.
   b. The file named *Eagle* contains the sample data. Develop a point estimate of the population proportion.
   c. Use $\alpha = 0.05$ to conduct your hypothesis test. Should Eagle go national with the promotion?

DATA *file*
LawSuit

42. One of the reasons health care costs have been rising rapidly in recent years is the increasing cost of malpractice insurance for physicians. Also, fear of being sued causes doctors to run more precautionary tests (possibly unnecessary) just to make sure they are not guilty of missing something. These precautionary tests also add to health care costs. Data in the file named *LawSuit* are consistent with findings in a *Reader's Digest* article and can be used to estimate the proportion of physicians over the age of 55 who have been sued at least once.
   a. Formulate hypotheses that can be used to see if these data can support a finding that more than half of physicians over the age of 55 have been sued at least once.
   b. Use Excel and the file named *LawSuit* to compute the sample proportion of physicians over the age of 55 who have been sued at least once. What is the *p* value for your hypothesis test?
   c. At $\alpha = 0.01$, what is your conclusion?

DATA *file*
PortAuthority

43. The Port Authority sells a wide variety of cables and adapters for electronic equipment online. Last year the mean value of orders placed with the Port Authority was $47.28, and management wants to assess whether the mean value of orders placed to date this year is the same as last year. The values of a sample of 49,896 orders placed this year are collected and recorded in the file *PortAuthority*.
   a. Formulate hypotheses that can be used to test whether the mean value of orders placed this year differs from the mean value of orders placed last year.
   b. Use the data in the file *PortAuthority* to conduct your hypothesis test. What is the *p* value for your hypothesis test? At $\alpha = 0.01$, what is your conclusion?

DATA *file*
PortAuthority

44. The Port Authority also wants to determine if the gender profile of its customers has changed since last year, when 59.4% of its orders placed were placed by males. The genders for a sample of 49,896 orders placed this year are collected and recorded in the file *PortAuthority*.
   a. Formulate hypotheses that can be used to test whether the proportion of orders placed by male customers this year differs from the proportion of orders placed by male customers placed last year.
   b. Use the data in the file *PortAuthority* to conduct your hypothesis test. What is the *p* value for your hypothesis test? At $\alpha = 0.05$, what is your conclusion?

CASE PROBLEM 1 YOUNG PROFESSIONAL MAGAZINE

Young Professional magazine was developed for a target audience of recent college graduates who are in their first 10 years in a business/professional career. In its two years of publication, the magazine has been fairly successful. Now the publisher is interested in expanding the magazine's advertising base. Potential advertisers continually ask about the demographics and interests of subscribers to *Young Professional*. To collect this information, the magazine commissioned a survey to develop a profile of its subscribers. The survey results will be used to help the magazine choose articles of interest and provide advertisers with a profile of subscribers. As a new employee of the magazine, you have been asked to help analyze the survey results, a portion of which are shown in the following table.

Age	Sex	Real Estate Purchases	Value of Investments($)	Number of Transactions	Broadband Access	Household Income($)	Children
38	Female	No	12200	4	Yes	75200	Yes
30	Male	No	12400	4	Yes	70300	Yes
41	Female	No	26800	5	Yes	48200	No
28	Female	Yes	19600	6	No	95300	No
31	Female	Yes	15100	5	No	73300	Yes
⋮	⋮	⋮	⋮	⋮	⋮	⋮	⋮

DATA *file*
Professional

Some of the survey questions follow:

1. What is your age?
2. Are you: Male_____ Female_____
3. Do you plan to make any real estate purchases in the next two years? Yes_____ No_____
4. What is the approximate total value of financial investments, exclusive of your home, owned by you or members of your household?
5. How many stock/bond/mutual fund transactions have you made in the past year?
6. Do you have broadband access to the Internet at home? Yes_____ No_____
7. Please indicate your total household income last year.
8. Do you have children? Yes_____ No_____

The file *Professional* contains the responses to these questions. The table shows the portion of the file pertaining to the first five survey respondents.

Managerial Report

Prepare a managerial report summarizing the results of the survey. In addition to statistical summaries, discuss how the magazine might use these results to attract advertisers. You might also comment on how the survey results could be used by the magazine's editors to identify topics that would be of interest to readers. Your report should address the following issues, but do not limit your analysis to just these areas.

1. Develop appropriate descriptive statistics to summarize the data.
2. Develop 95% confidence intervals for the mean age and household income of subscribers.
3. Develop 95% confidence intervals for the proportion of subscribers who have broadband access at home and the proportion of subscribers who have children.
4. Would *Young Professional* be a good advertising outlet for online brokers? Justify your conclusion with statistical data.
5. Would this magazine be a good place to advertise for companies selling educational software and computer games for young children?
6. Comment on the types of articles you believe would be of interest to readers of *Young Professional*.

CASE PROBLEM 2 QUALITY ASSOCIATES, INC.

Quality Associates, Inc., a consulting firm, advises its clients about sampling and statistical procedures that can be used to control their manufacturing processes. In one particular application, a client gave Quality Associates a sample of 800 observations taken while that client's process was operating satisfactorily. The sample standard deviation for these data was 0.21; hence, with so much data, the population standard deviation was assumed to be 0.21. Quality Associates then suggested that random samples of size 30 be taken periodically to monitor the process on an ongoing basis. By analyzing the new samples, the client could quickly learn whether the process was operating satisfactorily. When the process was not operating satisfactorily, corrective action could be taken to eliminate the problem. The design specification indicated the mean for the process should be 12. The hypothesis test suggested by Quality Associates follows:

$$H_0: \mu = 12$$
$$H_a: \mu \neq 12$$

Corrective action will be taken any time H_0 is rejected.

The samples listed in the following table were collected at hourly intervals during the first day of operation of the new statistical process control procedure. These data are available in the file *Quality*.

DATA *file*

Quality

Sample 1	Sample 2	Sample 3	Sample 4
11.55	11.62	11.91	12.02
11.62	11.69	11.36	12.02
11.52	11.59	11.75	12.05
11.75	11.82	11.95	12.18
11.90	11.97	12.14	12.11
11.64	11.71	11.72	12.07
11.64	11.71	11.72	12.07
11.80	11.87	11.61	12.05
12.03	12.10	11.85	11.64
11.94	12.01	12.16	12.39
11.92	11.99	11.91	11.65
12.13	12.20	12.12	12.11
12.09	12.16	11.61	11.90
11.93	12.00	12.21	12.22
12.21	12.28	11.56	11.88
12.32	12.39	11.95	12.03
11.93	12.00	12.01	12.35
11.85	11.92	12.06	12.09
11.76	11.83	11.76	11.77
12.16	12.23	11.82	12.20
11.77	11.84	12.12	11.79
12.00	12.07	11.60	12.30
12.04	12.11	11.95	12.27
11.98	12.05	11.96	12.29
12.30	12.37	12.22	12.47
12.18	12.25	11.75	12.03
11.97	12.04	11.96	12.17
12.17	12.24	11.95	11.94
11.85	11.92	11.89	11.97
12.30	12.37	11.88	12.23
12.15	12.22	11.93	12.25

Managerial Report

1. Conduct a hypothesis test for each sample at the 0.01 level of significance and determine what action, if any, should be taken. Provide the test statistic and *p* value for each test.

2. Compute the standard deviation for each of the four samples. Does the conjecture of 0.21 for the population standard deviation appear reasonable?
3. Compute limits for the sample mean $\bar{x}$ around $\mu = 12$ such that, as long as a new sample mean is within those limits, the process will be considered to be operating satisfactorily. If $\bar{x}$ exceeds the upper limit or if $\bar{x}$ is below the lower limit, corrective action will be taken. These limits are referred to as upper and lower control limits for quality-control purposes.
4. Discuss the implications of changing the level of significance to a larger value. What mistake or error could increase if the level of significance is increased?

Chapter 7

Linear Regression

CONTENTS

Alliance Data Systems*

DALLAS, TEXAS

Alliance Data Systems (ADS) provides transaction processing, credit services, and marketing services for clients in the rapidly growing customer relationship management (CRM) industry. ADS clients are concentrated in four industries: retail, petroleum/convenience stores, utilities, and transportation. In 1983, Alliance began offering end-to-end credit-processing services to the retail, petroleum, and casual dining industries; today the company employs more than 6,500 employees who provide services to clients around the world. Operating more than 140,000 point-of-sale terminals in the United States alone, ADS processes in excess of 2.5 billion transactions annually. The company ranks second in the United States in private-label credit services by representing 49 private label programs with nearly 72 million cardholders. In 2001, ADS made an initial public offering and is now listed on the New York Stock Exchange.

As one of its marketing services, ADS designs direct mail campaigns and promotions. With its database containing information on the spending habits of more than 100 million consumers, ADS can target consumers who are the most likely to benefit from a direct mail promotion. The Analytical Development Group uses regression analysis to build models that measure and predict the responsiveness of consumers to direct market campaigns. Some regression models predict the probability of purchase for individuals receiving a promotion, and others predict the amount spent by consumers who make purchases.

For one campaign, a retail store chain wanted to attract new customers. To predict the effect of the campaign, ADS analysts selected a sample from the consumer database, sent the sampled individuals promotional materials, and then collected transaction data on the consumers' responses. Sample data were collected on the amount of purchases made by the consumers responding to the campaign, as well as on a variety of consumer-specific variables thought to be useful in predicting sales. The consumer-specific variable that contributed most to predicting the amount purchased was the total amount of credit purchases at related stores over the past 39 months. ADS analysts developed an estimated regression equation relating the amount of purchase to the amount spent at related stores:

$$\hat{y} = 26.7 + 0.00205x,$$

where

$\hat{y}$ = predicted amount of purchase
x = amount spent at related stores

Using this equation, we could predict that someone spending \$10,000 over the past 39 months at related stores would spend \$47.20 when responding to the direct mail promotion. In this chapter, you will learn how to develop this type of estimated regression equation. The final model developed by ADS analysts also included several other variables that increased the predictive power of the preceding equation. Among these variables was the absence or presence of a bank credit card, estimated income, and the average amount spent per trip at a selected store. In this chapter, we will also learn how such additional variables can be incorporated into a multiple regression model.

*The authors are indebted to Philip Clemance, Director of Analytical Development at Alliance Data Systems, for providing this Analytics in Action.

Managerial decisions are often based on the relationship between two or more variables. For example, after considering the relationship between advertising expenditures and sales, a marketing manager might attempt to predict sales for a given level of advertising expenditures. In another case, a public utility might use the relationship between the daily high temperature and the demand for electricity to predict electricity usage on the basis of next month's anticipated daily high temperatures. Sometimes a manager will rely on intuition to judge how two variables are related. However, if data can be obtained, a statistical procedure called **regression analysis** can be used to develop an equation showing how the variables are related.

The statistical methods used in studying the relationship between two variables were first employed by Sir Francis Galton (1822–1911). Galton found that the heights of the sons of unusually tall or unusually short fathers tend to move, or "regress," toward the average height of the male population. Karl Pearson (1857–1936), a disciple of Galton, later confirmed this finding in a sample of 1,078 pairs of fathers and sons.

In regression terminology, the variable being predicted is called the **dependent variable**, or *response*, and the variables being used to predict the value of the dependent variable are called the **independent variables**, or *predictor variables*. For example, in analyzing the effect of advertising expenditures on sales, a marketing manager's desire to predict sales would suggest making sales the dependent variable. Advertising expenditure would be the independent variable used to help predict sales.

In this chapter, we begin by considering **simple linear regression**, in which the relationship between one dependent variable (denoted by y) and one independent variable (denoted by x) is approximated by a straight line. We then extend this concept to higher dimensions by introducing **multiple linear regression** to model the relationship between a dependent variable (y) and two or more independent variables ($x_1, x_2, \ldots, x_q$).

7.1 Simple Linear Regression Model

Butler Trucking Company is an independent trucking company in southern California. A major portion of Butler's business involves deliveries throughout its local area. To develop better work schedules, the managers want to estimate the total daily travel times for their drivers. The managers believe that the total daily travel times (denoted by y) are closely related to the number of miles traveled in making the daily deliveries (denoted by x). Using regression analysis, we can develop an equation showing how the dependent variable y is related to the independent variable x.

Regression Model

In the Butler Trucking Company example, a simple linear regression model hypothesizes that the travel time of a driving assignment (y) is linearly related to the number of miles traveled (x) as follows:

SIMPLE LINEAR REGRESSION MODEL

$$y = \beta_0 + \beta_1 x + \varepsilon \tag{7.1}$$

In equation (7.1), β_0 and β_1 are population parameters that describe the y-intercept and slope of the line relating y and x. The error term ε (Greek letter epsilon) accounts for the variability in y that cannot be explained by the linear relationship between x and y. The simple linear regression model assumes that the error term is a normally distributed random variable with a mean of zero and constant variance for all observations.

Estimated Regression Equation

In practice, the values of the population parameters β_0 and β_1 are not known and must be estimated using sample data. Sample statistics (denoted b_0 and b_1) are computed as estimates of the population parameters β_0 and β_1. Substituting the values of the sample statistics b_0 and b_1 for β_0 and β_1 in equation (7.1) and dropping the error term (because its expected value is zero), we obtain the **estimated regression** for simple linear regression:

ESTIMATED SIMPLE LINEAR REGRESSION EQUATION

$$\hat{y} = b_0 + b_1 x \tag{7.2}$$

The estimation of β_0 and β_1 is a statistical process much like the estimation of the population mean, μ, discussed in Chapter 6. β_0 and β_1 are the unknown parameters of interest, and b_0 and b_1 are the sample statistics used to estimate the parameters.

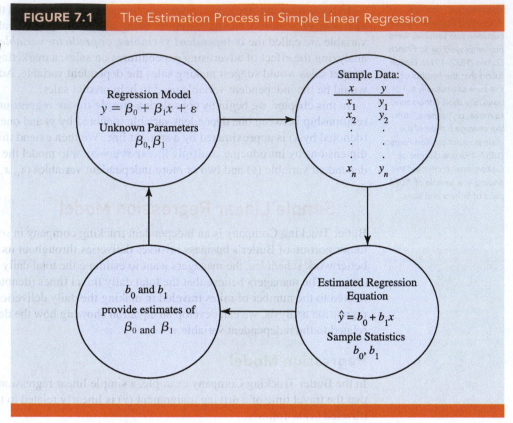

FIGURE 7.1   The Estimation Process in Simple Linear Regression

Regression Model
$$y = \beta_0 + \beta_1 x + \varepsilon$$
Unknown Parameters
β_0, β_1

Sample Data:

x	y
x_1	y_1
x_2	y_2
.	.
.	.
x_n	y_n

b_0 and b_1
provide estimates of
β_0 and β_1

Estimated Regression Equation
$$\hat{y} = b_0 + b_1 x$$
Sample Statistics
b_0, b_1

Figure 7.1 provides a summary of the estimation process for simple linear regression. Using equation (7.2), $\hat{y}$ provides an estimate for the mean value of y corresponding to a given value of x.

The graph of the estimated simple linear regression equation is called the *estimated regression line*; b_0 is the estimated y-intercept, and b_1 is the estimated slope. In the next section, we show how the least squares method can be used to compute the values of b_0 and b_1 in the estimated regression equation.

Examples of possible regression lines are shown in Figure 7.2. The regression line in Panel A shows that the estimated mean value of y is related positively to x, with larger values of $\hat{y}$ associated with larger values of x. In Panel B, the estimated mean value of y is related negatively to x, with smaller values of $\hat{y}$ associated with larger values of x. In Panel C, the estimated mean value of y is not related to x; that is, $\hat{y}$ is the same for every value of x.

In general, $\hat{y}$ is the **point estimator** of $E(y|x)$, the mean value of y for a given value of x. Thus, to estimate the mean or expected value of travel time for a driving assignment of 75 miles, Butler trucking would substitute the value of 75 for x in equation (7.2). In some cases, however, Butler Trucking may be more interested in predicting travel time for an upcoming driving assignment of a particular length. For example, suppose Butler Trucking would like to predict travel time for a new 75-mile driving assignment the company is considering. As it turns out, the best predictor of y for a given value of x is also provided by $\hat{y}$. Thus, to predict travel time for a new 75-mile driving assignment, Butler Trucking would also substitute the value of 75 for x in equation (7.3). The value of $\hat{y}$ provides both

A point estimator is a single value used as an estimate of the corresponding population parameter.

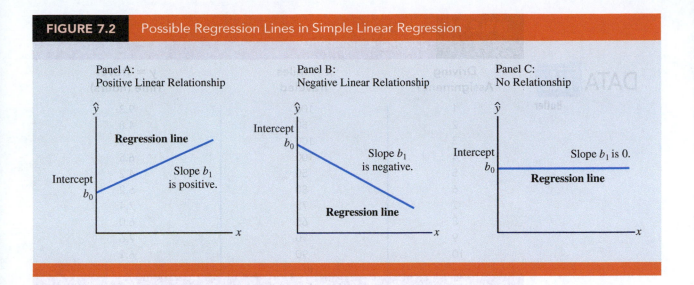

FIGURE 7.2   Possible Regression Lines in Simple Linear Regression

a point estimate of $E(y|x)$ for a given value of x and a prediction of an individual value of y for a given value of x. In most cases, we will refer to $\hat{y}$ simply as the predicted value of y.

7.2 Least Squares Method

The **least squares method** is a procedure for using sample data to find the estimated regression equation. To illustrate the least squares method, suppose data were collected from a sample of 10 Butler Trucking Company driving assignments. For the ith observation or driving assignment in the sample, x_i is the miles traveled and y_i is the travel time (in hours). The values of x_i and y_i for the 10 driving assignments in the sample are summarized in Table 7.1. We see that driving assignment 1, with $x_1 = 100$ and $y_1 = 9.3$, is a driving assignment of 100 miles and a travel time of 9.3 hours. Driving assignment 2, with $x_2 = 50$ and $y_2 = 4.8$, is a driving assignment of 50 miles and a travel time of 4.8 hours. The shortest travel time is for driving assignment 5, which requires 50 miles with a travel time of 4.2 hours.

Figure 7.3 is a scatter chart of the data in Table 7.1. Miles traveled is shown on the horizontal axis, and travel time (in hours) is shown on the vertical axis. Scatter charts for regression analysis are constructed with the independent variable x on the horizontal axis and the dependent variable y on the vertical axis. The scatter chart enables us to observe the data graphically and to draw preliminary conclusions about the possible relationship between the variables.

What preliminary conclusions can be drawn from Figure 7.3? Longer travel times appear to coincide with more miles traveled. In addition, for these data, the relationship between the travel time and miles traveled appears to be approximated by a straight line; indeed, a positive linear relationship is indicated between x and y. We therefore choose the simple linear regression model to represent this relationship. Given that choice, our next task is to use the sample data in Table 7.1 to determine the values of b_0 and b_1 in the estimated simple linear regression equation. For the ith driving assignment, the estimated regression equation provides:

$$\hat{y}_i = b_0 + b_1 x_i, \qquad (7.3)$$

where

$\hat{y}_i =$ predicted travel time (in hours) for the ith driving assignment
$b_0 =$ the y-intercept of the estimated regression line

TABLE 7.1	Miles Traveled and Travel Time for 10 Butler Trucking Company Driving Assignments	
Driving Assignment i	x = Miles Traveled	y = Travel Time (hours)
1	100	9.3
2	50	4.8
3	100	8.9
4	100	6.5
5	50	4.2
6	80	6.2
7	75	7.4
8	65	6.0
9	90	7.6
10	90	6.1

DATA *file*

Butler

b_1 = the slope of the estimated regression line
x_i = miles traveled for the ith driving assignment

With y_i denoting the observed (actual) travel time for driving assignment i and $\hat{y}_i$ in equation (7.3) representing the predicted travel time for driving assignment i, every driving assignment in the sample will have an observed travel time y_i and a predicted travel time $\hat{y}_i$. For the estimated regression line to provide a good fit to the data, the differences between the observed travel times y_i and the predicted travel times $\hat{y}_i$ should be small.

The least squares method uses the sample data to provide the values of b_0 and b_1 that minimize the sum of the squares of the deviations between the observed values of the

FIGURE 7.3	Scatter Chart of Miles Traveled and Travel Time for Sample of 10 Butler Trucking Company Driving Assignments

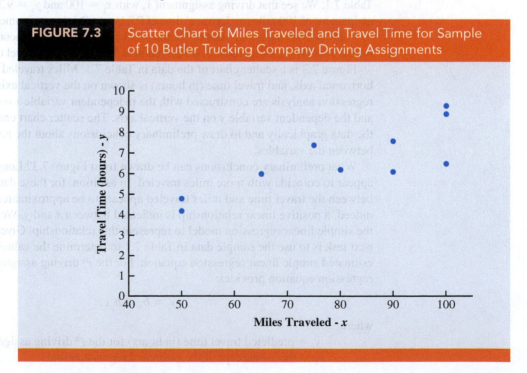

dependent variable y_i and the predicted values of the dependent variable $\hat{y}_i$. The criterion for the least squares method is given by equation (7.4).

LEAST SQUARES EQUATION

$$\min \sum_{i=1}^{n} (y_i - \hat{y}_i)^2 = \min \sum_{i=1}^{n} (y_1 - b_0 - b_1 x_i)^2 \qquad (7.4)$$

where

y_i = observed value of the dependent variable for the ith observation
$\hat{y}_i$ = predicted value of the dependent variable for the ith observation
n = total number of observations

This is known as the least squares method for estimating the regression equation.

The error we make using the regression model to estimate the mean value of the dependent variable for the ith observation is often written as $e_i = y_i - \hat{y}_i$ and is referred to as the ith **residual**. Using this notation, equation (7.4) can be rewritten as:

$$\min \sum_{i=1}^{n} e_i^2$$

and we say that we are finding the regression that minimizes the sum of squared errors.

Least Squares Estimates of the Regression Parameters

Although the values of b_0 and b_1 that minimize equation (7.3) can be calculated manually with equations (see note at end of this section), computer software such as Excel or XLMiner is generally used to calculate b_1 and b_0. For the Butler Trucking Company data in Table 7.1, an estimated slope of $b_1 = 0.0678$ and a y-intercept of $b_0 = 1.2739$ minimize the sum of squared errors (in the next section we show how to use Excel to obtain these values). Thus, our estimated simple linear regression model is $\hat{y} = 1.2739 + 0.0678x_1$.

We interpret b_1 and b_0 as we would the y-intercept and slope of any straight line. The slope b_1 is the estimated change in the mean of the dependent variable y that is associated with a one-unit increase in the independent variable x. For the Butler Trucking Company model, we therefore estimate that, if the length of a driving assignment were 1 unit (1 mile) longer, the mean travel time for that driving assignment would be 0.0678 unit (0.0678 hour, or approximately 4 minutes) longer. The y-intercept b_0 is the estimated value of the dependent variable y when the independent variable x is equal to 0. For the Butler Trucking Company model, we estimate that if the driving distance for a driving assignment was 0 units (0 miles), the mean travel time would be 1.2739 units (1.2739 hours, or approximately 76 minutes). Can we find a plausible explanation for this? Perhaps the 76 minutes represent the time needed to prepare, load, and unload the vehicle, which is required for all trips regardless of distance and which therefore does not depend on the distance traveled. However, we must use caution: To estimate the travel time for a driving distance of 0 miles, we have to extend the relationship we have found with simple linear regression well beyond the range of values for driving distance in our sample. Those sample values range from 50 to 100 miles, and this range represents the only values of driving distance for which we have empirical evidence of the relationship between driving distance and our estimated travel time.

It is important to note that the regression model is valid only over the **experimental region**, which is the range of values of the independent variables in the data used to estimate the model. Prediction of the value of the dependent variable outside the experimental region is called **extrapolation** and is risky. Because we have no empirical evidence that the relationship we have found holds true for values of x outside of the range of values of x in

The estimated value of the y-intercept often results from extrapolation.

the data used to estimate the relationship, extrapolation is risky and should be avoided if possible. For Butler Trucking, this means that any prediction outside the travel time for a driving distance less than 50 miles or greater than 100 miles is not a reliable estimate, and so for this model the estimate of β_0 is meaningless. However, if the experimental region for a regression problem includes zero, the y-intercept will have a meaningful interpretation.

We can now also use this model and our known values for miles traveled for a driving assignment (x) to estimate mean travel time in hours. For example, the first driving assignment in Table 7.1 has a value for miles traveled of $x = 100$. We estimate the mean travel time in hours for this driving assignment to be:

$$\hat{y}_i = 1.2739 + 0.0678(100) = 8.0539.$$

The point estimate $\hat{y}$ provided by the regression equation does not give us any information about the precision associated with the prediction. For that we must develop an interval estimate around the point estimate. In the appendix at the end of the chapter, we demonstrate how to generate interval estimates around the point estimates provided by a regression equation.

Since the travel time for this driving assignment was 9.3 hours, this regression estimate would have resulted in a residual of:

$$e_1 = y_1 - \hat{y}_1 = 9.3 - 8.0539 = 1.2461.$$

The simple linear regression model underestimated travel time for this driving assignment by 1.2461 hours (approximately 74 minutes). Table 7.2 shows the predicted mean travel times, the residuals, and the squared residuals for all 10 driving assignments in the sample data.

Note in Table 7.2 that:

- The sum of predicted values $\hat{y}_i$ is equal to the sum of the values of the dependent variable y.
- The sum of the residuals e_i is 0.
- The sum of the squared residuals e_i^2 has been minimized.

These three points will always be true for a simple linear regression that is determined by equations (7.6) and (7.7). Figure 7.4 shows the simple linear regression line $\hat{y}_i = 1.2739 + 0.0678x_i$ superimposed on the scatter chart for the Butler Trucking Company data in Table 7.1. This figure, which also highlights the residuals for driving assignment 3 (e_3) and driving assignment 5 (e_5), shows that the regression model underpredicts travel time for some driving assignments (such as driving assignment 3) and overpredicts travel time for others (such as driving assignment 5), but in general appears to fit the data relatively well.

TABLE 7.2	Predicted Travel Time and Residuals for 10 Butler Trucking Company Driving Assignments

Driving Assignment i	x = Miles Traveled	y = Travel Time (hours)	$\hat{y}_i = b_0 + b_1 x_i$	$e_i = y_i - \hat{y}_i$	e_i^2
1	100	9.3	8.0565	1.2435	1.5463
2	50	4.8	4.6652	0.1348	0.0182
3	100	8.9	8.0565	0.8435	0.7115
4	100	6.5	8.0565	−1.5565	2.4227
5	50	4.2	4.6652	−0.4652	0.2164
6	80	6.2	6.7000	−0.5000	0.2500
7	75	7.4	6.3609	1.0391	1.0797
8	65	6.0	5.6826	0.3174	0.1007
9	90	7.6	7.3783	0.2217	0.0492
10	90	6.1	7.3783	−1.2783	1.6341
Totals	67.0	67.0000		0.0000	8.0288

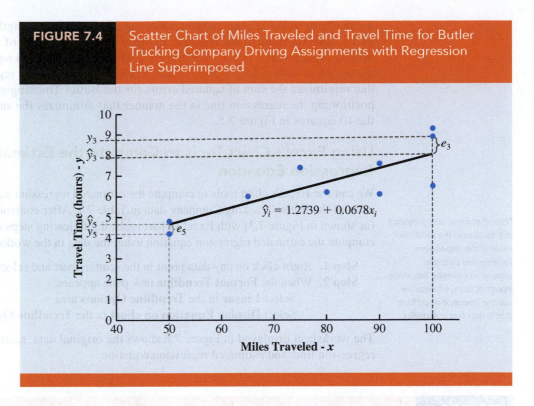

FIGURE 7.4   Scatter Chart of Miles Traveled and Travel Time for Butler Trucking Company Driving Assignments with Regression Line Superimposed

In Figure 7.5, a vertical line is drawn from each point in the scatter chart to the linear regression line. Each of these vertical lines represents the difference between the actual driving time and the driving time we predict using linear regression for one of the assignments in our data. The length of each vertical line is equal to the absolute value of the residual for one of the driving assignments. When we square a residual,

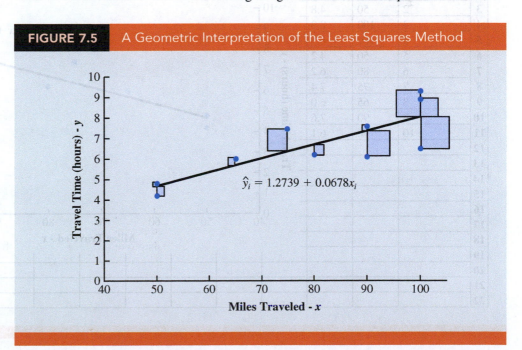

FIGURE 7.5   A Geometric Interpretation of the Least Squares Method

the resulting value is equal to the area of the square with the length of each side equal to the absolute value of the residual. In other words, the square of the residual for driving assignment 4 (e_4), $(-1.5565)^2 = 2.4227$, is the area of a square for which the length of each side is 1.5565. Thus, when we find the linear regression model that minimizes the sum of squared errors for the Butler Trucking example, we are positioning the regression line in the manner that minimizes the sum of the areas of the 10 squares in Figure 7.5.

Using Excel's Chart Tools to Compute the Estimated Regression Equation

Note that Excel uses y instead of ŷ to denote the predicted value of the dependent variable and puts the regression equation into slope-intercept form, whereas we use the intercept-slope form that is standard in statistics.

We can use Excel's chart tools to compute the estimated regression equation on a scatter chart of the Butler Trucking Company data in Table 7.1. After constructing a scatter chart (as shown in Figure 7.3) with Excel's chart tools, the following steps describe how to compute the estimated regression equation using the data in the worksheet:

Step 1. Right-click on any data point in the scatter chart and select **Add Trendline . . .**
Step 2. When the **Format Trendline** task pane appears:
      Select **Linear** in the **Trendline Options** area
      Select **Display Equation on chart** in the **Trendline Options** area

The worksheet displayed in Figure 7.6 shows the original data, scatter chart, estimated regression line, and estimated regression equation.

FIGURE 7.6   Scatter Chart and Estimated Regression Line for Butler Trucking Company

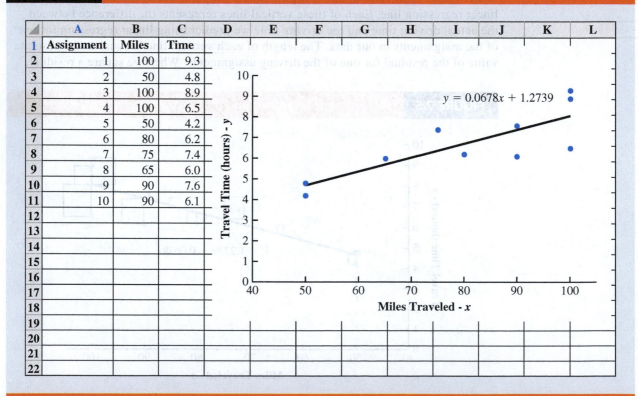

NOTES + COMMENTS

1. Differential calculus can be used to show that the values of b_0 and b_1 that minimize expression (7.5) are given by:

SLOPE EQUATION

$$b_1 = \frac{\sum_{i=1}^{n}(x_i - \bar{x})(y_i - \bar{y})}{\sum_{i=1}^{n}(x_i - \bar{x})^2}$$

y-INTERCEPT EQUATION

$$b_0 = \bar{y} - b_1\bar{x}$$

where

x_i = value of the independent variable for the ith observation

y_i = value of the dependent variable for the ith observation

$\bar{x}$ = mean value for the independent variable

$\bar{y}$ = mean value for the dependent variable

n = total number of observations

2. Equation 7.5 minimizes the sum of the squared deviations between the observed values of the dependent variable y_i and the predicted values of the dependent variable $\hat{y}_i$. One alternative is to simply minimize the sum of the deviations between the observed values of the dependent variable y_i and the predicted values of the dependent variable $\hat{y}_i$. This is not a viable option because then negative deviations (observations for which the regression forecast exceeds the actual value) and positive deviations (observations for which the regression forecast is less than the actual value) offset each other. Another alternative is to minimize the sum of the absolute value of the deviations between the observed values of the dependent variable y_i and the predicted values of the dependent variable $\hat{y}_i$. It is possible to compute estimated regression parameters that minimize this sum of the absolute value of the deviations, but this approach is more difficult than the least squares approach.

7.3 Assessing the Fit of the Simple Linear Regression Model

For the Butler Trucking Company example, we developed the estimated regression equation $\hat{y}_i = 1.2739 + 0.0678x_i$ to approximate the linear relationship between the miles traveled x and travel time in hours y. We now wish to assess how well the estimated regression equation fits the sample data. We begin by developing the intermediate calculations, referred to as sums of squares.

The Sums of Squares

Recall that we found our estimated regression equation for the Butler Trucking Company example by minimizing the sum of squares of the residuals. This quantity, also known as the *sum of squares due to error*, is denoted by SSE.

SUM OF SQUARES DUE TO ERROR

$$\text{SSE} = \sum_{i=1}^{n}(y_i - \hat{y}_i)^2 \tag{7.5}$$

The value of SSE is a measure of the error (in the same units as the dependent variable) that results from using the estimated regression equation to predict the values of the dependent variable in the sample.

We have already shown the calculations required to compute the sum of squares due to error for the Butler Trucking Company example in Table 7.2. The squared residual or error for each observation in the data is shown in the last column of that table. After computing and squaring

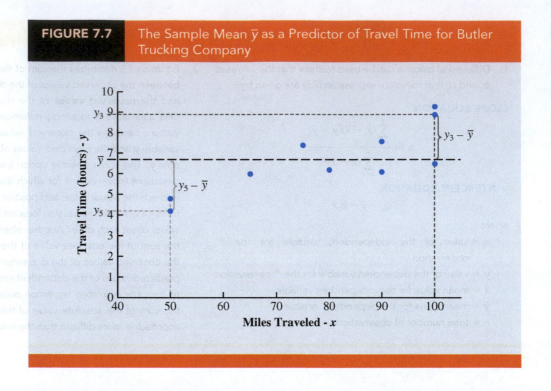

FIGURE 7.7   The Sample Mean $\bar{y}$ as a Predictor of Travel Time for Butler Trucking Company

the residuals for each driving assignment in the sample, we sum them to obtain SSE = 8.0288 hours. Thus, SSE = 8.0288 measures the error in using the estimated regression equation $\hat{y}_i = 1.2739 + 0.0678x_i$ to predict travel time for the driving assignments in the sample.

Now suppose we are asked to predict travel time in hours without knowing the miles traveled for a driving assignment. Without knowledge of any related variables, we would use the sample mean $\bar{y}$ as a predictor of travel time for any given driving assignment. To find $\bar{y}$, we divide the sum of the actual driving times y_i from Table 7.2 (67) by the number of observations n in the data (10); this yields $\bar{y} = 6.7$.

Figure 7.7 provides insight on how well we would predict the values of y_i in the Butler Trucking company example using $\bar{y} = 6.7$. From this figure, which again highlights the residuals for driving assignments 3 and 5, we can see that $\bar{y}$ tends to overpredict travel times for driving assignments that have relatively small values for miles traveled (such as driving assignment 5) and tends to underpredict travel times for driving assignments that have relatively large values for miles traveled (such as driving assignment 3).

In Table 7.3 we show the sum of squared deviations obtained by using the sample mean $\bar{y} = 6.7$ to predict the value of travel time in hours for each driving assignment in the sample. For the ith driving assignment in the sample, the difference $y_i - \bar{y}$ provides a measure of the error involved in using $\bar{y}$ to predict travel time for the ith driving assignment. The corresponding sum of squares, called the total sum of squares, is denoted SST.

TOTAL SUM OF SQUARES, SST

$$\text{SST} = \sum_{i=1}^{n} (y_i - \bar{y})^2 \tag{7.6}$$

TABLE 7.3	Calculations for the Sum of Squares Total for the Butler Trucking Simple Linear Regression			
Driving Assignment i	$x =$ Miles Traveled	$y =$ Travel Time (hours)	$y_i - \bar{y}$	$(y_i - \bar{y})^2$
1	100	9.3	2.6	6.76
2	50	4.8	−1.9	3.61
3	100	8.9	2.2	4.84
4	100	6.5	−0.2	0.04
5	50	4.2	−2.5	6.25
6	80	6.2	−0.5	0.25
7	75	7.4	0.7	0.49
8	65	6.0	−0.7	0.49
9	90	7.6	0.9	0.81
10	90	6.1	2.6	6.76
	Totals	67.0	0	23.9

The sum at the bottom of the last column in Table 7.3 is the total sum of squares for Butler Trucking Company: SST = 23.9.

Now we put it all together. In Figure 7.8 we show the estimated regression line $\hat{y}_i = 1.2739 + 0.0678x_i$ and the line corresponding to $\bar{y} = 6.7$. Note that the points cluster more closely around the estimated regression line $\hat{y}_i = 1.2739 + 0.0678x_i$ than they do about the horizontal line $\bar{y} = 6.7$. For example, for the third driving assignment in the sample, we see that the error is much larger when $\bar{y} = 6.7$ is used to predict y_3 than when $\hat{y}_3 = 1.2739 + 0.0678 (100) = 8.0539$ is used. We can think of SST as a measure of

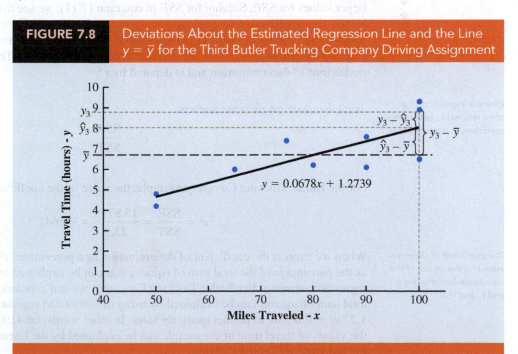

FIGURE 7.8 Deviations About the Estimated Regression Line and the Line $y = \bar{y}$ for the Third Butler Trucking Company Driving Assignment

how well the observations cluster about the $\bar{y}$ line and SSE as a measure of how well the observations cluster about the $\hat{y}$ line.

To measure how much the $\hat{y}$ values on the estimated regression line deviate from $\bar{y}$, another sum of squares is computed. This sum of squares, called the *sum of squares due to regression*, is denoted SSR.

SUM OF SQUARES DUE TO REGRESSION, SSR

$$\text{SSR} = \sum_{i=1}^{n}(\hat{y}_i - \bar{y})^2 \qquad (7.7)$$

From the preceding discussion, we should expect that SST, SSR, and SSE are related. Indeed, the relationship among these three sums of squares is:

$$\text{SST} = \text{SSR} + \text{SSE}, \qquad (7.8)$$

where

$\text{SST} = \text{total sum of squares}$
$\text{SSR} = \text{sum of squares due to regression}$
$\text{SSE} = \text{sum of squares due to error}$

The Coefficient of Determination

Now let us see how the three sums of squares, SST, SSR, and SSE, can be used to provide a measure of the goodness of fit for the estimated regression equation. The estimated regression equation would provide a perfect fit if every value of the dependent variable y_i happened to lie on the estimated regression line. In this case, $y_i - \hat{y}$ would be zero for each observation, resulting in SSE $= 0$. Because SST $=$ SSR $+$ SSE, we see that for a perfect fit SSR must equal SST, and the ratio (SSR/SST) must equal one. Poorer fits will result in larger values for SSE. Solving for SSE in equation (7.11), we see that SSE $=$ SST $-$ SSR. Hence, the largest value for SSE (and hence the poorest fit) occurs when SSR $= 0$ and SSE $=$ SST. The ratio SSR/SST, which will take values between zero and one, is used to evaluate the goodness of fit for the estimated regression equation. This ratio is called the **coefficient of determination** and is denoted by r^2.

In simple regression, r^2 is often referred to as the simple coefficient of determination.

COEFFICIENT OF DETERMINATION

$$r^2 = \frac{\text{SSR}}{\text{SST}} \qquad (7.9)$$

For the Butler Trucking Company example, the value of the coefficient of determination is:

$$r^2 = \frac{\text{SSR}}{\text{SST}} = \frac{15.8712}{23.9} = 0.6641.$$

The coefficient of determination r^2 is the square of the correlation between the y_i and $\hat{y}_i$, and $0 \le r^2 \le 1$.

When we express the coefficient of determination as a percentage, r^2 can be interpreted as the percentage of the total sum of squares that can be explained by using the estimated regression equation. For Butler Trucking Company, we can conclude that 66.41% of the total sum of squares can be explained by using the estimated regression equation $\hat{y}_i = 1.2739 + 0.0678x_i$ to predict quarterly sales. In other words, 66.41% of the variability in the values of travel time in our sample can be explained by the linear relationship between the miles traveled and travel time.

FIGURE 7.9   Scatter Chart and Estimated Regression Line with Coefficient of Determination r^2 for Butler Trucking Company

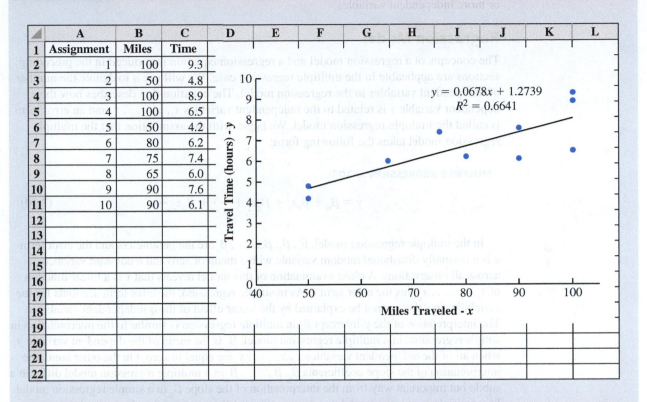

Using Excel's Chart Tools to Compute the Coefficient of Determination

In Section 7.1 we used Excel's chart tools to construct a scatter chart and compute the estimated regression equation for the Butler Trucking Company data. We will now describe how to compute the coefficient of determination using the scatter chart in Figure 7.3.

Step 1. Right-click on any data point in the scatter chart and select **Add Trendline. . .**
Step 2. When the **Format Trendline** task pane appears:
  Select **Display R-squared value on chart** in the **Trendline Options** area

Note that Excel notates the coefficient of determination as R².

Figure 7.9 displays the scatter chart, the estimated regression equation, the graph of the estimated regression equation, and the coefficient of determination for the Butler Trucking Company data. We see that $r^2 = 0.6641$.

N O T E S + C O M M E N T S

As a practical matter, for typical data in the social and behavioral sciences, values of r^2 as low as 0.25 are often considered useful. For data in the physical and life sciences, r^2 values of 0.60 or greater are often found; in fact, in some cases, r^2 values greater than 0.90 can be found. In business applications, r^2 values vary greatly, depending on the unique characteristics of each application.

7.4 The Multiple Regression Model

We now extend our discussion to the study of how a dependent variable y is related to two or more independent variables.

Regression Model

The concepts of a regression model and a regression equation introduced in the preceding sections are applicable in the multiple regression case. We will use q to denote the number of independent variables in the regression model. The equation that describes how the dependent variable y is related to the independent variables $x_1, x_2, \ldots, x_q$ and an error term is called the multiple regression model. We begin with the assumption that the multiple regression model takes the following form:

MULTIPLE REGRESSION MODEL

$$y = \beta_0 + \beta_1 x_1 + \beta_2 x_2 + \cdots + \beta_q x_q + \varepsilon \qquad (7.10)$$

In the multiple regression model, $\beta_0, \beta_1, \beta_2, \ldots, \beta_q$ are the parameters and the error term ε is a normally distributed random variable with a mean of zero and a constant variance across all observations. A close examination of this model reveals that y is a linear function of $x_1, x_2, \ldots, x_q$ plus the error term ε. As in simple regression, the error term accounts for the variability in y that cannot be explained by the linear effect of the q independent variables. The interpretation of the y-intercept β_0 in multiple regression is similar to the interpretation in simple regression; in a multiple regression model, β_0 is the mean of the dependent variable y when all of the independent variables $x_1, x_2, \ldots, x_q$ are equal to zero. On the other hand, the interpretation of the slope coefficients $\beta_1, \beta_2, \ldots, \beta_q$ in a multiple regression model differ in a subtle but important way from the interpretation of the slope β_1 in a simple regression model. In a multiple regression model the slope coefficient β_j represents the change in the mean value of the dependent variable y that corresponds to a one-unit increase in the independent variable x_j, *holding the values of all other independent variables in the model constant*. Thus, in a multiple regression model, the slope coefficient β_1 represents the change in the mean value of the dependent variable y that corresponds to a one-unit increase in the independent variable x_1, holding the values of $x_2, x_3, \ldots, x_q$ constant. Similarly, the slope coefficient β_2 represents the change in the mean value of the dependent variable y that corresponds to a one-unit increase in the independent variable x_2, holding the values of $x_1, x_3, \ldots, x_q$ constant.

Estimated Multiple Regression Equation

In practice, the values of the population parameters $\beta_0, \beta_1, \beta_2, \ldots, \beta_q$ are not known and so must be estimated from sample data. A simple random sample is used to compute sample statistics $b_0, b_1, b_2, \ldots, b_q$ that are then used as the point estimators of the parameters $\beta_0, \beta_1, \beta_2, \ldots, \beta_q$. These sample statistics provide the following estimated multiple regression equation.

ESTIMATED MULTIPLE REGRESSION EQUATION

$$\hat{y} = b_0 + b_1 x_1 + b_2 x_2 + \cdots + b_q x_q, \qquad (7.11)$$

where

$$b_0, b_1, b_2, \ldots, b_q = \text{the point estimates of } \beta_0, \beta_1, \beta_2, \ldots, \beta_q$$
$$\hat{y} = \text{estimated mean value of } y \text{ given values for } x_1, \ldots, x_q$$

Least Squares Method and Multiple Regression

As with simple linear regression, in multiple regression we wish to find a model that results in small errors over the sample data. We continue to use the least squares method to develop the estimated multiple regression equation; that is, we find b_0, b_1, b_2, . . . , b_q that minimize the sum of squared residuals (the deviations between the observed values of the dependent variable y_i and the estimated values of the dependent variable $\hat{y}$):

$$\min \sum_{i=1}^{n}(y_i - \hat{y}_i)^2 = \min \sum_{i=1}^{n}(y_i - b_0 - b_1x_1 - \cdots - b_qx_q)^2 = \min \sum_{i=1}^{n}e_i^2. \quad \textbf{(7.12)}$$

The estimation process for multiple regression is shown in Figure 7.10.

The estimated values of the dependent variable y are computed by substituting values of the independent variables x_1, x_2, . . . , x_q into the estimated multiple regression equation (7.11).

As in simple regression, it is possible to derive formulas that determine the values of the regression coefficients that minimize equation (7.12). However, these formulas involve the use of matrix algebra and are outside the scope of this text. Therefore, in presenting multiple regression, we focus on how computer software packages can be used to obtain the estimated regression equation and other information. The emphasis will be on how to construct and interpret a regression model.

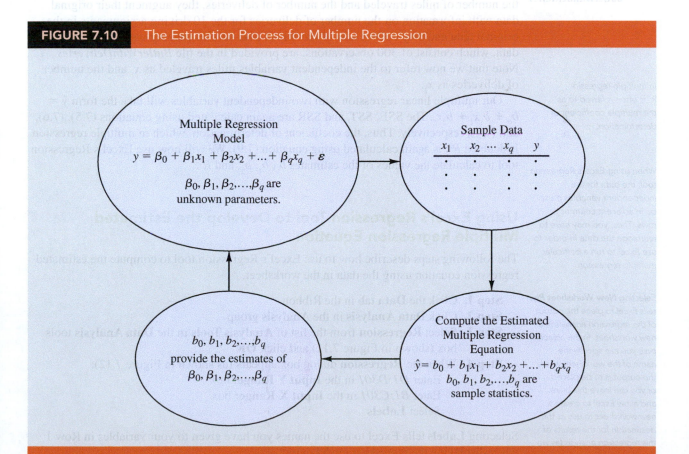

FIGURE 7.10   The Estimation Process for Multiple Regression

Multiple Regression Model
$$y = \beta_0 + \beta_1x_1 + \beta_2x_2 + \ldots + \beta_qx_q + \varepsilon$$
$\beta_0, \beta_1, \beta_2, \ldots, \beta_q$ are unknown parameters.

Sample Data

x_1	x_2	$\cdots$	x_q	y
·	·	·	·	·
·	·	·	·	·
·	·	·	·	·

Compute the Estimated Multiple Regression Equation
$$\hat{y} = b_0 + b_1x_1 + b_2x_2 + \ldots + b_qx_q$$
$b_0, b_1, b_2, \ldots, b_q$ are sample statistics.

$b_0, b_1, b_2, \ldots, b_q$ provide the estimates of $\beta_0, \beta_1, \beta_2, \ldots, \beta_q$

Butler Trucking Company and Multiple Regression

As an illustration of multiple regression analysis, recall that a major portion of Butler Trucking Company's business involves deliveries throughout its local area and that the managers want to estimate the total daily travel time for their drivers in order to develop better work schedules for the company's drivers.

Initially, the managers believed that the total daily travel time would be closely related to the number of miles traveled in making the daily deliveries. Based on a simple random sample of 10 driving assignments, we explored the simple linear regression model $y = \beta_0 + \beta_1 x + \varepsilon$ to describe the relationship between travel time (y) and number of miles (x). As Figure 7.9 shows, we found that the estimated simple linear regression equation for our sample data is $\hat{y}_i = 1.2739 + 0.0678 x_i$. With a coefficient of determination $r^2 = 0.6641$, the linear effect of the number of miles traveled explains 66.41% of the variability in travel time in the sample data, and so 33.59% of the variability in sample travel times remains unexplained. This result suggests to Butler's managers that other factors may contribute to the travel times for driving assignments. The managers might want to consider adding one or more independent variables to the model to explain some of the remaining variability in the dependent variable.

In considering other independent variables for their model, the managers felt that the number of deliveries made on a driving assignment also contributes to the total travel time. To support the development of a multiple regression model that includes both the number of miles traveled and the number of deliveries, they augment their original data with information on the number of deliveries for the 10 driving assignments in the original data and they collect new observations over several ensuing weeks. The new data, which consist of 300 observations, are provided in the file *ButlerWithDeliveries*. Note that we now refer to the independent variables miles traveled as x_1 and the number of deliveries as x_2.

Our multiple linear regression with two independent variables will take the form $\hat{y} = b_0 + b_1 x_1 + b_2 x_2$. The SSE, SST, and SSR are again calculated using equations (7.5), (7.6), and (7.7), respectively. Thus, the coefficient of determination, which in multiple regression is denoted R^2, is again calculated using equation (7.9). We will now use Excel's Regression tool to calculate the values of the estimates b_0, b_1, b_2, and R^2.

DATA file
ButlerWithDeliveries

In multiple regression, R^2 is often referred to as the multiple coefficient of determination.

When using Excel's Regression tool, the data for the independent variables must be in adjacent columns or rows. Thus, you may have to rearrange the data in order to use Excel to run a particular multiple regression.

Using Excel's Regression Tool to Develop the Estimated Multiple Regression Equation

The following steps describe how to use Excel's Regression tool to compute the estimated regression equation using the data in the worksheet.

*Selecting **New Worksheet Ply:** tells Excel to place the output of the regression analysis in a new worksheet. In the adjacent box, you can specify the name of the worksheet where the output is to be placed, or you can leave this blank and allow Excel to create a new worksheet to use as the destination for the results of this regression analysis (as we are doing here).*

Step 1. Click the **Data** tab in the Ribbon

Step 2. Click **Data Analysis** in the **Analysis** group

Step 3. Select **Regression** from the list of **Analysis Tools** in the **Data Analysis** tools box (shown in Figure 7.11) and click **OK**

Step 4. When the **Regression** dialog box appears (as shown in Figure 7.12):
Enter *D1:D301* in the **Input Y Range:** box
Enter *B1:C301* in the **Input X Range:** box
Select **Labels**

Selecting **Labels** tells Excel to use the names you have given to your variables in Row 1 when displaying the regression model output.

*If Data Analysis does not appear in your Analysis group, you will have to load the Analysis ToolPak add-in into Excel. To do so, click the **FILE** tab in the Ribbon, and click **Options**. When the **Excel Options** dialog box appears, click **Add-Ins** from the menu. Next to **Manage:**, select **Excel Add-ins**, and click **Go. . .** at the bottom of the dialog box. When the **Add-Ins** dialog box appears, select **Analysis ToolPak** and click **Go.** When the **Add-Ins** dialog box appears, check the box next to **Analysis Toolpak** and click **OK.***

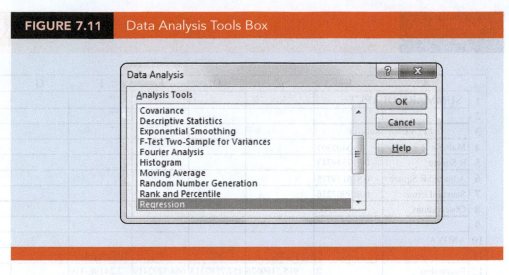

FIGURE 7.11   Data Analysis Tools Box

Select **Confidence Level:**
Enter *99* in the **Confidence Level:** box
Select **New Worksheet Ply:**
Click **OK**

In the Excel output shown in Figure 7.13, the label for the independent variable x_1 is Miles (see cell A18), and the label for the independent variable x_2 is Deliveries (see cell A19). The estimated regression equation is:

$$\hat{y} = 0.1273 + 0.0672x_1 + 0.6900x_2 \quad (7.13)$$

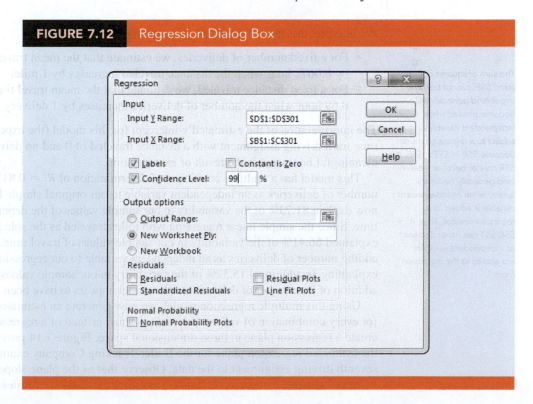

FIGURE 7.12   Regression Dialog Box

Excel Regression Output for the Butler Trucking Company with Miles and Deliveries as Independent Variables

	A	B	C	D	E	F	G	H	I
1	SUMMARY OUTPUT								
2									
3	*Regression Statistics*								
4	Multiple R	0.90407397							
5	R Square	0.817349743							
6	Adjusted R Square	0.816119775							
7	Standard Error	0.829967216							
8	Observations	300							
9									
10	ANOVA								
11		*df*	*SS*	*MS*	*F*	*Significance F*			
12	Regression	2	915.5160626	457.7580313	664.5292419	2.2419E-110			
13	Residual	297	204.5871374	0.68884558					
14	Total	299	1120.1032						
15									
16		*Coefficients*	*Standard Error*	*t Stat*	*P-value*	*Lower 95%*	*Upper 95%*	*Lower 99.0%*	*Upper 99.0%*
17	Intercept	0.127337137	0.20520348	0.620540826	0.53537766	–0.276499931	0.531174204	–0.404649592	0.659323866
18	Miles	0.067181742	0.002454979	27.36551071	3.5398E-83	0.062350385	0.072013099	0.06081725	0.073546235
19	Deliveries	0.68999828	0.029521057	23.37308852	2.84826E-69	0.631901326	0.748095234	0.613465414	0.766531147

We interpret this model in the following manner:

The sum of squares due to error, SSE, cannot become larger (and generally will become smaller) when independent variables are added to a regression model. Because SSR − SST = SSE, the SSR cannot become smaller (and generally becomes larger) when an independent variable is added to a regression model. Thus, $R^2 =$ SSR/SST can never decrease as independent variables are added to the regression model.

- For a fixed number of deliveries, we estimate that the mean travel time will increase by 0.0672 hour when the distance traveled increases by 1 mile.
- For a fixed distance traveled, we estimate that the mean travel time will increase by 0.69 hour when the number of deliveries increases by 1 delivery.

The interpretation of the estimated y-intercept for this model (the expected mean travel time for a driving assignment with a distance traveled of 0 and no deliveries) is not meaningful because it is the result of extrapolation.

This model has a multiple coefficient of determination of $R^2 = 0.8173$. By adding the number of deliveries as an independent variable to our original simple linear regression, we now explain 81.73% of the variability in our sample values of the dependent variable, travel time. Since the simple linear regression with miles traveled as the sole independent variable explained 66.41% of the variability in our sample values of travel time, we can see that adding number of deliveries as an independent variable to our regression model resulted in explaining an additional 15.32% of the variability in our sample values of travel time. The addition of the number of deliveries to the model appears to have been worthwhile.

Using this multiple regression model, we now generate an estimated mean value of y for every combination of values of x_1 and x_2. Thus, instead of a regression line, we now create a regression plane in three-dimensional space. Figure 7.14 provides the graph of the estimated regression plane for the Butler Trucking Company example and shows the seventh driving assignment in the data. Observe that as the plane slopes upward to larger values of estimated mean travel time ($\hat{y}$) as either the number of miles traveled (x_1) or

FIGURE 7.14	Graph of the Regression Equation for Multiple Regression Analysis with Two Independent Variables

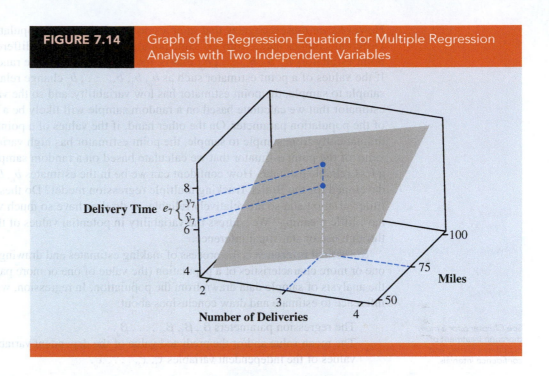

the number of deliveries (x_2) increases. Further, observe that the residual for a driving assignment when $x_1 = 75$ and $x_2 = 3$ is the difference between the observed y value and the estimated mean value of y given $x_1 = 75$ and $x_2 = 3$. Note that in Figure 7.14, the observed value lies above the regression plane, indicating that the regression model underestimates the expected driving time for the seventh driving assignment.

NOTES + COMMENTS

Although we use regression analysis to estimate relationships between independent variables and the dependent variable, it does not provide information on whether these are cause-and-effect relationships. The analyst can conclude that a cause-and-effect relationship exists between an independent variable and the dependent variable only if there is a theoretical justification that the relationship is in fact causal. In the Butler Trucking Company multiple regression, through regression analysis we have found evidence of a relationship between distance traveled and travel time and evidence of a relationship between number of deliveries and travel time. Nonetheless, we cannot

conclude from the regression model that changes in distance traveled x_1 cause changes in travel time y, and we cannot conclude that changes in number of deliveries x_2 cause changes in travel time y. The appropriateness of such cause-and-effect conclusions are left to supporting practical justification and to good judgment on the part of the analyst. Based on their practical experience, Butler Trucking's managers felt that increases in distance traveled and number of deliveries were likely causes of increased travel time. However, it is important to realize that the regression model itself provides no information about cause-and-effect relationships.

7.5 Inference and Regression

The statistics $b_0, b_1, b_2, \ldots, b_q$ are point estimators of the population parameters $\beta_0, \beta_1, \beta_2, \ldots, \beta_q$; that is, each of these $q + 1$ estimates is a single value used as an estimate of the corresponding population parameter. Similarly, we use $\hat{y}$ as a point estimator of $E(y \mid x_1, x_2, \ldots, x_q)$, the conditional expectation of y given values of $x_1, x_2, \ldots, x_q$.

However, we must recognize that samples do not replicate the population exactly. Different samples taken from the same population will result in different values of the point estimators $b_0, b_1, b_2, \ldots, b_q$; that is, the point estimators are random variables. If the values of a point estimator such as $b_0, b_1, b_2, \ldots, b_q$ change relatively little from sample to sample, the point estimator has low variability, and so the value of the point estimator that we calculate based on a random sample will likely be a reliable estimate of the population parameter. On the other hand, if the values of a point estimator change dramatically from sample to sample, the point estimator has high variability, and so the value of the point estimator that we calculate based on a random sample will likely be a less reliable estimate. How confident can we be in the estimates b_0, b_1, and b_2 that we developed for the Butler Trucking multiple regression model? Do these estimates have little variation and so are relatively reliable, or do they have so much variation that they have little meaning? We address the variability in potential values of the estimators through use of statistical inference.

Statistical inference is the process of making estimates and drawing conclusions about one or more characteristics of a population (the value of one or more parameters) through the analysis of sample data drawn from the population. In regression, we commonly use inference to estimate and draw conclusions about:

See Chapter 6 for a more thorough treatment of hypothesis testing and confidence intervals.

- The regression parameters $\beta_0, \beta_1, \beta_2, \ldots, \beta_q$.
- The mean value and/or the predicted value of the dependent variable y for specific values of the independent variables $x_1, x_2, \ldots, x_q$.

In our discussion of inference and regression, we will consider both **hypothesis testing** and **interval estimation**.

Conditions Necessary for Valid Inference in the Least Squares Regression Model

In conducting a regression analysis, we begin by making an assumption about the appropriate model for the relationship between the dependent and independent variable(s). For the case of linear regression, the assumed multiple regression model is:

$$y = \beta_0 + \beta_1 x_1 + \beta_2 x_2 + \cdots + \beta_q x_q + \varepsilon.$$

The least squares method is used to develop values for $b_1, b_2, \ldots, b_q$, the estimates of the model parameters $\beta_0, \beta_1, \beta_2, \ldots, \beta_p$, respectively. The resulting estimated multiple regression equation is:

$$\hat{y} = b_0 + b_1 x_1 + b_2 x_2 + \cdots + b_q x_q.$$

Although inference can provide greater understanding of the nature of relationships estimated through regression analysis, our inferences are valid only if the error term ε behaves in a certain way. Specifically, the validity of inferences in regression analysis depends on how well the following two conditions about the error term ε are met:

1. For any given combination of values of the independent variables $x_1, x_2, \ldots, x_q$, the population of potential error terms ε is normally distributed with a mean of 0 and a constant variance.
2. The values of ε are statistically independent.

The practical implication of normally distributed errors with a mean of zero and a constant variation for any given combination of values of $x_1, x_2, \ldots, x_q$ is that the regression estimates are unbiased (i.e., do not tend to over- or underpredict), possess

FIGURE 7.15 Illustration of the Conditions for Valid Inference in Regression

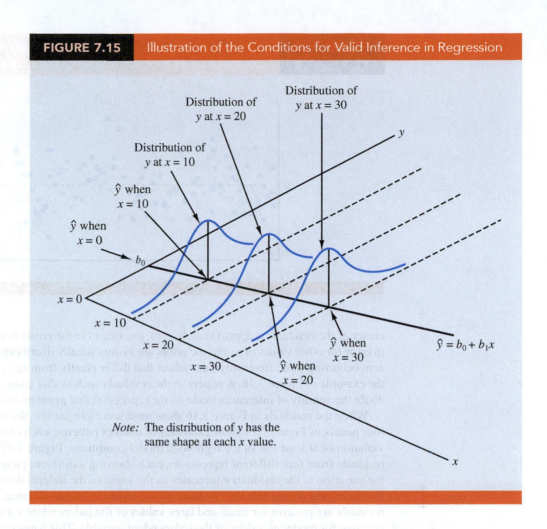

Distribution of
y at x = 30

Distribution of
y at x = 20

Distribution of
y at x = 10

$\hat{y}$ when
x = 10

$\hat{y}$ when
x = 0

b_0

x = 0

x = 10

x = 20

x = 30

$\hat{y}$ when
x = 30

$\hat{y}$ when
x = 20

y

$\hat{y} = b_0 + b_1 x$

x

Note: The distribution of y has the
same shape at each x value.

Keep in mind that we are also making an assumption or hypothesis about the form of the relationship between x and y. We assume that a straight line represented by $\beta_0 + \beta_1 x$ is the basis for the relationship between the variables. We must not lose sight of the fact that some other model, for instance $y = \beta_0 + \beta_1 x_1 + \beta_2 x_2 + \varepsilon$, may actually provide a better representation for the underlying population relationship.

consistent accuracy, and tend to err in small amounts rather than in large amounts. This first condition must be met for statistical inference in regression to be valid. The second condition is generally a concern when we collect data from a single entity over several periods of time and must also be met for statistical inference in regression to be valid in these instances. However, inferences in regression are generally reliable unless there are marked violations of these conditions.

Figure 7.15 illustrates these model conditions and their implications for a simple linear regression; note that in this graphical interpretation, the value of $E(y|x)$ changes linearly according to the specific value of x considered, and so the mean error is zero at each value of x. However, regardless of the x value, the error term ε and hence the dependent variable y are normally distributed, each with the same variance.

To evaluate whether the error of an estimated regression equation reasonably meets the two conditions, the sample residuals ($e_i = y_i - \hat{y}_i$ for observations $i = 1, \ldots n$) need to be analyzed. There are many sophisticated diagnostic procedures for detecting whether the sample errors violate these conditions, but simple scatter charts of the residuals and independent variables are an extremely effective method for assessing whether these conditions are violated. We should review the scatter chart for patterns in the residuals indicating that one or more of the conditions have been violated. At any given value of x, the

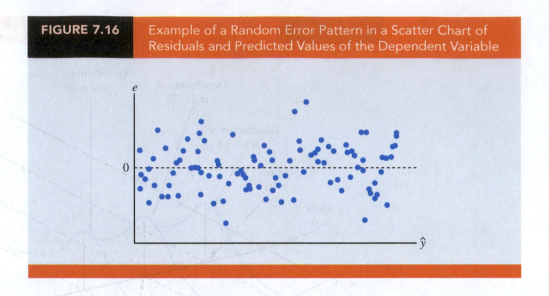

FIGURE 7.16   Example of a Random Error Pattern in a Scatter Chart of Residuals and Predicted Values of the Dependent Variable

center of the residuals is approximately zero, the spread in the errors is similar to the spread in error for other values of x, and the errors are symmetrically distributed with values near zero occurring more frequently than values that differ greatly from zero. This is shown in the example in Figure 7.16. A pattern in the residuals such as this gives us little reason to doubt the validity of inferences made on the regression that generated the residuals.

While the residuals in Figure 7.16 show no discernible pattern, the residuals in the four panels of Figure 7.17 show examples of distinct patterns, each of which suggests a violation of at least one of the regression model conditions. Figure 7.17 shows plots of residuals from four different regressions, each showing a different pattern. In panel (a), the variation in the residuals e increases as the value of the independent variable x increases, suggesting that the residuals do not have a constant variance. In panel (b), the residuals are positive for small and large values of the independent variable x but are negative for moderate values of the independent variable. This pattern suggests that the linear regression model underpredicts the value of dependent variable for small and large values of the independent variable and overpredicts the value of the dependent variable for intermediate values of the independent variable. In this case, the regression model does not adequately capture the relationship between the independent variable x and the dependent variable y. The residuals in panel (c) are not symmetrically distributed around 0; many of the negative residuals are relatively close to zero, while the relatively few positive residuals tend to be far from zero. This skewness suggests that the residuals are not normally distributed. Finally, the residuals in panel (d) are plotted over time t, which generally serves as an independent variable; that is, an observation is made at each of several (usually equally spaced) points in time. In this case, connected consecutive residuals allow us to see a distinct pattern across every set of four residuals; the second residual is consistently larger than the first and smaller than the third, whereas the fourth residual is consistently the smallest. This pattern, which occurs consistently over each set of four consecutive residuals in the chart in panel (d), suggests that the residuals generated by this model are not independent. A residual pattern such as this generally occurs when we have collected quarterly data and have not captured seasonal effects in the model. In each of these four instances, any inferences based on our regression will likely not be reliable.

Frequently, the residuals do not meet these conditions either because an important independent variable has been omitted from the model or because the functional form of

FIGURE 7.17 Examples of Diagnostic Scatter Charts of Residuals from Four Regressions

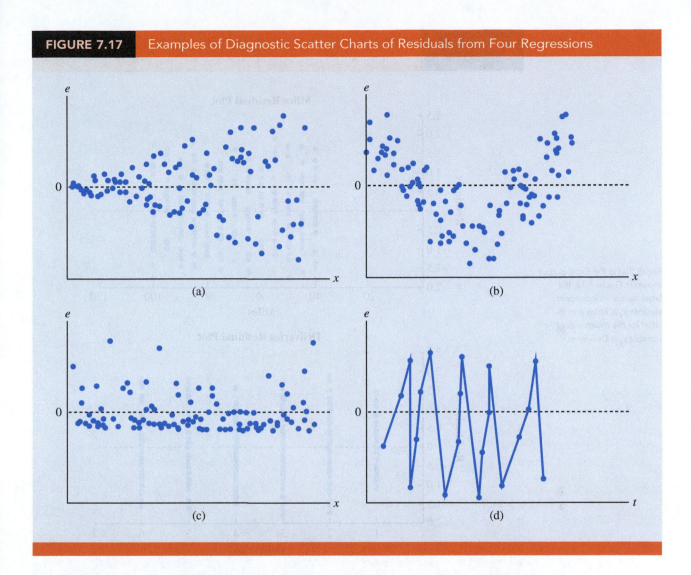

the model is inadequate to explain the relationships between the independent variables and the dependent variable. It is important to note that calculating the values of the estimates $b_0, b_1, b_2, \ldots, b_q$ does not require the errors to satisfy these conditions. However, the errors must satisfy these conditions in order for inferences (interval estimates for predicted values of the dependent variable and confidence intervals and hypothesis tests of the regression parameters $\beta_0, \beta_1, \beta_2, \ldots, \beta_q$) to be reliable.

You can generate scatter charts of the residuals against each independent variable in the model when using Excel's Regression tool; to do so, select the **Residual Plots** option in the **Residuals** area of the **Regression** dialog box. Figure 7.18 shows residual plots produced by Excel for the Butler Trucking Company example for which the independent variables are miles (x_1) and deliveries (x_2).

The residuals at each value of miles appear to have a mean of zero, to have similar variances, and to be concentrated around zero. The residuals at each value of deliveries also appear to have a mean of zero, to have similar variances, and to be concentrated around zero. Although there appears to be a slight pattern in the residuals across values of

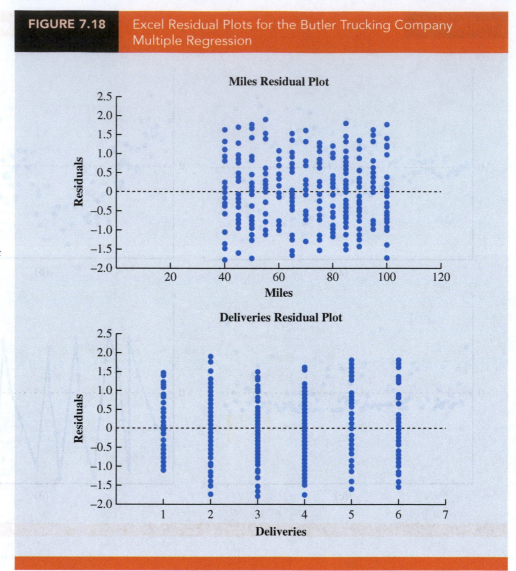

FIGURE 7.18 Excel Residual Plots for the Butler Trucking Company Multiple Regression

Recall that in the Excel output shown in Figure 7.13, the label for the independent variable x_1 is Miles and the label for the independent variable x_2 is Deliveries.

deliveries, it is negligible and could conceivably be the result of random variation. Thus, this evidence provides little reason for concern over the validity of inferences about the regression model that we may perform.

A scatter chart of the residuals e against the predicted values of the dependent variables is also commonly used to assess whether the residuals of the regression model satisfy the conditions necessary for valid inference. To obtain the data to construct a scatter chart of the residuals against the predicted values of the dependent variable using Excel's Regression tool, select the **Residuals** option in the **Residuals** area of the **Regression** dialog box (shown in Figure 7.12). This generates a table of predicted values of the dependent variable and residuals for the observations in the data; a partial list for the Butler Trucking multiple regression example is shown in Figure 7.19.

We can then use the Excel chart tool to create a scatter chart of these predicted values and residuals similar to the chart in Figure 7.20. The figure shows that the residuals at

FIGURE 7.19   Table of the First Several Predicted Values ŷ and Residuals e Generated by the Excel Regression Tool

23	RESIDUAL OUTPUT		
24			
25	*Observation*	*Predicted Time*	*Residuals*
26	1	9.605504464	−0.305504464
27	2	5.556419081	−0.756419081
28	3	9.605504464	−0.705504464
29	4	8.225507903	−1.725507903
30	5	4.8664208	−0.6664208
31	6	6.881873062	−0.681873062
32	7	7.235932632	0.164037368
33	8	7.254143492	−1.254143492
34	9	8.243688763	−0.643688763
35	10	7.553690482	−1.453690482
36	11	6.936415641	0.063584359
37	12	7.290505212	−0.290505212
38	13	9.287776613	0.312223387
39	14	5.874146931	0.625853069
40	15	6.954596501	0.245403499
41	16	5.556419081	0.443580919

FIGURE 7.20   Scatter Chart of Predicted Values ŷ and Residuals e

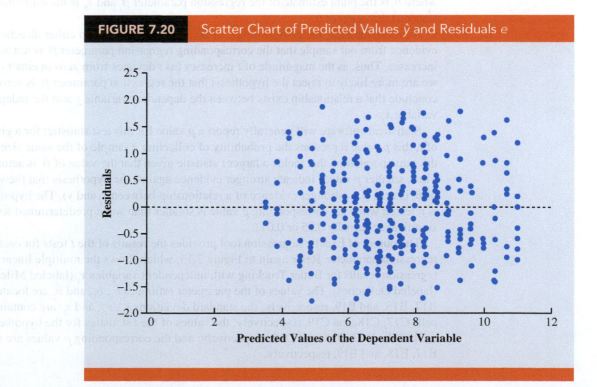

each predicted value of the dependent variable appear to have a mean of zero, to have similar variances, and to be concentrated around zero. This leads us to the same conclusion we reached when looking at the residuals plotted against the independent variables: The residuals provide little evidence that our regression model violates the conditions necessary for reliable inference. We can trust the inferences that we may wish to perform on our regression model.

Testing Individual Regression Parameters

Once we ascertain that our regression model satisfies the conditions necessary for reliable inference reasonably well, we can begin testing hypotheses and building confidence intervals. Specifically, we may then wish to determine whether statistically significant relationships exist between the dependent variable y and each of the independent variables $x_1, x_2, \ldots, x_q$ individually. Note that if a β_j is zero, then the dependent variable y does not change when the independent variable x_j changes, and there is no linear relationship between y and x_j. Alternatively, if a β_j is not zero, there is a linear relationship between the dependent variable y and the independent variable x_j.

See Chapter 6 for a more in-depth discussion of hypothesis testing.

We use a ***t* test** to test the hypothesis that a regression parameter β_j is zero. The corresponding null and alternative hypotheses are:

$$H_0: \beta = 0$$
$$H_a: \beta \neq 0$$

The standard deviation of b_j is often referred to as the standard error of b_j. Thus, s_{b_j} provides an estimate of the standard error of b_j.

The test statistic for this t test is:

$$t = \frac{b_j}{s_{b_j}},$$

(7.14)

where b_j is the point estimate of the regression parameter β_j and s_{b_j} is the estimated standard deviation of b_j.

As the value of b_j, the point estimate of β_j, deviates from zero in either direction, the evidence from our sample that the corresponding regression parameter β_j is not zero increases. Thus, as the magnitude of t increases (as t deviates from zero in either direction), we are more likely to reject the hypothesis that the regression parameter β_j is zero and so conclude that a relationship exists between the dependent variable y and the independent variable x_j.

Statistical software will generally report a p value for this test statistic; for a given value of t, this p value represents the probability of collecting a sample of the same size from the same population that yields a larger t statistic given that the value of β_j is actually zero. Thus, smaller p values indicate stronger evidence against the hypothesis that the value of β_j is zero (i.e., stronger evidence of a relationship between x_j and y). The hypothesis is rejected when the corresponding p value is smaller than some predetermined level of significance (usually 0.05 or 0.01).

The output of Excel's Regression tool provides the results of the t tests for each regression parameter. Refer again to Figure 7.13, which shows the multiple linear regression results for Butler Trucking with independent variables x_1 (labeled Miles) and x_2 (labeled Deliveries). The values of the parameter estimates b_0, b_1, and b_2 are located in cells B17, B18, and B19, respectively; the standard deviations s_{b_0}, s_{b_1}, and s_{b_2} are contained in cells C17, C18, and C19, respectively; the values of the t statistics for the hypothesis tests are in cells D17, D18, and D19, respectively; and the corresponding p values are in cells E17, E18, and E19, respectively.

Let's use these results to test the hypothesis that β_1 is zero. If we do not reject this hypothesis, we conclude that the mean value of y does not change when the value of x_1 changes, and so there is no relationship between driving time and miles traveled. We see in the Excel output in Figure 7.13 that the t statistic for this test is 27.3655 and that the associated p value is 3.5398E-83. This p value tells us that if the value of β_1 is actually zero, the probability we could collect a random sample of 300 observations from the population of Butler Trucking driving assignments that yields a t statistic with an absolute value greater than 27.3655 is practically zero. Such a small probability represents a highly unlikely scenario; thus, the small p value allows us to conclude that a relationship exists between driving time and miles traveled. (The p value is small enough to justify rejecting the hypothesis that $\beta_1 = 0$ for the Butler Trucking multiple regression example at a 0.01 level of significance or even at a far smaller level of significance.) Thus, this p value is sufficiently small to allow us to reject the hypothesis that there is no relationship between driving time and miles traveled at the 0.05 level of significance.

Similarly, we can test the hypothesis that β_2 is zero. If we do not reject this hypothesis, we conclude that the mean value of y does not change when the value of x_2 changes, and so there is no relationship between driving time and number of deliveries. We see in the Excel output in Figure 7.13 that the t statistic for this test is 23.3731 and that the associated p value is 2.84826E-69. This p value tells us that if the value of β_2 is actually zero, the probability we could collect a random sample of 300 observations from the population of Butler Trucking driving assignments that yields a t statistic with an absolute value greater than 23.3731 is practically zero. This is highly unlikely, and so the p value is sufficiently small to allow us to conclude that a relationship exists between driving time and number of deliveries. (The p value is small enough to justify rejecting the hypothesis that $\beta_2 = 0$ for the Butler Trucking multiple regression example at a 0.01 level of significance or even at a far smaller level of significance.) Thus, this p value is sufficiently small to allow us to reject the hypothesis that there is no relationship between driving time and number of deliveries at the 0.05 level of significance.

Finally, we can test the hypothesis that β_0 is zero in a similar fashion. If we do not reject this hypothesis, we conclude that the mean value of y is zero when the values of x_1 and x_2 are both zero, and so there is no driving time when a driving assignment is 0 miles and has 0 deliveries. We see in the Excel output that the t statistic for this test is 0.6205 and the associated p value is 0.5358. This p value tells us that if the value of β_0 is actually zero, the probability we could collect a random sample of 300 observations from the population of Butler Trucking driving assignments that yields a t statistic with an absolute value greater than 0.6205 is 0.5358. Thus, we do not reject the hypothesis that mean driving time is zero when a driving assignment is 0 miles and has 0 deliveries. However, the range of values for the independent variable distance traveled for the Butler Trucking multiple regression is 40 to 100, and the range of values for the independent variable number of deliveries is 1 to 6. Any prediction outside these ranges, such as the y-intercept for this model, is not a reliable estimate, and so a hypothesis test of β_0 is meaningless for this model. However, if the experimental region for a regression problem includes the origin, a hypothesis test of β_0 will be meaningful.

We can also execute each of these hypothesis tests through confidence intervals. A **confidence interval** for a regression parameter β_i is an estimated interval believed to contain the true value of β_i at some level of confidence. The level of confidence, or **confidence level**, indicates how frequently interval estimates based on samples of the same size taken from the same population using identical sampling techniques will contain the true value of β_i. Thus, when building a 95% confidence interval, we can expect that if we took samples of the same size from the same population using identical sampling

The estimated value of the y-intercept often results from extrapolation.

*See Chapter 6 for a more in-depth discussion of **confidence intervals**.*

techniques, the corresponding interval estimates would contain the true value of β_i for 95% of the samples.

Although the confidence intervals for $\beta_0, \beta_1, \beta_2, \ldots, \beta_q$ convey information about the variation in the estimates $b_1, b_2, \ldots, b_q$ that can be expected across repeated samples, they can also be used to test whether each of the regression parameters $\beta_0, \beta_1, \beta_2, \ldots, \beta_q$ is equal to zero in the following manner. To test that β_j is zero (i.e., there is no linear relationship between x_j and y) at some predetermined level of significance (say 0.05), first build a confidence interval at the $(1 - 0.05)100\%$ confidence level. If the resulting confidence interval does not contain zero, we conclude that β_j differs from zero at the predetermined level of significance.

The form of a confidence interval for β_j is as follows:

$$b_j \pm t_{\alpha/2} s_{b_j},$$

where b_j is the point estimate of the regression parameter β_j, s_{b_j} is the estimated standard deviation of b_j, and $t_{\alpha/2}$ is a multiplier term based on the sample size and specified $100(1 - \alpha)\%$ confidence level of the interval. More specifically, $t_{\alpha/2}$ is the t value that provides an area of $\alpha/2$ in the upper tail of a t distribution with $n - 2$ degrees of freedom.

Most software that is capable of regression analysis can also produce these confidence intervals. For example, the output of Excel's Regression tool for Butler Trucking, given in Figure 7.13, provides confidence intervals for β_1 (the slope coefficient associated with the independent variable x_1, labeled Miles) and β_2 (the slope coefficient associated with the independent variable x_2, labeled Deliveries), as well as the y-intercept β_0. The 95% confidence intervals for β_0, β_1, and β_2 are shown in cells F17:G17, F18:G18, and F19:G19, respectively; these 95% confidence intervals are automatically generated. Neither of the 95% confidence intervals for β_1 and β_2 includes zero, so we can conclude that β_1 and β_2 each differ from zero at the 0.05 level of significance. On the other hand, the 95% confidence interval for β_0 does include zero, so we conclude that β_0 does not differ from zero at the 0.05 level of significance. Again note that, for the Butler Trucking example, the estimated y-intercept results from extrapolation, and so the confidence interval for β_0 is meaningless. However, if the experimental region for a regression problem includes the origin, the confidence interval for β_0 will be meaningful.

The Regression tool dialog box offers the user the opportunity to generate confidence intervals for β_0, β_1, and β_2 at a confidence level other than 95%. In this example, we chose to create 99% confidence intervals for β_0, β_1, and β_2, which in Figure 7.13 are given in cells H17:I17, H18:I18, and H19:I19, respectively. Neither of the 99% confidence intervals for β_1 and β_2 includes zero, so we can conclude that β_1 and β_2 each differs from zero at the 0.01 level of significance. On the other hand, the 99% confidence interval for β_0 does include zero, so we conclude that β_0 does not differ from zero at the 0.01 level of significance.

Addressing Nonsignificant Independent Variables

If the data do not support rejection of the hypothesis that a β_j is zero, we conclude that there is no linear relationship between y and x_j. This leads to the question of how to handle the corresponding independent variable. Do we use the model as originally formulated with the nonsignificant independent variable, or do we rerun the regression without the nonsignificant independent variable and use the new result? The approach to be taken depends on a number of factors, but ultimately whatever model we use should have a theoretical basis. If practical experience dictates that the nonsignificant independent variable has a relationship with the dependent variable, the independent variable should be left in the model. On the other hand, if the model sufficiently explains the dependent variable without the nonsignificant independent variable, then we should consider rerunning the regression without the nonsignificant independent variable. Note that it is possible that the estimates of the other regression coefficients and their p values may change considerably when we remove the nonsignificant independent variable from the model.

The appropriate treatment of the inclusion or exclusion of the y-intercept when b_0 is not statistically significant may require special consideration. For example, in the Butler Trucking multiple regression model, recall that the p value for b_0 is 0.5354, suggesting that this estimate of β_0 is not statistically significant. Should we remove the y-intercept from this model because it is not statistically significant? Excel provides functionality to remove the y-intercept from the model by selecting **Constant is zero** in Excel's Regression tool. This will force the y-intercept to go through the origin (when the independent variables $x_1, x_2, \ldots, x_q$ all equal zero, the estimated value of the dependent variable will be zero). However, doing this can substantially alter the estimated slopes in the regression model and result in a less effective regression that yields less accurate predicted values of the dependent variable. The primary purpose of the regression model is to explain or predict values of the dependent variable for values of the independent variables that lie within the experimental region on which the model is based. Therefore, regression through the origin should not be forced unless there are strong *a priori* reasons for believing that the dependent variable is equal to zero when the values of all independent variables in the model are equal to zero. A common business example of regression through the origin is a model for which output in a labor-intensive production process is the dependent variable and hours of labor is the independent variable; because the production process is labor intense, we would expect no output when the value of labor hours is zero.

Multicollinearity

We use the term *independent variable* in regression analysis to refer to any variable used to predict or explain the value of the dependent variable. The term does not mean, however, that the independent variables themselves are independent in any statistical sense. On the contrary, most independent variables in a multiple regression problem are correlated with one another to some degree. For example, in the Butler Trucking example involving the two independent variables x_1 (miles traveled) and x_2 (number of deliveries), we could compute the sample correlation coefficient r_{x_1,x_2} to determine the extent to which these two variables are related. Doing so yields $r_{x_1,x_2} = 0.16$. Thus, we find some degree of linear association between the two independent variables. In multiple regression analysis, **multicollinearity** refers to the correlation among the independent variables.

To gain a better perspective of the potential problems of multicollinearity, let us consider a modification of the Butler Trucking example. Instead of x_2 being the number of deliveries, let x_2 denote the number of gallons of gasoline consumed. Clearly, x_1 (the miles traveled) and x_2 are now related; that is, we know that the number of gallons of gasoline used depends to a large extent on the number of miles traveled. Hence, we would conclude logically that x_1 and x_2 are highly correlated independent variables and that multicollinearity is present in the model. The data for this example are provided in the file *ButlerWithGasConsumption*.

Using Excel's Regression tool, we obtain the results shown in Figure 7.21 for our multiple regression. When we conduct a t test to determine whether β_1 is equal to zero, we find a p value of 3.1544E-07, and so we reject this hypothesis and conclude that travel time is related to miles traveled. On the other hand, when we conduct a t test to determine whether β_2 is equal to zero, we find a p value of 0.6588, and so we do not reject this hypothesis. Does this mean that travel time is not related to gasoline consumption? Not necessarily.

DATA *file*

ButlerWithGasConsumption

	A	B	C	D	E	F	G	H	I
1	SUMMARY OUTPUT								
2									
3	*Regression Statistics*								
4	Multiple R	0.69406354							
5	R Square	0.481724198							
6	Adjusted R Square	0.478234125							
7	Standard Error	1.398077545							
8	Observations	300							
9									
10	ANOVA								
11		*df*	*SS*	*MS*	*F*	*Significance F*			
12	Regression	2	539.5808158	269.7904079	138.0269794	4.09542E-43			
13	Residual	297	580.5223842	1.954620822					
14	Total	299	1120.1032						
15									
16		*Coefficients*	*Standard Error*	*t Stat*	*P-value*	*Lower 95%*	*Upper 95%*	*Lower 99.0%*	*Upper 99.0%*
17	Intercept	2.493095385	0.33669895	7.404523781	1.36703E-12	1.830477398	3.155713373	1.620208758	3.365982013
18	Miles	0.074701825	0.014274552	5.233216928	3.15444E-07	0.046609743	0.102793908	0.037695279	0.111708371
19	Gasoline Consumption	–0.067506102	0.152707928	–0.442060235	0.658767336	–0.368032789	0.233020584	–0.463398955	0.328386751

What it probably means in this instance is that, with x_1 already in the model, x_2 does not make a significant marginal contribution to predicting the value of y. This interpretation makes sense within the context of the Butler Trucking example; if we know the miles traveled, we do not gain much new information that would be useful in predicting driving time by also knowing the amount of gasoline consumed. We can see this in the scatter chart in Figure 7.22; miles traveled and gasoline consumed are strongly related.

Note that, even though we rejected the hypothesis that β_1 is equal to zero for this model, the value of the t statistic is much smaller and the p value substantially larger than in the multiple regression model that includes miles driven and number of deliveries as the independent variables. The evidence against the hypothesis that β_1 is equal to zero is weaker in the multiple regression that includes miles driven and gasoline consumed as the independent variables because of the high correlation between these two independent variables.

To summarize, in t tests for the significance of individual parameters, the difficulty caused by multicollinearity is that it is possible to conclude that a parameter associated with one of the multicollinear independent variables is not significantly different from zero when the independent variable actually has a strong relationship with the dependent variable. This problem is avoided when there is little correlation among the independent variables.

Statisticians have developed several tests for determining whether multicollinearity is strong enough to cause problems. In addition to the initial understanding of the nature of the relationships between the various pairs of variables that we can gain through scatter charts such as the chart shown in Figure 7.22, correlations between pairs of independent

If any estimated regression parameters $b_1, b_2, \ldots, b_q$ or associated p values change dramatically when a new independent variable is added to the model (or an existing independent variable is removed from the model), multicollinearity is likely present. Looking for changes such as these is sometimes used as a way to detect multicollinearity.

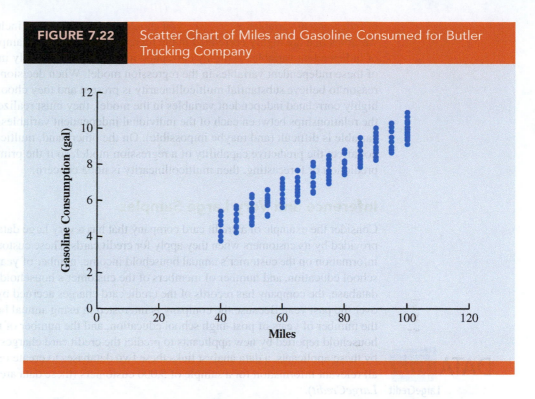

FIGURE 7.22   Scatter Chart of Miles and Gasoline Consumed for Butler Trucking Company

See Chapter 2 for a more in-depth discussion of correlation and how to compute it with Excel.

variables can be used to identify potential problems. According to a common rule-of-thumb test, multicollinearity is a potential problem if the absolute value of the sample correlation coefficient exceeds 0.7 for any two of the independent variables. We can place the Excel function:

=CORREL(B2:B301, C2:C301)

into any empty cell of the file *ButlerWithGasConsumption* to find that the correlation between Miles (in column B) and Gasoline Consumed (in column C) for the sample Butler Trucking data is $r_{\text{Miles, Gasoline Consumed}} = 0.9572$, which supports the conclusion that Miles and Gasoline Consumed are multicollinear. Similarly, by placing the Excel function:

=CORREL(B2:B301, D2:D301)

into any empty cell of the file *ButlerWithGasConsumption* shows that the correlation between Miles (in column B) and Deliveries (in column D) for the sample data is $r_{\text{Miles, Deliveries}} = 0.0258$. This supports the conclusion that Miles and Deliveries are not multicollinear. Other tests for multicollinearity are more advanced and beyond the scope of this text.

The primary consequence of multicollinearity is that it increases the standard deviation of $b_0, b_1, \ldots, b_q$ and predicted values of the dependent variable, and so inference based on these estimates is less precise than it should be. This means that confidence intervals for $\beta_0, \beta_1, \beta_2, \ldots, \beta_q$ and predicted values of the dependent variable are wider than they should be. Thus, we are less likely to reject the hypothesis that an individual parameter b_j is equal to zero than we otherwise would be, and multicollinearity leads us to conclude that an independent variable x_j is not related to the dependent variable y when they in fact are related. In addition, multicollinearity can result in confusing or misleading regression parameters $b_1, b_2, \ldots, b_q$. Therefore, if a primary objective of the regression analysis is inference, to explain the relationship between a dependent variable y and a set of independent variables $x_1, \ldots, x_q$, you should, if possible, avoid including independent variables that are highly correlated in the regression model. For example, when a pair of independent variables is highly correlated it is common to simply include only one of these independent variables in the regression model. When decision makers have reason to believe substantial multicollinearity is present and they choose to retain the highly correlated independent variables in the model, they must realize that separating the relationships between each of the individual independent variables and the dependent variable is difficult (and maybe impossible). On the other hand, multicollinearity does not affect the predictive capability of a regression model, so if the primary objective is prediction or forecasting, then multicollinearity is not a concern.

Inference and Very Large Samples

Consider the example of a credit card company that has a very large database of information provided by its customers when they apply for credit cards. These customer records include information on the customer's annual household income, number of years of post–high school education, and number of members of the customer's household. In a second database, the company has records of the credit card charges accrued by each customer over the past year. Because the company is interested in using annual household income, the number of years of post–high school education, and the number of members of the household reported by new applicants to predict the credit card charges that will be accrued by these applicants, a data analyst links these two databases to create one data set containing all relevant information for a sample of 5,000 customers (these data are available in the file *LargeCredit*).

The company has decided to apply multiple regression to these data to develop a model for predicting annual credit card charges for its new applicants. The dependent variable in the model is credit card charges accrued by a customer in the data set over the past year (y); the independent variables are the customer's annual household income (x_1), number of members of the household (x_2), and number of years of post–high school education (x_3). Figure 7.23 provides Excel output for the multiple regression model estimated using the data set the company has created.

The model has a coefficient of determination of 0.3635 (see cell B5 in Figure 7.23), indicating that this model explains approximately 36% of the variation in credit card charges accrued by the customers in the sample over the past year. The p value for each test of the individual regression parameters is also very small (see cells E18 through E20), indicating that for each independent variable we can reject the hypothesis of no relationship with the dependent variable. The estimated slopes associated with the dependent variables are all highly significant. The model estimates that:

- For a fixed number of members of the household and number of years of post–high school education, accrued credit card charges increase by \$120.63 when a customer's annual household income increases by \$1,000. This is shown in cell B18 of Figure 7.23.
- For a fixed annual household income and number of years of post–high school education, accrued credit card charges increase by \$533.85 when a customer's household increases by one member. This is shown in cell B19 of Figure 7.23.
- For a fixed annual household income and number of members of the household, accrued credit card charges decrease by \$505.63 when a customer's number of years of post–high school education increases by one year. This is shown in cell B20 of Figure 7.23.

Because the y-intercept is an obvious result of extrapolation (no customer in the data has values of zero for annual household income, number of members of the household, *and*

FIGURE 7.23   Excel Regression Output for Credit Card Company Example

	A	B	C	D	E	F	G	H	I
1	SUMMARY OUTPUT								
2									
3	*Regression Statistics*								
4	Multiple R	0.602946393							
5	R Square	0.363544353							
6	Adjusted R Square	0.363162174							
7	Standard Error	4847.563495							
8	Observations	5000							
9									
10	ANOVA								
11		*df*	*SS*	*MS*	*F*	*Significance F*			
12	Regression	3	67059251577	22353083859	951.2407238	0			
13	Residual	4996	1.174E+11	23498871.84					
14	Total	4999	1.8446E+11						
15									
16		*Coefficients*	*Standard Error*	*t Stat*	*P-value*	*Lower 95%*	*Upper 95%*	*Lower 99.0%*	*Upper 99.0%*
17	Intercept	2051.638735	258.2118129	7.945564971	2.37056E-15	1545.430245	2557.847226	1386.274984	2717.002486
18	Annual Income ($1000)	120.6315397	2.439500895	49.44927054	0	115.8490472	125.4140323	114.3454003	126.9176792
19	Household Size	533.8460243	33.07739782	16.13929932	3.6874E-57	468.9998058	598.6922428	448.6117306	619.080318
20	Years of Post-High School Education	−505.632418	45.54182323	−11.10259498	2.60612E-28	−594.9143812	−416.3504547	−622.9852144	−388.2796215

number of years of post–high school education), the estimated regression parameter b_0 is meaningless.

The small p values associated with a model that is fit on an extremely large sample do not imply that an extremely large sample solves all problems. Virtually all relationships between independent variables and the dependent variable will be statistically significant if the sample size is sufficiently large. That is, if the sample size is very large, there will be little difference in the b_j values generated by different random samples. Because we address the variability in potential values of our estimators through the use of statistical inference, and variability of our estimates b_j essentially disappears as the sample size grows very large, inference is of little use for estimates generated from very large samples. Thus, we generally are not concerned with the conditions a regression model must satisfy in order for inference to be reliable when we use a very large sample. Multicollinearity, on the other hand, can result in confusing or misleading regression parameters $b_1, b_2, \ldots, b_q$ and so is still a concern when we use a large data set to estimate a regression model that is to be used for explanatory purposes.

How much does sample size matter? Table 7.4 provides the regression parameter estimates and the corresponding p values for multiple regression models estimated on the first 50 observations, the second 50 observations, and so on for the *LargeCredit* data. Note that, even though the means of the parameter estimates for the regressions based on 50 observations are similar to the parameter estimates based on the full sample of 5,000 observations, the individual values of the estimated regression parameters in the regressions based on 50 observations show a great deal of variation. In these 10 regressions, the estimated values

TABLE 7.4	Regression Parameter Estimates and the Corresponding p values for 10 Multiple Regression Models, Each Estimated on 50 Observations from the *LargeCredit* Data

Observations	b_0	p value	b_1	p value	b_2	p value	b_3	p value
1–50	−805.182	0.7814	154.488	1.45E-06	234.664	0.5489	207.828	0.6721
51–100	894.407	0.6796	125.343	2.23E-07	822.675	0.0070	−355.585	0.3553
101–150	−2,191.590	0.4869	155.187	3.56E-07	674.961	0.0501	−25.309	0.9560
151–200	2,294.023	0.3445	114.734	1.26E-04	297.011	0.3700	−537.063	0.2205
201–250	8,994.040	0.0289	103.378	6.89E-04	−489.932	0.2270	−375.601	0.5261
251–300	7,265.471	0.0234	73.207	1.02E-02	−77.874	0.8409	−405.195	0.4060
301–350	2,147.906	0.5236	117.500	1.88E-04	390.447	0.3053	−374.799	0.4696
351–400	−504.532	0.8380	118.926	8.54E-07	798.499	0.0112	45.259	0.9209
401–450	1,587.067	0.5123	81.532	5.06E-04	1,267.041	0.0004	−891.118	0.0359
451–500	−315.945	0.9048	148.860	1.07E-05	1,000.243	0.0053	−974.791	0.0420
Mean	1,936.567		119.316		491.773		−368.637	

of b_0 range from −2,191.590 to 8,994.040, the estimated values of b_1 range from 73.207 to 155.187, the estimated values of b_2 range from −489.932 to 1,267.041, and the estimated values of b_3 range from −974.791 to 207.828. This is reflected in the p values corresponding to the parameter estimates in the regressions based on 50 observations, which are substantially larger than the corresponding p values in the regression based on 5,000 observations. These results underscore the impact that a very large sample size can have on inference.

For another example, suppose the credit card company also has a separate database of information on shopping and lifestyle characteristics that it has collected from its customers during a recent Internet survey. The data analyst notes in the results in Figure 7.23 that the original regression model fails to explain almost 65% of the variation in credit card charges accrued by the customers in the data set. In an attempt to increase the variation in the dependent variable explained by the model, the data analyst decides to augment the original regression with a new independent variable, number of hours per week spent watching television (which we will designate as x_4). After linking the databases so that all necessary information for each of the 5,000 customers is in a single data set, the analyst runs the new multiple regression and achieves the results shown in Figure 7.24.

The new model has a coefficient of determination of 0.3669 (see cell B5 in Figure 7.24), indicating the addition of number of hours per week spent watching television increased the explained variation in sample values of accrued credit card charges by less than 1%. The estimated regression parameters and associated p values for annual household income, number of members of the household, and number of years of post–high school education changed little after introducing into the model the number of hours per week spent watching television.

The estimated regression parameter for number of hours per week spent watching television is 20.44 (see cell B21 in Figure 7.24), suggesting a that 1-hour increase coincides with an increase of $20.44 in credit card charges accrued by each customer over the past year. The p value associated with this estimate is 2.3744E-07 (see cell E21 in Figure 7.24), so we can reject the hypothesis that there is no relationship between the number of hours per week spent watching television and credit card charges accrued. However, when the model is based on a very large sample, almost all relationships will be significant whether they are real or not, and statistical significance does not necessarily imply that a relationship is meaningful or useful.

FIGURE 7.24   Excel Regression Output for Credit Card Company Example after Adding Number of Hours per Week Spent Watching Television to the Model

	A	B	C	D	E	F	G	H	I
1	SUMMARY OUTPUT								
2									
3	*Regression Statistics*								
4	Multiple R	0.605753974							
5	R Square	0.366937877							
6	Adjusted R Square	0.36643092							
7	Standard Error	4835.106762							
8	Observations	5000							
9									
10	ANOVA								
11		*df*	*SS*	*MS*	*F*	*Significance F*			
12	Regression	4	67685219598	16921304900	723.8052269	0			
13	Residual	4995	1.16774E+11	23378257.4					
14	Total	4999	1.8446E+11						
15									
16		*Coefficients*	*Standard Error*	*t Stat*	*P-value*	*Lower 95%*	*Upper 95%*	*Lower 99.0%*	*Upper 99.0%*
17	Intercept	1440.385909	283.3464635	5.083479398	3.84109E-07	884.9024443	1995.869374	710.2547892	2170.51703
18	Annual Income ($1000)	120.4937794	2.433377775	49.51708715	0	115.7232906	125.2642681	114.2234176	126.7641412
19	Household Size	538.2043625	33.00314865	16.30766713	2.72804E-58	473.5037019	602.9050231	453.1613886	623.2473364
20	Years of Post-High School Education	−509.7777354	45.43185836	−11.22071062	7.12888E-29	−598.8441236	−420.7113472	−626.8471819	−392.7082889
21	Hours Per Week Watching Television	20.4413308	3.950382611	5.174519234	2.37441E-07	12.69684656	28.18581504	10.26192978	30.62073183

Is it reasonable to expect that the credit card charges accrued by a customer are related to the number of hours per week the consumer watches television? If not, the model that includes number of hours per week the consumer watches television as an independent variable may provide inaccurate or unreliable predictions of the credit card charges that will be accrued by new customers, even though we have found a significant relationship between these two variables. If the model is to be used to predict future amounts of credit charges, then the usefulness of including the number of hours per week the consumer watches television is best evaluated by measuring the accuracy of predictions for observations not included in the sample data used to construct the model. This use of out-of-sample data is common in data-mining applications and is covered in detail in Chapter 9.

N O T E S   +   C O M M E N T S

1. In multiple regression we can test the null hypothesis that the regression parameters $b_1, b_2, \ldots, b_q$ are all equal to zero ($H_0: \beta_1 = \beta_2 = \cdots = \beta_q = 0$, H_a: at least one $b_j \neq 0$ for $j = 1, \ldots, q$) with an F test based on the F probability distribution. The test statistic generated by the sample data for this test is:

$$F = \frac{SSR/q}{SSE/(n - q - 1)},$$

where SSR and SSE are as defined by equations (7.5) and (7.7), q is the number of independent variables in the regression model, and n is the number of observations in the sample. If the p value corresponding to the F statistic is smaller than some predetermined level of significance (usually 0.05 or 0.01), this leads us to reject the hypothesis that the values of $b_1, b_2, \ldots, b_q$ are all zero, and we would conclude that there is an overall regression relationship; otherwise, we conclude that there is no overall regression relationship.

The output of Excel's Regression tool provides the results of the F test; in Figure 7.13, which shows the multiple linear regression results for Butler Trucking with independent variables x_1 (labeled Miles) and x_2 (labeled Deliveries), the value of the F statistic and the corresponding p value are in cells E24 and F24, respectively. From the Excel output in Figure 7.13 we see tht the p value for the F test is essentially 0 (2.2419E-110, or 2.2419 with the decimal moved 110 places to the left). Thus, the p value is sufficiently small to allow us to reject the hypothesis that no overall regression relationship exists at the 0.05 level of significance.

2. Finding a significant relationship between an independent variable x_j and a dependent variable y in a linear regression does not enable us to conclude that the relationship is linear. We can state only that x_j and y are related and that a linear relationship explains a statistically significant portion of the variability in y over the range of values for x_j observed in the sample.

3. Note that a review of the correlations of pairs of independent variables is not always sufficient to entirely uncover multicollinearity. The problem is that sometimes one independent variable is highly correlated with some combination of several other independent variables. If you suspect that one independent variable is highly correlated with a combination of several other

independent variables, you can use multiple regression to assess whether the sample data support your suspicion. Suppose that your original regression model includes the independent variables $x_1, x_2, \ldots, x_q$ and that you suspect that x_1 is highly correlated with a subset of the other independent variables $x_2, \ldots, x_q$. Estimate the multiple linear regression for which x_1 is now the dependent variable; the subset of the independent variables $x_2, \ldots, x_q$ that you suspect are highly correlated with x_1 are now the independent variables. The coefficient of determination R^2 for this regression provides an estimate of the strength of the relationship between x_1 and the subset of the other independent variables $x_2, \ldots, x_q$ that you suspect are highly correlated with x_1. As a rule of thumb, if the coefficient of determination R^2 for this regression exceeds 0.50, multicollinearity between x_1 and the subset of the other independent variables $x_2, \ldots, x_q$ is a concern.

4. When working with a small number of observations, assessing the conditions necessary for inference to be valid in regression can be extremely difficult. Similarly, when working with a small number of observations, assessing multicollinearity can also be difficult. Under these conditions we generally proceed with inference unless we find strong evidence of a violation of the conditions necessary for inference to be valid in regression or a strong multicollinearity.

5. To determine the independent variables to be included in a regression model when working with an extremely large sample, one can partition the sample into a training set and a validation set. The training set is used to estimate the regression coefficients and the validation set is then used to estimate the accuracy of the model.

7.6 Categorical Independent Variables

Thus far, the examples we have considered have involved quantitative independent variables such as distance traveled and number of deliveries. In many situations, however, we must work with categorical independent variables such as sex (male, female), method of payment (cash, credit card, check), and so on. The purpose of this section is to show how categorical variables are handled in regression analysis. To illustrate the use and interpretation of a categorical independent variable, we will again consider the Butler Trucking Company example.

Butler Trucking Company and Rush Hour

Several of Butler Trucking's driving assignments require the driver to travel on a congested segment of a highway during the afternoon rush hour. Management believes this factor may also contribute substantially to variability in the travel times across driving assignments.

Dummy variables are sometimes referred to as indicator variables.

How do we incorporate information on which driving assignments include travel on a congested segment of a highway during the afternoon rush hour into a regression model?

The previous independent variables we have considered (such as miles traveled and number of deliveries) have been quantitative, but this new variable is categorical and will require us to define a new type of variable called a **dummy variable**. To incorporate a variable that indicates whether a driving assignment included travel on this congested segment of a highway during the afternoon rush hour into a model that currently includes the independent variables miles traveled (x_1) and number of deliveries (x_2), we define the following variable:

$$x_3 = \begin{cases} 0 \text{ if an assignment did not include travel on the congested segment of highway} \\ \quad \text{during afternoon rush hour} \\ 1 \text{ if an assignment included travel on the congested segment of highway} \\ \quad \text{during afternoon rush hour} \end{cases}$$

Once a value of one is input for each of the driving assignments that included travel on a congested segment of a highway during the afternoon rush hour and a value of zero is input for each of the remaining driving assignments in the sample data, the independent variable x_3 can be included in the model. The file *ButlerHighway* includes this dummy variable.

See Chapter 2 for step-by-step descriptions of how to construct charts in Excel.

Will this dummy variable add valuable information to the current Butler Trucking regression model? A review of the residuals produced by the current model may help us make an initial assessment. Using Excel chart tools, we can create a frequency distribution and a histogram of the residuals for driving assignments that included travel on a congested segment of a highway during the afternoon rush hour period. We then create a frequency distribution and a histogram of the residuals for driving assignments that did not include travel on a congested segment of a highway during the afternoon rush hour period. The two histograms are shown in Figure 7.25.

Recall that the residual for the ith observation is $e_i = y_i - \hat{y}_i$, which is the difference between the observed and predicted values of the dependent variable. The histograms in Figure 7.25 show that driving assignments that included travel on a congested segment of a highway during the afternoon rush hour period tend to have positive residuals, which means we are generally underpredicting the travel times for those driving assignments. Conversely, driving assignments that did not include travel on a congested segment of a highway during the afternoon rush hour period tend to have negative residuals, which means we are generally overpredicting the travel times for those driving assignments. These results suggest that the dummy variable could potentially explain a substantial proportion of the variance in travel time that is unexplained by the current model, and so we proceed by adding the dummy variable x_3 to the current Butler Trucking multiple regression model. Using Excel's Regression tool to develop the estimated regression equation, we obtained the Excel output in Figure 7.26. The estimated regression equation is:

ButlerHighway

$$\hat{y} = -0.3302 + 0.0672x_1 + 0.6735x_2 + 0.9980x_3. \tag{7.15}$$

Interpreting the Parameters

After checking to make sure this regression satisfies the conditions for inference and the model does not suffer from serious multicollinearity, we can consider inference on our results. The p values for the t tests of miles traveled (p value = 4.7852E-105), number of deliveries (p value = 6.7480E-87), and the rush hour driving dummy variable (p value = 6.4982E-31) are all extremely small, indicating that each of these independent variables has

FIGURE 7.25 Histograms of the Residuals for Driving Assignments That Included Travel on a Congested Segment of a Highway During the Afternoon Rush Hour and Residuals for Driving Assignments That Did Not

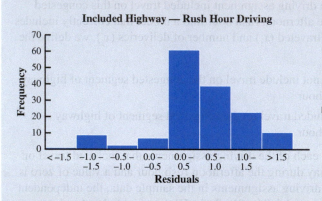

Included Highway — Rush Hour Driving

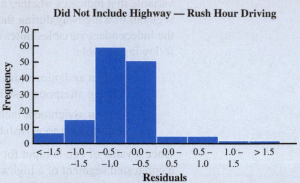

Did Not Include Highway — Rush Hour Driving

FIGURE 7.26 Excel Data and Output for Butler Trucking with Miles Traveled (x_1), Number of Deliveries (x_2), and the Highway Rush Hour Dummy Variable (x_3) as the Independent Variables

	A	B	C	D	E	F	G	H	I
1	SUMMARY OUTPUT								
2									
3	*Regression Statistics*								
4	Multiple R	0.940107228							
5	R Square	0.8838016							
6	Adjusted R Square	0.882623914							
7	Standard Error	0.663106426							
8	Observations	300							
9									
10	ANOVA								
11		*df*	*SS*	*MS*	*F*	*Significance F*			
12	Regression	3	989.9490008	329.9830003	750.455757	5.7766E–138			
13	Residual	296	130.1541992	0.439710132					
14	Total	299	1120.1032						
15									
16		*Coefficients*	*Standard Error*	*t Stat*	*P-value*	*Lower 95%*	*Upper 95%*	*Lower 99.0%*	*Upper 99.0%*
17	Intercept	–0.330229304	0.167677925	–1.969426232	0.04983651	–0.66022126	–0.000237349	–0.764941128	0.104482519
18	Miles	0.067220302	0.00196142	34.27125147	4.7852E-105	0.063360208	0.071080397	0.062135243	0.072305362
19	Deliveries	0.67351584	0.023619993	28.51465081	6.74797E-87	0.627031441	0.720000239	0.612280051	0.734751629
20	Highway	0.9980033	0.076706582	13.0106605	6.49817E-31	0.847043924	1.148962677	0.799138374	1.196868226

a statistical relationship with travel time. The model estimates that the mean travel time of a driving assignment increases by:

- 0.0672 hour for every increase of 1 mile traveled, holding constant the number of deliveries and whether the driving assignment route requires the driver to travel on the congested segment of a highway during the afternoon rush hour.
- 0.6735 hour for every delivery, holding constant the number of miles traveled and whether the driving assignment route requires the driver to travel on the congested segment of a highway during the afternoon rush hour.
- 0.9980 hour if the driving assignment route requires the driver to travel on the congested segment of a highway during the afternoon rush hour, holding constant the number of miles traveled and the number of deliveries.

In addition, $R^2 = 0.8838$ indicates that the regression model explains approximately 88.4% of the variability in travel time for the driving assignments in the sample. Thus, equation (7.15) should prove helpful in estimating the travel time necessary for the various driving assignments.

To understand how to interpret the regression when a categorical variable is present, let's compare the regression model for the case when $x_3 = 0$ (the driving assignment does not include travel on congested highways) and when $x_3 = 1$ (the driving assignment does include travel on congested highways). In the case that $x_3 = 0$, we have:

$$\hat{y} = -0.3302 + 0.0672x_1 + 0.6735x_2 + 0.9980(0)$$
$$= -0.3302 + 0.0672x_1 + 0.6735x_2. \tag{7.16}$$

In the case that $x_3 = 1$, we have:

$$\hat{y} = -0.3302 + 0.0672x_1 + 0.6735x_2 + 0.9980(1)$$
$$= 0.6678 + 0.0672x_1 + 0.6735x_2. \tag{7.17}$$

Comparing equations (7.16) and (7.17), we see that the mean travel time has the same linear relationship with x_1 and x_2 for both driving assignments that include travel on the congested segment of highway during the afternoon rush hour period and driving assignments that do not. However, the y-intercept is -0.3302 in equation (7.16) and $(-0.3302 + 0.9980)$ in equation (7.17). That is, 0.9980 is the difference between the mean travel time for driving assignments that include travel on the congested segment of highway during the afternoon rush hour and the mean travel time for driving assignments that do not.

In effect, the use of a dummy variable provides two estimated regression equations that can be used to predict the travel time: One that corresponds to driving assignments that include travel on the congested segment of highway during the afternoon rush hour period, and one that corresponds to driving assignments that do not include such travel.

More Complex Categorical Variables

The categorical variable for the Butler Trucking Company example had two levels: (1) driving assignments that include travel on the congested segment of highway during the afternoon rush hour, and (2) driving assignments that do not. As a result, defining a dummy variable with a value of zero indicating a driving assignment that does not include travel on the congested segment of highway during the afternoon rush hour and a value of one indicating a driving assignment that includes such travel was sufficient. However, when a categorical variable has more than two levels, care must be taken in both defining and interpreting the dummy variables. As we will show, if a categorical variable has k levels,

$k - 1$ dummy variables are required, with each dummy variable corresponding to one of the levels of the categorical variable and coded as 0 or 1.

For example, suppose a manufacturer of vending machines organized the sales territories for a particular state into three regions: A, B, and C. The managers want to use regression analysis to help predict the number of vending machines sold per week. With the number of units sold as the dependent variable, they are considering several independent variables (the number of sales personnel, advertising expenditures, etc.). Suppose the managers believe that sales region is also an important factor in predicting the number of units sold. Because sales region is a categorical variable with three levels (A, B, and C), we will need $3 - 1 = 2$ dummy variables to represent the sales region. Selecting Region A to be the "reference" region, each dummy variable can be coded 0 or 1 as follows:

$$x_1 = \begin{cases} 1 \text{ if sales Region B} \\ 0 \text{ otherwise} \end{cases}, x_2 = \begin{cases} 1 \text{ if sales Region C} \\ 0 \text{ otherwise} \end{cases}$$

With this definition, we have the following values of x_1 and x_2:

Region	x_1	x_2
A	0	0
B	1	0
C	0	1

The regression equation relating the estimated mean number of units sold to the dummy variables is written as:

$$\hat{y} = b_0 + b_1 x_1 + b_2 x_2.$$

Observations corresponding to Region A correspond to $x_1 = 0$, $x_2 = 0$, so the estimated mean number of units sold in Region A is:

$$\hat{y} = b_0 + b_1(0) + b_2(0) = b_0.$$

Observations corresponding to Region B are coded $x_1 = 1$, $x_2 = 0$, so the estimated mean number of units sold in Region B is:

$$\hat{y} = b_0 + b_1(1) + b_2(0) = b_0 + b_1.$$

Observations corresponding to Region C are coded $x_1 = 0$, $x_2 = 1$, so the estimated mean number of units sold in Region C is:

$$\hat{y} = b_0 + b_1(0) + b_2(1) = b_0 + b_2.$$

Thus, b_0 is the estimated mean sales for Region A, b_1 is the estimated difference between the mean number of units sold in Region B and the mean number of units sold in Region A, and b_2 is the estimated difference between the mean number of units sold in Region C and the mean number of units sold in Region A.

Dummy variables are often used to model seasonal effects in sales data. If the data are collected quarterly, we may use three dummy variables defined in the following manner:

$$x_1 = \begin{cases} 1 \text{ if spring;} \\ 0 \text{ otherwise} \end{cases}$$

$$x_2 = \begin{cases} 1 \text{ if summer;} \\ 0 \text{ otherwise} \end{cases}$$

$$x_3 = \begin{cases} 1 \text{ if fall} \\ 0 \text{ otherwise} \end{cases}$$

Two dummy variables were required because sales region is a categorical variable with three levels. But the assignment of $x_1 = 0$ and $x_2 = 0$ to indicate Region A, $x_1 = 1$ and $x_2 = 0$ to indicate Region B, and $x_1 = 0$ and $x_2 = 1$ to indicate Region C was arbitrary. For example, we could have chosen to let $x_1 = 1$ and $x_2 = 0$ indicate Region A, $x_1 = 0$ and $x_2 = 0$ indicate Region B, and $x_1 = 0$ and $x_2 = 1$ indicate Region C. In this case, b_0 is the mean or expected value of sales for Region B, b_1 is the difference between the mean number of units sold in Region A and the mean number of units sold in Region B, and b_2 is the difference between the mean number of units sold in Region C and the mean number of units sold in Region B.

The important point to remember is that when a categorical variable has k levels, $k - 1$ dummy variables are required in the multiple regression analysis. Thus, if the sales region example had a fourth region, labeled D, three dummy variables would be necessary. For example, these three dummy variables could then be coded as follows:

$$x_1 = \begin{cases} 1 \text{ if sales Region B} \\ 0 \text{ otherwise} \end{cases}, \quad x_2 = \begin{cases} 1 \text{ if sales Region C} \\ 0 \text{ otherwise} \end{cases}, \quad x_3 = \begin{cases} 1 \text{ if sales Region D} \\ 0 \text{ otherwise} \end{cases}$$

NOTES + COMMENTS

Detecting multicollinearity when a categorical variable is involved is difficult. The correlation coefficient that we used in Section 7.5 is appropriate only when assessing the relationship between two quantitative variables. However, recall that if any estimated regression parameters $b_1, b_2, \ldots, b_q$ or associated p values change dramatically when a new independent variable is added to the model (or an existing independent variable is removed from the model), multicollinearity is likely present. We can use our understanding of these ramifications of

multicollinearity to assess whether there is multicollinearity that involves a dummy variable. We estimate the regression model twice; once with the dummy variable included as an independent variable and once with the dummy variable omitted from the regression model. If we see relatively little change in the estimated regression parameters $b_1, b_2, \ldots, b_q$ or associated p values for the independent variables that have been included in both regression models, we can be confident there is not a strong multicollinearity involving the dummy variable.

7.7 Modeling Nonlinear Relationships

DATA *file*

Reynolds

Regression may be used to model more complex types of relationships. To illustrate, let us consider the problem facing Reynolds, Inc., a manufacturer of industrial scales and laboratory equipment. Managers at Reynolds want to investigate the relationship between length of employment of their salespeople and the number of electronic laboratory scales sold. The file *Reynolds* gives the number of scales sold by 15 randomly selected salespeople for the most recent sales period and the number of months each salesperson has been employed by the firm. Figure 7.27, the scatter chart for these data, indicates a possible curvilinear relationship between the length of time employed and the number of units sold.

FIGURE 7.27	Scatter Chart for the Reynolds Example

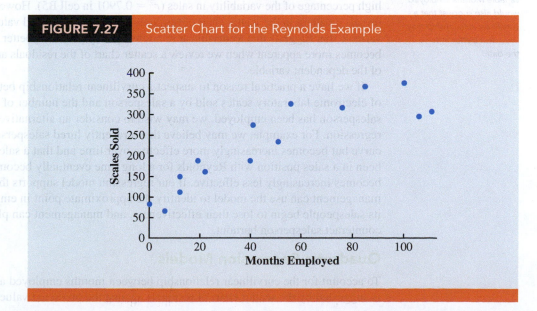

FIGURE 7.28	Excel Regression Output for the Reynolds Example

	A	B	C	D	E	F	G	H	I
1	SUMMARY OUTPUT								
2									
3	*Regression Statistics*								
4	Multiple R	0.888897515							
5	R Square	0.790138792							
6	Adjusted R Square	0.773995622							
7	Standard Error	48.49087146							
8	Observations	15							
9									
10	ANOVA								
11		*df*	*SS*	*MS*	*F*	*Significance F*			
12	Regression	1	115089.1933	115089.1933	48.94570268	9.39543E–06			
13	Residual	13	30567.74	2351.364615					
14	Total	14	145656.9333						
15									
16		*Coefficients*	*Standard Error*	*t Stat*	*P-value*	*Lower 95%*	*Upper 95%*	*Lower 95.0%*	*Upper 95.0%*
17	Intercept	113.7452874	20.81345608	5.464987985	0.000108415	68.78054927	158.7100256	68.78054927	158.7100256
18	Months Employed	2.367463621	0.338396631	6.996120545	9.39543E-06	1.636402146	3.098525095	1.636402146	3.098525095

The scatter chart of residuals against the independent variable Months Employed would also suggest that a curvilinear relationship may provide a better fit to the data.

Before considering how to develop a curvilinear relationship for Reynolds, let us consider the Excel output in Figure 7.28 for a simple linear regression; the estimated regression is:

$$\text{Sales} = 113.7453 + 2.3675 \text{ Months Employed.}$$

The computer output shows that the relationship is significant (p value = 9.3954E-06 in cell E18 of Figure 7.28 for the t test that $\beta_1 = 0$) and that a linear relationship explains a high percentage of the variability in sales ($r^2 = 0.7901$ in cell B5). However, Figure 7.29 reveals a pattern in the scatter chart of residuals against the predicted values of the dependent variable that suggests that a curvilinear relationship may provide a better fit to the data. This becomes more apparent when we review a scatter chart of the residuals and predicted values of the dependent variable.

If we have a practical reason to suspect a curvilinear relationship between number of electronic laboratory scales sold by a salesperson and the number of months the salesperson has been employed, we may wish to consider an alternative to simple linear regression. For example, we may believe that a recently hired salesperson faces a learning curve but becomes increasingly more effective over time and that a salesperson who has been in a sales position with Reynolds for a long time eventually becomes burned out and becomes increasingly less effective. If our regression model supports this theory, Reynolds management can use the model to identify the approximate point in employment when its salespeople begin to lose their effectiveness, and management can plan strategies to counteract salesperson burnout.

Quadratic Regression Models

To account for the curvilinear relationship between months employed and scales sold that is suggested by the scatter chart of residuals against the predicted values of the dependent

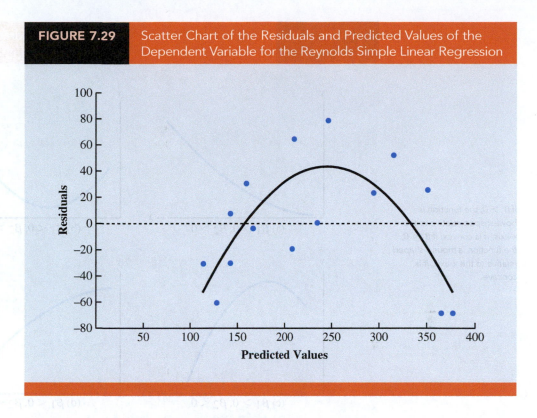

FIGURE 7.29   Scatter Chart of the Residuals and Predicted Values of the Dependent Variable for the Reynolds Simple Linear Regression

variable, we could include the square of the number of months the salesperson has been employed in the model as a second independent variable:

$$y = b_0 + b_1 x_1 + b_2 x_1^2 + e. \tag{7.18}$$

As we can see in Figure 7.30, quadratic regression models are flexible and are capable of representing a wide variety of nonlinear relationships between an independent variable and the dependent variable.

To develop an estimated regression equation corresponding to this model, referred to as a **quadratic regression model**, the statistical software package we are using needs the original data as well as the square of the number of months the employee has been with the firm. Figure 7.31 shows the Excel spreadsheet that includes the square of the number of months the employee has been with the firm. To create the variable, which we will call MonthsSq, we create a new column and set each cell in that column equal to the square of the associated value of the variable Months. These values are shown in Column B of Figure 7.31.

The regression output for the model in equation (7.18) is shown in Figure 7.32. The estimated regression equation is:

Sales = 61.4299 + 5.8198 Months Employed − 0.0310 MonthsSq,

where MonthsSq is the square of the number of months the salesperson has been employed. Because the value of b_1 (5.8198) is positive, and the value of b_2 (−0.0310) is negative, $\hat{y}$ will initially increase as the number of months the salesperson has been employed increases. As the value of the independent variable Months Employed increases, its squared value increases more rapidly, and eventually $\hat{y}$ will decrease as the number of months the salesperson has been employed increases.

The R^2 of 0.9013 indicates that this regression model explains approximately 90.2% of the variation in Scales Sold for our sample data. The lack of a distinct pattern in the scatter

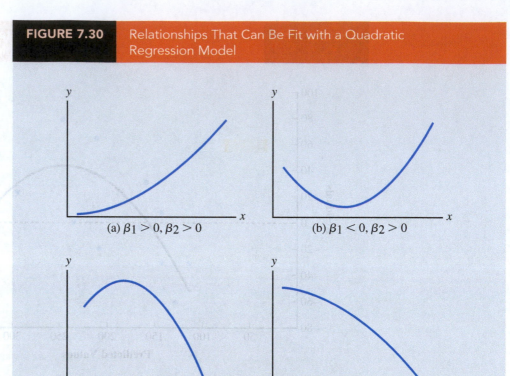

FIGURE 7.30 Relationships That Can Be Fit with a Quadratic Regression Model

If $\beta_2 > 0$, the function is bowl-shaped relative to the x-axis, it is convex; if $\beta_2 < 0$, the function is mound-shaped relative to the x-axis, it is concave.

(a) $\beta_1 > 0, \beta_2 > 0$

(b) $\beta_1 < 0, \beta_2 > 0$

(c) $\beta_1 > 0, \beta_2 < 0$

(d) $\beta_1 < 0, \beta_2 < 0$

FIGURE 7.31 Excel Data for the Reynolds Quadratic Regression Model

	A	B	C
1	**Months Employed**	**MonthsSq**	**Scales Sold**
2	41	1,681	275
3	106	11,236	296
4	76	5,776	317
5	100	10,000	376
6	22	484	162
7	12	144	150
8	85	7,225	367
9	111	12,321	308
10	40	1,600	189
11	51	2,601	235
12	0	0	83
13	12	144	112
14	6	36	67
15	56	3,136	325
16	19	361	189

FIGURE 7.32   Excel Output for the Reynolds Quadratic Regression Model

	A	B	C	D	E	F	G	H	I
1	SUMMARY OUTPUT								
2									
3	*Regression Statistics*								
4	Multiple R	0.949361402							
5	R Square	0.901287072							
6	Adjusted R Square	0.884834917							
7	Standard Error	34.61481184							
8	Observations	15							
9									
10	ANOVA								
11		*df*	*SS*	*MS*	*F*	*Significance F*			
12	Regression	2	131278.711	65639.35548	54.78231208	9.25218E-07			
13	Residual	12	14378.22238	1198.185199					
14	Total	14	145656.9333						
15									
16		*Coefficients*	*Standard Error*	*t Stat*	*P-value*	*Lower 95%*	*Upper 95%*	*Lower 99.0%*	*Upper 99.0%*
17	Intercept	61.42993467	20.57433536	2.985755485	0.011363561	16.60230882	106.2575605	−1.415187222	124.2750566
18	Months Employed	5.819796648	0.969766536	6.001234761	6.20497E-05	3.706856877	7.93273642	2.857606371	8.781986926
19	MonthsSq	−0.031009589	0.008436087	−3.675826286	0.003172962	−0.049390243	−0.012628935	−0.05677795	−0.005241228

The scatter chart of residuals against the independent variable Months Employed would also lead us to this conclusion.

chart of residuals against the predicted values of the dependent variable (Figure 7.33) suggests that the quadratic model fits the data better than the simple linear regression in the Reynolds example.

Although it is difficult to assess from a sample as small as this whether the regression model satisfies the conditions necessary for reliable inference, we see no marked violations of these conditions, so we will proceed with hypothesis tests of the regression parameters β_0, β_1, and β_2 for our quadratic regression model.

From the Excel output for the model in equation (7.18) provided in Figure 7.32, we see that the p values corresponding to the t statistics for Months Employed (6.2050E-05) and MonthsSq (0.0032) are both substantially less than 0.05, and hence we can conclude that adding MonthsSq to the model involving Months is significant. There is a nonlinear relationship between months and sales.

Note that if the estimated regression parameters b_1 and b_2 corresponding to the linear term x and the squared term x^2 are of the same sign, the estimated value of the dependent variable is either increasing over the experimental range of x (when $b_1 > 0$ and $b_2 > 0$) or decreasing over the experimental range of x (when $b_1 < 0$ and $b_2 < 0$). If the estimated regression parameters b_1 and b_2 corresponding to the linear term x and the squared term x^2 have different signs, the estimated value of the dependent variable has a maximum over the experimental range of x (when $b_1 > 0$ and $b_2 < 0$) or a minimum over the experimental range of x (when $b_1 < 0$ and $b_2 > 0$). In these instances, we can find the estimated maximum or minimum over the experimental range of x by finding the value of x at which the estimated value of the dependent variable stops increasing and begins decreasing (when a maximum exists) or stops decreasing and begins increasing (when a minimum exists).

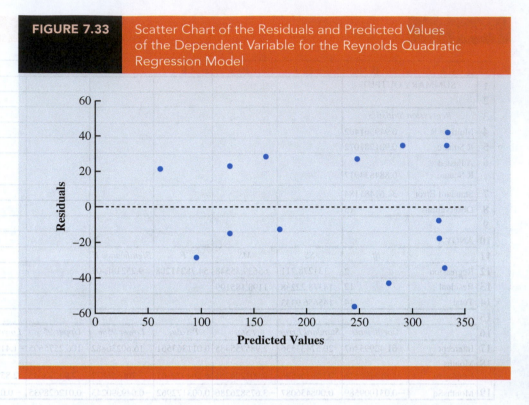

FIGURE 7.33   Scatter Chart of the Residuals and Predicted Values of the Dependent Variable for the Reynolds Quadratic Regression Model

For example, we estimate that when months employed increases by 1 from some value x ($x + 1$), sales changes by:

$$5.8198\,[(x + 1) - x] - 0.0310\,[(x + 1)^2 - x^2]$$
$$= 5.8198\,(x - x + 1) - 0.0310\,(x^2 + 2x + 1 - x^2)$$
$$= 5.8198 - 0.0310\,(2x + 1)$$
$$= 5.7888 - 0.0620x.$$

That is, estimated Sales initially increases as Months Employed increases and then eventually decreases as Months Employed increases. Solving this result for x:

$$5.7888 - 0.0620x = 0$$
$$-0.0620x = -5.7888$$
$$x = \frac{-5.7888}{-0.0620} = 93.3387$$

tells us that estimated maximum sales occurs at approximately 93 months (in about seven years nine months). We can then find the estimated maximum value of the dependent variable Sales by substituting this value of x into the estimated regression equation:

$$\text{Sales} = 61.58198 + 5.8198\,(93.3387) - 0.0310\,(93.3387^2) = 334.4909.$$

At approximately 93 months, the maximum estimated sales of approximately 334 scales occurs.

Piecewise Linear Regression Models

In business analytics applications, polynomial regression models of higher than second or third order are rarely used.

As an alternative to a quadratic regression model, we can recognize that below some value of Months Employed, the relationship between Months Employed and Sales appears to be positive and linear, whereas the relationship between Months Employed and Sales appears to be negative and linear for the remaining observations. A **piecewise linear regression model**

A piecewise linear regression model is sometimes referred to as a segment regression or a spline model.

FIGURE 7.34   Possible Position of Knot $x^{(k)}$

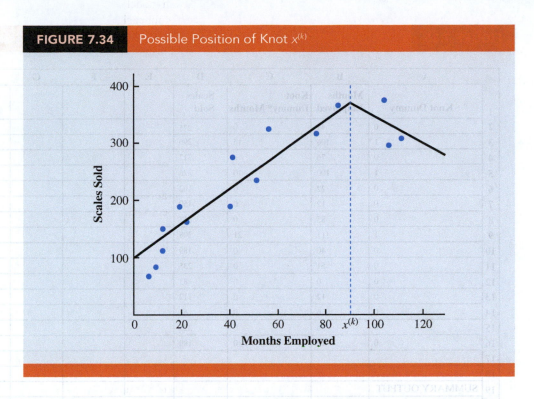

will allow us to fit these relationships as two linear regressions that are joined at the value of Months at which the relationship between Months Employed and Sales changes.

Our first step in fitting a piecewise linear regression model is to identify the value of the independent variable Months Employed at which the relationship between Months Employed and Sales changes; this point is called the **knot**, or *breakpoint*. Although theory should determine this value, analysts often use the sample data to aid in the identification of this point. Figure 7.34 provides the scatter chart for the Reynolds data with an indication of the possible location of the knot, which we have denoted $x^{(k)}$. From this scatter chart, it appears the knot is at approximately 90 months.

Once we have decided on the location of the knot, we define a dummy variable that is equal to zero for any observation for which the value of Months Employed is less than or equal to the value of the knot, and equal to one for any observation for which the value of Months Employed is greater than the value of the knot:

$$x_k = \begin{cases} 0 \text{ if } x_1 \leq x^{(k)} \\ 1 \text{ if } x_1 > x^{(k)} \end{cases} \qquad (7.19)$$

where

$x_1 =$ Months

$x^{(k)} =$ the value of the knot (90 months for the Reynolds example)

$x_k =$ the knot dummy variable

We then fit the following regression model:

$$y = b_0 + b_1 x_1 + b_2 (x_1 - x^{(k)}) x_k + e. \qquad (7.20)$$

The data and Excel output for the Reynolds piecewise linear regression model are provided in Figure 7.35. Because we placed the knot at $x^{(k)} = 90$, the estimated regression model is

$$\hat{y} = 87.2172 + 3.4094 x_1 - 7.8726(x_1 - 90)x_k$$

FIGURE 7.35 Data and Excel Output for the Reynolds Piecewise Linear Regression Model

	A	B	C	D	E	F	G	H	I
1	Knot Dummy	Months Employed	Knot Dummy* Months	Scales Sold					
2	0	41	0	275					
3	1	106	16	296					
4	0	76	0	317					
5	1	100	10	376					
6	0	22	0	162					
7	0	12	0	150					
8	0	85	0	367					
9	1	111	21	308					
10	0	40	0	189					
11	0	51	0	235					
12	0	0	0	83					
13	0	12	0	112					
14	0	6	0	67					
15	0	56	0	325					
16	0	19	0	189					
17									
18									
19	SUMMARY OUTPUT								
20									
21	*Regression Statistics*								
22	Multiple R	0.955796127							
23	R Square	0.913546237							
24	Adjusted R Square	0.899137276							
25	Standard Error	32.3941739							
26	Observations	15							
27									
28	ANOVA								
29		*df*	*SS*	*MS*	*F*	*Significance F*			
30	Regression	2	133064.3433	66532.17165	63.4012588	4.17545E-07			
31	Residual	12	12592.59003	1049.382502					
32	Total	14	145656.9333						
33									
34		*Coefficients*	*Standard Error*	*t Stat*	*P-value*	*Lower 95%*	*Upper 95%*	*Lower 99.0%*	*Upper 99.0%*
35	Intercept	87.21724231	15.31062519	5.696517369	9.9677E-05	53.85825572	120.5762289	40.45033153	133.9841531
36	Months Employed	3.409431979	0.338360666	10.07632484	3.2987E-07	2.67220742	4.146656538	2.375895931	4.442968028
37	Knot Dummy* Months	−7.872553259	1.902156543	−4.138751508	0.00137388	−12.01699634	−3.728110179	−13.68276572	−2.062340794

The output shows that the p value corresponding to the t statistic for knot term ($p = 0.0014$) is less than 0.05, and hence we can conclude that adding the knot to the model with Months Employed as the independent variable is significant.

But what does this model mean? For any value of Months less than or equal to 90, the knot term $7.8726(x_1 - 90)x_k$ is zero because the knot dummy variable $x_k = 0$, so the regression model is:

$$\hat{y} = 87.2172 + 3.4094x_1.$$

The variable Knot Dummy*Months is the product of the corresponding values of Knot Dummy and the difference between Months Employed and the knot value, i.e., C2 = A2 * (B2 − 90) in this Excel spreadsheet.

For any value of Months Employed greater than 90, the knot term is $-7.87(x_1 - 90)$ because the knot dummy variable $x_k = 1$, so the regression model is:

$$\hat{y} = 87.2172 + 3.4094x_1 - 7.8726(x_1 - 90)$$
$$= 87.2172 - 7.8726(-90) + (3.4094 - 7.8726)x_1 = 795.7512 - 4.4632x_1.$$

Note that if Months Employed is equal to 90, both regressions yield the same value of $\hat{y}$:

$$\hat{y} = 87.2172 + 3.4094(90) = 795.7512 - 4.4632(90) = 394.06.$$

So the two regression segments are joined at the knot.

Multiple knots can be used to fit complex piecewise linear regressions.

The interpretation of this model is similar to the interpretation of the quadratic regression model. A salesperson's sales are expected to increase by 3,409.4 electronic laboratory scales for each month of employment until the salesperson has been employed for 90 months. At that point the salesperson's sales are expected to decrease by 4,463.1 (because $3,409.4 - 7,872.5 = -4,463.1$) electronic laboratory scales for each additional month of employment.

Should we use the quadratic regression model or the piecewise linear regression model? These models fit the data equally well, and both have reasonable interpretations, so we cannot differentiate between the models on either of these criteria. Thus, we must consider whether the abrupt change in the relationship between Sales and Months Employed that is suggested by the piecewise linear regression model captures the real relationship between Sales and Months Employed better than the smooth change in the relationship between Sales and Months Employed suggested by the quadratic model.

Interaction Between Independent Variables

Often the relationship between the dependent variable and one independent variable is different at various values of a second independent variable. When this occurs, it is called an **interaction**. If the original data set consists of observations for y and two independent variables x_1 and x_2, we can incorporate an x_1x_2 interaction into the multiple linear regression in the following manner:

$$y = b_0 + b_1x_1 + b_2x_2 + b_3x_1x_2 + e. \tag{7.21}$$

To provide an illustration of interaction and what it means, let us consider the regression study conducted by Tyler Personal Care for one of its new shampoo products. The two factors believed to have the most influence on sales are unit selling price and advertising expenditure. To investigate the effects of these two variables on sales, prices of $2.00, $2.50, and $3.00 were paired with advertising expenditures of $50,000 and $100,000 in 24 test markets.

Tyler

The data collected by Tyler are provided in the file *Tyler*. Figure 7.36 shows the sample mean sales for the six price advertising expenditure combinations. Note that the sample mean sales corresponding to a price of $2.00 and an advertising expenditure of $50,000 is 461,000 units and that the sample mean sales corresponding to a price of $2.00 and an advertising expenditure of $100,000 is 808,000 units. Hence, with price held constant at $2.00, the difference in mean sales between advertising expenditures of $50,000 and $100,000 is $808,000 - 461,000 = 347,000$ units. When the price of the product is $2.50, the difference in mean sales between advertising expenditures of $50,000 and $100,000 is $646,000 - 364,000 = 282,000$ units. Finally, when the price is $3.00, the difference in mean sales between advertising expenditures of $50,000 and $100,000 is $375,000 - 332,000 = 43,000$ units. Clearly, the difference in mean sales between advertising expenditures of $50,000 and $100,000 depends on the price of the product. In other words, at higher selling prices, the effect of increased advertising expenditure diminishes. These

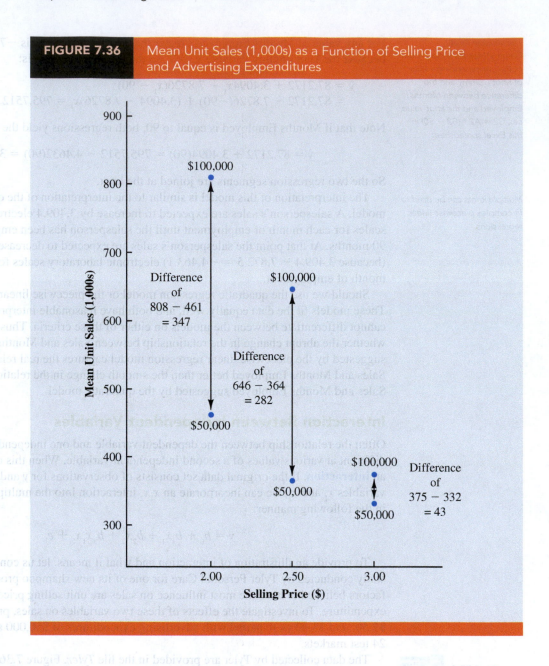

FIGURE 7.36   Mean Unit Sales (1,000s) as a Function of Selling Price and Advertising Expenditures

In the file Tyler, the data for the independent variable Price is in column A, the independent variable Advertising Expenditures is in column B, and the dependent variable Sales is in column D. We created the interaction variable Price*Advertising in column C by entering the function A2*B2 in cell C2, and then copying cell C2 into cells C3 through C25.

observations provide evidence of interaction between the price and advertising expenditure variables.

When interaction between two variables is present, we cannot study the relationship between one independent variable and the dependent variable y independently of the other variable. In other words, meaningful conclusions can be developed only if we consider the joint relationship that both independent variables have with the dependent variable. To account for the interaction, we use the regression model in equation (7.21), where:

$$y = \text{Unit Sales (1,000s)}$$
$$x_1 = \text{Price (\$)}$$
$$x_2 = \text{Advertising Expenditure (\$1,000s)}$$

FIGURE 7.37   Excel Output for the Tyler Personal Care Linear Regression Model with Interaction

	A	B	C	D	E	F	G	H	I
1	SUMMARY OUTPUT								
2									
3	*Regression Statistics*								
4	Multiple R	0.988993815							
5	R Square	0.978108766							
6	Adjusted R Square	0.974825081							
7	Standard Error	28.17386496							
8	Observations	24							
9									
10	ANOVA								
11		*df*	*SS*	*MS*	*F*	*Significance F*			
12	Regression	3	709316	236438.6667	297.8692	9.25881E-17			
13	Residual	20	15875.33333	793.7666667					
14	Total	23	725191.3333						
15									
16		*Coefficients*	*Standard Error*	*t Stat*	*P-value*	*Lower 95%*	*Upper 95%*	*Lower 99.0%*	*Upper 99.0%*
17	Intercept	−275.8333333	112.8421033	−2.444418575	0.023898351	−511.2178361	−40.44883053	−596.9074508	45.24078413
18	Price	175	44.54679188	3.928453489	0.0008316	82.07702045	267.9229796	48.24924412	301.7507559
19	Advertising Expenditure ($1,000s)	19.68	1.42735225	13.78776683	1.1263E-11	16.70259538	22.65740462	15.61869796	23.74130204
20	Price*Advertising	−6.08	0.563477299	−10.79014187	8.67721E-10	−7.255393049	−4.904606951	−7.683284335	−4.476715665

Note that the regression model in equation (7.21) reflects Tyler's belief that the number of units sold is related to selling price and advertising expenditure (accounted for by the $\beta_1 x_1$ and $\beta_2 x_2$ terms) and an interaction between the two variables (accounted for by the $\beta_3 x_1 x_2$ term).

The Excel output corresponding to the interaction model for the Tyler Personal Care example is provided in Figure 7.37.

The resulting estimated regression equation is:

Sales = −275.8333 + 175 Price + 19.68 Advertising − 6.08 Price*Advertising.

Because the *p* value corresponding to the *t* test for Price*Advertising is 8.6772E-10, we conclude that interaction is significant. Thus, the regression results show that the relationship between advertising expenditure and sales depends on the price (and the relationship between advertising expenditures and price depends on sales).

Our initial review of these results may alarm us: How can price have a positive estimated regression coefficient? With the exception of luxury goods, we expect sales to decrease as price increases. Although this result appears counterintuitive, we can make sense of this model if we work through the interpretation of the interaction. In other words, the relationship between the independent variable Price and the dependent variable Sales is different at various values of Advertising (and the relationship between the independent variable Advertising and the dependent variable Sales is different at various values of Price).

It becomes easier to see how the predicted value of Sales depends on Price by using the estimated regression model to consider the effect when Price increases by $1:

Sales After $1 Price Increase $= -275.8333 + 175$ (Price $+ 1$)
$$+ 19.68 \text{ Advertising} - 6.08 \text{ (Price} + 1) * \text{Advertising}.$$

Thus,

Sales After $1 Price Increase $-$ Sales Before $1 Price Increase $= 175 - 6.08$ Advertising Expenditure.

So the change in the predicted value of the dependent variable that occurs when the independent variable Price increases by $1 depends on how much was spent on advertising.

Consider a concrete example. If Advertising Expenditures is $50,000 when price is $2.00, we estimate sales to be:

Sales $= -275.8333 + 175$ (2) $+ 19.68$ (50) $- 6.08$ (2) (50) $= 450.1667$, or 450,167 units.

At the same level of Advertising Expenditures ($50,000) when price is $3.00, we estimate sales to be:

Sales $= -275.8333 + 175$ (3) $+ 19.68$ (50) $- 6.08$ (3) (50) $= 321.1667$, or 321,167 units.

So when Advertising Expenditures is $50,000, a change in price from $2.00 to $3.00 results in a $450,167 - 321,167 = 129,000$-unit decrease in estimated sales. However, if Advertising Expenditures is $100,000 when price is $2.00, we estimate sales to be:

Sales $= -275.8333 + 175$ (2) $+ 19.68$ (100) $- 6.08$ (2) (100) $= 826.1667$, or 826,167 units.

At the same level of Advertising Expenditures ($100,000) when price is $3.00, we estimate sales to be:

Sales $= -275.8333 + 175$ (3) $+ 19.68$ (100) $- 6.08$ (3) (100) $= 393.1667$, or 393,167 units.

So when Advertising Expenditures is $100,000, a change in price from $2.00 to $3.00 results in a $826,167 - 393,167 = 433,000$-unit decrease in estimated sales. When Tyler spends more on advertising, its sales are more sensitive to changes in price. Perhaps at larger Advertising Expenditures, Tyler attracts new customers who have been buying the product from another company and so are more aware of the prices charged for the product by Tyler's competitors.

There is a second and equally valid interpretation of the interaction; it tells us that the relationship between the independent variable Advertising Expenditure and the dependent variable Sales is different at various values of Price. Using the estimated regression model to consider the effect when Advertising Expenditure increases by $1,000:

Sales After $1K Advertising Increase $= -275.8333 + 175$ Price $+ 19.68$ (Advertising $+ 1$)
$$-6.08 \text{ Price} * \text{(Advertising} + 1).$$

Thus,

Sales After $1K Advertising Increase $-$ Sales Before $1K Advertising Increase $= 19.68$ $- 6.08$ Price.

So the change in the predicted value of the dependent variable that occurs when the independent variable Advertising Expenditure increases by $1,000 depends on the price.

Thus, if Price is $2.00 when Advertising Expenditures is $50,000, we estimate sales to be:

Sales $= -275.8333 + 175\,(2) + 19.68\,(50) - 6.08\,(2)\,(50) = 450.1667$, or 450,167 units.

At the same level of Price ($2.00) when Advertising Expenditures is $100,000, we estimate sales to be:

Sales $= -275.8333 + 175\,(2) + 19.68\,(100) - 6.08\,(2)\,(100) = 826.1667$, or 826,167 units.

So when Price is $2.00, a change in Advertising Expenditures from $50,000 to $100,000 results in a $826{,}167 - 450{,}167 = 376{,}000$-unit increase in estimated sales. However, if Price is $3.00 when Advertising Expenditures is 50,000, we estimate sales to be:

Sales $= -275.8333 + 175\,(3) + 19.68\,(50) - 6.08\,(3)\,(50) = 321.1667$, or 321,167 units.

At the same level of Price ($3.00) when Advertising Expenditures is $100,000, we estimate sales to be:

Sales $= -275.8333 + 175\,(3) + 19.68\,(100) - 6.08\,(3)\,(100) = 393.1667$, or 393,167 units.

So when Price is $3.00, a change in Advertising Expenditure from $50,000 to $100,000 results in a $393{,}167 - 321{,}167 = 72{,}000$-unit increase in estimated sales. When the price of Tyler's product is high, its sales are less sensitive to changes in advertising expenditure. Perhaps as Tyler increases its price, it must advertise more to convince potential customers that its product is a good value.

Note that we can combine a quadratic effect with interaction to produce a second-order polynomial model with interaction between the two independent variables. The model obtained is:

$$y = b_0 + b_1 x_1 + b_2 x_2 + b_3 x_1^2 + b_4 x_2^2 + b_5 x_1 x_2 + e. \qquad (7.22)$$

This model provides a great deal of flexibility in capturing nonlinear effects.

NOTES + COMMENTS

1. Just as a dummy variable can be used to allow for different y-intercepts for the two groups represented by the dummy, we can use an interaction between a dummy variable and a quantitative independent variable to allow for different relationships between independent and dependent variables for the two groups represented by the dummy. Consider the Butler Trucking example: Travel time is the dependent variable y, miles traveled and number of deliveries are the quantitative independent variables x_1 and x_2, and the dummy variable x_3 differentiates between driving assignments that included travel on a congested segment of a highway and driving assignments that did not. If we believe that the relationship between miles traveled and travel time differs for driving assignments that included travel on a congested segment of a highway and those that did not, we could create a new variable that is the interaction between miles

traveled and the dummy variable ($x_4 = x_1 * x_3$) and estimate the following model:

$$\hat{y} = b_0 + b_1 x_1 + b_2 x_2 + b_3 x_4.$$

If a driving assignment does not include travel on a congested segment of a highway, $x_4 = x_1 * x_3 = x_1 *(0) = 0$ and the regression model is:

$$\hat{y} = b_0 + b_1 x_1 + b_2 x_2.$$

If a driving assignment does include travel on a congested segment of a highway, $x_4 = x_1 * x_3 = x_1 *(1) = x_1$ and the regression model is:

$$\hat{y} = b_0 + b_1 x_1 + b_2 x_2 + b_3 x_1 (1)$$
$$= b_0 + (b_1 + b_3)x_1 + b_2 x_2.$$

So in this regression model b_1 is the estimate of the relationship between miles traveled and travel time for driving assignments that do not include travel on a congested segment of a highway, and $b_1 + b_3$ is the estimate of the relationship between miles traveled and travel time for driving assignments that do include travel on a congested segment of a highway.

2. Multicollinearity can be divided into two types. *Data-based multicollinearity* occurs when separate independent variables that are related are included in the model, whereas *structural multicollinearity* occurs when a new independent variable is created by taking a function of one or more existing independent variables. If we use ratings that consumers give on bread's aroma and taste as independent variables in a model for which the dependent variable is the overall rating of the bread, the multicollinearity that would exist between the aroma and taste ratings is an example of data-based multicollinearity. If we

build a quadratic model for which the independent variables are ratings that consumers give on bread's aroma and the square of the ratings that consumers give on bread's aroma, the multicollinearity that would exist is an example of structural multicollinearity.

3. Structural multicollinearity occurs naturally in polynomial regression models and regression models with interactions. You can greatly reduce the structural multicollinearity in a polynomial regression by centering the independent variable x (using $x - \bar{x}$ in place of x). In a regression model with interaction, you can greatly reduce the structural multicollinearity by centering both independent variables that interact. However, quadratic regression models and regression models with interactions are frequently used only for prediction; in these instances centering independent variables is not necessary because we are not concerned with inference.

7.8 Model Fitting

Finding an effective regression model can be challenging. Although we rely on theory to guide us, often we are faced with a large number of potential independent variables from which to choose. In this section we discuss common algorithms for building a regression model and the potential hazards of these and other similar algorithms.

Variable Selection Procedures

When there are many independent variables to consider, special procedures are sometimes employed to select the independent variables to include in the regression model. These variable selection procedures include **backward elimination**, **forward selection**, **stepwise selection**, and the **best subsets** procedure. Given a data set with several possible independent variables, we can use these procedures to identify which independent variables provide a model that best satisfies some criterion. The first four procedures are iterative; at each step of the procedure a single independent variable is added or removed and the new model is evaluated. The process continues until a stopping criterion indicates that the procedure cannot find a superior model. The best subsets procedure is not a one-variable-at-a-time procedure; it evaluates regression models involving different subsets of the independent variables.

The backward elimination procedure begins with the regression model that includes all of the independent variables under consideration. At each step of the procedure, backward elimination considers the removal of an independent variable according to some criterion. For example, if any independent variables currently in the model are not significant at a preselected level of significance, XLMiner removes the least significant of these independent variables from the model. The regression model is then refit with the remaining independent variables and statistical significance is reexamined. The backward elimination procedure stops when all independent variables in the model are significant at a preselected level of significance.

The forward selection procedure begins with none of the independent variables under consideration included in the regression model. At each step of the procedure, forward selection considers the addition of an independent variable according to some criterion. For example, if any independent variables currently not in the model are significant at a preselected level of significance, XLMiner adds the most significant of these independent variables to the model. The regression model is then refit with the additional independent variable and statistical significance is reexamined. The forward selection procedure stops when all of the independent variables not in the model are not significant at a preselected level of significance.

Similar to the forward selection procedure, the stepwise procedure begins with none of the independent variables under consideration included in the regression model. The analyst establishes both a criterion for allowing independent variables to enter the model and a criterion for allowing independent variables to remain in the model. For example, XLMiner adds the most significant variable and removes the least significant variable at each iteration. In the first step of the procedure, the most significant independent variable is added to the current model if its level of significance satisfies the entering threshold. Each subsequent step involves two intermediate steps. First, the remaining independent variables not in the current model are evaluated, and the most significant one is added to the model if its significance satisfies the entering threshold. Then the independent variables in the resulting model are evaluated, and the least significant variable is removed if its level of significance fails to satisfy the exiting threshold. The procedure stops when no independent variable not currently in the model has a level of significance that satisfies the entering threshold, and no independent variable currently in the model has a level of significance that fails to satisfy the exiting threshold.

In the best subsets procedure, simple linear regressions for each of the independent variables under consideration are generated, and then the multiple regressions with all combinations of two independent variables under consideration are generated, and so on. Once a regression model has been generated for every possible subset of the independent variables under consideration, the entire collection of regression models can be compared and evaluated by the analyst.

Although these algorithms are potentially useful when dealing with a large number of potential independent variables, they do not necessarily provide useful models. Once the procedure terminates, you should deliberate whether the combination of independent variables included in the final regression model makes sense from a practical standpoint and consider whether you can create a more useful regression model with more meaningful interpretation through the addition or removal of independent variables. Use your own judgment and intuition about your data to refine the results of these algorithms.

Overfitting

The objective in building a regression model (or any other type of mathematical model) is to provide the simplest accurate representation of the population. A model that is relatively simple will be easy to understand, interpret, and use, and a model that accurately represents the population will yield meaningful results.

When we base a model on sample data, we must be wary. Sample data generally do not perfectly represent the population from which they are drawn; if we attempt to fit a model too closely to the sample data, we risk capturing behavior that is idiosyncratic to the sample data rather than representative of the population. When the model is too closely fit to sample data and as a result does not accurately reflect the population, the model is said to have been overfit. **Overfitting** generally results from creating an overly complex model to explain idiosyncrasies in the sample data. In regression analysis, this often results from the use of complex functional forms or independent variables that do not have meaningful relationships with the dependent variable. If a model is overfit to the sample data, it will perform better on the sample data used to fit the model than it will on other data from the population. Thus, an overfit model can be misleading with regard to its predictive capability and its interpretation.

The stepwise procedure requires that the criterion for an independent variable to enter the regression model is more difficult to satisfy than the criterion for an independent variable to be removed from the regression model. This requirement prevents the same independent variable from exiting and then reentering the regression model in the same step.

XLMiner also provides a sequential replacement algorithm in which, for a given number of independent variables, individual independent variables are sequentially replaced and replacements that improve performance are retained.

The principle of using the simplest meaningful model possible without sacrificing accuracy is referred to as Ockham's razor, the law of parsimony, or the law of economy.

Overfitting is a difficult problem to detect and avoid. The following list summarizes one way to avoid overfitting and one way to determine how well a model will may generalize to new data.

- Use only independent variables that you expect to have real and meaningful relationships with the dependent variable.
- Use complex models, such as quadratic models and piecewise linear regression models, only when you have a reasonable expectation that such complexity provides a more accurate depiction of what you are modeling.
- Do not let software dictate your model. Use iterative modeling procedures, such as the stepwise and best-subsets procedures, only for guidance and not to generate your final model. Use your own judgment and intuition about your data and what you are modeling to refine your model.
- If you have access to a sufficient quantity of data, assess your model on data other than the sample data that were used to generate the model (this is referred to as **cross-validation**). The following list contains three possible ways to execute cross-validation.

Validation data sets are sometimes referred to as holdout samples. XLMiner allows the user to easily divide data sets into training and validation sets for use with regression models.

Holdout method: The sample data are randomly divided into mutually exclusive and collectively exhaustive training and validation sets. The **training set** is the data set used to build the candidate models that appear to make practical sense. The **validation set** is the set of data used to compare model performances and ultimately select a model for predicting values of the dependent variable. For example, we might randomly select half of the data for use in developing regression models. We could use these data as our training set to estimate a model or a collection of models that appear to perform well. Then we use the remaining half of the data as a validation set to assess and compare the models' performances and ultimately select the model that minimizes some measure of overall error when applied to the validation set. The advantages of the holdout method are that it is simple and quick. However, results of a holdout sample can vary greatly depending on which observations are randomly selected for the training set, the number of observations in the sample, and the number of observations that are randomly selected for the training and validation sets.

k-fold cross-validation: The sample data set are randomly divided into k equal-sized, mutually exclusive, and collectively exhaustive subsets called folds, and k iterations are executed. For each iteration, a different subset is designated as the validation set and the remaining $k - 1$ subsets are combined and designated as the training set. The model is estimated using the respective training set data and evaluated using the respective validation set. The results of the k iterations are then combined and evaluated. A common choice for the number of folds is $k = 10$. The k-fold cross-validation method is more complex and time consuming than the holdout method, but the results of the k-fold cross-validation method are less sensitive to how the observations are randomly assigned to the training validation sets.

Leave-one-out cross-validation: For a sample of n observations, an iteration consists of estimating the model on $n - 1$ observations and evaluating the model on the single observation that was omitted from the training data. This procedure is repeated for n total iterations so that the model is trained on each possible combination of $n - 1$ observations and evaluated on the single remaining observation in each case.

Observing these guidelines will reduce the risk of overfitting, but one must always be wary of the potential for overfitting when interpreting and assessing a model.

SUMMARY

In this chapter we showed how regression analysis can be used to determine how a dependent variable y is related to an independent variable x. In simple linear regression, the regression model is $y = \beta_0 + \beta_1 x_1 + \varepsilon$. We use sample data and the least squares method to develop the estimated regression equation $\hat{y} = b_0 + b_1 x_1$. In effect, b_0 and b_1 are the sample statistics used to estimate the unknown model parameters.

The coefficient of determination r^2 was presented as a measure of the goodness of fit for the estimated regression equation; it can be interpreted as the proportion of the variation in the sample values of the dependent variable y that can be explained by the estimated regression equation. We then extended our discussion to include multiple independent variables and reviewed how to use Excel to find the estimated multiple regression equation $\hat{y} = b_0 + b_1 x_1 + b_2 x_2 + \cdots + b_q x_q$, and we considered the interpretations of the parameter estimates in multiple regression and the ramifications of multicollinearity.

The assumptions related to the regression model and its associated error term ε were discussed. We reviewed the t test for determining whether there is a statistically significant relationship between the dependent variable and an individual independent variable given the other independent variables in the regression model. We showed how to use Excel to develop confidence interval estimates of the regression parameters $\beta_0, \beta_1, \ldots, \beta_q$, and we discussed the special case of inference with very large samples.

We showed how to incorporate categorical independent variables into a regression model through the use of dummy variables, and we discussed a variety of ways to use multiple regression to fit nonlinear relationships between independent variables and the dependent variable. We concluded with a discussion of various automated procedures for selecting independent variables to include in a regression model and consideration of the problem of overfitting a regression model.

GLOSSARY

Backward elimination An iterative variable selection procedure that starts with a model with all independent variables and considers removing an independent variable at each step.

Best subsets A variable selection procedure that constructs and compares all possible models with up to a specified number of independent variables.

Coefficient of determination A measure of the goodness of fit of the estimated regression equation. It can be interpreted as the proportion of the variability in the dependent variable y that is explained by the estimated regression equation.

Confidence interval An estimate of a population parameter that provides an interval believed to contain the value of the parameter at some level of confidence.

Confidence level An indication of how frequently interval estimates based on samples of the same size taken from the same population using identical sampling techniques will contain the true value of the parameter we are estimating.

Cross-validation Assessment of the performance of a model on data other than the data that were used to generate the model.

Dependent variable The variable that is being predicted or explained. It is denoted by y and is often referred to as the response.

Dummy variable A variable used to model the effect of categorical independent variables in a regression model; generally takes only the value zero or one.

Estimated regression The estimate of the regression equation developed from sample data by using the least squares method. The estimated simple linear regression equation is $\hat{y} = b_0 + b_1 x$, and the estimated multiple linear regression equation is $\hat{y} = b_0 + b_1 x_1 + b_2 x_2 + \cdots + b_q x_q$.

Experimental region The range of values for the independent variables $x_1, x_2, \ldots, x_q$ for the data that are used to estimate the regression model.

Extrapolation Prediction of the mean value of the dependent variable y for values of the independent variables $x_1, x_2, \ldots, x_q$ that are outside the experimental range.

Forward selection an iterative variable selection procedure that starts with a model with no variables and considers adding an independent variable at each step.

Holdout method Method of cross-validation in which sample data are randomly divided into mutually exclusive and collectively exhaustive sets, then one set is used to build the candidate models and the other set is used to compare model performances and ultimately select a model.

Hypothesis testing The process of making a conjecture about the value of a population parameter, collecting sample data that can be used to assess this conjecture, measuring the strength of the evidence against the conjecture that is provided by the sample, and using these results to draw a conclusion about the conjecture.

Independent variable(s) The variable(s) used for predicting or explaining values of the dependent variable. It is denoted by x and is often referred to as the predictor variable.

Interaction The relationship between the dependent variable and one independent variable is different at different values of a second independent variable.

Interval estimation The use of sample data to calculate a range of values that is believed to include the unknown value of a population parameter.

k-fold cross validation Method of cross-validation in which sample data set are randomly divided into k equal sized, mutually exclusive and collectively exhaustive subsets. In each of k iterations, one of the k subsets is used to build a candidate model and the remaining $k - 1$ sets are used evaluate the candidate model.

Knot The prespecified value of the independent variable at which its relationship with the dependent variable changes in a piecewise linear regression model; also called the breakpoint or the joint.

Least squares method A procedure for using sample data to find the estimated regression equation.

Leave-one-out cross validation Method of cross-validation in which candidate models are repeatedly fit using $n - 1$ observations and evaluated with the remaining observation.

Linear regression Regression analysis in which relationships between the independent variables and the dependent variable are approximated by a straight line.

Multicollinearity The degree of correlation among independent variables in a regression model.

Multiple linear regression Regression analysis involving one dependent variable and more than one independent variable.

Overfitting Fitting a model too closely to sample data, resulting in a model that does not accurately reflect the population.

p value The probability that a random sample of the same size collected from the same population using the same procedure will yield stronger evidence against a hypothesis than the evidence in the sample data given that the hypothesis is actually true.

Parameter A measurable factor that defines a characteristic of a population, process, or system.

Piecewise linear regression model Regression model in which one linear relationship between the independent and dependent variables is fit for values of the independent variable below a prespecified value of the independent variable, a different linear relationship between the independent and dependent variables is fit for values of the independent variable above the prespecified value of the independent variable, and the two regressions have the same estimated value of the dependent variable (i.e., are joined) at the prespecified value of the independent variable.

Point estimator A single value used as an estimate of the corresponding population parameter.

Quadratic regression model Regression model in which a nonlinear relationship between the independent and dependent variables is fit by including the independent variable and the square of the independent variable in the model: $\hat{y} = b_0 + b_1 x_1 + b_2 x_1^2$; also referred to as a second-order polynomial model.

Random variable The outcome of a random experiment (such as the drawing of a random sample) and so represents an uncertain outcome.

Regression analysis A statistical procedure used to develop an equation showing how the variables are related.

Regression model The equation that describes how the dependent variable y is related to an independent variable x and an error term; the *simple linear regression model* is $y = \beta_0 + \beta_1 x_1 + \varepsilon$, and the *multiple linear regression model* is $y = \beta_0 + \beta_1 x_1 + \beta_2 x_2 + \cdots + \beta_q x_q + \varepsilon$.

Residual The difference between the observed value of the dependent variable and the value predicted using the estimated regression equation; for the ith observation, the ith residual is $y_i - \hat{y}_i$.

Simple linear regression Regression analysis involving one dependent variable and one independent variable.

Statistical inference The process of making estimates and drawing conclusions about one or more characteristics of a population (the value of one or more parameters) through analysis of sample data drawn from the population.

Stepwise selection an iterative variable selection procedure that considers adding an independent variable and removing an independent variable at each step.

***t* test** Statistical test based on the Student's t probability distribution that can be used to test the hypothesis that a regression parameter β_j is zero; if this hypothesis is rejected, we conclude that there is a regression relationship between the jth independent variable and the dependent variable.

Training set The data set used to build the candidate models.

Validation set The data set used to compare model forecasts and ultimately pick a model for predicting values of the dependent variable.

PROBLEMS

1. *Bicycling World*, a magazine devoted to cycling, reviews hundreds of bicycles throughout the year. Its Road-Race category contains reviews of bicycles used by riders primarily interested in racing. One of the most important factors in selecting a bicycle for racing is its weight. The following data show the weight (pounds) and price ($) for ten racing bicycles reviewed by the magazine:

DATA *file*
BicyclingWorld

Model	Weight (lb)	Price ($)
Fierro 7B	17.9	2,200
HX 5000	16.2	6,350
Durbin Ultralight	15.0	8,470
Schmidt	16.0	6,300
WSilton Advanced	17.3	4,100
bicyclette vélo	13.2	8,700
Supremo Team	16.3	6,100
XTC Racer	17.2	2,680
D'Onofrio Pro	17.7	3,500
Americana #6	14.2	8,100

a. Develop a scatter chart with weight as the independent variable. What does the scatter chart indicate about the relationship between the weight and price of these bicycles?

b. Use the data to develop an estimated regression equation that could be used to estimate the price for a bicycle, given its weight. What is the estimated regression model?

c. Test whether each of the regression parameters β_0 and β_1 is equal to zero at a 0.05 level of significance. What are the correct interpretations of the estimated regression parameters? Are these interpretations reasonable?

d. How much of the variation in the prices of the bicycles in the sample does the regression model you estimated in part (b) explain?

e. The manufacturers of the D'Onofrio Pro plan to introduce the 15-lb D'Onofrio Elite bicycle later this year. Use the regression model you estimated in part (a) to predict the price of the D'Ononfrio Elite.

2. In a manufacturing process the assembly line speed (feet per minute) was thought to affect the number of defective parts found during the inspection process. To test this theory, managers devised a situation in which the same batch of parts was inspected visually at a variety of line speeds. They collected the following data:

Line Speed (ft/min)	No. of Defective Parts Found
20	21
20	19
40	15
30	16
60	14
40	17

a. Develop a scatter chart with line speed as the independent variable. What does the scatter chart indicate about the relationship between line speed and the number of defective parts found?

b. Use the data to develop an estimated regression equation that could be used to predict the number of defective parts found, given the line speed. What is the estimated regression model?

c. Test whether each of the regression parameters β_0 and β_1 is equal to zero at a 0.01 level of significance. What are the correct interpretations of the estimated regression parameters? Are these interpretations reasonable?

d. How much of the variation in the number of defective parts found for the sample data does the model you estimated in part (b) explain?

3. Jensen Tire & Auto is deciding whether to purchase a maintenance contract for its new computer wheel alignment and balancing machine. Managers feel that maintenance expense should be related to usage, and they collected the following information on weekly usage (hours) and annual maintenance expense (in hundreds of dollars).

Weekly Usage (hours)	Annual Maintenance Expense ($100s)
13	17.0
10	22.0
20	30.0
28	37.0
32	47.0
17	30.5
24	32.5
31	39.0
40	51.5
38	40.0

a. Develop a scatter chart with weekly usage hours as the independent variable. What does the scatter chart indicate about the relationship between weekly usage and annual maintenance expense?

b. Use the data to develop an estimated regression equation that could be used to predict the annual maintenance expense for a given number of hours of weekly usage. What is the estimated regression model?

c. Test whether each of the regression parameters β_0 and β_1 is equal to zero at a 0.05 level of significance. What are the correct interpretations of the estimated regression parameters? Are these interpretations reasonable?

d. How much of the variation in the sample values of annual maintenance expense does the model you estimated in part (b) explain?

e. If the maintenance contract costs $3,000 per year, would you recommend purchasing it? Why or why not?

4. A sociologist was hired by a large city hospital to investigate the relationship between the number of unauthorized days that employees are absent per year and the distance (miles) between home and work for the employees. A sample of 10 employees was chosen, and the following data were collected.

Distance to Work (miles)	No. of Days Absent
1	8
3	5
4	8
6	7
8	6
10	3
12	5
14	2
14	4
18	2

DATA *file*

Absent

a. Develop a scatter chart for these data. Does a linear relationship appear reasonable? Explain.

b. Use the data to develop an estimated regression equation that could be used to predict the number of days absent given the distance to work. What is the estimated regression model?

c. What is the 99% confidence interval for the regression parameter β_1? Based on this interval, what conclusion can you make about the hypotheses that the regression parameter β_1 is equal to zero?

d. What is the 99% confidence interval for the regression parameter β_0? Based on this interval, what conclusion can you make about the hypotheses that the regression parameter β_0 is equal to zero?

e. How much of the variation in the sample values of number of days absent does the model you estimated in part (b) explain?

5. The regional transit authority for a major metropolitan area wants to determine whether there is a relationship between the age of a bus and the annual maintenance cost. A sample of 10 buses resulted in the following data:

Age of Bus (years)	Annual Maintenance Cost ($)
1	350
2	370

(Continued)

DATA *file*

AgeCost

Age of Bus (years)	Annual Maintenance Cost ($)
2	480
2	520
2	590
3	550
4	750
4	800
5	790
5	950

   a. Develop a scatter chart for these data. What does the scatter chart indicate about the
      relationship between age of a bus and the annual maintenance cost?
   b. Use the data to develop an estimated regression equation that could be used to
      predict the annual maintenance cost given the age of the bus. What is the estimated
      regression model?
   c. Test whether each of the regression parameters β_0 and β_1 is equal to zero at a 0.05
      level of significance. What are the correct interpretations of the estimated regression
      parameters? Are these interpretations reasonable?
   d. How much of the variation in the sample values of annual maintenance cost does the
      model you estimated in part (b) explain?
   e. What do you predict the annual maintenance cost to be for a 3.5-year-old bus?

6. A marketing professor at Givens College is interested in the relationship between hours
   spent studying and total points earned in a course. Data collected on 156 students who
   took the course last semester are provided in the file *MktHrsPts*.

DATA *file*

MktHrsPts

   a. Develop a scatter chart for these data. What does the scatter chart indicate about the
      relationship between total points earned and hours spent studying?
   b. Develop an estimated regression equation showing how total points earned is related
      to hours spent studying. What is the estimated regression model?
   c. Test whether each of the regression parameters β_0 and β_1 is equal to zero at a 0.01
      level of significance. What are the correct interpretations of the estimated regression
      parameters? Are these interpretations reasonable?
   d. How much of the variation in the sample values of total point earned does the model
      you estimated in part (b) explain?
   e. Mark Sweeney spent 95 hours studying. Use the regression model you estimated in
      part (b) to predict the total points Mark earned.

7. The Dow Jones Industrial Average (DJIA) and the Standard & Poor's 500 (S&P 500)
   indexes are used as measures of overall movement in the stock market. The DJIA is
   based on the price movements of 30 large companies; the S&P 500 is an index composed
   of 500 stocks. Some say the S&P 500 is a better measure of stock market performance
   because it is broader based. The closing price for the DJIA and the S&P 500 for 15
   weeks, beginning with January 6, 2012, follow (*Barron's* web site, April 17, 2012).

DATA *file*

DJIAS&P500

Date	DJIA	S&P
January 6	12,360	1,278
January 13	12,422	1,289
January 20	12,720	1,315
January 27	12,660	1,316
February 3	12,862	1,345

February 10	12,801	1,343
February 17	12,950	1,362
February 24	12,983	1,366
March 2	12,978	1,370
March 9	12,922	1,371
March 16	13,233	1,404
March 23	13,081	1,397
March 30	13,212	1,408
April 5	13,060	1,398
April 13	12,850	1,370

a. Develop a scatter chart for these data with DJIA as the independent variable. What does the scatter chart indicate about the relationship between DJIA and S&P 500?

b. Develop an estimated regression equation showing how S&P 500 is related to DJIA. What is the estimated regression model?

c. What is the 95% confidence interval for the regression parameter β_1? Based on this interval, what conclusion can you make about the hypotheses that the regression parameter β_1 is equal to zero?

d. What is the 95% confidence interval for the regression parameter β_0? Based on this interval, what conclusion can you make about the hypotheses that the regression parameter β_0 is equal to zero?

e. How much of the variation in the sample values of S&P 500 does the model estimated in part (b) explain?

f. Suppose that the closing price for the DJIA is 13,500. Estimate the closing price for the S&P 500.

g. Should we be concerned that the DJIA value of 13,500 used to predict the S&P 500 value in part (f) is beyond the range of the DJIA used to develop the estimated regression equation?

8. The Toyota Camry is one of the best-selling cars in North America. The cost of a previously owned Camry depends on many factors, including the model year, mileage, and condition. To investigate the relationship between the car's mileage and the sales price for Camrys, the following data show the mileage and sale price for 19 sales (PriceHub web site, February 24, 2012).

DATA *file*
Camry

Miles (1,000s)	Price ($1,000s)
22	16.2
29	16.0
36	13.8
47	11.5
63	12.5
77	12.9
73	11.2
87	13.0
92	11.8
101	10.8
110	8.3
28	12.5

(Continued)

Miles (1,000s)	Price ($1,000s)
59	11.1
68	15.0
68	12.2
91	13.0
42	15.6
65	12.7
110	8.3

a. Develop a scatter chart for these data with miles as the independent variable. What does the scatter chart indicate about the relationship between price and miles?

b. Develop an estimated regression equation showing how price is related to miles. What is the estimated regression model?

c. Test whether each of the regression parameters β_0 and β_1 is equal to zero at a 0.01 level of significance. What are the correct interpretations of the estimated regression parameters? Are these interpretations reasonable?

d. How much of the variation in the sample values of price does the model estimated in part (b) explain?

e. For the model estimated in part (b), calculate the predicted price and residual for each automobile in the data. Identify the two automobiles that were the biggest bargains.

f. Suppose that you are considering purchasing a previously owned Camry that has been driven 60,000 miles. Use the estimated regression equation developed in part (b) to predict the price for this car. Is this the price you would offer the seller?

9. Dixie Showtime Movie Theaters, Inc., owns and operates a chain of cinemas in several markets in the southern United States. The owners would like to estimate weekly gross revenue as a function of advertising expenditures. Data for a sample of eight markets for a recent week follow:

DATA file
DixieShowtime

Market	Weekly Gross Revenue ($100s)	Television Advertising ($100s)	Newspaper Advertising ($100s)
Mobile	101.3	5.0	1.5
Shreveport	51.9	3.0	3.0
Jackson	74.8	4.0	1.5
Birmingham	126.2	4.3	4.3
Little Rock	137.8	3.6	4.0
Biloxi	101.4	3.5	2.3
New Orleans	237.8	5.0	8.4
Baton Rouge	219.6	6.9	5.8

a. Develop an estimated regression equation with the amount of television advertising as the independent variable. Test for a significant relationship between television advertising and weekly gross revenue at the 0.05 level of significance. What is the interpretation of this relationship?

b. How much of the variation in the sample values of weekly gross revenue does the model in part (a) explain?

c. Develop an estimated regression equation with both television advertising and newspaper advertising as the independent variables. Test whether each of the regression parameters β_0, β_1, and β_2 is equal to zero at a 0.05 level of significance. What are the correct interpretations of the estimated regression parameters? Are these interpretations reasonable?

d. How much of the variation in the sample values of weekly gross revenue does the model in part (c) explain?

e. Given the results in parts (a) and (c), what should your next step be? Explain.

f. What are the managerial implications of these results?

10. *Resorts & Spas,* a magazine devoted to upscale vacations and accommodations, published its Reader's Choice List of the top 20 independent beachfront boutique hotels in the world. The data shown are the scores received by these hotels based on the results from *Resorts & Spas'* annual Readers' Choice Survey. Each score represents the percentage of respondents who rated a hotel as excellent or very good on one of three criteria (comfort, amenities, and in-house dining). An overall score was also reported and used to rank the hotels. The highest ranked hotel, the Muri Beach Odyssey, has an overall score of 94.3, the highest component of which is 97.7 for in-house dining.

DATA *file*
BeachFrontHotels

Hotel	Overall	Comfort	Amenities	In-House Dining
Muri Beach Odyssey	94.3	94.5	90.8	97.7
Pattaya Resort	92.9	96.6	84.1	96.6
Sojourner's Respite	92.8	99.9	100.0	88.4
Spa Carribe	91.2	88.5	94.7	97.0
Penang Resort and Spa	90.4	95.0	87.8	91.1
Mokihana Hōkele	90.2	92.4	82.0	98.7
Theo's of Cape Town	90.1	95.9	86.2	91.9
Cap d'Agde Resort	89.8	92.5	92.5	88.8
Spirit of Mykonos	89.3	94.6	85.8	90.7
Turismo del Mar	89.1	90.5	83.2	90.4
Hotel Iguana	89.1	90.8	81.9	88.5
Sidi Abdel Rahman Palace	89.0	93.0	93.0	89.6
Sainte-Maxime Quarters	88.6	92.5	78.2	91.2
Rotorua Inn	87.1	93.0	91.6	73.5
Club Lapu-Lapu	87.1	90.9	74.9	89.6
Terracina Retreat	86.5	94.3	78.0	91.5
Hacienda Punta Barco	86.1	95.4	77.3	90.8
Rendezvous Kolocep	86.0	94.8	76.4	91.4
Cabo de Gata Vista	86.0	92.0	72.2	89.2
Sanya Deluxe	85.1	93.4	77.3	91.8

a. Determine the estimated multiple linear regression equation that can be used to predict the overall score given the scores for comfort, amenities, and in-house dining.

b. Use the *t* test to determine the significance of each independent variable. What is the conclusion for each test at the 0.01 level of significance?

c. Remove all independent variables that are not significant at the 0.01 level of significance from the estimated regression equation. What is your recommended estimated regression equation?

11. The American Association of Individual Investors (AAII) On-Line Discount Broker Survey polls members on their experiences with electronic trades handled by discount brokers. As part of the survey, members were asked to rate their satisfaction with the trade price and the speed of execution, as well as provide an overall satisfaction rating. Possible responses (scores) were no opinion (0), unsatisfied (1), somewhat satisfied (2), satisfied (3), and very satisfied (4). For each broker, summary scores were computed by computing a weighted average of the scores provided by each respondent. A portion the survey results follow (AAII web site, February 7, 2012).

DATA *file*

Broker

Brokerage	Satisfaction with Trade Price	Satisfaction with Speed of Execution	Overall Satisfaction with Electronic Trades
Scottrade, Inc.	3.4	3.4	3.5
Charles Schwab	3.2	3.3	3.4
Fidelity Brokerage Services	3.1	3.4	3.9
TD Ameritrade	2.9	3.6	3.7
E*Trade Financial	2.9	3.2	2.9
(Not listed)	2.5	3.2	2.7
Vanguard Brokerage Services	2.6	3.8	2.8
USAA Brokerage Services	2.4	3.8	3.6
Thinkorswim	2.6	2.6	2.6
Wells Fargo Investments	2.3	2.7	2.3
Interactive Brokers	3.7	4.0	4.0
Zecco.com	2.5	2.5	2.5
Firstrade Securities	3.0	3.0	4.0
Banc of America Investment Services	4.0	1.0	2.0

a. Develop an estimated regression equation using trade price and speed of execution to predict overall satisfaction with the broker. Interpret the coefficient of determination.
b. Use the *t* test to determine the significance of each independent variable. What are your conclusions at the 0.05 level of significance?
c. Interpret the estimated regression parameters. Are the relationships indicated by these estimates what you would expect?
d. Finger Lakes Investments has developed a new electronic trading system and would like to predict overall customer satisfaction assuming they can provide satisfactory service levels (3) for both trade price and speed of execution.
   Use the estimated regression equation developed in part (a) to predict overall satisfaction level for Finger Lakes Investments if they can achieve these performance levels.
e. What concerns (if any) do you have with regard to the possible responses the respondents could select on the survey.

12. The National Football League (NFL) records a variety of performance data for individuals and teams. To investigate the importance of passing on the percentage of games won by a team, the following data show the conference (Conf), average number of passing yards per attempt (Yds/Att), the number of interceptions thrown per attempt

(Int/Att), and the percentage of games won (Win%) for a random sample of 16 NFL teams for the 2011 season (NFL web site, February 12, 2012).

Team	Conf	Yds/Att	Int/Att	Win%
Arizona Cardinals	NFC	6.5	0.042	50.0
Atlanta Falcons	NFC	7.1	0.022	62.5
Carolina Panthers	NFC	7.4	0.033	37.5
Cincinnati Bengals	AFC	6.2	0.026	56.3
Detroit Lions	NFC	7.2	0.024	62.5
Green Bay Packers	NFC	8.9	0.014	93.8
Houston Texans	AFC	7.5	0.019	62.5
Indianapolis Colts	AFC	5.6	0.026	12.5
Jacksonville Jaguars	AFC	4.6	0.032	31.3
Minnesota Vikings	NFC	5.8	0.033	18.8
New England Patriots	AFC	8.3	0.020	81.3
New Orleans Saints	NFC	8.1	0.021	81.3
Oakland Raiders	AFC	7.6	0.044	50.0
San Francisco 49ers	NFC	6.5	0.011	81.3
Tennessee Titans	AFC	6.7	0.024	56.3
Washington Redskins	NFC	6.4	0.041	31.3

a. Develop the estimated regression equation that could be used to predict the percentage of games won, given the average number of passing yards per attempt. What proportion of variation in the sample values of proportion of games won does this model explain?

b. Develop the estimated regression equation that could be used to predict the percentage of games won, given the number of interceptions thrown per attempt. What proportion of variation in the sample values of proportion of games won does this model explain?

c. Develop the estimated regression equation that could be used to predict the percentage of games won, given the average number of passing yards per attempt and the number of interceptions thrown per attempt. What proportion of variation in the sample values of proportion of games won does this model explain?

d. The average number of passing yards per attempt for the Kansas City Chiefs during the 2011 season was 6.2, and the team's number of interceptions thrown per attempt was 0.036. Use the estimated regression equation developed in part (c) to predict the percentage of games won by the Kansas City Chiefs during the 2011 season. Compare your prediction to the actual percentage of games won by the Kansas City Chiefs. (*Note:* For the 2011 season, the Kansas City Chiefs' record was 7 wins and 9 losses.)

e. Did the estimated regression equation that uses only the average number of passing yards per attempt as the independent variable to predict the percentage of games won provide a good fit?

13. Johnson Filtration, Inc., provides maintenance service for water filtration systems throughout southern Florida. Customers contact Johnson with requests for maintenance service on their water filtration systems. To estimate the service time and the service cost, Johnson's managers want to predict the repair time necessary for each maintenance request. Hence, repair time in hours is the dependent variable. Repair time is believed to be related to three factors: the number of months since the last

maintenance service, the type of repair problem (mechanical or electrical), and the repairperson who performs the repair (Donna Newton or Bob Jones). Data for a sample of 10 service calls are reported in the following table:

DATA *file*

Repair

Repair Time in Hours	Months Since Last Service	Type of Repair	Repairperson
2.9	2	Electrical	Donna Newton
3.0	6	Mechanical	Donna Newton
4.8	8	Electrical	Bob Jones
1.8	3	Mechanical	Donna Newton
2.9	2	Electrical	Donna Newton
4.9	7	Electrical	Bob Jones
4.2	9	Mechanical	Bob Jones
4.8	8	Mechanical	Bob Jones
4.4	4	Electrical	Bob Jones
4.5	6	Electrical	Donna Newton

a. Develop the simple linear regression equation to predict repair time given the number of months since the last maintenance service, and use the results to test the hypothesis that no relationship exists between repair time and the number of months since the last maintenance service at the 0.05 level of significance. What is the interpretation of this relationship? What does the coefficient of determination tell you about this model?

b. Using the simple linear regression model developed in part (a), calculate the predicted repair time and residual for each of the 10 repairs in the data. Sort the data in ascending order by value of the residual. Do you see any pattern in the residuals for the two types of repair? Do you see any pattern in the residuals for the two repairpersons? Do these results suggest any potential modifications to your simple linear regression model? Now create a scatter chart with months since last service on the x-axis and repair time in hours on the y-axis for which the points representing electrical and mechanical repairs are shown in different shapes and/or colors. Create a similar scatter chart of months since last service and repair time in hours for which the points representing repairs by Bob Jones and Donna Newton are shown in different shapes and/or colors, Do these charts and the results of your residual analysis suggest the same potential modifications to your simple linear regression model?

c. Create a new dummy variable that is equal to zero if the type of repair is mechanical and one if the type of repair is electrical. Develop the multiple regression equation to predict repair time, given the number of months since the last maintenance service and the type of repair. What are the interpretations of the estimated regression parameters? What does the coefficient of determination tell you about this model?

d. Create a new dummy variable that is equal to zero if the repairperson is Bob Jones and one if the repairperson is Donna Newton. Develop the multiple regression equation to predict repair time, given the number of months since the last maintenance service and the repairperson. What are the interpretations of the estimated regression parameters? What does the coefficient of determination tell you about this model?

e. Develop the multiple regression equation to predict repair time, given the number of months since the last maintenance service, the type of repair, and the repairperson. What are the interpretations of the estimated regression parameters? What does the coefficient of determination tell you about this model?

f. Which of these models would you use? Why?

14. A study investigated the relationship between audit delay (the length of time from a company's fiscal year-end to the date of the auditor's report) and variables that describe the client and the auditor. Some of the independent variables that were included in this study follow:

Industry   A dummy variable coded 1 if the firm was an industrial company or 0 if the firm was a bank, savings and loan, or insurance company.

Public   A dummy variable coded 1 if the company was traded on an organized exchange or over the counter; otherwise coded 0.

Quality   A measure of overall quality of internal controls, as judged by the auditor, on a 5-point scale ranging from "virtually none" (1) to "excellent" (5).

Finished   A measure ranging from 1 to 4, as judged by the auditor, where 1 indicates "all work performed subsequent to year-end" and 4 indicates "most work performed prior to year-end."

A sample of 40 companies provided the following data:

DATA *file*
Audit

Delay (Days)	Industry	Public	Quality	Finished
62	0	0	3	1
45	0	1	3	3
54	0	0	2	2
71	0	1	1	2
91	0	0	1	1
62	0	0	4	4
61	0	0	3	2
69	0	1	5	2
80	0	0	1	1
52	0	0	5	3
47	0	0	3	2
65	0	0	2	3
60	0	0	1	3
81	1	0	1	2
73	1	0	2	2
89	1	0	2	1
71	1	0	5	4
76	1	0	2	2
68	1	0	1	2
68	1	0	5	2
86	1	0	2	2
76	1	1	3	1
67	1	0	2	3
57	1	0	4	2
55	1	1	3	2
54	1	0	5	2
69	1	0	3	3
82	1	0	5	1
94	1	0	1	1
74	1	1	5	2
75	1	1	4	3

(Continued)

Delay (Days)	Industry	Public	Quality	Finished
69	1	0	2	2
71	1	0	4	4
79	1	0	5	2
80	1	0	1	4
91	1	0	4	1
92	1	0	1	4
46	1	1	4	3
72	1	0	5	2
85	1	0	5	1

a. Develop the estimated regression equation using all of the independent variables included in the data.

b. How much of the variation in the sample values of delay does this estimated regression equation explain? What other independent variables could you include in this regression model to improve the fit?

c. Test the relationship between each independent variable and the dependent variable at the 0.05 level of significance, and interpret the relationship between each of the independent variables and the dependent variable.

d. On the basis of your observations about the relationships between the dependent variable Delay and the independent variables Quality and Finished, suggest an alternative model for the regression equation developed in part (a) to explain as much of the variability in Delay as possible.

15. The U.S. Department of Energy's Fuel Economy Guide provides fuel efficiency data for cars and trucks. A portion of the data for 311 compact, midsized, and large cars follows. The Class column identifies the size of the car: Compact, Midsize, or Large. The Displacement column shows the engine's displacement in liters. The FuelType column shows whether the car uses premium (P) or regular (R) fuel, and the HwyMPG column shows the fuel efficiency rating for highway driving in terms of miles per gallon. The complete data set is contained in the file *FuelData*:

DATA *file*

FuelData

Car	Class	Displacement	FuelType	HwyMPG
1	Compact	3.1	P	25
2	Compact	3.1	P	25
3	Compact	3.0	P	25
:	:	:	:	:
161	Midsize	2.4	R	30
162	Midsize	2.0	P	29
:	:	:	:	:
310	Large	3.0	R	25

a. Develop an estimated regression equation that can be used to predict the fuel efficiency for highway driving given the engine's displacement. Test for significance using the 0.05 level of significance. How much of the variation in the sample values of HwyMPG does this estimated regression equation explain?

b. Create a scatter chart with HwyMPG on the y-axis and displacement on the x-axis for which the points representing compact, midsize, and large automobiles are shown in different shapes and/or colors. What does this chart suggest about the relationship between the class of automobile (compact, midsize, and large) and HwyMPG?

c. Now consider the addition of the dummy variables ClassMidsize and ClassLarge to the simple linear regression model in part (a). The value of ClassMidsize is 1 if the car is a midsize car and 0 otherwise; the value of ClassLarge is 1 if the car is a large car and 0 otherwise. Thus, for a compact car, the value of ClassMidsize and the value of ClassLarge are both 0. Develop the estimated regression equation that can be used to predict the fuel efficiency for highway driving, given the engine's displacement and the dummy variables ClassMidsize and ClassLarge. How much of the variation in the sample values of HwyMPG is explained by this estimated regression equation?

d. Use significance level of 0.05 to determine whether the dummy variables added to the model in part (c) are significant.

e. Consider the addition of the dummy variable FuelPremium, where the value of FuelPremium is 1 if the car uses premium fuel and 0 if the car uses regular fuel. Develop the estimated regression equation that can be used to predict the fuel efficiency for highway driving given the engine's displacement, the dummy variables ClassMidsize and ClassLarge, and the dummy variable FuelPremium. How much of the variation in the sample values of HwyMPG does this estimated regression equation explain?

f. For the estimated regression equation developed in part (e), test for the significance of the relationship between each of the independent variables and the dependent variable using the 0.05 level of significance for each test.

16. A highway department is studying the relationship between traffic flow and speed during rush hour on Highway 193. The data in the file *TrafficFlow* were collected on Highway 193 during 100 recent rush hours.

DATA file
TrafficFlow

a. Develop a scatter chart for these data. What does the scatter chart indicate about the relationship between vehicle speed and traffic flow?

b. Develop an estimated simple linear regression equation for the data. How much variation in the sample values of traffic flow is explained by this regression model? Use a 0.05 level of significance to test the relationship between vehicle speed and traffic flow. What is the interpretation of this relationship?

c. Develop an estimated quadratic regression equation for the data. How much variation in the sample values of traffic flow is explained by this regression model? Test the relationship between each of the independent variables and the dependent variable at a 0.05 level of significance. How would you interpret this model? Is this model superior to the model you developed in part (b)?

d. As an alternative to fitting a second-order model, fit a model using a piecewise linear regression with a single knot. What value of vehicle speed appears to be a good point for the placement of the knot? Does the estimated piecewise linear regression provide a better fit than the estimated quadratic regression developed in part (c)? Explain.

e. Separate the data into two sets such that one data set contains the observations of vehicle speed less than the value of the knot from part (d) and the other data set contains the observations of vehicle speed greater than or equal to the value of the knot from part (d). Then fit a simple linear regression equation to each data set. How does this pair of regression equations compare to the single piecewise linear regression with the single knot from part (d)? In particular, compare predicted values of traffic flow for values of the speed slightly above and slightly below the knot value from part (d).

f. What other independent variables could you include in your regression model to explain more variation in traffic flow?

17. A sample containing years to maturity and (percent) yield for 40 corporate bonds is contained in the file named *CorporateBonds* (*Barron's*, April 2, 2012).

a. Develop a scatter chart of the data using years to maturity as the independent variable. Does a simple linear regression model appear to be appropriate?

b. Develop an estimated quadratic regression equation with years to maturity and squared values of years to maturity as the independent variables. How much variation in the sample values of yield is explained by this regression model? Test the relationship between each of the independent variables and the dependent variable at a 0.05 level of significance. How would you interpret this model?

c. Create a plot of the linear and quadratic regression lines overlaid on the scatter chart of years to maturity and yield. Does this helps you better understand the difference in how the quadratic regression model and a simple linear regression model fit the sample data? Which model does this chart suggest provides a superior fit to the sample data?

d. What other independent variables could you include in your regression model to explain more variation in yield?

18. In 2011, home prices and mortgage rates fell so far that in a number of cities the monthly cost of owning a home was less expensive than renting. The following data show the average asking rent for 10 markets and the monthly mortgage on the median priced home (including taxes and insurance) for 10 cites where the average monthly mortgage payment was less than the average asking rent (*The Wall Street Journal*, November 26–27, 2011).

City	Rent ($)	Mortgage ($)
Atlanta	840	539
Chicago	1,062	1,002
Detroit	823	626
Jacksonville	779	711
Las Vegas	796	655
Miami	1,071	977
Minneapolis	953	776
Orlando	851	695
Phoenix	762	651
St. Louis	723	654

a. Develop a scatter chart for these data, treating the average asking rent as the independent variable. Does a simple linear regression model appear to be appropriate?

b. Use a simple linear regression model to develop an estimated regression equation to predict the monthly mortgage on the median priced home given the average asking rent. Construct a plot of the residuals against the independent variable rent. Based on this residual plot, does a simple linear regression model appear to be appropriate?

c. Using a quadratic regression model, develop an estimated regression equation to predict the monthly mortgage on the median-priced home, given the average asking rent.

d. Do you prefer the estimated regression equation developed in part (a) or part (c)? Create a plot of the linear and quadratic regression lines overlaid on the scatter chart of the monthly mortgage on the median-priced home and the average asking rent to help you assess the two regression equations. Explain your conclusions.

19. A recent 10-year study conducted by a research team at the Great Falls Medical School was conducted to assess how age, systolic blood pressure, and smoking relate to the risk of strokes. Assume that the following data are from a portion of this study. Risk is interpreted as the probability (times 100) that the patient will have a stroke over the next 10-year period. For the smoking variable, define a dummy variable with 1 indicating a smoker and 0 indicating a nonsmoker.

Risk	Age	Systolic Blood Pressure	Smoker
12	57	152	No
24	67	163	No
13	58	155	No
56	86	177	Yes
28	59	196	No
51	76	189	Yes
18	56	155	Yes
31	78	120	No
37	80	135	Yes
15	78	98	No
22	71	152	No
36	70	173	Yes
15	67	135	Yes
48	77	209	Yes
15	60	199	No
36	82	119	Yes
8	66	166	No
34	80	125	Yes
3	62	117	No
37	59	207	Yes

DATA *file*

Stroke

a. Develop an estimated multiple regression equation that relates risk of a stroke to the person's age, systolic blood pressure, and whether the person is a smoker.
b. Is smoking a significant factor in the risk of a stroke? Explain. Use a 0.05 level of significance.
c. What is the probability of a stroke over the next 10 years for Art Speen, a 68-year-old smoker who has a systolic blood pressure of 175? What action might the physician recommend for this patient?
d. What other factors could be included in the model as independent variables?

DATA *file*

RugglesCollege

20. The Scholastic Aptitude Test (or SAT) is a standardized college entrance test that is used by colleges and universities as a means for making admission decisions. The critical reading and mathematics components of the SAT are reported on a scale from 200 to 800. Several universities believe these scores are strong predictors of an incoming student's potential success, and they use these scores as important inputs when making admission decisions on potential freshman. The file *RugglesCollege* contains freshman year GPA and the critical reading and mathematics SAT scores for a random sample of 200 students who recently completed their freshman year at Ruggles College.

a. Develop an estimated multiple regression equation that includes critical reading and mathematics SAT scores as independent variables. How much variation in freshman GPA is explained by this model? Test whether each of the regression parameters

β_0, β_1, and β_2 is equal to zero at a 0.05 level of significance. What are the correct interpretations of the estimated regression parameters? Are these interpretations reasonable?

b. Using the multiple linear regression model you developed in part (a), what is the predicted freshman GPA of Bobby Engle, a student who has been admitted to Ruggles College with a 660 SAT score on critical reading and at a 630 SAT score on mathematics?

c. The Ruggles College Director of Admissions believes that the relationship between a student's scores on the critical reading component of the SAT and the student's freshman GPA varies with the student's score on the mathematics component of the SAT. Develop an estimated multiple regression equation that includes critical reading and mathematics SAT scores and their interaction as independent variables. How much variation in freshman GPA is explained by this model? Test whether each of the regression parameters β_0, β_1, β_2, and β_3 is equal to zero at a 0.05 level of significance. What are the correct interpretations of the estimated regression parameters? Do these results support the conjecture made by the Ruggles College Director of Admissions?

d. Do you prefer the estimated regression model developed in part (a) or part (c)? Explain.

e. What other factors could be included in the model as independent variables?

21. Consider again the example introduced in Section 7.5 of a credit card company that has a database of information provided by its customers when they apply for credit cards. An analyst has created a multiple regression model for which the dependent variable in the model is credit card charges accrued by a customer in the data set over the past year (y), and the independent variables are the customer's annual household income (x_1), number of members of the household (x_2), and number of years of post–high school education (x_3). Figure 7.23 provides Excel output for a multiple regression model estimated using a data set the company created.

a. Estimate the corresponding simple linear regression with the customer's annual household income as the independent variable and credit card charges accrued by a customer over the past year as the dependent variable. Interpret the estimated relationship between the customer's annual household income and credit card charges accrued over the past year. How much variation in credit card charges accrued by a customer over the past year is explained by this simple linear regression model?

b. Estimate the corresponding simple linear regression with the number of members in the customer's household as the independent variable and credit card charges accrued by a customer over the past year as the dependent variable. Interpret the estimated relationship between the number of members in the customer's household and credit card charges accrued over the past year. How much variation in credit card charges accrued by a customer over the past year is explained by this simple linear regression model?

c. Estimate the corresponding simple linear regression with the customer's number of years of post–high school education as the independent variable and credit card charges accrued by a customer over the past year as the dependent variable. Interpret the estimated relationship between the customer's number of years of post–high school education and credit card charges accrued over the past year. How much variation in credit card charges accrued by a customer over the past year is explained by this simple linear regression model?

d. Recall the multiple regression in Figure 7.23 with credit card charges accrued by a customer over the past year as the dependent variable and customer's annual household income (x_1), number of members of the household (x_2), and number of years of post–high school education (x_3) as the independent variables. Do the estimated slopes differ substantially from the corresponding slopes that were estimated using simple linear regression in parts (a), (b), and (c)? What does this tell you about multicollinearity in the multiple regression model in Figure 7.23?

e. Add the coefficients of determination for the simple linear regression in parts (a), (b), and (c), and compare the result to the coefficient of determination for the multiple regression model in Figure 7.23. What does this tell you about multicollinearity in the multiple regression model in Figure 7.23?

f. Add age, a dummy variable for sex, and a dummy variable for whether a customer has exceeded his or her credit limit in the past 12 months as independent variables to the multiple regression model in Figure 7.23. Code the dummy variable for sex as 1 if the customer is female and 0 if male, and code the dummy variable for whether a customer has exceeded his or her credit limit in the past 12 months as 1 if the customer has exceeded his or her credit limit in the past 12 months and 0 otherwise. Do these variables substantially improve the fit of your model?

CASE PROBLEM ALUMNI GIVING

Alumni donations are an important source of revenue for colleges and universities. If administrators could determine the factors that could lead to increases in the percentage of alumni who make a donation, they might be able to implement policies that could lead to increased revenues. Research shows that students who are more satisfied with their contact with teachers are more likely to graduate. As a result, one might suspect that smaller class sizes and lower student/faculty ratios might lead to a higher percentage of satisfied graduates, which in turn might lead to increases in the percentage of alumni who make a donation. The following table shows data for 48 national universities. The Graduation Rate column is the percentage of students who initially enrolled at the university and graduated. The % of Classes Under 20 column shows the percentages of classes with fewer than 20 students that are offered. The Student/Faculty Ratio column is the number of students enrolled divided by the total number of faculty. Finally, the Alumni Giving Rate column is the percentage of alumni who made a donation to the university.

DATA *file*

AlumniGiving

	State	Graduation Rate	% of Classes Under 20	Student/ Faculty Ratio	Alumni Giving Rate
Boston College	MA	85	39	13	25
Brandeis University	MA	79	68	8	33
Brown University	RI	93	60	8	40
California Institute of Technology	CA	85	65	3	46
Carnegie Mellon University	PA	75	67	10	28
Case Western Reserve Univ.	OH	72	52	8	31
College of William and Mary	VA	89	45	12	27
Columbia University	NY	90	69	7	31
Cornell University	NY	91	72	13	35
Dartmouth College	NH	94	61	10	53
Duke University	NC	92	68	8	45
Emory University	GA	84	65	7	37

(Continued)

	State	Graduation Rate	% of Classes Under 20	Student/ Faculty Ratio	Alumni Giving Rate
Georgetown University	DC	91	54	10	29
Harvard University	MA	97	73	8	46
Johns Hopkins University	MD	89	64	9	27
Lehigh University	PA	81	55	11	40
Massachusetts Institute of Technology	MA	92	65	6	44
New York University	NY	72	63	13	13
Northwestern University	IL	90	66	8	30
Pennsylvania State Univ.	PA	80	32	19	21
Princeton University	NJ	95	68	5	67
Rice University	TX	92	62	8	40
Stanford University	CA	92	69	7	34
Tufts University	MA	87	67	9	29
Tulane University	LA	72	56	12	17
University of California–Berkeley	CA	83	58	17	18
University of California–Davis	CA	74	32	19	7
University of California–Irvine	CA	74	42	20	9
University of California–Los Angeles	CA	78	41	18	13
University of California–San Diego	CA	80	48	19	8
University of California–Santa Barbara	CA	70	45	20	12
University of Chicago	IL	84	65	4	36
University of Florida	FL	67	31	23	19
University of Illinois–Urbana Champaign	IL	77	29	15	23
University of Michigan–Ann Arbor	MI	83	51	15	13
University of North Carolina–Chapel Hill	NC	82	40	16	26
University of Notre Dame	IN	94	53	13	49
University of Pennsylvania	PA	90	65	7	41
University of Rochester	NY	76	63	10	23
University of Southern California	CA	70	53	13	22
University of Texas–Austin	TX	66	39	21	13
University of Virginia	VA	92	44	13	28
University of Washington	WA	70	37	12	12
University of Wisconsin–Madison	WI	73	37	13	13
Vanderbilt University	TN	82	68	9	31
Wake Forest University	NC	82	59	11	38
Washington University–St. Louis	MO	86	73	7	33
Yale University	CT	94	77	7	50

Managerial Report

1. Use methods of descriptive statistics to summarize the data.
2. Develop an estimated simple linear regression model that can be used to predict the alumni giving rate, given the graduation rate. Discuss your findings.
3. Develop an estimated multiple linear regression model that could be used to predict the alumni giving rate using the Graduation Rate, % of Classes Under 20, and Student/Faculty Ratio as independent variables. Discuss your findings.
4. Based on the results in parts (2) and (3), do you believe another regression model may be more appropriate? Estimate this model, and discuss your results.
5. What conclusions and recommendations can you derive from your analysis? What universities are achieving a substantially higher alumni giving rate than would be expected, given their Graduation Rate, % of Classes Under 20, and Student/Faculty Ratio? What universities are achieving a substantially lower alumni giving rate than would be expected, given their Graduation Rate, % of Classes Under 20, and Student/Faculty Ratio? What other independent variables could be included in the model?

Chapter 7 Appendix

Appendix 7.1 Regression with XLMiner

ButlerNewData

To show how XLMiner can be used for regression analysis, we again consider the Butler Trucking Company. The dependent variable is Travel Time (y), and the independent variables are Miles, Gasoline Consumption, and Deliveries. In the file *ButlerNewData*, there are two worksheets. The *Data* worksheet contains 300 observations from past routes. The *NewData* worksheet contains 10 additional observations corresponding to upcoming routes for which we have estimates on the miles driven, gasoline consumption, and number of deliveries. We would like to construct a regression model on the 300 observations in the *Data* worksheet and then use this model to predict the travel time for the 10 new observations in the *NewData* worksheet.

We use the following steps, accompanied by Figure 7.38, to execute a regression analysis for these data in XLMiner:

Step 1. Select any cell in the range of data (any cell in A1:D301)
Step 2. Click the **XLMiner Platform** tab in the Ribbon

FIGURE 7.38 XLMiner Regression Procedure

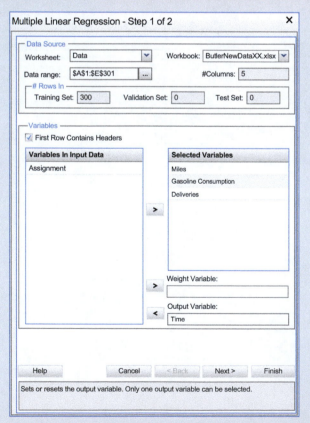
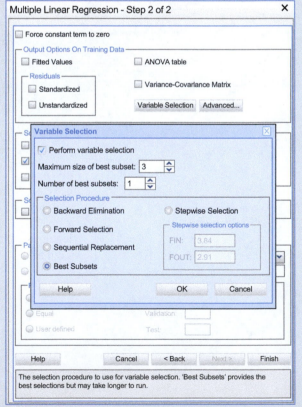

Sets or resets the output variable. Only one output variable can be selected.

The selection procedure to use for variable selection. 'Best Subsets' provides the best selections but may take longer to run.

Step 3. Click **Predict** in the **Data Mining** group, and select **Multiple Linear Regression**

Step 4. When the **Multiple Linear Regression–Step 1 of 2** dialog box appears:

In the Data Source area, confirm that the **Worksheet:**, **Workbook:**, and **Data range:** entries correspond to the appropriate data

In the **Variables In Input Data** box of the **Variables** area, select the **Miles**, **Gasoline Consumption**, and **Deliveries** variables, and click the > button to the left of the of the **Selected Variables** box to identify the independent variables

In the **Variables In Input Data** box of the **Variables** area, select **Time** and click the > button to the left of the of the **Output Variable** box to identify the dependent variable

Click **Next >**

Step 5. In the **Multiple Linear Regression–Step 2 of 2** dialog box:

Select **Summary report** in the **Score Training Data** area

In the **Output Options On Training Data** area, select **Variable Selection**

When the **Variable Selection** dialog box appears:

Select **Perform variable selection**

In the **Selection Procedure** area, select **Best Subsets**

Enter *3* in the **Maximum size of best subset:** box

Enter *1* in the **Number of best subsets:** box

Click **OK**

Click **Finish**

This procedure executes best-subsets variable selection by considering all multiple regression models with up to three variables. That is, XLMiner constructs all possible regression models with zero, one, two, and three independent variables (a total of $2^3 = 8$ models), and then outputs the best-fitting model of each respective size.

Figure 7.39 shows a portion of the output from the *MLR_Output* worksheet. The Regression Model table provides model information for the "full" regression model with all possible independent variables and the intercept (constant) term. The Variable Selection table lists the

FIGURE 7.39   XLMiner *MLR_Output* Worksheet

Regression Model

Input Variables	Coefficient	Std. Error	t-Statistic	P-Value	CI Lower	CI Upper	RSS Reduction
Intercept	0.237719	0.221644508	1.072522841	0.284359	-0.198479972	0.673917567	15917
Miles	0.077782	0.008464959	9.188649826	7.21E-18	0.061122415	0.094440676	539.1988
Gasoline Consumption	-0.1185	0.090572642	-1.30828857	0.19179	-0.296743085	0.059752779	0.381967
Deliveries	0.690926	0.029494272	23.42575518	2.25E-69	0.632880552	0.74897064	377.1115

Residual DF	296
R^2	0.8184
Adjusted R^2	0.816559
Std. Error Estimate	0.828975
RSS	203.4109

Variable Selection

Subset Link	#Coeffs	RSS	Cp	R^2	Adjusted R^2	Probability	Model 1	2	3	4
Choose Subset	1	1120.1032	1331.9546	0	0	0	Intercept			
Choose Subset	2	580.9044	549.3218	0.4814	0.4796	0	Intercept	Miles		
Choose Subset	3	204.5871	3.7116	0.8173	0.8161	0.1918	Intercept	Miles		Deliveries
Choose Subset	4	203.4109	4	0.8184	0.8166	1	Intercept	Miles	Gasoline Consumption	Deliveries

best-fitting regression model with one coefficient (corresponding to the constant or intercept term), two coefficients (corresponding to the y-intercept term and one independent variable), three coefficients (corresponding to the y-intercept term and two independent variables), and four coefficients (corresponding to the y-intercept term and three independent variables).

As Figure 7.39 shows, the model with the two independent variables Miles and Deliveries has only a slightly lower R^2 than the model with all three independent variables. Furthermore, as the Regression Model table shows, the Gasoline Consumption variable is statistically insignificant in the full regression model ($p = 0.19$) and has a counterintuitively negative effect on travel time (coefficient $= -0.1185$). These observations are due to the multicollinearity between Gasoline Consumption and Miles.

Based on the comparison of the various regression models, the regression model with three coefficients (the y-intercept, Miles, and Deliveries) seems to be the most appropriate. Therefore, we will use this model to predict the travel time for the 10 new observations in the NewData worksheet. We use the following steps to refit this regression model and generate predicted values in XLMiner:

Step 1. Click the link **Choose Subset** in cell C72 of the *MLR_Output* worksheet
Step 2. When the **Multiple Linear Regression–Step 1 of 2** dialog box appears, the confirm that the entries are prepopulated as in Figure 7.40 and click **Next**
Step 3. In the **Multiple Linear Regression–Step 2 of 2** dialog box:
   In the **Score New Data** area, select **In Worksheet**
   When the **Match Variables in the New Range** dialog box appears:
   In the **Data Source** area, enter *NewData* in the **Worksheet:** box and $A$1:$E$11 in the **Data Range:** box
   Confirm that the box next to **First Row Contains Headers** is checked
   In the **Variables** area, select **Match By Name**
   Click **OK**
   Click **Finish**

FIGURE 7.40   Predicting New Observations with XLMiner Regression Procedure

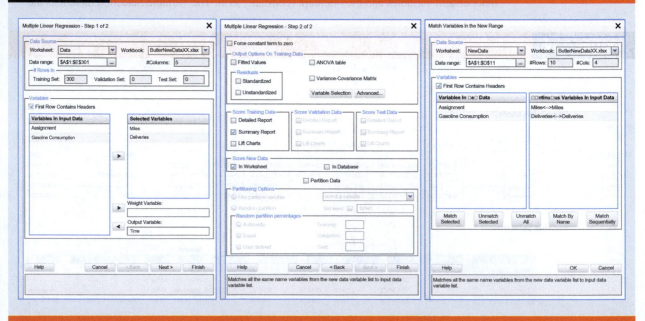

FIGURE 7.41	XLMiner Output for Two Variable Model

Regression Model

Input Variables	Coefficient	Std. Error	t-Statistic	P-Value	CI Lower	CI Upper	RSS Reduction
Intercept	0.127337	0.20520348	0.620540826	0.535378	-0.2765	0.531174	15917
Miles	0.067182	0.002454979	27.36551071	3.54E-83	0.06235	0.072013	539.1988
Deliveries	0.689998	0.029521057	23.37308852	2.85E-69	0.631901	0.748095	376.3172

Residual DF	297
R²	0.81735
Adjusted R²	0.81612
Std. Error Estimate	0.829967
RSS	204.5871

Training Data Scoring - Summary Report

Total sum of squared errors	RMS Error	Average Error
204.5871	0.825807	-3.31291E-15

This procedure constructs the regression model to predict travel time using miles driving and deliveries made. Figure 7.41 shows the fit information from the *MLR_Output1* worksheet; the corresponding regression equation is: Time = 0.1273 + 0.0672 Miles + 0.6900 Deliveries. Cells B16:B25 in Figure 7.42 contain the predictions for the travel time for the 10 new observations. For example, the predicted travel time for first observation (Row 16) is given by: Time = 0.1273 + 0.0672 (105) + 0.6900 (3) = 9.25 hours.

As Figure 7.42 shows, XLMiner also produces two types of interval estimates around the point estimate of the travel time for a new observation. Here, the 95% confidence interval is an interval estimate of the mean travel time for a route assignment with the given values of Miles and Deliveries. This is the appropriate interval estimate if we are interested in estimating the mean travel time for all route assignments with given mileage and number of deliveries. This confidence interval estimates the variability in the mean travel time.

Alternatively, the 95% prediction interval is an interval estimate on the prediction of travel time for an individual route assignment with the given values of Miles and Deliveries. This is the appropriate interval estimate if we are interested in predicting the travel time for an individual route assignment with the specified mileage and number of deliveries. This prediction interval estimates the variability inherent in a single route's travel time.

To illustrate, consider the first observation (Row 16) with 105 miles and 3 deliveries. The point estimate for the mean travel time as provided by the regression equation is 9.25 hours. For all 105-mile routes with 3 deliveries, a 95% confidence interval on the mean travel time ranges from 9.06 to 9.44 hours (cells C16 and D16 in Figure 7.42). That is, we are 95% confident that the true population mean travel time for 105-mile routes with 3 deliveries is between 9.06 and 9.44 hours.

Now suppose Butler Trucking is interested in predicting the travel time for an upcoming route assignment covering 105-miles and 3 deliveries. The best prediction for this route's travel time is 9.25 hours, as provided by the regression equation. However, a 95%

FIGURE 7.42   XLMiner Predictions of New Observations

Workbook	ButlerNewData.xlsx				
Worksheet	NewData				
Range	$A$1:$E$11				

Predicted Value	95% Confidence Intervals		95% Prediction Intervals		Miles	Deliveries
	Lower	Upper	Lower	Upper		
9.251415	9.058104	9.444725	7.606654	10.89618	105	3
6.918235	6.80624	7.030229	5.281038	8.555432	60	4
9.959594	9.786808	10.13238	8.317119	11.60207	95	5
7.53551	7.310045	7.760975	5.88666	9.184359	100	1
4.884602	4.707121	5.062082	3.241626	6.527578	40	3
7.571871	7.463385	7.680358	5.934911	9.208832	80	3
7.254143	7.151247	7.35704	5.617544	8.890743	65	4
5.892328	5.768443	6.016212	4.254275	7.530381	55	3
7.889599	7.714556	8.064642	6.246885	9.532314	95	2
8.579597	8.425884	8.733311	6.939019	10.22018	95	3

prediction interval for this travel time prediction ranges from 7.61 to 10.90 hours (cells E16 and F16 in Figure 7.42). That is, we are 95% confident that the travel time for a single 105-mile route with 3 deliveries will be between 7.61 and 10.90 hours.

Note that the 95% prediction interval for the travel time of a single route assignment with 105 miles and 3 deliveries is wider than the 95% confidence interval for the mean travel time of all route assignments with 105 miles and 3 deliveries. The difference reflects the fact that we are able to estimate the mean value of y more precisely than we can predict an individual value of y.

Finally, we point out that the width of the prediction (and confidence) intervals for the regression point estimate are not the same for each observation. Instead, the width of the interval depends on the corresponding values of the independent variables. Confidence intervals and prediction intervals are narrower when the values of the independent variables $x_1, x_2, \ldots,$ are closer to their respective means, $\bar{x}_1, \bar{x}_2, \ldots.$

For the Butler example, Table 7.5 shows the 10 new observations, the predicted travel times from the regression equation, and the corresponding 95% confidence intervals (CI) and prediction intervals (PI). Table 7.5 illustrates the varying width of the confidence and prediction intervals depending on the values of the independent variables Miles and Deliveries. For the 300 observations on which the regression equation model is based, the mean miles for a route assignment is 70.7 miles and the mean number of deliveries for a route assignment is 3.5. Assignment 307 has the mileage (65) and number of deliveries (4) that are closest to these means and correspondingly has the narrowest confidence and prediction intervals. Conversely, Assignment 304 has the widest confidence and prediction intervals because it has the mileage (100) and number of deliveries (1) that are the farthest from the average miles and average number of deliveries.

Table 7.5	Predicted Values and 95% Confidence Interval and Prediction Interval Half Widths for 10 New Observations				
Assignment	Miles	Deliveries	Predicted Value	95% CI Half-Width (+/–)	95% PI Half-Width (+/–)
301	105	3	9.25	0.193	1.645
302	60	4	6.92	0.112	1.637
303	95	5	9.96	0.173	1.642
304	100	1	7.54	0.225	1.649
305	40	3	4.88	0.177	1.643
306	80	3	7.57	0.108	1.637
307	65	4	7.25	0.103	1.637
308	55	3	5.89	0.124	1.638
309	95	2	7.89	0.175	1.643
310	95	3	8.58	0.154	1.641
	Avg. Miles = 70.7	Avg. Deliveries = 3.5			

Chapter 8

Time Series Analysis and Forecasting

CONTENTS

ANALYTICS IN ACTION

ACCO Brands*

ACCO Brands Corporation is one of the world's largest suppliers of branded office and consumer products and print finishing solutions. The company's brands include AT-A-GLANCE®, Day-Timer®, Five Star®, GBC®, Hilroy®, Kensington®, Marbig®, Mead®, NOBO, Quartet®, Rexel, Swingline®, Tilibra®, Wilson Jones®, and many others.

Because it produces and markets a wide array of products with myriad demand characteristics, ACCO Brands relies heavily on sales forecasts in planning its manufacturing, distribution, and marketing activities. By viewing its relationship in terms of a supply chain, ACCO Brands and its customers (which are generally retail chains) establish close collaborative relationships and consider each other to be valued partners. As a result, ACCO Brands' customers share valuable information and data that serve as inputs into ACCO Brands' forecasting process.

In her role as a forecasting manager for ACCO Brands, Vanessa Baker appreciates the importance of this additional information. "We do separate forecasts of demand for each major customer," said Baker, "and we generally use twenty-four to thirty-six months of history to generate monthly forecasts twelve to eighteen months into the future. While trends are important, several of our major product lines, including school, planning and organizing, and decorative calendars, are heavily seasonal, and seasonal sales make up the bulk of our annual volume."

Daniel Marks, one of several account-level strategic forecast managers for ACCO Brands, adds,

> The supply chain process includes the total lead time from identifying opportunities to making or procuring the product to getting the product on the shelves to align with the forecasted demand; this can potentially take several months, so the accuracy of our forecasts is critical throughout each step of the supply chain. Adding to this challenge is the risk of obsolescence. We sell many dated items, such as planners and calendars, which have a natural, built-in obsolescence. In addition, many of our products feature designs that are fashion-conscious or contain pop culture images, and these products can also become obsolete very quickly as tastes and popularity change. An overly optimistic forecast for these products can be very costly, but an overly pessimistic forecast can result in lost sales potential and give our competitors an opportunity to take market share from us.

In addition to looking at trends, seasonal components, and cyclical patterns, Baker and Marks must contend with several other factors. Baker notes, "We have to adjust our forecasts for upcoming promotions by our customers." Marks agrees and adds:

> We also have to go beyond just forecasting consumer demand; we must consider the retailer's specific needs in our order forecasts, such as what type of display will be used and how many units of a product must be on display to satisfy their presentation requirements. Current inventory is another factor—if a customer is carrying either too much or too little inventory, that will affect their future orders, and we need to reflect that in our forecasts. Will the product have a short life because it is tied to a cultural fad? What are the retailer's marketing and markdown strategies? Our knowledge of the environments in which our supply chain partners are competing helps us to forecast demand more accurately, and that reduces waste and makes our customers, as well as ACCO Brands, far more profitable.

———
*The authors are indebted to Vanessa Baker and Daniel Marks of ACCO Brands for providing input for this Analytics in Action.

The purpose of this chapter is to provide an introduction to time series analysis and forecasting. Suppose we are asked to provide quarterly **forecasts** of sales for one of our company's products over the coming one-year period. Production schedules, raw materials purchasing, inventory policies, marketing plans, and cash flows will all be affected by the quarterly forecasts we provide. Consequently, poor forecasts may result in poor planning and increased costs for the company. How should we go about providing the quarterly sales forecasts? Good judgment, intuition, and an awareness of the state of the economy may give us a rough idea, or feeling, of what is likely to happen in the future, but converting that feeling into a number that can be used as next year's sales forecast is challenging.

A forecast is simply a prediction of what will happen in the future. Managers must accept that regardless of the technique used, they will not be able to develop perfect forecasts.

Forecasting methods can be classified as qualitative or quantitative. Qualitative methods generally involve the use of expert judgment to develop forecasts. Such methods are appropriate when historical data on the variable being forecast are either unavailable or not applicable. Quantitative forecasting methods can be used when: (1) past information about the variable being forecast is available, (2) the information can be quantified, and (3) it is reasonable to assume that past is prologue (i.e., that the pattern of the past will continue into the future). We will focus exclusively on quantitative forecasting methods in this chapter.

If the historical data are restricted to past values of the variable to be forecast, the forecasting procedure is called a time series method and the historical data are referred to as *time series*. The objective of time series analysis is to uncover a pattern in the time series and then extrapolate the pattern to forecast the future; the forecast is based solely on past values of the variable and/or on past forecast errors.

Causal or exploratory forecasting methods are based on the assumption that the variable we are forecasting has a cause-and-effect relationship with one or more other variables. These methods help explain how the value of one variable impacts the value of another. For instance, the sales volume for many products is influenced by advertising expenditures, so regression analysis may be used to develop an equation showing how these two variables are related. Then, once the advertising budget is set for the next period, we could substitute this value into the equation to develop a prediction or forecast of the sales volume for that period. Note that if a time series method was used to develop the forecast, advertising expenditures would not be considered; that is, a time series method would base the forecast solely on past sales.

Modern data-collection technologies have enabled individuals, businesses, and government agencies to collect vast amounts of data that may be used for causal forecasting. For example, supermarket scanners allow retailers to collect point-of-sale data that can then be used to help aid in planning sales, coupon targeting, and other marketing and planning efforts. These data can help answer important questions like, "Which products tend to be purchased together?" One of the techniques used to answer such questions is regression analysis. In this chapter we discuss the use of regression analysis as a causal forecasting method.

In Section 8.1 we discuss the various kinds of time series that a forecaster might be faced with in practice. These include a constant or horizontal pattern, a trend, a seasonal pattern, both a trend and a seasonal pattern, and a cyclical pattern. To build a quantitative forecasting model it is also necessary to have a measurement of forecast accuracy. Different measurements of forecast accuracy, as well as their respective advantages and disadvantages, are discussed in Section 8.2. In Section 8.3 we consider the simplest case, which is a horizontal or constant pattern. For this pattern, we develop the classical moving average, weighted moving average, and exponential smoothing models. Many time series have a trend, and taking this trend into account is important; in Section 8.4 we provide regression models for finding the best model parameters when a linear trend is present, when the data show a seasonal pattern, or when the variable to be predicted has a causal relationship with other variables. Finally, in Section 8.5 we discuss considerations to be made when determining the best forecasting model to use.

NOTES + COMMENTS

Virtually all large companies today rely on enterprise resource planning (ERP) software to aid in their planning and operations. These software systems help the business run smoothly by collecting and efficiently storing company data, enabling it to be shared company-wide for planning at all levels: strategically, tactically, and operationally. Most ERP systems include a forecasting module to help plan for the future. SAP, one of the most widely used ERP systems, includes a forecasting component. This module allows the user to select from a number of forecasting techniques and/or have the system find a "best" model. The various forecasting methods and ways to measure the quality of a forecasting model discussed in this chapter are routinely available in software that supports forecasting.

8.1 Time Series Patterns

We limit our discussion to time series for which the values of the series are recorded at equal intervals. Cases in which the observations are made at unequal intervals are beyond the scope of this text.

A **time series** is a sequence of observations on a variable measured at successive points in time or over successive periods of time. The measurements may be taken every hour, day, week, month, year, or at any other regular interval. The pattern of the data is an important factor in understanding how the time series has behaved in the past. If such behavior can be expected to continue in the future, we can use it to guide us in selecting an appropriate forecasting method.

In Chapter 2 we discussed line charts, which are often used to graph time series.

To identify the underlying pattern in the data, a useful first step is to construct a *time series plot*, which is a graphical presentation of the relationship between time and the time series variable; time is represented on the horizontal axis and values of the time series variable are shown on the vertical axis. Let us first review some of the common types of data patterns that can be identified in a time series plot.

Horizontal Pattern

DATA *file*

Gasoline

A horizontal pattern exists when the data fluctuate randomly around a constant mean over time. To illustrate a time series with a horizontal pattern, consider the 12 weeks of data in Table 8.1. These data show the number of gallons of gasoline (in 1,000s) sold by a gasoline distributor in Bennington, Vermont, over the past 12 weeks. The average value, or mean, for this time series is 19.25 or 19,250 gallons per week. Figure 8.1 shows a time series plot for these data. Note how the data fluctuate around the sample mean of 19,250 gallons. Although random variability is present, we would say that these data follow a horizontal pattern.

The term **stationary time series** is used to denote a time series whose statistical properties are independent of time. In particular this means that:

1. The process generating the data has a constant mean.
2. The variability of the time series is constant over time.

For a formal definition of stationarity, see K. Ord and R. Fildes, Principles of Business Forecasting (Mason, OH: Cengage Learning, 2012), p. 155.

A time series plot for a stationary time series will always exhibit a horizontal pattern with random fluctuations. However, simply observing a horizontal pattern is not sufficient evidence to conclude that the time series is stationary. More advanced texts on forecasting

TABLE 8.1	Gasoline Sales Time Series
Week	**Sales (1,000s of gallons)**
1	17
2	21
3	19
4	23
5	18
6	16
7	20
8	18
9	22
10	20
11	15
12	22

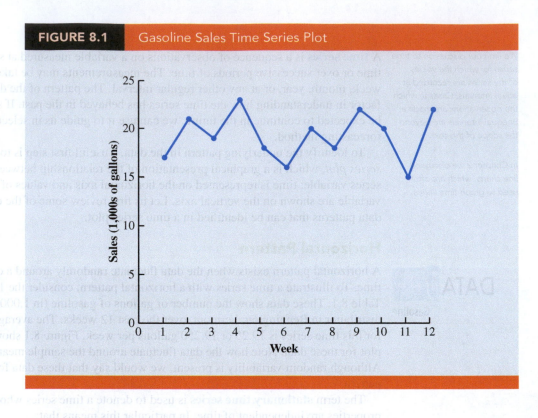

FIGURE 8.1 Gasoline Sales Time Series Plot

discuss procedures for determining whether a time series is stationary and provide methods for transforming a nonstationary time series into a stationary series.

Changes in business conditions often result in a time series with a horizontal pattern that shifts to a new level at some point in time. For instance, suppose the gasoline distributor signs a contract with the Vermont State Police to provide gasoline for state police cars located in southern Vermont beginning in week 13. With this new contract, the distributor naturally expects to see a substantial increase in weekly sales starting in week 13. Table 8.2

TABLE 8.2 Gasoline Sales Time Series after Obtaining the Contract with the Vermont State Police

DATA *file*

GasolineRevised

Week	Sales (1,000s of gallons)	Week	Sales (1,000s of gallons)
1	17	12	22
2	21	13	31
3	19	14	34
4	23	15	31
5	18	16	33
6	16	17	28
7	20	18	32
8	18	19	30
9	22	20	29
10	20	21	34
11	15	22	33

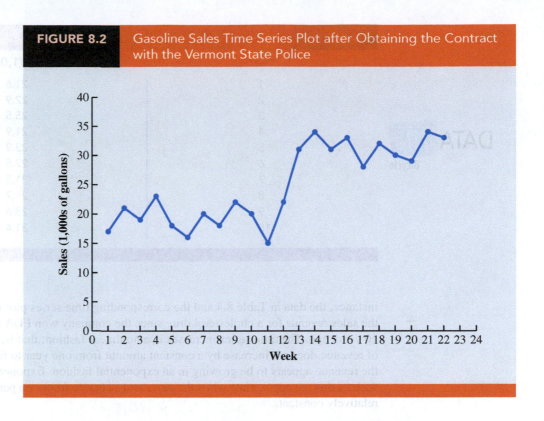

FIGURE 8.2 Gasoline Sales Time Series Plot after Obtaining the Contract with the Vermont State Police

shows the number of gallons of gasoline sold for the original time series and for the 10 weeks after signing the new contract. Figure 8.2 shows the corresponding time series plot. Note the increased level of the time series beginning in week 13. This change in the level of the time series makes it more difficult to choose an appropriate forecasting method. Selecting a forecasting method that adapts well to changes in the level of a time series is an important consideration in many practical applications.

Trend Pattern

Although time series data generally exhibit random fluctuations, a time series may also show gradual shifts or movements to relatively higher or lower values over a longer period of time. If a time series plot exhibits this type of behavior, we say that a **trend** pattern exists. A trend is usually the result of long-term factors such as population increases or decreases, shifting demographic characteristics of the population, improving technology, changes in the competitive landscape, and/or changes in consumer preferences.

To illustrate a time series with a linear trend pattern, consider the time series of bicycle sales for a particular manufacturer over the past 10 years, as shown in Table 8.3 and Figure 8.3. Note that a total of 21,600 bicycles were sold in year 1, a total of 22,900 in year 2, and so on. In year 10, the most recent year, 31,400 bicycles were sold. Visual inspection of the time series plot shows some up-and-down movement over the past 10 years, but the time series seems also to have a systematically increasing, or upward, trend.

The trend for the bicycle sales time series appears to be linear and increasing over time, but sometimes a trend can be described better by other types of patterns. For

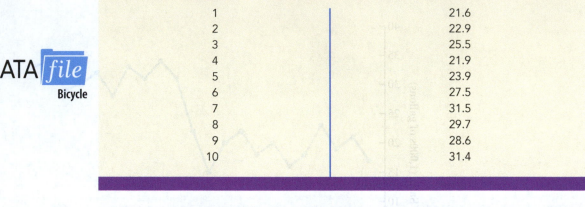

TABLE 8.3	Bicycle Sales Time Series
Year	**Sales (1,000s)**
1	21.6
2	22.9
3	25.5
4	21.9
5	23.9
6	27.5
7	31.5
8	29.7
9	28.6
10	31.4

DATA *file*

Bicycle

instance, the data in Table 8.4 and the corresponding time series plot in Figure 8.4 show the sales revenue for a cholesterol drug since the company won FDA approval for the drug 10 years ago. The time series increases in a nonlinear fashion; that is, the rate of change of revenue does not increase by a constant amount from one year to the next. In fact, the revenue appears to be growing in an exponential fashion. Exponential relationships such as this are appropriate when the *percentage* change from one period to the next is relatively constant.

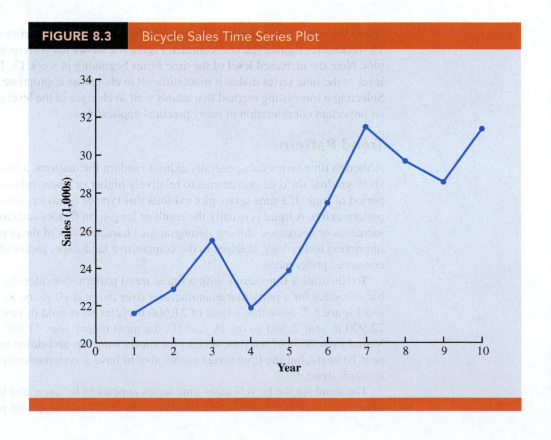

FIGURE 8.3 Bicycle Sales Time Series Plot

TABLE 8.4	Cholesterol Drug Revenue Time Series
Year	**Revenue ($ millions)**
1	23.1
2	21.3
3	27.4
4	34.6
5	33.8
6	43.2
7	59.5
8	64.4
9	74.2
10	99.3

DATA *file*

Cholesterol

Seasonal Pattern

The trend of a time series can be identified by analyzing movements in historical data over multiple time periods. **Seasonal patterns** are recognized by observing recurring patterns over successive periods of time. For example, a retailer who sells bathing suits expects low sales activity in the fall and winter months, with peak sales in the spring and summer months to occur every year. Retailers who sell snow removal equipment and heavy clothing, however, expect the opposite yearly pattern. Not surprisingly, the pattern for a time series plot that exhibits a recurring pattern over a one-year period due to seasonal influences is called a seasonal pattern. Although we generally think of seasonal movement in a time series as occurring within one year, time series data can also exhibit seasonal patterns of less than one year in duration. For example, daily traffic volume shows within-the-day "seasonal" behavior, with peak levels occurring during rush hours, moderate flow during the rest of the day and early evening, and light flow from midnight to early morning.

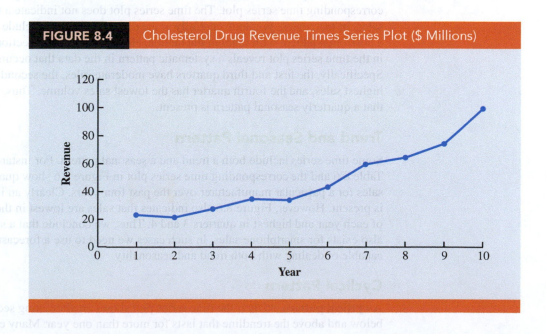

FIGURE 8.4	Cholesterol Drug Revenue Times Series Plot ($ Millions)

TABLE 8.5	Umbrella Sales Time Series	
Year	**Quarter**	**Sales**
1	1	125
	2	153
	3	106
	4	88
2	1	118
	2	161
	3	133
	4	102
3	1	138
	2	144
	3	113
	4	80
4	1	109
	2	137
	3	125
	4	109
5	1	130
	2	165
	3	128
	4	96

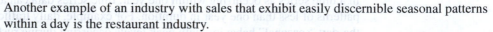

DATA *file*

Umbrella

Another example of an industry with sales that exhibit easily discernible seasonal patterns within a day is the restaurant industry.

As an example of a seasonal pattern, consider the number of umbrellas sold at a clothing store over the past five years. Table 8.5 shows the time series and Figure 8.5 shows the corresponding time series plot. The time series plot does not indicate a long-term trend in sales. In fact, unless you look carefully at the data, you might conclude that the data follow a horizontal pattern with random fluctuation. However, closer inspection of the fluctuations in the time series plot reveals a systematic pattern in the data that occurs within each year. Specifically, the first and third quarters have moderate sales, the second quarter has the highest sales, and the fourth quarter has the lowest sales volume. Thus, we would conclude that a quarterly seasonal pattern is present.

Trend and Seasonal Pattern

Some time series include both a trend and a seasonal pattern. For instance, the data in Table 8.6 and the corresponding time series plot in Figure 8.6 show quarterly smartphone sales for a particular manufacturer over the past four years. Clearly an increasing trend is present. However, Figure 8.6 also indicates that sales are lowest in the second quarter of each year and highest in quarters 3 and 4. Thus, we conclude that a seasonal pattern also exists for smartphone sales. In such cases we need to use a forecasting method that is capable of dealing with both trend and seasonality.

Cyclical Pattern

A **cyclical pattern** exists if the time series plot shows an alternating sequence of points below and above the trendline that lasts for more than one year. Many economic time series

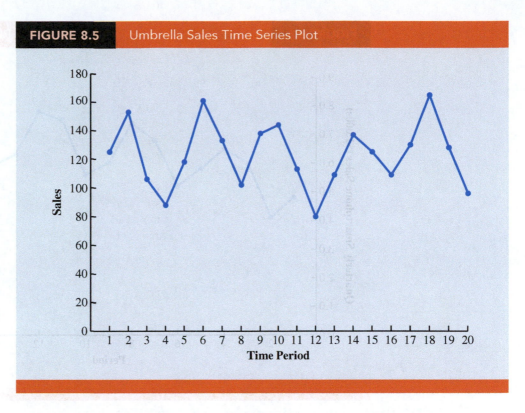

FIGURE 8.5   Umbrella Sales Time Series Plot

exhibit cyclical behavior with regular runs of observations below and above the trendline. Often the cyclical component of a time series is due to multiyear business cycles. For example, periods of moderate inflation followed by periods of rapid inflation can lead to a time series that alternates below and above a generally increasing trendline (e.g., a time series for housing costs). Business cycles are extremely difficult, if not impossible, to

TABLE 8.6   Quarterly Smartphone Sales Time Series

Year	Quarter	Sales ($1,000s)
1	1	4.8
	2	4.1
	3	6.0
	4	6.5
2	1	5.8
	2	5.2
	3	6.8
	4	7.4
3	1	6.0
	2	5.6
	3	7.5
	4	7.8
4	1	6.3
	2	5.9
	3	8.0
	4	8.4

DATA *file*

SmartPhoneSales

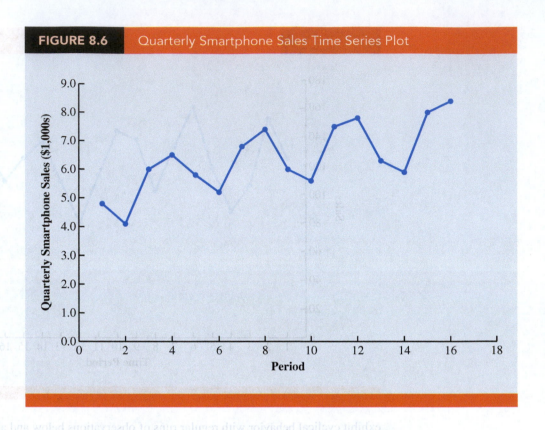

FIGURE 8.6 Quarterly Smartphone Sales Time Series Plot

forecast. As a result, cyclical effects are often combined with long-term trend effects and referred to as *trend-cycle effects*. In this chapter we do not deal with cyclical effects that may be present in the time series.

Identifying Time Series Patterns

The underlying pattern in the time series is an important factor in selecting a forecasting method. Thus, a time series plot should be one of the first analytic tools employed when trying to determine which forecasting method to use. If we see a horizontal pattern, then we need to select a method appropriate for this type of pattern. Similarly, if we observe a trend in the data, then we need to use a forecasting method that is capable of handling a trend effectively. In the next section we discuss methods for assessing forecast accuracy. We then consider forecasting models that can be used in situations for which the underlying pattern is horizontal; in other words, no trend or seasonal effects are present. We then consider methods appropriate when trend and/or seasonality are present in the data.

8.2 Forecast Accuracy

In this section we begin by developing forecasts for the gasoline time series shown in Table 8.1 using the simplest of all the forecasting methods. We use the most recent week's sales volume as the forecast for the next week. For instance, the distributor sold 17 thousand gallons of gasoline in week 1; this value is used as the forecast for week 2. Next, we use 21, the actual value of sales in week 2, as the forecast for week 3, and so on. The forecasts obtained for the historical data using this method are shown in Table 8.7 in

TABLE 8.7	Computing Forecasts and Measures of Forecast Accuracy Using the Most Recent Value as the Forecast for the Next Period					
Week	Time Series Value	Forecast	Forecast Error	Absolute Value of Forecast Error	Squared Forecast Error	Percentage Error	Absolute Value of Percentage Error
1	17						
2	21	17	4	4	16	19.05	19.05
3	19	21	−2	2	4	−10.53	10.53
4	23	19	4	4	16	17.39	17.39
5	18	23	−5	5	25	−27.78	27.78
6	16	18	−2	2	4	−12.50	12.50
7	20	16	4	4	16	20.00	20.00
8	18	20	−2	2	4	−11.11	11.11
9	22	18	4	4	16	18.18	18.18
10	20	22	−2	2	4	−10.00	10.00
11	15	20	−5	5	25	−33.33	33.33
12	22	15	7	7	49	31.82	31.82
		Totals	5	41	179	1.19	211.69

the Forecast column. Because of its simplicity, this method is often referred to as a **naïve forecasting method**.

How accurate are the forecasts obtained using this naïve forecasting method? To answer this question, we will introduce several measures of forecast accuracy. These measures are used to determine how well a particular forecasting method is able to reproduce the time series data that are already available. By selecting the method that is most accurate for the data already known, we hope to increase the likelihood that we will obtain more accurate forecasts for future time periods. The key concept associated with measuring forecast accuracy is **forecast error**. If we denote y_t and $\hat{y}_t$ as the actual and forecasted values of the time series for period t, respectively, the forecasting error for period t is:

FORECAST ERROR

$$e_t = y_t - \hat{y}_t \tag{8.1}$$

That is, the forecast error for time period t is the difference between the actual and the forecasted values for period t.

For instance, because the distributor actually sold 21 thousand gallons of gasoline in week 2, and the forecast, using the sales volume in week 1, was 17 thousand gallons, the forecast error in week 2 is:

$$e_2 = y_2 - \hat{y}_2 = 21 - 17 = 4.$$

A positive error such as this indicates that the forecasting method underestimated the actual value of sales for the associated period. Next we use 21, the actual value of sales in week 2, as the forecast for week 3. Since the actual value of sales in week 3 is 19, the forecast error for week 3 is $e_3 = 19 - 21 = -2$. In this case, the negative forecast error indicates that the forecast overestimated the actual value for week 3. Thus, the forecast error may be positive or negative, depending on whether the forecast is too low or too high.

A complete summary of the forecast errors for this naïve forecasting method is shown in Table 8.7 in the Forecast Error column. It is important to note that because we are using a past value of the time series to produce a forecast for period t, we do not have sufficient data to produce a naïve forecast for the first week of this time series.

A simple measure of forecast accuracy is the mean or average of the forecast errors. If we have n periods in our time series and k is the number of periods at the beginning of the time series for which we cannot produce a naïve forecast, the mean forecast error (MFE) is:

MEAN FORECAST ERROR (MFE)

$$\text{MFE} = \frac{\sum\limits_{t=k+1}^{n} e_t}{n - k} \tag{8.2}$$

Table 8.7 shows that the sum of the forecast errors for the gasoline sales time series is 5; thus, the mean, or average, error is $5/11 = 0.45$. Because we do not have sufficient data to produce a naïve forecast for the first week of this time series, we must adjust our calculations in both the numerator and denominator accordingly. This is common in forecasting; we often use k past periods from the time series to produce forecasts, and so we frequently cannot produce forecasts for the first k periods. In those instances the summation in the numerator starts at the first value of t for which we have produced a forecast (so we begin the summation at $t = k + 1$), and the denominator (which is the number of periods in our time series for which we are able to produce a forecast) will also reflect these circumstances. In the gasoline example, although the time series consists of $n = 12$ values, to compute the mean error we divided the sum of the forecast errors by 11 because there are only 11 forecast errors (we cannot generate forecast sales for the first week using this naïve forecasting method).

Also note that in the gasoline time series, the mean forecast error is positive, implying that the method is generally underforecasting; in other words, the observed values tend to be greater than the forecasted values. Because positive and negative forecast errors tend to offset one another, the mean error is likely to be small; thus, the mean error is not a very useful measure of forecast accuracy.

The **mean absolute error (MAE)** is a measure of forecast accuracy that avoids the problem of positive and negative forecast errors offsetting one another. As you might expect given its name, MAE is the average of the absolute values of the forecast errors:

The MAE is also referred to as the mean absolute deviation (MAD).

MEAN ABSOLUTE ERROR (MAE)

$$\text{MAE} = \frac{\sum\limits_{t=k+1}^{n} |e_t|}{n - k} \tag{8.3}$$

Table 8.7 shows that the sum of the absolute values of the forecast errors is 41; thus:

$$\text{MAE} = \text{average of the absolute value of the forecast errors} = \frac{41}{11} = 3.73.$$

Another measure that avoids the problem of positive and negative errors offsetting each other is obtained by computing the average of the squared forecast errors. This measure of forecast accuracy is referred to as the **mean squared error (MSE)**:

MEAN SQUARED ERROR (MSE)

$$\text{MSE} = \frac{\sum_{t=k+1}^{n} e_t^2}{n-k} \tag{8.4}$$

From Table 8.7, the sum of the squared errors is 179; hence:

$$\text{MSE} = \text{average of the square of the forecast errors} = \frac{179}{11} = 16.27.$$

The size of the MAE or MSE depends on the scale of the data. As a result, it is difficult to make comparisons for different time intervals (such as comparing a method of forecasting monthly gasoline sales to a method of forecasting weekly sales) or to make comparisons across different time series (such as monthly sales of gasoline and monthly sales of oil filters). To make comparisons such as these we need to work with relative or percentage error measures. The **mean absolute percentage error (MAPE)** is such a measure. To calculate MAPE we use the formula:

MEAN ABSOLUTE PERCENTAGE ERROR (MAPE)

$$\text{MAPE} = \frac{\sum_{t=k+1}^{n} \left| \left(\frac{e_t}{y_t} \right) 100 \right|}{n-k} \tag{8.5}$$

Table 8.7 shows that the sum of the absolute values of the percentage errors is:

$$\sum_{t=1+1}^{12} \left| \left(\frac{e_t}{y_t} \right) 100 \right| = 211.69.$$

Thus, the MAPE, which is the average of the absolute value of percentage forecast errors, is:

$$\frac{211.69}{11} = 19.24\%.$$

In summary, using the naïve (most recent observation) forecasting method, we obtain the following measures of forecast accuracy:

$$\text{MAE} = 3.73$$
$$\text{MSE} = 16.27$$
$$\text{MAPE} = 19.24\%$$

These measures of forecast accuracy simply measure how well the forecasting method is able to forecast historical values of the time series. Now, suppose we want to forecast sales for a future time period, such as week 13. The forecast for week 13 is 22, the actual value of the time series in week 12. Is this an accurate estimate of sales for week 13? Unfortunately, there is no way to address the issue of accuracy associated with forecasts for future time periods. However, if we select a forecasting method that works well for the historical data, and we have reason to believe the historical pattern will continue into the future, we should obtain forecasts that will ultimately be shown to be accurate.

Before closing this section, let us consider another method for forecasting the gasoline sales time series in Table 8.1. Suppose we use the average of all the historical data available as the forecast for the next period. We begin by developing a forecast for week 2. Because there is only one historical value available prior to week 2, the forecast for week 2 is just the time series value in week 1; thus, the forecast for week 2 is 17 thousand gallons of gasoline. To compute the forecast for week 3, we take the average of the sales values in weeks 1 and 2. Thus:

$$\hat{y}_3 = \frac{17 + 21}{2} = 19.$$

Similarly, the forecast for week 4 is:

$$\hat{y}_4 = \frac{17 + 21 + 19}{3} = 19.$$

The forecasts obtained using this method for the gasoline time series are shown in Table 8.8 in the Forecast column. Using the results shown in Table 8.8, we obtain the following values of MAE, MSE, and MAPE:

$$MAE = \frac{26.81}{11} = 2.44$$

$$MSE = \frac{89.07}{11} = 8.10$$

$$MAPE = \frac{141.34}{11} = 12.85\%$$

We can now compare the accuracy of the two forecasting methods we have considered in this section by comparing the values of MAE, MSE, and MAPE for each method.

TABLE 8.8   Computing Forecasts and Measures of Forecast Accuracy Using the Average of All the Historical Data as the Forecast for the Next Period

Week	Time Series Value	Forecast	Forecast Error	Absolute Value of Forecast Error	Squared Forecast Error	Percentage Error	Absolute Value of Percentage Error
1	17						
2	21	17.00	4.00	4.00	16.00	19.05	19.05
3	19	19.00	0.00	0.00	0.00	0.00	0.00
4	23	19.00	4.00	4.00	16.00	17.39	17.39
5	18	20.00	−2.00	2.00	4.00	−11.11	11.11
6	16	19.60	−3.60	3.60	12.96	−22.50	22.50
7	20	19.00	1.00	1.00	1.00	5.00	5.00
8	18	19.14	−1.14	1.14	1.31	−6.35	6.35
9	22	19.00	3.00	3.00	9.00	13.64	13.64
10	20	19.33	0.67	0.67	0.44	3.33	3.33
11	15	19.40	−4.40	4.40	19.36	−29.33	29.33
12	22	19.00	3.00	3.00	9.00	13.64	13.64
		Totals	4.52	26.81	89.07	2.75	141.34

	Naïve Method	Average of Past Values
MAE	3.73	2.44
MSE	16.27	8.10
MAPE	19.24%	12.85%

For each of these measures, the average of past values provides more accurate forecasts for the next period than using the most recent observation.

Evaluating different forecasts based on historical accuracy is helpful only if historical patterns continue into the future. As we note in Section 8.1, the 12 observations of Table 8.1 comprise a stationary time series. In Section 8.1 we also mentioned that changes in business conditions often result in a time series that is not stationary. We discussed a situation in which the gasoline distributor signed a contract with the Vermont State Police to provide gasoline for state police cars located in southern Vermont. Table 8.2 shows the number of gallons of gasoline sold for the original time series and for the 10 weeks after signing the new contract, and Figure 8.2 shows the corresponding time series plot. Note the change in level in week 13 for the resulting time series. When a shift to a new level such as this occurs, it takes several periods for the forecasting method that uses the average of all the historical data to adjust to the new level of the time series. However, in this case the simple naïve method adjusts very rapidly to the change in level because it uses only the most recent observation as the forecast.

Measures of forecast accuracy are important factors in comparing different forecasting methods, but we have to be careful not to rely too heavily on them. Good judgment and knowledge about business conditions that might affect the value of the variable to be forecast also have to be considered carefully when selecting a method. Historical forecast accuracy is not the sole consideration, especially if the pattern exhibited by the time series is likely to change in the future.

In the next section, we will introduce more sophisticated methods for developing forecasts for a time series that exhibits a horizontal pattern. Using the measures of forecast accuracy developed here, we will be able to assess whether such methods provide more accurate forecasts than we obtained using the simple approaches illustrated in this section. The methods that we will introduce also have the advantage that they adapt well to situations in which the time series changes to a new level. The ability of a forecasting method to adapt quickly to changes in level is an important consideration, especially in short-term forecasting situations.

8.3 Moving Averages and Exponential Smoothing

In this section we discuss two forecasting methods that are appropriate for a time series with a horizontal pattern: moving averages and exponential smoothing. These methods are capable of adapting well to changes in the level of a horizontal pattern such as the one we saw with the extended gasoline sales time series (Table 8.2 and Figure 8.2). However, without modification they are not appropriate when considerable trend, cyclical, or seasonal effects are present. Because the objective of each of these methods is to smooth out random fluctuations in the time series, they are referred to as *smoothing methods*. These methods are easy to use and generally provide a high level of accuracy for short-range forecasts, such as a forecast for the next time period.

Moving Averages

The **moving averages method** uses the average of the most recent k data values in the time series as the forecast for the next period. Mathematically, a moving average forecast of order k is:

MOVING AVERAGE FORECAST

$$\hat{y}_{t+1} = \frac{\sum (\text{most recent } k \text{ data values})}{k} = \frac{\sum_{i=t-k+1}^{t} y_i}{k}$$

$$= \frac{y_{t-k+1} + \cdots + y_{t-1} + y_t}{k} \tag{8.6}$$

where

$\hat{y}_{t+1}$ = forecast of the time series for period $t + 1$

y_t = actual value of the time series in period t

k = number of periods of time series data used to generate the forecast

The term *moving* is used because every time a new observation becomes available for the time series, it replaces the oldest observation in the equation and a new average is computed. Thus, the periods over which the average is calculated change, or move, with each ensuing period.

To illustrate the moving averages method, let us return to the original 12 weeks of gasoline sales data in Table 8.1 and Figure 8.1. The time series plot in Figure 8.1 indicates that the gasoline sales time series has a horizontal pattern. Thus, the smoothing methods of this section are applicable.

To use moving averages to forecast a time series, we must first select the order k, or the number of time series values to be included in the moving average. If only the most recent values of the time series are considered relevant, a small value of k is preferred. If a greater number of past values are considered relevant, then we generally opt for a larger value of k. As previously mentioned, a time series with a horizontal pattern can shift to a new level over time. A moving average will adapt to the new level of the series and continue to provide good forecasts in k periods. Thus a smaller value of k will track shifts in a time series more quickly (the naïve approach discussed earlier is actually a moving average for $k = 1$). On the other hand, larger values of k will be more effective in smoothing out random fluctuations. Thus, managerial judgment based on an understanding of the behavior of a time series is helpful in choosing an appropriate value of k.

To illustrate how moving averages can be used to forecast gasoline sales, we will use a three-week moving average ($k = 3$). We begin by computing the forecast of sales in week 4 using the average of the time series values in weeks 1 to 3:

$$\hat{y}_4 = \text{average for weeks 1 to 3} = \frac{17 + 21 + 19}{3} = 19.$$

Thus, the moving average forecast of sales in week 4 is 19, or 19,000 gallons of gasoline. Because the actual value observed in week 4 is 23, the forecast error in week 4 is $e_4 = 23 - 19 = 4$.

We next compute the forecast of sales in week 5 by averaging the time series values in weeks 2 to 4:

$$\hat{y}_5 = \text{average for weeks 2 to 4} = \frac{21 + 19 + 23}{3} = 21.$$

Hence, the forecast of sales in week 5 is 21 and the error associated with this forecast is $e_5 = 18 - 21 = -3$. A complete summary of the three-week moving average forecasts for the gasoline sales time series is provided in Table 8.9. Figure 8.7 shows the original time series plot and the three-week moving average forecasts. Note how the graph of the moving average forecasts has tended to smooth out the random fluctuations in the time series.

		TABLE 8.9	Summary of Three-Week Moving Average Calculations				

Week	Time Series Value	Forecast	Forecast Error	Absolute Value of Forecast Error	Squared Forecast Error	Percentage Error	Absolute Value of Percentage Error
1	17						
2	21						
3	19						
4	23	19	4	4	16	17.39	17.39
5	18	21	−3	3	9	−16.67	16.67
6	16	20	−4	4	16	−25.00	25.00
7	20	19	1	1	1	5.00	5.00
8	18	18	0	0	0	0.00	0.00
9	22	18	4	4	16	18.18	18.18
10	20	20	0	0	0	0.00	0.00
11	15	20	−5	5	25	−33.33	33.33
12	22	19	3	3	9	13.64	13.64
		Totals	0	24	92	−20.79	129.21

To forecast sales in week 13, the next time period in the future, we simply compute the average of the time series values in weeks 10, 11, and 12:

DATA *file*
Gasoline

$$\hat{y}_{13} = \text{average for weeks 10 to 12} = \frac{20 + 15 + 22}{3} = 19.$$

Thus, the forecast for week 13 is 19, or 19,000 gallons of gasoline.

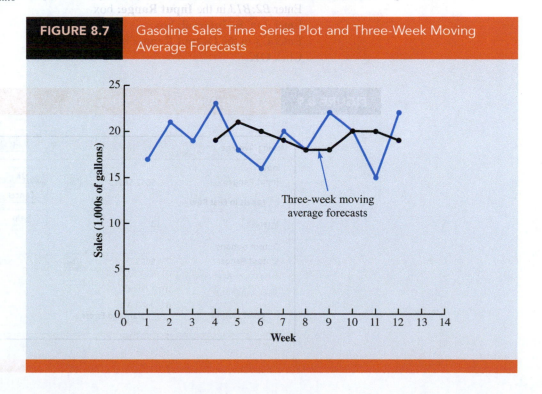

	FIGURE 8.7	Gasoline Sales Time Series Plot and Three-Week Moving Average Forecasts

Three-week moving average forecasts

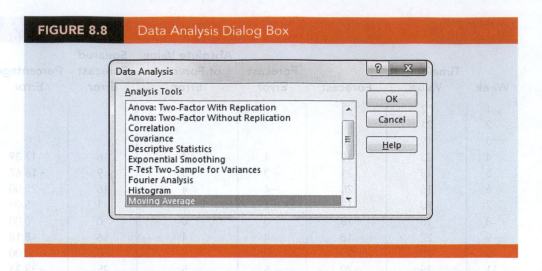

FIGURE 8.8   Data Analysis Dialog Box

To show how Excel can be used to develop forecasts using the moving averages method, we develop a forecast for the gasoline sales time series in Table 8.1 and Figure 8.1. We assume that the user has entered the week into rows 2 through 13 of column A and the sales data for the 12 weeks into worksheet rows 2 through 13 of column B.

The following steps can be used to produce a three-week moving average:

In versions of Excel prior to Excel 2016, the Data Analysis tool can be found in the Analysis group.

Step 1. Click the **Data** tab in the Ribbon
Step 2. Click **Data Analysis** in the **Analyze** group
Step 3. When the **Data Analysis** dialog box appears (Figure 8.8), select **Moving Average** and click **OK**
Step 4. When the **Moving Average** dialog box appears (Figure 8.9):
    Enter *B2:B13* in the **Input Range:** box
    Enter *3* in the **Interval:** box
    Enter *C3* in the **Output Range:** box
    Click **OK**

FIGURE 8.9   Moving Average Dialog Box

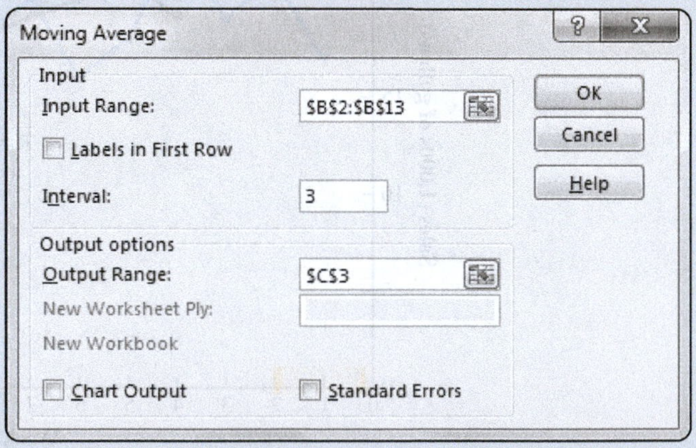

FIGURE 8.10	Excel Output for Moving Average Forecast for Gasoline Data

	A	B	C
1	**Week**	**Sales (1,000s of gallons)**	
2	1	17	
3	2	21	#N/A
4	3	19	#N/A
5	4	23	19
6	5	18	21
7	6	16	20
8	7	20	19
9	8	18	18
10	9	22	18
11	10	20	20
12	11	15	20
13	12	22	19
14	13		19

Once you have completed this step, the three-week moving average forecasts will appear in column C of the worksheet as shown in Figure 8.10. Note that forecasts for periods of other lengths can be computed easily by entering a different value in the **Interval:** box.

If **Data Analysis** does not appear in your **Analyze** group for Step 1 (or in the **Analysis** group in versions of Excel prior to Excel 2016), you will have to load the Analysis ToolPak add-in into Excel. To do so, click the **File** tab in the Ribbon and click **Options**. When the **Excel Options** dialog box appears, click **Add-Ins** from the menu. Next to **Manage**, select **Excel Add-ins** and click **Go...** at the bottom of the dialog box. When the **Add-Ins** dialog box appears select **Analysis ToolPak** and click **OK**.

Forecast Accuracy

In Section 8.2 we discussed three measures of forecast accuracy: mean absolute error (MAE), mean squared error (MSE), and mean absolute percentage error (MAPE). Using the three-week moving average calculations in Table 8.9, the values for these three measures of forecast accuracy are:

$$\text{MAE} = \frac{\sum_{t=k+1}^{n} |e_t|}{n - k} = \frac{24}{9} = 2.67$$

$$\text{MSE} = \frac{\sum_{t=k+1}^{n} e_t^2}{n - k} = \frac{92}{9} = 10.22$$

$$\text{MAPE} = \frac{\sum_{t=k+1}^{n} \left|\left(\frac{e_t}{y_t}\right)100\right|}{n - k} = \frac{129.21}{9} = 14.36\%$$

In Section 8.2 we showed that using the most recent observation as the forecast for the next week (a moving average of order $k = 1$) resulted in values of MAE = 3.73, MSE = 16.27, and MAPE = 19.24%. Thus, in each case the three-week moving average approach has provided more accurate forecasts than simply using the most recent observation as the forecast. Also note how we have revised the formulas for the MAE, MSE, and MAPE to reflect that our use of a three-week moving average leaves us with insufficient data to generate forecasts for the first three weeks of our time series.

If a large amount of data are available to build the forecast models, we suggest dividing the data into training and validation sets, and then determining the best value of k as the value that minimizes the MSE for the validation set. We discuss the use of training and validation sets in more detail in Section 8.5.

To determine whether a moving average with a different order k can provide more accurate forecasts, we recommend using trial and error to determine the value of k that minimizes the MSE. For the gasoline sales time series, it can be shown that the minimum value of MSE corresponds to a moving average of order $k = 6$ with MSE = 6.79. If we are willing to assume that the order of the moving average that is best for the historical data will also be best for future values of the time series, the most accurate moving average forecasts of gasoline sales can be obtained using a moving average of order $k = 6$.

Exponential Smoothing

Exponential smoothing uses a weighted average of past time series values as a forecast. The exponential smoothing model is:

EXPONENTIAL SMOOTHING FORECAST

$$\hat{y}_{t+1} = \alpha y_t + (1 - \alpha)\hat{y}_t \qquad (8.7)$$

where

$$\hat{y}_{t+1} = \text{forecast of the time series for period } t + 1$$
$$y_t = \text{actual value of the time series in period } t$$
$$\hat{y}_t = \text{forecast of the time series for period } t$$
$$\alpha = \text{smoothing constant } (0 \leq \alpha \leq 1)$$

Equation (8.7) shows that the forecast for period $t + 1$ is a weighted average of the actual value in period t and the forecast for period t. The weight given to the actual value in period t is the **smoothing constant** α, and the weight given to the forecast in period t is $1 - \alpha$. It turns out that the exponential smoothing forecast for any period is actually a weighted average of all the previous actual values of the time series. Let us illustrate by working with a time series involving only three periods of data: y_1, y_2, and y_3.

To initiate the calculations, we let $\hat{y}_1$ equal the actual value of the time series in period 1; that is, $\hat{y}_1 = y_1$. Hence, the forecast for period 2 is:

$$\hat{y}_2 = \alpha y_1 + (1 - \alpha)\hat{y}_1$$
$$= \alpha y_1 + (1 - \alpha)y_1$$
$$= y_1.$$

We see that the exponential smoothing forecast for period 2 is equal to the actual value of the time series in period 1.

The forecast for period 3 is:

$$\hat{y}_3 = \alpha y_2 + (1 - \alpha)\hat{y}_2 = \alpha y_2 + (1 - \alpha)y_1.$$

Finally, substituting this expression for $\hat{y}_3$ into the expression for $\hat{y}_4$, we obtain:

$$\hat{y}_4 = \alpha y_3 + (1 - \alpha)\hat{y}_3$$
$$= \alpha y_3 + (1 - \alpha)(\alpha y_2 + (1 - \alpha)y_1)$$
$$= \alpha y_3 + \alpha(1 - \alpha)y_2 + (1 - \alpha)^2 y_1.$$

We now see that $\hat{y}_4$ is a weighted average of the first three time series values. The sum of the coefficients, or weights, for y_1, y_2, and y_3 equals 1. A similar argument can be made to show that, in general, any forecast $\hat{y}_{t+1}$ is a weighted average of all the t previous time series values.

Despite the fact that exponential smoothing provides a forecast that is a weighted average of all past observations, all past data do not need to be retained to compute the forecast for the next period. In fact, equation (8.7) shows that once the value for the smoothing constant α is selected, only two pieces of information are needed to compute the forecast for period $t + 1$: y_t, the actual value of the time series in period t; and $\hat{y}_t$, the forecast for period t.

To illustrate the exponential smoothing approach to forecasting, let us again consider the gasoline sales time series in Table 8.1 and Figure 8.1. As indicated previously, to initialize the calculations we set the exponential smoothing forecast for period 2 equal to the actual value of the time series in period 1. Thus, with $y_1 = 17$, we set $\hat{y}_2 = 17$ to initiate the computations. Referring to the time series data in Table 8.1, we find an actual time series value in period 2 of $y_2 = 21$. Thus, in period 2 we have a forecast error of $e_2 = 21 - 17 = 4$.

Continuing with the exponential smoothing computations using a smoothing constant of $\alpha = 0.2$, we obtain the following forecast for period 3:

$$\hat{y}_3 = 0.2y_2 + 0.8\hat{y}_2 = 0.2(21) + 0.8(17) = 17.8.$$

Once the actual time series value in period 3, $y_3 = 19$, is known, we can generate a forecast for period 4 as follows:

$$\hat{y}_4 = 0.2y_3 + 0.8\hat{y}_3 = 0.2(19) + 0.8(17.8) = 18.04.$$

Continuing the exponential smoothing calculations, we obtain the weekly forecast values shown in Table 8.10. Note that we have not shown an exponential smoothing forecast or a forecast error for week 1 because no forecast was made (we used actual sales for week 1 as the forecasted sales for week 2 to initialize the exponential smoothing process). For week 12, we have $y_{12} = 22$ and $\hat{y}_{12} = 18.48$. We can we use this information to generate a forecast for week 13:

$$\hat{y}_{13} = 0.2y_{12} + 0.8\hat{y}_{12} = 0.2(22) + 0.8(18.48) = 19.18.$$

Thus, the exponential smoothing forecast of the amount sold in week 13 is 19.18, or 19,180 gallons of gasoline. With this forecast, the firm can make plans and decisions accordingly.

Figure 8.11 shows the time series plot of the actual and forecasted time series values. Note in particular how the forecasts smooth out the irregular or random fluctuations in the time series.

DATA *file*

Gasoline

To show how Excel can be used for exponential smoothing, we again develop a forecast for the gasoline sales time series in Table 8.1 and Figure 8.1. We use the file *Gasoline*, which has the week in rows 2 through 13 of column A and the sales data for the 12 weeks in rows 2 through 13 of column B. We use $\alpha = 0.2$. The following steps can be used to produce a forecast.

| | | TABLE 8.10 | Summary of the Exponential Smoothing Forecasts and Forecast Errors for the Gasoline Sales Time Series with Smoothing Constant $\alpha = 0.2$ | | |

Week	Time Series Value	Forecast	Forecast Error	Squared Forecast Error
1	17			
2	21	17.00	4.00	16.00
3	19	17.80	1.20	1.44
4	23	18.04	4.96	24.60
5	18	19.03	−1.03	1.06
6	16	18.83	−2.83	8.01
7	20	18.26	1.74	3.03
8	18	18.61	−0.61	0.37
9	22	18.49	3.51	12.32
10	20	19.19	0.81	0.66
11	15	19.35	−4.35	18.92
12	22	18.48	3.52	12.39
		Totals	10.92	98.80

Step 1. Click the **Data** tab in the Ribbon

Step 2. Click **Data Analysis** in the **Analyze** group

Step 3. When the **Data Analysis** dialog box appears (Figure 8.12), select **Exponential Smoothing** and click **OK**

| | | FIGURE 8.11 | Actual and Forecast Gasoline Time Series with Smoothing Constant $\alpha = 0.2$ |

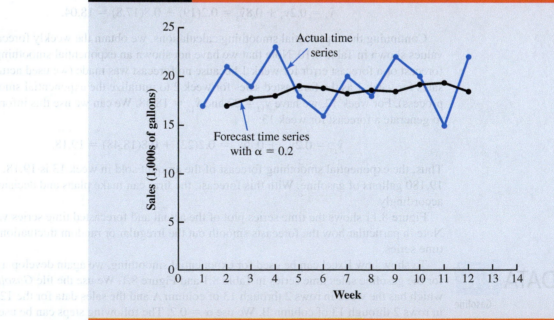

FIGURE 8.12   Data Analysis Dialog Box

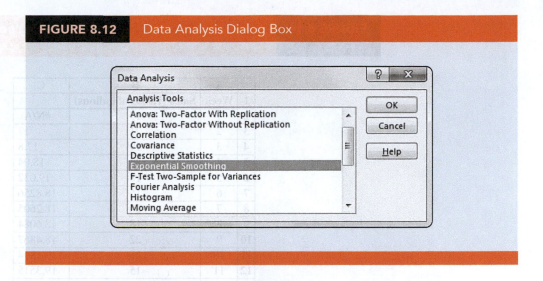

Step 4. When the **Exponential Smoothing** dialog box appears (Figure 8.13):
Enter *B2:B13* in the **Input Range:** box
Enter *0.8* in the **Damping factor:** box
Enter *C2* in the **Output Range:** box
Click **OK**

Once you have completed this step, the exponential smoothing forecasts will appear in column C of the worksheet as shown in Figure 8.14. Note that the value we entered in the **Damping factor:** box is $1 - \alpha$; forecasts for other smoothing constants can be computed easily by entering a different value for $1 - \alpha$ in the **Damping factor:** box.

Forecast Accuracy

In the preceding exponential smoothing calculations, we used a smoothing constant of $\alpha = 0.2$. Although any value of α between 0 and 1 is acceptable, some values will yield

FIGURE 8.13   Exponential Smoothing Dialog Box

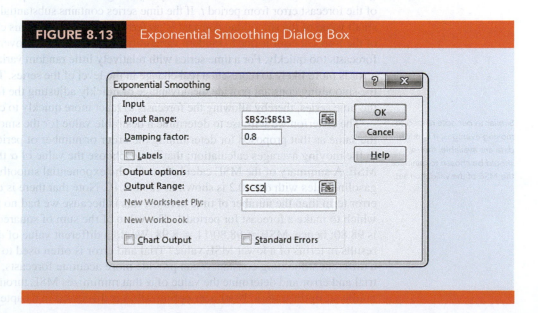

	A	B	C
1	Week	Sales (1,000s of gallons)	
2	1	17	#N/A
3	2	21	17
4	3	19	17.8
5	4	23	18.04
6	5	18	19.032
7	6	16	18.8256
8	7	20	18.2605
9	8	18	18.6084
10	9	22	18.4867
11	10	20	19.1894
12	11	15	19.3515
13	12	22	18.4812

more accurate forecasts than others. Insight into choosing a good value for α can be obtained by rewriting the basic exponential smoothing model as follows:

$$\hat{y}_{t+1} = \alpha y_t + (1 - \alpha)\hat{y}_t$$
$$= \alpha y_t + \hat{y}_t - \alpha \hat{y}_t$$
$$= \hat{y}_t + \alpha(y_t - \hat{y}_t) = \hat{y}_t + \alpha e_t.$$

Thus, the new forecast $\hat{y}_{t+1}$ is equal to the previous forecast $\hat{y}_t$ plus an adjustment, which is the smoothing constant α times the most recent forecast error, $e_t = y_t - \hat{y}_t$. In other words, the forecast in period $t + 1$ is obtained by adjusting the forecast in period t by a fraction of the forecast error from period t. If the time series contains substantial random variability, a small value of the smoothing constant is preferred. The reason for this choice is that if much of the forecast error is due to random variability, we do not want to overreact and adjust the forecasts too quickly. For a time series with relatively little random variability, a forecast error is more likely to represent a real change in the level of the series. Thus, larger values of the smoothing constant provide the advantage of quickly adjusting the forecasts to changes in the time series, thereby allowing the forecasts to react more quickly to changing conditions.

Similar to our note related to moving averages, if enough data are available, then α should be chosen to minimize the MSE of the validation set.

The criterion we will use to determine a desirable value for the smoothing constant α is the same as that proposed for determining the order or number of periods of data to include in the moving averages calculation; that is, we choose the value of α that minimizes the MSE. A summary of the MSE calculations for the exponential smoothing forecast of gasoline sales with $\alpha = 0.2$ is shown in Table 8.10. Note that there is one less squared error term than the number of time periods; this is because we had no past values with which to make a forecast for period 1. The value of the sum of squared forecast errors is 98.80; hence, MSE = 98.80/11 = 8.98. Would a different value of α provide better results in terms of a lower MSE value? Trial and error is often used to determine whether a different smoothing constant α can provide more accurate forecasts, but we can avoid trial and error and determine the value of α that minimizes MSE through the use of nonlinear optimization. Nonlinear optimization is discussed in Chapter 13.

NOTES + COMMENTS

1. Spreadsheet packages are effective tools for implementing exponential smoothing. With the time series data and the forecasting formulas in a spreadsheet such as the one shown in Table 8.10, you can use the MAE, MSE, and MAPE to evaluate different values of the smoothing constant α.
2. Moving averages and exponential smoothing provide the foundation for much of time series analysis, and many more sophisticated refinements of these methods have been developed. These include but are not limited to weighted moving averages, double moving averages, Brown's method for double exponential smoothing, and Holt-Winters exponential smoothing. Appendix 8.1 explains how to implement the Holt-Winters method using a new tool in Excel 2016 called Forecast Sheet. Appendix 8.2 demonstrates the use of the Excel add-in Analytic Solver Platform which allows for the use of additional forecasting models.

8.4 Using Regression Analysis for Forecasting

As we saw in Chapter 7, regression analysis is a statistical technique that can be used to develop a mathematical equation showing how variables are related. In regression terminology, the variable that is being predicted is called the *dependent*, or *response*, *variable*, and the variable or variables being used to predict the value of the dependent variable are called the *independent*, or *predictor*, *variables*. Regression analysis involving one independent variable and one dependent variable for which the relationship between the variables is approximated by a straight line is called *simple linear regression*. Regression analysis involving two or more independent variables is called *multiple regression analysis*. In this section we will show how to use regression analysis to develop forecasts for a time series that has a trend, a seasonal pattern, and both a trend and a seasonal pattern. We will also show how to use regression analysis to develop forecast models that include causal variables.

Linear Trend Projection

We now consider forecasting methods that are appropriate for time series that exhibit trend patterns and show how regression analysis can be used to forecast a time series with a linear trend. In Section 8.1 we used the bicycle sales time series in Table 8.3 and Figure 8.3 to illustrate a time series with a trend pattern. Let us now use this time series to illustrate how regression analysis can be used to forecast a time series with a linear trend. Although the time series plot in Figure 8.3 shows some up-and-down movement over the past 10 years, we might agree that the linear trendline shown in Figure 8.3 provides a reasonable approximation of the long-run movement in the series. We can use regression analysis to develop such a linear trendline for the bicycle sales time series.

Because simple linear regression analysis yields the linear relationship between the independent variable and the dependent variable that minimizes the MSE, we can use this approach to find a best-fitting line to a set of data that exhibits a linear trend. In finding a linear trend, the variable to be forecasted (y_t, the actual value of the time series in period t) is the dependent variable and the trend variable (time period t) is the independent variable. We will use the following notation for our linear trendline:

$$\hat{y}_t = b_0 + b_1 t, \tag{8.8}$$

where

$$\hat{y}_t = \text{forecast of sales in period } t$$
$$t = \text{time period}$$
$$b_0 = \text{the } y\text{-intercept of the linear trendline}$$
$$b_1 = \text{the slope of the linear trendline}$$

FIGURE 8.15 Excel Simple Linear Regression Output for Trendline Model for Bicycle Sales Data

	A	B	C	D	E	F	G	H	I
1	SUMMARY OUTPUT								
2									
3	*Regression Statistics*								
4	Multiple R	0.874526167							
5	R Square	0.764796016							
6	Adjusted R Square	0.735395518							
7	Standard Error	1.958953802							
8	Observations	10							
9									
10	ANOVA								
11		*df*	*SS*	*MS*	*F*	*Significance F*			
12	Regression	1	99.825	99.825	26.01302932	0.000929509			
13	Residual	8	30.7	3.8375					
14	Total	9	130.525						
15									
16		*Coefficients*	*Standard Error*	*t Stat*	*P-value*	*Lower 95%*	*Upper 95%*	*Lower 99.0%*	*Upper 99.0%*
17	Intercept	20.4	1.338220211	15.24412786	3.39989E-07	17.31405866	23.48594134	15.90975286	24.89024714
18	Year	1.1	0.215673715	5.100296983	0.000929509	0.60265552	1.59734448	0.376331148	1.823668852

In equation (8.8), the time variable begins at $t = 1$, corresponding to the first time series observation (year 1 for the bicycle sales time series). The time variable then continues until $t = n$, corresponding to the most recent time series observation (year 10 for the bicycle sales time series). Thus, for the bicycle sales time series $t = 1$ corresponds to the oldest time series value, and $t = 10$ corresponds to the most recent year.

Excel can be used to compute the estimated intercept b_0 and slope b_1. The Excel output for a regression analysis of the bicycle sales data is provided in Figure 8.15.

We see in this output that the estimated intercept b_0 is 20.4 (shown in cell B17) and the estimated slope b_1 is 1.1 (shown in cell B18). Thus,

$$\hat{y}_t = 20.4 + 1.1t \qquad (8.9)$$

is the regression equation for the linear trend component for the bicycle sales time series. The slope of 1.1 in this trend equation indicates that over the past 10 years the firm has experienced an average growth in sales of about 1,100 units per year. If we assume that the past 10-year trend in sales is a good indicator for the future, we can use equation (8.9) to project the trend component of the time series. For example, substituting $t = 11$ into equation (8.9) yields next year's trend projection, $\hat{y}_{11}$:

$$\hat{y}_{11} = 20.4 + 1.1(11) = 32.5.$$

Thus, the linear trend model yields a sales forecast of 32,500 bicycles for the next year.

We can also use the trendline to forecast sales farther into the future. Using equation (8.9), we develop annual forecasts of bicycle sales for two and three years into the future as follows:

$$\hat{y}_{12} = 20.4 + 1.1(12) = 33.6$$

$$\hat{y}_{13} = 20.4 + 1.1(13) = 34.7$$

The forecasted value increases by 1,100 bicycles in each year.

Note that in this example we are not using past values of the time series to produce forecasts, so we can produce a forecast for each period of the time series; that is, $k = 0$ in equations (8.3), (8.4), and (8.5) to calculate the MAE, MSE, and MAPE.

We can also use more complex regression models to fit nonlinear trends. For example, if we also include t^2 and t^3 as independent variables in our model, the estimated regression equation would become:

$$\hat{y}_t = b_0 + b_1 t + b_2 t^2 + b_3 t^3.$$

This model provides a forecast of a time series with curvilinear characteristics over time.

Another type of regression-based forecasting model occurs whenever all the independent variables are previous values of the same time series. For example, if the time series values are denoted $y_1, y_2, \ldots, y_n$, we might try to find an estimated regression equation relating y_t to the most recent time series values, y_{t-1}, y_{t-2}, and so on. If we use the actual values of the time series for the three most recent periods as independent variables, the estimated regression equation would be:

$$\hat{y}_t = b_0 + b_1 y_{t-1} + b_2 y_{t-2} + b_3 y_{t-3}.$$

Because autoregressive models typically violate the conditions necessary for inference in least squares regression, you must be careful when testing hypotheses or estimating confidence intervals in autoregressive models. There are special methods for constructing autoregressive models, but they are beyond the scope of this book.

Regression models such as this in which the independent variables are previous values of the time series are referred to as **autoregressive models**.

Seasonality

To the extent that seasonality exists, we need to incorporate it into our forecasting models to ensure accurate forecasts. We begin by considering a seasonal time series with no trend and then discuss how to model seasonality with a linear trend.

Seasonality Without Trend

Let us consider again the data from Table 8.5, the number of umbrellas sold at a clothing store over the past five years. As we see in the time series plot provided in Figure 8.5, the data do not suggest any long-term trend in sales. In fact, unless you look carefully at the data, you might conclude that the data follow a horizontal pattern with random fluctuation and that single exponential smoothing could be used to forecast sales. However, closer inspection of the time series plot reveals a pattern in the fluctuations. The first and third quarters have moderate sales, the second quarter the highest sales, and the fourth quarter the lowest sales. Thus, we conclude that a quarterly seasonal pattern is present.

We can model a time series with a seasonal pattern by treating the season as a dummy variable. As indicated in Chapter 7, categorical variables are data used to categorize observations of data, and $k - 1$ dummy variables are required to model a categorical variable that has k levels. Thus, we need three dummy variables to model four seasons. For instance, in the umbrella sales time series, the quarter to which each observation corresponds is treated as a season; it is a categorical variable with four levels: quarter 1, quarter 2, quarter 3, and quarter 4. Thus, to model the seasonal effects in the umbrella time series we need $4 - 1 = 3$ dummy variables. The three dummy variables can be coded as follows:

$$\text{Qtr1}_t = \begin{cases} 1 \text{ if period } t \text{ is a quarter 1} \\ 0 \text{ otherwise} \end{cases}$$

$$\text{Qtr2}_t = \begin{cases} 1 \text{ if period } t \text{ is a quarter 2} \\ 0 \text{ otherwise} \end{cases}$$

$$\text{Qtr3}_t = \begin{cases} 1 & \text{if period } t \text{ is a quarter 3} \\ 0 & \text{otherwise} \end{cases}$$

Using $\hat{y}_t$ to denote the forecasted value of sales for period t, the general form of the equation relating the number of umbrellas sold to the quarter the sales take place is as follows:

$$\hat{y}_t = b_0 + b_1\text{Qtr1}_t + b_2\text{Qtr2}_t + b_3\text{Qtr3}_t. \tag{8.10}$$

Note that the fourth quarter will be denoted by setting all three dummy variables to 0.

Table 8.11 shows the umbrella sales time series with the coded values of the dummy variables shown. We can use a multiple linear regression model to find the values of b_0, b_1, b_2, and b_3 that minimize the sum of squared errors. For this regression model, y_t is the dependent variable, and the quarterly dummy variables Qtr1_t, Qtr2_t, and Qtr3_t are the independent variables. Using the data in Table 8.11 and regression analysis, we obtain the following equation:

$$\hat{y}_t = 95.0 + 29.0\text{Qtr1}_t + 57.0\text{Qtr2}_t + 26.0\text{Qtr3}_t. \tag{8.11}$$

We can use equation (8.11) to forecast sales of every quarter for next year:

Quarter 1: Sales = 95.0 + 29.0(1) + 57.0(0) + 26.0(0) = 124
Quarter 2: Sales = 95.0 + 29.0(0) + 57.0(1) + 26.0(0) = 152
Quarter 3: Sales = 95.0 + 29.0(0) + 57.0(0) + 26.0(1) = 121
Quarter 4: Sales = 95.0 + 29.0(0) + 57.0(0) + 26.0(0) = 95

It is interesting to note that we could have obtained the quarterly forecasts for next year by simply computing the average number of umbrellas sold in each quarter. Nonetheless, for more complex problem situations, such as dealing with a time series that has both trend and seasonal effects, this simple averaging approach will not work.

TABLE 8.11	Umbrella Sales Time Series with Dummy Variables					
Period	Year	Quarter	Qtr1	Qtr2	Qtr3	Sales
1	1	1	1	0	0	125
2		2	0	1	0	153
3		3	0	0	1	106
4		4	0	0	0	88
5	2	1	1	0	0	118
6		2	0	1	0	161
7		3	0	0	1	133
8		4	0	0	0	102
9	3	1	1	0	0	138
10		2	0	1	0	144
11		3	0	0	1	113
12		4	0	0	0	80
13	4	1	1	0	0	109
14		2	0	1	0	137
15		3	0	0	1	125
16		4	0	0	0	109
17	5	1	1	0	0	130
18		2	0	1	0	165
19		3	0	0	1	128
20		4	0	0	0	96

Seasonality with Trend

We now consider situations for which the time series contains both seasonal effects and a linear trend by showing how to forecast the quarterly sales of smartphones introduced in Section 8.1. The data for the smartphone time series are shown in Table 8.6. The time series plot in Figure 8.6 indicates that sales are lowest in the second quarter of each year and increase in quarters 3 and 4. Thus, we conclude that a seasonal pattern exists for smartphone sales. However, the time series also has an upward linear trend that will need to be accounted for in order to develop accurate forecasts of quarterly sales. This is easily done by combining the dummy variable approach for handling seasonality with the approach for handling a linear trend discussed earlier in this section.

The general form of the regression equation for modeling both the quarterly seasonal effects and the linear trend in the smartphone time series is:

$$\hat{y}_t = b_0 + b_1 Qtr1_t + b_2 Qtr2_t + b_3 Qtr3_t + b_4 t, \tag{8.12}$$

where

$\hat{y}_t$ = forecast of sales in period t

$Qtr1_t$ = 1 if time period t corresponds to the first quarter of the year; 0 otherwise

$Qtr2_t$ = 1 if time period t corresponds to the second quarter of the year; 0 otherwise

$Qtr3_t$ = 1 if time period t corresponds to the third quarter of the year; 0 otherwise

t = time period (quarter)

For this regression model y_t is the dependent variable and the quarterly dummy variables $Qtr1_t$, $Qtr2_t$, and $Qtr3_t$ and the time period t are the independent variables.

Table 8.12 shows the revised smartphone sales time series that includes the coded values of the dummy variables and the time period t. Using the data in Table 8.12 with

TABLE 8.12		Smartphone Sales Time Series with Dummy Variables and Time Period				
Period	Year	Quarter	Qtr1	Qtr2	Qtr3	Sales (1,000s)
1	1	1	1	0	0	4.8
2		2	0	1	0	4.1
3		3	0	0	1	6.0
4		4	0	0	0	6.5
5	2	1	1	0	0	5.8
6		2	0	1	0	5.2
7		3	0	0	1	6.8
8		4	0	0	0	7.4
9	3	1	1	0	0	6.0
10		2	0	1	0	5.6
11		3	0	0	1	7.5
12		4	0	0	0	7.8
13	4	1	1	0	0	6.3
14		2	0	1	0	5.9
15		3	0	0	1	8.0
16		4	0	0	0	8.4

the regression model that includes both the seasonal and trend components, we obtain the following equation that minimizes our sum of squared errors:

$$\hat{y}_t = 6.07 - 1.36\text{Qtr1}_t - 2.03\text{Qtr2}_t - 0.304\text{Qtr3}_t + 0.146t. \qquad (8.13)$$

We can now use equation (8.13) to forecast quarterly sales for next year. Next year is year 5 for the smartphone sales time series, that is, time periods 17, 18, 19, and 20.

Forecast for time period 17 (quarter 1 in year 5):

$$\hat{y}_{17} = 6.07 - 1.36(1) - 2.03(0) - 0.304(0) + 0.146(17) = 7.19.$$

Forecast for time period 18 (quarter 2 in year 5):

$$\hat{y}_{18} = 6.07 - 1.36(0) - 2.03(1) - 0.304(0) + 0.146(18) = 6.67.$$

Forecast for time period 19 (quarter 3 in year 5):

$$\hat{y}_{19} = 6.07 - 1.36(0) - 2.03(0) - 0.304(1) + 0.146(19) = 8.54.$$

Forecast for time period 20 (quarter 4 in year 5):

$$\hat{y}_{20} = 6.07 - 1.36(0) - 2.03(0) - 0.304(0) + 0.146(20) = 8.99.$$

Thus, accounting for the seasonal effects and the linear trend in smartphone sales, the estimates of quarterly sales in year 5 are 7,190, 6,670, 8,540, and 8,990.

The dummy variables in the equation actually provide four equations, one for each quarter. For instance, if time period t corresponds to quarter 1, the estimate of quarterly sales is:

Quarter 1: Sales $= 6.07 - 1.36(1) - 2.03(0) - 0.304(0) + 0.146t = 4.71 + 0.146t.$

Similarly, if time period t corresponds to quarters 2, 3, and 4, the estimates of quarterly sales are:

Quarter 2: Sales $= 6.07 - 1.36(0) - 2.03(1) - 0.304(0) + 0.146t = 4.04 + 0.146t$

Quarter 3: Sales $= 6.07 - 1.36(0) - 2.03(0) - 0.304(1) + 0.146t = 5.77 + 0.146t$

Quarter 4: Sales $= 6.07 - 1.36(0) - 2.03(0) - 0.304(0) + 0.146t = 6.07 + 0.146t$

The slope of the trendline for each quarterly forecast equation is 0.146, indicating a consistent growth in sales of about 146 phones per quarter. The only difference in the four equations is that they have different intercepts.

In the smartphone sales example, we showed how dummy variables can be used to account for the quarterly seasonal effects in the time series. Because there were four levels for the categorical variable season, three dummy variables were required. However, many businesses use monthly rather than quarterly forecasts. For monthly data, season is a categorical variable with 12 levels, and thus $12 - 1 = 11$ dummy variables are required to capture monthly seasonal effects. For example, the 11 dummy variables could be coded as follows:

$$\text{Month1}_t = \begin{cases} 1 \text{ if period } t \text{ is January} \\ 0 \text{ otherwise} \end{cases}$$

$$\text{Month2}_t = \begin{cases} 1 \text{ if period } t \text{ is February} \\ 0 \text{ otherwise} \end{cases}$$

$$\vdots$$

$$\text{Month11}_t = \begin{cases} 1 \text{ if period } t \text{ is November} \\ 0 \text{ otherwise} \end{cases}$$

Other than this change, the approach for handling seasonality remains the same. Time series data collected at other intervals can be handled in a similar manner.

Using Regression Analysis as a Causal Forecasting Method

The methods discussed for estimating linear trends and seasonal effects make use of patterns in historical values of the variable to be forecast; these methods are classified as time series methods because they rely on past values of the variable to be forecast when developing the model. However, the relationship of the variable to be forecast with other variables may also be used to develop a forecasting model. Generally such models include only variables that are believed to cause changes in the variable to be forecast, such as:

- Advertising expenditures when sales is to be forecast.
- The mortgage rate when new housing construction is to be forecast.
- Grade point average when starting salaries for recent college graduates is to be forecast.
- The price of a product when the demand for the product is to be forecast.
- The value of the Dow Jones Industrial Average when the value of an individual stock is to be forecast.
- Daily high temperature when electricity usage is to be forecast.

Because these variables are used as independent variables when we believe they cause changes in the value of the dependent variable, forecasting models that include such variables as independent variables are referred to as **causal models**. It is important to note here that the forecasting model provides evidence only of association between an independent variable and the variable to be forecast. The model does not provide evidence of a causal relationship between an independent variable and the variable to be forecast; the conclusion that a causal relationship exists must be based on practical experience.

To illustrate how regression analysis is used as a causal forecasting method, we consider the sales forecasting problem faced by Armand's Pizza Parlors, a chain of Italian restaurants doing business in a five-state area. Historically, the most successful locations have been near college campuses. The managers believe that quarterly sales for these restaurants (denoted by y) are related positively to the size of the student population (denoted by x); that is, restaurants near campuses with a large population tend to generate more sales than those located near campuses with a small population.

Using regression analysis we can develop an equation showing how the dependent variable y is related to the independent variable x. This equation can then be used to forecast quarterly sales for restaurants located near college campuses given the size of the student population. This is particularly helpful for forecasting sales for new restaurant locations. For instance, suppose that management wants to forecast sales for a new restaurant that it is considering opening near a college campus. Because no historical data are available on sales for a new restaurant, Armand's cannot use time series data to develop the forecast. However, as we will now illustrate, regression analysis can still be used to forecast quarterly sales for this new location.

To develop the equation relating quarterly sales to the size of the student population, Armand's collected data from a sample of 10 of its restaurants located near college campuses. These data are summarized in Table 8.13. For example, restaurant 1, with $y = 58$ and $x = 2$, had \$58,000 in quarterly sales and is located near a campus with 2,000 students. Figure 8.16 shows a scatter chart of the data presented in Table 8.13, with the size of the student population shown on the horizontal axis and quarterly sales shown on the vertical axis.

What preliminary conclusions can we draw from Figure 8.16? Sales appear to be higher at locations near campuses with larger student populations. Also, it appears that the relationship

TABLE 8.13	Student Population and Quarterly Sales Data for 10 Armand's Pizza Parlors	
Restaurant	Student Population (1,000s)	Quarterly Sales ($1,000s)
1	2	58
2	6	105
3	8	88
4	8	118
5	12	117
6	16	137
7	20	157
8	20	169
9	22	149
10	26	202

DATA *file*

Armand's

between the two variables can be approximated by a straight line. In Figure 8.17, we can draw a straight line through the data that appears to provide a good linear approximation of the relationship between the variables. Observe that the relationship is not perfect. Indeed, few, if any, of the data fall exactly on the line. However, if we can develop the mathematical expression for this line, we may be able to use it to forecast the value of y corresponding to

FIGURE 8.16	Scatter Chart of Student Population and Quarterly Sales for Armand's Pizza Parlors

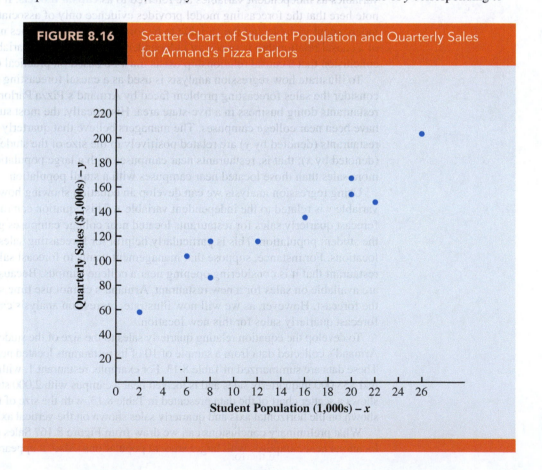

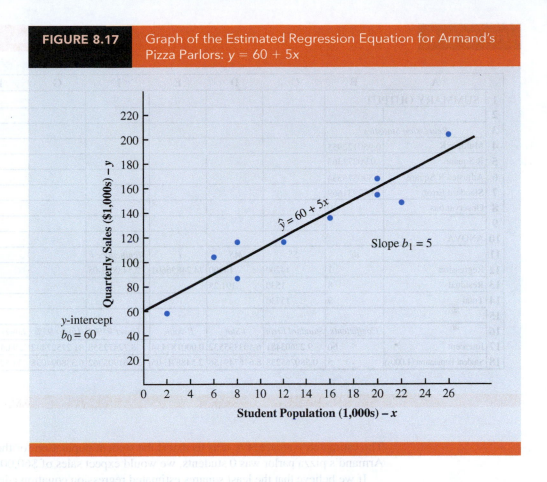

| **FIGURE 8.17** | Graph of the Estimated Regression Equation for Armand's Pizza Parlors: $y = 60 + 5x$ |

each possible value of x. The resulting equation of the line is called the estimated regression equation.

Using the least-squares method of estimation, the estimated regression equation is:

$$\hat{y}_i = b_0 + b_1 x_i, \qquad \textbf{(8.14)}$$

where

$\hat{y}_i$ = estimated value of the dependent variable (quarterly sales) for the ith observation
b_0 = intercept of the estimated regression equation
b_1 = slope of the estimated regression equation
x_i = value of the independent variable (student population) for the ith observation

The Excel output for a simple linear regression analysis of the Armand's Pizza data is provided in Figure 8.18.

We see in this output that the estimated intercept b_0 is 60 and the estimated slope b_1 is 5. Thus, the estimated regression equation is:

$$\hat{y}_i = 60 + 5x_i.$$

Note that the values of the independent variable range from 2,000 to 26,000; thus, as discussed in Chapter 7, the y-intercept in such cases is an extrapolation of the regression line and must be interpreted with caution.

The slope of the estimated regression equation ($b_1 = 5$) is positive, implying that, as student population increases, quarterly sales increase. In fact, we can conclude (because sales are measured in thousands of dollars and student population in thousands) that an increase in the student population of 1,000 is associated with an increase of $5,000 in expected quarterly sales; that is, quarterly sales are expected to increase by $5 per student.

FIGURE 8.18   Excel Simple Linear Regression Output for Armand's Pizza Parlors

	A	B	C	D	E	F	G	H	I
1	SUMMARY OUTPUT								
2									
3	*Regression Statistics*								
4	Multiple R	0.950122955							
5	R Square	0.90273363							
6	Adjusted R Square	0.890575334							
7	Standard Error	13.82931669							
8	Observations	10							
9									
10	ANOVA								
11		*df*	*SS*	*MS*	*F*	*Significance F*			
12	Regression	1	14200	14200	74.24836601	2.54887E-05			
13	Residual	8	1530	191.25					
14	Total	9	15730						
15									
16		*Coefficients*	*Standard Error*	*t Stat*	*P-value*	*Lower 95%*	*Upper 95%*	*Lower 99.0%*	*Upper 99.0%*
17	Intercept	60	9.22603481	6.503335532	0.000187444	38.72472558	81.27527442	29.04307968	90.95692032
18	Student Population (1,000s)	5	0.580265238	8.616749156	2.54887E-05	3.661905962	6.338094038	3.052985371	6.947014629

The estimated y-intercept b_0 tells us that if the student population for the location of an Armand's pizza parlor was 0 students, we would expect sales of $60,000.

If we believe that the least squares estimated regression equation adequately describes the relationship between x and y, using the estimated regression equation to forecast the value of y for a given value of x seems reasonable. For example, if we wanted to forecast quarterly sales for a new restaurant to be located near a campus with 16,000 students, we would compute:

$$\hat{y} = 60 + 5(16)$$
$$= 140.$$

Hence, we would forecast quarterly sales of $140,000.

The sales forecasting problem facing Armand's Pizza Parlors illustrates how simple linear regression analysis can be used to develop forecasts when a causal variable is available.

Combining Causal Variables with Trend and Seasonality Effects

Regression models are very flexible and can incorporate both causal variables and time series effects. Suppose we had a time series of several years of quarterly sales data and advertising expenditures for a single Armand's restaurant. If we suspected that sales were related to the causal variable advertising expenditures and that sales showed trend and seasonal effects, we could incorporate each into a single model by combining the approaches we have outlined. If we believe that the effect of advertising is not immediate, we might also try to find a relationship between sales in period t and advertising in the previous period, $t - 1$.

The value of an independent variable from the prior period is referred to as a lagged variable.

Multiple regression analysis also can be applied in these situations if additional data for other independent variables are available. For example, suppose that the management of Armand's Pizza Parlors also believes that the number of competitors near the college campus is related to quarterly sales. Intuitively, management believes that restaurants located near campuses with fewer competitors generate more sales revenue than those located near campuses with more competitors. With additional data, multiple regression analysis could be used to develop an equation relating quarterly sales to the size of the student population and the number of competitors.

Considerations in Using Regression in Forecasting

Although regression analysis allows for the estimation of complex forecasting models, we must be cautious about using such models and guard against the potential for overfitting our model to the sample data. Spyros Makridakis, a noted forecasting expert, conducted research showing that simple techniques usually outperform more complex procedures for short-term forecasting. Using a more sophisticated and expensive procedure will not guarantee better forecasts. However, many research studies, including those done by Makridakis, have also shown that quantitative forecasting models such as those presented in this chapter commonly outperform qualitative forecasts made by "experts." Thus, there is good reason to use quantitative forecasting methods whenever data are available.

Whether a regression approach provides a good forecast depends largely on how well we are able to identify and obtain data for independent variables that are closely related to the time series. Generally, during the development of an estimated regression equation, we will want to consider many possible sets of independent variables. Thus, part of the regression analysis procedure should focus on the selection of the set of independent variables that provides the best forecasting model.

8.5 Determining the Best Forecasting Model to Use

Given the variety of forecasting models and approaches, the obvious question is, "For a given forecasting study, how does one choose an appropriate model?" As discussed throughout this text, it is always a good idea to get descriptive statistics on the data and graph the data so that they can be visually inspected. In the case of times series data, a visual inspection can indicate whether seasonality appears to be a factor and whether a linear or nonlinear trend seems to exist. For causal modeling, scatter charts can indicate whether strong linear or nonlinear relationships exist between the independent and dependent variables. If certain relationships appear totally random, this may lead you to exclude these variables from the model.

As in regression analysis, you may be working with large data sets when generating a forecasting model. In such cases, it is recommended to divide your data into training and validation sets. For example, you might have five years of monthly data available to produce a time series forecast. You could use the first three years of data as a training set to estimate a model or a collection of models that appear to provide good forecasts. You might develop exponential smoothing models and regression models for the training set. You could then use the last two years as a validation set to assess and compare the models' performances. Based on the errors produced by the different models for the validation set, you could ultimately pick the model that minimizes some forecast error measure, such as MAE, MSE or MAPE. However, you must exercise caution in using the older portion of a time series for the training set and the more recent portion of the time series as the validation set; if the behavior of the time series has changed recently, the older portion of the time series may no longer show patterns similar to the more recent values of the time series, and a forecasting model based on such data will not perform well.

Some software packages try many different forecasting models on time series data (those included in this chapter and more) and report back optimal model parameters and error measures for each model tested. Although some of these software packages will even automatically select the best model to use, ultimately the user should decide which model to use going forward based on a combination of the software output and the user's managerial knowledge.

SUMMARY

This chapter provided an introduction to the basic methods of time series analysis and forecasting. First, we showed that to explain the behavior of a time series, it is often helpful to graph the time series and identify whether trend, seasonal, and/or cyclical components are present in the time series. The methods we have discussed are based on assumptions about which of these components are present in the time series.

We discussed how smoothing methods can be used to forecast a time series that exhibits no significant trend, seasonal, or cyclical effect. The moving averages approach consists of computing an average of past data values and then using that average as the forecast for the next period. In the exponential smoothing method, a weighted average of past time series values is used to compute a forecast.

For time series that have only a long-term trend, we showed how regression analysis could be used to make trend projections. For time series with seasonal influences, we showed how to incorporate the seasonality for more accurate forecasts. We described how regression analysis can be used to develop causal forecasting models that relate values of the variable to be forecast (the dependent variable) to other independent variables that are believed to explain (cause) the behavior of the dependent variable. Finally, we have provided guidance on how to select an appropriate model from the models discussed in this chapter.

GLOSSARY

Autoregressive model A regression model in which a regression relationship based on past time series values is used to predict the future time series values.

Causal models Forecasting methods that relate a time series to other variables that are believed to explain or cause its behavior.

Cyclical pattern The component of the time series that results in periodic above-trend and below-trend behavior of the time series lasting more than one year.

Exponential smoothing A forecasting technique that uses a weighted average of past time series values as the forecast.

Forecast A prediction of future values of a time series.

Forecast error The amount by which the forecasted value $\hat{y}_t$ differs from the observed value y_t, denoted $e_t = y_t - \hat{y}_t$.

Mean absolute error (MAE) A measure of forecasting accuracy; the average of the values of the forecast errors. Also referred to as mean absolute deviation (MAD).

Mean absolute percentage error (MAPE) A measure of the accuracy of a forecasting method; the average of the absolute values of the errors as a percentage of the corresponding forecast values.

Mean squared error (MSE) A measure of the accuracy of a forecasting method; the average of the sum of the squared differences between the forecast values and the actual time series values.

Moving averages method A method of forecasting or smoothing a time series that uses the average of the most recent n data values in the time series as the forecast for the next period.

Naïve forecasting method A forecasting technique that uses the value of the time series from the most recent period as the forecast for the current period.

Seasonal pattern The component of the time series that shows a periodic pattern over one year or less.

Smoothing constant A parameter of the exponential smoothing model that provides the weight given to the most recent time series value in the calculation of the forecast value.

Stationary time series A time series whose statistical properties are independent of time.

Time series A set of observations on a variable measured at successive points in time or over successive periods of time.

Trend The long-run shift or movement in the time series observable over several periods of time.

PROBLEMS

1. Consider the following time series data:

Week	1	2	3	4	5	6
Value	18	13	16	11	17	14

Using the naïve method (most recent value) as the forecast for the next week, compute the following measures of forecast accuracy:
   a. Mean absolute error
   b. Mean squared error
   c. Mean absolute percentage error
   d. What is the forecast for week 7?

2. Refer to the time series data in Problem 1. Using the average of all the historical data as a forecast for the next period, compute the following measures of forecast accuracy:
   a. Mean absolute error
   b. Mean squared error
   c. Mean absolute percentage error
   d. What is the forecast for week 7?

3. Problems 1 and 2 used different forecasting methods. Which method appears to provide the more accurate forecasts for the historical data? Explain.

4. Consider the following time series data:

Month	1	2	3	4	5	6	7
Value	24	13	20	12	19	23	15

 a. Compute MSE using the most recent value as the forecast for the next period. What is the forecast for month 8?
 b. Compute MSE using the average of all the data available as the forecast for the next period. What is the forecast for month 8?
 c. Which method appears to provide the better forecast?

5. Consider the following time series data:

Week	1	2	3	4	5	6
Value	18	13	16	11	17	14

 a. Construct a time series plot. What type of pattern exists in the data?
 b. Develop a three-week moving average for this time series. Compute MSE and a forecast for week 7.
 c. Use $\alpha = 0.2$ to compute the exponential smoothing values for the time series. Compute MSE and a forecast for week 7.
 d. Compare the three-week moving average forecast with the exponential smoothing forecast using $\alpha = 0.2$. Which appears to provide the better forecast based on MSE? Explain.
 e. Use trial and error to find a value of the exponential smoothing coefficient α that results in a smaller MSE than what you calculated for $\alpha = 0.2$.

6. Consider the following time series data:

Month	1	2	3	4	5	6	7
Value	24	13	20	12	19	23	15

 a. Construct a time series plot. What type of pattern exists in the data?
 b. Develop a three-week moving average for this time series. Compute MSE and a forecast for week 8.
 c. Use $\alpha = 0.2$ to compute the exponential smoothing values for the time series. Compute MSE and a forecast for week 8.
 d. Compare the three-week moving average forecast with the exponential smoothing forecast using $\alpha = 0.2$. Which appears to provide the better forecast based on MSE?
 e. Use trial and error to find a value of the exponential smoothing coefficient α that results in a smaller MSE than what you calculated for $\alpha = 0.2$.

7. Refer to the gasoline sales time series data in Table 8.1.
 a. Compute four-week and five-week moving averages for the time series.
 b. Compute the MSE for the four-week and five-week moving average forecasts.
 c. What appears to be the best number of weeks of past data (three, four, or five) to use in the moving average computation? Recall that the MSE for the three-week moving average is 10.22.

8. With the gasoline time series data from Table 8.1, show the exponential smoothing forecasts using $\alpha = 0.1$.
 a. Applying the MSE measure of forecast accuracy, would you prefer a smoothing constant of $\alpha = 0.1$ or $\alpha = 0.2$ for the gasoline sales time series?
 b. Are the results the same if you apply MAE as the measure of accuracy?
 c. What are the results if MAPE is used?

9. With a smoothing constant of $\alpha = 0.2$, equation (8.7) shows that the forecast for week 13 of the gasoline sales data from Table 8.1 is given by $\hat{y}_{13} = 0.2y_{12} + 0.8\hat{y}_{12}$. However, the forecast for week 12 is given by $\hat{y}_{12} = 0.2y_{11} + 0.8\hat{y}_{11}$. Thus, we could combine these two results to show that the forecast for week 13 can be written as:

$$\hat{y}_{13} = 0.2y_{12} + 0.8(0.2y_{11} + 0.8\hat{y}_{11}) = 0.2y_{12} + 0.16y_{11} + 0.64\hat{y}_{11}.$$

   a. Making use of the fact that $\hat{y}_{11} = 0.2y_{10} + 0.8\hat{y}_{10}$ (and similarly for $\hat{y}_{10}$ and $\hat{y}_{9}$), continue to expand the expression for $\hat{y}_{13}$ until it is written in terms of the past data values $y_{12}, y_{11}, y_{10}, y_{9}, y_{8}$, and the forecast for period 8, $\hat{y}_{8}$.
   b. Refer to the coefficients or weights for the past values $y_{12}, y_{11}, y_{10}, y_{9}, y_{8}$. What observation can you make about how exponential smoothing weights past data values in arriving at new forecasts? Compare this weighting pattern with the weighting pattern of the moving averages method.

10. United Dairies, Inc., supplies milk to several independent grocers throughout Dade County, Florida. Managers at United Dairies want to develop a forecast of the number of half gallons of milk sold per week. Sales data for the past 12 weeks are:

DATA *file*
UnitedDairies

Week	Sales	Week	Sales
1	2,750	7	3,300
2	3,100	8	3,100
3	3,250	9	2,950
4	2,800	10	3,000
5	2,900	11	3,200
6	3,050	12	3,150

   a. Construct a time series plot. What type of pattern exists in the data?
   b. Use exponential smoothing with $\alpha = 0.4$ to develop a forecast of demand for week 13. What is the resulting MSE?

11. For the Hawkins Company, the monthly percentages of all shipments received on time over the past 12 months are 80, 82, 84, 83, 83, 84, 85, 84, 82, 83, 84, and 83.

DATA *file*
Hawkins

   a. Construct a time series plot. What type of pattern exists in the data?
   b. Compare a three-month moving average forecast with an exponential smoothing forecast for $\alpha = 0.2$. Which provides the better forecasts using MSE as the measure of model accuracy?
   c. What is the forecast for next month?

12. Corporate triple A bond interest rates for 12 consecutive months are as follows:

9.5   9.3   9.4   9.6   9.8   9.7   9.8   10.5   9.9   9.7   9.6   9.6

DATA *file*
TripleABond

   a. Construct a time series plot. What type of pattern exists in the data?
   b. Develop three-month and four-month moving averages for this time series. Does the three-month or the four-month moving average provide the better forecasts based on MSE? Explain.
   c. What is the moving average forecast for the next month?

13. The values of Alabama building contracts (in millions of dollars) for a 12-month period are as follows:

DATA *file*
Alabama

240   350   230   260   280   320   220   310   240   310   240   230

   a. Construct a time series plot. What type of pattern exists in the data?
   b. Compare a three-month moving average forecast with an exponential smoothing forecast. Use $\alpha = 0.2$. Which provides the better forecasts based on MSE?
   c. What is the forecast for the next month using exponential smoothing with $\alpha = 0.2$?

14. The following time series shows the sales of a particular product over the past 12 months.

DATA *file*

MonthlySales

Month	Sales	Month	Sales
1	105	7	145
2	135	8	140
3	120	9	100
4	105	10	80
5	90	11	100
6	120	12	110

  a. Construct a time series plot. What type of pattern exists in the data?
  b. Use $\alpha = 0.3$ to compute the exponential smoothing values for the time series.
  c. Use trial and error to find a value of the exponential smoothing coefficient α that results in a relatively small MSE.

15. Ten weeks of data on the Commodity Futures Index are:

DATA *file*

CommodityFutures

    7.35 7.40 7.55 7.56 7.60 7.52 7.52 7.70 7.62 7.55

  a. Construct a time series plot. What type of pattern exists in the data?
  b. Use trial and error to find a value of the exponential smoothing coefficient α that results in a relatively small MSE.

16. The following table reports the percentage of stocks in a portfolio for nine quarters:

Quarter	Stock (%)
Year 1, Quarter 1	29.8
Year 1, Quarter 2	31.0
Year 1, Quarter 3	29.9
Year 1, Quarter 4	30.1
Year 2, Quarter 1	32.2
Year 2, Quarter 2	31.5
Year 2, Quarter 3	32.0
Year 2, Quarter 4	31.9
Year 3, Quarter 1	30.0

DATA *file*

Portfolio

  a. Construct a time series plot. What type of pattern exists in the data?
  b. Use trial and error to find a value of the exponential smoothing coefficient α that results in a relatively small MSE.
  c. Using the exponential smoothing model you developed in part (b), what is the forecast of the percentage of stocks in a typical portfolio for the second quarter of year 3?

17. Consider the following time series:

t	1	2	3	4	5
y_t	6	11	9	14	15

  a. Construct a time series plot. What type of pattern exists in the data?
  b. Use simple linear regression analysis to find the parameters for the line that minimizes MSE for this time series.
  c. What is the forecast for $t = 6$?

18. Consider the following time series:

t	1	2	3	4	5	6	7
y_t	120	110	100	96	94	92	88

    a. Construct a time series plot. What type of pattern exists in the data?

    b. Use simple linear regression analysis to find the parameters for the line that minimizes MSE for this time series.

    c. What is the forecast for $t = 8$?

19. Because of high tuition costs at state and private universities, enrollments at community colleges have increased dramatically in recent years. The following data show the enrollment for Jefferson Community College for the nine most recent years:

DATA *file*

Jefferson

Year	Period (t)	Enrollment (1,000s)
2001	1	6.5
2002	2	8.1
2003	3	8.4
2004	4	10.2
2005	5	12.5
2006	6	13.3
2007	7	13.7
2008	8	17.2
2009	9	18.1

    a. Construct a time series plot. What type of pattern exists in the data?

    b. Use simple linear regression analysis to find the parameters for the line that minimizes MSE for this time series.

    c. What is the forecast for year 10?

20. The Seneca Children's Fund (SCF) is a local charity that runs a summer camp for disadvantaged children. The fund's board of directors has been working very hard over recent years to decrease the amount of overhead expenses, a major factor in how charities are rated by independent agencies. The following data show the percentage of the money SCF has raised that was spent on administrative and fund-raising expenses over the past seven years:

DATA *file*

Seneca

Period (t)	Expense (%)
1	13.9
2	12.2
3	10.5
4	10.4
5	11.5
6	10.0
7	8.5

    a. Construct a time series plot. What type of pattern exists in the data?

    b. Use simple linear regression analysis to find the parameters for the line that minimizes MSE for this time series.

    c. Forecast the percentage of administrative expenses for year 8.

    d. If SCF can maintain its current trend in reducing administrative expenses, how long will it take SCF to achieve a level of 5% or less?

21. The president of a small manufacturing firm is concerned about the continual increase in manufacturing costs over the past several years. The following figures provide a time series of the cost per unit for the firm's leading product over the past eight years:

DATA *file*

ManufacturingCosts

Year	Cost/Unit ($)	Year	Cost/Unit ($)
1	20.00	5	26.60
2	24.50	6	30.00
3	28.20	7	31.00
4	27.50	8	36.00

a. Construct a time series plot. What type of pattern exists in the data?
b. Use simple linear regression analysis to find the parameters for the line that minimizes MSE for this time series.
c. What is the average cost increase that the firm has been realizing per year?
d. Compute an estimate of the cost/unit for next year.

22. Consider the following time series:

Quarter	Year 1	Year 2	Year 3
1	71	68	62
2	49	41	51
3	58	60	53
4	78	81	72

a. Construct a time series plot. What type of pattern exists in the data? Is there an indication of a seasonal pattern?
b. Use a multiple linear regression model with dummy variables as follows to develop an equation to account for seasonal effects in the data: Qtr1 = 1 if quarter 1, 0 otherwise; Qtr2 = 1 if quarter 2, 0 otherwise; Qtr3 = 1 if quarter 3, 0 otherwise.
c. Compute the quarterly forecasts for next year.

23. Consider the following time series data:

Quarter	Year 1	Year 2	Year 3
1	4	6	7
2	2	3	6
3	3	5	6
4	5	7	8

a. Construct a time series plot. What type of pattern exists in the data?
b. Use a multiple regression model with dummy variables as follows to develop an equation to account for seasonal effects in the data: Qtr1 = 1 if quarter 1, 0 otherwise; Qtr2 = 1 if quarter 2, 0 otherwise; Qtr3 = 1 if quarter 3, 0 otherwise.
c. Compute the quarterly forecasts for next year based on the model you developed in part (b).
d. Use a multiple regression model to develop an equation to account for trend and seasonal effects in the data. Use the dummy variables you developed in part (b) to capture seasonal effects and create a variable t such that $t = 1$ for quarter 1 in year 1, $t = 2$ for quarter 2 in year 1, . . . $t = 12$ for quarter 4 in year 3.
e. Compute the quarterly forecasts for next year based on the model you developed in part (d).
f. Is the model you developed in part (b) or the model you developed in part (d) more effective? Justify your answer.

24. The quarterly sales data (number of copies sold) for a college textbook over the past three years are as follows:

TextbookSales

Year	1	1	1	1	2	2	2	2	3	3	3	3
Quarter	1	2	3	4	1	2	3	4	1	2	3	4
Sales	1,690	940	2,625	2,500	1,800	900	2,900	2,360	1,850	1,100	2,930	2,615

a. Construct a time series plot. What type of pattern exists in the data?
b. Use a regression model with dummy variables as follows to develop an equation to account for seasonal effects in the data: Qtr1 = 1 if quarter 1, 0 otherwise; Qtr2 = 1 if quarter 2, 0 otherwise; Qtr3 = 1 if quarter 3, 0 otherwise.
c. Based on the model you developed in part (b), compute the quarterly forecasts for next year.
d. Let $t = 1$ to refer to the observation in quarter 1 of year 1; $t = 2$ to refer to the observation in quarter 2 of year 1; . . . ; and $t = 12$ to refer to the observation in quarter 4 of year 3. Using the dummy variables defined in part (b) and t, develop an equation to account for seasonal effects and any linear trend in the time series.
e. Based upon the seasonal effects in the data and linear trend, compute the quarterly forecasts for next year.
f. Is the model you developed in part (b) or the model you developed in part (d) more effective? Justify your answer.

25. Air pollution control specialists in southern California monitor the amount of ozone, carbon dioxide, and nitrogen dioxide in the air on an hourly basis. The hourly time series data exhibit seasonality, with the levels of pollutants showing patterns that vary over the hours in the day. On July 15, 16, and 17, the following levels of nitrogen dioxide were observed for the 12 hours from 6:00 a.m. to 6:00 p.m.:

Pollution

July 15	25	28	35	50	60	60	40	35	30	25	25	20
July 16	28	30	35	48	60	65	50	40	35	25	20	20
July 17	35	42	45	70	72	75	60	45	40	25	25	25

a. Construct a time series plot. What type of pattern exists in the data?
b. Use a multiple linear regression model with dummy variables as follows to develop an equation to account for seasonal effects in the data:

   Hour1 = 1 if the reading was made between 6:00 a.m. and 7:00 a.m.; 0 otherwise;
   Hour2 = 1 if the reading was made between 7:00 a.m. and 8:00 a.m.; 0 otherwise;
   :
   Hour11 = 1 if the reading was made between 4:00 p.m. and 5:00 p.m., 0 otherwise.

   Note that when the values of the 11 dummy variables are equal to 0, the observation corresponds to the 5:00 p.m. to 6:00 p.m. hour.
c. Using the equation developed in part (b), compute estimates of the levels of nitrogen dioxide for July 18.
d. Let $t = 1$ to refer to the observation in hour 1 on July 15; $t = 2$ to refer to the observation in hour 2 of July 15; . . . ; and $t = 36$ to refer to the observation in hour 12 of July 17. Using the dummy variables defined in part (b) and t, develop an equation to account for seasonal effects and any linear trend in the time series.

e. Based on the seasonal effects in the data and linear trend estimated in part (d), compute estimates of the levels of nitrogen dioxide for July 18.

f. Is the model you developed in part (b) or the model you developed in part (d) more effective? Justify your answer.

26. South Shore Construction builds permanent docks and seawalls along the southern shore of Long Island, New York. Although the firm has been in business only five years, revenue has increased from $308,000 in the first year of operation to $1,084,000 in the most recent year. The following data show the quarterly sales revenue in thousands of dollars:

DATA *file*

SouthShore

Quarter	Year 1	Year 2	Year 3	Year 4	Year 5
1	20	37	75	92	176
2	100	136	155	202	282
3	175	245	326	384	445
4	13	26	48	82	181

a. Construct a time series plot. What type of pattern exists in the data?

b. Use a multiple regression model with dummy variables as follows to develop an equation to account for seasonal effects in the data: Qtr1 = 1 if quarter 1, 0 otherwise; Qtr2 = 1 if quarter 2, 0 otherwise; Qtr3 = 1 if quarter 3, 0 otherwise.

c. Based on the model you developed in part (b), compute estimates of quarterly sales for year 6.

d. Let Period = 1 refer to the observation in quarter 1 of year 1; Period = 2 refer to the observation in quarter 2 of year 1; . . . and Period = 20 refer to the observation in quarter 4 of year 5. Using the dummy variables defined in part (b) and the variable Period, develop an equation to account for seasonal effects and any linear trend in the time series.

e. Based on the seasonal effects in the data and linear trend estimated in part (c), compute estimates of quarterly sales for year 6.

f. Is the model you developed in part (b) or the model you developed in part (d) more effective? Justify your answer.

27. Hogs & Dawgs is an ice cream parlor on the border of north-central Louisiana and southern Arkansas that serves 43 flavors of ice creams, sherbets, frozen yogurts, and sorbets. During the summer Hogs & Dawgs is open from 1:00 p.m. to 10:00 p.m. on Monday through Saturday, and the owner believes that sales change systematically from hour to hour throughout the day. She also believes her sales increase as the outdoor temperature increases. Hourly sales and the outside temperature at the start of each hour for the last week are provided in the file *IceCreamSales*.

DATA *file*

IceCreamSales

a. Construct a time series plot of hourly sales and a scatter plot of outdoor temperature and hourly sales. What types of relationships exist in the data?

b. Use a simple regression model with outside temperature as the causal variable to develop an equation to account for the relationship between outside temperature and hourly sales in the data. Based on this model, compute an estimate of hourly sales for today from 2:00 p.m. to 3:00 p.m. if the temperature at 2:00 p.m. is 93°F.

c. Use a multiple linear regression model with the causal variable outside temperature and dummy variables as follows to develop an equation to account for both seasonal effects and the relationship between outside temperature and hourly sales in the data in the data:

Hour1 = 1 if the sales were recorded between 1:00 p.m. and 2:00 p.m., 0 otherwise;
Hour2 = 1 if the sales were recorded between 2:00 p.m. and 3:00 p.m., 0 otherwise;
⋮
Hour8 = 1 if the sales were recorded between 8:00 p.m. and 9:00 p.m., 0 otherwise.

Note that when the values of the 8 dummy variables are equal to 0, the observation corresponds to the 9:00-to-10:00-p.m. hour.

Based on this model, compute an estimate of hourly sales for today from 2:00 p.m. to 3:00 p.m. if the temperature at 2:00 p.m. is 93°F.

d. Is the model you developed in part (b) or the model you developed in part (c) more effective? Justify your answer.

28. Donna Nickles manages a gasoline station on the corner of Bristol Avenue and Harpst Street in Arcata, California. Her station is a franchise, and the parent company calls her station every day at midnight to give her the prices for various grades of gasoline for the upcoming day. Over the past eight weeks Donna has recorded the price and sales (in gallons) of regular-grade gasoline at her station as well as the price of regular-grade gasoline charged by her competitor across the street. She is curious about the sensitivity of her sales to the price of regular gasoline she charges and the price of regular gasoline charged by her competitor across the street. She also wonders whether her sales differ systematically by day of the week and whether her station has experienced a trend in sales over the past eight weeks. The data collected by Donna for each day of the past eight weeks are provided in the file *GasStation*.

a. Construct a time series plot of daily sales, a scatter plot of the price Donna charges for a gallon of regular gasoline and daily sales at Donna's station, and a scatter plot of the price Donna's competitor charges for a gallon of regular gasoline and daily sales at Donna's station. What types of relationships exist in the data?

b. Use a multiple regression model with the price Donna charges for a gallon of regular gasoline and the price Donna's competitor charges for a gallon of regular gasoline as causal variables to develop an equation to account for the relationships between these prices and Donna's daily sales in the data. Based on this model, compute an estimate of sales for a day on which Donna is charging $3.50 for a gallon for regular gasoline and her competitor is charging $3.45 for a gallon of regular gasoline.

c. Use a multiple linear regression model with the trend and dummy variables as follows to develop an equation to account for both trend and seasonal effects in the data:

Monday = 1 if the sales were recorded on a Monday, 0 otherwise;
Tuesday = 1 if the sales were recorded on a Tuesday, 0 otherwise;
⋮
Saturday = 1 if the sales were recorded on a Saturday, 0 otherwise;

Note that when the values of the six dummy variables are equal to 0, the observation corresponds to Sunday.

Based on this model, compute an estimate of sales for Tuesday of the first week after Donna collected her data.

d. Use a multiple regression model with the price Donna charges for a gallon of regular gasoline and the price Donna's competitor charges for a gallon of regular gasoline as causal variables and the trend and dummy variables from part (c) to create an equation to account for the relationships between these prices and daily sales as well as the trend and seasonal effects in the data. Based on this model, compute an estimate of sales for Tuesday of the first week after Donna collected her data a day if Donna is charging $3.50 for a gallon for regular gasoline and her competitor is charging $3.45 for a gallon of regular gasoline.

e. Which of the three models you developed in parts (b), (c), and (d) is most effective? Justify your answer.

CASE PROBLEM: FORECASTING FOOD AND BEVERAGE SALES

The Vintage Restaurant, on Captiva Island near Fort Myers, Florida, is owned and operated by Karen Payne. The restaurant just completed its third year of operation. During those three years, Karen sought to establish a reputation for the restaurant as a high-quality dining establishment that specializes in fresh seafood. Through the efforts of Karen and her staff, her restaurant has become one of the best and fastest-growing restaurants on the island.

To better plan for future growth of the restaurant, Karen needs to develop a system that will enable her to forecast food and beverage sales by month for up to one year in advance. The following table shows the value of food and beverage sales ($1,000s) for the first three years of operation:

DATA *file*

Vintage

Month	First Year	Second Year	Third Year
January	242	263	282
February	235	238	255
March	232	247	265
April	178	193	205
May	184	193	210
June	140	149	160
July	145	157	166
August	152	161	174
September	110	122	126
October	130	130	148
November	152	167	173
December	206	230	235

Managerial Report

Perform an analysis of the sales data for the Vintage Restaurant. Prepare a report for Karen that summarizes your findings, forecasts, and recommendations. Include the following:

1. A time series plot. Comment on the underlying pattern in the time series.
2. Using the dummy variable approach, forecast sales for January through December of the fourth year.

How would you explain this model to Karen?

Assume that January sales for the fourth year turn out to be $295,000. What was your forecast error? If this error is large, Karen may be puzzled about the difference between your forecast and the actual sales value. What can you do to resolve her uncertainty about the forecasting procedure?

Chapter 8 Appendix

Appendix 8.1 Using the Excel Forecast Sheet

Excel 2016 features a new tool called Forecast Sheet. This interface automatically produces forecasts using the Holt–Winters additive seasonal smoothing model, which is an exponential smoothing approach to estimating additive linear trend and seasonal effects. It also generates a variety of other outputs that are useful in assessing the accuracy of the forecast model it produces.

Excel refers to the forecasting approach used by Forecast Sheet as the AAA exponential smoothing (ETS) algorithm, where AAA stands for additive error, additive trend, and additive seasonality.

We will demonstrate Forecast Sheet on the four years of quarterly smartphone sales that are provided in Table 8.6. A review of the time series plot of these data in Figure 8.6 provides clear evidence of an increasing linear trend and a seasonal pattern (sales are consistently lowest in the second quarter of each year and highest in quarters 3 and 4). We concluded in Section 8.4 that we need to use a forecasting method that is capable of dealing with both trend and seasonality when developing a forecasting model for this time series, and so it is appropriate to use Forecast Sheet to produce forecasts for these data.

We begin by putting the data into the format required by Forecast Sheet. The time series data must be collected on a consistent interval (i.e., annually, quarterly, monthly, etc.), and the spreadsheet must include two data series in contiguous columns or rows that include:

- a series with the dates or periods in the time series
- a series with corresponding time series values

DATA *file*

SmartPhoneSales

First, open the file *SmartPhoneSales*, then insert a column between column B (Quarter) and Column C (Sales (1,000s)). Enter *Period* into cell C1; this will be the heading for the column of values that will represent the periods in our data. Next enter *1* in cell C2, *2* in cell C3, *3* in cell C4, and so on, ending with *16* in Cell C17 as shown in Figure 8.19.

Now that the data are properly formatted for Forecast Sheet, the following steps can be used to produce forecasts for the next four quarters (periods 17 through 20) with Forecast Sheet:

Step 1. Highlight cells C1:D17 (the data in column C of this highlighted section is what Forecast Sheet refers to as the **Timeline Range** and the data in column D is the **Values Range**).

Step 2. Click the **Data** tab in the Ribbon

Step 3. Click **Forecast Sheet** in the **Forecast** group

Step 4. When the **Create Forecast Worksheet** dialog box appears (Figure 8.20):

Select **20** for **Forecast End**

Click **Options** to expand the **Create Forecast Worksheet** dialog box and show the options (Figure 8.20)

Forecast Sheet requires that the period selected for Forecast Start is one of the periods of the original time series.

Select **16** for **Forecast Start**

Select **95%** for **Confidence Interval**

Under **Seasonality**, click on **Set Manually** and select **4**

Select the checkbox for **Include forecast statistics**

Click **Create**

The results of Forecast Sheet will be output to a new worksheet as shown in Figure 8.21. The output of Forecast Sheet includes the following.

- The period for each of the 16 time series observations and the forecasted time periods in column A
- The actual time series data for periods 1 to 16 in column B

FIGURE 8.19   Smartphone Data Reformatted for Forecast Sheet

	A	B	C	D
1	**Year**	**Quarter**	**Period**	**Sales (1000s)**
2	1	1	1	4.8
3	1	2	2	4.1
4	1	3	3	6.0
5	1	4	4	6.5
6	2	1	5	5.8
7	2	2	6	5.2
8	2	3	7	6.8
9	2	4	8	7.4
10	3	1	9	6.0
11	3	2	10	5.6
12	3	3	11	7.5
13	3	4	12	7.8
14	4	1	13	6.3
15	4	2	14	5.9
16	4	3	15	8.0
17	4	4	16	8.4

- The forecasts for periods 16 to 20 in column C
- The lower confidence bounds for the forecasts for periods 16 to 20 in column D
- The upper confidence bounds for the forecasts for periods 16 to 20 in column E
- A line graph of the time series, forecast values, and forecast interval
- The values of the three parameters (alpha, beta, and gamma) used in the Holt–Winters additive seasonal smoothing model in cells H2:H4 (these values are determined by an algorithm in Forecast Sheet)
- Measures of forecast accuracy in cells H5:H8, including:
  - the MASE, or mean absolute scaled error, in cell H5; MASE, which was not discussed in this chapter, is defined as:

$$\text{MASE} = \frac{1}{n}\sum_{t=1}^{n}\frac{|e_t|}{\frac{1}{n-1}\sum_{t=2}^{n}|y_t - y_{t-1}|}$$

MASE compares the forecast error, e_t to a naïve forecast error given by $|y_t - y_{t-1}|$. If MASE > 1, then the forecast is considered inferior to a naïve forecast; if MASE < 1 the forecast is considered superior to a naïve forecast.

FIGURE 8.20	Create Forecast Worksheet Dialog Box with Options Open for Quarterly Smartphone Sales Data

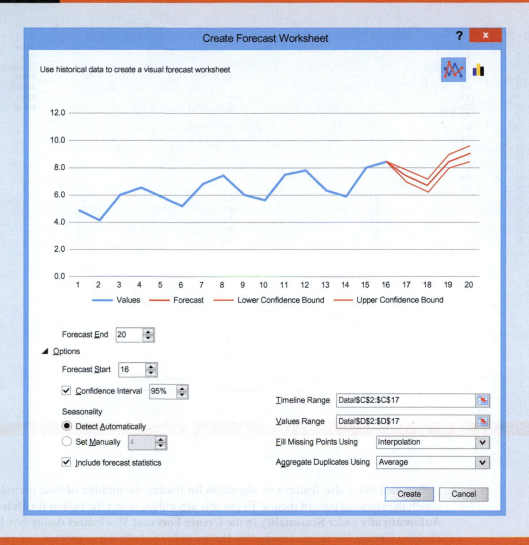

- the SMAPE, or symmetric mean absolute percentage error, in cell H6; SMAPE, which was not discussed in this chapter, is defined as:

$$\text{SMAPE} = \frac{1}{n}\sum_{t=1}^{n}\frac{|e_t|}{(|y_t| + |\hat{y}_t|)/2}$$

SMAPE is similar to mean absolute percentage error (MAPE), discussed in Section 8.2; both SMAPE and MAPE measure forecast error relative to actual values.

- the MAE, or mean absolute error, (as defined in equation 8.3) in cell H7
- the RMSE, or root mean squared error, (which is the square root of the MSE, defined in equation 8.4) in cell H8

FIGURE 8.21   Forecast Sheet Results for Quarterly Smartphone Sales Data

	A	B	C	D	E	F	G	H
1	Period	Sales (1000s)	Forecast(Sales (1000s))	Lower Confidence Bound(Sales (1000s))	Upper Confidence Bound(Sales (1000s))		Statistic	Value
2	1	4.8					Alpha	0.50
3	2	4.1					Beta	0.00
4	3	6.0					Gamma	0.00
5	4	6.5					MASE	0.22
6	5	5.8					SMAPE	0.03
7	6	5.2					MAE	0.20
8	7	6.8					RMSE	0.27
9	8	7.4						
10	9	6.0						
11	10	5.6						
12	11	7.5						
13	12	7.8						
14	13	6.3						
15	14	5.9						
16	15	8.0						
17	16	8.4	8.4	8.4	8.4			
18	17		7.3	6.9	7.8			
19	18		6.6	6.2	7.1			
20	19		8.4	7.9	9.0			
21	20		9.0	8.4	9.6			

Forecast Sheet also features an algorithm for finding the number of time periods over which the seasonal pattern recurs. To use this algorithm, select the option for **Detect Automatically** under **Seasonality** in the **Create Forecast Worksheet** dialog box before clicking **Create**. We suggest using this feature only to confirm a suspected seasonal pattern (Forecast Sheet actually does successfully detect a four-period seasonal pattern in the quarterly smartphone sales data). Using this feature to find a seasonal effect may lead to identification of a spurious pattern that does not actually reflect seasonality and cannot be expected to persist in future periods. This would result in a model that is overfit on the observed time series data and would likely produce very inaccurate forecasts. A forecast model with seasonality should only be fit when the modeler has reason to suspect a specific seasonal pattern.

Forecast Sheet is actually an interface that implements several functions that are new to Excel 2016. We can recreate the output from Forecast Sheet using these Excel functions. For example, after reformatting the data in the same manner as we did in preparation for using Forecast Sheet, we enter the values 17, 18, 19, and 20 into cells C18 through C21, respectively, to denote the periods for which we will be generating forecasts. We then enter the column titles *Forecast*, *Lower Confidence Interval*, *Upper Confidence Interval*, *Statistic*, and *Value* in cells E1 through I1, respectively. Next we enter the statistic

FIGURE 8.22   Smartphone Data Reformatted for Use with Excel Forecast Functions

	A	B	C	D	E	F	G	H	I
1	Year	Quarter	Period	Sales (1000s)	Forecast	Lower Confidence Bound	Upper Confidence Bound	Statistic	Value
2	1	1	1	4.8				Alpha	
3	1	2	2	4.1				Beta	
4	1	3	3	6.0				Gamma	
5	1	4	4	6.5				MASE	
6	2	1	5	5.8				SMAPE	
7	2	2	6	5.2				MAE	
8	2	3	7	6.8				RMSE	
9	2	4	8	7.4					
10	3	1	9	6.0					
11	3	2	10	5.6					
12	3	3	11	7.5				Seasonality	
13	3	4	12	7.8					
14	4	1	13	6.3					
15	4	2	14	5.9					
16	4	3	15	8.0					
17	4	4	16	8.4					
18			17						
19			18						
20			19						
21			20						

labels *Alpha*, *Beta*, *Gamma*, *MASE*, *SMAPE*, *MAE*, and *RMSE* in cells H2 through H8, respectively. Finally, we enter the label *Seasonality* in cell H12. This updated worksheet is shown in Figure 8.22.

We can now recreate the Forecast Sheet results in the updated worksheet shown in Figure 8.22 as follows:

- The forecast generated by Forecast Sheet for period 17 for the smartphone quarterly sales data can be found by using the formula:

$$\text{=FORECAST.ETS(C18,D2:D17,C2:C17,TRUE).}$$

The arguments for this function are the forecast period, the time series values, the timeline associated with the time series values, and a seasonality indicator that is TRUE if Excel is to automatically detect a seasonal pattern for the forecast and FALSE otherwise.

- The margin of error for the confidence bounds generated by Forecast Sheet for period 17 for the smartphone quarterly sales data can be found by using the formula:

$$\text{=FORECAST.ETS.CONFINT(C18,D2:D17,C2:C17,0.95,TRUE)}$$

The confidence bounds generated by Forecast Sheet for period 17 for the smartphone quarterly sales data can be found by using the formulas:

$$\text{=E18-FORECAST.ETS.CONFINT(C18,D2:D17,C2:C17,0.95,TRUE)}$$

and

$$\text{=E18+FORECAST.ETS.CONFINT(C18,D2:D17,C2:C17,0.95,TRUE).}$$

The arguments for this function are identical to the arguments for the FORECAST.ETS function.

- The statistics generated by Forecast Sheet for the smartphone quarterly sales data can be found by using the formulas:

  - Alpha

    =FORECAST.ETS.STAT(D2:D17,C2:C17,1,TRUE)

  - Beta

    =FORECAST.ETS.STAT(D2:D17,C2:C17,2,TRUE)

  - Gamma

    =FORECAST.ETS.STAT(D2:D17,C2:C17,3,TRUE)

  - MASE

    =FORECAST.ETS.STAT(D2:D17,C2:C17,4,TRUE)

  - SMAPE

    =FORECAST.ETS.STAT(D2:D17,C2:C17,5,TRUE)

  - MAE

    =FORECAST.ETS.STAT(D2:D17,C2:C17,6,TRUE)

  - RMSE

    =FORECAST.ETS.STAT(D2:D17,C2:C17,7,TRUE)

The arguments for this function are the time series values, the timeline associated with the time series values, the statistic type, and a seasonality indicator that is TRUE if Excel is to automatically detect a seasonal pattern for the forecast and FALSE otherwise. The statistic-type argument indicates which statistic will be produced by this function. Values for the statistic-type argument include the following:

- Statistic type = 1: requests the alpha parameter used in the Holt–Winters additive seasonal smoothing model
- Statistic type = 2: requests the beta parameter used in the Holt–Winters additive seasonal smoothing model
- Statistic type = 3: requests the gamma parameter used in the Holt–Winters additive seasonal smoothing model
- Statistic type = 4: requests the MASE that results when the Holt–Winters additive seasonal smoothing model is applied to the original time series data
- Statistic type = 5: requests the SMAPE that results when the Holt–Winters additive seasonal smoothing model is applied to the original time series data
- Statistic type = 6: requests the MAE that results when the Holt–Winters additive seasonal smoothing model is applied to the original time series data
- Statistic type = 7: requests the RMSE that results when the Holt–Winters additive seasonal smoothing model is applied to the original time series data

We can also use the formula FORECAST.ETS.SEASONALITY to determine the number of periods in the seasonal pattern detected by the FORECAST.ETS formula in the smartphone quarterly sales data by entering the following formula:

=FORECAST.ETS.SEASONALITY(D2:D17,C2:C17)

FIGURE 8.23	Forecast Results for Quarterly Smartphone Sales Data Using Excel Functions

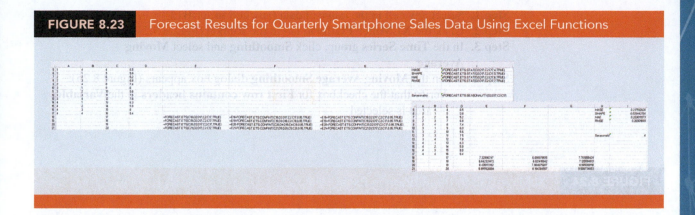

We now illustrate the use of these Excel functions on the smartphone quarterly sales data. We use the:

- FORECAST.ETS function to generate forecasts for periods 17 to 20 in cells E18:E21
- FORECAST.ETS.CONFINT function to generate confidence bounds for these four forecasts in cells F18:G21 (we subtract these values from the corresponding forecast values in cells E18:E21 to create lower confidence bounds, and we add these values to the corresponding forecast values in cells E18:E21 to create upper confidence bounds)
- FORECAST.ETS.STAT function with the appropriate values for the statistics type argument to generate the parameters of our Holt–Winters additive seasonal smoothing model and measures of forecast accuracy in cells I2:I8
- FORECAST.ETS.SEASONALITY function in cell I12 to determine the number of periods in the seasonal pattern detected by the =FORECAST.ETS function.

These results are provided in Figure 8.23.

Finally, note that:

- **Forecast Start** in the **Create Forecast Worksheet** dialog box controls both the first period to be forecasted and the last period to be used to generate the forecast model. If we had selected 15 for Forecast Start we would have generated a forecast model for the smartphone monthly sales data based on only the first 15 periods of data in the original time series.
- Forecast Sheet can accommodate multiple observations for a single period of the time series. The **Aggregate Duplicates Using** option in the **Create Forecast Worksheet** dialog box allows the user to select from several ways to deal with this issue.
- Forecast Sheet allows for up to 30% of the values for the time series variable to be missing. In the smartphone quarterly sales data, the value of sales for up to 30% of the 16 periods (or 4 periods) could be missing and Forecast Sheet will still produce forecasts. The **Fill Missing Points Using** option in the **Create Forecast Worksheet** dialog box allows the user to select whether the missing values will be replaced with zero or with the result of linearly interpolating existing values in the time series.

Appendix 8.2 Forecasting with XLMiner

To show how XLMiner can be used for forecasting, we again develop a three-week moving average for the original 12 weeks of gasoline sales data in Table 8.1 and Figure 8.1. Values for Week are in cells A2:A13 and Sales are in cells B2:B13.

Step 1. Select any cell in the range of data (any cell in A1:B13)
Step 2. Click the **XLMiner Platform** tab in the Ribbon (Figure 8.24)
Step 3. In the **Time Series** group, click **Smoothing** and select **Moving Average**
Step 4. When the **Moving Average Smoothing** dialog box appears (Figure 8.25):
Verify that the checkbox for **First row contains headers** in the **Variables** area is selected

---

FIGURE 8.24   XLMiner Tab in the Ribbon in Excel

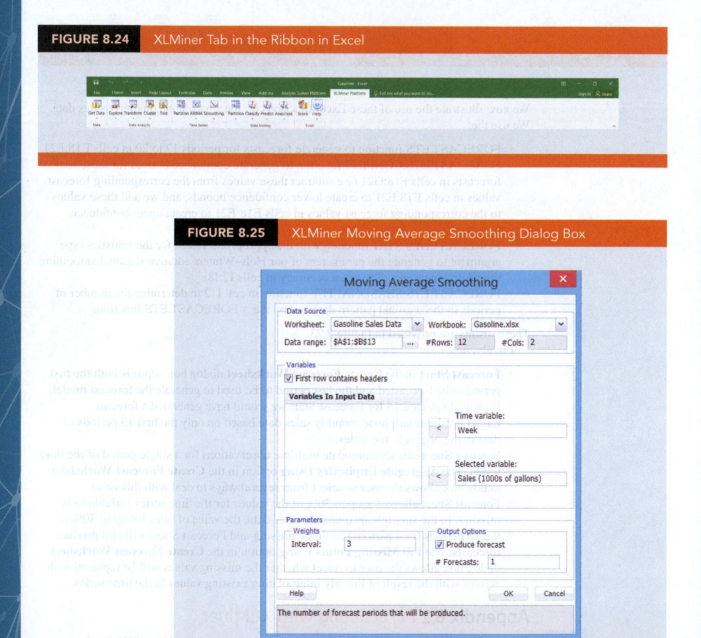

FIGURE 8.25   XLMiner Moving Average Smoothing Dialog Box

Select **Week** in the **Variables In Input Data** box and click the **>** button to move this variable into the **Time variable:** box (or verify that **Week** is in the **Time variable:** box)

Select **Sales (1000s of gallons)** in the **Variables In Input Data** box, and click the **>** button to move this variable into the **Selected variable:** box (or verify that **Sales (1000s of gallons)** is in the **Selected variable:** box)

Enter *3* in the **Interval:** box in the **Weights** area

Select the checkbox for **Produce forecast** in the **Output Options** area

Enter *1* in the **# Forecasts:** box to generate a forecast one period into the future

Click **OK**

XLMiner denotes the mean absolute deviation as the MAD.

The results are shown in Figure 8.26; they are found in the *MASmoothingOutput* worksheet. For this model the MAPE = 14.3566%, the MAD (or MAE) = 2.6667, and the MSE = 10.2222. The forecast for the next week is 19.

FIGURE 8.26   XLMiner Output for the Gasoline Sales Data Three-Period Moving Average Forecast

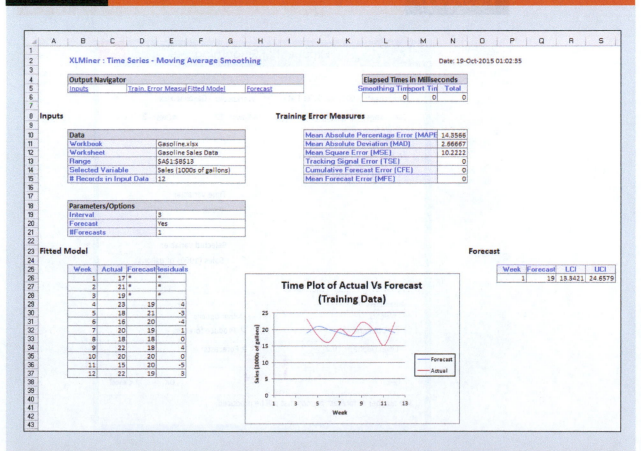

DATA *file*
Gasoline

To fit an exponential smoothing model with $\alpha = 0.2$ for the original 12 weeks of gasoline sales data in Table 8.1 and Figure 8.1, we follow the steps below. Recall again that values for Time are in cells A1:A13 and Sales are in cells B1:B13.

Step 1. Select any cell in the range of data (any cell in A1:B13)
Step 2. Click the **XLMiner Platform** tab in the Ribbon
Step 3. In the **Time Series** group, click **Smoothing** and select **Exponential**
Step 4. When the **Exponential Smoothing** dialog box appears (Figure 8.27):
   Verify that the check box for **First row contains headers** is selected
   Select **Week** in the **Variables In Input Data** box and click the **>** button to move this variable into the **Time variable:** box
   Select **Sales (1000s of gallons)** in the **Variables In Input Data** box and click the **>** button to move this variable into the **Selected Variable:** box
   Enter *0.2* in the **Level (Alpha):** box in the **Weights** area
   Select the check box for **Produce forecast** in the **Output Options** area
   Enter *1* in the **# Forecasts:** box
   Click **OK**

FIGURE 8.27   XLMiner Exponential Smoothing Dialog Box

Exponential Smoothing ✕

Data Source
Worksheet: Gasoline Sales Data ▾   Workbook: Gasoline.xlsx ▾
Data range: $A$1:$B$13 ...   #Rows: 12   #Cols: 2

Variables
☑ First row contains headers

Variables In Input Data

Time variable:
< | Week

Selected variable:
< | Sales (1000s of gallons)

Parameters
Weights
☐ Optimize
Level (Alpha): 0.2

Output Options
☑ Produce forecast
Forecasts: 1

Help   OK   Cancel

The number of forecast periods that will be produced.

The results are shown in Figure 8.28; they are found in the *ExponentialOutput* worksheet. For this model the MAPE = 13.4024%, the MAD (or MAE) = 2.5963, and the MSE = 8.9822. The forecast for the next week is 19.1850.

XLMiner can also be used to compute any of the regression models discussed in this chapter. Refer to Chapter 7 for instructions on how to use these tools.

FIGURE 8.28   XLMiner Output for the Gasoline Sales Data Exponential Smoothing Forecast with $\alpha = 0.2$

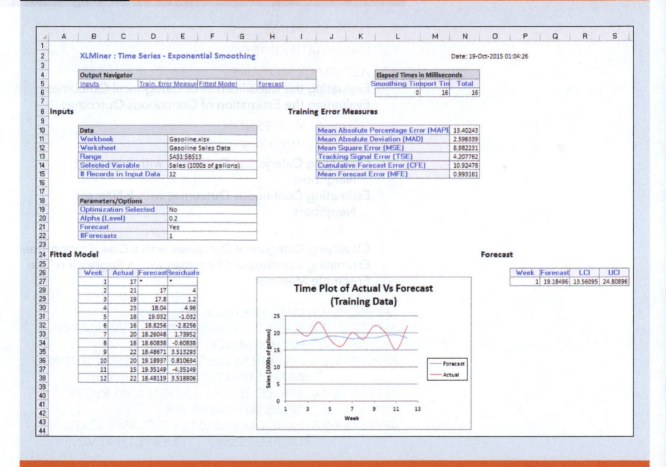

Chapter 9

Predictive Data Mining

CONTENTS

ANALYTICS IN ACTION

Orbitz*

Although they might not see their customers face to face, online retailers are getting to know their patrons to tailor the offerings on their virtual shelves. By mining web-browsing data collected in "cookies"—files that web sites use to track people's web-browsing behavior, online retailers identify trends that can potentially be used to improve customer satisfaction and boost online sales.

For example, consider Orbitz, an online travel agency that books flights, hotels, car rentals, cruises, and other travel activities for its customers. Tracking its patrons' online activities, Orbitz discovered that people who use Mac computers spend as much as

30% more per night on hotels. Orbitz's analytics team has uncovered other factors that affect purchase behavior, including how the shopper arrived at the Orbitz site (Did the user visit Orbitz directly or was he or she referred from another site?), previous booking history on Orbitz, and the shopper's geographic location. Orbitz can act on this and other information gleaned from the vast amount of web data to differentiate the recommendations for hotels, car rentals, flight bookings, etc.

*"On Orbitz, Mac Users Steered to Pricier Hotels" *Wall Street Journal* (2012, June 26).

In Chapter 4, we describe descriptive data-mining methods, such as clustering and association rules, that explore relationships between observations and/or variables.

Organizations are collecting an increasing amount of data, and one of the most pressing tasks is converting this data into actionable insights. A common challenge is to analyze this data to extract information on patterns and trends that can be used to assist decision makers in predicting future events. In this chapter, we discuss predictive methods that can be applied to leverage data to gain customer insights and to establish new business rules to guide managers.

We define an **observation**, or *record*, as the set of recorded values of **variables** associated with a single entity. An observation is often displayed as a row of values in a spreadsheet or database in which the columns correspond to the variables. For example, in direct-marketing data, an observation may correspond to a customer and contain information regarding her response to an e-mail advertisement as well as information regarding her demographic characteristics.

Estimation methods are also referred to as regression methods or prediction methods.

In this chapter, we focus on data-mining methods for predicting an outcome based on a set of input variables, or **features**. These methods are also referred to as **supervised learning**. Linear regression is a well-known supervised learning approach from classical statistics in which observations of a quantitative outcome (the dependent y variable) and one or more corresponding features (the independent variables $x_1, x_2, \ldots, x_q$) are used to create an equation for estimating y values. That is, in supervised learning the outcome variable "supervises" or guides the process of "learning" how to predict future outcomes. In this chapter, we focus on supervised learning

See Chapter 7 for a discussion of linear regression.

methods for the **estimation** of a continuous outcome (e.g., sales revenue) and for **classification** of a categorical outcomes (e.g., whether or not a customer defaults on a loan).

The data-mining process comprises the following steps:

1. *Data sampling.* Extract a sample of data that are relevant to the business problem under consideration.
2. *Data preparation.* Manipulate the data to put it in a form suitable for formal modeling. This step includes addressing missing and erroneous data, reducing the number of variables, and defining new variables. Data exploration is an important part of this step and may involve descriptive statistics, data visualization, and clustering.

Chapter 4 discusses the data-preparation process as well as clustering techniques often used to redefine variables. Chapters 2 and 3 discuss descriptive statistics and data-visualization techniques.

3. *Data partitioning.* Divide the sample data into three sets for the training, validation, and testing of the data-mining algorithm performance.
4. *Data exploration.* Apply descriptive statistics and data visualization to the training set to understand the data and assist in the selection of an appropriate technique.

5. *Model construction.* Apply the appropriate data-mining technique (e.g., *k*-nearest neighbors, regression trees) to the training data set to accomplish the desired data-mining task (classification or estimation).

6. *Model assessment.* Evaluate models by comparing performance on the training and validation data sets. Apply the chosen model to the test data as a final evaluation of model performance.

9.1 Data Sampling

Upon identifying a business problem, data on relevant variables must be obtained for analysis. Although access to large amounts of data offers the potential to unlock insight and improve decision making, it comes with the risk of drowning in a sea of data. Data repositories with millions of observations over hundreds of measured variables are now common. If the volume of relevant data is extremely large (thousands of observations or more), it is unnecessary (and computationally difficult) to use all the data in order to perform a detailed analysis. When dealing with large volumes of data (with hundreds of thousands or millions of observations), best practice is to extract a representative sample (with thousands or tens of thousands of observations) for analysis. A sample is representative if the analyst can make the same conclusions from it as from the entire population of data.

There are no definite rules to determine the size of a sample. The sample of data must be large enough to contain significant information, yet small enough to manipulate quickly. If the sample is too small, relationships in the data may be missed or spurious relationships may be suggested. Perhaps the best advice is to use enough data to eliminate any doubt about whether the sample size is sufficient; data-mining algorithms typically are more effective given more data. If we are investigating a rare event (e.g., click-through on an advertisement posted on a web site), the sample should be large enough to ensure several hundred to thousands of observations that correspond to click-throughs. That is, if the click-through rate is only 1%, then a representative sample would need to be approximately 50,000 observations in order to have about 500 observations corresponding to situations in which a person clicked on an ad.

When obtaining a representative sample, it is also important not to carelessly discard variables. It is generally best to include as many variables as possible in the sample. After exploring the data with descriptive statistics and visualization, the analyst can eliminate "uninteresting" variables.

For a more detailed description of sampling techniques, Appendix 9.1 illustrates how to create data sets for data mining analysis by sampling data from a larger volume using XLMiner.

NOTES + COMMENTS

1. XLMiner provides functionality to create data sets for data-mining analysis by sampling data from the larger volume residing in an Excel worksheet or a database (e.g., Access, SQL Server) by clicking the **Get Data** icon in the Data group of the **XLMiner Platform** ribbon and then choosing the appropriate source, **Worksheet**, **Database**, **File Folder** (to get data from a collection of files—often used in text mining), or **Big Data** (to get data from the Apache Spark cluster computing system).

2. After selecting from where to sample data, XLMiner offers several **Sampling Options** in its **Sampling** window. Users can specify a **Desired sample size**, and different random samples can be generated by varying the random seed in the box next to **Set seed**. XLMiner supports **Simple random sampling** with or without replacement. In simple random sampling without replacement, each observation is equally likely to be selected for the sample and an observation can be selected for the sample at most once. If **Sample with replacement** is selected, each observation is equally likely to be picked for the sample and an observation can be inserted more than once into the sample. One reason to sample with replacement is to artificially generate a larger sample in cases for which the number of observations observed is not large enough for the analysis desired. XLMiner also provides an option to execute **Stratified random sampling**, which allows the user to control the number of observations in the sample with certain values of a specified variable, called the *stratum variable*. One use of stratified sampling is to ensure that rare events of interest are adequately represented in the sample.

9.2 Data Partitioning

We begin by discussing how to partition a data set in order to appropriately evaluate the future accuracy of a predictive data-mining method. Consider a situation in which an analyst has relatively few data points from which to build a multiple regression model. To maintain the sample size necessary to obtain reliable estimates of slope coefficients, an analyst may have no choice but to use the entire data set to build a model. Even if measures such as R^2 and the standard error of the estimate suggest that the resulting linear regression model may fit the data set well, these measures only explain how well the model fits data it has "seen," and the analyst has little idea how well this model will fit other "unobserved" data points.

Multiple regression models are discussed in Chapter 7.

Classical statistics deals with a scarcity of data by determining the minimum sample size needed to draw legitimate inferences about the population. In contrast, data-mining applications deal with an abundance of data that simplifies the process of assessing the accuracy of data-based estimates of variable effects. However, the wealth of data can tempt the analyst the overfit the model. **Model overfitting** occurs when the analyst builds a model that does a great job of explaining the sample of data on which it is based, but fails to accurately predict outside the sample data. We can use the abundance of data to guard against the potential for overfitting by decomposing the data set into three partitions: the training set, the validation set, and the test set.

The **training set** consists of the data used to build the candidate models. For example, a training set may be used to estimate the slope coefficients in a multiple regression model. We use measures of accuracy of these models on the training set to identify a promising initial subset of models. However, since the training set consists of the data used to build the models, it cannot be used to clearly identify the best model for prediction when applied to new data (data outside the training set). Therefore, the promising subset of models is then applied to the **validation set** to identify which model may be the most accurate at predicting observations that were not used to build the model.

If the validation set is used to identify a "best" model through either comparison with other models or the tuning of model parameters. then the estimates of model accuracy are also biased (we tend to overestimate accuracy). Thus, the final model must be applied to the **test set** in order to conservatively estimate this model's effectiveness when applied to data that have not been used to build or select the model.

For example, suppose we have identified four models that fit the training set reasonably well. To evaluate how these models will handle predictions when applied to new data, we apply these four models to the validation set. After identifying the best of the four models, we apply this "best" model to the test set in order to obtain an unbiased estimate of this model's accuracy on future applications.

There are no definite rules for the size of the three partitions, but the training set is typically the largest. For estimation tasks, a rule of thumb is to have at least 10 times as many observations as variables. For classification tasks, a rule of thumb is to have at least $6 \times m \times q$ observations, where m is the number of outcome categories and q is the number of variables. When we are interested in predicting a rare event, such as a click-through on an advertisement posted on a web site or a fraudulent credit-card transaction, it is recommended that the training set oversample the number of observations corresponding to the rare events to provide the data-mining algorithm sufficient data to "learn" about the rare events. For example, if only one out of every 10,000 users clicks on an advertisement posted on a web site, we would not have sufficient information to distinguish between users who do not click-through and those who do if we constructed a representative training set consisting of one observation corresponding to a click-through and 9,999 observations with no click-through. In these cases, the training set should contain equal or nearly equal numbers of observations corresponding to the different values of the outcome variable. Note that we do not oversample the validation set and test sets; these samples should be representative of the overall population so that accuracy measures evaluated on these data sets appropriately reflect future performance of the data-mining model.

9.3 Accuracy Measures

DATA file
Optiva

There are different accuracy measures for methods classifying categorical outcomes than for methods estimating continuous outcomes. We describe each of these in the context of an example from the financial services industry. Optiva Credit Union wants to better understand its personal lending process and its loan customers. The file *Optiva* contains over 40,000 customer observations with information on whether the customer defaulted on a loan, customer age, average checking account balance, whether the customer had a mortgage, the customer's job status, the customer's marital status, and the customer's level of education. We will use these data to demonstrate the use of supervised learning methods to classify customers who are likely to default and to predict the average balance in a customer's bank accounts.

Evaluating the Classification of Categorical Outcomes

In our treatment of classification problems, we restrict our attention to problems for which we want to classify observations into one of two possible classes (e.g., loan default or no default), but the concepts generally extend to cases with more than two classes. A natural way to evaluate the performance of a classification method, or classifier, is to count the number of times that an observation is predicted to be in the wrong class. By counting the classification errors on a sufficiently large validation set and/or test set that is representative of the population, we will generate an accurate measure of classification performance of our model.

Classification error is commonly displayed in a **classification confusion matrix**, which displays a model's correct and incorrect classifications. Table 9.1 illustrates a classification confusion matrix resulting from an attempt to classify the customer observations in a subset of data from the file *Optiva*. In this table, Class 1 = loan default and Class 0 = no default. The classification confusion matrix is a cross-tabulation of the actual class of each observation and the predicted class of each observation. From the first row of the matrix in Table 9.1, we see that 146 observations corresponding to loan defaults were correctly identified as such, but another 89 actual loan defaults were classified as nondefault observations. From the second row, we observe that 5,244 actual nondefault observations were incorrectly classified as loan defaults, while 7,479 nondefaults were correctly identified.

TABLE 9.1	Classification Confusion Matrix		
		Predicted Class	
Actual Class		**1**	**0**
1		$n_{11} = 146$	$n_{10} = 89$
0		$n_{01} = 5{,}244$	$n_{00} = 7{,}479$

Many measures of classification accuracy are based on the classification confusion matrix. The percentage of misclassified observations is expressed as the **overall error rate** and is computed as:

$$\text{overall error rate} = \frac{n_{10} + n_{01}}{n_{11} + n_{10} + n_{01} + n_{00}}$$

The overall error rate of the classification in Table 9.1 is $(89 + 5{,}244)/(146 + 89 + 5{,}244 + 7{,}479) = 41.2\%$. One minus the overall error rate is often referred to as the **accuracy** of the model. The model accuracy based on Table 9.1 is 58.8%.

In Table 9.1, n_{01} is the number of false positives and n_{10} is the number of false negatives.

While overall error rate conveys an aggregate measure of misclassification, it counts misclassifying an actual Class 0 observation as a Class 1 observation (a **false positive**) the same as misclassifying an actual Class 1 observation as a Class 0 observation (a **false negative**). In many situations, the cost of making these two types of errors is not equivalent. For example, suppose we are classifying patient observations into two categories: Class 1 is cancer and Class 0 is healthy. The cost of incorrectly classifying a healthy patient observation as "cancer" will likely be limited to the expense (and stress) of additional testing. The cost of incorrectly classifying a cancer patient observation as "healthy" may result in an indefinite delay in treatment of the cancer and premature death of the patient.

To account for the assymetric costs in misclassification, we define the error rate with respect to the individual classes:

$$\textbf{Class 1 error rate} = \frac{n_{10}}{n_{11} + n_{10}}$$

$$\textbf{Class 0 error rate} = \frac{n_{01}}{n_{01} + n_{00}}$$

The Class 1 error rate of the classification in Table 9.1 is $89/(146 + 89) = 37.9\%$. The Class 0 error rate of the classification in Table 9.1 is $(5{,}244)/(5{,}244 + 7{,}479) = 41.2\%$. That is, the model that produced the classifications in Table 9.1 is slightly better at predicting Class 1 observations than Class 0 observations.

To understand the tradeoff between Class 1 error rate and Class 0 error rate, we must be aware of the criteria generally used by classification algorithms to classify observations. Most classification algorithms first estimate an observation's probability of Class 1 membership and then classify the observation into Class 1 if this probability meets or exceeds a specified **cutoff value** (default cutoff value, 0.5). The choice of cutoff value affects the type of classification error. As we decrease the cutoff value, more observations will be classified as Class 1, thereby increasing the likelihood that a Class 1 observation will be correctly classified as Class 1; that is, Class 1 error will decrease. However, as a side effect, more Class 0 observations will be incorrectly classified as Class 1; that is, Class 0 error will rise.

To demonstrate how the choice of cutoff value affects classification error, Table 9.2 shows a list of 50 observations (11 of which are actual Class 1 members) and an estimated probability of Class 1 membership produced by the classification algorithm. Table 9.3 shows classification confusion matrix and corresponding Class 1 error rates, Class 0 error rates, and overall error rates for cutoff values of 0.75, 0.5, and 0.25, respectively. As we decrease the cutoff value, more observations will be classified as Class 1, thereby increasing the likelihood that a Class 1 observation will be correctly classified as Class 1 (decreasing the Class 1 error rate). However, as a side effect, more Class 0 observations will be incorrectly classified as Class 1 (increasing the Class 0 error rate). That is, we can accurately identify more of the actual Class 1 observations by lowering the cutoff value, but we do so at a cost of misclassifying more actual Class 0 observations as Class 1

TABLE 9.2	Classification Probabilities		
Actual Class	**Probability of Class 1**	**Actual Class**	**Probability of Class 1**
1	1.00	0	0.66
1	1.00	0	0.65
0	1.00	1	0.64
1	1.00	0	0.62
0	1.00	0	0.60
0	0.90	0	0.51
1	0.90	0	0.49
0	0.88	0	0.49
0	0.88	1	0.46
1	0.88	0	0.46
0	0.87	1	0.45
0	0.87	1	0.45
0	0.87	0	0.45
0	0.86	0	0.44
1	0.86	0	0.44
0	0.86	0	0.30
0	0.86	0	0.28
0	0.85	0	0.26
0	0.84	1	0.25
0	0.84	0	0.22
0	0.83	0	0.21
0	0.68	0	0.04
0	0.67	0	0.04
0	0.67	0	0.01
0	0.67	0	0.00

observations. Figure 9.1 shows the Class 1 and Class 0 error rates for cutoff values ranging from 0 to 1. One common approach to handling the tradeoff between Class 1 and Class 0 error is to set the cutoff value to minimize the Class 1 error rate subject to a threshold on the maximum Class 0 error rate. Specifically, Figure 9.1 illustrates that for a maximum allowed Class 0 error rate of 70%, a cutoff value of 0.45 (depicted by the vertical dashed line) achieves a Class 1 error rate of 20%.

As we have mentioned, identifying Class 1 members is often more important than identifying Class 0 members. One way to evaluate a classifier's value is to compare its effectiveness in identifying Class 1 observations as compared with random classification. To gauge a classifier's added value, a **cumulative lift chart** compares the number of actual Class 1 observations identified if considered in decreasing order of their estimated probability of being in Class 1 and compares this to the number of actual Class 1 observations identified if randomly selected. The left panel of Figure 9.2 illustrates a cumulative lift chart. The point (10, 5) on the blue curve means that if the 10 observations with the largest estimated probabilities of being in Class 1 were selected from Table 9.2, 5 of these observations correspond to actual Class 1 members. In contrast, the point (10, 2.2) on the red curve means that if 10 observations were randomly selected, only $(11/50) \times 10 = 2.2$ of these

TABLE 9.3	Classification Confusion Matrices for Various Cutoff Values

Cutoff Value = 0.75

		Predicted Class	
Actual Class		1	0
1		$n_{11} = 6$	$n_{10} = 5$
0		$n_{01} = 15$	$n_{00} = 24$

Actual Class	No. of Cases	No. of Errors	Error Rate (%)
1	$n_{11} + n_{10} = 11$	$n_{10} = 5$	45.45
0	$n_{01} + n_{00} = 39$	$n_{01} = 15$	38.46
Overall	$n_{11} + n_{10} + n_{01} + n_{00} = 50$	$n_{10} + n_{01} = 20$	40.00

Cutoff Value = 0.50

		Predicted Class	
Actual Class		1	0
1		$n_{11} = 7$	$n_{10} = 4$
0		$n_{01} = 24$	$n_{00} = 15$

Actual Class	No. of Cases	No. of Errors	Error Rate (%)
1	11	4	36.36
0	39	24	61.54
Overall	50	28	56.00

Cutoff Value = 0.25

		Predicted Class	
Actual Class		1	0
1		$n_{11} = 10$	$n_{10} = 1$
0		$n_{01} = 33$	$n_{00} = 6$

Actual Class	No. of Cases	No. of Errors	Error Rate (%)
1	11	1	9.09
0	39	33	84.62
Overall	50	34	68.00

A decile is one of nine values that divide ordered data into ten equal parts. The deciles determine the values for 10%, 20%, 30% . . . 90% of the data.

observations would be Class 1 members. Thus, the better the classifier is at identifying responders, the larger the vertical gap between points on the red and blue curves.

Another way to view how much better a classifier is at identifying Class 1 observations than random classification is to construct a **decile-wise lift chart**. For a decile-wise lift chart, observations are ordered in decreasing probability of Class 1 membership and then considered in 10 equal-sized groups. For the data in Table 9.2, the first decile group corresponds to the

Figure 9.1 was created using a data table that varied the cutoff value and tracked the Class 1 error rate and Class 0 error rate. For instructions on how to construct data tables in Excel, see Chapter 10.

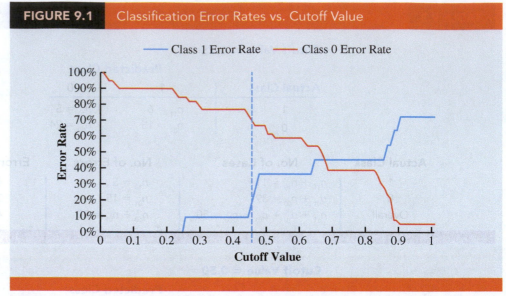

FIGURE 9.1   Classification Error Rates vs. Cutoff Value

$0.1 \times 50 = 5$ observations most likely to be in Class 1, the second decile group corresponds to the 6th through the 10th observations most likely to be in Class 1, and so on. For each of these deciles, the decile-wise lift chart compares the number of actual Class 1 observations to the number of Class 1 responders in a randomly selected group of $0.1 \times 50 = 5$ observations. In the first decile group from Table 9.2 (the top 10% of observations believed by the classifier to most likely to be in Class 1), there are three Class 1 observations. A random sample of 5 observations would be expected to have $5 \times (11/50) = 1.1$ observations in Class 1. Thus the first-decile lift of this classification is $3/1.1 = 2.73$, which corresponds to the height of the first bar in the chart in the right panel of Figure 9.2. The interpratation of this ratio is that in the first decile, the model correctly predicted three observations, whereas random sampling would, on average, correctly classify only 1.1. Visually, the taller the bar in a decile-wise lift chart, the better the classifier is at identifying responders in the respective decile group. The height of the bars for the 2nd through 10th deciles is computed and intepreted in a similar manner.

Lift charts are prominently used in direct-marketing applications that seek to identify customers who are likely to respond to a direct-mail promotion. In these applications, it is

FIGURE 9.2   Cumulative and Decile-Wise Lift Charts

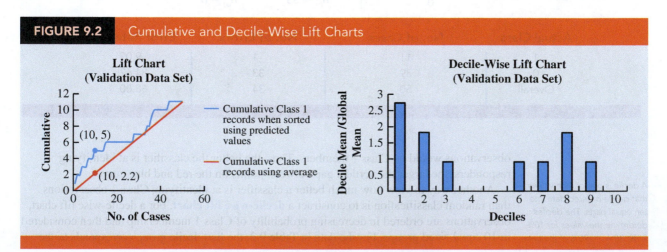

common to have a fixed budget and, therefore, a fixed number of customers to target. Lift charts identify how much better a data-mining model does at identifying responders than a mailing to a random set of customers.

In addition to the overall error rate, Class 1 error rate, and Class 0 error rate, there are a few other measures that express a classifier's performance. The ability to correctly predict Class 1 (positive) observations is commonly expressed by subtracting the Class 1 error rate from one. The resulting measure is referred to as the **sensitivity**, or **recall**, which is calculated as:

$$\text{Sensitivity} = 1 - \text{Class 1 error rate} = \frac{n_{11}}{n_{11} + n_{10}}.$$

Similarly, the ability to correctly predict Class 0 (negative) observations is commonly expressed by subtracting the Class 0 error rate from one. The resulting measure is referred to as the **specificity**, which is calculated as:

$$\text{Specificity} = 1 - \text{Class 0 error rate} = \frac{n_{00}}{n_{11} + n_{10}}.$$

The sensitivity of the model that produced the classifications in Table 9.1 is $146/(146 + 89) = 62.1\%$. The specificity of the model that produced the classifications in Table 9.1 is $7,479/(5,244 + 7,479) = 58.8\%$.

Precision is a measure that corresponds to the proportion of observations predicted to be Class 1 by a classifier that are actually in Class 1:

$$\text{Precision} = \frac{n_{11}}{n_{11} + n_{01}}.$$

The **F1 Score** combines precision and sensitivity into a single measure and is defined as:

$$\text{F1 Score} = \frac{2n_{11}}{2n_{11} + n_{01} + n_{10}}.$$

As we illustrated in Figure 9.1, decreasing the cutoff value will decrease the number of actual Class 1 observations misclassified as Class 0, but at the cost of increasing the number of Class 0 observations that are misclassfied as Class 1. The **receiver operating characteristic (ROC) curve** is an alternative graphical approach for displaying this tradeoff between a classifier's ability to correctly identify Class 1 observations and its Class 0 error rate. In a ROC curve, the vertical axis is the sensitivity of the classifier, and the horizontal axis is the Class 0 error rate (which is equal to $1 -$ specificity).

In Figure 9.3, the blue curve depicts the ROC curve corresponding to the classification probabilities in Table 9.2. The red diagonal line in Figure 9.3 represents random classification of observations. The point $(0, 0)$ on the curve occurs when the cutoff value is set so that all observations are classified as Class 0; for this set of 50 observations, a cutoff value greater than 1.0 will achieve this. That is, for a cutoff value greater than 1, for the observations in Table 9.2, sensitivity $= 0/(0 + 50) = 0$ and the Class 0 error rate $= 0/(0 + 50) = 0$. The point $(1, 1)$ on the curve occurs when the cutoff value is set so that all observations are classified as Class 1; for this set of 50 observations, a cutoff value of zero will achieve this. That is, for a cutoff value of 0, sensitivity $= 11/(11 + 0) = 1$ and the Class 0 error rate $= 39/(39 + 0) = 1$. Repeating these calculations for varying cutoff values and recording the resulting sensitivity and Class 0 error rate values, we can construct the ROC curve in Figure 9.3.

In general, we can evaluate the quality of a classifier by computing the area under the ROC curve. The more area under the ROC curve, the better the classifier performs. To understand why, suppose there exists a cutoff value such that a classifier correctly identifies each observation's actual class. Then, the ROC curve will pass through the point $(0, 1)$, which represents the case in which the Class 0 error rate is zero and the sensitivity is equal to one (which means that the Class 1 error rate is zero). In this case, the area under

FIGURE 9.3   Receiver Operating Characteristic (ROC) Curve

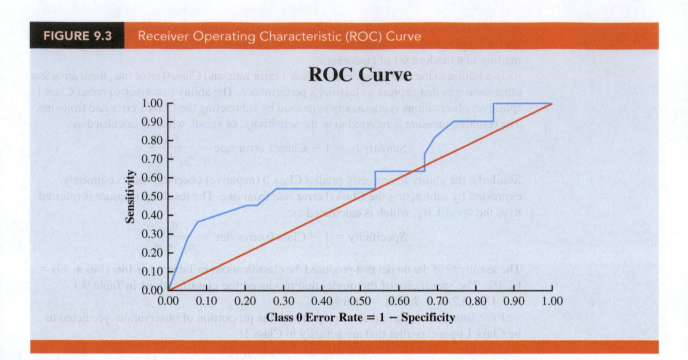

the ROC curve would be equal to one as the curve would extend from (0, 0) to (0, 1) to (1, 1). In Figure 9.3, note that the area under the red diagonal line representing random classification results is 0.5. In Figure 9.3, we observe that the classifier is providing value over a random classification, as the area under its ROC curve is greater than 0.5.

Evaluating the Estimation of Continuous Outcomes

There are several ways to measure accuracy when estimating a continuous outcome variable, but each of these measures is some function of the error in estimating an outcome for an observation i. Let e_i be the error in estimating an outcome for observation i, defined as $e_i = y_i - \hat{y}_i$, where y_i is the actual outcome for observation i and $\hat{y}_i$ is the predicted outcome for observation i. Two common measures are the **average error** $= \sum_{i=1}^{n} e_i / n$ and the **root mean squared error** (RMSE) $= \sqrt{\sum_{i=1}^{n} e_i^2 / n}$. The average error estimates the **bias** in a model's predictions. If the average error is negative, then the model tends to overestimate the value of the outcome variable; if the average error is positive, the model tends to underestimate the value of the outcome variable. The RMSE is similar to the standard error of the estimate for a regression model; it has the same units as the outcome variable predicted and provides a measure of how much the predicted value varies from the actual value.

Chapter 8 discusses additional measures, such as mean absolute error, mean absolute percentage error, and mean squared error, that also can be used to evaluate the accuracy of predictions.

Applying these measures (or others) to the model's predictions on the training set estimates the retrodictive accuracy or goodness-of-fit of the model, not the predictive accuracy. In estimating future performance, we are most interested in applying the accuracy measures to the model's predictions on the validation and test sets.

To demonstrate the computation and interpretation of average error and RMSE, we consider the challenge of predicting the average balance of Optiva Credit Union customers based on their features. Table 9.4 shows the error and squared error resulting from the predictions of the average balance for 10 observations. Using Table 9.4, we compute average error $= -80.1$ and the RSME $= 774$. Because the average error is negative, we observe that the model overestimates the actual balance of these 10 customers. Furthermore, if the performance of the model on these 10 observations is indicative of

TABLE 9.4	Computing Error in Estimates of Average Balance for 10 Customers		
Actual Average Balance	Estimated Average Balance	Error (e_i)	Squared Error (e_i^2)
3,793	3,784	9	9,054,081
1,800	1,460	340	16,384
900	1,381	−481	1,666,681
1,460	566	894	176,400
6,288	5,487	801	641,601
341	605	−264	69,696
506	760	−254	64,516
621	1,593	−972	944,784
1,442	3,050	−1,608	1,292,769
944	210	734	538,756

the accuracy on a larger set of observations, we should investigate improvements to the estimation model, as the RMSE of 774 is 43% of the average actual balance.

NOTES + COMMENTS

Lift charts analogous to those constructed for classification methods can also be applied to the continuous outcomes when using estimation methods. A lift chart for a continuous outcome variable is relevant for evaluating a model's effectiveness in identifying observations with the largest values of the outcome variable. This is similar to the way a lift chart for a categorical outcome variable helps evaluate a model's effectiveness in identifying observations that are most likely to be Class 1 members.

9.4 Logistic Regression

DATA file
OscarsDemo

Similar to how multiple linear regression predicts a continuous outcome variable, y, with a collection of explanatory variables, $x_1, x_2, \ldots, x_q$, via the linear equation $\hat{y} = b_0 + b_1 x_1 + \cdots + b_q x_q$, **logistic regression** attempts to classify a categorical outcome ($y = 0$ or 1) as a linear function of explanatory variables. However, directly trying to explain a categorical outcome via a linear function of the explanatory variables is not effective. To understand this, consider the task of predicting whether a movie wins the Academy Award for Best Picture using information on the total number of other Oscar nominations that a movie has received. Figure 9.4 shows a scatter chart of a sample of movie data found in the file *OscarsDemo*; each data point corresponds to the total number of Oscar nominations that a movie received and whether the movie won the best picture award (1 = movie won, 0 = movie lost). The diagonal line in Figure 9.4 corresponds to the simple linear regression fit. This linear function can be thought of as predicting the probability p of a movie winning the Academy Award for best picture via the equation $\hat{p} = -0.4054 + (0.0836 \times \text{total number of Oscar nominations})$. As Figure 9.4 shows, a linear regression model fails to appropriately explain a categorical outcome variable. This model predicts that a movie with fewer than 5 total Oscar nominations has a negative probability of winning the best picture award. For a movie with more than 17 total Oscar nominations, this model predicts a probability greater than 1.0 of winning the best picture award. Furthermore, the residual plot in

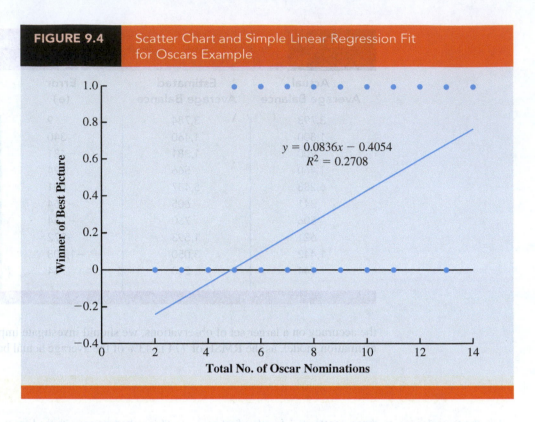

FIGURE 9.4   Scatter Chart and Simple Linear Regression Fit for Oscars Example

$y = 0.0836x - 0.4054$
$R^2 = 0.2708$

As discussed in Chapter 7, if a linear regression model is appropriate, the residuals should appear randomly dispersed with no discernible pattern.

Figure 9.5 shows an unmistakable pattern of systematic misprediction, suggesting that the simple linear regression model is not appropriate.

Estimating the probability p with the linear function $\hat{p} = b_0 + b_1 x_1 + \cdots + b_q x_q$ does not fit well because, although p is a continuous measure, it is restricted to the range $[0, 1]$; that is, a probability cannot be less than zero or larger than one. Figure 9.6 shows an S-shaped curve that appears to better explain the relationship between the probability p of winning the best picture award and the total number of Oscar nominations. Instead of extending off to positive and negative infinity, the S-shaped curve flattens and never goes above one or below zero. We can achieve this S-shaped curve by estimating an appropriate function of the probability p of winning the best picture award with a linear function rather than directly estimating p with a linear function.

As a first step, we note that there is a measure related to probability known as *odds* that is very prominent in gambling and epidemiology. If an estimate of the probability of an event is $\hat{p}$ then the equivalent odds measure is $\hat{p}/(1 - \hat{p})$. For example, if the probability of an event is $\hat{p} = 2/3$, then the odds measure would be $(2/3)/(1/3) = 2$, meaning that the odds are 2 to 1 that the event will occur. The odds metric ranges between zero and positive infinity, so by considering the odds measure rather than the probability $\hat{p}$, we eliminate the linear fit problem resulting from the upper bound on the probability $\hat{p}$. To eliminate the fit problem resulting from the remaining lower bound on $\hat{p}/(1 - \hat{p})$, we observe that the natural log of the odds for an event, also known as "log odds" or logit, $\ln(\hat{p}/(1 - \hat{p}))$, ranges from negative infinity to positive infinity. Estimating the logit with a linear function results in a logistic regression model:

$$\ln\left(\frac{\hat{p}}{1 - \hat{p}}\right) = b_0 + b_1 x_1 + \cdots + b_q x_q. \tag{9.1}$$

Given a training set of observations consisting of values for a set of explanatory variables, $x_1, x_2, \ldots, x_q$, and whether or not an event of interest occurred ($y = 0$ or 1), the logistic

FIGURE 9.5   Residuals for Simple Linear Regression on Oscars Data

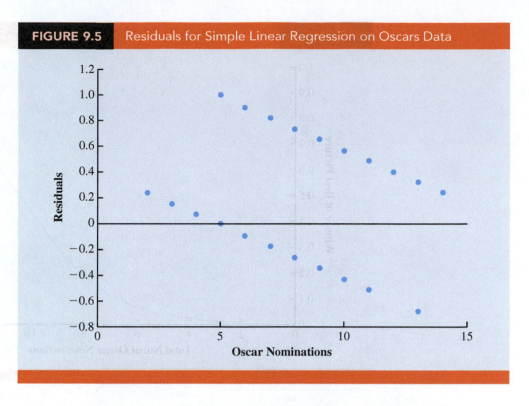

regression model fits values of $b_0, b_1, \ldots, b_q$ that best estimate the log odds of the event occurring. Fitting the logistic regression model to the data in the file *OscarsDemo* results in estimates of $b_0 = -6.214$ and $b_1 = 0.596$; that is, the log odds of a movie winning the best picture award is given by:

$$\ln\left(\frac{\hat{p}}{1-\hat{p}}\right) = -6.214 + 0.596 \times \text{total number of Oscar nominations.} \tag{9.2}$$

Software such as XLMiner is necessary to compute the estimates for the coefficients $b_0, b_1, b_2, \ldots, b_q$, of a logistic regression mode l that result in the best fit of the training data.

Unlike the coefficients in a multiple linear regression, the coefficients in a logistic regression do not have an intuitive interpretation. For example, $b_1 = 0.596$ means that for every additional Oscar nomination that a movie receives, its log odds of winning the best picture award increase by 0.596. In other words, the total number of Oscar nominations is linearly related to the log odds of a movie winning the best picture award. Unfortunately, a change in the log odds of an event is not as easy as to interpret as a change in the probability of an event. Algebraically solving equation (9.1) for *p*, we can express the relationship between the estimated probability of an event and the explanatory variables with an equation known as the logistic function:

LOGISTIC FUNCTION

$$\hat{p} = \frac{1}{1 + e^{-(b_0 + b_1 x_1 + \cdots + b_q x_q)}} \tag{9.3}$$

For the *OscarsDemo* data, equation (9.3) is

$$\hat{p} = \frac{1}{1 + e^{-(-6.214 + 0.596 \times \text{total number of Oscar nominations})}} \tag{9.4}$$

Plotting equation (9.4), we obtain the S-shaped curve of Figure 9.6. Clearly, the logistic regression fit implies a nonlinear relationship between the probability of winning the best picture award and the total number of Oscar nominations. The effect of increasing the total number of Oscar nominations on the probability of winning the best picture award

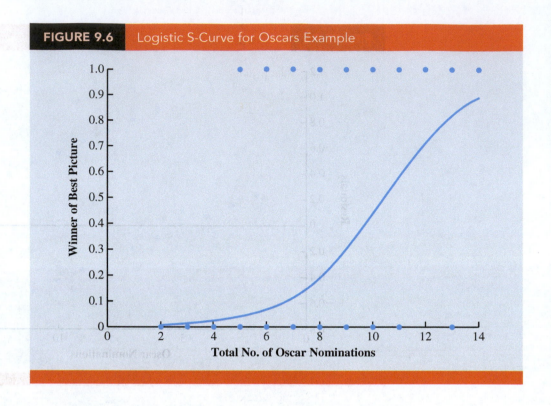

FIGURE 9.6   Logistic S-Curve for Oscars Example

depends on the original number of Oscar nominations. For instance, if the total number of Oscar nominations is four, an additional Oscar nomination increases the estimated

probability of winning the best picture award from $\hat{p} = \dfrac{1}{1 + e^{-(-6.214 + 0.596 \times 4)}} = 0.021$

to $\hat{p} = \dfrac{1}{1 + e^{-(-6.214 + 0.596 \times 5)}} = 0.038$, an increase of 0.017. But if the total number of Oscar nominations is eight, an additional Oscar nomination increases the estimated

probability of winning the best picture award from $\hat{p} = \dfrac{1}{1 + e^{-(-6.214 + 0.596 \times 8)}} = 0.191$ to

$\hat{p} = \dfrac{1}{1 + e^{-(-6.214 + 0.596 \times 9)}} = 0.299$, an increase of 0.108.

As with other classification methods, logistic regression classifies an observation by using equation (9.3) to compute the probability of an observation belonging to Class 1 and then comparing this probability to a cutoff value. If the probability exceeds the cutoff value (a typical value is 0.5), the observation is classified as Class 1 and otherwise it is classified as Class 0. Table 9.5 shows a subsample of the predicted probabilities computed using equation (9.3) and the subsequent classification.

The selection of variables to consider for a logistic regression model is similar to the approach in multiple linear regression. Especially when dealing with many variables, thorough data exploration via descriptive statistics and data visualization is essential in narrowing down viable candidates for explanatory variables. While a logistic regression model used for prediction should ultimately be judged based on its classification accuracy on validation and test sets, **Mallow's C_p statistic** is a measure commonly computed by statistical software that can be used to identify models with promising sets of variables. Models that achieve a small value of Mallow's C_p statistic tend to have smaller mean squared error and models with a value of Mallow's C_p statistic approximately equal to the number of coefficients in the model tend to have less bias (the tendency to systemically over- or under-predict).

See Chapter 7 for an in-depth discussion of variable selection in multiple regression models.

Appendix 9.2 demonstrates the construction of a logistic regression classifier using XLMiner.

TABLE 9.5	Predicted Probabilities by Logistic Regression for Oscars Example		
Total No. of Oscar Nominations	**Predicted Probability of Winning**	**Predicted Class**	**Actual Class**
14	0.89	Winner	Winner
11	0.58	Winner	Loser
10	0.44	Loser	Loser
6	0.07	Loser	Winner

NOTES + COMMENTS

As with multiple linear regression, strong collinearity between the independent variables $x_1, x_2, \ldots x_q$ in a logistic regression model can distort the estimation of the coefficients $b_1, b_2, \ldots b_q$ in equation (9.1). If we are constructing a logistic regression model to explain and quantify a relationship between the set of independent variables and the log odds of an event occurring, then it is recommended to avoid models that include independent variables that are highly correlated. However, if the purpose of a logistic regression model is to classify observations, multicollinearity does not affect predictive capability so correlated independent variables are not a concern and the model should be evaluated based on its classification accuracy on validation and test sets.

Appendix 9.3 demonstrates the use of XLMiner to apply k-NN for classification and estimation.

9.5 *k*-Nearest Neighbors

The *k*-Nearest Neighbor (*k*-NN) method can be used either to classify an outcome category or estimate a continuous outcome. In a *k*-NN approach, the predicted outcome for an observation in the validation set is based on the *k* most similar observations from the training set, where similarity is typically measured with Euclidean distance.

Classifying Categorical Outcomes with *k*-Nearest Neighbors

Unlike logistic regression, which uses a training set to build a classification model (the logistic equation) to apply to the observations in the validation and test sets, a nearest-neighbor classifier is a "lazy learner" that instead directly uses the entire training set to classify observations in the validation and test sets. When *k*-NN is used as a classification method, a new observation is classified as Class 1 if the percentage of its *k* nearest neighbors in Class 1 is greater than or equal to a specified cutoff value (a typical value is 0.5).

The value of *k* can plausibly range from 1 to *n*, the number of observations in the training set. If $k = 1$, then the classification of a new observation is set to be equal to the class of the single most similar observation from the training set. At the other extreme, if $k = n$, then the new observation's class is naïvely assigned to the most common class in the training set. Typical values of *k* range from 1 to 20. The best value of *k* can be determined by building models over a typical range ($k = 1, \ldots, 20$) and then selecting the value of k^* that results in the smallest classification error. Note that the use of the validation set to identify k^* in this manner implies that the method should be applied to a test set with this value of k^* to accurately estimate the classification error on future data.

To illustrate, suppose a training set consists of the 10 observations listed in Table 9.6. For this example, we will refer to an observation with Loan Default = 1 as a Class 1

TABLE 9.6	Training Set Observations for *k*-NN Classifier		
Observation	Average Balance	Age	Loan Default
1	49	38	1
2	671	26	1
3	772	47	1
4	136	48	1
5	123	40	1
6	36	29	0
7	192	31	0
8	6,574	35	0
9	2,200	58	0
10	2,100	30	0
Average:	1,285	38.2	
Standard Deviation:	2,029	10.2	

observation and an observation with Loan Default = 0 as a Class 0 observation. Our task is to classify a new observation with Average Balance = 900 and Age = 28 based on its similarity to the values of Average Balance and Age of the 10 observations in the training set.

Chapter 2 discusses z-scores.

Before computing the similarity between a new observation and the observations in the training set, it is common practice to normalize the values of all variables. By replacing the original values of each variable with the corresponding *z*-score, we avoid the computation of Euclidean distance being disproportionately affected by the scale of the variables. For example, the average value of the Average Balance variable in the training set is 1,285 and the standard deviation is 2,029. The average and standard deviation of the Age variable are 38.2 and 10.2, respectively. Thus, Observation 1's normalized value of Average Balance is $(49 - 1{,}285)/2{,}029 = -0.61$ and its normalized value of Age is $(38 - 38.2)/10.2 = -0.02$.

FIGURE 9.7	Scatter Chart for *k*-NN Classification

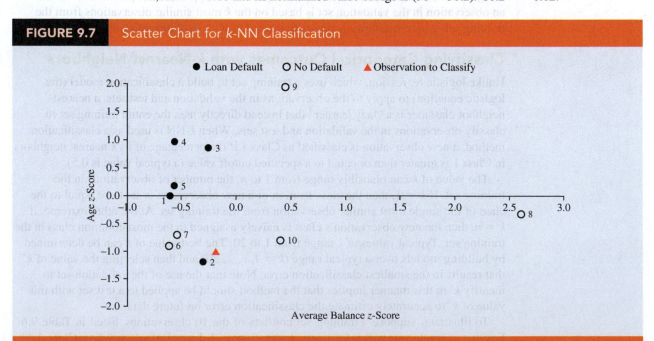

TABLE 9.7	Classification of Observation with Average Balance = 900 and Age = 28 for Different Values of *k*	
k	% of Class 1 Neighbors	Classification
1	1.00	1
2	0.50	1
3	0.33	0
4	0.25	0
5	0.40	0
6	0.50	1
7	0.57	1
8	0.63	1
9	0.56	1
10	0.50	1

Figure 9.7 displays the 10 training-set observations and the new observation to be classified plotted according to their normalized variable values. To classify the new observation, we will use a cutoff value of 0.5. For *k* = 1, this observation is classified as a Loan Default (Class 1) because its nearest neighbor (Observation 2) is in Class 1. For *k* = 2, we see that the two nearest neighbors are Observation 2 (Class 1) and Observation 7 (Class 0). Because at least 0.5 of the *k* = 2 neighbors are Class 1, the new observation is classified as Class 1. For *k* = 3, the three nearest neighbors are Observation 2 (Class 1), Observation 7 (Class 0), and Observation 6 (Class 0). Because only 1/3 of the neighbors are Class 1, the new observation is classified as Class 0 (.33 is less than the .5 cutoff value). Table 9.7 summarizes the classification of the new observation for values of *k* ranging from 1 to 10.

Estimating Continuous Outcomes with *k*-Nearest Neighbors

When *k*-NN is used to estimate a continuous outcome, a new observation's outcome value is predicted to be the *average* of the outcome values of its *k* nearest neighbors in the training set. The value of *k* can plausibly range from 1 to *n*, the number of observations in the training set. If *k* = 1, then the estimation of a new observation's outcome value is set equal to the outcome value of the single most similar observation from the training set. At the other extreme, if *k* = *n*, then the new observation's outcome value is estimated by the average outcome value over the entire training set. Typical values of *k* range from 1 to 20. The best value of *k* can be determined by building models over a typical range (*k* = 1, . . . , 20) and then selecting the value of k^* that results in the smallest estimation error. Note that the use of the validation set to identify k^* in this manner implies that the method should be applied to a test set with this value of k^* to accurately estimate the estimation error on future data.

To illustrate, we again consider the training set of 10 observations listed in Table 9.6. In this case, we are interested in estimating the value of Average Balance for a new observation based on its similarity with respect to Age to the 10 observations in the training set. Figure 9.8 displays the 10 training-set observations and a new observation with

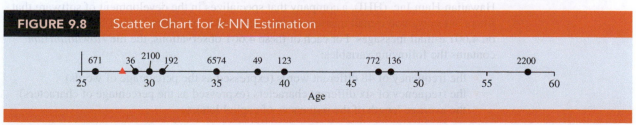

FIGURE 9.8 Scatter Chart for *k*-NN Estimation

TABLE 9.8	Estimation Average Balance for Observation with Age = 28 for Different Values of k	
k		**Average Balance Estimate**
1		$36
2		$936
3		$936
4		$750
5		$1,915
6		$1,604
7		$1,392
8		$1,315
9		$1,184
10		$1,285

Age = 28 for which we want to estimate the value of Average Balance. For $k = 1$, the new observation's average balance is estimated to be $36, which is the value of Average Balance for the nearest neighbor (Observation 6 in Table 9.6). For $k = 2$, we see that there is a tie between Observation 2 (Age = 26) and Observation 10 (Age = 30) for the second-closest observation to the new observation (Age = 28). Rather than employ an arbitrary tie-breaking rule, we will include all three observations to estimate the average balance of the new observation as $(36 + 671 + 2,100)/3 = 936. Table 9.8 summarizes the estimation of the new observation's average balance for values of k ranging from 1 to 10.

9.6 Classification and Regression Trees

Appendix 9.4 demonstrates how to construct classification and regression trees using XLMiner.

Classification and regression trees (CART) successively partition a data set of observations into increasingly smaller and more homogeneous subsets. At each iteration of the CART method, a subset of observations is split into two new subsets based on the values of a single variable. The CART method can be thought of as a series of questions that successively narrow down observations into smaller and smaller groups of decreasing **impurity**, which is the measure of the heterogeneity in a group of observations' outcome classes or outcome values.

Classifying Categorical Outcomes with a Classification Tree

For **classification trees**, the impurity of a group of observations is based on the proportion of observations belonging to the same class (where there is zero impurity if all observations in a group are in the same class). After a final tree is constructed, the classification of a new observation is then based on the final partition into which the new observation belongs (based on the variable splitting rules).

To demonstrate the classification tree method, we consider an example involving Hawaiian Ham Inc. (HHI), a company that specializes in the development of software that filters out unwanted e-mail messages (often referred to as "spam"). HHI has collected data on 4,601 e-mail messages. For each of these 4,601 observations, the file *HawaiianHam* contains the following variables:

- the frequency of 48 different words (expressed as the percentage of words)
- the frequency of six different characters (expressed as the percentage of characters)
- the average length of the sequences of capital letters

- the longest sequence of capital letters
- the total number of sequences with capital letters
- whether or not the e-mail was spam

DATA *file*
HawaiianHam

HHI would like to use these variables to classify e-mail messages as either "spam" (Class 1) or "not spam" (Class 0).

To explain how a classification tree categorizes observations, we use a small sample of data from **HHI** consisting of 46 observations and only two variables, Dollar and Exclamation, corresponding to the percentage of the $ character and the percentage of the ! character, respectively. The results of a classification tree analysis can be graphically displayed in a tree that explains the process of classifying a new observation. The tree outlines the values of the variables that result in an observation falling into a particular partition.

Let us consider the classification tree in Figure 9.9. At each step, the CART method identifies the split of the variable that results in the least impurity in the two resulting categories. In Figure 9.9, the number within the circle (or node) represents the value on which the variable (whose name is listed below the node) is split. The first partition is formed by splitting observations into two groups, observations with Dollar ≤ 0.0555 and observations with Dollar > 0.0555. The numbers on the left and right arc emanating from the node denote the number of observations in the Dollar ≤ 0.0555 and Dollar > 0.0555 partitions, respectively. There are 28 observations containing less than 5.55% of the '$' character and 18 observations containing more than 5.55% of the '$' character. The split on the variable

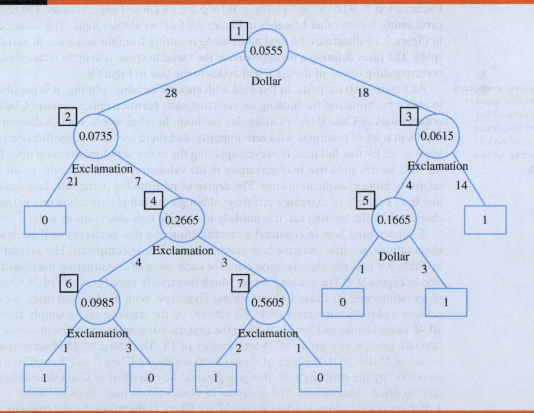

FIGURE 9.9   Construction Sequence of Branches in a Classification Tree

Dollar at the value 0.0555 is selected because it results in the two subsets of the original 46 observations with the least impurity. The splitting process is then repeated on these two newly created groups of observations in a manner that again results in an additional subset with the least impurity. In this tree, the second split is applied to the group of 28 observations with Dollar $\leq$ 0.0555 using the variable Exclamation; 21 of the 28 observations in this subset have Exclamation $\leq$ 0.0735, while 7 have Exclamation $>$ 0.0735. After this second variable splitting, there are three total partitions of the original 46 observations. There are 21 observations with values of Dollar $\leq$ 0.0555 and Exclamation $\leq$ 0.0735, 7 observations with values of Dollar $\leq$ 0.0555 and Exclamation $>$ 0.0735, and 18 observations with values of Dollar $>$ 0.0555. No further partitioning of the 21-observation group with values of Dollar $\leq$ 0.0555 and Exclamation $\leq$ 0.0735 is necessary since this group consists entirely of Class 0 (nonspam) observations (i.e., this group has zero impurity). The 7-observation group with values of Dollar $\leq$ 0.0555 and Exclamation $>$ 0.0735 and 18-observation group with values of Dollar $>$ 0.0555 are successively partitioned in the order as denoted by the boxed numbers in Figure 9.9 until subsets with zero impurity are obtained.

For example, the group of 18 observations with Dollar $>$ 0.0555 is further split into two groups using the variable Exclamation; 4 of the 18 observations in this subset have Exclamation $\leq$ 0.0615, while the other 14 observations have Exclamation $>$ 0.0615. That is, 4 observations have Exclamation $>$ 0.0555 and Exclamation $\leq$ 0.0615. This subset of 4 observations is further decomposed into 1 observation with Dollar $\leq$ 0.1665 and 3 with Dollar $>$ 0.1665. At this point, there is no further branching in this portion of the tree since corresponding subsets have zero impurity. That is, the subset of 1 observation with Dollar $>$ 0.0555, Exclamation $\leq$ 0.0615 and Dollar $\leq$ 0.1665 is a Class 0 observation (nonspam) and the subset of 3 observations with Dollar $>$ 0.0555, Exclamation $\leq$ 0.0615 , and Dollar $>$ 0.1665 are all Class 1 observations. The recursive partitioning for the other branches in Figure 9.9 follows similar logic. The scatter chart in Figure 9.10 illustrates the final partitioning resulting from the sequence of variable splits. The rules defining a partition divide the variable space into eight rectangles, each corresponding to one of the eight leaf nodes in the tree in Figure 9.9.

As Figure 9.10 suggests, in this case with enough variable splitting, it is possible to obtain partitions on the training set such that each partition either contains Class 1 observations or Class 0 observations, but not both. In other words, enough decomposition results in a set of partitions with zero impurity, and there are no misclassifications of the training set by this full tree. However, applying the entire set of partitioning rules from the full classification tree to observations in the validation set will typically result in a relatively large classification error. The degree of partitioning in the full classification tree is an example of extreme overfitting; although the full classification tree perfectly characterizes the training set, it is unlikely to classify new observations well.

Unless there exist observations that have identical values of all the input variables but different outcome classes, the leaf nodes of the full classification tree will have zero impurity.

To understand how to construct a classification tree that performs well on new observations, we first examine how classification error is computed. The second column of Table 9.9 lists the classification error for each stage of constructing the classification tree in Figure 9.9. The training set on which this tree is based consists of 26 Class 0 observations and 20 Class 1 observations. Therefore, with no decision rules, we can achieve a classification error of 43.5% (20/46) on the training set by simply classifying all 46 observations as Class 0. Adding the first decision node separates the observations into two groups, one group of 28 and another of 18. The group of 28 observations has values of Dollar $\leq$ 0.0555; 25 of these observations are Class 0 and 3 are Class 1; therefore, by the majority rule, this group would be classified as Class 0, resulting in three misclassified observations. The group of 18 observations has values of Dollar $>$ 0.0555; 1 of these observations is Class 0, and 17 are Class 1; therefore, by the majority rule, this group would be classified as Class 1, resulting in one misclassified observation.

9.6   Classification and Regression Trees   **459**

FIGURE 9.10	Geometric Illustration of Full Classification Tree Partitions

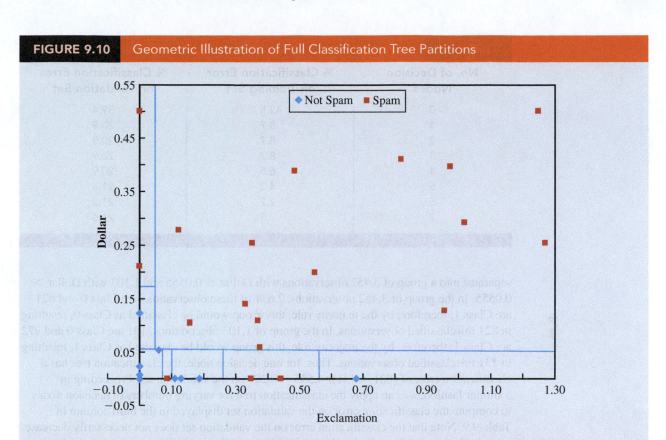

Thus, for one decision node, the classification tree has a classification error of $(3 + 1)/46 = 0.087$.

When the second decision node is added, the 28 observations with values of Dollar $\leq$ 0.0555 are further decomposed into a group of 21 observations and a group of 7 observations. The classification tree with two decision nodes has three groups: a group of 18 observations with Dollar > 0.0555, a group of 21 observations with Dollar $\leq$ 0.0555 and Exclamation ≤ 0.0735, and a group of 7 observations with Dollar ≤ 0.0555 and Exclamation > 0.0735. As before, the group of 18 observations would be classified as Class 1 and misclassify a single observation that is actually Class 0. In the group of 21 observations, all of these observations are Class 0, so there is no misclassification error for this group. In the group of seven observations, four are Class 0 and three are Class 1. Therefore, by the majority rule, this group would be classified as Class 0, resulting in three misclassified observations. Thus, for the classification tree with two decision nodes (and three partitions), the classification error is $(1 + 0 + 3)/46 = 0.087$. Proceeding in a similar fashion, we can compute the classification error on the training set for classification trees with varying numbers of decision nodes to complete the second column of Table 9.9. Table 9.9 shows that the classification error on the training set decreases as we add more decision nodes and split the observations into smaller partitions.

To evaluate how well the decision rules of the classification tree in Figure 9.9 established from the training set extend to other data, we apply it to a validation set of 4,555 observations consisting of 2,762 Class 0 observations and 1,793 Class 1 observations. Without any decision rules, we can achieve a classification error of 39.4% (1,793/4,555) on the training set by simply classifying all 4,555 observations as Class 0. Applying the first decision node

TABLE 9.9	Classification Error Rates on Sequence of Pruned Trees	
No. of Decision Nodes	% Classification Error on Training Set	% Classification Error on Validation Set
0	43.5	39.4
1	8.7	20.9
2	8.7	20.9
3	8.7	20.9
4	6.5	20.9
5	4.3	21.3
6	2.2	21.3
7	0	21.6

separates into a group of 3,452 observations with Dollar ≤ 0.0555 and 1,103 with Dollar > 0.0555. In the group of 3,452 observations, 2,631 of these observations are Class 0 and 821 are Class 1; therefore, by the majority rule, this group would be classified as Class 0, resulting in 821 misclassified observations. In the group of 1,103 observations, 131 are Class 0 and 972 are Class 1; therefore, by the majority rule, this group would be classified as Class 1, resulting in 131 misclassified observations. Thus, for one decision node, the classification tree has a classification error of $(821 + 131)/4,555 = 0.209$ on the validation set. Proceeding in a similar fashion, we can apply the classification tree for varying numbers of decision nodes to compute the classification error on the validation set displayed in the third column of Table 9.9. Note that the classification error on the validation set does not necessarily decrease as more decision nodes split the observations into smaller partitions.

To identify a classification tree with good performance on new data, we "prune" the full classification tree by removing decision nodes in the reverse order in which they were added. In this manner, we seek to eliminate the decision nodes corresponding to weaker rules. Figure 9.11 illustrates the tree resulting from pruning the last variable splitting rule (Exclamation ≤ 0.5605 or Exclamation > 0.5605) from Figure 9.9. By pruning this rule, we obtain a partition defined by Dollar ≤ 0.0555, Exclamation > 0.0735, and Exclamation > 0.2665 that contains three observations. Two of these observations are Class 1 (spam) and one is Class 0 (nonspam), so this pruned tree classifies observations in this partition as Class 1 observations, since the proportion of Class 1 observations in this partition (two-thirds) exceeds the default cutoff value of 0.5. Therefore, the classification error of this pruned true on the training set is $1/46 = 0.022$, an increase over the zero classification error of the full tree on the training set. However, Table 9.9 shows that applying the six decision rules of this pruned tree to the validation set achieves a classification error of 0.213, which is less than the classification error of 0.216 of the full tree on the validation set. Compared to the full tree with seven decision rules, the pruned tree with six decision rules is less likely to be overfit to the training set.

Sequentially removing decision nodes, we can obtain six pruned trees. These pruned trees have one to six variable splits (decision nodes). However, while adding decision nodes at first decreases the classification error on the validation set, too many decision nodes overfits the classification tree to the training data and results in increased error on the validation set. For each of these pruned trees, each observation belongs to a single partition defined by a sequence of decision rules and is classified as Class 1 if the proportion of Class 1 observations in the partition exceeds the cutoff value (default value, 0.5) and Class 0 otherwise.

One common approach for identifying the best-pruned tree is to begin with the full classification tree and prune decision rules until the classification error on the validation set

---

FIGURE 9.11   Classification Tree with One Pruned Branch

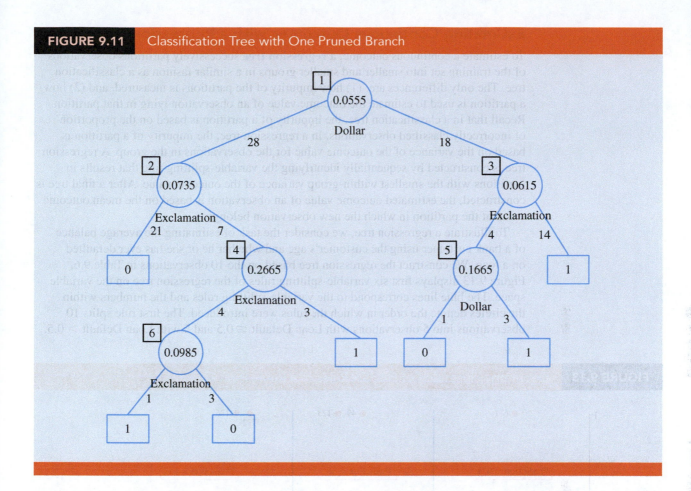

---

increases. Following this procedure, Table 9.9 suggests that a classification tree partitioning observations into two subsets with a single decision node (Dollar $\leq$ 0.0555 or Dollar > 0.0555) is just as reliable at classifying the validation data as any other tree. As Figure 9.12 shows, this classification tree classifies e-mails with '!' accounting for $\leq$ 5.55% of the characters as nonspam and e-mails as spam if the '$' character accounts for more than 5.55% of the total characters in the email, otherwise the email is classified as nonspam. This best-pruned classification tree results in a classification error of 20.9% on the validation set.

FIGURE 9.12   Best-Pruned Classification Tree

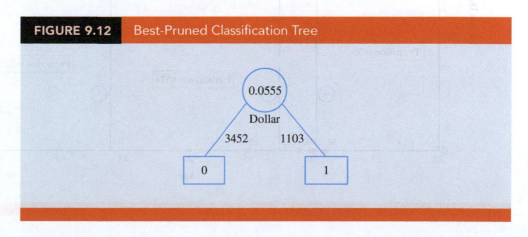

Estimating Continuous Outcomes with a Regression Tree

To estimate a continuous outcome, a **regression tree** successively partitions observations of the training set into smaller and smaller groups in a similar fashion as a classification tree. The only differences are: (1) how impurity of the partitions is measured, and (2) how a partition is used to estimate the outcome value of an observation lying in that partition. Recall that in a classification tree, the impurity of a partition is based on the proportion of incorrectly classified observations. In a regression tree, the impurity of a partition is based on the variance of the outcome value for the observations in the group. A regression tree is constructed by sequentially identifying the variable-splitting rule that results in partitions with the smallest within-group variance of the outcome value. After a final tree is constructed, the estimated outcome value of an observation is based on the mean outcome value of the partition in which the new observation belongs.

To illustrate a regression tree, we consider the task of estimating the average balance of a bank customer using the customer's age and whether he or she has ever defaulted on a loan. We construct the regression tree based on the 10 observations in Table 9.6. Figure 9.13 displays first six variable-splitting rules of the regression tree on the variable space. The blue lines correspond to the variable-splitting rules and the numbers within the circles denote the order in which the rules were introduced. The first rule splits 10 observations into 5 observations with Loan Default $\leq$ 0.5 and 5 with Loan Default $>$ 0.5.

FIGURE 9.13 Geometric Illustration of First Six Rules of a Regression Tree

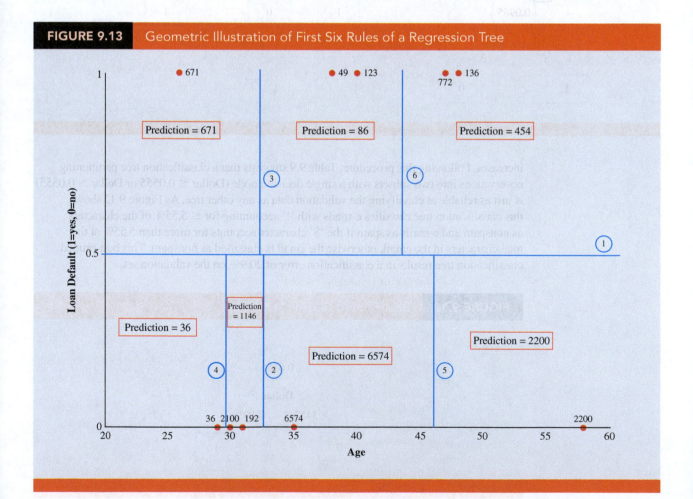

Unless there exist observations that have identical values of all the input variables but different values of the outcome variable, the leaf nodes of the full regression tree will have zero impurity.

This rule results in two groups of observations such that the variance in Average Balance within the groups is as small as possible. The second rule further splits the 5 observations with Loan Default ≤ 0.5 into a partition with 3 with Age ≤ 33 and 2 with Age > 33. Again, this rule results in the largest reduction in variance within any partition. Four more rules further split the observations into partitions with smaller Average Balance variance as illustrated by Figure 9.13. This six-rule regression tree would then sets its prediction estimate of each partition to be the average of the Average Balance variable (depicted in the red boxes in Figure 9.13).

Note that the full regression tree would continue to partition the variable space into smaller rectangles until the Average Balance variable was the same in each partition. Then, similar to the classification tree, rules are pruned from this full regression tree in order to obtain the simplest tree that obtained the least amount of prediction error.

Ensemble Methods

Up to this point, we have demonstrated the prediction of a new observation (either classification in the case of a categorical outcome or estimation in the case of a continuous outcome) based on the decision rules of a single constructed tree. In this section, we discuss the notion of ensemble methods. In an **ensemble method**, predictions are made based on the combination of a collection of models. For example, instead of basing the classification of a new observation on a single classification tree, an ensemble method generates a collection of different classification trees and then predicts the class of a new observation based on the collective voting of this collection.

To gain an intuitive grasp of why an ensemble of prediction models may outperform, on average, any single prediction model, let's consider the task of predicting the value of the S&P 500 Index one year in the future. Suppose there are 100 financial analysts independently developing their own forecast based on a variety of information. One year from now, there certainly will be one analyst (or more in the case of a tie) whose forecast will prove to be the most accurate. However, identifying beforehand which of the 100 analysts will be the most accurate may be virtually impossible. Therefore, instead of trying to pick one of the analysts and depending solely on their forecast, an ensemble approach would combine their forecasts (e.g., taking an average of the 100 forecast values) and use this as the predicted value of the S&P 500 Index. The two necessary conditions for an ensemble to perform better than a single model are: (1) The individual base models are constructed independently of each other (analysts don't base their forecasts on the forecasts of other analysts), and (2) the individual models perform better than just randomly guessing.

A neural network is also typically an unstable prediction method, but this method is beyond the scope of this book.

There are two primary steps to an ensemble approach: (1) the development of a committee of individual base models, and (2) the combination of the individual base models' predictions to form a composite prediction. While an ensemble can be composed of various individual classification or estimation models, the ensemble approach works better with an unstable prediction method. A classification or estimation method is **unstable** if relatively small changes in the training set cause its predictions to fluctuate substantially. As classification and regression trees are known to be unstable, our discussion of ensemble methods will involve CART. Specifically, we discuss three different ways to construct an ensemble of classification or regression trees: bagging, boosting, and random forests.

In the **bagging** approach, the committee of individual base models is generated by first constructing multiple training sets by repeated random sampling of the *n* observations in the original data *with replacement*. Because the sampling is done with replacement, some observations may appear multiple times in a single training set, while other observations will not appear at all. If each generated training set consists of *n* observations, then the probability of an observation from the original data *not* being selected for a specific

TABLE 9.10		Original 10-Observation Training Data							
Age	29	31	35	38	47	48	53	54	58	70
Loan default	0	0	0	1	1	1	1	0	0	0

training set is $((n - 1)/n)^n$. Therefore, the average proportion of a training set of size n that are unique observations from the original data is $1 - ((n - 1)/n)^n$. The bagging approach then trains a predictive model on each of the m training sets and generates the ensemble prediction based on the average of the m individual predictions.

To demonstrate bagging, we consider the task of classifying customers as defaulting or not defaulting on their loan, using only their age. Table 9.10 contains the 10 observations in the original training data. Table 9.11 shows the results of generating 10 new training sets by randomly sampling from the original data with replacement. For each of these training sets, we construct a one-rule classification tree that minimizes the impurity of the resulting partition. The two partitions of each training set are illustrated with a vertical red line and accompanying decision rule.

Table 9.12 shows the results of applying this ensemble of 10 classification trees to a validation set consisting of 10 observations. The ensemble method bases its classification on the average of the 10 individual classifications trees; if at least half of the individual trees classify an observation as Class 1, so does the ensemble. Note from Table 9.12 that the 20% classification error rate of the ensemble is lower than any of the individual trees, illustrating the potential advantage of using ensemble methods.

Similar to bagging, the **boosting** method generates its committee of individual base models by sampling multiple training sets. However, boosting iteratively adapts how it samples the original data when constructing a new training set based on the prediction error of the models constructed on the previous training sets. To generate the first training set, each of the n observations in the original data is initially given equal weight of being selected. That is, each observation i has weight $w_i = 1/n$. A classification or estimation model is then trained on this training set and is used to predict the outcome of the n observations in the original data. The weight of each observation i is then adjusted based on the degree of its prediction error. For example, in a classification problem, if an observation i is misclassified by a classifier, then its weight w_i is increased, but if it is correctly classified, then its weight w_i is decreased. The next training set is then generated by sampling the observations according to the updated weights. In this manner, the next training set is more likely to contain observations that have been mispredicted in early iterations.

XLMiner offers three different variants of the AdaBoost boosting algorithm that differ in the weighting of individual models' predictions when they are averaged.

To combine the predictions of the m individual models from the m training sets, boosting weights the vote of each individual model based on its overall prediction error. For example, suppose that the classifier associated with the jth training set has a large prediction error and the classifier associated with the kth training set has a small prediction error. Then the classification votes of the jth classifier will be weighted less than the classification votes of the kth classifer when they are combined. Note that this method differs from bagging, in which each of the individual classifiers has an equally weighted vote.

Random forests (also called *random trees*) can be viewed as a variation of bagging specifically tailored for use with classification or regression trees. As in bagging, the random forests approach generates multiple training sets by randomly sampling (with replacement) the n observations in the original data. However, when constructing a tree model for each separate training set, each tree is restricted to using only a fixed number of randomly selected input variables. For example, suppose we are attempting to classify a

TABLE 9.11 Bagging: Generation of 10 New Training Sets and Corresponding Classification Trees

Iteration 1 — Age ≤ 36.5

Age	29	31	31	35	38	38	47	48	58	58
Loan default	0	0	0	0	1	1	1	1	0	0
Prediction	0	0	0	0	1	1	1	1	1	1

Iteration 2 — Age ≤ 50.5

Age	29	31	35	38	47	54	58	70	70	70
Loan default	0	0	0	1	1	0	0	0	0	0
Prediction	0	0	0	0	0	0	0	0	0	0

Iteration 3 — Age ≤ 36.5

Age	29	31	35	38	38	47	53	53	54	58
Loan default	0	0	0	1	1	1	1	1	0	0
Prediction	0	0	0	1	1	1	1	1	1	1

Iteration 4 — Age ≤ 34.5

Age	29	29	31	38	38	47	47	53	54	58
Loan default	0	0	0	1	1	1	1	1	0	0
Prediction	0	0	0	1	1	1	1	1	1	1

Iteration 5 — Age ≤ 39

Age	29	29	31	47	48	48	48	70	70	70
Loan default	0	0	0	1	1	1	1	0	0	0
Prediction	0	0	0	1	1	1	1	1	1	1

Iteration 6 — Age ≤ 53.5

Age	31	38	47	48	53	53	53	54	58	70
Loan default	0	1	1	1	1	1	1	0	0	0
Prediction	1	1	1	1	1	1	1	0	0	0

Iteration 7 — Age ≤ 53.5

Age	29	38	38	48	53	54	58	58	58	70
Loan default	0	1	1	1	1	0	0	0	0	0
Prediction	1	1	1	1	1	0	0	0	0	0

Iteration 8 — Age ≤ 53.5

Age	29	31	47	47	47	53	53	54	58	70
Loan default	0	0	1	1	1	1	1	0	0	0
Prediction	1	1	1	1	1	1	1	0	0	0

Iteration 9 — Age ≤ 53.5

Age	29	35	38	38	48	53	53	54	70	70
Loan default	0	0	1	1	1	1	1	0	0	0
Prediction	1	1	1	1	1	1	1	0	0	0

Iteration 10 — Age ≤ 14.5

Age	29	29	29	29	35	35	54	54	58	58
Loan default	0	0	0	0	0	0	0	0	0	0
Prediction	0	0	0	0	0	0	0	0	0	0

TABLE 9.12   Classification of 10 Observations from Validation Set with Bagging Ensemble

Age	26	29	30	32	34	37	42	47	48	54	Overall Error Rate
Loan default	1	0	0	0	0	1	0	1	1	0	
Tree 1	0	0	0	0	0	1	1	1	1	1	30%
Tree 2	0	0	0	0	0	0	0	0	0	0	40%
Tree 3	0	0	0	0	0	1	1	1	1	1	30%
Tree 4	0	0	0	0	0	1	1	1	1	1	30%
Tree 5	0	0	0	0	0	0	1	1	1	1	40%
Tree 6	1	1	1	1	1	1	1	1	1	0	50%
Tree 7	1	1	1	1	1	1	1	1	1	0	50%
Tree 8	1	1	1	1	1	1	1	1	1	0	50%
Tree 9	1	1	1	1	1	1	1	1	1	0	50%
Tree 10	0	0	0	0	0	0	0	0	0	0	40%
Average Vote	0.4	0.4	0.4	0.4	0.4	0.7	0.8	0.8	0.8	0.4	
Bagging Ensemble	0	0	0	0	0	1	1	1	1	0	20%

The default seting in XLMiner's random trees procedure is for each individual classification tree to be based on $f = \sqrt{q}$ variables and each individual regression tree to be based on $f = q/3$ variables.

tax return as fraudulent or not and there are q input variables. For each of the m generated training sets, a classification tree is constructed based on splitting rules based on f randomly selected input variables, where f is much smaller than q.

For most problems, the predictive accuracy of boosting ensembles exceeds the predictive accuracy of bagging ensembles. Boosting achieves its performance advantage because: (1) It evolves its committee of models by focusing on observations that are mispredicted, and (2) the member models' votes are weighted by their accuracy. However, boosting is more computationally expensive than bagging. Because there is no adaptive feedback in a bagging approach, all m training sets and corresponding models can be implemented simultaneously. However, in boosting, the first training set and predictive model guide the construction of the second training set and predictive model, and so on. The random forests approach has performance similar to boosting, but maintains the computational simplicity of bagging.

SUMMARY

In this chapter, we introduced the concepts and techniques in predictive data mining. Predictive data mining methods, also called supervised learning, classify a categorical outcome or estimate a continuous outcome. We described how to partition data into training, validation, and test sets in order to construct and evaluate predictive data mining models. We discussed various accuracy measures for classification and estimation methods. We discussed three common data mining methods: logistic regression, k-nearest neighbors, and classification/regression trees. We explained how logistic regression is analogous to multiple linear regression for the case when the outcome variable is binary. We demonstrated how to use logistic regression, as well as k-nearest neighbors and classification trees, to classify a binary categorical outcome. We also discussed the use of k-nearest neighbors and regression trees to estimate a continuous outcome. In our discussion of ensemble methods, we presented the concept of generating multiple prediction models and combining their predictions. We illustrated the use of ensemble methods within the context of classification trees

TABLE 9.13	Overview of Supervised Learning Methods	
	Strengths	**Weaknesses**
k-NN	Simple	Requires large amounts of data relative to number of variables
Classification and Regression Trees	Provides easy-to-interpret business rules; can handle data sets with missing data	May miss interactions between variables since splits occur one at a time; sensitive to changes in data entries
Multiple Linear Regression	Provides easy-to-interpret relationship between dependent and independent variables	Assumes linear relationship between outcome and variables
Logistic Regression	Classification analog of the familiar multiple regression modeling procedure	Coefficients not easily interpretable in terms of probability
Discriminant Analysis	Allows classification based on interaction effects between variables	Assumes variables are normally distributed with equal variance
Naïve Bayes	Simple and effective at classifying	Requires a large amount of data; restricted to categorical variables
Neural Networks	Flexible and often effective	Many difficult decisions to make when building the model; results cannot be easily explained, i.e., "black box"

and noted that ensemble methods based on committees of "weak" prediction models generally outperform a single "strong" prediction model. Table 9.13 provides a comparative summary of common supervised learning approaches. We provide brief descriptions of discriminant analysis, the naïve Bayes method, and neural networks in the following Notes + Comments section.

NOTES + COMMENTS

1. XLMiner provides functionality for the **Discriminant Analysis** classification procedure under **Classify** in the **Data Mining** group on the **XLMiner** Ribbon. Like logistic regression, discriminant analysis assumes a functional form to describe the probability that an observation belongs to a class and then uses data to develop estimates of the parameters of the function. Specifically, P(observation i belongs to Class 1) $= \frac{e^{c_1(i)}}{e^{c_0(i)} + e^{c_1(i)}}$, where $c_0(i)$ and $c_1(i)$ are classification scores for Class 0 and Class 1 that are computed by the algorithm. The strengths of discriminant analysis are its computational simplicity and its ability to provide estimates of the effect of each variable on the probability of class membership. However, while discriminant analysis is useful for small data sets, on large data sets its performance is typically dominated by other classification methods.

2. XLMiner provides functionality for the **Naïve Bayes** classification procedure under **Classify** in the **Data Mining** group on the **XLMiner** Ribbon. The naïve Bayes method is based on Bayes' Theorem from classical statistics. However, it is limited to using only categorical predictor variables to classify an observation and requires a very large number of observations to be effective.

3. XLMiner provides functionality for neural networks for both classification and estimation. Neural networks are based on the biological model of brain activity. Well-structured neural networks have been shown to possess accurate classification and estimation performance in many application domains. However, the use of neural networks is a "black box" method that does not provide any interpretable explanation to accompany its classifications or estimates. Adjusting the parameters to tune the neural network performance is largely trial and error guided by rules of thumb and user experience.

GLOSSARY

Accuracy Measure of classification success defined as 1 minus the overall error rate.

Average error The average difference between the actual values and the predicted values of observations in a data set.

Bagging An ensemble method that generates a committee of models based on different random samples and makes predictions based on the average prediction of the set of models.

Bias The tendency of a predictive model to overestimate or underestimate the value of a continuous outcome.

Boosting An ensemble method that iteratively samples from the original training data to generate individual models that target observations that were mispredicted in previously generated models. Its predictions are based on the weighted average of the predictions of the individual models, where the weights are proportional to the individual models' accuracy.

Class 0 error rate The percentage of Class 0 observations misclassified by a model in a data set.

Class 1 error rate The percentage of actual Class 1 observations misclassified by a model in a data set.

Classification confusion matrix A matrix showing the counts of actual versus predicted class values.

Classification tree A tree that classifies a categorical outcome variable by splitting observations into groups via a sequence of hierarchical rules.

Classification A predictive data mining task requiring the prediction of an observation's outcome class or category.

Cumulative lift chart A chart used to present how well a model performs in identifying observations most likely to be in Class 1 as compared with random classification.

Cutoff value The smallest value that the predicted probability of an observation can be for the observation to be classified as Class 1.

Decile-wise lift chart A chart used to present how well a model performs at identifying observations for each of the top k deciles most likely to be in Class 1 versus a random selection.

Ensemble method A predictive data-mining approach in which a committee of individual classification or estimation models are generated and a prediction is made by combining these individual predictions.

Estimation A predictive data mining task requiring the prediction of an observation's continuous outcome value.

F1 Score A measure combining precision and sensitivity into a single metric.

False negative The misclassification of a Class 1 observation as Class 0.

False positive The misclassification of a Class 0 observation as Class 1.

Features A set of input variables used to predict an observation's outcome class or continuous outcome value.

Impurity Measure of the heterogeneity of observations in a classification tree.

k-Nearest neighbors A classification method that classifies an observation based on the class of the k observations most similar or nearest to it.

Logistic regression A generalization of linear regression for predicting a categorical outcome variable.

Mallow's C_p statistic A measure in which small values approximately equal to the number of coefficients suggest promising logistic regression models.

Model overfitting A situation in which a model explains random patterns in the data on which it is trained rather than just the relationships, resulting in training-set accuracy that far exceeds accuracy for the new data.

Observation (record) A set of observed values of variables associated with a single entity, often displayed as a row in a spreadsheet or database.

Overall error rate The percentage of observations misclassified by a model in a data set.

Precision The percentage of observations predicted to be Class 1 that actually are Class 1.

Random forests A variant of the bagging ensemble method that generates a committee of classification or regression trees based on different random samples but restricts each individual tree to a limited number of randomly selected features (variables)

Receiver operating characteristic (ROC) curve A chart used to illustrate the tradeoff between a model's ability to identify Class 1 observations and its Class 0 error rate.

Regression tree A tree that predicts values of a continuous outcome variable by splitting observations into groups via a sequence of hierarchical rules.

Root mean squared error A measure of the accuracy of an estimation method defined as the square root of the sum of squared deviations between the actual values and predicted values of observations.

Sensitivity (recall) The percentage of actual Class 1 observations correctly identified.

Specificity The percentage of actual Class 1 observations correctly identified.

Supervised learning Category of data-mining techniques in which an algorithm learns how to predict or classify an outcome variable of interest.

Test set Data set used to compute unbiased estimate of final predictive model's accuracy.

Training set Data used to build candidate predictive models.

Unstable When small changes in the training set cause its predictions to fluctuate substantially.

Validation set Data used to evaluate candidate predictive models.

Variable (feature) A characteristic or quantity of interest that can take on different values.

PROBLEMS

Due to the realistic size of these data sets, XLMiner may take several minutes to complete execution for some of these problems. Where relevant, we used the default seed of 12345 when applying XLMiner.

Salmons

1. Salmons Stores operates a national chain of women's apparel stores. Five thousand copies of an expensive four-color sales catalog have been printed, and each catalog includes a coupon that provides a $50 discount on purchases of $200 or more. Salmons would like to send the catalogs only to customers who have the highest probability of using the coupon. The file *Salmons* contains data from an earlier promotional campaign. For each of 1,000 Salmons customers, three variables are tracked: last year's total spending at Salmons, whether they have a Salmons store credit card, and whether they used the promotional coupon they were sent.

   Create a standard partition of the data with all the tracked variables and 50% of observations in the training set, 30% in the validation set, and 20% in the test set. Use logistic regression to classify observations as a promotion-responder or not by using Spending and Card as input variables and Coupon as the output variable. Perform **Variable Selection** with the best subsets procedure with the number of best subsets equal to two.

   a. Evaluate the logistic regression models based on their classification error. Recommend a final model and express the model as a mathematical equation relating the output variable to the input variables.

   b. For the model selected in part (a), interpret the meaning of the first-decile lift in the decile-wise lift chart on the test set.

c. What is the area under the ROC curve on the test set? To achieve a sensitivity of at least 0.80, how much Class 0 error rate must be tolerated?

Sandhills

2. Sandhills Bank would like to increase the number of customers who use payroll direct deposit as part of the rollout of its new e-banking platform. Management has proposed offering an increased interest rate on a savings account if customers sign up for direct deposit into a checking account. To determine whether this proposal is a good idea, management would like to estimate how many of the 200 current customers who do not use direct deposit would accept the offer. In the *Data* worksheet of the file *Sandhills*, the IT company that handles Sandhills Bank's e-banking has provided anonymized data from one of its other client banks that made a similar promotion to increase direct deposit participation. For 1,000 customers, this data lists the average monthly checking account balance and whether the customer signed up for direct deposit. The *Customer* worksheet contains the average monthly balance data for Sandhill's 200 customers that would be the target of the direct-deposit promotion. Sandhills would like to estimate the likelihood of these customers signing up for direct deposit.

Create a standard partition of the data in the *Data* worksheet with 60% of observations in the training set and 40% in the validation set. Classify the data using *k*-Nearest Neighbors with up to *k* = 20. Use Balance the as input variable and Direct as the output variable. In Step 2 of XLMiner's *k*-Nearest Neighbors Classification procedure, be sure to **Normalize Input Data**, **Score on best k between 1 and specified value**, and assign prior class probabilities **According to relative occurrences in training data**. In Step 3, specify the data in the *Customer* worksheet by selecting **In Worksheet** in the **Score New Data** area.

a. For the cutoff probability value 0.5, what value of *k* minimizes the overall error rate on the validation data?

b. What is the area under the ROC curve on the validation set? To achieve a sensitivity of 0.80, how much Class 0 error rate must be tolerated?

c. Using the default cutoff value of 0.5, how many of Sandhills Bank's 200 customers does *k*-Nearest Neighbors classify as enrolling in direct deposit?

Dana

3. Over the past few years the percentage of students who leave Dana College at the end of their first year has increased. Last year, Dana started voluntary one-credit hour-long seminars with faculty to help first-year students establish an on-campus connection. If Dana is able to show that the seminars have a positive effect on retention, college administrators will be convinced to continue funding this initiative. Dana's administration also suspects that first-year students with lower high school GPAs have a higher probability of leaving Dana at the end of the first year. The file *Dana* contains data on the 500 first-year students from last year. Each observation consists of a first-year student's high school GPA, whether they enrolled in a seminar, and whether they dropped out and did not return to Dana. Create a standard partition of the data with all the tracked variables and 60% of observations in the training set and 40% in the validation set. Use logistic regression to classify observations as dropped out or not dropped out by using GPA and Seminar as input variables and Dropped as the output variable. Perform **Variable Selection** with the best subsets procedure with the number of best subsets equal to two.

a. Evaluate the logistic regression models based on their predictive accuracy on the validation set. Recommend a final model and express the model as a mathematical equation relating the output variable to the input variables.

b. The data analyst team realized that they jumped directly into building a predictive model without exploring the data. Using descriptive statistics and charts, investigate any relationships in the data that may explain the unsatisfactory result in part (a).

For next year's first-year class, what could Dana's administration do regarding the enrollment of the seminars to better determine whether they have an effect on retention?

DATA *file*
BlueOrRed

4. Campaign organizers for both the Republican and Democratic parties are interested in identifying individual undecided voters who would consider voting for their party in an upcoming election. The file *BlueOrRed* contains data on a sample of voters with tracked variables, including whether or not they are undecided regarding their candidate preference, age, whether they own a home, gender, marital status, household size, income, years of education, and whether they attend church.

Create a standard partition of the data with all the tracked variables and 50% of observations in the training set, 30% in the validation set, and 20% in the test set. Classify the data using k-Nearest Neighbors with up to $k = 20$. Use Age, HomeOwner, Female, HouseholdSize, Income, Education, and Church as input variables and Undecided as the output variable. In Step 2 of XLMiner's k-Nearest Neighbors Classification procedure, be sure to **Normalize Input Data, Score on best k between 1 and specified value**, and assign prior class probabilities **According to relative occurrences in training data**.

a. For $k = 1$, what is the overall error rate on the training set and the validation set, respectively? Explain the difference in magnitude of these two measures.

The k-Nearest Neighbors procedure is computationally intensive. Depending on your computer's capability, you may have to reduce the number of observations in the training set (by repartitioning the original data and reducing the percentage allocated to the training set) in order to successfully execute the k-Nearest Neighbors procedure.

b. For the cutoff probability value of 0.5, what value of k minimizes the overall error rate on the validation data? Explain the difference in the overall error rate on the training, validation, and test set.

c. Examine the decile-wise lift chart for the test set. What is the first decile lift? Interpret this value.

d. In the effort to identify undecided voters, a campaign is willing to accept an increase in the misclassification of decided voters as undecided if it can correctly classify more undecided voters. For cutoff probability values of 0.5, 0.4, 0.3, and 0.2, what are the corresponding Class 1 error rates and Class 0 error rates on the validation data?

5. Refer to the scenario in Problem 4 using the file *BlueOrRed*. Create a standard partition of the data with all the tracked variables and 50% of observations in the training set, 30% in the validation set, and 20% in the test set. Fit a single classification tree using Age, HomeOwner, Female, Married, HouseholdSize, Income, Education, and Church as input variables and Undecided as the output variable. In Step 2 of XLMiner's Classification Tree procedure, be sure to **Normalize Input Data** and to set the **Minimum # records in a terminal node** to 100. Generate the **Full tree** and **Best pruned tree**.

a. From the *CT_Output* worksheet, what is the overall error rate of the full tree on the training set? Explain why this is not necessarily an indication that the full tree should be used to classify future observations and the role of the best-pruned tree.

b. Consider a 50-year-old man who attends church, has 15 years of education, owns a home, is married, lives in a household of four people, and has an annual income of $150,000. Using the *CT_PruneTree* worksheet, does the best-pruned tree classify this observation as undecided?

c. For the default cutoff value of 0.5, what are the overall error rate, Class 1 error rate, and Class 0 error rate of the best-pruned tree on the test set?

d. Examine the decile-wise lift chart for the best-pruned tree on the test set. What is the first decile lift? Interpret this value.

6. Refer to scenario in Problem 4 using the file *BlueOrRed*. Create a standard partition of the data with all the tracked variables and 50% of observations in the training set,

30% in the validation set, and 20% in the test set. Apply the random trees procedure to create an ensemble of classification trees using Age, HomeOwner, Female, Married, HouseholdSize, Income, Education, and Church as input variables and Undecided as the output variable. In Step 2 of XLMiner's Random Trees Classification procedure, be sure to **Normalize Input Data**, to set **Number of weak learners** to 20, to set the **Number of randomly selected features** to 3, and to set the **Minimum # records in a terminal node** to 100.

   a. What is the most important variable in terms of reducing the classification error of the ensemble?

   b. For the default cutoff value of 0.5, compare the overall error rate, Class 1 error rate, and Class 0 error rate of the random trees on the test set to the corresponding measures of the single best-pruned tree from Problem 5.

7. Refer to the scenario in Problem 4 using the file *BlueOrRed*. Create a standard partition of the data with all the tracked variables and 50% of observations in the training set, 30% in the validation set, and 20% in the test set. Use logistic regression to classify observations as undecided (or decided) using Age, HomeOwner, Female, Married, HouseholdSize, Income, Education, and Church as input variables and Undecided as the output variable. Perform **Variable Selection** with the best subsets procedure with the number of best subsets equal to two.

   a. From the generated set of logistic regression models, use Mallow's C_p statistic to identify a pair of candidate models. Then evaluate these candidate models based on their classification error and decile-wise lift on the validation set. Recommend a final model and express the model as a mathematical equation relating the output variable to the input variables.

   b. Increases in which variables increase the chance of a voter being undecided? Increases in which variables decrease the chance of a voter being decided?

   c. Using the default cutoff value of 0.5 for your logistic regression model, what is the overall error rate on the test set?

8. Telecommunications companies providing cell-phone service are interested in customer retention. In particular, identifying customers who are about to churn (cancel their service) is potentially worth millions of dollars if the company can proactively address the reason that customer is considering cancellation and retain the customer. The DATAfile *Cellphone* contains customer data to be used to classify a customer as a churner or not.

    Using XLMiner's Partition with Oversampling procedure, partition the data with all the variables so there is 50% successes (churners) in the training set and 40% of the validation data are taken away as test set. Use 12345 as the seed in the randomized sampling. Classify the data using k-Nearest Neighbors with up to $k = 20$. Use Churn as the output variable and all the other variables as input variables. In Step 2 of XLMiner's k-Nearest Neighbors Classification procedure, be sure to **Normalize Input Data, Score on best k between 1 and specified value**, and specify prior probabilities that correspond to the Class 0 and Class 1 probabilities in the original data set (see cell F21 in the *Data_Partition* worksheet).

   a. Why is partitioning with oversampling advised in this case?

   b. For the cutoff probability value of 0.5, what value of k minimizes the overall error rate on the validation data?

   c. Referring to *KNNC_Output*, what is the overall error rate on the test set?

   d. Referring to *KNNC_Output*, what are the Class 1 and Class 0 error rates on the test set?

   e. Compute and interpret the sensitivity and specificity for the test set.

f. How many false positives and false negatives did the model commit on the test set? What percentage of predicted churners were false positives? What percentage of predicted nonchurners were false negatives?

g. Examine the decile-wise lift chart on the test set. What is the first decile lift on the test set? Interpret this value.

9. Refer to scenario in Problem 8 using the file *Cellphone*. Using XLMiner's Partition with Oversampling procedure, partition the data with all the variables so there is 50% successes (churners) in the training set and 40% of the validation data are taken away as test set. Use 12345 as the seed in the randomized sampling. Fit a single classification tree using Churn as the output variable and all the other variables as input variables. In Step 2 of XLMiner's Classification Tree procedure, be sure to **Normalize Input Data** and to set the **Minimum # records in a terminal node** to 1. Generate the **Full tree**, **Best pruned tree**, and **Minimum error tree**.

a. Why is partitioning with oversampling advised in this case?

b. From the *CT_Output* worksheet, what is the overall error rate of the full tree on the training set? Explain why this is not necessarily an indication that the full tree should be used to classify future observations and the role of the best pruned tree.

c. Consider the minimum error tree in the *CT_MinErrorTree* worksheet. List and interpret the set of rules that characterize churners.

d. For the default cutoff value of 0.5, what are the overall error rate, Class 1 error rate, and Class 0 error rate of the best-pruned tree on the test set?

e. Examine the decile-wise lift chart for the best-pruned tree on the test set. What is the first decile lift? Interpret this value.

10. Refer to the scenario in Problem 8 using the file *Cellphone*. Using XLMiner's Partition with Oversampling procedure, partition the data with all the variables so there is 50% successes (churners) in the training set and 40% of the validation data are taken away as test set. Use 12345 as the seed in the randomized sampling. Apply the random trees ensemble approach using Churn as the output variable and all the other variables as input variables. In Step 2 of XLMiner's Random Trees Classification procedure, be sure to **Normalize Input Data**, to set **Number of weak learners** to 20, and to set the **Minimum # records in a terminal node** to 1.

a. What is the most important variable in terms of reducing the classification error of the ensemble?

b. For the default cutoff value of 0.5, compare the overall error rate, Class 1 error rate, and Class 0 error rate of the random trees on the test set to the corresponding measures of the single best-pruned tree from Problem 5.

11. Refer to the scenario in Problem 8 using the file *Cellphone*. In XLMiner's Partition with Oversampling procedure, partition the data with all the variables so there is 50% successes (churners) in the training set and 40% of the validation data are taken away as a test set. Use 12345 as the seed in the randomized sampling. Construct a logistic regression model using Churn as the output variable and all the other variables as input variables. Perform **Variable Selection** with the best subsets procedure with the number of best subsets equal to two.

a. Why is partitioning with oversampling advised in this case?

b. From the generated set of logistic regression models, use Mallow's C_p statistic to identify a pair of candidate models. Then evaluate these candidate models based on their classification error on the validation set and decile-wise lift on the validation set. Recommend a final model and express the model as a mathematical equation relating the output variable to the input variables. Do the relationships suggested by the model make sense? Try to explain them.

c. Using the default cutoff value of 0.5 for your logistic regression model, what is the overall error rate on the test set?

DATA *file*
CreditScore

12. A consumer advocacy agency, Equitable Ernest, is interested in providing a service in which an individual can estimate their own credit score (a continuous measure used by banks, insurance companies, and other businesses when granting loans, quoting premiums, and issuing credit). The file *CreditScore* contains data on an individual's credit score and other variables.

Create a standard partition of the data with all the tracked variables and 50% of observations in the training set, 30% in the validation set, and 20% in the test set. Predict the individuals' credit scores using k-Nearest Neighbors with up to $k = 20$. Use CreditScore as the output variable and all the other variables as input variables. In Step 2 of XLMiner's k-Nearest Neighbors Prediction procedure, be sure to **Normalize input data** and to **Score on best k between 1 and specified value**. Generate a **Detailed Report** for all three sets of data.

a. What value of k minimizes the RMSE on the validation data?
b. How does the RMSE on the test set compare to the RMSE on the validation set?
c. What is the average error on the test set? Analyze the distribution of the residual output in the *KNNP_TestScore* worksheet by constructing a histogram.

13. Refer to the scenario in Problem 11 using the file *CreditScore*. Create a standard partition of the data with all the tracked variables and 50% of observations in the training set, 30% in the validation set, and 20% in the test set. Predict the individuals' credit scores using a single regression tree. Use CreditScore as the output variable and all the other variables as input variables. In Step 2 of XLMiner's Regression Tree procedure, be sure to **Normalize Input Data**, to specify **Using Best Pruned Tree** as the scoring option, and to set the **Minimum # records in a terminal node** to 244. Generate the **Full tree**, **Best pruned tree**, and **Minimum error tree**. Generate a **Detailed Report** for the training, validation, and test sets.

a. What is the RMSE of the best-pruned tree on the validation data and on the test set? Discuss the implication of these calculations.
b. Consider an individual who has had 5 credit bureau inquiries, has used 10% of her available credit, has $14,500 of total available credit, has no collection reports or missed payments, is a homeowner, has an average credit age of 6.5 years, and has worked continuously for the past 5 years. What is the best-pruned tree's predicted credit score for this individual?
c. Repeat the construction of a single regression tree following the previous instructions, but in Step 2 of XLMiner's Regression Tree procedure, set the **Minimum # records in a terminal node** to 1. How does the RMSE of the best pruned tree on the test set compare to the analogous measure from part (a)? In terms of number of decision nodes, how does the size of the best-pruned tree compare to the size of the best-pruned tree from part (a)?

14. Refer to scenario in Problem 11 using the file *CreditScore*. Create a standard partition of the data with all the tracked variables and 50% of observations in the training set, 30% in the validation set, and 20% in the test set. Apply the random trees ensemble approach using CreditScore as the output variable and all the other variables as input variables. In Step 2 of XLMiner's Random Trees Classification procedure, be sure to **Normalize Input Data**, to set **Number of weak learners** to 20, and to set the **Minimum # records in a terminal node** to 244. Compare the root mean squared error of the random trees on the test set to the root mean squared error of the single best-pruned tree from part (a) of Problem 13.

Oscars

15. Each year, the American Academy of Motion Picture Arts and Sciences recognizes excellence in the film industry by honoring directors, actors, and writers with awards (called "Oscars") in different categories. The most notable of these awards is the Oscar for Best Picture. The *Data* worksheet in the file *Oscars* contains data on a sample of movies nominated for the Best Picture Oscar. The variables include total number of Oscar nominations across all award categories, number of Golden Globe awards won (the Golden Globe award show precedes the Academy Awards), whether or not the movie is a comedy, and whether or not the movie won the Best Picture Oscar award.

There is also a variable called ChronoPartition that specifies how to partition the data into training, validation, and test sets. The value "t" identifies observations that belong to the training set, the value "v" identifies observations that belong to the validation set, and the value "s" identifies observations that belong to the test set. Create a standard partition of the data containing all the variables (except the partition variable ChronoPartition) using XLMiner's **Standard Partition** routine by selecting **Use partition variable** in the **Partitioning options area** and specifying the variable ChronoPartition.

Construct a logistic regression model to classify winners of the Best Picture Oscar. Use Winner as the output variable and OscarNominations, GoldenGlobeWins, and Comedy as input variables. Perform **Variable Selection** with the best subsets procedure with the number of best subsets equal to 2. Generate a **Detailed Report** for the training and validation sets.

a. From the generated set of logistic regression models, use Mallow's C_p statistic to identify a pair of candidate models. Then evaluate these candidate models based on their classification error on the validation set. Recommend a final model and express the model as a mathematical equation relating the output variable to the input variables. Do the relationships suggested by the model make sense? Try to explain them.

b. Using the default cutoff value of 0.5, what is the sensitivity of the logistic regression model on the validation set? Why is this a good metric to use for this problem?

c. Note that each year there is only one winner of the Best Picture Oscar. Knowing this, what is wrong with classifying a movie based on a cutoff value? (*Hint*: Investigate the results on the *LR_ValidationScore* worksheet and investigate the predicted results on an annual basis.)

d. What is the best way to use the model to predict the annual winner? Out of the six years in the validation data, how many does the model correctly "identify" as the winner?

e. Use the model from part (a) to predict the 2014 nominees for Best Picture; in Step 3 of XLMiner's Logistic Regression procedure, check the box next to **In worksheet** in the **Score new data** area. In the **Match Variable in the New Range** dialog box: (1) Specify *NewDataToPredict* in the **Worksheet**: field, (2) enter the cell range C1:E9 in the **Data range:** field, and (3) click **Match By Name**. When completing the procedure, this will result in a *LR_NewScore* worksheet, which will contain the predicted probability that each 2014 nominee will win the Best Picture. What film did the model believe was the most likely to win the 2014 Academy Award for Best Picture? Was the model correct?

HousingBubble

16. As an intern with the local home builder's association, you have been asked to analyze the state of the local housing market, which has suffered during a recent economic crisis. You have been provided two data sets in the file *HousingBubble*. The *Pre-Crisis* worksheet contains information on 1,978 single-family homes sold during the one-year period before the burst of the "housing bubble." The *Post-Crisis* worksheet contains

information on 1,657 single-family homes sold during the one-year period after the burst of the housing bubble. The *NewDataToPredict* worksheet contains information on homes currently for sale.

a. Consider the *Pre-Crisis* worksheet data. Create a standard partition of the data with all the tracked variables and 50% of observations in the training set, 30% in the validation set, and 20% in the test set. Predict the sale price using *k*-Nearest Neighbors with up to *k* = 20. Use Price as the output variable and all the other variables as input variables. In Step 2 of XLMiner's *k*-Nearest Neighbors Prediction procedure, be sure to **Normalize Input Data** and to **Score on best k between 1 and specified value**. Check the box next to **In worksheet** in the **Score New Data** area. In the **Match Variables in the New Range** dialog box: (1) Specify the *NewDataToPredict* worksheet in the **Worksheet:** field, (2) enter the cell range A1:P2001 in the **Data range:** field, and (3) click **Match By Name**. When completing the procedure, this will result in a *KNNP_NewScore* worksheet, which will contain the predicted sales price for each home in *NewDataToPredict*.

   i.   What value of *k* minimizes the RMSE on the validation data?
   ii. What is the RMSE on the validation data and test set?
   iii. What is the average error on the validation data and test set? What does this suggest?

b. Repeat part (a) with the *Post-Crisis* worksheet data.

c. The *KNNP_NewScore* and *KNNP_NewScore* worksheets contain the sales price predictions for the 2,000 homes in the *NewDataToPredict* using the pre-crisis and post-crisis data, respectively. For each of these 2,000 homes, compare the two predictions by computing the percentage change in predicted price between the pre-crisis and post-crisis models. Let percentage change = (post-crisis predicted price − pre-crisis predicted price)/pre-crisis predicted price. Summarize these percentage changes with a histogram. What is the average percentage change in predicted price between the pre-crisis and post-crisis model?

17. Refer to scenario in Problem 16 using the file *HousingBubble*.

a. Consider the *Pre-Crisis* worksheet data. Create a standard partition of the data with all the tracked variables and 50% of observations in the training set, 30% in the validation set, and 20% in the test set. Predict the sale price using a single regression tree. Use Price as the output variable and all the other variables as input variables. In Step 2 of XLMiner's Regression Tree procedure, be sure to **Normalize Input Data**, to set the **Minimum # records in a terminal node** to 1, and to specify **Using Best Pruned Tree** as the scoring option. In Step 3 of XLMiner's Regression Tree procedure, generate the **Pruned tree**. Generate the **Full tree** and **Pruned tree**. Check the box next to **In worksheet** in the **Score New Data** area. In the **Match Variables in the New Range** dialog box: (1) Specify the *NewDataToPredict* worksheet in the **Worksheet:** field, (2) enter the cell range A1:P2001 in the **Data range:** field, and (3) click **Match By Name.** When completing the procedure, this will result in a *RT_NewScore1* worksheet, which will contain the predicted sales price for each home in *NewDataToPredict*.

   i.   In terms of number of decision nodes, compare the size of the full tree to the size of the best-pruned tree.
   ii. What is the RMSE of the best-pruned tree on the validation data and on the test set?
   iii. What is the average error on the validation data and the test set? What does this suggest?

iv. By examining the best-pruned tree, what are the critical variables in predicting the price of a home?

b. Repeat part (a) with the *Post-Crisis* worksheet data.

c. The *RT_NewScore1* and *RT_NewScore2* worksheets contain the sales price predictions for the 2,000 homes in the *NewDataToPredict* using the pre-crisis and post-crisis data, respectively. For each of these 2,000 homes, compare the two predictions by computing the percentage change in predicted price between the pre-crisis and post-crisis model. Let percentage change = (post-crisis predicted price − pre-crisis predicted price)/pre-crisis predicted price. Summarize these percentage changes with a histogram. What is the average percentage change in predicted price between the pre-crisis and post-crisis model? What does this suggest about the impact of the bursting of the housing bubble?

18. Refer to scenario in Problem 14 using the file *HousingBubble*.

a. Consider the *Pre-Crisis* worksheet data. Create a standard partition of the data with all the tracked variables and 50% of observations in the training set, 30% in the validation set, and 20% in the test set. Predict the sale price using multiple linear regression. Use Price as the output variable and all the other variables as input variables. Perform **Variable Selection** with the **Best Subsets** procedure with the number of best subsets equal to two.

   i. From the generated set of multiple linear regression models, select one that you believe is a good fit. Select **Choose Subset** of the corresponding model and refit the model to obtain the coefficients. In Step 2 of XLMiner's Multiple Linear Regression procedure, check the box next to **In worksheet** in the **Score New Data** area. In the **Match Variables in the New Range** dialog box: (1) Specify the *NewDataToPredict* worksheet in the **Worksheet:** field, (2) enter the cell range A1:P2001 in the **Data range:** field, and (3) click **Match By Name**.

   ii. For the model you selected, what is the RMSE on the validation data and the test set?

   iii. What is the average error on the validation data and test set? What does this suggest?

b. Repeat part (a) with the *Post-Crisis* worksheet data.

c. The *MLR_NewScore* worksheets generated in parts (a) and (b) contain the sales price predictions for the 2,000 homes in the *NewDataToPredict* using the pre-crisis and post-crisis data, respectively. For each of these 2,000 homes, compare the two predictions by computing the percentage change in predicted price between the pre-crisis and post-crisis model. Let percentage change = (post-crisis predicted price − pre-crisis predicted price)/pre-crisis predicted price. Summarize these percentage changes with a histogram. What is the average percentage change in predicted price between the pre-crisis and post-crisis model?

CASE PROBLEM: GREY CODE CORPORATION

Grey Code Corporation (GCC) is a media and marketing company involved in magazine and book publishing and in television broadcasting. GCC's portfolio of home and family magazines has been a long-running strength, but they have expanded to become a provider of a spectrum of services (market research, communications planning, web site advertising, etc.) that can enhance their clients' brands.

GCC's relational database contains over a terabyte of data encompassing 75 million customers. GCC uses the data in its database to develop campaigns for new customer acquisition, customer reactivation, and the identification of cross-selling opportunities for products. For example, GCC will generate separate versions of a monthly issue of a magazine that will differ only by the advertisements they contain. They will mail a subscribing customer the version with the print ads identified by their database as being of most interest to that customer.

One particular problem facing GCC is how to boost the customer response rate to renewal offers that it mails to its magazine subscribers. The industry response rate is about 2%, but GCC has historically performed better than that. However, GCC must update its model to correspond to recent changes. GCC's director of database marketing, Chris Grey, wants to make sure GCC maintains its place as one of the top achievers in targeted marketing. The file *GCC* contains 99 variables (columns) and 50,000 rows (distinct customers).

Play the role of Chris Grey and construct a classification model to identify customers who are likely to respond to a mailing. Write a report that documents the following steps:

1. Explore the data. This includes addressing any missing data as well as treatment of variables. Variables may need to be transformed. Also, because of the large number of variables, you must identify appropriate means to reduce the dimension of the data. In particular, it may be helpful to filter out unnecessary and redundant variables.
2. Partition the data into training, validation, and test sets.
3. Experiment with various classification methods and propose a final model for identifying customers who will respond to the targeted marketing.
   a. Your report should include a chart of the Class 1 and Class 0 error rates for various values of the cutoff probability.
   b. Recommend a cutoff probability value. For the test set, what is the overall error rate at this value? What are the Class 1 and Class 0 error rates at this value?
   c. If GCC sends the targeted marketing to the model's top decile, what is the expected response rate? How does that compare to the average industry rate?

Chapter 9 Appendix

Appendix 9.1 Data Partitioning with XLMiner

Before a classification or estimation method can be constructed, the data must be partitioned into training, validation, and test sets. We demonstrate this using the Optiva Credit Union example. In the file *Optiva* we observe that only 1.8% of the customer observations correspond to a default. Thus, the task of classifying loan customers as either "default" or "no default" involves a rare event. To provide sufficient information on loan defaults, we will create a training set with 50% loan default observations. The validation set and test set will be formed to have approximately 1.8% loan default observations in order to be representative of the overall population. The following steps and Figure 9.14 demonstrate this process. We have saved the standard partition of the Optiva data set resulting from executing the following steps in the file *OptivaPartOS*.

DATA *file*

Optiva

Step 1. Select any cell in the range of the data
Step 2. Click the **XLMiner Platform** tab on the Ribbon
Step 3. Click **Partition** from the **Data Mining** group
Step 4. Click **Partition with Oversampling**
Step 5. In the **Data Source** area, confirm that the **Worksheet:**, **Workbook:**, and **Data range:** entries correspond to the appropriate data (see Figure 9.14)
Step 6. In the **Variables** area, select **First Row Contains Headers**
Step 7. In the **Variables** box of the **Variables** area, select **CustomerID**, **LoanDefault**, **AverageBalance**, **Age**, **Entrepreneur**, **Unemployed**, **Married**, **Divorced**, **High School**, and **College** variables and click the > button to populate the **Variables in the Partition Data** box
Step 8. Select **LoanDefault** in the **Variables in the Partition Data** box of the **Variables** area
Step 9. Click the > button to populate the **Output variable:** box
Step 10. In the **Randomization Options** area, select the box next to **Set seed:** and enter *12345*
Step 11. In the **Output options** area, select **1** from the pulldown menu of the **Specify Success class**:
Step 12. In the **Output options** area, enter *2* in the **# Classes** box, enter *50* in the **Specify % success in training set** box, and enter *40* in the **Specify % validation data to be taken away as test data**
Step 13. Click **OK**

To partition the data in the file *Optiva* for the purposes of predicting a customer's average balance, we use XLMiner's Standard Data Partition procedure. The following steps and Figure 9.15 demonstrate the process of partitioning a data set so that 23.15% of the observations compose the training set, 46.11% of the observations compose the validation set, and 30.74% of the observations compose the test set. We have saved the standard partition of the Optiva data set resulting from executing the following steps in the file *OptivaStandard*.

Step 1. Select any cell in the range of the data
Step 2. Click the **XLMiner Platform** tab on the Ribbon
Step 3. Click **Partition** from the **Data Mining** group
Step 4. Click **Standard Partition**

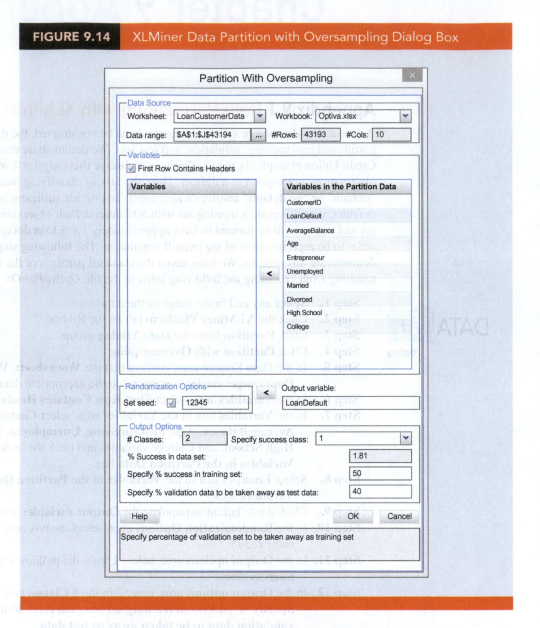

FIGURE 9.14   XLMiner Data Partition with Oversampling Dialog Box

Step 5.   In the **Data Source** area, confirm that the **Worksheet:**, **Workbook:**, and **Data range:** entries correspond to the appropriate data (see Figure 9.15)

Step 6.   In the **Variables** area, select **First Row Contains Headers**

Step 7.   In the **Variables** box of the **Variables** area, select **CustomerID**, **AverageBalance**, **Age**, **Entrepreneur**, **Unemployed**, **Married**, **Divorced**, **High School**, and **College** variables and click the > button to populate the **Variables in the partitioned data** box

Step 8.   In the **Partitioning options** area, select **Pick up rows randomly**, select the box next to **Set seed:**, and enter *12345*

Step 9.   In the **Partitioning percentages when picking up rows randomly** area, select **Specify percentages**, enter *23.15* in the **Training Set** box, enter *46.11* in the **Validation Set** box, and enter *30.74* in the **Test Set** box

Step 10. Click **OK**

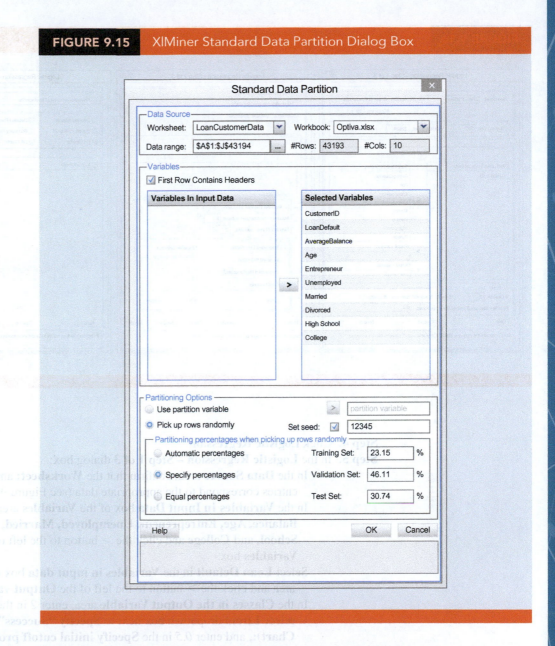

FIGURE 9.15   XlMiner Standard Data Partition Dialog Box

Appendix 9.2 Logistic Regression Classification with XLMiner

We demonstrate how XLMiner facilitates the construction of a logistic regression model by using the Optiva Credit Union problem of classifying customer observations as either a loan default (Class 1) or no default (Class 0). The following steps and Figure 9.16 demonstrate this process.

Step 1. In the *Data_Partition* worksheet, select any cell (such as cell B26) in the range of data listed below **Selected Variables**

Step 2. Click the **XLMiner Platform** tab on the Ribbon

Step 3. Click **Classify** from the **Data Mining** group

FIGURE 9.16   XLMiner Steps for Logistic Regression

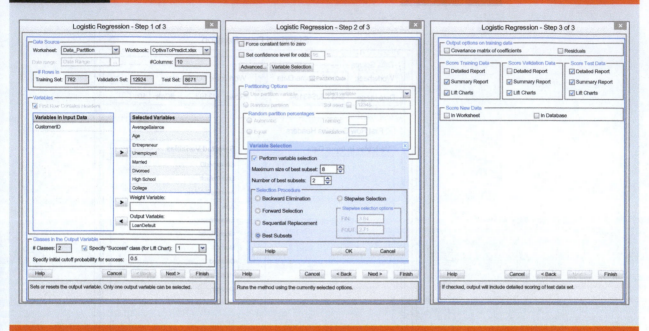

Step 4. Click **Logistic Regression**
Step 5. In the **Logistic Regression – Step 1 of 3** dialog box:

In the **Data Source** area, confirm that the **Worksheet:** and **Workbook:** entries correspond to the appropriate data (see Figure 9.16)

In the **Variables In Input Data** box of the **Variables** area, select **Average Balance, Age, Entrepreneur, Unemployed, Married, Divorced, High School,** and **College** and click the > button to the left of the **Selected Variables** box

Select **Loan Default** in the **Variables in input data** box of the **Variables** area and click the > button to the left of the **Output variable:** box

In the **Classes in the Output Variable** area, enter *2* in the **# Classes** box, select **1** from dropdown box next to **Specify "Success" class (for Lift Chart):**, and enter *0.5* in the **Specify initial cutoff probability for success:** box

Click **Next**

Step 6. In the **Logistic Regression – Step 2 of 3** dialog box:

Click **Variable Selection** and when the **Variable Selection** dialog box appears:

Select the checkbox for **Perform variable selection**

Set the **Maximum size of best subset:** box to **8**

In the **Selection Procedure** area, select **Best Subsets**

Above the **Selection Procedure area,** set the **Number of best subsets:** box to **2**

Click **OK**

Click **Next**

Step 7. In the **Logistic Regression – Step 3 of 3** dialog box:

In the **Score Test Data** area, select the checkboxes for **Detailed Report**, **Summary Report**, and **Lift Charts**. Leave all other checkboxes unchanged.

Click **Finish**

XLMiner provides several options for selecting variables to include in alternative logistic regression models. Best subsets is the most comprehensive method; it considers every possible combination of the variables but is typically appropriate only when dealing with fewer than 10 explanatory variables. When dealing with many variables, best subsets may be too computationally expensive, as it will require constructing hundreds of alternative models. In cases with a moderate number of variables, 10 to 20, backward selection is effective at eliminating the unhelpful variables. Backward elimination begins with all possible variables and sequentially removes the least useful variable (with respect to statistical significance). When dealing with more than 20 variables, forward selection is often appropriate, as it identifies the most helpful variables.

This procedure builds several logistic regression models for consideration. In the *LR_Output* worksheet displayed in Figure 9.17, the area titled **Regression Model** lists the statistical information on the logistic regression model using all of the selected explanatory variables. This information corresponds to the logistic regression fit of:

$$\ln(\hat{p}/(1 - \hat{p})) = 0.6745 - 0.0005 \times \text{Average Balance} + \cdots$$
$$+ 0.5262 \times \text{Divorced} + \cdots - 0.2428 \times \text{College}$$

FIGURE 9.17   XLMiner Logistic Regression Output in *LR_Output* Worksheet

While these coefficients do not have a direct intuitive interpretation, the sign of a coefficient in the logistic regression is meaningful. For example, the negative coefficient of the Average Balance variable means that as a customer's average balance increases, the probability of default decreases. Similarly, the positive coefficient of the binary Divorced variable means that a divorced customer is more likely to default than a nondivorced customer. The p value information reflects the statistical significance of each coefficient. While a logistic regression model used for predictive purposes should ultimately be judged by its classification error on the validation and test sets, the p value information can provide some guidance about which models to evaluate further (i.e., large p values suggest that the corresponding variable may be less helpful in accurately classifying observations).

In addition to fitting the logistic regression model with all the selected explanatory variables, XLMiner also provides summary measures on models with combinations of the variables. The **Variable Selection** area in Figure 9.17 lists (Maximum size of best subset $\times$ Number of best subsets) $= 8 \times 2 = 16$ models. To sort through these models, typically there is a preference for models with fewer coefficients (cells D92 through D107) and with a Mallow's C_p statistic value (cells F92 through F107) that is small and near the number of coefficients in the model. RSS stands for residual sum of squares and computes the sum of squared deviations between the predicted probability of success and the actual value (1 or 0). Models with a smaller RSS are preferred, but as more variables are added, the additional decrease in RSS is not as large.

After identifying one or more models for further analysis, we can then evaluate each of them with respect to how well they classify the observations in the validation set. Evaluating the models listed in Figure 9.17, we see that there appear to be several similar models. For example, the model in row 94 with 2 coefficients (the constant and the variable AverageBalance) may be a good candidate for closer examination.

Clicking on **Choose Subset** in cell C94 of the *LR_Output* worksheet activates the XLMiner procedure to refit the logistic regression model with explanatory variable AverageBalance. The following steps and Figure 9.18 explain how to construct this logistic regression model and use it to predict the loan default probability of 30 new customers.

> **Step 1.** Click on **Choose Subset** in cell C94 of *LR_Output* worksheet
> **Step 2.** In the **Logistic Regression – Step 1 of 3** dialog box, click **Next >**
> **Step 3.** In the **Logistic Regression – Step 2 of 3** dialog box, click **Next**
> **Step 4.** In the **Logistic Regression – Step 3 of 3** dialog box:
>> In the **Score Test Data** area, select the checkboxes for **Detailed Report, Summary Report, Lift Charts;** leave all other checkboxes unchanged
>> In the **Score New Data** area, select **In worksheet**
>> When the **Match Variables in the New Range** dialog box appears:
>> In the **Data Source** area, select the worksheet name **New Data To Predict** from the pulldown menu next to **Worksheet;** enter *$A$1:$J$31* in the **Data Range:** box
>> In the **Variables** area, select the checkbox for **First Row Contains Headers** and click **Match By Name**
>> Click **OK**
>> Click **Finish**

The preceding steps produce a worksheet titled *LR_Output1* that lists the classification confusion matrices for the logistic regression model with AverageBalance as the explanatory variable. Figure 9.19 displays the classification confusion matrices for the validation and test sets. Using the cutoff value of 0.5, we observe that the logistic

FIGURE 9.18   XLMiner Steps for Refitting the Logistic Regression Model and Predicting New Data

---

Logistic Regression - Step 1 of 3

Data Source
Worksheet: Data_Partition   Workbook: OptivaToPredict.xlsx
Data range: Data Range   # Columns: 10

Rows In
Training Set: 782   Validation Set: 12924   Test Set: 8671

Variables
☑ First Row Contains Headers

Variables In Input Data	Selected Variables
CustomerID	AverageBalance
Age	
Entrepreneur	
Unemployed	
Married	
Divorced	
High School	
College	

Weight Variable:

Output Variable:
LoanDefault

Classes in the Output Variable
Classes: 2   ☑ Specify "Success" class (for Lift Chart): 1
Specify initial cutoff probability for success: 0.5

Help   Cancel   < Back   Next >   Finish
View help.

Logistic Regression - Step 2 of 3

☐ Force constant term to zero
☐ Set confidence level for odds: 95 %
Advanced...   Variable Selection

☐ Partition Data

Partitioning Options
○ Use partition variable   select variable
○ Random partition   Set seed: ☐ 12345
Random partition percentages
○ Automatic   Training:
○ Equal   Validation:
○ User defined   Test:

Help   Cancel   < Back   Next >   Finish
Move to the next step.

Logistic Regression - Step 3 of 3

Output options on training data
☐ Covariance matrix of coefficients   ☐ Residuals

Score Training Data	Score Validation Data	Score Test Data
☐ Detailed Report	☐ Detailed Report	☑ Detailed Report
☑ Summary Report	☑ Summary Report	☑ Summary Report
☑ Lift Charts	☑ Lift Charts	☑ Lift Charts

Score New Data
☐ In Worksheet   ☐ In Database

Help   Cancel   < Back   Next >   Finish
Cancels the current operation.

Match Variables in the New Range

Data Source
Worksheet: NewDataToPredict   Workbook: OptivaToPredict.xlsx
Data range: $A$1:$J$31   #Rows: 30   #Cols: 10

Variables
☑ First Row Contains Headers

Variables In New Data	Continuous Variables in Input Data
CustomerID	AverageBalance<=>AverageBalance
Age	
Entrepreneur	
Unemployed	
Married	
Divorced	
High School	
College	
LoanDefault	

Match Selected   Unmatch Selected   Unmatch All   Match By Name   Match Sequentially

Help   OK   Cancel
Matches all the same name variables from the new data variable list to input data variable list.

FIGURE 9.19   Classification Error for Logistic Regression Model in *LR_Output* Worksheet

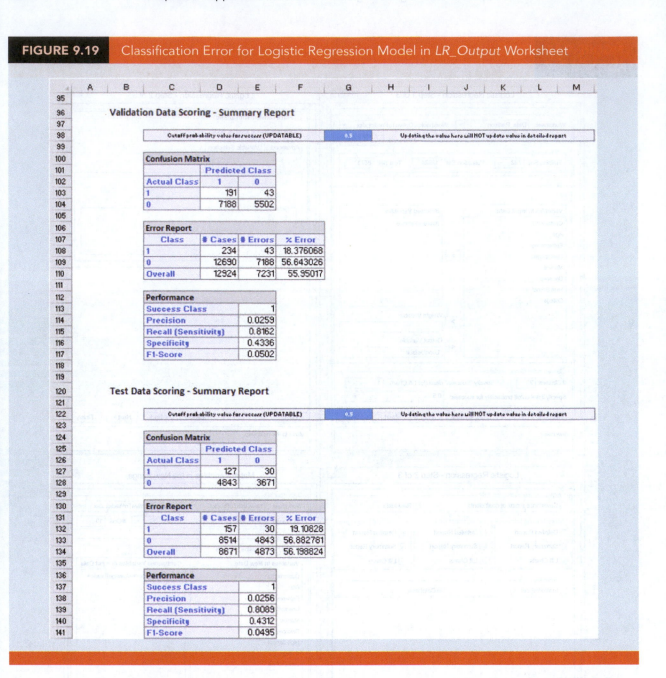

regression model has a Class 1 error rate of 18.38% and a Class 0 error rate of 56.64% on the validation data; on the test set, the Class 1 error rate is 19.11% and the Class 0 error rate is 56.88%. Optiva can expect a Class 1 error rate of approximately 19% and a Class 0 error rate of approximately of 57% when using this model on new customer observations.

The preceding steps also produce a worksheet titled *LR_NewScore1* that lists the logistic regression model's classification of the 30 new customer observations in the *NewDataToPredict* worksheet. Figure 9.20 displays the estimated probability of Class 1 membership (loan default) and the classification using the cutoff value of 0.5. For example, the first observation has an estimated probability of 0.4135 for defaulting on a loan. Based on the cutoff value of 0.5, we predict that this observation is Class 0 or a nondefaulter on a loan.

FIGURE 9.20   Classification of 30 New Customer Observations (*LR_Newscore* Worksheet)

	Predicted Class	Prob. for 0	Prob. for 1	AverageBalance
15	0	0.5864874	0.41351259	1467
16	1	0.438304	0.56169598	386
17	0	0.5888982	0.41110178	1485
18	1	0.4806967	0.51930328	695
19	1	0.4823527	0.51764733	707
20	1	0.3932268	0.60677317	50
21	0	0.9128765	0.08712349	5085
22	0	0.6476437	0.35235626	1936
23	0	0.7582661	0.24173389	2903
24	1	0.4682931	0.53170691	605
25	0	0.9911537	0.00884632	9372
26	1	0.4277195	0.5722805	308
27	0	0.7742013	0.22579872	3064
28	0	0.5623052	0.4376948	1288
29	0	0.5769387	0.42306135	1396
30	1	0.3890146	0.61098537	18
31	1	0.4351767	0.56482335	363
32	1	0.3969256	0.60307439	78
33	1	0.4940913	0.50590868	792
34	1	0.4080913	0.59190873	162
35	1	0.3933587	0.60664127	51
36	0	0.7255977	0.2744023	2594
37	1	0.4233956	0.57660436	276
38	0	0.9406896	0.0593104	5835
39	1	0.455106	0.54489403	509
40	1	0.3993097	0.60069035	96
41	1	0.4255561	0.57444386	292
42	1	0.4095608	0.59043924	173
43	1	0.4790412	0.52095881	683
44	1	0.4553801	0.54461987	511

NOTES + COMMENTS

1. Other XLMiner alternatives for selecting variables in a regression model include stepwise selection and sequential replacement. Stepwise selection starts with no variables, but at each step considers both the insertion and removal of a variable based on the *F*-statistics FIN and FOUT, respectively. To prevent cycling, FIN ≥ FOUT, with typical values of 6.5 and 3, respectively. Sequential replacement considers models with a fixed number of values by inserting a new variable whenever one is removed.

2. XLMiner provides functionality for multiple linear regression that greatly enhances the basic regression capabilities provided by Excel's Data Analysis Toolpak. The **Multiple Linear Regression** procedure is listed under **Prediction** in the **Data Mining** group on the XLMiner Ribbon. This functionality is described in the appendix to Chapter 7.

Appendix 9.3 *k*-Nearest Neighbor Classification and Estimation with XLMiner

XLMiner provides the capability to apply the *k*-Nearest Neighbors method for classifying a 0–1 categorical outcome and for estimating a continuous outcome. We begin by demonstrating how to use *k*-Nearest Neighbors as a classification method.

We apply this *k*-Nearest Neighbors method on the data partitioned with oversampling from *Optiva* to classify observations as either loan default (Class 1) or no default (Class 0). The following steps and Figure 9.21 demonstrate this process.

DATA *file*

OptivaPartOS

Step 1. In the *Data_Partition* worksheet, select any cell (such as cell B26) in the range of data listed below **Selected Variables**

Step 2. Click the **XLMiner Platform** tab on the Ribbon

Step 3. Click **Classify** from the **Data Mining** group

Step 4. Click *k*-**Nearest Neighbors**

Step 5. In the *k*-**Nearest Neighbors Classification – Step 1 of 3** dialog box:

In the **Data Source** area, confirm that the **Worksheet:**, **Workbook:**, and **Data range:** entries correspond to the appropriate data (see Figure 9.21)

In the **Variables in Input Data** box of the **Variables** area, select **Average Balance**, **Age**, **Entrepreneur**, **Unemployed**, **Married**, and **Divorced**, **High School**, and **College** variables and click the > button to the left of the **Selected Variables** box

In the **Variables in Input Data** box of the **Variables** area, select **Loan Default** and click the > button to the left of the **Output Variable:** box

In the **Classes in the Output Variable** area, enter *2* in the **# Classes** box, select **1** from dropdown box next to **Specify "Success" class (for Lift Chart):**, and enter *0.5* in the **Specify initial cutoff probability value for success** box

Click **Next**

Step 6. In the *k*-**Nearest Neighbors Classification – Step 2 of 3** dialog box:

Select the checkbox for **Normalize input data**

Enter *20* in the **Number of nearest neighbors (k):** box

In the **Scoring Option** area, select **Score on best k between 1 and specified value**

In the **Prior Class Probabilities** area, select **User specified prior probabilities**, and enter *0.9819* for the probabilty of Class 0 and *0.0181* for the probability of Class 1 by double-clicking the corresponding entry in the table

Click **Next**

Step 7. In the *k*-**Nearest Neighbors Classification – Step 3 of 3** dialog box:

In the **Score Test Data** area, select the checkboxes for **Detailed Report, Summary Report**, and **Lift Charts;** leave all other checkboxes unchanged

Click **Finish**

If there are not k distinct nearest neighbors of an observation because this observation has several neighboring observations equidistant from it, then the procedure must break this tie. To do this, XLMiner randomly selects from the set of equidistant neighbors, the needed number of observations to assemble a set of k-nearest neighbors. The likelihood of an equidistant neighboring observation being selected depends on the prior probability of the observation's class.

This procedure runs the *k*-Nearest Neighbors method for values of *k* ranging from 1 to 20 on both the training set and validation set. The procedure generates a worksheet titled *KNNC_Output* that contains the overall error rate on the training set and the validation set for various values of *k*. As Figure 9.22 shows, *k* = 1 achieves the smallest

FIGURE 9.21   XLMiner Steps for *k*-Nearest Neighbors Classification

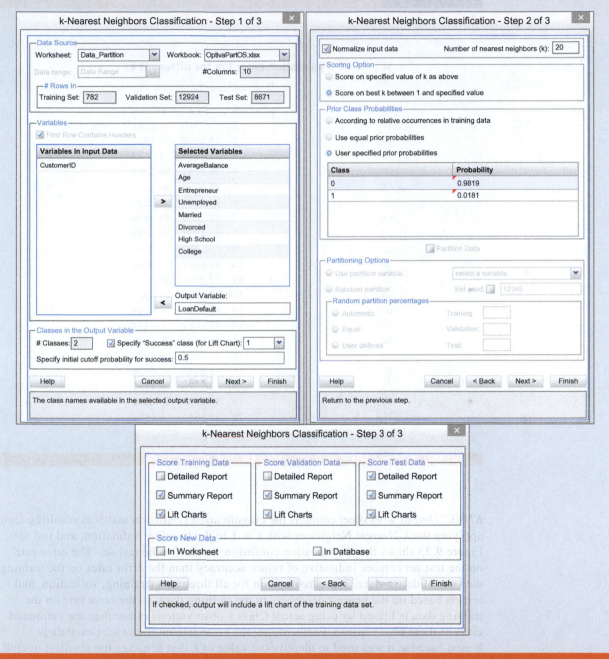

overall error rate on the validation set. This suggests that Optiva should classify a customer as "default or no default" based on the category of the most similar customer in the training set.

XLMiner applies *k*-Nearest Neighbors to the test set using the value of *k* that achieves the smallest overall error rate on the validation set (*k* = 1 in this case). The

FIGURE 9.22	KNNC_Output Worksheet: Classification Error Rates for Range of k Values for k-Nearest Neighbors

	A	B	C	D	E	F
54		**Validation error log for different k**				
55						
56			Value of k	% Error Training	% Error Validation	
57			1	0	43.2297	<- Best k
58			2	23.1458	62.9913	
59			3	21.4834	44.692	
60			4	26.7263	59.0994	
61			5	25.7033	46.9514	
62			6	29.9233	59.1535	
63			7	29.2839	48.8626	
64			8	31.4578	58.5809	
65			9	31.202	50.3637	
66			10	32.6087	58.5036	
67			11	32.9923	49.2572	
68			12	32.4808	55.0913	
69			13	32.8645	48.584	
70			14	32.6087	55.424	
71			15	31.9693	49.6828	
72			16	33.6317	55.4395	
73			17	32.8645	51.6326	
74			18	33.376	56.1281	
75			19	34.0153	51.0368	
76			20	35.1662	56.6852	

KNNC_Output worksheet contains the classification confusion matrices resulting from applying the *k*-Nearest Neighbors with *k* = 1 to the training, validation, and test sets. Figure 9.23 shows the classification confusion matrix for the test set. The error rate on the test set is more indicative of future accuracy than the error rates on the training data or validation data. The classification for all three sets (training, validation, and test) is based on the nearest neighbors in the training data, so the error rate on the training data is biased by using actual Class 1 observations rather than the estimated class of these observations. Furthermore, the error rate on the validation data is biased because it was used to identify the value of *k* that achieves the smallest overall error rate.

To demonstrate how to use *k*-Nearest Neighbors to estimate a continuous outcome, we consider a partitioned sample of data from *Optiva* and the task of predicting an observation's average balance. The following steps and Figure 9.24 demonstrate this process.

Step 1. In the *Data_Partition* worksheet, select any cell (such as cell B21) in the range of data listed below **Selected Variables**

FIGURE 9.23	Classification Confusion Matrix for *k*-Nearest Neighbors

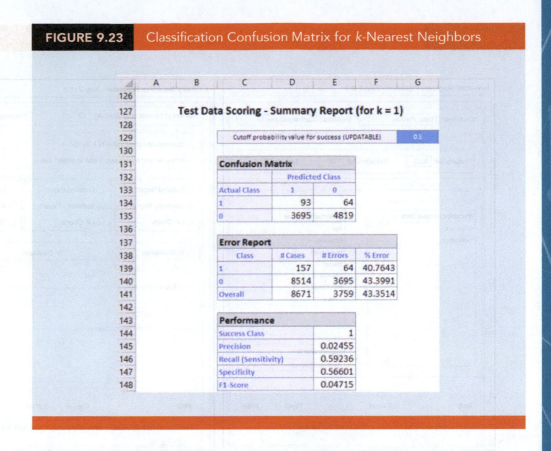

Test Data Scoring - Summary Report (for k = 1)

Cutoff probability value for success (UPDATABLE)	0.5

Confusion Matrix

Actual Class	Predicted Class	
	1	0
1	93	64
0	3695	4819

Error Report

Class	# Cases	# Errors	% Error
1	157	64	40.7643
0	8514	3695	43.3991
Overall	8671	3759	43.3514

Performance

Success Class	1
Precision	0.02455
Recall (Sensitivity)	0.59236
Specificity	0.56601
F1-Score	0.04715

The k-Nearest Neighbors procedure is computationally intense. Depending on your computer's capability, you may have to reduce the number of observations in the training set (by repartitioning the original data and reducing the percentage allocated to the training set) in order to successfully execute the k-Nearest Neighbors procedure.

Step 2. Click the **XLMiner Platform** tab on the Ribbon

Step 3. Click **Predict** from the **Data Mining** group

Step 4. Click *k*-**Nearest Neighbors**

Step 5. In the *k*-**Nearest Neighbors Prediction – Step 1 of 2** dialog box:

In the **Data Source** area, confirm that the **Worksheet:**, **Workbook:**, and **Data range:** entries correspond to the appropriate data

In the **Variables in Input Data** box of the **Variables** area, select **Age**, **Entrepreneur**, **Unemployed**, **Married**, **Divorced**, **High School**, and **College** variables and click the > button to the left of the **Selected Variables** box

Select **Average Balance** in the **Variables in input data** box of the **Variables** area and click the > button to the left of the **Output variable:** box

Click **Next**

Step 6. In the *k*-**Nearest Neighbors Prediction – Step 2 of 2** dialog box:

Enter *20* in the **Number of nearest neighbors (k)** box

Select the checkbox for **Normalize input data**

In the **Scoring Option** area, select **Score on best k between 1 and specified value**

In the **Score Test Data** area, select **Detailed Report**, **Summary Report**, and **Lift Charts**

Click **Finish**

FIGURE 9.24   XLMiner Steps for *k*-Nearest Neighbors Prediction

This procedure runs the *k*-Nearest Neighbors method for values of *k* ranging from 1 to 20 on both the training set and the validation set. The procedure generates a worksheet titled *KNNP_Output* that contains the RMSE on the training set and validation set for various values of *k*. As Figure 9.25 shows, *k* = 20 achieves the smallest RMSE on the validation set. This suggests that Optiva should estimate a customer's average balance with the average balance of the 20 most similar customers in the training set.

XLMiner applies *k*-Nearest Neighbors to the test set using the value of *k* that achieves the smallest RMSE on the validation set (*k* = 20 in this case). The *KNNP_Output* worksheet contains the RMSE and average error resulting from applying the *k*-Nearest Neighbors with *k* = 20 to the training, validation, and test sets. Figure 9.26 shows the RMSE for the training validation and test sets. The RMSE of $3,534.98 on the test set provides Optiva an estimate of how accurate the estimates will be on new data. The average error of −81.46 on the test set suggests a slight tendency to overestimate the average balance of observation in the test set.

FIGURE 9.25   Prediction Error for Range of *k* Values for *k*-Nearest Neighbors

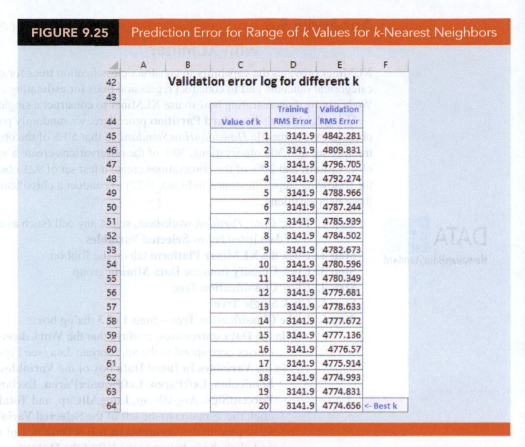

Validation error log for different k

Value of k	Training RMS Error	Validation RMS Error	
1	3141.9	4842.281	
2	3141.9	4809.831	
3	3141.9	4796.705	
4	3141.9	4792.274	
5	3141.9	4788.966	
6	3141.9	4787.244	
7	3141.9	4785.939	
8	3141.9	4784.502	
9	3141.9	4782.673	
10	3141.9	4780.596	
11	3141.9	4780.349	
12	3141.9	4779.681	
13	3141.9	4778.633	
14	3141.9	4777.672	
15	3141.9	4777.136	
16	3141.9	4776.57	
17	3141.9	4775.914	
18	3141.9	4774.993	
19	3141.9	4774.831	
20	3141.9	4774.656	<- Best k

FIGURE 9.26   Prediction Accuracy for *k*-Nearest Neighbors

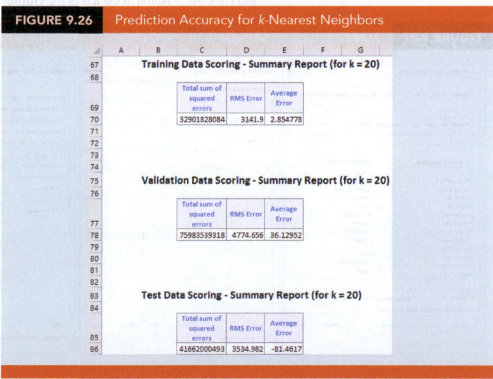

Training Data Scoring - Summary Report (for k = 20)

Total sum of squared errors	RMS Error	Average Error
32901828084	3141.9	2.854778

Validation Data Scoring - Summary Report (for k = 20)

Total sum of squared errors	RMS Error	Average Error
75983539318	4774.656	36.12952

Test Data Scoring - Summary Report (for k = 20)

Total sum of squared errors	RMS Error	Average Error
41662000493	3534.982	-81.4617

Appendix 9.4 Single Classification and Regression Trees with XLMiner

XLMiner provides the capability to construct classification trees for classifying a 0–1 categorical outcome and to construct regression trees for estimating a continuous outcome. We begin by demonstrating how to use XLMiner to construct a single classification tree.

Using XLMiner's **Standard Partition** procedure, we randomly partition the 4,601 observations in the file *HawaiianHamStandard* so that 50% of the observations create a training set of 2,300 observations, 30% of the observations create a validation set of 1,380 observations, and 20% of the observations create a test set of 921 observations. We apply the following steps (illustrated in Figure 9.27) to conduct a classification tree analysis on these data partitions.

Step 1. In the *Data_Partition* worksheet, select any cell (such as cell B21) in the range of data listed below **Selected Variables**

Step 2. Click the **XLMiner Platform** tab on the Ribbon

Step 3. Click **Classify** from the **Data Mining** group

Step 4. Click **Classification Tree**

Step 5. Click **Single Tree**

Step 6. In the **Classification Tree – Step 1 of 3** dialog box:

In the **Data source** area, confirm that the **Worksheet:** and **Workbook:** entries correspond to the appropriate data (see Figure 9.27)

In the **Variables In Input Data** box of the **Variables** area, select **Semicolon, LeftParen, LeftSquareParen, Exclamation, Dollar, PercentSign, AvgAllCap, LongAllCap,** and **TotalAllCap** and click the > button to the left of the **Selected Variables** box.

Select **Spam** in the **Variables In Input Data** box of the **Variables** area and click the > button to the left of the **Output variable:** box

FIGURE 9.27   XLMiner Steps for Classification Trees

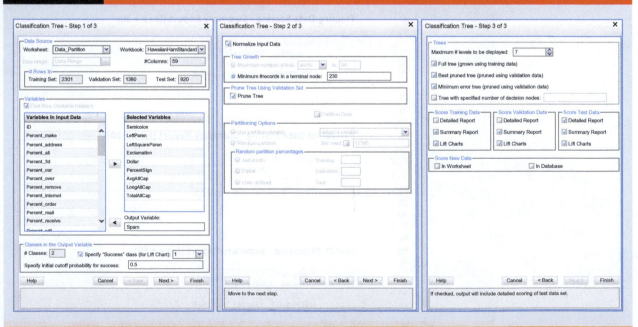

In the **Classes in the output variable** area, enter *2* for **# Classes:**, select **1** from dropdown box next to **Specify "Success" class (for Lift Chart)**, and enter *0.5* in the **Specify initial cutoff probability for success** box
Click **Next >**

Step 7. In the **Classification Tree – Step 2 of 3** dialog box:
Select the checkbox for **Normalize Input Data**
In the **Tree Growth** area, enter *230* in the box next to **Minimum # records in a terminal node:**
In the **Prune Tree Using Validation Set** area, select the checkbox for **Prune tree**
Click **Next**

Step 8. In the **Classification Tree – Step 3 of 3** dialog box:
In the **Trees** area, set the **Maximum # levels to be displayed:** box to **7**
In the **Trees** area, select the checkboxes for **Full tree (grown using training data)**, **Best pruned tree (pruned using validation data)**, and **Minimum error tree (pruned using validation data)**
In the **Score Test Data** area, select **Detailed Report**, **Summary Report**, and **Lift charts;** leave all other checkboxes unchanged
Click **Finish**

This procedure first constructs a "full" classification tree on the training data, that is, a tree that is successively partitioned by variable splitting rules until the resultant branches contain less than the minimum number of observations (230 observations in this example) or the number of displayed tree levels is reached (7 in this example). Figure 9.28 displays the first seven levels of the full tree, which XLMiner provides in a worksheet titled *CT_FullTree*. XLMiner sequentially prunes this full tree in varying degrees to investigate overfitting the

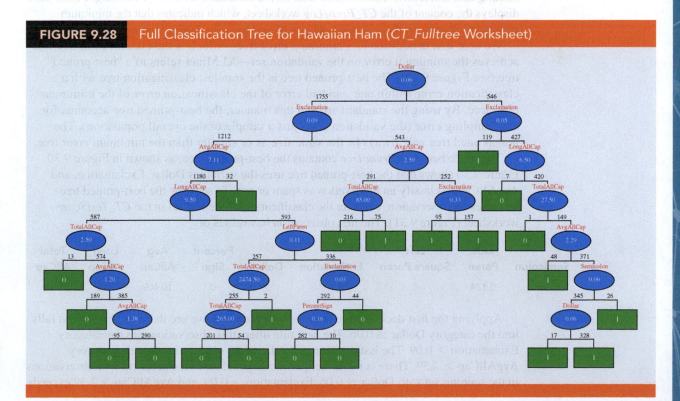

FIGURE 9.29	Prune Log for Classification Tree (*CT_PruneLog* Worksheet)

# Decision Nodes	% Error		% Std. Error	
21	13.98551			
20	13.98551			
19	13.98551			
18	13.98551			
17	13.98551			
16	13.98551			
15	13.98551			
14	13.98551			
13	13.98551			
12	13.98551			
11	13.98551			
10	13.98551			
9	13.98551			
8	13.98551	<-- Min Error Tree	% Std. Error	0.933653
7	14.34783			
6	14.34783			
5	14.34783			
4	14.34783			
3	14.13043	<-- Best Pruned		
2	19.92754			
1	19.92754			
0	39.85507			

training data and records classification error on the validation set in *CT_PruneLog*. Figure 9.29 displays the content of the *CT_PruneLog* worksheet, which indicates that the minimum classification error on the validation set is achieved by an eight-decision-node tree.

We note that in addition to a minimum error tree—which is the classification tree that achieves the minimum error on the validation set—XLMiner refers to a "best pruned" tree (see Figure 9.29). The best-pruned tree is the smallest classification tree with a classification error within one standard error of the classification error of the minimum error tree. By using the standard error in this manner, the best-pruned tree accounts for any sampling error (the validation set is just a sample of the overall population). The best-pruned tree will always be the same size as or smaller than the minimum error tree.

The worksheet *CT_PruneTree* contains the best-pruned tree, as shown in Figure 9.30. Figure 9.30 shows that the best-pruned tree uses the variables Dollar, Exclamation, and AvgAllCap to classify an observation as spam or not. To see how the best-pruned tree classifies an observation, consider the classification of the test set in the *CT_TestScore* worksheet (Figure 9.31). The first observation has values of:

Semicolon	Left Paren	Left Square Paren	Exclamation	Dollar	Percent Sign	Avg AllCap	Long AllCap	Total AllCap
0	0.124	0	0.207	0	0	10.409	343	635

Applying the first decision rule in the best-pruned tree, we see that this observation falls into the category Dollar $\leq$ 0.06. The next rule filters this observation into the category Exclamation > 0.09. The last decision node places the observation into the category AvgAllCap > 2.59. There is no further partitioning and since the proportion of observations in the training set with Dollar $\leq$ 0.06, Exclamation > 0.09, and AvgAllCap > 2.59 exceeds

FIGURE 9.30   Best-Pruned Classification Tree for Hawaiian Ham (*CT_PruneTree* Worksheet)

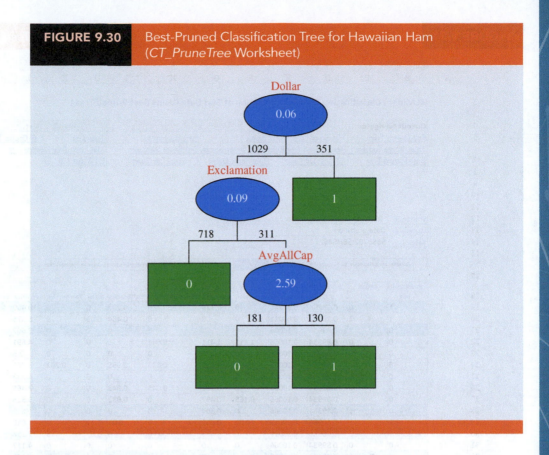

the cutoff value of 0.5, the best-pruned tree classifies this observation as Class 1 (spam). As Figure 9.31 shows, this is a misclassification, as the actual class for this observation is Class 0 (not spam). The overall classification accuracy for the best-pruned tree on the test set can be found in the *CT_Output* worksheet as shown in Figure 9.32.

To demonstrate how to construct a single regression tree with XLMiner for continuous estimation, we consider the partitioned data from the Optiva Credit Union problem to predict a customer's average checking account balance. The following steps and Figure 9.33 demonstrate this process.

DATA *file*

OptivaStandard

Step 1. In the *Data_Partition* worksheet, select any cell (such as cell B21) in the range of data listed below **Selected Variables**

Step 2. Click the **XLMiner Platform** tab on the Ribbon

Step 3. Click **Predict** from the **Data Mining** group

Step 4. Click **Regression Tree**

Step 5. Click **Single Tree**

Step 6. In the **Regression Tree – Step 1 of 3** dialog box:

In the **Data Source** area, confirm that the **Worksheet:** and **Workbook:** entries correspond to the appropriate data (see Figure 9.33)

In the **Variables In Input Data** box of the **Variables** area, select **Age**, **Entrepreneur**, **Unemployed**, **Married**, **Divorced**, **High School**, and **College** variables and click the > to the left of the **Input Variables** box.

Select **AverageBalance** in the **Variables In Input Data** box of the **Variables** area, and click the > button to the left of the **Output variable:** box

Click **Next**

FIGURE 9.31 Best-Pruned Tree Classification of Test Set for Hawaiian Ham (*CT_TestScore* Worksheet)

XLMiner : Classification Tree - Classification of Test Data (Using Best Pruned Tree)

Output Navigator					
Full-Grown Tree	Min-Error Tree	Inputs	Prior class probs	Train Log	Full-Grown Tree Rul
Train. Score Summary	Best-Pruned Tree Rule	Valid. Score Summa	Test Score Summary	Min-Error Tree R	Prune Log
Best-Pruned Tree	CT Test Lift Chart	Test Score Detail	CT Train. Lift Chart	CT Valid. Lift Ch	

Workbook	HawaiianHamStandard.xlsx
Worksheet	Data_Partition
Range	$B$3702:$BH$4621

Cutoff probability value for success (UPDATABLE)	0.5	Updating the value here will NOT update value in summary report

Predicted Class	Actual Class	Prob. for 0	Prob. for 1(success)	Semicolon	LeftParen	LeftSquareParen	Exclamation	Dollar	PercentSign	AvgAllCap	LongAllCap	TotalAllCap
1	0	0.18254	0.81746	0	0.124	0	0.207	0	0	10.409	343	635
1	1	0.10989	0.89011	0	0	0	0.484	0.08	0	8.375	85	201
0	1	0.89934	0.10066	0	0	0	0	0	0	2.307	16	30
0	0	0.89934	0.10066	1.411	1.411	0.041	0	0	0	4.891	20	675
0	0	0.89934	0.10066	0	0	0	0	0	0	2.5	9	15
0	0	0.89934	0.10066	0.607	0.064	0.036	0.055	0	0.202	3.766	43	1789
0	0	0.89934	0.10066	0	0	0	0	0	0	4.333	11	13
0	0	0.89934	0.10066	0	0.131	0.043	0.043	0	0	2.468	15	195
0	0	0.89934	0.10066	0.165	0.497	0	0.082	0	0	3.525	20	208
0	1	0.89934	0.10066	0	0.307	0	0	0	0	3.39	45	139
1	1	0.10989	0.89011	0.01	0.052	0	0.01	0.17	0	1.818	13	462
1	0	0.10989	0.89011	0	0	0	0	0.07	0	2.216	44	215
0	0	0.89934	0.10066	0	0	0	0	0	0	4.117	47	70
0	1	0.89934	0.10066	0	0	0	0	0	0	3.642	8	51
1	1	0.18254	0.81746	0.094	0.189	0.284	0.662	0	0	10.068	131	292

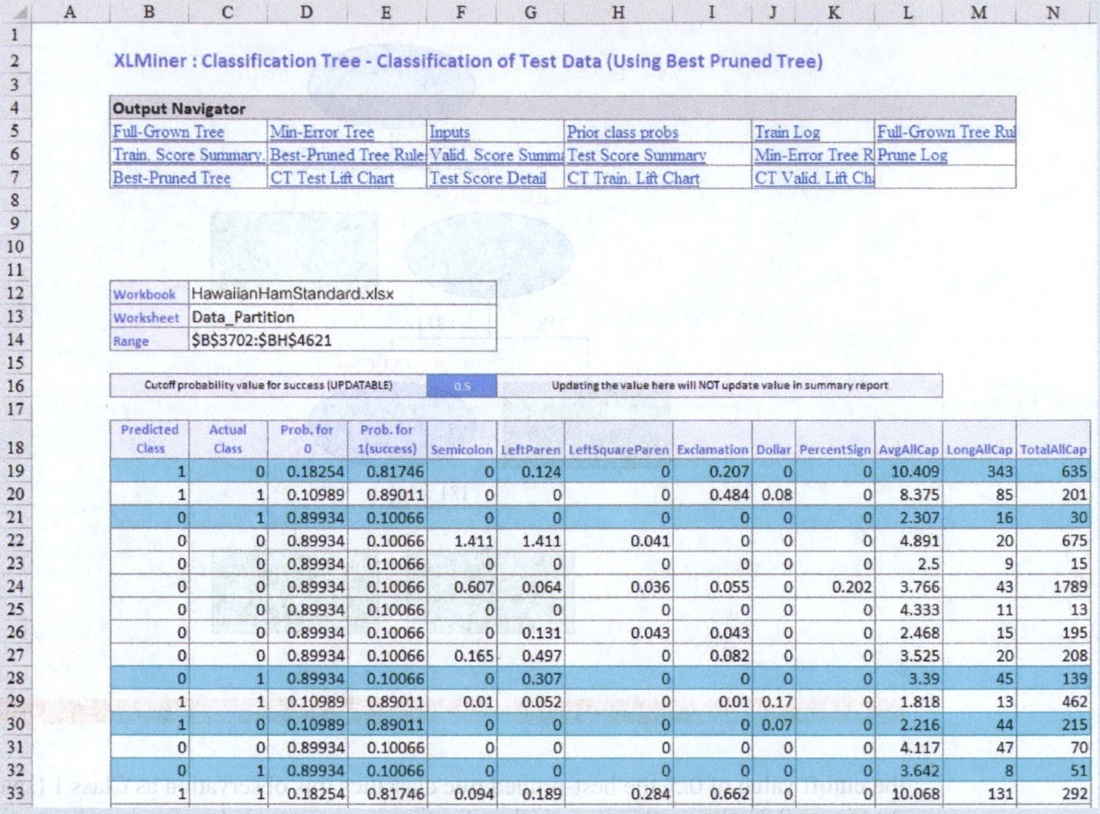

Step 7. In the **Regression Tree – Step 2 of 3** dialog box:
Select the checkbox for **Normalize input data**
In the **Tree Growth** area, enter *999* in the box next to **Minimum # records in a terminal node:**
In the **Scoring option** area, select **Using Best Pruned Tree**
Click **Next**

Step 8. In the **Regression Tree – Step 3 of 3** dialog box:
Increase the **Maximum # levels to be displayed:** box to **7**
In the **Trees** area, select **Full tree (grown using training data)**, **Pruned tree (pruned using validation data)**, and **Minimum error tree (pruned using validation data)**
In the **Score Test Data** area, select **Detailed Report** and **Summary Report**
Click **Finish**

This procedure first constructs a "full" regression tree on the training data, that is, a tree that successively partitions the variable space via variable splitting rules until the resultant branches contain less than the specified minimum number of observations (999 observations in this example) or the number of displayed tree levels is reached (7 in this example). The worksheet *RT_FullTree* (shown in Figure 9.34) displays the full

FIGURE 9.32   Best-Pruned Tree Classification Confusion Matrix on Test Set (*CT_Output* Worksheet)

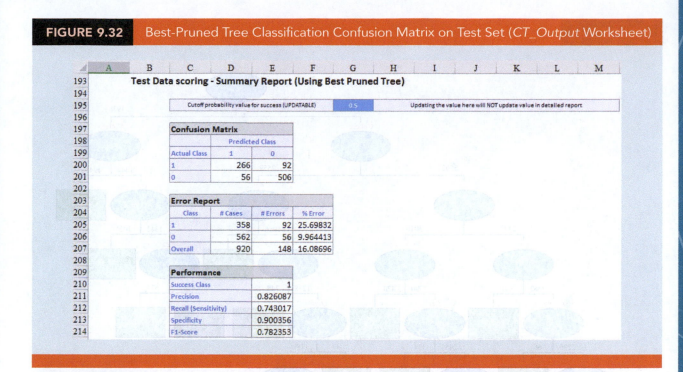

FIGURE 9.33   XLMiner Steps for Regression Trees

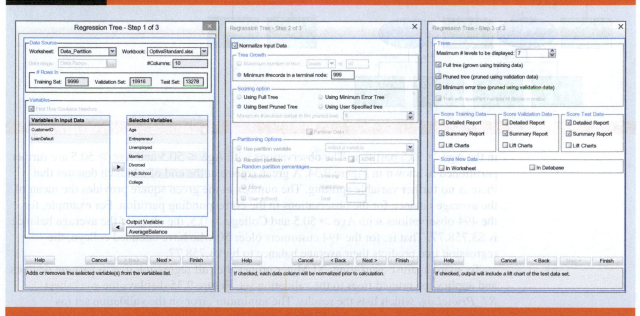

regression tree. In this tree, the number within the node represents the value on which the variable (whose name is listed above the node) is split. The first partition is formed by splitting observations into two groups, observations with Age ≤ 50.5 and observations with Age > 50.5. The numbers on the left and right arcs emanating from the blue oval node denote that there are 8,061 observations in the Age ≤ 50.5 partition and 1,938 observations

FIGURE 9.34   Full Regression Tree for Optiva Credit Union (*RT_FullTree* Worksheet)

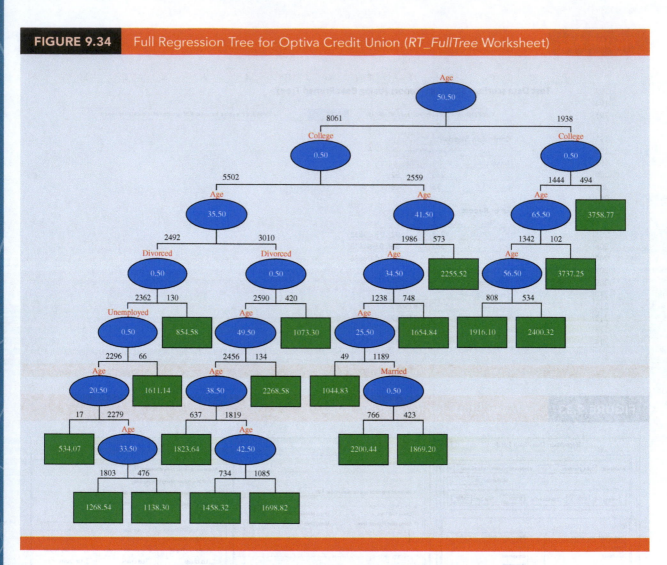

in the Age > 50.5 partition. The observations with Age ≤ 50.5 and Age > 50.5 are further partitioned as shown in Figure 9.34. A green square at the end of a branch denotes that there is no further variable splitting. The number in the green square provides the mean of the average balance for the observations in the corresponding partition. For example, for the 494 observations with Age > 50.5 and College > 0.5, the mean of the average balance is $3,758.77. That is, for the 494 customers older 50 who have attended college, the regression tree predicts their average balance to be $3,758.77.

To guard against overfitting, XLMiner prunes the full regression tree to varying degrees and applies the pruned trees to the validation set. Figure 9.35 displays the worksheet *RT_PruneLog,* which lists the results. The minimum error on the validation set (as measured by the sum of squared error between the regression tree predictions and actual observation values) is achieved by the seven-decision-node tree shown in Figure 9.36.

We note that in addition to a "minimum error tree"—which is the regression tree that achieves the minimum error on the validation set—XLMiner also refers to a "best pruned" tree (see Figure 9.35). The best-pruned tree is the smallest regression tree with a prediction error within one standard error of the prediction error of the minimum error tree. By using the standard error in this manner, the best-pruned tree accounts for any sampling error

FIGURE 9.35   Errors From the Validation Set (*RT_PruneLog* Worksheet)

# Decision Nodes	Cost Complexity	Train. MSE	Valid. MSE			
18	0	14,434,284	14,798,745			
17	11,500	14,436,817	14,796,021			
16	14,351	14,437,456	14,796,338			
15	14,439	14,440,446	14,795,740			
14	28,405	14,442,769	14,798,168			
13	31,559	14,443,613	14,790,154			
12	31,559	14,448,682	14,790,154			
11	35,883	14,453,399	14,789,452			
10	51,890	14,454,301	14,795,661			
9	50,688	14,461,841	14,801,872			
8	50,900	14,468,813	14,788,238			
7	50,900	14,482,597	14,788,238	<-- Best Pruned & Min Error Tree	Std. Error	3845.548
6	52,775	14,484,490	14,797,493			
5	82,700	14,509,632	14,799,763			
4	97,685	14,515,384	14,812,024			
3	100,566	14,534,921	14,851,006			
2	154,621	14,621,654	14,956,908			
1	173,465	14,673,194	14,949,313			
0	159,208	14,832,402	14,983,561			

FIGURE 9.36   Best-Pruned Regression Tree for Optiva Credit Union (*RT_PruneTree* Worksheet)

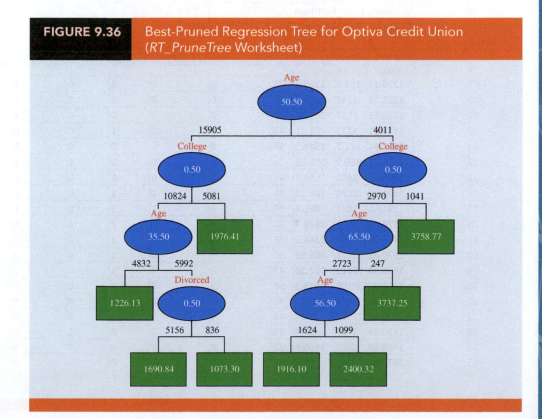

(the validation set is just a sample of the overall population). The best-pruned tree will always be the same size as or smaller than the minimum error tree.

To see how the best-pruned tree predicts an outcome for an observation, consider the classification of the test set in the *RT_TestScore* worksheet (Figure 9.37). The first observation in Figure 9.37 has values of Age = 22, Entrepreneur = 0, Unemployed = 0, Married = 1, Divorced = 0, High School = 1, and College = 0. Applying the first decision

FIGURE 9.37   Best-Pruned Tree Prediction of Test Set for Optiva Credit Union (*RT_TestScore* Worksheet)

XLMiner : Regression Tree - Prediction of Test Data (Using Best Pruned Tree)

Output Navigator

Full-Grown Tree	Min-Error Tree	Inputs		Full-Grown Tree	Best Pruned Tree
Min-Error Tree	Train. Score -	Valid. Score - Summary		Test Score - Sum	Prune Log
Best-Pruned Tree	RT Test Lift C	Test Score Detail			

Workbook	OptivaStandard.xlsx
Workshee	Data_Partition
Range	$B$29936:$K$43213

Predicted Value	Actual Value	Residual	Age	Entrepreneur	Unemployed	Married	Divorced	High School	College
1226.13	107.9	-1118.2	22	0	0	1	0	1	0
1226.13	2146	920.17	34	0	0	1	0	1	0
1226.13	1017	-209.53	30	0	0	0	0	1	0
1976.41	1275	-701.11	42	0	0	1	0	0	1
1690.84	141.7	-1549.1	36	0	0	0	0	0	0
1226.13	666.9	-559.23	34	0	0	0	0	1	0
1976.41	3883	1906.7	46	0	0	0	0	0	1
1976.41	1070	-906.51	34	0	0	1	0	0	1
1916.1	1065	-851.4	56	0	0	1	0	1	0
1976.41	10500	8523.7	34	0	0	1	0	0	1
2400.32	56	-2344.3	59	0	0	1	0	1	0
1976.41	1671	-305.91	35	0	0	1	0	0	1
1690.84	2613	922.16	47	0	0	1	0	1	0
3758.77	8108	4349.3	58	1	0	1	0	0	1
1690.84	202.8	-1488	42	0	0	0	0	0	0
1976.41	27963	25987	43	0	0	1	0	0	1
1690.84	7067	5376	36	0	0	0	0	1	0
1690.84	289.9	-1400.9	37	0	0	0	0	1	0
1976.41	49.4	-1927	38	0	0	0	0	0	1

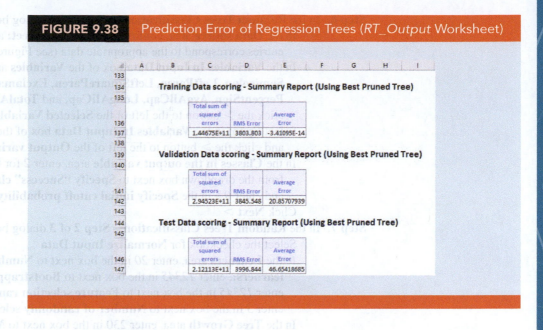

FIGURE 9.38   Prediction Error of Regression Trees (*RT_Output* Worksheet)

Training Data scoring - Summary Report (Using Best Pruned Tree)

Total sum of squared errors	RMS Error	Average Error
1.44675E+11	3803.803	-3.41095E-14

Validation Data scoring - Summary Report (Using Best Pruned Tree)

Total sum of squared errors	RMS Error	Average Error
2.94523E+11	3845.548	20.85707939

Test Data scoring - Summary Report (Using Best Pruned Tree)

Total sum of squared errors	RMS Error	Average Error
2.12113E+11	3996.844	46.65418685

rule in the best-pruned tree, we see that this observation falls into the Age $\leq$ 50.5 category. The next rule applies to the College variable, and we see that this observation falls into the College $\leq$ 0.5. The next rule places the observation in the Age $\leq$ 35.5 partition. There is no further partitioning, and the mean observation value of average balance for observations in the training set with Age $\leq$ 50.5, College $\leq$ 0.5, and Age $\leq$ 35.5 is $1,226. Therefore, the best-pruned regression tree predicts that the observation's average balance will be $1,226. As Figure 9.37 shows, the observation's actual average balance is $108, resulting in an error of −$1,118.

Reducing the minimum number of records required for a terminal node in XLMiner's regression tree procedure may result in more accurate predictions at the expense of increased time to construct the tree.

The *RT_Output* worksheet (Figure 9.38) provides the prediction error of the best-pruned tree on the training, validation, and test sets. Specifically, the RMSE of the best-pruned tree on the validation set and test set is $3,846 and $3,997, respectively. Using this best-pruned tree, which characterizes a customer based only on their age and whether they attended colleage, Optiva can expect that the RMSE will be approximately $3,997 when estimating the average balance of new customer data.

Appendix 9.5 Random Forests of Classification or Regression Trees with XLMiner

In this appendix, we demonstrate XLMiner's functionality for implementing the random forests (random trees) ensemble method for both classification and estimation problems. We begin by constructing a random forest of classification trees for classifying an observation as spam or not spam in the Hawaiian Ham example.

DATA *file*
HawaiianHamStandard

Step 1. In the *Data_Partition* worksheet, select any cell (such as cell B21) in the range of data listed below **Selected Variables**
Step 2. Click the **XLMiner Platform** tab on the Ribbon
Step 3. Click **Classify** from the **Data Mining** group
Step 4. Click **Classification Tree**
Step 5. Click **Random Trees**

Step 6. In the **Random Trees Classification – Step 1 of 3** dialog box:

In the **Data source** area, confirm that the **Worksheet:** and **Workbook:** entries correspond to the appropriate data (see Figure 9.39)

In the **Variables In Input Data** box of the **Variables** area, select **Semicolon, LeftParen, LeftSquareParen, Exclamation, Dollar, PercentSign, AvgAllCap, LongAllCap,** and **TotalAllCap** and click the > button to the left of the **Selected Variables** box.

Select **Spam** in the **Variables In Input Data** box of the **Variables** area and click the > button to the left of the **Output variable:** box

In the **Classes in the output variable** area, enter *2* for **# Classes:**, select **1** from the dropdown box next to **Specify "Success" class (for Lift Chart)**, and enter *0.5* in the **Specify initial cutoff probability for success** box

Click **Next >**

Step 7. In the **Random Trees Classification – Step 2 of 3** dialog box:

Select the checkbox for **Normalize Input Data**

In the **Learners** area, enter *20* in the box next to **Number of weak learners:**, enter *12345* in the box next to **Bootstrapping random seed:**, enter *12345* in the box next to **Feature selection random seed:**, and enter *3* in the box next to **Number of randomly selected features:**

In the **Tree Growth** area, enter 230 in the box next to **Minimum # records in a terminal node:**

Click **Next**

Step 8. In the **Random Trees Classification – Step 3 of 3** dialog box:

In the **Score Test Data** area, select **Detailed Report, Summary Report,** and **Lift charts;** leave all other checkboxes unchanged

Click **Finish**

FIGURE 9.39   XLMiner Steps for Random Trees Classification

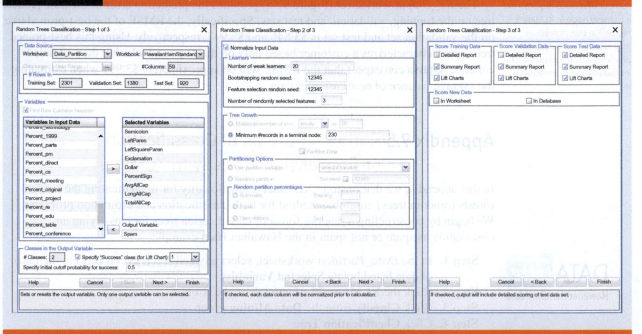

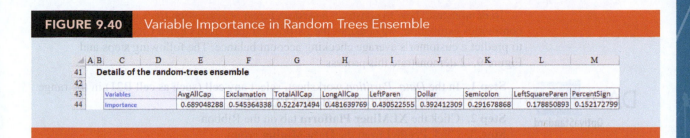

FIGURE 9.40   Variable Importance in Random Trees Ensemble

	A	B	C	D	E	F	G	H	I	J	K	L	M
41			**Details of the random-trees ensemble**										
42													
43			Variables		AvgAllCap	Exclamation	TotalAllCap	LongAllCap	LeftParen	Dollar	Semicolon	LeftSquareParen	PercentSign
44			Importance		0.689048288	0.545364338	0.522471494	0.481639769	0.430522555	0.392412309	0.291678868	0.178850893	0.152172799

This procedure generates six worksheets of output. Figures 9.40 and 9.41 display two key pieces of information from the *CTRandTrees_Output* worksheet. Figure 9.40 lists each variable's importance, in decreasing order, a measure between 0 and 1 that describes a variable's contribution in reducing the total misclassification error of the ensemble's prediction. Figure 9.41 displays the classification accuracy measures of the 20 random trees. Comparing Figure 9.41 to Figure 9.32, we observe that the random trees ensemble approach outperforms the single classification tree constructed in Appendix 9.4.

The other five worksheets are analogous to the XLMiner output for the single classification tree method of Appendix 9.4. The *CTRandTrees_TestScore* worksheet lists the ensemble's classification of each observation in test set. The *CTRandTrees_TrainLiftChart*, *CTRandTrees_ValidLiftChart*, and *CTRandTrees_TestLiftChart* worksheets contain lift charts, decile-wise lift charts, and ROC curves for the random trees classifier on the training set, validation set, and test set, respectively. The *CTRandTrees_Stored* lists the variable-splitting rules for the 20 individual classification trees composing the random forest ensemble.

FIGURE 9.41   Random Trees Classification Confusion Matrix on Test Set

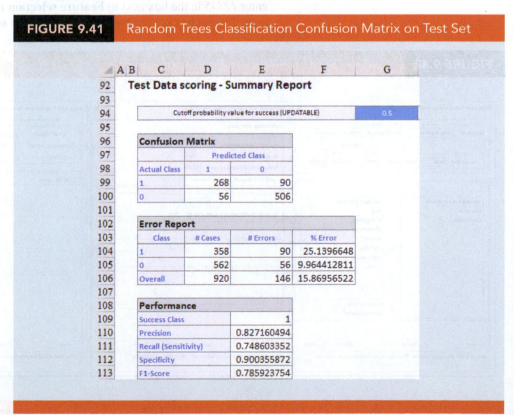

	A	B	C	D	E	F	G
92			**Test Data scoring - Summary Report**				
93							
94			Cutoff probability value for success (UPDATABLE)				0.5
95							
96			**Confusion Matrix**				
97					Predicted Class		
98			Actual Class	1	0		
99			1	268	90		
100			0	56	506		
101							
102			**Error Report**				
103			Class	# Cases	# Errors	% Error	
104			1	358	90	25.1396648	
105			0	562	56	9.964412811	
106			Overall	920	146	15.86956522	
107							
108			**Performance**				
109			Success Class		1		
110			Precision		0.827160494		
111			Recall (Sensitivity)		0.748603352		
112			Specificity		0.900355872		
113			F1-Score		0.785923754		

To demonstrate how to construct a random forest of regression trees with XLMiner for continuous estimation, we consider the partitioned data from Optiva Credit Union problem to predict a customer's average checking account balance. The following steps and Figure 9.42 demonstrate this process.

DATA file
OptivaStandard

Step 1. In the *Data_Partition* worksheet, select any cell (such as cell B21) in the range of data listed below **Selected Variables**

Step 2. Click the **XLMiner Platform** tab on the Ribbon

Step 3. Click **Predict** from the **Data Mining** group

Step 4. Click **Regression Tree**

Step 5. Click **Single Tree**

Step 6. In the **Regression Tree Random Trees – Step 1 of 3** dialog box:

In the **Data Source** area, confirm that the **Worksheet:** and **Workbook:** entries correspond to the appropriate data (see Figure 9.42)

In the **Variables In Input Data** box of the **Variables** area, select **Age**, **Entrepreneur**, **Unemployed**, **Married**, **Divorced**, **High School**, and **College** variables and click the > to the left of the **Input Variables** box.

Select **Average Balance** in the **Variables In Input Data** box of the **Variables** area, and click the > button to the left of the **Output variable:** box

Click **Next**

Step 7. In the **Regression Tree Random Trees – Step 2 of 3** dialog box:

Select the checkbox for **Normalize input data**

In the **Learners** area, enter *20* in the box next to **Number of weak learners:**, enter *12345* in the box next to **Bootstrapping random seed:**, enter *12345* in the box next to **Feature selection random seed:**, and enter *2* in the box next to **Number of randomly selected features:**

FIGURE 9.42   XLMiner Steps for Random Regression Trees

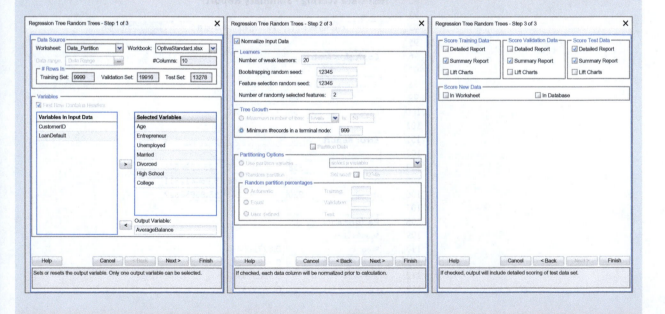

In the **Tree Growth** area, enter *999* in the box next to **Minimum # records in a terminal node:**
Click **Next**

Step 8. In the **Regression Tree Random Trees – Step 3 of 3** dialog box:
In the **Score Test Data** area, select **Detailed Report** and **Summary Report**
Click **Finish**

This procedure outputs three worksheets. As Figure 9.43 shows, the *RTRandTrees_Output* worksheet contains the estimation error on the training set, validation set, and test set for the predictions based on the 20 random regression trees. The *RTRandTrees_TestScore* worksheet compares the predicted value to the actual value for each observation in the test set. The *RTRandTrees_Stored* worksheet lists the variable-splitting rules for each of the 20 regression trees in the ensemble.

| FIGURE 9.43 | Random Regression Trees Prediction Error |

Training Data scoring - Summary Report

Total sum of squared errors	RMS Error	Average Error
1.44373E+11	3799.841	9.107265

Validation Data scoring - Summary Report

Total sum of squared errors	RMS Error	Average Error
2.94001E+11	3842.139	37.29935

Test Data scoring - Summary Report

Total sum of squared errors	RMS Error	Average Error
2.12644E+11	4001.849	62.10917

Chapter 10

Spreadsheet Models

CONTENTS

ANALYTICS IN ACTION

Procter & Gamble*

Procter & Gamble (P&G) is a Fortune 500 consumer goods company headquartered in Cincinnati, Ohio. P&G produces well-known brands such as Tide detergent, Gillette razors, Swiffer cleaning products, and many other consumer goods. P&G is a global company and has been recognized for its excellence in business analytics, including supply chain analytics and market research.

With operations around the world, P&G must do its best to maintain inventory at levels that meet its high customer service requirements. A lack of on-hand inventory can result in a stockout of a product and an inability to meet customer demand. This not only results in lost revenue for an immediate sale but can also cause customers to switch permanently to a competing brand. On the other hand, excessive inventory forces P&G to invest cash in inventory when that money could be invested in other opportunities, such as research and development.

To ensure that the inventory of its products around the world is set at appropriate levels, P&G analytics personnel developed and deployed a series of spreadsheet inventory models. These spreadsheets implement mathematical inventory models to tell business units when and how much to order to keep inventory levels where they need to be in order to maintain service and keep investment as low as possible.

The spreadsheet models were carefully designed to be easily understood by the users and easy to use and interpret. Their users can also customize the spreadsheets to their individual situations.

Over 70% of the P&G business units use these models, with a conservative estimate of a 10% reduction in inventory around the world. This equates to a cash savings of nearly $350 million.

*I. Farasyn, K. Perkoz, and W. Van de Velde, "Spreadsheet Model for Inventory Target Setting at Procter & Gamble, *Interfaces* 38, no. 4 (July–August 2008): 241–250.

Numerous specialized software packages are available for descriptive, predictive, and prescriptive business analytics. Because these software packages are specialized, they usually provide the user with numerous options and the capability to perform detailed analyses. However, they tend to be considerably more expensive than a spreadsheet package such as Excel. Also, specialized packages often require substantial user training. Because spreadsheets are less expensive, often come preloaded on computers, and are fairly easy to use, they are without question the most used business analytics tool. Every day, millions of people around the world use spreadsheet decision models to perform risk analysis, inventory tracking and control, investment planning, breakeven analysis, and many other essential business planning and decision tasks. A well-designed, well-documented, and accurate spreadsheet model can be a very valuable tool in decision making.

If you have never used a spreadsheet or have not done so recently, we suggest you first familiarize yourself with the material in Appendix A. It provides basic information that is fundamental to using Excel.

Spreadsheet models are mathematical and logic-based models. Their strength is that they provide easy-to-use, sophisticated mathematical and logical functions, allowing for easy instantaneous recalculation for a change in model inputs. This is why spreadsheet models are often referred to as **what-if models**. What-if models allow you to answer questions such as, "If the per unit cost is $4, what is the impact on profit?" Changing data in a given cell has an impact not only on that cell but also on any other cells containing a formula or function that uses that cell.

In this chapter we discuss principles for building reliable spreadsheet models. We begin with a discussion of how to build a conceptual model of a decision problem, how to convert the conceptual model to a mathematical model, and how to implement the model in a spreadsheet. We introduce two analysis tools available in Excel, Data Tables and Goal Seek, and we discuss some Excel functions that are useful for building spreadsheet models for decision making. Finally, we present how to audit a spreadsheet model to ensure its reliability.

10.1 Building Good Spreadsheet Models

Let us begin our discussion of spreadsheet models by considering the cost of producing a single product. The total cost of manufacturing a product can usually be defined as the sum of two costs: fixed cost and variable cost. *Fixed cost* is the portion of the total cost that does not depend on the production quantity; this cost remains the same no matter how much is produced. *Variable cost*, on the other hand, is the portion of the total cost that is dependent on and varies with the production quantity. To illustrate how cost models can be developed, we will consider a manufacturing problem faced by Nowlin Plastics.

Nowlin Plastics produces a line of cell phone covers. Nowlin's best-selling cover is its Viper model, a slim but very durable black and gray plastic cover. The annual fixed cost for the Viper cover is $234,000. This fixed cost includes management time and other costs that are incurred regardless of the number of units eventually produced. In addition, the total variable cost, including labor and material costs, is $2 for each unit produced.

Nowlin is considering outsourcing the production of some products for next year, including the Viper. Nowlin has a bid from an outside firm to produce the Viper for $3.50 per unit. Although it is more expensive per unit to outsource the Viper ($3.50 versus $2.00), the fixed cost can be avoided if Nowlin purchases rather than manufactures the product. Next year's exact demand for Viper is not yet known. Nowlin would like to compare the costs of manufacturing the Viper in-house to those of outsourcing its production to another firm, and management would like to do that for various production quantities. Many manufacturers face this type of decision, which is known as a **make-versus-buy decision**.

Influence Diagrams

It is often useful to begin the modeling process with a conceptual model that shows the relationships between the various parts of the problem being modeled. The conceptual model helps in organizing the data requirements and provides a road map for eventually constructing a mathematical model. A conceptual model also provides a clear way to communicate the model to others. An **influence diagram** is a visual representation of which entities influence others in a model. Parts of the model are represented by circular or oval symbols called *nodes*, and arrows connecting the nodes show influence.

Figure 10.1 shows an influence diagram for Nowlin's total cost of production for the Viper. Total manufacturing cost depends on fixed cost and variable cost, which in turn depends on the variable cost per unit and the quantity required.

An expanded influence diagram that includes an outsourcing option is shown in Figure 10.2. Note that the influence diagram in Figure 10.1 is a subset of the influence diagram in Figure 10.2. Our method here—namely, to build an influence diagram for a portion of the problem and then expand it until the total problem is conceptually modeled—is usually a good way to proceed. This modular approach simplifies the process and reduces the likelihood of error. This is true not just for influence diagrams but for the construction of the mathematical and spreadsheet models as well. Next we turn our attention to using the influence diagram in Figure 10.2 to guide us in the construction of the mathematical model.

Building a Mathematical Model

The task now is to use the influence diagram to build a mathematical model. Let us first consider the cost of manufacturing the required units of the Viper. As the influence diagram shows, this cost is a function of the fixed cost, the variable cost per unit, and the quantity required. In general, it is best to define notation for every node in the influence diagram. Let us define the following:

q = quantity (number of units) required
FC = the fixed cost of manufacturing

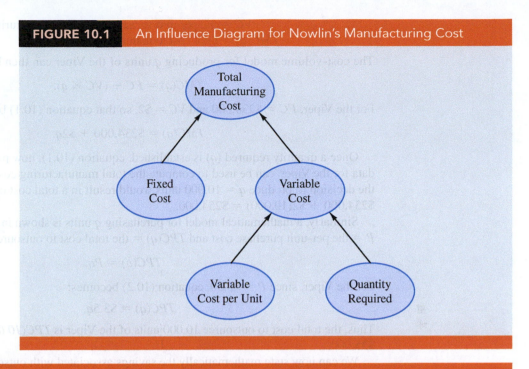

FIGURE 10.1   An Influence Diagram for Nowlin's Manufacturing Cost

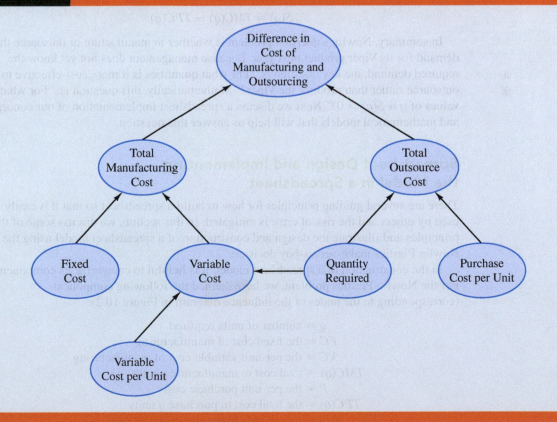

FIGURE 10.2   An Influence Diagram for Comparing Manufacturing Versus Outsourcing Cost for Nowlin Plastics

$$VC = \text{the per-unit variable cost of manufacturing}$$
$$TMC(q) = \text{total cost to manufacture } q \text{ units}$$

The cost-volume model for producing q units of the Viper can then be written as follows:

$$TMC(q) = FC + (VC \times q). \tag{10.1}$$

For the Viper, $FC = \$234{,}000$ and $VC = \$2$, so that equation (10.1) becomes:

$$TMC(q) = \$234{,}000 + \$2q.$$

Once a quantity required (q) is established, equation (10.1), now populated with the data for the Viper, can be used to compute the total manufacturing cost. For example, the decision to produce $q = 10{,}000$ units would result in a total cost of $TMC(10{,}000) = \$234{,}000 + \$2(10{,}000) = \$254{,}000$.

Similarly, a mathematical model for purchasing q units is shown in equation (10.2). Let $P = $ the per-unit purchase cost and $TPC(q) = $ the total cost to outsource or purchase q units:

$$TPC(q) = Pq. \tag{10.2}$$

For the Viper, since $P = \$3.50$, equation (10.2) becomes:

$$TPC(q) = \$3.5q.$$

Thus, the total cost to outsource 10,000 units of the Viper is $TPC(10{,}000) = 3.5(10{,}000) = \$35{,}000$.

We can now state mathematically the savings associated with outsourcing. Let $S(q) = $ the savings due to outsourcing, that is, the difference between the total cost of manufacturing q units and the total cost of buying q units:

$$S(q) = TMC(q) - TPC(q). \tag{10.3}$$

In summary, Nowlin's decision problem is whether to manufacture or outsource the demand for its Viper product next year. Because management does not yet know the required demand, the key question is, "For what quantities is it more cost-effective to outsource rather than produce the Viper?" Mathematically, this question is, "For what values of q is $S(q) > 0$?" Next we discuss a spreadsheet implementation of our conceptual and mathematical models that will help us answer this question.

Spreadsheet Design and Implementing the Model in a Spreadsheet

There are several guiding principles for how to build a spreadsheet so that it is easily used by others and the risk of error is mitigated. In this section, we discuss some of those principles and illustrate the design and construction of a spreadsheet model using the Nowlin Plastics make-versus-buy decision.

In the construction of a spreadsheet model, it is helpful to categorize its components. For the Nowlin Plastics problem, we have defined the following components (corresponding to the nodes of the influence diagram in Figure 10.2):

$$q = \text{number of units required}$$
$$FC = \text{the fixed cost of manufacturing}$$
$$VC = \text{the per-unit variable cost of manufacturing}$$
$$TMC(q) = \text{total cost to manufacture } q \text{ units}$$
$$P = \text{the per-unit purchase cost}$$
$$TPC(q) = \text{the total cost to purchase } q \text{ units}$$
$$S(q) = \text{the savings from outsourcing } q \text{ units}$$

Note that q, FC, VC, and P each is the beginning of a path in the influence diagram in Figure 10.2. In other words, they have no inward-pointing arrows.

Several points are in order. Some of these components are a function of other components (*TMC*, *TPC*, and *S*), and some are not (*q*, *FC*, *VC*, and *P*). *TMC*, *TPC*, and *S* will be formulas involving other cells in the spreadsheet model, whereas *q*, *FC*, *VC*, and *P* will just be entries in the spreadsheet. Furthermore, the value we can control or choose is *q*. In our analysis, we seek the value of *q*, such that $S(q) > 0$; that is, the savings associated with outsourcing is positive. The number of Vipers to make or buy for next year is Nowlin's decision. So we will treat *q* somewhat differently than we will *FC*, *VC*, and *P* in the spreadsheet model, and we refer to the quantity *q* as a **decision variable**. *FC*, *VC*, and *P* are measurable factors that define characteristics of the process we are modeling and so are *uncontrollable inputs* to the model, which we refer to as **parameters** of the model.

Figure 10.3 shows a spreadsheet model for the Nowlin Plastics make-versus-buy decision.

Column A is reserved for labels, including cell A1, where we have named the model "Nowlin Plastics." The input parameters (*FC*, *VC*, and *P*) are placed in cells B4, B5, and B7, respectively. We offset *P* from *FC* and *VC* because it is for outsourcing. We have created a parameters section in the upper part of the sheet. Below the parameters section, we have created the Model section. The first entry in the Model section is the quantity *q*— the number of units of Viper produced or purchased in cell B11—and shaded it to signify that this is a decision variable. We have placed the formulas corresponding to equations (10.1) to (10.3) in cells B13, B15, and B17. Cell B13 corresponds to equation (10.1), cell B15 to (10.2), and cell B17 to (10.3).

As described in Appendix A, Excel formulas always begin with an equal sign.

In cell B11 of Figure 10.3, we have set the value of *q* to 10,000 units. The model shows that the cost to manufacture 10,000 units is $254,000, the cost to purchase the 10,000 units is $35,000, and the savings from outsourcing is $219,000. At a quantity of 10,000 units, we see that it is better to incur the higher variable cost ($3.50 versus $2) than to manufacture and have to incur the additional fixed cost of $234,000. It will take a value of *q* larger than 10,000 units to make up the fixed cost incurred when Nowlin manufactures the product. At this point, we could increase the value of *q* by placing a value higher than 10,000 in cell B11 and see how much the savings in cell B17 decreases, doing this until the savings are close to zero. This is called a *trial-and-error approach*. Fortunately, Excel has what-if analysis tools that will help us use our model to further analyze the problem. We will discuss these what-if analysis tools in Section 10.2. Before doing so, let us first review what we have learned in constructing the Nowlin spreadsheet model.

The general principles of spreadsheet model design and construction are:

- Separate the parameters from the model.
- Document the model, and use proper formatting and color as needed.
- Use simple formulas.

Let us discuss the general merits of each of these points.

Separate the parameters from the model Separating the parameters from the model enables the user to update the model parameters without the risk of mistakenly creating an error in a formula. For this reason, it is good practice to have a parameters section at the top of the spreadsheet. A separate model section should contain all calculations. For a what-if model or an optimization model, some cells in the model section might also correspond to controllable inputs or decision variables (values that are not parameters or calculations but are the values we choose). The Nowlin model in Figure 10.3 is an example of this. The parameters section is in the upper part of the spreadsheet, followed by the model section, below which are the calculations and a decision cell (B11 for *q* in our model). Cell B11 is shaded to signify that it is a decision cell.

FIGURE 10.3　Nowlin Plastics Make-Versus-Buy Spreadsheet Model

	A	B	C
1	**Nowlin Plastics**		
2			
3	**Parameters**		
4	Manufacturing Fixed Cost	234000	
5	Manufacturing Variable Cost per Unit	2	
6			
7	Outsourcing Cost per Unit	3.5	
8			
9			
10	**Model**		
11	Quantity	10000	
12			
13	Total Cost to Produce	=B4+B11*B5	
14			
15	Total Cost to Outsource	=B7*B11	
16			
17	Savings due to Outsourcing	=B13−B15	
18			
19			

MODEL *file*

Nowlin

	A	B
1	**Nowlin Plastics**	
2		
3	**Parameters**	
4	Manufacturing Fixed Cost	$234,000.00
5	Manufacturing Variable Cost per Unit	$2.00
6		
7	Outsourcing Cost per Unit	$3.50
8		
9		
10	**Model**	
11	Quantity	10,000
12		
13	Total Cost to Produce	$254,000.00
14		
15	Total Cost to Outsource	$35,000.00
16		
17	Savings due to Outsourcing	$219,000.00
18		
19		

Document the model and use proper formatting and color as needed A good spreadsheet model is well documented. Clear labels and proper formatting and alignment facilitate navigation and understanding. For example, if the values in a worksheet are cost, currency formatting should be used. Also, no cell with content should be unlabeled. A new user should be able to easily understand the model and its calculations. If color makes a model easier to understand and navigate, use it for cells and labels.

Use simple formulas Clear, simple formulas can reduce errors and make it easier to maintain the spreadsheet. Long and complex calculations should be divided into several cells. This makes the formula easier to understand and easier to edit. Avoid using numbers in a formula (separate the data from the model). Instead, put the number in a cell in the parameters section of your worksheet and refer to the cell location in the formula. Building the formula in this manner avoids having to edit the formula for a simple data change. For example, equation (10.3), the savings due to outsourcing, can be calculated as follows: $S(q) = TMC(q) - TPC(q) = FC + (VC)q - Pq = FC + (VC - P)q$. Since $VC - P = 3.50 - 2 = 1.50$, we could have just entered the following formula in a single cell: $=234{,}000 - 1.50 * B11$. This is a very bad idea because if any of the input data change, the formula must be edited. Furthermore, the user would not know the values of VC and P, only that, for the current values, the difference is 1.50. The approach in Figure 10.3 is more transparent, is simpler, lends itself better to analysis of changes in the parameters, and is less likely to contain errors.

N O T E S   +   C O M M E N T S

1. Some users of influence diagrams recommend using different symbols for the various types of model entities. For example, circles might denote known inputs, ovals might denote uncertain inputs, rectangles might denote decisions or controllable inputs, triangles might denote calculations, and so forth.

2. The use of color in a spreadsheet model is an effective way to draw attention to a cell or set of cells. For example, we shaded cell B11 in Figure 10.3 to draw attention to the fact that q is a controllable input. However, avoid using too much color. Overdoing it may overwhelm users and actually have a negative impact on their ability to understand the model.

3. Holding down the **Ctrl** key and pressing the ~ key (usually located above the Tab key) in Excel will toggle between displaying the formulas in a spreadsheet and the values.

10.2 What-If Analysis

Excel offers a number of tools to facilitate what-if analysis. In this section we introduce two such tools, Data Tables and Goal Seek. Both of these tools are designed to rid the user of the tedious manual trial-and-error approach to analysis. Let us see how these two tools can help us analyze Nowlin's make-versus-buy decision.

Data Tables

An Excel **Data Table** quantifies the impact of changing the value of a specific input on an output of interest. Excel can generate either a **one-way data table**, which summarizes a single input's impact on the output, or a **two-way data table**, which summarizes two inputs' impact on the output.

Let us consider how savings due to outsourcing changes as the quantity of Vipers changes. This should help us answer the question, "For which values of q is outsourcing more cost-effective?" A one-way data table changing the value of quantity and reporting savings due to outsourcing would be very useful. We will use the previously developed Nowlin spreadsheet for this analysis.

The first step in creating a one-way data table is to construct a sorted list of the values you would like to consider for the input. Let us investigate the quantity q over a range from 0 to 300,000 in increments of 25,000 units. Figure 10.4 shows the data entered in cells D5 through D17, with a column label in D4. This column of data is the set of values that Excel will use as inputs for q. Since the output of interest is savings due to outsourcing (located in cell B17), we have entered the formula $=B17$ in cell E4. In general, set the cell to the right of the label to the cell location of the output variable of interest. Once the basic structure is in place, we invoke the Data Table tool using the following steps:

	A	B	C	D	E	F	G
1	**Nowlin Plastics**						
2							
3	**Parameters**						
4	Manufacturing Fixed Cost	$234,000.00		Quantity	$219,000.00		
5	Manufacturing Variable Cost per Unit	$2.00		0			
6				25,000			
7	Outsourcing Cost per Unit	$3.50		50,000			
8				75,000			
9				100,000			
10	**Model**			125,000			
11	Quantity	10,000		150,000			
12				175,000			
13	Total Cost to Produce	$254,000.00		200,000			
14				225,000			
15	Total Cost to Outsource	$35,000.00		250,000			
16				275,000			
17	Savings due to Outsourcing	$219,000.00		300,000			
18							

Data Table dialog box:
Row input cell: [ ]
Column input cell: B11
OK   Cancel

In versions of Excel prior to Excel 2016, the What-If Analysis tool can be found in the Data Tools group.

Step 1. Select cells D4:E17
Step 2. Click the **Data** tab in the Ribbon
Step 3. Click **What-If Analysis** in the **Forecast** group, and select **Data Table**
Step 4. When the **Data Table** dialog box appears, enter *B11* in the **Column input cell:** box
Click **OK**

Entering B11 in the Column input cell: box indicates that the column of data corresponds to different values of the input located in cell B11.

As shown in Figure 10.5, the table will be populated with the value of savings due to outsourcing for each value of quantity of Vipers in the table. For example, when $q = 25,000$ we see that $S(25,000) = \$196,500$, and when $q = 250,000$, $S(250,000) = -\$141,000$. A negative value for savings due to outsourcing means that manufacturing is cheaper than outsourcing for that quantity.

We have learned something very valuable from this table. Not only have we quantified the savings due to outsourcing for a number of quantities, we know too that, for quantities of 150,000 units or less, outsourcing is cheaper than manufacturing and that, for quantities of 175,000 units or more, manufacturing is cheaper than outsourcing. Depending on Nowlin's confidence in their demand forecast for the Viper product for next year, we have likely satisfactorily answered the make-versus-buy question. If, for example, management is highly confident that demand will be at least 200,000 units of Viper, then clearly they should manufacture the Viper rather than outsource. If management believes that Viper demand next year will be close to 150,000 units, they might still decide to manufacture rather than outsource. At 150,000 units, the savings due to outsourcing is only $9,000. That might not justify outsourcing if, for example, the quality assurance standards at the outsource firm are not at an acceptable level. We have provided management with valuable information that they may use to decide whether to make or buy. Next we illustrate how to construct a two-way data table.

In versions of Excel prior
to Excel 2016, the *What-If
Analysis* tool can be found in
the Data Tools group

FIGURE 10.5   Results of One-Way Data Table for Nowlin Plastics

	A	B	C	D	E
1	**Nowlin Plastics**				
2					
3	**Parameters**				
4	Manufacturing Fixed Cost	$234,000.00		Quantity	$219,000.00
5	Manufacturing Variable Cost per Unit	$2.00		0	$234,000
6				25,000	$196,500
7	Outsourcing Cost per Unit	$3.50		50,000	$159,000
8				75,000	$121,500
9				100,000	$84,000
10	**Model**			125,000	$46,500
11	Quantity	10,000		150,000	$9,000
12				175,000	–$28,500
13	Total Cost to Produce	$254,000.00		200,000	–$66,000
14				225,000	–$103,500
15	Total Cost to Outsource	$35,000.00		250,000	–$141,000
16				275,000	–$178,500
17	Savings due to Outsourcing	$219,000.00		300,000	–$216,000
18					

Suppose that Nowlin has now received five different bids on the per-unit cost for outsourcing the production of the Viper. Clearly, the lowest bid provides the greatest savings. However, the selection of the outsource firm—if Nowlin decides to outsource—will depend on many factors, including reliability, quality, and on-time delivery. So it would be instructive to quantify the differences in savings for various quantities and bids. The five current bids are $2.89, $3.13, $3.50, $3.54, and $3.59. We may use the Excel Data Table to construct a two-way data table with quantity as a column and the five bids as a row, as shown in Figure 10.6.

In Figure 10.6, we have entered various quantities in cells D5 through D17, as in the one-way table. These correspond to cell B11 in our model. In cells E4 through I4, we have entered the bids. These correspond to B7, the outsourcing cost per unit. In cell D4, above the column input values and to the left of the row input values, we have entered the formula =B17, the location of the output of interest, in this case, savings due to outsourcing. Once the table inputs have been entered into the spreadsheet, we perform the following steps to construct the two-way Data Table.

Step 1. Select cells D4:I17
Step 2. Click the **Data** tab in the Ribbon
Step 3. Click **What-If Analysis** in the **Forecast** group, and select **Data Table**
Step 4. When the **Data Table** dialog box appears:
Enter *B7* in the **Row input cell:** box
Enter *B11* in the **Column input cell:** box
Click **OK**

Figure 10.6 shows the selected cells and the **Data Table** dialog box. The results are shown in Figure 10.7.

We now have a table that shows the savings due to outsourcing for each combination of quantity and bid price. For example, for 75,000 Vipers at a cost of $3.13 per unit, the

FIGURE 10.6   The Input for Constructing a Two-Way Data Table for Nowlin Plastics

	A	B	C	D	E	F	G	H	I	J	K	L	M
1	Nowlin Plastics												
2													
3	Parameters												
4	Manufacturing Fixed Cost	$234,000.00		$219,000.00	$2.89	$3.13	$3.50	$3.54	$3.59				
5	Manufacturing Variable Cost per Unit	$2.00		0									
6				25,000									
7	Outsourcing Cost per Unit	$3.50		50,000									
8				75,000									
9				100,000									
10	Model			125,000									
11	Quantity	10,000		150,000									
12				175,000									
13	Total Cost to Produce	$254,000.00		200,000									
14				225,000									
15	Total Cost to Outsource	$35,000.00		250,000									
16				275,000									
17	Savings due to Outsourcing	$219,000.00		300,000									
18													
19													

Data Table

Row input cell: B7

Column input cell: B11

OK   Cancel

FIGURE 10.7   Results of a Two-Way Data Table for Nowlin Plastics

	A	B	C	D	E	F	G	H	I
1	Nowlin Plastics								
2									
3	Parameters								
4	Manufacturing Fixed Cost	$234,000.00		$219,000.00	$2.89	$3.13	$3.50	$3.54	$3.59
5	Manufacturing Variable Cost per Unit	$2.00		0	$234,000	$234,000	$234,000	$234,000	$234,000
6				25,000	$211,750	$205,750	$196,500	$195,500	$194,250
7	Outsourcing Cost per Unit	$3.50		50,000	$189,500	$177,500	$159,000	$157,000	$154,500
8				75,000	$167,250	$149,250	$121,500	$118,500	$114,750
9				100,000	$145,000	$121,000	$84,000	$80,000	$75,000
10	Model			125,000	$122,750	$92,750	$46,500	$41,500	$35,250
11	Quantity	10,000		150,000	$100,500	$64,500	$9,000	$3,000	–$4,500
12				175,000	$78,250	$36,250	–$28,500	–$35,500	–$44,250
13	Total Cost to Produce	$254,000.00		200,000	$56,000	$8,000	–$66,000	–$74,000	–$84,000
14				225,000	$33,750	–$20,250	–$103,500	–$112,500	–$123,750
15	Total Cost to Outsource	$35,000.00		250,000	$11,500	–$48,500	–$141,000	–$151,000	–$163,500
16				275,000	–$10,750	–$76,750	–$178,500	–$189,500	–$203,250
17	Savings due to Outsourcing	$219,000.00		300,000	–$33,000	–$105,000	–$216,000	–$228,000	–$243,000
18									

savings from buying versus manufacturing the units is $149,250. We can also see the range for the quantity for each bid price that results in a negative savings. For these quantities and bid combinations, it is better to manufacture than to outsource.

Using the Data Table allows us to quantify the savings due to outsourcing for the quantities and bid prices specified. However, the table does not tell us the exact number at which the transition occurs from outsourcing being cheaper to manufacturing being cheaper. For example, although it is clear from the table that for a bid price of $3.50 the savings due to outsourcing goes from positive to negative at some quantity between 150,000 units and 175,000 units, we know only that this transition occurs somewhere in that range. As we illustrate next, the what-if analysis tool Goal Seek can tell us the precise number at which this transition occurs.

Goal Seek

Excel's **Goal Seek** tool allows the user to determine the value of an input cell that will cause the value of a related output cell to equal some specified value (the *goal*). In the case of Nowlin Plastics, suppose we want to know the value of the quantity of Vipers at which it becomes more cost-effective to manufacture rather than outsource. For example, we see from the table in Figure 10.7 that, for a bid price of $3.50 and some quantity between 150,000 units and 175,000 units, savings due to outsourcing goes from positive to negative. Somewhere in this range of quantity, the savings due to outsourcing is zero, and that is the point at which Nowlin would be indifferent to manufacturing and outsourcing. We may use Goal Seek to find the quantity of Vipers that satisfies the goal of zero savings due to outsourcing for a bid price of $3.50. The following steps describe how to use Goal Seek to find this point.

In versions of Excel prior to Excel 2016, the What-If Analysis tool can be found in the Data Tools group

Step 1. Click the **Data** tab in the Ribbon
Step 2. Click **What-If Analysis** in the **Forecast** group, and select **Goal Seek**
Step 3. When the **Goal Seek** dialog box appears (Figure 10.8):
   Enter *B17* in the **Set cell:** box

FIGURE 10.8   Goal Seek Dialog Box for Nowlin Plastics

▲	A	B	C	D	E	F
1	**Nowlin Plastics**					
2						
3	**Parameters**					
4	Manufacturing Fixed Cost	$234,000.00				
5	Manufacturing Variable Cost per Unit	$2.00				
6						
7	Outsourcing Cost per Unit	$3.50				
8						
9						
10	**Model**					
11	Quantity	10,000				
12						
13	Total Cost to Produce	$254,000.00				
14						
15	Total Cost to Outsource	$35,000.00				
16						
17	Savings due to Outsourcing	$219,000.00				
18						

Goal Seek dialog box:
Set cell: B17
To value: 0
By changing cell: B11

[OK] [Cancel]

FIGURE 10.9   Results from Goal Seek for Nowlin Plastics

	A	B	C	D	E	F
1	Nowlin Plastics					
2						
3	Parameters					
4	Manufacturing Fixed Cost	$234,000.00				
5	Manufacturing Variable Cost per Unit	$2.00				
6						
7	Outsourcing Cost per Unit	$3.50				
8						
9						
10	Model					
11	Quantity	156,000				
12						
13	Total Cost to Produce	$546,000.00				
14						
15	Total Cost to Outsource	$546,000.00				
16						
17	Savings due to Outsourcing	$0.00				
18						

Goal Seek Status

Goal Seeking with Cell B17 found a solution.

Target value: 0
Current value: $0.00

Step   Pause   OK   Cancel

Enter *0* in the **To value:** box
Enter *B11* in the **By changing cell:** box
Click **OK**
Step 4. When the **Goal Seek Status** dialog box appears, click **OK**

The completed Goal Seek dialog box is shown in Figure 10.8.

The results from Goal Seek are shown in Figure 10.9. The savings due to outsourcing in cell B17 is zero, and the quantity in cell B11 has been set by Goal Seek to 156,000. When the annual quantity required is 156,000, it costs $564,000 either to manufacture the product or to purchase it. We have already seen that lower values of the quantity required favor outsourcing. Beyond the value of 156,000 units it becomes cheaper to manufacture the product.

NOTES + COMMENTS

1. We emphasize the location of the reference to the desired output in a one-way versus a two-way Data Table. For a one-way table, the reference to the output cell location is placed in the cell above and to the right of the column of input data so that it is in the cell just to the right of the label of the column of input data. For a two-way table, the reference to the output cell location is placed above the column of input data and to the left of the row input data.

2. Notice that in Figures 10.5 and 10.7, the tables are formatted as currency. This must be done manually after the table is constructed using the options in the **Number** group under the **Home** tab in the Ribbon. It also a good idea to label the rows and the columns of the table.

3. For very complex functions, Goal Seek might not converge to a stable solution. Trying several different initial values (the actual value in the cell referenced in the **By changing cell:** box) when invoking Goal Seek may help.

10.3 Some Useful Excel Functions for Modeling

In this section we use several examples to introduce additional Excel functions that have proven useful in modeling decision problems. Many of these functions will be used in the chapters on optimization, simulation, and decision analysis.

SUM and SUMPRODUCT

Two very useful functions are SUM and SUMPRODUCT. The SUM function adds up all of the numbers in a range of cells. The SUMPRODUCT function returns the sum of the products of elements in a set of arrays. As we shall see in Chapter 11, SUMPRODUCT is very useful for linear optimization models.

Let us illustrate the use of SUM and SUMPRODUCT by considering a transportation problem faced by Foster Generators. This problem involves the transportation of a product from three plants to four distribution centers. Foster Generators operates plants in Cleveland, Ohio; Bedford, Indiana; and York, Pennsylvania. Production capacities for the three plants over the next three-month planning period are known.

The firm distributes its generators through four regional distribution centers located in Boston, Massachusetts; Chicago, Illinois; St. Louis, Missouri; and Lexington, Kentucky. Foster has forecasted demand for the three-month period for each of the distribution centers. The per-unit shipping cost from each plant to each distribution center is also known. Management would like to determine how much of its products should be shipped from each plant to each distribution center.

A transportation analyst developed a what-if spreadsheet model to help Foster develop a plan for how to ship its generators from the plants to the distribution centers to minimize cost. Of course, capacity at the plants must not be exceeded, and forecasted demand must be satisfied at each of the four distribution centers. The what-if model is shown in Figure 10.10.

The parameters section is rows 2 through 10. Cells B5 through E7 contain the per-unit shipping cost from each origin (plant) to each destination (distribution center). For example, it costs $2.00 to ship one generator from Bedford to St. Louis. The plant capacities are given in cells F5 through F7, and the distribution center demands appear in cells B8 through E8.

The model is in rows 11 through 20. Trial values of shipment amounts from each plant to each distribution center appear in the shaded cells, B17 through E19. The total cost of shipping for this proposed plan is calculated in cell B13 using the SUMPRODUCT function. The general form of the SUMPRODUCT function is:

$$=\text{SUMPRODUCT}(array1,\ array2).$$

The arrays used as arguments in the SUMPRODUCT function must be of the same dimension. For example, in the Foster Generator model, B5:E7 is an array of three rows and four columns. B17:E19 is an array of the same dimensions.

The function pairs each element of the first array with its counterpart in the second array, multiplies the elements of the pairs together, and adds the results. In cell B13, =SUMPRODUCT(B5:E7,B17:E19) pairs the per-unit cost of shipping for each origin-destination pair with the proposed shipping plan for that and adds their products:

$$\text{B5*B17} + \text{C5*C17} + \text{D5*D17} + \text{E5*E17} + \text{B6*B18} + \cdots + \text{E7*E19}.$$

In cells F17 through F19, the SUM function is used to add up the amounts shipped for each plant. The general form of the SUM function is

$$=\text{SUM}(range),$$

where *range* is a range of cells. For example, the function in cell F17 is =SUM(B17:E17), which adds the values in B17, C17, D17, and E17: 5000 + 0 + 0 + 0 = 5000. The SUM function in cells B20 through E20 does the same for the amounts shipped to each distribution center.

FIGURE 10.10   What-If Model for Foster Generators

	A	B	C	D	E	F	G
1	Foster Generators						
2	Parameters						
3	Shipping Cost/Unit			Destination			
4	Origin	Boston	Chicago	St. Louis	Lexington	Supply	
5	Cleveland	3	2	7	6	5000	
6	Bedford	6	5	2	3	6000	
7	York	2	5	4	5	2500	
8	Demand	6000	4000	2000	1500		
9							
10							
11	Model						
12							
13	Total Cost	=SUMPRODUCT(B5:E7,B17:E19)					
14							
15				Destination			
16	Origin	Boston	Chicago	St. Louis	Lexington	Total	
17	Cleveland	5000	0	0	0	=SUM(B17:E17)	
18	Bedford	1000	4000	1000	0	=SUM(B18:E18)	
19	York	0	0	1000	1500	=SUM(B19:E19)	
20	Total	=SUM(B17:B19)	=SUM(C17:C19)	=SUM(D17:D19)	=SUM(E17:E19)		
21							

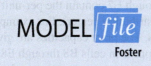

MODEL *file*

Foster

	A	B	C	D	E	F	G
1	Foster Generators						
2	Parameters						
3	Shipping Cost/Unit			Destination			
4	Origin	Boston	Chicago	St. Louis	Lexington	Supply	
5	Cleveland	$3.00	$2.00	$7.00	$6.00	5000	
6	Bedford	$6.00	$5.00	$2.00	$3.00	6000	
7	York	$2.00	$5.00	$4.00	$5.00	2500	
8	Demand	6000	4000	2000	1500		
9							
10							
11	Model						
12							
13	Total Cost	$54,500.00					
14							
15				Destination			
16	Origin	Boston	Chicago	St. Louis	Lexington	Total	
17	Cleveland	5000	0	0	0	5000	
18	Bedford	1000	4000	1000	0	6000	
19	York	0	0	1000	1500	2500	
20	Total	6000	4000	2000	1500		
21							

By comparing the amounts shipped from each plant to the capacity for that plant, we see that no plant violates its capacity. Likewise, by comparing the amounts shipped to each distribution center to the demand at that center, we see that all demands are met. The total shipping cost for the proposed plan is $54,500. Is this the lowest-cost plan? It is not clear. We will revisit the Foster Generators problem in Chapter 11, where we discuss linear optimization models.

IF and COUNTIF

Gambrell Manufacturing produces car stereos. Stereos are composed of a variety of components that the company must carry in inventory to keep production running smoothly. However, because inventory can be a costly investment, Gambrell generally likes to keep its components inventory to a minimum. To help monitor and control its inventory, Gambrell uses an inventory policy known as an *order-up-to policy*.

The order-up-to policy is as follows. Whenever the inventory on hand drops below a certain level, enough units are ordered to return the inventory to that predetermined level. If the current number of units in inventory, denoted by H, drops below M units, enough inventory is ordered to get the level back up to M units. M is called the *order-up-to point*. Stated mathematically, if Q is the amount we order, then:

$$Q = M - H.$$

An inventory model for Gambrell Manufacturing appears in Figure 10.11. In the upper half of the worksheet, the component ID number, inventory on hand (H), order-up-to point (M), and cost per unit are given for each of four components. Also given in this sheet is the fixed cost per order. The fixed cost is interpreted as follows: Each time a component is ordered, it costs Gambrell $120 to process the order. The fixed cost of $120 is incurred whenever an order is placed, regardless of how many units are ordered.

The model portion of the worksheet calculates the order quantity for each component. For example, for component 570, $M = 100$ and $H = 5$, so $Q = M - H = 100 - 5 = 95$. For component 741, $M = 70$ and $H = 70$ and no units are ordered because the on-hand inventory of 70 units is equal to the order-up-to point of 70. The calculations are similar for the other two components.

Depending on the number of units ordered, Gambrell receives a discount on the cost per unit. If 50 or more units are ordered, there is a quantity discount of 10% on every unit purchased. For example, for component 741, the cost per unit is $4.50, and 95 units are ordered. Because 95 exceeds the 50-unit requirement, there is a 10% discount, and the cost per unit is reduced to $4.50 - 0.1($4.50) = $4.50 - $0.45 = $4.05. Not including the fixed cost, the cost of goods purchased is then $4.05(95) = $384.75.

The Excel functions used to perform these calculations are shown in Figure 10.11 (for clarity, we show formulas for only the first three columns). The IF function is used to calculate the purchase cost of goods for each component in row 17. The general form of the IF function is:

=IF(*condition, result if condition is true, result if condition is false*).

For example, in cell B17 we have =IF(B16 >= $B$10, $B$11*B6, B6)*B16. This statement says that, if the order quantity (cell B16) is greater than or equal to minimum amount required for a discount (cell B10), then the cost per unit is B11*B6 (there is a 10% discount, so the cost is 90% of the original cost); otherwise, there is no discount, and the cost per unit is the amount given in cell B6. The cost per unit computed by the IF function is then multiplied by the order quantity (B16) to obtain the total purchase cost of component 570. The purchase cost of goods for the other components are computed in a like manner.

The total cost in cell B23 is the sum of the total fixed ordering costs (B21) and the total cost of goods (B22). Because we place three orders (one each for components 570, 578, and 755), the fixed cost of the orders is 3*120 = $360.

FIGURE 10.11	Gambrell Manufacturing Component Ordering Model

▲	A	B	C
1	**Gambrell Manufacturing**		
2	**Parameters**		
3	Component ID	**570**	**578**
4	Inventory On-Hand	5	30
5	Order-up-to Point	100	55
6	Cost per Unit	4.5	12.5
7			
8	Fixed Cost per Order	120	
9			
10	Minimum Order Size for Discount	50	
11	Discounted to	0.9	
12			
13	**Model**		
14			
15	Component ID	=B3	=C3
16	Order Quantity	=B5–B4	=C5–C4
17	Cost of Goods	=IF(B16 >= $B$10, $B$11*B6,B6)*B16	=IF(C16 >= $B$10, $B$11*C6,C6)*C16
18			
19	Total Number of Orders	=COUNTIF(B16:E16,">0")	
20			
21	Total Fixed Costs	=B19*B8	
22	Total Cost of Goods	=SUM(B17:E17)	
23	Total Cost	=SUM(B21:B22)	
24			

Notice the use of absolute references to B10 and B11 in row 17. As discussed in Appendix A, this facilitates copying cell B17 to cells C17, D17, and E17.

MODEL *file*
Gambrell

▲	A	B	C	D	E
1	**Gambrell Manufacturing**				
2	**Parameters**				
3	Component ID	570	578	741	755
4	Inventory On-Hand	5	30	70	17
5	Order-up-to Point	100	55	70	45
6	Cost per Unit	$4.50	$12.50	$3.26	$4.15
7					
8	Fixed Cost per Order	$120			
9					
10	Minimum Order Size for Discount	50			
11	Discounted to	90%			
12					
13	**Model**				
14					
15	Component ID	570	578	741	755
16	Order Quantity	95	25	0	28
17	Cost of Goods	$384.75	$312.50	$0.00	$116.20
18					
19	Total Number of Orders	3			
20					
21	Total Fixed Costs	$360.00			
22	Total Cost of Goods	$813.45			
23	Total Cost	$1,173.45			
24					

The COUNTIF function in cell B19 is used to count how many times we order. In particular, it counts the number of components having a positive order quantity. The general form of the COUNTIF function (which was discussed in Chapter 2 for creating frequency distributions) is:

=COUNTIF(*range, condition*).

The *range* is the range to search for the *condition*. The condition is the test to be counted when satisfied. In the Gambrell model in Figure 10.11, cell B19 counts the number of cells that are greater than zero in the range of cells B16:E16 via the syntax =COUNTIF(B16:E16, ">0"). Note that quotes are required for the condition with the COUNTIF function. In the model, because only cells B16, C16, and E16 are greater than zero, the COUNTIF function in cell B19 returns 3.

As we have seen, IF and COUNTIF are powerful functions that allow us to make calculations based on a condition holding (or not). There are other such conditional functions available in Excel. In a problem at the end of this chapter, we ask you to investigate one such function, the SUMIF function. Another conditional function that is extremely useful in modeling is the VLOOKUP function, which is illustrated with an example in the next section.

VLOOKUP

The director of sales at Granite Insurance needs to award bonuses to her sales force based on performance. There are 15 salespeople, each with his or her own territory. Based on the size and population of the territory, each salesperson has a sales target for the year.

The measure of performance for awarding bonuses is the percentage achieved above the sales target. Based on this metric, a salesperson is placed into one of five bonus bands and awarded bonus points. After all salespeople are placed in a band and awarded points, each is awarded a percentage of the bonus pool, based on the percentage of the total points awarded. The sales director has created a spreadsheet model to calculate the bonuses to be awarded. The spreadsheet model is shown in Figure 10.12 (note that we have hidden rows 19–28).

As shown in cell E3 in Figure 10.12, the bonus pool is $250,000 for this year. The bonus bands are in cells A7:C11. In this table, column A gives the lower limit of the bonus band, column B the upper limit, and column C the bonus points awarded to anyone in that bonus band. For example, salespeople who achieve 56% above their sales target would be awarded 15 bonus points.

As shown in Figure 10.12, the name and percentage above the target achieved for each salesperson appear below the bonus-band table in columns A and B. In column C, the VLOOKUP function is used to look in the bonus band table and automatically assign the number of bonus points to each salesperson.

The VLOOKUP function allows the user to pull a subset of data from a larger table of data based on some criterion. The general form of the VLOOKUP function is:

$$=VLOOKUP(value, table, index, range),$$

where

$value$ = the value to search for in the first column of the table
$table$ = the cell range containing the table
$index$ = the column in the table containing the value to be returned
$range$ = TRUE if looking for the first approximate match of $value$ and FALSE if looking for an exact match of $value$ (We will explain the difference between approximate and exact matches in a moment.)

VLOOKUP assumes that the first column of the table is sorted in ascending order. The VLOOKUP function for salesperson Choi in cell C18 is as follows:

$$=VLOOKUP(B18,\$A\$7:\$C\$11,3,TRUE).$$

If the range in the VLOOKUP function is FALSE, the only change is that Excel searches for an exact match of the first argument in the first column of the data.

This function uses the percentage above target sales from cell B18 and searches the first column of the table defined by A7:C11. Because the *range* is set to TRUE, indicating

FIGURE 10.12	Granite Insurance Bonus Model

	A	B	C	D	E
1	Granite Insurance Bonus Awards				
2					
3	Parameters			Bonus Pool	250000
4					
5	Bonus Bands to be awarded for percentage above target sales.				
6	Lower Limit	Upper Limit	Bonus Points		
7	0	0.1	0		
8	0.11	0.5	10		
9	0.51	0.79	15		
10	0.8	0.99	25		
11	1	100	40		
12					
13	Model				
14	Last Name	% Above Target Sales	Bonus Points	% of Pool	Bonus Amount
15	Barth	0.83	=VLOOKUP(B15,$A$7:$C$11,3,TRUE)	=C15/$C$30	=D15*$E$3
16	Benson	0	=VLOOKUP(B16,$A$7:$C$11,3,TRUE)	=C16/$C$30	=D16*$E$3
17	Capel	1.18	=VLOOKUP(B17,$A$7:$C$11,3,TRUE)	=C17/$C$30	=D17*$E$3
18	Choi	0.44	=VLOOKUP(B18,$A$7:$C$11,3,TRUE)	=C18/$C$30	=D18*$E$3
29	Ruebush	0.85	=VLOOKUP(B29,$A$7:$C$11,3,TRUE)	=C29/$C$30	=D29*$E$3
30		Total	=SUM(C15:C29)	=SUM(D15:D29)	=SUM(E15:E29)

	A	B	C	D	E
1	Granite Insurance Bonus Awards				
2					
3	Parameters			Bonus Pool	$250,000
4					
5	Bonus Bands to be awarded for percentage above target sales.				
6	Lower Limit	Upper Limit	Bonus Points		
7	0%	10%	0		
8	11%	50%	10		
9	51%	79%	15		
10	80%	99%	25		
11	100%	10000%	40		
12					
13	Model				
14	Last Name	% Above Target Sales	Bonus Points	% of Pool	Bonus Amount
15	Barth	83%	25	8.5%	$21,186.44
16	Benson	0%	0	0.0%	$0.00
17	Capel	118%	40	13.6%	$33,898.31
18	Choi	44%	10	3.4%	$8,474.58
29	Ruebush	85%	25	8.5%	$21,186.44
30		Total	295	100%	$250,000.00

MODEL *file*

Granite

a search for the first approximate match, Excel searches in the first column of the table from the top until it finds a number strictly greater than the value of B18. B18 is 44%, and the first value in the table in column A larger than 44% is in cell A9 (51%). It then backs up one row (to row 8). In other words, it finds the last value in the first column less than or equal to 44%. Because a 3 is in the third argument of the VLOOKUP function, it takes the element in row 8 of the third column of the table, which is 10 bonus points. In summary, the VLOOKUP with *range* set to TRUE takes the first argument and searches the first column of the table for the last row that is less than or equal the first argument. It then selects from that row, the element in the column number of the third argument.

Once all salespeople are awarded bonus points based on VLOOKUP and the bonus-band table, the total number of bonus points awarded is given in cell C30 using the SUM function. Each person's bonus points as a percentage of the total awarded is calculated in column D, and in column E each person is awarded that percentage of the bonus pool. As a check, cells D30 and E30 give the total percentages and dollar amounts awarded.

Numerous mathematical, logical, and financial functions are available in Excel. In addition to those discussed here, we will introduce you to other functions, as needed, in examples and end-of-chapter problems. Having already discussed principles for building good spreadsheet models and after having seen a variety of spreadsheet models, we turn now to how to audit Excel models to ensure model integrity.

10.4 Auditing Spreadsheet Models

Excel contains a variety of tools to assist you in the development and debugging of spreadsheet models. These tools are found in the **Formula Auditing** group of the **Formulas** tab, as shown in Figure 10.13. Let us review each of the tools available in this group.

Trace Precedents and Dependents

After selecting cells, the Trace Precedents button creates arrows pointing to the selected cell from cells that are part of the formula in that cell. The Trace Dependents button, on the other hand, shows arrows pointing from the selected cell to cells that depend on the selected cell. Both of the tools are excellent for quickly ascertaining how parts of a model are linked.

An example of Trace Precedents is shown in Figure 10.14. Here we have opened the Foster Generators Excel file, selected cell B13, and clicked the **Trace Precedents** button in the **Formula Auditing** group. Recall that the cost in cell B13 is calculated as the SUMPRODUCT of the per-unit shipping cost and units shipped. In Figure 10.14, to show this relationship, arrows are drawn to these areas of the spreadsheet to cell B13. These arrows may be removed by clicking on the **Remove Arrows** button in the **Auditing Tools** group.

An example of Trace Dependents is shown in Figure 10.15. We have selected cell E18, the units shipped from Bedford to Lexington, and clicked on the **Trace Dependents** button

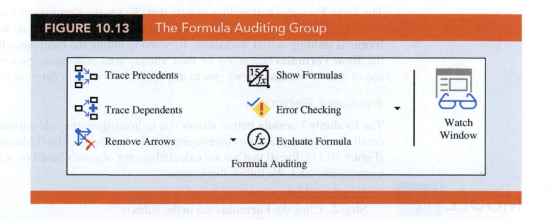

FIGURE 10.13   The Formula Auditing Group

- Trace Precedents
- Trace Dependents
- Remove Arrows
- Show Formulas
- Error Checking
- Evaluate Formula
- Watch Window

Formula Auditing

FIGURE 10.14	Trace Precedents for Foster Generator

	A	B	C	D	E	F	G
1	Foster Generators						
2	Parameters						
3	Shipping Cost/Unit		**Destination**				
4	Origin	Boston	Chicago	St. Louis	Lexington	Supply	
5	Cleveland	$3.00	$2.00	$7.00	$6.00	5000	
6	Bedford	$6.00	$5.00	$2.00	$3.00	6000	
7	York	$2.00	$5.00	$4.00	$5.00	2500	
8	Demand	6000	4000	2000	1500		
9							
10							
11	Model						
12							
13	Total Cost	$54,500.00					
14							
15			**Destination**				
16	Origin	Boston	Chicago	St. Louis	Lexington	Total	
17	Cleveland	5000	0	0	0	5000	
18	Bedford	1000	4000	1000	0	6000	
19	York	0	0	1000	1500	2500	
20	Total	6000	4000	2000	1500		
21							
22							

in the **Formula Auditing** group. As shown in Figure 10.15, units shipped from Bedford to Lexington impacts the cost function in cell B13, the total units shipped from Bedford given in cell F18, as well as the total units shipped to Lexington in cell E20. These arrows may be removed by clicking on the **Remove Arrows** button in the **Auditing Tools** group.

Trace Precedents and Trace Dependents can highlight errors in copying and formula construction by showing that incorrect sections of the worksheet are referenced.

Show Formulas

The Show Formulas button does exactly that. To see the formulas in a worksheet, simply click on any cell in the worksheet and then click on **Show Formulas**. You will see the formulas residing in that worksheet. To revert to hiding the formulas, click again on the **Show Formulas** button. As we have already seen in our examples in this chapter, the use of Show Formulas allows you to inspect each formula in detail in its cell location.

Evaluate Formulas

The **Evaluate Formula** button allows you to investigate the calculations of a cell in great detail. As an example, let us investigate cell B17 of the Gambrell Manufacturing model (Figure 10.11). Recall that we are calculating cost of goods based on whether there is a quantity discount. We follow these steps:

Step 1. Select cell B17
Step 2. Click the **Formulas** tab in the Ribbon
Step 3. Click the **Evaluate Formula** button in the **Formula Auditing** group

MODEL *file*

Gambrell

FIGURE 10.15   Trace Dependents for the Foster Generators Model

	A	B	C	D	E	F	G
1	Foster Generators						
2	Parameters						
3	Shipping Cost/Unit		Destination				
4	Origin	Boston	Chicago	St. Louis	Lexington	Supply	
5	Cleveland	$3.00	$2.00	$7.00	$6.00	5000	
6	Bedford	$6.00	$5.00	$2.00	$3.00	6000	
7	York	$2.00	$5.00	$4.00	$5.00	2500	
8	Demand	6000	4000	2000	1500		
9							
10							
11	Model						
12							
13	Total Cost	$54,500.00					
14							
15			Destination				
16	Origin	Boston	Chicago	St. Louis	Lexington	Total	
17	Cleveland	5000	0	0	0	5000	
18	Bedford	1000	4000	1000	0	6000	
19	York	0	0	1000	1500	2500	
20	Total	6000	4000	2000	1500		
21							
22							

Step 4. When the **Evaluate Formula** dialog box appears (Figure 10.16), click the **Evaluate** button

Step 5. Repeat Step 4 until the formula has been completely evaluated

Step 6. Click **Close**

Figure 10.17 shows the **Evaluate Formula** dialog box for cell B17 in the Gambrell Manufacturing spreadsheet model after four clicks of the **Evaluate** button.

The Evaluate Formula tool provides an excellent means of identifying the exact location of an error in a formula.

Error Checking

The **Error Checking** button provides an automatic means of checking for mathematical errors within formulas of a worksheet. Clicking on the **Error Checking** button causes Excel to check every formula in the sheet for calculation errors. If an error is found, the **Error Checking** dialog box appears. An example for a hypothetical division by zero error is shown in Figure 10.18. From this box, the formula can be edited, the calculation steps can be observed (as in the previous section on Evaluate Formulas), or help can be obtained through the Excel help function. The Error Checking procedure is particularly helpful for large models where not all cells of the model are visible.

Watch Window

The **Watch Window**, located in the Formula Auditing group, allows the user to observe the values of cells included in the Watch Window box list. This is useful for large models when

FIGURE 10.16   The Evaluate Formula Dialog Box for Gambrell Manufacturing

	A	B	C	D	E	F	G	H	I	J
1	**Gambrell Manufacturing**									
2	**Parameters**									
3	Component ID	**570**	**578**	**741**	**755**					
4	Inventory On-Hand	5	30	70	17					
5	Order Up to Point	100	55	70	45					
6	Cost per Unit	$4.50	$12.50	$3.26	$4.15					
7										
8	Fixed Cost per Order	$120								
9										
10	Minimum Order Size for Discount	50								
11	Discounted to	90%								
12										
13	**Model**									
14										
15	Component ID	**570**								
16	Order Quantity	95								
17	Cost of Goods	$384.75								
18										
19	Total Number of Orders	3								
20										
21	Total Fixed Costs	$360.00								
22	Total Cost of Goods	$813.45								
23	Total Cost	$1,173.45								
24										

Evaluate Formula dialog box:

Reference: Model!$B$17

Evaluation: = IF(B16 >= $B$10, $B$11*B6,B6)*B16

To show the result of the underlined expression, click Evaluate. The most recent result appears italicized.

[Evaluate] [Step In] [Step Out] [Close]

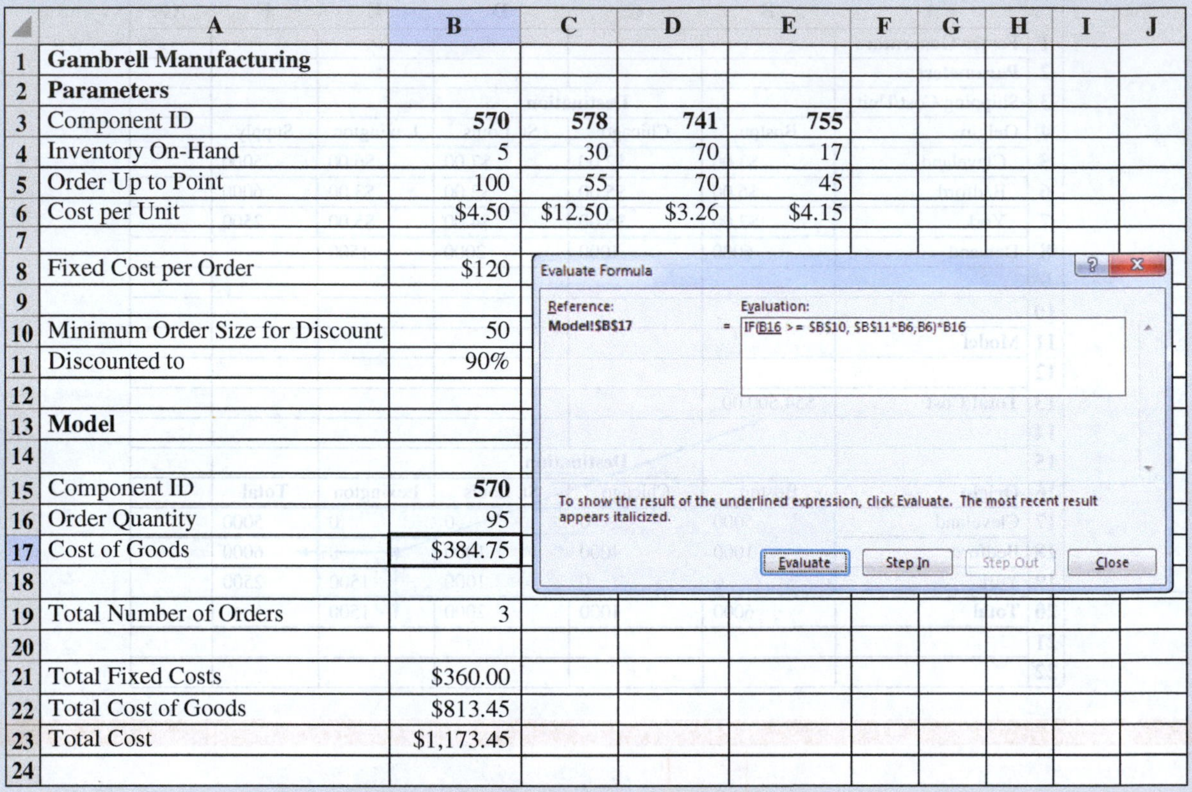

FIGURE 10.17   The Evaluate Formula Dialog Box for Gambrell Manufacturing Cell B17 after Four Clicks of the Evaluate Button

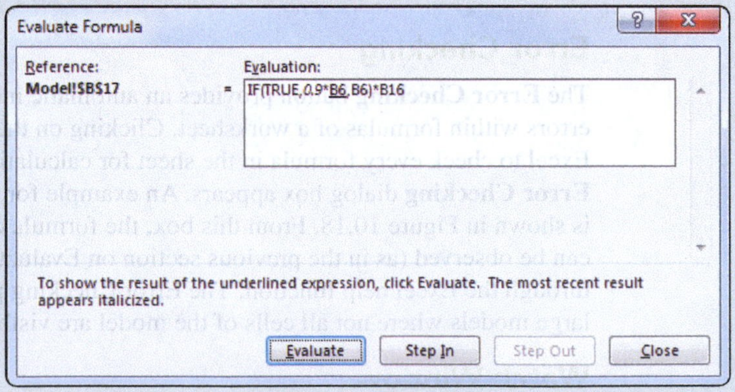

Evaluate Formula dialog box:

Reference: Model!$B$17

Evaluation: = IF(TRUE,0.9*B6, B6)*B16

To show the result of the underlined expression, click Evaluate. The most recent result appears italicized.

[Evaluate] [Step In] [Step Out] [Close]

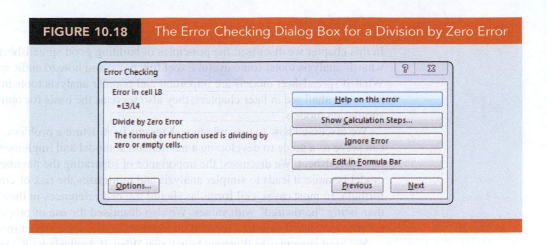

FIGURE 10.18 The Error Checking Dialog Box for a Division by Zero Error

not all of the model is observable on the screen or when multiple worksheets are used. The user can monitor how the listed cells change with a change in the model without searching through the worksheet or changing from one worksheet to another.

A Watch Window for the Gambrell Manufacturing model is shown in Figure 10.19. The following steps were used to add cell B17 to the watch list:

Step 1. Click the **Formulas** tab in the Ribbon
Step 2. Click **Watch Window** in the **Formula Auditing** group to display the **Watch Window**
Step 3. Click **Add Watch...**
Step 4. Select the cell you would like to add to the watch list (in this case B17)

As shown in Figure 10.19, the list gives the workbook name, worksheet name, cell name (if used), cell location, cell value, and cell formula. To delete a cell from the watch list, click on the entry from the list, and then click on the **Delete Watch** button that appears in the upper part of the **Watch Window**.

The Watch Window, as shown in Figure 10.19, allows us to monitor the value of B17 as we make changes elsewhere in the worksheet. Furthermore, if we had other worksheets in this workbook, we could monitor changes to B17 of the worksheet even from these other worksheets. The Watch Window is observable regardless of where we are in any worksheet of a workbook.

FIGURE 10.19 The Watch Window for Cell B17 of the Gambrell Manufacturing Model

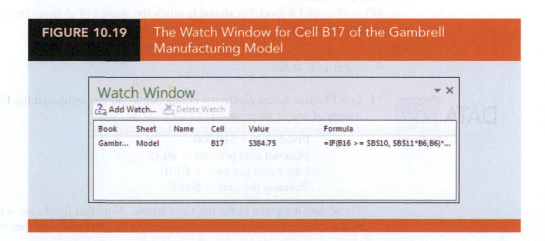

SUMMARY

In this chapter we discussed the principles of building good spreadsheet models, several what-if analysis tools, some useful Excel functions, and how to audit spreadsheet models. What-if spreadsheet models are important and popular analysis tools in and of themselves, but as we shall see in later chapters, they also serve as the basis for optimization and simulation models.

We discussed how to use influence diagrams to structure a problem. Influence diagrams can serve as a guide to developing a mathematical model and implementing the model in a spreadsheet. We discussed the importance of separating the parameters from the model because it leads to simpler analysis and minimizes the risk of creating an error in a formula. In most cases, cell formulas should use cell references in their arguments rather than being "hardwired" with values. We also discussed the use of proper formatting and color to enhance the ease of use and understanding of a spreadsheet model.

We used examples to illustrate how Excel What-If Analysis tools Data Tables and Goal Seek can be used to perform detailed and efficient what-if analysis. We also discussed a number of Excel functions that are useful for business analytics. Finally, we discussed Excel Formula Auditing tools that may be used to debug and monitor spreadsheet models to ensure that they are error-free and accurate.

GLOSSARY

Data Table An Excel tool that quantifies the impact of changing the value of a specific input on an output of interest.

Decision variable A model input the decision maker can control.

Goal Seek An Excel tool that allows the user to determine the value for an input cell that will cause the value of a related output cell to equal some specified value, called the *goal*.

Influence diagram A visual representation that shows which entities influence others in a model.

Make-versus-buy decision A decision often faced by companies that have to decide whether they should manufacture a product or outsource its production to another firm.

One-way data table An Excel Data Table that summarizes a single input's impact on the output of interest.

Parameter In a what-if model, the uncontrollable model input.

Two-way data table An Excel Data Table that summarizes two inputs' impact on the output of interest.

What-if model A model designed to study the impact of changes in model inputs on model outputs.

PROBLEMS

1. Cox Electric makes electronic components and has estimated the following for a new design of one of its products:

> Fixed cost = \$10,000
> Material cost per unit = \$0.15
> Labor cost per unit = \$0.10
> Revenue per unit = \$0.65

These data are given in the file *CoxElectric*. Note that fixed cost is incurred regardless of the amount produced. Per-unit material and labor cost together make up the variable cost per unit. Assuming that Cox Electric sells all that it produces, profit is calculated by subtracting the fixed cost and total variable cost from total revenue.

a. Build an influence diagram that illustrates how to calculate profit.

b. Using mathematical notation similar to that used for Nowlin Plastics, give a mathematical model for calculating profit.

c. Implement your model from part (b) in Excel using the principles of good spreadsheet design.

d. If Cox Electric makes 12,000 units of the new product, what is the resulting profit?

2. Use the spreadsheet model constructed to answer Problem 1 to answer this problem.

a. Construct a one-way data table with production volume as the column input and profit as the output. Breakeven occurs when profit goes from a negative to a positive value; that is, breakeven is when total revenue = total cost, yielding a profit of zero. Vary production volume from 0 to 100,000 in increments of 10,000. In which interval of production volume does breakeven occur?

b. Use Goal Seek to find the exact breakeven point. Assign **Set cell:** equal to the location of profit, **To value:** = 0, and **By changing cell:** equal to the location of the production volume in your model.

3. Eastman Publishing Company is considering publishing an electronic textbook about spreadsheet applications for business. The fixed cost of manuscript preparation, textbook design, and web-site construction is estimated to be $160,000. Variable processing costs are estimated to be $6 per book. The publisher plans to sell single-user access to the book for $46.

a. Build a spreadsheet model to calculate the profit/loss for a given demand. What profit can be anticipated with a demand of 3500 copies?

b. Use a data table to vary demand from 1000 to 6000 in increments of 200 to assess the sensitivity of profit to demand.

c. Use Goal Seek to determine the access price per copy that the publisher must charge to break even with a demand of 3500 copies.

4. The University of Cincinnati Center for Business Analytics is an outreach center that collaborates with industry partners on applied research and continuing education in business analytics. One of the programs offered by the center is a quarterly Business Intelligence Symposium. Each symposium features three speakers on the real-world use of analytics. Each corporate member of the center (there are currently 10) receives five free seats to each symposium. Nonmembers wishing to attend must pay $75 per person. Each attendee receives breakfast, lunch, and free parking. The following are the costs incurred for putting on this event:

Rental cost for the auditorium	$150
Registration processing	$8.50 per person
Speaker costs	3 @ $800 = $2400
Continental breakfast	$4.00 per person
Lunch	$7.00 per person
Parking	$5.00 per person

a. Build a spreadsheet model that calculates a profit or loss based on the number of nonmember registrants.

b. Use Goal Seek to find the number of nonmember registrants that will make the event break even.

5. Consider again the scenario described in Problem 4.

a. The Center for Business Analytics is considering a refund policy for no-shows. No refund would be given for members who do not attend, but nonmembers who do not attend will be refunded 50% of the price. Extend the model you developed in Problem 4 for the Business Intelligence Symposium to account for the fact that, historically, 25% of members who registered do not show and 10% of registered nonmembers do not attend. The center pays the caterer for breakfast and lunch based on the number of registrants (not the number of attendees). However, the center pays for parking only for those who attend. What is the profit if each corporate member registers their full allotment of tickets and 127 nonmembers register?

b. Use a two-way data table to show how profit changes as a function of number of registered nonmembers and the no-show percentage of nonmembers. Vary the number of nonmember registrants from 80 to 160 in increments of 5 and the percentage of nonmember no-shows from 10 to 30% in increments of 2%.

6. Consider again Problem 3. Through a series of web-based experiments, Eastman has created a predictive model that estimates demand as a function of price. The predictive model is demand $= 4,000 - 6p$, where p is the price of the e-book.

a. Update your spreadsheet model constructed for Problem 3 to take into account this demand function.

b. Use Goal Seek to calculate the price that results in breakeven.

c. Use a data table that varies price from $50 to $400 in increments of $25 to find the price that maximizes profit.

7. Lindsay is 25 years old and has a new job in web development. She wants to make sure that she is financially sound in 30 years, so she plans to invest the same amount into a retirement account at the end of every year for the next 30 years. Construct a data table that will show Lindsay the balance of her retirement account for various levels of annual investment and return. Develop the two-way table for annual investment amounts of $5,000 to $20,000 in increments of $1,000 and for returns of 0 to 12% in increments of 1%. Note that because Lindsay invests at the end of the year, there is no interest earned on the contribution for the year in which she contributes.

8. Consider again Lindsay's investment in Problem 7. The real value of Lindsay's account after 30 years of investing will depend on inflation over that period. In the Excel function $=NPV(rate, value1, value2, ...)$, $rate$ is called the discount rate, and $value1$, $value 2$, etc. are incomes (positive) or expenditures (negative) over equal periods of time. Update your model from Problem 7 using the NPV function to get the net present value of Lindsay's retirement fund. Construct a data table that shows the net present value of Lindsay's retirement fund for various levels of return and inflation (discount rate). Use a data table to vary the return from 0 to 12% in increments of 1% and the discount rate from 0 to 4% in increments of 1% to show the impact on the net present value. (*Hint:* Calculate the total amount added to the account each year, and discount that stream of payments using the NPV function.)

9. Newton Manufacturing produces scientific calculators. The models are N350, N450, and the N900. Newton has planned its distribution of these products around eight customer zones: Brazil, China, France, Malaysia, U.S. Northeast, U.S. Southeast, U.S. Midwest, and U.S. West. Data for the current quarter (volume to be shipped in thousands of units) for each product and each customer zone are given in the file *Newton*. Newton would like to know the total number of units going to each customer zone and also the total units of each product shipped. There are several ways to get this information from the data set. One way is to use the SUMIF function.

The SUMIF function extends the SUM function by allowing the user to add the values of cells meeting a logical condition. The general form of the function is:

$$=\text{SUMIF}(test\ range,\ condition,\ range\ to\ be\ summed).$$

The *test range* is an area to search to test the *condition,* and the *range to be summed* is the position of the data to be summed. So, for example, using the file *Newton*, we use the following function to get the total units sent to Malaysia:

$$=\text{SUMIF}(A3:A26,A3,C3:C26).$$

Cell A3 contains the text "Malaysia"; A3:A26 is the range of customer zones; and C3:C26 are the volumes for each product for these customer zones. The SUMIF looks for matches of "Malaysia" in column A and, if a match is found, adds the volume to the total. Use the SUMIF function to get total volume by each zone and total volume by each product.

10. Consider the transportation model in the file *Williamson*, which is very similar to the Foster Generators model discussed in this chapter. Williamson produces a single product and has plants in Atlanta, Lexington, Chicago, and Salt Lake City and warehouses in Portland, St. Paul, Las Vegas, Tuscon, and Cleveland. Each plant has a capacity, and each warehouse has a demand. Williamson would like to find a low-cost shipping plan. Mr. Williamson has reviewed the results and notices right away that the total cost is way out of line. Use the **Formula Auditing** tool under the **Formulas** tab in Excel to find any errors in this model. Correct the errors. (*Hint:* The model contains two errors. Be sure to check every formula.)

11. Professor Rao would like to accurately calculate the grades for the 58 students in his Operations Planning and Scheduling class (OM 455). He has thus far constructed a spreadsheet, part of which follows:

	A	B	C	D	E
1	OM 455				
2	Section 001				
3	Course Grading Scale Based on Course Average:				
4		Lower	Upper	Course	
5		Limit	Limit	Grade	
6		0	59	F	
7		60	69	D	
8		70	79	C	
9		80	89	B	
10		90	100	A	
11					
12		Midterm	Final	Course	Course
13	Last Name	Score	Score	Average	Grade
14	Alt	70	56	63.0	
15	Amini	95	91	93.0	
16	Amoako	82	80	81.0	
17	Apland	45	78	61.5	
18	Bachman	68	45	56.5	
19	Corder	91	98	94.5	
20	Desi	87	74	80.5	
21	Dransman	60	80	70.0	
22	Duffuor	80	93	86.5	
23	Finkel	97	98	97.5	
24	Foster	90	91	90.5	

a. The Course Average is calculated by weighting the Midterm Score and Final Score 50% each. Use the VLOOKUP function with the table shown to generate the Course Grade for each student in cells E14 through E24.

b. Use the COUNTIF function to determine the number of students receiving each letter grade.

12. Richardson Ski Racing (RSR) sells equipment needed for downhill ski racing. One of RSR's products is fencing used on downhill courses. The fence product comes in 150-foot rolls and sells for $215 per roll. However, RSR offers quantity discounts. The following table shows the price per roll depending on order size:

RSR

Quantity Ordered		
From	**To**	**Price per Roll**
1	50	$215
51	100	$195
101	200	$175
201	and up	$155

The file *RSR* contains 172 orders that have arrived for the coming six weeks.

a. Use the VLOOKUP function with the preceding pricing table to determine the total revenue from these orders.

b. Use the COUNTIF function to determine the number of orders in each price bin.

13. A put option in finance allows you to sell a share of stock at a given price in the future. There are different types of put options. A European put option allows you to sell a share of stock at a given price, called the exercise price, at a particular point in time after the purchase of the option. For example, suppose you purchase a six-month European put option for a share of stock with an exercise price of $26. If six months later, the stock price per share is $26 or more, the option has no value. If in six months the stock price is lower than $26 per share, then you can purchase the stock and immediately sell it at the higher exercise price of $26. If the price per share in six months is $22.50, you can purchase a share of the stock for $22.50 and then use the put option to immediately sell the share for $26. Your profit would be the difference, $26 − $22.50 = $3.50 per share, less the cost of the option. If you paid $1.00 per put option, then your profit would be $3.50 − $1.00 = $2.50 per share.

a. Build a model to calculate the profit of this European put option.

b. Construct a data table that shows the profit per share for a share price in six months between $10 and $30 per share in increments of $1.00.

14. Consider again Problem 13. The point of purchasing a European option is to limit the risk of a decrease in the per-share price of the stock. Suppose you purchased 200 shares of the stock at $28 per share and 75 six-month European put options with an exercise price of $26. Each put option costs $1.

a. Using data tables, construct a model that shows the value of the portfolio with options and without options for a share price in six months between $15 and $35 per share in increments of $1.00.

b. Discuss the value of the portfolio with and without the European put options.

15. The Camera Shop sells two popular models of digital SLR cameras. The sales of these products are not independent; if the price of one increases, the sales of the other increases. In economics, these two camera models are called *substitutable products*. The store wishes to establish a pricing policy to maximize revenue from these products.

A study of price and sales data shows the following relationships between the quantity sold (N) and price (P) of each model:

$$N_A = 195 - 0.6P_A + 0.25P_B$$
$$N_B = 301 + 0.08P_A - 0.5P_B$$

a. Construct a model for the total revenue and implement it on a spreadsheet.

b. Develop a two-way data table to estimate the optimal prices for each product in order to maximize the total revenue. Vary each price from $250 to $500 in increments of $10.

16. A few years back, Dave and Jana bought a new home. They borrowed $230,415 at an annual fixed rate of 5.49% (15-year term) with monthly payments of $1,881.46. They just made their 25th payment, and the current balance on the loan is $208,555.87.

   Interest rates are at an all-time low, and Dave and Jana are thinking of refinancing to a new 15-year fixed loan. Their bank has made the following offer: 15-year term, 3.0%, plus out-of-pocket costs of $2,937. The out-of-pocket costs must be paid in full at the time of refinancing.

   Build a spreadsheet model to evaluate this offer. The Excel function:

$$=\text{PMT}(rate, nper, pv, fv, type)$$

calculates the payment for a loan based on constant payments and a constant interest rate. The arguments of this function are:

   $rate$ = the interest rate for the loan
   $nper$ = the total number of payments
   pv = present value (the amount borrowed)
   fv = future value [the desired cash balance after the last payment (usually 0)]
   $type$ = payment type (0 = end of period, 1 = beginning of the period)

   For example, for Dave and Jana's original loan, there will be 180 payments ($12*15 = 180$), so we would use $=\text{PMT}(0.0549/12, 180, 230415,0,0) = \$1,881.46$. Note that because payments are made monthly, the annual interest rate must be expressed as a monthly rate. Also, for payment calculations, we assume that the payment is made at the end of the month.

   The savings from refinancing occur over time, and therefore need to be discounted back to current dollars. The formula for converting K dollars saved t months from now to current dollars is:

$$\frac{K}{(1 + r)^{t-1}}$$

   where r is the monthly inflation rate. Assume that $r = 0.002$ and that Dave and Jana make their payment at the end of each month.

   Use your model to calculate the savings in current dollars associated with the refinanced loan versus staying with the original loan.

17. Consider again the mortgage refinance problem in Problem 16. Assume that Dave and Jana have accepted the refinance offer of a 15-year loan at 3% interest rate with out-of-pocket expenses of $2,937. Recall that they are borrowing $208,555.87. Assume that there is no prepayment penalty, so that any amount over the required payment is applied to the principal. Construct a model so that you can use Goal Seek to determine the monthly payment that will allow Dave and Jana to pay off the loan in 12 years. Do the same for 10 and 11 years. Which option for prepayment, if any, would you choose and why? (*Hint:* Break each monthly payment up into interest and principal

[the amount that is deducted from the balance owed]. Recall that the monthly interest that is charged is the monthly loan rate multiplied by the remaining loan balance.)

DATA *file*
Floyds

18. Floyd's Bumpers has distribution centers in Lafayette, Indiana; Charlotte, North Carolina; Los Angeles, California; Dallas, Texas; and Pittsburgh, Pennsylvania. Each distribution center carries all products sold. Floyd's customers are auto repair shops and larger auto parts retail stores. You are asked to perform an analysis of the customer assignments to determine which of Floyd's customers should be assigned to each distribution center. The rule for assigning customers to distribution centers is simple: A customer should be assigned to the closest center. The file *Floyds* contains the distance from each of Floyd's 1,029 customers to each of the five distribution centers. Your task is to build a list that tells which distribution center should serve each customer. The following functions will be helpful:

$$=MIN(array).$$

The MIN function returns the smallest value in a set of numbers. For example, if the range A1:A3 contains the values 6, 25, and 38, then the formula =MIN(A1:A3) returns the number 6, because it is the smallest of the three numbers:

$$=MATCH(lookup\_value, lookup\_array, match\ type).$$

The MATCH function searches for a specified item in a range of cells and returns the relative position of that item in the range. The *lookup_value* is the value to match, the *lookup_array* is the range of search, and *match type* indicates the type of match (use 0 for an exact match).

For example, if the range A1:A3 contains the values 6, 25, and 38, then the formula =MATCH(25,A1:A3,0) returns the number 2, because 25 is the second item in the range.

$$=INDEX(array, column\_num).$$

The INDEX function returns the value of an element in a position of an array. For example, if the range A1:A3 contains the values 6, 25, and 38, then the formula =INDEX(A1:A3, 2) = 25, because 25 is the value in the second position of the array A1:A3. (*Hint:* Create three new columns. In the first column, use the MIN function to calculate the minimum distance for the customer in that row. In the second column use the MATCH function to find the position of the minimum distance. In the third column, use the position in the previous column with the INDEX function referencing the row of distribution center names to find the name of the distribution center that should service that customer.)

DATA *file*
FloydsMay

19. Refer to Problem 18. Floyd's Bumpers pays a transportation company to ship its product in full truckloads to its customers. Therefore, the cost for shipping is a function of the distance traveled and a fuel surcharge (also on a per-mile basis). The cost per mile is $2.42, and the fuel surcharge is $0.56 per mile. The file *FloydsMay* contains data for shipments for the month of May (each record is simply the customer zip code for a given truckload shipment) as well as the distance table from the distribution centers to each customer. Use the MATCH and INDEX functions to retrieve the distance traveled for each shipment, and calculate the charge for each shipment. What is the total amount that Floyd's Bumpers spends on these May shipments? (*Hint:* The INDEX function may be used with a two-dimensional array: =INDEX(*array, row_num, column_num*), where *array* is a matrix, *row_num* is the row number, and *column_num* is the column position of the desired element of the matrix.)

20. An auto dealership is advertising that a new car with a sticker price of $35,208 is on sale for $25,995 if payment is made in full, or it can be financed at 0% interest

for 72 months with a monthly payment of $489. Note that 72 payments $\times$ $489 per payment = $35,208, which is the sticker price of the car. By allowing you to pay for the car in a series of payments (starting one month from now) rather than $25,995 now, the dealer is effectively loaning you $25,995. If you choose the 0% financing option, what is the effective interest rate that the auto dealership is earning on your loan? (*Hint:* Discount the payments back to current dollars [see Problem 16 for a discussion of discounting], and use Goal Seek to find the discount rate that makes the net present value of the payments = $25,995.)

CASE PROBLEM: RETIREMENT PLAN

Tim is 37 years old and would like to establish a retirement plan. Develop a spreadsheet model that could be used to assist Tim with retirement planning. Your model should include the following input parameters:

Tim's current age = 37 years
Tim's current total retirement savings = $259,000
Annual rate of return on retirement savings = 4%
Tim's current annual salary = $145,000
Tim's expected annual percentage increase in salary = 2%
Tim's percentage of annual salary contributed to retirement = 6%
Tim's expected age of retirement = 65
Tim's expected annual expenses after retirement (current dollars) = $90,000
Rate of return on retirement savings after retirement = 3%
Income tax rate postretirement = 15%

Assume that Tim's employer contributes 6% of Tim's salary to his retirement fund. Tim can make an additional annual contribution to his retirement fund before taxes (tax free) up to a contribution of $16,000. Assume that he contributes $6,000 per year. Also, assume an inflation rate of 2%.

Managerial Report

Your spreadsheet model should provide the accumulated savings at the onset of retirement as well as the age at which funds will be depleted (given assumptions on the input parameters).

As a feature of your spreadsheet model, build a data table to demonstrate the sensitivity of the age at which funds will be depleted to the retirement age and additional pre-tax contributions. Similarly, consider other factors you think might be important.

Develop a report for Tim outlining the factors that will have the greatest impact on his retirement.

Chapter 11

Linear Optimization Models

CONTENTS

ANALYTICS IN ACTION

MeadWestvaco Corporation*

MeadWestvaco Corporation is a major producer of premium papers for periodicals, books, commercial printing, and business forms. The company also produces pulp and lumber; designs and manufactures packaging systems for beverage and other consumables markets; and is a world leader in the production of coated board and shipping containers. Quantitative analyses at MeadWestvaco are developed and implemented by the company's Decision Analysis Department. The department assists decision makers by providing them with analytical tools as well as personal analysis and recommendations.

MeadWestvaco uses analytical models to assist with the long-range management of the company's timberland. Through the use of large-scale linear programs, timber harvesting plans are developed to cover a substantial time horizon. These models

consider wood market conditions, mill pulpwood requirements, harvesting capacities, and general forest management principles. Within these constraints, the model arrives at an optimal harvesting and purchasing schedule based on discounted cash flow. Alternative schedules reflect changes in the various assumptions concerning forest growth, wood availability, and general economic conditions.

Business analytics is also used in the development of the inputs for the linear programming models. Timber prices and supplies, as well as mill requirements, must be forecast over the time horizon, and advanced sampling techniques are used to evaluate land holdings and to project forest growth. The harvest schedule is then developed using a linear optimization model.

*Based on information provided by Dr. Edward P. Winkofsky of MeadWestvaco Corporation.

This chapter begins our discussion of *prescriptive analytics* and how optimization models can be used to support and improve managerial decision making. Optimization problems maximize or minimize some function, called the **objective function**, and usually have a set of restrictions known as **constraints**. Consider the following typical applications of optimization:

1. A manufacturer wants to develop a production schedule and an inventory policy that will satisfy demand in future periods. Ideally, the schedule and policy will enable the company to satisfy demand and at the same time *minimize* the total production and inventory costs.
2. A financial analyst must select an investment portfolio from a variety of stock and bond investment alternatives. The analyst would like to establish the portfolio that *maximizes* the return on investment.
3. A marketing manager wants to determine how best to allocate a fixed advertising budget among alternative advertising media such as web, radio, television, newspaper, and magazine. The manager would like to determine the media mix that *maximizes* advertising effectiveness.
4. A company has warehouses in a number of locations. Given specific customer demands, the company would like to determine how much each warehouse should ship to each customer so that total transportation costs are *minimized*.

Each of these examples has a clear objective. In example 1, the manufacturer wants to minimize costs; in example 2, the financial analyst wants to maximize return on investment; in example 3, the marketing manager wants to maximize advertising effectiveness; and in example 4, the company wants to minimize total transportation costs.

Likewise, each problem has constraints that limit the degree to which the objective can be pursued. In example 1, the manufacturer is restricted by the constraints requiring

Linear programming was initially referred to as "programming in a linear structure." In 1948, Tjalling Koopmans suggested to George Dantzig that the name was much too long: Koopman's suggestion was to shorten it to linear programming. George Dantzig agreed, and the field we now know as linear programming was named.

product demand to be satisfied and limiting production capacity. The financial analyst's portfolio problem is constrained by the total amount of investment funds available and the maximum amounts that can be invested in each stock or bond. The marketing manager's media selection decision is constrained by a fixed advertising budget and the availability of the various media. In the transportation problem, the minimum-cost shipping schedule is constrained by the supply of product available at each warehouse.

Optimization models can be linear or nonlinear. We begin with linear optimization models, also known as linear programs. Linear programming is a problem-solving approach developed to help managers make better decisions. Numerous applications of linear programming can be found in today's competitive business environment. For instance, GE Capital uses linear programming to help determine optimal lease structuring, and Marathon Oil Company uses linear programming for gasoline blending and to evaluate the economics of a new terminal or pipeline.

11.1 A Simple Maximization Problem

Par, Inc. is a small manufacturer of golf equipment and supplies whose management has decided to move into the market for medium- and high-priced golf bags. Par's distributor is enthusiastic about the new product line and has agreed to buy all the golf bags Par produces over the next three months.

After a thorough investigation of the steps involved in manufacturing a golf bag, management determined that each golf bag produced will require the following operations:

1. Cutting and dyeing the material
2. Sewing
3. Finishing (inserting umbrella holder, club separators, etc.)
4. Inspection and packaging

The director of manufacturing analyzed each of the operations and concluded that if the company produces a medium-priced standard model, each bag will require $7/10$ hour in the cutting and dyeing department, $1/2$ hour in the sewing department, 1 hour in the finishing department, and $1/10$ hour in the inspection and packaging department. The more expensive deluxe model will require 1 hour for cutting and dyeing, $5/6$ hour for sewing, $2/3$ hour for finishing, and $1/4$ hour for inspection and packaging. This production information is summarized in Table 11.1.

Par's production is constrained by a limited number of hours available in each department. After studying departmental workload projections, the director of manufacturing estimates that 630 hours for cutting and dyeing, 600 hours for sewing, 708 hours for finishing, and 135 hours for inspection and packaging will be available for the production of golf bags during the next three months.

TABLE 11.1	Production Requirements Per Golf Bag	
	Production Time (hours)	
Department	**Standard Bag**	**Deluxe Bag**
Cutting and Dyeing	$7/10$	1
Sewing	$1/2$	$5/6$
Finishing	1	$2/3$
Inspection and Packaging	$1/10$	$1/4$

It is important to understand that we are maximizing profit contribution, not profit. Overhead and other shared costs must be deducted before arriving at a profit figure.

The accounting department analyzed the production data, assigned all relevant variable costs, and arrived at prices for both bags that will result in a profit contribution[1] of $10 for every standard bag and $9 for every deluxe bag produced. Let us now develop a mathematical model of the Par, Inc. problem that can be used to determine the number of standard bags and the number of deluxe bags to produce in order to maximize total profit contribution.

Problem Formulation

Problem formulation, or **modeling**, is the process of translating the verbal statement of a problem into a mathematical statement. Formulating models is an art that can be mastered only with practice and experience. Even though every problem has some unique features, most problems also have common features. As a result, *some* general guidelines for optimization model formulation can be helpful, especially for beginners. We will illustrate these general guidelines by developing a mathematical model for Par, Inc.

Understand the problem thoroughly We selected the Par, Inc. problem to introduce linear programming because it is easy to understand. However, more complex problems will require much more effort to identify the items that need to be included in the model. In such cases, read the problem description to get a feel for what is involved. Taking notes will help you focus on the key issues and facts.

Describe the objective The objective is to maximize the total contribution to profit.

Describe each constraint Four constraints relate to the number of hours of manufacturing time available; they restrict the number of standard bags and the number of deluxe bags that can be produced.

- *Constraint 1:* The number of hours of cutting and dyeing time used must be less than or equal to the number of hours of cutting and dyeing time available.
- *Constraint 2:* The number of hours of sewing time used must be less than or equal to the number of hours of sewing time available.
- *Constraint 3:* The number of hours of finishing time used must be less than or equal to the number of hours of finishing time available.
- *Constraint 4:* The number of hours of inspection and packaging time used must be less than or equal to the number of hours of inspection and packaging time available.

Define the decision variables The controllable inputs for Par, Inc. are: (1) the number of standard bags produced, and (2) the number of deluxe bags produced. Let:

$$S = \text{number of standard bags}$$

$$D = \text{number of deluxe bags}$$

In optimization terminology, S and D are referred to as the **decision variables**.

Write the objective in terms of the decision variables Par's profit contribution comes from two sources: (1) the profit contribution made by producing S standard bags, and (2) the profit contribution made by producing D deluxe bags. If Par makes $10 for every standard bag, the company will make $10S$ if S standard bags are produced. Also, if Par makes $9 for every deluxe bag, the company will make $9D$ if D deluxe bags are produced. Thus, we have:

$$\text{Total profit contribution} = 10S + 9D.$$

---

[1]From an accounting perspective, profit contribution is more correctly described as the contribution margin per bag since overhead and other shared costs are not allocated.

Because the objective—maximize total profit contribution—is a function of the decision variables S and D, we refer to $10S + 9D$ as the *objective function*. Using *Max* as an abbreviation for maximize, we write Par's objective as follows:

$$\text{Max } 10S + 9D.$$

Write the constraints in terms of the decision variables

Constraint 1:

The units of measurement on the left-hand side of the constraint must match the units of measurement on the right-hand side.

$$\begin{pmatrix} \text{Hours of cutting and} \\ \text{dyeing time used} \end{pmatrix} \leq \begin{pmatrix} \text{Hours of cutting and} \\ \text{dyeing time available} \end{pmatrix}$$

Every standard bag Par produces will use $7/10$ hour cutting and dyeing time; therefore, the total number of hours of cutting and dyeing time used in the manufacture of S standard bags is $7/10\, S$. In addition, because every deluxe bag produced uses 1 hour of cutting and dyeing time, the production of D deluxe bags will use $1D$ hours of cutting and dyeing time. Thus, the total cutting and dyeing time required for the production of S standard bags and D deluxe bags is given by:

$$\text{Total hours of cutting and dyeing time used} = 7/10\, S + 1D.$$

The director of manufacturing stated that Par has at most 630 hours of cutting and dyeing time available. Therefore, the production combination we select must satisfy the requirement:

$$7/10\, S + 1D \leq 630. \tag{11.1}$$

Constraint 2:

$$\begin{pmatrix} \text{Hours of sewing} \\ \text{time used} \end{pmatrix} \leq \begin{pmatrix} \text{Hours of sewing} \\ \text{time available} \end{pmatrix}.$$

From Table 11.1 we see that every standard bag manufactured will require $1/2$ hour for sewing, and every deluxe bag will require $5/6$ hour for sewing. Because 600 hours of sewing time are available, it follows that

$$1/2\, S + 5/6\, D \leq 600. \tag{11.2}$$

Constraint 3:

$$\begin{pmatrix} \text{Hours of finishing} \\ \text{time used} \end{pmatrix} \leq \begin{pmatrix} \text{Hours of finishing} \\ \text{time available} \end{pmatrix}.$$

Every standard bag manufactured will require 1 hour for finishing, and every deluxe bag will require $2/3$ hour for finishing. With 708 hours of finishing time available, it follows that:

$$1S + 2/3\, D \leq 708. \tag{11.3}$$

Constraint 4:

$$\begin{pmatrix} \text{Hours of inspection and} \\ \text{packaging time used} \end{pmatrix} \leq \begin{pmatrix} \text{Hours of inspection and} \\ \text{packaging time available} \end{pmatrix}.$$

Every standard bag manufactured will require $1/10$ hour for inspection and packaging, and every deluxe bag will require $1/4$ hour for inspection and packaging. Because 135 hours of inspection and packaging time are available, it follows that:

$$1/10\, S + 1/4\, D \leq 135. \tag{11.4}$$

We have now specified the mathematical relationships for the constraints associated with the four departments. Have we forgotten any other constraints? Can Par produce a negative number of standard or deluxe bags? Clearly, the answer is no. Thus, to prevent the decision variables S and D from having negative values, two constraints must be added:

$$S \geq 0 \quad \text{and} \quad D \geq 0. \tag{11.5}$$

These constraints ensure that the solution to the problem will contain only nonnegative values for the decision variables and are thus referred to as the **nonnegativity constraints**. Nonnegativity constraints are a general feature of many linear programming problems and may be written in the abbreviated form:

$$S, D \geq 0.$$

Mathematical Model for the Par, Inc. Problem

The mathematical statement, or mathematical formulation, of the Par, Inc. problem is now complete. We succeeded in translating the objective and constraints of the problem into a set of mathematical relationships, referred to as a **mathematical model**. The complete mathematical model for the Par, Inc. problem is as follows:

$$\text{Max} \quad 10S + 9D$$
$$\text{subject to (s.t.)}$$

$\frac{7}{10}S + 1D \leq 630$	Cutting and dyeing
$\frac{1}{2}S + \frac{5}{6}D \leq 600$	Sewing
$1S + \frac{2}{3}D \leq 708$	Finishing
$\frac{1}{10}S + \frac{1}{4}D \leq 135$	Inspection and packaging
$S, D \geq 0$	

Our job now is to find the product mix (i.e., the combination of values for S and D) that satisfies all the constraints and at the same time yields a value for the objective function that is greater than or equal to the value given by any other feasible solution. Once these values are calculated, we will have found the optimal solution to the problem.

This mathematical model of the Par, Inc. problem is a **linear programming model**, or **linear program**, because the objective function and all constraint functions (the left-hand sides of the constraint inequalities) are linear functions of the decision variables.

Mathematical functions in which each variable appears in a separate term and is raised to the first power are called **linear functions**. The objective function ($10S + 9D$) is linear because each decision variable appears in a separate term and has an exponent of 1. The amount of production time required in the cutting and dyeing department ($\frac{7}{10}S + 1D$) is also a linear function of the decision variables for the same reason. Similarly, the functions on the left-hand side of all the constraint inequalities (the constraint functions) are linear functions. Thus, the mathematical formulation of this problem is referred to as a linear program.

Linear programming has nothing to do with computer programming. The use of the word programming means "choosing a course of action." Linear programming involves choosing a course of action when the mathematical model of the problem contains only linear functions.

NOTES + COMMENTS

The three assumptions necessary for a linear programming model to be appropriate are proportionality, additivity, and divisibility. *Proportionality* means that the contribution to the objective function and the amount of resources used in each constraint are proportional to the value of each decision variable. *Additivity* means that the value of the objective function and the total resources used can be found by summing the objective function contribution and the resources used for all decision variables. *Divisibility* means that the decision variables are continuous. The divisibility assumption plus the nonnegativity constraints mean that decision variables can take on any value greater than or equal to zero.

11.2 Solving the Par, Inc. Problem

Now that we have modeled the Par, Inc. problem as a linear program, let us discuss how we might find the optimal solution. The optimal solution must be a feasible solution. A **feasible solution** is a setting of the decision variables that satisifies all of the constraints of the problem. The optimal solution also must have an objective function value as good as any other feasible solution. For a maximization problem like Par, Inc., this means that the solution must be feasible and achieve the highest objective function value of any feasible solution. To solve a linear program then, we must search over the **feasible region**, which is the set of all feasible solutions, and find the solution that gives the best objective function value.

Because the Par, Inc. model has two decision variables, we are able to graph the feasible region. Discussing the geometry of the feasible region of the model will help us better understand linear programming and how we are able to solve much larger problems on the computer.

The Geometry of the Par, Inc. Problem

Recall that the feasible region is the set of points that satisfies all of the constraints of the problem. When we have only two decision variables and the functions of these variables are linear, they form lines in two-dimensional space. If the constraints are inequalities, the constraint cuts the space into two, with the line and the area on one side of the line being the space that satisfies that constraint. These subregions are called *half spaces*. The *intersection* of these half spaces makes up the feasible region.

The feasible region for the Par, Inc. problem is shown in Figure 11.1. Notice that the horizontal axis corresponds to the value of S and the vertical axis to the value of D. The

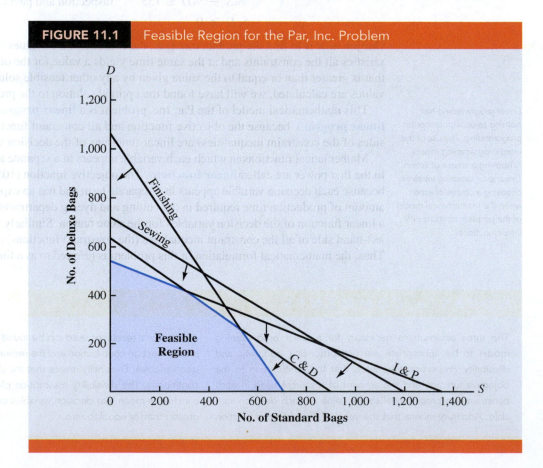

FIGURE 11.1   Feasible Region for the Par, Inc. Problem

nonnegativity constraints define that the feasible region is in the area bounded by the horizontal and vertical axes. Each of the four constraints is graphed as equality (a line), and arrows show the direction of the half space that satisfies the inequality constraint. The intersection of the four half spaces in the area bounded by the axes is the shaded region; this is the feasible region for the Par, Inc. problem. Any point in the shaded region satisfies all four constraints of the problem and nonnegativity.

To solve the Par, Inc. problem, we must find the point in the feasible region that results in the highest possible objective function value. A contour line is a set of points on a map, all of which have the same elevation. Similar to the way contour lines are used in geography, we may define an *objective function contour* to be a set of points (in this case a line) that yield a fixed value of the objective function. By choosing a fixed value of the objective function, we may plot contour lines of the objective function over the feasible region (Figure 11.2). In this case, as we move away from the origin we see higher values of the objective function and the highest such contour is $10S + 9D = 7{,}668$, after which we leave the feasible region. The highest value contour intersects the feasible region at a single point—point ③.

Of course, this geometric approach to solving a linear program is limited to problems with only two variables. What have we learned that can help us solve larger linear optimization problems?

Based on the geometry of Figure 11.2, to solve a linear optimization problem we only have to search over the **extreme points** of the feasible region to find an optimal solution. The extreme points are found where constraints intersect on the boundary of the feasible region. In Figure 11.2, points ①, ②, ③, ④, and ⑤ are the extreme points of the feasible region.

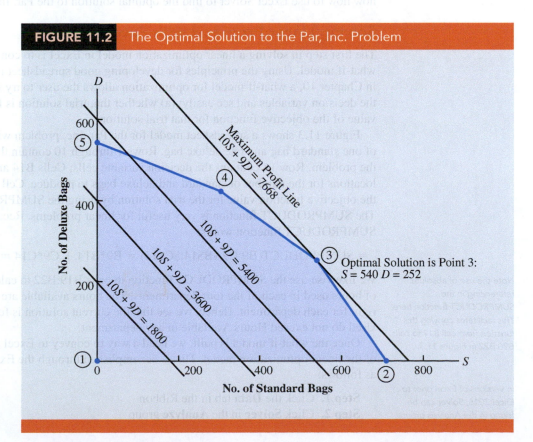

FIGURE 11.2   The Optimal Solution to the Par, Inc. Problem

Maximum Profit Line
$10S + 9D = 7668$

$10S + 9D = 5400$

$10S + 9D = 3600$

$10S + 9D = 1800$

Optimal Solution is Point 3:
$S = 540$ $D = 252$

No. of Deluxe Bags

No. of Standard Bags

Because each extreme point lies at the intersection of two constraint lines, we may obtain the values of S and D by solving simultaneously as equalities, the pair of constraints that form the given point. The values of S and D and the objective function value at points 1 through 5 are as follows:

Point	S	D	Profit = 10S + 9D
1	0	0	10(0) + 9(0) = 0
2	708	0	10(708) + 9(0) = 7,080
3	540	252	10(540) + 9(252) = 7,668
4	300	420	10(300) + 9(420) = 6,780
5	0	540	10(0) + 9(540) = 4,860

The highest profit is achieved at point ③. Therefore, the optimal plan is to produce 540 standard bags and 252 deluxe bags, as shown in Figure 11.2.

It turns out that this approach of investigating only extreme points works well and generalizes for larger problems. The simplex algorithm, developed by George Dantzig, is quite effective at investigating extreme points in an intelligent way to find the optimal solution to even very large linear programs.

Excel Solver is software that utilizes Dantzig's simplex algorithm to solve linear programs by systematically finding which set of constraints form the optimal extreme point of the feasible region. Once it finds an optimal solution, Solver then reports the optimal values of the decision variables and the optimal objective function value. Let us illustrate now how to use Excel Solver to find the optimal solution to the Par, Inc. problem.

Solving Linear Programs with Excel Solver

The first step in solving a linear optimization model in Excel is to construct the relevant what-if model. Using the principles for developing good spreadsheet models discussed in Chapter 10, a what-if model for optimization allows the user to try different values of the decision variables and see easily: (a) whether that trial solution is feasible, and (b) the value of the objective function for that trial solution.

Figure 11.3 shows a spreadsheet model for the Par, Inc. problem with a trial solution of one standard bag and one deluxe bag. Rows 1 through 10 contain the parameters for the problem. Row 14 contains the decision variable cells: Cells B14 and C14 are the locations for the number of standard and deluxe bags to produce. Cell B16 calculates the objective function value for the trial solution by using the SUMPRODUCT function. The SUMPRODUCT function is very useful for linear problems. Recall how the SUMPRODUCT function works:

$$= \text{SUMPRODUCT(B9:C9,\$B\$14:\$C\$14)} = \text{B9*B14} + \text{C9*C14} = 10(1) + 9(1) = 19.$$

Note the use of absolute referencing in the SUMPRODUCT function here. This facilitates copying this function from cell B19 to cells B20:B22 in Figure 11.3.

We likewise use the SUMPRODUCT function in cells B19:B22 to calculate the number of hours used in each of the four departments. The hours available are immediately to the right for each department. Hence, we see that the current solution is feasible, since Hours Used do not exceed Hours Available in any department.

Once the what-if model is built, we need a way to convey to Excel Solver the structure of the linear optimization model. This is accomplished through the Excel Solver dialog box as follows:

In versions of Excel prior to Excel 2016, Solver can be found in the Analysis group.

Step 1. Click the **Data** tab in the Ribbon

Step 2. Click **Solver** in the **Analyze** group

FIGURE 11.3   What-If Spreadsheet Model for Par, Inc.

	A	B	C	D
1	Par, Inc.			
2	Parameters			
3		Production Time (Hours)		Time Available
4	Operation	Standard	Deluxe	Hours
5	Cutting and Dyeing	=7/10	1	630
6	Sewing	=5/10	=5/6	600
7	Finishing	1	=2/3	708
8	Inspection and Packaging	=1/10	=1/4	135
9	Profit Per Bag	10	9	
10				
11	Model			
12				
13		Standard	Deluxe	
14	Bags Produced	1	1	
15				
16	Total Profit	=SUMPRODUCT(B9:C9,$B$14:$C$14)		
17				
18	Operation	Hours Used	Hours Available	
19	Cutting and Dyeing	=SUMPRODUCT(B5:C5,$B$14:$C$14)	=D5	
20	Sewing	=SUMPRODUCT(B6:C6,$B$14:$C$14)	=D6	
21	Finishing	=SUMPRODUCT(B7:C7,$B$14:$C$14)	=D7	
22	Inspection and Packaging	=SUMPRODUCT(B8:C8,$B$14:$C$14)	=D8	

MODEL *file*

Par

	A	B	C	D
1	Par, Inc.			
2	Parameters			
3		Production Time (Hours)		Time Available
4	Operation	Standard	Deluxe	Hours
5	Cutting and Dyeing	0.7	1	630
6	Sewing	0.5	0.83333	600
7	Finishing	1	0.66667	708
8	Inspection and Packaging	0.1	0.25	135
9	Profit Per Bag	10	9.00	
10				
11	Model			
12				
13		Standard	Deluxe	
14	Bags Produced	1.00	1.00	
15				
16	Total Profit	$19.00		
17				
18	Operation	Hours Used	Hours Available	
19	Cutting and Dyeing	1.7	630	
20	Sewing	1.33333	600	
21	Finishing	1.66667	708	
22	Inspection and Packaging	0.35	135	

FIGURE 11.4   Solver Dialog Box and Solution to the Par, Inc. Problem

	A	B	C	D	E	F	G	H	I	J	K	L	M
1	Par, Inc.												
2	Parameters												
3		Production Time (Hours)		Time Available									
4	Operation	Standard	Deluxe	Hours									
5	Cutting and Dyeing	0.7	1	630									
6	Sewing	0.5	0.83333	600									
7	Finishing	1	0.66667	708									
8	Inspection and Packaging	0.1	0.25	135									
9	Profit Per Bag	10	9.00										
10													
11	Model												
12													
13		Standard	Deluxe										
14	Bags Produced	540.00	252.00										
15													
16	Total Profit	$7,668.00											
17													
18	Operation	Hours Used	Hours Available										
19	Cutting and Dyeing	630	630										
20	Sewing	480.00000	600										
21	Finishing	708.00000	708										
22	Inspection and Packaging	117	135										
23													
24													
25													
26													
27													
28													
29													
30													

Solver Parameters

Set Objective: $B$16

To: ● Max   ○ Min   ○ Value Of: 0

By Changing Variable Cells:
$B$14:$C$14

Subject to the Constraints:
$B$19:$B$22 <= $C$19:$C$22

Add
Change
Delete
Reset All
Load/Save

☑ Make Unconstrained Variables Non-Negative

Select a Solving Method: Simplex LP   Options

Solving Method
Select the GRG Nonlinear engine for Solver Problems that are smooth nonlinear. Select the LP Simplex engine for linear Solver Problems, and select the Evolutionary engine for Solver problems that are non-smooth.

Help   Solve   Close

Step 3. When the **Solver Parameters** dialog box appears (Figure 11.4):
  Enter *B16* in the **Set Objective:** box
  Select **Max** for the **To:** option
  Enter *B14:C14* in the **By Changing Variable Cells:** box
Step 4. Click the **Add** button
  When the **Add Constraint** dialog box appears:
  Enter *B19:B22* in the left-hand box under **Cell Reference:**
  Select **<=** from the dropdown button
  Enter *C19:C22* in the **Constraint:** box
  Click **OK**
Step 5. Select the checkbox for **Make Unconstrained Variables Non-Negative**
Step 6. From the drop-down menu for **Select a Solving Method:**, choose **Simplex LP**

FIGURE 11.5	The Solver Answer Report for the Par, Inc. Problem

◢	A	B	C	D	E	F	G
13							
14	Objective Cell (Max)						
15		Cell	Name	Original Value	Final Value		
16		$B$16	Total Profit	$19.00	$7,668.00		
17							
18							
19	Variable Cells						
20		Cell	Name	Original Value	Final Value	Integer	
21		$B$14	Bags Produced Standard	1.000	540.000	Contin	
22		$C$14	Bags Produced Deluxe	1.000	252.000	Contin	
23							
24							
25	Constraints						
26		Cell	Name	Cell Value	Formula	Status	Slack
27		$B$19	Cutting and Dyeing Hours Used	630	$B$19<=$C$19	Binding	0
28		$B$20	Sewing Hours Used	480	$B$20<=$C$20	Not Binding	120
29		$B$21	Finishing Hours Used	708	$B$21<=$C$21	Binding	0
30		$B$22	Inspection and Packaging Hours Used	117	$B$22<=$C$22	Not Binding	18
31							

Step 7. Click **Solve**

Step 8. When the **Solver Results** dialog box appears:
>   Select **Keep Solver Solution**
>   In the **Reports** section, select **Answer Report**
>   Click **OK**

The completed Solver dialog box and solution for the Par, Inc. problem are shown in Figure 11.4. The optimal solution is to make 540 standard bags and 252 deluxe bags (see cells B14 and C14) for a profit of $7,688 (see cell B16). This corresponds to point 3 in Figure 11.2. Also note that, from cells B19:B22 compared to C19:C22, we use all cutting and dyeing time as well as all finishing time. This is, of course, consistent with what we have seen in Figures 11.1 and 11.2: The cutting, dyeing, and finishing constraints intersect to form point 3 in the graph.

The Excel Solver Answer Report appears in Figure 11.5. The Answer Report contains three sections: Objective Cell, Variable Cells, and Constraints. In addition to some other information, each section gives the cell location, name, and value of the cell(s). The Objective Cell section indicates that the optimal (Final Value) of Total Profit is $7,668.00. In the Variable Cells section, the two far-right columns indicate the optimal values of the decision cells and whether or not the variables are required to be integer (here they are labeled "Contin" for continuous). Note that Solver generates a Name for a cell by concatenating the text to the left and above that cell. Hence, the name of cell $B$14 is created by combining the labels "Bags Produced" and "Standard" to produce the name "Bags Produced Standard."

Variable cells that are required to be integer will be discussed in Chapter 12.

The Constraints section gives the left-hand side value for each constraint (in this case the hours used), the formula showing the constraint relationship, the status (Binding or Not Binding), and the Slack value. A **binding constraint** is one that holds as an equality at the optimal solution. Geometrically, binding constraints intersect to form the optimal point. We see in Figure 11.5 that the cutting and dyeing and finishing constraints are designated as binding, consistent with our geometric study of this problem.

The **slack** value for each less-than-or-equal-to constraint indicates the difference between the left-hand and right-hand values for a constraint. Of course, by definition, binding constraints have zero slack. Consider for example the sewing department constraint. By adding a nonnegative **slack variable,** we can make the constraint equality:

$$\tfrac{1}{2}S + \tfrac{5}{6}D \leq 600$$
$$\tfrac{1}{2}S + \tfrac{5}{6}D + slack_{sewing} = 600$$
$$slack_{sewing} = 600 - \tfrac{1}{2}(540) + \tfrac{5}{6}(252) = 600 - 270 - 210 = 120$$

The slack value for the inspecting and packaging constraint is calculated in a similar way. For resource constraints like departmental hours available, the slack value gives the amount of unused resource, in this case, time measured in hours.

NOTES + COMMENTS

1. Notice in the data section for the Par, Inc. spreadsheet shown in Figure 11.3, that we have entered fractions in cells C6: =5/6 and C7: =2/3. We do this to make sure we maintain accuracy because rounding these values could have an impact on our solution.

2. By selecting **Make Unconstrained Variables Non-Negative** in the **Solver Parameters** dialog box, all decision variables are declared to be nonnegative.

3. Although we have shown the Answer Report and how to interpret it, we will usually show the solution to an

optimization problem directly in the spreadsheet. A well-designed spreadsheet that follows the principles discussed in Chapter 10 should make it easy for the user to interpret the optimal solution directly from the spreadsheet.

4. In addition to the Answer Report, Solver also allows you to generate two other reports. The Sensitivity Report will be discussed in Section 11.5. The Limits Report gives information on the objective function value when variables are set to their limits.

11.3 A Simple Minimization Problem

M&D Chemicals produces two products that are sold as raw materials to companies that manufacture bath soaps and laundry detergents. Based on an analysis of current inventory levels and potential demand for the coming month, M&D's management specified that the combined production for products A and B must total at least 350 gallons. Separately, a major customer's order for 125 gallons of product A must also be satisfied. Product A requires 2 hours of processing time per gallon, and product B requires 1 hour of processing time per gallon. For the coming month, 600 hours of processing time are available. M&D's objective is to satisfy these requirements at a minimum total production cost. Production costs are $2 per gallon for product A and $3 per gallon for product B.

Problem Formulation

To find the minimum-cost production schedule, we will formulate the M&D Chemicals problem as a linear program. Following a procedure similar to the one used for the Par, Inc. problem, we first define the decision variables and the objective function for the problem. Let:

$$A = \text{number of gallons of product A to produce}$$
$$B = \text{number of gallons of product B to produce}$$

With production costs at $2 per gallon for product A and $3 per gallon for product B, the objective function that corresponds to the minimization of the total production cost can be written as:

$$\text{Min } 2A + 3B.$$

Next consider the constraints placed on the M&D Chemicals problem. To satisfy the major customer's demand for 125 gallons of product A, we know A must be at least 125. Thus, we write the constraint:

$$1A \geq 125.$$

For the combined production for both products, which must total at least 350 gallons, we can write the constraint:

$$1A + 1B \geq 350.$$

Finally, for the limitation of 600 hours on available processing time, we add the constraint:

$$2A + 1B \leq 600.$$

After adding the nonnegativity constraints $(A, B \geq 0)$, we arrive at the following linear program for the M&D Chemicals problem:

$$\text{Min} \quad 2A + 3B$$

s.t.

$1A$		≥ 125	Demand for product A
$1A$	$+ 1B$	≥ 350	Total production
$2A$	$+ 1B$	≤ 600	Processing time
A, B	≥ 0		

Solution for the M&D Chemicals Problem

M&DModel

A spreadsheet model for the M&D Chemicals problem along with the Solver dialog box are shown in Figure 11.6. The complete linear programming model for the M&D Chemicals problem in Excel Solver is contained in the file *M&DModel*. We use the SUMPRODUCT function to calculate total cost in cell B16 and also to calculate total processing hours used in cell B23. The optimal solution, which is shown in the spreadsheet and in the Answer Report in Figure 11.7, is to make 250 gallons of product A and 100 gallons of product B, for a total cost of $800. Both the total production constraint and the processing time constraints are binding (350 gallons are provided, the same as required, and all 600 processing hours are used). The requirement that at least 125 gallons of Product A be produced is not binding. For greater-than-or-equal-to constraints, we can define a nonnegative variable called a surplus variable. A **surplus variable** tells how much over the right-hand side the left-hand side of a greater-than-or-equal-to constraint is for a solution. A surplus variable is subtracted from the left-hand side of the constraint. For example:

$$1A \geq 125$$
$$1A - \text{surplus}_A = 125$$
$$\text{surplus}_A = 1A - 125 = 250 - 125 = 125$$

As was the case with less-than-or-equal-to constraints and slack variables, a positive value for a surplus variable indicates that the constraint is not binding.

NOTES + COMMENTS

1. In the spreadsheet and Solver model for the M&D Chemicals problem, we separated the greater-than-or-equal-to constraints and the less-than-or-equal-to constraints. This allows for easier entry of the constraints into the Add Constraint dialog box.

2. In the Excel Answer Report, both slack and surplus variables are labeled "Slack."

FIGURE 11.6   Solver Dialog Box and Solution to the M&D Chemical Problem

	A	B	C	D
1	**M&D Chemicals**			
2	**Parameters**			
3		Product A	Product B	Time Available
4	Processing Time (hours)	2	1	600
5	Production Cost	$2.00	$3.00	
6				
7	Minimum Total Production	350		
8	Product A Minimum	125		
9				
10				
11	**Model**			
12				
13		Product A	Product B	
14	Gallons Produced	250	100	
15				
16	Minimize Total Cost	$800.00		
17				
18		Provided	Required	
19	Product A	250	125	
20	Total Production	350	350	
21				
22		Hours Used	Hours Available	Unused Hours
23	Processing Time	600	600	0
24				
25				
26				
27				
28				
29				
30				

MODEL *file*

M&DModel

Solver Parameters

Se_t Objective: $B$16

To: ○ _Max   ● Mi_n   ○ _Value Of: 0

_By Changing Variable Cells:

$B$14:$C$14

Su_bject to the Constraints:

$B$19:$B$20 >= $C$19:$C$20
$B$23 <= $C$23

[_Add]
[_Change]
[_Delete]
[_Reset All]
[Load/_Save]

☑ _Make Unconstrained Variables Non-Negative

_Select a Solving Method: Simplex LP   [O_ptions]

Solving Method

Select the GRG Nonlinear engine for Solver Problems that are smooth nonlinear. Select the LP Simplex engine for linear Solver Problems, and select the Evolutionary engine for Solver problems that are non-smooth.

[_Help]   [_Solve]   [Cl_ose]

FIGURE 11.7	The Solver Answer Report for the M&D Chemicals Problem

◢	A	B	C	D	E	F	G
13							
14		Objective Cell (Min)					
15		Cell	Name	Original Value	Final Value		
16		$B$16	Minimize Total Cost	$0.00	$800.00		
17							
18							
19		Variable Cells					
20		Cell	Name	Original Value	Final Value	Integer	
21		$B$14	Gallons Produced Product A	0	250	Contin	
22		$C$14	Gallons Produced Product B	0	100	Contin	
23							
24							
25		Constraints					
26		Cell	Name	Cell Value	Formula	Status	Slack
27		$B$19	Product A Provided	250	$B$19>=$C$19	Not Binding	125
28		$B$20	Total Production Provided	350	$B$20>=$C$20	Binding	0
29		$B$23	Processing Time Hours Used	600	$B$23<=$C$23	Binding	0
30							

11.4 Special Cases of Linear Program Outcomes

In this section we discuss three special situations that can arise when we attempt to solve linear programming problems.

Alternative Optimal Solutions

From the discussion of the graphical solution procedure, we know that optimal solutions can be found at the extreme points of the feasible region. Now let us consider the special case in which the optimal objective function contour line coincides with one of the binding constraint lines on the boundary of the feasible region. We will see that this situation can lead to the case of **alternative optimal solutions**; in such cases, more than one solution provides the optimal value for the objective function.

To illustrate the case of alternative optimal solutions, we return to the Par, Inc. problem. However, let us assume that the profit for the standard golf bag (S) has been decreased to $6.30. The revised objective function becomes $6.3S + 9D$. The graphical solution of this problem is shown in Figure 11.8. Note that the optimal solution still occurs at an extreme point. In fact, it occurs at two extreme points: extreme point ④ ($S = 300, D = 420$) and extreme point ③ ($S = 540, D = 252$).

The objective function values at these two extreme points are identical; that is:

$$6.3S + 9D = 6.3(300) + 9(420) = 5670$$

and

$$6.3S + 9D = 6.3(540) + 9(252) = 5670.$$

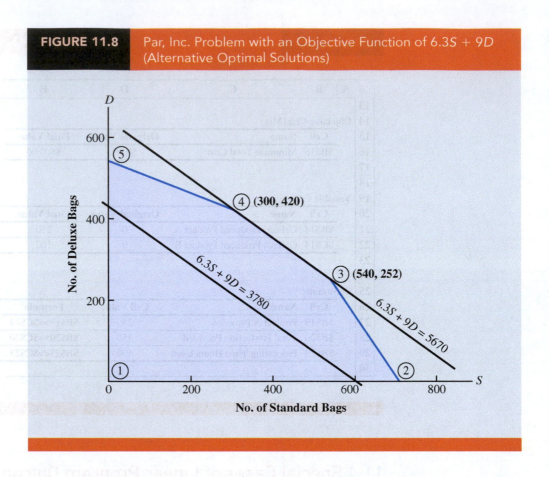

FIGURE 11.8   Par, Inc. Problem with an Objective Function of 6.3S + 9D (Alternative Optimal Solutions)

Furthermore, any point on the line connecting the two optimal extreme points also provides an optimal solution. For example, the solution point ($S = 420$, $D = 336$), which is halfway between the two extreme points, also provides the optimal objective function value of:

$$6.3S + 9D = 6.3(420) + 9(336) = 5670.$$

A linear programming problem with alternative optimal solutions is generally a good situation for the manager or decision maker. It means that several combinations of the decision variables are optimal and that the manager can select the most desirable optimal solution. Unfortunately, determining whether a problem has alternative optimal solutions is not a simple matter. In Section 11.7, we discuss an approach for finding alternative optima.

Infeasibility

Problems with no feasible solution do arise in practice, most often because management's expectations are too high or because too many restrictions have been placed on the problem.

Infeasibility means that no solution to the linear programming problem satisfies all the constraints, including the nonnegativity conditions. Graphically, infeasibility means that a feasible region does not exist; that is, no points satisfy all the constraints and the nonnegativity conditions simultaneously. To illustrate this situation, let us look again at the problem faced by Par, Inc.

Suppose that management specified that at least 500 of the standard bags and at least 360 of the deluxe bags must be manufactured. The graph of the solution region may now be constructed to reflect these new requirements (see Figure 11.9). The shaded area in the lower left-hand portion of the graph depicts the points that satisfy the departmental constraints on the availability of time. The shaded area in the upper right-hand portion depicts the points

FIGURE 11.9	No Feasible Region for the Par, Inc. Problem with Minimum Production Requirements of 500 Standard and 360 Deluxe Bags

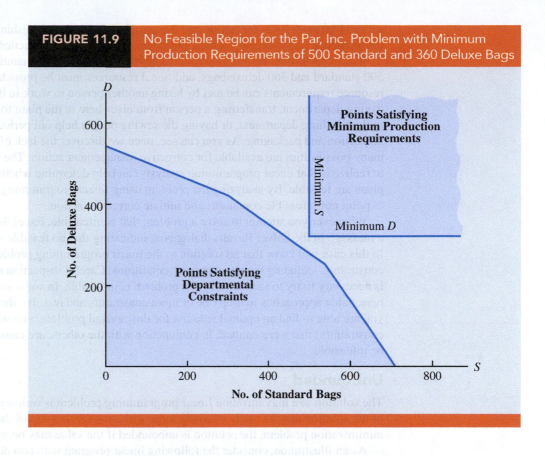

that satisfy the minimum production requirements of 500 standard and 360 deluxe bags. But no points satisfy both sets of constraints. Thus, we see that if management imposes these minimum production requirements, no feasible region exists for the problem.

How should we interpret infeasibility in terms of this current problem? First, we should tell management that, given the resources available (i.e., production time for cutting and dyeing, sewing, finishing, and inspection and packaging), it is not possible to make 500 standard bags and 360 deluxe bags. Moreover, we can tell management exactly how much of each resource must be expended to make it possible to manufacture these numbers of bags. Table 11.2 shows the minimum amounts of resources that must be available, the amounts currently available, and additional amounts that would be required to accomplish this level of production. Thus,

TABLE 11.2	Resources Needed to Manufacture 500 Standard Bags and 360 Deluxe Bags

Operation	Minimum Required Resources (hours)	Available Resources (hours)	Additional Resources Needed (hours)
Cutting and dyeing	$7/10$ (500) + 1(360) = 710	630	80
Sewing	$1/2$ (500) + $5/6$ (360) = 550	600	None
Finishing	1(500) + $2/3$ (360) = 740	708	32
Inspection and packaging	$1/10$ (500) + $1/4$ (360) = 140	135	5

we need 80 more hours for cutting and dyeing, 32 more hours for finishing, and 5 more hours for inspection and packaging to meet management's minimum production requirements.

If after reviewing this information, management still wants to manufacture 500 standard and 360 deluxe bags, additional resources must be provided. Perhaps the resource requirements can be met by hiring another person to work in the cutting and dyeing department, transferring a person from elsewhere in the plant to work part-time in the finishing department, or having the sewing people help out periodically with the inspection and packaging. As you can see, once we discover the lack of a feasible solution, many possibilities are available for corrective management action. The important thing to realize is that linear programming analysis can help determine whether management's plans are feasible. By analyzing the problem using linear programming, we are often able to point out infeasible conditions and initiate corrective action.

Whenever you attempt to solve a problem that is infeasible, Excel Solver will return a message in the Solver Results dialog box, indicating that no feasible solutions exists. In this case you know that no solution to the linear programming problem will satisfy all constraints, including the nonnegativity conditions. Careful inspection of your formulation is necessary to try to identify why the problem is infeasible. In some situations, the only reasonable approach is to drop one or more constraints and re-solve the problem. If you are able to find an optimal solution for this revised problem, you will know that the constraint(s) that were omitted, in conjunction with the others, are causing the problem to be infeasible.

Unbounded

The solution to a maximization linear programming problem is **unbounded** if the value of the solution may be made infinitely large without violating any of the constraints; for a minimization problem, the solution is unbounded if the value may be made infinitely small.

As an illustration, consider the following linear program with two decision variables, X and Y:

$$\text{Max} \quad 20X + 10Y$$
$$\text{s.t.}$$
$$1X \quad\quad \geq 2$$
$$1Y \leq 5$$
$$X, Y \geq 0$$

In Figure 11.10 we graph the feasible region associated with this problem. Note that we can indicate only part of the feasible region because the feasible region extends indefinitely in the direction of the X-axis. Looking at the objective function lines in Figure 11.10, we see that the solution to this problem may be made as large as we desire. In other words, no matter which solution we pick, we will always be able to reach some feasible solution with a larger value. Thus, we say that the solution to this linear program is *unbounded*.

Whenever you attempt to solve an unbounded problem using Excel Solver, you will receive a message in the Solver Results dialog box telling you that the "Objective Cell values do not converge." In linear programming models of real problems, the occurrence of an unbounded solution means that the problem has been improperly formulated. We know it is not possible to increase profits indefinitely. Therefore, we must conclude that if a profit maximization problem results in an unbounded solution, the mathematical model does not sufficiently represent the real-world problem. In many cases, this error is the result of inadvertently omitting a constraint during problem formulation.

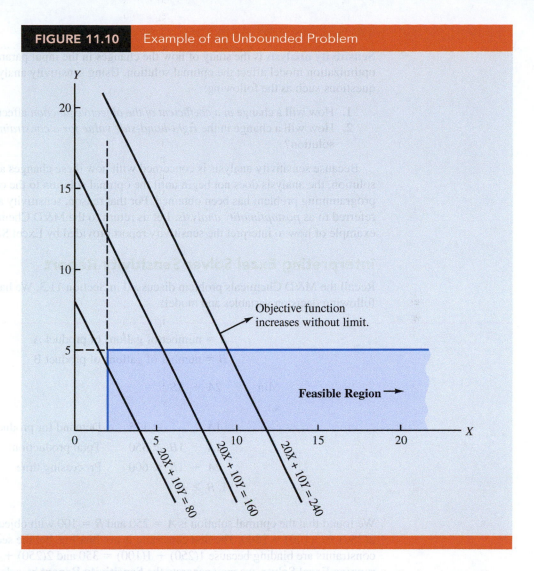

FIGURE 11.10   Example of an Unbounded Problem

Objective function increases without limit.

Feasible Region

$20X + 10Y = 80$

$20X + 10Y = 160$

$20X + 10Y = 240$

The parameters for optimization models are often less than certain. In the next section, we discuss the sensitivity of the optimal solution to uncertainty in the model parameters. In addition to the optimal solution, Excel Solver can provide some useful information on the sensitivity of that solution to changes in the model parameters.

NOTES + COMMENTS

1. Infeasibility is independent of the objective function. It exists because the constraints are so restrictive that no feasible region for the linear programming model is possible. Thus, when you encounter infeasibility, making changes in the coefficients of the objective function will not help; the problem will remain infeasible.

2. The occurrence of an unbounded solution is often the result of a missing constraint. However, a change in the objective function may cause a previously unbounded problem to become bounded with an optimal solution. For example, the graph in Figure 11.10 shows an unbounded solution for the objective function Max $20X + 10Y$. However, changing the objective function to Max $-20X - 10Y$ will provide the optimal solution $X = 2$ and $Y = 0$ even though no changes have been made in the constraints.

11.5 Sensitivity Analysis

Sensitivity analysis is the study of how the changes in the input parameters of an optimization model affect the optimal solution. Using sensitivity analysis, we can answer questions such as the following:

1. How will a change *in a coefficient of the objective function* affect the optimal solution?
2. How will a change in the *right-hand-side value for a constraint* affect the optimal solution?

Because sensitivity analysis is concerned with how these changes affect the optimal solution, the analysis does not begin until the optimal solution to the original linear programming problem has been obtained. For that reason, sensitivity analysis is often referred to as *postoptimality analysis*. Let us return to the M&D Chemicals problem as an example of how to interpret the sensitivity report provided by Excel Solver.

Interpreting Excel Solver Sensitivity Report

Recall the M&D Chemicals problem discussed in Section 11.3. We had defined the following decision variables and model:

$$A = \text{number of gallons of product A}$$
$$B = \text{number of gallons of product B}$$

$$
\begin{aligned}
\text{Min} \quad & 2A + 3B \\
\text{s.t.} \quad & \\
& 1A \qquad\qquad \geq 125 \qquad \text{Demand for product A} \\
& 1A + 1B \geq 350 \qquad \text{Total production} \\
& 2A + 1B \leq 600 \qquad \text{Processing time} \\
& A, B \geq 0
\end{aligned}
$$

We found that the optimal solution is $A = 250$ and $B = 100$ with objective function value = $2(250) + 3(100) = \$800$. The first constraint is not binding, but the second and third constraints are binding because $1(250) + 1(100) = 350$ and $2(250) + 100 = 600$. After running Excel Solver, we may generate the **Sensitivity Report** by selecting **Sensitivity** from the **Reports** section of the **Solver Results** dialog box and then selecting **OK**. The Sensitivity report for the M&D Chemicals problem appears in Figure 11.11. There are two sections in this report: one for decision variables (Variable Cells) and one for Constraints.

Let us begin by interpreting the Constraints section. The cell location of the left-hand side of the constraint, the constraint name, and the value of the left-hand side of the constraint at optimality are given in the first three columns. The fourth column gives the shadow price for each constraint. The **shadow price** for a constraint is the change in the optimal objective function value if the right-hand side of that constraint is increased by one. Let us interpret each shadow price given in the report in Figure 11.11.

The first constraint is: $1A \geq 125$. This is a nonbinding constraint because $250 > 125$. If we change the constraint to $1A \geq 126$, there will be no change in the objective function value. The reason for this is that the constraint will remain nonbinding at the optimal solution, because $1A = 250 > 126$. Hence, the shadow price is zero. In fact, *nonbinding constraints will always have a shadow price of zero.*

The second constraint is binding and its shadow price is 4. The interpretation of the shadow price is as follows. If we change the constraint from $1A + 1B \geq 350$ to

FIGURE 11.11 Solver Sensitivity Report for the M&D Chemicals Problem

	A	B	C	D	E	F	G	H
4								
5								
6	Variable Cells							
7				Final	Reduced	Objective	Allowable	Allowable
8		Cell	Name	Value	Cost	Coefficient	Increase	Decrease
9		$B$14	Gallons Produced Product A	250	0	2	1	1E + 30
10		$C$14	Gallons Produced Product B	100	0	3	1E + 30	1
11								
12	Constraints							
13				Final	Shadow	Constraint	Allowable	Allowable
14		Cell	Name	Value	Price	R.H. Side	Increase	Decrease
15		$B$19	Product A Provided	250	0	125	125	1E + 30
16		$B$20	Total Production Provided	350	4	350	125	50
17		$B$23	Processing Time Hours Used	600	−1	600	100	125
18								

$1A + 1B \geq 351$, the optimal objective function value will increase by $4; that is, the new optimal solution will have an objective function value equal to $800 + $4 = $804.

The third constraint is also binding and has a shadow price of -1. The interpretation of the shadow price is as follows. If we change the constraint from $2A + 1B \leq 600$ to $2A + 1B \leq 601$, the objective function value will decrease by $1; that is, the new optimal solution will have an objective function value equal to $800 − $1 = $799.

Note that the shadow price for the second constraint is positive, but for the third it is negative. Why is this? The sign of the shadow price depends on whether the problem is a maximization or a minimization and the type of constraint under consideration. The M&D Chemicals problem is a cost minimization problem. The second constraint is a greater-than-or-equal-to constraint. By increasing the right-hand side, we make the constraint even *more* restrictive. This results in an increase in cost. Contrast this with the third constraint. The third constraint is a less-than-or-equal-to constraint. By increasing the right-hand side, we make more hours available. We have made the constraint less restrictive. Because we have made the constraint *less* restrictive, there are more feasible solutions from which to choose. Therefore, cost drops by $1.

Making a constraint more restrictive is often referred to as tightening the constraint. Making a constraint less restrictive is often referred to as relaxing, or loosening, the constraint.

When observing shadow prices, the following general principle holds: *Making a binding constraint more restrictive degrades or leaves unchanged the optimal objective function value, and making a binding constraint less restrictive improves or leaves unchanged the optimal objective function.* We shall see several more examples of this later in this chapter. Also, shadow prices are symmetric; so the negative of the shadow price is the change in the objective function for a *decrease* of one in the right-hand side.

In Figure 11.11, the Allowable Increase and the Allowable Decrease are the allowable changes in the right-hand side for which the current shadow price remains valid. For example, because the allowable increase in the processing time is 100, if we increase the processing time hours by 50 to 600 + 50 = 650, we can say with certainty that the optimal objective function value will change by (−1)50 = −50. Hence, we know that the optimal objective function value will be $800 − $50 = $750. If we increase the right-hand side of the processing time beyond the allowable increase of 100, we cannot predict what will happen. Likewise, if we decrease the right-hand side of the processing time constraint by 50, we know the optimal objective function value will change by the negative of the shadow price: $-(-1)50 = 50$. Cost will increase by \$50. If we change the right-hand side by more than the allowable increase or decrease, the shadow price is no longer valid.

Let us now turn to the Variable Cells section of the Sensitivity Report. As in the constraint section, the cell location, variable name, and final (optimal) value for each variable are given. The fourth column is Reduced Cost. The **reduced cost** for a decision variable is the shadow price of the nonnegativity constraint for that variable. In other words, the reduced cost indicates the change in the optimal objective function value that results from changing the right-hand side of the nonnegativity constraint from 0 to 1.

In the fifth column of the report, the objective function coefficient for the variable is given. The Allowable Increase and Allowable Decrease indicate the change in the objective function coefficient for which the *current optimal solution will remain optimal*. The value $1E + 30$ in the report is essentially infinity. So long as the cost of product A, is greater than or equal to negative infinity and less than or equal to $2 + 1 = 3$, the current solution remains optimal. For example, if the cost of product A is really \$2.50 per gallon, we do not need to re-solve the model. Because the increase in cost of \$0.50 is less than the allowable increase of \$1.00, the current solution of 250 gallons of product A and 100 gallons of product B remains optimal.

As we have seen, the Excel Solver Sensitivity Report can provide useful information about the sensitivity of the optimal solution to changes in the model input data. However, this type of classical sensitivity analysis is somewhat limited. Classical sensitivity analysis is based on the assumption that only one piece of input data has changed; it is assumed that all other parameters remain as stated in the original problem. In many cases, however, we are interested in what would happen if two or more pieces of input data are changed simultaneously. The easiest way to examine the effect of simultaneous changes is to make the changes and rerun the model.

NOTES + COMMENTS

We defined the reduced cost as the shadow price of the nonnegativity constraint for that variable. When there is a binding simple upper-bound constraint for a variable, the reduced cost reported by Solver is the shadow price of that upper-bound constraint. Likewise, if there is a binding nonzero lower bound for a variable, the reduced cost is the shadow price for that lower-bound constraint. So to be more general, the reduced cost for a decision variable is the shadow price of the binding simple lower- or upper-bound constraint for that variable.

11.6 General Linear Programming Notation and More Examples

Earlier in this chapter we showed how to formulate linear programming models for the Par, Inc. and M&D Chemicals problems. To formulate a linear programming model of the Par, Inc. problem, we began by defining two decision variables: S = number of standard bags and D = number of deluxe bags. In the M&D Chemicals problem, the two decision variables were defined as A = number of gallons of product A and B = number of gallons of product B. We selected decision-variable names of S and D in the Par, Inc. problem and A and B in the M&D Chemicals problem to make it easier to recall what these decision variables represented in the problem. Although this approach works well for linear programs involving a small number of decision variables, it can become difficult when dealing with problems involving a large number of decision variables.

A more general notation that is often used for linear programs uses the letter x with a subscript. For instance, in the Par, Inc. problem, we could have defined the decision variables as follows:

$$x_1 = \text{number of standard bags}$$
$$x_2 = \text{number of deluxe bags}$$

In the M&D Chemicals problem, the same variable names would be used, but their definitions would change:

$$x_1 = \text{number of gallons of product A}$$
$$x_2 = \text{number of gallons of product B}$$

A disadvantage of using general notation for decision variables is that we are no longer able to easily identify what the decision variables actually represent in the mathematical model. However, the advantage of general notation is that formulating a mathematical model for a problem that involves a large number of decision variables is much easier. For instance, for a linear programming model with three decision variables, we would use variable names of x_1, x_2, and x_3; for a problem with four decision variables, we would use variable names of x_1, x_2, x_3, and x_4; and so on. Clearly, if a problem involved 1,000 decision variables, trying to identify 1,000 unique names would be difficult. However, using the general linear programming notation, the decision variables would be defined as $x_1, x_2, x_3, \ldots, x_{1000}$.

Using this new general notation, the Par, Inc. model would be written:

$$\text{Max} \quad 10x_1 + 9x_2$$
s.t.
$$\begin{array}{llll} \tfrac{7}{10}x_1 + 1x_2 & \leq 630 & \text{Cutting and dyeing} \\ \tfrac{1}{2}x_1 + \tfrac{5}{6}x_2 & \leq 600 & \text{Sewing} \\ 1x_1 + \tfrac{2}{3}x_2 & \leq 708 & \text{Finishing} \\ \tfrac{1}{10}x_1 + \tfrac{1}{4}x_2 & \leq 135 & \text{Inspection and packaging} \\ x_1, x_2 & \geq 0 \end{array}$$

In some of the examples that follow in this section and in Chapters 12 and 13, we will use this type of subscripted notation.

Investment Portfolio Selection

In finance, linear programming can be applied in problem situations involving capital budgeting, make-or-buy decisions, asset allocation, portfolio selection, financial planning, and many more. Next, we describe a portfolio selection problem.

Portfolio selection problems involve situations in which a financial manager must select specific investments—for example, stocks and bonds—from a variety of investment alternatives. Managers of mutual funds, credit unions, insurance companies, and banks frequently encounter this type of problem. The objective function for portfolio selection problems usually is maximization of expected return or minimization of risk. The constraints usually take the form of restrictions on the type of permissible investments, state laws, company policy, maximum permissible risk, and so on. Problems of this type have been formulated and solved using a variety of optimization techniques. In this section we formulate and solve a portfolio selection problem as a linear program.

Consider the case of Welte Mutual Funds, Inc., located in New York City. Welte just obtained $100,000 by converting industrial bonds to cash and is now looking for other

TABLE 11.3	Investment Opportunities for Welte Mutual Funds
Investment	**Projected Rate of Return (%)**
Atlantic Oil	7.3
Pacific Oil	10.3
Midwest Steel	6.4
Huber Steel	7.5
Government bonds	4.5

investment opportunities for these funds. Based on Welte's current investments, the firm's top financial analyst recommends that all new investments be made in the oil industry, steel industry, or government bonds. Specifically, the analyst identified five investment opportunities and projected their annual rates of return. The investments and rates of return are shown in Table 11.3.

The management at Welte imposed the following investment guidelines:

1. Neither industry (oil or steel) should receive more than $50,000.
2. The amount invested in government bonds should be at least 25% of the steel industry investments.
3. The investment in Pacific Oil, the high-return but high-risk investment, cannot be more than 60% of the total oil industry investment.

What portfolio recommendations—investments and amounts—should be made for the available $100,000? Given the objective of maximizing projected return subject to the budgetary and managerially imposed constraints, we can answer this question by formulating and solving a linear programming model of the problem. The solution will provide investment recommendations for the management of Welte Mutual Funds.

Let us define the following decision variables:

$$X_1 = \text{dollars invested in Atlantic Oil}$$
$$X_2 = \text{dollars invested in Pacific Oil}$$
$$X_3 = \text{dollars invested in Midwest Steel}$$
$$X_4 = \text{dollars invested in Huber Steel}$$
$$X_5 = \text{dollars invested in government bonds}$$

Using the projected rates of return shown in Table 11.3, we write the objective function for maximizing the total return for the portfolio as:

$$\text{Max} \quad 0.073X_1 + 0.103X_2 + 0.064X_3 + 0.075X_4 + 0.045X_5.$$

The constraint specifying investment of the available $100,000 is:

$$X_1 + X_2 + X_3 + X_4 + X_5 = 100,000.$$

The requirements that neither the oil nor steel industry should receive more than $50,000 are:

$$X_1 + X_2 \leq 50,000$$
$$X_3 + X_4 \leq 50,000$$

The requirement that the amount invested in government bonds be at least 25% of the steel industry investment is expressed as:

$$X_5 \geq 0.25(X_3 + X_4).$$

Finally, the constraint that Pacific Oil cannot be more than 60% of the total oil industry investment is:

$$X_2 \leq 0.60(X_1 + X_2).$$

By adding the nonnegativity restrictions, we obtain the complete linear programming model for the Welte Mutual Funds investment problem:

Max $0.073 X_1 + 0.103 X_2 + 0.064 X_3 + 0.075 X_4 + 0.045 X_5$

s.t.

$X_1 +$	$X_2 +$	$X_3 +$	$X_4 +$	$X_5 =$	100,000	Available funds
$X_1 +$	X_2			$\leq$	50,000	Oil industry maximum
		$X_3 +$	X_4	$\leq$	50,000	Steel industry maximum
	$X_5 \geq 0.25 (X_3 + X_4)$					Government bonds minimum
	$X_2 \leq 0.60 (X_1 + X_2)$					Pacific Oil restriction
	$X_1, X_2, X_3, X_4, X_5 \geq 0$					

MODEL *file*

Welte

The optimal solution to this linear program is shown in Figure 11.12. Note that the optimal solution indicates that the portfolio should be diversified among all the investment opportunities except Midwest Steel. The projected annual return for this portfolio is $8,000, which is an overall return of 8%. Except for the upper bound on the Steel investment, all constraints are binding.

NOTES + COMMENTS

1. The optimal solution to the Welte Mutual Funds problem indicates that $20,000 should be spent on the Atlantic Oil stock. If Atlantic Oil sells for $75 per share, we would have to purchase exactly 266⅔ shares in order to spend exactly $20,000. The difficulty of purchasing fractional shares can be handled by purchasing the largest possible integer number of shares with the allotted funds (e.g., 266 shares of Atlantic Oil). This approach guarantees that the budget constraint will not be violated. This approach, of course, introduces the possibility that the solution will no longer be optimal, but the danger is slight if a large number of securities are involved. In cases in which the analyst believes that the

decision variables *must* have integer values, the problem must be formulated as an integer linear programming model (the topic of Chapter 12).

2. Financial portfolio theory stresses obtaining a proper balance between risk and return. In the Welte problem, we explicitly considered return in the objective function. Risk is controlled by choosing constraints that ensure diversity among oil and steel stocks and a balance between government bonds and the steel industry investment. In Chapter 13, we discuss investment portfolio models that control risk as measured by the variance of returns on investment.

Transportation Planning

The *transportation problem* arises frequently in planning for the distribution of goods and services from several supply locations to several demand locations. Typically, the quantity of goods available at each supply location (origin) is limited, and the quantity of goods needed at each of several demand locations (destinations) is known. The usual objective in a transportation problem is to minimize the cost of shipping goods from the origins to the destinations.

Let us revisit the transportation problem faced by Foster Generators, discussed in Chapter 10. This problem involves the transportation of a product from three plants to

FIGURE 11.12 The Solution for the Welte Mutual Funds Problem

	A	B	C	D	E	F
1	Welte Mutual Funds Problem					
2						
3	Parameters					
4	Investment	Projected Rate of Return				
5	Atlantic Oil	0.073		Available Funds	100000	
6	Pacific Oil	0.103		Oil Max	50000	
7	Midwest Steel	0.064		Steel Max	50000	
8	Huber Steel	0.075		Pacific Oil Max	0.6	
9	Gov't Bonds	0.045		Gov't Bonds Min	0.25	
10						
11	Model					
12						
13	Investment	Amount Invested				
14	Atlantic Oil	20000				
15	Pacific Oil	30000				
16	Midwest Steel	0				
17	Huber Steel	40000				
18	Gov't Bonds	10000				
19						
20	Max Total Return	=SUMPRODUCT(B5:B9, B14:B18)				
21						
22		Funds Invested	Funds Available	Unused Funds		
23	Total	=SUM(B14:B18)	=E5	= C23−B23		
24						
25		Funds Invested	Max Allowed			
26	Oil	=SUM(B14:B15)	=E6			
27	Steel	=SUM(B16:B17)	=E7			
28	Pacific Oil	=B15	=E8*(B14+B15)			
29						
30		Funds Invested	Min Required			
31	Gov't Bonds	=B18	=E9*(B16+B17)			

	A	B	C	D	E
1	Welte Mutual Funds Problem				
2					
3	Parameters				
4	Investment	Projected Rate of Return			
5	Atlantic Oil	0.073		Available Funds	$100,000.00
6	Pacific Oil	0.103		Oil Max	$50,000.00
7	Midwest Steel	0.064		Steel Max	$50,000.00
8	Huber Steel	0.075		Pacific Oil Max	0.6
9	Gov't Bonds	0.045		Gov't Bonds Min	0.25
10					
11	Model				
12					
13	Investment	Amount Invested			
14	Atlantic Oil	$20,000.00			
15	Pacific Oil	$30,000.00			
16	Midwest Steel	$0.00			
17	Huber Steel	$40,000.00			
18	Gov't Bonds	$10,000.00			
19					
20	Max Total Return	$8,000.00			
21					
22		Funds Invested	Funds Available	Unused Funds	
23	Total	$100,000.00	$100,000.00	$0.00	
24					
25		Funds Invested	Max Allowed		
26	Oil	$50,000.00	$50,000.00		
27	Steel	$40,000.00	$50,000.00		
28	Pacific Oil	$30,000.00	$30,000.00		
29					
30		Funds Invested	Min Required		
31	Gov't Bonds	$10,000.00	$10,000.00		

four distribution centers. Foster Generators operates plants in Cleveland, Ohio; Bedford, Indiana; and York, Pennsylvania. Production capacities over the next three-month planning period for one type of generator are as follows:

Origin	Plant	Three-Month Production Capacity (units)
1	Cleveland	5,000
2	Bedford	6,000
3	York	2,500
	Total	13,500

The firm distributes its generators through four regional distribution centers located in Boston, Massachusetts; Chicago, Illinois; St. Louis, Missouri; and Lexington, Kentucky; the three-month forecast of demand for the distribution centers is as follows:

Destination	Distribution Center	Three-Month Demand Forecast (units)
1	Boston	6,000
2	Chicago	4,000
3	St. Louis	2,000
4	Lexington	1,500
		Total 13,500

Management would like to determine how much of its production should be shipped from each plant to each distribution center. Figure 11.13 shows graphically the 12 distribution routes Foster can use. Such a graph is called a *network*; the circles are referred to as *nodes*, and the lines connecting the nodes as *arcs*. Each origin and destination is represented by a node, and each possible shipping route is represented by an arc. The amount of the supply is written next to each origin node, and the amount of the demand is written next to each destination node. The goods shipped from the origins to the destinations represent the flow in the network. Note that the direction of flow (from origin to destination) is indicated by the arrows.

For Foster's transportation problem, the objective is to determine the routes to be used and the quantity to be shipped via each route that will provide the minimum total transportation cost. The cost for each unit shipped on each route is given in Table 11.4 and is shown on each arc in Figure 11.13.

A linear programming model can be used to solve this transportation problem. We use *double-subscripted* decision variables, with x_{11} denoting the number of units shipped from origin 1 (Cleveland) to destination 1 (Boston), x_{12} denoting the number of units shipped from origin 1 (Cleveland) to destination 2 (Chicago), and so on. In general, the decision variables for a transportation problem having m origins and n destinations are written as follows:

$$x_{ij} = \text{number of units shipped from origin } i \text{ to destination } j$$
$$\text{where } i = 1, 2, \ldots, m \text{ and } j = 1, 2, \ldots, n.$$

Because the objective of the transportation problem is to minimize the total transportation cost, we can use the cost data in Table 11.4 or on the arcs in Figure 11.13 to develop the following cost expressions:

Transportation costs for
  units shipped from Cleveland $= 3x_{11} + 2x_{12} + 7x_{13} + 6x_{14}$

Transportation costs for
  units shipped from Bedford $\quad= 6x_{21} + 5x_{22} + 2x_{23} + 3x_{24}$

Transportation costs for
  units shipped from York $\quad\quad= 2x_{31} + 5x_{32} + 4x_{33} + 5x_{34}$

The sum of these expressions provides the objective function showing the total transportation cost for Foster Generators.

Transportation problems need constraints because each origin has a limited supply and each destination has a demand requirement. We consider the supply constraints first. The capacity at the Cleveland plant is 5,000 units. With the total number of units shipped from the Cleveland plant expressed as $x_{11} + x_{12} + x_{13} + x_{14}$, the supply constraint for the Cleveland plant is:

$$x_{11} + x_{12} + x_{13} + x_{14} \leq 5,000 \quad \text{Cleveland supply}$$

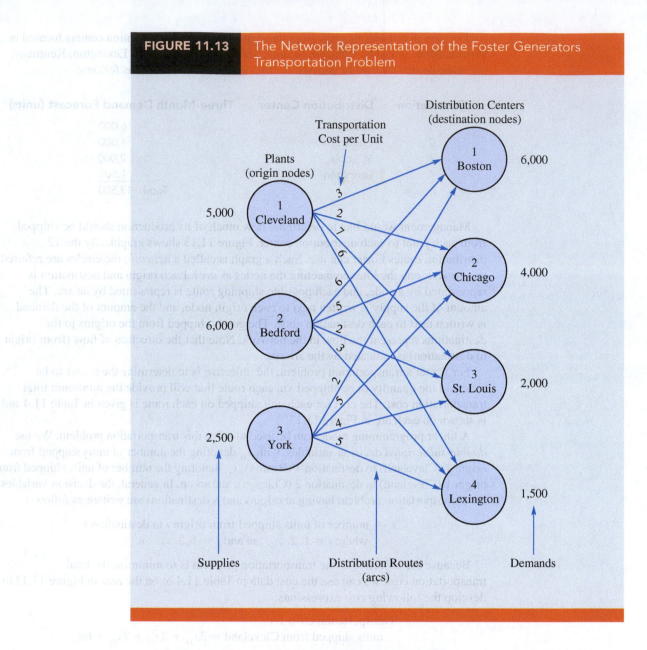

FIGURE 11.13   The Network Representation of the Foster Generators Transportation Problem

Transportation Cost per Unit

Distribution Centers (destination nodes)

Plants (origin nodes)

5,000   1 Cleveland

6,000   2 Bedford

2,500   3 York

1 Boston   6,000

2 Chicago   4,000

3 St. Louis   2,000

4 Lexington   1,500

3
2
7
6
6
5
2
3
2
5
4
5

Supplies   Distribution Routes (arcs)   Demands

TABLE 11.4   Transportation Cost Per Unit for the Foster Generators Transportation Problem ($)

	Destination			
Origin	Boston	Chicago	St. Louis	Lexington
Cleveland	3	2	7	6
Bedford	6	5	2	3
York	2	5	4	5

With three origins (plants), the Foster transportation problem has three supply constraints. Given the capacity of 6,000 units at the Bedford plant and 2,500 units at the York plant, the two additional supply constraints are:

$$x_{21} + x_{22} + x_{23} + x_{24} \leq 6{,}000 \quad \text{Bedford supply}$$
$$x_{31} + x_{32} + x_{33} + x_{34} \leq 2{,}500 \quad \text{York supply}$$

With the four distribution centers as the destinations, four demand constraints are needed to ensure that destination demands will be satisfied:

$$x_{11} + x_{21} + x_{31} = 6{,}000 \quad \text{Boston demand}$$
$$x_{12} + x_{22} + x_{32} = 4{,}000 \quad \text{Chicago demand}$$
$$x_{13} + x_{23} + x_{33} = 2{,}000 \quad \text{St. Louis demand}$$
$$x_{14} + x_{24} + x_{34} = 1{,}500 \quad \text{Lexington demand}$$

Combining the objective function and constraints into one model provides a 12-variable, 7-constraint linear programming formulation of the Foster Generators transportation problem:

$$
\begin{aligned}
\text{Min} \quad & 3x_{11} + 2x_{12} + 7x_{13} + 6x_{14} + 6x_{21} + 5x_{22} + 2x_{23} + 3x_{24} + 2x_{31} + 5x_{32} + 4x_{33} + 5x_{34} \\
\text{s.t.} \quad & \\
& x_{11} + x_{12} + x_{13} + x_{14} \leq 5{,}000 \\
& x_{21} + x_{22} + x_{23} + x_{24} \leq 6{,}000 \\
& x_{31} + x_{32} + x_{33} + x_{34} \leq 2{,}500 \\
& x_{11} + x_{21} + x_{31} = 6{,}000 \\
& x_{12} + x_{22} + x_{32} = 4{,}000 \\
& x_{13} + x_{23} + x_{33} = 2{,}000 \\
& x_{14} + x_{24} + x_{34} = 1{,}500 \\
& x_{ij} \geq 0 \quad \text{for } i = 1, 2, 3 \text{ and } j = 1, 2, 3, 4
\end{aligned}
$$

Comparing the linear programming formulation to the network in Figure 11.13 leads to several observations. All the information needed for the linear programming formulation is on the network. Each node has one constraint, and each arc has one variable. The sum of the variables corresponding to arcs from an origin node must be less than or equal to the origin's supply, and the sum of the variables corresponding to the arcs into a destination node must be equal to the destination's demand.

A spreadsheet model and the solution to the Foster Generators problem (Figure 11.14) shows that the minimum total transportation cost is $39,500. The values for the decision variables show the optimal amounts to ship over each route. For example, 1,000 units should be shipped from Cleveland to Boston, and 4,000 units should be shipped from Cleveland to Chicago. Other values of the decision variables indicate the remaining shipping quantities and routes.

Advertising Campaign Planning

Applications of linear programming to marketing are numerous. Advertising campaign planning, marketing mix, and market research are just a few areas of application. In this section we consider an advertising campaign planning application.

Advertising campaign planning applications of linear programming are designed to help marketing managers allocate a fixed advertising budget to various advertising media. Potential media include newspapers, magazines, radio, television, and direct mail. In these applications, the objective is to maximize reach, frequency, and quality of exposure. Restrictions on

FIGURE 11.14   Spreadsheet Model and Solution for the Foster Generator Problem

	A	B	C	D	E	F
1	Foster Generators					
2	Parameters					
3	Shipping Cost/Unit		Destination			
4	Origin	Boston	Chicago	St. Louis	Lexington	Supply
5	Cleveland	3	2	7	6	5000
6	Bedford	6	5	2	3	6000
7	York	2	5	4	5	2500
8	Demand	6000	4000	2000	1500	
9						
10						
11	Model					
12						
13	Total Cost	=SUMPRODUCT(B5:E7,B17:E19)				
14						
15			Destination			
16	Origin	Boston	Chicago	St. Louis	Lexington	Total
17	Cleveland	1000	4000	0	0	=SUM(B17:E17)
18	Bedford	2500	0	2000	1500	=SUM(B18:E18)
19	York	2500	0	0	0	=SUM(B19:E19)
20	Total	=SUM(B17:B19)	=SUM(C17:C19)	=SUM(D17:D19)	=SUM(E17:E19)	
21						

MODEL *file*

Foster

	A	B	C	D	E	F	G
1	Foster Generators						
2	Parameters						
3	Shipping Cost/Unit		Destination				
4	Origin	Boston	Chicago	St. Louis	Lexington	Supply	
5	Cleveland	$3.00	$2.00	$7.00	$6.00	5000	
6	Bedford	$6.00	$5.00	$2.00	$3.00	6000	
7	York	$2.00	$5.00	$4.00	$5.00	2500	
8	Demand	6000	4000	2000	1500		
9							
10							
11	Model						
12							
13	Total Cost	$39,500.00					
14							
15			Destination				
16	Origin	Boston	Chicago	St. Louis	Lexington	Total	
17	Cleveland	1000	4000	0	0	5000	
18	Bedford	2500	0	2000	1500	6000	
19	York	2500	0	0	0	2500	
20	Total	6000	4000	2000	1500		
21							

the allowable allocation usually arise during consideration of company policy, contract requirements, and media availability. In the application that follows, we illustrate how a media selection problem might be formulated and solved using a linear programming model.

Relax-and-Enjoy Lake Development Corporation is developing a lakeside community at a privately owned lake. The primary market for the lakeside lots and homes includes all middle- and upper-income families within approximately 100 miles of the development. Relax-and-Enjoy employed the advertising firm of Boone, Phillips, and Jackson (BP&J) to design the promotional campaign.

After considering possible advertising media and the market to be covered, BP&J recommended that the first month's advertising be restricted to five media. At the end of the month, BP&J will then reevaluate its strategy based on the month's results. BP&J collected data on the number of potential customers reached, the cost per advertisement, the maximum number of times each medium is available, and the exposure quality rating for each of the five media. The quality rating is measured in terms of an exposure quality unit, a measure of the relative value of one advertisement in each of the media. This measure, based on BP&J's experience in the advertising business, takes into account factors such as audience demographics (age, income, and education of the audience reached), image presented, and quality of the advertisement. The information collected is presented in Table 11.5.

Relax-and-Enjoy provided BP&J with an advertising budget of \$30,000 for the first month's campaign. In addition, Relax-and-Enjoy imposed the following restrictions on how BP&J may allocate these funds: At least 10 television commercials must be used, at least 50,000 potential customers must be reached, and no more than \$18,000 may be spent on television advertisements. What advertising media selection plan should be recommended?

The decision to be made is how many times to use each medium. We begin by defining the decision variables:

$$DTV = \text{number of times daytime TV is used}$$
$$ETV = \text{number of times evening TV is used}$$
$$DN = \text{number of times daily newspaper is used}$$
$$SN = \text{number of times Sunday newspaper is used}$$
$$R = \text{number of times radio is used}$$

The data on quality of exposure in Table 11.5 show that each daytime TV (DTV) advertisement is rated at 65 exposure quality units. Thus, an advertising plan with DTV advertisements will provide a total of $65DTV$ exposure quality units. Continuing with the data in Table 11.5, we find evening TV (ETV) rated at 90 exposure quality units, daily newspaper (DN) rated at 40 exposure quality units, Sunday newspaper (SN) rated at 60 exposure quality units, and radio (R) rated at 20 exposure quality units. With the objective of maximizing the total exposure quality units for the overall media selection plan, the objective function becomes:

$$\text{Max}\quad 65DTV + 90ETV + 40DN + 60SN + 20R \qquad \text{Exposure quality}$$

TABLE 11.5	Advertising Media Alternatives for the Relax-and-Enjoy Lake Development Corporation			
Advertising Media	No. of Potential Customers Reached	Cost (\$) per Advertisement	Maximum Times Available per Month*	Exposure Quality Units
1. Daytime TV (1 min), station WKLA	1,000	1,500	15	65
2. Evening TV (30 sec), station WKLA	2,000	3,000	10	90
3. Daily newspaper (full page), *The Morning Journal*	1,500	400	25	40
4. Sunday newspaper magazine (½ page color), *The Sunday Press*	2,500	1,000	4	60
5. Radio, 8:00 a.m. or 5:00 p.m. news (30 sec), station KNOP	300	100	30	20

*The maximum number of times the medium is available is either the maximum number of times the advertising medium occurs (e.g., four Sundays per month) or the maximum number of times BP&J recommends that the medium is used.

We now formulate the constraints for the model from the information given:

Each medium has a maximum availability:

$$DTV \leq 15$$
$$ETV \leq 10$$
$$DN \leq 25$$
$$SN \leq 4$$
$$R \leq 30$$

A total of $30,000 is available for the media campaign:

$$1500DTV + 3000ETV + 400DN + 1000SN + 100R \leq 30,000$$

At least 10 television commercials must be used:

$$DTV + ETV \geq 10.$$

At least 50,000 potential customers must be reached:

$$1000DTV + 2000ETV + 1500DN + 2500SN + 300R \geq 50,000$$

No more than $18,000 may be spent on television advertisements:

$$1500DTV + 3000ETV \leq 18,000.$$

By adding the nonnegativity restrictions, we obtain the complete linear programming model for the Relax-and-Enjoy advertising campaign planning problem:

$$\text{Max} \quad 65\,DTV + 90\,ETV + 40\,DN + 60\,SN + 20\,R \qquad \text{Exposure quality}$$

s.t.

DTV					≤ 15	
	ETV				≤ 10	
		DN			≤ 25	Availability of media
			SN		≤ 4	
				R	≤ 30	
$1500\,DTV +$	$3000\,ETV +$	$400\,DN +$	$1000\,SN +$	$100\,R$	$\leq 30,000$	Budget
$DTV +$	ETV				≥ 10	Television
$1500\,DTV +$	$3000\,ETV$				$\leq 18,000$	restrictions
$1000\,DTV +$	$2000\,ETV +$	$1500\,DN +$	$2500\,SN +$	$300\,R$	$\geq 50,000$	Customers reached
		DTV, ETV, DN, SN, R			≥ 0	

A spreadsheet model and the optimal solution to this linear programming model are shown in Figure 11.15.

The optimal solution calls for advertisements to be distributed among daytime TV, daily newspaper, Sunday newspaper, and radio. The maximum number of exposure quality units is 2,370, and the total number of customers reached is 61,500.

Let us consider now the Sensitivity Report for the Relax-and-Enjoy advertising campaign planning problem shown in Figure 11.16. We begin by interpreting the Constraints section.

Note that the overall budget constraint has a shadow price of 0.060. Therefore, a $1.00 increase in the advertising budget will lead to an increase of 0.06 exposure quality unit. The shadow price of -25 for the number of TV ads indicates that increasing the number of television commercials required by 1 will decrease the exposure quality of the advertising

FIGURE 11.15 A Spreadsheet Model and the Solution for the Relax-and-Enjoy Lake Development Corporation Problem

	A	B	C	D	E	F	G	H	I
1	Relax-and-Enjoy Lake Development Corporation								
2	Parameters								
3			Media						
4		DTV	ETV	DN	SN	R			
5	Cust Reach	1000	2000	1500	2500	300		Min Cust Reach	50000
6	Cost/Ad	1500	3000	400	1000	100		Min TV Ads	10
7	Availability	15	10	25	4	30		Max TV Budget	18000
8	Exposure/Ad	65	90	40	60	20		Budget	30000
9									
10									
11	Model								
12		DTV	ETV	DN	SN	R			
13	Ads Placed	10	0	25	2	30			
14									
15	Max Exposure	=SUMPRODUCT(B8:F8,B13:F13)							
16									
17		Achieved	Min Required						
18	Reach	=SUMPRODUCT(B5:F5,B13:F13)	=I5						
19	Num TV Ads	=B13+C13	=I6						
20									
21		Used	Limit						
22	TV Budget	=SUMPRODUCT(B6:C6,B13:C13)	=I17						
23	Budget	=SUMPRODUCT(B6:F6,B13:F13)	=I18						

MODEL *file*

Relax

	A	B	C	D	E	F	G	H	I
1	Relax-and-Enjoy Lake Development Corporation								
2	Parameters								
3			Media						
4		DTV	ETV	DN	SN	R			
5	Cust Reach	1,000	2,000	1,500	2,500	300		Min Cust Reach	50,000
6	Cost/Ad	$1,500	$3,000	$400	$1,000	$100		Min TV Ads	10
7	Availability	15	10	25	4	30		Max TV Budget	$18,000
8	Exposure/Ad	65	90	40	60	20		Budget	$30,000
9									
10									
11	Model								
12		DTV	ETV	DN	SN	R			
13	Ads Placed	10	0	25	2	30			
14									
15	Max Exposure	2370							
16									
17		Achieved	Min Required						
18	Reach	61,500	50,000						
19	Num TV Ads	10	10						
20									
21		Used	Limit						
22	TV Budget	$15,000	$18,000						
23	Budget	$30,000	$30,000						

plan by 25 units. Alternatively, decreasing the number of television commercials by 1 will increase the exposure quality of the advertising plan by 25 units. Thus, Relax-and-Enjoy should consider reducing the requirement of having at least 10 television commercials.

Note that the availability-of-media constraints are not listed in the constraint section. These types of constraints, simple upper (or lower) bounds on a decision variable, are not listed in the report, just as nonnegativity constraints are not listed. There is information

FIGURE 11.16   The Excel Sensitivity Report for the Relax-and-Enjoy Lake Development Corporation Problem

Variable Cells

Cell	Name	Final Value	Reduced Cost	Objective Coefficient	Allowable Increase	Allowable Decrease
$B$13	Ads Placed DTV	10	0	65	25	65
$C$13	Ads Placed ETV	0	−65	90	65	1E + 30
$D$13	Ads Placed DN	25	16	40	1E + 30	16
$E$13	Ads Placed SN	2	0	60	40	16.6666667
$F$13	Ads Placed R	30	14	20	1E + 30	14

Constraints

Cell	Name	Final Value	Shadow Price	Constraint R.H. Side	Allowable Increase	Allowable Decrease
$B$18	Reach Achieved	61500	0	50000	11500	1E + 30
$B$19	Num TV Ads Achieve	10	−25	10	1.33333333	1.33333333
$B$22	TV Budget Used	$15,000.00	0	18000	1E + 30	3000
$B$23	Budget Used	$30,000.00	0.06	30000	2000	2000

about these constraints in the variables section under reduced cost. Let us therefore turn our attention to the Variable Cells section of the report.

Let us interpret each of the three nonzero reduced costs in Figure 11.16. The variable *ETV*, the number of evening TV ads, is currently at its lower bound of zero. Therefore, the reduced cost of −65 is the shadow price of the nonnegativity constraint, which we interpret as follows. If we change the requirement that $ETV \geq 0$ to $ETV \geq 1$, exposure will drop by 65. Notice that for the other variables that have a nonzero reduced cost, *DN* and *R*, the number of daily newspaper ads and radio ads respectively, are at their upper bounds of 25 and 30. In these cases, the reduced cost is the shadow price of the upper-bound constraint on each of these variables. For example, allowing 31 rather than only 30 radio ads will increase exposures by 14.

The allowable increase and decrease for the objective function coefficients are interpreted as discussed in Section 11.5. For example, as long as the number of exposures per ad for daytime TV does not increase by more than 25 or decrease by more than 65, the current plan shown in Figure 11.15 remains optimal.

NOTES + COMMENTS

1. The media selection model required subjective evaluations of the exposure quality for the media alternatives. Marketing managers may have substantial data concerning exposure quality, but the final coefficients used in the objective function may also include considerations based primarily on managerial judgment.

2. The media selection model presented in this section uses exposure quality as the objective function and places a constraint on the number of customers reached. An alternative formulation of this problem would be to use the number of customers reached as the objective function and to add a constraint indicating the minimum total exposure quality required for the media plan.

11.7 Generating an Alternative Optimal Solution for a Linear Program

The goal of business analytics is to provide information to management for improved decision making. If a linear program has more than one optimal solution, as discussed in Section 11.4, it would be good for management to know this. There might be factors external to the model that make one optimal solution preferable to another. For example, in a portfolio optimization problem, perhaps more than one strategy yields the maximum expected return. However, those strategies might be quite different in terms of their risk to the investor. Knowing the optimal alternatives and then assessing the risk of each, the investor could then pick the least risky alternative from the optimal solutions. In this section, we discuss how to generate an alternative optimal solution if one exists.

Let us reconsider the Foster Generators transportation problem from the previous section. If one exists, how might we generate an alternative optimal solution for this problem? From Figure 11.14 we know the following is an optimal solution:

$$x_{11} = 1{,}000, x_{12} = 4{,}000, x_{13} = 0, x_{14} = 0$$
$$x_{21} = 2{,}500, x_{22} = 0, x_{23} = 2{,}000, x_{24} = 1{,}500$$
$$x_{31} = 2{,}500, x_{32} = 0, x_{33} = 0, x_{34} = 0$$

The optimal cost is \$39,500. With this information, we may revise our previous model to try to find an alternative optimal solution. We know that any alternative solution must be feasible, so it must satisfy all of the constraints of the original model. Also, to be optimal, the solution must give a total cost of \$39,500. We can enforce this by taking the objective function and making it a constraint equal to \$39,500:

$$3x_{11} + 2x_{12} + 7x_{13} + 6x_{14} + 6x_{21} + 5x_{22} + 2x_{23} + 3x_{24} + 2x_{31} + 5x_{32} + 4x_{33} + 5x_{34} = 39{,}500.$$

But, what should our objective function be for the revised problem? In the solution we previously found:

$$x_{13} = x_{14} = x_{22} = x_{32} = x_{33} = x_{34} = 0.$$

If we maximize the sum of these variables and if the optimal objective function value of this revised problem is positive, we have found a different feasible solution that is also optimal. The revised model is:

$$\text{Max} \quad x_{13} + x_{14} + x_{22} + x_{32} + x_{33} + x_{34}$$

s.t.

$$
\begin{array}{lcr}
x_{11} + x_{12} + x_{13} + x_{14} & & \leq 5{,}000 \\
x_{21} + x_{22} + x_{23} + x_{24} & & \leq 6{,}000 \\
x_{31} + x_{32} + x_{33} + x_{34} & & \leq 2{,}500 \\
x_{11} \qquad\qquad + x_{21} \qquad\qquad + x_{31} & & = 6{,}000 \\
x_{12} \qquad\qquad + x_{22} \qquad\qquad + x_{32} & & = 4{,}000 \\
x_{13} \qquad\qquad + x_{23} \qquad\qquad + x_{33} & & = 2{,}000 \\
x_{14} \qquad\qquad + x_{24} \qquad\qquad + x_{34} & & = 1{,}500 \\
\end{array}
$$

$$3x_{11} + 2x_{12} + 7x_{13} + 6x_{14} + 6x_{21} + 5x_{22} + 2x_{23} + 3x_{24} + 2x_{31} + 5x_{32} + 4x_{33} + 5x_{34} = 39{,}500$$

$$x_{ij} \geq 0$$

$$\text{for } i = 1, 2, 3 \text{ and } j = 1, 2, 3, 4$$

TABLE 11.6	An Alternative Optimal Solution to the Foster Generators Transportation Problem				

Total Cost = $39,500

		Amount Shipped To:				
		Boston	Chicago	St. Louis	Lexington	Total
From:	Cleveland	3,500	1,500	0	0	5,000
	Bedford	0	2,500	2,000	1,500	6,000
	York	2,500	0	0	0	2,500
	Total	6,000	4,000	2,000	1,500	

The solution to this problem has objective function value = 2,500, indicating that the variables that were zero in the previous solution now add up to 2,500. The new solution is shown in Table 11.6.

Comparing Figure 11.14 and Table 11.6, we see that in this new solution, Bedford ships 2,500 units to Chicago instead of to Boston.

What types of issues might make management prefer one of these solutions over the other? Notice that the original solution has the Boston distribution center sourced from all three plants, whereas each of the other distribution centers is sourced by one plant. This would imply that the manager in the Boston distribution center has to deal with three different plant managers, whereas each of the other distribution center managers has only one plant manager. The Boston manager might feel disadvantaged, having to spend too much time coordinating among the plants. The alternative solution provides a more balanced solution. Managers in Boston and Chicago each deal with two plants, and those in St. Louis and Lexington, which have lower total volumes, deal with only one plant. Because the alternative solution seems to be more equitable, it might be preferred. Recall that both solutions give a total cost of $39,500.

In summary, the general approach for trying to find an alternative optimal solution to a linear program is:

Step 1: Solve the linear program
Step 2: Make a new objective function to be maximized. It is the sum of those variables that were equal to zero in the solution from Step 1
Step 3: Keep all the constraints from the original problem. Add a constraint that forces the original objective function to be equal to the optimal objective function value from Step 1
Step 4: Solve the problem created in Steps 2 and 3. If the objective function value is positive, you have found an alternative optimal solution

SUMMARY

We formulated linear programming models for the Par, Inc. maximization problem and the M&D Chemicals minimization problem. For the Par, Inc. problem, we showed how a graphical solution procedure could be used to solve a two-variable problem to help us better understand how the computer can solve large linear programs. We discussed how Excel Solver can be used to solve linear optimization problems. In formulating a linear programming model of the Par, Inc. and M&D problems, we developed a general definition of a linear program.

A linear program is a mathematical model with the following qualities:

1. A linear objective function that is to be maximized or minimized
2. A set of linear constraints
3. Variables restricted to nonnegative values

Slack variables may be used to write less-than-or-equal-to constraints in equality form, and surplus variables may be used to write greater-than-or-equal-to constraints in equality form. The value of a slack variable can usually be interpreted as the amount of unused resource, whereas the value of a surplus variable indicates the amount over and above some stated minimum requirement. Binding constraints have zero slack or surplus.

If the solution to a linear program is infeasible or unbounded, no optimal solution to the problem can be found. In the case of infeasibility, no feasible solutions are possible. In the case of an unbounded solution, the objective function can be made infinitely large for a maximization problem and infinitely small for a minimization problem. In the case of alternative optimal solutions, two or more optimal extreme points exist.

We also discussed sensitivity analysis and the interpretation of the Sensitivity Report generated by Excel Solver and how the impact of changes in the objective function coefficients and right-hand side values of constraints can be assessed. We showed how to write a mathematical model using general linear programming notation and presented three additional examples of linear programming applications: portfolio selection, transportation planning, and media selection. Finally, we concluded the chapter with a procedure for finding an alternative optimal solution when one exists.

GLOSSARY

Alternative optimal solutions The case in which more than one solution provides the optimal value for the objective function.

Binding constraint A constraint that holds as an equality at the optimal solution.

Constraints Restrictions that limit the settings of the decision variables.

Decision variable A controllable input for a linear programming model.

Extreme point Graphically speaking, the feasible solution points occurring at the vertices, or "corners," of the feasible region. With two-variable problems, extreme points are determined by the intersection of the constraint lines.

Feasible region The set of all feasible solutions.

Feasible solution A solution that satisfies all the constraints simultaneously.

Infeasibility The situation in which no solution to the linear programming problem satisfies all the constraints.

Linear function A mathematical function in which each variable appears in a separate term and is raised to the first power.

Linear programming model (linear program) A mathematical model with a linear objective function, a set of linear constraints, and nonnegative variables.

Mathematical model A representation of a problem in which the objective and all constraint conditions are described by mathematical expressions.

Nonnegativity constraints A set of constraints that requires all variables to be nonnegative.

Objective function The expression that defines the quantity to be maximized or minimized in a linear programming model.

Objective function coefficient allowable increase (decrease) The allowable increase/decrease of an objective function coefficient is the amount the coefficient may increase (decrease) without causing any change in the values of the decision variables in the optimal solution. The allowable increase/decrease for the objective function coefficients can be used to calculate the range of optimality.

Problem formulation (modeling) The process of translating a verbal statement of a problem into a mathematical statement called the *mathematical model*.

Reduced cost If a variable is at its lower bound of zero, the reduced cost is equal to the shadow price of the nonnegativity constraint for that variable. In general, if a variable is at its lower or upper bound, the reduced cost is the shadow price for that simple lower- or upper-bound constraint.

Right-hand side allowable increase (decrease) The amount the right-hand side may increase (decrease) without causing any change in the shadow price for that constraint. The allowable increase and decrease for the right-hand side can be used to calculate the range of feasibility for that constraint.

Sensitivity analysis The study of how changes in the input parameters of a linear programming problem affect the optimal solution.

Shadow price The change in the optimal objective function value per unit increase in the right-hand side of a constraint.

Slack The difference between the right-hand-side and the left-hand-side of a less-than-or-equal-to constraint.

Slack variable A variable added to the left-hand side of a less-than-or-equal-to constraint to convert the constraint into an equality. The value of this variable can usually be interpreted as the amount of unused resources.

Surplus variable A variable subtracted from the left-hand side of a greater-than-or-equal-to constraint to convert the constraint into an equality. The value of this variable can usually be interpreted as the amount over and above some required minimum level.

Unbounded The situation in which the value of the solution may be made infinitely large in a maximization linear programming problem or infinitely small in a minimization problem without violating any of the constraints.

PROBLEMS

1. Kelson Sporting Equipment, Inc., makes two types of baseball gloves: a regular model and a catcher's model. The firm has 900 hours of production time available in its cutting and sewing department, 300 hours available in its finishing department, and 100 hours available in its packaging and shipping department. The production time requirements and the profit contribution per glove are given in the following table:

| | Production Time (hours) | | | |
Model	Cutting and Sewing	Finishing	Packaging and Shipping	Profit/Glove
Regular model	1	½	⅛	$5
Catcher's model	3/2	⅓	¼	$8

Assuming that the company is interested in maximizing the total profit contribution, answer the following:

a. What is the linear programming model for this problem?

b. Develop a spreadsheet model and find the optimal solution using Excel Solver. How many of each model should Kelson manufacture?

c. What is the total profit contribution Kelson can earn with the optimal production quantities?

d. How many hours of production time will be scheduled in each department?

e. What is the slack time in each department?

2. The Sea Wharf Restaurant would like to determine the best way to allocate a monthly advertising budget of $1,000 between newspaper advertising and radio advertising. Management decided that at least 25% of the budget must be spent on each type of media and that the amount of money spent on local newspaper advertising must be at least twice the amount spent on radio advertising. A marketing consultant developed an index that measures audience exposure per dollar of advertising on a scale from 0 to 100, with higher values implying greater audience exposure. If the value of the index for local newspaper advertising is 50 and the value of the index for spot radio advertising is 80, how should the restaurant allocate its advertising budget to maximize the value of total audience exposure?
   a. Formulate a linear programming model that can be used to determine how the restaurant should allocate its advertising budget in order to maximize the value of total audience exposure.
   b. Develop a spreadsheet model and solve the problem using Excel Solver.

3. Blair & Rosen, Inc. (B&R) is a brokerage firm that specializes in investment portfolios designed to meet the specific risk tolerances of its clients. A client who contacted B&R this past week has a maximum of $50,000 to invest. B&R's investment advisor decides to recommend a portfolio consisting of two investment funds: an Internet fund and a Blue Chip fund. The Internet fund has a projected annual return of 12%, and the Blue Chip fund has a projected annual return of 9%. The investment advisor requires that at most $35,000 of the client's funds should be invested in the Internet fund. B&R services include a risk rating for each investment alternative. The Internet fund, which is the more risky of the two investment alternatives, has a risk rating of 6 per $1,000 invested. The Blue Chip fund has a risk rating of 4 per $1,000 invested. For example, if $10,000 is invested in each of the two investment funds, B&R's risk rating for the portfolio would be 6(10) + 4(10) = 100. Finally, B&R developed a questionnaire to measure each client's risk tolerance. Based on the responses, each client is classified as a conservative, moderate, or aggressive investor. Suppose that the questionnaire results classified the current client as a moderate investor. B&R recommends that a client who is a moderate investor limit his or her portfolio to a maximum risk rating of 240.
   a. Formulate a linear programming model to find the best investment strategy for this client.
   b. Build a spreadsheet model and solve the problem using Solver. What is the recommended investment portfolio for this client? What is the annual return for the portfolio?
   c. Suppose that a second client with $50,000 to invest has been classified as an aggressive investor. B&R recommends that the maximum portfolio risk rating for an aggressive investor is 320. What is the recommended investment portfolio for this aggressive investor?
   d. Suppose that a third client with $50,000 to invest has been classified as a conservative investor. B&R recommends that the maximum portfolio risk rating for a conservative investor is 160. Develop the recommended investment portfolio for the conservative investor.

4. Adirondack Savings Bank (ASB) has $1 million in new funds that must be allocated to home loans, personal loans, and automobile loans. The annual rates of return for the three types of loans are 7% for home loans, 12% for personal loans, and 9% for automobile loans. The bank's planning committee has decided that at least 40% of the new funds must be allocated to home loans. In addition, the planning committee has specified that the amount allocated to personal loans cannot exceed 60% of the amount allocated to automobile loans.

      a. Formulate a linear programming model that can be used to determine the amount of funds ASB should allocate to each type of loan to maximize the total annual return for the new funds.

      b. How much should be allocated to each type of loan? What is the total annual return? What is the annual percentage return?

      c. If the interest rate on home loans increases to 9%, would the amount allocated to each type of loan change? Explain.

      d. Suppose the total amount of new funds available is increased by $10,000. What effect would this have on the total annual return? Explain.

      e. Assume that ASB has the original $1 million in new funds available and that the planning committee has agreed to relax the requirement that at least 40% of the new funds must be allocated to home loans by 1%. How much would the annual return change? How much would the annual percentage return change?

5. Round Tree Manor is a hotel that provides two types of rooms with three rental classes: Super Saver, Deluxe, and Business. The profit per night for each type of room and rental class is as follows:

| | Rental Class | | |
Room	Super Saver	Deluxe	Business
Type I	$30	$35	—
Type II	$20	$30	$40

Type I rooms do not have high-speed wireless Internet access and are not available for the Business rental class. Round Tree's management makes a forecast of the demand by rental class for each night in the future. A linear programming model developed to maximize profit is used to determine how many reservations to accept for each rental class. The demand forecast for a particular night is 130 rentals in the Super Saver class, 60 in the Deluxe class, and 50 in the Business class. Round Tree has 100 Type I rooms and 120 Type II rooms.

      a. Formulate and solve a linear program to determine how many reservations to accept in each rental class and how the reservations should be allocated to room types.

      b. For the solution in part (a), how many reservations can be accommodated in each rental class? Is the demand for any rental class not satisfied?

      c. With a little work, an unused office area could be converted to a rental room. If the conversion cost is the same for both types of rooms, would you recommend converting the office to a Type I or a Type II room? Why?

      d. Could the linear programming model be modified to plan for the allocation of rental demand for the next night? What information would be needed and how would the model change?

6. Industrial Designs has been awarded a contract to design a label for a new wine produced by Lake View Winery. The company estimates that 150 hours will be required to complete the project. The firm's three graphic designers available for assignment to this project are Lisa, a senior designer and team leader; David, a senior designer; and Sarah, a junior designer. Because Lisa has worked on several projects for Lake View Winery, management specified that Lisa must be assigned at least 40% of the total number of hours assigned to the two senior designers. To provide label designing experience for Sarah, the junior designer must be assigned at least 15% of the total project time. However, the number of hours assigned to Sarah must not exceed 25%

of the total number of hours assigned to the two senior designers. Due to other project commitments, Lisa has a maximum of 50 hours available to work on this project. Hourly wage rates are $30 for Lisa, $25 for David, and $18 for Sarah.

   a. Formulate a linear program that can be used to determine the number of hours each graphic designer should be assigned to the project to minimize total cost.
   b. How many hours should be assigned to each graphic designer? What is the total cost?
   c. Suppose Lisa could be assigned more than 50 hours. What effect would this have on the optimal solution? Explain.
   d. If Sarah were not required to work a minimum number of hours on this project, would the optimal solution change? Explain.

7. Vollmer Manufacturing makes three components for sale to refrigeration companies. The components are processed on two machines: a shaper and a grinder. The times (in minutes) required on each machine are as follows:

	Machine	
Component	Shaper	Grinder
1	6	4
2	4	5
3	4	2

The shaper is available for 120 hours, and the grinder for 110 hours. No more than 200 units of component 3 can be sold, but up to 1,000 units of each of the other components can be sold. In fact, the company already has orders for 600 units of component 1 that must be satisfied. The profit contributions for components 1, 2, and 3 are $8, $6, and $9, respectively.

   a. Formulate and solve for the recommended production quantities.
   b. What are the objective coefficient ranges for the three components? Interpret these ranges for company management.
   c. What are the right-hand-side ranges? Interpret these ranges for company management.
   d. If more time could be made available on the grinder, how much would it be worth?
   e. If more units of component 3 can be sold by reducing the sales price by $4, should the company reduce the price?

8. Photon Technologies, Inc., a manufacturer of batteries for mobile phones, signed a contract with a large electronics manufacturer to produce three models of lithium-ion battery packs for a new line of phones. The contract calls for the following:

Battery Pack	Production Quantity
PT-100	200,000
PT-200	100,000
PT-300	150,000

Photon Technologies can manufacture the battery packs at manufacturing plants located in the Philippines and Mexico. The unit cost of the battery packs differs at the two plants because of differences in production equipment and wage rates. The unit costs for each battery pack at each manufacturing plant are as follows:

	Plant	
Product	**Philippines**	**Mexico**
PT-100	$0.95	$0.98
PT-200	$0.98	$1.06
PT-300	$1.34	$1.15

The PT-100 and PT-200 battery packs are produced using similar production equipment available at both plants. However, each plant has a limited capacity for the total number of PT-100 and PT-200 battery packs produced. The combined PT-100 and PT-200 production capacities are 175,000 units at the Philippines plant and 160,000 units at the Mexico plant. The PT-300 production capacities are 75,000 units at the Philippines plant and 100,000 units at the Mexico plant. The cost of shipping from the Philippines plant is $0.18 per unit, and the cost of shipping from the Mexico plant is $0.10 per unit.

a. Develop a linear program that Photon Technologies can use to determine how many units of each battery pack to produce at each plant to minimize the total production and shipping cost associated with the new contract.

b. Solve the linear program developed in part (a), to determine the optimal production plan.

c. Use sensitivity analysis to determine how much the production and/or shipping cost per unit would have to change to produce additional units of the PT-100 in the Philippines plant.

d. Use sensitivity analysis to determine how much the production and/or shipping cost per unit would have to change to produce additional units of the PT-200 in the Mexico plant.

9. The Westchester Chamber of Commerce periodically sponsors public service seminars and programs. Currently, promotional plans are under way for this year's program. Advertising alternatives include television, radio, and online. Audience estimates, costs, and maximum media usage limitations are as shown:

Constraint	Television	Radio	Online
Audience per advertisement	100,000	18,000	40,000
Cost per advertisement	$2,000	$300	$600
Maximum media usage	10	20	10

To ensure a balanced use of advertising media, radio advertisements must not exceed 50% of the total number of advertisements authorized. In addition, television should account for at least 10% of the total number of advertisements authorized.

a. If the promotional budget is limited to $18,200, how many commercial messages should be run on each medium to maximize total audience contact? What is the allocation of the budget among the three media, and what is the total audience reached?

b. By how much would audience contact increase if an extra $100 were allocated to the promotional budget?

10. The management of Hartman Company is trying to determine the amount of each of two products to produce over the coming planning period. The following information concerns labor availability, labor utilization, and product profitability:

Department	Product 1	Product 2	Hours Available
A	1.00	0.35	100
B	0.30	0.20	36
C	0.20	0.50	50
Profit contribution/unit	$30.00	$15.00	

a. Develop a linear programming model of the Hartman Company problem. Solve the model to determine the optimal production quantities of products 1 and 2.

b. In computing the profit contribution per unit, management does not deduct labor costs because they are considered fixed for the upcoming planning period. However, suppose that overtime can be scheduled in some of the departments. Which departments would you recommend scheduling for overtime? How much would you be willing to pay per hour of overtime in each department?

c. Suppose that 10, 6, and 8 hours of overtime may be scheduled in departments A, B, and C, respectively. The cost per hour of overtime is $18 in department A, $22.50 in department B, and $12 in department C. Formulate a linear programming model that can be used to determine the optimal production quantities if overtime is made available. What are the optimal production quantities, and what is the revised total contribution to profit? How much overtime do you recommend using in each department? What is the increase in the total contribution to profit if overtime is used?

11. The employee credit union at State University is planning the allocation of funds for the coming year. The credit union makes four types of loans to its members. In addition, the credit union invests in risk-free securities to stabilize income. The various revenue-producing investments, together with annual rates of return, are as follows:

Type of Loan/Investment	Annual Rate of Return (%)
Automobile loans	8
Furniture loans	10
Other secured loans	11
Signature loans	12
Risk-free securities	9

The credit union will have $2 million available for investment during the coming year. State laws and credit union policies impose the following restrictions on the composition of the loans and investments:

- Risk-free securities may not exceed 30% of the total funds available for investment.
- Signature loans may not exceed 10% of the funds invested in all loans (automobile, furniture, other secured, and signature loans).
- Furniture loans plus other secured loans may not exceed the automobile loans.
- Other secured loans plus signature loans may not exceed the funds invested in risk-free securities.

How should the $2 million be allocated to each of the loan/investment alternatives to maximize total annual return? What is the projected total annual return?

12. The Atlantic Seafood Company (ASC) is a buyer and distributor of seafood products that are sold to restaurants and specialty seafood outlets throughout the Northeast. ASC has a frozen storage facility in New York City that serves as the primary distribution point for all products. One of the ASC products is frozen large black tiger shrimp, which are sized at 16 to 20 pieces per pound. Each Saturday, ASC can purchase more tiger shrimp or sell the tiger shrimp at the existing New York City warehouse market price. ASC's goal is to buy tiger shrimp at a low weekly price and sell it later at a higher price. ASC currently has 20,000 pounds of tiger shrimp in storage. Space is available to store a maximum of 100,000 pounds of tiger shrimp each week. In addition, ASC developed the following estimates of tiger shrimp prices for the next four weeks:

Week	Price/lb
1	$6.00
2	$6.20
3	$6.65
4	$5.55

ASC would like to determine the optimal buying/storing/selling strategy for the next four weeks. The cost to store a pound of shrimp for one week is $0.15, and to account for unforeseen changes in supply or demand, management also indicated that 25,000 pounds of tiger shrimp must be in storage at the end of week 4. Determine the optimal buying/storing/selling strategy for ASC. What is the projected four-week profit? (*Hint:* Define variables for buying, selling, and inventory held in each week. Then use a constraint to define the relationship between these: inventory from end of previous period + bought this period − sold this period = inventory at end of this period. This type of constraint is referred to as an inventory balance constraint.)

13. The Silver Star Bicycle Company will manufacture both men's and women's models for its Easy-Pedal bicycles during the next two months. Management wants to develop a production schedule indicating how many bicycles of each model should be produced in each month. Current demand forecasts call for 150 men's and 125 women's models to be shipped during the first month and 200 men's and 150 women's models to be shipped during the second month. Additional data are as follows:

Production Model	Costs	Labor Requirements (hours) Manufacturing	Assembly	Current Inventory
Men's	$120	2.0	1.5	20
Women's	$90	1.6	1.0	30

Last month, the company used a total of 1,000 hours of labor. The company's labor relations policy will not allow the combined total hours of labor (manufacturing plus assembly) to increase or decrease by more than 100 hours from month to month. In addition, the company charges monthly inventory at the rate of 2% of the production cost based on the inventory levels at the end of the month. The company would like to have at least 25 units of each model in inventory at the end of the two months. (*Hint:* Define variables for production and inventory held in each period for each product.

Then use a constraint to define the relationship between these: inventory from end of previous period + produced this period − demand this period = inventory at end of this period.)

a. Establish a production schedule that minimizes production and inventory costs and satisfies the labor-smoothing, demand, and inventory requirements. What inventories will be maintained and what are the monthly labor requirements?

b. If the company changed the constraints so that monthly labor increases and decreases could not exceed 50 hours, what would happen to the production schedule? How much will the cost increase? What would you recommend?

14. The Clark County Sheriff's Department schedules police officers for 8-hour shifts. The beginning times for the shifts are 8:00 a.m., noon, 4:00 p.m., 8:00 p.m., midnight, and 4:00 a.m. An officer beginning a shift at one of these times works for the next 8 hours. During normal weekday operations, the number of officers needed varies depending on the time of day. The department staffing guidelines require the following minimum number of officers on duty:

Time of Day	Minimum No. of Officers on Duty
8:00 a.m.–noon	5
Noon–4:00 p.m.	6
4:00 p.m.–8:00 p.m.	10
8:00 p.m.–midnight	7
Midnight–4:00 a.m.	4
4:00 a.m.–8:00 a.m.	6

Determine the number of police officers that should be scheduled to begin the 8-hour shifts at each of the six times to minimize the total number of officers required. (*Hint:* Let x_1 = the number of officers beginning work at 8:00 a.m., x_2 = the number of officers beginning work at noon, and so on.)

15. Bay Oil produces two types of fuel (regular and super) by mixing three ingredients. The major distinguishing feature of the two products is the octane level required. Regular fuel must have a minimum octane level of 90, whereas super must have a level of at least 100. The cost per barrel, octane levels, and available amounts (in barrels) for the upcoming two-week period appear in the following table, along with the maximum demand for each end product and the revenue generated per barrel:

Ingredient	Cost/Barrel	Octane	Available (barrel)
1	$16.50	100	110,000
2	$14.00	87	350,000
3	$17.50	110	300,000

	Revenue/Barrel	Max Demand (barrel)
Regular	$18.50	350,000
Super	$20.00	500,000

Develop and solve a linear programming model to maximize contribution to profit. What is the optimal contribution to profit?

16. Consider the following network representation of a transportation problem:

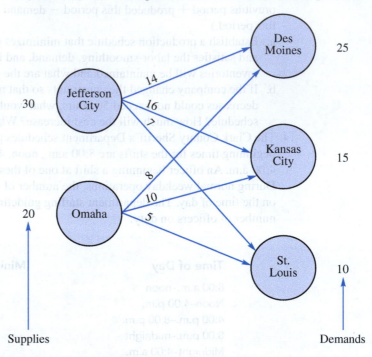

Supplies   Demands

The supplies, demands, and transportation costs per unit are shown on the network. What is the optimal (cost minimizing) distribution plan?

17. Refer to the transportation problem described in Problem 16. Use the procedure described in Section 11.7 to try to find an alternative optimal solution.

18. Aggie Power Generation supplies electrical power to residential customers for many U.S. cities. Its main power generation plants are located in Los Angeles, Tulsa, and Seattle. The following table shows Aggie Power Generation's major residential markets, the annual demand in each market (in Megawatts or MWs), and the cost to supply electricity to each market from each power generation plant (prices are in $/MW).

Distribution Costs ($/MW)			
City	Los Angeles	Tulsa	Seattle	Demand (MWs)
Seattle	$356.25	$593.75	$ 59.38	950.00
Portland	$356.25	$593.75	$178.13	831.25
San Francisco	$178.13	$475.00	$296.88	2,375.00
Boise	$356.25	$475.00	$296.88	593.75
Reno	$237.50	$475.00	$356.25	950.00
Bozeman	$415.63	$415.63	$296.88	593.75
Laramie	$356.25	$415.63	$356.25	1,187.50
Park City	$356.25	$356.25	$475.00	712.50
Flagstaff	$178.13	$475.00	$593.75	1,187.50
Durango	$356.25	$296.88	$593.75	1,543.75

a. If there are no restrictions on the amount of power that can be supplied by any of the power plants, what is the optimal solution to this problem? Which cities should be supplied by which power plants? What is the total annual power distribution cost for this solution?

b. If at most 4,000 MWs of power can be supplied by any one of the power plants, what is the optimal solution? What is the annual increase in power distribution cost that results from adding these constraints to the original formulation?

19. The Calhoun Textile Mill is in the process of deciding on a production schedule. It wishes to know how to weave the various fabrics it will produce during the coming quarter. The sales department has confirmed orders for each of the 15 fabrics produced by Calhoun. These demands are given in the following table. Also given in this table is the variable cost for each fabric. The mill operates continuously during the quarter: 13 weeks, 7 days a week, and 24 hours a day.

There are two types of looms: dobbie and regular. Dobbie looms can be used to make all fabrics and are the only looms that can weave certain fabrics, such as plaids. The rate of production for each fabric on each type of loom is also given in the table. Note that if the production rate is zero, the fabric cannot be woven on that type of loom. Also, if a fabric can be woven on each type of loom, then the production rates are equal. Calhoun has 90 regular looms and 15 dobbie looms. For this problem, assume that the time requirement to change over a loom from one fabric to another is negligible.

Management would like to know how to allocate the looms to the fabrics and which fabrics to buy on the market so as to minimize the cost of meeting demand.

Fabric	Demand (yd)	Dobbie (yd/hr)	Regular (yd/hr)	Mill Cost ($/yd)	Sub. Cost ($/yd)
1	16,500	4.653	0.00	0.6573	0.80
2	52,000	4.653	0.00	0.5550	0.70
3	45,000	4.653	0.00	0.6550	0.85
4	22,000	4.653	0.00	0.5542	0.70
5	76,500	5.194	5.194	0.6097	0.75
6	110,000	3.809	3.809	0.6153	0.75
7	122,000	4.185	4.185	0.6477	0.80
8	62,000	5.232	5.232	0.4880	0.60
9	7,500	5.232	5.232	0.5029	0.70
10	69,000	5.232	5.232	0.4351	0.60
11	70,000	3.733	3.733	0.6417	0.80
12	82,000	4.185	4.185	0.5675	0.75
13	10,000	4.439	4.439	0.4952	0.65
14	380,000	5.232	5.232	0.3128	0.45
15	62,000	4.185	4.185	0.5029	0.70

20. Refer to the Calhoun Textile Mill production problem described in Problem 19. Use the procedure described in Section 11.7 to try to find an alternative optimal solution. If you are successful, discuss the differences in the solution you found versus that found in Problem 19.

CASE PROBLEM: INVESTMENT STRATEGY

J. D. Williams, Inc. is an investment advisory firm that manages more than $120 million in funds for its numerous clients. The company uses an asset allocation model that recommends the portion of each client's portfolio to be invested in a growth stock fund, an income fund, and a money market fund. To maintain diversity in each client's portfolio, the firm places limits on the percentage of each portfolio that may be invested in each of the three funds. General guidelines indicate that the amount invested in the growth fund must be between 20 and 40% of the total portfolio value. Similar percentages for the other two funds stipulate that between 20 and 50% of the total portfolio value must be in the income fund and that at least 30% of the total portfolio value must be in the money market fund.

In addition, the company attempts to assess the risk tolerance of each client and adjust the portfolio to meet the needs of the individual investor. For example, Williams just contracted with a new client who has $800,000 to invest. Based on an evaluation of the client's risk tolerance, Williams assigned a maximum risk index of 0.05 for the client. The firm's risk indicators show the risk of the growth fund at 0.10, the income fund at 0.07, and the money market fund at 0.01. An overall portfolio risk index is computed as a weighted average of the risk rating for the three funds, where the weights are the fraction of the client's portfolio invested in each of the funds.

Additionally, Williams is currently forecasting annual yields of 18% for the growth fund, 12.5% for the income fund, and 7.5% for the money market fund. Based on the information provided, how should the new client be advised to allocate the $800,000 among the growth, income, and money market funds? Develop a linear programming model that will provide the maximum yield for the portfolio. Use your model to develop a managerial report.

Managerial Report

1. Recommend how much of the $800,000 should be invested in each of the three funds. What is the annual yield you anticipate for the investment recommendation?
2. Assume that the client's risk index could be increased to 0.055. How much would the yield increase, and how would the investment recommendation change?
3. Refer again to the original situation, in which the client's risk index was assessed to be 0.05. How would your investment recommendation change if the annual yield for the growth fund were revised downward to 16% or even to 14%?
4. Assume that the client expressed some concern about having too much money in the growth fund. How would the original recommendation change if the amount invested in the growth fund is not allowed to exceed the amount invested in the income fund?
5. The asset allocation model you developed may be useful in modifying the portfolios for all of the firm's clients whenever the anticipated yields for the three funds are periodically revised. What is your recommendation as to whether use of this model is possible?

Chapter 11 Appendix

Appendix 11.1 Solving Linear Optimization Models Using Analytic Solver Platform

In this appendix, we illustrate how to use Analytic Solver Platform (ASP) to solve linear programs in Excel. We assume that ASP has been installed.

Recall the M&D Chemicals problem. The linear optimization model we developed is:

$$A = \text{number of gallons of product A}$$
$$B = \text{number of gallons of product B}$$

$$
\begin{array}{lll}
\text{Min} & 2A + 3B & \\
\text{s.t.} & & \\
& 1A \qquad \geq 125 & \text{Demand for product A} \\
& 1A + 1B \geq 350 & \text{Total production} \\
& 2A + 1B \leq 600 & \text{Processing time} \\
& A, B \geq 0 &
\end{array}
$$

The spreadsheet model is as shown in Figure 11.17.

Open the file *M&D*. To solve the M&D Chemicals problem using ASP, follow these steps:

Step 1. Click the **Analytic Solver Platform** tab in the Ribbon

Step 2. When the **Solver Options and Model Specifications** task pane appears, click the ⊞ next to **Optimization** to expand the tree structure (If the task pane is not visible, click **Model** in the **Model** group to activate this pane.)

Step 3. When the optimization tree structure appears (Figure 11.18):
   Select **Objective**
   Select cell B16
   Click the **Add** button ➕ in the **Solver Options and Model Specifications** task pane (Figure 11.18)
   Select **$B$16 (Max)** under **Objective**
   Right click and select **Edit**
   When the **Change Objective** dialog box appears, select **Min** for **To:**
   Click **OK**

Step 4. Under **Variables,** select **Normal**
   Select cells B14:C14
   Click the **Add** button ➕ in the **Solver Options and Model Specifications** task pane

Step 5. Under **Constraints**, select **Normal**
   Select cells B19:B20
   Click the **Add** button ➕ in the **Solver Options and Model Specifications** task pane
   When the **Add Constraint** dialog box appears:
   Select **>=** from the drop-down button
   Enter *C19:C20* in the **Constraint:** area
   Click **OK**

FIGURE 11.17   Excel Spreadsheet Model for M&D Chemicals

	A	B	C	D
1	M&D Chemicals			
2	Parameters			
3		Product A	Product B	Time Available
4	Processing Time (hours)	2	1	600
5	Production Cost	2	3	
6				
7	Minimum Total Production	350		
8	Product A Minimum	125		
9				
10				
11	Model			
12				
13		Product A	Product B	
14	Gallons Produced	250	100	
15				
16	Minimize Total Cost	=SUMPRODUCT(B5:C5,B14:C14)		
17				
18		Provided	Required	
19	Product A	=B14	=B8	
20	Total Production	=B14+C14	=B7	
21				
22		Hours Used	Hours Available	Unused Hours
23	Processing Time	=SUMPRODUCT(B4:C4,B14:C14)	=D4	=C23–B23
24				

MODEL *file*

M&D

	A	B	C	D
1	M&D Chemicals			
2	Parameters			
3		Product A	Product B	Time Available
4	Processing Time (hours)	2	1	600
5	Production Cost	$2.00	$3.00	
6				
7	Minimum Total Production	350		
8	Minimize Total Cost	125		
9				
10				
11	Model			
12				
13		Product A	Product B	
14	Gallons Produced	250	100	
15				
16	Minimize Total Cost	$800.00		
17				
18		Provided	Required	
19	Product A	250	125	
20	Total Production	350	350	
21				
22		Hours Used	Hours Available	Unused Hours
23	Processing Time	600	600	0

FIGURE 11.18   The Optimization Tree Structure in the Solver Options and Model Specifications Dialog Box

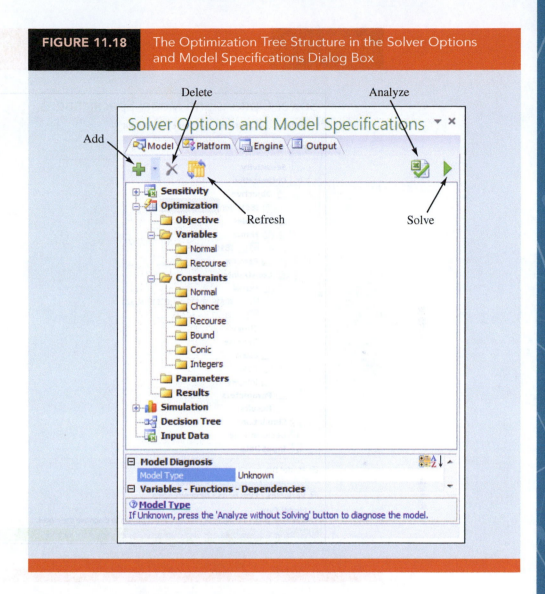

Step 6. Under **Constraints**, select **Normal**

Select cell B23

Click the **Add** button ✚ in the **Solver Options and Model Specifications** task pane

When the **Add Constraint** dialog box appears:

Select **<=** from the drop-down button

Enter *C23* in the **Constraint:** area

Click **OK**

The **Solver Options and Model Specifications** dialog box should now appear as shown in Figure 11.19

Step 7. Click the **Engine** tab in the **Solver Options and Model Specifications** task pane

Select the checkbox for **Automatically Select Engine**

In the **General** area click **Assume Non-Negative**

Select **True** from the drop-down menu

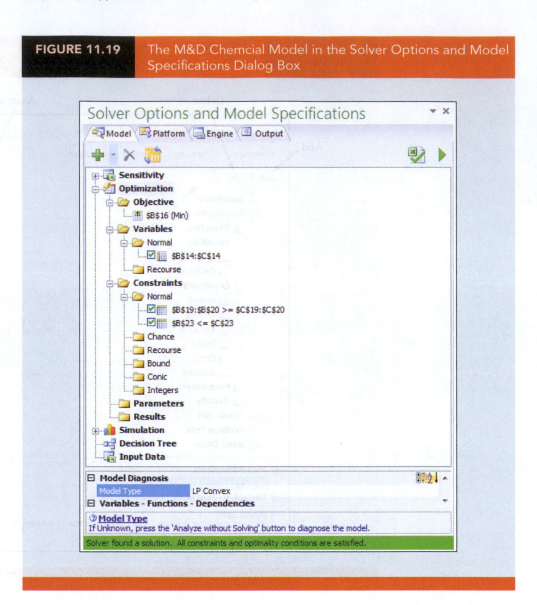

FIGURE 11.19 The M&D Chemcial Model in the Solver Options and Model Specifications Dialog Box

Upon clicking the Solve button, the Guided Mode dialog box will appear if ASP's Guided Mode is turned on. ASP's Guided Mode assists the analyst through the optimization process and can be turned off at the analyst's discretion.

Step 8. Click the **Model** tab in the **Solver Options and Model Specifications** task pane

Step 9. To solve the problem, click the **Solve** button ▶ in the **Solver Options and Model Specifications** task pane (Figure 11.18)

The solution is sent to the spreadsheet, and the output appears under the **Output** tab in the **Solver Options and Model Specifications** task pane (Figure 11.20). The output indicates that the optimal solution was found and that all constraints were satisfied. The solution should be the same as when we solved the M&D Chemicals problem using standard Excel Solver as shown in Figure 11.6. The complete linear programming model for the M&D Chemicals problem can be found in the file *M&DModel*.

MODEL *file*

M&DModel

FIGURE 11.20   The Output from the Optimization from Analytic Solver Platform

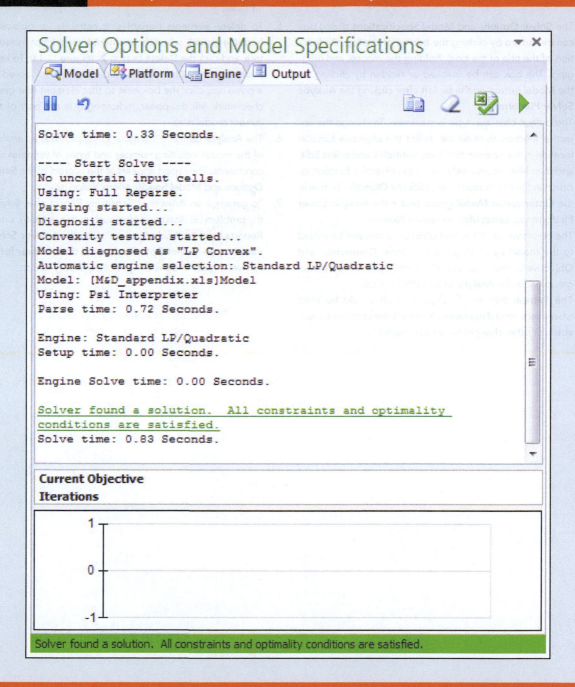

NOTES + COMMENTS

1. The **Solver Options and Model Specifications** dialog box can be moved by clicking the banner at the top (the location of the title of the box), holding the mouse, and dragging. The box can be invoked or hidden by clicking on the **Model** button on the far left after clicking the **Analytic Solver Platform** tab.

2. The default objective type is maximize. To change the objective function to minimize, select the objective function location in the optimization tree, right-click and select **Edit**, and then **Min.** Alternatively, select the objective function location in the optimization tree, click the **Objective** button in the **Optimization Model** group under the **Analytic Solver Platform** tab, select **Min**, and select **Normal**.

3. The objective, variables, and constraints can also be added to the model by clicking the **Decisions**, **Constraints**, and **Objective** buttons, respectively, in the **Optimization Model** group under the **Analytic Solver Platform** tab.

4. The **Refresh** button [icon] (Figure 11.18) should be used whenever a model has been changed (new constraints, variables, or other changes have been made).

5. To delete elements (variables, constraints, or objective) from the model, select the element from the optimization tree, and click the **Delete** button ✕ (Figure 11.18). To keep a variable or constraint in the model but have it ignored for a given run, click the box next to that element (the green checkmark will disappear, indicating it is not part of the current model run).

6. The **Analyze** button [icon] (Figure 11.18) provides an analysis of the model including number and types of variables and constraints. The report appears at the bottom of the **Solver Options and Model Specifications** dialog box.

7. To generate an Answer or Sensitivity Report after solving the problem (as discussed previously in this chapter), select **Reports** from the **Analysis** group under the **Analytic Solver Platform** tab. Select **Optimization** and then **Answer** for an Answer Report or **Sensitivity** for a Sensitivity Report.

Chapter 12

Integer Linear Optimization Models

CONTENTS

ANALYTICS IN ACTION

Petrobras*

Petrobras, the largest corporation in Brazil, operates approximately 80 offshore oil production and exploration platforms in the oil-rich Campos Basin. One of Petrobras's biggest challenges is planning its logistics, including how to efficiently and safely transport nearly 1,900 employees per day from its four mainland bases to the offshore platforms and then back to the mainland. Every day, planners must route and schedule the helicopters used for this purpose. This routing and scheduling problem is challenging because there are over a billion possible combinations of schedules and routes.

Petrobras uses mixed integer linear optimization to solve its helicopter transport scheduling and routing problem. The objective function of the optimization model is a weighted function designed to ensure safety, minimize unmet demand, and minimize the cost of the transport of its crews. Because offshore landings are the riskiest part of the transport, the safety objective is met by minimizing the number of offshore landings

required in the schedule. Numerous constraints must be met in planning these routes and schedule. These include limiting the number of departures from a platform at certain times; ensuring no time conflicts for a given helicopter and pilot; ensuring proper breaks for pilots; and limiting the number of flights per day for a given helicopter as well as routing restrictions. The decision variables include binary variables for assigning helicopters to flights and pilots to break times, as well as variables on the number of passengers per flight.

Compared to the previously used manual approach to this problem, the new approach using the integer optimization model transports the same number of passengers but with 18% fewer offshore landings, 8% less flight time, and a reduction in cost of 14%. The annual cost savings is estimated to be approximately $24 million.

---

*Based on F. Menezes et al., "Optimizing Helicopter Transport of Oil Rig Crews at Petrobras," *Interfaces* 40. no. 5 (September–October 2010): 408–416.

In this chapter we discuss a class of problems that are modeled as linear programs with the additional requirement that one or more variables must be an integer. Such problems are called **integer linear programs**.

The objective of this chapter is to provide an applications-oriented introduction to integer linear programming. First, in Section 12.1, we discuss the different types of integer linear programming models. In Section 12.2, we discuss an example, Eastborne Realty and the geometry of all-integer linear programs, and in Section 12.3, we show how to use Excel Solver to solve integer optimization problems. In Section 12.4, we discuss four applications of integer linear programming that make use of binary variables: capital budgeting, fixed cost, bank location, and market share optimization problems. In Section 12.5, we provide additional illustrations of the modeling flexibility provided by binary variables. In Section 12.6, we discuss ways to generate useful alternative solutions in integer linear optimization. The chapter appendix discusses how to use Analytic Solver Platform to solve integer linear optimization problems.

12.1 Types of Integer Linear Optimization Models

The only difference between the problems in this chapter and the problems in Chapter 11 on linear programming is that one or more variables are required to be an integer. If all variables are required to be an integer, we have an **all-integer linear program**. The following is a two-variable, all-integer linear programming model:

$$\text{Max}\quad 2x_1 + 3x_2$$
$$\text{s.t.}$$
$$3x_1 + 3x_2 \leq 12$$
$$\tfrac{2}{3}x_1 + 1x_2 \leq 4$$
$$1x_1 + 2x_2 \leq 6$$
$$x_1, x_2 \geq 0 \text{ and integer}$$

If we drop the phrase *and integer* from the last line of this model, we have the familiar two-variable linear program. The linear program that results from dropping the integer requirements is called the linear programming relaxation, or **LP Relaxation**, of the integer linear program.

If some, but not necessarily all, variables are required to be integer, we have a **mixed-integer linear program**. The following is a two-variable, mixed-integer linear program:

$$\text{Max}\quad 3x_1 + 4x_2$$
$$\text{s.t.}$$
$$-1x_1 + 2x_2 \leq 8$$
$$1x_1 + 2x_2 \leq 12$$
$$2x_1 + 1x_2 \leq 16$$
$$x_1, x_2 \geq 0 \text{ and } x_2 \text{ integer}$$

We obtain the LP Relaxation of this mixed-integer linear program by dropping the requirement that x_2 be integer.

In some applications, the integer variables may take on only the values 0 or 1. Then we have a **binary integer linear program**. As we see later in the chapter, binary variables provide additional modeling capability.

12.2 Eastborne Realty, An Example of Integer Optimization

Eastborne Realty has $2 million available for the purchase of new rental property. After an initial screening, Eastborne reduced the investment alternatives to townhouses and apartment buildings. Each townhouse can be purchased for $282,000, and five are available. Each apartment building can be purchased for $400,000, and the developer will construct as many buildings as Eastborne wants to purchase.

Eastborne's property manager can devote up to 140 hours per month to these new properties; each townhouse is expected to require 4 hours per month, and each apartment building is expected to require 40 hours per month. The annual cash flow, after deducting mortgage payments and operating expenses, is estimated to be $10,000 per townhouse and $15,000 per apartment building. Eastborne's owner would like to determine the number of townhouses and the number of apartment buildings to purchase to maximize annual cash flow.

We begin by defining the decision variables:

$$T = \text{number of townhouses}$$
$$A = \text{number of apartment buildings}$$

The objective function for cash flow (in thousands of dollars) is:

$$\text{Max } 10T + 15A.$$

Three constraints must be satisfied:

$$282T + 400A \leq 2{,}000 \quad \text{Funds available (\$1,000s)}$$
$$4T + 40A \leq 140 \quad \text{Manager's time (hours)}$$
$$T \leq 5 \quad \text{Townhouses available}$$

The variables T and A must be nonnegative. In addition, the purchase of a fractional number of townhouses and/or a fractional number of apartment buildings is unacceptable. Thus, T and A must be integer. The model for the Eastborne Realty problem is the following all-integer linear program:

$$\text{Max} \quad 10T + 15A$$
$$\text{s.t.}$$
$$282T + 400A \leq 2{,}000$$
$$4T + 40A \leq 140$$
$$T \leq 5$$
$$T, A \geq 0 \text{ and integer}$$

The model for Eastborne Realty is a linear all-integer program. Next we discuss the geometry of this model.

The Geometry of Linear All-Integer Optimization

The geometry of the feasible region for the Eastborne Reality problem is shown in Figure 12.1. The lightly shaded region is the feasible region of the LP Relaxation. The optimal linear programming solution is point b, which is $T = 2.479$ townhouses and $A = 3.252$ apartment buildings. The optimal value of the objective function is 73.574,

FIGURE 12.1   The Geometry of the Eastborne Realty Problem

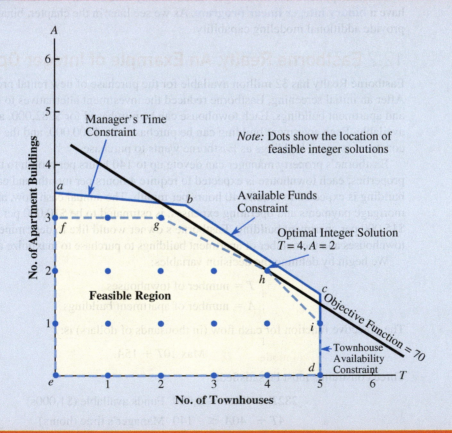

which indicates an annual cash flow of $73,574. Point *b* is formed by the intersection of the Manager's Time constraint and the Available Funds constraint. Unfortunately, because Eastborne cannot purchase fractional numbers of townhouses and apartment buildings, further analysis is necessary.

In many cases, a noninteger solution can be rounded to obtain an acceptable integer solution. For instance, a linear programming solution to a production scheduling problem might call for the production of 15,132.4 cases of breakfast cereal. The rounded integer solution of 15,132 cases would probably have minimal impact on the value of the objective function and the feasibility of the solution. Rounding would be a sensible approach. Indeed, whenever rounding has a minimal impact on the objective function and constraints, most managers find it acceptable; a near-optimal solution is satisfactory.

However, rounding may not always be a good strategy. When the decision variables take on small values that have a major impact on the value of the objective function or feasibility, an optimal integer solution is needed. Let us return to the Eastborne Realty problem and examine the impact of rounding. The optimal solution to the LP Relaxation for Eastborne Realty resulted in $T = 2.479$ townhouses and $A = 3.252$ apartment buildings. Because each townhouse costs $282,000 and each apartment building costs $400,000, rounding to an integer solution can be expected to have a substantial economic impact on the problem.

Suppose that we round the solution to the LP Relaxation to obtain the integer solution $T = 2$ and $A = 3$, with an objective function value of $10(2) + 15(3) = 65$. The annual cash flow of $65,000 is substantially less than the annual cash flow of $73,574 provided by the solution to the LP Relaxation. Do other rounding possibilities exist? Exploring other rounding alternatives shows that the integer solution $T = 3$ and $A = 3$ is infeasible because it requires $282,000(3) + $400,000(3) = $3,738,000, which is more than the $2 million that Eastborne has available. The rounded solution of $T = 2$ and $A = 4$ is also infeasible for the same reason. At this point, rounding has led to two townhouses and three apartment buildings with an annual cash flow of $65,000 as the best feasible integer solution to the problem. Unfortunately, we don't know whether this solution is the best integer solution to the problem.

Rounding to an integer solution is a trial-and-error approach. Each rounded solution must be evaluated for feasibility as well as for its impact on the value of the objective function. Even when a rounded solution is feasible, we have no guarantee that we have found the optimal integer solution. We will see shortly that the rounded solution ($T = 2$ and $A = 3$) is not optimal for Eastborne Realty.

What is the true feasible region for the Eastborne Realty problem? As shown in Figure 12.1, the feasible region is the set of integer points that lie within the feasible region of the LP Relaxation. There are 20 such feasible solutions (designated by blue dots in the figure). The region bounded by the dashed lines is known as the **convex hull** of the set of feasible integer solutions. The convex hull of a set of points is the smallest intersection of linear inequalities that contain the set of points. Notice that the convex hull in Figure 12.1 has integer extreme points (points *d, e, f, g, h,* and *i*). If we knew the convex hull, we could use linear programming to find the optimal integer corner point. Unfortunately, identifying the convex hull can be very time consuming. This is somewhat counterintuitive because there are only 20 feasible solutions, but solving an integer optimization problem such as that for Eastborne Realty may require solving numerous linear programs to find the optimal integer solution. Therefore, an integer optimization problem can be much more time consuming to solve than solving a linear program of comparable size.

It is true that the optimal solution to the integer program will be an extreme point of the convex hull, so one or more of the extreme points *d, e, f, g, h,* and *i* are optimal. The objective function contour shown in Figure 12.1 with an objective function value equal to

70 shows that point h is the optimal solution. As a check, let us evaluate each of the corner points of the convex hull in Figure 12.1:

Point	$T =$	$A =$	Annual Cash Flow ($000) =
d	5	0	$10(5) + 15(0) = 50$
e	0	0	$10(0) + 15(0) = \ \ 0$
f	0	3	$10(0) + 15(3) = 45$
g	2	3	$10(2) + 15(3) = 65$
h	4	2	$10(4) + 15(2) = 70$
i	5	1	$10(5) + 15(1) = 65$

This confirms that the optimal integer solution occurs at point h, where $T = 4$ townhouses and $A = 2$ apartment buildings. The objective function value is an annual cash flow of \$70,000. This solution is substantially better than the best solution found by rounding: $T = 2$, $A = 3$ with an annual cash flow of \$65,000. Thus, we see that rounding would not have been the best strategy for Eastborne Realty.

NOTES + COMMENTS

1. An important observation can be made from the analysis of the Eastborne Realty problem. It has to do with the relationship between the value of the optimal integer solution and the value of the optimal solution to the LP Relaxation. For integer linear programs involving maximization, the value of the optimal solution to the LP Relaxation provides an upper bound on the value of the optimal integer solution. This observation is valid for the Eastborne Realty problem. The value of the optimal integer solution is \$70,000, and the value of the optimal solution to the LP Relaxation is \$73,574. Thus, we know from the LP Relaxation solution that the upper bound for the value of the objective function is \$73,574. For integer linear programs involving minimization, the value of the optimal solution to the LP Relaxation provides a lower bound on the value of the optimal integer solution.

2. The two popular approaches to solving integer linear optimization problems are branch-and-bound and cutting planes. Both solve a series of LP relaxations to arrive at an optimal integer solution. The *branch-and-bound approach* breaks the feasible region of the LP Relaxation into subregions until the subregions have integer solutions or it is determined that the solution cannot be in the subregion. *Cutting plane* approaches try to identify the convex hull by adding a series of new constraints that do not exclude any feasible integer points. Indeed, most software for integer optimization, including Excel Solver, employs a combination of these two approaches.

12.3 Solving Integer Optimization Problems with Excel Solver

The worksheet formulation and solution for integer linear programs is similar to that for linear programming problems. Actually the worksheet formulation is exactly the same, but some additional information must be provided when setting up the Solver Parameters and Options dialog boxes. Constraints must be added in the Solver Parameters dialog box to identify the integer variables. In addition, the value for Tolerance in the Integer Options dialog box may need to be adjusted to obtain a solution.

Let us demonstrate the Excel solution of an integer linear program by showing how Excel Solver can be used to solve the Eastborne Realty problem. The worksheet with the optimal solution is shown in Figure 12.2. We will describe the key elements of the worksheet and how to obtain the solution, and then we will interpret the solution.

The parameters and descriptive labels appear in cells A1:G7 of the worksheet in Figure 12.2. The cells in the lower portion of the worksheet contain the information required by the Excel Solver (decision variables, objective function, constraint left-hand sides, and constraint right-hand sides).

MODEL *file*

Eastborne

FIGURE 12.2 Eastborne Realty Spreadsheet Model

	A	B	C	D	E	F	G
1	Eastborne Realty Problem						
2	Parameters						
3		Townhouse	Apt. Bldg.				
4	Price (000)	282	400			Funds Avl. ($000)	2000
5	Mgr. Time	4	40			Mgr. Time Avl. (Hours)	140
6						Townhouses Avl.	5
7	Ann. Cash Flow ($000)	10	15				
8							
9							
10							
11	Model						
12		Number of					
13		Townhouses	Apt. Bldgs.				
14	Purchase Plan	4	2			Total Used	Total Available
15					Funds ($000)	=SUMPRODUCT(B4:C4,$B$14:$C$14)	=G4
16					Funds (Hours)	=SUMPRODUCT(B5:C5,$B$14:$C$14)	=G5
17	Max Cash Flow ($000)	=SUMPRODUCT(B7:C7,B14:C14)			Townhouses	=B14	=G6
18							

	A	B	C	D	E	F	G	H
1	Eastborne Realty Problem							
2	Parameters							
3		Townhouse	Apt. Bldg.					
4	Price (000)	$282	$400			Funds Avl. ($000)	$2,000	
5	Mgr. Time	4	40			Mgr. Time Avl. (Hours)	140	
6						Townhouses Avl.	5	
7	Ann. Cash Flow ($000)	$10	$15					
8								
9								
10								
11	Model							
12		Number of						
13		Townhouses	Apt. Bldgs.					
14	Purchase Plan	4	2			Total Used	Total Available	
15					Funds ($000)	$1,928	$2,000	
16					Time (Hours)	96	140	
17	Max Cash Flow ($000)	$70			Townhouses	4	5	
18								

Decision variables	Cells B14:C14 are reserved for the decision variables.
Objective function	The formula =SUMPRODUCT(B7:C7,B14:C14) has been placed into cell B17 to reflect the annual cash flow associated with the solution.
Left-hand sides	The left-hand sides for the three constraints are placed into cells F15:F17.
	Cell F15 =SUMPRODUCT(B4:C4, $B$14:$C$14) (Copy to cell F16)
	Cell F17 =B14
Right-hand sides	The right-hand sides for the three constraints are placed into cells G15:G17.
	Cell G15 =G4 (Copy to cells G16:G17)

To solve the Eastborne Realty problem, we follow these steps:

Step 1. Click the **Data** tab in the Ribbon
Step 2. In the **Analyze** group, click **Solver**
Step 3. When the **Solver Parameters** dialog box appears (Figure 12.3):
  Enter *B17* in the **Set Objective:** box
    Select **Max** for the **To:** option
    Enter *B14:C14* in the **By Changing Variable Cells:** box

---

FIGURE 12.3   Solver Parameters Dialog Box for Eastborne Realty

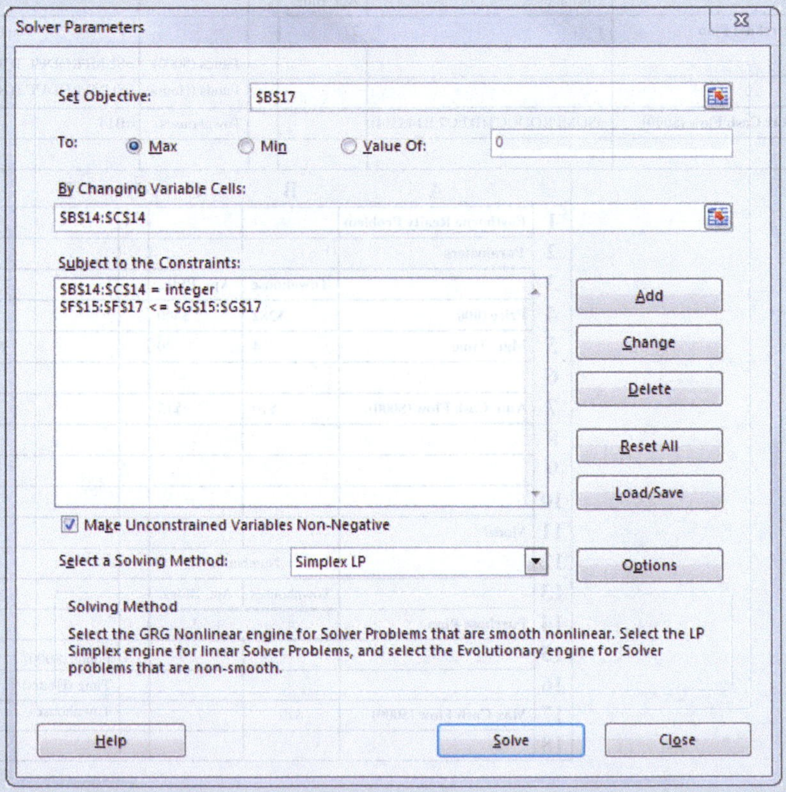

Step 4. Click the **Add** button

When the **Add Constraint** dialog box appears:

Enter *B14:C14* in the **Cell Reference:** box

Select **int** from the drop-down menu

Binary variables are identified with the bin designation in the Solver Parameters dialog box.

When **int** is selected, the term "integer" automatically appears in the **Constraint:** box. This constraint tells Solver that the decision variables in cells B14 and C14 must be integers.

Step 5. Click the **Add** button

When the **Add Constraint** dialog box appears:

Enter *F15:F17* in the **Cell Reference:** box

Select ≤ from the drop-down menu

Enter *G15:G17* in the **Constraint:** area

Click **OK**

Step 6. Select the **Make Unconstrained Variables Non-Negative** option

Select **Simplex LP** from the **Select a Solving Method:** drop-down menu

Step 7. Click the **Options** button

Select the **All Methods** tab, and set the **Integer Optimality (%):** to *0*, as shown in Figure 12.4. This ensures that we find the optimal integer solution.

Click **OK** to close the **Options** dialog box

FIGURE 12.4   Solver Options Dialog Box

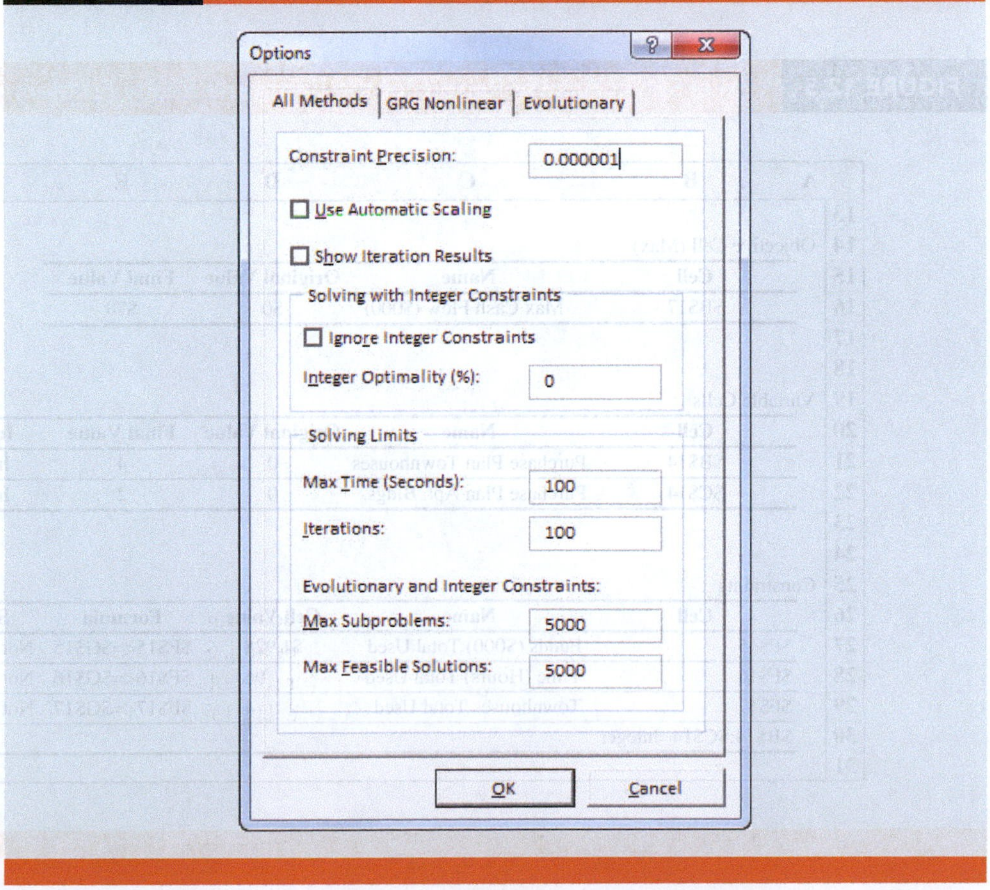

Step 8. When the **Solver Parameters** dialog box reappears, click **Solve**

Step 9. When the **Solver Results** dialog box appears, select **Answer** in the **Reports** area and click **OK**

MODEL *file*

EastborneModel

The completed linear integer optimization model for the Eastborne Realty problem is contained in the file *EastborneModel*.

Figure 12.5 shows the Eastborne Realty Answer Report. The structure of the Answer Report from Excel Solver for integer programs is the same as that described in Chapter 11 for linear programs. The first section gives information regarding the objective function. It shows that the objective function is located in cell B17 and that the optimal (Final Value) of the objective function is $70,000. The Variable Cells section gives the location, name, and original and optimal values (Final Value) of the decision variables, as well as an indication that the decision variables have been designated as integers. For the Eastborne problem, in Figure 12.5, we see that the optimal solution is to purchase four townhouses and two apartment buildings. Finally, the Constraints section gives us detail on the status of each constraint at optimality. We see that none of the three constraints is binding, and from the slack column, we see that we have $72,000 unused from budget and 44 unused hours and that we are under the limit of 5 townhouses by 1.

As this example illustrates, and as we have seen in Figure 12.1, unlike in a linear program, the solution to an integer program can be such that none of the constraints is binding at the optimal point.

A Cautionary Note About Sensitivity Analysis

The classical sensitivity analysis discussed in Chapter 11 for linear programs is not available for integer programs. Because of the discrete nature of integer optimization, it is

---

FIGURE 12.5 Excel Solver Answer Report for the Eastborne Realty Problem

	A	B	C	D	E	F	G
13							
14		Objective Cell (Max)					
15		**Cell**	**Name**	**Original Value**	**Final Value**		
16		$B$17	Max Cash Flow ($000)	$0	$70		
17							
18							
19		Variable Cells					
20		**Cell**	**Name**	**Original Value**	**Final Value**	**Integer**	
21		$B$14	Purchase Plan Townhouses	0	4	Integer	
22		$C$14	Purchase Plan Apt. Bldgs.	0	2	Integer	
23							
24							
25		Constraints					
26		**Cell**	**Name**	**Cell Value**	**Formula**	**Status**	**Slack**
27	$F$15		Funds ($000) Total Used	$1,928	$F$15<=$G$15	Not Binding	72
28	$F$16		Time (Hours) Total Used	96	$F$16<=$G$16	Not Binding	44
29	$F$17		Townhouses Total Used	4	$F$17<=$G$17	Not Binding	1
30	$B$14:$C$14=Integer						
31							

not possible to easily calculate objective function coefficient ranges, shadow prices, and right-hand-side ranges. However, this does not mean that the sensitivity analysis is not important for integer programs. Sensitivity analysis often is more crucial for integer linear programming problems than for linear programming problems. A small change in one of the coefficients in the constraints can cause a relatively large change in the value of the optimal solution. To understand why, consider the following integer programming model of a simple capital budgeting problem involving four projects and a budgetary constraint for a single time period:

$$\text{Max} \quad 40x_1 + 60x_2 + 70x_3 + 160x_4$$
$$\text{s.t.}$$
$$16x_1 + 35x_2 + 45x_3 + 85x_4 \leq 100$$
$$x_1, x_2, x_3, x_4 = 0, 1$$

Sensitivity reports are not available for integer optimization problems. To determine the sensitivity of the solution to changes in model inputs, you must change the data and re-solve the problem.

The optimal solution to this problem is $x_1 = 1$, $x_2 = 1$, $x_3 = 1$, and $x_4 = 0$, with an objective function value of $170. However, note that if the available budget is increased by $1 (from $100 to $101), the optimal solution changes to $x_1 = 1$, $x_2 = 0$, $x_3 = 0$, and $x_4 = 1$, with an objective function value of $200. In other words, one additional dollar in the budget would lead to a $30 increase in the return. Surely management, when faced with such a situation, would increase the budget by $1. Because of the extreme sensitivity of the value of the optimal solution to the constraint coefficients, practitioners usually recommend re-solving the integer linear program several times with variations in the coefficients before attempting to choose the best solution for implementation.

N O T E S   +   C O M M E N T S

The time required to obtain an optimal solution can be highly variable for integer linear programs. If an optimal solution cannot be found within a reasonable amount of time, the **Integer Optimality (%)** can be reset to 5% or some higher value so that the search procedure may stop when a near-optimal solution (within the tolerance of being optimal) has been found. This can shorten the solution time because, if the **Integer Optimality (%)** is set to 5%, Solver can stop when it knows it is within 5% of optimal rather than having to complete the search. In general, unless you are experiencing excessive run times, we recommend you set the **Integer Optimality (%)** to 0.

12.4 Applications Involving Binary Variables

Much of the modeling flexibility provided by integer linear programming is due to the use of binary variables. In many applications, binary variables provide selections or choices with the value of the variable equal to one if a corresponding activity is undertaken and equal to zero if the corresponding activity is not undertaken. The capital budgeting, fixed cost, bank location, and product design and market share optimization applications presented in this section make use of binary variables.

Capital Budgeting

The estimated net present value is the net cash flow discounted back to the beginning of year 1.

The Ice-Cold Refrigerator Company is considering investing in several projects that have varying capital requirements over the next four years. Faced with limited capital each year, management would like to select the most profitable projects that it can afford. The estimated net present value for each project, the capital requirements, and the available capital over the four-year period are shown in Table 12.1.

TABLE 12.1 Project Net Present Value, Capital Requirements, and Available Capital for the Ice-Cold Refrigerator Company

	Project				
	Plant Expansion ($)	Warehouse Expansion ($)	New Machinery ($)	New Product Research ($)	Total Capital Available ($)
Present Value	90,000	40,000	10,000	37,000	
Year 1 Cap Rqmt	15,000	10,000	10,000	15,000	40,000
Year 2 Cap Rqmt	20,000	15,000		10,000	50,000
Year 3 Cap Rqmt	20,000	20,000		10,000	40,000
Year 4 Cap Rqmt	15,000	5,000	4,000	10,000	35,000

Let us define four binary decision variables:

$P = 1$ if the plant expansion project is accepted; 0 if rejected
$W = 1$ if the warehouse expansion project is accepted; 0 if rejected
$M = 1$ if the new machinery project is accepted; 0 if rejected
$R = 1$ if the new product research project is accepted; 0 if rejected

In a **capital budgeting problem**, the company's objective function is to maximize the net present value of the capital budgeting projects. This problem has four constraints: one for the funds available in each of the next four years.

A binary integer linear programming model with dollars in thousands is:

$$\text{Max} \quad 90P + 40W + 10M + 37R$$

s.t.

$$
\begin{aligned}
15P + 10W + 10M + 15R &\le 40 \quad \text{(Year 1 capital available)} \\
20P + 15W \phantom{{}+ 10M} + 10R &\le 50 \quad \text{(Year 2 capital available)} \\
20P + 20W \phantom{{}+ 10M} + 10R &\le 40 \quad \text{(Year 3 capital available)} \\
15P + 5W + 4M + 10R &\le 35 \quad \text{(Year 4 capital available)} \\
P, W, M, R &= 0, 1
\end{aligned}
$$

The Ice-Cold spreadsheet model and Solver dialog box are shown in Figure 12.6. The SUMPRODUCT function is used to calculate the amount of capital used in each year as well as the net present value.

The Excel Solver Answer Report is shown in Figure 12.7. The optimal solution is $P = 1$, $W = 1$, $M = 1$, $R = 0$, with a total estimated net present value of $140,000. Thus, the company should fund the plant expansion, warehouse expansion, and new machinery projects. The new product research project should be put on hold unless additional capital funds become available. The values of the slack variables (Figure 12.7) show that the company will have $5,000 remaining in year 1, $15,000 remaining in year 2, and $11,000 remaining in year 4. Checking the capital requirements for the new product research project, we see that enough funds are available for this project in years 2 and 4. However, the company would have to find additional capital funds of $10,000 in year 1 and $10,000 in year 3 to fund the new product research project.

Fixed Cost

In many applications, the cost of production has two components: a fixed setup cost and a variable cost directly related to the production quantity. The use of binary variables makes including the setup cost possible in a model for a production application.

FIGURE 12.6   Ice-Cold Spreadsheet Model and Solver Dialog Box

	A	B	C	D	E	F	G
1	**Ice-Cold Refrigerator**						
2	**Parameters**						
3				Financial Data ($1000s)			
4			Plant	Warehouse	New	New Prod.	
5			Expansion	Expansion	Machinery	Research	Capital
6		Net Present Value	$90	$40	$10	$37	Available
7		Year 1 Capital	$15	$10	$10	$15	$40
8		Year 2 Capital	$20	$15		$10	$50
9		Year 3 Capital	$20	$20		$10	$40
10		Year 4 Capital	$15	$5	$4	$10	$35
11							
12							
13							
14	**Model**						
15							
16		Net Present Value ($1000s)		$140.00			
17							
18			Plant	Warehouse	New	New Prod.	
19			Expansion	Expansion	Machinery	Research	
20		Investment Plan	1	1	1	0	
21							
22		Amount ($1000s)					
23		Spent	Available				
24	Year 1	$35	$40				
25	Year 2	$35	$50				
26	Year 3	$40	$40				
27	Year 4	$24	$35				

MODEL *file*

IceCold

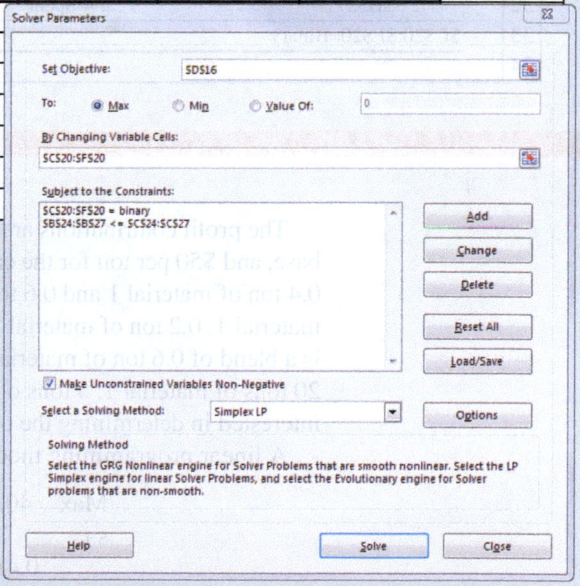

Solver Parameters

Se_t_ Objective: $D$16

To: ● Ma_x_   ○ Mi_n_   ○ _V_alue Of: 0

_B_y Changing Variable Cells:

$C$20:$F$20

S_u_bject to the Constraints:

$C$20:$F$20 = binary
$B$24:$B$27 <= $C$24:$C$27

Add
Change
_D_elete
_R_eset All
Load/Save

☑ Ma_k_e Unconstrained Variables Non-Negative

S_e_lect a Solving Method: Simplex LP   ▾   O_p_tions

Solving Method

Select the GRG Nonlinear engine for Solver Problems that are smooth nonlinear. Select the LP Simplex engine for linear Solver Problems, and select the Evolutionary engine for Solver problems that are non-smooth.

_H_elp   _S_olve   Cl_o_se

As an example of a **fixed-cost problem**, consider the production problem faced by RMC Inc. Three raw materials are used to produce three products: a fuel additive, a solvent base, and a carpet cleaning fluid. The following decision variables are used:

F = tons of fuel additive produced
S = tons of solvent base produced
C = tons of carpet cleaning fluid produced

FIGURE 12.7   Answer Report for Ice-Cold Refrigerator

	A	B	C	D	E	F	G
13							
14		Objective Cell (Max)					
15		Cell	Name	Original Value	Final Value		
16		$D$16	Net Present Value ($1000s) Expansion	$0.00	$140.00		
17							
18							
19		Variable Cells					
20		Cell	Name	Original Value	Final Value	Integer	
21		$C$20	Investment Plan Plant Expansion	0	1	Binary	
22		$D$20	Investment Plan WH Expansion	0	1	Binary	
23		$E$20	Investment Plan Machinery	0	1	Binary	
24		$F$20	Investment Plan Research	0	0	Binary	
25							
26							
27		Constraints					
28		Cell	Name	Cell Value	Formula	Status	Slack
29		$B$24	Year 1 Spent	$35	$B$24<=$C$24	Not Binding	5
30		$B$25	Year 2 Spent	$35	$B$25<=$C$25	Not Binding	15
31		$B$26	Year 3 Spent	$40	$B$26<=$C$26	Binding	0
32		$B$27	Year 4 Spent	$24	$B$27<=$C$27	Not Binding	11
33		$C$20:$F$20=Binary					
34							

The profit contributions are $40 per ton for the fuel additive, $30 per ton for the solvent base, and $50 per ton for the carpet cleaning fluid. Each ton of fuel additive is a blend of 0.4 ton of material 1 and 0.6 ton of material 3. Each ton of solvent base requires 0.5 ton of material 1, 0.2 ton of material 2, and 0.3 ton of material 3. Each ton of carpet cleaning fluid is a blend of 0.6 ton of material 1, 0.1 ton of material 2, and 0.3 ton of material 3. RMC has 20 tons of material 1, 5 tons of material 2, and 21 tons of material 3, and management is interested in determining the optimal production quantities for the upcoming planning period.

A linear programming model of the RMC problem is:

$$\text{Max} \quad 40F + 30S + 50C$$

s.t.

$$0.4F + 0.5S + 0.6C \leq 20 \quad \text{Material 1}$$
$$0.2S + 0.1C \leq 5 \quad \text{Material 2}$$
$$0.6F + 0.3S + 0.3C \leq 21 \quad \text{Material 3}$$
$$F, S, C \geq 0$$

Using Excel Solver, we obtain an optimal solution consisting of 27.5 tons of fuel additive, 0 tons of solvent base, and 15 tons of carpet cleaning fluid, with a value of $1,850.

This linear programming formulation of the RMC problem does not include a fixed cost for production setup of the products. Suppose that the following data are available concerning the setup cost and the maximum production quantity for each of the three products:

Product	Setup Cost ($)	Maximum Production (tons)
Fuel additive	200	50
Solvent base	50	25
Carpet cleaning fluid	400	40

The modeling flexibility provided by binary variables can now be used to incorporate the fixed setup costs into the production model. The binary variables are defined as follows:

$SF = 1$ if the fuel additive is produced; 0 if not
$SS = 1$ if the solvent base is produced; 0 if not
$SC = 1$ if the carpet cleaning fluid is produced; 0 if not

Using these setup variables, the total setup cost is:

$$200SF + 50SS + 400SC.$$

We can now rewrite the objective function to include the setup cost. Thus, the net profit objective function becomes:

$$\text{Max } 40F + 30S + 50C - 200SF - 50SS - 400SC.$$

Next, we must write production capacity constraints so that, if a setup variable equals 0, production of the corresponding product is not permitted, and if a setup variable equals 1, production is permitted up to the maximum quantity. For the fuel additive, we do so by adding the following constraint:

$$F \leq 50SF.$$

Note that, with this constraint present, production of the fuel additive is not permitted when $SF = 0$. When $SF = 1$, production of up to 50 tons of fuel additive is permitted. We can think of the setup variable as a switch. When it is off ($SF = 0$), production is not permitted; when it is on ($SF = 1$), production is permitted.

Similar production capacity constraints, using binary variables, are added for the solvent base and carpet cleaning products:

$$S \leq 25SS$$
$$C \leq 40SC$$

In summary, we have the following fixed-cost model for the RMC problem with setups:

$$\text{Max } 40F + 30S + 50C - 200SF - 50SS - 400SC$$

s.t.

$0.4F + 0.5S + 0.6C$	≤ 20	Material 1
$0.2S + 0.1C$	≤ 5	Material 2
$0.6F + 0.3S + 0.3C$	≤ 21	Material 3
F	$\leq 50SF$	Maximum Fuel Additive
S	$\leq 25SS$	Maximum Solvent Base
C	$\leq 40SC$	Maximum Carpet Cleaning

$$F, S, C \geq 0; SF, SS, SC = 0 \text{ or } 1$$

A spreadsheet model and Solver dialog box for the RMC problem are shown in Figure 12.8. The SUMPRODUCT function is used to calculate the material used, and cells D31, D32, and D33 contain the capacity multiplied by the appropriate binary variable (=B11*B22 in cell D31, =C11*C22 in cell D32 and =D11*D22 in cell D33).

FIGURE 12.8   RMC with Setups Spreadsheet Model and Solver Dialog Box

	A	B	C	D	E
1	RMC				
2	Parameters				
3			Material Requirements (tons)		
4		Fuel	Solvent	Cleaning	Tons
5	Materials	Additive	Base	Fluid	Available
6	Material 1	0.4	0.5	0.6	20
7	Material 2		0.2	0.1	5
8	Material 3	0.6	0.3	0.3	21
9	Profit per Ton	$40	$30	$50	
10	Setup Cost	$200	$50	$400	
11	Capacity (Tons)	50	25	40	
12					
13					
14	Model				
15					
16					
17		Max Net Profit	$1,350.00		
18					
19					
20		Fuel	Solvent	Cleaning	
21	Tons Produced	25.0	20.0	0.0	
22	Setup	1	1	0	
23					
24					
25			Used	Available	
26		Material 1	20	20	
27		Material 2	4	5	
28		Material 3	21	21	
29					
30			Tons Produced	Max Tons	
31		Max F	25	50	
32		Max S	20	25	
33		Max C	0.0	0	

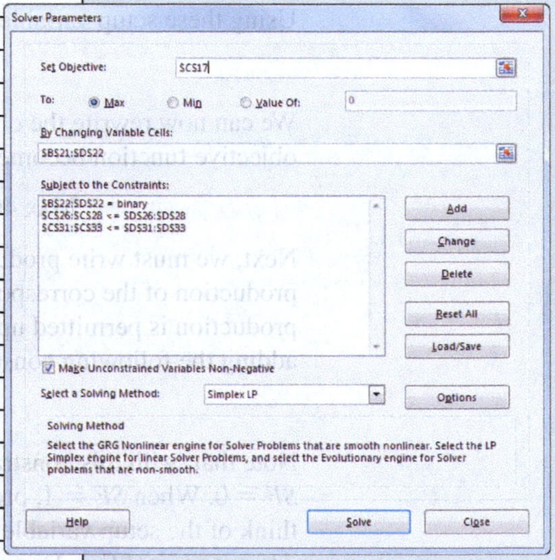

Solver Parameters

Se_t Objective: $C$17

To: ● Ma_x   ○ Mi_n   ○ _Value Of: 0

_By Changing Variable Cells:
$B$21:$D$22

Subject to the Constraints:
$B$22:$D$22 = binary
$C$26:$C$28 <= $D$26:$D$28
$C$31:$C$33 <= $D$31:$D$33

[Add]
[Change]
[Delete]
[Reset All]
[Load/Save]

☑ Make Unconstrained Variables Non-Negative

S_elect a Solving Method: Simplex LP   [▼]   [Options]

Solving Method
Select the GRG Nonlinear engine for Solver Problems that are smooth nonlinear. Select the LP Simplex engine for linear Solver Problems, and select the Evolutionary engine for Solver problems that are non-smooth.

[Help]   [Solve]   [Close]

The Excel Answer Report is shown in Figure 12.9. The optimal solution requires 25 tons of fuel additive and 20 tons of solvent base. The value of the objective function after deducting the setup cost is $1,350. The setup cost for the fuel additive and the solvent base is $200 + $50 = $250. The optimal solution includes $SC = 0$, which indicates that the more expensive $400 setup cost for the carpet cleaning fluid should be avoided. Thus, the carpet cleaning fluid is not produced.

The key to developing a fixed-cost model is the introduction of a binary variable for each fixed cost and the specification of an upper bound for the corresponding production variable. For a production quantity x, a constraint of the form $x \leq My$ can then be used to allow production when the setup variable $y = 1$ and not to allow production when the setup

FIGURE 12.9	Answer Report for RMC Production Problem

	A	B	C	D	E	F	G
13							
14		Objective Cell (Max)					
15		**Cell**	**Name**	**Original Value**	**Final Value**		
16		$C$17	Max Net Profit	$0.00	$1,350.00		
17							
18							
19		Variable Cells					
20		**Cell**	**Name**	**Original Value**	**Final Value**	**Integer**	
21		$B$21	Tons Produced Fuel	0.0	25.0	Contin	
22		$C$21	Tons Produced Solvent	0.0	20.0	Contin	
23		$D$21	Tons Produced Cleaning	0.0	0.0	Contin	
24		$B$22	Setup Fuel	0	1	Binary	
25		$C$22	Setup Solvent	0	1	Binary	
26		$D$22	Setup Cleaning	0	0	Binary	
27							
28							
29		Constraints					
30		**Cell**	**Name**	**Cell Value**	**Formula**	**Status**	**Slack**
31		$C$26	Material 1 Used	20	$C$26<=$D$26	Binding	0
32		$C$27	Material 2 Used	4	$C$27<=$D$27	Not Binding	1
33		$C$28	Material 3 Used	21	$C$28<=$D$28	Binding	0
34		$C$31	Max F Tons Produced	25	$C$31<=$D$31	Not Binding	25
35		$C$32	Max S Tons Produced	20	$C$32<=$D$32	Not Binding	5
36		$C$33	Max C Tons Produced	0.0	$C$33<=$D$33	Binding	0
37		$B$22:$D$22=Binary					
38							

MODEL *file*
RMCSetup

variable $y = 0$. The value of the maximum production quantity M should be large enough to allow for all reasonable levels of production, but choosing excessively large values of M will slow the solution procedure.

Bank Location

The long-range planning department for the Ohio Trust Company is considering expanding its operation into a 20-county region in northeastern Ohio (Figure 12.10). Currently, Ohio Trust does not have a principal place of business in any of the 20 counties. According to the banking laws in Ohio, if a bank establishes a principal place of business (PPB) in any county, branch banks can be established in that county and in any of the adjacent counties. However, to establish a new principal place of business, Ohio Trust must either obtain approval for a new bank from the state's superintendent of banks or purchase an existing bank.

Table 12.2 lists the 20 counties in the region and adjacent counties. For example, Ashtabula County is adjacent to Lake, Geauga, and Trumbull counties; Lake County is adjacent to Ashtabula, Cuyahoga, and Geauga counties; and so on.

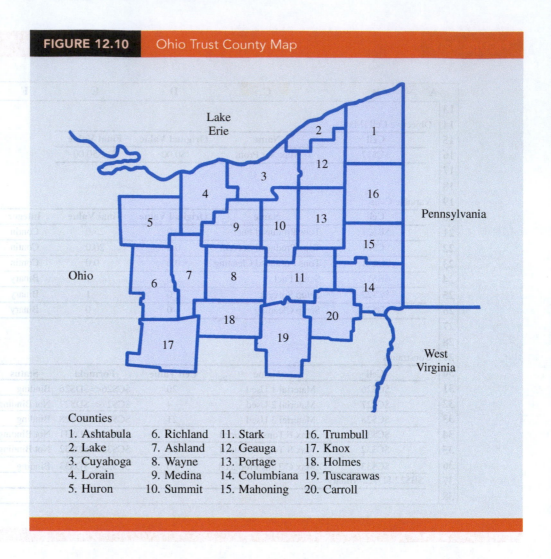

FIGURE 12.10 Ohio Trust County Map

Counties

1. Ashtabula	6. Richland	11. Stark	16. Trumbull
2. Lake	7. Ashland	12. Geauga	17. Knox
3. Cuyahoga	8. Wayne	13. Portage	18. Holmes
4. Lorain	9. Medina	14. Columbiana	19. Tuscarawas
5. Huron	10. Summit	15. Mahoning	20. Carroll

As an initial step in its planning, Ohio Trust would like to determine the minimum number of PPBs necessary to do business throughout the 20-county region. A binary integer programming model can be used to solve this location problem for Ohio Trust. We define the variables as:

x_i = 1 if a PBB is established in county i; 0 otherwise.

To minimize the number of PPBs needed, we write the objective function as:

$$\text{Min } x_1 + x_2 + \cdots + x_{20}.$$

The bank may locate branches in a county if the county contains a PPB or is adjacent to another county with a PPB. Thus, the binary linear program will need one constraint for each county. For example, the constraint for Ashtabula County is:

$$x_1 + x_2 + x_{12} + x_{16} \geq 1 \text{ Ashtabula}$$

Note that satisfaction of this constraint ensures that a PPB will be placed in Ashtabula County *or* in one or more of the adjacent counties. This constraint thus guarantees that Ohio Trust will be able to place branch banks in Ashtabula County.

TABLE 12.2	Counties in the Ohio Trust Expansion Region
Counties Under Consideration	**Adjacent Counties (by Number)**
1. Ashtabula	2, 12, 16
2. Lake	1, 3, 12
3. Cuyahoga	2, 4, 9, 10, 12, 13
4. Lorain	3, 5, 7, 9
5. Huron	4, 6, 7
6. Richland	5, 7, 17
7. Ashland	4, 5, 6, 8, 9, 17, 18
8. Wayne	7, 9, 10, 11, 18
9. Medina	3, 4, 7, 8, 10
10. Summit	3, 8, 9, 11, 12, 13
11. Stark	8, 10, 13, 14, 15, 18, 19, 20
12. Geauga	1, 2, 3, 10, 13, 16
13. Portage	3, 10, 11, 12, 15, 16
14. Columbiana	11, 15, 20
15. Mahoning	11, 13, 14, 16
16. Trumbull	1, 12, 13, 15
17. Knox	6, 7, 18
18. Holmes	7, 8, 11, 17, 19
19. Tuscarawas	11, 18, 20
20. Carroll	11, 14, 19

The complete statement of the bank location problem is:

OhioTrust

$$\text{Min} \quad x_1 + x_2 + \quad \ldots \quad + x_{20}$$

s.t.

$$x_1 + x_2 \quad + x_{12} + x_{16} \qquad \geq 1 \quad \text{Ashtabula}$$
$$x_1 + x_2 + x_3 + x_{12} \qquad \geq 1 \quad \text{Lake}$$
$$\vdots$$
$$x_{11} + x_{14} + x_{19} + x_{20} \geq 1 \quad \text{Carroll}$$
$$x_i = 0, 1 \quad i = 1, 2, \ldots, 20$$

In Problem 10, we ask you to solve this problem for the entire state of Ohio.

We use Excel Solver to solve this 20-variable, 20-constraint problem formulation. In Figure 12.11, we show the optimal solution. The optimal solution calls for principal places of business in Ashland, Stark, and Geauga counties. With PPBs in these three counties, Ohio Trust can place branch banks in all 20 counties. Clearly the integer programming model could be enlarged to allow for expansion into a larger area or throughout the entire state.

Product Design and Market Share Optimization

Conjoint analysis is a market research technique that can be used to learn how prospective buyers of a product value the product's attributes. In this section, we will show how the results of conjoint analysis can be used in an integer programming model of a **product design and market share optimization problem**. We illustrate the approach by considering a problem facing Salem Foods, a major producer of frozen foods.

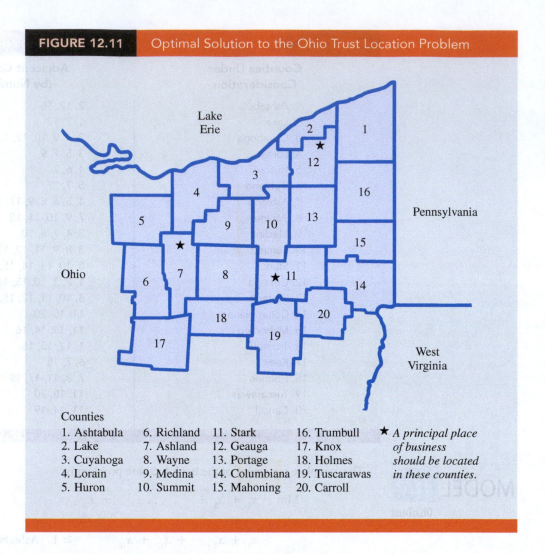

FIGURE 12.11 Optimal Solution to the Ohio Trust Location Problem

Counties

1. Ashtabula	6. Richland	11. Stark	16. Trumbull	★ *A principal place*
2. Lake	7. Ashland	12. Geauga	17. Knox	*of business*
3. Cuyahoga	8. Wayne	13. Portage	18. Holmes	*should be located*
4. Lorain	9. Medina	14. Columbiana	19. Tuscarawas	*in these counties.*
5. Huron	10. Summit	15. Mahoning	20. Carroll	

Salem Foods is planning to enter the frozen pizza market. Currently, two existing brands, Antonio's and King's, have the major share of the market. In trying to develop a sausage pizza that will capture a substantial share of the market, Salem determined that the four most important attributes when consumers purchase a frozen sausage pizza are crust, cheese, sauce, and sausage flavor. The crust attribute has two levels (thin and thick); the cheese attribute has two levels (mozzarella and blend); the sauce attribute has two levels (smooth and chunky); and the sausage flavor attribute has three levels (mild, medium, and hot).

In a typical conjoint analysis, a sample of consumers is asked to express their preference for a product with chosen levels for the attributes. Then regression analysis is used to determine the part-worth for each of the attribute levels. In essence, the **part-worth** is the utility value that a consumer attaches to each level of each attribute. Provided part-worths from regression analysis, we will show how they can be used to determine the overall value a consumer attaches to a particular product.

Table 12.3 shows the part-worths for each level of each attribute provided by a sample of eight potential Salem customers who are currently buying either King's or Antonio's pizza. For consumer 1, the part-worths for the crust attribute are 11 for thin crust and 2 for thick crust, indicating a preference for thin crust. For the cheese attribute, the part-worths

TABLE 12.3		Part-Worths for the Salem Foods Problem							
	Crust		**Cheese**		**Sauce**		**Sausage Flavor**		
Consumer	**Thin**	**Thick**	**Mozzarella**	**Blend**	**Smooth**	**Chunky**	**Mild**	**Medium**	**Hot**
1	11	2	6	7	3	17	26	27	8
2	11	7	15	17	16	26	14	1	10
3	7	5	8	14	16	7	29	16	19
4	13	20	20	17	17	14	25	29	10
5	2	8	6	11	30	20	15	5	12
6	12	17	11	9	2	30	22	12	20
7	9	19	12	16	16	25	30	23	19
8	5	9	4	14	23	16	16	30	3

are 6 for the mozzarella cheese and 7 for the cheese blend; thus, consumer 1 has a slight preference for the cheese blend. From the other part-worths, we see that consumer 1 shows a strong preference for the chunky sauce over the smooth sauce (17 to 3) and has a slight preference for the medium-flavored sausage. Note that consumer 2 shows a preference for the thin crust, the cheese blend, the chunky sauce, and mild-flavored sausage. The part-worths for the others consumers are interpreted similarly.

The part-worths can be used to determine the overall value (utility) that each consumer attaches to a particular type of pizza. For instance, consumer 1's current favorite pizza is the Antonio's brand, which has a thick crust, mozzarella cheese, chunky sauce, and medium-flavored sausage. We can determine consumer 1's utility for this particular type of pizza using the part-worths in Table 12.3. For consumer 1, the part-worths are 2 for thick crust, 6 for mozzarella cheese, 17 for chunky sauce, and 27 for medium-flavored sausage. Thus, consumer 1's utility for the Antonio's brand pizza is $2 + 6 + 17 + 27 = 52$. We can compute consumer 1's utility for a King's brand pizza similarly. The King's brand pizza has a thin crust, a cheese blend, smooth sauce, and mild-flavored sausage. Because the part-worths for consumer 1 are 11 for thin crust, 7 for cheese blend, 3 for smooth sauce, and 26 for mild-flavored sausage, consumer 1's utility for the King's brand pizza is $11 + 7 + 3 + 26 = 47$. In general, each consumer's utility for a particular type of pizza is the sum of the part-worths for the attributes of that type of pizza.

Utility values are discussed in more detail in Chapter 15.

To be successful with its brand, Salem Foods realizes that it must entice consumers in the marketplace to switch from their current favorite brand of pizza to the Salem product. In other words, Salem must design a pizza (choose the type of crust, cheese, sauce, and sausage flavor) that will have the highest utility for enough people to ensure sufficient sales to justify making the product. Assuming the sample of eight consumers in the current study is representative of the marketplace for frozen sausage pizza, we can formulate and solve an integer programming model that can help Salem come up with such a design. In marketing literature, the problem being solved is called the *share of choice* problem.

The decision variables are defined as follows:

l_{ij} = 1 if Salem chooses level i for attribute j; 0 otherwise
y_k = 1 if consumer k chooses the Salem brand; 0 otherwise

The objective is to choose the levels of each attribute that will maximize the number of consumers who prefer the Salem brand pizza. Because the number of consumers who prefer the Salem brand pizza is just the sum of the y_k variables, the objective function is:

$$\text{Max } y_1 + y_2 + \cdots + y_8.$$

One constraint is needed for each consumer in the sample. To illustrate how the constraints are formulated, let us consider the constraint corresponding to consumer 1. For consumer 1, the utility of a particular type of pizza can be expressed as the sum of the part-worths:

$$\text{Utility for consumer } 1 = 11l_{11} + 2l_{21} + 6l_{12} + 7l_{22} + 3l_{13} + 17l_{23} + 26l_{14} + 27l_{24} + 8l_{34}.$$

For consumer 1 to prefer the Salem pizza, the utility for the Salem pizza must be greater than the utility for consumer 1's current favorite. Recall that consumer 1's current favorite brand of pizza is Antonio's, with a utility of 52. Thus, consumer 1 will purchase the Salem brand only if the levels of the attributes for the Salem brand are chosen such that:

$$11l_{11} + 2l_{21} + 6l_{12} + 7l_{22} + 3l_{13} + 17l_{23} + 26l_{14} + 27l_{24} + 8l_{34} > 52.$$

Given the definitions of the y_k decision variables, we want $y_1 = 1$ when the consumer prefers the Salem brand and $y_1 = 0$ when the consumer does not prefer the Salem brand. Thus, we write the constraint for consumer 1 as follows:

$$11l_{11} + 2l_{21} + 6l_{12} + 7l_{22} + 3l_{13} + 17l_{23} + 26l_{14} + 27l_{24} + 8l_{34} \geq 1 + 52y_1.$$

With this constraint, y_1 cannot equal 1 unless the utility for the Salem design (the left-hand side of the constraint) exceeds the utility for consumer 1's current favorite by at least 1. Because the objective function is to maximize the sum of the y_k variables, the optimization will seek a product design that will allow as many y_k variables as possible to equal 1.

A similar constraint is written for each consumer in the sample. The coefficients for the l_{ij} variables in the utility functions are taken from Table 12.3, and the coefficients for the y_k variables are obtained by computing the overall utility of the consumer's current favorite brand of pizza. The following constraints correspond to the eight consumers in the study:

$$11l_{11} + 2l_{21} + 6l_{12} + 7l_{22} + 3l_{13} + 17l_{23} + 26l_{14} + 27l_{24} + 8l_{34} \geq 1 + 52y_1$$
$$11l_{11} + 7l_{21} + 15l_{12} + 17l_{22} + 16l_{13} + 26l_{23} + 14l_{14} + 1l_{24} + 10l_{34} \geq 1 + 58y_2$$
$$7l_{11} + 5l_{21} + 8l_{12} + 14l_{22} + 16l_{13} + 7l_{23} + 29l_{14} + 16l_{24} + 19l_{34} \geq 1 + 66y_3$$
$$13l_{11} + 20l_{21} + 20l_{12} + 17l_{22} + 17l_{13} + 14l_{23} + 25l_{14} + 29l_{24} + 10l_{34} \geq 1 + 83y_4$$
$$2l_{11} + 8l_{21} + 6l_{12} + 11l_{22} + 30l_{13} + 20l_{23} + 15l_{14} + 5l_{24} + 12l_{34} \geq 1 + 58y_5$$
$$12l_{11} + 17l_{21} + 11l_{12} + 9l_{22} + 2l_{13} + 30l_{23} + 22l_{14} + 12l_{24} + 20l_{34} \geq 1 + 70y_6$$
$$9l_{11} + 19l_{21} + 12l_{12} + 16l_{22} + 16l_{13} + 25l_{23} + 30l_{14} + 23l_{24} + 19l_{34} \geq 1 + 79y_7$$
$$5l_{11} + 9l_{21} + 4l_{12} + 14l_{22} + 23l_{13} + 16l_{23} + 16l_{14} + 30l_{24} + 3l_{34} \geq 1 + 59y_8$$

Antonio's brand is the current favorite pizza for consumers 1, 4, 6, 7, and 8. King's brand is the current favorite pizza for consumers 2, 3, and 5.

Four more constraints must be added, one for each attribute. These constraints are necessary to ensure that one and only one level is selected for each attribute. For attribute 1 (crust), we must add the constraint:

$$l_{11} + l_{21} = 1.$$

Because l_{11} and l_{21} are both binary variables, this constraint requires that one of the two variables equals one, and the other equals zero. The following three constraints ensure that one and only one level is selected for each of the other three attributes:

$$l_{12} + l_{22} = 1$$
$$l_{13} + l_{23} = 1$$
$$l_{14} + l_{24} + l_{34} = 1$$

MODEL *file*

Salem

The data, model, and solution for the Salem pizza problem may be found in the file *Salem*. The optimal solution to this 17-variable, 12-constraint integer linear program is $l_{11} = l_{22} = l_{23} = l_{14} = 1$ and $y_2 = y_5 = y_6 = y_7 = 1$. The value of the optimal solution is 4, indicating that if Salem makes this type of pizza, it will be preferable to the current favorite for four of the eight consumers. With $l_{21} = l_{22} = l_{23} = l_{14} = 1$, the pizza design that obtains the largest market share for Salem has a thin crust, a cheese blend, a chunky sauce, and mild-flavored sausage. Note also that with $y_2 = y_5 = y_6 = y_7 = 1$, consumers 2, 5, 6, and 7 will prefer the Salem pizza. This information may lead Salem to choose to market this type of pizza.

12.5   Modeling Flexibility Provided by Binary Variables

In Section 12.4, we presented four applications involving binary integer variables. In this section, we continue the discussion of the use of binary integer variables in modeling. First, we show how binary integer variables can be used to model multiple-choice and mutually exclusive constraints. Then we show how binary integer variables can be used to model situations in which k projects out of a set of n projects must be selected, as well as situations in which the acceptance of one project is conditional on the acceptance of another project.

Multiple-Choice and Mutually Exclusive Constraints

Recall the Ice-Cold Refrigerator capital budgeting problem introduced in Section 12.4. The decision variables were defined as:

$P = 1$ if the plant expansion project is accepted; 0 if rejected
$W = 1$ if the warehouse expansion project is accepted; 0 if rejected
$M = 1$ if the new machinery project is accepted; 0 if rejected
$R = 1$ if the new product research project is accepted; 0 if rejected

Suppose that, instead of one warehouse expansion project, the Ice-Cold Refrigerator Company actually has three warehouse expansion projects under consideration. One of the warehouses *must* be expanded because of increasing product demand, but new demand is not sufficient to make expansion of more than one warehouse necessary. The following variable definitions and **multiple-choice constraint** could be incorporated into the previous binary integer linear programming model to reflect this situation. Let:

$W_1 = 1$ if the original warehouse expansion project is accepted; 0 if rejected
$W_2 = 1$ if the second warehouse expansion project is accepted; 0 if rejected
$W_3 = 1$ if the third warehouse expansion project is accepted; 0 if rejected

The multiple-choice constraint reflecting the requirement that exactly one of these projects must be selected is:

$$W_1 + W_2 + W_3 = 1.$$

If W_1, W_2, and W_3 are allowed to assume only the values 0 or 1, then one and only one of these projects will be selected from among the three choices.

If the requirement that one warehouse must be expanded did not exist, the multiple-choice constraint could be modified as follows:

$$W_1 + W_2 + W_3 \leq 1.$$

This modification allows for the case of no warehouse expansion ($W_1 = W_2 = W_3 = 0$) but does not permit more than one warehouse to be expanded. This type of constraint is often called a **mutually exclusive constraint**.

k Out of *n* Alternatives Constraint

An extension of the notion of a multiple-choice constraint can be used to model situations in which *k out of a set of n* projects must be selected—a *k* **out of *n* alternatives**

constraint. Suppose that W_1, W_2, W_3, W_4, and W_5 represent five potential warehouse expansion projects and that two of the five projects must be accepted. The constraint that satisfies this new requirement is:

$$W_1 + W_2 + W_3 + W_4 + W_5 = 2.$$

If no more than two of the projects are to be selected, we would use the following less-than-or-equal-to constraint:

$$W_1 + W_2 + W_3 + W_4 + W_5 \leq 2.$$

Again, each of these variables must be restricted to binary values.

Conditional and Corequisite Constraints

Sometimes the acceptance of one project is conditional on the acceptance of another. For example, suppose that for the Ice-Cold Refrigerator Company, the warehouse expansion project was conditional on the plant expansion project. In other words, management will not consider expanding the warehouse unless the plant is expanded. With P representing plant expansion and W representing warehouse expansion, a **conditional constraint** could be introduced to enforce this requirement:

$$W \leq P.$$

P and W must each be 0 or 1; when P is 0, W will be forced to 0. When P is 1, W is allowed to be 1; thus, both the plant and the warehouse can be expanded. However, we note that the preceding constraint does not force the warehouse expansion project (W) to be accepted if the plant expansion project (P) is accepted.

If the warehouse expansion project had to be accepted whenever the plant expansion project was, and vice versa, we would say that P and W represented **corequisite constraint** projects. To model such a situation, we simply write the preceding constraint as an equality:

$$W = P.$$

The constraint forces P and W to take on the same value.

12.6 Generating Alternatives in Binary Optimization

If alternative optimal solutions exist, it would be good for management to know this because some factors that make one alternative preferred over another might not be included in the model. Also, if the solution is a unique optimal solution, it would be good to know how much worse the second-best solution is than the unique optimal solution. If the second-best solution is very close to optimal, it might be preferred over the true optimal solution because of factors outside the model.

As an example, let us reconsider the Ohio Trust location problem presented in Section 12.4. The solution for the minimum number of principle places of business (PPBs) is three. As shown in Figure 12.11, the solution is to place PPBs in county 7 (Ashland), county 11 (Stark), and county 12 (Geauga). However, suppose when Ohio Trust tries to implement this solution, it is not possible to find a suitable location for a PPB in one of these three counties. Are there other alternative solutions of three counties, or is this a unique optimal solution? By adding a special constraint based on the current solution and then resolving the model, we may answer this question.

The current solution for Ohio Trust can be broken into two sets of variables: those that are set to one and those that are set to zero. Let the set O denote the set of variables set to one and the set Z those that are set to zero. For the Ohio Trust solution, these sets are as follows:

Set O: x_7, x_{11}, x_{12}

Set Z: $x_1, x_2, x_3, x_4, x_5, x_6, x_8, x_9, x_{10}, x_{13}, x_{14}, x_{15}, x_{16}, x_{17}, x_{18}, x_{19}, x_{20}$

We may add the following constraint:

(Sum of variables in the set O) − (sum of variables in the set Z) ≤ (number of variables in the set O) − 1,

which for our current solution is:

$$x_7 + x_{11} + x_{12} - x_1 - x_2 - x_3 - x_4 - x_5 - x_6 - x_8 - x_9 - x_{10} - x_{13} -$$
$$x_{14} - x_{15} - x_{16} - x_{17} - x_{18} - x_{19} - x_{20} \leq 3 - 1 = 2.$$

This constraint has the very special property that it makes the current solution infeasible, but keeps feasible all other solutions that are feasible to the original problem. This constraint will force (at least) one of the variables in set O to change from one to zero or will force (at least) one of the variables in set Z to change from zero to one.

When we append this new constraint to the original model, we obtain the solution displayed in Figure 12.12. Notice that the optimal objective function value has increased to

FIGURE 12.12   A Second-Best Solution to the Ohio Trust Location Problem

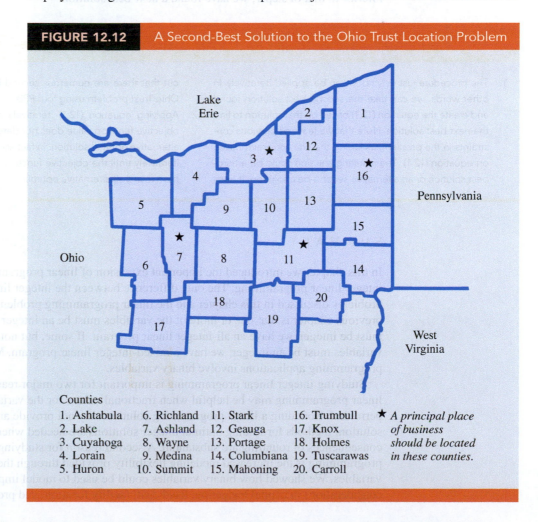

Counties

1. Ashtabula   6. Richland   11. Stark   16. Trumbull   ★ *A principal place*
2. Lake   7. Ashland   12. Geauga   17. Knox   *of business*
3. Cuyahoga   8. Wayne   13. Portage   18. Holmes   *should be located*
4. Lorain   9. Medina   14. Columbiana   19. Tuscarawas   *in these counties.*
5. Huron   10. Summit   15. Mahoning   20. Carroll

four. This tells us that the solution we found in Section 12.4 with objective function value equal to 3 is a unique optimal solution. Any other feasible solution will require four or more PBBs to cover the entire 20-county region. So, if for any of the three counties in the original solution we cannot find a suitable location for a PBB, the next best solution will require PBBs in four counties and the solution in Figure 12.10 is a second-best alternative. Note that if the optimal objective functions of the new problem with constraint added had been 3, we would have found an alternative optimal solution.

We can summarize the procedure for finding an alternative solution as follows:

Step 1: Solve the original problem
Step 2: Create two sets:
  O = the set of variables equal to one in Step 1
  Z = the set of variables equal to zero in Step 1
Step 3: Add the following constraint to the original problem, and solve

$$\text{(Sum of variables in the set O)} - \text{(sum of variables in the set Z)}$$
$$\leq \text{(number of variables in the set O)} - 1 \tag{12.1}$$

If the objective function value in step 3 is equal to the objective function value of step 1, we have found an alternative optimal solution. If the objective function value of step 3 is inferior to that of step 1, we have found a next-best solution.

NOTES + COMMENTS

1. The procedure just described can be applied iteratively. In other words, we can take the second-best solution found and create the equation (12.1) based on that solution to find the next-best solution. Note that we leave all previous constraints in the problem, including the first constraint based on equation (12.1). The resulting solution could be a third-best solution or an alternative second-best solution. It turns

out that there are numerous second-best solutions to the Ohio Trust problem using four PPBs.

2. Applying equation (12.1) iteratively and finding that the objective function value does not deteriorate generates an alternative optimal solution. In fact applying equation (12.1) iteratively until the objective function changes ensures you have found all alternative optima.

SUMMARY

In this chapter we introduced the important extension of linear programming referred to as integer linear programming. The only difference between the integer linear programming problems discussed in this chapter and the linear programming problems studied in the previous chapter is that one or more of the variables must be an integer. If all variables must be integer, we have an all-integer linear program. If some, but not necessarily all, variables must be an integer, we have a mixed-integer linear program. Most integer programming applications involve binary variables.

Studying integer linear programming is important for two major reasons. First, integer linear programming may be helpful when fractional values for the variables are not permitted. Rounding a linear programming solution may not provide an optimal integer solution; methods for finding optimal integer solutions are needed when the economic consequences of rounding are substantial. A second reason for studying integer linear programming is the increased modeling flexibility provided through the use of binary variables. We showed how binary variables could be used to model important managerial considerations in capital budgeting, fixed cost, facility location, and product design/

market share applications. We showed how to generate second-best solutions or alternative optima if they exist by adding a constraint based on those solutions. This is important for providing alternatives for management.

The number of applications of integer linear programming continues to grow rapidly, partly because of the availability of good integer linear programming software packages. As researchers develop solution procedures capable of solving larger integer linear programs and as computer speed increases, a continuation of the growth of integer programming applications is expected.

GLOSSARY

All-integer linear program An integer linear program in which all variables are required to be integers.

Binary integer linear program An all-integer or mixed-integer linear program in which the integer variables are permitted to assume only the values 0 or 1. Also called *binary integer program*.

Capital budgeting problem A binary integer programming problem that involves choosing which possible projects or activities provide the best investment return.

Conditional constraint A constraint involving binary variables that does not allow certain variables to equal one unless certain other variables are equal to one.

Conjoint analysis A market research technique that can be used to learn how prospective buyers of a product value the product's attributes.

Convex hull The smallest intersection of linear inequalities that contain a certain set of points.

Corequisite constraint A constraint requiring that two binary variables be equal and that they are both either in or out of the solution.

Fixed-cost problem A binary mixed-integer programming problem in which the binary variables represent whether an activity, such as a production run, is undertaken (variable = 1) or not (variable = 0).

Integer linear program A linear program with the additional requirement that one or more of the variables must be an integer.

k out of n alternatives constraint An extension of the multiple-choice constraint that requires that the sum of *n* binary variables equals *k*.

Location problem A binary integer programming problem in which the objective is to select the best locations to meet a stated objective. Variations of this problem (see the bank location problem in Section 12.4) are known as *covering problems*.

LP Relaxation The linear program that results from dropping the integer requirements for the variables in an integer linear program.

Mixed-integer linear program An integer linear program in which some, but not necessarily all, variables are required to be integers.

Multiple-choice constraint A constraint requiring that the sum of two or more binary variables equals one. Thus, any feasible solution makes a choice of which variable to set equal to one.

Mutually exclusive constraint A constraint requiring that the sum of two or more binary variables be less than or equal to one. Thus, if one of the variables equals one, the others must equal zero. However, all variables could equal zero.

Part-worth The utility value that a consumer attaches to each level of each attribute in a conjoint analysis model.

Product design and market share optimization problem Sometimes called the share of choice problem, the choice of a product design that maximizes the number of consumers that prefer it.

PROBLEMS

1. STAR Co. provides paper to smaller companies with volumes that are not large enough to warrant dealing directly with the paper mill. STAR receives 100-feet-wide paper rolls from the mill and cuts the rolls into smaller rolls of widths 12, 15, and 30 feet. The demands for these widths vary from week to week. The following cutting patterns have been established:

Pattern Number	12-ft	15-ft	30-ft	Trim Loss (ft)
1	0	6	0	10
2	0	0	3	10
3	8	0	0	4
4	2	1	2	1
5	7	1	0	1

Trim loss is the leftover paper from a pattern (e.g., for pattern 4, $2(12) + 1(15) + 2(30) = 99$ feet used results in $100 - 99 = 1$ foot of trim loss). Demands this week are 5,670 12-foot rolls, 1,680 15-foot rolls, and 3,350 30-foot rolls. Develop an all-integer model that will determine how many 100-foot rolls to cut into each of the five patterns in order to meet demand and minimize trim loss (leftover paper from a pattern).

2. The following questions refer to a capital budgeting problem with six projects represented by binary variables x_1, x_2, x_3, x_4, x_5, and x_6.
   a. Write a constraint modeling a situation in which two of the projects 1, 3, 5, and 6 must be undertaken.
   b. Write a constraint modeling a situation in which, if project 3 or 5 is undertaken, they must both be undertaken.
   c. Write a constraint modeling a situation in which project 1 or 4 must be undertaken, but not both.
   d. Write constraints modeling a situation in which project 4 cannot be undertaken unless projects 1 and 3 also are undertaken.
   e. Revise the requirement in part (d) to accommodate the case in which, when projects 1 and 3 are undertaken, project 4 also must be undertaken.

3. Spencer Enterprises is attempting to choose among a series of new investment alternatives. The potential investment alternatives, the net present value of the future stream of returns, the capital requirements, and the available capital funds over the next three years are summarized as follows:

Alternative	Net Present Value ($)	Capital Requirements ($) Year 1	Year 2	Year 3
Limited warehouse expansion	4,000	3,000	1,000	4,000
Extensive warehouse expansion	6,000	2,500	3,500	3,500
Test market new product	10,500	6,000	4,000	5,000
Advertising campaign	4,000	2,000	1,500	1,800
Basic research	8,000	5,000	1,000	4,000
Purchase new equipment	3,000	1,000	500	900
Capital funds available		10,500	7,000	8,750

   a. Develop and solve an integer programming model for maximizing the net present value.
   b. Assume that only one of the warehouse expansion projects can be implemented. Modify your model from part (a).

c. Suppose that if test marketing of the new product is carried out, the advertising campaign also must be conducted. Modify your formulation from part (b) to reflect this new situation.

4. Hawkins Manufacturing Company produces connecting rods for 4- and 6-cylinder automobile engines using the same production line. The cost required to set up the production line to produce the 4-cylinder connecting rods is $2,000, and the cost required to set up the production line for the 6-cylinder connecting rods is $3,500. Manufacturing costs are $15 for each 4-cylinder connecting rod and $18 for each 6-cylinder connecting rod. There is no production on weekends, so on Friday the line is disassembled and cleaned. On Monday, the line must be set up to run whichever product will be produced that week. Once the line has been set up, the weekly production capacities are 6,000 6-cylinder connecting rods and 8,000 4-cylinder connecting rods. Let

x_4 = the number of 4-cylinder connecting rods produced next week
x_6 = the number of 6-cylinder connecting rods produced next week
s_4 = 1 if the production line is set up to produce the 4-cylinder connecting rods;
  0 if otherwise
s_6 = 1 if the production line is set up to produce the 6-cylinder connecting rods;
  0 if otherwise

a. Using the decision variables x_4 and s_4, write a constraint that sets next week's maximum production of the 4-cylinder connecting rods to either 0 or 8,000 units.

b. Using the decision variables x_6 and s_6, write a constraint that sets next week's maximum production of the 6-cylinder connecting rods to either 0 or 6,000 units.

c. Write a constraint that requires that production be set up for exactly one of the two rods.

d. Write the cost function to be minimized.

5. Grave City is considering the relocation of several police substations to obtain better enforcement in high-crime areas. The locations under consideration together with the areas that can be covered from these locations are given in the following table:

Potential Locations for Substations	Areas Covered
A	1, 5, 7
B	1, 2, 5, 7
C	1, 3, 5
D	2, 4, 5
E	3, 4, 6
F	4, 5, 6
G	1, 5, 6, 7

a. Formulate an integer programming model that could be used to find the minimum number of locations necessary to provide coverage to all areas.

b. Solve the problem in part (a).

6. Hart Manufacturing makes three products. Each product requires manufacturing operations in three departments: A, B, and C. The labor-hour requirements, by department, are as follows:

Department	Product 1	Product 2	Product 3
A	1.50	3.00	2.00
B	2.00	1.00	2.50
C	0.25	0.25	0.25

During the next production period the labor-hours available are 450 in department A, 350 in department B, and 50 in department C. The profit contributions per unit are $25 for product 1, $28 for product 2, and $30 for product 3.

a. Formulate a linear programming model for maximizing total profit contribution.

b. Solve the linear program formulated in part (a). How much of each product should be produced, and what is the projected total profit contribution?

c. After evaluating the solution obtained in part (b), one of the production supervisors noted that production setup costs had not been taken into account. She noted that setup costs are $400 for product 1, $550 for product 2, and $600 for product 3. If the solution developed in part (b) is to be used, what is the total profit contribution after taking into account the setup costs?

d. Management realized that the optimal product mix, taking setup costs into account, might be different from the one recommended in part (b). Formulate a mixed-integer linear program that takes setup costs provided in part (c) into account. Management also stated that we should not consider making more than 175 units of product 1, 150 units of product 2, or 140 units of product 3.

e. Solve the mixed-integer linear program formulated in part (d). How much of each product should be produced and what is the projected total profit contribution? Compare this profit contribution to that obtained in part (c).

7. Offhaus Manufacturing produces office supplies but outsources the delivery of its products to third-party carriers. Offhaus ships to 20 cities from its Dayton, Ohio, manufacturing facility and has asked a variety of carriers to bid on its business. Seven carriers have responded with bids. The resulting bids (in dollars per truckload) are shown in the table. For example, the table shows that carrier 1 bid on the business to cities 11 to 20. The right side of the table provides the number of truckloads scheduled for each destination in the next quarter.

Bid S/Truckload	Carrier 1	Carrier 2	Carrier 3	Carrier 4	Carrier 5	Carrier 6	Carrier 7	Destination	Demand (truckloads)
City 1					$2,188	$1,666	$1,790	City 1	30
City 2		$1,453			$2,602	$1,767		City 2	10
City 3		$1,534			$2,283	$1,857	$1,870	City 3	20
City 4		$1,687			$2,617	$1,738		City 4	40
City 5		$1,523			$2,239	$1,771	$1,855	City 5	10
City 6		$1,521			$1,571		$1,545	City 6	10
City 7		$2,100		$1,922	$1,938		$2,050	City 7	12
City 8		$1,800		$1,432	$1,416		$1,739	City 8	25
City 9		$1,134		$1,233	$1,181		$1,150	City 9	25
City 10		$672		$610	$669		$678	City 10	33
City 11	$724		$723	$627	$657		$706	City 11	11
City 12	$766		$766	$721	$682		$733	City 12	29
City 13	$741		$745		$682		$733	City 13	12
City 14	$815	$800	$828		$745		$832	City 14	24
City 15	$904		$880		$891		$914	City 15	10
City 16	$958		$933		$891		$914	City 16	10
City 17	$925		$929		$937		$984	City 17	23
City 18	$892		$869	$822	$829		$864	City 18	25
City 19	$927		$969		$967		$1,008	City 19	12
City 20	$963		$938		$955		$995	City 20	10
No. of Bids	10	10	10	7	20	5	18		

DATA *file*

Offhaus

Because dealing with too many carriers can be cumbersome, Offhaus would like to limit the number of carriers it uses to three. Also, for customer relationship reasons Offhaus wants each city to be assigned to only one carrier (i.e., no splitting of the demand to a given city across carriers).

a. Develop a model that will yield the three selected carriers and the city-carrier assignments that minimize the cost of shipping. Solve the model and report the solution.

b. Offhaus is not sure whether three is the correct number of carriers to select. Run the model you developed in part (a) for allowable carriers varying from one to seven. Based on results, how many carriers would you recommend and why?

8. The Martin-Beck Company operates a plant in St. Louis with an annual capacity of 30,000 units. Product is shipped to regional distribution centers located in Boston, Atlanta, and Houston. Because of an anticipated increase in demand, Martin-Beck plans to increase capacity by constructing a new plant in one or more of the following cities: Detroit, Toledo, Denver, or Kansas City. The estimated annual fixed cost and the annual capacity for the four proposed plants are as follows:

Proposed Plant	Annual Fixed Cost	Annual Capacity
Detroit	$175,000	10,000
Toledo	$300,000	20,000
Denver	$375,000	30,000
Kansas City	$500,000	40,000

The company's long-range planning group developed forecasts of the anticipated annual demand at the distribution centers as follows:

Distribution Center	Annual Demand
Boston	30,000
Atlanta	20,000
Houston	20,000

The shipping cost per unit from each plant to each distribution center is as follows:

| Plant Site | Distribution Centers | | |
	Boston	Atlanta	Houston
Detroit	5	2	3
Toledo	4	3	4
Denver	9	7	5
Kansas City	10	4	2
St. Louis	8	4	3

a. Formulate a mixed-integer programming model that could be used to help Martin-Beck determine which new plant or plants to open in order to satisfy anticipated demand.

b. Solve the model you formulated in part (a). What is the optimal cost? What is the optimal set of plants to open?

c. Using equation (12.1), find a second-best solution. What is the increase in cost versus the best solution from part (b)?

9. Galaxy Cloud Services operates several data centers across the United States containing servers that store and process the data on the Internet. Suppose that Galaxy Cloud Services currently has five outdated data centers: one each in Michigan, Ohio, and California and two in New York. Management is considering increasing the capacity of these data centers to keep up with increasing demand. Each data center contains servers that are dedicated to Secure data and to Super Secure data. The cost to update each data center and the resulting increase in server capacity for each type of server are as follows:

Data Center	Cost ($ millions)	Secure Servers	Super Secure Servers
Michigan	2.5	50	30
New York 1	3.5	80	40
New York 2	3.5	40	80
Ohio	4.0	90	60
California	2.0	20	30

The projected needs are for a total increase in capacity of 90 Secure servers and 90 Super Secure servers. Management wants to determine which data centers to update to meet projected needs and, at the same time, minimize the total cost of the added capacity.

a. Formulate a binary integer programming model that could be used to determine the optimal solution to the capacity increase question facing management.

b. Solve the model formulated in part (a) to provide a recommendation for management.

10. CHB, Inc., a bank holding company, is evaluating the potential for expanding into the state of Ohio. State law permits establishing branches in any county that is adjacent to a county in which a PPB (principal place of business) is located. The following map shows the State of Ohio. The file *CHB* contains an adjacency matrix with a one in the *i*th row and *j*th column indicating that the counties represented by the *i*th row and the *j*th column share a border. A zero indicates that the two counties do not share a border.

DATA *file*

CHB

Ohio

Formulate and solve a linear binary model that will tell CHB the minimum number of PPBs required and their location in order to allow CHB to put a branch in every county in Ohio.

11. For Problem 10, use equation (12.1) to determine whether your solution to Problem 10 is unique. If your solution is not unique, use equation (12.1) iteratively to find all alternative optimal solutions. How many are there?

12. Consider again the CHB, Inc. problem described in Problem 10. Suppose only a limted number of PPBs can be placed. CHB would like to place this limited number of PPBs in counties so that the allowable branches can reach the maximum possible population. The file *CHBPop* contains the county adjacency matrix described in Problem 10 as well as the population of each county.
    a. Assume that only a fixed number of PPBs, denoted k, can be established. Formulate a linear binary integer program that will tell CHB, Inc. where to locate the fixed number of PPBs in order to maximize the population reached. (*Hint:* Review the Ohio Trust formulation in Section 12.4. Introduce variable $y_i = 1$ if it is possible to establish a branch in county i, and $y_i = 0$ otherwise; that is, if county i is covered by a PPB, then the population can be counted as covered.).
    b. Suppose that two PPBs can be established. Where should they be located to maximize the population served?
    c. Solve your model from part (a) for an allowable number of PPBs ranging from 1 to 10. In other words, solve the model 10 times, k set to 1, 2, ..., 10. Record the population reached for each value of k. Graph the results of part (b) by plotting the population reached versus the number of PPBs allowed. Based on their cost calculations, CHB considers an additional PPB to be fiscally prudent only if it increases the population reached by at least 500,000 people. Based on this graph, how many PPBs do you recommend to implement?

13. The Northshore Bank is working to develop an efficient work schedule for full-time and part-time tellers. The schedule must provide for efficient operation of the bank, including adequate customer service, employee breaks, and so on. On Fridays, the bank is open from 9:00 a.m. to 7:00 p.m. The number of tellers necessary to provide adequate customer service during each hour of operation is summarized here:

Time	No. of Tellers	Time	No. of Tellers
9:00 a.m.–10:00 a.m.	6	2:00 p.m.–3:00 p.m.	6
10:00 a.m.–11:00 a.m.	4	3:00 p.m.–4:00 p.m.	4
11:00 a.m.–Noon	8	4:00 p.m.–5:00 p.m.	7
Noon–1:00 p.m.	10	5:00 p.m.–6:00 p.m.	6
1:00 p.m.–2:00 p.m.	9	6:00 p.m.–7:00 p.m.	6

Each full-time employee starts on the hour and works a 4-hour shift, followed by a 1-hour break and then a 3-hour shift. Part-time employees work one 4-hour shift beginning on the hour. Considering salary and fringe benefits, full-time employees cost the bank $15 per hour ($105 a day), and part-time employees cost the bank $8 per hour ($32 per day).
    a. Formulate an integer programming model that can be used to develop a schedule that will satisfy customer service needs at a minimum employee cost. (*Hint:* Let x_i = number of full-time employees coming on duty at the beginning of hour i and y_i = number of part-time employees coming on duty at the beginning of hour i.)
    b. Solve the LP Relaxation of your model in part (a).
    c. Solve your model in part (a) for the optimal schedule of tellers. Comment on the solution.

d. After reviewing the solution to part (c), the bank manager realized that some additional requirements must be specified. Specifically, she wants to ensure that one full-time employee is on duty at all times and that there is a staff of at least five full-time employees. Revise your model to incorporate these additional requirements, and solve for the optimal solution.

14. Burnside Marketing Research conducted a study for Barker Foods on several formulations for a new dry cereal. Three attributes were found to be most influential in determining which cereal had the best taste: ratio of wheat to corn in the cereal flake, type of sweetener (sugar, honey, or artificial), and the presence or absence of flavor bits. Seven children participated in taste tests and provided the following part-worths for the attributes (see Section 12.4 for a discussion of part-worths):

	Wheat/Corn		Sweetener			Flavor Bits	
Child	Low	High	Sugar	Honey	Artificial	Present	Absent
1	15	35	30	40	25	15	9
2	30	20	40	35	35	8	11
3	40	25	20	40	10	7	14
4	35	30	25	20	30	15	18
5	25	40	40	20	35	18	14
6	20	25	20	35	30	9	16
7	30	15	25	40	40	20	11

DATA *file*
Burnside

a. Suppose the overall utility (sum of part-worths) of the current favorite cereal is 75 for each child. What product design will maximize the share of choice for the seven children in the sample?

b. Assume that the overall utility of the current favorite cereal for children 1 to 4 is 70, and the overall utility of the current favorite cereal for children 5 to 7 is 80. What product design will maximize the share of choice for the seven children in the sample?

15. The Bayside Art Gallery is considering installing a video camera security system to reduce its insurance premiums. A diagram of Bayside's eight exhibition rooms is shown in the following figure; the openings between the rooms are numbered 1 to 13. A security firm proposed that two-way cameras be installed at some room openings. Each camera has the ability to monitor the two rooms between which the camera is located. For example, if a camera were located at opening number 4, rooms 1 and 4 would be covered; if a camera were located at opening 11, rooms 7 and 8 would be covered; and so on. Management decided not to locate a camera system at the entrance to the display rooms. The objective is to provide security coverage for all eight rooms using the minimum number of two-way cameras.

a. Formulate a binary integer linear programming model that will enable Bayside's management to determine the locations for the camera systems.

b. Solve the model formulated in part (a) to determine how many two-way cameras to purchase and where they should be located.

c. Suppose that management wants to provide additional security coverage for room 7. Specifically, management wants room 7 to be covered by two cameras. How would the model you formulated in part (a) have to change to accommodate this policy restriction?

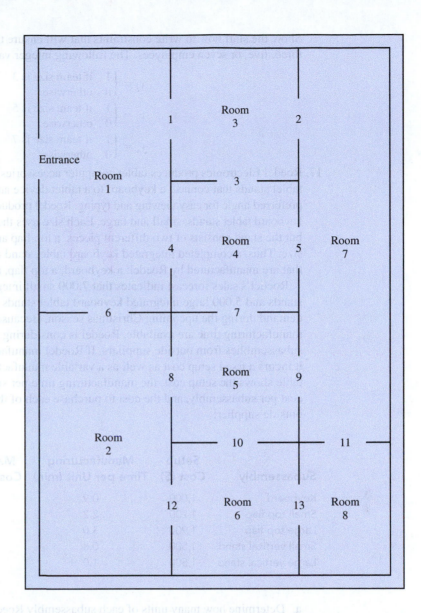

d. With the policy restriction specified in part (c), determine how many two-way camera systems will need to be purchased and where they will be located.

16. The Delta Group is a management consulting firm specializing in the health care industry. A team is being formed to study possible new markets, and a linear programming model has been developed for selecting team members. However, one constraint the president imposed is that the team size should be three, five, or seven members. The staff cannot figure out how to incorporate this requirement in the model. The current model requires that team members be selected from three departments and uses the following variable definitions:

x_1 = the number of employees selected from department 1
x_2 = the number of employees selected from department 2
x_3 = the number of employees selected from department 3

Show the staff how to write constraints that will ensure that the team will consist of three, five, or seven employees. The following integer variables should be helpful:

$$y_1 = \begin{cases} 1 & \text{if team size is 3} \\ 0 & \text{otherwise} \end{cases}$$

$$y_2 = \begin{cases} 1 & \text{if team size is 5} \\ 0 & \text{otherwise} \end{cases}$$

$$y_3 = \begin{cases} 1 & \text{if team size is 7} \\ 0 & \text{otherwise} \end{cases}$$

17. Roedel Electronics produces tablet computer accessories, including integrated keyboard tablet stands that connect a keyboard to a tablet device and holds the device at a preferred angle for easy viewing and typing. Roedel produces two sizes of integrated keyboard tablet stands, small and large. Each size uses the same keyboard attachment, but the stand consists of two different pieces, a top flap and a vertical stand that differ by size. Thus, a completed integrated keyboard tablet stand consists of three subassemblies that are manufactured by Roedel: a keyboard, a top flap, and a vertical stand.

   Roedel's sales forecast indicates that 7,000 small integrated keyboard tablet stands and 5,000 large integrated keyboard tablet stands will be needed to satisfy demand during the upcoming Christmas season. Because only 500 hours of in-house manufacturing time are available, Roedel is considering purchasing some, or all, of the subassemblies from outside suppliers. If Roedel manufactures a subassembly in-house, it incurs a fixed setup cost as well as a variable manufacturing cost. The following table shows the setup cost, the manufacturing time per subassembly, the manufacturing cost per subassembly, and the cost to purchase each of the subassemblies from an outside supplier:

Subassembly	Setup Cost ($)	Manufacturing Time per Unit (min)	Manufacturing Cost per Unit ($)	Purchase Cost per Unit ($)
Keyboard	1,000	0.9	0.40	0.65
Small top flap	1,200	2.2	2.90	3.45
Large top flap	1,900	3.0	3.15	3.70
Small vertical stand	1,500	0.8	0.30	0.50
Large vertical stand	1,500	1.0	0.55	0.70

   a. Determine how many units of each subassembly Roedel should manufacture and how many units of each subassembly Roedel should purchase. What is the total manufacturing and purchase cost associated with your recommendation?

   b. Suppose Roedel is considering purchasing new machinery to produce large top flaps. For the new machinery, the setup cost is $3,000; the manufacturing time is 2.5 minutes per unit, and the manufacturing cost is $2.60 per unit. Assuming that the new machinery is purchased, determine how many units of each subassembly Roedel should manufacture and how many units of each subassembly Roedel should purchase. What is the total manufacturing and purchase cost associated with your recommendation? Do you think the new machinery should be purchased? Explain.

18. Suppose that management of Valley Cinemas would like to investigate the potential of using a scheduling system for their chain of multiple-screen theaters. Valley selected a small two-screen movie theater for the pilot testing and would like to develop an integer programming model to help schedule the movies. Six movies are available.

The first week each movie is available, the last week each movie can be shown, and the maximum number of weeks that each movie can run are shown here:

Movie	First Week Available	Last Week Available	Max. Run (weeks)
1	1	2	2
2	1	3	2
3	1	1	1
4	2	4	2
5	3	6	3
6	3	5	3

The overall viewing schedule for the theater is composed of the individual schedules for each of the six movies. For each movie, a schedule must be developed that specifies the week the movie starts and the number of consecutive weeks it will run. For instance, one possible schedule for movie 2 is for it to start in week 1 and run for two weeks. Theater policy requires that once a movie is started, it must be shown in consecutive weeks. It cannot be stopped and restarted again. To represent the schedule possibilities for each movie, the following decision variables were developed:

$$y_{ijw} = \begin{cases} 1 & \text{if movie } i \text{ is scheduled to start in week } j \text{ and run for } w \text{ weeks} \\ 0 & \text{otherwise} \end{cases}$$

For example, $x_{532} = 1$ means that the schedule selected for movie 5 is to begin in week 3 and run for two weeks. For each movie, a separate variable is given for each possible schedule.

a. Three schedules are associated with movie 1. List the variables that represent these schedules.

b. Write a constraint requiring that only one schedule be selected for movie 1.

c. Write a constraint requiring that only one schedule be selected for movie 5.

d. What restricts the number of movies that can be shown in week 1? Write a constraint that restricts the number of movies selected for viewing in week 1.

e. Write a constraint that restricts the number of movies selected for viewing in week 3.

19. East Coast Trucking provides service from Boston to Miami using regional offices located in Boston, New York, Philadelphia, Baltimore, Washington, Richmond, Raleigh, Florence, Savannah, Jacksonville, and Tampa. The number of miles between the regional offices is provided in the following table:

	New York	Philadelphia	Baltimore	Washington	Richmond	Raleigh	Florence	Savannah	Jacksonville	Tampa	Miami
Boston	211	320	424	459	565	713	884	1,056	1,196	1,399	1,669
New York		109	213	248	354	502	673	845	985	1,188	1,458
Philadelphia			104	139	245	393	564	736	876	1,079	1,349
Baltimore				35	141	289	460	632	772	975	1,245
Washington					106	254	425	597	737	940	1,210
Richmond						148	319	491	631	834	1,104
Raleigh							171	343	483	686	956
Florence								172	312	515	785
Savannah									140	343	613
Jacksonville										203	473
Tampa											270

The company's expansion plans involve constructing service facilities in some of the cities where regional offices are located. Each regional office must be within 400 miles of a service facility. For instance, if a service facility is constructed in Richmond, it can provide service to regional offices located in New York, Philadelphia, Baltimore, Washington, Richmond, Raleigh, and Florence. Management would like to determine the minimum number of service facilities needed and where they should be located.

a. Formulate an integer linear program that can be used to determine the minimum number of service facilities needed and their locations.

b. Solve the integer linear program formulated in part (a). How many service facilities are required, and where should they be located?

c. Suppose that each service facility can provide service only to regional offices within 300 miles. Re-solve the integer linear program with the 300-mile requirement. How many service facilities are required and where should they be located?

20. Dave has $100,000 to invest in 10 mutual fund alternatives with the following restrictions. For diversification, no more than $25,000 can be invested in any one fund. If a fund is chosen for investment, then at least $10,000 will be invested in it. No more than two of the funds can be pure growth funds, and at least one pure bond fund must be selected. The total amount invested in pure bond funds must be at least as much as the amount invested in pure growth funds. Using the following expected returns, formulate and solve a model that will determine the investment strategy that will maximize expected annual return. What assumptions have you made in your model? How often would you expect to run your model?

Fund	Type	Expected Return (%)
1	Growth	6.70
2	Growth	7.65
3	Growth	7.55
4	Growth	7.45
5	Growth & Income	7.50
6	Growth & Income	6.45
7	Growth & Income	7.05
8	Stock & Bond	6.90
9	Bond	5.20
10	Bond	5.90

CASE PROBLEM: APPLECORE CHILDREN'S CLOTHING

Applecore Children's Clothing is a retailer that sells high-end clothes for toddlers (ages 1 to 3), primarily in shopping malls. Applecore also has a successful Internet-based sales division. Recently Dave Walker, vice-president of the e-commerce division, has been given the directive to expand the company's Internet sales. He commissioned a major study on the effectiveness of Internet ads placed on news web sites. The results were favorable: Current patrons who purchased via the Internet and saw the ads on news web sites spent more, on average, than did comparable Internet customers who did not see the ads.

With this new information on Internet ads, Walker continued to investigate how new Internet customers could most effectively be reached. One of these ideas involved strategically purchasing ads on news web sites prior to and during the holiday season.

To determine which news sites might be the most effective for ads, Walker conducted a follow-up study. An e-mail questionnaire was administered to a sample of 1,200 current Internet customers to ascertain which of 30 news sites they regularly visit. The idea is that web sites with high proportions of current customer visits would be viable sources of future customers for Applecore products.

Walker would like to ascertain which news sites should be selected for ads. The problem is complicated because Walker does not want to count multiple exposures. So, if a respondent visits multiple sites with Applecore ads or visits a given site multiple times, that respondent should be counted as reached but not more than once. In other words, a customer is considered reached if he or she has visited at least one web site with an Applecore ad.

Data from the customer e-mail survey have begun to trickle in. Walker wants to develop a prototype model based on the current survey results. So far, 53 surveys have been returned. To keep the prototype model manageable, Walker wants to proceed with model development using the data from the 53 returned surveys and using only the first 10 news sites in the questionnaire. The costs of ads per week for the 10 web sites are given in the following table, and the budget is $10,000 per week. For each of the 53 responses received, the 10 web sites visited regularly are shown below. For a given customer–web site pair, a one indicates that the customer regularly visits that web site, and a zero indicates that the customer does not regularly visit that site.

Data for Applecore Customer Visits to News Web sites (respondents 5 to 33 hidden)

DATA *file*

Applecore

	Web Site									
	1	2	3	4	5	6	7	8	9	10
Cost/Wk ($000)	$5.0	$8.0	$3.5	$5.5	$7.0	$4.5	$6.0	$5.0	$3.0	$2.2
	Web Site									
Customer	1	2	3	4	5	6	7	8	9	10
1	0	0	0	0	0	0	0	0	0	1
2	1	0	0	1	0	0	0	0	0	0
3	1	0	0	0	0	0	0	0	0	0
4	0	0	0	0	1	1	0	0	0	0
34	0	0	0	1	1	0	0	0	0	0
35	1	0	0	0	1	1	0	0	0	0
36	1	0	1	0	0	0	0	0	0	0
37	0	0	1	0	1	0	0	1	0	0
38	0	0	1	0	0	0	0	0	0	0
39	0	1	0	0	0	0	1	0	0	0
40	0	1	0	0	0	0	1	0	0	0
41	0	0	0	0	0	0	1	0	0	0
42	0	0	0	1	1	1	0	0	0	0
43	0	0	0	0	0	0	0	0	0	0
44	0	0	0	0	1	0	0	0	0	1
45	1	1	0	0	0	0	0	0	0	0
46	0	0	0	0	0	0	1	0	0	0
47	1	0	0	0	1	0	0	0	0	1
48	0	0	1	0	0	0	0	0	0	0
49	1	0	1	1	0	0	0	0	0	0
50	0	0	0	0	0	0	0	0	0	0
51	0	1	0	0	0	1	0	0	0	0
52	0	0	0	0	0	0	0	0	0	0
53	0	1	0	0	1	0	0	1	1	1

Managerial Report

1. Develop a model that will allow Applecore to maximize the number of customers reached for a budget of $10,000 for one week of promotion.
2. Solve the model. What is the maximum number of customers reached for the $10,000 budget?
3. Perform a sensitivity analysis on the budget for values from $5,000 to $35,000 in increments of $5,000. Construct a graph of percentage reach versus budget. Is the additional increase in percentage reach monotonically decreasing as the budget allocation increases? Why or why not? What is your recommended budget? Explain.

Chapter 12 Appendix

Appendix 12.1 Solving Integer Linear Optimization Problems Using Analytic Solver Platform

In this appendix, we illustrate how to use Analytic Solver Platform (ASP) to solve integer linear programs in Excel.

Recall the Eastborne Realty integer programming model:

$$T = \text{number of townhouses}$$
$$A = \text{number of apartment buildings}$$

$$\text{Max} \quad 10T + 15A$$
$$\text{s.t.}$$
$$282T + 400A \leq 2000$$
$$4T + 40A \leq 140$$
$$T \leq 5$$
$$T, A \geq 0, \text{ and integer}$$

The spreadsheet model is shown in Figure 12.13.

DATA *file*

Eastborne

If the Solver Options and Model Specifications task pane is not visible, click Model in the Model group under the ANALYTIC SOLVER PLATFORM tab to activate this pane.

Step 1. Click the **Analytic Solver Platform** tab in the Excel Ribbon

Step 2. When the **Solver Options and Model Specifications** task pane appears, select the ⊞ next to **Optimization** to expand the tree structure

Step 3. When the optimization tree structure appears (see Figure 12.14):
   Select **Objective**
   Select cell B17
   Click the **Add** button ✚ in the **Solver Options and Model Specifications** task pane (Figure 12.14)

Step 4. Under **Variables**, select **Normal**
   Select cells B14:C14
   Click the **Add** button ✚ in the **Solver Options and Model Specifications** task pane

Step 5. Under **Constraints,** select **Normal**
   Select cells F15:F17
   Click the **Add** button ✚ in the **Solver Options and Model Specifications** task pane
   When the **Add Constraint** dialog box appears:
   Select **<=** from the drop-down button
   Enter *G15:G17* in the **Constraint:** area
   Click **OK**

Step 6. Under **Constraints**, select **Integers**
   Select cells B14:C14
   Click the **Add** button ✚ in the **Solver Options and Model Specifications** task pane
   In the **Add Constraint** dialog box, from the drop down list select **int**
   Click **OK**

FIGURE 12.13 Eastborne Realty Spreadsheet Model

	A	B	C	D	E	F	G
1	Eastborne Realty Problem						
2	Parameters						
3		Townhouse	Apt. Bldg.				
4	Price ($000)	282	400			Funds Avl. ($000)	2000
5	Mgr. Time	4	40			Mgr. Time Avl. (Hours)	140
6						Townhouses Avl.	5
7	Ann. Cash Flow ($000)	10	15				
8							
9							
10							
11	Model						
12		Number of					
13		Townhouses	Apt. Bldgs.				
14	Purchase Plan	4	2			Total Used	Total Available
15					Funds ($000)	=SUMPRODUCT(B4:C4,$B$14:$C$14)	=G4
16					Time (Hours)	=SUMPRODUCT(B5:C5,$B$14:$C$14)	=G5
17	Max Cash Flow ($000)	=SUMPRODUCT (B7:C7,B14:C14)			Townhouses	=B14	=G6
18							

	A	B	C	D	E	F	G
1	Eastborne Realty Problem						
2	Parameters						
3		Townhouse	Apt. Bldg.				
4	Price ($000)	$282	$400			Funds Avl. ($000)	$2,000
5	Mgr. Time	4	40			Mgr. Time Avl. (Hours)	140
6						Townhouses Avl.	5
7	Ann. Cash Flow ($000)	$10	$15				
8							
9							
10							
11	Model						
12		Number of					
13		Townhouses	Apt. Bldgs.				
14	Purchase Plan	4	2			Total Used	Total Available
15					Funds ($000)	$1,928	$2,000
16					Time (Hours)	96	140
17	Max Cash Flow ($000)	$70			Townhouses	4	5
18							

FIGURE 12.14	The Optimization Tree Structure in the Solver Options and Model Specifications Dialog Box

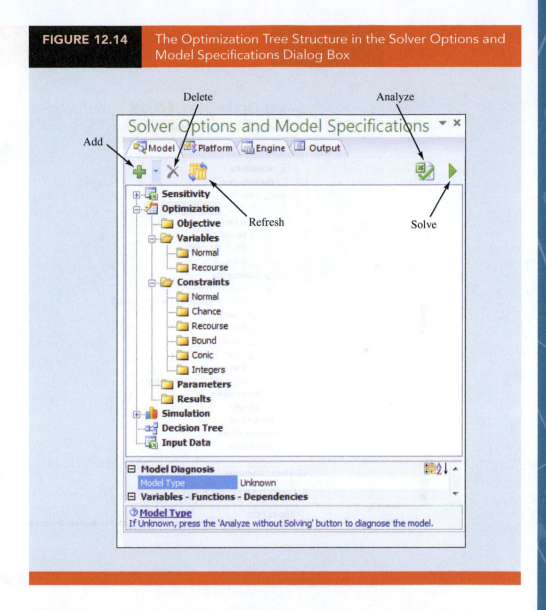

The **Solver Options and Model Specifications** pane should now appear as shown in Figure 12.15.

Upon clicking the Solve button, the Guided Mode dialog box will appear if ASP's Guided Mode is turned on. ASP's Guided Mode assists the analyst through the optimization process and can be turned off at the analyst's discretion.

Step 7. Click the **Engine** tab in the **Solver Options and Model Specifications** task pane
    Select the checkbox for **Automatically Select Engine**
       In the **General** area, click **Assume Non-Negative**
          Select **True** from the drop-down menu
Step 8. Click the **Model** tab in the **Solver Options and Model Specifications** task pane
Step 9. Click the **Solve** button ▶ in the **Solver Options and Model Specifications** task pane (see Figure 12.14)

The solution is sent to the spreadsheet, and the output appears under the **Output** tab in the **Solver Options and Model Specifications** pane, as shown in Figure 12.16.

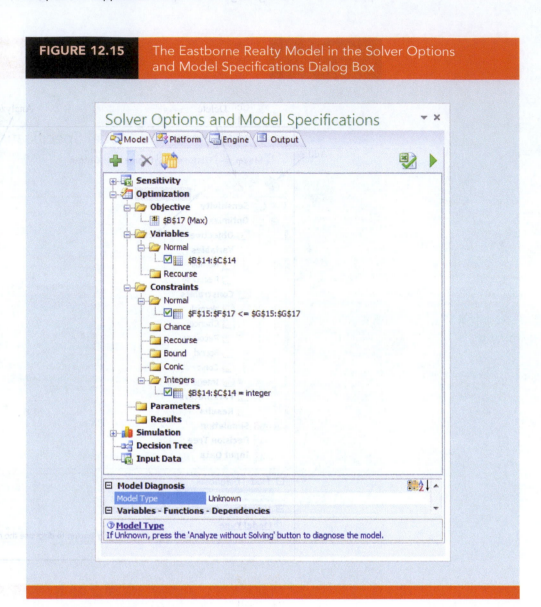

FIGURE 12.15   The Eastborne Realty Model in the Solver Options and Model Specifications Dialog Box

The output indicates that the optimal solution was found and that all constraints were satisfied. The solution should be same as when we solve the Eastborne Realty problem using standard Excel Solver as shown in Figure 12.2. The completed linear integer optimization model for the Eastborne Realty problem is contained in the file *EastborneModel*.

FIGURE 12.16   The Output from the Optimization from Analytic Solver Platform

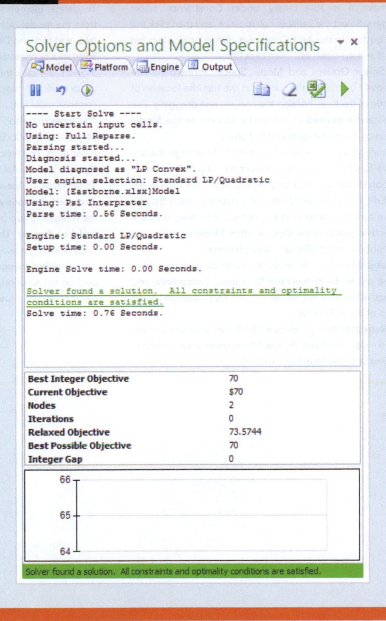

NOTES + COMMENTS

1. To make a variable binary, under **Constraints**, select **Integers**. Select the variable cell location and then click the **Add** button. In the **Add Constraint** dialog box, select *bin* from the drop-down list. Then click OK.

2. The **Solver Options and Model Specifications** pane can be moved by clicking the banner at the top (the location of the title of the box), holding the mouse, and dragging. The pane can be invoked or hidden by clicking on the **Model** button on the far left of the ASP Ribbon.

3. The default objective type is maximize. To change the objective function to minimize, select the objective function location in the optimization tree, right-click the mouse, select **Edit**, and then select **Min**. Alternatively, select the objective function location in the optimization tree, click the **Objective** button in the **Optimization Model** group in the ASP Ribbon, select **Min**, and select **Normal**.

4. The objective, variables, and constraints can also be added to the model by clicking the **Decisions**, **Constraints**, and **Objective** buttons, respectively, in the **Optimization Model** group of the ASP Ribbon.

5. The **Refresh** button 🔁 (Figure 12.14) should be used whenever a model has been changed (new constraints, variables, or other changes have been made).

6. To delete elements (variables, constraints, or objective) from the model, select the element from the optimization tree, and click the **Delete** button ✕ (Figure 12.14). To keep a variable or constraint in the model but have it ignored for a given run, click the box next to that element (the green check mark will disappear, indicating that it is not part of the current model run).

7. The **Analyze** button 📊 (Figure 12.14) provides an analysis of the model including number and types of variables and constraints. The report appears at the bottom of the **Solver Options and Model Specifications pane**.

8. To generate an Answer Report after solving the problem (as discussed previously in this chapter), select **Reports** from the Analysis group of the ASP Ribbon. Select **Optimization** and then **Answer**. The Sensitivity Report available for linear programs is not available for integer programs. To determine whether changes in the input parameters have an impact on the solution, the model must be resolved with the new parameter values.

Chapter 13

Nonlinear Optimization Models

CONTENTS

Intercontinental Hotels*

InterContinental Hotel Group (IHG) owns, leases, or franchises over 4,500 hotels in about 100 countries around the world. It offers over 700,000 guest rooms, more than any other hotel. InterContinental Hotels, Crowne Plaza Hotels and Resorts, Holiday Inn Hotels and Resorts, and Holiday Inn Express are some of InterContinental's brands.

Like airlines and rental car companies, hotels offer a perishable good; that is, hotels have a limited time window in which to sell the product, after which the value perishes. For example, an empty seat on an airline flight is of no value, as is a hotel room that goes empty overnight. In dealing with perishable goods, how to price them in such a way as to maximize revenue is a challenge. Price the hotel room too high, and it will sit empty overnight and generate zero revenue. Price the hotel room too low, the hotel will be filled, but revenue likely will be lower than it could

have been with higher pricing, even if fewer rooms were booked. *Revenue management* (RM) is a term used to describe analytical approaches to this pricing problem.

IHG developed a novel approach to the hotel room pricing problem that uses a nonlinear optimization model to determine prices to charge for its rooms. Each day, IHG searches the Internet to acquire competitors' prices. The competitors' prices are factored into IHG's pricing optimization model, which is run daily. The model is nonlinear because the objective function is to maximize contribution (revenue − cost), but both demand and revenue are a function of the price variable. Over 2,000 IHG hotels have started using this pricing model, and its use has led to increased revenue in excess of $145 million.

*Based on D. Kosuhik, J. A. Higbie, and C. Eister, "Retail Price Optimization at InterContinental Hotels Group," *Interfaces* 42, no. 1, (January–February 2012): 45–57.

Many business processes behave in a nonlinear manner. For example, the price of a bond is a nonlinear function of interest rates, and the price of a stock option is a nonlinear function of the price of the underlying stock. The marginal cost of production often decreases with the quantity produced, and the quantity demanded for a product is usually a nonlinear function of the price. These and many other nonlinear relationships are present in many business applications.

A **nonlinear optimization problem** is any optimization problem in which at least one term in the objective function or a constraint is nonlinear. In Section 13.1, we examine a production problem in which the objective function is a nonlinear function of the decision variables, similar to the Analytics in Action: Intercontinental Hotels. In Section 13.2, we discuss issues that make nonlinear optimization very different from linear optimization. Section 13.3 presents a nonlinear model for facility location. In Section 13.4, we present the Nobel Prize–winning Markowitz model for managing the trade-off between risk and return in the construction of an investment portfolio. In Section 13.5, we consider a well-known model that effectively forecasts sales or adoptions of a new product. The chapter appendix describes how to solve nonlinear optimization models using the Analytic Solver Platform.

13.1 A Production Application: Par, Inc. Revisited

We introduce constrained and unconstrained nonlinear optimization problems by considering an extension of the Par, Inc. linear program introduced in Chapter 11. We first consider the case in which the relationship between price and quantity sold causes the objective function to be nonlinear. The resulting unconstrained nonlinear program is then solved. As we shall see, the unconstrained optimal solution does not satisfy the production constraints of the original problem. Adding the production constraints back into the problem allows us to show the formulation and solution of a constrained nonlinear optimization model.

An Unconstrained Problem

Let us consider a revision of the Par, Inc. problem discussed in Chapter 11. Recall that Par, Inc. decided to manufacture standard and deluxe golf bags. In formulating the linear programming model for the Par, Inc. problem, we assumed that the company could sell all of the standard and deluxe bags it could produce. However, depending on the price of the golf bags, this assumption may not hold. An inverse relationship usually exists between price and demand. As price increases, the quantity demanded decreases. Let P_S denote the price Par, Inc. charges for each standard bag and P_D denote the price for each deluxe bag. Assume that the demand for standard bags, S, and the demand for deluxe bags, D, are given by:

$$S = 2{,}250 - 15P_S \qquad \text{(13.1)}$$

$$D = 1{,}500 - 5P_D \qquad \text{(13.2)}$$

The revenue generated from standard bags is the price of each standard bag, P_S, times the number of standard bags sold, S. If the cost to produce a standard bag is \$70, then the cost to produce S standard bags is 70S. Thus, the profit contribution for producing and selling S standard bags (revenue − cost) is:

$$P_S S - 70S = (P_S - 70)S. \qquad \text{(13.3)}$$

We can solve equation (13.1) for P_S to show how the price of a standard bag is related to the number of standard bags sold: $P_S = 150 - (1/15)S$. Substituting $150 - (1/15)S$ for P_S in equation (13.3), the profit contribution for standard bags is:

$$(P_S - 70)S = [150 - (1/15)S - 70]S = 80S - (1/15)S^2. \qquad \text{(13.4)}$$

Suppose that the cost to produce each deluxe golf bag is \$150. Using the same logic we used to develop equation (13.4), the profit contribution for deluxe bags is:

$$(P_D - 150)D = [300 - (1/5)D - 150]D = 150D - (1/5)D^2.$$

Total profit contribution is the sum of the profit contribution for standard bags and the profit contribution for deluxe bags. Thus, total profit contribution is written as:

$$\text{Total profit contribution} = 80S - (1/15)S^2 + 150D - (1/5)D^2. \qquad \text{(13.5)}$$

Note that the two linear demand functions, equations (13.1) and (13.2), give a nonlinear total profit contribution function, equation (13.5). This function is an example of a **quadratic function** because the nonlinear terms have an exponent of 2 (S^2 and D^2).

Details of how to use Excel Solver for nonlinear optimization are discussed in the next section.

Using Excel Solver, we find that the values of S and D that maximize the profit contribution function are $S = 600$ and $D = 375$. The corresponding prices are \$110 for standard bags and \$225 for deluxe bags, and the profit contribution is \$52,125. If all production constraints are also satisfied, these values provide the optimal solution for Par, Inc.

A Constrained Problem

In calculating the unconstrained optimal solution, we have ignored the production constraints discussed in Chapter 11. Recall that Par, Inc. has limited amounts of time available in each of four departments (cutting and dyeing, sewing, finishing, and inspection and packaging). We must enforce constraints that ensure that the amount of time used does not exceed the amount of time available in each of these departments. The problem that Par, Inc. must solve is to maximize the total profit contribution subject to all of the departmental labor hour constraints given in Chapter 11. The complete mathematical model for the Par, Inc. constrained nonlinear maximization problem is as follows:

$$\text{Max} \quad 80S - \tfrac{1}{15}S^2 + 150D - \tfrac{1}{5}D^2$$

s.t.

$\tfrac{7}{10}S +$	$1D \leq 630$	Cutting and dyeing
$\tfrac{1}{2}S +$	$\tfrac{5}{6}D \leq 600$	Sewing
$1S +$	$\tfrac{2}{3}D \leq 708$	Finishing
$\tfrac{1}{10}S +$	$\tfrac{1}{4}D \leq 135$	Inspection and packaging
$S, D \geq 0$		

The feasible region for the original Par, Inc. problem, along with the unconstrained optimal solution point (600, 375), is shown in Figure 13.1. The unconstrained optimum of (600, 375) is obviously outside the feasible region.

This maximization problem is exactly the same as the Par, Inc. problem in Chapter 11 except for the nonlinear objective function. The solution to this new constrained nonlinear maximization problem is shown in Figure 13.2.

In Figure 13.2 we see three profit contribution contour lines. Each point on the same contour line is a point of equal profit. Here, the contour lines show profit contributions of

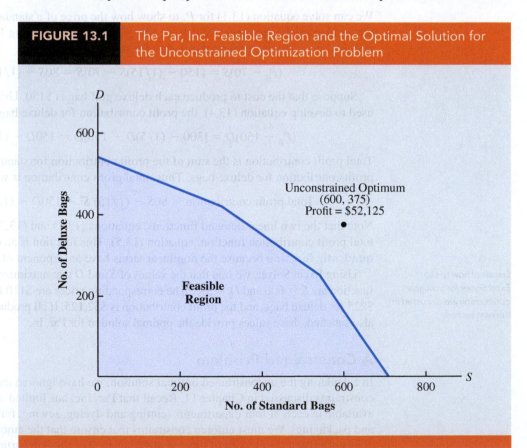

FIGURE 13.1   The Par, Inc. Feasible Region and the Optimal Solution for the Unconstrained Optimization Problem

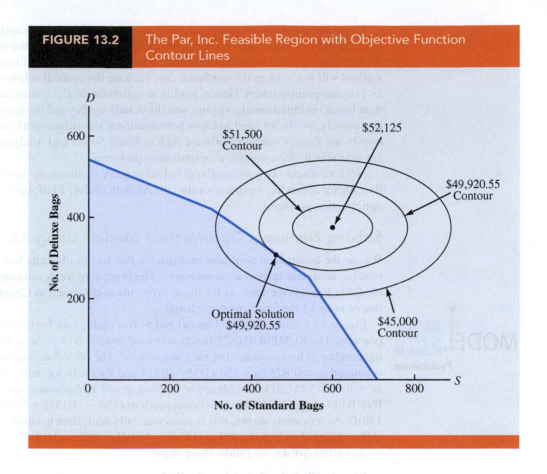

FIGURE 13.2   The Par, Inc. Feasible Region with Objective Function Contour Lines

$45,000, $49,920.55, and $51,500. In the original Par, Inc. problem described in Chapter 11, the objective function is linear, and thus the profit contours are straight lines. However, for the Par, Inc. problem with a quadratic objective function, the profit contours are ellipses.

Because part of the $45,000 profit contour line cuts through the feasible region, we know that an infinite number of combinations of standard and deluxe bags will yield a profit of $45,000. An infinite number of combinations of standard and deluxe bags also provide a profit of $51,500. However, none of the points on the $51,500 contour profit line is in the feasible region. As the contour lines move farther out from the unconstrained optimum of (600, 375) the profit contribution associated with each contour line decreases. The contour line representing a profit of $49,920.55 intersects the feasible region at a single point. Without showing all of the details in solving for this point, the point of intersection is 459.717 standard bags and 308.198 deluxe bags. This solution provides the maximum possible profit. No contour line that has a profit contribution greater than $49,920.55 will intersect the feasible region. Because the contour lines are nonlinear, the contour line with the highest profit can touch the boundary of the feasible region at any point, not just an extreme point. In the Par, Inc. case, the optimal solution is on the cutting and dyeing constraint line partway between two extreme points.

It is also possible for the optimal solution to a nonlinear optimization problem to lie in the interior of the feasible region. For instance, if the right-hand sides of the constraints in the Par, Inc. problem were all increased by a sufficient amount, the feasible region would expand so that the optimal unconstrained solution point of (600, 375) with a profit contribution of $52,125 in Figure 13.2 would be in the interior of the feasible region.

Many linear optimization algorithms (e.g., the simplex method) optimize by examining only the extreme points and selecting the extreme point that gives the best solution value. As the solution to the constrained nonlinear problem for Par, Inc. illustrates, such a method will not work in the nonlinear case because the optimal solution is generally not an extreme-point solution. Hence, nonlinear optimization algorithms are more complex than linear optimization algorithms, and the details are beyond the scope of this text. Fortunately, we do not need to know how nonlinear algorithms work; we just need to know how to use them. Computer software such as Excel Solver and Analytic Solver Platform are available to solve nonlinear optimization problems.

Next we discuss how to use Excel Solver to solve nonlinear optimization problems. In the chapter appendix, we discuss using the Analytic Solver Platform to solve nonlinear optimization problems.

Solving Nonlinear Optimization Models Using Excel Solver

We use the constrained nonlinear problem for Par, Inc. to illustrate how to use Excel Solver to solve nonlinear optimization problems. The procedure for developing and entering the model in Excel is the same as for linear problems as discussed in Chapter 11, except that one or more of the functions is nonlinear.

ParNonlinear

Figure 13.3 shows the Excel model and Solver dialog box for the nonlinear Par, Inc. problem. The SUMPRODUCT function is used in cells B19 through B22 to calculate the number of hours required in each department. The price function for standard bags is entered in cell B25 as =150-(1/15)*$B$14 and similarly for deluxe bags in cell D26 as =300-(1/5)*$C$14. The objective function in cell B16 contains the formula =(B25-B9)*B14+(B26-C9)*C14, which corresponds to $(150 - (1/15)S - 70)S + (300 - (1/5)D - 150)D$. As previously shown, this is mathematically equivalent to equation (13.5) because

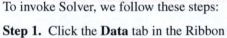

$(150 - (1/15)S - 70)S + (300 - (1/5)D - 150)D = 80S - (1/15) S^2 + 150D - (1/5) D^2$.

To invoke Solver, we follow these steps:

Step 1. Click the **Data** tab in the Ribbon
Step 2. Click **Solver** in the **Analyze** group
Step 3. When the **Solver Parameters** dialog box appears:
    Enter *B16* into the **Set Objective:** box
Step 4. Enter *B14:C14* into the **By Changing Variable Cells:** box area
Step 5. Click the **Add** button
    Enter *B19:B22* in the **Cell Reference:** box
    Select ≤ from the drop-down menu
    Enter *C19:C22* in the **Constraint:** box
    Click **OK**
Step 6. Select the **Make Unconstrained Variables Non-negative** option
Step 7. For **Select a Solving Method:** select **GRG Nonlinear** from the drop-down menu
Step 8. Click **Solve**
Step 9. When the **Solver Results** dialog box appears, click **OK**

ParNonlinearModel

The complete model for the constrained nonlinear Par, Inc. problem is contained in the file *ParNonlinearModel*.

The Answer Report generated by Excel Solver has the same structure as that of linear programs. Rather than show the Answer Report here, we refer to the optimal values shown in the spreadsheet in Figure 13.3. The optimal value of the objective function is $49,920.55, and this is achieved by producing 459.717 Standard bags and 308.198 Deluxe bags. This is the optimal point shown geometrically in Figure 13.2. Also, comparing cells C19 through C22 with D19 through D22 shows that only the cutting and dyeing constraint is binding, which is consistent with Figure 13.2.

FIGURE 13.3

FIGURE 13.3	Spreadsheet Model and Solver Parameters Dialog Box for the Nonlinear Par, Inc. Problem

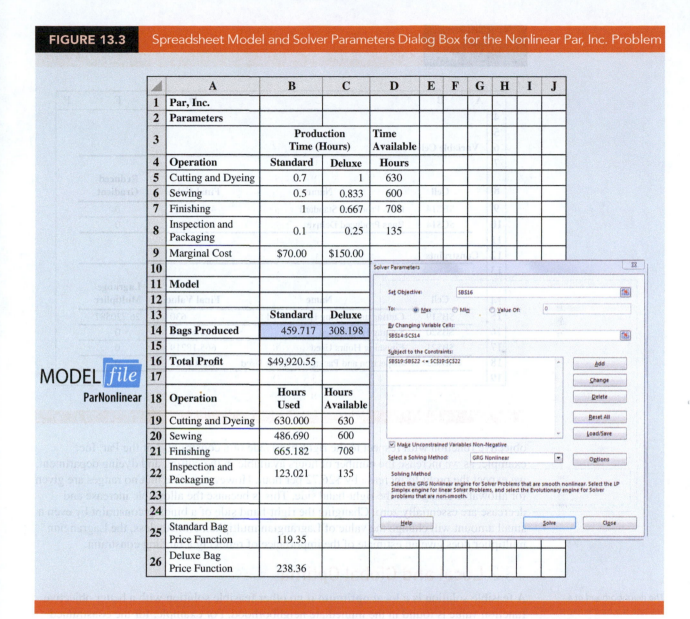

MODEL *file*

ParNonlinear

Sensitivity Analysis and Shadow Prices in Nonlinear Models

The Sensitivity Report for the nonlinear Par, Inc. problem is shown in Figure 13.4. As in the linear case, there are two sections: one for the variables and the other for constraints. The variables section gives the cell location, name, final (optimal) value, and **reduced gradient** for each variable. The reduced gradient is analogous to the reduced cost for linear models. It is essentially the shadow price of the nonnegativity constraint or, more generally, the shadow price of a binding simple lower or upper bound on the decision variable.

The constraint section gives the cell location, name, and final value for the left-hand side of each constraint. For the Par, Inc. problem, the final values are the amount of time in hours used in each of the four departments. The far right column gives the **Lagrangian multiplier** for each constraint. The Lagrangian multiplier is the shadow price for a constraint in a nonlinear problem. In other words, the Lagrangian multiplier is the rate of change of the

	Cell	Name	Final Value	Reduced Gradient
Variable Cells				
	$B$14	Bags Produced Standard	459.7166	0
	$C$14	Bags Produced Deluxe	308.19838	0

	Cell	Name	Final Value	Lagrange Multiplier
Constraints				
	$B$19	Cutting and Dyeing Hours Used	630	26.720587
	$B$20	Sewing Hours Used	486.69028	0
	$B$21	Finishing Hours Used	665.18219	0
	$B$22	Inspection and Packaging Hours Used	123.02126	0

objective function with respect to the right-hand side of a constraint. For the Par, Inc. example, as we increase the number of hours available in the cutting and dyeing department, we expect the profit to increase by $26.72 per hour. However, notice that no ranges are given for allowable changes to the right-hand side. This is because the allowable increase and decrease are essentially zero. Changing the right-hand side of a binding constraint by even a small amount will change the value of Lagrangian multiplier. Nonetheless, the Lagrangian multiplier does give an estimate of the importance of relieving a binding constraint.

13.2 Local and Global Optima

The neighborhood of a solution is a mathematical concept that refers to the set of points within a relatively close proximity of the solution. See Figure 13.7 for a graphical example of local minimums and local maximums.

All global optimal solutions are local optimal solutions, but not all local optimal solutions are global optimal solutions.

A feasible solution is a **local optimum** if no other feasible solution with a better objective function value is found in the immediate neighborhood. For example, for the constrained Par, Inc. problem, the local optimum corresponds to a local maximum; a point is a **local maximum** if no other feasible solution with a larger objective function value is in the immediate neighborhood. Similarly, for a minimization problem, a point is a **local minimum** if no other feasible solution with a smaller objective function value is in the immediate neighborhood.

Nonlinear optimization problems can have multiple local optimal solutions, which means we are concerned with finding the best of the local optimal solutions. A feasible solution is a **global optimum** if no other feasible point with a better objective function value is found in the feasible region. In the case of a maximization problem, the global optimum corresponds to a **global maximum**. A point is a global maximum if no other point in the feasible region gives a strictly larger objective function value. For a minimization problem, a point is a **global minimum** if no other feasible point with a strictly smaller objective function value is in the feasible region. A global maximum is also a local maximum, and a global minimum is also a local minimum.

FIGURE 13.5   A Concave Function $f(X, Y) = -X^2 - Y^2$

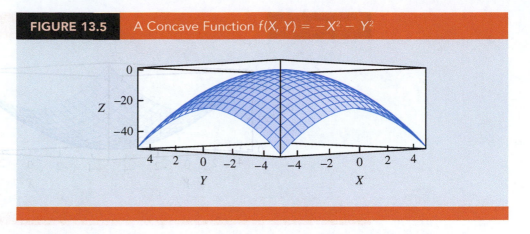

Nonlinear problems with multiple local optima are difficult to solve. But in many nonlinear applications, a single local optimal solution is also the global optimal solution. For such problems, we need to find only a local optimal solution. We will now present some of the more common classes of nonlinear problems of this type.

Consider the function $f(X, Y) = -X^2 - Y^2$. The shape of this function is illustrated in Figure 13.5. A function that is bowl-shaped down is called a **concave function**. The maximum value for this particular function is 0, and the point (0, 0) gives the optimal value of 0. The point (0, 0) is a local maximum; but it is also a global maximum because no point gives a larger function value. In other words, no values of X and Y result in an objective function value greater than 0. Functions that are concave, such as $f(X, Y) = -X^2 - Y^2$, have a single local maximum that is also a global maximum. This type of nonlinear problem is relatively easy to maximize.

The objective function for the nonlinear Par, Inc. problem is an example of a concave function:

$$80S - 1/15\, S^2 + 150D - 1/5D^2.$$

In general, if all the squared terms in a quadratic function have a negative coefficient and there are no cross-product terms, such as xy (or for the Par, Inc. problem, SD), then the function is a concave quadratic function. Thus, for the Par, Inc. problem, we are assured that the local maximum identified by Excel Solver in Figure 13.3 is the global maximum.

Let us now consider another type of function with a single local optimum that is also a global optimum. Consider the function $f(X, Y) = X^2 + Y^2$. The shape of this function is illustrated in Figure 13.6. It is bowl-shaped up and called a **convex function**. The minimum value for this particular function is 0, and the point (0, 0) gives the minimum value of 0. The point (0, 0) is a local minimum and a global minimum because no values of X and Y give an objective function value less than 0. Convex functions, such as $f(X, Y) = X^2 + Y^2$, have a single local minimum and are relatively easy to minimize.

For a concave function, we can be assured that if our computer software finds a local maximum, it has found a global maximum. Similarly, for a convex function, we know that if our computer software finds a local minimum, it has found a global minimum. However, some nonlinear functions have multiple local optima. For example, Figure 13.7 shows the graph of the following function over the feasible regions: $0 \leq X \leq 1, 0 \leq Y \leq 1$:

$$f(X,Y) = X\sin(5\pi X) + Y\sin(5\pi Y),$$

where sin is the trigonometric sine function, and π is approximately 3.1416. The hills and valleys in this graph show that this function has a number of local maximums and local minimums.

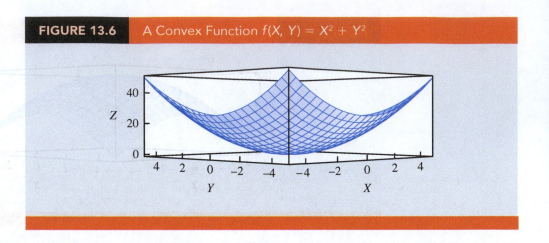

FIGURE 13.6 A Convex Function $f(X, Y) = X^2 + Y^2$

From a technical standpoint, functions with multiple local optima pose a serious challenge for optimization software; most nonlinear optimization software methods can get stuck and terminate at a local optimum. Unfortunately, many applications can be nonlinear with multiple local optima, and the objective function value for a local optimum may be much worse than the objective function value for a global optimum. Developing algorithms capable of finding the global optimum is currently an active research area.

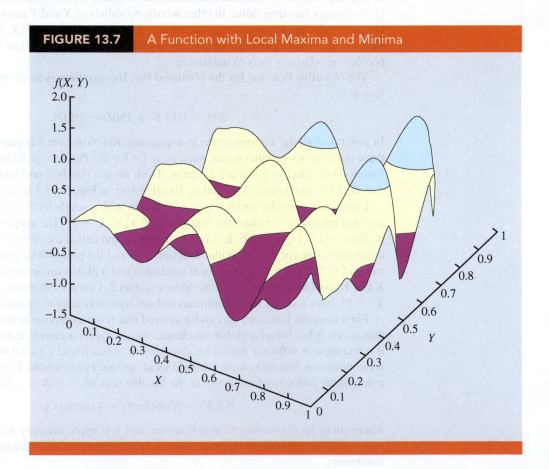

FIGURE 13.7 A Function with Local Maxima and Minima

Next we discuss a very practical approach to dealing with local maximums and local minimums when using Excel Solver for nonlinear problems.

Overcoming Local Optima with Excel Solver

How do you know when multiple local optima exist? The mathematical ways to determine this are beyond the scope of this text. From a practical point of view, if the solution obtained by optimization software depends on the starting point, then there are multiple local optima. Thus, when using Excel Solver, if the solution returned from Solver is different when starting from different values in the decision variable cells, then there are local optima. The converse is not necessarily true; that is, if the same solution is returned when starting from a different set of starting points, this does not necessarily mean that you have found the global optimal solution.

MODEL *file*

LocalOptima

Let us consider the problem shown in Figure 13.7:

$$\text{Max } f(X,Y) = X \sin(5\pi X) + Y \sin(5\pi Y)$$

s.t.

$$0 \leq X \leq 1$$

$$0 \leq Y \leq 1$$

Table 13.1 shows the results returned from Excel Solver for different starting points (values in the decision variable cells when Solver is invoked). In each of the five cases in Table 13.1, Solver returns with the message, "Solver has converged to the current solution. All constraints are satisfied."

Excel Solver does provide an option that allows you to increase the confidence that you have found a global optimal solution. Clicking **Options** on the **Solver Parameters** dialog box and then selecting the **GRG Nonlinear** tab results in the dialog box shown in Figure 13.8. Clicking the **Use Multistart** option in the **Multistart** section causes Solver to use multiple starting solutions and report the best solution found from all of the starting points. The **Population Size** is the number of starting points used. Solver selects starting points randomly using the **Random Seed** (an integer value) such that the points are within the bounds specified. Although providing simple lower and upper bounds is not required (unless the **Require Bounds on the Variables** option is selected), the procedure is much more effective when bounds are provided. We recommend selecting the **Require Bounds on the Variables** checkbox and providing bounds before you use the Multistart option.

TABLE 13.1	Solutions from Excel Solver for a Problem with Multiple Local Optima				
Starting Point			**Solution Returned**		
					Objective Function
X	**Y**		**X**	**Y**	**Value**
0.000	0.000		0.129	0.129	0.231
1.000	0.000		0.905	0.000	0.902
0.000	1.000		0.000	0.905	0.902
0.500	0.500		0.508	0.508	1.008
1.000	1.000		0.905	0.905	1.805

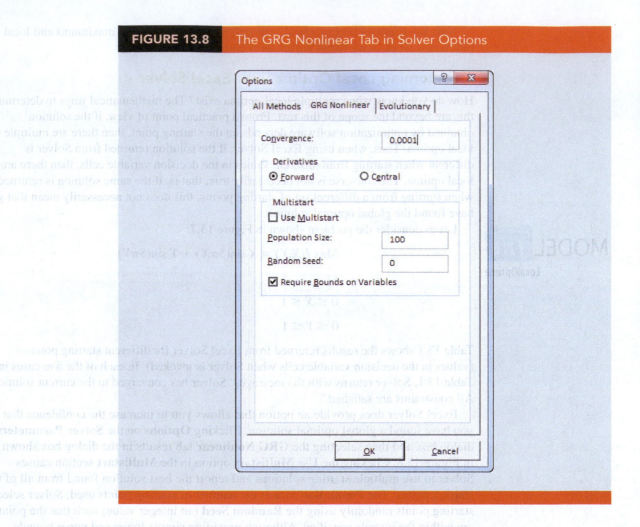

FIGURE 13.8   The GRG Nonlinear Tab in Solver Options

If the solution to a problem appears to depend on the starting values for the decision variables, we recommend you use the Multistart option.

In Figure 13.8, randomly generated starting points will be used and simple bounds of 0 and 1 have been specified as constraints in the Solver dialog box. The result reported by Solver is $X = 0.90447$, $Y = 0.90447$, with objective function = 1.804. The message provided by Solver is, "Solver converged in probability to a global solution."

N O T E S   +   C O M M E N T S

1. The Multistart option works best with bounds specified on each decision variable. It is often easy to calculate effective upper and lower bounds for the decision variables. For example, if you have a linear less-than-or-equal-to constraint with positive coefficients, upper bounds can be a calculated by simply dividing the right-hand side by the coefficient for each variable. Using the cutting and dyeing constraint from the Par, Inc. problem, $7/10\,S + 1D \le 630$, we can deduce the following upper bounds: $S \le 630/(7/10) = 900$ and $D \le 630/1 = 630$.

2. In addition to GRG Nonlinear, Excel Solver provides another solution method, Evolutionary Solver, to solve nonlinear problems with local optimal solutions. Evolutionary Solver is based on a method that searches for an optimal solution by iteratively adjusting a population of candidate solutions. In this text, we limit our discussion for nonlinear problems to GRG Nonlinear, which is based on more classical optimization techniques. However, Evolutionary Solver may be useful for more complex nonlinear models that involve Excel functions such as VLOOKUP and IF.

13.3 A Location Problem

Let us consider the case of LaRosa Machine Shop (LMS). LMS is studying where to locate its tool bin facility on the shop floor. The locations of the five production stations appear in Figure 13.9. In an attempt to be fair to the workers in each of the production stations, management has decided to try to find the position of the tool bin that would *minimize the sum of the distances* from the tool bin to the five production stations. We define the following decision variables:

$$X = \text{horizontal location of the tool bin}$$
$$Y = \text{vertical location of the tool bin}$$

MODEL *file*

LaRosa

We may measure the distance from a station to the tool bin located at (X, Y) by using Euclidean (straight-line) distance. For example, the distance from fabrication located at the coordinates $(1, 4)$ to the tool bin located at the coordinates (X, Y) is given by:

$$\sqrt{(X - 1)^2 + (Y - 4)^2}$$

The unconstrained optimization problem is as follows:

$$\text{Min} \quad (\sqrt{(X - 1)^2 + (Y - 4)^2} + \sqrt{(X - 1)^2 + (Y - 2)^2} + \sqrt{(X - 2.5)^2 + (Y - 2)^2} + \sqrt{(X - 3)^2 + (Y - 5)^2} + \sqrt{(X - 4)^2 + (Y - 4)^2})$$

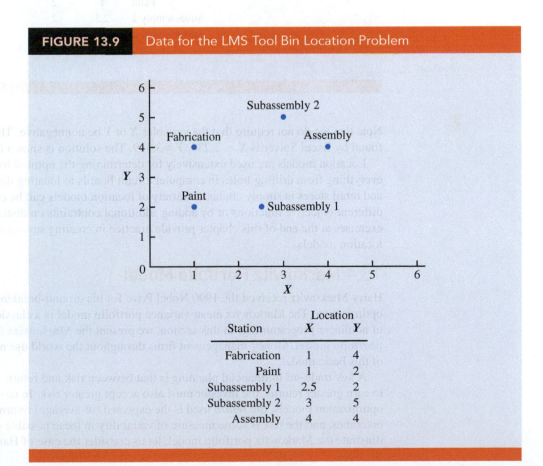

FIGURE 13.9 Data for the LMS Tool Bin Location Problem

Station	Location X	Y
Fabrication	1	4
Paint	1	2
Subassembly 1	2.5	2
Subassembly 2	3	5
Assembly	4	4

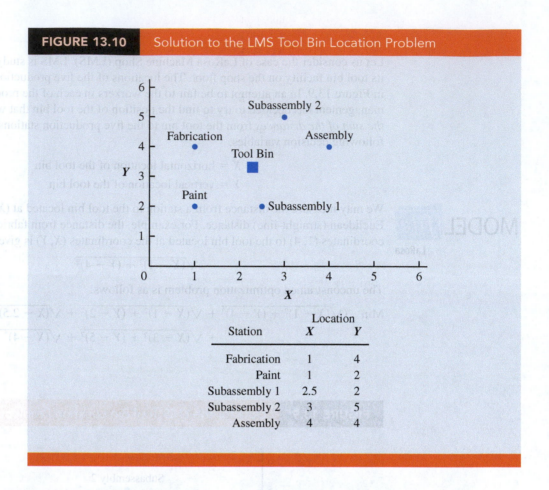

FIGURE 13.10 Solution to the LMS Tool Bin Location Problem

Station	Location	
	X	**Y**
Fabrication	1	4
Paint	1	2
Subassembly 1	2.5	2
Subassembly 2	3	5
Assembly	4	4

Note that we do not require that the variables X or Y be nonnegative. The optimal solution found by Excel Solver is $X = 2.230$, $Y = 3.349$. The solution is shown in Figure 13.10.

Location models are used extensively for determining the optimal locations for everything from drilling holes in computer circuit boards to locating distribution centers and retail stores in supply chains. A variety of location models can be created by using different objective functions or by adding additional contraints on distances traveled. The exercises at the end of this chapter provide practice in creating several different forms of location models.

13.4 Markowitz Portfolio Model

Harry Markowitz received the 1990 Nobel Prize for his ground-breaking work in portfolio optimization. The Markowitz mean-variance portfolio model is a classic application of nonlinear programming. In this section, we present the **Markowitz mean-variance portfolio model**. Money management firms throughout the world use numerous variations of this basic model.

A key trade-off in financial planning is that between risk and return. For a chance to earn greater returns, the investor must also accept greater risk. In most portfolio optimization models, the *return* used is the expected (or average) return of the possible outcomes, and the *risk* is some measure of variability in these possible outcomes. To illustrate the Markowitz portfolio model, let us consider the case of Hauck Investment Services.

TABLE 13.2	Mutual Fund Performances in Five Selected Years (Used as Planning Scenarios for the Next 12 Months)				
	Annual Return (%)				
Mutual Fund	**Year 1**	**Year 2**	**Year 3**	**Year 4**	**Year 5**
Foreign Stock	10.06	13.12	13.47	45.42	−21.93
Intermediate-Term Bond	17.64	3.25	7.51	−1.33	7.36
Large-Cap Growth	32.41	18.71	33.28	41.46	−23.26
Large-Cap Value	32.36	20.61	12.93	7.06	−5.37
Small-Cap Growth	33.44	19.40	3.85	58.68	−9.02
Small-Cap Value	24.56	25.32	−6.70	5.43	17.31

Hauck Investment Services designs annuities, IRAs, 401(k) plans, and other investment vehicles for investors with a variety of risk tolerances. Hauck would like to develop a portfolio model that can be used to determine an optimal portfolio involving a mix of six mutual funds. Table 13.2 shows the annual return (percent) for five 1-year periods for the six mutual funds. Year 1 represents a year in which all mutual funds yield good returns. Year 2 is also a good year for most of the mutual funds. But year 3 is a bad year for the small-cap value fund, year 4 is a bad year for the intermediate-term bond fund, and year 5 is a bad year for four of the six mutual funds.

It is not possible to predict the exact returns for any of the funds over the next 12 months, but the portfolio managers at Hauck Financial Services think that the returns for the five years shown in Table 13.2 are scenarios that can be used to represent the possibilities for the next year. For the purpose of building portfolios for their clients, Hauck's portfolio managers will choose a mix of these six mutual funds and assume that one of the five possible scenarios will describe the return over the next 12 months.

The portfolio construction problem is to determine how much of the portfolio to invest in each investment alternative. To determine the proportion of the portfolio that will be invested in each of the mutual funds we use the following decision variables:

FS = proportion of portfolio invested in the foreign stock mutual fund

IB = proportion of portfolio invested in the intermediate-term bond fund

LG = proportion of portfolio invested in the large-cap growth fund

LV = proportion of portfolio invested in the large-cap value fund

SG = proportion of portfolio invested in the small-cap growth fund

SV = proportion of portfolio invested in the small-cap value fund

Because the sum of these proportions must equal one, we need the following constraint:

$$FS + IB + LG + LV + SG + SV = 1.$$

The other constraints are concerned with the return that the portfolio will earn under each of the planning scenarios in Table 13.2.

The portfolio return over the next 12 months depends on which of the possible scenarios (years 1 through 5) in Table 13.2 occurs. Let R_1 denote the portfolio return if the scenario represented by year 1 occurs, R_2 denote the portfolio return if the scenario represented by year 2 occurs, and so on. The portfolio returns for the five planning years (scenarios) are as follows:

Scenario 1 return:

$$R_1 = 10.06FS + 17.64IB + 32.41LG + 32.36LV + 33.44SG + 24.56SV$$

Scenario 2 return:

$$R_2 = 13.12FS + 3.25IB + 18.71LG + 20.61LV + 19.40SG + 25.32SV$$

Scenario 3 return:

$$R_3 = 13.47FS + 7.51IB + 33.28LG + 12.93LV + 3.85SG - 6.70SV$$

Scenario 4 return:

$$R_4 = 45.42FS - 1.33IB + 41.46LG + 7.06LV + 58.68SG + 5.43SV$$

Scenario 5 return:

$$R_5 = -21.93FS + 7.36IB - 23.26LG - 5.37LV - 9.02SG + 17.31SV$$

If p_s is the probability of scenario s, among n possible scenarios, then the *expected* return for the portfolio is $\bar{R}$, where:

$$\bar{R} = \sum_{s=1}^{n} p_s R_s. \qquad (13.6)$$

If we assume that the five planning scenarios in the Hauck Financial Services model are equally likely to occur, then:

$$\bar{R} = \sum_{s=1}^{5} \tfrac{1}{5} R_s = \tfrac{1}{5} \sum_{s=1}^{5} R_s.$$

Measuring risk is a bit more difficult. Entire books are devoted to the topic of risk measurement. The measure of risk most often associated with the Markowitz portfolio model is the variance of the portfolio's return. If the expected return is defined by equation (13.6), the variance of the portfolio's return is:

$$Var = \sum_{s=1}^{n} p_s (R_s - \bar{R})^2. \qquad (13.7)$$

For the Hauck Financial Services example, the five planning scenarios are equally likely, thus:

$$Var = \sum_{s=1}^{n} \tfrac{1}{5} (R_s - \bar{R})^2 = \tfrac{1}{5} \sum_{s=1}^{n} (R_s - \bar{R})^2.$$

The portfolio variance is the average of the sum of the squares of the deviations from the mean value under each scenario. The larger this number, the more widely dispersed the scenario returns are about the average value. If the portfolio variance were equal to zero, then every scenario return R_i would be equal, and there would be no risk.

Two basic ways to formulate the Markowitz model are: (1) to minimize the variance of the portfolio subject to a constraint on the expected return of the portfolio, and (2) to maximize the expected return of the portfolio subject to a constraint on variance. Consider the first case. Assume that Hauck clients would like to construct a portfolio from the six mutual funds listed in Table 13.2 that will minimize their risk as measured by the portfolio variance. However, the clients also require the expected portfolio return to be at least 10%. In our notation, the objective function is:

$$\text{Min} \quad \tfrac{1}{5} \sum_{s=1}^{n} (R_s - \overline{R})^2.$$

The constraint on expected portfolio return is $\overline{R} \geq 10$. The complete Markowitz model involves 12 variables and 8 constraints (excluding the nonnegativity constraints).

$$\text{Min } \tfrac{1}{5} \sum_{s=1}^{5} (R_s - \overline{R})^2 \tag{13.8}$$

s.t.

$$10.06FS + 17.64IB + 32.41LG + 32.36LV + 33.44SG + 24.56SV = R_1 \tag{13.9}$$

$$13.12FS + 3.25IB + 18.71LG + 20.61LV + 19.40SG + 25.32SV = R_2 \tag{13.10}$$

$$13.47FS + 7.51IB + 33.28LG + 12.93LV + 3.85SG - 6.70SV = R_3 \tag{13.11}$$

$$45.42FS - 1.33IB + 41.46LG + 7.06LV + 58.68SG + 5.43SV = R_4 \tag{13.12}$$

$$-21.93FS + 7.36IB - 23.26LG - 5.37LV - 9.02SG + 17.31SV = R_5 \tag{13.13}$$

$$FS + IB + LG + LV + SG + SV = 1 \tag{13.14}$$

$$\tfrac{1}{5} \sum_{s=1}^{5} R_s = \overline{R} \tag{13.15}$$

$$\overline{R} \geq 10 \tag{13.16}$$

$$FS, IB, LG, LV, SG, SV \geq 0 \tag{13.17}$$

The objective for the Markowitz model is to minimize portfolio variance. Equations (13.9) through (13.13) define the return for each scenario. Equation (13.14) requires all of the money to be invested in the mutual funds; this constraint is often called the *unity constraint*. Equation (13.15) defines $\overline{R}$, which is the expected return of the portfolio. Equation (13.16) requires the portfolio return to be at least 10%. Finally, equation (13.17) requires a nonnegative investment in each Hauck mutual fund. Note that $R_1, R_2, R_3, R_4,$ and R_5, as well as $\overline{R}$, are not required to be nonnegative. It is possible that the return in a given scenario or the expected return of the portfolio is negative.

The solution for this model using a required return of at least 10% appears in Figure 13.11. The minimum value for the portfolio variance is 27.136. This solution implies that the clients will get an expected return of 10% ($\overline{R} \geq 10$) and minimize their risk as measured by portfolio variance by investing approximately 16% of the portfolio in the foreign stock fund (FS = 0.158), 53% in the intermediate bond fund (IB = 0.525), 4% in the large-cap growth fund (LG = 0.042), and 27% in the small-cap value fund (SV = 0.274).

The **Solver Parameters** dialog box is also shown in Figure 13.11. Note that we have selected **GRG Nonlinear** as the method and we have *not* selected **Make Unconstrained Variables Non-Negative**. Instead we have entered as an explicit constraint set that B17 through B22 must be ≥ 0.

MODEL *file*

HauckMarkowitz

The Markowitz portfolio model provides a convenient way for an investor to trade off risk versus return. In practice, this model is typically solved iteratively for different values of return. Figure 13.12 is a graph of the minimum portfolio variances versus required expected returns as required expected return is varied from 8% to 12% in increments of 1%. In finance, this graph is called the **efficient frontier**. Each point on the efficient frontier is the minimum possible risk (measured by portfolio variance) for the given return. By looking at the graph of the efficient frontier, investors can select the mean-variance combination with which they are most comfortable.

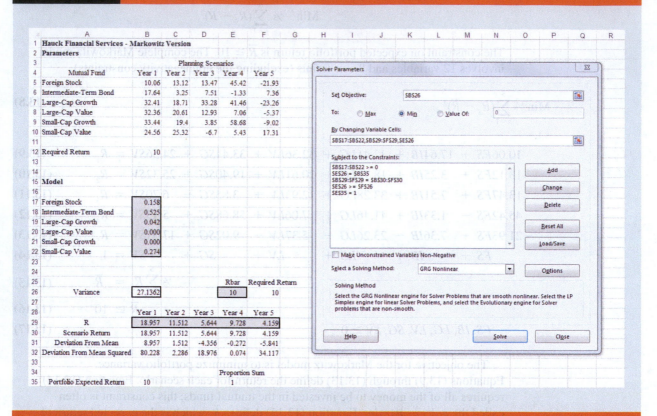

FIGURE 13.11 Solution for the Hauck Minimum Variance Portfolio with a Required Return of at Least 10%

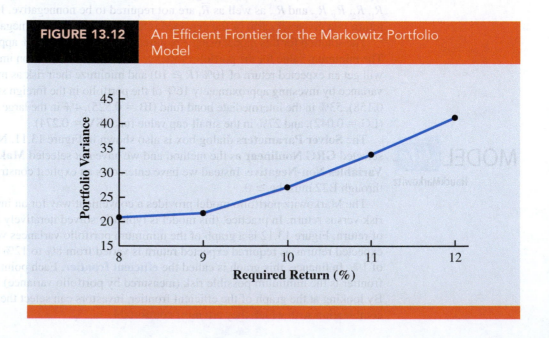

FIGURE 13.12 An Efficient Frontier for the Markowitz Portfolio Model

1. Notice that the solution given in Figure 13.11 has more than 50% of the portfolio invested in the intermediate-term bond fund. It may be unwise to let one asset contribute so heavily to the portfolio. Upper and lower bounds on the amount of an asset type in the portfolio can be easily modeled. Hence, upper bounds are often placed on the percentage of the portfolio invested in a single asset. Likewise, it might be undesirable to include an extremely small quantity of an asset in the portfolio. Thus, there may be constraints that require nonzero amounts of an asset to be at least a minimum percentage of the portfolio.

2. In the Hauck example, 100% of the available portfolio was invested in mutual funds. However, risk-averse investors often prefer to have some of their money in a so-called risk-free asset, such as U.S. Treasury bills. Thus, many portfolio optimization models allow funds to be invested in a risk-free asset.

3. In this section, portfolio variance was used to measure risk. However, variance, as it is defined, counts deviations both above and below the mean. Most investors are happy with returns above the mean but wish to avoid returns below the mean. Hence, numerous portfolio models allow for flexible risk measures. A problem at the end of this chapter illustrates the use of alternative risk measures.

4. In practice, both brokers and mutual fund companies adjust portfolios as new information becomes available. However, constantly adjusting a portfolio may lead to large transaction costs. The case problem at the end of this chapter requires you to develop a modification of the Markowitz portfolio selection problem to account for transaction costs.

13.5 Forecasting Adoption of a New Product

Forecasting new adoptions after a product introduction is an important marketing problem. In this section, we introduce a forecasting model developed by Frank Bass[1] that has proven to be particularly effective in forecasting the adoption of innovative and new technologies in the marketplace. Nonlinear optimization is used to estimate the parameters of the Bass forecasting model. The model has three parameters that must be estimated.

m = the number of people estimated to eventually adopt the new product.

A company introducing a new product is obviously interested in the value of parameter m.

q = the coefficient of imitation.

Parameter q measures the likelihood of adoption due to a potential adopter being influenced by someone who has already adopted the product. It measures the word-of-mouth or social media effect influencing purchases.

p = the coefficient of innovation.

Parameter p measures the likelihood of adoption, assuming no influence from someone who has already purchased (adopted) the product. It is the likelihood of someone adopting the product because of her or his own interest in the innovation.

Using these parameters, let us now develop the forecasting model. Let C_{t-1} denote the number of people who have adopted the product through time $t - 1$. Because m is the number of people estimated to eventually adopt the product, $m - C_{t-1}$ is the number of potential adopters remaining at time $t - 1$. We refer to the time interval between time $t - 1$ and time t as period t. During period t, some percentage of the remaining number of potential adopters, $m - C_{t-1}$, will adopt the product. This value depends on the likelihood of a new adoption.

---

[1]See Frank M. Bass, "A New Product Growth Model for Consumer Durables," *Management Science* 15 (1969).

Loosely speaking, the likelihood of a new adoption is the likelihood of adoption due to imitation plus the likelihood of adoption due to innovation. The likelihood of adoption due to imitation is a function of the number of people who have already adopted the product. The larger the current pool of adopters, the greater their influence through word of mouth. Because C_{t-1}/m is the fraction of the number of people estimated to adopt the product by time $t - 1$, the likelihood of adoption due to imitation is computed by multiplying this fraction by q, the coefficient of imitation. Thus, the likelihood of adoption due to imitation is:

$$q(C_{t-1}/m).$$

The likelihood of adoption due to innovation is simply p, the coefficient of innovation. Thus, the likelihood of adoption is:

$$p + q(C_{t-1}/m).$$

The Bass forecasting model given in equation (13.18) can be rigorously derived from statistical principles. Rather than providing such a derivation, we have emphasized the intuitive aspects of the model.

Using the likelihood of adoption we can develop a forecast of the remaining number of potential customers that will adopt the product during time period t. Thus, F_t, the forecast of the number of new adopters during time period t, is:

$$F_t = (p + q[C_{t-1}/m]) \, (m - C_{t-1}). \tag{13.18}$$

In developing a forecast of new adoptions in period t using the Bass model, the value of C_{t-1} will be known from past sales data. But we also need to know the values of the parameters to use in the model. Let us now see how nonlinear optimization is used to estimate the parameter values m, p, and q.

Consider Figure 13.13. This figure shows the graph of box office revenues (in $ millions) for two different films, an independent studio film and a summer blockbuster action movie, over the first 12 weeks after release. Strictly speaking, box office revenues for time period t are not the same as the number of adopters during time period t. However, the number of repeat customers is usually small, and box office revenues are a multiple of the number of moviegoers. The Bass forecasting model seems appropriate here.

FIGURE 13.13   Weekly Box Office Revenues for an Independent Studio Film and a Summer Blockbuster Movie

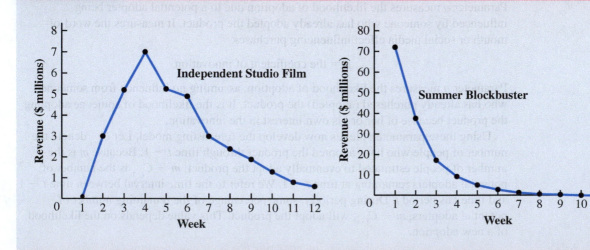

These two films illustrate drastically different adoption patterns. Note that revenues for the independent studio film grow until the revenues peak in week four and then decline. For this film, much of the revenue is obviously due to word-of-mouth influence. In terms of the Bass model, the imitation factor dominates the innovation factor, and we expect $q > p$. However, for the summer blockbuster, revenues peak in week 1 and drop sharply afterward. The innovation factor dominates the imitation factor, and we expect $q < p$.

The forecasting model given in equation (13.18) can be incorporated into a nonlinear optimization problem to find the values of p, q, and m that give the best forecasts for a set of data. Assume that N periods of data are available. Let us denote the actual number of adopters (or a multiple of that number, such as sales) in period t as C_t for $t = 1, \ldots, N$. Then the forecast in each period and the corresponding forecast error E_t is defined by:

$$F_t = (p + q[C_{t-1}/m])(m - C_{t-1}) \quad \text{and} \quad E_t = F_t - C_t.$$

Notice that the forecast error is the difference between the forecast value F_t and the actual value C_t. It is common statistical practice to estimate the parameters p, q, and m by minimizing the sum of squared errors.

Doing so for the Bass forecasting model leads to the following nonlinear optimization problem:

$$\text{Min} \sum_{t=1}^{N} E_t^2 \tag{13.19}$$

s.t.

$$F_t = (p + q[C_{t-1}/m])(m - C_{t-1}) \qquad t = 1, 2, \ldots, N \tag{13.20}$$

$$E_t = F_t - C_t \qquad t = 1, 2, \ldots, N \tag{13.21}$$

Because equations (13.19) and (13.20) both contain nonlinear terms, this model is a nonlinear minimization problem.

Note that the parameters of the Bass forecasting model are the decision variables in this nonlinear optimization model.

The data in Table 13.3 provide the revenue and cumulative revenues for the independent studio film in weeks 1–12. Using these data, the nonlinear model to estimate the parameters of the Bass forecasting model for the independent studio film follows:

$$\text{Min} \quad E_1^2 + E_2^2 + \cdots + E_{12}^2$$

$$\text{s.t.} \quad F_1 = (p)m$$

$$F_2 = [p + q(0.10/m)](m - 0.10)$$

$$F_3 = [p + q(3.10/m)](m - 3.10)$$

$$\vdots$$

$$F_{12} = [p + q(34.85/m)](m - 34.85)$$

$$E_1 = F_1 - 0.10$$

$$E_2 = F_2 - 3.00$$

$$\vdots$$

$$E_{12} = F_{12} - 0.60$$

The solutions to this nonlinear model and to a similar nonlinear model for the summer blockbuster are given in Table 13.4.

TABLE 13.3	Box Office Revenues and Cumulative Revenues in $ Millions for Independent Studio Film	
Week	**Revenues S_t**	**Cumulative Revenues C_t**
1	0.10	0.10
2	3.00	3.10
3	5.20	8.30
4	7.00	15.30
5	5.25	20.55
6	4.90	25.45
7	3.00	28.45
8	2.40	30.85
9	1.90	32.75
10	1.30	34.05
11	0.80	34.85
12	0.60	35.45

MODEL *file*

Bass

The optimal forecasting parameter values given in Table 13.4 are intuitively appealing and consistent with Figure 13.13. For the independent studio film, which has the largest revenues in week 4, the value of the imitation parameter q is 0.49; this value is substantially larger than the innovation parameter $p = 0.074$. The film picks up momentum over time because of favorable word of mouth. After week 4, revenues decline as more and more of the potential market for the film has already seen it. Contrast these data with the summer blockbuster movie, which has a negative value of -0.018 for the imitation parameter q and an innovation parameter p of 0.49. The greatest number of adoptions is in week 1, and new adoptions decline afterward. Obviously the word-of-mouth influence is not favorable.

In Figure 13.14, we show the forecast values based on the parameters in Table 13.4 and the observed values in the same graph. The Bass forecasting model does a good job of tracking revenue for the independent small-studio film. For the summer blockbuster, the Bass model does an outstanding job; it is virtually impossible to distinguish the forecast line from the actual adoption line.

You may wonder what good a forecasting model is if we must wait until after the adoption cycle is complete to estimate the parameters. One way to use the Bass forecasting model for a new product is to assume that sales of the new product will behave in a way that is similar to a previous product for which p and q have been calculated and to subjectively estimate m, the potential market for the new product. For example, one might assume that box office receipts for movies next summer will behave similarly to box office receipts for movies last summer. Then the p and q used for next summer's movies would be the p and q values calculated from the actual box office receipts last summer.

TABLE 13.4	Optimal Forecast Parameters for Independent Studio Film and Summer Blockbuster Movie	
Parameter	**Independent Studio Film**	**Summer Blockbuster**
p	0.074	0.460
q	0.490	−0.018
m	34.850	149.540

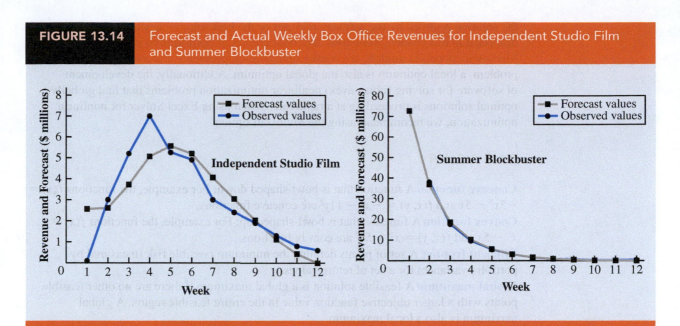

FIGURE 13.14 Forecast and Actual Weekly Box Office Revenues for Independent Studio Film and Summer Blockbuster

A second approach is to wait until several periods of data for the new product are available. For example, if five periods of data are available, the sales data for these five periods could be used to forecast demand for period 6. Then, after six periods of sales are observed, a forecast for period 7 is made. This method is often called *a rolling-horizon* approach.

N O T E S   +   C O M M E N T S

The optimization model used to determine the parameter values for the Bass forecasting model is an example of a difficult nonlinear optimization problem. It is neither convex nor concave. For such models, local optima may give values that are much worse than the global optimum. We recommend using the Multistart option in Excel Solver when solving such problems.

S U M M A R Y

In this chapter we introduced nonlinear optimization models. A nonlinear optimization model is a model with at least one nonlinear term in either a constraint or the objective function. Because so many applications of business analytics involve nonlinear functions, allowing nonlinear terms greatly increases the number of important applications that can be modeled as an optimization problem. Numerous problems in portfolio optimization, option pricing, marketing, economics, facility location, forecasting, and scheduling lend themselves to nonlinear models.

Unfortunately, nonlinear optimization models are not as easy to solve as linear optimization models, or even integer linear optimization models. As a rule of thumb, if a problem can be modeled realistically as a linear or integer linear problem, then it is probably best to do so. Many nonlinear formulations have local optima that are not globally optimal. Because most nonlinear optimization software terminates with a local optimum, the solution returned by the software may not be the best solution available. However, as discussed in this chapter, numerous important classes of optimization problems, such as the Markowitz portfolio models, are convex optimization problems. For a convex optimization problem, a local optimum is also the global optimum. Additionally, the development of software for solving (nonconvex) nonlinear optimization problems that find globally optimal solutions is proceeding at a rapid rate. When using Excel Solver for nonlinear optimization, we recommend using the Multistart option.

GLOSSARY

Concave function A function that is bowl-shaped down: For example, the functions $f(x) = -5x^2 - 5x$ and $f(x, y) = -x^2 - 11y^2$ are concave functions.

Convex function A function that is bowl-shaped up: For example, the functions $f(x) = x^2 - 5x$ and $f(x, y) = x^2 + 5y^2$ are convex functions.

Efficient frontier A set of points defining the minimum possible risk (measured by portfolio variance) for a set of return values.

Global maximum A feasible solution is a global maximum if there are no other feasible points with a larger objective function value in the entire feasible region. A global maximum is also a local maximum.

Global minimum A feasible solution is a global minimum if there are no other feasible points with a smaller objective function value in the entire feasible region. A global minimum is also a local minimum.

Global optimum A feasible solution is a global optimum if there are no other feasible points with a better objective function value in the entire feasible region. A global optimum may be either a global maximum or a global minimum.

Lagrangian multiplier The shadow price for a constraint in a nonlinear problem, that is, the rate of change of the objective function with respect to the right-hand side of a constraint.

Local maximum A feasible solution is a local maximum if there are no other feasible solutions with a larger objective function value in the immediate neighborhood.

Local minimum A feasible solution is a local minimum if there are no other feasible solutions with a smaller objective function value in the immediate neighborhood.

Local optimum A feasible solution is a local optimum if there are no other feasible solutions with a better objective function value in the immediate neighborhood. A local optimum may be either a local maximum or a local minimum.

Markowitz mean-variance portfolio model An optimization model used to construct a portfolio that minimizes risk subject to a constraint requiring a minimum level of return.

Nonlinear optimization problem An optimization problem that contains at least one nonlinear term in the objective function or a constraint.

Quadratic function A nonlinear function with terms to the power of two.

Reduced gradient Value associated with a variable in a nonlinear model that is analogous to the reduced cost in a linear model; the shadow price of a binding simple lower or upper bound on the decision variable.

PROBLEMS

1. GreenLawns provides a lawn fertilizing and weed control service. The company is adding a special aeration treatment as a low-cost extra service option that it hopes will help attract new customers. Management is planning to promote this new service in two media: radio and direct-mail advertising. A media budget of $3,000 is available for

this promotional campaign. Based on past experience in promoting its other services, GreenLawns has obtained the following estimate of the relationship between sales and the amount spent on promotion in these two media:

$$S = -2R^2 - 10M^2 - 8RM + 18R + 34M,$$

where

S = total sales in thousands of dollars

R = thousands of dollars spent on radio advertising

M = thousands of dollars spent on direct-mail advertising

GreenLawns would like to develop a promotional strategy that will lead to maximum sales subject to the restriction provided by the media budget.

a. What is the value of sales if $2,000 is spent on radio advertising and $1,000 is spent on direct-mail advertising?

b. Formulate an optimization problem that can be solved to maximize sales subject to the media budget of spending no more than $3,000 on total advertising.

c. Determine the optimal amount to spend on radio and direct-mail advertising. How much in sales will be generated?

2. The Cobb-Douglas production function is a classic model from economics used to model output as a function of capital and labor. It has the form:

$$f(L,C) = c_0 L^{c_1} C^{c_2},$$

where c_0, c_1, and c_2 are constants. The variable L represents the units of input of labor, and the variable C represents the units of input of capital.

a. In this example, assume $c_0 = 5$, $c_1 = 0.25$, and $c_2 = 0.75$. Assume each unit of labor costs $25 and each unit of capital costs $75. With $75,000 available in the budget, develop an optimization model to determine how the budgeted amount should be allocated between capital and labor in order to maximize output.

b. Find the optimal solution to the model you formulated in part (a). (*Hint:* When using Excel Solver, use the Multistart option with bounds $0 \leq L \leq 3,000$ and $0 \leq C \leq 1,000$.)

3. Let S represent the amount of steel produced (in tons). Steel production is related to the amount of labor used (L) and the amount of capital used (C) by the following function:

$$S = 20 L^{0.30} C^{0.70}.$$

In this formula L represents the units of labor input and C the units of capital input. Each unit of labor costs $50, and each unit of capital costs $100.

a. Formulate an optimization problem that will determine how much labor and capital are needed to produce 50,000 tons of steel at minimum cost.

b. Solve the optimization problem you formulated in part (a). (*Hint:* When using Excel Solver, start with an initial $L > 0$ and $C > 0$.)

4. The profit function for two products is:

$$\text{Profit} = -3x_1^2 + 42 x_1 - 3x_2^2 + 48x_2 + 700,$$

where x_1 represents units of production of product 1, and x_2 represents units of production of product 2. Producing one unit of product 1 requires 4 labor-hours, and producing one unit of product 2 requires 6 labor-hours. Currently, 24 labor-hours are available. The cost of labor-hours is already factored into the profit function, but it is possible to schedule overtime at a premium of $5 per hour.

a. Formulate an optimization problem that can be used to find the optimal production quantity of products 1 and 2 and the optimal number of overtime hours to schedule.

b. Solve the optimization model you formulated in part (a). How much should be produced and how many overtime hours should be scheduled?

5. Jim's Camera shop sells two high-end cameras, the Sky Eagle and Horizon. The demand for these two cameras are as follows: D_S = demand for the Sky Eagle, P_S is the selling price of the Sky Eagle, D_H is the demand for the Horizon, and P_H is the selling price of the Horizon.

$$D_S = 222 - 0.60P_S + 0.35P_H$$

$$D_H = 270 + 0.10P_S - 0.64P_H$$

The store wishes to determine the selling price that maximizes revenue for these two products. Develop the revenue function for these two models, and find the prices that maximize revenue.

6. Heller Manufacturing has two production facilities that manufacture baseball gloves. Production costs at the two facilities differ because of varying labor rates, local property taxes, type of equipment, capacity, and so on. The Dayton plant has weekly costs that can be expressed as a function of the number of gloves produced:

$$TCD(X) = X^2 - X + 5,$$

where X is the weekly production volume in thousands of units, and $TCD(X)$ is the cost in thousands of dollars. The Hamilton plant's weekly production costs are given by:

$$TCH(Y) = Y^2 + 2Y + 3,$$

where Y is the weekly production volume in thousands of units, and $TCH(Y)$ is the cost in thousands of dollars. Heller Manufacturing would like to produce 8,000 gloves per week at the lowest possible cost.

a. Formulate a mathematical model that can be used to determine the optimal number of gloves to produce each week at each facility.

b. Solve the optimization model to determine the optimal number of gloves to produce at each facility.

7. Many forecasting models use parameters that are estimated using nonlinear optimization. A good example is the Bass model introduced in this chapter. Another example is the exponential smoothing forecasting model discussed in Chapter 8. The exponential smoothing model is common in practice and is described in further detail in Chapter 8. For instance, the basic exponential smoothing model for forecasting sales is:

$$\hat{y}_{t+1} = \alpha y_t + (1 - \alpha)\hat{y}_t$$

where

$\hat{y}_{t+1}$ = forecast of sales for period $t + 1$

y_t = actual sales for period t

$\hat{y}_t$ = forecast of sales for period t

α = smoothing constant, $0 \leq \alpha \leq 1$

This model is used recursively; the forecast for time period $t + 1$ is based on the forecast for period t, $\hat{y}_t$, the observed value of sales in period t, y_t, and the smoothing parameter α. The use of this model to forecast sales for 12 months is illustrated in the following table with the smoothing constant $\alpha = 0.3$. The forecast errors, $y_t - \hat{y}_t$, are

Week (t)	Observed Value (y_t)	Forecast ($\hat{y}_t$)	Forecast Error ($y_t - \hat{y}_t$)	Squared Forecast Error ($y_t - \hat{y}_t)^2$
1	17	17.00	0.00	0.00
2	21	17.00	4.00	16.00
3	19	18.20	0.80	0.64
4	23	18.44	4.56	20.79
5	18	19.81	−1.81	3.27
6	16	19.27	−3.27	10.66
7	20	18.29	1.71	2.94
8	18	18.80	−0.80	0.64
9	22	18.56	3.44	11.83
10	20	19.59	0.41	0.17
11	15	19.71	−4.71	22.23
12	22	18.30	3.70	13.69
				SUM = 102.86

calculated in the fourth column. The value of α is often chosen by minimizing the sum of squared forecast errors. The last column of the table shows the square of the forecast error and the sum of squared forecast errors.

In using exponential smoothing models, one tries to choose the value of α that provides the best forecasts.

a. The file *ExpSmooth* contains the observed data shown here. Construct this table using the formula above. Note that we set the forecast in period 1 to the observed in period 1 to get started ($\hat{y}_1 = y_1 = 17$), then the formula above for $\hat{y}_{t+1}$ is used starting in period 2. Make sure to have a single cell corresponding to α in your spreadsheet model. After confirming the values in the table below with $\alpha = 0.3$, try different values of α to see if you can get a smaller sum of squared forecast errors.

b. Use Excel Solver to find the value of α that minimizes the sum of squared forecast errors.

8. Andalus Furniture Company has two manufacturing plants, one at Aynor and another at Spartanburg. The cost in dollars of producing a kitchen chair at each of the two plants is given here. The cost of producing Q_1 chairs at Aynor is:

$$75Q_1 + 5Q_1^2 + 100$$

and the cost of producing Q_2 kitchen chairs at Spartanburg is:

$$25Q_2 + 2.5Q_2^2 + 150.$$

Andalus needs to manufacture a total of 40 kitchen chairs to meet an order just received. How many chairs should be made at Aynor, and how many should be made at Spartanburg in order to minimize total production cost?

9. The economic order quantity (EOQ) model is a classical model used for controlling inventory and satisfying demand. Costs included in the model are holding cost per unit, ordering cost, and the cost of goods ordered. The assumptions for that model are that only a single item is considered, that the entire quantity ordered arrives at one time, that the demand for the item is constant over time, and that no shortages are allowed.

Suppose we relax the first assumption and allow for multiple items that are independent except for a budget restriction. The following model describes this situation:

Let D_j = annual demand for item j

C_j = unit cost of item j

S_j = cost per order placed for item j

i = inventory carrying charge as a percentage of the cost per unit

B = the maximum amount of investment in goods

N = number of items

The decision variables are Q_j, the amount of item j to order. The model is:

$$\text{Minimize} \sum_{j=1}^{N}\left[C_j D_j + \frac{S_j D_j}{Q_j} + iC_j\frac{Q_j}{2}\right]$$

s.t.

$$\sum_{j=1}^{N} C_j Q_j \leq B$$

$$Q_j \geq 0 \, j = 1, 2, \ldots, N$$

In the objective function, the first term is the annual cost of goods, the second is the annual ordering cost (D_j/Q_j is the number of orders), and the last term is the annual inventory holding cost ($Q_j/2$ is the average amount of inventory).

a. Set up a spreadsheet model for the following data:

	Item 1	Item 2	Item 3
Annual Demand	2,000	2,000	1,000
Item Cost	$100	$50	$80
Order Cost	$150	$135	$125
B = $20,000			
i = 0.20			

b. Solve the problem using Excel Solver. (*Hint:* For Solver to find a solution, you need to start with decision variable values that are greater than 0.)

10. Phillips Inc. produces two distinct products, A and B. The products do not compete with each other in the marketplace; that is, neither cost, price, nor demand for one product will impact the demand for the other. Phillips' analysts have collected data on the effects of advertising on profits. These data suggest that, although higher advertising correlates with higher profits, the marginal increase in profits diminishes at higher advertising levels, particularly for product B. Analysts have estimated the following functions:

Annual profit for product A = $1.2712 \, LN(X_A) + 17.414$

Annual profit for product B = $0.3970 \, LN(X_B) + 16.109$

where X_A and X_B are the advertising amount allocated to products A and B, respectively, in thousands of dollars, profit is in millions of dollars, and LN is the natural logarithm function. The advertising budget is $500,000, and management has dictated that at least $50,000 must be allocated to each of the two products.

(*Hint:* To compute a natural logarithm for the value X in Excel, use the formula = $LN(X)$. For Solver to find an answer, you also need to start with decision variable values greater than 0 in this problem.)

a. Build an optimization model that will prescribe how Phillips should allocate its marketing budget to maximize profit.

b. Solve the model you constructed in part (a) using Excel Solver.

DATA *file*
LaRosaDemand

11. Let us consider again the data from the LaRosa tool bin location problem discussed in Section 13.3.

a. Suppose we know the average number of daily trips made to the tool bin from each production station. The average number of trips per day are 12 for fabrication, 24 for Paint, 13 for Subassembly 1, 7 for Subassembly 2, and 17 for Assembly. It seems as though we would want the tool bin closer to those stations with high average numbers of trips. Develop a new unconstrained model that minimizes the sum of the *demand-weighted distance* defined as the product of the demand (measured in number of trips) and the distance to the station.

b. Solve the model you developed in part (a). Comment on the differences between the unweighted distance solution given in Section 13.3 and the demand-weighted solution.

12. TN Communications provides cellular telephone services. The company is planning to expand into the Cincinnati area and is trying to determine the best location for its transmission tower. The tower transmits over a radius of 10 miles. The locations that must be reached by this tower are shown in the following figure.

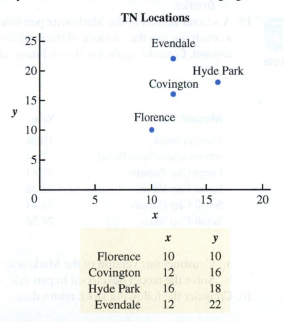

TN Locations

	x	y
Florence	10	10
Covington	12	16
Hyde Park	16	18
Evendale	12	22

TN Communications would like to find the tower location that reaches each of these cities and minimizes the sum of the distances to all locations from the new tower.

a. Formulate a model to find the optimal location.

b. Formulate and solve a model that minimizes the maximum distance from the transmission tower location to the city locations.

DATA *file*
Wedding

13. The distance between two cities in the United States can be approximated by the following formula, where lat_1 and $long_1$ are the latitude and longitude of city 1 and lat_2 and $long_2$ are the latitude and longitude of city 2:

$$69\sqrt{(lat_1 - lat_2)^2 + (long_1 - long_2)^2}$$

Ted's daughter is getting married, and he is inviting relatives from 15 different locations in the United States. The file *Wedding* gives the longitude, latitude, and number of relatives in each of the 15 locations. Ted would like to find a wedding location that minimizes the demand-weighted distance, where demand is the number of relatives at each location. Find the optimal location. (*Hint:* Notice that all longitude values given for this problem are negative. Make sure that you do *not* check the option for **Make Unconstrained Variables Non-Negative** in Solver.)

StockReturn1

14. Consider the stock return scenarios for Apple Computer (APPL), Advanced Micro Devices (AMD), and Oracle Corporation (ORCL) shown in the following table:

	1	2	3	4	5	6	7	8
APPL	−39.80	10.10	124.90	151.80	−58.30	14.30	−41.90	57.10
AMD	−42.50	13.60	56.90	36.70	−34.80	−67.40	183.60	6.30
ORCL	−10.20	137.90	170.60	16.60	−40.70	−30.30	15.20	−0.60

a. Develop the Markowitz portfolio model for these data with a required expected return of 25 percent. Assume that the eight scenarios are equally likely to occur.

b. Solve the model developed in part (a).

c. Vary the required return in 1% increments from 25% to 30%, and plot the efficient frontier.

HauckData

15. A second version of the Markowitz portfolio model maximizes expected return subject to a constraint that the variance of the portfolio must be less than or equal to some specified amount. Consider again the Hauck Financial Service data given in Section 13.4.

Mutual Fund	**Annual Return (%)**				
	Year 1	Year 2	Year 3	Year 4	Year 5
Foreign Stock	10.06	13.12	13.47	45.42	−21.93
Intermediate-Term Bond	17.64	3.25	7.51	−1.33	7.36
Large-Cap Growth	32.41	18.71	33.28	41.46	−23.26
Large-Cap Value	32.36	20.61	12.93	7.06	−5.37
Small-Cap Growth	33.44	19.40	3.85	58.68	−9.02
Small-Cap Value	24.56	25.32	−6.70	5.43	17.31

a. Construct this version of the Markowitz model for a maximum variance of 30.

b. Solve the model developed in part (a).

16. Consider the following stock return data:

	1	2	3	4	5	6
Stock 1	0.300	0.103	0.216	−0.046	−0.071	0.056
Stock 2	0.225	0.290	0.216	−0.272	0.144	0.107
Stock 3	0.149	0.260	0.419	−0.078	0.169	−0.035

StockReturn2

	7	8	9	10	11	12
Stock 1	0.038	0.089	0.090	0.083	0.035	0.176
Stock 2	0.321	0.305	0.195	0.390	−0.072	0.715
Stock 3	0.133	0.732	0.021	0.131	0.006	0.908

a. Construct the Markowitz portfolio model using a required expected return of 15%. Assume that the 12 scenarios are equally likely to occur.

b. Solve the model using Excel Solver.

c. Solve the model for various values of required expected return and plot the efficient frontier.

17. Let us consider again the investment data from Hauck Financial Services used in Section 13.4 to illustrate the Markowitz portfolio model. The data are shown below, along with the return of the S&P 500 Index. Hauck would like to create a portfolio using the funds listed, so that the resulting portfolio matches the return of the S&P 500 index as closely as possible.

Mutual Fund	Year 1	Year 2	Year 3	Year 4	Year 5
Foreign Stock	10.060	13.120	13.470	45.420	−21.930
Intermediate-Term Bond	17.640	3.250	7.510	−1.330	7.360
Large-Cap Growth	32.410	18.710	33.280	41.460	−23.260
Large-Cap Value	32.360	20.610	12.930	7.060	−5.370
Small-Cap Growth	33.440	19.400	3.850	58.680	−9.020
Small-Cap Value	24.560	25.320	−6.700	5.430	17.310
S&P 500 Return	25.000	20.000	8.000	30.000	−10.000

a. Develop an optimization model that will give the fraction of the portfolio to invest in each of the funds so that the return of the resulting portfolio matches as closely as possible the return of the S&P 500 Index. (*Hint:* Minimize the sum of the squared deviations between the portfolio's return and the S&P 500 Index return for each year in the data set.)

b. Solve the model developed in part (a).

18. As discussed in Section 13.4, the Markowitz model uses the variance of the portfolio as the measure of risk. However, variance includes deviations both below and above the mean return. Semivariance includes only deviations below the mean and is considered by many to be a better measure of risk.

a. Develop a model that minimizes semivariance for the Hauck Financial data given in the file *HauckData* with a required return of 10%. (*Hint:* Modify model (13.8)–(13.17). Define a variable d_s for each scenario and let $d_s \geq \overline{R} - R_s$ with $d_s \geq 0$. Then make the objective function: Min $\frac{1}{5} \sum_{s=1}^{5} d_s^2$.)

b. Solve the model you developed in part (a) with a required expected return of 10%.

19. Refer to Problem 15. Use the model developed there to construct an efficient frontier by varying the maximum allowable variance from 20 to 60 in increments of 5 and solving for the maximum return for each. Plot the efficient frontier and compare it to Figure 13.12.

20. The weekly box office revenues (in $ millions) for the summer blockbuster movie discussed in Section 13.5 follow. Use these data in the Bass forecasting model given by equations (13.19)–(13.21) to estimate the parameters p, q, and m.

Week	Revenues
1	72.39
2	37.93
3	17.58
4	9.57
5	5.39
6	3.13
7	1.62
8	0.87
9	0.61
10	0.26
11	0.19
12	0.35

DATA *file*

Blockbuster

The Bass forecasting model is a good example of a difficult-to-solve nonlinear program, and the answer you get may be a local optimum that is not nearly as good as the result given in Table 13.4. Solve the model using Excel Solver with the Multistart option, and see whether you can duplicate the results in Table 13.4.

CASE PROBLEM: PORTFOLIO OPTIMIZATION WITH TRANSACTION COSTS

Hauck Financial Services has a number of passive, buy-and-hold clients. For these clients, Hauck offers an investment account whereby clients agree to put their money into a portfolio of mutual funds that is rebalanced once a year. When the rebalancing occurs, Hauck determines the mix of mutual funds in each investor's portfolio by solving an extension of the Markowitz portfolio model that incorporates transaction costs. Investors are charged a small transaction cost for the annual rebalancing of their portfolio. For simplicity, assume the following:

- At the beginning of the time period (in this case one year), the portfolio is rebalanced by buying and selling Hauck mutual funds.
- The transaction costs associated with buying and selling mutual funds are paid at the beginning of the period when the portfolio is rebalanced, which, in effect, reduces the amount of money available to reinvest.
- No further transactions are made until the end of the time period, at which point the new value of the portfolio is observed.
- The transaction cost is a linear function of the dollar amount of mutual funds bought or sold.

Jean Delgado is one of Hauck's buy-and-hold clients. We briefly describe the model as it is used by Hauck for rebalancing her portfolio. The mix of mutual funds that are being considered for her portfolio are a foreign stock fund (*FS*), an intermediate-term bond fund (*IB*), a large-cap growth fund (*LG*), a large-cap value fund (*LV*), a small-cap growth fund (*SG*), and a small-cap value fund (*SV*). In the traditional Markowitz model, the variables are usually interpreted as the proportion of the portfolio invested in the asset represented by the variable. For example, *FS* is the proportion of the portfolio invested in the foreign stock fund.

However, it is equally correct to interpret FS as the dollar amount invested in the foreign stock fund. Then $FS = 25{,}000$ implies that $25{,}000 is invested in the foreign stock fund. Based on these assumptions, the initial portfolio value must equal the amount of money spent on transaction costs plus the amount invested in all the assets after rebalancing; that is:

$$\text{Initial portfolio value} = \text{amount invested in all assets after rebalancing}$$
$$+ \text{transaction costs.}$$

The extension of the Markowitz model that Hauck uses for rebalancing portfolios requires a balance constraint for each mutual fund. This balance constraint is:

$$\text{Amount invested in fund } i = \text{initial holding of fund } i$$
$$+ \text{amount of fund } i \text{ purchased} - \text{amount of fund } i \text{ sold.}$$

Using this balance constraint requires three additional variables for each fund: one for the amount invested prior to rebalancing, one for the amount sold, and one for the amount purchased. For instance, the balance constraint for the foreign stock fund is:

$$FS = FS\_START + FS\_BUY - FS\_SELL.$$

Jean Delgado has $100,000 in her account prior to the annual rebalancing, and she has specified a minimum acceptable return of 10%. Hauck plans to use the following model to rebalance Ms. Delgado's portfolio. The complete model with transaction costs is:

$$\text{Min } \tfrac{1}{5} \sum_{s=1}^{5} (R_S - \overline{R})^2$$

s.t.

$$0.1006FS + 0.1764IB + 0.3241LG + 0.3236LV + 0.3344SG + 0.2456SV = R_1$$
$$0.1312FS + 3.2500IB + 0.1871LG + 0.2061LV + 0.1940SG + 0.2532SV = R_2$$
$$0.1347FS + 0.0751IB + 0.3328LG + 0.1293LV + 0.385SG - 0.0670SV = R_3$$
$$0.4542FS - 0.0133IB + 0.4146LG + 0.0706LV + 0.5868SG + 0.0543SV = R_4$$
$$-0.2193FS + 0.0736IB - 0.2326LG - 0.0537LV - 0.0902SG + 0.1731SV = R_5$$

$$\tfrac{1}{5} \sum_{s=1}^{5} R_S = \overline{R}$$

$$\overline{R} \geq 10{,}000$$

$$FS + IB + LG + LV + SG + SV + TRANS\_COST = 100{,}000$$

$$FS\_START + FS\_BUY - FS\_SELL = FS$$
$$IB\_START + IB\_BUY - IB\_SELL = IB$$
$$LG\_START + LG\_BUY - LG\_SELL = LG$$
$$LV\_START + LV\_BUY - LV\_SELL = LV$$
$$SG\_START + SG\_BUY - SG\_SELL = SG$$
$$SV\_START + SV\_BUY - SV\_SELL = SV$$

$$TRANS\_FEE * (FS\_BUY + FS\_SELL + IB\_BUY + IB\_SELL +$$
$$LG\_BUY + LG\_SELL + LV\_BUY + LV\_SELL + SG\_BUY +$$
$$SG\_SELL + SV\_BUY + SV\_SELL) = TRANS\_COST$$

$$FS\_START = 10{,}000$$
$$IB\_START = 10{,}000$$

$$LG\_START = 10{,}000$$
$$LV\_START = 40{,}000$$
$$SG\_START = 10{,}000$$
$$SV\_START = 20{,}000$$
$$TRANS\_FEE = 0.01$$
$$FS, IB, LG, LV, SG, SV \geq 0$$

Notice that the transaction fee is set at 1% in the model (the last constraint) and that the transaction cost for buying and selling shares of the mutual funds is a linear function of the amount bought and sold. With this model, the transaction costs are deducted from the client's account at the time of rebalancing and thus reduce the amount of money invested. The solution for Ms. Delgado's rebalancing problem is shown as part of the Managerial Report.

Managerial Report

Assume that you are a financial analytics specialist newly hired by Hauck Financial Services. One of your first tasks is to review the portfolio rebalancing model in order to resolve a dispute with Jean Delgado. Ms. Delgado has had one of the Hauck passively managed portfolios for the past five years and has complained that she is not getting the rate of return of 10% that she specified. After reviewing her annual statements for the past five years, she feels that she is actually getting less than 10% on average.

1. According to the following Model Solution, $IB\_BUY = \$41{,}268.51$. How much in transaction costs did Ms. Delgado pay for purchasing additional shares of the intermediate-term bond fund?

MODEL SOLUTION

Optimal	Objective Value
	27219457.356

Variable	Value	Variable	Value
R_1	18953.280	IB_START	10000.000
$\overline{R}$	10000.000	IB_BUY	41268.510
R_2	11569.210	IB_SELL	0.000
R_3	5663.961	LG_START	10000.000
R_4	9693.921	LG_BUY	0.000
R_5	4119.631	LG_SELL	5060.688
FS	15026.860	LV_START	40000.000
IB	51268.510	LV_BUY	0.000
LG	4939.312	LV_SELL	40000.000
LV	0.000	SG_START	10000.000
SG	0.000	SG_BUY	0.000
SV	27675.000	SG_SELL	10000.000
TRANS_COST	1090.311	SV_START	20000.000
FS_START	10000.000	SV_BUY	7675.004
FS_BUY	5026.863	SV_SELL	0.000
FS_SELL	0.000	TRANS_FEE	0.010

2. Based on the Model Solution, what is the total transaction cost associated with rebalancing Ms. Delgado's portfolio?
3. After paying transactions costs, how much did Ms. Delgado have invested in mutual funds after her portfolio was rebalanced?
4. According to the Model Solution, $IB = \$51,268.51$. How much can Ms. Delgado expect to have in the intermediate-term bond fund at the end of the year?
5. According to the Model Solution, the expected return of the portfolio is $10,000. What is the expected dollar amount in Ms. Delgado's portfolio at the end of the year? Can she expect to earn 10% on the $100,000 she had at the beginning of the year?
6. It is now time to prepare a report to management to explain why Ms. Delgado did not earn 10% each year on her investment. Make a recommendation in terms of a revised portfolio model that can be used so that Jean Delgado can have an expected portfolio balance of $110,000 at the end of next year. Prepare a report that includes a modified optimization model that will give an expected return of 10% on the amount of money available at the beginning of the year before paying the transaction costs. Explain why the current model does not do this.
7. Solve the formulation in part (6) for Jean Delgado. How does the portfolio composition differ from that of the Model Solution?

Chapter 13 Appendix

Appendix 13.1 Solving Nonlinear Optimization Problems with Analytic Solver Platform

In this appendix, we illustrate how to use Analytic Solver Platform (ASP) to solve nonlinear optimization problems in Excel. We assume that ASP has been installed.

In the Par, Inc. problem, the nonlinear optimization model we developed is:

Let S = the number of standard bags to produce
D = the number of deluxe bags to produce

$$\text{Max} \quad 80S - \tfrac{1}{15}S^2 + 150D - \tfrac{1}{5}D^2$$

s.t.

$$\tfrac{7}{10}S + 1D \le 630 \qquad \text{Cutting and dyeing}$$
$$\tfrac{1}{2}S + \tfrac{5}{6}D \le 600 \qquad \text{Sewing}$$
$$1S + \tfrac{2}{3}D \le 708 \qquad \text{Finishing}$$
$$\tfrac{1}{10}S + \tfrac{1}{4}D \le 135 \qquad \text{Inspection and packaging}$$
$$S, D \ge 0$$

The spreadsheet model is shown in Figure 13.15.

Open the file *ParNonlinear*. To solve the Par, Inc. problem using ASP, follow these steps:

Step 1. Click the **Analytic Solver Platform** tab in the Ribbon

Step 2. When the **Solver Options and Model Specifications** task pane appears, select the ⊞ next to **Optimization** to expand the tree structure (If the task pane is not visible, click **Model** in the **Model** group to activate this pane.)

Step 3. When the optimization tree structure appears (Figure 13.16):
Select **Objective**
Select cell B16
Click the **Add** button ✚ in the **Solver Options and Model Specifications** task pane (Figure 13.16)

Step 4. Under **Variables**, select **Normal**
Select cells B14:C14
Click the **Add** button ✚ in the **Solver Options and Model Specifications** task pane

Step 5. Under **Constraints**, select **Normal**
Select cells B19:B22
Click the **Add** button ✚ in the **Solver Options and Model Specifications** task pane
When the **Add Constraint** dialog box appears:
Select <= from the drop-down button
Enter *C19:C22* in the **Constraint** area
Click **OK**

MODEL *file*

ParNonlinear

FIGURE 13.15 Excel Spreadsheet Model for Par, Inc.

	A	B	C	D
1	Par, Inc.			
2	Parameters			
3		Production Time (Hours)		Time Available
4	Operation	Standard	Deluxe	(Hours)
5	Cutting and Dyeing	0.7	1	630
6	Sewing	0.5	=5/6	600
7	Finishing	1	=2/3	708
8	Inspection and Packaging	0.1	0.25	135
9	Marginal Cost	70	150	
10				
11	Model			
12				
13		Standard	Deluxe	
14	Bags Produced	459.716599481298	308.198380121294	
15				
16	Total Profit	=(B25-B9)*B14+(B26-C9)*C14		
17				
18	Operation	Hours Used	Hours Available	
19	Cutting and Dyeing	=SUMPRODUCT(B5:C5,$B$14:$C$14)	=D5	
20	Sewing	=SUMPRODUCT(B6:C6,$B$14:$C$14)	=D6	
21	Finishing	=SUMPRODUCT(B7:C7,$B$14:$C$14)	=D7	
22	Inspection and Packaging	=SUMPRODUCT(B8:C8,$B$14:$C$14)	=D8	
23				
24				
25	Standard Bag Price Function	=150-(1/15)*$B$14		
26	Deluxe Bag Price Function	=300-(1/5)*$C$14		
27				

	A	B	C	D
1	Par, Inc.			
2	Parameters			
3		Production Time (Hours)		Time Available
4	Operation	Standard	Deluxe	(Hours)
5	Cutting and Dyeing	0.7	1	630
6	Sewing	0.5	0.833333333	600
7	Finishing	1	0.666666667	708
8	Inspection and Packaging	0.1	0.25	135
9	Marginal Cost	$70.00	$150.00	
10				
11	Model			
12				
13		Standard	Deluxe	
14	Bags Produced	459.7166	308.1984	
15				
16	Total Profit	$49,920.55		
17				
18	Operation	Hours Used	Hours Available	
19	Cutting and Dyeing	630.00	630	
20	Sewing	486.69	600	
21	Finishing	665.18	708	
22	Inspection and Packaging	123.02	135	
23				
24				
25	Standard Bag Price Function	119.35		
26	Deluxe Bag Price Function	238.36		

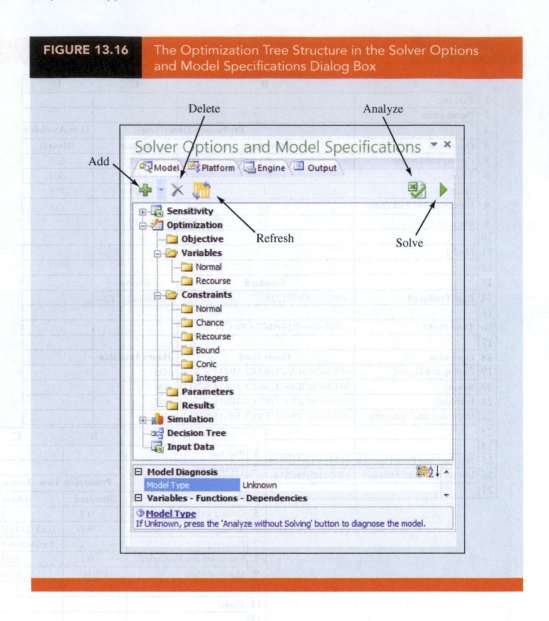

FIGURE 13.16   The Optimization Tree Structure in the Solver Options and Model Specifications Dialog Box

The **Solver Options and Model Specifications** dialog box should now appear as shown in Figure 13.17.

Upon clicking the Solve button, the Guided Mode dialog box will appear if ASP's Guided Mode is turned on. ASP's Guided Mode assists the analyst in the optimization process and can be turned off at the analyst's discretion.

Step 6. Click the **Engine** tab in the **Solver Options and Model Specifications** task pane
   Select the checkbox for **Automatically Select Engine**
   In the **General** area click **Assume Non-Negative**
      Select **True** from the drop-down menu
Step 7. Click the **Model** tab in the **Solver Options and Model Specifications** task pane
Step 8. To solve the problem, click the **Solve** button ▶ in the **Solver Options and Model Specifications** task pane (Figure 13.16)

The Par, Inc. Model in the Solver Options and Model Specifications Dialog Box

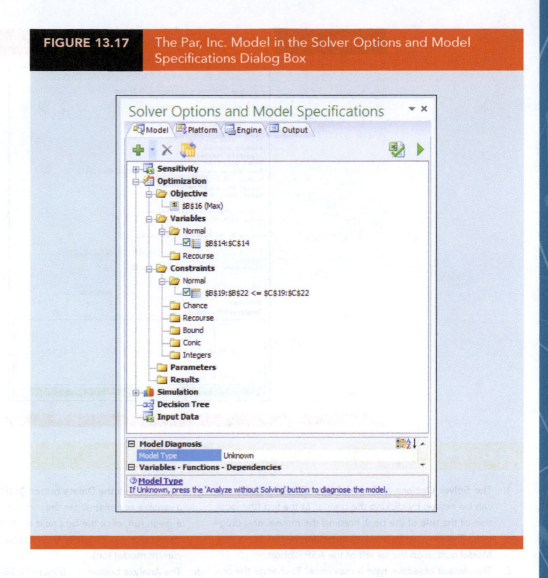

MODEL *file*

ParNonlinearModel

The solution is sent to the spreadsheet, and the output appears under the **Output** tab in the **Solver Options and Model Specifications** dialog box, as shown in Figure 13.18. The output indicates that the optimal solution was found and all constraints were satisfied. The solution should be the same as when we solved the problem using standard Excel Solver as shown in Figure 13.3. The complete model for the constrained nonlinear Par, Inc. problem is contained in the file *ParNonlinearModel*.

| FIGURE 13.18 | The Output from the Optimization from Analytic Solver Platform |

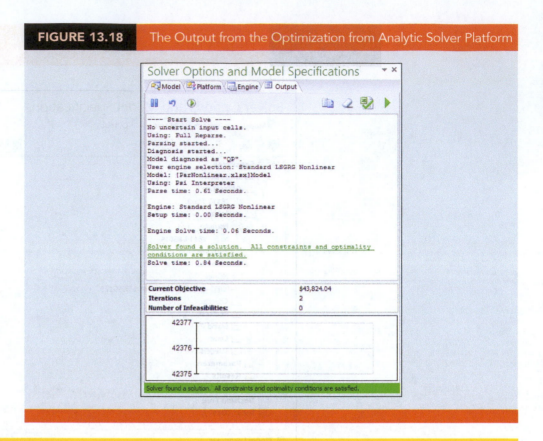

NOTES + COMMENTS

1. The **Solver Options and Model Specifications** task pane can be moved by clicking the banner at the top (the location of the title of the box), holding the mouse, and dragging. The box can be invoked or hidden by clicking on the **Model** button on the far left of the ASP Ribbon.

2. The default objective type is maximize. To change the objective function to minimize, select the objective function location in the optimization tree, right-click the mouse, select **Edit**, and then select **Min**. Alternatively, select the objective function location in the optimization tree, click the **Objective** button in the **Optimization Model** group in the ASP Ribbon, select **Min**, and select **Normal**.

3. The objective, variables, and constraints can also be added to the model by clicking the **Decisions**, **Constraints**, and **Objective** buttons, respectively, in the **Optimization Model** group of the ASP Ribbon.

4. The **Refresh** button 🔄 (Figure 13.16) should be used whenever a model has been changed (new constraints, variables, or other changes have been made).

5. To delete elements (variables, constraints, or objective) from the model, select the element from the optimization tree, and click the **Delete** button ✖ (Figure 13.16). To keep a variable or constraint in the model but have it ignored for a given run, click the box next to that element (the green checkmark will disappear, indicating it is not part of the current model run).

6. The **Analyze** button 📈 (Figure 13.16) provides an analysis of the model, including the number and types of variables and constraints. The report appears at the bottom of the **Solver Options and Model Specifications** dialog box.

7. To generate an Answer or Sensitivity Report as discussed in this chapter, after solving the problem, select **Reports** from the **Analysis** group of the ASP Ribbon. Select **Optimization** and then **Answer** for an Answer Report or **Sensitivity** for a Sensitivity Report.

8. To invoke the MultiStart option in ASP, click on the **Engine** tab, select **Standard LSGRG Nonlinear Engine** from the drop-down menu, and then, in the **Global Optimization** section, select **True** from the drop-down menu next to **MultiStart**.

Chapter 14

Monte Carlo Simulation

CONTENTS

ANALYTICS IN ACTION

Cook County Hospital ICU*

Every year in the United States, approximately two million patients acquire an infection after being admitted to a hospital. More than 100,000 of these patients die as a result of their hospital-acquired infections. This problem is expected to worsen as pathogens continue to develop greater resistance to antibiotics.

Two methods of decreasing the rate of hospital-acquired infections are: (1) patient isolation, and (2) greater adherence to hand-washing hygiene. If infected patients can be identified quickly, they can be quarantined to prevent larger outbreaks. Furthermore, proper hand washing can greatly reduce the number of pathogens present on the skin and thereby lead to fewer infections. Yet previous studies have found that less than half of all health workers completely and correctly follow hand-hygiene protocols.

A group of researchers used data from the intensive care unit (ICU) at Cook County Hospital in Chicago, Illinois, to create a simulation model of the movements of patients, health care workers, hospital visitors, and actual pathogens that lead to infections. The researchers were able to simulate both the creation of a new isolation ward in the ICU and better hand-hygiene habits. The simulation estimated rates of infection and impacts on hospital costs in each scenario.

The simulation showed that both patient isolation and better hand hygiene can greatly reduce infection rates. Improving hand hygiene is considerably cheaper than building and maintaining additional quarantine facilities, but the researchers point out that even the best simulations do not consider the psychological responses of health care workers. The simulation cannot detect why hand-hygiene compliance is currently low, so improving adherence in practice could be challenging.

*From R. Hagtvedt, P. Griffin, P. Keskinocak, and R. Roberts, "A Simulation Model to Compare Strategies for the Reduction of Health-Care-Associated Infections," *Interfaces* 39, no. 3 (May–June 2009).

Monte Carlo simulation originated during World War II as part of the Manhattan Project to develop nuclear weapons. "Monte Carlo" was selected as the code name for the classified method in reference to the famous Monte Carlo casino in Monaco and the uncertainties inherent in gambling.

Uncertainty pervades decision making in business, government, and our personal lives. This chapter introduces the use of **Monte Carlo simulation** to evaluate the impact of uncertainty on a decision. Simulation models have been successfully used in a variety of disciplines. Financial applications include investment planning, project selection, and option pricing. Marketing applications include new product development and the timing of market entry for a product. Management applications include project management, inventory ordering (especially important for seasonal products), capacity planning, and revenue management (prominent in the airline, hotel, and car rental industries). In each of these applications, uncertain quantities complicate the decision process.

As we will demonstrate, a spreadsheet simulation analysis requires a model foundation of logical formulas that correctly express the relationships between parameters and decisions to generate outputs of interest. A simulation model extends the spreadsheet modeling approach of Chapter 10 by replacing the use of single values for parameters with a range of possible values. For example, a simple spreadsheet model may compute a clothing retailer's profit, given values for the number of ski jackets ordered from the manufacturer and the number of ski jackets demanded by customers. A simulation analysis extends this model by replacing the single value used for ski jacket demand with a **probability distribution** of possible values of ski jacket demand. A probability distribution of ski jacket demand represents not only the range of possible values but also the relative likelihood of various levels of demand.

To evaluate a decision with a Monte Carlo simulation, an analyst identifies parameters that are not known with a high degree of certainty and treats these parameters as random, or uncertain, variables. The values for the **random variables** are randomly generated from the specified probability distributions. The simulation model uses the randomly generated values of the random variables and the relationships between parameters and decisions to compute the corresponding values of an output. Specifically, a simulation experiment produces a *distribution* of output values that correspond to the randomly generated values of the uncertain input variables. This probability distribution of the output values describes the range of possible outcomes, as well as the relative likelihood of each outcome. After reviewing the simulation results, the analyst is often able to make decision recommendations for the **controllable inputs** that address not only the *average* output but also the *variability* of the output.

In this chapter, we construct spreadsheet simulation models using only native Excel functionality. As we will show, the fundamental elements of simulation modeling can be executed in native Excel. However, there are many simulation software products that provide sophisticated simulation modeling features and automate the generation of outputs such as charts and summary statistics. Some of these software packages can be installed as Excel add-ins, including @RISK, Crystal Ball, and Analytic Solver Platform. In the appendices to this chapter, we demonstrate the features of the Excel add-in Analytic Solver Platform to construct spreadsheet simulation models.

14.1 Risk Analysis for Sanotronics LLC

When making a decision in the presence of uncertainty, the decision maker should be interested not only in the average, or expected, outcome, but also in information regarding the range of possible outcomes. In particular, decision makers are interested in **risk analysis**, that is, quantifying the likelihood and magnitude of an undesirable outcome. In this section, we show how to perform a risk analysis study for a medical device company called Sanotronics.

Sanotronics LLC is a start-up company that manufactures medical devices for use in hospital clinics. Inspired by experiences with family members who have battled cancer, Sanotronics's founders have developed a prototype for a new device that limits health care workers' exposure to chemotherapy treatments while they are preparing, administering, and disposing of these hazardous medications. The new device features an innovative design and has the potential to capture a substantial share of the market.

Sanotronics would like an analysis of the first-year profit potential for the device. Because of Sanotronics's tight cash flow situation, management is particularly concerned about the potential for a loss. Sanotronics has identified the key parameters in determining first-year profit: selling price per unit (p), first-year administrative and advertising costs (c_a), direct labor cost per unit (c_i), parts cost per unit (c_p), and first-year demand (d). After conducting market research and a financial analysis, Sanotronics estimates with a high level of certainty that the device's selling price will be $249 per unit and that the first-year administrative and advertising costs will total $1,000,000.

Sanotronics is not certain about the values for the cost of direct labor, the cost of parts, and the first-year demand. At this stage of the planning process, Sanotronics's base estimates of these inputs are $45 per unit for the direct labor cost, $90 per unit for the parts cost, and 15,000 units for the first-year demand. We begin our risk analysis by considering a small set of what-if scenarios.

Base-Case Scenario

Sanotronics's first-year profit is computed by:

$$\text{Profit} = (p - c_i - c_p) \times d - c_a. \tag{14.1}$$

Recall that Sanotronics is certain of a selling price of $249 per unit, and administrative and advertising costs total $1,000,000. Substituting these values into equation (14.1) yields:

$$\text{Profit} = (249 - c_i - c_p) \times d - 1,000,000. \tag{14.2}$$

Sanotronics's base-case estimates of the direct labor cost per unit, the parts cost per unit, and first-year demand are $45, $90, and 15,000 units, respectively. These values constitute the **base-case scenario** for Sanotronics. Substituting these values into equation (14.2) yields the following profit projection:

$$\text{Profit} = (249 - 45 - 90)(15{,}000) - 1{,}000{,}000 = 710{,}000.$$

Thus, the base-case scenario leads to an anticipated profit of $710,000.

Although the base-case scenario looks appealing, Sanotronics is aware that the values of direct labor cost per unit, parts cost per unit, and first-year demand are uncertain, so the base-case scenario may not occur. To help Sanotronics gauge the impact of the uncertainty, the company may consider performing a what-if analysis. A **what-if analysis** involves considering alternative values for the random variables (direct labor cost, parts cost, and first-year demand) and computing the resulting value for the output (profit).

Sanotronics is interested in what happens if the estimates of the direct labor cost per unit, parts cost per unit, and first-year demand do not turn out to be as expected under the base-case scenario. For instance, suppose that Sanotronics believes that direct labor costs could range from $43 to $47 per unit, parts cost could range from $80 to $100 per unit, and first-year demand could range from 0 to 30,000 units. Using these ranges, what-if analysis can be used to evaluate a **worst-case scenario** and a **best-case scenario**.

Worst-Case Scenario

The worst-case scenario for the direct labor cost is $47 (the highest value), the worst-case scenario for the parts cost is $100 (the highest value), and the worst-case scenario for demand is 0 units (the lowest value). Substituting these values into equation (14.2) leads to the following profit projection:

$$\text{Profit} = (249 - 47 - 100)(0) - 1{,}000{,}000 = -1{,}000{,}000.$$

So, the worst-case scenario leads to a projected *loss* of $1,000,000.

Best-Case Scenario

The best-case value for the direct labor cost is $43 (the lowest value), for the parts cost it is $80 (the lowest value), and for demand it is 30,000 units (the highest value). Substituting these values into equation (14.2) leads to the following profit projection:

$$\text{Profit} = (249 - 43 - 80)(30{,}000) - 1{,}000{,}000 = 2{,}780{,}000.$$

So the best-case scenario leads to a projected *profit* of $2,780,000.

At this point, the what-if analysis provides the conclusion that profits may range from a loss of $1,000,000 to a profit of $2,780,000 with a base-case profit of $710,000. Although the base-case profit of $710,000 is possible, the what-if analysis indicates that either a substantial loss or a substantial profit is also possible. Sanotronics can repeat this what-if analysis for other scenarios. However, simple what-if analyses do not indicate the likelihood of the various profit or loss values. In particular, we do not know anything about the probability of a loss. To conduct a more thorough evaluation of risk by obtaining insight on the potential magnitude and probability of undesirable outcomes, we now turn to developing a spreadsheet simulation model.

In Chapter 10, we discuss the use of Data Tables and Goal Seek in Excel for what-if analysis. However, these methods do not indicate the relative likelihood of the occurrence of different scenarios.

Sanotronics Spreadsheet Model

The first step in constructing a spreadsheet simulation model is to express the relationship between the inputs and the outputs with appropriate formula logic. Figure 14.1 provides

FIGURE 14.1   Excel Worksheet for Sanotronics

	A	B
1	**Sanotronics**	
2		
3	**Parameters**	
4	Selling Price per Unit	249
5	Administrative & Advertising Cost	1000000
6	Direct Labor Cost Per Unit	45
7	Parts Cost Per Unit	90
8	Demand	15000
9		
10	**Model**	
11	Profit	=((B4-B6-B7)*B8)-B5
12		

	A	B
1	**Sanotronics**	
2		
3	**Parameters**	
4	Selling Price per Unit	$249.00
5	Administrative & Advertising Cost	$1,000,000
6	Direct Labor Cost Per Unit	$45.00
7	Parts Cost Per Unit	$90.00
8	Demand	15,000
9		
10	**Model**	
11	Profit	$710,000.00

DATA *file*

Sanotronics

the formula and value views for the Sanotronics spreadsheet. Data on selling price per unit, administrative and advertising cost, direct labor cost per unit, parts cost per unit, and demand are in cells B4 to B8. The profit calculation, corresponding to equation (14.1), is expressed in cell B11 using appropriate cell references and formula logic. For the values shown in Figure 14.1, the spreadsheet model computes profit for the base-case scenario. By changing one or more values for the input parameters, the spreadsheet model can be used to conduct a manual what-if analysis (e.g., the best-case and worst-case scenarios).

Use of Probability Distributions to Represent Random Variables

Using the what-if approach to risk analysis, we manually select values for the random variables (direct labor cost per unit, parts cost per unit, and first-year demand), and then compute the resulting profit. Instead of manually selecting the values for the random variables, a Monte Carlo simulation randomly generates values for the random variables so that the values used reflect what we might observe in practice. A probability distribution describes the possible values of a random variable and the relative likelihood of the random variable realizing these values. The analyst can use historical data and knowledge of the random variable (range, mean, mode, standard deviation) to specify the probability distribution for a random variable. As we describe in the following paragraphs, Sanotronics researched the direct labor cost per unit, the parts cost per unit, and first-year demand to identify the respective probability distributions for these three random variables.

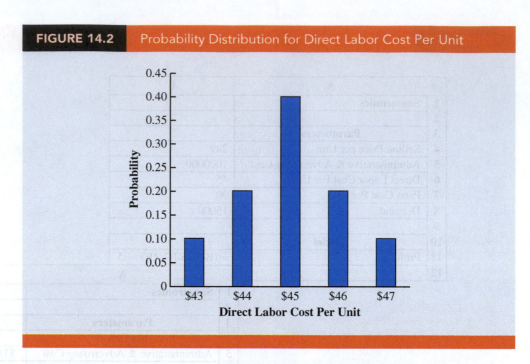

FIGURE 14.2   Probability Distribution for Direct Labor Cost Per Unit

Probability distributions are covered in more detail in Chapter 5.

Based on recent wage rates and estimated processing requirements of the device, Sanotronics believes that the direct labor cost will range from $43 to $47 per unit and is described by the discrete probability distribution shown in Figure 14.2. Thus, we see that there is a 0.1 probability that the direct labor cost will be $43 per unit, a 0.2 probability that the direct labor cost will be $44 per unit, and so on. The highest probability, 0.4, is associated with a direct labor cost of $45 per unit. Because we have assumed that the direct labor cost per unit is best described by a **discrete probability distribution**, the direct labor cost per unit can take on *only* the values of $43, $44, $45, $46, or $47.

Sanotronics is relatively unsure of the parts cost because it depends on many factors, including the general economy, the overall demand for parts, and the pricing policy of Sanotronics's parts suppliers. Sanotronics is confident that the parts cost will be between $80 and $100 per unit but is unsure as to whether any particular values between $80 and $100 are more likely than others. Therefore, Sanotronics decides to describe the uncertainty in parts cost with a uniform probability distribution, as shown in Figure 14.3.

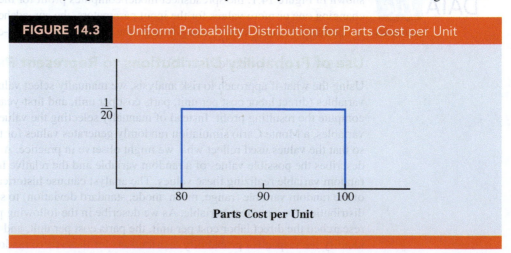

FIGURE 14.3   Uniform Probability Distribution for Parts Cost per Unit

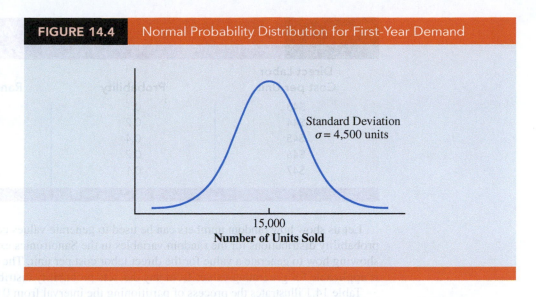

FIGURE 14.4   Normal Probability Distribution for First-Year Demand

Standard Deviation
$\sigma = 4{,}500$ units

15,000
Number of Units Sold

One advantage of simulation is that the analyst can adjust the probability distributions of the random variables to determine the impact of the assumptions about the shape of the uncertainty on the output measures.

Costs per unit between $80 and $100 are equally likely. A uniform probability distribution is an example of a **continuous probability distribution**, which means that the parts cost can take on *any* value between $80 and $100.

Based on sales of comparable medical devices, Sanotronics believes that first-year demand is described by the normal probability distribution shown in Figure 14.4. The mean or expected value of first-year demand is 15,000 units. The standard deviation of 4,500 units describes the variability in the first-year demand. The normal probability distribution is a continuous probability distribution in which any value is possible, but values extremely larger or smaller than the mean are increasingly unlikely.

Generating Values for Random Variables with Excel

To simulate the Sanotronics problem, we must generate values for the three random variables and compute the resulting profit. A set of values for the random variables is called a *trial*. Then we generate another trial, compute a second value for profit, and so on. We continue this process until we are satisfied that enough trials have been conducted to describe the probability distribution for profit. Put simply, simulation is the process of generating values of random variables and computing the corresponding output measures.

In the Sanotronics model, representative values must be generated for the random variables corresponding to direct labor cost per unit, the parts cost per unit, and the first-year demand. To illustrate how to generate these values, we need to introduce the concept of computer-generated random numbers.

Computer-generated random numbers[1] are randomly selected numbers from 0 up to, but not including, 1; this interval is denoted [0, 1). All values of the computer-generated random numbers are equally likely and so the values are uniformly distributed over the interval from 0 to 1. Computer-generated random numbers can be obtained using built-in functions available in computer simulation packages and spreadsheets. For example, placing the formula =RAND() in a cell of an Excel worksheet will result in a random number between 0 and 1 being placed into that cell.

---

[1]Computer-generated random numbers are formally called pseudorandom numbers because they are generated through the use of mathematical formulas and are therefore not technically random. The difference between random numbers and pseudorandom numbers is primarily philosophical, and we use the term *random numbers* even when they are generated by a computer.

TABLE 14.1 Random Number Intervals for Generating Value of Direct Labor Cost per Unit

Direct Labor Cost per Unit	Probability	Interval of Random Numbers
$43	0.1	[0.0, 0.1)
$44	0.2	[0.1, 0.3)
$45	0.4	[0.3, 0.7)
$46	0.2	[0.7, 0.9)
$47	0.1	[0.9, 1.0)

Let us show how random numbers can be used to generate values corresponding to the probability distributions for the random variables in the Sanotronics example. We begin by showing how to generate a value for the direct labor cost per unit. The approach described is applicable for generating values from any discrete probability distribution.

Table 14.1 illustrates the process of partitioning the interval from 0 to 1 into subintervals so that the probability of generating a random number in a subinterval is equal to the probability of the corresponding direct labor cost. The interval of random numbers from 0 up to but not including 0.1, [0, 0.1), is associated with a direct labor cost of $43; the interval of random numbers from 0.1 up to but not including 0.3, [0.1, 0.3), is associated with a direct labor cost of $44, and so on. With this assignment of random number intervals to the possible values of the direct labor cost, the probability of generating a random number in any interval is equal to the probability of obtaining the corresponding value for the direct labor cost. Thus, to select a value for the direct labor cost, we generate a random number between 0 and 1 using the RAND function in Excel. If the random number is at least 0.0 but less than 0.1, we set the direct labor cost equal to $43. If the random number is at least 0.1 but less than 0.3, we set the direct labor cost equal to $44, and so on.

Each trial of the simulation requires a value for the direct labor cost. Suppose that on the first trial the random number is 0.9109. From Table 14.1, because 0.9109 is in the interval [0.9, 1.0), the corresponding simulated value for the direct labor cost would be $47 per unit. Suppose that on the second trial the random number is 0.2841. From Table 14.1, the simulated value for the direct labor cost would be $44 per unit.

Each trial in the simulation also requires a value of the parts cost and first-year demand. Let us now turn to the issue of generating values for the parts cost. The probability distribution for the parts cost per unit is the uniform distribution shown in Figure 14.3. Because this random variable has a different probability distribution than direct labor cost, we use random numbers in a slightly different way to generate simulated values for parts cost. To generate a value for a random variable characterized by a continuous uniform distribution, the following Excel formula is used:

$$\text{Value of uniform random variable} = \text{lower bound} + (\text{upper bound} - \text{lower bound}) \times \text{RAND}(). \quad (14.3)$$

For Sanotronics, the parts cost per unit is a uniformly distributed random variable with a lower bound of $80 and an upper bound of $100. Applying equation (14.3) leads to the following formula for generating the parts cost:

$$\text{Parts cost} = 80 + 20 \times \text{RAND}(). \quad (14.4)$$

By closely examining equation (14.4), we can understand how it uses random numbers to generate uniformly distributed values for parts cost. The first term of equation (14.4) is 80 because Sanotronics is assuming that the parts cost will never drop below $80 per unit.

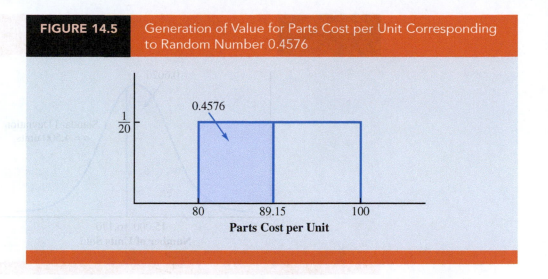

FIGURE 14.5 Generation of Value for Parts Cost per Unit Corresponding to Random Number 0.4576

Since RAND is between 0 and 1, the second term, $20 \times$ RAND(), corresponds to how much more than the lower bound the simulated value of parts cost is. Because RAND is equally likely to be any value between 0 and 1, the simulated value for the parts cost is equally likely to be between the lower bound $(80 + 0 = 80)$ and the upper bound $(80 + 20 = 100)$. For example, suppose that a random number of 0.4576 is obtained. As illustrated by Figure 14.5, the value for the parts cost would be:

$$\text{Parts cost} = 80 + 20 \times 0.4576 = 80 + 9.15 = 89.15 \text{ per unit.}$$

Suppose that a random number of 0.5842 is generated on the next trial. The value for the parts cost would be:

$$\text{Parts cost} = 80 + 20 \times 0.5842 = 80 + 11.68 = 91.68 \text{ per unit.}$$

With appropriate choices of the lower and upper bounds, equation (14.3) can be used to generate values for any uniform probability distribution.

Lastly, we need a procedure for generating the first-year demand from computer-generated random numbers. Because first-year demand is normally distributed with a mean of 15,000 units and a standard deviation of 4,500 units (see Figure 14.4), we need a procedure for generating random values from this normal probability distribution.

Once again we will use random numbers between 0 and 1 to simulate values for first-year demand. To generate a value for a random variable characterized by a normal distribution with a specified mean and standard deviation, the following Excel formula is used:

Equation (14.5) can be used to generate values for any normal probability distribution by changing the values specified for the mean and standad deviation, respectively.

$$\text{Value of normal random variable} = \text{NORM.INV(RAND(), mean, standard deviation).} \quad \textbf{(14.5)}$$

For Sanotronics, first-year demand is a normally distributed random variable with a mean of 15,000 and a standard deviation of 4,500. Applying equation (14.5) leads to the following formula for generating the first-year demand:

$$\text{Demand} = \text{NORM.INV(RAND(), 15000, 4500).} \quad \textbf{(14.6)}$$

Suppose that the random number of 0.6026 is produced by the RAND function; applying equation (14.6) then results in Demand = NORM.INV(0.6026, 15000, 4500) = 16,170 units. To understand how equation (14.6) uses random numbers to generate normally distributed values for first-year demand, we note that the Excel expression =NORM.INV(0.6026, 15000, 4500) provides the value for a normal distribution with a mean of 15,000 and a standard deviation of 4,500, such that 60.26 percent of the area under

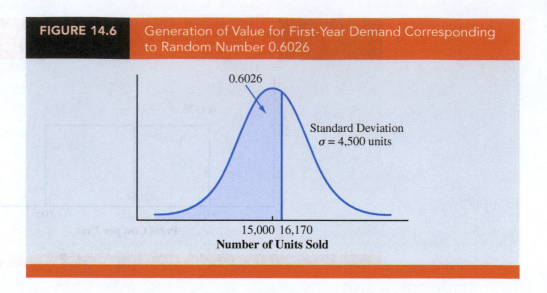

FIGURE 14.6   Generation of Value for First-Year Demand Corresponding to Random Number 0.6026

the normal curve is to the left of this value (Figure 14.6). Now suppose that the random number produced by the RAND function is 0.3551; applying equation (14.6) then results in Demand = NORM.INV(0.3551, 15000, 4500) = 13,328 units. Because half of this normal distribution lies below the mean of 15,000 and half lies above it, RAND values less than 0.5 result in values of first-year demand below the average of 15,000 units, and RAND values above 0.5 correspond to values of first-year demand above the average of 15,000 units.

Now that we know how to randomly generate values for the random variables (direct labor cost, parts cost, first-year demand) from their respective probability distributions, we modify the spreadsheet by adding this information. The static values in Figure 14.1 for these parameters in cells B6, B7, and B8 are replaced with cell formulas that will randomly generate values whenever the spreadsheet is recalculated (as shown in Figure 14.7). Corresponding to Table 14.1, cell B6 uses a random number generated by the RAND function and looks up the corresponding direct labor cost per unit by applying the VLOOKUP function to the table of intervals contained in cells A15:C19 (which corresponds to Table 14.1). Cell B7 executes equation (14.4) using references to the lower bound and upper bound of the uniform distribution of the parts cost in cells F14 and F15, respectively.[2] Cell B8 executes equation (14.6) using references to the mean and standard deviation of the normal distribution of the first-year demand in cells F18 and F19, respectively.[3]

For further description of the VLOOKUP function, refer to Chapter 10.

Executing Simulation Trials with Excel

Each trial in the simulation involves randomly generating values for the random variables (direct labor cost, parts cost, and first-year demand) and computing profit. To facilitate the execution of multiple simulation trials, we use Excel's Data Table functionality in an

---

[2]Technically, random variables modeled with continuous probability distributions should be appropriately rounded to avoid modeling error. For example, the simulated values of parts cost per unit should be rounded to the nearest penny. To simplify exposition, we do not worry about the small amount of error that occurs in this case. To model these random variables more accurately, the formula in cell B7 should be =ROUND(F12+(F13-F12)*RAND(),2).

[3]In addition to being a continuous distribution that technically requires rounding when applied to discrete phenomena (like units of medical device demand), the normal distribution also allows negative values. The probability of a negative value is quite small in the case of first-year demand, and we simply ignore the small amount of modeling error for the sake of simplicity. To model first-year demand more accurately, the formula in cell B8 should be =MAX(ROUND(NORM.INV(RAND(),F16,F17),0),0).

FIGURE 14.7   Formula Worksheet for Sanotronics

	A	B	C	D	E	F
1	**Sanotronics**					
2						
3	**Parameters**					
4	Selling Price per Unit	249				
5	Administrative & Advertising Cost	1000000				
6	Direct Labor Cost per Unit	=VLOOKUP(RAND(),A15:C19,3,TRUE)				
7	Parts Cost per Unit	=F14+(F15-F14)*RAND()				
8	Demand	=NORM.INV(RAND(),F18,F19)				
9						
10	**Model**					
11	Profit	=((B4-B6-B7)*B8)-B5				
12						
13	**Direct Labor Cost**				**Parts Cost (Uniform Distribution)**	
14	**Lower End of Interval**	**Upper End of Interval**	**Cost per Unit**	**Probability**	Lower Bound	80
15	0	=D15+A15	43	0.1	Upper Bound	100
16	=B15	=D16+A16	44	0.2		
17	=B16	=D17+A17	45	0.4	**Demand (Normal Distribution)**	
18	=B17	=D18+A18	46	0.2	Mean	15000
19	=B18	1	47	0.1	Standard Deviation	4500
20						

These steps iteratively select the simulation trial number from the range A22 through A1021 and substitute it into the blank cell selected in Step 4 (D1). This substitution has no bearing on the spreadsheet, but it forces Excel to recalculate the spreadsheet each time, thereby generating new random numbers with the RAND functions in cells B6, B7, and B8.

unorthodox, but effective, manner. To set up the spreadsheet for the execution of 1,000 simulation trials, we structure a table as shown in cells A21 through E1021 in Figure 14.8. As Figure 14.8 shows, A22:A1021 numbers the 1,000 simulation trials (rows 43 through 1020 are hidden). To populate the table of simulation trials in cells A22 through E1021, we execute the following steps:

Step 1. Select cell range A22:E1021
Step 2. Click the **Data** tab in the Ribbon
Step 3. Click **What-If Analysis** in the **Forecast** group and select **Data Table...**
Step 4. When the **Data Table** dialog box appears, leave the **Row input cell:** box blank and enter any empty cell in the spreadsheet (e.g., D1) into the **Column input cell:** box
Step 5. Click **OK**

Figure 14.9 shows the results of a set of 1,000 simulation trials. After executing the simulation with the data table, each row in this table corresponds to a distinct simulation trial consisting of different values of the random variables. In Trial 1 (row 22 in the spreadsheet), we see that the direct labor cost is $45 per unit, the parts cost is $86.29 per unit, and first-year demand is 19,976 units, resulting in profit of $1,351,439. In Trial 2 (row 23 in the spreadsheet), we observe random variables of $45 for the direct labor cost, $81.02 for the parts cost, and 14,910 for first-year demand. These values provide a simulated profit of $833,700 on the second simulation trial. Note that the values shown when you run your simulation will be different due to the random inputs.

Pressing the F9 key recalculates the spreadsheet, thereby generating a new set of simulation trials.

FIGURE 14.8 Setting Up Sanotronics Spreadsheet for 1,000 Simulation Trials

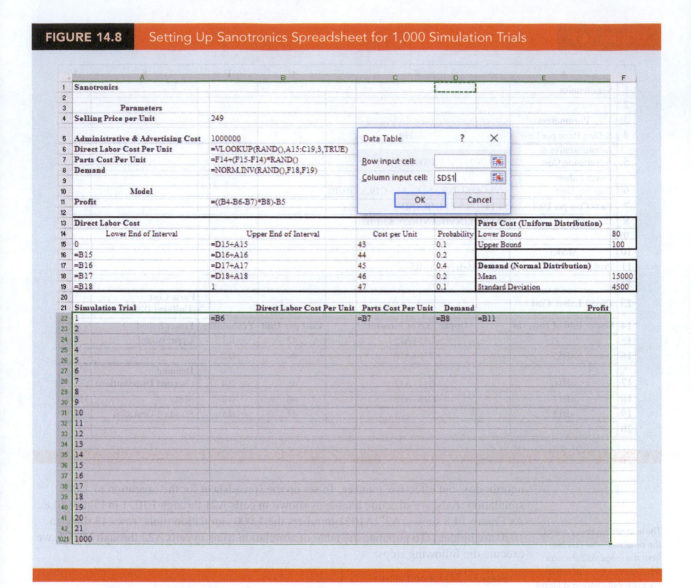

Measuring and Analyzing Simulation Output

The analysis of the output observed over the set of simulation trials is a critical part of the simulation process. For the collection of simulation trials, it is helpful to compute descriptive statistics such as sample average, sample standard deviation, minimum, maximum, and sample proportion. To compute these statistics for the Sanotronics example, we use the following Excel functions:

Cell H22	=AVERAGE(E22:E1021)
Cell H23	=STDEV.S(E22:E1021)
Cell H24	=MIN(E22:E1021)
Cell H25	=MAX(E22:E1021)
Cell H26	=COUNTIF(E22:E1021,"<0")/COUNT(E22:E1021)

FIGURE 14.9 Output from Sanotronics Simulation

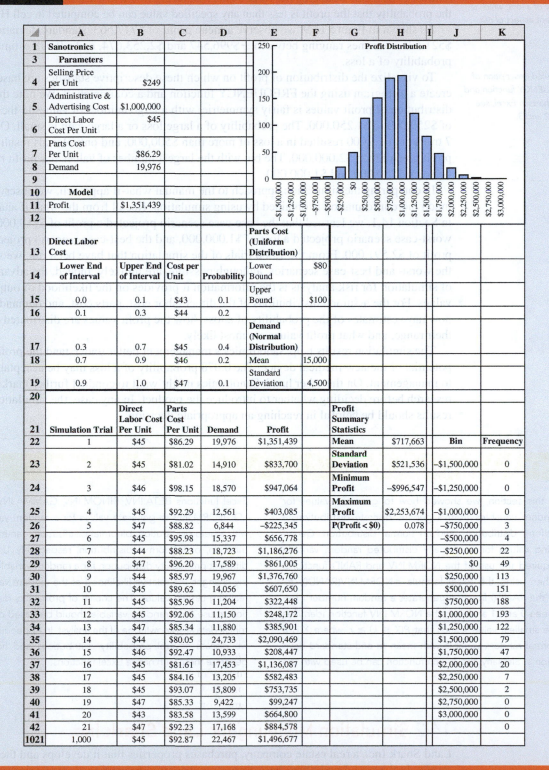

	A	B	C	D	E	F	G	H	I	J	K
1	Sanotronics										
3	Parameters										
4	Selling Price per Unit	$249									
5	Administrative & Advertising Cost	$1,000,000									
6	Direct Labor Cost Per Unit	$45									
7	Parts Cost Per Unit	$86.29									
8	Demand	19,976									
9											
10	Model										
11	Profit	$1,351,439									
12											
13	Direct Labor Cost				Parts Cost (Uniform Distribution)						
14	Lower End of Interval	Upper End of Interval	Cost per Unit	Probability	Lower Bound	$80					
15	0.0	0.1	$43	0.1	Upper Bound	$100					
16	0.1	0.3	$44	0.2							
17	0.3	0.7	$45	0.4	Demand (Normal Distribution)						
18	0.7	0.9	$46	0.2	Mean	15,000					
19	0.9	1.0	$47	0.1	Standard Deviation	4,500					
20											
21	Simulation Trial	Direct Labor Cost Per Unit	Parts Cost Per Unit	Demand	Profit		Profit Summary Statistics			Bin	Frequency
22	1	$45	$86.29	19,976	$1,351,439		Mean	$717,663			
23	2	$45	$81.02	14,910	$833,700		Standard Deviation	$521,536		-$1,500,000	0
24	3	$46	$98.15	18,570	$947,064		Minimum Profit	-$996,547		-$1,250,000	0
25	4	$45	$92.29	12,561	$403,085		Maximum Profit	$2,253,674		-$1,000,000	0
26	5	$47	$88.82	6,844	-$225,345		P(Profit < $0)	0.078		-$750,000	3
27	6	$45	$95.98	15,337	$656,778					-$500,000	4
28	7	$44	$88.23	18,723	$1,186,276					-$250,000	22
29	8	$47	$96.20	17,589	$861,005					$0	49
30	9	$44	$85.97	19,967	$1,376,760					$250,000	113
31	10	$45	$89.62	14,056	$607,650					$500,000	151
32	11	$45	$85.96	11,204	$322,448					$750,000	188
33	12	$45	$92.06	11,150	$248,172					$1,000,000	193
34	13	$47	$85.34	11,880	$385,901					$1,250,000	122
35	14	$44	$80.05	24,733	$2,090,469					$1,500,000	79
36	15	$46	$92.47	10,933	$208,447					$1,750,000	47
37	16	$45	$81.61	17,453	$1,136,087					$2,000,000	20
38	17	$45	$84.16	13,205	$582,483					$2,250,000	7
39	18	$45	$93.07	15,809	$753,735					$2,500,000	2
40	19	$47	$85.33	9,422	$99,247					$2,750,000	0
41	20	$43	$83.58	13,599	$664,800					$3,000,000	0
42	21	$47	$92.23	17,168	$884,578						0
1021	1,000	$45	$92.87	22,467	$1,496,677						

*Simulation studies enable
an objective estimate of the
probability of a loss, which is
an important aspect of risk
analysis.*

Cell H26 computes the ratio of the number of trials whose profit is less than zero over the total number of trials. By changing the value of the second argument in the COUNTIF function, the probability that the profit is less than any specified value can be computed in cell H26.

As shown in Figure 14.9, we observe a mean profit of $717,663, standard deviation of $521,536, extremes ranging between −$996,547 and $2,253,674, and a 0.078 estimated probability of a loss.

*For a detailed description of
the FREQUENCY function and
creating charts in Excel, see
Chapters 2 and 3.*

To visualize the distribution of profit on which these descriptive statistics are based, we create a histogram using the FREQUENCY function and a column chart. We note that the distribution of profit values is fairly symmetric, with a large number of values in the range of $250,000 to $1,250,000. The probability of a large loss or a large gain is small. Only 7 trials out of 1,000 resulted in a loss of more than $500,000, and only 9 trials resulted in a profit greater than $2,000,000. The bin with the largest number of values has profit ranging between $750,000 and $1,000,000.

In comparing the simulation approach to the manual what-if approach, we observe that much more information is obtained by using simulation. Recall from the what-if analysis in Section 14.1, we learned that the base-case scenario projected a profit of $710,000. The worst-case scenario projected a loss of $1,000,000, and the best-case scenario projected a profit of $2,591,000. From the 1,000 trials of the simulation that have been run, we see that the worst- and best-case scenarios, although possible, are unlikely. Indeed, the advantage of simulation for risk analysis is the information it provides on the likelihood of output values. For the assumed distributions of the direct labor cost, parts cost, and demand, we now have estimates of the probability of a loss, how the profit values are distributed over their range, and what profit values are most likely.

The simulation results help Sanotronics's management better understand the profit/loss potential of the new medical device. The 0.078 probability of a loss may be acceptable to management. On the other hand, Sanotronics might want to conduct further market research before deciding whether to introduce the product. In any case, the simulation results should be helpful in reaching an appropriate decision.

NOTES + COMMENTS

In this section, we showed how to generate values for random variables from a generic discrete distribution, a uniform distribution, and a normal distribution. Generating values for a normally distributed random variable required the use of the NORM.INV and RAND functions. When using the Excel formula =NORM.INV(RAND(), *m*, *s*), the RAND() function generates a random number *r* between 0 and 1 and then the NORM.INV function identifies the smallest value *k* such that $P(X \leq k) \geq r$, where *X* is a normal random variable with mean *m* and standard deviation *s*. Similarly, the RAND function can be used with the

Excel functions BETA.INV, BINOM.INV, GAMMA.INV, and LOGNORM.INV to generate values for a random variable with a beta distribution, binomial distribution, gamma distribution, or lognormal distribution, respectively. Using a different probability distribution for a random variable simply changes the relative likelihood of the random variable realizing certain values. The choice of probability distribution to use for a random variable should be based on historical data and knowledge of the analyst. In Appendix 14.5, we discuss several probability distributions and how to generate them with native Excel functions.

14.2 Simulation Modeling for Land Shark Inc.

Land Shark Inc., a real estate company, purchases properties that it develops and then resells. In the past, Land Shark has successfully acquired properties via first-price sealed-bid auctions involving commercial and residential properties. In such auctions, each bidder

TABLE 14.2	Bid Data on Commercial Property Auctions							
Bid Amount (as a Fraction of Estimated Property Value)								
Property No.	**Bid 1**	**Bid 2**	**Bid 3**	**Bid 4**	**Bid 5**	**Bid 6**	**Bid 7**	**Bid 8**
1	0.830	0.797	0.833	0.878	0.839	0.843		
2	0.835	0.823	0.781	0.892	0.767	0.787		
3	0.763	0.862	0.814	0.895				
4	0.771	0.859	0.867	0.850	0.833			
5	0.836	0.898	0.831	0.897	0.831	0.657	0.846	
6	0.850	0.863	0.825	0.910	0.848			
7	0.890	0.820	0.874	0.877	0.818			
8	0.804	0.881	0.786	0.884	0.773	0.819	0.824	
9	0.819	0.851	0.786	0.896	0.784	0.792		
10	0.860	0.756	0.876	0.887	0.866			
11	0.880	0.834	0.831	0.871	0.857	0.759		
12	0.810	0.870						
13	0.887	0.716	0.817	0.9	0.869	0.885	0.856	0.761

submits a single concealed bid. The submitted bids are then compared, and the party with the highest bid wins the property and pays the bid amount. In case of a tie (a rare occurrence), a coin flip decides the winner.

DATA *file*

LandShark

Land Shark has been reviewing upcoming property auctions and has identified a commercial property of interest. Land Shark estimates the value of this property to be $1,389,000. Using bidding data disclosed to the public, Land Shark has maintained a file summarizing 50 previous auctions that it believes are similar to the upcoming property auction. Table 14.2 displays bid data for a portion of Land Shark's data. The data for all 50 auctions is in the *Auctions* worksheet of the file *LandShark*. Because the property value up for sale varies between auctions, Land Shark expresses the submitted bid amounts as a percentage of the respective property's value (as estimated by Land Shark) to make the bids in different auctions comparable. Land Shark is considering a bid of $1,250,000 but would like to evaluate its chances of winning the upcoming auction with this bid.

Spreadsheet Model for Land Shark

To evaluate Land Shark's chances of winning the auction, we develop a simulation model for the auction. Our first step in modeling the upcoming property auction is to identify the input parameters and output measures. The next step is to develop a spreadsheet model that conveys the logical relationships between the input parameters and the output measures. Then we prepare the spreadsheet model for simulation analysis by replacing the static values of the input parameters that Land Shark does not know with certainty with probability distributions of possible values.

The relevant input parameters for the upcoming auction are the estimated value of the property, the number of bidders, and the submitted bid amounts. The output data in which we are interested are whether Land Shark wins the simulated auction given its specified amount and Land Shark's net return. If Land Shark wins the auction, its return is computed as the difference between the estimated value of the property and its bid amount. If Land Shark does not win the auction, its return is $0.

Whether Land Shark wins the simulated auction can be determined by comparing Land Shark's bid amount to that of the largest competitor. Based on Land Shark's data on

50 past auctions, we assume that the number of submitted bid amounts may range from two to eight. Therefore, to determine the bid amount of the largest competitor, the spreadsheet model must be able to compute the maximum bid from a varying number of bids.

Figure 14.10 shows the formula view and value view of the spreadsheet model. Cell B4 contains the estimated value of the property (Land Shark is relatively certain of this value), cell B5 contains a value for the number of bidders (Land Shark is uncertain of this value), and cells B8 through B15 contain values of eight possible competing bids expressed as percentages of the property's estimated value (Land Shark is uncertain of these values). Cells C8 through C15 express the corresponding bid percentages in cells B8 through B15 as dollar amounts. If the number of bidders in cell B5 is less than the eight possible bids listed in cells B8 through B15, the IF formulas in cells C8 through C15 set the bid amount to $0 for all the excess bids (effectively eliminating these bids). For example, consider the formula in cell C8, =IF(A8>$B$5, 0, B8*$B$4). This formula compares the bid index in cell A8 to the number of bidders in cell B5, and if the bid index exceeds the number of bidders, a bid amount of $0 is calculated so that the bid is not considered. Otherwise, the bid amount is calculated by multiplying the bid percentage by the estimated value of the property.

For a detailed discussion of the IF function in Excel, see Chapter 10; for a discussion of relative and absolute cell references, see Appendix A.

FIGURE 14.10 Base Spreadsheet Model for Land Shark

	A	B	C
1	Land Shark		
2			
3	Parameters		
4	Estimated Value	1389000	
5	Number of Bidders	4	
6			
7	Bid Index	Bid (% of Estimated Value)	Bid Amount
8	1	0.887	=IF(A8>$B$5,0,B8*$B$4)
9	2	0.716	=IF(A9>$B$5,0,B9*$B$4)
10	3	0.817	=IF(A10>$B$5,0,B10*$B$4)
11	4	0.9	=IF(A11>$B$5,0,B11*$B$4)
12	5	0.869	=IF(A12>$B$5,0,B12*$B$4)
13	6	0.885	=IF(A13>$B$5,0,B13*$B$4)
14	7	0.856	=IF(A14>$B$5,0,B14*$B$4)
15	8	0.761	=IF(A15>$B$5,0,B15*$B$4)
16			
17	Model		
18	Land Shark Bid Amount	1230000	
19	Largest Competitor Bid	=MAX(C8:C15)	
20	Land Shark Win Auction?	=IF(B18>B19,1,0)	
21	Land Shark Return	=B20*(B4-B18)	

	A	B	C
1	Land Shark		
2			
3	Parameters		
4	Estimated Value	$1,389,000	
5	Number of Bidders	4	
6			
7	Bid Index	Bid (% of Estimated Value)	Bid Amount
8	1	0.887	$1,232,043
9	2	0.716	$994,524
10	3	0.817	$1,134,813
11	4	0.900	$1,250,100
12	5	0.869	$0
13	6	0.885	$0
14	7	0.856	$0
15	8	0.761	$0
16			
17	Model		
18	Land Shark Bid Amount	$1,230,000	
19	Largest Competitor Bid	$1,250,100	
20	Land Shark Win Auction?	0	
21	Land Shark Return	$0	

Cell B18 contains Land Shark's bid amount (highlighted in gray to denote that this is a controllable decision). Cell B19 computes the largest competitor bid by taking the maximum value over the range C8:C15. Land Shark tracks two output measures: whether it wins the auction and the return from the auction. By comparing Land Shark's bid amount in cell B18 to the largest competitor bid in cell B19, the logic =IF(B18>B19,1,0) in cell B20 indicates that Land Shark wins the auction by returning the value of 1 and the Land Shark loses the auction by returning the value of 0. The value of 1 or 0 in Cell B20 to denote a Land Shark win or loss allows the simulation model to count the number of times Land Shark wins the auction over a set of simulation trials. The formula in cell B21, =B20*(B4-B18), computes the return from the auction; if Land Shark wins the auction, the return is equal to the estimated value minus the bid amount, otherwise the return is zero because the value of cell B20 will be zero.

Generating Values for Land Shark's Random Variables

In the Land Shark simulation model constructed in Figure 14.10, there are several uncertain quantities: the number of competing bidders and how much the competitors will bid (as a percentage of property's estimated value). In this section, we discuss how to specify probability distributions for these uncertain quantities or random variables.

First, consider the number of bidders. Figure 14.11 contains the frequency distribution of the number of bidders for the 50 previous auctions that Land Shark has tracked in the *Auctions* worksheet of the file *LandShark*. The number of bidders has ranged from two to eight over the past 50 auctions. Unless Land Shark has reason to believe that there may be fewer than two bids on an upcoming auction, it is probably safe to assume that there will be a minimum of two competing bids. There has not been an auction with more than eight

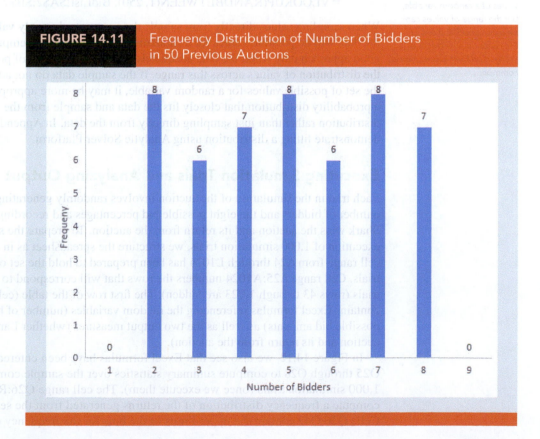

FIGURE 14.11   Frequency Distribution of Number of Bidders in 50 Previous Auctions

*For a detailed discussion of
frequency distributions, see
Chapter 2.*

*The integer uniform
distribution is a special
case of the discrete uniform
distribution discussed
in Chapter 5. In both
distributions, all values are
equally likely. However, in the
integer uniform distribution,
the possible values are
consecutive integers over the
defined range. In a general
discrete uniform distribution,
the possible values do not
have to be consecutive
integers (or even integers),
but rather just a set of distinct,
discrete values.*

*When an analyst knows
little about the likelihood of
values of a random variable,
but the range of values can
be ascertained, the use of
the continuous or discrete
(integer) uniform distribution is
common.*

bidders, so eight is a reasonable assumption for the maximum number of competing bids unless Land Shark's experience with the local real estate market suggests that more than eight competing bids is possible.

Figure 14.11 suggests that the relative likelihood of different values for the number of bidders is nearly equal and that differences are likely due to the fact that this frequency distribution is based on only 50 auction observations. Thus, Land Shark decides to model the number of bidders to be 2, 3, 4, 5, 6, 7, or 8 with equal probability. In this case, the integer uniform distribution is the appropriate choice, as it is characterized by a series of equally likely consecutive integers over a specified range.

To generate a value for a random variable characterized by an integer uniform distribution, the following Excel formula is used:

Value of integer uniform random variable = RANDBETWEEN(lower integer value, upper integer value). (14.7)

For Land Shark, the lower integer value is 2 and the upper integer value is 8. Applying equation (14.7), we enter the formula =RANDBETWEEN(2, 8) into cell B5.

Each competitor's bid percentage is also a random variable. From the past 50 auctions, there has been a total of 250 observations of how competitors have bid (as a percentage of the estimated value). These 250 bid amounts from the *Auctions* worksheet have been relisted in the *BidList* worksheet in the file *LandShark*. Land Shark believes that these 250 bid values are an accurate representation of the distribution of future bids. Thus, we will simulate the bids for the upcoming auction by randomly selecting a value from 1 of these 250 bid values. To sample a value for a random variable from a set of possible values, we use the Excel formula:

=VLOOKUP(RANDBETWEEN(1, 250), BidList!$A$2:$B$73, 2, FALSE).

When sampling values directly from sample data, we note that only values that exist in the data will be possible values for a simulation trial. Resampling empirical data is a good approach only when the data adequately represent the range of possible values and the distribution of values across this range. If the sample data do not adequately describe the set of possible values for a random variable, it may be more appropriate to identify a probability distribution that closely fits the data and sample from the fitted probability distribution rather than just sampling directly from the data. In Appendix 14.2, we demonstrate fitting a distribution using Analytic Solver Platform.

Executing Simulation Trials and Analyzing Output

Each trial in the simulation of the auction involves randomly generating values for the number of bidders and the eight possible bid percentages and recording whether Land Shark wins the auction and its return from the auction. To prepare the spreadsheet for the execution of 1,000 simulation trials, we structure the spreadsheet as in Figure 14.12. The cell range from A24 through L1024 has been prepared to hold the set of 1,000 simulation trials. Cell range A25:A1024 numbers the rows that will correspond to the 1,000 simulation trials (rows 43 through 1,023 are hidden). The first row of the table (cells B25 through L25) contains Excel formulas referencing the random variables (number of bidders and the eight possible bid amounts) as well as the two output measures (whether Land Shark wins the auction and its return from the auction).

In Figure 14.12, we also see that Excel formulas have been entered into cells O25 through O28 to compute summary statistics over the sample composed of the 1,000 simulation trials (once we execute them). The cell range Q26:R42 is set up to compute a frequency distribution of the returns generated from the set of 1,000 trials. Cells Q26:Q42 contain the upper limits of the bins for the frequency distribution.

FIGURE 14.12   Setting Up Land Shark Spreadsheet for 1,000 Simulation Trials

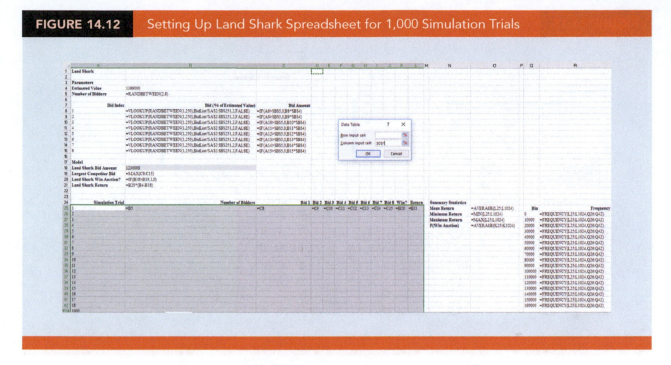

Cells R26:R42 contain the array formula FREQUENCY that computes the number of observations in each bin.

To populate the table of simulation trials, we execute the following steps:

For a detailed description of the FREQUENCY function, see Chapter 2.

Step 1. Select cell range A25:A1024
Step 2. Click the **Data** tab in the Ribbon
Step 3. Click **What-If Analysis** in the **Forecast** group and select **Data Table...**
Step 4. When the **Data Table** dialog box appears, leave the **Row input cell:** box blank and enter any empty cell in the spreadsheet (e.g., *D1*) into the **Column input cell:** box
Step 5. Click **OK**

Figure 14.13 shows the results of a set of 1,000 simulation trials. After executing the simulation with the Data Table, each row of this table corresponds to a distinct simulation trial consisting of different values of the random variables. We see that Land Shark does not win the simulated auction corresponding to Trial 1 because one of the four competing bids (Bid 1 = $1,241,766) is larger than its bid of $1,230,000. In Trial 4, we observe that Land Shark wins the auction because its bid of $1,230,000 is larger than the two competing bids of $1,177,872 and $1,080,642.

Figure 14.13 also shows that based on this set of 1,000 simulation trials, Land Shark's estimated mean return is $36,888 and the estimated probability that it wins the auction is 0.232. In this simulation experiment, when Land Shark bids $1,230,000, there are only two outcomes: either it wins the auction and earns a return of $159,000 or it loses the auction and earns of return of $0. Out of the 1,000 simulated auctions, the frequency table shows that Land Shark does not win the auction ($0 return) in 768 auctions and wins the auction (earns $159,000) in 232 auctions. We note that a different set of 1,000 simulation trials can be generated by pressing the **F9** key, and this may result in varying values of the summary statistics because these will now be based on a different sample. To gauge how much sampling error exists in the output statistics, press the **F9** key and observe how much the output statistics vary. When

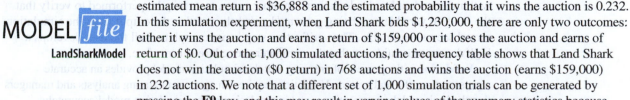

MODEL *file*

LandSharkModel

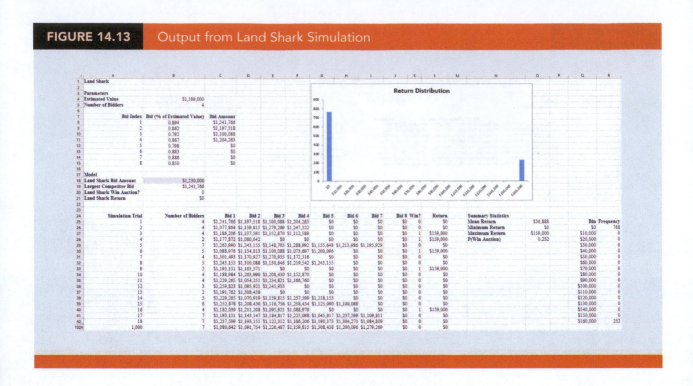

FIGURE 14.13   Output from Land Shark Simulation

When you run your LandShark simulation, the values you see will be different. This is to be expected with simulation models. Each time the simulation is executed, the values may vary because different random numbers are being used.

using 1,000 trials, the estimated mean return consistently varies between $30,000 and $42,000 and the estimated probability of winning the auction consistently varies between 0.20 and 0.26. In general, increasing the number of trials in a simulation experiment will decrease the variability in the summary statistics from one set of simulation trials to the next. Therefore, if we wish to decrease the sampling error in the output statistics, we should increase the number of simulation trials and re-execute the simulation experiment via Excel's Data Table tool.

14.3 Simulation Considerations

Verification and Validation

An important aspect of any simulation study involves confirming that the simulation model accurately describes the real system. Inaccurate simulation models cannot be expected to provide worthwhile information. Thus, before using simulation results to draw conclusions about a real system, one must take steps to verify and validate the simulation model.

Verification is the process of determining that the computer procedure that performs the simulation calculations is logically correct. Verification is largely a debugging task to make sure that no errors are in the computer procedure that implements the simulation. In some cases, an analyst may compare computer results for a limited number of events with independent hand calculations. In other cases, tests may be performed to verify that the random variables are being generated correctly and that the output from the simulation model seems reasonable. The verification step is not complete until the user develops a high degree of confidence that the computer procedure is error free.

Validation is the process of ensuring that the simulation model provides an accurate representation of a real system. Validation requires an agreement among analysts and managers that the logic and the assumptions used in the design of the simulation model accurately reflect how the real system operates. The first phase of the validation process is done prior to or in conjunction with the development of the computer procedure for the simulation process.

Validation continues after the computer program has been developed, with the analyst reviewing the simulation output to see whether the simulation results closely approximate the performance of the real system. If possible, the output of the simulation model is compared to the output of an existing real system to make sure that the simulation output closely approximates the performance of the real system. If this form of validation is not possible, an analyst can experiment with the simulation model and have one or more individuals experienced with the operation of the real system review the simulation output to determine whether it is a reasonable approximation of what would be obtained with the real system under similar conditions.

Verification and validation are not tasks to be taken lightly. They are key steps in any simulation study and are necessary to ensure that decisions and conclusions based on the simulation results are appropriate for the real system.

Advantages and Disadvantages of Using Simulation

The primary advantages of simulation are that it is easy to understand and that the methods can be used to model and learn about the behavior of complex systems that would be difficult, if not impossible, to deal with analytically. Simulation models are flexible; they can be used to describe systems without requiring the assumptions that are often required by mathematical models. In general, the larger the number of random variables a system has, the more likely it is that a simulation model will provide the best approach for studying the system. Another advantage is that a simulation model provides a convenient experimental laboratory for the real system. Changing assumptions or operating policies in the simulation model and rerunning it can provide results that help predict how such changes will affect the operation of the real system. Experimenting directly with a real system is often not feasible. Simulation models frequently warn against poor decision strategies by projecting disastrous outcomes such as system failures, large financial losses, and so on.

Simulation is not without disadvantages. For complex systems, the process of developing, verifying, and validating a simulation model can be time consuming and expensive (however, the process of developing the model generally leads to a better understanding of the system, which is an important benefit). Like all mathematical models, the analyst must be conscious of the assumptions of the model in order to understand its limitations. In addition, each simulation run provides only a sample of how the real system will operate. As such, the summary of the simulation data provides only estimates or approximations about the real system. Nonetheless, the danger of obtaining poor solutions is greatly mitigated if the analyst exercises good judgment in developing the simulation model and follows proper verification and validation steps and if the simulation process is run long enough under a wide variety of conditions so that the analyst has sufficient data to predict how the real system will operate.

SUMMARY

Simulation is a method for learning about a real system by experimenting with a model that represents the system. Some of the reasons simulation is frequently used are:

1. It can be used for a wide variety of practical problems.
2. The simulation approach is relatively easy to explain and understand. As a result, management confidence is increased, and of the results are more easily accepted.
3. Spreadsheet add-in software and specialized software packages have made it easier to develop and implement simulation models for increasingly complex problems.

In this chapter, we showed how native Excel functions can be used to execute a simulation on a pair of examples. For the Sanotronics problem, we used simulation to evaluate the risk involving the development of a new product. Then we developed a simulation model to help Land Shark Inc. estimate how varying its bid amount affects the likelihood of winning a property auction. With the steps below, we summarize the procedure for developing a simulation model involving controllable inputs, uncertain inputs represented by random variables, and output measures.

Summary of Steps for Conducting a Simulation Analysis

1. *Construct a spreadsheet model that computes output measures for given values of inputs.* The foundation of a good simulation model is logic that correctly relates input values to outputs. Audit the spreadsheet to ensure that the cell formulas correctly evaluate the outputs over the entire range of possible input values.

2. *Identify inputs that are uncertain, and specify probability distributions for these cells* (rather than just static numbers). Note that all inputs may not have a degree of uncertainty sufficient to require modeling with a probability distribution. Other inputs may actually be decision variables, which are not random and should not be modeled with probability distributions; rather, these are values that the decision maker can control.

3. *Select one or more outputs to record over the simulation trials.* Typical information recorded for an output includes a histogram of output values over all simulation trials and summary statistics such as the mean, standard deviation, maximum, minimum, and percentile values.

4. *Execute the simulation for a specified number of trials.* For most small to moderate-sized simulation problems, we recommend the use of 10,000 trials. The amount of sampling error can be monitored by observing how much simulation output measures fluctuate across multiple simulation runs.

5. *Analyze the outputs and interpret the implications on the decision-making process.* In addition to estimates of the mean output, simulation allows us to construct a distribution of possible output values. Analyzing the simulation results allows the decision-maker to draw conclusions about the operation of the real system.

In this chapter, we have focused on Monte Carlo simulation consisting of independent trials in which the results for one trial do not affect what happens in subsequent trials. Another style of simulation, called **discrete-event simulation**, involves trials that represent how a system evolves over time. One common application of discrete-event simulation is the analysis of waiting lines. In a waiting-line simulation, the random variables are the interarrival times of the customers and the service times of the servers, which together determine the waiting and completion times for the customers. Although it is possible to conduct small discrete-event simulations with native Excel functionality or with a Monte Carlo simulation Excel add-in such as Analytic Solver Platform, discrete-event simulation modeling is best conducted with special-purpose software such as Arena®, ProModel®, and Simio®. These packages have built-in simulation clocks, simplified methods for generating random variables, and procedures for collecting and summarizing the simulation output.

Problems 21, 22, and 23 involve small waiting-line simulation models.

GLOSSARY

Base-case scenario Output resulting from the most likely values for the random variables of a model.

Best-case scenario Output resulting from the best values that can be expected for the random variables of a model.

Continuous probability distribution A probability distribution for which the possible values for a random variable can take any value in an interval or collection of intervals. An interval can include negative and positive infinity.

Controllable input Input to a simulation model that is selected by the decision maker.

Discrete probability distribution A probability distribution for which the possible values for a random variable can take on only specified discrete values.

Discrete-event simulation A simulation method that describes how a system evolves over time by using events that occur at discrete points in time.

Monte Carlo simulation A simulation method that uses repeated random sampling to represent uncertainty in a model representing a real system and that computes the values of model outputs.

Probability distribution A description of the range and relative likelihood of possible values of a random variable (uncertain quantity).

Random variable (uncertain variable) Input to a simulation model whose value is uncertain and described by a probability distribution.

Risk analysis The process of evaluating a decision in the face of uncertainty by quantifying the likelihood and magnitude of an undesirable outcome.

Simulation optimization The process of applying optimization techniques to identify optimal (or near-optimal) values of the decision variables in a simulation model.

Validation The process of determining that a simulation model provides an accurate representation of a real system.

Verification The process of determining that a computer program implements a simulation model as it is intended.

What-if analysis A trial-and-error approach to learning about the range of possible outputs for a model. Trial values are chosen for the model inputs (these are the what-ifs) and the value of the output(s) is computed.

Worst-case scenario Output resulting from the worst values that can be expected for the random variables of a model.

PROBLEMS

Most of these problems can be solved using only native Excel functionality. We note the problems that require the use of a simulation add-in such as ASP, Crystal Ball, or @RISK. We recommend the use of ASP with 10,000 trials per simulation.

1. The management of Brinkley Corporation is interested in using simulation to estimate the profit per unit for a new product. The selling price for the product will be $45 per unit. Probability distributions for the purchase cost, the labor cost, and the transportation cost are estimated as follows:

Procurement Cost ($)	Probability	Labor Cost ($)	Probability	Transportation Cost ($)	Probability
10	0.25	20	0.10	3	0.75
11	0.45	22	0.25	5	0.25
12	0.30	24	0.35		
		25	0.30		

a. Compute profit per unit for base-case (most likely), worst-case, and best-case scenarios.

b. Construct a simulation model to estimate the mean profit per unit.

c. Why is the simulation approach to risk analysis preferable to generating a variety of what-if scenarios?

d. Management believes that the project may not be sustainable if the profit per unit is less than $5. Use simulation to estimate the probability that the profit per unit will be less than $5.

2. Construct a spreadsheet simulation model to simulate 10,000 rolls of a die with the six sides numbered 1, 2, 3, 4, 5 and 6.
   a. Construct a histogram of the 10,000 observed dice rolls.
   b. For each roll of two dice, record the sum of the dice. Construct a histogram of the 10,000 observations of the sum of two dice.
   c. For each roll of three dice, record the sum of the dice. Construct a histogram of the 10,000 observations of the sum of three dice.
   d. Compare the histograms in parts (a) to (c). What statistical phenomenon does this sequence of charts illustrate? (*Hint:* see Appendix 14.2)

3. The management of Madeira Manufacturing Company is considering the introduction of a new product. The fixed cost to begin the production of the product is $30,000. The variable cost for the product is expected to be between $16 and $24, with a most likely value of $20 per unit. The product will sell for $50 per unit. Demand for the product is expected to range from 300 to 2,100 units, with 1,200 units the most likely.
   a. Develop a what-if spreadsheet model computing profit for this product in the base-case, worst-case, and best-case scenarios.
   b. Discuss why simulation would be appropriate for this situation. Would simulation be a preferable approach to analyze this situation? Why or why not?

4. Refer to the Madeira Manufacturing spreadsheet analysis in Problem 3. Model the variable cost as a uniform random variable with a minimum of $16 and maximum of $24. Model product demand as 1,000 times the value of a gamma random variable with the shape parameter (alpha) of 4 and a scale parameter (beta) of 3.
   a. Perform a simulation analysis to compute the mean profit and the probability that the project will result in a loss.
   b. What is your recommendation with regard to the introduction of the product?

5. Statewide Auto Insurance believes that for every trip longer than 10 minutes that a teenager drives, there is a 1 in 1,000 chance that the drive will results in an auto accident. Assume that the cost of an accident can be modeled with a beta distribution with a *shape1* (alpha) parameter of 1.5, a *shape2* (beta) parameter of 3, a minimum value of $500, and a maximum value of $20,000. Construct a simulation model to answer the following questions.
   a. If a teenager drives 500 trips longer than 10 minutes, what is the mean cost resulting from accidents?
   b. If a teenager drives 500 trips longer than 10 minutes, what is the probability that the total cost from accidents will exceed $8,000?

6. Galaxy Co. distributes wireless routers to Internet service providers. Galaxy procures each router for $75 from its supplier and sells each router for $125. Monthly demand for the router is a normal random variable with a mean of 100 units and a standard deviation of 20 units. At the beginning of each month, Galaxy orders enough routers from its supplier to bring the inventory level up to 100 routers. If the monthly demand is less than 100, Galaxy pays $15 per router that remains in inventory at the end of the month. If the monthly demand exceeds 100, Galaxy sells only the 100 routers in stock. Galaxy assigns a shortage cost of $30 for each unit of demand that is unsatisfied to represent a loss-of-goodwill among its customers. Management would like to use a simulation model to analyze this situation.
   a. What is the average monthly profit resulting from its policy of stocking 100 routers at the beginning of each month?
   b. What percentage of total demand is satisfied?

7. Using simulation software such as Analytic Solver Platform, develop a simulation model for the Sanotronics problem that was presented in Section 14.2 using native Excel functionality.
   a. Obtain estimates for the mean profit, maximum profit, minimum profit, and standard deviation of profit.
   b. What is your estimate of the probability of a loss?

8. Grear Tire Company has produced a new tire with an estimated mean lifetime mileage of 36,500 miles. Management also believes that the standard deviation is 5,000 miles and that tire mileage is normally distributed. To promote the new tire, Grear has offered to refund some money if the tire fails to reach 30,000 miles before the tire needs to be replaced. Specifically, for tires with a lifetime below 30,000 miles, Grear will refund a customer $1 per 100 miles short of 30,000.
   a. For each tire sold, what is the expected cost of the promotion?
   b. What is the probability that Grear will refund more than $50 for a tire?
   c. At what mileage should Grear set the promotion claim if it wants the expected cost to be $2?

9. To generate leads for new business, Gustin Investment Services offers free financial planning seminars at major hotels in Southwest Florida. Gustin conducts seminars for groups of 25 individuals. Each seminar costs Gustin $3,500, and the average first-year commission for each new account opened is $5,000. Gustin estimates that for each individual attending the seminar, there is a 0.01 probability that he/she will open a new account.
   a. Determine the equation for computing Gustin's profit per seminar, given values of the relevant parameters.
   b. What type of random variable is the number of new accounts opened? (*Hint:* Review Appendix 14.5 for descriptions of various types of probability distributions.)
   c. Construct a spreadsheet simulation model to analyze the profitability of Gustin's seminars. Would you recommend that Gustin continue running the seminars?
   d. How large of an audience does Gustin need before a seminar's expected profit is greater than zero?

10. Baseball's World Series is a maximum of seven games, with the winner being the first team to win four games. Assume that the Atlanta Braves are playing the Minnesota Twins in the World Series and that the first two games are to be played in Atlanta, the next three games at the Twins' ballpark, and the last two games, if necessary, back in Atlanta. Taking into account the projected starting pitchers for each game and the home field advantage, the probabilities of Atlanta winning each game are as follows:

Game	1	2	3	4	5	6	7
Probability of Win	0.60	0.55	0.48	0.45	0.48	0.55	0.50

   a. Set up a spreadsheet simulation model in which the possibility of Atlanta winning each game is a random variable.
   b. What is the probability that the Atlanta Braves win the World Series?
   c. What is the average number of games played regardless of the winner?

11. Suppose that the price of a share of a particular stock listed on the New York Stock Exchange is currently $39. The following probability distribution shows how the price per share is expected to change over a three-month period:

Stock Price Change ($)	Probability
−2	0.05
−1	0.10
0	0.25
+1	0.20
+2	0.20
+3	0.10
+4	0.10

   a. Construct a spreadsheet simulation model that computes the value of the stock price in 3 months, 6 months, 9 months, and 12 months under the assumption that the change in stock price over any 3-month period is independent of the change in stock price over any other 3-month period.

  b. With the current price of $39 per share, simulate the price per share for the next four 3-month periods. What is the average stock price per share in 12 months? What is the standard deviation of the stock price in 12 months?

  c. Based on the model assumptions, what are the lowest and highest possible prices for this stock in 12 months? Based on your knowledge of the stock market, how valid do you think this is? Propose an alternative to modeling how stock prices evolve over 3-month periods.

12. The Iowa Energy are scheduled to play against the Maine Red Claws in an upcoming game in the National Basketball Association Developmental League (NBA-DL). Because a player in the NBA-DL is still developing his skills, the number of points he scores in a game can vary. Assume that each player's point production can be represented as an integer uniform variable with the ranges provided in the following table:

Player	Iowa Energy	Maine Red Claws
1	[5,20]	[7,12]
2	[7,20]	[15,20]
3	[5,10]	[10,20]
4	[10,40]	[15,30]
5	[6,20]	[5,10]
6	[3,10]	[1,20]
7	[2,5]	[1,4]
8	[2,4]	[2,4]

  a. Develop a spreadsheet model that simulates the points scored by each team.
  b. What are the average and standard deviation of points scored by the Iowa Energy? What is the shape of the distribution of points scored by the Iowa Energy?
  c. What are the average and standard deviation of points scored by the Maine Red Claws? What is the shape of the distribution of points scored by the Maine Red Claws?
  d. Let Point Differential = Iowa Energy points − Maine Red Claw points. What is the average point differential between the Iowa Energy and Maine Red Claws? What is the standard deviation in the point differential? What is the shape of the point differential distribution? How is the average point differential related to the average points scored by Iowa and Maine? How is the variance in the point differential related to the variance in points scored by Iowa and Maine?
  e. What is the probability that the Iowa Energy scores more points than the Maine Red Claws?
  f. The coach of the Iowa Energy feels that they are the underdog and is considering a riskier game strategy. The effect of this strategy is that the range of each Energy player's point production increases symmetrically so that the new range is [0, original upper bound + original lower bound]. For example, Energy player 1's range with the risky strategy is [0,25]. How does the new strategy affect the average and standard deviation of the Energy point total? How does that affect the probability of the Iowa Energy scoring more points that the Maine Red Claws?

13. A project has four activities (A, B, C, and D) that must be performed sequentially. The probability distributions for the time required to complete each of the activities are as follows:

Activity	Activity Time (weeks)	Probability
A	5	0.25
	6	0.35
	7	0.25
	8	0.15
B	3	0.20
	5	0.55
	7	0.25
C	10	0.10
	12	0.25
	14	0.40
	16	0.20
	18	0.05
D	8	0.60
	10	0.40

a. Construct a spreadsheet simulation model to estimate the average length of the project and the standard deviation of the project length.

b. What is the estimated probability that the project will be completed in 35 weeks or less?

14. Over the past year, a financial analyst has tracked the daily change in the price per share of common stock for a major oil company. Using simulation software such as Analytic Solver Platform, develop a simulation model to analyze the stock price at the end of the next quarter. Assume 63 trading days and a current price per share of $51.60.

a. Based on the data in the *DataToFit* worksheet of the file *DailyStock*, use software such as Analytic Solver Platform to fit a distribution to represent the daily change in stock price.

b. When fitting the distribution in part (a), you made the implicit assumption that each day's change in stock price is independent of every other day's change in stock price. See if this assumption is justifiable by estimating the correlation of consecutive days' change in stock price using the Excel formula =CORREL(B3:B313, B4:B314) in the *DataToFit* worksheet.

c. Using the distribution that you fit in part (a), use the simulation model to estimate the expected price per share at the end of the quarter. What is the probability that the stock price will be below $26.55?

d. The *WhatReallyHappened* worksheet of the file *DailyStock* contains the 63 values of the daily change in stock price that actually occurred during the quarter. (You can plug these 63 values into your model to confirm the calculations.) What does this reveal about the limitations of simulation modeling?

e. Based on the observation that many distributions underestimate the possibility of extreme values, some experts suggest the use of a "heavy-tailed" distribution to model the change in stock price. The Cauchy distribution is one such heavy-tailed distribution in which the likelihood of extreme daily changes in stock price are much more likely than with other distributions (such as the normal distribution). Fit a Cauchy distribution to the data in the *DataToFit* worksheet and observe the impact on the analysis. (*Hint:* To avoid unrealistic swings in stock price, truncate the possible values from the Cauchy distribution by setting the lower cutoff and upper cutoff values to −1 and 1, respectively.)

15. In preparing for the upcoming holiday season, Fresh Toy Company (FTC) designed a new doll called The Dougie that teaches children how to dance. The fixed cost

to produce the doll is $100,000. The variable cost, which includes material, labor, and shipping costs, is $34 per doll. During the holiday selling season, FTC will sell the dolls for $42 each. If FTC overproduces the dolls, the excess dolls will be sold in January through a distributor who has agreed to pay FTC $10 per doll. Demand for new toys during the holiday selling season is extremely uncertain. Forecasts are for expected sales of 60,000 dolls with a standard deviation of 15,000. The normal probability distribution is assumed to be a good description of the demand. FTC has tentatively decided to produce 60,000 units (the same as average demand), but it wants to conduct an analysis regarding this production quantity before finalizing the decision.

a. Create a what-if spreadsheet model using formulas that relate the values of production quantity, demand, sales, revenue from sales, amount of surplus, revenue from sales of surplus, total cost, and net profit. What is the profit corresponding to average demand (60,000 units)?

b. Modeling demand as a normal random variable with a mean of 60,000 and a standard deviation of 15,000, simulate the sales of The Dougie doll using a production quantity of 60,000 units. What is the estimate of the average profit associated with the production quantity of 60,000 dolls? How does this compare to the profit corresponding to the average demand (as computed in part a)?

c. Before making a final decision on the production quantity, management wants an analysis of a more aggressive 70,000-unit production quantity and a more conservative 50,000-unit production quantity. Run your simulation with these two production quantities. What is the mean profit associated with each?

d. Besides mean profit, what other factors should FTC consider in determining a production quantity? Compare the four production quantities (40,000; 50,000; 60,000; and 70,000) using all these factors. What trade-offs occur? What is your recommendation?

16. South Central Airlines (SCA) operates a commuter flight between Atlanta and Charlotte. The regional jet holds 50 passengers, and currently SCA books only up to 50 reservations. Past data shows that SCA always sells all 50 reservations but that, on average, two passengers do not show up. As a result, with 50 reservations, the flight is often being flown with empty seats. To capture additional profit, SCA is considering an overbooking strategy in which they would accept 52 reservations even though the airplane holds only 50 passengers. SCA believes that it will be able to always book all 52 reservations. The probability distribution for the number of passengers showing up when 52 reservations are accepted is estimated as follows:

Passengers Showing Up	Probability
48	0.05
49	0.25
50	0.50
51	0.15
52	0.05

SCA receives a marginal profit of $100 for each passenger who books a reservation (regardless of whether or not they show up). The airline will also incur a cost for any passenger denied seating on the flight. This cost, which covers the added expenses of rescheduling the passenger as well as loss of goodwill, is estimated to be $150 per passenger. Develop a spreadsheet simulation model for this overbooking system. Simulate the number of passengers showing up for a flight.

a. What is the average net profit for each flight with the overbooking strategy?

b. What is the probability that the net profit with the overbooking strategy will be less than the net profit without overbooking (50*$100 = $5,000)?

c. Explain how your simulation model could be used to evaluate other overbooking levels such as 51, 53, and 54 and for recommending a best overbooking strategy.

17. The wedding date for a couple is quickly approaching, and the wedding planner must provide the caterer an estimate of how many people will attend the reception so that the appropriate quantity of food is prepared for the buffet. The following table contains information on the number of RSVPs for the 145 invitations. Unfortunately, the number of guests who actually attend does not always correspond to the number of RSVPs.

Based on her experience, the wedding planner knows that it is extremely rare for guests to attend a wedding if they affirmed that they will not be attending. Therefore, the wedding planner will assume that no one from these 50 invitations will attend. The wedding planner estimates that the each of the 25 guests planning to come alone has a 75% chance of attending alone, a 20% chance of not attending, and a 5% chance of bringing a companion. For each of the 60 RSVPs who plan to bring a companion, there is a 90% chance that she or he will attend with a companion, a 5% chance of attending alone, and a 5% chance of not attending at all. For the 10 people who have not responded, the wedding planner assumes that there is an 80% chance that each will not attend, a 15% chance they will attend alone, and a 5% chance they will attend with a companion.

RSVPs	No. of Invitations
0	50
1	25
2	60
No response	10

a. Assist the wedding planner by constructing a spreadsheet simulation model to determine the expected number of guests who will attend the reception.

b. To be accommodating hosts, the couple has instructed the wedding planner to use the Monte Carlo simulation model to determine X, the minimum number of guests for which the caterer should prepare the meal, so that there is at least a 90% chance that the actual attendance is less than or equal to X. What is the best estimate for the value of X?

18. OuRx, a retail pharmacy chain, is faced with the decision of how much flu vaccine to order for the next flu season. OuRx has to place a single order for the flu vaccine several months before the beginning of the season because it takes four to five months for the supplier to create the vaccine. OuRx wants to more closely examine the ordering decision because, over the past few years, the company has ordered too much vaccine or too little. OuRx pays a wholesale price of $12 per dose to obtain the flu vaccine from the supplier and then sells the flu shot to their customers at a retail price of $20. Based on industry trends as feedback from their marketing managers, OuRx has generated a rough estimate of flu vaccine demand at their retail pharmacies. OuRx is confident that demand will range from 800,000 doses to 4,500,000 doses. The following table lists weights for demand values within this range.

Demand	1,000,000	2,000,000	3,000,000	4,000,000
Weight	0.05	0.20	0.50	0.25

Because OuRx earns a profit on flu shots that it sells and it can't sell more than its supply, the appropriate profit computation depends on whether demand exceeds the order quantity or vice versa. Similarly, the number of lost sales and excess doses depends on whether demand exceeds the order quantity or vice versa.

a. Construct a spreadsheet model that computes net profit corresponding to a given level of demand and specified order quantity. What is the expected net profit corresponding to an order quantity of 3,000,000?

b. Determine the order quantity that maximizes expected profit. What is the probability of running out of flu vaccine at this order quantity?

c. How many doses does OuRx need to order so that the probability of running out of flu vaccine is only 25%? How much expected profit will OuRx lose if it orders this amount rather than the amount from part (b)?

19. Recall the Land Shark example within the chapter.

MODEL *file*

LandSharkModel
or LandSharkASP

a. Determine Land Shark's bid amount that would maximize its expected return on the upcoming auction.

b. What is Land Shark's probability of winning the auction at the bid amount from part (a)?

20. At a local university, the Student Commission on Programming and Entertainment (SCOPE) is preparing to host its first music concert of the school year. To successfully produce this music concert, SCOPE has to complete several activities. The following table lists information regarding each activity. An activity's immediate predecessors are the activities that must be completed before the considered activity can begin. The table also lists duration estimates (in days) for each activity.

Activity	Immediate Predecessors	Minimum Time	Likely Time	Maximum Time
A: Negotiate contract with selected musicians	—	5	6	9
B: Reserve site	—	8	12	15
C: Logistical arrangements for music group	A	5	6	7
D: Screen and hire security personnel	B	3	3	3
E: Advertising and ticketing	B, C	1	5	9
F: Hire parking staff	D	4	7	10
G: Arrange concession sales	E	3	8	10

If you use simulation software other than Analytic Solver Platform, you may model the duration of each activity as a beta distribution with the minimum, most likely, and maximum times listed in the table associated with the problem. The beta distribution generalizes the PERT distribution.

The following network illustrates the precedence relationships in the SCOPE project. The project begins with activities A and B, which can start immediately (time 0) because they have no predecessors. On the other hand, activity E cannot be started until activities B and C are both completed. The project is not complete until all activities are completed.

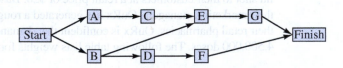

a. Using the PERT distribution in Analytic Solver Platform or another simulation software package to represent the duration of each activity, construct a simulation model to estimate the expected amount of time to complete the concert preparations.

b. What is the likelihood that the project will be complete in 23 days?

BurgerDome

21. Burger Dome is a fast-food restaurant currently evaluating its customer service. In its current operation, an employee takes a customer's order, tabulates the cost, receives payment from the customer, and then fills the order. Once the customer's order is filled, the employee takes the order of the next customer waiting for service. Assume that time between each customer's arrival is an exponential random variable with a mean of 1.35 minutes. Assume that the time for the employee to complete the customer's service is an exponential random variable with a mean of 1 minute. Use the file *BurgerDome* to complete a simulation model for the waiting line at Burger Dome for a 14-hour workday. Note that you will need to use native Excel functionality to solve this problem because the educational version of ASP has a limit of 100 random variables. As Appendix 14.5 describes, Excel formula =LN(RAND())*(-m) generates a value for an exponential random variable with mean m. Using the summary statistics gathered at the bottom of the spreadsheet model, answer the following questions.
    a. What is the average wait time experienced by a customer?
    b. What is the longest wait time experienced by a customer?
    c. What is the probability that a customer waits more than 2 minutes?
    d. Create a histogram depicting the wait time distribution.
    e. By pressing the **F9** key to generate a new set of simulation trials, you can observe the variability in the summary statistics from simulation to simulation. Typically, this variability can be reduced by increasing the number of trials. Why is this approach not appropriate for this problem?

22. One advantage of simulation is that a simulation model can be altered easily to reflect a change in the assumptions. Refer to the Burger Dome analysis in Problem 21. Assume that the service time is more accurately described by a normal distribution with a mean of 1 minute and a standard deviation of 0.2 minute. This distribution has less variability than the exponential distribution originally used. What is the impact of this change on the output measures?

BurgerDomeTwoServers

23. Refer to the Burger Dome analysis in Problem 21. Burger Dome wants to consider the effect of hiring a second employee to serve customers (in parallel with the first employee). Use the file *BurgerDomeTwoServers* to complete a simulation model that accounts for the second employee. (*Hint:* The time that a customer begins service will depend on the availability of employees.) What is the impact of this change on the output measures?

LandSharkASP

24. Land Shark is investigating the sensitivity of its model to the assumptions it made on the random variables. In particular, Land Shark is interested in modeling how it generates its competitor's bid percentages.
    a. Rather than generating a competitor's bid percentage by resampling from the 250 observed bid amounts, use simulation software such as Analytic Solver Platform to fit an appropriate distribution based on these 250 data points and rerun the simulation model. In addition to considering the fit of the distribution to the data, when selecting a distribution, keep in mind the range of bid amounts that would be reasonable.
    b. For Land Shark's bid amount of $1,230,000, how does the estimate of its probability of winning the auction from the model in part a differ from the resampling approach for the model in Section 14.2 (and Appendix 14.1)?
    c. Comment on the implications of modeling random variables and which approach you feel is more appropriate in this case.

25. For this problem, use the Land Shark simulation model from Problem 24 that fits a distribution to data in order to simulate competitor bid amounts.
    a. Determine Land Shark's bid amount (rounded to the nearest $1,000) that maximizes its expected return. What is the probability that Land Shark wins the auction at this bid amount?

b. If Land Shark bids $5,000 more than the amount in part (a), what is the likelihood that it wins the auction? How much expected return does Land Shark sacrifice by increasing its bid in this manner?

OrangeTech

26. Orange Tech (OT) is a software company that provides a suite of programs that are essential to everyday business computing. OT has just enhanced its software and released a new version of its programs. For financial planning purposes, OT needs to forecast its revenue over the next few years. To begin this analysis, OT is considering one of its largest customers. This customer always eventually upgrades to the newest software version, but the number of years that pass before the customer purchases an upgrade varies. Up to the year that the customer actually upgrades, assume there is a 0.50 probability that the customer upgrades in any particular year. In other words, the upgrade year of the customer is a random variable. For guidance on an appropriate way to model upgrade year, refer to Appendix 14.5. Furthermore, the revenue that OT earns from the customer's upgrade also varies (depending on the number of programs the customer decides to upgrade). Assume that the revenue from an upgrade obeys a normal distribution with a mean of $100,000 and a standard deviation of $25,000. Using the template in the file *OrangeTech*, complete a simulation model that analyzes the net present value of the revenue from the customer upgrade. Use an annual discount rate of 10%.

a. What is the average net present value that OT earns from this customer? [*Hint:* Excel's NPV function computes the net present value for a sequence of cash flows. To correctly use this function, use the formula =NPV(discount rate, flow range) + initial amount, where *discount rate* is the annual discount rate, *flow range* is the cell range containing cash flows for years 1 through *n*, and *initial amount* is the cash flow in the initial period (year 0)].

b. What is the standard deviation of net present value? How does this compare to the standard deviation of the revenue? Explain.

27. To boost holiday sales, Ginsberg jewelry store is advertising the following promotion: "If more than 7 inches of snow fall in the first 7 days of the year (January 1 through January 7), purchases made between Thanksgiving and Christmas are free!"

Based on historical sales records as well as experience with past promotions, the store manager believes that the total holiday sales between Thanksgiving and Christmas could range anywhere between $200,000 and $400,000 but is unsure of anything more specific. Ginsberg has collected data on snowfall from December 17 to January 16 for the past several winters.

Ginsberg

a. Construct a simulation model to assess potential refund amounts so that Ginsberg can evaluate the option of purchasing an insurance policy to cover potential losses. Using simulation software such as Analytic Solver Platform, incorporate the correlation in snowfall on consecutive days (as outlined in Appendix 14.4). To aid the computation of correlation in consecutive days, the file *Ginsberg* has been organized so that one column contains the snowfall amount on the day corresponding to the Day column and another column contains snowfall amount on the following day. You may safely ignore any correlation between every second day, every third day, and so on.

b. What is the probability that Ginsberg will have to refund sales?

c. What is the expected refund? Why is this a poor measure to use to assess risk?

d. What is the expected refund if snowfall exceeds 7 inches?

28. A creative entrepreneur has created a novelty soap called Jackpot. Inside each bar of Jackpot soap is a rolled-up bill of U.S. currency. There are 1,000 bars of soap in the initial offering of the soap. Although the denomination of the bill inside a bar of soap is unknown, the distribution of bills in these first 1,000 bars is given in the following table:

Bill Denomination	Number of Bills
$1	520
$5	260
$10	130
$20	60
$50	29
$100	1
Total	1,000

How many bars of soap does a customer have to buy so that, on average, she has purchased two bars of soap containing a $50 or $100 bill? (*Hint:* Use the hypergeometric distribution in simulation software such as Analytic Solver Platform to answer this question.)

29. Refer to the Jackpot soap scenario in Problem 28. After the sale of the original 1,000 bars of soap, Jackpot soap went viral, and the soap has become wildly popular. Production of the soap has been ramped up so that now millions of bars have been produced. However, the distribution of the bills in the soap obeys the same distribution as outlined in Problem 28. On average, how many bars of soap will a customer have to buy before purchasing three bars of soap each containing a bill of at least $20 value? Use the negative binomial distribution in simulation software such as Analytic Solver Platform to answer this question.

30. Press Teag Worldwide (PTW) has investments around the world that generate revenue in the British pound, the New Zealand dollar, and the Japanese yen. The quarterly revenue generated in British pounds, New Zealand dollars, and Japanese yen are £100,000, NZD 250,000, and ¥10,000,000, respectively. At the end of each quarter, PTW converts the revenue from these three international operations back into U.S. dollars, exposing PTW to exchange rate risk. The current exchange rates are $1.60 per £1, $0.82 per NZD 1, and $0.02 per ¥1. PTW wants to construct a simulation model to assess its vulnerability to the uncertain exchange rate fluctuations. The first step is to construct a spreadsheet model that appropriately captures the relationships between the various inputs. To model the fluctuation in the exchange rate between the American dollar and British pound, PTW expresses the number of U.S. dollars ($) per British Pound (£) one quarter from now by:

ExchangeRates

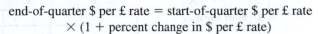

end-of-quarter $ per £ rate = start-of-quarter $ per £ rate
× (1 + percent change in $ per £ rate)

That is, given the start-of-quarter exchange rate and the percent change in the exchange rate over the quarter, this equation computes the end-of-quarter exchange rate. Analogous equations can be constructed to compute the fluctuation in the $ per New Zealand dollar (NZD) exchange rate and $ per Japanese yen (¥) in a similar manner.

a. Construct a spreadsheet model that, given the start-of-quarter exchange rate and the percent change in the exchange rate over the quarter, computes the end-of-quarter exchange rate for each of the three foreign currencies. Using these three end-of-quarter exchange rates, the spreadsheet model should then compute PTW's total quarterly revenue in U.S. dollars. If the percent change in each of three exchange rates is 0%, and thus the exchange rates stay at their current values, what is the total quarterly revenue in the U.S. dollars?

b. The percent change in the exchange rate between pairs of currencies is not known with certainty at the start of a quarter. Therefore, PTW would like to model the percent change in $ per £ rate, the percent change in $ per NZD rate, and the percent change in $ per ¥ rate as random variables. Based on the data in *Data* worksheet of the file *ExchangeRates*, use software such as Analytic Solver Platform to fit a distribution for the percent changes in the exchange rate for the three foreign currencies. Assume the exchange rate changes are independent random variables. What is the probability that the total quarterly revenue will be less than $450,000?

c. PTW realizes that the analysis in part (b) ignored potential dependency between the exchange rate fluctuations. For example, if the U.S. dollar weakens against the British pound, it may be more likely to also weaken against the New Zealand dollar. Using software such as Analytic Solver Platform, incorporate the correlation between the percent changes in the exchange rate for the three currencies (see Appendix 14.4). After accounting for any correlation, what is the probability that the total quarterly revenue will be less than $450,000?

CASE PROBLEM: FOUR CORNERS

What will your portfolio be worth in 10 years? In 20 years? When you stop working? The Human Resources Department at Four Corners Corporation was asked to develop a financial planning model that would help employees address these questions. Tom Gifford was asked to lead this effort and decided to begin by developing a financial plan for himself. Tom has a degree in business and, at the age of 40, is making $85,000 per year. Through contributions to his company's retirement program and the receipt of a small inheritance, Tom has accumulated a portfolio valued at $50,000. Tom plans to work 20 more years and hopes to accumulate a portfolio valued at $1,000,000. Can he do it?

Tom began with a few assumptions about his future salary, his new investment contributions, and his portfolio growth rate. He assumed a 5% annual salary growth rate and plans to make new investment contributions at 6% of his salary. After some research on historical stock market performance, Tom decided that a 10% annual portfolio growth rate was reasonable. Using these assumptions, Tom developed the following Excel worksheet:

	A	B	C	D	E	F	G
1	Four Corners						
2							
3	Age	40					
4	Current Salary	$85,000					
5	Current Portfolio	$50,000					
6	Annual Investment Rate	6%					
7	Salary Growth Rate	5%					
8	Portfolio Growth Rate	10%					
9							
10	Year	Beginning Balance	Salary	New Investment	Earnings	Ending Balance	Age
11	1	$50,000	$85,000	$5,100	$5,255	$60,355	41
12	2	$60,355	$89,250	$5,355	$6,303	$72,013	42
13	3	$72,013	$93,713	$5,623	$7,482	$85,118	43
14	4	$85,118	$98,398	$5,904	$8,807	$99,829	44
15	5	$99,829	$103,318	$6,199	$10,293	$116,321	45
16							

The worksheet provides a financial projection for the next five years. In computing the portfolio earnings for a given year, Tom assumed that his new investment contribution would occur evenly throughout the year, and thus half of the new investment could be included in the computation of the portfolio earnings for the year. From the worksheet, we see that, at age 45, Tom is projected to have a portfolio valued at $116,321.

Tom's plan was to use this worksheet as a template to develop financial plans for the company's employees. The data in the spreadsheet would be tailored for each employee, and rows would be added to it to reflect the employee's planning horizon. After adding another 15 rows to the worksheet, Tom found that he could expect to have a portfolio of $772,722 after 20 years. Tom then took his results to show his boss, Kate Krystkowiak.

Although Kate was pleased with Tom's progress, she voiced several criticisms. One of the criticisms was the assumption of a constant annual salary growth rate. She noted that most employees experience some variation in the annual salary growth rate from year to year. In addition, she pointed out that the constant annual portfolio growth rate was unrealistic and that the actual growth rate would vary considerably from year to year. She further suggested that a simulation model for the portfolio projection might allow Tom to account for the random variability in the salary growth rate and the portfolio growth rate.

After some research, Tom and Kate decided to assume that the annual salary growth rate would vary from 0 to 5% and that a uniform probability distribution would provide a realistic approximation. Four Corners' accountants suggested that the annual portfolio growth rate could be approximated by a normal probability distribution with a mean of 10% and a standard deviation of 5%. With this information, Tom set off to redesign his spreadsheet so that it could be used by the company's employees for financial planning.

Managerial Report

Play the role of Tom Gifford, and develop a simulation model for financial planning. Write a report for Tom's boss and, at a minimum, include the following:

For a review of Goal Seek, refer to Chapter 10.

1. Without considering the random variability, extend the current worksheet to 20 years. Confirm that by using the constant annual salary growth rate and the constant annual portfolio growth rate, Tom can expect to have a 20-year portfolio of $772,722. What would Tom's annual investment rate have to increase to in order for his portfolio to reach a 20-year, $1,000,000 goal? (*Hint:* Use Goal Seek.)

2. Redesign the spreadsheet model to incorporate the random variability of the annual salary growth rate and the annual portfolio growth rate into a simulation model. Assume that Tom is willing to use the annual investment rate that predicted a 20-year, $1,000,000 portfolio in part 1. Show how to simulate Tom's 20-year financial plan. Use results from the simulation model to comment on the uncertainty associated with Tom reaching the 20-year, $1,000,000 goal.

3. What recommendations do you have for employees with a current profile similar to Tom's after seeing the impact of the uncertainty in the annual salary growth rate and the annual portfolio growth rate?

4. Assume that Tom is willing to consider working 25 more years instead of 20 years. What is your assessment of this strategy if Tom's goal is to have a portfolio worth $1,000,000?

5. Discuss how the financial planning model developed for Tom Gifford can be used as a template to develop a financial plan for any of the company's employees.

Chapter 14 Appendix

Appendix 14.1 Land Shark Inc. Simulation with Analytic Solver Platform

In this appendix, we demonstrate the process of building a spreadsheet simulation model for the Land Shark problem in Section 14.2 with the Excel add-in Analytic Solver Platform (ASP). This Excel add-in facilitates the generation of random values from a variety of probability distributions, eases the process of executing simulation trials (no need to use Excel's Data Table tool as in Sections 14.1 and 14.2), and offers a wide array of measures and charts describing the simulation output. In the construction of a spreadsheet-based simulation model, the construction of the base spreadsheet model describing the relationships between the inputs and outputs is the same regardless of whether the analyst relies only on native Excel (as we did within the chapter) or utilizes an Excel add-in such as Analytic Solver Platform (ASP), @RISK, or Crystal Ball. Therefore, we begin our discussion of applying ASP to solve the Land Shark problem starting from the base spreadsheet model in the file *LandShark*.

Generating Values for Land Shark's Random Variables

Appendix 14.5 provides an overview of many of the various probability distributions used in ASP.

ASP provides the analyst flexibility in characterizing the possible values of the random variables in a simulation model by providing a gallery of probability distributions. ASP uses the term **uncertain variable** to refer to a random variable. These terms are synonyms referring to an uncertain quantity in a simulation model. We next demonstrate the use of ASP to specify probability distributions for the Land Shark problem.

Instead of using the ASP Ribbon buttons, the Solver Options and Model Specifications pane that appears on the right side of the spreadsheet can also be used to directly set up a simulation and/or optimization model.

First consider the number of bidders. The number of bidders has ranged from two to eight over the past 50 auctions. Unless Land Shark has reason to believe that there may be fewer than two bids on an upcoming auction, it is probably safe to assume that there will be a minimum of two competing bids. There has not been an auction with more than eight bidders, so eight is a reasonable assumption for the maximum number of competing bids unless Land Shark's experience with the local real estate market suggests that more than eight competing bids is possible.

With only 50 data points, there is limited information on the relative likelihood of different values for the number of bidders in the range from two to eight. Due to this lack of information, Land Shark decides to use an integer uniform distribution in which the number of bidders is equally likely to be 2, 3, 4, 5, 6, 7, or 8. To implement this probability distribution in the Land Shark simulation model, we follow these steps:

DATA *file*

LandShark

Placing the mouse pointer over a cell that contains an ASP probability distribution displays a mini-dialog box with a chart that illustrates the distribution in the cell. Clicking the upper right-hand corner of this box will open a larger dialog box for this distribution.

Step 1. Select cell B5 in the *Model* worksheet (corresponding to the number of bidders)
Step 2. Click the **Analytic Solver Platform** tab in the Ribbon
Step 3. Click **Distributions** in the **Simulation Model** group
Step 4. Select **Discrete** and click **IntUniform**
Step 5. When the **$B$5** dialog box appears (Figure 14.14), in the **Parameters** area:
Enter 2 in the box to the right of **lower**
Enter 8 in the box to the right of **upper**
Step 6. Click **Save**

Each competitor's bid percentage is also a random variable. From the past 50 auctions, Land Shark has gathered 250 observations of how competitors have bid (as a percentage

The Distribution Wizard option under the Distributions button in the Simulation Model group of the Analytic Solver Platform tab guides the user through the steps of identifying an appropriate probability distribution for a random variable.

| FIGURE 14.14 | Entering an Integer Uniform Distribution |

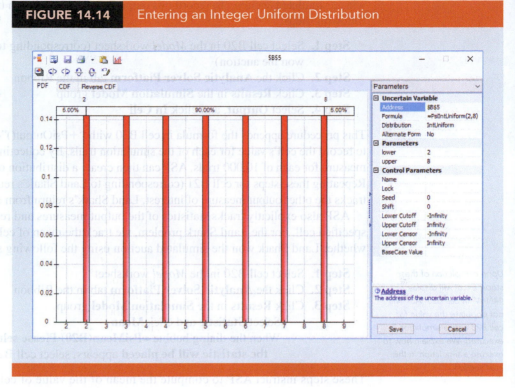

If the sample data do not adequately characterize the set of values for a random variable, it may be more appropriate to fit a distribution using the Fit procedure in the Tools group of the Analytic Solver Platform tab. We demonstrate fitting a distribution in Appendix 14.2.

of the estimated value). Land Shark believes that these 250 bid values are an accurate representation of the distribution of future bids. Thus, we will simulate the bids for the upcoming auction by randomly selecting a value from one of these 250 bid values using the Resample distribution in ASP. When using the Resample distribution on sample data, we note that only values that exist in the data will be possible values for a simulation trial. Resampling empirical data is a good approach only when the data adequately represents the range of possible values and the distribution of values across this range.

The following steps demonstrate how to simulate values of competing bids by resampling empirical data:

The argument BidList!$B$2:$B$251 in Step 5 tells ASP to look in cells B2:B251 of the BidList worksheet to find the possible values for the random variable.

Step 1. Select cell B8 in the *Model* worksheet
Step 2. Click the **Analytic Solver Platform** tab in the Ribbon
Step 3. Click **Distributions** in the **Simulation Model** group
Select **Custom,** and click **Resample**
Step 4. When the dialog bubble **=PsiResample(Range) Please select a Range** appears, select the range B2:B251 in the *BidList* worksheet
Step 5. In cell B8 of the *Model* worksheet, change the relative referencing to absolute referencing so the formula reads =PsiResample(BidList!$B$2:$B$251)
Step 6. Copy cell B8 and paste into cells B9 through B15 (see Figure 14.15)

Tracking Output Measures for Land Shark

After defining all the random variables with ASP, we are ready to use ASP to track output measures. For Land Shark, one output measure of interest is whether Land Shark wins a simulated auction. To record this output over the simulation trials, we apply the following steps:

Step 1. Select cell B20 in the *Model* worksheet (corresponding to whether Land Shark won the auction)
Step 2. Click the **Analytic Solver Platform** tab in the Ribbon
Step 3. Click **Results** in the **Simulation Model** group
Step 4. Select **Output**, and click **In Cell**

This procedure appends the formula in cell B20 with "+PsiOutput()"—which triggers ASP to record the cell's value for each of the simulation trials. By collecting the value of an output measure for each of 10,000 trials, ASP can then create a distribution of the output measure. Repeating these steps for cell B21 (corresponding to Land Shark's return on the auction) tracks the other output measure of interest, Land Shark's return from a simulated auction.

ASP also explicitly tracks statistics of the output measures and records them in a specified cell. For the Land Shark problem, we track the mean of cell B20, which indicates whether Land Shark won the simulated auction using the following steps:

Upon completion of these steps, Excel will display "#N/A" in cell B23. ASP will not populate the value for cell B23 until a simulation is executed. We explain how to execute a simulation in the next section.

Step 1. Select cell B20 in the *Model* worksheet
Step 2. Click the **Analytic Solver Platform** tab in the Ribbon
Step 3. Click **Results** in the **Simulation Model** group
  Select **Statistic** and click **Mean**
  When the dialog bubble **=PsiMean(B20) Please select the cell where the statistic will be placed** appears, select cell B23

These steps instruct ASP to compute the mean of the value of cell B20 over the simulation trials and place it in cell B23. Computing the mean of a function that is one if Land Shark wins the auction and zero if Land Shark loses the auction is equivalent to counting the number of trials in which Land Shark wins the simulated auction and dividing by the number of auctions; in other words, this mean (or expected value) corresponds to a probability estimate that Land Shark wins the upcoming auction.

To track the mean of Land Shark's return from the set of simulated auctions, we execute the following steps:

Upon completion of these steps, Excel will display "#N/A" in cell B24. ASP will not populate the value for cell B24 until a simulation is executed. We explain how to execute the simulation in the next section.

Step 1. Select cell B21 in the *Model* worksheet
Step 2. Click the **Analytic Solver Platform** tab in the Ribbon
Step 3. Click **Results** in the **Simulation Model** group
  Select **Statistic** and click **Mean**
  When the dialog bubble **=PsiMean(B21) Please select the cell where the statistic will be placed** appears, select cell B24

Figure 14.15 shows the formula view of the Land Shark simulation model after its construction via ASP.

Executing Simulation Trials and Analyzing Output for Land Shark

When there is more than one uncertain function in the model, the Chart Wizard dialog box will appear and display histograms of up to six cells corresponding to uncertain functions and uncertain variables.

ASP provides many user options for executing a simulation. For the Land Shark problem, the following steps explain how to set the number of trials to 10,000.

Step 1. Click the **Analytic Solver Platform** tab in the Ribbon
Step 2. In the **Tools** group, enter *10000* in the box next to **Trials:**

The following steps describe how to execute the set of 10,000 simulation trials, to analyze simulation output, and then to interactively observe the effect of varying Land Shark's bid amount (or any fixed value in the spreadsheet model).

FIGURE 14.15	Land Shark Simulation Model

	A	B	C
1	Land Shark		
2			
3	Parameters		
4	Estimated Value	1389000	
5	Number of Bidders	=PsiIntUniform(2,8)	
6			
7	Bid Index	Bid (% of Estimated Value)	Bid Amount
8	1	=PsiResample(BidList!$B$2:$B$251)	=IF(A8>$B$5,0,B8*$B$4)
9	2	=PsiResample(BidList!$B$2:$B$251)	=IF(A9>$B$5,0,B9*$B$4)
10	3	=PsiResample(BidList!$B$2:$B$251)	=IF(A10>$B$5,0,B10*$B$4)
11	4	=PsiResample(BidList!$B$2:$B$251)	=IF(A11>$B$5,0,B11*$B$4)
12	5	=PsiResample(BidList!$B$2:$B$251)	=IF(A12>$B$5,0,B12*$B$4)
13	6	=PsiResample(BidList!$B$2:$B$251)	=IF(A13>$B$5,0,B13*$B$4)
14	7	=PsiResample(BidList!$B$2:$B$251)	=IF(A14>$B$5,0,B14*$B$4)
15	8	=PsiResample(BidList!$B$2:$B$251)	=IF(A15>$B$5,0,B15*$B$4)
16			
17	Model		
18	Land Shark Bid Amount	1230000	
19	Largest Competitor Bid	=MAX(C8:C15)	
20	Land Shark Win Auction?	=IF(B18>B19,1,0) + PsiOutput()	
21	Land Shark Return	=B20*(B4-B18) + PsiOutput()	
22			
23	P(Land Shark Wins Auction)	=PsiMean(B20)	
24	Expected Return	=PsiMean(B21)	

When interactive simulation in ASP is activated, the spreadsheet will automatically rerun the simulation to evaluate changes to any of the values in the spreadsheet.

Step 1. Click the **Analytic Solver Platform** tab in the Ribbon

Step 2. Click the arrow under **Simulate** from the **Solve Action** group
From the drop-down menu that appears, select **Interactive**

Step 3. When the **Chart Wizard** dialog box appears (Figure 14.16), double-click on the **$B$21(func)** histogram in the top row to activate the **$B$21** dialog box (Figure 14.17)

Step 4. Select cell B18 and enter *1300000* (Figure 14.18)

This histogram for $B$21 displays the distribution of Land Shark's return over the 10,000 simulation trials. As Figure 14.17 illustrates, if Land Shark bids $1,230,000 on the property, it has a probability of approximately 0.2368 of winning the auction and an expected return of $37,651. Figure 14.18 shows that if Land Shark increases its bid amount to $1,300,000, its estimated probability of winning the auction increases to 0.786 and its expected return increases to $69,954.

Increasing the number of trials per simulation reduces the sampling error of the estimates of the output. We typically use 10,000 trials, but you may use up to 100,000 trials in the educational version of ASP. To get an idea of how much noise is in the output statistics, rerun the simulation, and observe how much output statistics change. For example, in the Land Shark problem, the probability that Land Shark wins the auction when bidding $1,250,000 is consistently between 0.4900 and 0.5050, whereas the expected

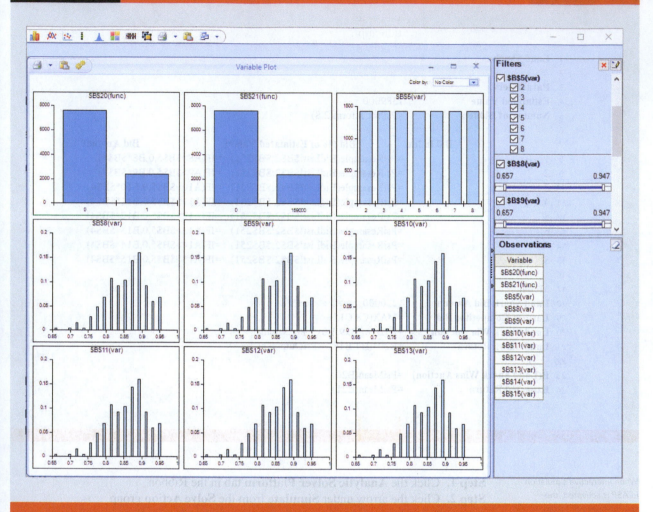

Pressing F9 in Excel will rerun the specified number of simulation trials (10,000 in our example).

return is consistently between $77,500 and $78,500, suggesting that the 10,000 trials is sufficient for obtaining a precise estimate.

Recall that when you run your simulation in the file *LandSharkASP*, the values you see will be different; this is to be expected when running a simulation. To create a reproducible experiment, you can fix the set of random numbers used in a simulation. In ASP, this is accomplished by selecting the **Options** tab in the **Options** group, clicking the **Simulation** tab in the **Analytic Solver Platform Options** dialog box, and then setting the **Sim. Random Seed** to a positive number of your choice.

As an alternative to manually varying the value of an input such as the Land Shark bid amount, ASP allows an analyst to execute a set of parameterized simulations, in which each simulation run is executed with a different specified value of the input. We demonstrate this functionality on the Land Shark example. Suppose we are interested in evaluating how varying Land Shark's bid amount affects its expected return. As shown in Figure 14.19, we enter a table of values for the Land Shark bid amount ranging from $1,250,000 to $1,340,000 in cells D19:D28.

FIGURE 14.17   Land Shark Simulation Output

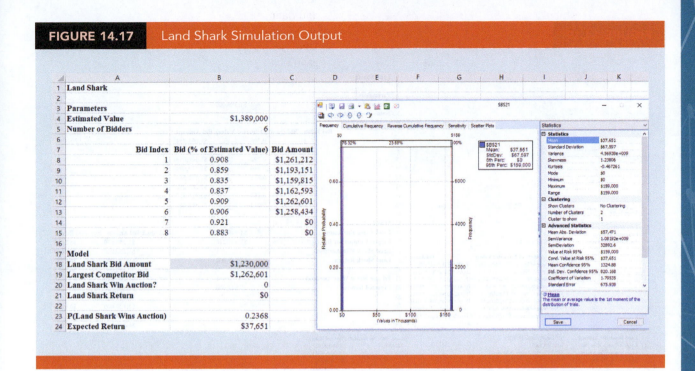

FIGURE 14.18   Land Shark Simulation Output with Adjusted Bid Amount

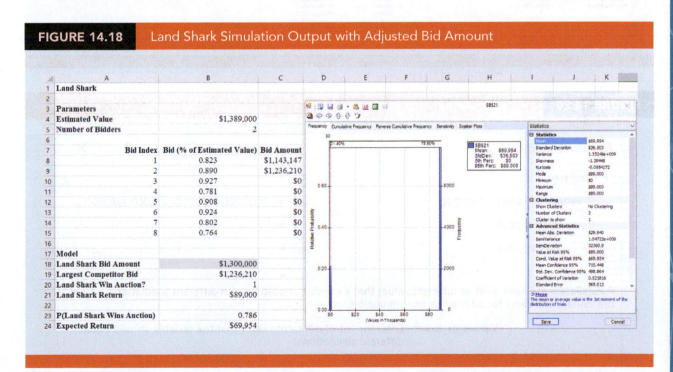

MODEL *file*

LandSharkASP

To execute the 10,000 trials with the bid amount at each of the 10 bid amount values shown in Figure 14.19, we implement the following steps:

Step 1. Click the **Analytic Solver Platform** tab in the Ribbon

Step 2. Select cell B18 (which contains Land Shark's bid amount)

FIGURE 14.19   Executing a Set of Simulations with Varying Land Shark Bid Amount

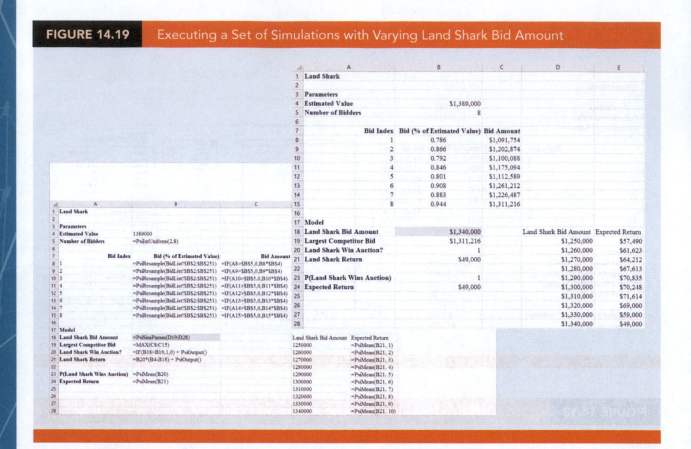

FIGURE 14.20   Function Arguments Dialog Box

Function Arguments   ?   ✕

PsiSimParam

Values_or_lower	D19:D28	=	{1250000;1260000;1270000;1280000;...
Upper		=	
Base_case		=	

        =   1250000

PsiSimParam provides a list of different values that a variable should have in different simulations, where the value is the same for all trials in one simulation.

        Values_or_lower   Enter the list of different values that the variable should equal in different simulations.

Formula result = $1,250,000

Help on this function   OK   Cancel

FIGURE 14.21   Simulation Options Dialog Box

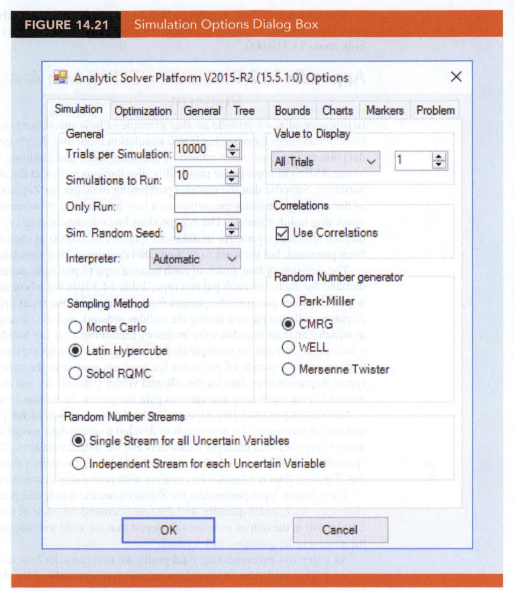

*Setting **Sim. Random Seed**
to a positive number will fix
the sequence of random
variables generated in a
series of simulation trials
allowing the analyst to conduct
reproducible experiments.*

Step 3. Click **Parameters** in the **Parameters** group
  Select **Simulation**
  When the **Function Arguments** dialog box appears (Figure 14.20), in the
  box next to **Values_or_lower**, enter *D19:D28*
Step 4. Click **OK**
Step 5. Click **Options** in the **Options** group
  When the **Analytic Solver Platform Options** dialog box appears
  (Figure 14.21), enter *10* in the box next to **Simulations to Run:**
Step 6. Click **OK**
Step 7. Select cell B21 (which contains Land Shark's return)
Step 8. Click **Results** in the **Simulation Model** group
  Select **Statistic** and click **Mean**
  When the dialog bubble **=PsiMean(B21) Please select the cell where the
  statistic will be placed** appears, select the cell range E19:E28

When modeling the competitor's bids by resampling the 250 bids in the *BidList* worksheet, Figure 14.19 shows that Land Shark's expected return is maximized when it bids about $1,310,000.

Appendix 14.2 Distribution Fitting with Analytic Solver Platform

In this appendix, we provide another example of how specialized simulation software such as ASP facilitates more sophisticated simulation modeling. Motivated by the purchasing decision facing Zapatoes, a retailer of women's shoes and clothing, we demonstrate how to use ASP to fit appropriate probability distributions to model the associated random variables. Suppose that the regional purchasing manager for Zapatoes is in the process of determining the order quantities for a new product line of women's sleepwear for the upcoming holiday season. The new product line consists of four types of pajamas: cotton, flannel, silk, and velour. An initial order quantity of 10,000 of each type of pajama has been proposed, but we want to evaluate this decision with a simulation model.

The decision of how much of each pajama type to purchase depends on the pricing and demand for each. For each pajama type, Table 14.3 lists the wholesale price (the price at which Zapatoes procures the pajama from its supplier), the retail price (the price at which Zapatoes sells the pajama during the holiday season), and the clearance price (the price at which Zapatoes liquidates the inventory remaining after the holiday season). To help estimate the demand for each pajama type, Zapatoes' marketing department has gathered a representative sample of past sales for products similar to the cotton and flannel pajama types. Representative data for the silk and velour pajamas are not available, so we must work with the marketing managers to gain insight on the demand for these products.

Our first step in modeling Zapatoes' ordering decision is to identify the input parameters and output measures. The next step is to develop a spreadsheet model that conveys the logical relationships between the input parameters and the output measures. Then we prepare the spreadsheet model for simulation analysis by replacing the static values of the input parameters that Zapatoes does not know with certainty with probability distributions of possible values.

The relevant input parameters for Zapatoes are the wholesale price, retail price, clearance price, order quantity, and the retail demand for each of the four pajama types. Total profit is the output measure of interest that we want to compute for given values of the prices, order quantity, and demand.

As a step toward computing total profit, we first consider how to compute the retail sales volume. The retail sales volume for a pajama type depends on the demand and the order quantity.

$$\text{Retail sales} = \text{minimum}\{\text{demand, order quantity}\} \tag{14.7}$$

In other words, the amount of a pajama type sold at retail price is the minimum of the amount demanded and the amount available.

TABLE 14.3	Pajama Price Information		
	Wholesale Price	**Retail Price**	**Clearance Price**
Cotton Pajama	$25	$30	$10
Flannel Pajama	$25	$40	$10
Silk Pajama	$35	$60	$30
Velour Pajama	$30	$55	$20

Pajamas not sold at retail price during the selling season are sold at their respective clearance prices in the weeks after the holidays. The clearance sales volume for a pajama type is computed as:

$$\text{Clearance sales} = \text{order quantity} - \text{retail sales}. \qquad (14.8)$$

Profit corresponding to the sales of a pajama type is computed from the retail sales and clearance sales by multiplying each by their corresponding profit margin. The profit margin for a retail sale is the retail price (p_r) minus the wholesale price (p_w). The profit margin for a clearance sale is the clearance price (p_c) minus the wholesale price (p_w). Thus, the profit resulting from a pajama type is:

$$\text{Profit} = \text{retail sales} \times (p_r - p_w) + \text{clearance sales} \times (p_c - p_w). \qquad (14.9)$$

Figure 14.22 shows the Excel formula logic of the spreadsheet model. Cells H5 through H8 apply equation (14.7) to compute the retail sales volume for each pajama type. Cells I5 through I8 apply equation (14.8) to compute the clearance sales volume for each pajama type. Cells J5 through J8 apply equation (14.9) to compute the profit corresponding to each pajama type. We compute the total profit across all pajama types with the Excel formula =SUM(J5:J8) in cell J9; this is the output measure that Zapatoes wants to track. Cells G5 through G8 contain the order quantities (highlighted in gray to denote that these are controllable decisions).

Modeling Random Variables for Zapatoes

Zapatoes

Cells E5 through E8 of Figure 14.22 contain values for the demand for each pajama type. The demand for each pajama type is a random variable whose value is not known with certainty at the time Zapatoes must determine their order quantities. In this section, we demonstrate several different ways to model the uncertainty in the demand for the four pajama types.

The cotton and flannel pajamas are similar to other products that Zapatoes has sold in the past. The marketing department has compiled representative samples of cotton and

---

FIGURE 14.22   Zapatoes Spreadsheet Model

	A	B	C	D	E	F	G	H	I	J
1	Zapatoes									
2										
3	Parameters						Model			
4		Wholesale Price	Retail Price	Clearance Price	Demand		Order Quantity	Retail Sales	Clearance Sales	Profit
5	Cotton Pajama	25	30	10	25000		10000	=MIN(E5,G5)	=G5-H5	=(H5*(C5-B5))+(I5*(D5-B5))
6	Flannel Pajama	25	40	10	15000		10000	=MIN(E6,G6)	=G6-H6	=(H6*(C6-B6))+(I6*(D6-B6))
7	Silk Pajama	35	60	30	10000		10000	=MIN(E7,G7)	=G7-H7	=(H7*(C7-B7))+(I7*(D7-B7))
8	Velour Pajama	30	55	20	5000		10000	=MIN(E8,G8)	=G8-H8	=(H8*(C8-B8))+(I8*(D8-B8))
9									Total Profit:	=SUM(J5:J8)
10										
11	Silk Pajama Demand							Mean Total Profit:		
12	Minimum value	0								
13	Maximum value	30000								
14										
15	Values	Likelihood								
16	5000	0.1								
17	10000	0.4								
18	15000	0.2								
19	20000	0.25								
20	25000	0.05								
21										
22										
23	Velour Pajama Demand									
24	Minimum value	2500								
25	Most likely value	10000								
26	Maximum value	25000								

FIGURE 14.23   Fit Options Dialog Box for Cotton Pajamas

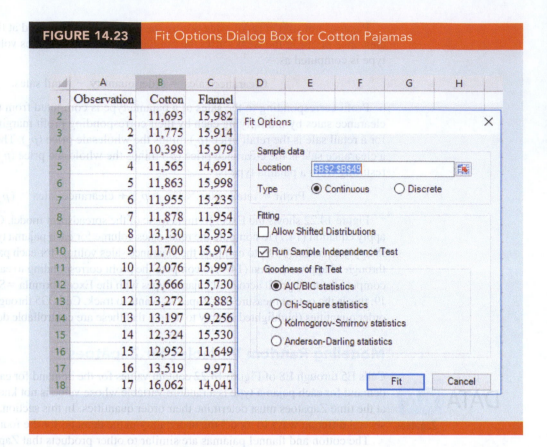

flannel pajama demand, respectively. These data are provided in the worksheet labeled *Data* in the file *Zapatoes*. The following steps demonstrate how to use ASP to fit a probability distribution to characterize the demand for cotton pajamas.

DATA *file*

Zapatoes

Step 1. Select cells B2:B49 in the *Data* worksheet
Step 2. Click the **Analytic Solver Platform** tab in the Ribbon
Step 3. Click **Fit** in the **Tools** group
Step 4. When the **Fit Options** dialog box appears (Figure 14.23):
         Verify that $B$2:$B$49 is entered in the box next to **Location** and the checkbox for **Allow Shifted Distributions** is *not* selected
         Click **Fit**

At this point, a **Fit Results** dialog box appears (Figure 14.24). In the left pane of the **Fit Results** dialog box, ASP lists the distributions fit to the data in order of decreasing goodness-of-fit. ASP attempts to fit many distributions to the data, including several exotic distributions. To view the fit of a distribution, click the box next to the distribution. For example, Figure 14.24 shows that, by clicking the box next to the **MaxExtreme** and **BetaGeneral** distributions, we can visually compare the maximum extreme value and beta distributions to the uniform distribution, which mathematically is the best-fitting.

In addition to the statistical fit of the various distributions to the sample data, it is important to emphasize that the analyst should also take into consideration qualitative factors in selecting a distribution (particularly when fitting a distribution to a small sample of data). By clicking on **Uniform** in the upper-right pane of the **Fit Results** dialog box, we can view statistical properties about the fitted uniform distribution. This fitted uniform distribution has a minimum value of 10,398, a maximum value of 24,172, a mean of 17,285, and a standard deviation of

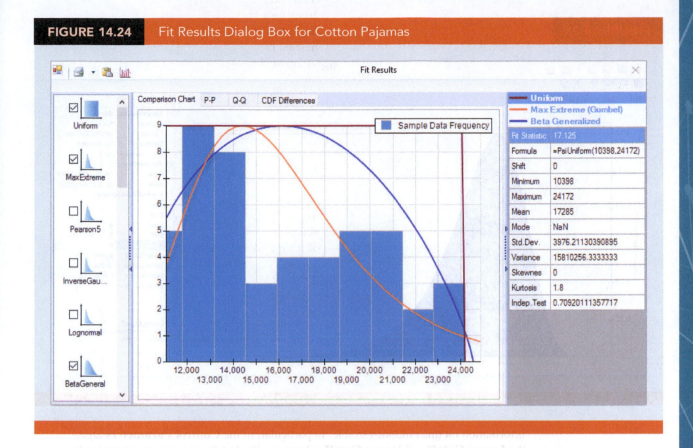

FIGURE 14.24   Fit Results Dialog Box for Cotton Pajamas

3,976. If we want to allow levels of demand outside this range, then the uniform distribution is not appropriate (or should be adjusted). Clicking on **Max Extreme (Gumbel)** in the upper-right pane of the **Fit Results** dialog box, we observe that the fitted maximum extreme value distribution ranges from negative infinity to positive infinity and has a mean and standard deviation of 16,152 and 3,919, respectively. Clicking on **Beta Generalized** in the upper-right pane of the Fit Results dialog box, we observe that the fitted beta distribution ranges from 9,231 to 24,536 and has a mean and standard deviation of 16,550 and 3,608, respectively.

In this case, Zapatoes believes that the fitted maximum extreme value distribution appropriately captures the behavior of cotton pajama demand. Regardless, it is generally a good idea to test the impact of the distribution choice by running the simulation with various distributions for the random variables and observing the impact on the output measures. To complete the process of modeling the cotton pajama demand as a maximum extreme value random variable, we execute the following steps:

Step 5. In the left pane of the **Fit Results** dialog box, uncheck the boxes to the left of all distributions except **MaxExtreme** so that it is the only distribution selected

Step 6. Close the **Fit Results** dialog box by clicking the [✕] in the upper right corner of the dialog box

Step 7. Click **Yes** in response to the query **Do you wish to accept the fitted distribution?**

Step 8. Select cell E5 in the *Model* worksheet (this cell corresponds to the demand for cotton pajamas)

Step 9. When the **$E$5** dialog box appears, click **Save**

Setting the lower cutoff to zero for a probability distribution prevents negative values from being sampled from the distribution by effectively rescaling the distribution.

To view the distribution of cotton pajama demand, double-click cell E5 to open the **$E$5** dialog box. As Figure 14.25 illustrates, the right pane of this dialog box contains

FIGURE 14.25   Modeling Cotton Pajama Demand

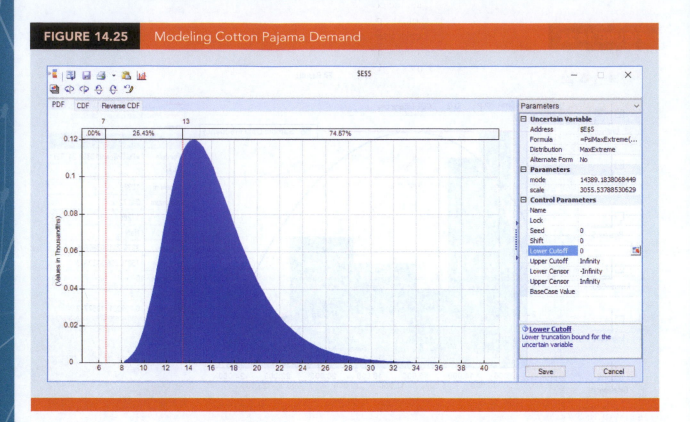

information on this random variable. In particular, in the **Control Parameters** area, the **Lower Cutoff** and **Upper Cutoff** values specify that the maximum extreme value distribution is unbounded (extremely large and small values are possible, although unlikely). To reflect the fact that negative values of cotton pajama demand are not possible, we enter *0* in the box to the right of **Lower Cutoff** and click **Save**.

Now we turn to fitting a distribution for flannel pajama demand by following steps similar to those for fitting a distribution for cotton pajama demand:

Step 1. Select cells C2:C49 in the *Data* worksheet

Step 2. Click the **Analytic Solver Platform** tab in the Ribbon

Step 3. Click **Fit** in the **Tools** group

Step 4. When the **Fit Options** dialog box appears:

Verify that $C$2:$C$49 is entered in the box next to **Location** and the checkbox for **Allow Shifted Distributions** is *not* selected

Click **Fit**

At this point, a **Fit Results** dialog box appears (Figure 14.26). For flannel pajama demand, the beta (**BetaGeneral**) distribution provides the best mathematical fit to the sample of 48 observations. As Figure 14.26 illustrates, we compare the **BetaGeneral** distribution, **Normal** distribution, and **Gamma** distribution by selecting the checkbox next to each of these distributions in the left pane of the **Fit Results** dialog box. Each of these distributions would imply different characteristics for the flannel pajama demand. For the beta distribution fit to this data, small values close to the minimum of 2,172 or large values close to maximum of 15,999 are the most likely and values in between are less likely. For the normal distribution fit to this data, values near the mean of 8,763 are most likely, with more extreme values being less likely. The gamma distribution fit to this data is positively

FIGURE 14.26   Comparing Distribution Fits to Flannel Pajama Demand

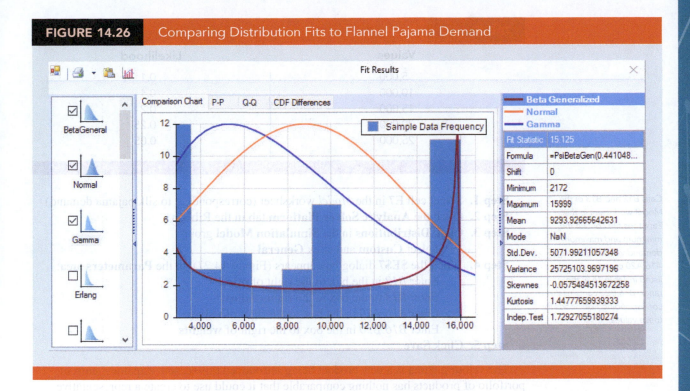

skewed, with the most likely values being less than the mean of 8,763, but a higher probability of extremely large values than the normal distribution fit to this data.

Zapatoes is satisfied that the minimum (2,172) and maximum (15,999) of the fitted distribution sufficiently captures the range of outcomes. Furthermore, based on awareness of the boom-and-bust nature of flannel pajamas, Zapatoes decides that the near-minimum or near-maximum values being the most likely is accurate. Regardless, it is a good modeling practice to test the sensitivity of the output measures to the choice of distribution by running the simulation with various distributions for the random variables.

To complete the process of modeling the cotton pajama demand as a beta random variable, we complete the following steps:

Step 5. In the left pane of the **Fit Results** dialog box, uncheck the boxes to the left of all distributions except **BetaGeneral** so that it is the only distribution selected

Step 6. Close the **Fit Results** dialog box by cliking the ☒ in upper right corner of the dialog box

Step 7. Click **Yes** in response to the query **Do you wish to accept the fitted distribution?**

Step 8. Select cell E6 in the *Model* worksheet (this cell corresponds to the demand for cotton pajamas)

Step 9. Click **Save**

Because the silk pajama's design is different from that of all other Zapatoes' existing products, the marketing department does not believe that we should use past retail sales of other silk attire to estimate the demand distribution for the new silk pajama type. However, Zapatoes has conducted extensive marketing surveys to estimate likely demand scenarios for silk pajamas. Based on these marketing surveys, Zapatoes produced Table 14.4. Zapatoes also estimates a minimum silk pajama demand of 0 and a maximum possible demand of 30,000. We use this information to construct a custom (continuous) general distribution for silk pajama demand with the following steps.

TABLE 14.4	Estimates of Silk Pajama Demand	
Values		**Likelihood**
5,000		0.1
10,000		0.4
15,000		0.2
20,000		0.25
25,000		0.05

Cells B12 and B13 of the Model worksheet in the Zapatoes file contain the minimum and maximum demand values. The range A16:A20 contains the values listed in Table 14.4; the range B16:B20 contains the corresponding likelihoods for these values.

Step 1. Select cell E7 in the *Model* worksheet (corresponding to silk pajama demand)

Step 2. Click the **Analytic Solver Platform** tab in the Ribbon

Step 3. Click **Distributions** in the **Simulation Model** group
   Select **Custom** and click **General**

Step 4. When the **$E$7** dialog box appears (Figure 14.27), in the **Parameters** area:
   Enter *B12* in the box to the right of **min**
   Enter *B13* in the box to the right of **max**
   Enter *A16:A20* in the box to the right of **values**
   Enter *B16:B20* in the box to the right of **weights**

Step 5. Click **Save**

The velour pajama is a new product being introduced this season. Zapatoes' current portfolio of products has nothing comparable that it could use to create a representative

FIGURE 14.27   Custom General Distribution for Silk Pajama Demand

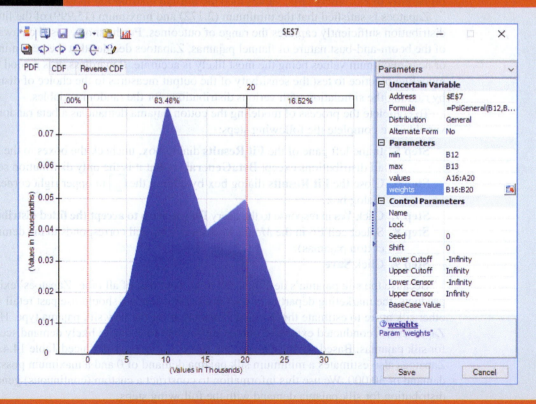

The velour pajama demand parameters (minimum, most likely, and maximum) are contained in cells B24:B26 of the Model worksheet of the Zapatoes file.

sample, and little information is known on potential demand for the product. However, a panel of Zapatoes' most experienced marketing managers has estimated that the minimum, likely, and maximum values of velour pajama demand are 2,500 units, 10,000 units, and 25,000 units, respectively. We use these values to model the velour pajama demand with a triangular distribution with the following steps:

Step 1. Select cell E8 in the *Model* worksheet (corresponding to velour pajama demand)
Step 2. Click the **Analytic Solver Platform** tab in the Ribbon
Step 3. Click **Distributions** in the **Simulation Model** group
　　　　Select **Common** and click **Triangular**

The triangular probability distribution is also discussed in Chapter 5. ASP uses the term likely to refer to the mode of the triangular distribution.

Step 4. In the **Parameters** area of the **$E$8** dialog box (Figure 14.28):
　　　　Enter *B24* in the box to the right of **min**
　　　　Enter *B25* in the box to the right of **likely**
　　　　Enter *B26* in the box to the right of **max**
Step 5. Click **Save**

Tracking Output Measures for Zapatoes

After defining all the random variables with ASP, we are ready to use ASP to track output measures. For Zapatoes, the primary output measure of interest is the total profit summed across all four pajama types. To record this output over the simulation trials, we apply the following steps:

Step 1. Select cell J9 in the *Model* worksheet (corresponding the total profit summed across pajama types)
Step 2. Click the **Analytic Solver Platform** tab in the Ribbon
Step 3. Click **Results** in the **Simulation Model** group
　　　　Select **Output** and click **In Cell**

This procedure appends the formula in cell J9 with "+PsiOutput()"—which triggers the ASP to record the cell's value for each of the simulation trials. By collecting the value of total profit for each of 10,000 trials, ASP then can create a distribution of total profit.

FIGURE 14.28　　Triangular Distribution for Velour Pajama Demand

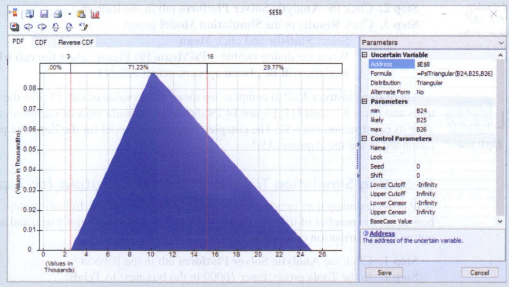

FIGURE 14.29 Zapatoes Simulation Model

	A	B	C	D	E	F	G	H	I	J
1	Zapatoes									
2										
3	Parameters						Model			
4		Wholesale Price	Retail Price	Clearance Price	Demand		Order Quantity	Retail Sales	Clearance Sales	Profit
5	Cotton Pajama	25	30	10	=PsiMaxExtreme(14389,3056,PsiTruncate(0, 1E+30))		10000	=MIN(E5,G5)	=G5-H5	=(H5*(C5-B5))+(I5*(D5-B5))
6	Flannel Pajama	25	40	10	=PsiBetaGen(0.441,0.4152,2172,15999)		10000	=MIN(E6,G6)	=G6-H6	=(H6*(C6-B6))+(I6*(D6-B6))
7	Silk Pajama	35	60	30	=PsiGeneral(B12,B13,A16:A20,B16:B20)		10000	=MIN(E7,G7)	=G7-H7	=(H7*(C7-B7))+(I7*(D7-B7))
8	Velour Pajama	30	55	20	=PsiTriangular(B24,B25,B26)		10000	=MIN(E8,G8)	=G8-H8	=(H8*(C8-B8))+(I8*(D8-B8))
9									Total Profit:	=SUM(J5:J8) + PsiOutput()
10										
11	Silk Pajama Demand								Mean Total Profit:	=PsiMean(J9)
12	Minimum value	0								
13	Maximum value	30000								
14										
15	Values	Likelihood								
16	5000	0.1								
17	10000	0.4								
18	15000	0.2								
19	20000	0.25								
20	25000	0.05								
21										
22										
23	Velour Pajama Demand									
24	Minimum value	2500								
25	Most likely value	10000								
26	Maximum value	25000								

ASP also allows us to explicitly track statistics of the output measures and record them in a specified cell. We track the mean total profit using the following steps:

On completion of these steps, Excel will display "#N/A" in cell J11. ASP will not populate the value for cell J11 until a simulation is executed.

Step 1. Select cell J9 in the *Model* worksheet
Step 2. Click the **Analytic Solver Platform** tab in the Ribbon
Step 3. Click **Results** in the **Simulation Model** group
Select **Statistic** and click **Mean**
When the dialog bubble **=PsiMean(J9) Please select the cell where the statistic will be placed** appears, select cell J11

MODEL *file*
ZapatoesASP

These steps instruct ASP to compute the mean of the value of cell J9 over the simulation trials and place it in cell J11. Figure 14.29 shows the formula view of the simulation model after its construction via ASP. The complete simulation model for the Zapatoes problem is contained in the file *ZapatoesASP*.

Executing Simulation Trials and Analyzing Output for Zapatoes

ASP provides many user options for executing a simulation. The following steps illustrate how to set the number of trials to 10,000, execute a set of simulation trials, and analyze the output (the distribution of total profit).

Step 1. Click the **Analytic Solver Platform** tab in the Ribbon
Step 2. In the **Tools** group, enter *10000* in the box next to **Trials:**
Step 3. Click the arrow under **Simulate** in the **Solve Action** group
From the drop-down menu that appears, click **Interactive**

FIGURE 14.30   Distribution of Total Profit with Order Quantities = 10,000

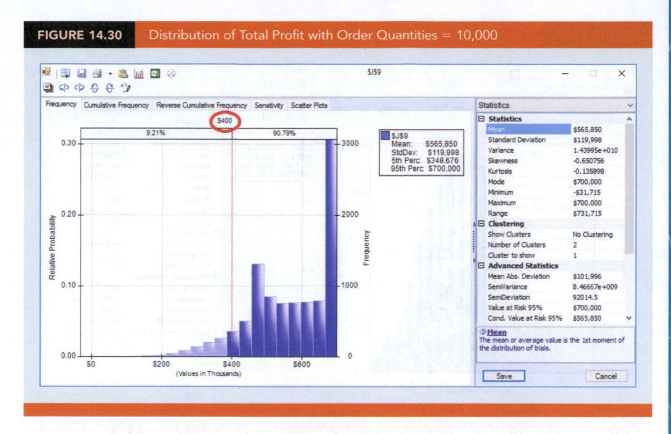

Step 4. When the **$J$9** dialog box appears, click on the number at the top of the chart (above the red dotted line) and enter *400* (see red circle in Figure 14.30)
Click **Save**

Due to differences in the random numbers generated, simulation results will vary.

Figure 14.30 shows the output of one set of 10,000 simulation trials when Zapatoes orders 10,000 of each pajama type. From Figure 14.30, we see that the mean total profit is $565,850. In addition, the minimum profit over 10,000 simulation trials is −$31,715 and the maximum profit is $700,000. By specifying a value of 400 in Step 4 above, we observe that there is an estimated 0.9079 probability that Zapatoes will make more than $400,000 (and hence a 0.0921 probability that Zapatoes will make less than $400,000). At first glance, the shape of the total profit distribution is a bit surprising (with a large number of trials resulting in the maximum value of $700,000 profit). This maximum value occurs when demand exceeds the order quantity for all four pajama types and sells all the pajamas ordered; Zapatoes can never sell more pajamas than it orders!

To see how the distribution of total profit is affected by the order quantity, we can rerun the simulation for different order quantities. For example, we can change the order quantities of each type of pajama by entering 18,000 in cells G5, G6, G7, and G8. Figure 14.31 shows the distribution of total profit for one possible set of 10,000 simulation trials. We now observe that the mean total profit is $585,447, which is an increase of $19,597 over the case when ordering 10,000 units of each pajama type. The minimum profit over 10,000 simulation trials is −$217,765, and the maximum profit is $1,199,968. There is an estimated 0.7596 probability that Zapatoes will make more than $400,000 (and hence a 0.2404 probability that Zapatoes will make less than $400,000). This analysis indicates that doubling the order quantity increases the mean total profit and increases the upside (in terms of chance of larger profits) but also exposes Zapatoes to a larger chance of smaller profits.

We see from Figure 14.31 that the distribution of total profit is bell-shaped. When order quantities are sufficiently high (so that they do not limit profit potential), low profit contributions

FIGURE 14.31   Distribution of Total Profit with Order Quantities = 18,000

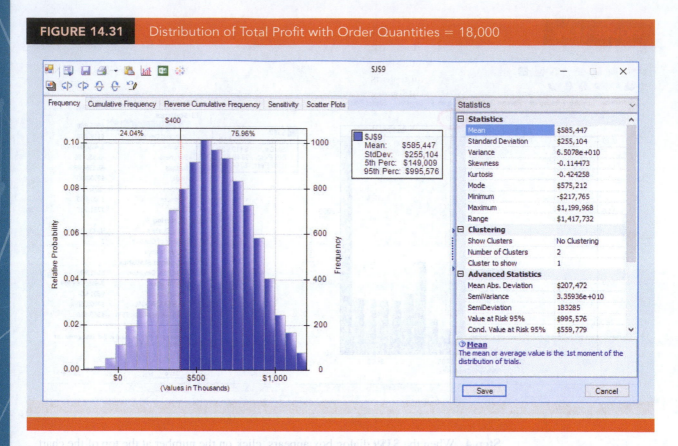

from one pajama type are often offset by high profit contributions from another pajama type. The result of the offsetting profit contributions among pajama types is that moderate total profit amounts are more common than extremely low or high total profit amounts.

The resulting bell-shaped histogram in Figure 14.31 is the result of the general statistical concept known as the central limit theorem. The central limit theorem states that the sum of independent random variables can be approximated by a normal probability distribution as the number of random variables being added gets large. In this case, the total profit is the sum of the uncertain profits from the four pajama types, which we have assumed are independent.

Appendix 14.3 Simulation Optimization with Analytic Solver Platform

In Appendix 14.2, we demonstrated how to evaluate different order quantities for the Zapatoes problem by rerunning simulations for different values of the decision variables. In this appendix, we demonstrate how to use ASP to apply optimization techniques in spreadsheet simulation models with random variables. This approach is called **simulation optimization**. A simulation optimization model is an optimization problem complicated by the presence of random variables. In general, ASP searches for optimal values of the decision variables by iteratively adjusting the values of the decision variables. For each set of decision variable values, ASP evaluates the quality of the solution over a set of simulation trials. Therefore, solving a simulation optimization model can be very computationally expensive and take a long time. Furthermore, ASP cannot guarantee an optimal solution to a simulation optimization model because of sampling error resulting from the simulation trials and because the

MODEL *file*

ZapatoesSimOpt

optimization problem may have multiple local optimal solutions due to nonlinear relationships. Therefore, it is helpful to solve the model multiple times and compare the solutions across runs.

For the Zapatoes problem, we want to determine the order quantities for the four types of pajamas that maximize the mean (expected) total profit. Although the forecasted demand looks promising, Zapatoes wants to be conservative and spend no more than $1,150,000 on the wholesale procurement of the pajamas. As Figure 14.32 shows, we add the constraint on wholesale expenditures to the Zapatoes spreadsheet model by first entering the computation of the wholesale expenditures into cell G12 using the Excel formula =SUMPRODUCT(B5:B8,G5:G8). Then we enter the value $1,150,000 into cell H12 to reflect the budget. The algorithms that ASP employs to solve simulation optimization models work best when bounds on the decision variable values are provided. Management wants to order at least 1,000 units of each type of pajama. Furthermore, management does not want to order more than 20,000 units of any single type of pajama.

To enter the simulation optimization model into ASP, we execute the following steps:

Step 1. Click the **Analytic Solver Platform** tab in the Ribbon

Step 2. Click **Model** in the **Model** group to display the **Solver Options and Model Specifications** pane on the right-hand side of the spreadsheet

Step 3. In the **Solver Options and Model Specifications** pane, click the ⊞ to the left of **Optimization** to expand the optimization tree structure (Figure 14.33)

Click **Objective**

Select cell J9 (which contains the computation of total profit for a single scenario)

Click the **Add** button ✚ in the **Solver Options and Model Specifications** pane

Double-click **$J$9 (Max)** listed under **Objective**

When the **Change Objective** dialog box appears (Figure 14.34), select **Expected** from the drop-down menu to the right of **Set Cell:**

Click **OK**

FIGURE 14.32   Setting Up Zapatoes' Simulation Optimization

	A	B	C	D	E	F	G	H	I	J
1	**Zapatoes**									
2										
3	**Parameters**						**Model**			
4		**Wholesale Price**	**Retail Price**	**Clearance Price**	**Demand**		**Order Quantity**	**Retail Sales**	**Clearance Sales**	**Profit**
5	**Cotton Pajama**	$25	$30	$10	13,463		10,000	10,000	0	$50,000
6	**Flannel Pajama**	$25	$40	$10	3,634		10,000	3,634	6,366	-$40,967
7	**Silk Pajama**	$35	$60	$30	6,232		10,000	6,232	3,768	$136,972
8	**Velour Pajama**	$30	$55	$20	8,852		10,000	8,852	1,148	$209,823
9									**Total Profit:**	**$355,828**
10										
11	**Silk Pajama Demand**						**Expenditures**	**Budget**		
12	Minimum value	0					=SUMPRODUCT(B5:B8,G5:G8)	$1,150,000		
13	Maximum value	30000								
14										
15	**Values**	**Likelihood**								
16	5,000	0.1								
17	10,000	0.4								
18	15,000	0.2								
19	20,000	0.25								
20	25,000	0.05								
21										
22										
23	**Velour Pajama Demand**									
24	Minimum value	2,500								
25	Most likely value	10,000								
26	Maximum value	25,000								

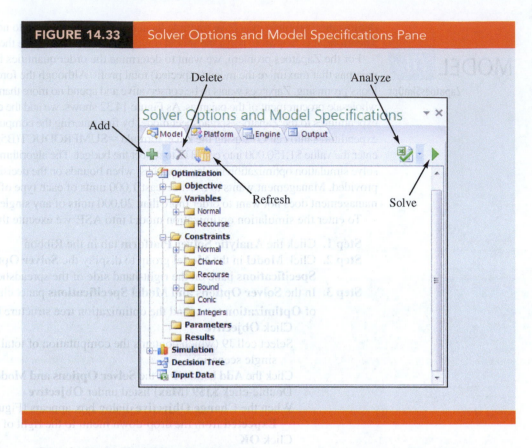

FIGURE 14.33   Solver Options and Model Specifications Pane

Step 4. Under **Variables,** click **Normal**

Select the range G5:G8 (which contains the four order quantities)

Click the **Add** button ✚ in the **Solver Options and Model Specifications** pane

Step 5. Under **Constraints,** click **Normal**

Select cell G12

Click the **Add** button ✚ in the **Solver Options and Model Specifications** pane

When the **Add Constraint** dialog box appears (Figure 14.35):

Select **<=** from the drop-down button

Enter *H12* in the **Constraint:** area

Click **OK**

Step 6. Under **Constraints,** select **Normal**

Select cells G5:G8

Click the **Add** button ✚ in the **Solver Options and Model Specifications** pane

When the **Add Constraint** dialog box appears:

Select **<=** from the drop-down button

Enter *20000* in the **Constraint:** area

Click **Add**

When the **Add Constraint** dialog box appears:

Enter *G5:G8* in the **Cell Reference:** area

Select **>=** from the drop-down button

Enter *1000* in the **Constraint:** area

Click **OK**

Step 5 constrains the total expenditures (cell G12) to be less than or equal to the budget (cell H12). Step 6 requires that all order quantities (cells G5:G8) are less than or equal to 20,000. Step 7 forces Zapatoes to order at least 1,000 units of each type of pajama.

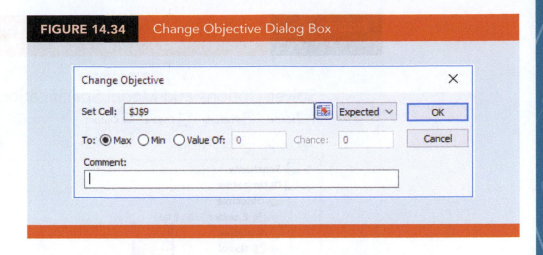

FIGURE 14.34   Change Objective Dialog Box

MODEL *file*

ZapatoesSimOpt

Upon clicking the Solve button, the Guided Mode dialog box will appear if ASP's Guided Mode is turned on. ASP's Guided Mode assists the analyst in the optimization process and can be turned off by clicking Help in the Help group of the Analytic Solver Platform Ribbon and then under Operating Mode, selecting Expert Mode.

Figure 14.36 shows the completed simulation optimization model as contained in the file *ZapatoesSimOpt*. The following steps prepare settings for the simulation model for optimization and execute the simulation optimization:

Step 1. Click the **Analytic Solver Platform** tab in the Ribbon

Step 2. If the **Solver Options and Model Specifications** pane is not visible, click **Model** in the **Model** group

Step 3. Click the **Engine** tab in the **Solver Options and Model Specifications** pane (Figure 14.37)

> Deselect the **Automatically Select Engine** checkbox
>
> Select **Standard Evolutionary Engine** from the drop-down menu at the top of the pane
>
> In the **General** area, click **Global Search** and then select **Genetic Algorithm** from the drop-down box

Step 4. Click the **Output** tab in the **Solver Options and Model Specifications** pane

> Click the **Solve** button ▶ to begin the simulation-optimization procedure

FIGURE 14.35   Adding Constraint on Wholesale Expenditure

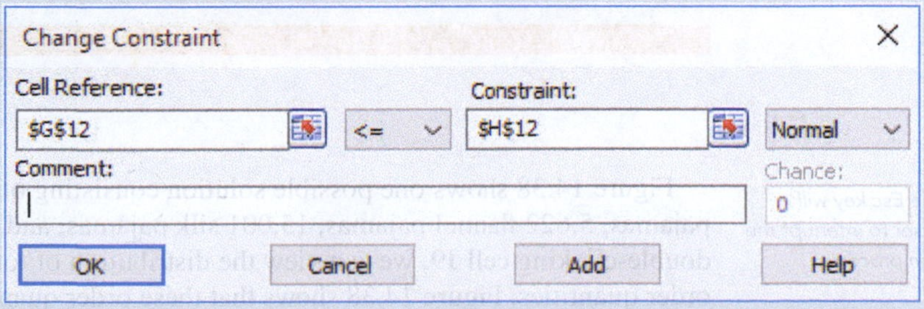

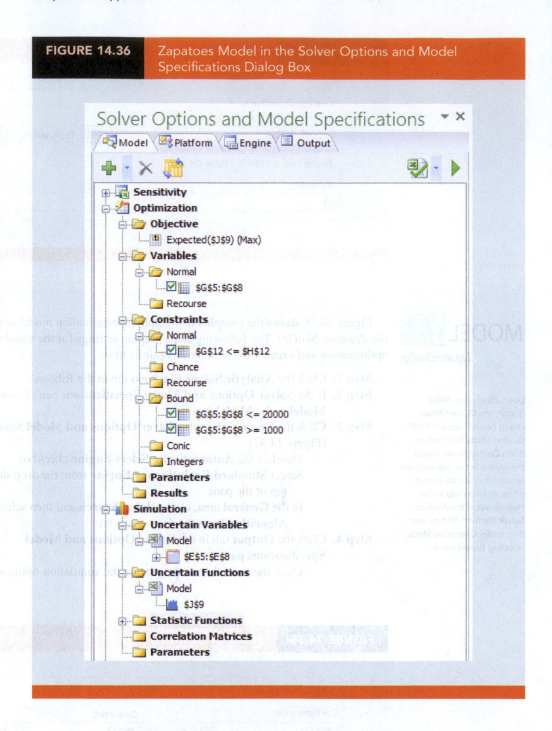

FIGURE 14.36   Zapatoes Model in the Solver Options and Model Specifications Dialog Box

*Pressing the Esc key will
allow the user to interrupt the
optimization process.*

Figure 14.38 shows one possible solution consisting of order quantities of 4,282 cotton pajamas, 5,622 flannel pajamas, 15,001 silk pajamas, and 12,579 velour pajamas. By double-clicking cell J9, we can view the distribution of total profit resulting from these order quantities. Figure 14.38 shows that these order quantities achieve an estimated

We recommend testing both the *Scatter Search* and *Genetic Algorithm* options for the **Global Search** setting in the **General** area of the **Engine** menu.

FIGURE 14.37	Settings for Simulation Optimization

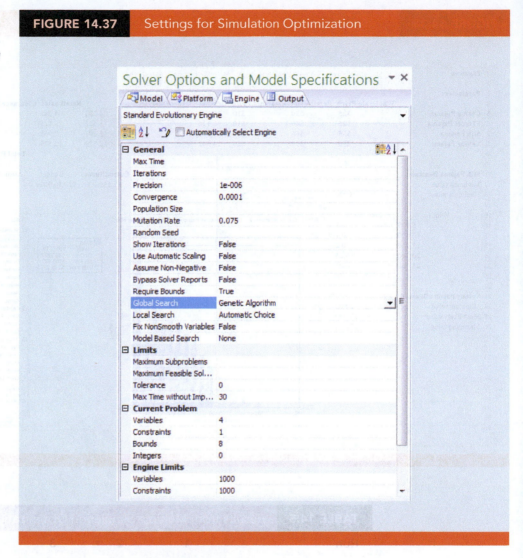

average total profit of \$607,774. At this solution, there is a 0.9121 probability of a total profit greater than \$400,000 (and hence a 0.0879 probability of a profit less than \$400,000).

ASP (or any software) cannot generally guarantee obtaining the optimal solution to a simulation optimization model because this type of problem can be very difficult to solve. Furthermore, ASP may terminate with different best-found solutions when re-solving the model. Therefore, we recommend re-solving a simulation optimization model several times and comparing the solutions. For example, Table 14.5 shows results from five optimization runs on the Zapatoes problem. Although the values of the decision variables are not exactly the same, the estimated average total profit is nearly identical for each of the five solutions and there is clear guidance on the relative values of the order quantities.

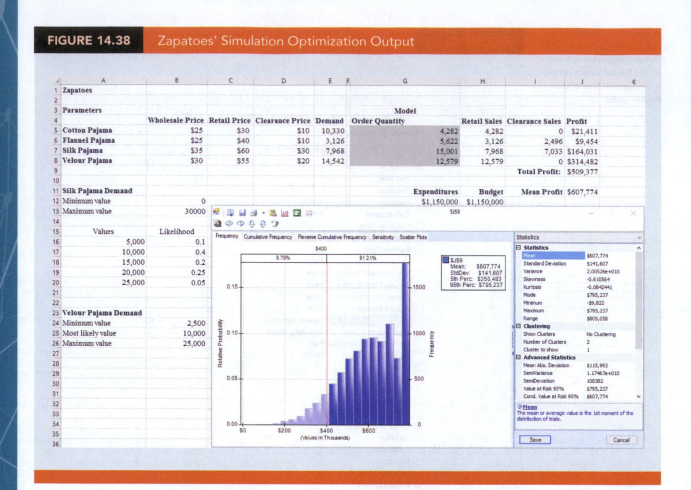

FIGURE 14.38   Zapatoes' Simulation Optimization Output

TABLE 14.5   Results from Multiple Simulation Optimization Runs

Run	1	2	3	4	5
Cotton	4,282	4,283	4,284	4,283	4,282
Flannel	5,622	5,622	5,622	5,623	5,623
Silk	15,001	15,000	15,000	15,000	15,000
Velour	12,579	12,579	12,579	12,579	12,579
Average Total Profit	$607,774	$607,773	$607,772	$607,773	$607,773

Appendix 14.4 Correlating Random Variables with Analytic Solver Platform

Chapter 5 covers independence of random variables in additional detail.

In all the simulation models considered thus far, we have represented all random variables with independent probability distributions. In other words, the values of the random variables have been generated independently and have no dependence on each other. There are many situations in which the values of two or more random variables have strong interrelationships. Consider two complementary products such as razors and replacement blades. Above-average sales of razors are often associated with above-average sales of replacement blades. In finance, the notion of diversification is based on investing in assets such that when one asset provides a below-average return, another asset often provides an above-average return.

Through the measure of the correlation, ASP provides the ability to model the dependence between pairs of random variables. In Chapter 2, we presented the most common correlation measure, the Pearson product moment correlation coefficient. The Pearson product moment correlation coefficient ranges between -1 and $+1$. Values closer to -1 denote a stronger negative linear relationship between a pair of random variables. Values closer to $+1$ denote a stronger positive linear relationship between a pair of random variables. A correlation measure close to 0 denotes the absence of a linear relationship between a pair of random variables.

ASP's use of the Spearman rank correlation coefficent allows it to generate interrelated values between pairs of random variables which have different probability distributions.

ASP employs a slightly different measure of correlation called the Spearman rank correlation. Like the Pearson product moment correlation coefficient, the Spearman rank correlation coefficeint ranges between -1 and $+1$. However, Spearman rank correlation measures the degree of monotonicity in the relationship between two variables; in a monotonic relationship, either the first variable never decreases as the second variable increases or the first variable never increases as the second variable increases. Thus, the Spearman rank coefficient differs from the Pearson product moment correlation (discussed in Chapter 2), which measures the strength of a linear relationship between two variables.

The left panel of Figure 14.39 illustrates a negative monotonic relationship (Spearman rank correlation coefficient $= -1$). The right panel illustrates a positive monotonic relationship (Spearman rank correlation coefficient $= +1$). On a scatter chart of two variables with a monotonic relationship, the slope of the lines connecting consecutive data points will never change sign; that is, the slopes will either be all less than or equal to zero, or all greater than or equal to zero.

Recall the Zapatoes problem from Appendix 14.2. Our original simulation model treats the demand for the four pajama products as independent random variables. However, it is

FIGURE 14.39   Monotonic Decreasing Relationship (Left Pane) and Monotonic Increasing Relationship (Right Pane)

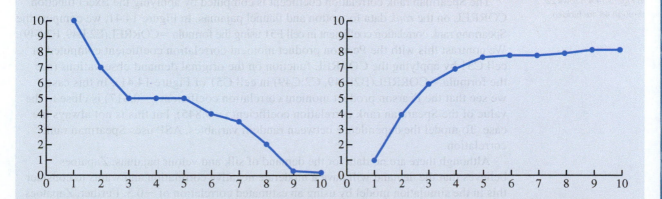

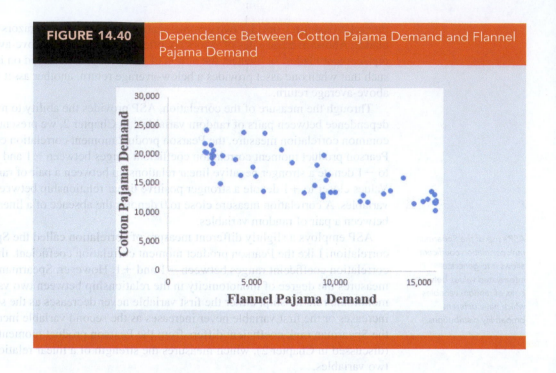

FIGURE 14.40 Dependence Between Cotton Pajama Demand and Flannel Pajama Demand

likely that the demand for these products is not independent in reality. Suppose that market research suggests that cotton and flannel pajamas are often substitutes; that is, customers often buy one or the other, but rarely both. Based on the sample data on cotton and pajama demand in the *Data* worksheet of the file *Zapatoes*, Figure 14.40 illustrates the evidence of a negative relationship between cotton and flannel pajama demand.

To compute the Spearman rank correlation coefficient to measure the dependence between cotton and flannel pajama demand, we first find the rank of each observation of cotton pajama demand and the rank of each observation of flannel pajama demand using the Excel function RANK.AVG. Columns E and F in Figure 14.41 show the rank of each observed value of cotton pajama demand and flannel pajama demand, respectively. For example, cell E2 contains the formula =RANK.AVG(B2, $B$2:$B$49) and returns the value of 46 to denote that demand of 11,693 cotton pajamas is the 46th largest observation in the list of 48 values.

> When a value occurs more than once, the RANK.AVG function returns the average rank of the value.

The Spearman rank correlation coefficent is computed by applying the Excel function CORREL on the *rank* data for cotton and flannel pajamas. In Figure 14.41, we compute the Spearman rank correlation coefficient in cell F51 using the formula =CORREL(E2:E49, F2:F49). We contrast this with the Pearson product moment correlation coefficient computed in cell C51 by applying the CORREL function on the original demand observations (see the formula =CORREL(B2:B49, C2:C49) in cell C51 of Figure 14.41). In this case, we see that the Pearson product moment correlation coefficient (-0.817) is close to the value of the Spearman rank correlation coefficient (-0.845), but this is not always the case. To model the dependence between random variables, ASP uses Spearman rank correlation.

> In Figure 14.41, rows 22 through 48 are hidden.

Although there are no data for the demand of silk and velour pajamas, Zapatoes believes that the demand will have a moderate negative correlation and wants to consider this in the simulation model by using an estimated correlation of -0.5. Further, Zapatoes believes that cotton pajama demand will have a slight positive correlation with both silk and velour pajamas and wants to use an estimate of 0.25 for the correlation between

FIGURE 14.41   Calculating Spearman Rank Correlation Coefficient

	A	B	C	D	E	F
1	Observation	Cotton	Flannel		Cotton Rank	Flannel Rank
2	1	11693	15982		=RANK.AVG(B2,$B$2:$B$49)	=RANK.AVG(C2,$C$2:$C$49)
3	2	11775	15914		=RANK.AVG(B3,$B$2:$B$49)	=RANK.AVG(C3,$C$2:$C$49)
4	3	10398	15979		=RANK.AVG(B4,$B$2:$B$49)	=RANK.AVG(C4,$C$2:$C$49)
5	4	11565	14691		=RANK.AVG(B5,$B$2:$B$49)	=RANK.AVG(C5,$C$2:$C$49)
6	5	11863	15998		=RANK.AVG(B6,$B$2:$B$49)	=RANK.AVG(C6,$C$2:$C$49)
7	6	11955	15235		=RANK.AVG(B7,$B$2:$B$49)	=RANK.AVG(C7,$C$2:$C$49)
8	7	11878	11954		=RANK.AVG(B8,$B$2:$B$49)	=RANK.AVG(C8,$C$2:$C$49)
9	8	13130	15935		=RANK.AVG(B9,$B$2:$B$49)	=RANK.AVG(C9,$C$2:$C$49)
10	9	11700	15974		=RANK.AVG(B10,$B$2:$B$49)	=RANK.AVG(C10,$C$2:$C$49)
11	10	12076	15997		=RANK.AVG(B11,$B$2:$B$49)	=RANK.AVG(C11,$C$2:$C$49)
12	11	13666	15730		=RANK.AVG(B12,$B$2:$B$49)	=RANK.AVG(C12,$C$2:$C$49)
13	12	13272	12883		=RANK.AVG(B13,$B$2:$B$49)	=RANK.AVG(C13,$C$2:$C$49)
14	13	13197	9256		=RANK.AVG(B14,$B$2:$B$49)	=RANK.AVG(C14,$C$2:$C$49)
15	14	12324	15530		=RANK.AVG(B15,$B$2:$B$49)	=RANK.AVG(C15,$C$2:$C$49)
16	15	12952	11649		=RANK.AVG(B16,$B$2:$B$49)	=RANK.AVG(C16,$C$2:$C$49)
17	16	13519	9971		=RANK.AVG(B17,$B$2:$B$49)	=RANK.AVG(C17,$C$2:$C$49)
18	17	16062	14041		=RANK.AVG(B18,$B$2:$B$49)	=RANK.AVG(C18,$C$2:$C$49)
19	18	14732	8755		=RANK.AVG(B19,$B$2:$B$49)	=RANK.AVG(C19,$C$2:$C$49)
20	19	12016	11494		=RANK.AVG(B20,$B$2:$B$49)	=RANK.AVG(C20,$C$2:$C$49)
21	20	13807	13304		=RANK.AVG(B21,$B$2:$B$49)	=RANK.AVG(C21,$C$2:$C$49)
49	48	24172	2285		=RANK.AVG(B49,$B$2:$B$49)	=RANK.AVG(C49,$C$2:$C$49)
50						
51		Pearson:	=CORREL(B2:B49,C2:C49)		Spearman:	=CORREL(E2:E49,F2:F49)

	A	B	C	D	E	F
1	Observation	Cotton	Flannel		Cotton Rank	Flannel Rank
2	1	11,693	15,982		46	3
3	2	11,775	15,914		44	7
4	3	10,398	15,979		48	4
5	4	11,565	14,691		47	11
6	5	11,863	15,998		43	1
7	6	11,955	15,235		41	10
8	7	11,878	11,954		42	15
9	8	13,130	15,935		35	6
10	9	11,700	15,974		45	5
11	10	12,076	15,997		39	2
12	11	13,666	15,730		28	8
13	12	13,272	12,883		33	14
14	13	13,197	9,256		34	24
15	14	12,324	15,530		38	9
16	15	12,952	11,649		36	16
17	16	13,519	9,971		30	18
18	17	16,062	14,041		23	12
19	18	14,732	8,755		26	26
20	19	12,016	11,494		40	17
21	20	13,807	13,304		27	13
49	48	24,172	2,285		1	46
50						
51		Pearson:	-0.817		Spearman:	-0.845

cotton and silk pajama demand, as well as between cotton and velour pajama demand. Zapatoes does not have a strong evidence regarding the interdependence between flannel pajamas and silk or velour pajamas, respectively. Based on intuition, Zapatoes will set the correlation between flannel and velour to 0.25 and the correlation between flannel and silk to zero. To set up a correlation matrix that captures these interrelationships, we execute the following steps:

MODEL *file*

ZapatoesRank

Clicking on the arrow under the Correlations icon opens a drop-down menu. Clicking Matrices from this menu is equivalent to clicking on the Correlations icon.

Step 1. Starting from the *Model* worksheet in the file *ZapatoesRank,* click the **Analytic Solver Platform** tab in the Ribbon

Step 2. Click the **Correlations** icon in the **Simulation Model** group

Step 3. When the **Create new correlation matrix** dialog box opens, click the **>>** button to populate the **Preview** area

Step 4. In the **Preview** area of the Create new correlations matrix dialog box:
Click the matrix entry in the $E$5 row and $E$6 column and enter −0.845
Click the matrix entry in the $E$5 row and $E$7 column and enter 0.25

FIGURE 14.42   Constructing a Correlation Matrix in ASP

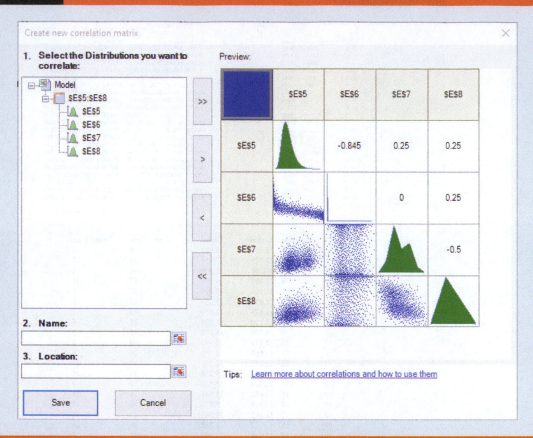

The entry in row i and column j in the lower diagonal of the correlation matrix in Figure 14.42 displays a scatter chart of data for the two variables with the corresponding correlation measure in row j and column i.

Click the matrix entry in the $E$5 row and $E$8 column and enter *0.25*
Click the matrix entry in the $E$6 row and $E$7 column and enter *0*
Click the matrix entry in the $E$6 row and $E$8 column and enter *0.25*
Click the matrix entry in the $E$7 row and $E$8 column and enter *−0.5*

Step 5. Click **Save**

Step 6. When the dialog bubble **Please select the location of the Matrix** appears, select cell A28

When subjectively estimating correlation coefficients, it is possible to define values that are mathematically inconsistent. For example, if stock A's return is positively correlated with stock B's return, and stock B's return is positively correlated with stock C's return, then stock C's return cannot be negatively correlated with stock A's return. ASP validates and, if necessary, adjusts the correlation matrix to maintain mathematical consistency. Continuing from the previous steps, we execute this validation by means of the following steps:

If correlation coefficients are defined in a manner that is mathematically consistent, the correlation matrix is said to be positive definite. After clicking Validate, if the correlation matrix is not positive definite, ASP will alert the analyst and offer to adjust the correlation coefficients so that the correlation matrix is positive definite.

Step 7. In the **Manage correlation matrices** dialog box, click **Validate**

Step 8. Click **Yes** in the dialog box **The Correlation Matrix is not Positive Definite. Do you want Analytic Solver Platform to help you fix the matrix?**

Step 9. In the **Make your matrix valid** dialog box (see Figure 14.43)
Click the **Largest Change** button and click the matrix entry in the $E$6 row and $E$7 column (shading this entry green)

FIGURE 14.43   Making Correlation Matrix Mathematically Consistent

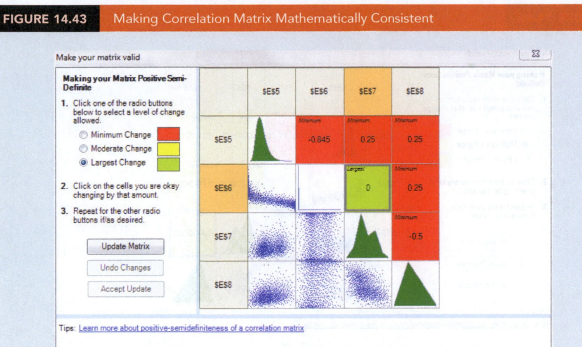

Click the **Moderate Change** button and click the matrix entry in the $E$6
row and $E$8 column, the matrix entry in the $E$5 row and $E$7
column, the matrix entry in the $E$5 row and $E$8 column, and the
matrix entry in the $E$7 row and $E$8 column (shading these respective
entries yellow)

Step 10. Click **Update Matrix**

Step 11. Click **Accept Update** (Figure 14.44)

Step 12. Close **Manage correlation matrices** dialog box

In this case, the qualitative estimates of correlation are not mathematically consistent.
As Figure 14.43 shows, we adjust this by instructing ASP which estimates we will allow
it to adjust in order to maintain mathematical consistency. In this case, Zapatoes is not at
all confident in the pairwise correlations that it subjectively estimated. Figure 14.44 shows
the correlation matrix after adjustment, and we see that the changes are very minor, so we
accept them without reservation.

The effect of modeling correlation can be analyzed by running the simulation with
and without correlations by clicking on the drop-down arrow below the **Correlations**
button in the **Simulations Model** group of the **Analytic Solver Platform** tab in
the Ribbon and then checking (and unchecking) the box next to **Use Correlations**.
Running a simulation with the correlations (and order quantities of 10,000 units of
each pajama type), we obtain the distribution of total profit shown in Figure 14.45.
Comparing Figure 14.30 to Figure 14.45, we see that considering the correlation
between demands has a negligible effect on the average profit when ordering 10,000
units each pajama type. However, the likelihood of earning profit less than $400,000
increases about a percentage point. Repeating the simulation trials shows that these
observations are consistent.

FIGURE 14.44   Adjusted Correlation Matrix

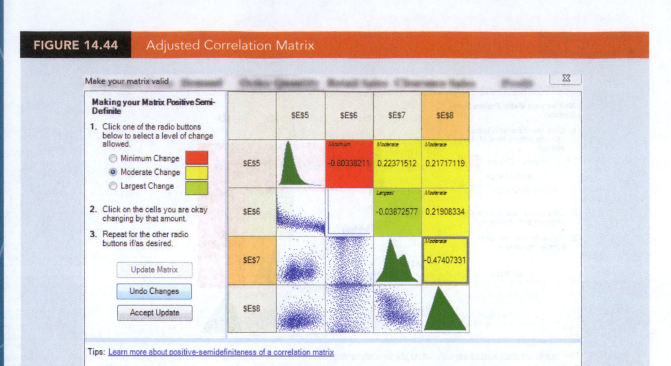

FIGURE 14.45   Total Profit Distribution with Correlated Demand

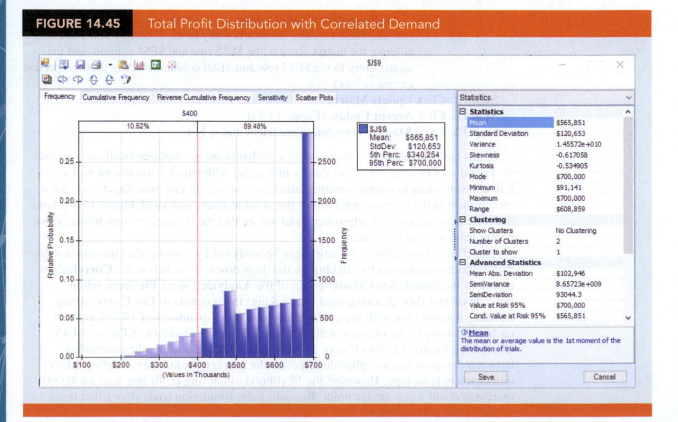

Appendix 14.5 Probability Distributions for Random Variables

Selecting the appropriate probability distribution to characterize a random variable in a simulation model can be a critical modeling decision. In this appendix, we review several of the distributions provided by Analytic Solver Platform in Excel. For each distribution, the parameters are the values required to completely specify the distribution. The range provides the minimum and maximum values that can be taken by a random variable that follows the given distribution. We also provide a short description of the overall shape and/or common uses of the distribution.

Continuous Probability Distributions

Random variables that can be many possible values (even if the values are discrete) are often modeled with a continuous probability distribution.

Normal Distribution

Parameters: mean (m), stdev (s)

Range: $-\infty$ to $+\infty$

Description: The normal distribution is a bell-shaped, symmetric distribution centered at its mean m. The normal distribution is often a good way to characterize a quantity that is the sum of many independent random variables.

Example: In human resource management, employee performance is often well represented by a normal distribution. Typically, the performance of 68% of employees is within one standard deviation of the average performance, and the performance of 95% of the employees is within two standard deviations. Employees with exceptionally low or high performance are rare.

Native Excel function: NORM.INV(RAND(), m, s)

Beta Distribution

Parameters (for BetaGen): shape1 (α-alpha), shape2 (β-beta), min (a), max (b)

Range: a to b

Description: Over the range specified by values a and b, the beta distribution has a very flexible shape that can be manipulated by adjusting α and β. The beta distribution is useful in modeling an uncertain quantity that has a known minimum and maximum value.

Example: Setting $a = 0$ and $b = 1$, the beta distribution can be used to describe the likelihood of values for the true proportion of drivers in an age group who would favor one model of car over another.

Native Excel function: BETA.INV(RAND(), alpha, beta, a, b)

PERT Distribution

Parameters: min (a), likely (m), max (b)

Range: a to b

Description: The PERT distribution is a special case of the beta distribution in which the most likely value is specified instead of shape parameters. The PERT distribution is used specifically for project management applications.

Example: In estimating the time to complete an activity, a project manager often uses the PERT distribution by specifying the minimum time to complete the activity, the most likely time to complete an activity, and the maximum time it will take to complete the activity.

Exponential Distribution

Parameters: mean (m)

Range: 0 to $+\infty$

Description: The exponential distribution is characterized by a mean value equal to its standard deviation and a long right tail stretching from a mode value of 0.

Example: The time between events, such as customer arrivals or customer defaults on bill payment, are commonly modeled with an exponential distribution. An exponential random variable possesses the "memoryless" property; the probability that there will be 25 or more minutes between customer arrivals if 10 minutes have passed since the last customer arrival is the same as the probability that there will be more than 15 minutes until the next arrival if a customer just arrived. In other words, the probability of a customer arrival occurring in the next x minutes does not depend on how long it's been since the last arrival.

Native Excel function: LN(RAND())*$(-m)$

Triangular Distribution

Parameters: min (a), likely (m), max (b)

Range: a to b

Description: The triangular distribution is often used when little is known about a random variable besides its range, but it is thought to have a single mode. The distribution is shaped like a triangle with vertices at a, m, and b.

Example: In corporate finance, a triangular distribution may be used to model a project's revenue growth in a net present value analysis if the analyst can reliably provide minimum, most likely, and maximum estimates of growth.

Uniform Distribution

Parameters: min (a), max (b)

Range: a to b

Description: The uniform distribution is appropriate when a random variable is equally likely to be any value between a and b. When little is known about a phenomenon other than its minimum and maximum possible values, the uniform distribution can be a safe choice to model an uncertain quantity.

Example: A service technician making a house call may quote a 4-hour time window in which he will arrive. If the technician is equally likely to arrive any time during this time window, then the arrival time of the technician in this time window may be described with a uniform distribution.

Native Excel function: $a + (b - a)$*RAND()

Log-Normal Distribution

Parameters: log_mean (m), log_stdev (s)

Range: 0 to $+\infty$

*This parameterization of the log-normal distribution corresponds to the **LogNorm2** distribution in ASP.*

Description: The log-normal distribution is a unimodal distribution (like the normal distribution) that has a minimum value of 0 and a long right tail (unlike the normal distribution). The log-normal distribution is often a good way to characterize a quantity that is the product of many independent, positive random variables. The logarithm of a log-normally distributed random variable is normally distributed.

Example: The income distribution of a population is often well described using a log-normal distribution.

Native Excel function: LOGNORM.INV(RAND(), log_mean, log_stdev), where log_mean and log_stdev are the mean and standard deviation of the normally distributed random variable obtained when taking the logarithm of the log-normally distributed random variable.

Custom General Distribution

Parameters: min (a), max (b), and a set of values $\{v_1, v_2, v_3, \ldots, v_k\}$ and corresponding weights $\{w_1, w_2, w_3, \ldots, w_k\}$

Range: a to b

Description: A custom general distribution can be used to shape a tailored distribution to model any continuous uncertain quantity. The relative likelihood of values between the minimum and maximum are based on interpolations of the weights specified for the provided set of values.

Example: The boom-or-bust nature of the revenue generated by a movie from a polarizing director may be described by a custom general (continuous) distribution. The relevant values (in millions of dollars) are a minimum of $a = 0$, a maximum of $b = 70$, and other values of $\{5, 25, 45, 65\}$ with respective weights of $\{0.6, 0.05, 0.05, 0.3\}$. This particular distribution is U-shaped, and extreme values are more likely than moderate values—a phenomenon not well captured by other distributions.

Discrete Probability Distributions

Random variables that can be only a relatively small number of discrete values are often best modeled with a discrete distribution. The appropriate choice of discrete distribution relies on the specific situation. For discrete distributions, we provide the parameters required to specify the distribution, the possible values taken by a random variable that follows the distribution, and a short description of the distribution and example of a possible application.

Binomial Distribution

Parameters: trials (n), prob (p)

Possible values: $0, 1, 2, \ldots, n$

Description: A binomial random variable corresponds to the number of times an event successfully occurs in n trials, and the probability of a success at each trial is p and independent of whether a success occurs on other trials. Note that for $n = 1$, the binomial is equivalent to the Bernoulli distribution.

Example: In a portfolio of 20 similar stocks, each of which has the same probability of increasing in value of $p = 0.6$, the total number of stocks that increase in value can be described by a binomial distribution with parameters $n = 20$ and $p = 0.6$.

Native Excel function: BINOM.INV(n, p, RAND())

A Bernoulli random variable is the same as a binomial random variable with one trial ($n = 1$)

Bernoulli Distribution

Parameters: prob (p)

Possible values: 0 (event doesn't happen) or 1 (event successfully occurs)

Description: A Bernoulli random variable corresponds to whether an event successfully occurs given a probability p of successfully occurring.

Example: Whether a particular stock increases in value over a defined length of time is a Bernoulli random variable.

Native Excel function: BINOM.INV(1, p, RAND())

Hypergeometric Distribution

Parameters: trials (n), suc (s), pop (N)

Possible values: $\max\{0, n + s - N\}, \ldots, \min\{n, s\}$

Description: A hypergeometric random variable corresponds to the number of times an element labeled a success is selected out of n trials in the situation where there are N total elements, s of which are labeled a success and, once selected, cannot be selected again. Note that this is similar to the binomial distribution except that now the trials are dependent because removing the selected element changes the probabilities of selecting an element labeled a success on subsequent trials.

Example: A certain company produces circuit boards to sell to computer manufacturers. Because of a quality defect in the manufacturing process, it is known that exactly 70 circuit boards out of a lot of 100 have been produced incorrectly and are faulty. If a company orders 40 circuit boards, the number of faulty circuit boards that the company will receive in their order is a hypergeometric random variable with $n = 40$, $s = 70$, and $N = 100$. Note that, in this case, at least 10 circuit boards will be faulty, but no more than 40 (because at most 30 circuit boards are not faulty).

Geometric Distribution

Parameters: prob (p)

Possible values: 0, 1, 2, . . . ,

Description: A geometric random variable corresponds to the number of times that an event fails to occur until the first trial that an event successfully occurs, given that the probability of an event successfully occurring at each trial is p.

Example: Consider the research and development (R&D) division of a large company. An R&D division may invest in several projects that fail before investing in a project succeeds. If each project has a probability of success of p, the number of projects that fail before a successful project occurs is a geometric random variable with parameter p.

Negative Binomial Distribution

Parameters: suc (s), prob (p)

Possible values: 0, 1, 2, . . .

Description: A negative binomial random variable corresponds to the number of times that an event fails to occur until an event successfully occurs s times, given that the probability of an event successfully occurring at each trial is p. Note that for $s = 1$, the negative binomial is equivalent to the geometric distribution.

Example: The number of projects that fail in the R&D division before experiencing three successful projects is a negative binomial random variable.

Poisson Distribution

Parameters: mean (m)

Possible values: 0, 1, 2, . . .

Description: A Poisson random variable corresponds to the number of times that an event occurs within a specified period of time given that m is the average number of events within the specified period of time.

Example: The number of patients arriving at a health care clinic in a hour can be modeled with a Poisson random variable with $m = 5$, if on average 5 customers arrive to the store in a hour.

Integer Uniform Distribution

Parameters: lower (l), upper (u)

Possible values: $l, l + 1, l + 2, . . . , u - 2, u - 1, u$

Description: An integer uniform random variable assumes that the integer values between l and u are equally likely.

Example: The number of philanthropy volunteers from a class of 10 students may be an integer uniform variable with values 0, 1, 2, . . . , 10.

Native Excel function: RANDBETWEEN(l, u)

Discrete Uniform Distribution

Parameters: set of values $\{v_1, v_2, v_3, . . . , v_k\}$

Possible values: $v_1, v_2, v_3, . . . , v_k$

Description: A discrete uniform random variable is equally likely to be any of the specified set of values $\{v_1, v_2, v_3, \ldots, v_k\}$.

Example: Consider a game show that awards a contestant a cash prize from an envelope randomly selected from six possible envelopes. If the envelopes contain $1, $5, $10, $20, $50, and $100, respectively, then the prize is a discrete uniform random variable with values {1, 5, 10, 20, 50, 100}.

Native Excel function: VLOOKUP(RANDBETWEEN(1,k), range, 2, false) where range corresponds to the cell range of a two-column table in which the first column numbers the rows from 1 to k and the second column contains the k distinct values.

Custom Discrete Distribution

Parameters: set of values $\{v_1, v_2, v_3, \ldots, v_k\}$ and corresponding weights $\{w_1, w_2, w_3, \ldots, w_k\}$ such that $w_1 + w_2 + \cdots + w_k = 1$.

Possible values: $v_1, v_2, v_3, \ldots, v_k$

Description: A custom discrete distribution can be used to create a tailored distribution to model a discrete, uncertain quantity. The value of a custom discrete random variable is equal to the value v_i with probability w_i.

Example: The number of qualified proposals submitted for consideration of venture capital funding may be described by a custom discrete distribution with values of {2, 3, 4, 6} with respective weights of {0.2, 0.1, 0.35, 0.35}.

Native Excel function: Use the RAND() function in conjunction with the VLOOKUP function referencing a table in which each row lists a possible value and a segment of the interval [0, 1) representing the likelihood of the corresponding value. For an example, consider the generation of values for the direct labor cost per unit in the Sanotronics LLC problem of Section 14.1; Figure 14.7 illustrates the implementation.

Chapter 15

Decision Analysis

CONTENTS

ANALYTICS IN ACTION

Phytopharm*

As a pharmaceutical development and functional food company, Phytopharm's primary revenue streams come from licensing agreements with larger companies. After Phytopharm establishes proof of principle for a new product by successfully completing early clinical trials, it seeks to reduce its risk by licensing the product to a large pharmaceutical or nutrition company that will further develop and market it.

There is substantial uncertainty regarding the future sales potential of early stage products; only 1 in 10 of such products makes it to market, and only 30% of these yield a healthy return. Phytopharm and its licensing partners would often initially propose very different terms for the licensing agreement. Therefore, Phytopharm employed a team of researchers to develop a flexible method for appraising a product's potential and subsequently supporting the negotiation of the lump-sum payments for development milestones and royalties on eventual sales that comprise the licensing agreement.

Using computer simulation, the resulting decision analysis model allows Phytopharm to perform sensitivity analysis on estimates of development cost, the probability of successful Food and Drug Administration clearance, launch date, market size, market share, and patent expiry. In particular, a decision tree model allows Phytopharm and its licensing partner to mutually agree on the number of development milestones. Depending on the status of the project at a milestone, the licensing partner can opt to abandon the project or continue development. Laying out these sequential decisions in a decision tree allows Phytopharm to negotiate milestone payments and royalties that equitably split the project's value between Phytopharm and its potential licensee.

---

*Based on P. Crama, B. De Ryck, Z. Degraeve, and W. Chong, "Research and Development Project Valuation and Licensing Negotiations at Phytopharm plc," *Interfaces,* 37 no. 5 (September– October 2007): 472–487.

Ultimately, business analytics is about making better decisions. The tools and techniques we have introduced previously are designed to aid a decision maker in analyzing existing data, predicting future behavior, and recommending decisions. This chapter introduces a field known as decision analysis that can be used to develop an optimal strategy when a decision maker is faced with several decision alternatives and an uncertain or risk-filled pattern of future events. For example, by evaluating the different naming options and understanding the potential sources of uncertainty, Procter & Gamble used decision analysis techniques to help choose the best brand name when they introduced Crest White Strips.

Decision analysis techniques are used widely in many different settings. The Analytics in Action, Phytopharm, discusses the use of decision analysis to manage Phytopharm's pipeline of pharmaceutical products, which have long development times and relatively high levels of uncertainty. Federal agencies in the United States have used decision analysis to evaluate the potential risks from terrorist attacks and to recommend counterterrorism strategies. The State of North Carolina used decision analysis in evaluating whether to implement a medical screening test to detect metabolic disorders in newborns.

Even when a careful decision analysis has been conducted, uncertainty about future events means that the final outcome is not completely under the control of the decision maker. In some cases, the selected decision alternative may provide good or excellent results. In other cases, a relatively unlikely future event may occur, causing the selected decision alternative to provide only fair or even poor results. The risk associated with any decision alternative is a direct result of the uncertainty associated with the final outcome. A good decision analysis includes careful consideration of risk. Through risk analysis, the decision maker is provided with probability information about the favorable as well as the unfavorable outcomes that may occur.

We begin the study of decision analysis by considering problems that involve reasonably few decision alternatives and reasonably few possible future events. Payoff tables and decision trees are introduced to provide a structure for the decision problem and to illustrate the fundamentals of decision analysis. Decision trees are used to analyze more complex problems and to identify an optimal sequence of decisions, referred to as an *optimal decision strategy*. Sensitivity analysis shows how changes in various aspects of the problem affect the recommended decision alternative. We return to the use of Bayes' theorem (first seen in Chapter 5) for calculating the probabilities of future events and incorporating additional information about the decisions. We conclude this chapter with a discussion of utility and decision analysis that expands on different attitudes toward risk taken by decision makers.

15.1 Problem Formulation

The first step in the decision analysis process is problem formulation. We begin with a verbal statement of the problem. We then identify the **decision alternatives**; the uncertain future events, referred to as **chance events**; and the **outcomes** associated with each combination of decision alternative and chance event outcome. Let us begin by considering a construction project of the Pittsburgh Development Corporation.

Pittsburgh Development Corporation (PDC) purchased land that will be the site of a new luxury condominium complex. The location provides a spectacular view of downtown Pittsburgh and the Golden Triangle, where the Allegheny and Monongahela Rivers meet to form the Ohio River. PDC plans to price the individual condominium units between $300,000 and $1,400,000.

PDC commissioned preliminary architectural drawings for three different projects: one with 30 condominiums, one with 60 condominiums, and one with 90 condominiums. The financial success of the project depends on the size of the condominium complex and the chance event concerning the demand for the condominiums. The statement of the PDC decision problem is to select the size of the new luxury condominium project that will lead to the largest profit given the uncertainty concerning the demand for the condominiums.

Given the statement of the problem, it is clear that the decision is to select the best size for the condominium complex. PDC has the following three decision alternatives:

$$d_1 = \text{a small complex with 30 condominiums}$$
$$d_2 = \text{a medium complex with 60 condominiums}$$
$$d_3 = \text{a large complex with 90 condominiums}$$

A factor in selecting the best decision alternative is the uncertainty associated with the chance event concerning the demand for the condominiums. When asked about the possible demand for the condominiums, PDC's president acknowledged a wide range of possibilities but decided that it would be adequate to consider two possible chance event outcomes: a strong demand and a weak demand.

In decision analysis, the possible outcomes for a chance event are referred to as the **states of nature**. The states of nature are defined so that they are mutually exclusive (no more than one can occur) and collectively exhaustive (at least one must occur); thus, one and only one of the possible states of nature will occur. For the PDC problem, the chance event concerning the demand for the condominiums has two states of nature:

$$s_1 = \text{strong demand for the condominiums}$$
$$s_2 = \text{weak demand for the condominiums}$$

Management must first select a decision alternative (complex size); then a state of nature follows (demand for the condominiums), and finally an outcome will occur. In this case, the outcome is PDC's profit.

TABLE 15.1	Payoff Table for the PDC Condominium Project ($ Millions)	
	State of Nature	
Decision Alternative	**Strong Demand, s_1**	**Weak Demand, s_2**
Small complex, d_1	8	7
Medium complex, d_2	14	5
Large complex, d_3	20	−9

Payoff Tables

Payoffs can be expressed in terms of profit, cost, time, distance, or any other measure appropriate for the decision problem being analyzed.

Given the three decision alternatives and the two states of nature, which complex size should PDC choose? To answer this question, PDC will need to know the outcome associated with each possible combination of decision alternative and state of nature. In decision analysis, we refer to the outcome resulting from a specific combination of a decision alternative and a state of nature as a **payoff**. A table showing payoffs for all combinations of decision alternatives and states of nature is a **payoff table**.

Because PDC wants to select the complex size that provides the largest profit, profit is used as the outcome. The payoff table with profits (in millions of dollars) is shown in Table 15.1. Note, for example, that if a medium complex is built and demand turns out to be strong, a profit of $14 million will be realized. We will use the notation V_{ij} to denote the payoff associated with decision alternative i and state of nature j. Using Table 15.1, $V_{31} = 20$ indicates that a payoff of $20 million occurs if the decision is to build a large complex (d_3) and the strong demand state of nature (s_1) occurs. Similarly, $V_{32} = −9$ indicates a loss of $9 million if the decision is to build a large complex (d_3) and the weak demand state of nature (s_2) occurs.

Decision Trees

A **decision tree** provides a graphical representation of the decision-making process. Figure 15.1 presents a decision tree for the PDC problem. Note that the decision tree shows the natural or logical progression that will occur over time. First, PDC must make a decision regarding the size of the condominium complex (d_1, d_2, or d_3). Then, after the decision is implemented, either state of nature s_1 or s_2 will occur. The number at each end point of the tree indicates that the payoff associated with a particular sequence. For example, the topmost payoff of 8 indicates that an $8 million profit is anticipated if PDC constructs a small condominium complex (d_1) and demand turns out to be strong (s_1). The next payoff of 7 indicates an anticipated profit of $7 million if PDC constructs a small condominium complex (d_1) and demand turns out to be weak (s_2). Thus, the decision tree provides a graphical depiction of the sequences of decision alternatives and states of nature that provide the six possible payoffs for PDC.

The decision tree in Figure 15.1 shows four nodes, numbered 1 to 4. **Nodes** are used to represent decisions and chance events. Squares are used to depict **decision nodes**, circles are used to depict **chance nodes**. Thus, node 1 is a decision node, and nodes 2, 3, and 4 are chance nodes. The **branches** connect the nodes; those leaving the decision node correspond to the decision alternatives. The branches leaving each chance node correspond to the states of nature. The outcomes (payoffs) are shown at the end of the states-of-nature branches. We now turn to the question: How can the decision maker use the information in the payoff table or the decision tree to select the best decision alternative? Several approaches may be used and are covered in the remaining sections of this chapter.

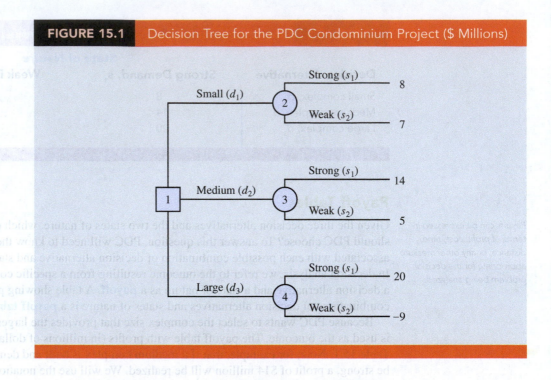

FIGURE 15.1   Decision Tree for the PDC Condominium Project ($ Millions)

15.2 Decision Analysis Without Probabilities

In this section we consider approaches to decision analysis that do not require knowledge of the probabilities of the states of nature. These approaches are appropriate in situations in which a simple best-case and worst-case analysis is sufficient and in which the decision maker has little confidence in his or her ability to assess the probabilities. Because different approaches sometimes lead to different decision recommendations, the decision maker must understand the approaches available and then select the specific approach that, according to the judgment of the decision maker, is the most appropriate.

Optimistic Approach

For a maximization problem, the optimistic approach often is referred to as the maximax approach; for a minimization problem, the corresponding terminology is minimin.

The **optimistic approach** evaluates each decision alternative in terms of the *best* payoff that can occur. The decision alternative that is recommended is the one that provides the best possible payoff. For a problem in which maximum profit is desired, as in the PDC problem, the optimistic approach would lead the decision maker to choose the alternative corresponding to the largest profit. For problems involving minimization, this approach leads to choosing the alternative with the smallest payoff.

TABLE 15.2	Maximum Payoff for Each PDC Decision Alternative
Decision Alternative	**Maximum Payoff**
Small complex, d_1	8
Medium complex, d_2	14
Large complex, d_3	20 ←———— Maximum of the maximum payoff values

To illustrate the optimistic approach, we use it to develop a recommendation for the PDC problem. First, we determine the maximum payoff for each decision alternative; then we select the decision alternative that provides the overall maximum payoff. These steps systematically identify the decision alternative that provides the largest possible profit. Table 15.2 illustrates these steps.

Because 20, corresponding to d_3, is the largest payoff, the decision to construct the large condominium complex is the recommended decision alternative using the optimistic approach.

Conservative Approach

For a maximization problem, the conservative approach often is referred to as the maximin approach; for a minimization problem the corresponding terminology is minimax.

The **conservative approach** evaluates each decision alternative in terms of the *worst* payoff that can occur. The decision alternative recommended is the one that provides the best of the worst possible payoffs. For a problem in which the output measure is profit, as in the PDC problem, the conservative approach would lead the decision maker to choose the alternative that maximizes the minimum possible profit that could be obtained. For problems involving minimization (for example, when the output measure is cost instead of profit), this approach identifies the alternative that will minimize the maximum payoff.

To illustrate the conservative approach, we use it to develop a recommendation for the PDC problem. First, we identify the minimum payoff for each of the decision alternatives; then we select the decision alternative that maximizes the minimum payoff. Table 15.3 illustrates these steps for the PDC problem.

Because 7, corresponding to d_1, yields the maximum of the minimum payoffs, the decision alternative of a small condominium complex is recommended. This decision approach is considered conservative because it identifies the worst possible payoffs and then recommends the decision alternative that avoids the possibility of extremely "bad" payoffs. In the conservative approach, PDC is guaranteed a profit of at least $7 million. Although PDC may make more, it *cannot* make less than $7 million.

Minimax Regret Approach

In decision analysis, **regret** is the difference between the payoff associated with a *particular* decision alternative and the payoff associated with the decision that would yield the most desirable payoff for a given state of nature. Thus, regret represents how much potential

TABLE 15.3	Minimum Payoff for Each PDC Decision Alternative
Decision Alternative	**Minimum Payoff ($ Millions)**
Small complex, d_1	7 ←———— Maximum of the minimum payoff values
Medium complex, d_2	5
Large complex, d_3	−9

payoff one would forgo by selecting a *particular* decision alternative, given that a specific state of nature will occur. This is why regret is often referred to as **opportunity loss**.

As its name implies, under the **minimax regret approach** to decision analysis, one would choose the decision alternative that minimizes the maximum state of regret that could occur over all possible states of nature. This approach is neither purely optimistic nor purely conservative. Let us illustrate the minimax regret approach by showing how it can be used to select a decision alternative for the PDC problem.

Suppose that PDC constructs a small condominium complex (d_1) and demand turns out to be strong (s_1). Table 15.1 showed that the resulting profit for PDC would be $8 million. However, given that the strong demand state of nature (s_1) has occurred, we realize that the decision to construct a large condominium complex (d_3), yielding a profit of $20 million, would have been the best decision. The difference between the payoff for the best decision alternative ($20 million) and the payoff for the decision to construct a small condominium complex ($8 million) is the regret or opportunity loss associated with decision alternative d_1 when state of nature s_1 occurs; thus, for this case, the opportunity loss or regret is $20 million − $8 million = $12 million. Similarly, if PDC makes the decision to construct a medium condominium complex (d_2) and the strong demand state of nature (s_1) occurs, the opportunity loss, or regret, associated with d_2 would be $20 million − $14 million = $6 million. Of course, if PDC chooses to construct a large complex (d_3) and demand is strong, they would have no regret.

In general, the following expression represents the opportunity loss, or regret:

REGRET (OPPORTUNITY LOSS)

$$R_{ij} = |V_j^* - V_{ij}| \tag{15.1}$$

where

R_{ij} = the regret associated with decision alternative d_i and state of nature s_j
V_j^* = the payoff value corresponding to the best decision for the state of nature s_j
V_{ij} = the payoff corresponding to decision alternative d_i and state of nature s_j

Note the role of the absolute value in equation (15.1). For minimization problems, the best payoff, V_j^*, is the smallest entry in column j. Because this value always is less than or equal to V_{ij}, the absolute value of the difference between V_j^* and V_{ij} ensures that the regret is always the magnitude of the difference.

Using equation (15.1) and the payoffs in Table 15.1, we can compute the regret associated with each combination of decision alternative d_i and state of nature s_j. Because the PDC problem is a maximization problem, V_j^* will be the largest entry in column j of the payoff table. Thus, to compute the regret, we simply subtract each entry in a column from the largest entry in the column. Table 15.4 shows the opportunity loss, or regret, table for the PDC problem.

TABLE 15.4	Opportunity Loss, or Regret, Table for the PDC Condominium Project ($ Millions)	
	State of Nature	
Decision Alternative	**Strong Demand s_1**	**Weak Demand s_2**
Small complex, d_1	12	0
Medium complex, d_2	6	2
Large complex, d_3	0	16

TABLE 15.5	Maximum Regret for Each PDC Decision Alternative

Decision Alternative	Maximum Regret ($ millions)	
Small complex, d_1	12	
Medium complex, d_2	6	← Minimum of the maximum regret
Large complex, d_3	16	

The next step in applying the minimax regret approach is to list the maximum regret for each decision alternative; Table 15.5 shows the results for the PDC problem. Selecting the decision alternative with the *minimum* of the *maximum* regret values—hence, the name *minimax regret*—yields the minimax regret decision. For the PDC problem, the alternative to construct the medium condominium complex, with a corresponding maximum regret of $6 million, is the recommended minimax regret decision.

Note that the three approaches discussed in this section provide different recommendations, which in itself is not bad. It simply reflects the difference in decision-making philosophies that underlie the various approaches. Ultimately, the decision maker will have to choose the most appropriate approach and then make the final decision accordingly. The main criticism of the approaches discussed in this section is that they do not consider any information about the probabilities of the various states of nature. In the next section, we discuss an approach that utilizes probability information in selecting a decision alternative.

15.3 Decision Analysis with Probabilities

Expected Value Approach

In many decision-making situations, we can obtain probability assessments for the states of nature. When such probabilities are available, we can use the **expected value approach** to identify the best decision alternative. Let us first define the expected value of a decision alternative and then apply it to the PDC problem.

Let:

$$N = \text{the number of states of nature}$$
$$P(s_j) = \text{the probability of state of nature } s_j$$

Because one and only one of the N states of nature can occur, the probabilities must satisfy two conditions:

$$P(s_j) \geq 0 \qquad \text{for all states of nature}$$

$$\sum_{j=1}^{N} P(s_j) = P(s_1) + P(s_2) + \cdots + P(s_N) = 1$$

The **expected value (EV)** of decision alternative d_i is defined as follows:

EXPECTED VALUE OF DECISION ALTERNATIVE d_i

$$EV(d_i) = \sum_{j=1}^{N} P(s_j)V_{ij} \tag{15.2}$$

In words, the expected value of a decision alternative is the sum of weighted payoffs for the decision alternative. The weight for a payoff is the probability of the associated state of nature and therefore the probability that the payoff will occur. Let us return to the PDC problem to see how the expected value approach can be applied.

PDC is optimistic about the potential for the luxury high-rise condominium complex. Suppose that this optimism leads to an initial subjective probability assessment of 0.8 that demand will be strong (s_1) and a corresponding probability of 0.2 that demand will be weak (s_2). Thus, $P(s_1) = 0.8$ and $P(s_2) = 0.2$. Using the payoff values in Table 15.1 and equation (15.2), we compute the expected value for each of the three decision alternatives as follows:

$$EV(d_1) = 0.8\,(8) + 0.2\,(7) = 7.8$$
$$EV(d_2) = 0.8\,(14) + 0.2\,(5) = 12.2$$
$$EV(d_3) = 0.8\,(20) + 0.2\,(-9) = 14.2$$

Thus, using the expected value approach, we find that the large condominium complex, with an expected value of $14.2 million, is the recommended decision.

Computer packages are available to help in constructing more complex decision trees. In the chapter appendix, we discuss the use of Analytic Solver Platform to create decision trees.

The calculations required to identify the decision alternative with the best expected value can be conveniently carried out on a decision tree. Figure 15.2 shows the decision tree for the PDC problem with state-of-nature branch probabilities. Working backward through the decision tree, we first compute the expected value at each chance node. In other words, at each chance node, we weight each possible payoff by its probability of occurrence. By doing so, we obtain the expected values for nodes 2, 3, and 4, as shown in Figure 15.3.

Because the decision maker controls the branch leaving decision node 1 and because we are trying to maximize the expected profit, the best decision alternative at node 1 is d_3. Thus, the decision tree analysis leads to a recommendation of d_3, with an expected value of $14.2 million. Note that this recommendation is also obtained with the expected value approach in conjunction with the payoff table.

Other decision problems may be substantially more complex than the PDC problem, but if a reasonable number of decision alternatives and states of nature are present, you can use the decision tree approach outlined here. First, draw a decision tree consisting of decision nodes, chance nodes, and branches that describe the sequential nature of the problem. If

---

FIGURE 15.2   PDC Decision Tree with State-of-Nature Branch Probabilities

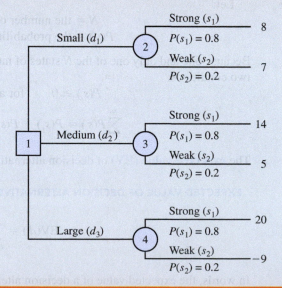

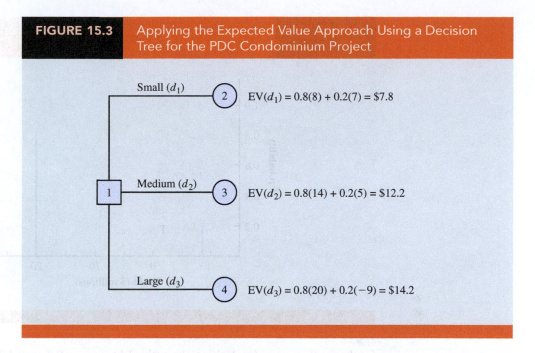

FIGURE 15.3   Applying the Expected Value Approach Using a Decision Tree for the PDC Condominium Project

Small (d_1) ② $EV(d_1) = 0.8(8) + 0.2(7) = \$7.8$

Medium (d_2) ③ $EV(d_2) = 0.8(14) + 0.2(5) = \$12.2$

Large (d_3) ④ $EV(d_3) = 0.8(20) + 0.2(-9) = \$14.2$

you use the expected value approach, the next step is to determine the probabilities for each of the states of nature and compute the expected value at each chance node. Then select the decision branch leading to the chance node with the best expected value. The decision alternative associated with this branch is the recommended decision.

In practice, obtaining precise estimates of the probabilities for each state of nature is often impossible. In some cases where similar decisions have been made many times in the past, one may use historical data to estimate the probabilities for the different states of nature. However, often there are little, or no, historical data to guide the estimates of these probabilities. In these cases, we may have to rely on subjective estimates to determine the probabilities for the states of nature. When relying on subjective estimates, we often want to get more than one estimate because many studies have shown that even knowledgeable experts are often overly optimistic in their estimates. It is also particularly important when dealing with subjective probability estimates to perform risk analysis and sensitivity analysis, as we will explain.

Risk Analysis

Risk analysis helps the decision maker recognize the difference between the expected value of a decision alternative and the payoff that may actually occur. A decision alternative and a state of nature combine to generate the payoff associated with a decision. The **risk profile** for a decision alternative shows the possible payoffs along with their associated probabilities.

Let us demonstrate risk analysis and the construction of a risk profile by returning to the PDC condominium construction project. Using the expected value approach, we identified the large condominium complex (d_3) as the best decision alternative. The expected value of $14.2 million for d_3 is based on a 0.8 probability of obtaining a $20 million profit and a 0.2 probability of obtaining a $9 million loss. The 0.8 probability for the $20 million payoff and the 0.2 probability for the −$9 million payoff provide the risk profile for the large complex decision alternative. This risk profile is shown graphically in Figure 15.4.

Sometimes a review of the risk profile associated with an optimal decision alternative may cause the decision maker to choose another decision alternative even though the expected value of the other decision alternative is not as good. For example, the risk profile

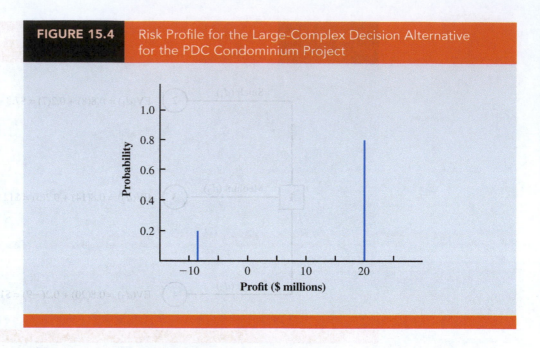

FIGURE 15.4   Risk Profile for the Large-Complex Decision Alternative for the PDC Condominium Project

for the medium-complex decision alternative (d_2) shows a 0.8 probability for a $14 million payoff and a 0.2 probability for a $5 million payoff. Because no probability of a loss is associated with decision alternative d_2, the medium-complex decision alternative would be judged less risky than the large-complex decision alternative. As a result, a decision maker might prefer the less risky medium-complex decision alternative even though it has an expected value of $2 million less than the large-complex decision alternative.

Sensitivity Analysis

Sensitivity analysis can be used to determine how changes in the probabilities for the states of nature or changes in the payoffs affect the recommended decision alternative. In many cases, the probabilities for the states of nature and the payoffs are based on subjective assessments. Sensitivity analysis helps the decision maker understand which of these inputs are critical to the choice of the best decision alternative. If a small change in the value of one of the inputs causes a change in the recommended decision alternative, the solution to the decision analysis problem is sensitive to that particular input. Extra effort and care should be taken to make sure the input value is as accurate as possible. On the other hand, if a modest-to-large change in the value of one of the inputs does not cause a change in the recommended decision alternative, the solution to the decision analysis problem is not sensitive to that particular input. No extra time or effort would be needed to refine the estimated input value.

One approach to sensitivity analysis is to select different values for the probabilities of the states of nature and the payoffs and then resolve the decision analysis problem. If the recommended decision alternative changes, we know that the solution is sensitive to the changes made. For example, suppose that in the PDC problem the probability for a strong demand is revised to 0.2 and the probability for a weak demand is revised to 0.8. Would the recommended decision alternative change? Using $P(s_1) = 0.2$, $P(s_2) = 0.8$, and equation (15.2), the revised expected values for the three decision alternatives are:

$$EV(d_1) = 0.2 (8) + 0.8 (7) = 7.2$$
$$EV(d_2) = 0.2 (14) + 0.8 (5) = 6.8$$
$$EV(d_3) = 0.2 (20) + 0.8 (-9) = -3.2$$

With these probability assessments, the recommended decision alternative is to construct a small condominium complex (d_1), with an expected value of \$7.2 million. The probability of strong demand is only 0.2, so constructing the large condominium complex (d_3) is the least preferred alternative, with an expected value of $-$\$3.2 million (a loss).

Thus, when the probability of strong demand is large, PDC should build the large complex; when the probability of strong demand is small, PDC should build the small complex. Obviously, we could continue to modify the probabilities of the states of nature and learn even more about how changes in the probabilities affect the recommended decision alternative. Sensitivity analysis calculations can also be made for the values of the payoffs. We can easily change the payoff values and resolve the problem to see if the best decision changes.

NOTES + COMMENTS

1. The definition of expected value given in this chapter is consistent with that given in Chapter 5, but here we use the notation and terminology specific to decision analysis. In both cases, the expected value is defined as the weighted average of possible values.

2. The drawback to the sensitivity analysis approach described in this section is the numerous calculations required to evaluate the effect of several possible changes in the state-of-nature probabilities and/or payoff values. In the chapter appendix we demonstrate how to use Analytic Solver Platform and a Data Table in Excel to generate sensitivity analysis for decision problems.

15.4 Decision Analysis with Sample Information

Frequently, decision makers have the ability to collect additional information about the states of nature. It is worthwhile for the decision maker to consider the potential value of this additional information and how it can affect the decision analysis process. Most often, additional information is obtained through experiments designed to provide **sample information** about the states of nature. Raw material sampling, product testing, and market research studies are examples of experiments (or studies) that may enable management to revise or update the state-of-nature probabilities.

To analyze the potential benefit of additional information, we must first introduce a few additional terms related to decision analysis. The preliminary or **prior probability** assessments for the states of nature that are the best probability values available prior to obtaining additional information. These revised probabilities after obtaining additional information are called **posterior probabilities**.

Let us return to the PDC problem and assume that management is considering a 6-month market research study designed to learn more about potential market acceptance of the PDC condominium project. Management anticipates that the market research study will provide one of the following two results:

1. *Favorable report:* A substantial number of the individuals contacted express interest in purchasing a PDC condominium.
2. *Unfavorable report:* Very few of the individuals contacted express interest in purchasing a PDC condominium.

The decision tree for the PDC problem with sample information shows the logical sequence for the decisions and the chance events in Figure 15.5. By introducing the possibility of conducting a market research study, the PDC problem becomes more complex. First, PDC's management must decide whether the market research should be conducted. If it is conducted, PDC's management must be prepared to make a decision about the size of the condominium

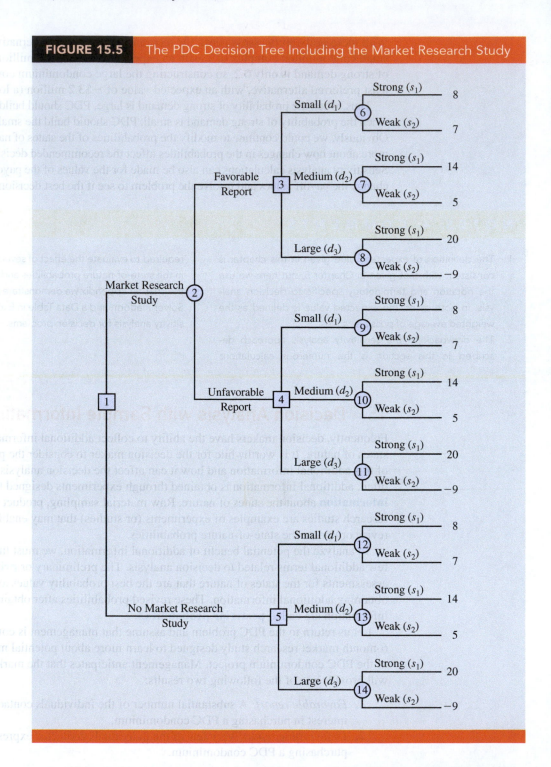

FIGURE 15.5   The PDC Decision Tree Including the Market Research Study

project if the market research report is favorable and, possibly, a different decision about the size of the condominium project if the market research report is unfavorable. In Figure 15.5, the squares are decision nodes and the circles are chance nodes. At each decision node, the branch of the tree that is taken is based on the decision made. At each chance node, the branch of the tree that is taken is based on probability or chance. For example, decision node 1 shows that PDC must first make the decision of whether to conduct the market research study. If the market research study is undertaken, chance node 2 indicates that both the favorable report branch and the unfavorable report branch are not under PDC's control and will be determined by chance. Node 3 is a decision node, indicating that PDC must make the decision to construct the small, medium, or large complex if the market research report is favorable. Node 4 is a decision node showing that PDC must make the decision to construct the small, medium, or large complex if the market research report is unfavorable. Node 5 is a decision node indicating that PDC must make the decision to construct the small, medium, or large complex if the market research is not undertaken. Nodes 6 to 14 are chance nodes indicating that the strong demand or weak demand state-of-nature branches will be determined by chance.

Analysis of the decision tree and the choice of an optimal strategy require that we know the branch probabilities corresponding to all chance nodes. PDC has developed the following branch probabilities:

The branch probabilities for P(favorable report) and P(unfavorable report) are calculated using Bayes' rule, first introduced in Chapter 5. We illustrate these calculations in Section 15.5.

If the market research study is undertaken:

$$P(\text{favorable report}) = 0.77$$
$$P(\text{unfavorable report}) = 0.23$$

If the market research report is favorable, the posterior probabilities are:

$$P(\text{strong demand given a favorable report}) = 0.94$$
$$P(\text{weak demand given a favorable report}) = 0.06$$

If the market research report is unfavorable, the posterior probabilities are:

$$P(\text{strong demand given an unfavorable report}) = 0.35$$
$$P(\text{weak demand given an unfavorable report}) = 0.65$$

If the market research report is not undertaken, the prior probabilities are applicable:

$$P(\text{strong demand}) = 0.80$$
$$P(\text{weak demand}) = 0.20$$

The branch probabilities are shown on the decision tree in Figure 15.6.

A **decision strategy** is a sequence of decisions and chance outcomes in which the decisions chosen depend on the yet-to-be-determined outcomes of chance events. The approach used to determine the optimal decision strategy is based on a rollback of the expected values in the decision tree using the following steps:

1. At chance nodes, compute the expected value by multiplying the payoff at the end of each branch by the corresponding branch probabilities.
2. At decision nodes, select the decision branch that leads to the best expected value. This expected value becomes the expected value at the decision node.

Starting the rollback calculations by computing the expected values at chance nodes 6 to 14 provides the following results:

$$
\begin{aligned}
\text{EV(Node 6)} &= 0.94(8) + 0.06(7) &&= 7.94 \\
\text{EV(Node 7)} &= 0.94(14) + 0.06(5) &&= 13.46 \\
\text{EV(Node 8)} &= 0.94(20) + 0.06(-9) &&= 18.26 \\
\text{EV(Node 9)} &= 0.35(8) + 0.65(7) &&= 7.35 \\
\text{EV(Node 10)} &= 0.35(14) + 0.65(5) &&= 8.15 \\
\text{EV(Node 11)} &= 0.35(20) + 0.65(-9) &&= 1.15 \\
\text{EV(Node 12)} &= 0.80(8) + 0.20(7) &&= 7.80 \\
\text{EV(Node 13)} &= 0.80(14) + 0.20(5) &&= 12.20 \\
\text{EV(Node 14)} &= 0.80(20) + 0.20(-9) &&= 14.20 \\
\end{aligned}
$$

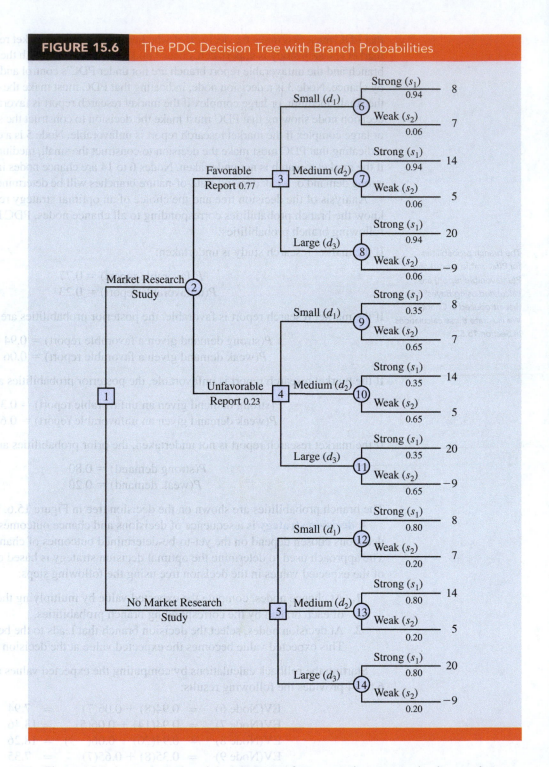

Figure 15.7 shows the reduced decision tree after computing expected values at these chance nodes.

Next, move to decision nodes 3, 4, and 5. For each of these nodes, we select the decision alternative branch that leads to the best expected value. For example, at node 3 we have the choice of the small complex branch with EV(Node 6) = 7.94, the medium complex branch

FIGURE 15.7 PDC Decision Tree after Computing Expected Values at Chance Nodes 6 to 14

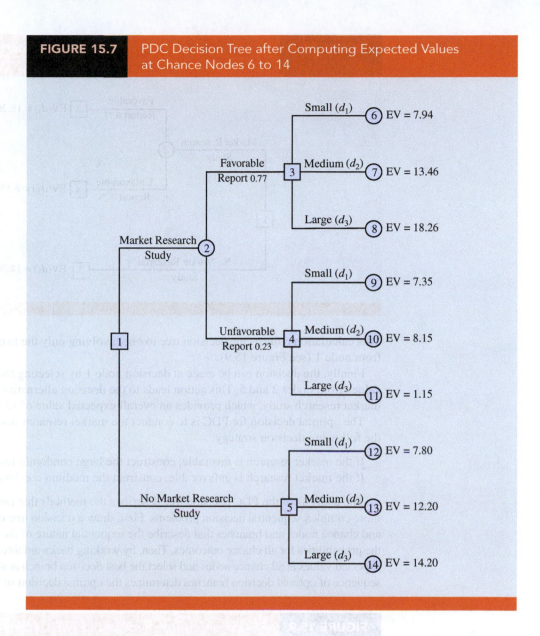

with EV(Node 7) = 13.46, and the large complex branch with EV(Node 8) = 18.26. Thus, we select the large complex decision alternative branch and the expected value at node 3 becomes EV(Node 3) = 18.26.

For node 4, we select the best expected value from nodes 9, 10, and 11. The best decision alternative is the medium complex branch that provides EV(Node 4) = 8.15. For node 5, we select the best expected value from nodes 12, 13, and 14. The best decision alternative is the large complex branch that provides EV(Node 5) = 14.20. Figure 15.8 shows the reduced decision tree after choosing the best decisions at nodes 3, 4, and 5 and rolling back the expected values to these nodes.

The expected value at chance node 2 can now be computed as follows:

$$EV(\text{Node 2}) = 0.77EV(\text{Node 3}) + 0.23EV(\text{Node 4})$$
$$= 0.77(18.26) + 0.23(8.15) = 15.93$$

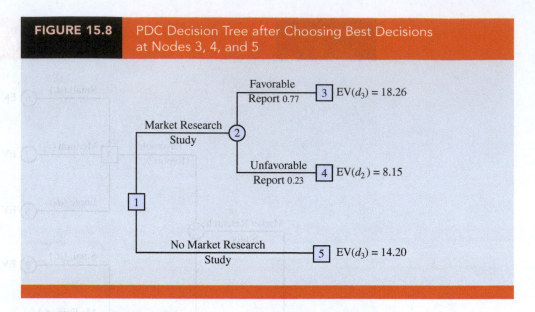

This calculation reduces the decision tree to one involving only the two decision branches from node 1 (see Figure 15.9).

Finally, the decision can be made at decision node 1 by selecting the best expected values from nodes 2 and 5. This action leads to the decision alternative to conduct the market research study, which provides an overall expected value of 15.93.

The optimal decision for PDC is to conduct the market research study and then carry out the following decision strategy:

If the market research is favorable, construct the large condominium complex.
If the market research is unfavorable, construct the medium condominium complex.

The analysis of the PDC decision tree describes the methods that can be used to analyze more complex sequential decision problems. First, draw a decision tree consisting of decision and chance nodes and branches that describe the sequential nature of the problem. Determine the probabilities for all chance outcomes. Then, by working backward through the tree, compute expected values at all chance nodes and select the best decision branch at all decision nodes. The sequence of optimal decision branches determines the optimal decision strategy for the problem.

FIGURE 15.9   PDC Decision Tree Reduced to Two Decision Branches

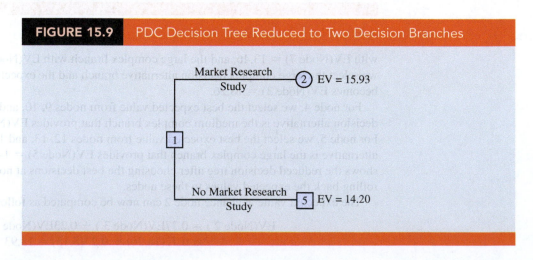

Expected Value of Sample Information

The EVSI = $1.73 million suggests PDC should be willing to pay up to $1.73 million to conduct the market research study.

In the PDC problem, the market research study is the sample information used to determine the optimal decision strategy. The expected value associated with the market research study is 15.93. Previously, we showed that the best expected value if the market research study is *not* undertaken is 14.20. Thus, we can conclude that the difference, 15.93 − 14.20 = 1.73, is the **expected value of sample information (EVSI)**. In other words, conducting the market research study adds $1.73 million to the PDC expected value. In general, the expected value of sample information is as follows:

EXPECTED VALUE OF SAMPLE INFORMATION (EVSI)

$$EVSI = |EVwSI - EVwoSI| \qquad (15.3)$$

where

EVSI = expected value of sample information
EVwSI = expected value *with* sample information about the states of nature
EVwoSI = expected value *without* sample information about the states of nature

Expected Value of Perfect Information

A special case of gaining additional information related to a decision problem is when the sample information provides **perfect information** on the states of nature. In other words, consider a case in which the marketing study undertaken by PDC would determine exactly which state of nature will occur. Clearly, such a result is highly unlikely from a marketing study, but such an analysis provides a best-case analysis of the benefit provided by the marketing study. If the investment required for the additional information exceeds the expected value of perfect information, then we would not want to invest in procuring the additional information.

To illustrate the calculation of the expected value of perfect information, we return to the PDC decision. We assume for the moment that PDC could determine with certainty, prior to making a decision, which state of nature is going to occur. To make use of this perfect information, we will develop a decision strategy that PDC should follow once it knows which state of nature will occur.

To help determine the decision strategy for PDC, we reproduced PDC's payoff table as Table 15.6. If PDC knew for sure that state of nature s_1 would occur, the best decision alternative would be d_3, with a payoff of $20 million. Similarly, if PDC knew for sure that state of nature s_2 would occur, the best decision alternative would be d_1, with a payoff of $7 million. Thus, we can state PDC's optimal decision strategy when the perfect information becomes available as follows:

If s_1, select d_3 and receive a payoff of $20 million.
If s_2, select d_1 and receive a payoff of $7 million.

It would be worth $3.2 million for PDC to learn the level of market acceptance before selecting a decision alternative. This represents the maximum that PDC should invest in any market research to provide additional information on the states of nature because no market research study can be expected to provide perfect information.

TABLE 15.6	Payoff Table for the PDC Condominium Project ($ Millions)	
	State of Nature	
Decision Alternative	**Strong Demand s_1**	**Weak Demand s_2**
Small complex, d_1	8	7
Medium complex, d_2	14	5
Large complex, d_3	20	−9

What is the expected value for this decision strategy? To compute the expected value with perfect information, we return to the original probabilities for the states of nature: $P(s_1) = 0.8$ and $P(s_2) = 0.2$. Thus, there is a 0.8 probability that the perfect information will indicate state of nature s_1, and the resulting decision alternative d_3 will provide a \$20 million profit. Similarly, with a 0.2 probability for state of nature s_2, the optimal decision alternative d_1 will provide a \$7 million profit. Thus, from equation (15.2) the expected value of the decision strategy that uses perfect information is $0.8(20) + 0.2(7) = 17.4$.

We refer to the expected value of \$17.4 million as the *expected value with perfect information* (EVwPI).

Earlier in this section we showed that the recommended decision using the expected value approach is decision alternative d_3, with an expected value of \$14.2 million. Because this decision recommendation and expected value computation were made without the benefit of perfect information, \$14.2 million is referred to as the *expected value without perfect information* (EVwoPI).

The expected value with perfect information is \$17.4 million, and the expected value without perfect information is \$14.2; therefore, the expected value of the perfect information (EVPI) is $17.4 - \$14.2 = \$3.2$ million. In other words, \$3.2 million represents the additional expected value that can be obtained if perfect information were available about the states of nature.

In general, the **expected value of perfect information (EVPI)** is computed as follows:

EXPECTED VALUE OF PERFECT INFORMATION (EVPI)

$$EVPI = |EVwPI - EVwoPI| \qquad \text{(15.4)}$$

where

   EVPI = expected value of perfect information
   EVwPI = expected value *with* perfect information about the states of nature
   EVwoPI = expected value *without* perfect information about the states of nature

15.5 Computing Branch Probabilities with Bayes' Theorem

In Section 15.4 the branch probabilities for the PDC decision tree chance nodes were provided in the problem description. No computations were required to determine these probabilities. In this section, we show how **Bayes' theorem** can be used to compute branch probabilities for decision trees.

We first introduced Bayes' theorem in Chapter 5 as a means of calculating posterior probabilities as updates of prior probabilities once additional information is obtained. For the PDC problem, the branch probabilities are the posterior probabilities for demand that have been updated based on the sample information of whether the market research report is favorable or unfavorable.

The PDC decision tree is shown again in Figure 15.10. Let:

$$F = \text{favorable market research report}$$
$$U = \text{unfavorable market research report}$$
$$s_1 = \text{strong demand (state of nature 1)}$$
$$s_2 = \text{weak demand (state of nature 2)}$$

At chance node 2, we need to know the branch probabilities $P(F)$ and $P(U)$. At chance nodes 6, 7, and 8, we need to know the branch probabilities $P(s_1|F)$, which is read as "the probability of state of nature 1 given a favorable market research report," and $P(s_2|F)$,

FIGURE 15.10   The PDC Decision Tree

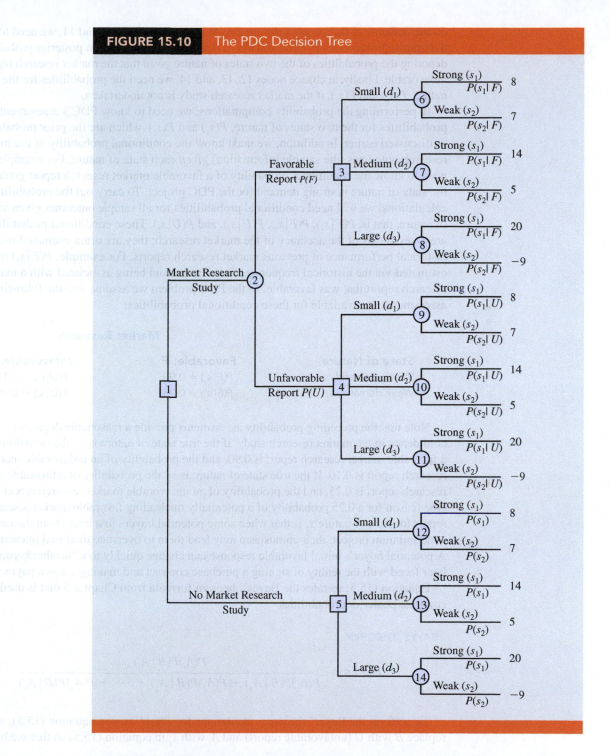

which is the probability of state of nature 2 given a favorable market research report. As described in Chapter 5, the notation | in $P(s_1|F)$ and $P(s_2|F)$ is read as "given" and indicates a **conditional probability** because we are interested in the probability of a particular state of nature "conditioned" on the fact that we receive a favorable market report. $P(s_1|F)$ and $P(s_2|F)$ are referred to as *posterior probabilities* because they are conditional probabilities based on the outcome of the sample information. At chance nodes 9, 10, and 11, we need to know the branch probabilities $P(s_1|U)$ and $P(s_2|U)$; note that these are also posterior probabilities, denoting the probabilities of the two states of nature *given* that the market research report is unfavorable. Finally, at chance nodes 12, 13, and 14, we need the probabilities for the states of nature, $P(s_1)$ and $P(s_2)$, if the market research study is not undertaken.

In performing the probability computations, we need to know PDC's assessment of the probabilities for the two states of nature, $P(s_1)$ and $P(s_2)$, which are the prior probabilities as discussed earlier. In addition, we must know the conditional probability of the market research outcomes (the sample information) *given* each state of nature. For example, we need to know the conditional probability of a favorable market research report given that the state of nature is strong demand for the PDC project. To carry out the probability calculations, we will need conditional probabilities for all sample outcomes given all states of nature, that is, $P(F|s_1)$, $P(F|s_2)$, $P(U|s_1)$, and $P(U|s_2)$. These conditional probabilities are assessments of the accuracy of the market research; they are often estimated using historical performance of previous market research reports. For example, $P(F|s_1)$ may be estimated via the historical frequency of strong demand being associated with a market research report that was favorable. In the PDC problem we assume that the following assessments are available for these conditional probabilities:

	Market Research	
State of Nature	**Favorable, F**	**Unfavorable, U**
Strong demand, s_1	$P(F|s_1) = 0.90$	$P(U|s_1) = 0.10$
Weak demand, s_2	$P(F|s_2) = 0.25$	$P(U|s_2) = 0.75$

Note that the preceding probability assessments provide a reasonable degree of confidence in the market research study. If the true state of nature is s_1, the probability of a favorable market research report is 0.90, and the probability of an unfavorable market research report is 0.10. If the true state of nature is s_2, the probability of a favorable market research report is 0.25, and the probability of an unfavorable market research report is 0.75. One reason for a 0.25 probability of a potentially misleading favorable market research report for state of nature s_2 is that when some potential buyers first hear about the new condominium project, their enthusiasm may lead them to overstate their real interest in it. A potential buyer's initial favorable response can change quickly to a "no-thank-you" when later faced with the reality of signing a purchase contract and making a down payment.

Equation (15.5) restates the Bayes' theorem formula from Chapter 5 that is used to compute posterior probabilities.

BAYES' THEOREM

$$P(A_i|B) = \frac{P(A_i)P(B|A_i)}{P(A_1)P(B|A_1) + P(A_2)P(B|A_2) + \cdots + P(A_n)P(B|A_n)} \tag{15.5}$$

To perform the Bayes' theorem calculations for $P(s_1|U)$ using equation (15.5), we replace B with U (unfavorable report) and A_i with s_1 in equation (15.5) so that we have:

$$P(s_1|U) = \frac{P(U|s_1)P(s_1)}{P(U|s_1)P(s_1) + P(U|s_2)P(s_2)}$$

$$= \frac{0.10 \times 0.80}{(0.10 \times 0.80) + (0.20 \times 0.75)} = 0.35$$

which indicates that the probability of strong demand given an unfavorable market research report is 0.35. We can also calculate the probability of weak demand given an unfavorable market research report as shown below:

$$P(s_2|U) = \frac{P(U|s_2)P(s_2)}{P(U|s_1)P(s_1) + P(U|s_2)P(s_2)} = \frac{0.75 \times 0.20}{(0.10 \times 0.80) + (0.75 \times 0.20)} = 0.65.$$

Similarly, we can calculate the posterior probabilities for strong and weak demand given a favorable market research report using equation (15.5):

$$P(s_1|F) = \frac{P(F|s_1)P(s_1)}{P(F|s_1)P(s_1) + P(F|s_2)P(s_2)} = \frac{0.90 \times 0.80}{(0.90 \times 0.80) + (0.25 \times 0.20)} = 0.94$$

and

$$P(s_2|F) = \frac{P(F|s_2)P(s_2)}{P(F|s_1)P(s_1) + P(F|s_2)P(s_2)} = \frac{0.25 \times 0.20}{(0.90 \times 0.80) + (0.25 \times 0.20)} = 0.06.$$

This indicates that a favorable research report leads to a posterior probability of 0.94 that the demand will be strong and a posterior probability of only 0.06 that demand will be weak.

The discussion in this section shows an underlying relationship between the probabilities on the various branches in a decision tree. It would be inappropriate to assume different prior probabilities, $P(s_1)$ and $P(s_2)$, without determining how these changes would alter $P(F)$ and $P(U)$, as well as the posterior probabilities $P(s_1|F)$, $P(s_2|F)$, $P(s_1|U)$, and $P(s_2|U)$.

15.6 Utility Theory

The decision analysis situations presented so far in this chapter expressed outcomes (payoffs) in terms of monetary values. With probability information available about the outcomes of the chance events, we defined the optimal decision alternative as the one that provides the best expected value. However, in some situations the decision alternative with the best expected value may not be the preferred alternative. A decision maker may also wish to consider intangible factors such as risk, image, or other nonmonetary criteria in order to evaluate the decision alternatives. When monetary value does not necessarily lead to the most preferred decision, expressing the value (or worth) of a consequence in terms of its utility will permit the use of expected utility to identify the most desirable decision alternative. The discussion of utility and its application in decision analysis is presented in this section.

Utility is a measure of the total worth or relative desirability of a particular outcome; it reflects the decision maker's attitude toward a collection of factors such as profit, loss, and risk. Researchers have found that as long as the monetary value of payoffs stays within a range that the decision maker considers reasonable, selecting the decision alternative with the best expected value usually leads to selection of the most preferred decision. However, when the payoffs are extreme, decision makers are often unsatisfied or uneasy with the decision that simply provides the best expected value.

As an example of a situation in which utility can help in selecting the best decision alternative, let us consider the problem faced by Swofford, Inc., a relatively small real estate investment firm located in Atlanta, Georgia. Swofford currently has two investment opportunities that require approximately the same cash outlay. The cash requirements necessary prohibit Swofford from making more than one investment at this time. Consequently, three possible decision alternatives may be considered.

TABLE 15.7   Payoff Table for Swofford, Inc.

Decision Alternative	State of Nature		
	Prices Go Up s_1	Prices Stable s_2	Prices Go Down s_3
Investment A, d_1	$30,000	$20,000	-$50,000
Investment B, d_2	$50,000	-$20,000	-$30,000
Do not invest, d_3	0	0	0

The three decision alternatives, denoted d_1, d_2, and d_3, are:

$$d_1 = \text{make investment A}$$
$$d_2 = \text{make investment B}$$
$$d_3 = \text{do not invest}$$

The monetary payoffs associated with the investment opportunities depend on the investment decision and on the direction of the real estate market during the next six months (the chance event). Real estate prices will go up, remain stable, or go down. Thus, the states of nature, denoted s_1, s_2, and s_3, are:

$$s_1 = \text{real estate prices go up}$$
$$s_2 = \text{real estate prices remain stable}$$
$$s_3 = \text{real estate prices go down}$$

Using the best information available, Swofford has estimated the profits, or payoffs, associated with each decision alternative and state-of-nature combination. The resulting payoff table is shown in Table 15.7.

The best estimate of the probability that real estate prices will go up is 0.3; the best estimate of the probability that prices will remain stable is 0.5; and the best estimate of the probability that prices will go down is 0.2. Thus, the expected values for the three decision alternatives are:

$$\text{EV}(d_1) = 0.3(30,000) + 0.5(20,000) + 0.2(-50,000) = 9000$$
$$\text{EV}(d_2) = 0.3(50,000) + 0.5(-20,000) + 0.2(-30,000) = -11,000$$
$$\text{EV}(d_3) = 0.3(0) + 0.5(0) + 0.2(0) = 0$$

Using the expected value approach, the optimal decision is to select investment A with an expected value of $9,000. Is it really the best decision alternative? Let us consider some other relevant factors that relate to Swofford's capability for absorbing the loss of $50,000 if investment A is made and prices actually go down.

Actually, Swofford's current financial position is weak. This condition is partly reflected in Swofford's ability to make only one investment. More important, however, the firm's president believes that, if the next investment results in a substantial loss, Swofford's future will be in jeopardy. Although the expected value approach leads to a recommendation for d_1, do you think the firm's president would prefer this decision? We suspect that the president would select d_2 or d_3 to avoid the possibility of incurring a $50,000 loss. In fact, a reasonable conclusion is that, if a loss of even $30,000 could drive Swofford out of business, the president would select d_3, believing that both investments A and B are too risky for Swofford's current financial position.

The way we resolve Swofford's dilemma is first to determine Swofford's utility for the various outcomes. Recall that the utility of any outcome is the total worth of that outcome, taking into account all risks and consequences involved. If the utilities for the various consequences are assessed correctly, the decision alternative with the highest expected utility is the most preferred, or best, alternative. We next show how to determine the utility of the outcomes so that the alternative with the highest expected utility can be identified.

Utility and Decision Analysis

The procedure we use to establish a utility for each of the payoffs in Swofford's situation requires that we first assign a utility to the best and worst possible payoffs. Any values will work as long as the utility assigned to the best payoff is greater than the utility assigned to the worst payoff. In this case, $50,000 is the best payoff and −$50,000 is the worst. Suppose, then, that we arbitrarily make assignments to these two payoffs as follows:

Utility values of 0 and 1 could have been selected here; we selected 0 and 10 to avoid any possible confusion between the utility value for a payoff and the probability p.

$$\text{Utility of } -\$50,000 = U(-50,000) = 0$$
$$\text{Utility of } \$50,000 = U(50,000) = 10$$

Let us now determine the utility associated with every other payoff.

Consider the process of establishing the utility of a payoff of $30,000. First we ask Swofford's president to state a preference between a guaranteed $30,000 payoff and an opportunity to engage in the following lottery, or bet, for some probability of p that we select:

p is often referred to as the indifference probability.

Lottery: Swofford obtains a payoff of $50,000 with probability p and a payoff of −$50,000 with probability $(1 − p)$.

Obviously, if p is very close to 1, Swofford's president would prefer the lottery to the guaranteed payoff of $30,000 because the firm would virtually ensure itself a payoff of $50,000. If p is very close to 0, Swofford's president would clearly prefer the guarantee of $30,000. In any event, as p increases continuously from 0 to 1, the preference for the guaranteed payoff of $30,000 decreases and at some point is equal to the preference for the lottery. At this value of p, Swofford's president would have equal preference for the guaranteed payoff of $30,000 and the lottery; at greater values of p, Swofford's president would prefer the lottery to the guaranteed $30,000 payoff. For example, let us assume that when $p = 0.95$, Swofford's president is indifferent between the guaranteed payoff of $30,000 and the lottery. For this value of p, we can compute the utility of a $30,000 payoff as follows:

$$U(30,000) = pU(50,000) + (1 − p)U(−50,000)$$
$$= 0.95(10) + (0.05)(0)$$
$$= 9.5.$$

Obviously, if we had started with a different assignment of utilities for a payoff of $50,000 and −$50,000, the result would have been a different utility for $30,000. For example, if we had started with an assignment of 100 for $50,000 and 10 for −$50,000, the utility of a $30,000 payoff would be:

$$U(30,000) = 0.95(100) + 0.05(10)$$
$$= 95.0 + 0.5$$
$$= 95.5.$$

Hence, we must conclude that the utility assigned to each payoff is not unique but merely depends on the initial choice of utilities for the best and worst payoffs.

Before computing the utility for the other payoffs, let us consider the implication of Swofford's president assigning a utility of 9.5 to a payoff of $30,000. Clearly, when $p = 0.95$, the expected value of the lottery is:

$$EV(\text{lottery}) = 0.95(\$50,000) + 0.05(−\$50,000)$$
$$= \$47,500 − \$2,500$$
$$= \$45,000.$$

The difference between the expected value of the lottery and the guaranteed payoff can be viewed as the risk premium the decision maker is willing to pay.

Although the expected value of the lottery when $p = 0.95$ is $45,000, Swofford's president is indifferent between the lottery (and its associated risk) and a guaranteed payoff of $30,000. Thus, Swofford's president is taking a conservative, or risk-avoiding, viewpoint. A decision maker who would choose a guaranteed payoff over a lottery with a superior expected payoff is a **risk avoider** (or is said to be risk-averse). The president would rather have $30,000 for certain than risk anything greater than a 5% chance of incurring a loss of $50,000. In other words, the difference between the EV of $45,000 and the guaranteed payoff of $30,000 is the risk premium that Swofford's president would be willing to pay to avoid the 5% chance of losing $50,000.

To compute the utility associated with a payoff of −$20,000, we must ask Swofford's president to state a preference between a guaranteed −$20,000 payoff and an opportunity to engage again in the following lottery:

Lottery: Swofford obtains a payoff of $50,000 with probability p and a payoff of −$50,000 with probability $(1 − p)$.

Note that this lottery is exactly the same as the one we used to establish the utility of a payoff of $30,000 (in fact, we can use this lottery to establish the utility for any value in the Swofford payoff table). We need to determine the value of p that would make the president indifferent between a guaranteed payoff of −$20,000 and the lottery. For example, we might begin by asking the president to choose between a certain loss of $20,000 and the lottery with a payoff of $50,000 with probability $p = 0.90$ and a payoff of −$50,000 with probability $(1 − p) = 0.10$. What answer do you think we would get? Surely, with this high probability of obtaining a payoff of $50,000, the president would elect the lottery. Next, we might ask whether $p = 0.85$ would result in indifference between the loss of $20,000 for certain and the lottery. Again the president might prefer the lottery. Suppose that we continue until we get to $p = 0.55$, at which point the president is indifferent between the payoff of −$20,000 and the lottery. In other words, for any value of p less than 0.55, the president would take a loss of $20,000 for certain rather than risk the potential loss of $50,000 with the lottery; and for any value of p above 0.55, the president would choose the lottery. Thus, the utility assigned to a payoff of −$20,000 is:

$$U(-\$20,000) = pU(\$50,000) + (1 - p)U(-\$50,000)$$
$$= 0.55(10) + 0.45(0)$$
$$= 5.5.$$

Again let us assess the implication of this assignment by comparing it to the expected value approach. When $p = 0.55$, the expected value of the lottery is:

$$EV(\text{lottery}) = 0.55(\$50,000) + 0.45(-\$50,000)$$
$$= \$27,500 - \$22,500$$
$$= \$5,000.$$

Thus, Swofford's president would just as soon absorb a certain loss of $20,000 as take the lottery and its associated risk, even though the expected value of the lottery is $5,000. Once again this preference demonstrates the conservative, or risk-avoiding, point of view of Swofford's president.

In these two examples, we computed the utility for the payoffs of $30,000 and −$20,000. We can determine the utility for any payoff M in a similar fashion. First, we must find the probability p for which the decision maker is indifferent between a guaranteed payoff of M and a lottery with a payoff of $50,000 with probability p and −$50,000 with probability $(1 − p)$. The utility of M is then computed as follows:

$$U(M) = pU(\$50,000) + (1 - p)U(-\$50,000)$$
$$= p(10) + (1 - p)0$$
$$= 10p.$$

TABLE 15.8	Utility of Monetary Payoffs for Swofford, Inc.		
Monetary Value	**Indifference Value of *p***		**Utility**
$50,000	Does not apply		10.0
30,000	0.95		9.5
20,000	0.90		9.0
0	0.75		7.5
−20,000	0.55		5.5
−30,000	0.40		4.0
−50,000	Does not apply		0

Using this procedure we developed a utility for each of the remaining payoffs in Swofford's problem. The results are presented in Table 15.8.

Now that we have determined the utility of each of the possible monetary values, we can write the original payoff table in terms of utility. Table 15.9 shows the utility for the various outcomes in the Swofford problem. The notation we use for the entries in the utility table is U_{ij}, which denotes the utility associated with decision alternative d_i and state of nature s_j. Using this notation, we see that $U_{23} = 4.0$.

We can now compute the **expected utility (EU)** of the utilities in Table 15.9 in a similar fashion as we computed expected value in Section 15.3. In other words, to identify an optimal decision alternative for Swofford, Inc., the expected utility approach requires the analyst to compute the expected utility for each decision alternative and then select the alternative yielding the highest expected utility. With N possible states of nature, the expected utility of a decision alternative d_i is given by:

EXPECTED UTILITY (EU)

$$EU(d_i) = \sum_{j=1}^{N} P(s_j)U_{ij} \qquad (15.6)$$

The expected utility for each of the decision alternatives in the Swofford problem is:

$$EU(d_1) = 0.3\,(9.5) + 0.5\,(9.0) + 0.2\,(0) = 7.35$$
$$EU(d_2) = 0.3\,(10) + 0.5\,(5.5) + 0.2\,(4.0) = 6.55$$
$$EU(d_3) = 0.3\,(7.5) + 0.5\,(7.5) + 0.2\,(7.5) = 7.50$$

TABLE 15.9	Utility Table for Swofford, Inc.		
		State of Nature	
Decision Alternative	**Prices Up s_1**	**Prices Stable s_2**	**Prices Down s_3**
Investment A, d_1	9.5	9.0	0
Investment B, d_2	10.0	5.5	4.0
Do not invest, d_3	7.5	7.5	7.5

Note that the optimal decision using the expected utility approach is d_3, do not invest. The ranking of alternatives according to the president's utility assignments and the associated monetary values are as follows:

Ranking of Decision Alternatives	Expected Utility	Expected Value
Do not invest	7.50	0
Investment A	7.35	9,000
Investment B	6.55	−1,000

Note that, although investment A had the highest expected value of $9,000, the analysis indicates that Swofford should decline this investment. The rationale behind not selecting investment A is that the 0.20 probability of a $50,000 loss was considered by Swofford's president to involve a serious risk. The seriousness of this risk and its associated impact on the company were not adequately reflected by the expected value of investment A. We assessed the utility for each payoff to assess this risk adequately.

The following steps state in general terms the procedure used to solve the Swofford, Inc., investment problem:

Step 1. Develop a payoff table using monetary values

Step 2. Identify the best and worst payoff values in the table and assign each a utility, with U(best payoff) > U(worst payoff)

Step 3. For every other monetary value M in the original payoff table, do the following to determine its utility:

    a. Define the lottery such that there is a probability p of the best payoff and a probability $(1 − p)$ of the worst payoff

    b. Determine the value of p such that the decision maker is indifferent between a guaranteed payoff of M and the lottery defined in step 3(a)

    c. Calculate the utility of M as follows:

$$U(M) = pU(\text{best payoff}) + (1 − p)U(\text{worst payoff})$$

Step 4. Convert each monetary value in the payoff table to a utility

Step 5. Apply the expected utility approach to the utility table developed in step 4 and select the decision alternative with the highest expected utility

The procedure we described for determining the utility of monetary consequences can also be used to develop a utility measure for nonmonetary consequences. Assign the best consequence a utility of 10 and the worst a utility of 0. Then create a lottery with a probability of p for the best consequence and $(1 − p)$ for the worst consequence. For each of the other consequences, find the value of p that makes the decision maker indifferent between the lottery and the consequence. Then calculate the utility of the consequence in question as follows:

$$U(\text{consequence}) = pU(\text{best consequence}) + (1 − p)U(\text{worst consequence}).$$

Utility Functions

Next we describe how different decision makers may approach risk in terms of their assessment of utility. The financial position of Swofford, Inc., was such that the firm's president evaluated investment opportunities from a conservative, or risk-avoiding, point of view. However, if the firm had a surplus of cash and a stable future, Swofford's president might have been looking for investment alternatives that, although perhaps risky, contained a potential for substantial profit. That type of behavior would demonstrate that the president is a risk taker with respect to this decision.

TABLE 15.10   Revised Utilities for Swofford, Inc., Assuming a Risk Taker

Monetary Value	Indifference Value of p	Utility
$50,000	Does not apply	10.0
30,000	0.50	5.0
20,000	0.40	4.0
0	0.25	2.5
−20,000	0.15	1.5
−30,000	0.10	1.0
−50,000	Does not apply	0

A **risk taker** is a decision maker who would choose a lottery over a guaranteed payoff when the expected value of the lottery is inferior to the guaranteed payoff. In this section, we analyze the decision problem faced by Swofford from the point of view of a decision maker who would be classified as a risk taker. We then compare the conservative point of view of Swofford's president (a risk avoider) with the behavior of a decision maker who is a risk taker.

For the decision problem facing Swofford, Inc., using the general procedure for developing utilities as discussed previously, a risk taker might express the utility for the various payoffs shown in Table 15.10. As before, $U(50,000) = 10$ and $U(-50,000) = 0$. Note the difference in behavior reflected in Table 15.10 and Table 15.8. In other words, in determining the value of p at which the decision maker is indifferent between a guaranteed payoff of M and a lottery in which $50,000 is obtained with probability p and −$50,000 with probability $(1 - p)$, the risk taker is willing to accept a greater risk of incurring a loss of $50,000 in order to gain the opportunity to realize a profit of $50,000.

To help develop the utility table for the risk taker, we have reproduced the Swofford, Inc. payoff table in Table 15.11. Using these payoffs and the risk taker's utilities given in Table 15.10, we can write the risk taker's utility table as shown in Table 15.12. Using the

TABLE 15.11   Payoff Table for Swofford, Inc.

Decision Alternative	State of Nature		
	Prices Up s_1	Prices Stable s_2	Prices Down s_3
Investment A, d_1	$30,000	$20,000	−$50,000
Investment B, d_2	$50,000	−$20,000	−$30,000
Do not invest, d_3	0	0	0

TABLE 15.12   Utility Table of a Risk Taker for Swofford, Inc.

Decision Alternative	State of Nature		
	Prices Up s_1	Prices Stable s_2	Prices Down s_3
Investment A, d_1	5.0	4.0	0
Investment B, d_2	10.0	1.5	1.0
Do not invest, d_3	2.5	2.5	2.5

state-of-nature probabilities $P(s_1) = 0.3$, $P(s_2) = 0.5$, and $P(s_3) = 0.2$, the expected utility for each decision alternative is:

$$EU(d_1) = 0.3\,(5.0) + 0.5\,(4.0) + 0.2\,(0) = 3.50$$
$$EU(d_2) = 0.3\,(10) + 0.5\,(1.5) + 0.2\,(1.0\,) = 3.95$$
$$EU(d_3) = 0.3\,(2.5) + 0.5\,(2.5) + 0.2\,(2.5) = 2.50$$

What is the recommended decision? Perhaps somewhat to your surprise, the analysis recommends investment B, with the highest expected utility of 3.95. Recall that this investment has a −$1,000 expected value. Why is it now the recommended decision? Remember that the decision maker in this revised problem is a risk taker. Thus, although the expected value of investment B is negative, utility analysis has shown that this decision maker is enough of a risk taker to prefer investment B and its potential for the $50,000 profit.

Ranking by the expected utilities generates the following order of preference of the decision alternatives for the risk taker and the associated expected values:

Ranking of Decision Alternatives	Expected Utility	Expected Value
Investment B	3.95	−$1,000
Investment A	3.50	$9,000
Do not invest	2.50	0

Comparing the utility analysis for a risk taker with the more conservative preferences of the president of Swofford, Inc., who is a risk avoider, we see that, even with the same decision problem, different attitudes toward risk can lead to different recommended decisions. The utilities established by Swofford's president indicated that the firm should not invest at this time, whereas the utilities established by the risk taker showed a preference for investment B. Note that both of these decisions differ from the best expected value decision, which was investment A.

We can obtain another perspective of the difference between behaviors of a risk avoider and a risk taker by developing a graph that depicts the relationship between monetary value and utility. We use the horizontal axis of the graph to represent monetary values and the vertical axis to represent the utility associated with each monetary value. Now, consider the data in Table 15.8, with a utility corresponding to each monetary value for the original Swofford, Inc., problem. These values can be plotted on a graph to produce the top curve in Figure 15.11. The resulting curve is the **utility function for money** for Swofford's president. Recall that these points reflected the conservative, or risk-avoiding, nature of Swofford's president. Hence, we refer to the top curve in Figure 15.11 as a utility function for a risk avoider. Using the data in Table 15.10 developed for a risk taker, we can plot these points to produce the bottom curve in Figure 15.11. The resulting curve depicts the utility function for a risk taker.

By looking at the utility functions in Figure 15.11, we can begin to generalize about the utility functions for risk avoiders and risk takers. Although the exact shape of the utility function will vary from one decision maker to another, we can see the general shape of these two types of utility functions. The utility function for a risk avoider shows a diminishing marginal return for money. For example, the increase in utility going from a monetary value of −$30,000 to $0 is $7.5 − 4.0 = 3.5$, whereas the increase in utility in going from $0 to $30,000 is only $9.5 − 7.5 = 2.0$.

However, the utility function for a risk taker shows an increasing marginal return for money. For example, in Figure 15.11, the increase in utility for the risk taker in going from −$30,000 to $0 is $2.5 − 1.0 = 1.5$, whereas the increase in utility in going from $0 to $30,000 for the risk taker is $5.0 − 2.5 = 2.5$. Note also that in either case the utility

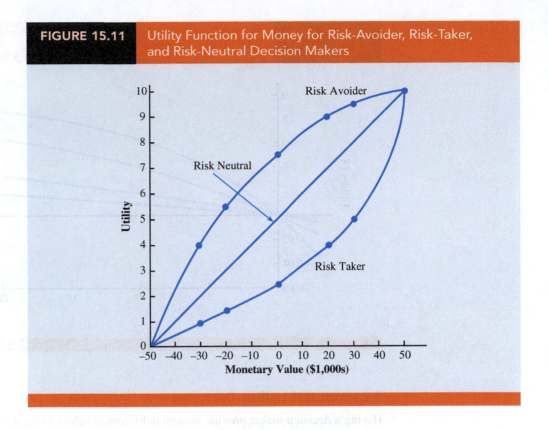

FIGURE 15.11   Utility Function for Money for Risk-Avoider, Risk-Taker, and Risk-Neutral Decision Makers

function is always increasing; that is, more money leads to more utility. All utility functions possess this property.

We concluded that the utility function for a risk avoider shows a diminishing marginal return for money and that the utility function for a risk taker shows an increasing marginal return. When the marginal return for money is neither decreasing nor increasing but remains constant, the corresponding utility function describes the behavior of a decision maker who is neutral to risk. The following characteristics are associated with a **risk-neutral** decision maker:

1. The utility function can be drawn as a straight line connecting the "best" and the "worst" points.
2. The expected utility approach and the expected value approach applied to monetary payoffs result in the same action.

The straight, diagonal line in Figure 15.11 depicts the utility function of a risk-neutral decision maker using the Swofford, Inc., problem data.

Generally, when the payoffs for a particular decision-making problem fall into a reasonable range—the best is not too good and the worst is not too bad—decision makers tend to express preferences in agreement with the expected value approach. Thus, we suggest asking the decision maker to consider the best and worst possible payoffs for a problem and assess their reasonableness. If the decision maker believes that they are in the reasonable range, the decision alternative with the best expected value can be used. However, if the payoffs appear unreasonably large or unreasonably small (e.g., a huge loss) and if the decision maker believes that monetary values do not adequately reflect her or his true preferences for the payoffs, a utility analysis of the problem should be considered.

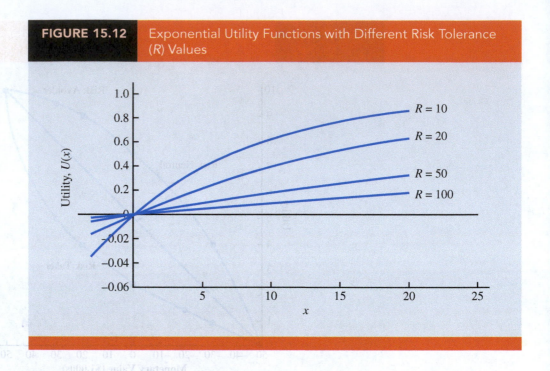

FIGURE 15.12   Exponential Utility Functions with Different Risk Tolerance (R) Values

Exponential Utility Function

Having a decision maker provide enough indifference values to create a utility function can be time consuming. An alternative is to assume that the decision maker's utility is defined by an exponential function. Figure 15.12 shows examples of different exponential utility functions. Note that all the exponential utility functions indicate that the decision maker is risk averse. The form of the exponential utility function is as follows.

In equation (15.7), the number e ≈ 2.718282... is a mathematical constant corresponding to the base of the natural logarithm. In Excel, e^x can be evaluated for any power x using the function EXP(x).

EXPONENTIAL UTILITY FUNCTION

$$U(x) = 1 - e^{-x/R} \qquad (15.7)$$

The R parameter in equation (15.7) represents the decision maker's risk tolerance; it controls the shape of the exponential utility function. Larger R values create flatter exponential functions, indicating that the decision maker is less risk averse (closer to risk neutral). Smaller R values indicate that the decision maker has less risk tolerance (is more risk averse). A common method to determine an approximate risk tolerance is to ask the decision maker to consider a scenario in which he or she could win $R with probability 0.5 and lose $R/2 with probability 0.5. The R value to use in equation (15.7) is the largest $R for which the decision maker would accept this gamble. For instance, if the decision maker is comfortable accepting a gamble with a 50% chance of winning $2,000 and a 50% chance of losing $1,000, but not with a gamble with a 50% chance of winning $3,000 and a 50% chance of losing $1,500, then we would use R = $2,000 in equation (15.7). Determining the maximum gamble that a decision maker is willing to take and then using this value in the exponential utility function can be much less time-consuming than generating a complete table of indifference probabilities. One should remember that using an exponential utility function assumes that the decision maker is risk averse; however, this is often true in practice for business decisions.

NOTES + COMMENTS

1. In the Swofford problem, we have been using a utility of 10 for the best payoff and 0 for the worst. We could have chosen any values as long as the utility associated with the best payoff exceeds the utility associated with the worst payoff. Alternatively, a utility of 1 can be associated with the best payoff and a utility of 0 associated with the worst payoff. Had we made this choice, the utility for any monetary value M would have been the value of p at which the decision maker was indifferent between a guaranteed payoff of M and a lottery in which the best payoff is obtained with probability p and the worst payoff is obtained with probability $(1 - p)$. Thus, the utility for any monetary value would have been equal to the probability of earning the best payoff. Often this choice is made because of the ease in computation. We chose not to do so to emphasize the distinction between the utilities and the indifference probabilities for the lottery.

2. Circumstances often dictate whether one acts as a risk avoider or a risk taker when making a decision. For example, you may think of yourself as a risk avoider when faced with financial decisions, but if you have ever purchased a lottery ticket, you have actually acted as a risk taker. For example, suppose you purchase a $1 lottery ticket for a simple lottery in which the object is to pick the six numbers that will be drawn from 50 potential numbers. Also suppose that the winner (who correctly choses all six numbers that are drawn) will receive $1,000,000. There are 15,890,700 possible winning combinations, so your probability of winning is 1/15890700 = 0.000000062929889809763 (i.e., *very low*) and the expected value of your ticket is:

$$\frac{1}{15,890,700}(\$1,000,000 - \$1) + \left(1 - \frac{1}{15,890,700}\right)(-\$1)$$

$$= -\$0.93707$$

or about −$0.94.

If a lottery ticket has a negative expected value, why does anyone play? The answer is in utility; most people who play lotteries associate great utility with the possiblity of winning the $1,000,000 prize and relatively little utility with the $1 cost for a ticket, and so the expected value of the utility of the lottery ticket is positive even though the expected value of the ticket is negative.

SUMMARY

Decision analysis can be used to determine a recommended decision alternative or an optimal decision strategy when a decision maker is faced with an uncertain and risk-filled pattern of future events. The goal of decision analysis is to identify the best decision alternative or the optimal decision strategy, given information about the uncertain events and the possible consequences or payoffs. The "best" decision should consider the risk preference of the decision maker in evaluating outcomes.

We showed how payoff tables and decision trees could be used to structure a decision problem and describe the relationships among the decisions, the chance events, and the consequences. We presented three approaches to decision making without probabilities: the optimistic approach, the conservative approach, and the minimax regret approach. When probability assessments are provided for the states of nature, the expected value approach can be used to identify the recommended decision alternative or decision strategy.

Even though the expected value approach can be used to obtain a recommended decision alternative or optimal decision strategy, the payoff that actually occurs will usually have a value different from the expected value. A risk profile provides a probability distribution for the possible payoffs and can assist the decision maker in assessing the risks associated with different decision alternatives. Sensitivity analysis can be conducted to determine the effect changes in the probabilities for the states of nature and changes in the values of the payoffs have on the recommended decision alternative.

In cases in which sample information about the chance events is available, a sequence of decisions has to be made. First we must decide whether to obtain the sample information. If the answer is yes, an optimal decision strategy based on the specific sample information must be developed. In this situation, decision trees and the expected value approach can be used to determine the optimal decision strategy.

Bayes' theorem can be used to compute branch probabilities for decision trees. Bayes' theorem updates a decision maker's prior probabilities regarding the states of nature using sample information to compute revised posterior probabilities.

We showed how utility could be used in decision-making situations in which monetary value did not provide an adequate measure of the payoffs. Utility is a measure of the total worth of an outcome. As such, utility takes into account the decision maker's assessment of all aspects of a consequence, including profit, loss, risk, and perhaps additional nonmonetary factors. The examples showed how the use of expected utility can lead to decision recommendations that differ from those based on expected value.

A decision maker's judgment must be used to establish the utility for each consequence. We presented a step-by-step procedure to determine a decision maker's utility for monetary payoffs. We also discussed how conservative, risk-avoiding decision makers assess utility differently from more aggressive, risk-taking decision makers.

GLOSSARY

Bayes' theorem A theorem that enables the use of sample information to revise prior probabilities.

Branch Lines showing the alternatives from decision nodes and the outcomes from chance nodes.

Chance event An uncertain future event affecting the consequence, or payoff, associated with a decision.

Chance nodes Nodes indicating points at which an uncertain event will occur.

Conditional probabilities The probability of one event, given the known outcome of a (possibly) related event.

Conservative approach An approach to choosing a decision alternative without using probabilities. For a maximization problem, it leads to choosing the decision alternative that maximizes the minimum payoff; for a minimization problem, it leads to choosing the decision alternative that minimizes the maximum payoff.

Decision alternatives Options available to the decision maker.

Decision nodes Nodes indicating points at which a decision is made.

Decision strategy A strategy involving a sequence of decisions and chance outcomes to provide the optimal solution to a decision problem.

Decision tree A graphical representation of the decision problem that shows the sequential nature of the decision-making process.

Expected utility (EU) The weighted average of the utilities associated with a decision alternative. The weights are the state-of-nature probabilities.

Expected value (EV) For a chance node, the weighted average of the payoffs. The weights are the state-of-nature probabilities.

Expected value approach An approach to choosing a decision alternative based on the expected value of each decision alternative. The recommended decision alternative is the one that provides the best expected value.

Expected value of perfect information (EVPI) The difference between the expected value of an optimal strategy based on perfect information and the "best" expected value without any sample information.

Expected value of sample information (EVSI) The difference between the expected value of an optimal strategy based on sample information and the "best" expected value without any sample information.

Minimax regret approach An approach to choosing a decision alternative without using probabilities. For each alternative, the maximum regret is computed, which leads to choosing the decision alternative that minimizes the maximum regret.

Node An intersection or junction point of a decision tree.

Optimistic approach An approach to choosing a decision alternative without using probabilities. For a maximization problem, it leads to choosing the decision alternative corresponding to the largest payoff; for a minimization problem, it leads to choosing the decision alternative corresponding to the smallest payoff.

Outcome The result obtained when a decision alternative is chosen and a chance event occurs.

Payoff A measure of the outcome of a decision such as profit, cost, or time. Each combination of a decision alternative and a state of nature has an associated payoff.

Payoff table A tabular representation of the payoffs for a decision problem.

Perfect information A special case of sample information in which the information tells the decision maker exactly which state of nature is going to occur.

Posterior (revised) probabilities The probabilities of the states of nature after revising the prior probabilities based on sample information.

Prior probabilities The probabilities of the states of nature prior to obtaining sample information.

Regret (opportunity loss) The amount of loss (lower profit or higher cost) from not making the best decision for each state of nature.

Risk analysis The study of the possible payoffs and probabilities associated with a decision alternative or a decision strategy in the face of uncertainty.

Risk avoider A decision maker who would choose a guaranteed payoff over a lottery with a better expected payoff.

Risk-neutral A decision maker who is neutral to risk. For this decision maker, the decision alternative with the best expected value is identical to the alternative with the highest expected utility.

Risk profile The probability distribution of the possible payoffs associated with a decision alternative or decision strategy.

Risk taker A decision maker who would choose a lottery over a better guaranteed payoff.

Sample information New information obtained through research or experimentation that enables updating or revising the state-of-nature probabilities.

Sensitivity analysis The study of how changes in the probability assessments for the states of nature or changes in the payoffs affect the recommended decision alternative.

States of nature The possible outcomes for chance events that affect the payoff associated with a decision alternative.

Utility A measure of the total worth of a consequence reflecting a decision maker's attitude toward considerations such as profit, loss, and risk.

Utility function for money A curve that depicts the relationship between monetary value and utility.

PROBLEMS

1. The following payoff table shows profit for a decision analysis problem with two decision alternatives and three states of nature:

Decision Alternative	State of Nature		
	s_1	s_2	s_3
d_1	250	100	25
d_2	100	100	75

  a. Construct a decision tree for this problem.

  b. If the decision maker knows nothing about the probabilities of the three states of nature, what is the recommended decision using the optimistic, conservative, and minimax regret approaches?

2. Southland Corporation's decision to produce a new line of recreational products resulted in the need to construct either a small plant or a large plant. The best selection of plant size depends on how the marketplace reacts to the new product line. To conduct an analysis, marketing management has decided to view the possible long-run demand as low, medium, or high. The following payoff table shows the projected profit in millions of dollars:

Plan Size	Long-Run Demand		
	Low	Medium	High
Small	150	200	200
Large	50	200	500

  a. What is the decision to be made, and what is the chance event for Southland's problem?

  b. Construct a decision tree.

  c. Recommend a decision based on the use of the optimistic, conservative, and minimax regret approaches.

3. Amy Lloyd is interested in leasing a new Honda and has contacted three automobile dealers for pricing information. Each dealer offered Amy a closed-end 36-month lease with no down payment due at the time of signing. Each lease includes a monthly charge and a mileage allowance. Additional miles receive a surcharge on a per-mile basis. The monthly lease cost, the mileage allowance, and the cost for additional miles follow:

Dealer	Monthly Cost	Mileage Allowance	Cost per Additional Mile
Hepburn Honda	$299	36,000	$0.15
Midtown Motors	$310	45,000	$0.20
Hopkins Automotive	$325	54,000	$0.15

Amy decided to choose the lease option that will minimize her total 36-month cost. The difficulty is that Amy is not sure how many miles she will drive over the next three years. For purposes of this decision, she believes it is reasonable to assume that she will drive 12,000 miles per year, 15,000 miles per year, or 18,000 miles per year. With this assumption Amy estimated her total costs for the three lease options. For example, she figures that the Hepburn Honda lease will cost her 36($299) + $0.15(36,000 − 36,000) = $10,764 if she drives 12,000 miles per year, 36($299) + $0.15(45,000 − 36,000) = $12,114 if she drives 15,000 miles per year, or 36($299) + $0.15(54,000 − 36,000) = $13,464 if she drives 18,000 miles per year.

a. What is the decision, and what is the chance event?

b. Construct a payoff table for Amy's problem.

c. If Amy has no idea which of the three mileage assumptions is most appropriate, what is the recommended decision (leasing option) using the optimistic, conservative, and minimax regret approaches?

d. Suppose that the probabilities that Amy drives 12,000, 15,000, and 18,000 miles per year are 0.5, 0.4, and 0.1, respectively. What option should Amy choose using the expected value approach?

e. Develop a risk profile for the decision selected in part (d). What is the most likely cost, and what is its probability?

f. Suppose that, after further consideration, Amy concludes that the probabilities that she will drive 12,000, 15,000, and 18,000 miles per year are 0.3, 0.4, and 0.3, respectively. What decision should Amy make using the expected value approach?

4. Investment advisors estimated the stock market returns for four market segments: computers, financial, manufacturing, and pharmaceuticals. Annual return projections vary depending on whether the general economic conditions are improving, stable, or declining. The anticipated annual return percentages for each market segment under each economic condition are as follows:

Market Segment	Economic Condition		
	Improving	Stable	Declining
Computers	10	2	−4
Financial	8	5	−3
Manufacturing	6	4	−2
Pharmaceuticals	6	5	−1

a. Assume that an individual investor wants to select one market segment for a new investment. A forecast shows improving to declining economic conditions with the following probabilities: improving (0.2), stable (0.5), and declining (0.3). What is the preferred market segment for the investor, and what is the expected return percentage?

b. At a later date, a revised forecast shows a potential for an improvement in economic conditions. New probabilities are as follows: improving (0.4), stable (0.4), and declining (0.2). What is the preferred market segment for the investor based on these new probabilities? What is the expected return percentage?

5. Hudson Corporation is considering three options for managing its data warehouse: continuing with its own staff, hiring an outside vendor to do the managing, or using a combination of its own staff and an outside vendor. The cost of the operation depends on future demand. The annual cost of each option (in thousands of dollars) depends on demand as follows:

Staffing Options	Demand		
	High	Medium	Low
Own staff	650	650	600
Outside vendor	900	600	300
Combination	800	650	500

a. If the demand probabilities are 0.2, 0.5, and 0.3, which decision alternative will minimize the expected cost of the data warehouse? What is the expected annual cost associated with that recommendation?

b. Construct a risk profile for the optimal decision in part (a). What is the probability of the cost exceeding $700,000?

6. The following payoff table shows the profit for a decision problem with two states of nature and two decision alternatives:

Decision Alternative	State of Nature	
	s_1	s_2
d_1	10	1
d_2	4	3

a. Suppose $P(s_1) = 0.2$ and $P(s_2) = 0.8$. What is the best decision using the expected value approach?

b. Perform sensitivity analysis on the payoffs for decision alternative d_1. Assume the probabilities are as given in part (a), and find the range of payoffs under states of nature s_1 and s_2 that will keep the solution found in part (a) optimal. Is the solution more sensitive to the payoff under state of nature s_1 or s_2?

7. Myrtle Air Express decided to offer direct service from Cleveland to Myrtle Beach. Management must decide between a full-price service using the company's new fleet of jet aircraft and a discount service using smaller-capacity commuter planes. It is clear that the best choice depends on the market reaction to the service Myrtle Air offers. Management developed estimates of the contribution to profit for each type of service based on two possible levels of demand for service to Myrtle Beach: strong and weak. The following table shows the estimated quarterly profits (in thousands of dollars):

Service	Demand for Service	
	Strong	Weak
Full price	$960	−$490
Discount	$670	$320

a. What is the decision to be made, what is the chance event, and what is the consequence for this problem? How many decision alternatives are there? How many outcomes are there for the chance event?

b. If nothing is known about the probabilities of the chance outcomes, what is the recommended decision using the optimistic, conservative, and minimax regret approaches?

c. Suppose that management of Myrtle Air Express believes that the probability of strong demand is 0.7 and the probability of weak demand is 0.3. Use the expected value approach to determine an optimal decision.

d. Suppose that the probability of strong demand is 0.8 and the probability of weak demand is 0.2. What is the optimal decision using the expected value approach?

e. Use sensitivity analysis to determine the range of demand probabilities for which each of the decision alternatives has the largest expected value.

8. Video Tech is considering marketing one of two new video games for the coming holiday season: Battle Pacific or Space Pirates. Battle Pacific is a unique game and appears to have no competition. Estimated profits (in thousands of dollars) under high, medium, and low demand are as follows:

Battle Pacific	Demand		
	High	Medium	Low
Profit	$1,000	$700	$300
Probability	0.2	0.5	0.3

Video Tech is optimistic about its Space Pirates game. However, the concern is that profitability will be affected by a competitor's introduction of a video game viewed as similar to Space Pirates. Estimated profits (in thousands of dollars) with and without competition are as follows:

| Space Pirates | Demand | | |
With Competition	High	Medium	Low
Profit	$800	$400	$200
Probability	0.3	0.4	0.3

| Space Pirates | Demand | | |
Without Competition	High	Medium	Low
Profit	$1,600	$800	$400
Probability	0.5	0.3	0.2

a. Develop a decision tree for the Video Tech problem.
b. For planning purposes, Video Tech believes there is a 0.6 probability that its competitor will produce a new game similar to Space Pirates. Given this probability of competition, the director of planning recommends marketing the Battle Pacific video game. Using expected value, what is your recommended decision?
c. Show a risk profile for your recommended decision.
d. Use sensitivity analysis to determine what the probability of competition for Space Pirates would have to be for you to change your recommended decision alternative.

9. Seneca Hill Winery recently purchased land for the purpose of establishing a new vineyard. Management is considering two varieties of white grapes for the new vineyard: Chardonnay and Riesling. The Chardonnay grapes would be used to produce a dry Chardonnay wine, and the Riesling grapes would be used to produce a semidry Riesling wine. It takes approximately four years from the time of planting before new grapes can be harvested. This length of time creates a great deal of uncertainty concerning future demand and makes the decision about the type of grapes to plant difficult. Three possibilities are being considered: Chardonnay grapes only; Riesling grapes only; and both Chardonnay and Riesling grapes. Seneca management decided that for planning purposes it would be adequate to consider only two demand possibilities for each type of wine: strong or weak. With two possibilities for each type of wine, it was necessary to assess four probabilities. With the help of some forecasts in industry publications, management made the following probability assessments:

| Chardonnay Demand | Riesling Demand | |
	Weak	Strong
Weak	0.05	0.50
Strong	0.25	0.20

Revenue projections show an annual contribution to profit of $20,000 if Seneca Hill plants only Chardonnay grapes and demand is weak for Chardonnay wine, and $70,000 if Seneca plants only Chardonnay grapes and demand is strong for Chardonnay wine. If Seneca plants only Riesling grapes, the annual profit projection is $25,000 if demand is weak for Riesling grapes and $45,000 if demand is strong for Riesling grapes. If Seneca plants both types of grapes, the annual profit projections are shown in the following table:

| Chardonnay Demand | Riesling Demand | |
	Weak	Strong
Weak	$22,000	$40,000
Strong	$26,000	$60,000

a. What is the decision to be made, what is the chance event, and what is the consequence? Identify the alternatives for the decisions and the possible outcomes for the chance events.

b. Develop a decision tree.

c. Use the expected value approach to recommend which alternative Seneca Hill Winery should follow in order to maximize expected annual profit.

d. Suppose management is concerned about the probability assessments when demand for Chardonnay wine is strong. Some believe it is likely for Riesling demand to also be strong in this case. Suppose that the probability of strong demand for Chardonnay and weak demand for Riesling is 0.05 and that the probability of strong demand for Chardonnay and strong demand for Riesling is 0.40. How does this change the recommended decision? Assume that the probabilities when Chardonnay demand is weak are still 0.05 and 0.50.

e. Other members of the management team expect the Chardonnay market to become saturated at some point in the future, causing a fall in prices. Suppose that the annual profit projections fall to $50,000 when demand for Chardonnay is strong and only Chardonnay grapes are planted. Using the original probability assessments, determine how this change would affect the optimal decision.

10. Hemmingway, Inc. is considering a $5 million research and development (R&D) project. Profit projections appear promising, but Hemmingway's president is concerned because the probability that the R&D project will be successful is only 0.50. Furthermore, the president knows that even if the project is successful, it will require that the company build a new production facility at a cost of $20 million in order to manufacture the product. If the facility is built, uncertainty remains about the demand and thus uncertainty about the profit that will be realized. Another option is that if the R&D project is successful, the company could sell the rights to the product for an estimated $25 million. Under this option, the company would not build the $20 million production facility.

   The decision tree follows. The profit projection for each outcome is shown at the end of the branches. For example, the revenue projection for the high demand outcome is $59 million. However, the cost of the R&D project ($5 million) and the cost of the production facility ($20 million) show the profit of this outcome to be $59 − $5 − $20 = $34 million. Branch probabilities are also shown for the chance events.

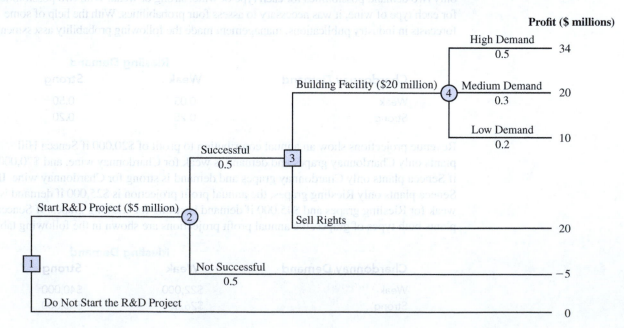

Profit ($ millions)

a. Analyze the decision tree to determine whether the company should undertake the R&D project. If it does, and if the R&D project is successful, what should the company do? What is the expected value of your strategy?

b. What must the selling price be for the company to consider selling the rights to the product?

c. Develop a risk profile for the optimal strategy.

11. Dante Development Corporation is considering bidding on a contract for a new office building complex. The following figure shows the decision tree prepared by one of Dante's analysts. At node 1, the company must decide whether to bid on the contract. The cost of preparing the bid is $200,000. The upper branch from node 2 shows that the company has a 0.8 probability of winning the contract if it submits a bid. If the company wins the bid, it will have to pay $2 million to become a partner in the project. Node 3 shows that the company will then consider doing a market research study to forecast demand for the office units prior to beginning construction. The cost of this study is $150,000. Node 4 is a chance node showing the possible outcomes of the market research study.

Nodes 5, 6, and 7 are similar in that they are the decision nodes for Dante to either build the office complex or sell the rights in the project to another developer. The decision to build the complex will result in an income of $5 million if demand is high and $3 million if demand is moderate. If Dante chooses to sell its rights in the project to another developer, income from the sale is estimated to be $3.5 million. The probabilities shown at nodes 4, 8, and 9 are based on the projected outcomes of the market research study.

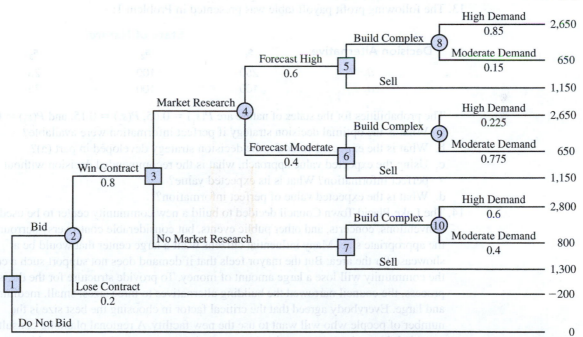

a. Verify Dante's profit projections shown at the ending branches of the decision tree by calculating the payoffs of $2,650,000 and $650,000 for first two outcomes.

b. What is the optimal decision strategy for Dante, and what is the expected profit for this project?

c. What would the cost of the market research study have to be before Dante would change its decision about the market research study?

d. Develop a risk profile for Dante.

12. Embassy Publishing Company received a six-chapter manuscript for a new college textbook. The editor of the college division is familiar with the manuscript and estimated a 0.65 probability that the textbook will be successful. If successful, a profit of $750,000 will be realized. If the company decides to publish the textbook and it is unsuccessful, a loss of $250,000 will occur.

Before making the decision to accept or reject the manuscript, the editor is considering sending the manuscript out for review. A review process provides either a favorable (F) or unfavorable (U) evaluation of the manuscript. Past experience with the review process suggests that probabilities $P(F) = 0.7$ and $P(U) = 0.3$ apply. Let s_1 = the textbook is successful, and s_2 = the textbook is unsuccessful. The editor's initial probabilities of s_1 and s_2 will be revised based on whether the review is favorable or unfavorable. The revised probabilities are as follows:

$$P(s_1|F) = 0.75 \qquad P(s_1|U) = 0.417$$
$$P(s_2|F) = 0.25 \qquad P(s_2|U) = 0.583$$

a. Construct a decision tree assuming that the company will first make the decision as to whether to send the manuscript out for review and then make the decision to accept or reject the manuscript.

b. Analyze the decision tree to determine the optimal decision strategy for the publishing company.

c. If the manuscript review costs $5,000, what is your recommendation?

d. What is the expected value of perfect information? What does this EVPI suggest for the company?

13. The following profit payoff table was presented in Problem 1:

Decision Alternative	State of Nature		
	s_1	s_2	s_3
d_1	250	100	25
d_2	100	100	75

The probabilities for the states of nature are $P(s_1) = 0.65$, $P(s_2) = 0.15$, and $P(s_3) = 0.20$.

a. What is the optimal decision strategy if perfect information were available?

b. What is the expected value for the decision strategy developed in part (a)?

c. Using the expected value approach, what is the recommended decision without perfect information? What is its expected value?

d. What is the expected value of perfect information?

14. The Lake Placid Town Council decided to build a new community center to be used for conventions, concerts, and other public events, but considerable controversy surrounds the appropriate size. Many influential citizens want a large center that would be a showcase for the area. But the mayor feels that if demand does not support such a center, the community will lose a large amount of money. To provide structure for the decision process, the council narrowed the building alternatives to three sizes: small, medium, and large. Everybody agreed that the critical factor in choosing the best size is the number of people who will want to use the new facility. A regional planning consultant provided demand estimates under three scenarios: worst case, base case, and best case. The worst-case scenario corresponds to a situation in which tourism drops substantially; the base-case scenario corresponds to a situation in which Lake Placid continues to attract visitors at current levels; and the best-case scenario corresponds to a substantial increase in tourism. The consultant has provided probability assessments of 0.10, 0.60, and 0.30 for the worst-case, base-case, and best-case scenarios, respectively.

The town council suggested using net cash flow over a five-year planning horizon as the criterion for deciding on the best size. The following projections of net cash flow (in thousands of dollars) for a five-year planning horizon have been developed. All costs, including the consultant's fee, have been included.

Center Size	Demand Scenario		
	Worst Case	Base Case	Best Case
Small	400	500	660
Medium	−250	650	800
Large	−400	580	990

a. What decision should Lake Placid make using the expected value approach?
b. Construct risk profiles for the medium and large alternatives. Given the mayor's concern over the possibility of losing money and the result of part (a), which alternative would you recommend?
c. Compute the expected value of perfect information. Do you think it would be worth trying to obtain additional information concerning which scenario is likely to occur?
d. Suppose the probability of the worst-case scenario increases to 0.2, the probability of the base-case scenario decreases to 0.5, and the probability of the best-case scenario remains at 0.3. What effect, if any, would these changes have on the decision recommendation?
e. The consultant has suggested that an expenditure of $150,000 on a promotional campaign over the planning horizon will effectively reduce the probability of the worst-case scenario to zero. If the campaign can be expected to also increase the probability of the best-case scenario to 0.4, is it a good investment?

15. A real estate investor has the opportunity to purchase land currently zoned as residential. If the county board approves a request to rezone the property as commercial within the next year, the investor will be able to lease the land to a large discount firm that wants to open a new store on the property. However, if the zoning change is not approved, the investor will have to sell the property at a loss. Profits (in thousands of dollars) are shown in the following payoff table:

Decision Alternative	State of Nature	
	Rezoning Approved s_1	Rezoning Not Approved s_2
Purchase, d_1	600	−200
Do not purchase, d_2	0	0

a. If the probability that the rezoning will be approved is 0.5, what decision is recommended? What is the expected profit?
b. The investor can purchase an option to buy the land. Under the option, the investor maintains the rights to purchase the land anytime during the next three months while learning more about possible resistance to the rezoning proposal from area residents. Probabilities are as follows:

Let H = high resistance to rezoning
L = low resistance to rezoning

$$P(H) = 0.55 \quad P(s_1|H) = 0.18 \quad P(s_2|H) = 0.82$$
$$P(L) = 0.45 \quad P(s_1|L) = 0.89 \quad P(s_2|L) = 0.11$$

What is the optimal decision strategy if the investor uses the option period to learn more about the resistance from area residents before making the purchase decision?

c. If the option will cost the investor an additional $10,000, should the investor purchase the option? Why or why not? What is the maximum that the investor should be willing to pay for the option?

16. Suppose that you are given a decision situation with three possible states of nature: s_1, s_2, and s_3. The prior probabilities are $P(s_1) = 0.2$, $P(s_2) = 0.5$, and $P(s_3) = 0.3$. With sample information I, $P(I|s_1) = 0.1$, $P(I|s_2) = 0.05$, and $P(I|s_3) = 0.2$. Compute the revised (or posterior) probabilities: $P(s_1|I)$, $P(s_2|I)$, and $P(s_3|I)$.

17. To save on expenses, Rona and Jerry agreed to form a carpool for traveling to and from work. Rona prefers to use the somewhat longer but more consistent Queen City Avenue. Although Jerry prefers the quicker expressway, he agreed with Rona that they should take Queen City Avenue if the expressway has a traffic jam. The following payoff table provides the one-way time estimate in minutes for traveling to or from work:

	State of Nature	
	Expressway Open	Expressway Jammed
Decision Alternative	s_1	s_2
Queen City Avenue, d_1	30	30
Expressway, d_2	25	45

Based on their experience with traffic problems, Rona and Jerry agreed on a 0.15 probability that the expressway would be jammed.

In addition, they agreed that weather seemed to affect the traffic conditions on the expressway. Let

C = clear
O = overcast
R = rain

The following conditional probabilities apply:

$$P(C|s_1) = 0.8 \qquad P(O|s_1) = 0.2 \qquad P(R|s_1) = 0.0$$
$$P(C|s_2) = 0.1 \qquad P(O|s_2) = 0.3 \qquad P(R|s_2) = 0.6$$

a. Use Bayes' theorem for probability revision to compute the probability of each weather condition and the conditional probability of the expressway being open, s_1, or jammed, s_2, given each weather condition.
b. Show the decision tree for this problem.
c. What is the optimal decision strategy, and what is the expected travel time?

18. The Gorman Manufacturing Company must decide whether to manufacture a component part at its Milan, Michigan, plant or purchase the component part from a supplier. The resulting profit is dependent on the demand for the product. The following payoff table shows the projected profit (in thousands of dollars):

	State of Nature		
	Low Demand	Medium Demand	High Demand
Decision Alternative	s_1	s_2	s_3
Manufacture, d_1	−20	40	100
Purchase, d_2	10	45	70

The state-of-nature probabilities are $P(s_1) = 0.35$, $P(s_2) = 0.35$, and $P(s_3) = 0.30$.

a. Use a decision tree to recommend a decision.
b. Use EVPI to determine whether Gorman should attempt to obtain a better estimate of demand.

c. A test market study of the potential demand for the product is expected to report either a favorable (F) or unfavorable (U) condition. The relevant conditional probabilities are as follows:

$$P(F|s_1) = 0.10 \quad P(U|s_1) = 0.90$$
$$P(F|s_2) = 0.40 \quad P(U|s_2) = 0.60$$
$$P(F|s_3) = 0.60 \quad P(U|s_3) = 0.40$$

Joint probabilities are discussed in Chapter 5.

What is the probability that the market research report will be favorable? [*Hint:* We can find this value by summing the joint probability values as follows: $P(F) = P(F \cap s_1) + P(F \cap s_2) + P(F \cap s_3) = P(s_1)P(F|s_1) + P(s_2)P(F|s_2) + P(s_3)P(F|s_3)$.]

d. What is Gorman's optimal decision strategy?

e. What is the expected value of the market research information?

19. A firm has three investment alternatives. Payoffs are in thousands of dollars.

	Economic Conditions		
	Up	Stable	Down
Decision Alternative	s_1	s_2	s_3
Investment A, d_1	100	25	0
Investment B, d_2	75	50	25
Investment C, d_3	50	50	50
Probabilities	0.40	0.30	0.30

a. Using the expected value approach, which decision is preferred?

b. For the lottery having a payoff of $100,000 with probability p and $0 with probability $(1 - p)$, two decision makers expressed the following indifference probabilities. Find the most preferred decision for each decision maker using the expected utility approach.

	Indifference Probability (p)	
Profit	Decision Maker A	Decision Maker B
$75,000	0.80	0.60
$50,000	0.60	0.30
$25,000	0.30	0.15

c. Why don't decision makers A and B select the same decision alternative?

20. Alexander Industries is considering purchasing an insurance policy for its new office building in St. Louis, Missouri. The policy has an annual cost of $10,000. If Alexander Industries doesn't purchase the insurance and minor fire damage occurs, a cost of $100,000 is anticipated; the cost if major or total destruction occurs is $200,000. The costs, including the state-of-nature probabilities, are as follows:

	Damage		
	None	Minor	Major
Decision Alternative	s_1	s_2	s_3
Purchase insurance, d_1	10,000	10,000	10,000
Do not purchase insurance, d_2	0	100,000	200,000
Probabilities	0.96	0.03	0.01

a. Using the expected value approach, what decision do you recommend?

b. What lottery would you use to assess utilities? (*Note:* Because the data are costs, the best payoff is $0.)

c. Assume that you found the following indifference probabilities for the lottery defined in part (b). What decision would you recommend?

Cost	Indifference Probability
10,000	$p = 0.99$
100,000	$p = 0.60$

   d. Do you favor using expected value or expected utility for this decision problem? Why?

21. In a certain state lottery, a lottery ticket costs $2. In terms of the decision to purchase or not to purchase a lottery ticket, suppose that the following payoff table applies:

	State of Nature	
	Win	**Lose**
Decision Alternatives	s_1	s_2
Purchase lottery ticket, d_1	300,000	−2
Do not purchase lottery ticket, d_2	0	0

   a. A realistic estimate of the chances of winning is 1 in 250,000. Use the expected value approach to recommend a decision.

   b. If a particular decision maker assigns an indifference probability of 0.000001 to the $0 payoff, would this individual purchase a lottery ticket? Use expected utility to justify your answer.

22. Three decision makers have assessed utilities for the following decision problem (payoff in dollars):

	State of Nature		
Decision Alternative	s_1	s_2	s_3
d_1	20	50	−20
d_2	80	100	−100

The indifference probabilities are as follows:

	Indifference Probability (p)		
Payoff	**Decision Maker A**	**Decision Maker B**	**Decision Maker C**
100	1.00	1.00	1.00
80	0.95	0.70	0.90
50	0.90	0.60	0.75
20	0.70	0.45	0.60
−20	0.50	0.25	0.40
−100	0.00	0.00	0.00

   a. Plot the utility function for money for each decision maker.

   b. Classify each decision maker as a risk avoider, a risk taker, or risk-neutral.

   c. For the payoff of 20, what is the premium that the risk avoider will pay to avoid risk? What is the premium that the risk taker will pay to have the opportunity of the high payoff?

23. In Problem 22, if $P(s_1) = 0.25$, $P(s_2) = 0.50$, and $P(s_3) = 0.25$, find a recommended decision for each of the three decision makers. (*Note:* For the same decision problem, different utilities can lead to different decisions.)

24. Translate the following monetary payoffs into utilities for a decision maker whose utility function is described by an exponential function with $R = 250$: −$200, −$100, $0, $100, $200, $300, $400, $500.

25. Consider a decision maker who is comfortable with an investment decision that has a 50% chance of earning $25,000 and a 50% chance of losing $12,500, but not with any larger investments that have the same relative payoffs.
   a. Write the equation for the exponential function that approximates this decision maker's utility function.
   b. Plot the exponential utility function for this decision maker for x values between $-20,000$ and $35,000$. Is this decision maker risk-seeking, risk-neutral, or risk-averse?
   c. Suppose the decision maker decides that she would actually be willing to make an investment that has a 50% chance of earning $30,000 and a 50% chance of losing $15,000. Plot the exponential function that approximates this utility function and compare it to the utility function from part (b). Is the decision maker becoming more risk-seeking or more risk-averse?

CASE PROBLEM: PROPERTY PURCHASE STRATEGY

Glenn Foreman, president of Oceanview Development Corporation, is considering submitting a bid to purchase property that will be sold by sealed-bid auction at a county tax foreclosure. Glenn's initial judgment is to submit a bid of $5 million. Based on his experience, Glenn estimates that a bid of $5 million will have a 0.2 probability of being the highest bid and securing the property for Oceanview. The current date is June 1. Sealed bids for the property must be submitted by August 15. The winning bid will be announced on September 1.

If Oceanview submits the highest bid and obtains the property, the firm plans to build and sell a complex of luxury condominiums. However, a complicating factor is that the property is currently zoned for single-family residences only. Glenn believes that a referendum could be placed on the voting ballot in time for the November election. Passage of the referendum would change the zoning of the property and permit construction of the condominiums.

The sealed-bid procedure requires the bid to be submitted with a certified check for 10% of the amount bid. If the bid is rejected, the deposit is refunded. If the bid is accepted, the deposit is the down payment for the property. However, if the bid is accepted and the bidder does not follow through with the purchase and meet the remainder of the financial obligation within six months, the deposit will be forfeited. In this case, the county will offer the property to the next highest bidder.

To determine whether Oceanview should submit the $5 million bid, Glenn conducted some preliminary analysis. This preliminary work provided an assessment of 0.3 for the probability that the referendum for a zoning change will be approved and resulted in the following estimates of the costs and revenues that will be incurred if the condominiums are built:

Costs and Revenue Estimates	
Revenue from condominium sales	$15,000,000
Costs	
Property	$5,000,000
Construction expenses	$8,000,000

If Oceanview obtains the property and the zoning change is rejected in November, Glenn believes that the best option would be for the firm not to complete the purchase of the property. In this case, Oceanview would forfeit the 10% deposit that accompanied the bid.

Because the likelihood that the zoning referendum will be approved is such an important factor in the decision process, Glenn suggested that the firm hire a market research service to conduct a survey of voters. The survey would provide a better estimate of the likelihood that the referendum for a zoning change would be approved. The market research firm that Oceanview Development has worked with in the past has agreed to do the study for $15,000. The results of the study will be available August 1, so that Oceanview will have this information before the August 15 bid deadline. The results of the survey will be a prediction either that the zoning change will be approved or that the zoning change will be rejected. After considering the record of the market research service in previous studies conducted for Oceanview, Glenn developed the following probability estimates concerning the accuracy of the market research information:

$$P(A|s_1) = 0.9 \quad P(N|s_1) = 0.1$$
$$P(A|s_2) = 0.2 \quad P(N|s_2) = 0.8$$

where

A = prediction of zoning change approval
N = prediction that zoning change will not be approved
s_1 = the zoning change is approved by the voters
s_2 = the zoning change is rejected by the voters

Managerial Report

Perform an analysis of the problem facing the Oceanview Development Corporation, and prepare a report that summarizes your findings and recommendations. Include the following items in your report:

1. A decision tree that shows the logical sequence of the decision problem
2. A recommendation regarding what Oceanview should do if the market research information is not available
3. A decision strategy that Oceanview should follow if the market research is conducted
4. A recommendation as to whether Oceanview should employ the market research firm, along with the value of the information provided by the market research firm

Include the details of your analysis as an appendix to your report.

Chapter 15 Appendix

Appendix 15.1 Using Analytic Solver Platform to Create Decision Trees

In this appendix, we describe how Analytic Solver Platform can be used to develop a decision tree for the PDC problem presented in Section 15.3. The decision tree for the PDC problem is shown in Figure 15.13.

Getting Started: An Initial Decision Tree

To build a decision tree for the PDC problem using Analytic Solver Platform, follow these steps in a blank workbook in Excel:

Step 1. Select cell A1
Step 2. Click the **Analytic Solver Platform** tab on the Ribbon
Step 3. Click **Decision Tree** in the **Tools** group
    Select **Node**, and click **Add Node**
Step 4. When the **Decision Tree** dialog box appears, verify that **Decision** is selected for **Node Type**, and click **OK**

A decision tree with one decision node and two branches (initially labeled as "Decision 1" and "Decision 2") appears, as shown in Figure 15.14.

FIGURE 15.13 Decision Tree for the PDC Condominium Project (Payoffs in Millions of $)

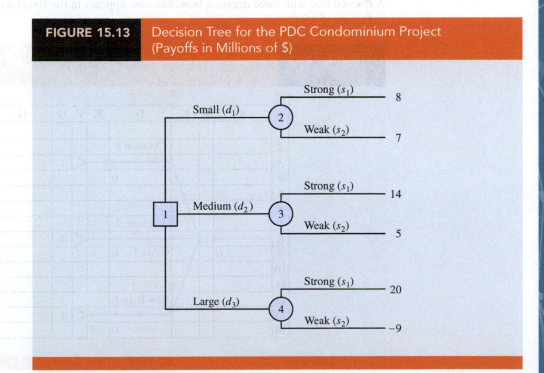

FIGURE 15.14   Decision Tree with One Decision Node and Two Branches Created with Analytic Solver Platform

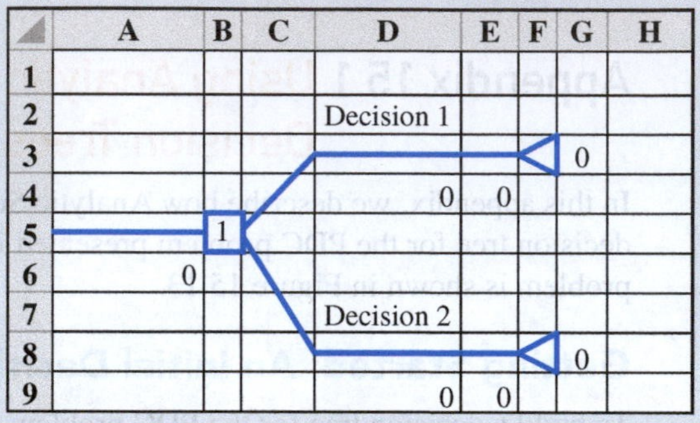

Adding a Branch

The PDC problem has three decision alternatives (small, medium, and large condominium complexes), so we must add another decision branch to the tree.

Step 1. Select cell B5
Step 2. Click the **Analytic Solver Platform** tab in the Ribbon
Step 3. Click **Decision Tree** in the **Tools** group
Select **Branch**, and click **Add Branch**
Step 4. When the **Decision Tree** dialog box appears, verify that **Decision** is selected for **Node Type**, and click **OK**

A revised tree with three decision branches now appears in the Excel worksheet as shown in Figure 15.15.

FIGURE 15.15   Decision Tree for the PDC Problem with Three Branches Created with Analytic Solver Platform

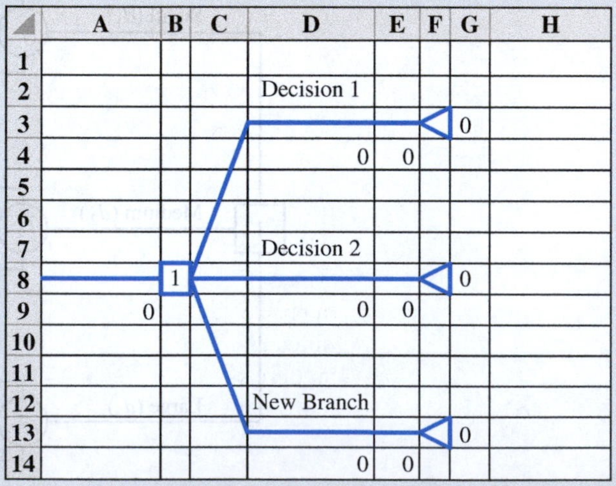

FIGURE 15.16   Decision Tree for the PDC Problem with Renamed Branches Created with Analytic Solver Platform

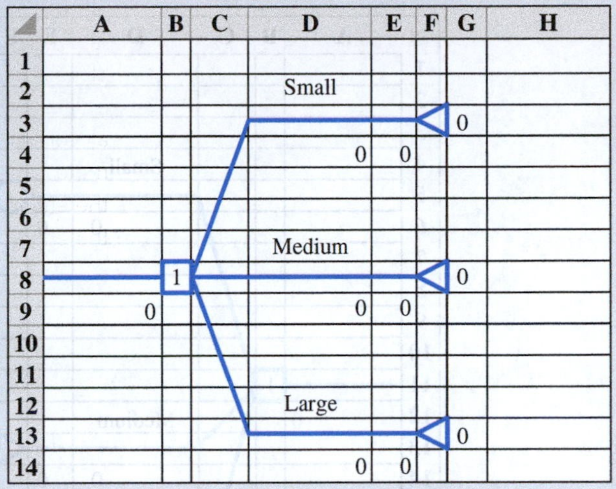

Naming the Decision Alternatives

The decision alternatives can be named by selecting the cells containing the labels "Decision 1," "Decision 2," and "New Branch," and then entering the corresponding PDC names *Small*, *Medium*, and *Large* (cells D2, D7, and D12). After naming the alternatives, the PDC tree with three decision branches appears as shown in Figure 15.16.

Adding Chance Nodes

The chance event for the PDC problem is the demand for the condominiums, which may be either strong or weak. Thus, a chance node with two branches must be added at the end of each decision alternative branch. To add a chance node with two branches to the top decision alternative branch:

Step 1. Select cell F3
Step 2. Click the **Analytic Solver Platform** tab in the Ribbon
Step 3. Select **Decision Tree** from the **Tools** group
Select **Node**, and click **Add Node**
Step 4. When the **Decision Tree** dialog box appears, select **Event/Chance** in the **Node Type** area
Click **OK**

The tree now appears as shown in Figure 15.17.

We next select the cells containing "Event 1" and "Event 2" (cells H2 and H7) and rename them *Strong* and *Weak* to provide the proper names for the PDC states of nature. After doing so, we can copy the subtree for the chance node in cell F5 to the other two decision branches to complete the structure of the PDC decision tree as follows:

Step 1. Select cell F5
Step 2. Click the **Analytic Solver Platform** tab in the Ribbon
Step 3. Click **Decision Tree** in the **Tools** group
Select **Node**, and click **Copy Node**

FIGURE 15.17   Decision Tree for the PDC Problem with an Added Chance Node Created with Analytic Solver Platform

	A	B	C	D	E	F	G	H	I	J	K	L
1								50%				
2								Event 1				
3											0	
4				Small					0	0		
5												
6					0	0		50%				
7								Event 2				
8											0	
9									0	0		
10												
11			1									
12		0		Medium								
13											0	
14					0	0						
15												
16												
17				Large								
18											0	
19					0	0						

Step 4. Select cell F13
Step 5. Click the **Analytic Solver Platform** tab in the Ribbon
Step 6. Click **Decision Tree** in the **Tools** group
Select **Node**, and click **Paste Node**

This copy-and-paste procedure places a chance node at the end of the Medium decision branch. Repeating the same copy-and-paste procedure for the Large decision branch completes the structure of the PDC decision tree, as shown in Figure 15.18.

Inserting Probabilities and Payoffs

We now insert probabilities and payoffs into the decision tree. In Figure 15.18, we see that an equal probability of 0.5 is assigned automatically to each of the chance outcomes. For PDC, the probability of strong demand is 0.8 and the probability of weak demand is 1 minus the probability of strong demand, $1 - 0.8 = 0.2$. We can enter *0.8* into cell H1 and the formula =1−H1 into cell H6. We enter the formula =H1 into cells H11 and H21, and we enter the formula =H6 into cells H16 and H26. In this way, all probabilities will be updated correctly if we change the value in cell H1.

To insert the payoffs, we enter *8* in H4, *7* in cell H9, *14* in cell H14, *5* in cell H19, *20* in cell H24, and −*9* in cell H29. Note in Figure 15.19 that the payoffs also appear in the right-hand margin of the decision tree. The payoffs in the right margin are computed by a formula that adds the payoffs on all of the branches leading to the associated terminal node. For the PDC problem, no payoffs are associated with the decision alternatives branches, so we leave the default values of zero in cells D6, D16, and D26. The PDC decision tree

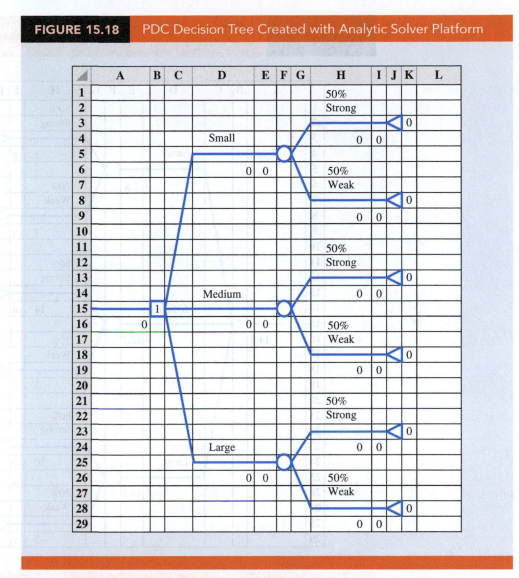

FIGURE 15.18   PDC Decision Tree Created with Analytic Solver Platform

is now complete. After inserting the PDC probabilities and payoffs, the PDC decision tree appears as shown in Figure 15.19.

Interpreting the Result

When probabilities and payoffs are inserted, Analytic Solver Platform automatically makes the rollback computations necessary to determine the optimal solution. Optimal decisions are identified by the number in the corresponding decision node. In the PDC decision tree in Figure 15.19, cell B15 contains the decision node. Note that a 3 appears in this node, which tells us that decision alternative branch 3 provides the optimal decision. We can also easily identify the best decision using the Highlight function in Analytic Solver Platform. To highlight the best decision follow these steps:

Step 1. Click the **Analytic Solver Platform** tab in the Ribbon
Step 2. Click **Decision Tree** in the **Tools** group
Select **Highlight**, and click **Highlight Best**

	FIGURE 15.19		PDC Decision Tree with Branch Probabilities and Payoffs Created with Analytic Solver Platform

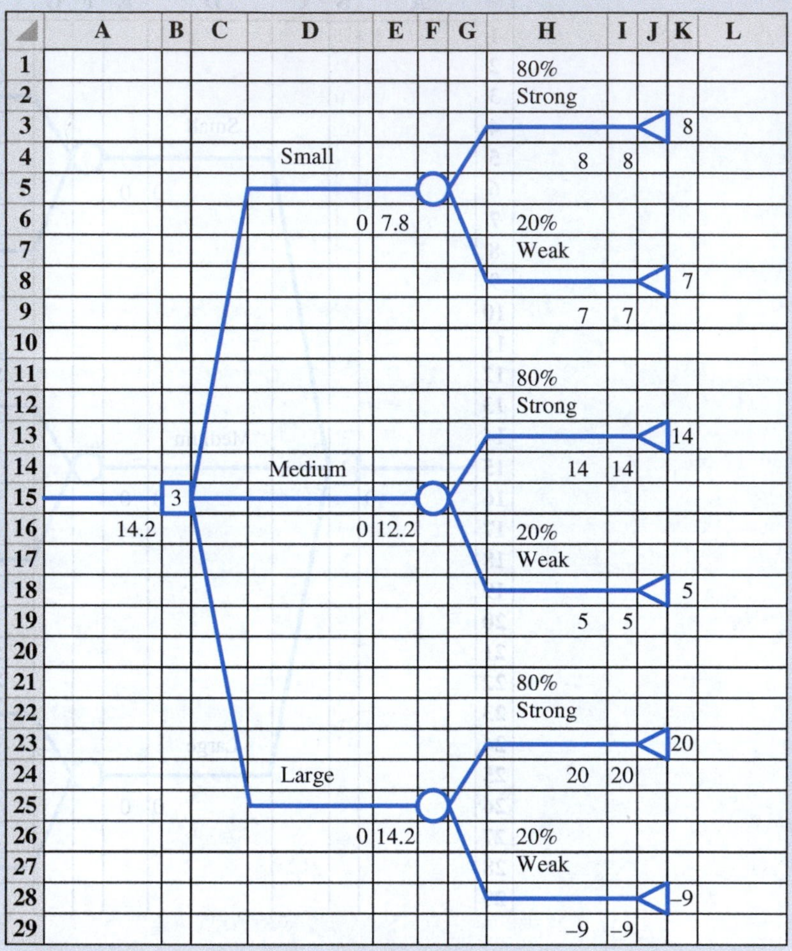

Analytic Solver Platform highlights the best decision for the PDC problem. From Figure 15.20, we see that decision analysis recommends that PDC construct the large condominium complex. The expected value of this decision appears at the beginning of the tree in cell A16. Thus, we see that the optimal expected value is $14.2 million. The expected values of the other decision alternatives are displayed at the end of the corresponding decision branch. Thus, referring to cells E6 and E16, we see that the expected value of the small complex is $7.8 million and the expected value of the medium complex is $12.2 million.

Using software such as Analytic Solver Platform to develop decision trees allows for quick and easy sensitivity analysis. We can easily analyze the impact of changing branch probabilities and payoffs by simply changing these values in Excel and observing the impact on the optimal decision using Analytic Solver Platform. For

FIGURE 15.20   Decision Tree for the PDC Problem with Best Decision Highlighted Created with Analytic Solver Platform

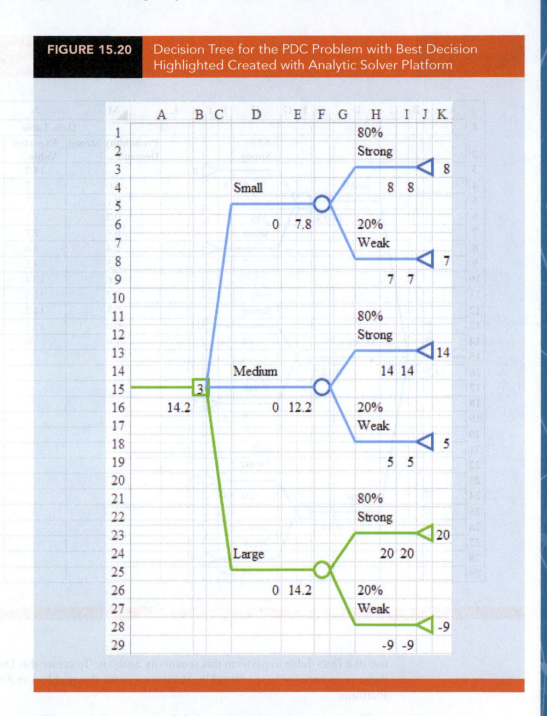

instance, if we want to examine the impact of different values of Strong demand on our decision, we can change the value of cell H1 and see whether this changes the optimal decision.

A convenient way to summarize the sensitivity of a decision to a particular parameter is to combine the decision tree from Analytic Solver Platform with a Data Table in Excel. Suppose we want to evaluate the impact of different probabilities of strong demand over a wide range of possibilities. The Excel worksheet shown in Figure 15.21 demonstrates the

FIGURE 15.21 Decision Tree and Data Table Illustrating Sensitivity Analysis for the PDC Problem Created with Analytic Solver Platform

					Data Table		
					Probability Strong Demand	**Expected Value**	**Best Decision**
						14.2	Large
	Small		8	8	0.0	7	Small
					0.1	7.1	Small
	0 7.8	20% Weak			0.2	7.2	Small
					0.3	7.7	Medium
			7	7	0.4	8.6	Medium
					0.5	9.5	Medium
					0.6	10.4	Medium
		80% Strong			0.7	11.3	Medium
			14	14	0.8	14.2	Large
	Medium				0.9	17.1	Large
3					1.0	20	Large
14.2	0 12.2	20% Weak					
			5	5			
		80% Strong					
	Large		20	20			
	0 14.2	20% Weak					
			−9	−9			

use of a Data Table to perform this sensitivity analysis. To create this Data Table, we follow these steps once we have created the decision tree for this problem in Analytic Solver Platform:

Step 1. Enter the values *0.0, 0.1, 0.2,* etc. into cells M4 to M14, as shown in Figure 15.20, to represent the different scenarios for the probability of Strong demand

Step 2. Enter =A16 into cell N3 to keep track of the optimal expected value in each scenario

Step 3. Enter the formula =CHOOSE(B15,"Small","Medium","Large") into cell O3. This will return the best decision in each scenario

What-If Analysis can be found in the Data Tools group in versions of Excel prior to Excel 2016.

The use of Data Tables in Excel is covered in more detail in Chapter 10.

Step 4. Select cells M3:O14
Step 5. Click the **Data** tab in the Ribbon
Step 6. Click **What-If Analysis** in the **Forecast** group
        Select **Data Table. . .**
Step 7. When the **Data Table** dialog box opens, enter =H1 into the **Column input cell:** box
        Click **OK**

The Excel function CHOOSE in Step 3 chooses a value from a list of possibilities based on the index in the referenced cell. In Step 3, the CHOOSE function enters "Small" in cell O3 if the value in cell B15 is 1; it enters "Medium" if the value in cell B15 is 2; and it enters "Large" if the value in cell B15 is 3. By entering =H1 in Step 7, we tell Excel to substitute the values of 0, 0.1, 0.2, and so on for the probability of strong demand and then return the related outputs.

Figure 15.21 shows the completed decision tree and Data Table. From Figure 15.21, we see that the best decision is to construct the Small complex if the probability of strong demand is 0, 0.1, or 0.2, the Medium complex if the probability is any value shown between 0.3 and 0.7, and the Large complex if the probability of strong demand is 0.8 or greater. The Data Table also provides the expected values for these decisions in each scenario. Such sensitivity analysis can be greatly beneficial in demonstrating which values should be clarified, if possible, by procuring additional information.

Using the Exponential Utility Function in Analytic Solver Platform

By default, the decision trees created in Analytic Solver Platform use the expected value approach for calculating the best decisions. However, we can easily change this setting so that Analytic Solver Platform will use an exponential utility function to calculate utilities and determine the best decisions. To do this, we will modify the settings using the Solver Options and Model Specifications task pane of Analytic Solver Platform. To change the settings in a decision tree to use exponential utility functions, we use the following steps.

If the Solver Options and Model Specifications task pane is not visible, it can be activated by clicking the Model button in the Model group under the Analytic Solver Platform tab in the Ribbon.

Step 1. Click the **Analytic Solver Platform** tab in the Ribbon to reveal the **Solver Options and Model Specifications** task pane
Step 2. In the **Solver Options and Model Specifications** task pane, click the **Model** tab
        Select **Decision Tree** in the **Solver Options and Model Specifications** task pane (Figure 15.22)
Step 3. In the **Decision Tree** area at the bottom of the **Solver Options and Model Specifications** task pane, click **Expected Values** next to **Certainty Equivalents**
        Change this value to **Exponential Utility Function**
Step 4. We also must provide the risk tolerance value (*R* in equation 15.7) to be used in the exponential utility function. In the **Decision Tree** area at the bottom of the **Solver Options and Model Specifications** task pane, change the value next to **Risk Tolerance** to *1*

Figure 15.22 shows the completed decision tree using the exponential utility function. Step 4 indicates that we are using a value of \$1 million as the *R* value in equation (15.7). We know that the units here are in millions of dollars because those are the units used by the values in our decision tree. Recall that a small risk tolerance (*R* value), relative to the payoff values in the decision tree, indicates that the decision maker is very risk averse.

FIGURE 15.22   Decision Tree in Analytic Solver Platform Using an Exponential Utility Function with $R = \$1$ Million

▲	A	B	C	D	E	F	G	H	I	J	K	L	M	N	O
1														Data Table	
2								80% Strong					Probability Strong Demand	Expected Value	Best Decision
3												8		7.7046	Small
4				Small				8	8				0.0	7.0000	Small
5									0.9997				0.1	7.0653	Small
6				0	7.7046			20%					0.2	7.1352	Small
7					0.9995			Weak					0.3	7.2103	Small
8												7	0.4	7.2915	Small
9								7	7				0.5	7.3799	Small
10									0.9991				0.6	7.4769	Small
11								80%					0.7	7.5843	Small
12								Strong					0.8	7.7046	Small
13												14	0.9	7.8414	Small
14				Medium				14	14				1.0	20.0000	Large
15			1						1.0000						
16	7.7046			0	6.6089			20%							
17	0.9995				0.9987			Weak							
18												5			
19								5	5						
20									0.9933						
21								80%							
22								Strong							
23												20			
24				Large				20	20						
25									1.0000						
26				0	−7.3906			20%							
27					−1619.6168			Weak							
28												−9			
29								−9	−9						
30									−8102.0839						

Once we make this change in Analytic Solver Platform, the decision tree calculations are done using utilities based on the exponential function rather than using the expected value method.

In the Data Table in Figure 15.22, we see that the decision maker often prefers to build the Small complex to limit downside risk due to the decision maker being very risk averse. However, if we change the risk tolerance (R) to be \$9 million, this means that the decision maker is less risk averse. Figure 15.23 shows the decision tree with an exponential utility function and $R = \$9$ million; here we see that the decision maker is more likely to choose the Medium complex for many different probabilities of Strong demand as compared to the

FIGURE 15.23   Decision Tree in Analytic Solver Platform Using an Exponential Utility Function with $R = \$9$ Million

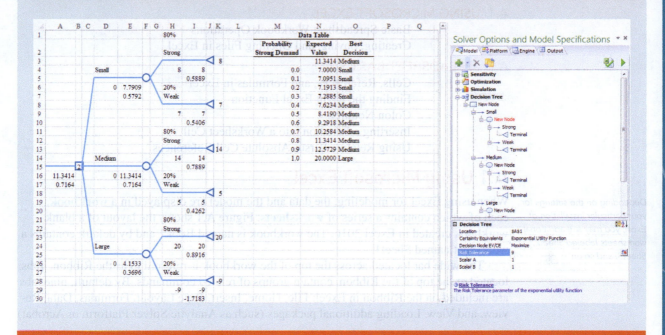

more risk averse decision maker shown in Figure 15.22. Figure 15.23 reflects a decision maker who is less risk averse and more willing to accept decisions that could have higher payoffs but that also have higher likelihoods of worse payoffs.

The complete decision tree and data table for the PDC problem are contained in the file *PDCModel*.

DATA *file*

PDCModel

Appendix A–Basics of Excel

CONTENTS

A.1 Using Microsoft Excel

Depending on the settings for your particular installation of Excel, you may see additional worksheets labeled Sheet2, Sheet3, and so on.

When using Excel for modeling, the data and the model are displayed in a **workbook**, each of which contains a series of **worksheets**. Figure A.1 shows the layout of a blank workbook created in Excel 2016. The workbook is named Book1 and by default contains a worksheet named Sheet1.

The wide bar located across the top of the workbook is referred to as the Ribbon. Tabs, located at the top of the Ribbon, contain groups of related commands. By default, nine tabs are included on the Ribbon in Excel: File, Home, Insert, Page Layout, Formulas, Data, Review, and View. Loading additional packages (such as Analytic Solver Platform or Acrobat)

FIGURE A.1   Blank Workbook in Excel

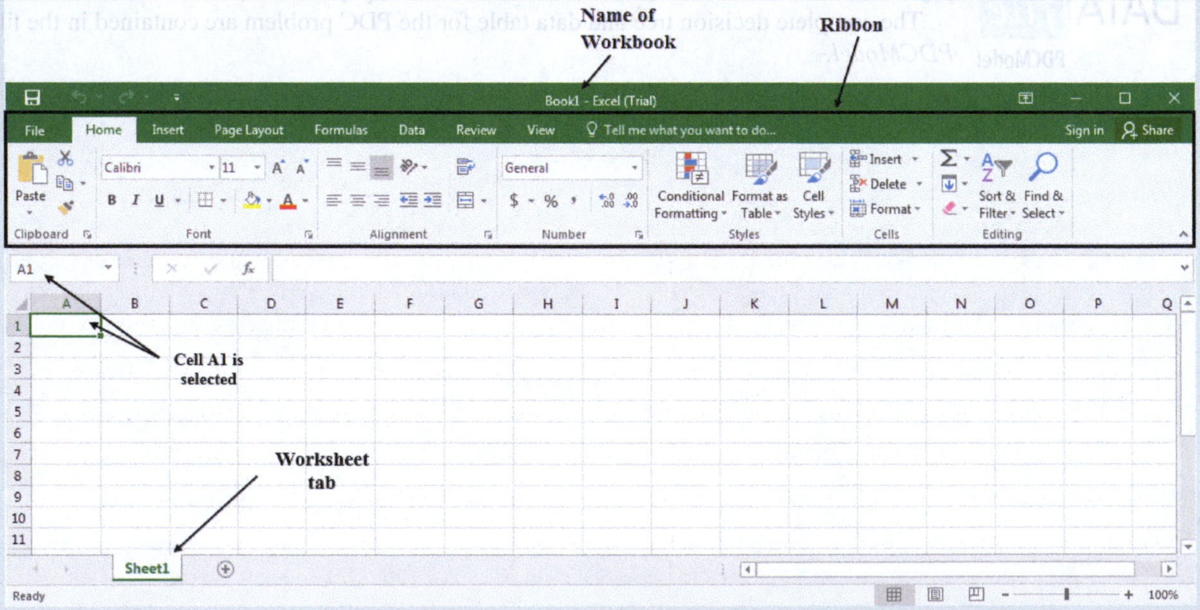

FIGURE A.2   Groups on the Home tab in the Ribbon of an Excel Workbook

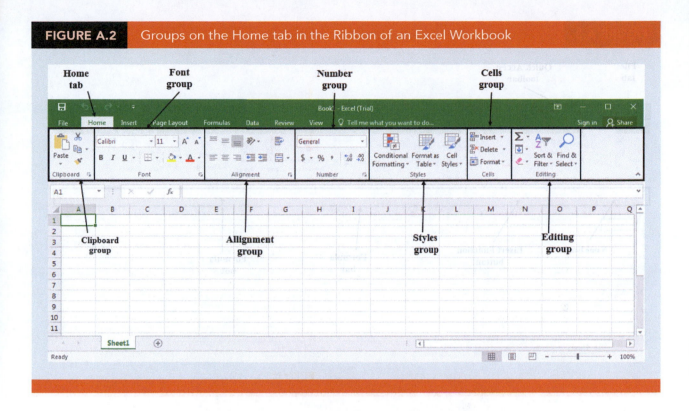

may create additional tabs. Each tab contains several groups of related commands. The File tab is used to Open, Save, and Print files as well as to change the Options being used by Excel and to load Add-ins. Note that the Home tab is selected when a workbook is opened. Figure A.2 displays the seven groups located in the Home tab: Clipboard, Font, Alignment, Number, Styles, Cells, and Editing. Commands are arranged within each group.

Keyboard shortcut: pressing Ctrl-B will change the font of the text in the selected cell to bold. We include a full list of keyboard shortcuts for Excel at the end of this appendix.

For example, to change selected text to boldface, click the **Home** tab and click the **Bold** button **B** in the **Font** group. The other tabs in the Ribbon are used to modify data in your spreadsheet or to perform analysis.

Figure A.3 illustrates the location of the File tab, the Quick Access Toolbar, and the Formula Bar. The Quick Access Toolbar allows you to quickly access commonly used workbook functions.

For instance, the Quick Access Toolbar shown in Figure A.3 includes a **Save** button ⊟ that can be used to save files without having to first click the **File** tab. To add or remove features on the Quick Access Toolbar, click the **Customize Quick Access Toolbar** button ▾ on the Quick Access Toolbar.

The Formula Bar contains a Name box, the Insert Function button *fx*, and a Formula box. In Figure A.3, "A1" appears in the Name box because cell A1 is selected. You can select any other cell in the worksheet by using the mouse to move the cursor to another cell and clicking or by typing the new cell location in the name box and pressing the Enter key. The Formula box is used to display the formula in the currently selected cell. For instance, if you had entered $=A1+A2$ into cell A3, whenever you select cell A3, the formula $=A1+A2$ will be shown in the Formula box. This feature makes it very easy to see and edit a formula in a cell. The Insert Function button allows you to quickly access all of the functions available in Excel. Later, we show how to find and use a particular function with the Insert Function button.

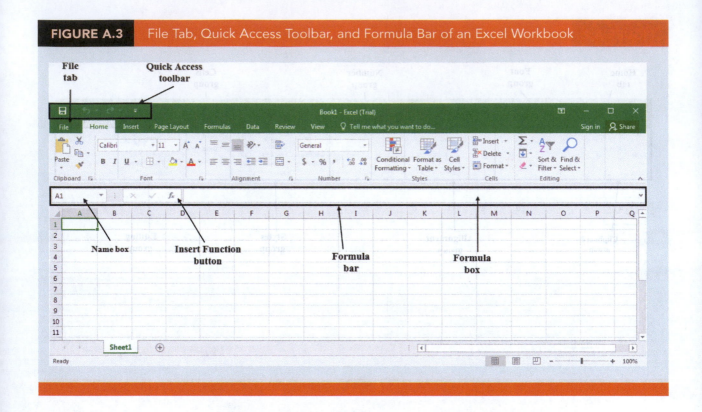

FIGURE A.3   File Tab, Quick Access Toolbar, and Formula Bar of an Excel Workbook

Basic Spreadsheet Workbook Operations

To change the name of the current worksheet, we take the following steps:

Step 1. Right-click on the worksheet tab named **Sheet1**

Step 2. Select the **Rename** option

Step 3. Enter *Nowlin* to rename the worksheet and press **Enter**

You can create a copy of the newly renamed Nowlin worksheet by following these steps:

Step 1. Right-click the worksheet tab named **Nowlin**

Step 2. Select the **Move or Copy…** option

Step 3. When the **Move or Copy** dialog box appears, select the checkbox for **Create a Copy**, and click **OK**

The name of the copied worksheet will appear as "Nowlin (2)." You can then rename it, if desired, by following the steps outlined previously. Worksheets can also be moved to other workbooks or to a different position in the current workbook by using the Move or Copy option.

To create additional worksheets follow these steps:

Step 1. Right-click on the tab of any existing worksheet

Step 2. Select **Insert…**

Step 3. When the **Insert** dialog box appears, select **Worksheet** from the **General** area, and click **OK**

New worksheets can also be created using the insert worksheet button ⊕ at the bottom of the screen.

Worksheets can be deleted by right-clicking the worksheet tab and choosing **Delete**. After clicking Delete, a window may appear, warning you that any data appearing in the worksheet will be lost. Click **Delete** to confirm that you do want to delete the worksheet.

Creating, Saving, and Opening Files in Excel

To illustrate manually entering, saving, and opening a file, we will use the Nowlin Plastics make-versus-buy model from Chapter 10. The objective is to determine whether Nowlin should manufacture or outsource production for its Viper product next year. Nowlin must pay a fixed cost of $234,000 and a variable cost per unit of $2 to manufacture the product. Nowlin can outsource production for $3.50 per unit.

We begin by assuming that Excel is open and a blank worksheet is displayed. The Nowlin data can now be entered manually by simply typing the manufacturing fixed cost of $234,000, the variable cost of $2, and the outsourcing cost of $3.50 into the worksheet.

We will place the data for the Nowlin example in the top portion of Sheet1 of the new workbook. First, we enter the label *Nowlin Plastics* in cell A1 and click the Bold button in the font group. Next we enter the label Parameters and click on the Bold button in the Font group. To identify each of the three data values, we enter the label *Manufacturing Fixed Cost* in cell A4, the label *Manufacturing Variable Cost per Unit* in cell A5, and the label *Outsourcing Cost per Unit* in cell A7. Next, we enter the actual data into the corresponding cells in column B: the value of *$234,000* in cell B4; the value of *$2* in cell B5; and the value of *$3.50* in cell B7. Figure A.4 shows a portion of the worksheet we have just developed.

Before we begin the development of the model portion of the worksheet, we recommend that you first save the current file; this will prevent you from having to reenter the data in case something happens that causes Excel to close. To save the workbook using the filename *Nowlin*, we perform the following steps:

Step 1. Click the **File** tab on the Ribbon
Step 2. Click **Save** in the list of options
Step 3. Select **This PC** under **Save As**, and click **Browse**
Step 4. When the **Save As** dialog box appears
       Select the location where you want to save the file
       Enter the file name *Nowlin* in the **File name:** box
       Click **Save**

Keyboard shortcut: To save the file, press Ctrl-S.

Excel's Save command is designed to save the file as an Excel workbook. As you work with and build models in Excel, you should follow the practice of periodically saving the file so that you will not lose any work. After you have saved your file for the first time,

FIGURE A.4	Nowlin Plastics Data

	A	B	C
1	**Nowlin Plastics**		
2			
3	**Parameters**		
4	Manufacturing Fixed Cost	$234,000.00	
5	Manufacturing Variable Cost per Unit	$2.00	
6			
7	Outsourcing Cost per Unit	$3.50	
8			

the Save command will overwrite the existing version of the file, and you will not have to perform Steps 3 and 4.

Sometimes you may want to create a copy of an existing file. For instance, suppose you change one or more of the data values and would like to save the modified file using the filename *NowlinMod*. The following steps show how to save the modified workbook using filename *NowlinMod*:

Step 1. Click the **File** tab in the Ribbon
Step 2. Click **Save As** in the list of options
Step 3. Select **This PC** under **Save As**, and click **Browse**
Step 4. When the **Save As** dialog box appears:
  Select the location where you want to save the file
  Type the file name *NowlinMod* in the **File name:** box
  Click **Save**

Once the *NowlinMod* workbook has been saved, you can continue to work with the file to perform whatever type of analysis is appropriate. When you are finished working with the file, simply click the close-window button ✕ located at the top right-hand corner of the Ribbon.

Later, you can easily access a previously saved file. For example, the following steps show how to open the previously saved Nowlin workbook:

Step 1. Click the **File** tab in the Ribbon
Step 2. Click **Open** in the list of options
Step 3. Select **This PC** under **Open** and click **Browse**
Step 4. When the **Open** dialog box appears:
  Find the location where you previously saved the *Nowlin* file
  Click on the filename **Nowlin** so that it appears in the **File name:** box
  Click **Open**

A.2 Spreadsheet Basics
Cells, References, and Formulas in Excel

We begin by assuming that the Nowlin workbook is open again and that we would like to develop a model that can be used to compute the manufacturing and outsourcing cost given a certain required volume. We will use the bottom portion of the worksheet shown in Figure A.4 to develop the model. The model will contain formulas that refer to the location of the data cells in the upper section of the worksheet. By putting the location of the data cells in the formula, we will build a model that can be easily updated with new data.

We enter the label *Model* into cell A10 and press the **Bold** button in the **Font** group. To provide a visual reminder that the bottom portion of this worksheet will contain the model. In cell A11, we enter the label *Quantity*. Next, we enter the labels *Total Cost to Produce* in cell A13, *Total Cost to Outsource* in cell A15, and *Savings due to Outsourcing* in cell A17.

To display all formulas in the cells of a worksheet, hold down the Ctrl key and then press the ~ key (usually located above the Tab key).

In cell B11 we enter *10000* to represent the quantity produced/outsourced by Nowlin Plastics. We will now enter formulas in cells B13, B15, and B17 that use the quantity in cell B11 to compute the values for production cost, outsourcing cost, and savings from outsourcing. The total cost to produce is the sum of the manufacturing fixed cost (cell B4) and the manufacturing variable cost. The manufacturing variable cost is the product of the production volume (cell B11) and the variable cost per unit (cell B5). Thus, the formula for total variable cost is B11*B5; to compute the value of total cost, we enter the formula =B4+B11*B5 in cell B13. Next, total cost to outsource is the product of the outsourcing cost per unit (cell B7) and the quantity (cell B11); this is computed by entering the formula =B7*B11 in cell B15. Finally, the savings due to outsourcing is computed by subtracting the cost of outsourcing (cell B15) from the production cost (cell B13). Thus, in cell B17 we enter the formula =B13-B15. Figure A.5 shows the Excel worksheet values and formulas used for these calculations.

We can now compute the savings due to outsourcing by entering a value for the quantity to be manufactured or outsourced in cell B11. Figure A.5 shows the results after entering a value of 10,000 in cell B11. We see that a quantity of 10,000 units results in a production cost of $254,000 and outsourcing of 35,000. Thus, the savings due to outsourcing is $219,000.

FIGURE A.5   Nowlin Plastics Data and Model

	A	B	C
1	Nowlin Plastics		
2			
3	Parameters		
4	Manufacturing Fixed Cost	234000	
5	Manufacturing Variable Cost per Unit	2	
6			
7	Outsourcing Cost per Unit	3.5	
8			
9			
10	Model		
11	Quantity	10000	
12			
13	Total Cost to Produce	=B4+B11*B5	
14			
15	Total Cost to Outsource	=B7*B11	
16			
17	Savings due to Outsourcing	=B13-B15	
18			

MODEL *file*

Nowlin

	A	B	C
1	Nowlin Plastics		
2			
3	Parameters		
4	Manufacturing Fixed Cost	$234,000.00	
5	Manufacturing Variable Cost per Unit	$2.00	
6			
7	Outsourcing Cost per Unit	$3.50	
8			
9			
10	Model		
11	Quantity	10,000	
12			
13	Total Cost to Produce	$254,000.00	
14			
15	Total Cost to Outsource	$35,000.00	
16			
17	Savings due to Outsourcing	$219,000.00	
18			

Finding the Right Excel Function

Excel provides a variety of built-in formulas or functions for developing mathematical models. If we know which function is needed and how to use it, we can simply enter the function into the appropriate worksheet cell. However, if we are not sure which functions are available to accomplish a task or are not sure how to use a particular function, Excel can provide assistance.

To identify the functions available in Excel click the **Insert Function** button *fx* on the formula bar; this opens the **Insert Function** dialog box shown in Figure A.6. The **Search for a function:** box at the top of the dialog box enables us to type a brief description for what we want to do. After doing so and clicking **Go**, Excel will search for and display, in the **Select a function** box, the functions that may accomplish our task. In many situations, however, we may want to browse through an entire category of functions to see what is available. For this task, the **Or select a category:** box is helpful. It contains a drop-down list of several categories of functions provided by Excel. Figure A.6 shows that we selected the **Math & Trig** category. As a result, Excel's Math & Trig functions appear in alphabetical order in the **Select a function:** area. We see the ABS function listed first, followed by the ACOS function, and so on.

The ABS function calculates the absolute value of a number. The ACOS function calculates the arccosine of a number.

Colon Notation

Although many functions, such as the ABS function, have a single argument, some Excel functions depend on arrays. **Colon notation** provides an efficient way to convey arrays and matrices of cells to functions. The colon notation may be described as follows:

FIGURE A.6	Insert Function Dialog Box

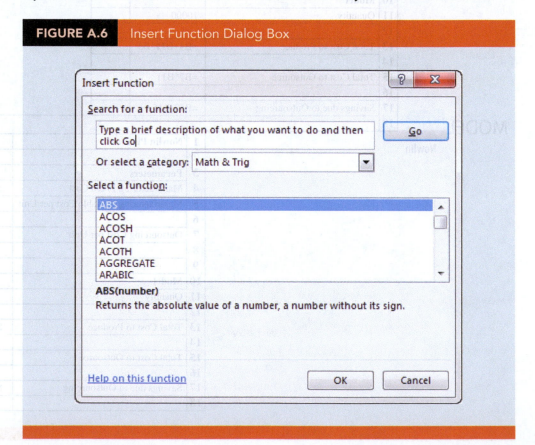

B1:B5 means cell B1 "through" cell B5, namely the array of values stored in the locations (B1,B2,B3,B4,B5). Consider, for example, the following function =SUM(B1:B5). The sum function adds up the elements contained in the function's argument. Hence, =SUM(B1:B5) evaluates the following formula:

$$=B1+B2+B3+B4+B5.$$

To illustrate the use of colon notation, we will consider the financial data for Nowlin Plastics contained in the DATAfile *NowlinFinancial* and shown in Figure A.7. Column A contains the name of each month, column B the revenue for each month, and column C

FIGURE A.7   Nowlin Plastics Monthly Revenues and Costs

	A	B	C
1	Month	Revenue	Cost
2	January	3459000	3250000
3	February	2873000	2640000
4	March	3195000	3021000
5	April	2925000	3015000
6	May	3682000	3150000
7	June	3436000	3240000
8	July	3410000	3185000
9	August	3782000	3237000
10	September	3548000	3196000
11	October	3136000	2997000
12	November	3028000	2815000
13	December	2845000	2803000
14			
15	Total:	=SUM(B2:B13)	=SUM(C2:C13)
16			
17	Average:	=AVERAGE(B2:B13)	=AVERAGE(C2:C13)

	A	B	C
1	Month	Revenue	Cost
2	January	$ 3,459,000	$ 3,250,000
3	February	$ 2,873,000	$ 2,640,000
4	March	$ 3,195,000	$ 3,021,000
5	April	$ 2,925,000	$ 3,015,000
6	May	$ 3,682,000	$ 3,150,000
7	June	$ 3,436,000	$ 3,240,000
8	July	$ 3,410,000	$ 3,185,000
9	August	$ 3,782,000	$ 3,237,000
10	September	$ 3,548,000	$ 3,196,000
11	October	$ 3,136,000	$ 2,997,000
12	November	$ 3,028,000	$ 2,815,000
13	December	$ 2,845,000	$ 2,803,000
14			
15	Total:	$39,319,000	$36,549,000
16			
17	Average:	$ 3,276,583	$ 3,045,750

the cost data. In row 15, we compute the total revenues and costs for the year. To do this we first enter *Total:* in cell A15. Next, we enter the formula =SUM(B2:B13) in cell B15 and =SUM(C2:C13) in cell C15. This shows that the total revenues for the company are $39,319,000 and the total costs are $36,549,000.

Inserting a Function into a Worksheet Cell

Continuing with the Nowlin financial data, we will now show how to use the Insert Function and Function Arguments dialog boxes to select a function, develop its arguments, and insert the function into a worksheet cell. We wish to calculate the average monthly revenue and cost at Nowlin. To do so, we take the following steps.

The Function Arguments dialog box contains a link Help on this function in case you need additional guidance on the use of a particular function in Excel.

Step 1. Select cell B17 in the DATAfile *NowlinFinancial*
Step 2. Click the Insert Function button *fx.*
      Select **Statistical** in the **Or select a category:** box
      Select **AVERAGE** from the **Select a function:** options
Step 3. When the **Function Arguments** dialog box appears:
      Enter *B2:B13* in the **Number1** box
      Click **OK**
Step 4. Repeat Steps 1 through 3 for the cost data in column C

Figure A.7 shows that the average monthly revenue is $3,276,583 and the average monthly cost is $3,045,750.

Using Relative Versus Absolute Cell References

NowlinFinancial

One of the most powerful abilities of spreadsheet software such as Excel is the ability to use relative references in formulas. Use of a **relative reference** allows the user to enter a formula once into Excel and then copy and paste that formula to other places so that the formula will update with the correct data without having to retype the formula. We will demonstrate the use of relative references in Excel by calculating the monthly profit at Nowlin Plastics using the following steps:

After completing Step 2, a shortcut to copying the formula to the range D3:D13 is to place the pointer in the bottom-right corner of cell D2 and then double-click.

Step 1. Enter the label *Profit* in cell D1 and press the **Bold** button in the **Font** group of the Home tab
Step 2. Enter the formula =B2-C2 in cell D2
Step 3. Copy the formula from cell D2 by selecting cell D2 and clicking **Copy** from the **Clipboard** group of the **Home** tab
Step 4. Select cells D3:D13
Step 5. Paste the formula from cell D2 by clicking **Paste** from the **Clipboard** group of the **Home** tab

Keyboard shortcut: You can copy in Excel by pressing Ctrl-C. You can paste in Excel by pressing Ctrl-V.

The result of these steps is shown in Figure A.8, where we have calculated the profit for each month. Note that even though the only formula we entered was =B2-C2 in cell D2, the formulas in cells D3 through D13 have been updated correctly to calculate the profit of each month using that month's revenue and cost.

In some situations, however, we do not want to use relative referencing in formulas. The alternative is to use an absolute reference, which we indicate to Excel by putting "$" before the row and/or column locations of the cell location. An **absolute reference** does *not* update to a new cell reference when the formula is copied to another location. We illustrate the use of an absolute reference by continuing to use the Nowlin financial data. Nowlin calculates an after-tax profit each month by multiplying its actual monthly profit by one minus its tax rate, which is currently estimated to be 30%. Cell B19 in

FIGURE A.8   Nowlin Plastics Profit Calculation

	A	B	C	D
1	Month	Revenue	Cost	Profit
2	January	3459000	3250000	=B2-C2
3	February	2873000	2640000	=B3-C3
4	March	3195000	3021000	=B4-C4
5	April	2925000	3015000	=B5-C5
6	May	3682000	3150000	=B6-C6
7	June	3436000	3240000	=B7-C7
8	July	3410000	3185000	=B8-C8
9	August	3782000	3237000	=B9-C9
10	September	3548000	3196000	=B10-C10
11	October	3136000	2997000	=B11-C11
12	November	3028000	2815000	=B12-C12
13	December	2845000	2803000	=B13-C13
14				
15	Total:	=SUM(B2:B13)	=SUM(C2:C13)	
16				
17	Average:	=AVERAGE(B2:B13)	=AVERAGE(C2:C13)	

	A	B	C	D
1	Month	Revenue	Cost	Profit
2	January	$ 3,459,000	$ 3,250,000	$ 209,000
3	February	$ 2,873,000	$ 2,640,000	$ 233,000
4	March	$ 3,195,000	$ 3,021,000	$ 174,000
5	April	$ 2,925,000	$ 3,015,000	$ (90,000)
6	May	$ 3,682,000	$ 3,150,000	$ 532,000
7	June	$ 3,436,000	$ 3,240,000	$ 196,000
8	July	$ 3,410,000	$ 3,185,000	$ 225,000
9	August	$ 3,782,000	$ 3,237,000	$ 545,000
10	September	$ 3,548,000	$ 3,196,000	$ 352,000
11	October	$ 3,136,000	$ 2,997,000	$ 139,000
12	November	$ 3,028,000	$ 2,815,000	$ 213,000
13	December	$ 2,845,000	$ 2,803,000	$ 42,000
14				
15	Total:		$39,319,000	$36,549,000	
16				
17	Average:	$ 3,276,583	$ 3,045,750	

In some cases, you may want Excel to use relative referencing for either the column or row location and absolute referencing for the other. For instance, to force Excel to always refer to column A but use relative referencing for the row, you would enter =$A1 into, say, cell B1. If this formula is copied into cell C3, the updated formula would be =$A3 (whereas it would be updated to =B3 if relative referencing was used for both the column and row location).

Figure A.9 contains this tax rate. In column E, we calculate the after-tax profit for Nowlin in each month by using the following steps:

Step 1. Enter the label *After-Tax Profit* in cell E1 and press the **Bold** Button in the **Font** group of the **Home** tab.

Step 2. Enter the formula =D2*(1-$B$19) in cell E2

Step 3. Copy the formula from cell E2 by selecting cell E2 and clicking **Copy** from the **Clipboard** group of the **Home** tab

Step 4. Select cells E3:E13

Step 5. Paste the formula from cell E2 by clicking **Paste** from the **Clipboard** group of the **Home** tab

Figure A.9 shows the after-tax profit in each month. Using $B$19 in the formula in cell E2 forces Excel to always refer to cell $B$19, even if we copy and paste this formula

FIGURE A.9   Nowlin Plastics After-Tax Profit Calculation Illustrating Relative Versus Absolute References

	A	B	C	D	E
1	Month	Revenue	Cost	Profit	After-Tax Profit
2	January	3459000	3250000	=B2-C2	=D2*(1-$B$19)
3	February	2873000	2640000	=B3-C3	=D3*(1-$B$19)
4	March	3195000	3021000	=B4-C4	=D4*(1-$B$19)
5	April	2925000	3015000	=B5-C5	=D5*(1-$B$19)
6	May	3682000	3150000	=B6-C6	=D6*(1-$B$19)
7	June	3436000	3240000	=B7-C7	=D7*(1-$B$19)
8	July	3410000	3185000	=B8-C8	=D8*(1-$B$19)
9	August	3782000	3237000	=B9-C9	=D9*(1-$B$19)
10	September	3548000	3196000	=B10-C10	=D10*(1-$B$19)
11	October	3136000	2997000	=B11-C11	=D11*(1-$B$19)
12	November	3028000	2815000	=B12-C12	=D12*(1-$B$19)
13	December	2845000	2803000	=B13-C13	=D13*(1-$B$19)
14					
15	Total:	=SUM(B2:B13)	=SUM(C2:C13)		
16					
17	Average:	=AVERAGE(B2:B13)	=AVERAGE(C2:C13)		
18					
19	Tax Rate:	0.3			

DATA *file*

NowlinFinancialComplete

	A	B	C	D	E
1	Month	Revenue	Cost	Profit	After-Tax Profit
2	January	$ 3,459,000	$ 3,250,000	$ 209,000	$ 146,300
3	February	$ 2,873,000	$ 2,640,000	$ 233,000	$ 163,100
4	March	$ 3,195,000	$ 3,021,000	$ 174,000	$ 121,800
5	April	$ 2,925,000	$ 3,015,000	$ (90,000)	$ (63,000)
6	May	$ 3,682,000	$ 3,150,000	$ 532,000	$ 372,400
7	June	$ 3,436,000	$ 3,240,000	$ 196,000	$ 137,200
8	July	$ 3,410,000	$ 3,185,000	$ 225,000	$ 157,500
9	August	$ 3,782,000	$ 3,237,000	$ 545,000	$ 381,500
10	September	$ 3,548,000	$ 3,196,000	$ 352,000	$ 246,400
11	October	$ 3,136,000	$ 2,997,000	$ 139,000	$ 97,300
12	November	$ 3,028,000	$ 2,815,000	$ 213,000	$ 149,100
13	December	$ 2,845,000	$ 2,803,000	$ 42,000	$ 29,400
14					
15	Total:	$39,319,000	$36,549,000		
16					
17	Average:	$ 3,276,583	$ 3,045,750		
18					
19	Tax Rate:	30%			

somewhere else in our worksheet. Notice that D2 continues to be a relative reference and is updated to D3, D4, and so on when we copy this formula to cells E3, E4, etc., respectively.

SUMMARY

In this appendix we have reviewed the basics of using Microsoft Excel. We have discussed the basic layout of Excel, file creation, saving, and editing as well as how to reference cells, use formulas, and use the copy and paste functions in an Excel worksheet. We have illustrated how to find and enter Excel functions and described the difference between relative and absolute cell references. In Chapter 10, we give a detailed treatment of how to create more advanced business analytics models in Excel. We conclude this appendix with Table A.1, which shows commonly used keyboard shortcut keys in Excel. Keyboard shortcut keys can save considerable time when entering data into Excel.

GLOSSARY

Absolute reference The reference to a cell location in an Excel worksheet formula or function. This reference does not update according to its relative position when copied.

Colon notation Notation used in an Excel worksheet to denote "through." For example, =SUM(B1:B4) implies sum cells B1 through B4, or equivalently, B1+B2+B3+B4.

Relative reference The reference to a cell location in an Excel worksheet formula or function. This reference updates according to its relative position when copied.

Workbook An Excel file that contains a series of worksheets.

Worksheet A single page in Excel containing a matrix of cells defined by their column and row locations in an Excel workbook.

TABLE A.1	Keyboard Shortcut Keys in Excel
Keyboard Shortcut Key	**Task Description**
Ctrl-S	Save
Ctrl-C	Copy
Ctrl-V	Paste
Ctrl-F	Find (can be used to find text both within a cell and within a formula in Excel)
Ctrl-P	Print
Ctrl-A	Selects all cells in the current data region
Ctrl-B	Changes the selected text to/from bold font
Ctrl-I	Changes the selected text to/from italic font
Ctrl-~ (usually located above the Tab key)	Toggles between displaying values and formulas in the Worksheet.
Ctrl-↓ (down arrow key)	Moves to the bottom-most cell of the current data region
Ctrl-↑ (up arrow key)	Moves to the top-most cell of the current data region
Ctrl-→ (right arrow key)	Moves to the right-most cell of the current data region
Ctrl-← (left arrow key)	Moves to the left-most cell of the current data region
Ctrl-Home	Moves to the top-left-most cell of the current data region
Ctrl-End	Moves to the bottom-left-most cell of the current data region
Shift-↓	Selects the current cell and the cell below
Shift-↑	Selects the current cell and the cell above
Shift-→	Selects the current cell and the cell to the right
Shift-←	Selects the current cell and the cell to the left
Ctrl-Shift-↓	Selects all cells from the current cell to the bottom-most cell of the data region
Ctrl-Shift-↑	Selects all cells from the current cell to the top-most cell of the data region
Ctrl-Shift-→	Selects all cells from the current cell to the right-most cell in the data region
Ctrl-Shift-←	Selects all cells from the current cell to the left-most cell in the data region
Ctrl-Shift-Home	Selects all cells from the current cell to the top-left-most cell in the data region
Ctrl-Shift-End	Selects all cells from the current cell to the bottom-right-most cell in the data region
Ctrl-Spacebar	Selects the entire current column
Shift-Spacebar	Selects the entire current row

A data region refers to all adjacent cells that contain data in an Excel worksheet.

Holding down the Ctrl key and clicking on multiple cells allows you to select multiple nonadjacent cells. Holding down the Shift key and clicking on two nonadjacent cells selects all cells between the two cells.

Appendix B—Database Basics with Microsoft Access

CONTENTS

Data are the cornerstone of analytics; without accurate and timely data on relevant aspects of a business or organization, analytic techniques are useless, and the resulting analyses are meaningless (or worse yet, potentially misleading). The data used by organizations to make decisions are not static, but rather are dynamic and constantly changing, usually at a rapid pace. Every change or addition to a database represents a new opportunity to introduce errors into the data, so it is important to be capable of searching for duplicate entries or entries with errors. Furthermore, related data may be stored in different locations to simplify data entry or increase security. Because an analysis frequently requires information from several sets of data, an analyst must be able to efficiently combine information from multiple data sets in a logical manner. In this appendix, we will review tools in Microsoft Access® that can be used for these purposes.

B.1 Database Basics

A **database** is a collection of logically related data that can be retrieved, manipulated, and updated to meet a user's or organization's needs. By providing centralized access to data efficiently and consistently, a database serves as an electronic warehouse of information on some specific aspect of an organization. A database allows for the systematic accumulation, management, storage, retrieval, and analysis of the information it contains while reducing inaccuracies that routinely result from manual record keeping. Organizations of all sizes maintain databases that contain information about their customers, markets, suppliers, and employees. Throughout this appendix, we will consider issues that arise in the creation and maintenance of a database for Stinson's MicroBrew Distributor, a licensed regional independent distributor of beer and a member of the National Beer Wholesalers Association. Stinson's provides refrigerated storage, transportation, and delivery of premium beers produced by several local microbreweries, so the company's facilities include a state-of-the-art temperature-controlled warehouse and a fleet of temperature-controlled trucks. Stinson's also employs sales, receiving, warehousing/inventory, and delivery personnel. When making a delivery, Stinson's monitors the retailer's shelves, taps, and keg lines to ensure the freshness and quality of the product. Because beer is perishable and because microbreweries often do not have the capacity to store, transport, and deliver large quantities of the products they produce, Stinson's holds a critical position in this supply chain.

Stinson's needs to develop a faster, more efficient, and more accurate means of recording, maintaining, and retrieving data related to various aspects of its business. The company's management team has identified three broad key areas of data management: personnel (information on Stinson's employees); supplier (information on purchases of beer made by Stinson's from its suppliers); and retailer (information on sales to Stinson's retail customers). We will use Microsoft Access 2016 in designing Stinson's database. Access is a *relational* database management system (RDBMS), which is the most commonly used type of database system in business. Data in a relational database are stored in tables, which are the fundamental components of a database. A relational database allows the user to retrieve subsets of data from tables and retrieve and combine data that are stored in related tables.

In this section we will learn how to use Access to create a database and perform some basic database operations. Access is a database management system that is commonly used by businesses to manage databases. In Access, a database is defined as a collection of related objects that are saved as a single file. An object in Access can be a:

- **Table**: Data arrayed in rows and columns (similar to a worksheet in an Excel spreadsheet) in which rows correspond to **records** (the individual units from which the data have been collected) and columns correspond to **fields** (the variables on which data have been collected from the records)
- **Form**: An object that is created from a table to simplify the process of entering data
- **Query**: A question posed by a user about the data in the database
- **Report**: Output from a table or a query that has been put into a specific prespecified format

In this appendix, we will focus on tables and queries. You can refer to a wide variety of books on database design to learn about forms, reports, and other database objects.

Tables are the foundation of an Access database. Each field in a table has a data type. The most commonly used are:

- *Short Text:* A field that contains words (such as the field *Gender* that may be used to record whether a Stinson's employee is female or male); can contain no more than 255 alphanumeric characters
- *Long Text:* A larger field that contains words and is generally used for recording lengthy descriptive entries (such as the field *Notes on Special Circumstances for a Transaction* that may be used to record detailed notes about unique aspects of specific transactions between Stinson's and its retail customers); can contain no more than to 65,536 alphanumeric characters.
- *Number*: A field that contains numerical values. There are several sizes of Number fields, which include:
  - *Byte:* Stores whole numbers from 0 to 255
  - *Decimal:* Stores numbers from $-10^{28} + 1$ to $10^{28} - 1$
  - *Integer:* Stores nonfractional numbers from $-32,768$ to $32,767$
  - *Long Integer:* Stores nonfractional numbers from $-2,147,483,648$ to $2,147,483,647$
  - *Single:* Stores numbers from -3.402823×10^{38} to 3.402823×10^{38}
  - *Double:* Stores numbers from $-1.79769313 \times 10^{308}$ to $1.79769313 \times 10^{308}$
- *Currency:* A field that contains monetary values (such as the field *Transaction Amount* that may be used to record payments for goods that have been ordered by Stinson's retail customers)
- *Yes/No:* A field that contains binary variables (such as the field *Sunday Deliveries?* that may be used to record whether Stinson's retail customers accept deliveries on Sundays)

Microsoft Access 2016 is virtually identical to Microsoft Access 2013 and 2010, so the instructions provided in this appendix also apply to Access 2010 and Access 2013.

In versions of Access prior to Access 2013 the Long Text field type is referred to as the Memo field type.

- *Date/Time:* A field that contains dates and times (such as the field *Date of Order* that may be used to record the date of an order placed by Stinson's with one of its suppliers)

Once you create a field and set its data type, you can set additional field properties. For example, for a numerical field you can define the data size to be Byte, Integer, Long Integer, Single, Double, Replication ID, or Decimal.

A database may consist of several tables that are maintained separately for a variety of reasons. We have already mentioned that Stinson's maintains information on its personnel, its suppliers and orders and its retail customers and sales. With regard to its retail customers, Stinson's may maintain information on the company name, street address, city, state, zip code, telephone number, and e-mail address; the dates of orders placed and quantities ordered; and the dates of actual deliveries and quantities delivered. In this example, we may consider establishing a table on Stinson's retailer customers; in this table each record corresponds to a retail customer, and the fields include the retail customer's company name, street address, city, state, zip code, telephone number, and e-mail address. Maintenance of this table is relatively simple; these data likely are not updated frequently for existing retail customers, and when Stinson's begins selling to a new retail customer, it has to establish only a single new record containing the information for the new retail customer in each field.

Stinson's may maintain other tables in this database. To track purchases made by its retail customers, the company may maintain a table of retail orders that includes the retail customer's name and the dollar value, date, and number of kegs and cases of beer for each order received by Stinson's. Because this table contains one record for each order placed with Stinson's, this table must be updated much more frequently than the table of information on Stinson's retailer customers.

A user who submits a query is effectively asking a question about the information in one or more tables in a database. For example, suppose Stinson's has determined that it has surplus kegs of Fine Pembrook Ale in inventory and is concerned about potential spoilage. As a result, the Marketing Department decides to identify all retail customers who have ordered kegs of Fine Pembrook Ale during the previous three months so that Stinson's can call these retailers and offer them a discounted price on additional kegs of this beer. A query could be designed to search the Retail Orders table for retail customers who meet this criterion. When the query is run, the output of the query provides the answer.

More complex queries may require data to be retrieved from multiple tables. For these queries, the tables must be connected by a join operation that links the records of the tables by their values in some common field. The common field serves as a bridge between the two tables, and the bridged tables are then treated by the query as a large single table comprising the fields of the original tables that have been joined. In designing a database for Stinson's, we may include the customer ID as a field in both the table of retail customers and table of retail orders; values in the field customer ID would then provide the basis for linking records in these two tables. Thus, even though the table of retail orders does not contain the information on each of Stinson's retail customers that is contained in the table of Stinson's retail customers, if the database is well designed, the information in these two tables can easily be combined whenever necessary.

Each table in a database generally contains a **primary key field** that has a unique value for each record in the table. A primary key field is used to identify how records from several tables in a database are logically related. In our previous example, Customer ID is the primary key field for the table of Stinson's retail customers. To facilitate the linking of records in the table of Stinson's retail customers with logically related records in the table of retail orders, the two tables must share a primary key. Thus, a field for Customer ID may be included in the table of retail orders so that information in this table can

A Replication ID field is used for storing a globally unique identifier to prevent duplication of an identifier (such as customer number) when multiple copies of the same database are in use in different locations.

In addition to answering a user's questions about the data in one or more tables, a query can also be used to add a record to the end of a table, delete a record from a table, or change the values for one or more records in a table. These functions are accomplished through append, delete, and update queries. We discuss queries in more detail later in this appendix.

For tables that do not include a primary key field, a unique identifier for each record in the table may be formed by combining two or more fields (if the combination of these two fields will yield a unique value for each record that may be included in the table); the result is called a compound primary key and is used in the same way a primary key is used.

be linked to information on each of Stinson's retail customers; when a field is included in a table for the sole purpose of facilitating links with records from another table, the field is referred to as a **foreign key field**.

Considerations When Designing a Database

Before creating a new database, we should carefully consider the following issues:

- What is the purpose of this database?
- Who will use this database?
- What queries and reports do the users of this database need?
- What information or data (fields) will this database include?
- What tables must be created, and how will the fields be allocated to these tables?
- What are the relationships between these tables?
- What are the fields that will be used to link related tables?
- What forms does the organization need to create to support the use of this database?

The answers to these questions will enable us to efficiently create a more effective and useful database. Let us consider these issues within the context of designing Stinson's database. Stinson's has several reasons for developing and implementing a database. Quick access to reliable and current data will enable Stinson's to monitor inventory and place orders from the microbreweries so that it can meet the demand of the retailers it supplies, while avoiding excess quantities and potential spoilage of inventory. These data can also be used to monitor the age of the product in inventory, which is a critical issue for a perishable product. Patterns in the orders of various beers placed by Stinson's retail customers can be analyzed to determine forecasts of future demand. Employees' salaries, federal and state tax withholding, vacation and sick days taken/remaining for the current year, and contributions to retirement funds can be tracked. Orders received from retail customers and Stinson's deliveries can be better coordinated. In summary, Stinson's can use a database to utilize information about its business in numerous ways that will potentially improve the efficiency and profitability of the company.

If we were to create a database for Stinson's MicroBrew Distributor, who within the company might need to use information from the database? A quick review of Stinson's reasons for developing and implementing a database provides the answer. Warehousing/inventory can use the database to control inventory. Delivery can create efficient delivery routes for the drivers on a daily basis and assess the on-time performance of the delivery system. Receiving can anticipate and prepare to receive daily deliveries of microbrews. Human resources can administer payroll, taxes, and benefits. Marketing can identify and exploit potential sales opportunities.

By considering the users and uses for the database, we can make a preliminary determination of the queries and reports the users of this database will need and the data (fields) this database must include. At this point we can consider the tables to be created, how the fields will be allocated to the tables, and the potential relationships between these tables. We can see that we will need to incorporate data on:

- Each microbrewery for which Stinson's distributes beer (Stinson's suppliers).
- Each order placed with and delivery received from the microbreweries (Stinson's supplies).
- Each retailer to which Stinson's distributes beer (Stinson's customers).
- Each order received from and delivery made to Stinson's retail customers (Stinson's sales).

- Each of Stinson's employees (Stinson's workforce).

As we design these tables and allocate fields to the tables we design, we must ensure that our database stores Stinson's data in the correct formats and is capable of outputting the queries, forms, and reports that Stinson's employees need.

With these considerations in mind, we decide to begin with the following 11 tables and associated fields in designing a database for Stinson's MicroBrew Distributor:

- TblEmployees
  - EmployeeID
  - EmpFirstName
  - EmpLastName
  - Gender
  - DOB
  - Street Address
  - City
  - State
  - Zip Code
  - Phone Number

- TblJobTitle
  - Job ID
  - Job Title

- TblEmployHist
  - EmployeeID
  - Start Date
  - End Date
  - Job ID
  - Salary
  - Hourly Rate

- TblBrewers
  - BrewerID
  - Brewery Name
  - Street Address
  - City
  - State
  - Zip Code
  - Phone Number

- TblSOrders
  - SOrder Number
  - BrewerID
  - Date of SOrder
  - EmployeeID
  - Keg or Case?
  - SQuantity Ordered

- TblSDeliveries
  - SOrder Number
  - BrewerID
  - EmployeeID
  - Date of SDelivery
  - SQuantity Delivered

- TblPurchasePrices
  - BrewerID
  - KegPurchasePrice
  - CasePurchasePrice

- TblRetailers
  - CustID
  - Name
  - Class
  - Street Address
  - City
  - State
  - Zip Code
  - Phone Number

- TblROrders
  - ROrder Number
  - Name
  - CustID
  - BrewerID
  - Date of ROrder
  - Keg or Case?
  - RQuantity Ordered
  - Rush?

- TblRDeliveries
  - CustID
  - Name
  - ROrder Number
  - EmployeeID
  - Date of RDelivery
  - RQuantity Delivered
- TblSalesPrices
  - BrewerID
  - KegSalesPrice
  - CaseSalesPrice

Each table contains information about a particular aspect of Stinson's business operations:

Note that the name of each table begins with the three letter designation Tbl; this is consistent with the Leszynski/ Reddick guidelines, a common set of standards for naming database objects.

- *TblEmployees*: Information about each Stinson's employee, primarily obtained when the employee is hired
- *TblJobTitle*: Information about each type of position held by Stinson's employees
- *TblEmployHist*: Information about the employment history of each Stinson's employee
- *TblBrewers*: Information about each microbrewery that supplies Stinson's with beer
- *TblSOrders*: Information about each order that Stinson's has placed with the microbreweries that supply Stinson's with beer
- *TblSDeliveries*: Information about each delivery that Stinson's has received from the microbreweries that supply Stinson's with beer
- *TblPurchasePrices*: Information about the price charged by each microbrewery that supplies Stinson's with beer
- *TblRetailers*: Information about each retailer that Stinson's supplies with beer
- *TblROrders*: Information about each order that Stinson's has received from the retailers that Stinson's supplies with beer
- *TblRDeliveries*: Information about each delivery that Stinson's has made to the retailers that Stinson's supplies with beer
- *TblSalesPrices*: Information about the price charged to retailers by Stinson's for each of the microwbrews it distributes

The first three tables deal with personnel information, the next four with product supply/purchasing information, and the last four with demand/sales information. Figure B.1 shows how these tables are related.

The relationships among the tables define how they can be linked. For example, suppose Stinson's Shipping Manager needs information on the orders placed by Stinson's retail customers that are to be filled tomorrow so that she can solve an optimization model that provides the optimal routes for Stinson's delivery trucks. The Shipping Manager needs to generate a report that includes the amount of various beers ordered and the address of each retail customer that has placed an order. To do so, she can use the common field CustID to link records from the TblRetailers. When the delivery has been made, the relevant information is input into the TblRDeliveries table. If the Shipping Manager needs to generate a report of deliveries made by each driver for the past week, she can use the common field EmpoyeeID to link records from the TblEmployees table with related records from the TblRDeliveries table.

Once Stinson's is satisfied that the planned database will provide the organization with the capability to collect and manage its data, and Stinson's is also confident that the database is capable of outputting the queries, forms, and reports that its employees need, we can proceed by using Access to create the new database. However, it is important to realize that it is unusual for a new database to meet all of the potential needs of its users. A well-designed database allows for augmentation and revision when needs that the current database does not meet are identified.

FIGURE B.1 Tables and Relationships for Stinson's Microbrew Distributor Database

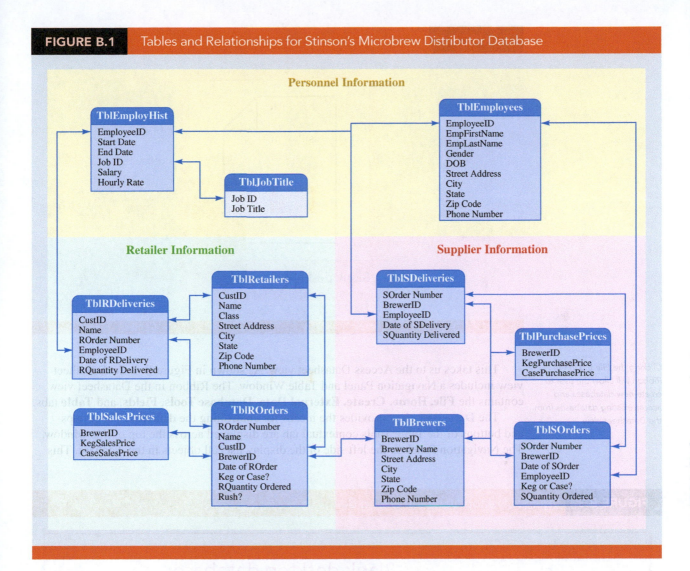

Creating a Database in Access

When you open Access, the left pane provides links to databases you have recently opened as well as a means for opening existing database documents. The available document templates are provided in the right pane; these preinstalled templates can be used to create new databases that utilize common formats. Because we are focusing on building a fairly generic database, we will use the Blank desktop database tool. We are now ready to create a new database by following these steps:

Step 1. Click the **Blank desktop database** icon (Figure B.2)
Step 2. When the **Blank desktop database** dialog box (Figure B.3) appears:
  Enter the name of the new database in the **File Name** box (we will call our new database *Stinsons.accdb*)
  Indicate the location where the new database will be saved by clicking the **Browse** button 📂 (we will save the database called *Stinsons.accdb* in the folder *C:\Stinson Files*)
Step 3. Click **Create**

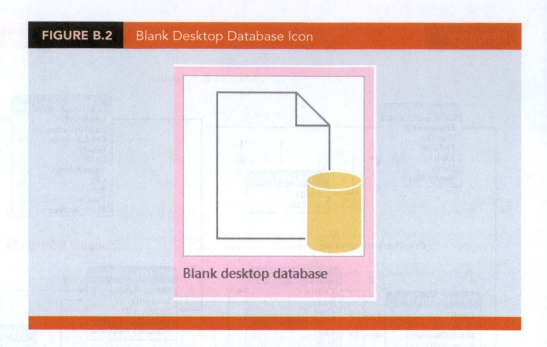

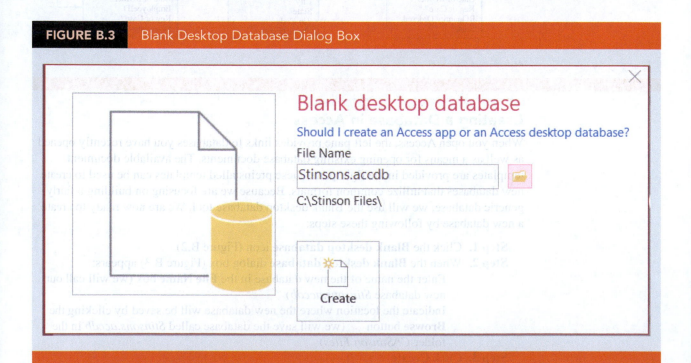

Clicking the File tab in the Ribbon will allow the user to create new databases and access existing databases from the Datasheet view.

This takes us to the Access Datasheet view. As shown in Figure B.4, the Datasheet view includes a Navigation Panel and Table Window. The Ribbon in the Datasheet view contains the **File, Home, Create, External Data, Database Tools, Fields**, and **Table** tabs.

The **Datasheet view** provides the means for controlling the database. The groups and buttons of the Table Tools contextual tab are displayed across the top of this window. The Navigation Panel on the left side of the display lists all objects in the database. This

---

FIGURE B.4 Datasheet View and Table Tools Contextual Tab

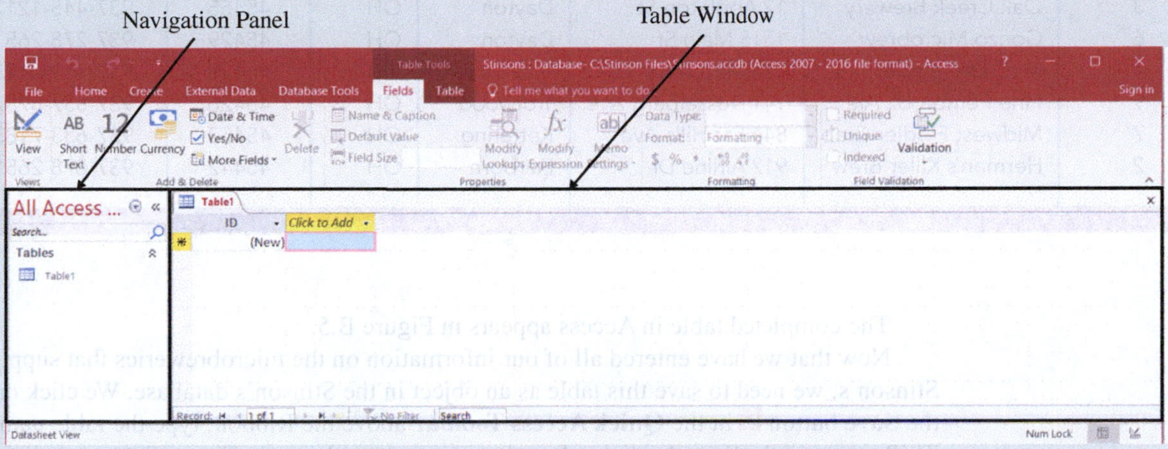

Navigation Panel

Table Window

[Access application screenshot showing the Datasheet View with the Navigation Panel on the left labeled "All Access..." listing Tables > Table1, and the Table Window on the right showing Table1 with ID and "Click to Add" columns. The Table Tools Fields contextual tab ribbon is visible at the top.]

---

provides a user with direct access to tables, reports, queries, forms, and so on that make up the currently open database. On the right side of the display is the Table Window; the tab in the upper left corner of the Table Window shows the name of the current table (Table1 in Figure B.4). In the Table Window, we can enter data directly into the table or modify data in an existing table.

The first step in creating a new database is to create one or more tables. Because tables store the information contained in a database, they are the foundation of a database and must be created prior to the creation of any other objects in the database. There are two options for manually creating a table: We can enter data directly in Datasheet view, or we can design a table in **Design view**. We will create our first table, TblBrewers, by entering data directly in Datasheet view. You can review an example database comprising all of the objects and relationships between the objects that we create throughout this appendix for the Stinson's database in the file *Stinsons*.

In Datasheet view the data are entered by field, one record at a time. In Figure B.1 we see that the fields for TblBrewers are BrewerID, Brewery Name, Street Address, City, State, Zip Code, and Phone Number. From Stinson's current filing system, we have been able to retrieve the information in Table B.1 on the breweries that supply Stinson's.

We can enter these data into our new database in Datasheet view by following these steps:

Step 1. Enter the first record from Table B.1 into the first row of the **Table Window** in Access by entering a *3* in the top row next to (**New**), pressing the **Tab** key, entering *Oak Creek Brewery* in the next column, pressing the **Tab** key, entering *12 Appleton St* in the next column, pressing the **Tab** key, entering *Dayton* in the next column, pressing the **Tab** key, etc.

Step 2. Enter the second record from Table B.1 by repeating Step 1 for the Gonzo Microbrew data and entering these data into the second row of the **Table Window** in Access

Continue entering data for the remaining microbreweries in this manner

DATA *file*

Stinsons

You can click the Help button ⓘ *to find detailed instructions on creating a table (or using any other Access functionality).*

When we enter 3 in Step 1, this establishes a new field with the generic name "Field1" and generates a value for the ID column. Pressing Tab moves to the next field entry box for the same record.

TABLE B.1	Raw Data for Table TblBrewers					
BrewerID	**Brewery Name**	**Street Address**	**City**	**State**	**Zip Code**	**Phone Number**
3	Oak Creek Brewery	12 Appleton St	Dayton	OH	45455	937-445-1212
6	Gonzo Microbrew	1515 Main St	Dayton	OH	45429	937-278-2651
4	McBride's Pride	425 Mad River Rd	Miamisburg	OH	45459	937-439-0123
9	Fine Pembrook Ale	141 Dusselberg Ave	Trotwood	OH	45426	937-837-8752
7	Midwest Fiddler Crab	844 Far Hills Ave	Kettering	OH	45453	937-633-7183
2	Herman's Killer Brew	912 Airline Dr	Fairborn	OH	45442	937-878-2651

The completed table in Access appears in Figure B.5.

Now that we have entered all of our information on the microbreweries that supply Stinson's, we need to save this table as an object in the Stinson's database. We click on the **Save** button 🖫 in the **Quick Access Toolbar** above the Ribbon, type the table name *TblBrewers* in the **Save As** dialog box that appears (as shown in Figure B.6), and click **OK**. The name in the Table Name tab on the Table Window now reads "TblBrewers."

We can now use the Design view to provide meaningful names for our fields and specify each field's properties. We switch to Design view by first clicking on the arrow below the **View** button 🗹 in the **Views** group of the Ribbon. This will open a pull-down menu with options for various views (recall that we are currently in the Datasheet view). Clicking on the **Design View** option opens the Design view for the current table as shown in Figure B.7. From the Design view we can define or edit the table's fields and field properties as well as rearrange the order of the fields if we wish. The name of the current table is again identified in the Name Tab, and the Table Window is replaced with two sections: the Table Design Grid on top and the Field Properties Pane on the bottom of this window.

FIGURE B.5   Records for Six Microbreweries Entered into an Access Table

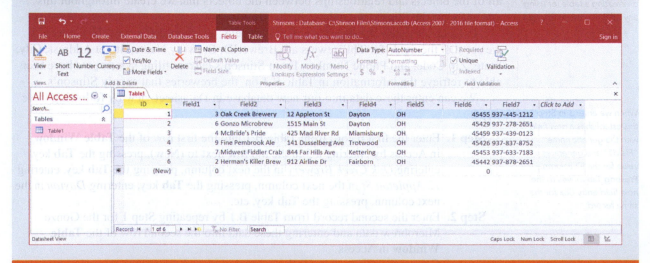

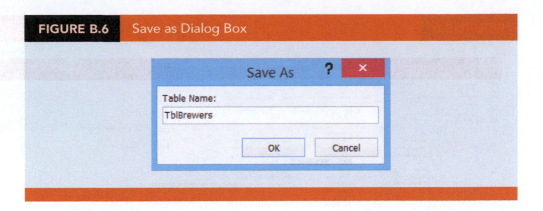

FIGURE B.6   Save as Dialog Box

*Note that Field Names used
in Access cannot exceed
64 characters, cannot begin
with a space, and can include
any combination of letters,
numbers, spaces, and special
characters except for a
period (.), an accent grave ('),
an exclamation point (!), or
square brackets ([and]).*

We can now replace the generic field names (Field1, Field2, etc.) in the column on the right side of the Table Design Grid of TblBrewers with the names we established from our original database design and then move to defining the field type for each field. To change the data type for a field in design view, we follow these steps:

Step 1. Click on the cell in the **Data Type** column (the middle column) in the **Table Design Grid** in the row of the field for which you want to change the data type

Step 2. Click on the drop-down arrow ⏷ in the upper right-hand corner of the selected cell

Step 3. Define the data type for the field using the drop-down menu (Figure B.8)

FIGURE B.7   Design View for the Table TblBrewers

Navigation Panel   Table Design Grid   Field Properties Pane

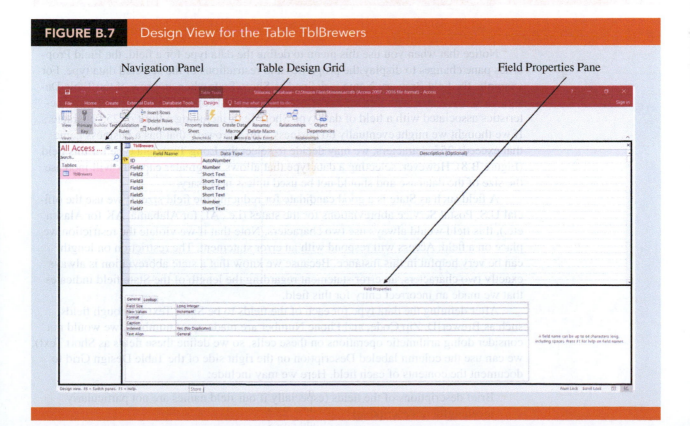

FIGURE B.8   Changing the Data Type for the Brewery Name Field in the Table TblBrewers

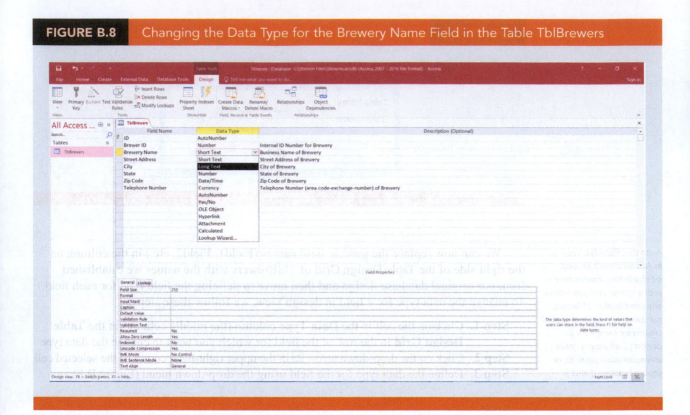

Notice that when you use this menu to define the data type for a field, the Field Properties pane changes to display the properties and restrictions of the selected data type. For example, the field Brewery Name is defined as Short Text; when any row of the Table Design Grid associated with this field is selected, the Field Property Pane shows the characteristics associated with a field of data type Short Text, including a limit of 255 characters. If we thought we might eventually do business with a brewery that has a business name that exceeds 255 characters, we may decide to select the Long Text data type for this field (Figure B.8). However, selecting a data type that allows for greater capacity will increase the size of the database and should not be used unless necessary.

A field such as State is a good candidate for reducing the field size. If we use the official U.S. Postal Service abbreviations for the states (i.e., AL for Alabama, AK for Alaska, etc.), this field would always use two characters. Note that if we violate the restriction we place on a field, Access will respond with an error statement. The restriction on length can be very helpful in this instance. Because we know that a state abbreviation is always exactly two characters, an error statement regarding the length of the State field indicates that we made an incorrect entry for this field.

After defining the data type for each of the fields to be Short Text (although fields such as BrewerID, Zip Code, and Phone Number are made up of numbers, we would not consider doing arithmetic operations on these cells, so we define these fields as Short Text), we can use the column labeled Description on the right side of the Table Design Grid to document the contents of each field. Here we may include:

- Brief descriptions of the fields (especially if our field names are not particularly meaningful or descriptive)

FIGURE B.9 — Drop-Down Menu for Deleting Fields in the Design View

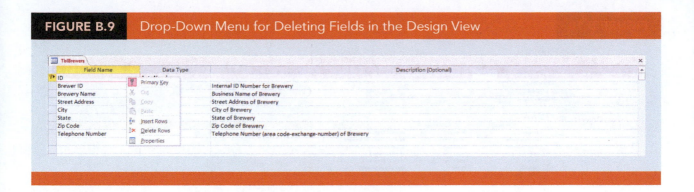

- Instructions for entering data into the fields (e.g., we may indicate that a telephone number is entered area code-exchange-number)
- Indications of whether a field acts as a primary or foreign key

To change the primary key from the default field ID to BrewerID, we use the following steps:

Step 1. Click on any cell in the BrewerID row
Step 2. Click the **Design** tab in the Ribbon
Step 3. Click the **Primary Key** icon in the **Tools** group

This changes the primary key from the ID field to the BrewerID field. We can now delete the ID field because it is no longer needed.

Step 4. Right-click any cell in the ID row and click **Delete Rows** (Figure B.9)
Click **Yes** when the dialog box appears to confirm that you want to delete this row

We have now created the table TblBrewers by entering the data in Datasheet view (Figure B.10) and: (1) changed the name of each field, (2) identified the correct data type for each field, (3) revised properties for some fields, (4) added a description for each field, and (5) changed the primary key field to BrewerID in Design view. Alternatively, we could create a table in Design view. We first enter the field names, data types, and descriptions in the Table Design grid. After saving this table as TblSOrders, we then move to the Database Window, which now has defined fields, and enter the information in the appropriate cells. Suppose we take this approach to create the table TblSOrders, which contains information on orders Stinson's places with the microbreweries. We have the following data for orders from the past week (Table B.2) that we will use to initially populate this table (new orders will be added to the table as they are placed).

The fields represent Stinson's internal number assigned to each order placed with a brewery (SOrderNumber), Stinson's internal identification number assigned to the microbrewery with which the order has been placed (BrewerID), the date on which Stinson's placed the order (Date of SOrder), the identification number of the Stinson's employee who placed the order (EmployeeID), an indication of whether the order was for kegs or cases of beer (Keg or Case?), and the quantity (in units) ordered (SQuantity Ordered). As before, we enter the information into the Field Name, Data Type, and Description columns of the Table Design grid, remove the ID field, change the primary key field (this time to the field SOrderNumber), and revise the properties of the fields as necessary in the Field Properties area as shown in Figure B.11.

FIGURE B.10 Design View of Table Design for TblBrewers

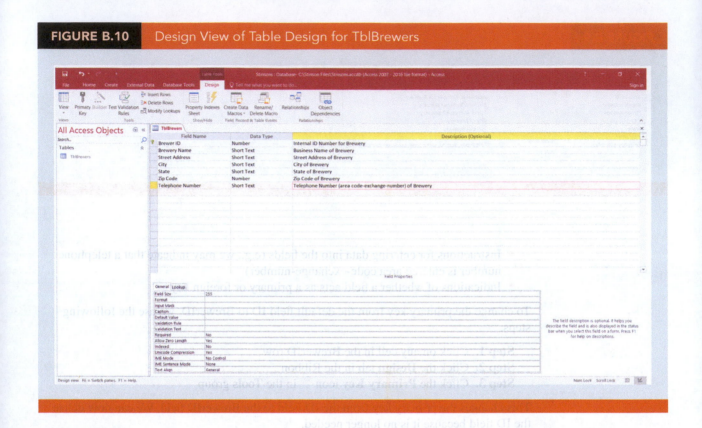

TABLE B.2 Raw Data for Table TblSOrders

SOrderNumber	BrewerID	Date of SOrder	EmployeeID	Keg or Case?	SQuantity Ordered
17351	3	11/5/2012	135	Keg	3
17352	9	11/5/2012	94	Case	6
17353	7	11/5/2012	94	Keg	2
17354	3	11/6/2012	94	Keg	3
17355	3	11/6/2012	135	Keg	2
17356	6	11/6/2012	135	Case	5
17358	2	11/7/2012	94	Keg	3
17359	4	11/7/2012	135	Keg	2
17360	3	11/8/2012	94	Case	8
17361	2	11/8/2012	94	Keg	1
17362	7	11/8/2012	94	Keg	2
17363	9	11/8/2012	135	Keg	4
17364	2	11/8/2012	94	Keg	2
17365	3	11/9/2012	135	Case	5
17366	2	11/9/2012	135	Keg	4
17367	7	11/9/2012	94	Case	4
17368	9	11/9/2012	135	Keg	4
17369	4	11/9/2012	94	Keg	3

Appendix B—Database Basics with Microsoft Ac...

FIGURE B.11 Design View of Table Design for TblSOrders

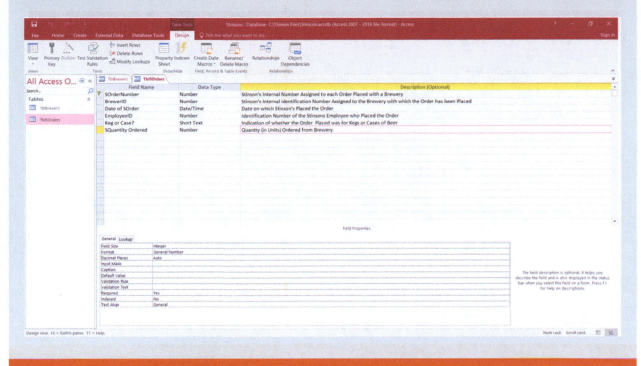

Now we return to the Database window and manually input the data from Table B.2 into the table TblSOrders as shown in Figure B.12. Note that in both Datasheet view and Design view, we now have separate tabs with the table names TblBrewers and TblSOrders and that these two tables are listed in the Navigation Panel. We can use either Datasheet view or Design view to move between our tables.

We can also create a table by reading information from an external file. Access is capable of reading information from several types of external files. Here we demonstrate by reading data from an Excel file into a new table TblSDeliveries. The Excel file *SDeliveries.xlsx* contains the information on deliveries received by Stinson's from various microbreweries during a recent week. The fields of this table, as shown in Figure B.12, will correspond to the column headings in the Excel worksheet displayed in Figure B.13.

The columns in Figure B.13 represent: Stinson's internal number assigned to each order placed with a microbrewery (SOrderNumber), Stinson's internal identification number assigned to the microbrewery with which the order has been placed (BrewerID), the identification number of the Stinson's employee who received the delivery (EmployeeID), the date on which Stinson's received the delivery (Date of Sdelivery), and the quantity (in units) received in the delivery (SQuantity Delivered). To import these data directly into the table TblSDeliveries, we follow these steps:

Step 1. Click the **External Data** tab in the Ribbon
Step 2. Click the **Excel** icon in the **Import & Link** group (Figure B.14)

FIGURE B.12   Datasheet View for TblSOrders

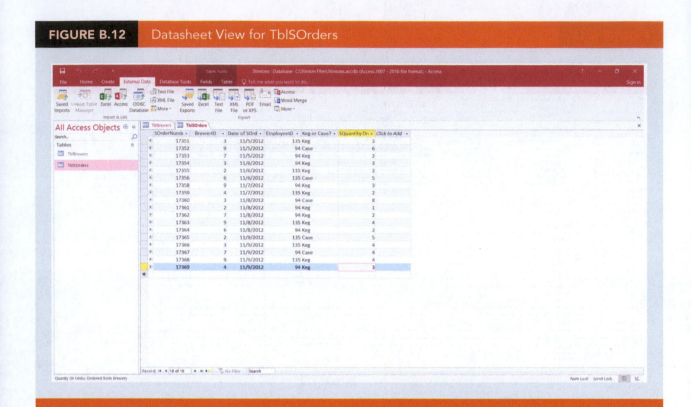

FIGURE B.13   Excel Spreadsheet SDeliveries.xlsx

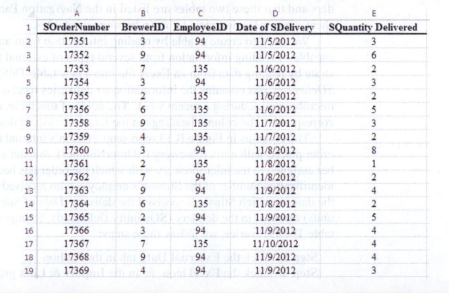

	A	B	C	D	E
1	SOrderNumber	BrewerID	EmployeeID	Date of SDelivery	SQuantity Delivered
2	17351	3	94	11/5/2012	3
3	17352	9	94	11/5/2012	6
4	17353	7	135	11/6/2012	2
5	17354	3	94	11/6/2012	3
6	17355	2	135	11/6/2012	2
7	17356	6	135	11/6/2012	5
8	17358	9	135	11/7/2012	3
9	17359	4	135	11/7/2012	2
10	17360	3	94	11/8/2012	8
11	17361	2	135	11/8/2012	1
12	17362	7	94	11/8/2012	2
13	17363	9	94	11/9/2012	4
14	17364	6	135	11/8/2012	2
15	17365	2	94	11/9/2012	5
16	17366	3	94	11/9/2012	4
17	17367	7	135	11/10/2012	4
18	17368	9	94	11/9/2012	4
19	17369	4	94	11/9/2012	3

FIGURE B.14   External Data Tab on the Access Ribbon

Verify that the check box for First Row Contains Column Headings

If the Excel worksheet from which we are importing the data does not contain column headings, Access will assign dummy names to the fields that can later be changed in the Table Design grid of Design view.

Step 3. When the **Get External Data—Excel Spreadsheet** dialog box appears (Figure B.15), click the **Browse…** button

Navigate to the location of the Excel file to be imported into Access (in this case, *SDeliveries.xlsx*), and indicate the manner in which we want to import the information in this Excel file by selecting the appropriate radio button (we are importing these data to a new table, TblSDeliveries, in the current database)

Step 4. Click **OK**

FIGURE B.15   Get External Data—Excel Spreadsheet Dialog Box

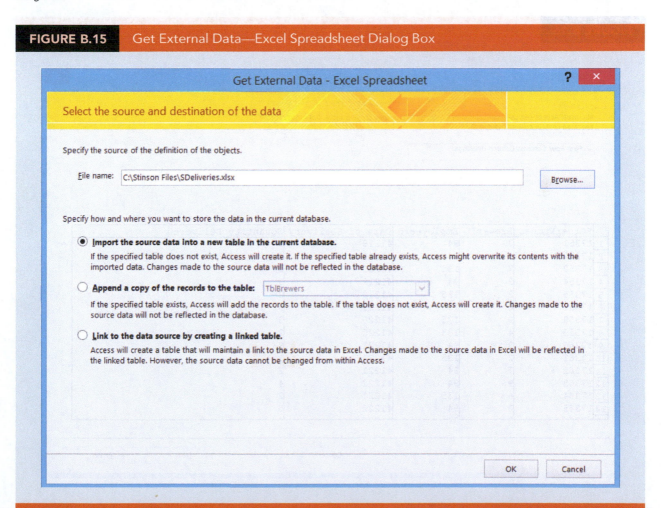

Step 5. When the **Import Spreadsheet Wizard** dialog box opens (Figure B.16), arrange the information as shown in Figure B.16

Verify that the check box for **First Row Contains Column Headings** is selected because the worksheet from which we are importing the data contains column headings

Click **Next >** to open the second screen of the **Import Spreadsheet Wizard** dialog box (Figure B.17)

Step 6. Indicate the format for the first field (in this case, SOrderNumber) and whether this field is the primary key field for the new table (it is in this case)

Click **Next >**

If your Excel file contains multiple worksheets, you will be prompted by the Import Spreadsheet Wizard to select the worksheet from which you want to import data. After you have selected a worksheet and clicked on Next, you will automatically proceed to the screen in Figure B.16.

We continue to work through the ensuing screens of the **Import Spreadsheet Wizard** dialog box, indicating the format for each field and identifying the primary key field (SOrderNumber) for the new table. When we have completed the final screen, we click **Finish** and add the table TblSDeliveries to our database. Note that in both Datasheet view (Figure B.18) and Design view, we now have separate tabs with the table names TblBrewers, TblSOrders, and TblSDeliveries, and that these three tables are listed in the Navigation Panel.

FIGURE B.16   First Screen of Import Spreadsheet Wizard Dialog Box

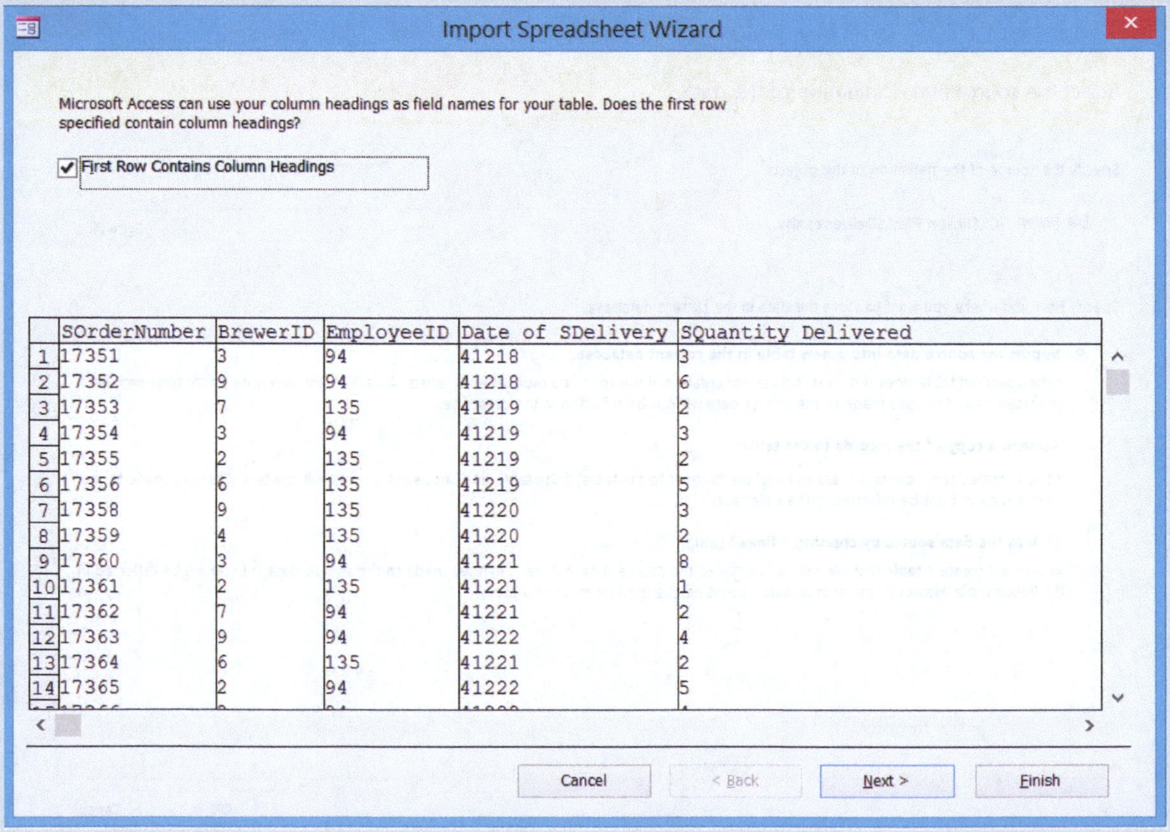

FIGURE B.17   Second Screen of Import Spreadsheet Wizard Dialog Box

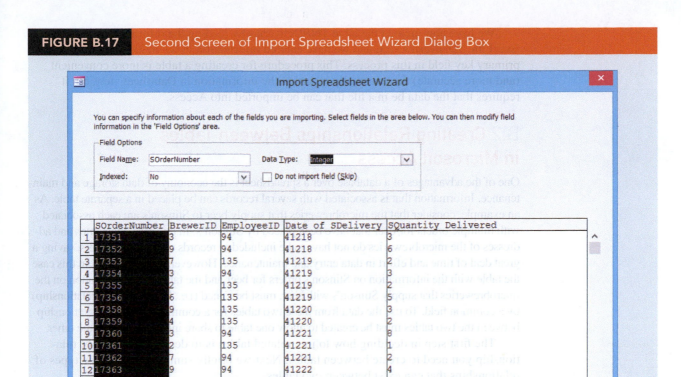

FIGURE B.18   Datasheet View for TblSDeliveries

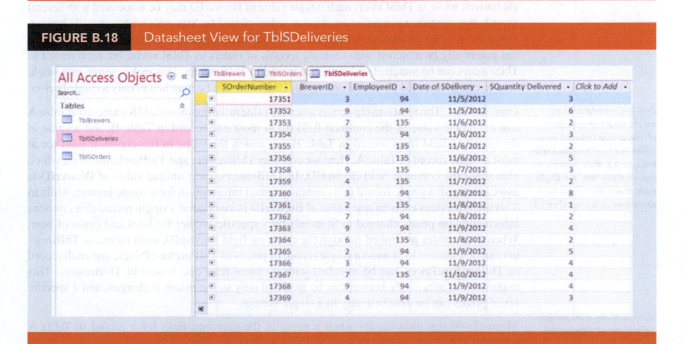

We have now created the table TblSDeliveries by reading the information from the Excel file *SDeliveries.xlsx*, and we have entered information in the fields and identified the primary key field in this process. This procedure for creating a table is more convenient (and more accurate) than manually inputting the information in Datasheet view, but it requires that the data be in a file that can be imported into Access.

B.2 Creating Relationships Between Tables in Microsoft Access

One of the advantages of a database over a spreadsheet is the economy of data storage and maintenance. Information that is associated with several records can be placed in a separate table. As an example, consider that the microbreweries that supply beer to Stinson's are each associated with multiple orders for beer that have been placed by Stinson's. In this case, the names and addresses of the microbreweries do not have to be included in records of Stinson's orders, saving a great deal of time and effort in data entry and maintenance. However, the two tables, in this case the table with the information on Stinson's orders for beer and the table with information on the microbreweries that supply Stinson's with beer, must be joined (i.e., have a defined relationship) by a common field. To use the data from these two tables for a common purpose, a relationship between the two tables must be created to allow one table to share information with the other.

The first step in deciding how to join related tables is to decide what type of relationship you need to create between tables. Next we briefly summarize the three types of relationships that can exist between two tables.

One-To-Many relationships are the most common type of relationship between two tables in a relational database; these relationships are sometimes abbreviated as 1:∞.

One-To-Many This relationship occurs between two tables, which we will label as Table A and Table B, when the value in the common field for a record in Table A can match the value in the common field for multiple records in Table B, but a value in the common field for a record in Table B can match the value in the common field for at most a single record in Table A. Consider TblBrewers and TblSOrders with the common field BrewerID. In TblBrewers, each unique value of BrewerID is associated with a single record that contains contact information for a single brewer, while in TblSOrders each unique value of BrewerID may be associated with several records that contain information on various orders placed by Stinson's with a specific brewer. When these tables are linked through the common field BrewerID, each record in TblBrewers can potentially be matched with multiple records of orders in TblSOrders, but each record in TblSOrders can be matched with only one record in TblBrewers. This makes sense, as a single brewer can be matched to several orders, but each order can be matched to only a single brewer.

One-To-One relationships are the least common form of relationship between two tables in a relational database because it is often possible to include these data in a single table; these relationships are sometimes abbreviated as 1:1.

One-To-One This relationship occurs when the value in the common field for a record in Table A can match the value in the common field for at most one record in Table B, and a value in the common field for a record in Table B can match the value in the common field for at most a single record in Table A. Here we consider TblBrewers and TblPurchasePrices, which also share the common field BrewerID. In TblBrewers, each unique value of BrewerID is associated with a single record that contains contact information for a single brewer, while in TblPurchasePrices each unique value of BrewerID is associated a single record that contains information on prices charged to Stinson's by a specific brewer for kegs and cases of beer. When these tables are linked through the common field BrewerID, each record in TblBrewers can be matched to at most a single record of prices in TblPurchasePrices, and each record in TblPurchasePrices can be matched with no more than one record in TblBrewers. This makes sense, as a single brewer can be matched only to the prices it charges, and a specific set of prices can be matched only to a single brewer.

Many-To-Many relationships are sometimes abbreviated as ∞:∞.

Many-To-Many This occurs when a value in the common field for a record in Table A can match the value in the common field for multiple records in Table B, and a value in the common field for a record in Table B can match the value in the common field for several records in Table A. Many-To-Many relationships are not directly supported by Access but can be facilitated by creating a third table, called an *associate table*, that contains a primary key and a foreign key to each of the original tables. This ultimately results in one-to-many relationships between the associate table and the two original tables. Our design for Stinson's database does not include any many-to-many relationships.

To create any of these three types of relationships between two tables, we must satisfy the rules of integrity. Recall that the primary key field for a table is a field that has (and will have throughout the life of the database) a unique value for each record. Defining a primary key field for a table ensures that the table will have **entity integrity**, which means that the table will have no duplicate records.

Note that when the primary key field for one table is a foreign key field in another table, it is possible for a value of this field to occur several times in the table for which it is a foreign key field. For example, Job ID is the primary key field in the table TblJobTitle and will have a unique value for each record in this table. But Job ID is a foreign field in the table TblEmployHist, so a value of Job ID can occur several times in TblEmployHist.

Referential integrity is the rule that establishes the relationship between two tables. For referential integrity to be established, when the foreign key field in one table (say, Table B) and the primary key field in the other table (say, Table A) are matched, each value that occurs in the foreign key field in Table B must also occur in the primary key field in Table A. For instance, to preserve referential integrity for the relationship between TblEmployHist and TblJobTitle, each employee record in TblEmployHist must have a value in the Job ID field that exactly matches a value of the Job ID field in TblJobTitle. If a record in TblEmployHist has a value for the foreign key field (Job ID) that does not occur in the primary key field (Job ID) of TblJobTitle, the record is said to be **orphaned** (in this case, this would occur if we had an employee who has been assigned a job that does not exist in our database). An orphaned record would be lost in any table that results from joining TblJobTitle and TblEmployHist. Enforcing referential integrity through Access prevents records from becoming orphaned and lost when tables are joined.

Violations of referential integrity lead to inconsistent data, which results in meaningless and potentially misleading analyses. Enforcement of referential integrity is critical not only for ensuring the quality of the information in the database but also for ensuring the validity of all conclusions based on these data.

We are now ready to establish relationships between tables in our database. We will first establish a relationship between the tables TblBrewers and TblSOrders. To establish a relationship between these two tables, take the following steps:

Step 1.   Click the **Database Tools** tab in the Ribbon (Figure B.19)

Step 2.   From the Navigation Panel select one of the tables for which you want to establish a relationship (we will click on **TblBrewers**)

Step 3.   Click the **Relationships** icon ▦ in the **Relationships** group
This will open the contextual tab **Relationship Tools** in the Ribbon and a new display with a tab labeled **Relationships** in the workspace, as shown in Figure B.20. A box listing all fields in the table you selected before clicking the **Relationships** icon will be provided

Step 4.   Click **Show Table** in the **Relationships** group
When the **Show Table** dialog box opens (Figure B.21), select the second table for which you want to establish a relationship (in our example, this is **TblSOrders**) to establish a relationship between these two tables
Click **Add**
Click **Close**

You can select multiple tables in the Show Table dialog box by holding down the Ctrl key and selecting multiple tables.

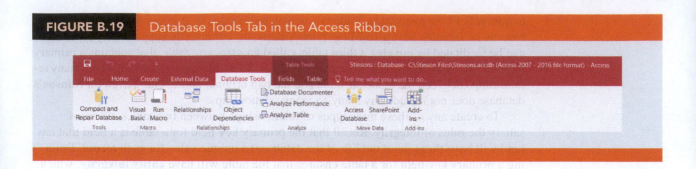

Once we have selected the two tables (TblBrewers and TblSOrders) for which we are establishing a relationship, boxes showing the fields for the two tables will appear in the workspace. If Access can identify a common field, it will also suggest a relationship between these two tables. In our example, Access has identified BrewerID as a common field between TblBrewers and TblSOrders and is showing a relationship between these two tables based on this field (Figure B.22).

In this instance, Access has correctly identified the relationship we want to establish between TblBrewers and TblSOrders. However, if Access does not correctly identify the relationship, we can modify the relationship between these tables. If we double-click on the line connecting TblBrewers to TblSOrders, we open the relationship's **Edit Relationships** dialog box, as shown in Figure B.23.

Note here that Access has correctly identified the relationship between TblBrewers and TblSOrders to be one-to-many and that we have several options from which to select. We can use the pull-down menu under the name of each table in the relationship to select different fields to use in the relationship between the two tables.

By selecting the **Enforce Referential Integrity** option in the **Edit Relationships** dialog box, we can indicate that we want Access to monitor this relationship to ensure that it satisfies relational integrity. This means that every unique value in the BrewerID field in TblSOrders also appears in the BrewerID field of TblBrewers; that is, there is a one-to-many relationship between TblBrewers and TblSOrders, and Access will revise the display of the relationship as shown in Figure B.22 to reflect that this is a one-to-many relationship.

If Access does not suggest a relationship between two tables, you can click Create New... in the Edit Relationships dialog box to open the Create New dialog box, which then will allow you to specify the tables to be related and the fields in these tables to be used to establish the relationship.

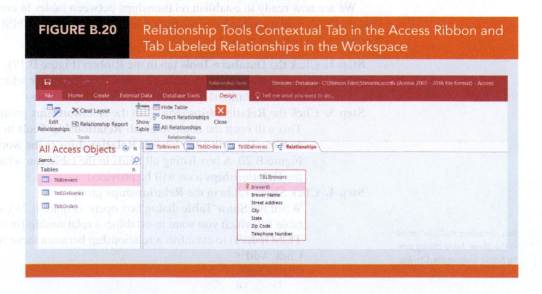

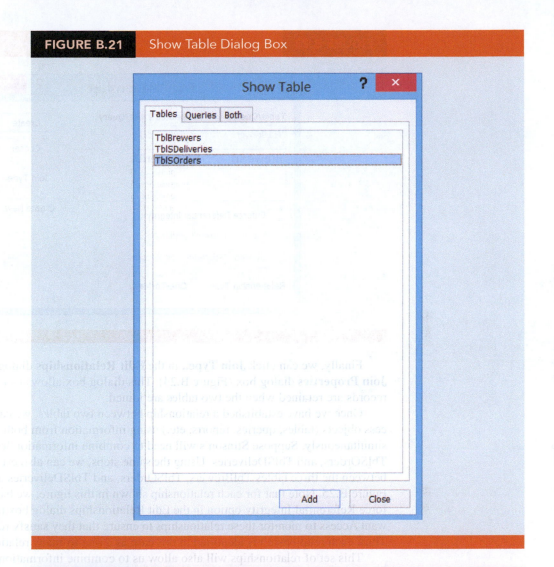

FIGURE B.21   Show Table Dialog Box

FIGURE B.22   Upper Portion of the Relationships Workspace Showing the Relationship Between TblBrewers and TblSOrders

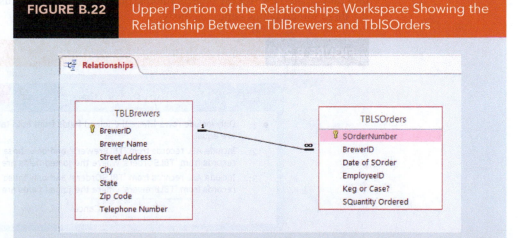

FIGURE B.23   Edit Relationships Dialog Box

Edit Relationships

Table/Query: Related Table/Query:

TBLBrewers   ▾   TBLSOrders   ▾

BrewerID   ▾   BrewerID   ▲

☐ Enforce Referential Integrity

☐ Cascade Update Related Fields

☐ Cascade Delete Related Records

Relationship Type: One-To-Many

Create
Cancel
Join Type..
Create New..

Finally, we can click **Join Type..** in the **Edit Relationships** dialog box to open the **Join Properties** dialog box (Figure B.24). This dialog box allows us to specify which records are retained when the two tables are joined.

Once we have established a relationship between two tables, we can create new Access objects (tables, queries, reports, etc.) using information from both of the joined tables simultaneously. Suppose Stinson's will need to combine information from TblBrewers, TblSOrders, and TblSDeliveries. Using the same steps, we can also establish relationships between the three tables TblBrewers, TblSOrders, and TblSDeliveries as shown in Figure B.25. Note that for each relationship shown in this figure, we have used the Enforce Referential Integrity option in the Edit Relationships dialog box to indicate that we want Access to monitor these relationships to ensure that they satisfy relational integrity. Thus, each relationship is identified in this case as a one-to-many relationship.

This set of relationships will also allow us to combine information from all three tables and create new Access objects (tables, queries, reports, etc.) using information from the three joined tables simultaneously.

FIGURE B.24   Join Properties Dialog Box

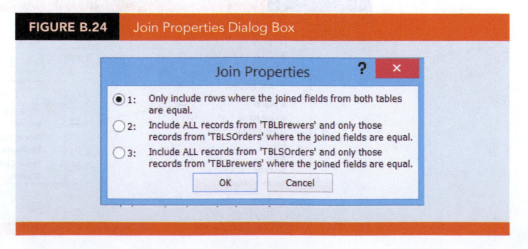

Join Properties

◉ 1: Only include rows where the joined fields from both tables are equal.

○ 2: Include ALL records from 'TBLBrewers' and only those records from 'TBLSOrders' where the joined fields are equal.

○ 3: Include ALL records from 'TBLSOrders' and only those records from 'TBLBrewers' where the joined fields are equal.

OK   Cancel

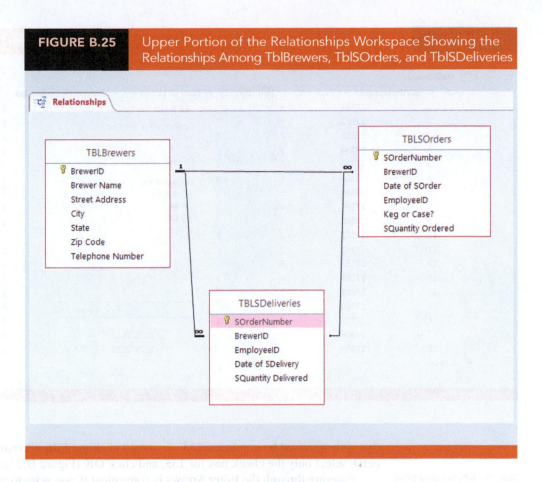

FIGURE B.25   Upper Portion of the Relationships Workspace Showing the Relationships Among TblBrewers, TblSOrders, and TblSDeliveries

B.3 Sorting and Filtering Records

As our tables inevitably grow or are joined to form larger tables, the number of records can become overwhelming. One of the strengths of relational database software such as Access is that they provide tools, such as sorting and filtering, for dealing with large quantities of data. Access provides several tools for sorting the records in a table into a desired sequence and filtering the records in a table to generate a subset of your data that meets specific criteria. We begin by considering sorting the records in a table to improve the organization of the data and increase the value of information in the table by making it easier to find records with specific characteristics. Access allows for records to be sorted on values of one or more fields, called the *sort fields*, in either ascending or descending order. To sort on a single field, we click on the Filter Arrow in the field on which we wish to sort.

Note that different data types have different sort options.

Suppose that Stinson's Manager of Receiving wants to review a list of all deliveries received by Stinson's, and she wants the list sorted by the Stinson's employee who received the orders. To accomplish this, we first open the table TblSDeliveries in Datasheet view. We then click on the **Filter Arrow** ▾ for the field EmployeeID (the sort field), as shown in Figure B.26; to sort the data in ascending order by values in the EmployeeID field, we click on ↑↓ **Sort Smallest to Largest** (clicking on ↓↑ **Sort Largest to Smallest** will sort the data in descending order by values in the EmployeeID field). By using the Filter Arrows, we can sort the data in a table on values of any of the table's fields.

We can also use this pull-down menu to filter our data to generate a subset of data in a table that satisfies specific conditions. If we want to create a display of only deliveries

Pull-Down Menu for Sorting and Filtering Records in a Table with the Filter Arrow

that were received by employee 135, we would click the **Filter Arrow** next to EmployeeID, select only the check box for **135**, and click **OK** (Figure B.27).

Note that different data types have different filter options.

Filtering through the Filter Arrows is convenient if you want to retain records associated with several different values in a field. For example, if we want to generate a display of the records in the table TblSDeliveries associated with breweries with BrewerIDs 3, 4, and 9, we would click on the **Filter Arrow** next to BrewerID, deselect the check boxes for **2, 4, 6**, and **7**, and click **OK**.

Top Rows of the Tabular Display of Results of Filtering

Clicking Selection in the Sort & Filter group will also filter on values of a single field.

The **Sort & Filter** group in the **Home** tab also provides tools for sorting and filtering records in a table. To quickly sort all records in a table on values for a field, open the table to be sorted in Datasheet view, and click on any cell in the field to be sorted. Then click on ↓ **Ascending** to sort records from smallest to largest values in the sort field or on ↓ **Descending** to sort records from largest to smallest in the sort field.

Access also allows for simultaneous sorting and filtering through the Advanced function in the Sort & Filter group of the Home tab; the advanced Filter/Sort display for the table TblSDeliveries is shown in Figure B.28. Once we have opened the table to be filtered and sorted in Datasheet view, we click on **Advanced** in the **Sort & Filter** group of the **Home** tab, as shown in Figure B.28. We then select **Advanced Filter/Sort…**. From this display, we double-click on the first field in the field list on which we wish to filter. The field we have selected will appear in the heading of the first column in the tabular display at the bottom of the screen. We can then indicate in the appropriate portion of this display the sorting and filtering to be done on this field. We continue this process for every field for which we want to apply a filter and/or sort, remembering that the sorting will be nested (the table will be sorted on the first sort field, and then the sort for the second sort field will be executed within each unique value of the first sort field, and so on).

Suppose we wish to create a new tabular display of all records for deliveries from breweries with BrewerIDs of 4 or 7 for which fewer than 7 units were delivered, and we want the records in this display sorted in ascending order first on values of the field BrewerID and then on values of the field SQuantity Delivered. To execute these criteria, we perform the following steps:

We can toggle between a display of the filtered/sorted data and a display of the original table by clicking on Toggle Filter in the Sort & Filter group of the Home tab.

Step 1. Click the **Home** tab in the Ribbon

Step 2. Click **Advanced** in the **Sort & Filter** group, and select **Advanced Filter/Sort…**

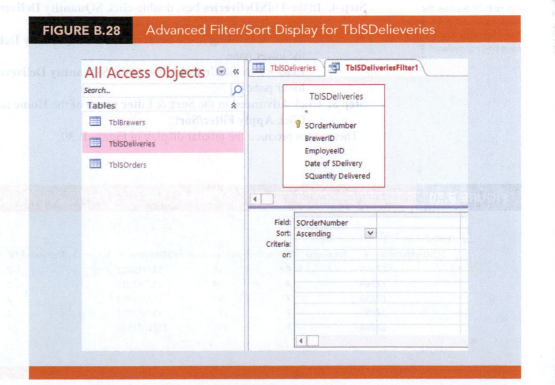

| FIGURE B.28 | Advanced Filter/Sort Display for TblSDelieveries |

B.2   Sorting and

FIGURE B.29   Tabular Display of Criteria for Simultaneous Filtering and Sorting Using Advanced Filter/Sort

Field:	BrewerID	SQuantity Delivered
Sort:	Ascending	Ascending
Criteria:	4	<7
or:	7	

Figure B.29 displays the lower pane of the Advanced Filter/Sort after Steps 1 to 4 have been completed.

Step 3. In the **TblSDeliveries** box, double-click **BrewerID** to add this field to the first column in the lower pane of the screen

Select **Ascending** in the **Sort:** row of the **BrewerID** column in the lower pane

Enter *4* in the **Criteria:** row of the **BrewerID** column in the lower pane

Enter *7* in the **or:** row of the **BrewerID** column in the lower pane

Step 4. In the **TblSDeliveries** box, double-click **SQuantity Delivered** to add this to the second column in the lower pane of the screen

Select **Ascending** in the **Sort:** row of the **SQuantity Delivered** column in the lower pane

Enter *<7* in the **Criteria:** row of the **SQuantity Delivered** column in the lower pane

Step 5. Click **Advanced** in the **Sort & Filter** group of the **Home** tab

Click **Apply Filter/Sort**

These steps produce the tabular display in Figure B.30.

FIGURE B.30   Tabular Display of Filtered and Sorted Data Using Advanced Filter/Sort

SOrderNumber	BrewerID	EmployeeID	Date of SDelivery	SQuantity Delivered	Click to Add
17359	4	135	11/7/2012	2	
17369	4	94	11/9/2012	3	
17362	7	94	11/8/2012	2	
17353	7	135	11/6/2012	2	
17367	7	135	11/10/2012	4	

Note that the data, after being filtered to show only records with breweries that do have values of 4 or 7 in the BrewerID field and all records with deliveries of 7 or fewer units, are sorted first in ascending order on the BrewerID field. Within each unique value in the BrewerID field, the records are sorted in ascending order on the SQuanity Delivered field.

NOTES + COMMENTS

1. We can use wildcard symbols when filtering by substituting an asterisk symbol (*) for any portion of the value of a field you want to represent with a wildcard. For example, if we wanted to create a table of information on all Stinson employees whose last names started with the letter B, we would filter the field EmpLastName in the table TblEmployees by entering *B** in the **Criteria:** row of the Advanced Filter/Sort. This filter will return all records that have the combination of the first letter "B" and any other following characters in the EmpLastName field.

B.4 Queries

Queries are a way of searching for and compiling data that meet specific criteria from one or more tables. They enable you to extract particular fields from a table or create a new table that combines information from several related tables.

Although there are similarities between queries and simple searches or filters, queries are far more powerful because they can be used to extract information from multiple tables. For example, although you could use a search in the table TblBrewers to find the name of a brewer that supplies beer to Stinson's or a filter on the table TblSOrders to view only orders placed by Stinson's for kegs of beer, neither of those approaches would let you simultaneously view both the names of brewers and orders placed for kegs of beer. However, you could easily run a query to create a record of every order Stinson's has placed for kegs of beer that includes the name of the brewer and the corresponding order that was placed. By taking advantage of the relationships among the tables of a database, a well-designed query can yield information that would be cumbersome or difficult to discern by examining the data in individual tables.

Access allows for several types of queries. The three most commonly used are:

- **Select queries**: These are the simplest and most commonly used queries; they are used to extract the subset of data from a table that satisfy one or more criteria. For example, Stinson's Manager of Receiving may want to review a list of all deliveries received by Stinson's that includes the Stinson's employee who received each order over some period of time. A select query could be applied to the table TblSDeliveries (shown in the original database design illustrated in Figure B.1) to create the subset of this table containing only the fields SOrderNumber and EmployeeID.

Action queries are also known as Data Manipulation Language (DML) statements.

- **Action queries**: These queries are used to change data in existing tables. For example, the sales manager may want to increase the prices charged to retailers by Stinson's for the kegs of microbrews that Stinson's sells. The sales manager can quickly make this change through an action query applied to the table TblSalesPrices to quickly perform these calculations and modify these prices in the database. Action queries allow the user to modify many records quickly and efficiently. Access provides four types of action queries:

- *Update* allows the values of one or more fields in the result set to be modified.
- *Make table* creates a new table based on the results of the query.
- *Append* is similar to a make table query, except that the results of the query are appended to an existing table.
- *Delete* deletes all the records in the results of the query from the underlying table.

- **Crosstab queries**: These perform calculations on information in a table. Stinson's Manager of Receiving may be interested in how many kegs and cases of beer have been delivered to Stinson's and which Stinson's employee received the shipment. The manager could find this information by applying a crosstab query to the table TblSDeliveries (shown in the original database design in Figure B.1) to create a table that shows number of kegs and cases delivered by the Stinson's employee who received the shipment.

We next review how to execute each of these types of queries in Access.

Select Queries

We start by considering the needs of Stinson's Manager of Receiving, who wants to review a list of all deliveries received by Stinson's and the Stinson's employee who received the orders during some recent week. This requires us to perform a select query on the table TblSDeliveries to create a subset of this table that includes only the fields SOrderNumber and EmployeeID for deliveries to Stinson's during the past week (the only week for which we have data in our new database) and display this subset in Datasheet view. To execute this select query, we take the following steps:

Step 1. Click the **Create** tab in the Ribbon (Figure B.31)

Step 2. Click **Query Wizard** in the **Queries** group

Step 3. When the **New Query** dialog box appears (Figure B.32)
Select **Simple Query Wizard**
Click **OK**

Step 4. When the next **Simple Query Wizard** dialog box appears (see Figure B.33):
Select **Table: TblSDeliveries** in the **Tables/Queries** box
Select the fields **SOrderNumber** and **EmployeeID** from the **Available Fields:** box and move these to the **Selected Fields:** box using the 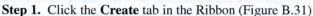 button (Figure B.33)
Click **Next >**

Step 5. When the next **Simple Query Wizard** dialog box appears (Figure B.34):
Select **Detail (shows every field of every record)**
Click **Next >**

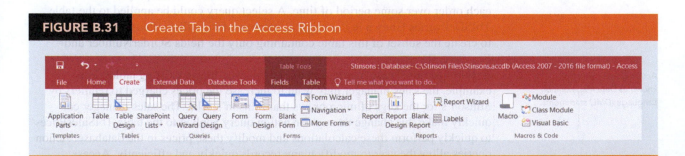

FIGURE B.31   Create Tab in the Access Ribbon

| FIGURE B.32 | New Query Dialog Box |

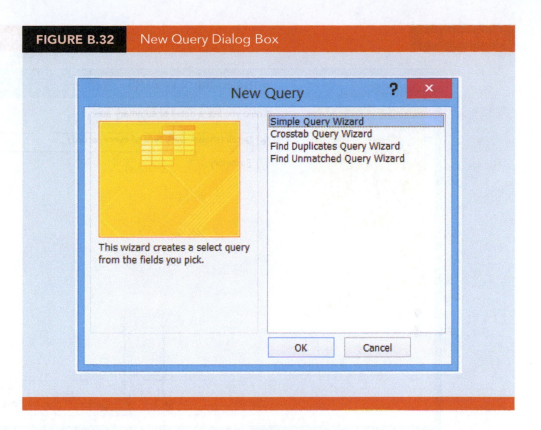

| FIGURE B.33 | First Step of the Simple Query Wizard |

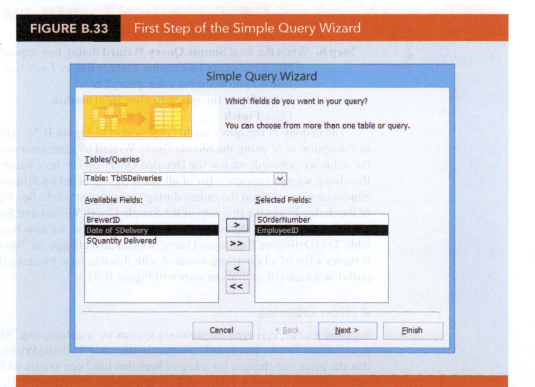

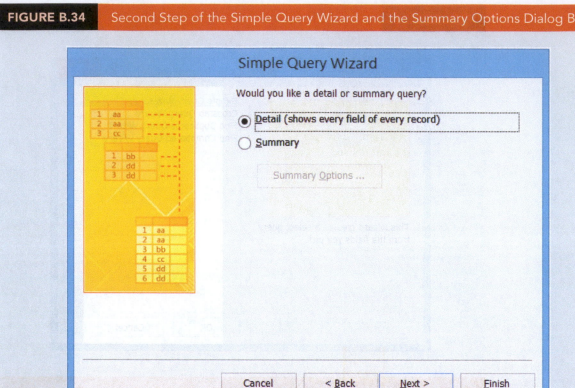

FIGURE B.34   Second Step of the Simple Query Wizard and the Summary Options Dialog Box

Step 6. When the final **Simple Query Wizard** dialog box appears (Figure B.35):
Name our query by entering *TblSDeliveries Employee Query* in the **What title do you want for your query?** box
Select **Open the query to view information**
Click **Finish**

The display of the query results is provided in Figure B.36. Although Step 5 offers us the option of of using the Simple Query Wizard to generate a summary display of the fields we selected, we use the Detailed Query option here because the Manager of Receiving wants to review a list of all deliveries received by Stinson's and the Stinson's employee who received the orders during some recent week. See Figure B.34 for displays of the dialog boxes for this step of the Simple Query Wizard and Summary Options.

Note that in both Datasheet view and Design view, we now have a new tab with the table TblSDeliveries Employee Query. We can also change the Navigation Panel so that it shows a list of all queries associated with this database by using the Navigation Panel's pull-down menu of options as shown in Figure B.37.

Action Queries

Suppose that in reviewing the database system we are designing, Stinson's Sales Manager notices that we have made an error in the table TblSalesPrices. She shares with us that the price she charges for a keg of beer that has been produced by the Midwest Fiddler Crab microbrewery (value of 7 for BrewerID) should be $240, not the $230 we have

FIGURE B.35 Final Step of the Simple Query Wizard

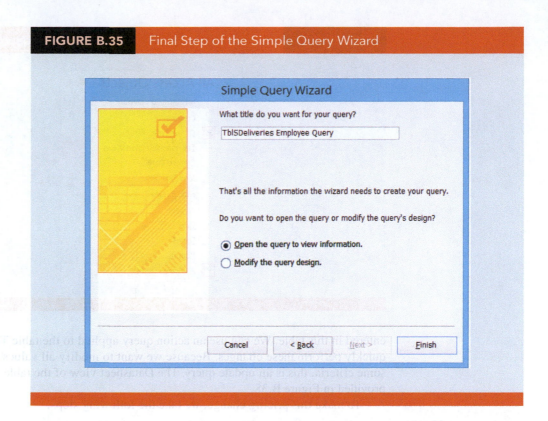

Simple Query Wizard

What title do you want for your query?

TblSDeliveries Employee Query

That's all the information the wizard needs to create your query.

Do you want to open the query or modify the query's design?

- ⦿ Open the query to view information.
- ◯ Modify the query design.

Cancel   < Back   Next >   Finish

FIGURE B.36 Display of Results of a Simple Query

SOrderNumber	EmployeeID
17351	94
17352	94
17353	135
17354	94
17355	135
17356	135
17358	135
17359	135
17360	94
17361	135
17362	94
17363	94
17364	135
17365	94
17366	94
17367	135
17368	94
17369	94

Tabs: TblSDeliveries | **TblSDeliveries Employee Query**

| FIGURE B.37 | Pull-Down Menu of Options in the Navigation Panel |

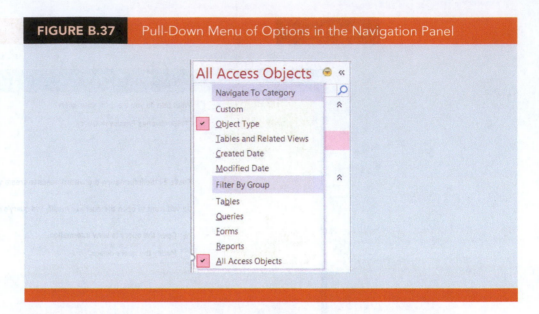

entered in this table. We can use an action query applied to the table TblSalesPrices to quickly perform these changes. Because we want to modify all values of a field that meet some criteria, this is an update query. The Datasheet view of the table TblSalesPrices is provided in Figure B.38.

To make this pricing change, we take the following steps:

Stinsons

This step produces the TblSalesPrices box that contains a list of fields in this table.

Step 1. Click the **Create** tab in the Ribbon

Step 2. Click **Query Design** in the **Queries** group. This opens the **Query Design** window and the **Query Tools** contextual tab (Figure B.39)

Step 3. When the **Show Table** dialog box appears, select **TblSalesPrices** and click **Add** Click **Close**

Step 4. In the **TblSalesPrices** box, double-click on **KegSalesPrice**. This opens a column labeled KegSalesPrice in the **Field:** row at the bottom pane of the display

Click **Update**, , in the **Query Type** group of the **Design** tab

Enter *240* in the **Update To:** row of the **KegSalesPrice** column in the bottom pane of the display

| FIGURE B.38 | Datasheet View of TblSalesPrices |

TblSalesPrices

BrewerID	KegSalesPrice	CaseSalesPrice	Click to Add
2	$225.00	$47.00	
3	$249.00	$52.00	
4	$210.00	$40.00	
6	$255.00	$55.00	
7	$230.00	$49.00	
9	$220.00	$45.00	

FIGURE B.39   Query Tools Contextual Tab

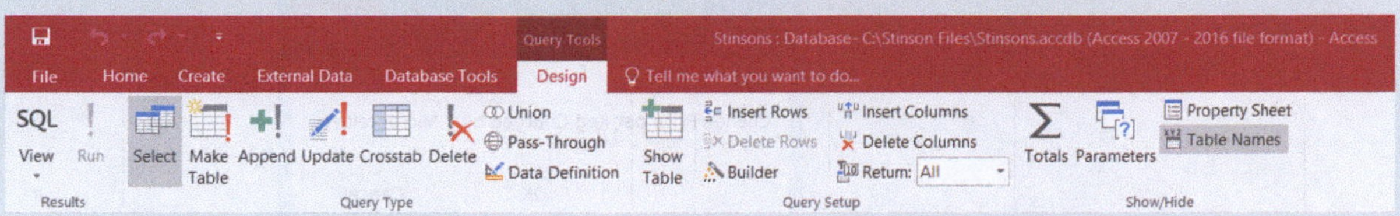

Step 5. In the **TblSalesPrices** box, double-click on **BrewerID** to open a second column in the bottom pane of the display labeled BrewerID

Enter *7* in the **Criteria:** row of the **BrewerID** column (Figure B.40)

Step 6. Click the **Run** button **!** in the **Results** group of the Design tab

When the dialog box alerting us that we are about to update one row of the table appears, click **Yes**

Once we click **Yes** in the dialog box, the price charged to Stinson's for a keg of beer supplied by the Midwest Fiddler Crab microbrewery (BrewerID equal to 7) in the table TblSalesPrices is changed from $230.00 to $240.00.

Once saved, a query can be modified and saved again to use later.

Step 7. To save this query, click the **Save** icon 🖫 in the **Quick Access** toolbar

When the **Save As** dialog box opens (Figure B.41), enter the name *Change Price per Keg Charged by a Microbrewery* for **Query Name:**

Click **OK**

Opening the table TblSalesPrices in Datasheet view (Figure B.42) shows that the price of a keg charged to Stinson's for a keg of beer supplied by the Midwest Fiddler Crab microbrewery (BrewerID equal to 7) has been revised from $230 to $240.

Crosstab Queries

We use crosstab queries to summarize data in one field by values of one or more other fields. In our example, we will consider an issue faced by Stinson's Inventory Manager, who wants to know how many kegs and cases of beer have been ordered by each Stinson's employee from each microbrewery. To provide the manager with this information,

FIGURE B.40   Display of Information for the Update Query

Field:	KegSalesPrice	BrewerID
Table:	TblSalesPrices	TblSalesPrices
Update To:	240	
Criteria:		7
or:		

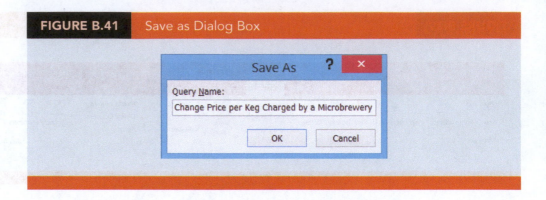

FIGURE B.41   Save as Dialog Box

we apply a crosstab query to the table TblSOrders (shown in the original database design illustrated in Figure B.1) to create a table that shows the number of kegs and cases ordered by each Stinson's employee from each microbrewery. To create this crosstab query, we take the following steps:

Step 3 produces the TblSOrders box in Access that contains a list of fields in this table.

Step 1.   Click the **Create** tab in the Ribbon

Step 2.   Click **Query Design** in the **Queries** group. This opens the **Query Design** window and the **Query Tools** contextual tab

Step 3.   When the **Show Table** dialog box opens, select **TblSOrders**, click **Add**, then click **Close**

Step 4.   In the **TblSOrders** box, double-click **BrewerID**, **Keg or Case?**, and **SQuantity Ordered** to add these fields to the columns in the lower pane of the window

Step 5.   In the **Query Type** group of the **Design** tab, click **Crosstab**

Step 6.   In the **BrewerID** column of the window's lower pane,
Select **Row Heading** in the **Crosstab:** row
Select **Ascending** in the **Sort:** row

Step 7.   In the **Keg or Case?** column of the window's lower pane,
Select **Column Heading** in the **Crosstab:** row
Select **Ascending** in the **Sort:** row

FIGURE B.42   TblSalesPrices in Datasheet View After Running the Update Query

	BrewerID	KegSalesPrice	CaseSalesPrice	Click to Add
⊞	2	$225.00	$47.00	
⊞	3	$249.00	$52.00	
⊞	4	$210.00	$40.00	
⊞	6	$255.00	$55.00	
⊞	7	$240.00	$49.00	
⊞	9	$220.00	$45.00	

Tabs: **TblSalesPrices** | Change Price per Keg Charged by a Microbrewery

FIGURE B.43 Display of Design of the Crosstab Query

Field:	BrewerID	Keg or Case?	SQuantity Ordered
Table:	TblSOrders	TblSOrders	TblSOrders
Total:	Group By	Group By	Sum
Crosstab:	Row Heading	Column Heading	Value
Sort:	Ascending	Ascending	
Criteria:			
or:			

Step 8. In the **SQuantity Ordered** column of the window's lower pane,
Select **Sum** in the **Total:** row
Select **Value** in the **Crosstab:** row

Step 9. In the **Results** group of the **Design** tab, click the **Run** button, **!**, to execute the crosstab query

Figure B.43 displays the results of completing Steps 1 to 8 to create our crosstab query. In the first column, we have indicated we want values of the field BrewerID to act as the row headings of our table (in ascending order), whereas in the second column we have indicated that we want values of the field Keg or Case? to act as the column headings of our table (again, in ascending order). In the third column, we have indicated that values of the field SQuantity Ordered will be summed for every combination of row (value of the field BrewerID) and column (value of the field Keg or Case?).

The results of the crosstab query appear in Figure B.44. From Figure B.44, we see that we have ordered 8 cases and 10 kegs of beer from the microbrewery with a value of 3 for the BrewerID field (the Oak Creek Brewery).

Step 10. To save the results of this query, click the **Save** icon, 🖫, in the **Quick Access** toolbar
When the **Save As** dialog box opens, enter *Brewer Orders Query* for **Query Name:**
Click **OK**

FIGURE B.44 Results of Crosstab Query

BrewerID	Case	Keg
2	5	3
3	8	10
4		5
6	5	2
7	4	4
9	6	11

NOTES + COMMENTS

1. Action queries permanently change the data in a database, so we suggest that you back up the database before performing an action query. After you have reviewed the results of the action query and are satisfied that the query worked as desired, you can then save the database with the results of the action query. Some cautious users save the original database under a different name so that they can revert to the original pre–action query database if they later find that the action query has had an undesirable effect on the database.

2. Crosstab queries do not permanently change the data in a database.

3. The Make Table, Append, and Delete action queries work in manners similar to Update action queries and are also useful ways to modify tables to better suit the user's needs.

B.5 Saving Data to External Files

You can open the file Stinsons and follow these steps to reproduce an external Excel file of the data in TblSOrders.

After we complete Step 4, another dialog box asks us if we want to save the steps we used to export the information in this table; this can be handy to have later if we have to export similar data again.

Access can export data to external files in formats that are compatible with a wide variety of software. To export the information from the table TblSOrders to an external Excel file, we take the following steps:

Step 1. Click the **External Data** tab in the Ribbon (Figure B.45)
Step 2. In the **Navigation Panel**, click **TblSOrders**
Step 3. In the **Export** group of the **External Data** tab, click the **Excel** icon, 📊
Step 4. When the **Export—Excel Spreadsheet** dialog box opens (Figure B.46), click the **Browse…** button
Find the destination where you want to save your exported file and then click the **Save** button
Verify that the correct path and file name are listed in the **File Name**: box (*TblSOrders.xlsx* in this example)
Verify that the **File format:** is set to **Excel Workbook (*.xlsx)**
Select the check boxes for **Export data with formatting and layout.** and **Open the designation file after the export operation is complete.**
Click **OK**

Exporting information to an external file is particularly useful when applied to tables that have been linked or to query results.

The preceding steps export the table TblSOrders from Access into an Excel file named *TblSOrders.xlsx*. Exporting information from a relational database such as Access to Excel allows one to apply the tools and techniques covered throughout this textbook to a subset of a large data set. This can be much more efficient than using Excel to clean and filter large data sets.

FIGURE B.45　　　External Data Tab in Access

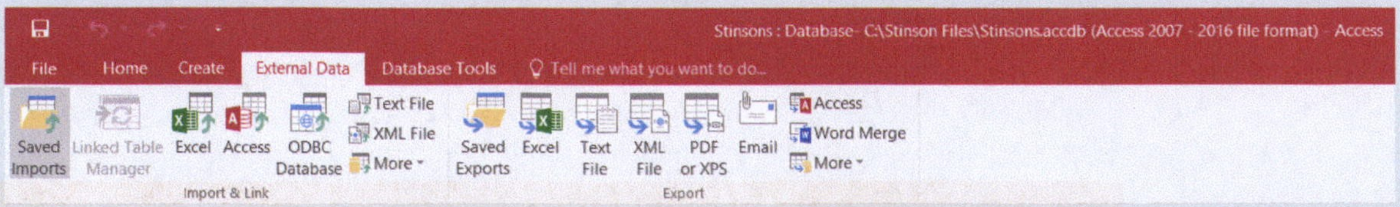

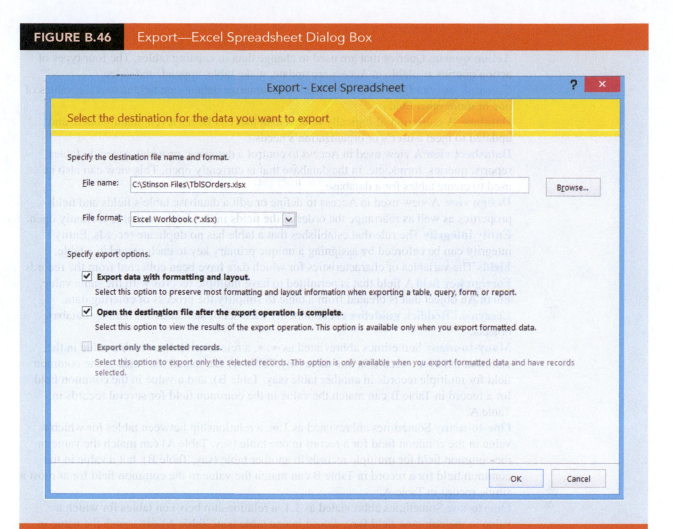

FIGURE B.46   Export—Excel Spreadsheet Dialog Box

SUMMARY

The amount of data available for analyses is increasing at a rapid rate, and this trend will not change in the foreseeable future. Furthermore, the data used by organizations to make decisions are dynamic, and they change rapidly. Thus, it is critical that a data analyst understand how data are stored, revised, updated, retrieved, and manipulated. We have reviewed tools in Microsoft Access® that can be used for these purposes.

In this appendix we have reviewed basic concepts of database creation and management that are important to consider when using data from a database in an analysis. We have discussed several ways to create a database in Microsoft Access®, and we have demonstrated Access tools for preparing data in an existing database for analysis. These include tools for reading data from external sources into tables, creating relationships between tables, sorting and filtering records, designing and executing queries, and saving data to external files.

GLOSSARY

Action queries Queries that are used to change data in existing tables. The four types of action queries available in Access are update, make table, append, and delete.

Crosstab queries Queries that are used to summarize data in one field across the values of one or more other fields.

Database A collection of logically related data that can be retrieved, manipulated, and updated to meet a user's or organization's needs.

Datasheet view A view used in Access to control a database; provides access to tables, reports, queries, forms, etc. in the database that is currently open. This view can also be used to create tables for a database.

Design view A view used in Access to define or edit a database table's fields and field properties as well as rearrange the order of the fields in the database that is currently open.

Entity integrity The rule that establishes that a table has no duplicate records. Entity integrity can be enforced by assigning a unique primary key to each record in a table.

Fields The variables or characteristics for which data have been collected from the records.

Foreign key field A field that is permitted to have multiple records with the same value.

Form An object that is created from a table to simplify the process of entering data.

Leszynski/Reddick guidelines A commonly used set of standards for naming database objects.

Many-to-many Sometimes abbreviated as $\infty:\infty$, a relationship for which a value in the common field for a record in one table (say, Table A) can match the value in the common field for multiple records in another table (say, Table B), and a value in the common field for a record in Table B can match the value in the common field for several records in Table A.

One-to-many Sometimes abbreviated as $1:\infty$, a relationship between tables for which a value in the common field for a record in one table (say, Table A) can match the value in the common field for multiple records in another table (say, Table B), but a value in the common field for a record in Table B can match the value in the common field for at most a single record in Table A.

One-to-one Sometimes abbreviated as $1:1$, a relationship between tables for which a value in the common field for a record in one table (say, Table A) can match the value in the common field for at most one record in another table (say, Table B), and a value in the common field for a record in Table B can match the value in the common field for at most a single record in Table A.

Orphaned A record in a table that has a value for the foreign key field of a table that does not match the value in the primary key field for any record of a related table. Enforcing referential integrity prevents the creation of orphaned records.

Primary key field A field that must have a unique value for each record in the table and is used to identify how records from several tables in a database are logically related.

Query A question posed by a user about the data in the database.

Records The individual units from which the data for a database have been collected.

Referential integrity The rule that establishes the proper relationship between two tables.

Report Output from a table or a query that has been put into a specific prespecified format.

Select queries Queries that are used to extract the subset of data that satisfy one or more criteria from a table.

Table Data arrayed in rows and columns (similar to a worksheet in an Excel spreadsheet) in which rows correspond to records and columns correspond to fields.

References

Data Management and Microsoft Access

Adamski, J. J., K. T. Finnegan, and S. Scollard *New Perspectives on Microsoft® Access 2013, Comprehensive*. Cengage Learning, 2014.

Alexander, M. *The Excel Analyst's Guide to Access*, Wiley, 2010.

Alexander, M. *Access 2013 Bible*, 1st ed. Wiley, 2013.

Balter, A. *Using Microsoft Access 2010*. Que Publishing, 2010.

Carter, J., and J. Juarez. *Microsoft Office Access 2010: A Lesson Approach, Complete*. McGraw-Hill, 2011.

Conrad, J. *Microsoft Access 2013 Inside Out*, 1st ed. Microsoft Press, 2013.

Friedrichsen, L. *Microsoft® Access 2013: Illustrated Complete*. Cengage Learning, 2014.

Jennings, R. *Microsoft Access 2010 in Depth*. Que Publishing, 2010.

MacDonald, *Access 2013: The Missing Manual*, 1st ed. O'Reilly Media, 2013.

Owen, G. *Using Microsoft Excel and Access 2013 for Accounting*, 4th ed. South-Western College/West, 2014.

Pratt, P. J., and M. Z. Last. *Microsoft® Access 2013: Complete*. Cengage Learning, 2014.

Data Mining

Linoff, G. S., and M. J. Berry. *Data Mining Techniques: For Marketing, Sales, and Customer Relationship Management*, 3rd ed. Wiley, 2011.

Berthold, M., and D. J. Hand. *Intelligent Data Analysis*. Springer (Berlin), 1999.

Hand, D. J., H. Mannila, and P. Smyth. *Principles of Data Mining*. MIT Press, 2001.

Hastie, T., R. Tibshirani, and J. Friedman. *The Elements of Statistical Learning*, 2nd ed. Springer (Berlin), 2009.

Schmueli, G., N. R. Patel, and P. C. Bruce. *Data Mining for Business Intelligence*, 2nd ed. Wiley, 2010.

Tan, P.-N., M. Steinbach, and V. Kumar, *Introduction to Data Mining*. Addison-Wesley, 2006.

Data Visualization

Alexander, M., and J. Walkenbach. *Excel Dashboards and Reports*. Wiley, 2010.

Cleveland, W. S. *Visualizing Data*. Hobart Press, 1993.

Cleveland, W. S. *The Elements of Graphing Data*, 2nd ed. Hobart Press, 1994.

Entrepreneur, 2012 Annual Ranking of America's Top Franchise Opportunities, 2012.

Few, S. *Show Me the Numbers: Designing Tables and Graphs to Enlighten*. Analytics Press, 2004.

Few, S. *Information Dashboard Design: The Effective Visual Communication of Data*. O'Reilly Media, 2006.

Few, S. *Now You See It: Simple Visualization Techniques for Quantitative Analysis*. Analytics Press, 2009.

Longley, P. A., M. Goodchild, D. J. Maguire, and D. W. Rhind. *Geographic Information Systems and Science*. Wiley, 2010.

The Pew Research Center, Internet & American Life Project, 2011.

Robbins, N. B. *Creating More Effective Graphs*. Wiley, 2004.

Telea, A. C. *Data Visualization Principles and Practice*. A. K. Peters, 2008.

Tufte, E. R. *Envisioning Information*. Graphics Press, 1990.

Tufte, E. R. *Visual and Statistical Thinking: Displays of Evidence for Making Decisions*. Graphics Press, 1997.

Tufte, E. R. *Visual Explanations: Images and Quantities, Evidence and Narrative*. Graphics Press, 1997.

Tufte, E. R. *The Visual Display of Quantitative Information,* 2nd ed. Graphics Press, 2001.

Tufte, E. R. *Beautiful Evidence*. Graphics Press, 2006.

Wong, D. M. *The Wall Street Journal Guide to Information Graphics*. Norton, 2010.

Young, F. W., P. M. Valero-Mora, and M. Friendly. *Visual Statistics: Seeing Data with Dynamic Interactive Graphics*. Wiley, 2006.

Decision Analysis

Clemen, R. T., and T. Reilly. *Making Hard Decisions with DecisionTools*. Cengage Learning, 2004.

Golub, A. L. *Decision Analysis: An Integrated Approach*. Wiley, 1997.

Goodwin, P., and G. Wright. *Decision Analysis for Management Judgment,* 4th ed. Wiley, 2009.

Peterson, M. *An Introduction to Decision Theory*. Cambridge, 2009.

Pratt, J. W., H. Raiffa, and R. Schlaiter. *Introduction to Statistical Decision Theory*. MIT Press, 2008.

Raiffa, H. *Decision Analysis*. McGraw-Hill, 1997.

Time Series and Forecasting

Bowerman, B. L., R. T. O'Connell and A. Koehler. *Forecasting, Time Series, and Regression*, 4th ed. Cengage, 2005.

Box, G. E. P., G. M. Jenkins, and G. C. Reinsel. *Time Series Analysis: Forecasting and Control,* 4th ed. Wiley, 2008.

Hanke, J. E., and D. Wichern. *Business Forecasting,* 9th ed., Prentice Hall, 2009.

Makridakis, S. G., S. C. Wheelwright, and R. J. Hyndman. *Forecasting Methods and Applications,* 3rd ed. Wiley, 1997.

Ord, K., and R. Fildes. *Principles of Business Forecasting*. Cengage Learning, 2013.

Wilson, J. H., B. Keating, and John Galt Solutions, Inc. *Business Forecasting with Accompanying Excel-Based Forecast X™ Software*, 5th ed. McGraw-Hill/Irwin, 2007.

General Business Analytics

Ayres, I. *Super Crunchers: Why Thinking-by-Numbers Is the New Way to Be Smart.* Bantam, 2008.

Baker, S. *The Numerati.* Mariner Books, 2009.

Davenport, T. H., and J. G. Harris, *Competing on Analytics.* Harvard Business School Press, 2007.

Davenport, T. H., J. G. Harris, and R. Morrison, *Analytics at Work.* Harvard Business School Press, 2010.

Davenport, T. H., Ed. *Enterprise Analytics.* FT Press, 2012.

Fisher, M., and A. Raman. *The New Science of Retailing.* Harvard Business Press, 2010.

Lewis, M. *Moneyball: The Art of Winning an Unfair Game.* Norton, 2004.

Wind, J., P. E. Green, D. Shifflet, and M. Scarbrough. "Courtyard by Marriott: Designing a Hotel Facility with Consumer-Based Marketing Models," *Interfaces* 19, no. 1 (January–February 1989): 25–47.

Optimization

Baker, K. R. *Optimization Modeling with Spreadsheets,* 2nd ed. Wiley, 2011.

Bazaraa, M. S., H. D. Sherali, and C.M. Shetty. *Nonlinear Programming: Theory and Algorithms.* Wiley Interscience, 2006.

Bazaraa, M. S., J. J. Jarvis, and H. D. Sherali. *Linear Programming and Network Flows.* Wiley, 2009.

Chen, D., R. G. Batson, and Y. Dang. *Applied Integer Programming.* Wiley, 2010.

Sashihara, S. *The Optimization Edge.* McGraw-Hill, 2011.

Winston, W. L. *Financial Models Using Simulation and Optimization,* 2nd ed. Palisade Corporation, 2008.

Probability

Anderson, D., D. Sweeney and T. Williams. *Essentials of Modern Business Statistics*, 6th ed. Cengage, 2016.

Anderson, D., D. Sweeney, T. Williams, J. Camm and J. Cochran. *An Introduction to Statistics for Business and Economics*, 13th ed. Cengage, 2015.

Ross, S. M. *An Introduction to Probability Models*, 11th ed. Academic Press, 2014.

Regression Analysis

Chatterjee, S., and A. S. Hadi. *Regression Analysis by Example,* 4th ed. Wiley, 2006.

Draper, N. R., and H. Smith. *Applied Regression Analysis,* 3rd ed. Wiley, 1998.

Graybill, F. A., and H. K. Iyer. *Regression Analysis: Concepts and Applications.* Wadsworth, 1994.

Hosmer, D. W., and S. Lemeshow. *Applied Logistic Regression,* 3rd ed. Wiley, 2013.

Kleinbaum, D. G., L. L. Kupper, A. Nizam, and E. Rosenberg. *Applied Regression Analysis and Multivariate Methods,* 5th ed. Cengage Learning, 2013.

Mendenhall, M., T. Sincich, and T. R. Dye. *A Second Course in Statistics: Regression Analysis,* 7th ed. Prentice Hall, 2011.

Montgomery, D. C., E. A. Peck, and G. G. Vining. *Introduction to Linear Regression Analysis,* 5th ed. Wiley, 2012.

Neter, J., W. Wasserman, M. H. Kutner, and C. Nashtsheim. *Applied Linear Statistical Models,* 5th ed. McGraw-Hill, 2004.

Monte Carlo Simulation

Bell, P. *Brent-Harbridge Developments, Inc.* Richard Ivey School of Business, University of Western Ontario, 1998.

Law, A. M. *Simulation Modeling and Analysis,* 4th ed. McGraw-Hill, 2006.

Ross, S. *Simulation.* Academic Press, 2013.

Savage, S. L. *Flaw of Averages.* Wiley, 2012.

Talib, N. N. *Fooled by Randomness.* Random House, 2004.

Wainer, H. *Picturing the Uncertain World.* Princeton University Press, 2009.

Winston, W. *Decision Making Under Uncertainty.* Palisade Corporation, 2007.

Spreadsheet Modeling

Leong, T., and M. Cheong. *Business Modeling with Spreadsheets: Problems, Principles, and Practice,* 2nd ed. McGraw-Hill (Asia), 2010.

Powell, S. G., and R. J. Batt. *Modeling for Insight.* Wiley, 2008.

Winston, W. *Excel 2013 Data Analysis and Business Modeling.* Microsoft Press, 2014.

Statistical Inference

Barnett, V. *Comparative Statistical Inference*, 3rd ed. Wiley, 1999.

Casella, G. and R. L. Berger. *Statistical Inference*, 2nd ed. Duxbury, 2002.

Roussas, G. G. *An Introduction to Probability and Statistical Inference*, 1st ed. Elsevier, 2003.

Wasserman, L. *All of Statistics: A Concise Course in Statistical Inference* (Springer Texts in Statistics) 1st ed. Springer, 2004.

Welsh, A. H. *Aspects of Statistical Inference*, 1st ed. Wiley, 1996.

Young, G. A. and R. L. Smith. *Essentials of Statistical Inference*, 1st ed. Cambridge 2005.

Index